A DICTIONARY
OF THE
SECOND WORLD WAR

A DICTIONARY
OF THE
SECOND WORLD WAR

Elizabeth-Anne Wheal
Stephen Pope
and
James Taylor

GRAFTON BOOKS
A Division of the Collins Publishing Group

LONDON GLASGOW
TORONTO SYDNEY AUCKLAND

Grafton Books
A Division of the Collins Publishing Group
8 Grafton Street, London W1X 3LA

Published by Grafton Books 1989

British Library Cataloguing in Publication Data

Wheal, Elizabeth-Anne
Dictionary of the Second World War
1. World War 2
I. Title   II. Pope, Stephen
III. Taylor, James
940.53

ISBN 0-246-13391-0

Photoset by Rowland Phototypesetting Ltd,
Bury St Edmunds, Suffolk
Printed in Great Britain by
William Collins Sons & Co. Ltd, Glasgow

Contents

Acknowledgements

The authors owe special thanks to several people who have contributed greatly to the production of this book: to David O'Leary for invaluable research, advice and encouragement throughout; to John Hughes and Diana Talbot of ICL for their expert assistance on the typescript; to Ken and Pat Pope for their crucial logistic contributions; and to Phyllis Wheal and Owen and Michael Appleton for their unflagging support and indispensable help in compilation.

How to Use This Book

Although the actions and events, personalities and politics, men and machines of the Second World War are dealt with individually in this book, the complexity and scope of fighting in the major war theatres and the contrasting qualities, formations and organizations of men and *matériel* demand some comprehensive generic entries to provide a narrative background to the complex detail described. Thus, each of the major war theatres has been given its own general descriptive entry, which gives a broad campaign background and refers the reader to the more detailed battle and other entries relevant to it.

The major theatre entries are: **THE WESTERN OFFENSIVE**: The German Campaign in France, the Netherlands and Belgium in 1940; **EAST AFRICA, Campaign for**; **THE DESERT WAR**; **TORCH**; **TUNISIA, Campaign for**: The Allied and Axis Campaigns in Africa, 1940 –3; **CHINA, Campaigns in**: The conflict between Japanese and US and Chinese forces, 1937–45; **BURMA, Campaigns in**: The Allied campaigns against the Japanese, 1941–5; **THE PACIFIC WAR**: The Allied war against Japan, 1941–5; **THE EASTERN FRONT**: The conflict in the Soviet Union and Eastern Europe between Russian and German forces, 1941–5; **NORTHWEST EUROPE, Allied Campaigns in**: The Allied liberation of western Europe and invasion of Germany, 1944–5; **ATLANTIC, Battle of the**: The German war against Allied ocean trade, 1939–5; **MEDITERRANEAN SEA**: The naval conflict, 1940–3.

To supplement these, comprehensive entries on armed forces and decisive weapons of the combatants add an important second dimension to the background. Major navies and air forces are given some extra emphasis in recognition of the highly mechanized nature of warfare in WW2. Their important aircraft types and warships are described individually, and the importance of tanks in ground operations is similarly recognized. Other weapons and tactics are generically discussed (e.g. **SUBMARINE**; **RADAR**; **AIRBORNE OPERATIONS**; **AMPHIBIOUS WARFARE**). Taken together, these generic entries outline a clear, comprehensive skeleton of the conflict which will enhance the reader's appreciation of the subject.

A system of cross-referencing, represented by a *, indicates further sources of information to expand the reader's knowledge. The asterisk is generally only included where a reference aids comprehension and is placed only against the first appearance of the subject in the text of an entry. Other relevant information, if it is not named in the text, is referred to at the end of each entry.

Introduction

Between the wars which broke out in the third decade of the twentieth century and the peace of 1945, most nations, most of the world's manufacturing capacity and most of the Earth's people, were directly or indirectly involved in the conflict which is known as the Second World War. This description of the period is, of course, mostly a convenient shorthand: neither Japan's invasion of Manchuria, Italy's attack on Abyssinia nor the Spanish Civil War are normally included under the umbrella of world war. The events so described are usually those which began with the German invasion of Poland on 1 September 1939 and ended with the Japanese surrender in August 1945.

Ignorance and propaganda formed most ideas of the nature of the conflict. But as the number of belligerents increased from 1941 onwards, a broad view emerged among the nations fighting Nazi Germany or Japan that these two countries represented a unique political evil. Conversely, largely as a result of the eloquence of Churchill and Roosevelt, the Allied cause was increasingly seen as a democratic crusade, and a great tyranny like Stalin's Russia was able to assume a mantle to which it had no possible claim.

This general view of WW2 barely survived the peace. Many nations soon found it inadequate on many counts; few historians had ever accepted it as anything but a propaganda device. Today, only if we look at the war as a number of separately motivated wars gradually engulfing most of the globe, can we make any sense at all of the complex events of the time.

The difficulty of any other approach is easily demonstrated. France, an early belligerent, sometimes chooses to see itself as involved in two separate wars, one in 1939 –440 and another in 1942–45; two great powers, Italy and the Soviet Union, changed sides during the course of hostilities, and the latter only joined the war against Japan in the very last days. Some nations were brought into war as a result of the invasion of their territory, the Netherlands and Belgium by the Germans, Norway by the British and French, Finland by the Russians. While genuinely neutral countries existed, neutral Spain supplied a division to fight in Russia and the neutral Irish government was unable to prevent thousands of young Irishmen from enlisting in the British Army. So daunting and complex is the route by which over fifty nations reached a state of war on one side or the other, that (within the limits of this introduction) some simplifications are necessary.

Essentially, therefore, we shall consider the outbreak of two separate but overlapping wars, one with its epicentre in Europe, the other in the Pacific. In both of these, the United States took a leading role; in both of these, the fate of the British Empire hung in the balance. In this sense, only Britain and America could be said to have fought a world war. To say this is not to diminish the vast sacrifices of others, the Soviet people, the Jews, the Germans themselves and finally the Japanese, as the victims of the first atomic bomb to be used in warfare. It is simply to underline the fact that WW2 is basically an Anglo-Saxon interpretation of events.

In Europe, the experience of war in the late 1930s is inseparable from the personality of Adolf Hitler. But it would nevertheless be untrue to say that from 1933 the European part of the world war was inevitable. At many stages the serpentine movement of history towards Armageddon might have been stopped. It was not, and a major part of what followed must be laid at the door of Hitler.

But others, notably the victors of WW1, had made it possible for the roots of Nazism to grow in fertile soil. The peace treaties which followed the First World War were felt to be unsatisfactory by some victor nations, such as Italy, and disastrous by others, by vanquished states such as Germany and Hungary. In Germany's case this was a conviction widely indulged by its population. The loss of territory, impossible levels of reparations, the transfer of German colonies, the restriction on the size of German land and sea forces and the total air force ban, were all seen as a calculated attempt to reduce Germany to the level of a Rumania or Bulgaria.

The concept of the 'Versailles Diktat' was invented; the idea, fiercely exploited by the Nazis, of the November Criminals was born. Germany had been stabbed in the back. Her politicians had betrayed the Army. A German had no further to look than this for explanations of the vertiginous inflation of the 20s or the bitter unemployment of the early 30s. The exclusion of Germany from the benefit of empire and the greedy exploitation of the Western Allies had led to what Germans saw around them in the first years of the thirties. Such was the widely held view. It was Adolf Hitler's particular gift to graft onto this genuine despair the long strand of intense anti-Semitism in central Europe. Jewish capitalism organized from London, Paris or New York, or Jewish Bolshevism in Moscow, was held responsible for the German condition. Evident contradictions in the thesis were brushed aside.

Adolf Hitler's solution was simple to understand: to destroy the power of the Jews in Germany; to rebuild the armed forces and to acquire by rough diplomacy and war, if appropriate, *Lebensraum*, living space, in the East. It seemed, to many Germans, to make sense.

On the French and British side, reactions to the rise of Hitler were complicated. Nearly all the politicians saw the Führer as a threat to peace. In Moscow he was similarly perceived. The problem in the West, however, was that most French and British governments between 1919 and 1939 saw the Soviet Union as at least as great a threat to peace as the new Germany.

Paralysed therefore by uncertainty, by an almost equal fear of Germany and Russia, the Western Allies saw appeasement of Adolf Hitler as the first card to play. In treaties like the Anglo-German Naval Treaty and the Munich Agreement, the 'legitimate' aspirations of the new Germany were recognized. The Western Allies soon realized they were riding a tiger. And the tiger itself now quickly devoured Czechoslovakia in two bites, Austria and finally Poland.

But Hitler had first taken an important step before he risked everything by crossing the Polish border on 1 September 1939. He had recognized and exploited the Allies' fear of the Soviet Union. He had equally recognized the Soviet Union's belief that London and Paris would never sign a mutual defence treaty. By signing a pact with his own arch enemy, Hitler believed that he had ensured the safe execution of his next step, the invasion of Poland.

In the event, a reluctant Britain and an even more reluctant France declared war. Germany seized most of Poland; Russia took her agreed portion. Italy hesitated between the benefit of belligerency and the prestige of mediation. The United States government under Roosevelt took every step short of war to support what had become Britain's struggle for survival.

Within little over two years, all of Europe but Sweden and Switzerland, Portugal and Spain were at war. Forces were fighting in North Africa and Iraq, at the gates of

Moscow, and in the North Atlantic. Warsaw, Rotterdam, London and Berlin had been bombed. Throughout eastern Poland, camps were being constructed for the Final Solution of the Jewish problem. War had entered too deeply into the spirit of Europeans for an attempt at negotiated peace to be more than the dream of a few liberal Germans.

In the Pacific, the war between Japan and the United States and the British Commonwealth developed from quite other origins. Any examination of the causes of the Pacific War must trace the steps by which the Japanese Empire rose, via the tutelage of the United States and the naval alliance with Britain. Her rapid growth throughout the twentieth century brought her, within less than 50 years, into serious contention with the Anglo-Saxon powers for the fabled China trade.

By the beginning of the century, the commercial interests of the United States and Europe had first fostered the illusion of the overwhelming profits to be made in the Chinese market, then proclaimed its necessity to the industrial economies of the West. Its function was to absorb what was seen as American and European manufacturing overcapacity and to provide an economic panacea which was to save the industrial countries from depression. The United States, with Britain's agreement, took the lead in ensuring that the commercial exploitation of China would be open to all. In the years following the Washington conferences, shortly after WW1, this 'Open Door' policy had become the keystone of American commercial and political strategy in the Pacific.

But the Open Door had from the outset conceded Japan's 'special interests' in China. Originally envisaged as a policy linked to a strong US and British presence in the Pacific, it was comprised from its inception by this proviso. In the years preceding WW1, and to an even greater extent after the war, Britain was increasingly unable, and American Senates unwilling, to maintain the naval strength which underpinned the Open Door. There was therefore no response available to the West when Japan exploited the European crisis in 1914 to take over German possessions in the Pacific. Now in control of the Caroline and Marshall islands, the Japanese Navy sat astride the US fleet's route from its western coast to the Philippines, complacently regarded as the key to American naval power in the Pacific.

When America herself joined the war in 1917, a further accommodation with Japan became necessary. The 1917 accord affirmed the Open Door, but again acknowledged Japan's special interests. Post-war, the Washington Naval Treaties, which imposed a 3:5:5 ratio of Japanese, US and British fleet strength in the Pacific, appeared to America to cement the cornerstone of a moral 'Pax Americana' on Japanese expansion in the Far East.

But, as the Australian government had pointed out at the Imperial Conference in 1922, the ratio agreement had not solved the problem of Japan's expansion – it had merely contained it. The trap had been set for succeeding Presidents. Unless the warship ratio could be carefully maintained, and this was to prove impossible as US fleet strength fell prey to economic pressures, Japan was increasingly in a position to enforce her claims.

The 1922 Four Power Treaty, which replaced the Anglo-Japanese alliance, appeared to affirm the Open Door, but again, it recognized Japan's extensive railway and industrial interests in Manchuria. Most importantly, the Treaty signalled the end of the Anglo-Japanese alliance, from which overtaxed British governments had been increasingly anxious to retire. Although the Treaty presented a gentlemanly way of progressing Britain's withdrawal from Far Eastern power politics, moderate opinion in Japan was shocked and depressed by the apparent evasion of a friendship which the Japanese had valued. By terminating the alliance, Britain relinquished the option of influencing policy-making in Tokyo, while it did nothing to strengthen the security of the US, and greatly undermined the strategic situation of Australia and New Zealand, Hong Kong and other British possessions. The illusory success of the Pax Americana, was soon to be tested more seriously.

During the twenties, the US Navy declined as the American consumer industry boomed. While the endemic instability in China proved a major disincentive to US investors, who preferred to put their money into flourishing Japanese industries instead, Japan massively increased its investment in Manchuria and expanded its special interests. From 1919, these were protected by the Kwantung Army, an outpost garrison at the time, but already the spawning ground for the fanatical young proponents of Japanese military expansionism such as Hideki Tojo.

By 1930, London and Tokyo shared equal control of 70 per cent of all foreign investment in China, to the United States' 6 per cent. In turn, Japan's economy expanded rapidly, becoming increasingly dependent on US oil and strategic raw materials. The urban youth in Japan proclaimed their enthusiasm for the resulting westernization and liberalization of Japan during the twenties, and *mogo* and *moba* (Japanese contractions from modern girl and modern boy) became the 'in' thing to be. The effects of modernization were also reflected in governments of the period. Kato Takaaki (1924–6) and his successor Wakatsuki appeared to be moving Japan into an era of party government and of real, if modified, liberalism. Although reactionary conservatism and ultra-nationalism remained forces to contend with in Japan and traditional political corruption remained a feature of Japanese politics, the government's strong connections with big business (in particular, Mitsubishi, who, like other *zaibatsu*, saw a reduction in armaments as an imperative for commercial growth) reinforced this view.

But in China, the prostrate giant whose exploitation was the *raison d'être* of the Open Door policy, the clouds of the future political storm were already gathering. Chiang Kai-shek, successor in 1925 to the presidency of the young Chinese republic proclaimed by Sun Yat-sen, was a ruthless young general whose brand of armed nationalism had propelled China into a period of violent modernization. Beyond the struggle against the Chinese communists, this meant ridding China of foreign interference.

To the West it seemed a sign of progress in the Far East, if an enigmatic one, and the major powers enthusiastically endorsed China's right to sovereignty. To the Japanese Army, however, and notably to the Kwantung Army stationed on China's doorstep, it represented a new threat to territorial security and expansionist ambitions. Among the ultra-nationalists, liberalism and weakness were increasingly denounced as part and parcel.

The world banking crisis of the late twenties propelled these various tensions into crisis. In Japan, the plummeting value of the Yen, the high tariff barriers imposed by the West, and enormous consequent losses to farmers and small businessmen brought desperate and angry protests against the *zaibatsu* – the huge family industrial and banking conglomerates like Mitsubishi – and a general indictment of moderate government as the cause of the disaster. As in Germany, the political articulation of these protests was increasingly spearheaded by calls to expand aggressively Japanese interests abroad – in this case on the Asian mainland. Finally, the crisis exposed the division which had been growing throughout the twenties, between the military bureaucracy, with its unique supreme control over the Army, Navy and national security, and the moderate civilians in government. From this point, democracy in Japan was to face a severe test.

The total loss of control of the Army in foreign policy was demonstrated dramatically to the world in 1931, when a fabricated incident led to the Kwantung Army's occupation of Manchuria. Uninformed and unable to force the Army back from its position, the Japanese government was emasculated. From 1933, successive Tokyo cabinets struggled against international suspicion on the one hand, and conspiracy, threatened coups, assassinations and political chaos on the other. As the Army watched the growing strength of Chiang in China and made its own decisions about the way to answer it, Japanese cabinets were held in political limbo, between increasing international hostility to Japan and the thrall of the Army.

China's appeal to the League of Nations and the resulting Lytton Commission to investigate the Japanese puppet state in Manchuria, now renamed Manchukuo, were ignored by the Japanese Army. While Japanese troops advanced into Inner Mongolia and compelled the Chinese to accept a demilitarized zone between Peking and the Manchurian border, the League's refusal to recognize Manchukuo equally failed to disrupt the political and commercial penetration of north China demanded by Japanese militarism.

In the face of this obvious new threat to peace, the new American President, Franklin Roosevelt, was unable to spring himself from the trap laid earlier in the century. Committed to the 'sanctity of international treaties' while lacking the military strength to guarantee it, his slow drift towards a policy of major naval expansion lagged behind events in Japan.

The military eruption in Tokyo in 1936, the culmination of a factional struggle between warring ultra-nationalist groups, set the final seal on the political hegemony of the Army in Japan. The signing of the Anti-Comintern Pact with Germany in December of that year made explicit the new orientation of global diplomatic relationships. Negotiated by the Army rather than the Foreign Ministry, it reinforced the Kwantung Army's position on its northwestern flank against Russia, which threatened a military advance south into China. Within six weeks of the formation

in June 1937 of Prince Konoe's first cabinet, which many in Japan had hoped would inhibit increasing Army extremism, incidents at Shanghai led to the *de facto* outbreak of war against China. League protests were utterly ignored by Japan. Instead, the announcement of the 'New Order in East Asia' proclaimed Japan's destiny as political and economic guardian of a vast East Asian empire whose huge resources would release it from dependence on the West.

The outbreak of war in Europe provided the final impetus to Japanese expansionism. Isolated from the United States and Britain, and encouraged by German successes which appeared to have devastated the fighting strength of Japan's imperial rivals, the opportunity to expand into her newly claimed sphere of interest gave the militarist cause new momentum. The conclusion of the Tripartite Pact in September 1940 with Germany and Italy tied Japan's fortunes to the Axis. At that moment, with the Allied war effort clearly foundering, the Pact appeared to guarantee US and British non-interference in the establishment of the New Order.

Too late, and still without adequate military power to back it up, the oil embargo declared by America, the Dutch and British as a response to Japanese moves into Indochina in mid-1941 imposed a countdown to war. Unable to count on its own reserves for more than two years, Japan was now committed to choosing a direction from strictly limited options. Faced with the choices of international loss of face, unacceptable terms, or war, Japan imposed its own timetable for the resolution of the problem by negotiation. With the appointment of ultra-nationalist leader General Tojo to the Premiership in October 1941, the decision was effectively made.

This war was an experience unlike any other. Among the incalculable numbers of people affected, millions had been killed or displaced from their homes. Nothing remotely like it had been seen in the history of the world. In China, whole peasant populations were driven before the Japanese; in France in 1940, some 6 million Dutch, Belgians and northern French poured southwards before the advancing German armies; Poles were driven east by the Germans then west by the Russians. Incalculable numbers of men and women were transferred from Poland, France, the Channel Islands and Russia, to work as slave labour for the Reich. By 1944 millions of German civilians were fleeing from the advancing Soviet armies. Huge numbers of soldiers were also moved to distant battle-fields: thousands of young Australians found themselves in the desert in Africa, or on a mid-ocean island in the Pacific; some 8 million young Americans found themselves strung out across the globe at Guadalcanal, or Norfolk, England, Normandy or on the Rhine. In the last days Siberians took Berlin; a Polish Army found itself in Persia, a Brazilian division in Italy. British soldiers were engaged from Narvik to Rangoon; Italians fought at Stalingrad. An estimated 55 million people died as a result of the conflict.

In sharp contrast to the bleak images of trench attrition and the biplane amateurishness of WW1, the images of warfare in WW2, embellished by Hollywood and glamorized by the epic nature of the struggle, often appear highly sophisticated. Certainly mechanization, systemization, new technologies, all transformed the strategic possibilities of warfare, and the conflict in turn propelled technology and science into a dynamic post-war phase. The same apparent sophistication was applied by the Nazi state, as it set about the systematic destruction of whole racial populations and employed technology to increase the efficacy of the programme.

But these veneered images conceal the actual nature and ultimate determinants of the conflict. The first, quite simply, was wealth. The incalculable economic might of the United States sustained the Allied war effort to a level which ultimately overwhelmed the resources of Germany and Japan.

The second was chaos. This is not to deny the staggering feats of co-ordination and co-operation achieved during the conflict, or to belittle the extraordinary endurance of its participants. It is a measure of those achievements that they were made in the face of the destructive dynamics of the conflict. That millions all over the world, civilian as well as military, survived this widespread and ruthless chaos – the dislocation of societies, the devastation of economies, the brutal demands of warfare itself – is little short of miraculous, though it was done at incalculable cost. The confusions and fortuities of war, as well as its destructiveness, formed a great part of its momentum. Mistakes and miscalculations often played as great a part as strategy and tactics. Hindsight should not allow us to diminish this ruthless chaos, which presided over the action on all levels during WW2.

Note on Technical Data

Entries for aircraft, tanks and major warships are accompanied by a brief summary of the weapon's specifications. Abbreviations used are as follows: AA – antiaircraft; b – beam; DP – dual purpose (air/surface); FD – flight deck; hp – horsepower; lb – pound weight; lgth – length; m – miles; mg – machine-gun; o/a – overall; pdr – pounder; TT – torpedo tube. Measures are given in feet and inches; ships' displacements are standard unless stated and all figures for operational range give normal range unless stated. Aircraft are entered under the name of the designer/manufacturer (e.g. *Heinkel* He111, *Bristol* Beaufighter), except for US bombers, fighters and transports which were most commonly known by their B-, P- or C- prefix (e.g. B-17, P-40). This has been done for ease of textual reference.

A

Aachen The first German city to fall to the Allies in the autumn of 1944. Units of the US 1st Army crossed the German frontier on 11 September and troops of the 7th Corps penetrated the first two belts of fortified West Wall defences which encompassed the city. German reinforcements were quickly brought up. Although encircled and subjected to heavy air and artillery* bombardment, the local commander at Aachen did not surrender until 21 October.

ABDA Command Allied command for forces in the Far East (American, British, Dutch and Australian) established in December 1941, and commanded by British General Wavell*, C-in-C India. In control of forces in Burma*, Malaya*, the Dutch East Indies* and the Philippines* and charged with the defence of Malaya, Burma and Australia, Wavell had neither the forces, logistical support nor the authority to mount any effective defence against the Japanese offensive in the Southwest Pacific, launched before the start of the new year. The command was dissolved in February 1942. It was reconstituted as Southwest Pacific Command in March 1942 with headquarters in Australia.

Abetz, Otto (1903–58) German ambassador to the Vichy* French government, 1940–4, Abetz had been a protégé of Ribbentrop* and was loyally supported by Pierre Laval*. After the German occupation of southern France he became responsible for SD* operations throughout France and initiated anti-Jewish drives.

Abetz received a 20-year prison sentence for war crimes from a French military tribunal. Released in 1958, his death in a motor accident was widely believed to be a revenge killing by former members of the French resistance*.

Absolute National Defence Sphere of Japan See Pacific War. See Map 10.

Abwehr The German military intelligence organization. Before the war, the Abwehr came into frequent conflict with Nazi intelligence departments, the Gestapo* and SD*. Following his appointment as Abwehr chief in 1935, Admiral Canaris* reached an agreement with Gestapo chief Heydrich* which resolved the conflicting spheres of interest. The two organizations ran in parallel – both had spy schools and ran spies overseas. After the outbreak of war, Abwehr stations, based on army districts, opened throughout occupied Europe and in tolerant neutral countries including Portugal*, Spain, Sweden*, Switzerland and Turkey. The Hamburg office supervised agents in Britain and the US.

As a military rather than party organization, the Abwehr attracted non-Nazi and anti-Nazi members. With the encouragement of Canaris, whose chief assistant Hans Oster* actively promoted resistance activities using Abwehr contacts, Abwehr personnel were an important element of the opposition to Hitler's regime. They were deeply involved in the preparations for the July Bomb* attempt on Hitler's life in 1944, although by this time the organization's loyalty was crucially compromised and its functions heavily eroded by the SD. Finally, in 1944, the defection of two German agents to the British in Turkey following the Abwehr's failure to predict Allied moves in Northwest Europe gave Himmler* an opportunity to take over. In June Kaltenbrunner absorbed the Abwehr into his SS* RSHA department and the Abwehr was formally dissolved. See also Resistance: Germany.

Accolade Code-name for an Allied plan, encouraged by Churchill*, to capture the Greek island of Rhodes, along with other Aegean islands, after the conquest of Sicily* in 1943. The plan was opposed by American military chiefs, notably General Marshall*, American Chief of Staff.

Ace Generally used to describe a fighter pilot credited with destroying more than five hostile aircraft in combat. Credits for confirmed 'kills' were often claimed by more than one pilot which produced anomalies in the international scoring system. French pilots, for example, were given a full credit for each victory in which they were involved, but US air forces and the RAF* divided victories into fractions. Shared 'kills' were tallied separately in Russia and Italy. In Japan and Britain there were recognized aces but their importance was played down, both preferring to promote group rather than individual successes. The Luftwaffe*, which used a one credit, one victory system for points scoring but counted aeroengines for decoration purposes, completely dominated the lists of the war's top-scoring aces. This is partly explained by the comprehensive nature of the Luftwaffe's early victories, particularly on the Eastern Front* during 1941, and the inclusion of pre-war Spanish totals.

Several dozen German pilots were credited with over 100 victories and the leading ace – Major Erich Hartmann – had 352 confirmed 'kills', all but seven of them Soviet aircraft. In Japan, Chief Warrant Officer Hiroyashi Nishizawa scored 104 victories; the top Finnish ace, Captain Hans Wind, scored 75. The top Red Air Force* pilot was Major Ivan Kozhedub (62 kills) and the highest scoring American was Major Richard Bong of the USAAF* (40). The French *Armée de l'Air** lost most of its records during the Battle of France, but credits Captain Pierre Clostermann with 33 victories. The RAF's highest scorer was Group Captain J. E. Johnson (38), although loss of records probably denied Squadron Leader M. Pattle a higher total.

The term 'ace' was also applied to successful submarine commanders on both sides. Again, German officers scored most highly (see Kretschmer, Otto), while many British and US submariners, led by Commander Richard O'Kane of the USS *Tang**, also qualified as 'aces'.

Achilles, HMNZS See Ajax, HMS.

Achse (Axis) Code-name for a German plan developed in July 1943 for a military takeover of Italy*, in the event of defection by the Italian government. The Axis plan, an extension of an earlier plan Alarich*, was set in motion on the orders of Field Marshal Kesselring* from his HQ at Frascati, after news reached him of the Italian surrender* to the Allies on 8 September. Rome* was occupied by German troops and large Italian forces there, as well as in northern and southern Italy and occupied France, were disarmed or dispersed, though this ignored Hitler's specific order that all Italian forces be taken prisoner. Italian garrisons in the Balkans*, Greece* and the Aegean were similarly dissolved.

Acrobat, Operation Code-name for the planned British offensive into Tripolitania, following the success of Operation Crusader* in late 1941. Rommel's* counter-offensive of January 1942 drove the 8th Army quickly back to Gazala* before Acrobat could be launched.

Adachi, Lieutenant General Hatazo (1890–1947) Graduate of the Japanese Military Academy and the War College, Adachi was appointed to lead the Japanese 18th Army in November 1942, a command which he retained until the end of the war. Adachi led the fighting to retain New Guinea*, commanding forces retreating to Buna*, Sio and then to Madang against General MacArthur's* forces, which finally pinned down the 18th Army at Wewak in mid-1944. Adachi committed suicide in September 1947, an act which demonstrated his acceptance of personal responsibility for war crimes charged to his subordinates at the Rabaul* prison camp.

Adak See Aleutian Islands.

Adenauer, Konrad (1876–1967) Mayor of Cologne from 1917 to 1933 when he was dismissed by the Nazis, Adenauer was among those arrested following the July Bomb* attempt on Hitler's life in 1944, but avoided sentence to a concentration camp. He was placed in charge of Cologne's administration by the US Army* when it was occupied in December. The British military government dismissed Adenauer in September 1945. He subsequently became first Chancellor of the new German *Bundesrepublik*.

Admiral Graf Spee Launched in 1934, the *Graf Spee* was the third and last of the German Navy's* 'pocket battleships', and was built to the same design as her sister the *Admiral Scheer** (see Deutschland). She was at sea in the South Atlantic in September 1939, and in two months of commerce raiding sank nine ships totalling 50,089 tons. She was caught off Uruguay on 13 December by a Royal Navy* force comprising the heavy cruiser *Exeter** and the light cruisers *Ajax** and *Achilles*. In the ensuing Battle of the River Plate*, the *Graf Spee* initially concentrated her guns on the *Exeter* and damaged her badly without sinking her. Meanwhile the two light cruisers followed standard Royal Navy procedure and repeatedly attacked the *Graf Spee* from both sides, using their 5-knot speed advantage to avoid her clumsy 11-inch guns.

Damaged, the German ship broke off the action and put into neutral Montevideo for repairs. Convinced that stronger British forces were close at hand (which they were not), and anxious to forestall the propaganda defeat of surrendering so famous a warship, Captain Hans Langsdorff scuttled the *Admiral Graf Spee* with the agreement of his High Command on 17 December. Nevertheless the battle had been a victory for the British and was a timely boost to Royal Navy morale, exploding the myth of invincibility which had surrounded the famous 'pocket battleships'.
BRIEF DATA See Admiral Scheer.

Admiral Hipper German Navy* heavy cruiser launched in 1937. The *Admiral Hipper* and her sister the *Blücher** were Germany's first modern heavy cruisers and their design showed that much had been learned from the notorious failings of earlier types developed by other navies. They were well protected and armed, with powerful and well-sited anti-aircraft batteries, but their main weakness was the limited range and unreliability of their turbine engines. Both ships were announced as 10,000 tonners, placing them within international treaty limits.

The *Admiral Hipper* was rammed by the British destroyer *Glowworm** during the Norwegian campaign, but was repaired and in 1941 sank 12 merchantmen during Atlantic cruises interrupted by regular machinery breakdowns. Not an ideal long-range raider, she was transferred to northern waters. After her failure (along with the *Lützow*) at the Battle of the Barents Sea in December 1942 (see Deutschland), the *Admiral Hipper* was sent to the Baltic for training duties. After receiving heavy bomb damage, she was scuttled at Kiel on 3 May 1945.
BRIEF DATA (1939) Displacement: 13,900 tons; Dimensions: o/a lgth – 675' 9", b – 70'; Speed 32.5 knots; Armament: 8 × 8" gun (4 × 2), 12 × 4.1" AA gun, 12 × 37mm AA, 4 × 20mm AA, 12 × 21" TT, 3 aircraft.

Admiral Scheer The second of the German Navy's* *Panzerschiffe*, launched in 1933 (see Deutschland). The *Admiral Scheer* and her sister the *Admiral Graf Spee** were slight modifications of the original design with a broader beam and thicker belt armour, resulting in a marginally reduced operational radius. The *Scheer's* commerce raiding career was highly successful. Between November 1940, when she broke out into the Atlantic*, and her return to Germany the following April, she sank 17 merchant ships and the Armed Merchant Cruiser* HMS *Jervis Bay*, repeatedly escaping Royal Navy* warships deployed to track her down. In 1942 the *Scheer* operated from Norway against Arctic convoys* but was eventually transferred to the Baltic for training and army support operations. On 9 April 1945, she was sunk in Kiel dockyard by RAF* bombers.
BRIEF DATA (1939) Displacement: 12,200 tons; Dimensions: o/a lgth 616' 9", b – 71' 3"; Speed: 26 knots; Armament: 6 × 11" gun (2 × 3), 8 × 5.9" gun, 6 × 4.1" AA gun, 8 × 37mm AA gun, 10 × 20mm AA gun, 8 × 21" TT, 2 aircraft.

Admiralty Islands An island chain on the northwest perimeter of the Bismarck Sea* in the Southwest Pacific, it was attacked by an American task force, formed from the US 1st Cavalry Division, at the end of February 1944. The attack began with a landing on Los Negros, one of the largest islands of the group. Organized fighting ended on 25 March. On 18 May, an American naval and air base was established on Manus, which provided a significant advantage to American forces in the Southwest Pacific during operations to tighten the ring around the important Japanese base at Rabaul*. See also Pacific War.

Afrika Korps The *Deutsches Afrika Korps* (DAK) was formed in early 1941 to assist the Italian war effort in North Africa. It comprised the 15th Panzer and 5th Light (later renamed 21st Panzer) Divisions under the command of Lt General E. Rommel*. Although the term was popularly used to describe all Axis forces in Africa, it technically applied only to these two armoured divisions which served under several commanders after Rommel's promotion to overall command in the theatre in 1942. See also Desert War; Tunisia, Campaign in.

Agaki The *Agaki* was laid down in 1921 as a battlecruiser – part of the Japanese naval expansion programme halted by the Washington Naval Treaty. Instead of being scrapped she was chosen for conversion as an aircraft carrier along with her sister, the *Amagi*. The latter was replaced by the *Kaga** in 1923, and the two near-sisters emerged similarly well-armed and geared to high aircraft capacity, which was further increased during modernization from 1936 –8. The *Agaki* was the flagship of Admiral Nagumo's* Carrier Fleet at the start of the Pacific War*, and took part in the attack on Pearl Harbor*. She was sunk by Japanese destroyers at the Battle of Midway* on 5 June 1942, after being fatally damaged by bombs and torpedoes from American aircraft.
BRIEF DATA (1941) Displacement: 36,500 tons; Dimensions: o/a lgth – 885' 4", b – 102' 9"; Speed: 31.2 knots; Armament: 6 × 8" gun (6 × 1), 12 × 4.7" gun, 28 × 25mm AA gun, 91 aircraft.

Agano Japanese light cruiser and Class, which also included the *Noshiro*, *Yahagi* and *Sakawa*. Designed in the late 1930s but not completed until 1942–4, they were thinly armoured and undergunned, although their anti-aircraft* defences were subsequently improved. The *Agano* was sunk by the US submarine *Skate* off Truk* in February 1944, and her sister the *Noshiro* was sunk off Samar* in October as part of Admiral Kurita's* force at the Battle of the Leyte Gulf*. The *Yahagi* was destroyed as part of the suicide mission to Okinawa* centred on the battleship *Yamato** in April 1945, and only the *Sakawa* (last of the class to be completed) survived to be surrendered to the Allies.

BRIEF DATA (Agano, 1942) Displacement: 6,652 tons; Dimensions: o/a lgth – 571', b – 49' 9"; Speed: 35 knots; Armament: 6 × 6.1" gun (3 × 2), 4 × 3" AA gun, 32 × 25mm AA gun, 8 × 24" TT, 16 depth charges, 2 aircraft.

A Go Code-name for the Japanese counter-attack which was the blueprint for the Battle of the Philippine Sea* (June 1944). The plan called for aircraft based in the strategically important Mariana* Islands to attack the American invasion force headed there in combination with strikes by carrier aircraft positioned at maximum range.

Aichi B7A2 Shooting Star (Ryusei) Japanese Navy* aircraft designed to combine high performance attack capability and fighter manoeuvrability. The Shooting Star encountered serious engine trouble at the prototype stage and was not produced until the summer of 1944. Aircraft carriers capable of deploying such a long machine had not been developed in time, and the plane saw only limited action from shore bases. Just over 100 were built.

BRIEF DATA (B7A2) Type: 2-man carrier bomber; Engine: 1 × 2,000hp Nakajima Homare; Max speed: 352mph; Ceiling: 37,000'; Range: 1,150m; Arms: 2 × 20mm cannon, 1 × 13mm mg; Bomb load: 1,760lb or torpedo*; Allied code-name: Grace.

Aichi D3A Similar in appearance to the German Junkers Ju87* *Stuka*, the D3A1 entered production in late 1939 and was Japan's main naval dive-bomber in the first years of the Pacific War*. The plane was a success at Pearl Harbor*, but was increasingly confined to shore bases following Japanese carrier losses at the battles of Coral Sea* and Midway*. The faster D3A2s were first produced in August 1942, but these suffered heavy losses during 1944 and were reduced to training or suicide attack

missions in the later stages of the war. A total of about 1,270 D3As were built and some were still being manufactured when hostilities ended.

BRIEF DATA (D3A2) Type: 2-man carrier dive-bomber; Engine: 1 × 1,300hp Mitsubishi Kinsei; Max speed: 267mph; Ceiling: 34,500'; Range: 969m; Arms: 3 × 7.7mm mg; Bomb load: 550lb internal, 130lb external; Allied code-name: Val.

Aichi E13A1 Designed for catapult-launched armed reconnaissance, the E13A1 seaplane also served the Japanese Navy* in strike-bombing, Kamikaze*, air/sea rescue* and command liaison roles – often operating from improvised anchorages. Later E13A1b versions mounted primitive air-to-surface radar*, and the plane remained in production from early 1941 until the end of the war, by which time about 1,400 had been delivered.

BRIEF DATA (E13A1) Type: 3-man reconnaissance seaplane; Engine: 1 × 1,060hp Mitsubishi Kinsei; Max speed: 233mph; Ceiling: 28,000'; Range: 1,380m; Arms: 1 × 7.7mm mg; Bomb load: 550lb; Allied code-name: Jake.

Aichi E16A1 Auspicious Cloud (Zuium) First flown in 1942 and produced from January 1944, the E16A1 was an attempt by the Japanese Navy* to redefine the role of seaplanes, and was designed from the outset as a dive-bomber. About 260 were built, and they were shot down in large numbers during 1944. Survivors were later used for suicide attack missions. An improved E16A2 was still in the prototype stage when the war ended.

BRIEF DATA (E16A1) Type: 2-man floatplane dive-bomber; Engine: 1 × 1,300hp Mitsubishi Kinsei; Max speed: 273mph; Ceiling: 33,000'; Range: 730m; Arms: 2 × 20mm cannon, 1 × 13mm mg; Bomb load: 550lb; Allied code-name: Paul.

Airborne Operations Operations involving the delivery of ground forces by air landing, glider or parachute. The US Army* had planned to use parachutists in 1918, but the end of WW1 had prevented development of the idea. The Red Army* in fact became the first to try out airborne troops in 1927, but their programme lapsed following the execution of its leading proponent, Tukhachevsky, in 1937. Thus, although the Russians possessed about 100,000 paratroops in 1941, they were hardly used at all in their designated role. The British War Office, informed of Russian progress by Wavell* in 1936, showed no real interest in the field, but in Germany an experimental airborne staff had been set up under Student* in 1935, and the 7th Fliegerkorps (Airborne Division) was ready for action by 1939.

German forces had been transported to Austria* by air in 1938, and small numbers of paratroops took part in the attacks on Poland* and Norway*. The first major airborne operation of the war took place in May 1940, when gliders were used for the first time, and a total of 4,000 German troops dropped or landed from 450 aircraft for the invasions of Belgium and the Netherlands (see Western Offensive). About 8,000 airborne troops were envisaged for the invasion of Britain, and some 11,000 – including all the Luftwaffe's* paratroops – were involved in the battle for Crete* in May 1941. Heavy losses in this operation contributed to Hitler's* disenchantment with the concept, and German airborne forces were never again used in an offensive role. Instead, they operated as a highly mobile strike force, dropped into important combat zones but not risked behind enemy lines.

Churchill* was a strong advocate of airborne warfare, and General Sir Frederick Browning was given the task of forming a British airborne division in October 1940. The first British paratroops saw action the following February, when 38 of them blew an aqueduct in Italy. The first US Army battalion of parachutists had been formed in September 1940, and a Provisional Parachute Group was established in 1941. By 1945 the Allies had a total of six airborne divisions (four of them American) as well as several independent brigades (GB) or regiments (US) of paratroops.

The Allied divisions combined glider and parachute forces and were alway used *en masse* – in the invasions of Sicily* and Normandy*, for the attack on Arnhem* and for the crossing of the Rhine*. Smaller-scale units like the SAS* were employed to seize or sabotage tactical objectives, while still smaller groups or individuals were dropped into Axis-occupied territories in aid of resistance* groups.

Most airborne operations were confined to the European theatre and relatively little use of airborne forces was made in the Pacific. The US 11th Airborne Division was in the Pacific from 1944, but fought primarily as a ground force, and the Japanese conducted only small-scale operations with their few paratroops. Even in Europe, the pace of ground advances was often so rapid that airborne operations could not be fully planned before their objectives were overrun.

The main advantage of paratroops was the speed with which they could be deployed on long-range operations. Their major weaknesses were their vulnerability while in the air and their dependence on good supply routes once in position. Without these, their light purpose-designed equipment was no match for that of conventional ground forces. By the end of the war, all sides had concluded that major offensive airborne operations were prohibitively complex and costly.

Air-Sea Rescue All sides used aircraft for sea rescue purposes in WW2, and the practice was first begun on a large scale by British and German forces in 1940. The Luftwaffe* employed some veteran floatplanes for the task, and the British sent out Westland Lysander* liaison planes (with fighter escort) to drop rubber rafts to airmen downed in the Channel during Battle of Britain* engagements. Pick-ups were mostly performed by motor boats. German air-sea rescue in the region remained the prerogative of the Luftwaffe and many of their innovations – such as one-man dinghies for fighters and yellow water-marker dye for spotting – were copied by the British, who set up an Air-Sea Rescue Service early in 1941. This had no aircraft of its own but concentrated on liaison and co-ordination between naval and air-force units (the RAF* controlled British coastal aircraft throughout the war). In June 1943, USAAF* forces in England introduced their own system specifically for the theatre, which made much greater use of aircraft. P-47* fighter-bombers spotted liferafts and protected the rescue craft, while converted B-17* bombers patrolled the area dropping liferafts. The rescue craft itself was frequently a US Navy* flying boat. British experience contributed to the formulation of this system and in the Mediterranean all Allied air-sea rescue remained under British organizational control. Elsewhere, in theatres dominated by United States forces, air-sea rescue remained a matter of co-ordination between the individual army and navy commands and a unified overall air-sea rescue command was never created by the United States.

Aitape See New Guinea.

Ajax, HMS British cruiser, completed in 1935 as the fastest of five light *Leander* Class units, which replaced 10,000-ton heavy cruisers in the Royal Navy's* construction programmes at the end of the 1920s. In need of greater trade protection facilities and thus more cruisers than their competitors, the British sought to maximize the number of ships available to them under the overall tonnage limitations of the London Naval Treaty (1930), while relying on the same treaty to enforce a moratorium on bigger cruisers with 8-inch guns. With hindsight Britain's faith in naval limitation treaties seems naive, and the state of cruiser art had left the *Leanders* obsolete by 1939. Nevertheless, despite thin deck armour and the paucity of their anti-aircraft* defences,

they displayed a useful wartime combination of resilience and good fortune.

In December 1939, the *Ajax* and her sister ship HMNZS *Achilles* played a vital part in driving the German 'pocket battleship' *Admiral Graf Spee** into Montevideo harbour at the Battle of the River Plate. Repairs and refits apart, *Ajax* served the remainder of the war in the Mediterranean* and survived to be scrapped in 1949. Her sisters the *Leander, Achilles* (both manned by New Zealanders) and *Orion* also survived, but the *Neptune*, which ran into a minefield off Tripoli* in December 1941, was lost. During the war, surviving units were fitted with improved radar* and light anti-aircraft* facilities, while spotter aircraft and catapult were removed.
BRIEF DATA (Ajax, 1939) Displacement: 6,985 tons; Dimensions: o/a lgth – 554' 3", b – 55' 9"; Speed: 32.5 knots; Armament: 8 × 6" gun (4 × 2), 8 × 4" AA gun, 12 × 0.5" AA mg, 8 × 21" TT, one aircraft.

Alamein, El Egyptian coastal town about 50 miles west of Alexandria*, guarding a 40-mile-wide bottleneck between the sea and the impassable Qattara Depression. After its defeat at Gazala* in June 1942, the British 8th Army was in full retreat and vital bases at Cairo and Alexandria were threatened by Rommel's* swift armoured advance. On 25 June, General Auchinleck* – British C-in-C, Middle East – took direct control of the 8th Army and ordered a withdrawal from planned defensive positions at Mersa Matruh* to the Alamein area. The Alamein line then formed the North African front over the next four months, and three vitally important battles were fought that turned the campaign.

Rommel arrived at the Alamein line with the remains of his forces (see Gazala) on 30 June, and launched the first battle of Alamein the following day. British defences consisted of four fortified 'boxes' stretched across the bottleneck, connected by small mobile columns. Most of their armour was only just arriving back at Alamein, but Rommel was unaware of this or of the existence of the newest fort, at Dier el Shein, a few miles south of Alamein. His main armoured thrust did not capture the position until nightfall, after which the panzers were halted by air attacks on their meagre supply lines. While panic was breaking out in Cairo, Auchinleck remained convinced of Rommel's underlying weakness, and a strong armoured counter-attack the next day prevented further advance by the Afrika Korps*. On 3 July, after a converging move by an Italian division had been routed, Rommel broke off the battle. He had only 26 tanks fit for action, little fuel and his troops were exhausted. Auchinleck sought to press home his advantage by a series of armoured thrusts over the next few weeks, but these were ill-co-ordinated at field level and the attacks were called off as reinforcements reached Rommel at the end of the month.

Auchinleck had won an important, if partial, victory. His prime objective, to halt Rommel's advance on the Nile Delta, had been achieved and his decision to withdraw to a strong defensive position vindicated. The eventual stalemate resulting from the relative failure of his follow-up attacks gave the British time to reinforce their positions on a scale that Axis Mediterranean supply routes could not hope to match. As men and equipment poured into Alamein in August, Churchill replaced Auchinleck with General Alexander* as C-in-C and Lt General Montgomery* in command of the 8th Army. The new leadership maintained and strengthened Auchinleck's defensive plan for the position, which offered only one possible attack point for Rommel's next offensive at the end of August, known as the battle of Alam Halfa.

On the night of 30 August the Afrika Korps attacked to the south, between the Alam Nayil ridge and the Qattara Depression. Rommel now had 200 German tanks and 240 vulnerable Italian tanks, while Montgomery could call on 700. Many of the British tanks were American-built Grants* and Shermans*, which outper-

formed Rommel's standard Panzerkampf-wagen IIIs*. Rommel hoped to surprise the British by a dawn raid in their rear after a drive eastwards, but the Afrika Korps got bogged down in a deep minefield and was caught by the RAF* next morning only a few miles beyond it. Abandoning his eastward advance, Rommel turned north across difficult soft ground towards the British position at Alam Halfa, guarded by the 22nd Armoured Brigade. Attacking the position, the panzer divisions were pinned down by perpetual bombing and accurate artillery*, while their fuel shortages became critical. When Montgomery brought up his other two armoured brigades on 2 September, Rommel began a gradual withdrawal.

Unwilling to risk his armour in pursuit, Montgomery ordered the New Zealanders on the Alam Nayil ridge to close off the retreat, but their attack on the night of 3 September was disrupted by armoured units guarding Rommel's flank and the withdrawal was otherwise unhindered. By 6 September the Axis forces were encamped on high ground six miles east of the original front and the British command called off the battle. Although another opportunity had been missed to inflict a decisive defeat on Rommel, Alam Halfa marked an important watershed in the Desert War*. Axis forces never again came so close to material parity in North Africa and with both sides aware that Rommel could no longer hope for outright victory, the balance of morale swung permanently in the 8th Army's favour.

Despite Churchill's impatience for action, Alexander and Montgomery spent weeks meticulously planning their offensive – Operation Lightfoot – which opened the third and most famous battle of Alamein on the night of 23 October. By now the 8th Army had 230,000 men available against less than 80,000 Axis troops. More than 500 of the 1,200 tanks at Montgomery's disposal were Grants or Shermans, while of Rommel's 540 tanks, 280 were obsolete Italian types and only 38 were

PzKpfw IVs*, which could match the American tanks. Similarly outnumbered in the air, the Axis forces were short of fuel and ammunition, and the spread of sickness had claimed Rommel himself, under treatment in an Austrian hospital when the battle began. In the Mediterranean*, renewed air and submarine activity from Malta* had virtually paralysed supply operations.

The main British attack was concentrated to the north, along a narrow front a few miles south of the coast. This punched a wedge into German positions but became bogged down by minefields and defensive fire, while a diversionary attack in the south broke down on 21 October. After two days of mutual attrition, Montgomery switched his attack north to pinch off Axis coastal forces, but Rommel – recalled when Stumme, his replacement, died on 24 October – had rushed his southern armoured forces to the scene. This attack (Operation Supercharge) also became bogged down in a battle of attrition, so Montgomery returned to his original, narrow line of assault on 2 November. After resisting this for the first day, Rommel – with only about 30 German tanks left – began a withdrawal west to Fuka that night. Ordered back onto the offensive by Hitler*, Rommel's forces were split by the approaching 8th Army's armour, now with a 20 to 1 superiority in tanks. On 4 November Rommel finally retreated, avoiding Montgomery's cautious attempts to cut him off and escaping to Tripolitania when bad weather broke up the coastal plain on 6 November. Two days later the Allied Torch* landings began in Northwest Africa and Axis forces found themselves squeezed between two much larger armies. See Map 9.

Alam Halfa, Battle of See Alamein, El.

Alarich Code-name for a German plan, issued on 22 May 1943, which provided for the occupation of northern Italy* and evacuation of the southern peninsula in the event of Italian capitulation to the Allies.

After Mussolini's* fall on 25 July, Operation Copenhagen to seize the Mont Cenis Pass, and Operation Siegfried, to occupy the southern French coastal area where the Italian 4th Army was stationed, were both successfully completed. See also Achse.

Alaska, USS The *Alaska* and her sister the *Guam* were the last battlecruisers ever completed. They were built for the US Navy* in response to an imagined Japanese class similar to the German *Scharnhorst**. Somewhere between a battleship and a cruiser in size and armament, they had no true role in the Pacific War* and, although they only joined the fleet in late 1944, they were decommissioned in 1946.
BRIEF DATA (1944) Displacement: 27,500 tons; Dimensions: o/a lgth – 808' 6", b – 90' 9"; Speed: 33 knots; Armament: 9 × 12" gun (3 × 3), 12 × 5" DP gun, 56 × 40mm AA gun, 34 × 20mm AA gun, 4 aircraft.

Albacore, USS US Navy* *Gato* Class submarine commissioned in June 1942. By the time she went down with all hands after striking a mine* in November 1944, the *Albacore* had sunk eight Japanese ships in ten completed Pacific patrols. These included the aircraft carrier *Taiho**, a light cruiser and two destroyers.
BRIEF DATA (*Gato* Class) Displacement: (surface) 1,525 tons; Dimensions: lgth – 311' 9", b – 27' 3"; Speed: 20.25 knots (10 submerged); Armament: 1 × 5" gun, 1 × 40mm AA gun, 10 × 21" TT.

Albania, Italian Invasion of (1939) Italy had enjoyed virtual control over Albanian military and economic affairs since the defensive alliance between the two states of 1927. At that time, King Ahmed Zogu (he changed his name to King Zog in 1928) regarded his other neighbour, Yugoslavia, as the greater threat, but on 7 April 1939, the Italians invaded. After only minimal resistance, Zog was chased into exile and a puppet government installed – with Victor Emmanuel III* of Italy becoming king.

It was from Albanian positions that Mussolini launched attacks on Greece* and Yugoslavia, and much of the Greek campaign was, in fact, fought on Albanian soil. When Italy surrendered to the Allies in 1943, Albanian independence was restored by Germany, and communist partisans led by Enver Hoxha controlled most of the country before the end of WW2. Hoxha's regime was recognized by the Soviet Union, Britain and the United States on 10 November 1945. See Greece, Italian invasion of; Balkans, German invasion of; Map 26.

Aleutian Islands A string of bleak, rocky, American-owned islands stretching out from the Alaskan peninsula across the northern rim of the Pacific, of which two (Kiska and Attu) were occupied against little opposition by Japanese forces landed from two light carriers on 7 June 1942. Conceived as a diversionary measure in support of the Midway* operation, the Japanese later made considerable propaganda* use of this success, to divert attention from their significant setback at Midway.

Although the islands' geography and local weather conditions severely limited their strategic value to either American or Japanese forces, the occupation provoked the launch of a large and uneconomic American operation (at a time when US resources were still limited) to retake the islands and reassure the increasingly nervous American public about the threat to Alaska's security.

Operations began in August 1942 with a bombardment of Kiska. By the end of July 1943, two American air bases had been established in Adak (Kiska) and Amchitka. Attu was attacked in May 1943 and Japanese forces there collapsed by the end of the month, though at a large cost in casualties on both sides. A final amphibious* attempt to capture Kiska involving 35,000 American and Canadian troops was launched in mid-August against the Japanese garrison of 6,000 men, only to discover that the last of the garrison had been evacuated in submarines* and surface ships two weeks before.

Alexander, Field Marshal Harold (1891 –1969) One of the most respected and successful British military leaders of the war, Alexander had entered the Army in 1911, rising rapidly to become a lieutenant colonel in 1918. At the start of WW2, he was in command of the 1st Division, British Expeditionary Force, enhancing his reputation by his handling of the rearguard at Dunkirk*. He was subsequently promoted to command 1st Corps, and in December 1940 transferred to Southern Command, where he won Churchill's* confidence. In March 1942, Alexander flew to Burma* as the Japanese invasion armies advanced on Rangoon*. Unable to hold the Burmese capital, Alexander nevertheless fulfilled his prime objective in directing Lt General Slim's* lengthy tactical withdrawal from Burma into India.

In August 1942, Alexander succeeded to yet another command in crisis when he replaced Auchinleck* as C-in-C, Middle East. Alexander's partnership with 8th Army commander Montgomery* in the Desert War* was highly successful. While this success owed much to Auchinleck's well organized defences at El Alamein*, to Montgomery's tactical flexibility and to the enormous disparity in strength between the two sides, Alexander deserves credit for the supply and support he made available to Montgomery. In February 1943, as Allied armies converged on Tunisia*, Alexander was given operational control of all ground forces in the theatre as Commander 18th Army Group and Supreme Allied Commander Eisenhower's* deputy. In this capacity, Alexander oversaw the final conquest of North Africa, and subsequently the Allied invasions of Sicily* and Italy*.

Of all the major campaigns which Alexander directed during the war, the Allied campaign in Italy was the most blighted and frustrating of his career. Disadvantaged from the outset by a lack of Allied consensus over the strategic worth and status of the campaign, the Allied effort in Italy was also hampered by poor choice of landing sites, and the exceptional tactical defence directed by overall German commander in Italy, Field Marshal Kesselring*. During 1944, Alexander's progress was also hindered by the loss of forces, equipment, and many of his most experienced field commanders to Britain, in preparation for the projected invasion of Normandy*, scheduled for the late spring.

But it is arguable that, as 1944 wore on, Alexander's and Churchill's arguments for renewed offensives to break the stalemate on the Italian peninsula, in preference to a diversionary landing in the south of France (favoured by US service chiefs), were less and less well-founded. Clearly, both were unwilling to lose the opportunity to ensure a major, and largely British, victory in the Mediterranean theatre.

The capitulation of Rome* to the Allies on 4 June 1944 was an encouraging, if largely symbolic achievement. Alexander was promoted to Field Marshal in recognition of his service. When Eisenhower was transferred to London as Supreme Commander Allied European Forces to supervise the invasion of Northwest Europe*, he requested that Alexander – a sure-footed military diplomat – accompany him. This was vetoed by Churchill, however, and Alexander remained in command of the 15th Army Group in Italy until December 1944, when he was appointed Supreme Allied Commander in the Mediterranean theatre. On 29 April 1945 he accepted the German surrender in Italy.

After the war, Alexander served as Governor-General of Canada, then as Minister of Defence in Churchill's second government in 1952. He was created Earl Alexander of Tunis in that year.

Alexandria Egyptian port and the main base for the British Mediterranean Fleet. Alexandria was not an ideal choice, since it was difficult to defend both from land and sea, but it was the Royal Navy's* only large port facility in the Eastern Mediter-

ranean. In December 1941 the harbour was penetrated by Italian human torpedoes (see Midget Submarines), which sank the battleships *Queen Elizabeth** and *Valiant* in the shallows. Rommel's* Desert War* offensive of 1942 threatened the port by land, and all unessential shipping was evacuated for a time before the decisive victories at El Alamein* pushed the front line westward.

Algiers The easternmost point of the Allied Torch* invasion of 8 November 1942. Although the landings themselves were hampered by poor co-ordination and inexperience, troops met no organized resistance on the beaches around Algiers and only token hostility inland. A small frontal assault on the main harbour was nevertheless pinned down and disarmed. The most important action at Algiers, however, took place in the conference rooms, where Admiral Darlan* and General Mark Clark* finally agreed a general armistice with French North African forces by 11 November. Two weeks later the C-in-C of Torch, General Eisenhower*, established his headquarters in Algiers. The following June the French Committee of National Liberation was formed there (see Free France).

Alsace, German Offensive in, 1944 Initially Hitler's preferred site for the launch of a German winter counter-offensive in 1944, Alsace was eventually chosen as the target of a subsidiary attack, code-named Nordwind, in support of the major offensive in the Ardennes (see Battle of the Bulge). The Nordwind offensive began on 31 December, with a surprise attack on thinly stretched American 7th Army positions by the German 13th SS, 89th and 90th Corps. Attacking south from the Saar region, they hoped to gain the Saverne Gap, and meet the northward drive of the 64th Corps from the Colmar pocket, which made a ten-mile advance towards Bitche to threaten the historic city of Strasbourg, on the Rhine*. Allied commanding general Eisenhower responded to the anxiety of General De

Gaulle* by ordering 7th Army Group commander Devers* to hold Strasbourg at all costs, despite his initial inclination to withdraw the US 7th and 1st French Armies to the Vosges. While American counter-attacks stalled the drive from the Saar, renewed German attacks on 7 and 17 January, including the forcing of a small bridgehead across the Rhine north of Strasbourg, forced an American withdrawal to the Moder River on 20 January. Nevertheless American and French reserve forces halted both German drives from the north and south and the action was ended decisively with concentric attacks on German 19th Army units which had been holding out in the Colmar pocket for over two months. Resistance ended on 9 February. See Northwest Europe, Allied Invasion of; Map 37.

Altmark Incident A German supply ship for the *Admiral Graf Spee**, the *Altmark* was pursued into Jösing Fjord in neutral Norwegian waters, on the night of 16 February 1940, by the British destroyer *Cossack**, whose commander knew of the presence of prisoners secretly transferred to the *Altmark* from the *Graf Spee*. A boarding party from the *Cossack* rescued 299 British seamen and then withdrew. The Norwegian government protested at the violation of their neutrality but allowed the *Altmark* to return to German waters.

Ambon (Amboina) The second largest naval base in the Dutch East Indies*, it was captured by Japanese forces in February 1942.

Amchitka See Aleutian Islands.

American Volunteer Group See Chennault, Major General Claire.

Amphibious Warfare An amphibious operation involves the co-ordination of military and naval forces to effect a landing on a hostile shore. In 1939 such assaults were poorly regarded in Europe – a legacy of the disastrous Dardanelles campaign of 1915 and a recognition of advances in military aviation. On the other hand, Japan and the US were forced to plan for amphibious landings, since most strategic targets in the Pacific Ocean could only be reached by combined operations. In the 1930s the US Navy's* Marine Corps was experimenting with light landing craft, and the Japanese had developed amphibious techniques and equipment for operations against China*. During the Pacific War* amphibious operations became the primary offensive tactic. They were also the medium through which the Allies began their major offensives in Africa and Europe.

The first large-scale landing on a hostile coast in WW2 was the German invasion of Norway* in 1940. Six army divisions were successfully put ashore under air and naval cover, although on a scale that was minuscule by later Allied standards. Impressed by German success, the British set up a Combined Operations Command under Royal Navy* control shortly after the fall of France, and work on the design of specialist landing craft was speeded up. During 1941 minor raids were undertaken against positions on the French and Norwegian coasts (see Commandos), and the experience gained in these was used to effect in the more ambitious assault on St Nazaire* of March 1942.

It had been assumed since 1940 that any Allied military offensive in Europe would require large-scale landings, a premise reinforced by US entry into the war and the subsequent clamour for the opening of a 'Second Front' to relieve pressure on the Soviet Union. That much remained to be learned in the field was clear from the disastrous failure of a raid on Dieppe* in August 1942, that was repulsed with appalling losses. Destroyers* had provided the main bombardment support for the operation and fighters formed the air cover. In future, heavy warships and bombers would be used to disable shore defences, and landing troops were to be supported by a variety of special-purpose engineering vehicles, most of which were developed by the British after 1942.

Production of troop-carrying landing craft was largely the responsibility of US industry. These were needed in enormous numbers for the large-scale landings in Africa and Europe in 1942–4. The Torch* landings in Northwest Africa demonstrated that the size and complexity of naval support requirements had been grasped and mastered, although direct assaults on fortified harbours proved costly and there was a great deal of confusion ashore, particularly among inexperienced American units.

The amphibious invasion of Sicily* (Operation Husky) employed airborne* troops in advance of the main landings for the first time, along with an enormous pre-invasion bombardment and a fleet of over 1,700 landing craft of various sizes, including new armoured (and armed) types. Operation Avalanche, the invasion of Italy* that took place in September, followed a similar pattern although some landing craft were withdrawn to prepare for the Normandy* landings. The British tested their special-purpose vehicles on the Italian coast, and the improvised airstrips characteristic of the Pacific War made their first European appearance. By June 1944 Allied confidence in amphibious warfare had increased enormously, and the invasion of Normandy was the biggest combined operation of the war. Planned with great caution, it incorporated the full body of Anglo-American experience gained since 1940 and introduced innovations in command organization and technology (e.g. Mulberries*). Its success marked the climax of amphibious warfare in Europe.

In the Pacific, amphibious operations were basic to both American and Japanese offensive plans, and most of the naval battles in this theatre were directly concerned with landings or their supply. The Japanese demonstrated their mastery of the form in the first days of the war, although they could never transport forces on the scale of later Allied operations. They also proved highly skilled and fanatically determined in the art of defence against amphibious assault. Against this the first American operations in the Pacific were plagued by inexperience, lack of confidence and difficult conditions, with high seas and coral reefs wrecking many landing craft.

The amphibious landing vehicle was if anything even more precious in the Pacific than in Europe. Vast distances between strategic targets made supply difficult and repair was almost impossible on remote and non-industrialized islands. Supplies were further limited by the demands of European operations. This was felt particularly in Southeast Asia Command (SEAC), which achieved little in the field of amphibious warfare until 1944. Elsewhere, the Americans were quick learners, mastering the geographical conditions and developing the use of naval bombardment and air supremacy in a prolonged series of island-hopping offensives which spanned the whole Pacific theatre. Fast carrier task forces, supported by a mass of heavy naval artillery and supplied by US Navy* Fleet Trains, enabled Allied troops to seize targets far beyond advanced Japanese strongholds, although the ingenuity and dedication of garrisons meant that extension of beachheads was often a costly and drawn out business. The climactic amphibious operation of the Pacific War was the attack on Okinawa* in April 1945, involving 1,200 warships. By the end of the war, the techniques of amphibious warfare had been perfected by the Allies, but the original objection to its use – heavy loss of life among the attackers – remained. Thus Allied leaders, anticipating the dedication of its defenders, predicted the loss of a million men in landings on Japan itself – an important factor in determining the fate of Hiroshima* and Nagasaki*. See also Landing Vehicle Tracked; Special-purpose Vehicles.

Amtrac See Landing Vehicle Tracked.

Anakim Code-name for a proposed British plan, discussed during late 1942/early 1943, to launch amphibious* assaults on Rangoon*, in conjunction with combined land offensives into Burma* by Chinese and British troops from India and by the Nationalist Army from China*. The plan was finally abandoned in the spring of 1943 when it became clear that neither the agreement nor the resources were available.

Anami, General Korechika (1887–1945) Japanese Vice Minister of War under Konoe* in 1940, Anami took part in the political intrigues which brought the extreme militarist General Tojo* to power as Prime Minister of Japan in October 1941. (See Introduction; Pacific War). During much of WW2, Anami commanded forces fighting in China*, Dutch East Indies* and New Guinea*. Appointed War Minister in Kantaro Suzuki's cabinet in April 1945, Anami sought to delay surrender to the Americans, though he clearly appreciated the inevitability of Japan's eventual defeat.

His final refusal to join a group of officers planning a coup to forestall the Emperor's declaration of surrender was influential in ensuring the acceptance of surrender by most of the highest ranking Japanese officers. He nevertheless committed hara-kiri at his official residence in August 1945, shortly before the broadcast of Emperor Hirohito's* acceptance of the Allied peace terms.

Anders, General Wladyslaw (1892–1970) Polish military commander, captured with his retreating army by the Russians at the fall of Poland* in September 1939. Anders was imprisoned in the Lubianka after his refusal to join the Red Army* (a choice made by many Polish soldiers), but was released in 1941 as part of an agreement between Russia and the Polish government-in-exile* forced by the German invasion of Russia (see Eastern Front). Anders was given permission to trace and recruit Polish POWs held in Russian labour camps. He subsequently arranged the evacuation of nearly 160,000 men to Persia* (Iran) and Palestine, where they were trained by British military staff and later integrated into the British 8th Army as the 2nd Polish Corps.

Landed in Italy* as part of the 8th Army invasion force in September 1943, the 2nd Corps fought with particular distinction, most notably at Monte Cassino*, which was captured at enormous cost in casualties after three attempts by other units had failed. General Anders then led 2nd Corps in the battles up the Adriatic coast and in the clearance of the Po valley.

After the German surrender in 1945, Anders was appointed C-in-C of the Polish Army by the Polish government-in-exile, though 'Ander's Army' itself was now a political embarrassment to the United States and Britain in their relations with Russia and was therefore disbanded. Moreover, Anders' loyalty to Stanislaw Mikolajczyk*, Prime Minister of the exiled government, made his return to post-war Poland impossible. Thus, most of Anders' demobilized troops chose, like Anders himself, to settle in western Europe. Of 112,000 men, only 80 officers and less than 20,000 troops returned home. In the years following the war, General Anders increasingly became a national figure and political focus for Polish exiles in Britain. He remained so until his death in 1970.

Anderson, General Sir Kenneth (1891–1959) British soldier who commanded a division during the British Army's evacuation of Dunkirk* in June, 1940. Two years later, as a Lt General, he was chosen to command the Allied 1st Army for the campaigns in Northwest Africa. After the Axis surrender in Tunisia*, he was given command of the 2nd Army in preparation for the Allied invasion of Normandy*, but was replaced by Lt General Dempsey* before it took place. After a spell in home commands he became C-in-C, East Africa in 1945. Anderson served as Governor of Gibraltar from 1947–52 and was promoted to full general in 1949.

Anglo-German Naval Treaty In 1935, following Hitler's denunciation of the Treaty of Versailles, Britain came to a unilateral naval agreement with Germany. The Anglo-German Naval Treaty allowed Germany to build up to 35 per cent of total Royal Navy* strength. This was expressed only in overall tonnage, which meant that the German Navy* could produce larger numbers of any class provided compensatory reductions were made in other areas. With this in mind the German government agreed to state that it would not build above 45 per cent of Royal Navy submarine tonnage. Germany had claimed the right to full submarine equality, but settled for an escape clause which made this possible in the event of hostile construction by a third party.

Hailed within the German Navy as a masterstroke, the treaty provoked considerable international criticism. The French in particular were outraged, but in the complete absence of concerted or individual action from either the signatories of Versailles or the League of Nations, the British had at least found a way to bring Germany within the scope of existing international naval agreements.

A second naval agreement was signed by Britain and Germany in 1937, which effectively secured the latter's adherence to the international qualitative restrictions of the 2nd London Naval Treaty (1936), which in themselves were short-lived and ineffectual. The following year Russian cruiser and submarine construction was invoked by Germany to activate the submarine equality clause and permit the construction of cruisers above the new permitted levels. On 28 April 1939, Hitler denounced the Anglo-German Naval Treaty.

Anglo-Polish Alliance Signed on 25 August 1939, this alliance formalized the British assurances of military aid to Poland* in the event of attack by a European power. The wisdom of making such a guarantee of Poland's sovereignty was widely assumed by British politicians at the time (Lloyd George was its only critic in the British Parliament), but has since been strongly criticized by some commentators, who argue that the opportunity to safeguard Eastern Europe from German expansionism had already been sacrificed to Prime Minister Neville Chamberlain's* policy of appeasement*. In his *History of the Second World War*, Winston Churchill* gives a characteristically hyperbolic, though highly persuasive interpretation of the Anglo-Polish Alliance: 'History, which, we are told, is mainly the record of crimes, follies and miseries of mankind, may be scoured and ransacked to find a parallel to this sudden and complete reversal of . . . appeasement, and its transformation almost overnight into a readiness to accept an obviously imminent war . . . Here was a decision at last, taken at the worst possible moment and on the least satisfactory ground, which must surely lead to the slaughter of tens of millions of people.' (It is notable, however, that Churchill proclaimed himself firmly in favour at the time.) Though military leaders held a more pessimistic view of Britain's ability to defend Polish interests, the desire for a diplomatic solution to the crisis in Europe overrode practical objections. When Hitler invaded Poland on 1 September 1939, the Anglo-Polish Alliance provided the basis for Britain's declaration of war against Germany on 3 September. See also Introduction; Poland, German Campaign in.

Anschluss The movement in Germany and Austria* for the union of the two countries in a Greater Germany, which resulted in Austria's forced annexation by Hitler* in March 1938. Although such a union had been specifically forbidden by the post-WW1 Treaty of Versailles, agitation for Anschluss continued in both countries during the 1920s and early 30s. Nazi parties in both states strongly supported the political union. In 1934 Austrian Nazis murdered Chancellor Dollfuss in an attempted coup, though it was defeated by government forces and Hitler was forced to withdraw active support for the putchists.

In February 1938, however, Hitler called Austrian Chancellor Schuschnigg to a meeting at Berchtesgaden during which he used intimidating tactics to underpin his extensive demands: the lifting of the ban on the Austrian Nazi Party; the promotion of covert Nazi Dr Seyss-Inquart* as Minister of the Interior and another Nazi, Glaise-Horstenau, as Minister of War; the absorption of Austria in the German economic system.

Unable to counter the threat of force posed by Hitler at Berchtesgaden, the Austrian government and President assented to the changes. Implementation was accompanied by an emotive speech from Hitler to the Reichstag on Germany's responsibility for its Austrian adherents and a significant rise in carefully orchestrated and often violent Nazi demonstrations in Vienna, Graz and elsewhere. In control of the police, Seyss-Inquart did nothing to counter these.

With his government on the verge of collapse, Schuschnigg made a final attempt to stop Hitler using force, by calling for a plebiscite on the issue of union, but as pressure from Germany and Nazis in the Austrian government increased, Schuschnigg was unable to maintain his position. On 11 March, having telephoned Seyss-Inquart to announce the cancellation of the plebiscite, Schuschnigg was powerless to stop a series of Berlin-organized Austrian SS attacks on Social Democrats, Jews and other anti-Nazis that provided Seyss-Inquart with the pretext to appeal to Berlin for help in restoring order. Along with the German troops that crossed the frontier on 12 March, Gestapo* and SD* arrived to begin their brutal suppression of the population. Schuschnigg was one of the first of 76,000 Austrians sent to Dachau* in the first weeks of the Anschluss. As the terror continued, an Austrian concentration camp* was established at Mauthausen, where at least 35,000 people were executed during the Anschluss.

The leader of the Austrian SS attacks, Kaltenbrunner*, was made Minister of State Security, in what was now renamed Ostmark and Globocnik (later to acquire a reputation for unparalleled brutality in Poland) became Gauleiter of Vienna. A wave of anti-Semitism, on a scale not seen in Austria before, followed the Nazi seizure of power. Now in a position to revive the device of a plebiscite as a final seal on force and illegality, Hitler announced a ballot on the Anschluss for 10 April, confident that he could determine its outcome. A total vote in favour of 99 per cent reflected the brutal efficacy of the Nazi takeover.

Anthropoids Code-name for Czech soldiers flown from London to Czechoslovakia* in the spring of 1942 to assassinate Reinhard Heydrich*, Protector of Bohemia.

Anti-aircraft Defence Anti-aircraft guns were deployed with field units, on ships and around important defensive areas in WW2. They ranged in size from light machine-guns*, for use against low-flying craft, through rapid-firing 20–40mm cannon (see Bofors; Oerlikon) with a maximum effective ceiling of about 6,000ft, to heavy pieces which were aimed at aircraft in the 10–25,000ft range. These latter were usually used for static defence, fired a weightier projectile at a slower rate and grew larger as the war progressed. In 1939 75mm weapons were regarded as 'heavies', although Germany had an excellent 88mm design (see Eighty-Eight), but by the later war years 120–150mm calibre guns were needed to reach the increased ceilings of contemporary bombers.

The first specialist AA guns had been introduced in 1916. Long-barrelled, high-velocity weapons on a pedestal mount with 360 degree traverse, they had been relatively successful and their basic design remained unaltered in WW2. Similarly the major problem for AA gunners was the same in 1939 as it had been in 1918 – the difficulty of aiming at a distant target capable of performing rapid three-dimensional manoeuvres. The problem had in fact worsened between the wars as refinements to mechanical targeting aids had failed to keep pace with the great strides made in aircraft performance. Therefore the major tactic employed by all sides against high-flying aircraft in WW2 was to throw up an enormous barrage of time-fused shells in front of a bomber formation and hope that some of the planes would fly into it.

This was both inefficient and expensive. Anything better than one hit per 2,000 shells fired could be regarded as good shooting, and this assumed that approaching aircraft could be spotted in time to aim accurately. Thus in Germany the Luftwaffe* controlled deep fields of the heaviest 'flak' weapons, sited for the protection of the homeland against bombers by the effective saturation shelling of their approach routes. All sides used barrage balloons to channel aircraft into corridors of fire, and searchlights were employed to pick out individual targets at night. These concentrations of firepower could be effective given the right geographical conditions to restrict aerial approach routes, but important sites like the Ploesti* oilfields in Rumania could only be safeguarded at great cost in manpower and munitions. Fire control and command systems became increasingly sophisticated during the war to enable such concentrations to be brought quickly to bear.

That anti-aircraft gunners achieved any significant success against high altitude aircraft owed a great deal to the development of radar*. Its use for early warning purposes was pioneered by the British, whose Chain Home defence system was installed across southern England just before the war. As the Allies built up a big lead in the field, more sophisticated radar enabled gunners to calculate quickly and accurately the speed and course of their targets. By the end of the war sets were available for aiming even light AA mountings, and could be used to provide continuous information for tracking while firing.

This still did not solve the problem of efficiently destroying the target. Direct hits were rare but a near miss was often enough, and so shells were detonated by timed rather than contact fuses, which left little margin for error and none for evasive changes of altitude. The Allied development of the proximity fuse – containing a small radio transmitter which detonated the shell on interference from a nearby aircraft – greatly improved the strike rate. By the time it was introduced in 1943, Allied air supremacy over land and sea was such that it was mainly employed against V-1* rockets and Kamikaze* attacks.

Air superiority also meant that many Allied field AA units had been disbanded by 1944. For the same reason German ground forces in Europe were compelled to rely more than ever on anti-aircraft guns, and to employ specialist AA tanks (Flakwagen) built as an unwelcome distraction from battle tank* production. The US Army* nevertheless continued to fit light AA mountings to virtually all of its field vehicles throughout the war, a trend not followed by other armies.

At sea all sides, particularly the European powers, found that they had underestimated the scale of anti-aircraft defence needed for warships, which were generally fitted with vastly increased AA capability as the war progressed. On major fleet units machine-guns gave way to 20–40mm cannon for use against dive-bombers. Often in multiple mounts, these were crammed into every available space, and superstructures were modified to offer greater arc of fire. Cannon were not usually available for smaller vessels, and every conceivable type of machine-gun was pressed into some sort of naval AA service. Later in the war, the Japanese Navy* experimented with large numbers of wire-trailing phosphorus rockets* for use against aircraft, but they proved quite ineffectual.

Heavier naval weapons were usually of 100–130mm calibre, but on modern Allied warships secondary surface armament was replaced by dual purpose air/surface weapons, the best of which was the US Navy's 5-inch (127mm) DP gun. Specialist AA cruisers were built to protect fleets, and were usually deployed around the edge of a battle formation. Major warships also benefitted greatly from multiple radar installation although the best protection against bombers remained the deployment of shipborne fighter aircraft. By the end of the war, only a well co-ordinated mass attack by various types of bomber from many heights and directions could expect to succeed against a properly protected major warship.

Anti-Comintern Pact German treaties with Japan and Italy against the 'Comintern', the Soviet-controlled system of international Communist parties. The treaty with Japan, signed by German Foreign Minister Ribbentrop* in November 1936, included secret protocols pledging diplomatic and economic assistance in any war against Russia. Hitler* contrived to justify the alliance on racial grounds: 'the blood of Japan contains virtues close to the pure Nordic'. The second signatory of the pact, Mussolini*, was already an Axis* partner when persuaded to sign in November 1937.

Anti-Semitism Although hatred and fear of Jews had been a major force in the development of Nazism, it was not exclusive to the NSDAP, nor was it by any means started by them. From age to age throughout Europe, 'religious' anti-Semitism had been practised by governments and peoples, alternating between tolerance (or even encouragement) of Jewish communities and violent 'scapegoat' attacks on them. The most notorious anti-Semitic practices of the nineteenth century were the 'pogroms', organized by Russian imperial authorities, which destroyed whole communities. During this century racial motives replaced religious anti-Semitism, as theories of 'Aryan' or 'Nordic' superiority were developed by 'racial theorists' such as Houston Stewart Chamberlain, based on a crude assimilation of Darwinian

notions of the survival of the fittest. In Russia, anti-Semitism was practised by the state – ghettos (designated areas) were decreed for Jews in many cities and towns. Generally in Europe anti-Semitism became linked with conservative and right-wing politics, and often to the closely associated church movements.

In Germany after WW1, the frustrations of defeat and economic collapse often resulted in acts of violence linked with anti-Semitism. The 1919 murders of Rosa Luxemburg in Berlin and Kurt Eisner in Munich were an indication of anti-Semitic as well as anti-Bolshevik feeling. The murder of Foreign Minister Rathenau in 1922 can be similarly viewed. With the rise of the NSDAP, 'racial' anti-Semitism, which was justified in countless crude pseudo-scientific statements and violent propaganda, became a key element and function of Nazi ideology. Once in power in 1933, the Nazis sought to exclude Jews from public life, business activity, and finally from life itself. The stages are clearly signposted in the Nuremberg Laws, Crystal Night and the Final Solution*. The following is a brief chronology of the fate of Jews in Nazi Germany.

1933 Official boycott of Jewish shops
1935 Nuremberg Laws promulgated: Law of Reich Citizenship; Aryan a precondition for public appointments; marriage between Aryan and Jew forbidden
1937 Confiscation of Jewish businesses without legal justification
1938 Destruction of Munich synagogue; destruction of Nuremberg synagogue; Crystal Night pogrom, more than 20,000 Jews imprisoned; expulsion of all Jews from schools; Aryans to take over all Jewish companies
1939 Law on tenancies envisaging Jews living together in 'Jewish Houses'; night-time curfew for Jews
1940 First deportation of Jews from Germany and newly occupied Alsace-Lorraine, Saar and Baden

1941 Jews used for forced labour; yellow star compulsory; general deportation of German Jews begins

1942 Conference on 'Final Solution' at Wannsee, a Berlin suburb; Jews banned from public transport; food · rations reduced

1944 As Russians advance, concentration camp inmates marched to the West

1945 Russians liberate Auschwitz; an estimated 50 per cent (250,000) of the pre-war German Jewish population had perished since 1939.

See also Hitler, Adolf; Concentration Camps.

Anti-submarine Warfare The ability of air and surface forces to detect and destroy submarines grew dramatically during WW2, and the field was thoroughly dominated by Britain and the US. The most pressing need was to protect convoys*, and for this purpose escort warships and aircraft were vital. These were not available to the Allies in effective quantities at the start of the war and it was not until 1943 that the output of US shipyards and the availability of long-range air cover combined to offer Allied merchant shipping constant protection.

At the same time the quality of equipment enabling Allied escort forces to destroy predators was improving greatly. In 1939, the depth charge was the main weapon against submarines. This was a 200 −300lb charge of high explosive detonated by pressure at a preset depth. It was thrown from the side or the stern of a destroyer* or smaller specialist warship. Depth charges remained in use throughout the war, but they underwent many refinements. More powerful explosives were developed, their shape was redesigned for greater flexibility of depth and plunging speed, and a type was successfully developed for aircraft use.

A major weakness in all anti-submarine tactics in 1939 was the primitive nature of underwater detection equipment. Between the wars, hydrophones had been used to listen for a submarine's engines, but by 1939 all sides possessed operational sonar equipment. Sonar stands for *sound navigation and ranging*, and is a term covering all underwater listening devices using the principle of measuring reflected sound waves to produce a picture of the ocean below. ASDIC is the British name (derived from the initials of a WW1 research body) for the same thing, and the Royal Navy* placed great faith in the system at the start of the war. Unfortunately ASDIC proved insufficient defence against the U-boats. Too few sets and operators were available, while the night surface attacks favoured by German commanders remained undetectable.

By 1942, Anglo-American co-operation had enabled the refinement of sonar equipment and training to a far higher degree of accuracy, and the parallel development of short-wave radar* sets, which could be fitted to aircraft, rendered extended surface operation virtually suicidal for Axis submarines. The Ultra* intelligence unit performed vital work decrypting transactions and rerouting convoys, and the British developed the HF/DF (Huff-Duff) high frequency radio direction finder, which could pinpoint the briefest broadcasts from submarines. Ahead-throwing depth-charge mortars (see Squid) solved the problem of attacking from directly above submarines, which had hitherto nullified the sonar equipment of surface escorts at a vital moment.

From 1943 enormous numbers of Allied escort warships and aircraft carriers reached the ocean battlegrounds and, provided with advanced equipment, were formed into hunter-killer groups, seeking out Axis boats with great efficiency. U-boats in the Atlantic were forced decisively onto the defensive and the Japanese submarine service was decimated. By contrast most British submarine losses were to mines* in the Mediterranean*, while Japanese anti-submarine measures were virtually non-existent, allowing US Navy* boats almost complete freedom of the Pacific. See also Atlantic, Battle of the; Radar; Submarine.

Anti-tank Artillery In 1939, all major armies used two-wheeled anti-tank guns of 37–40mm calibre, firing solid shot shells. These could defeat any tank* that they were likely to meet up to a maximum range of about 500 yards. Rapid wartime advances in tank design led all the main belligerents to develop ever larger and more powerful anti-tank weapons. Combined with improvements in shell design, this trend produced late-war weapons (e.g. the US 90mm gun, British 17 pounder and German 88mm Pak 43) able to pierce 230–250mm of stationary armour at up to 1,000 yards. An important step was the use of high-velocity anti-aircraft* guns in the anti-tank role. The German Army* used its 88mm AA gun (see Eighty-Eight) against armour to great effect from 1942, and Soviet AA defences were generally treated as dual-purpose batteries.

The penalty for increased firepower was lack of mobility. Pre-war anti-tank guns weighed about 1,000lb, but weapons of over ten tons were planned by 1945. These were clearly obsolete in terms of contemporary warfare and all sides devoted considerable effort to producing self-propelled tank destroyers (see Self-propelled Artillery) and shoulder-fired rocket launchers (see Hollow Charge Weapons) as alternatives. Experimental taper-bored, cone-bored and recoilless guns of various types were also produced in small quantities, although none was ever entirely successful. After the war, the missile replaced artillery as the standard field defence against armour.

Antonescu, Ion (1880–1946) Rumanian right-wing politician and national leader from 1940–4. Antonescu served as Minister of Defence (1934) and Chief of General Staff (1937) in the dictatorial regime of King Carol, the erstwhile 'playboy monarch'. In 1938 his association with the extreme right-wing Iron Guard got him into trouble, and he was imprisoned for conspiracy against the pro-French government. The collapse of France in June 1940, and the Soviet seizure of Bessarabia and Bukovina at the end of that month, made an arrangement with Germany inevitable. Restored to favour, Antonescu was named Prime Minister on 4 September 1940. Two days later, King Carol abdicated and was exiled to Spain at Hitler's* suggestion. The new premier immediately established a pro-German dictatorship – the 'National Legionary State' – and proclaimed himself 'Conducator'.

At first he enjoyed considerable support. Iron Guard elements were removed from the new government of their former associate after only a few weeks, and Antonescu modelled himself on the Fascism of Mussolini* rather than the aggressive racism of the German government. Popular sentiment supported his anti-Soviet stance and Hitler, concerned for the safety of the Ploesti* oilfields, encouraged Rumanian participation in the German invasion of Russia*. Meetings between the two dictators began in November and, fortified by the promise of Russian territory 'up to the Dneiper', 30 Rumanian divisions took the field in June 1941. In October, when Rumanian forces took Odessa*, the port was renamed in honour of their leader.

Antonescu's standing declined with failing German fortunes and mounting Rumanian casualties on the Eastern Front*. By April 1944, the Red Army* was at the River Prut and the Allies were bombing Bucharest*. When Soviet forces began their advance into Rumania on 20 August, Stalin's diligent peace overtures to Rumania finally paid off. On the night of 23 August the regent, Prince Michael*, led a *coup d'état* in Bucharest and imprisoned Antonescu's cabinet. Rumania changed sides at once, greatly easing the progress of the Russian armies, and eventually committed 150,000 men to fighting against the Axis. Antonescu was later sentenced to death by the Russians, and executed as a collaborator on 1 June 1946.

Antonov, General Aleksei I (1896–1962) Red Army* officer who commanded the Transcaucasian Front* in 1941–2, before being appointed General Vasilevsky's* representative in Moscow. Posted as GHQ representative on the Voronezh Front by Stalin*, with whom he was apparently not popular, Antonov's service there led to his promotion as Deputy Chief of the General Staff and Operations Chief, with orders to act as liaison between Stalin and the front commanders. Deputizing for Vasilevsky during his frequent absences, Antonov directed the preparation of Operation Bagration* and the final Russian offensive against Berlin*. In 1944 he was chief Russian spokesman at the Allied Conferences* in Moscow and later Potsdam. He was appointed Chief of the General Staff in April 1945.

Antwerp Major Belgian port at the head of the Scheldt estuary which was retaken with wharves and docks intact by Allied forces under General Montgomery* on 4 September 1944. It was intended to be used as a major supply point in support of the Allied drive into Germany, following the explosive Allied breakout across the Seine and the retreat of the German 15th Army across northern France to Belgium in late August. Montgomery's eagerness to exploit his success and drive his forces directly towards Germany, however, ignored a serious tactical omission. His failure to clear the seaward access to the port (the 60-mile stretch of the estuary itself, without which the port was useless) held up supply of the Allied armies at a critical point and necessitated a prolonged and costly clearing operation. As a result, Antwerp was the focus of fighting throughout the autumn of 1944 and delayed the development of the Allied offensive into Germany sufficiently to allow time for the launch of a large-scale German counter-offensive in the Ardennes (see Battle of the Bulge). See Northwest Europe, Allied Invasion of.

Anvil/Dragoon, Operation Successive code-names for the supplementary Allied amphibious landings in southern France, between Cannes and Toulon, launched on 15 August 1944, in support of the Normandy* invasion begun on 6 June. Originally planned to precede the main invasion of France (Operation Overlord), Operation Anvil had been delayed due to drawn-out Anglo-American disagreements over the relative strategic importance of the campaigns in Italy and in France (see Conferences; Italy, Campaign in). Compromise arrangements among the Combined Chiefs of Staff* over the extension of the Italian campaign, heavily pressed for by Churchill* and the British military chiefs, came to an end at the beginning of July on the intervention of President Roosevelt* and General Eisenhower*, whose unequivocal belief in the greater military value of the Anvil operation was acceded to only grudgingly by Churchill. The question has remained controversial.

Now (perhaps significantly) renamed Dragoon by Churchill, the operation was mounted by a Franco-American force of seven divisions under the overall command of 7th Army commander, Lt General Alexander Patch*, beginning with a sea and airborne* assault behind the beaches to disrupt defence and communications. Little opposition was offered by the withdrawing German 19th Army to the 86,000 men landed on the first day. A follow-up French force under General Lattre de Tassigny* encountered and overcame the fiercest resistance at Toulon* and Marseilles (captured on 28 August), while the Allied forces chased the withdrawing German column up the Rhone Valley, though too late to stop the escape of most Germans to Alsace-Lorraine. In mid-September, forward patrols joined up with counterparts of Eisenhower's northern force near Dijon, and subsequently the southern force, redesignated the 6th Army Group under Lt General Devers*, came under Eisenhower's command for the Allied drive into Germany. See Northwest Europe, Allied Invasion of.

Anzio Small port on the west coast of Italy which was the site of an Anglo-American amphibious* assault (code-name Shingle) on 22 January 1944 during the Allied campaign in Italy* and has since come to be regarded as one of the most notorious lost opportunities of the Allied war effort. It was one of the largest Allied operations of the war, but the landing, by units of the US 5th Army under Major General John Lucas*, failed in its primary objective – to cut the communications lines of the German 10th Army and force a withdrawal from their strongly-held defensive positions south of Anzio on the Gustav Line*.

First conceived by General Eisenhower* in the autumn of 1943, Operation Shingle had been abandoned on logistical grounds but was revived at the Cairo and Tehran conferences*, largely on the insistence of Winston Churchill*, who was passionately committed to the campaign in Italy and the possibility of a largely British victory in the Mediterranean theatre. Bartering approval of the Allied invasion of southern France (Anvil/Dragoon*) for the necessary landing craft to proceed with the Anzio landing, Churchill ensured that planning went ahead for the launch of an amphibious 'end run' at Anzio to be co-ordinated with a direct assault on the Gustav Line concentrated at Cassino*.

Attacks on the formidable German positions at Cassino* on 17 and 20 January drew German commander Field Marshal Kesselring's* reserves to the Gustav Line, enabling Lucas's 6th Corps to land at Anzio and Nettuno largely unopposed. Lucas's decision at this critical point, backed by US General Mark Clark*, not to exploit the opportunity and push inland to the first objective, the Alban Hills, enabled German reinforcements to contain 6th Corps on the Anzio bridgehead and then mount counter-attacks which jeopardized the whole operation. Although the bridgehead was finally stabilized, 6th Corps (now commanded by Major General Truscott*) remained trapped for a further four months. Resupplied and reinforced by a shuttle ser-vice of landing craft from Naples, the Anglo-American force engaged in one of the most bitterly fought defensive battles of the war against General Mackensen's 14th Army.

On the Gustav Line a renewed spring offensive (Operation Diadem) began with a highly courageous penetration by French and Moroccan forces, under General Juin*, across trackless, mountainous terrain, exploited by Polish forces under General Anders*, who stormed Monte Cassino and opened a corridor for the American advance near the coast. On 24 May 5th Army units made contact with the Anzio forces as the German defence disintegrated. Ignoring Allied commander Alexander's* order to cut the main highways to Rome (routes 6 and 7) and trap the withdrawing German forces, Mark Clark led the Anzio forces direct to Rome*, entering the Italian capital on 4 June, though this triumph was diminished in the long term by the failure to encircle the German forces and ensure a swift victory in Italy. Instead the Allied armies were forced to continue the slow and costly campaign, described by military historian Liddell-Hart as 'gnawing' up the leg of the Italian peninsula.

Anzio Annie Nickname given by American troops to one of two German 280mm K5(E) railway guns (the other nicknamed Anzio Express) which fired their 564lb shells on the Anzio* beachhead in Italy* during the winter of 1944. Named Leopold and Robert by their German crews, these 135-foot long, 215-ton monsters were Germany's best designed rail guns of the war, with a range of 38.64 miles (improved in its final version, with fin-stabilized arrow shells, to over 90 miles) and were housed in a railway tunnel and rolled out for firing. Anzio Annie was later salvaged and is now on display at the US Army Ordnance Museum in Aberdeen, Maryland. See also Artillery, Heavy.

Aoba Japanese heavy cruiser and Class. The *Aoba* and her sister the *Kinugasa* were improved versions of the *Furutaka** Class, completed in the late 1920s and modernized in 1940. Along with the *Furutakas* they formed the 6th Cruiser Squadron with the South Sea Force at the start of the Pacific War*. The *Kinugasa* was sunk by aircraft from the USS *Enterprise** off Guadalcanal* on 14 November 1942, but the *Aoba* survived until July 1945, when she was destroyed by bombs in Kure dockyard. BRIEF DATA (Aoba, 1941) Displacement: 9,000 tons; Dimensions: o/a lgth – 602' 6", b – 57' 9"; Speed: 33.3 knots; Armament: 6 × 8" gun (3 × 2), 4 × 4.7" AA gun, 8 × 25mm AA gun, 4 × 13mm AA gun, 8 × 24" TT, 2 aircraft.

Aosta, Amadeo, Duke of (1898–1942) A cousin of the King of Italy, the Duke was Governor-General of Italian East Africa and Viceroy of Ethiopia in 1940. As C-in-C he conducted the Italian campaign in the region, surrendering his surrounded and depleted forces at Amba Alagi on 17 May 1941. He was imprisoned by the British in Nairobi, Kenya, where he died in 1942. See East Africa, Campaign in.

Aparri Small port on the north coast of the Philippine* island of Luzon*, where Japanese forces landed unopposed on 10 December 1941 and retained a garrison throughout most of the war in the Pacific*. Air bases inland were also maintained to support operations in Luzon.

Appeasement British and French foreign policy of the 1930s which sought to propitiate the European Fascist powers by concession over matters otherwise thought to carry the risk of war. Generally a pejorative term as now applied to the policy of Prime Minister Neville Chamberlain* and French leaders of the period (most notably Edouard Daladier*), the usage of the time was meant specifically, by appeasers, to suggest those steps which might be taken to prevent Hitler* taking the law into his own hands. The policy had its roots in a general and desperate commitment to peace in post-WW1 Europe, and the growing feeling in the early 1930s in Britain (and, to a lesser extent, in France), that the terms imposed on Germany by the Versailles Treaty had been impossibly harsh (see Introduction). The justice of Adolf Hitler's demand for a rearmed Germany and the restoration of 'German' territories (such as the Rhineland) was largely accepted by Chamberlain. By appeasing Hitler, and reaching direct agreements over these demands, Chamberlain believed he could lay the basis for a lasting European peace.

In practice, however, appeasement was quickly compromised by the increasingly blatant opportunism of Hitler, Mussolini* and even Franco*. By 1938, Chamberlain had recognized Mussolini's bloody conquest of Ethiopia (Abyssinia), accepted international intervention in the Spanish Civil War and tolerated the German annexation of Austria* (see Anschluss). At Munich* in 1938, having clearly decided privately to accede to Hitler on the issue of the Sudeten Germans months before, Chamberlain performed his most notorious last act of appeasement (see Czechoslovakia; Henlein). Persuaded that this would be Hitler's last demand, he returned from Munich in September announcing 'Peace with honour!' to reporters at the airport. This final act of appeasement surprised Hitler, who had expected a confrontation over the Sudetenland, and dismayed his critics in Germany, who had hoped for outside support to overthrow the Nazi regime (see Halder; Beck; Kleist). When Hitler marched into Czechoslovakia in March 1939 it was finally clear to Chamberlain that appeasement had failed.

Arado Ar196 The Ar196A1 was introduced in 1939 as a spotter plane aboard the German Navy's* principal warships, and was followed early in 1940 by the more powerfully armed Ar196A3. Intended primarily for coastal reconnaissance and patrol, it also flew as a convoy* escort and as the 'eyes' of auxiliary commerce raiders (see Hilfskreuzer). A useful and popular aircraft, it remained in front-line service almost until the end of the war. Before production ended in 1944, 593 machines were built, including a small number manufactured in the Netherlands and France.

BRIEF DATA (Ar196A3) Type: 2-seat reconnaissance/patrol floatplane; Engine: 1 × 970hp BMW; Max speed: 193mph; Ceiling: 23,000'; Range: 670m; Arms: 2 × 20mm cannon, 3 × 7.9mm mg; Bomb load: 220lb.

Arado Ar234 Blitz The world's first operational jet bomber. The German Blitz incorporated many technological features not then available to the Allies and began Luftwaffe* service in August 1944 as the Ar234B1 reconnaissance aircraft. Operating over Britain and Italy*, these proved virtually impossible for Allied fighters to catch or shoot down, and the few Ar234B2 bombers which entered the war at the Battle of the Bulge* in December 1944 were equally elusive. Although a four-engined Ar234C model was developed, large-scale production of new aircraft designs was impossible in Germany in the last year of the war and only 38 Ar234s of all types (including two night fighters) were in service by April 1945.

BRIEF DATA (Ar234B2) Type: single-seat reconnaissance/bomber; Engines: 2 × Junkers 004B turbojet; Max speed: 461mph; Range: 700m (full); Arms: 2 × 20mm cannon; Bomb load: 3,300lb (external).

Arakan Southwestern coastal area of Burma*, on the Bay of Bengal, and initially the site of a limited and unsuccessful counter-offensive against Japanese occupying forces by Allied forces under British General Wavell* (then Supreme Allied Commander in Southeast Asia). By May 1942, the Japanese 15th Army under Lt General Iida* had decisively driven the Allies out of Burma and achieved the planned frontier of Japanese expansion in Southeast Asia (see Pacific War). While the monsoons halted further operations,

Japan consolidated her positions, and General Wavell (in uneasy collaboration with Chiang Kai-shek* and his abrasive deputy, General Stilwell*, in China*) made plans for the reconquest of Burma, to begin in November with the onset of the dry season. Subject to the wider political and military problems facing the Combined Chiefs of Staff*, who allocated a low priority to this theatre, the Arakan offensive also faced command problems in dealing with General Stilwell and Chiang Kai-shek. Although Wavell gave initial approval to a Chinese plan to converge on Japanese forces in Burma with 15 Chinese divisions from Assam and Yunnan and ten British and Indian divisions, Chiang withdrew his support at the last minute. Exasperated by what he saw as Wavell's faltering commitment, Chiang was unprepared to accept Wavell's hesitation, though it was chiefly based on his concern that there was insufficient air and naval support to cover the planned land operations.

In September 1942 Wavell nevertheless made the decision to mount a limited Arakan offensive, aiming to launch a force south from Chittagong on a drive down the Mayu peninsula, in combination with a seaborne assault on Akyab island, to recapture air bases for further operations. The plan for the amphibious* assault had to be abandoned due to lack of equipment and naval support, but the attack down the Mayu Peninsula was launched in mid-December. It was halted across the estuary of the Mayu River within two weeks by a reinforced Japanese force under General Iida.

Despite protests during February from General Irwin, the British Commander of the Eastern Army, that his troops were suffering too badly from the malarial conditions to continue, Wavell, under pressure from Churchill*, ordered the advance to continue. Outflanked by Japanese forces under Lt General Koga* and left stranded as the Japanese advanced northwards from the Mayu River towards the Maungdaw–Buthidaung line, the offensive collapsed.

An attempt by Lt General Slim*, who took over command of the remains of the Arakan forces on 14 April, to trap the Japanese proved too much for his exhausted troops. At the beginning of May Buthidaung and Maungdaw were abandoned to the Japanese, who halted their offensive on that line. By the end of the month the Allied troops were back on the line they had held six months before. See Map 24.

Arcadia (1st Washington) Conference See Conferences, Allied.

Arctic Convoys Allied convoys* carrying war supplies to Russia from Great Britain, taking the shortest route to Murmansk (northern Russia's only major ice-free port) or Archangel round the western tip of Norway. Their main value was political rather than material. Arctic convoys provided tangible proof of the Western Allies' commitment to the Soviet Union, and maintained some sort of running response to Stalin's urgent demands for a 'Second Front'. Militarily they were almost indefensible. The threat of German air and naval forces based in Norway* combined with appalling weather conditions to make the Arctic runs among the most dangerous operations of the war.

The first Arctic convoy sailed from Britain in September 1941, and only one merchant ship was lost that year. Thirteen convoys sailed in 1942, and they were subjected to a series of powerful attacks from heavily reinforced German U-boat and aircraft forces, backed by the threat of major surface warships. The sinking of 60 ships from these attacks was compounded by heavy loss of life in waters too cold for human survival.

The most disastrous convoy of 1942 was eastbound PQ17, which sailed in June with 34 ships. Believing incorrectly that PQ17 was about to be attacked by the German battleship *Tirpitz**, the British Admiralty ordered the convoy to scatter on 4 July. The result was a massacre and only 13 ships reached their destination. The next

convoy, PQ18, did not sail until September and was given a much stronger escort. Although 13 out of 40 ships were sunk, Luftwaffe* and U-boat losses were also serious. The German surface warships in Norway remained a largely unseen threat, but their mere presence kept a considerable Royal Navy* force in the area.

Only six convoys sailed in 1943, none at all during the longer days from March to November. The increase in Allied antisubmarine* strength which reversed the situation in the Battle of the Atlantic* also substantially improved the chances of merchantmen in the Arctic. Luftwaffe strength declined in Norway and by 1944 the major German naval surface units had been put out of action. Thirteen more convoys sailed in 1944–5 and only 13 more ships were sunk in total.

In all, 4 million tons of supplies were shipped to the Soviet Union by the Arctic route, including 5,000 tanks and over 7,000 aircraft. Eighteen Allied warships were sunk defending the convoys and the German Navy* lost 38 U-boats, a battlecruiser (the *Scharnhorst**) and two destroyers. Despite constant Russian demands for more Arctic convoys throughout the war, the Red Navy* played only a small part in the running battle which surrounded them, offering only limited protection in Russian coastal waters.

Ardennes Heavily wooded and semimountainous frontier region of southern Belgium on the border with Germany, north of the Maginot Line*, it was shortsightedly considered impassable to tanks* by British and French military chiefs at the start of the war. Weakly garrisoned with reserve divisions of the Belgian 2nd and 9th Armies, the Ardennes was penetrated on 10 May 1940, by seven panzer divisions, (including General Guderian's* 19th Corps and General Rommel's* 7th Panzer Division) at the spearhead of General Rundstedt's* Army Group A, driving across the Belgian and Luxembourg borders along the narrow Ardennes roadways, in accordance with the German attack plan for the Western Offensive* (see Manstein Plan). Reaching the Meuse River at Dinant on 12 May, Rommel's division crossed it the following day against Corap's withdrawing 9th Army, followed by a successful assault crossing further south at Sédan by Guderian's forces. Despite stubborn resistance from Belgian and French forces, which held up General Hoth's panzers on the Meuse at Montherme and Mézières until 15 May, the armoured German advance westward towards the coast could not be halted (see Map 3).

In 1944, following the successful Allied invasion of Northwest Europe*, the Ardennes was chosen by Hitler as the location of a last-ditch winter counter-offensive against the invading Allied forces (see Battle of the Bulge).

Area Bombing The strategy of night-time blanket bombing of urban areas, often of civilian population, formed a significant and controversial part of the Allied air war against Germany. The policy had roots in the British air doctrine between the wars, which also had its proponents in Europe and the US. This emphasized the potential of large-scale bombing offensives as a means to achieve victory independently of armies and navies, and the RAF* was primarily developed to carry them out.

At the outbreak of the war both the RAF and the Luftwaffe* were restricted to attacking military targets. Both expected to succeed with daylight raids but were forced to switch to night bombing because of crippling bomber losses suffered in large-scale strategic attacks. This dramatically reduced accuracy and, when the British sought an offensive role in the European air war after the Battle of Britain*, gave rise to the policy of area bombing in the absence of any other viable role for Bomber Command's strategic forces. Its object was to devastate large, often heavily-populated areas in order to undermine the morale of the German people and dislocate German industry.

Area bombing was seen within the RAF as an opportunity to win the war quickly and without the need for an invasion of mainland Europe, a view particularly associated with Air Marshal Sir Arthur Harris*, head of RAF Bomber Command from February 1942, but also shared by many outside the service who feared a repetition of the costly trench warfare of 1917 or who sought revenge for the Luftwaffe's blitz* on British cities.

Throughout 1942 and 1943 this devastating air campaign killed an estimated 600,000 civilians and destroyed or damaged some 6 million homes in the Ruhr, Hamburg, Nuremberg, Munich, Cologne and Berlin. Discussion about the moral acceptability of the strategy was little in evidence, although Churchill* and US air chiefs (notably General Eaker*, Commander of the US 8th Air Force) did occasionally question its effectiveness, which fell well below RAF expectations. Nevertheless, it was maintained until the end of the war, and interrupted only by the temporary diversion of strategic bombing forces to direct support for the invasion of Normandy* in mid-1944.

The culmination of the policy came in early 1945. A massive attack on Dresden in February, one of the most controversial of the war, was followed in March by USAAF* attacks on Japanese cities. Both offensives caused enormous loss of life. In Germany few believed that 'terror bombing' had any other object than the highest possible civilian casualties, and it is strongly argued today that the destruction of cities as advocated by Harris was a major war crime. See also Strategic Bombing Offensive.

Argentan-Falaise The Argentan-Falaise Gap described the distance separating US and Canadian forces attempting to close the Falaise pocket, in northern France, in August 1944. Thirty-five thousand Germans escaped from the pocket before it was closed, trapping roughly 50,000 troops and much of the equipment. Failure to close the gap sooner caused antagonism among the Allies. See Northwest Europe, Allied Invasion of.

Arima, Rear Admiral Masafumi (1895–1944) Commander of the Japanese 26th Naval Air Flotilla, he has posthumously come to be regarded as the first Kamikaze* pilot of the Japanese Navy*. Immediately before the launch of a strike against the American carrier force which had been bombing Formosa prior to the Luzon* landings, Rear Admiral Arima dramatically declared his intention to crash into a US carrier and not return alive by ripping off his badges of rank. The force of 86 aircraft dive-bombed but did not sink the US carrier *Franklin**. Twenty pilots, including Arima, were lost in the attack.

Arizona, USS. See Pennsylvania, USS.

Arkansas, USS. Commissioned in 1912, and rebuilt in 1925–7, the *Arkansas* was the US Navy's* oldest battleship in 1941. Her sister ship, the *Wyoming*, had been retired in 1932, but the *Arkansas* had her retirement postponed by the outbreak of WW2. She served at first in the Atlantic on training and troop convoy duties, but returned to front-line action in 1944, providing shore bombardment in support of Allied landings in Normandy* and the Anvil/Dragoon* invasion of southern France. Like all American battleships before 1941, she was built for strength at the expense of speed. Along with wartime improvements in radar* and anti-aircraft* capability, this well-equipped her for the gunnery support role, which she repeated at Iwo Jima* and Okinawa* in 1945, before ending her days as a target vessel at Bikini Atoll the following year.
BRIEF DATA (1941) Displacement: 26,100 tons; Dimensions: o/a lgth – 562' 6", b – 106' 3"; Speed: 20.5 knots; Armament: 12 × 12" gun (6 × 2), 16 × 5" gun, 8 × 3" AA gun, 4 × 3pdr AA gun, 3 aircraft.

Ark Royal, HMS The only modern aircraft carrier available to the Royal Navy* in 1939. The *Ark Royal* was begun in 1934 and built comfortably within the relatively generous tonnage limits applied to individual carriers by the current Washington and London Naval Treaties. She benefitted greatly from the wealth of design experience gained by the British through their many experimental carrier conversions, and was the world's outstanding ship of her type at the time of her completion in 1938. She was fast, manoeuvrable, well-armed and a stable platform for a large force of aircraft. In view of the poor quality of British naval aircraft development, she needed to be (see Fleet Air Arm).

The *Ark Royal's* war career was short but distinctly high-profile. In 1940 she saw action off Norway* before joining Force H* based on Gibraltar* in time for the attacks on French bases at Mers-el-Kébir* and Dakar*. In May the following year the *Ark Royal* played a prominent part in the sinking of the *Bismarck**, her aircraft fatally wrecking the German battleship's steering gear. Involved also in numerous Mediterranean* operations, she was the subject of a loud propaganda* campaign, sparked by an optimistic German report of her demise early in the war. The *Ark Royal* was eventually destroyed by a single torpedo* from the *U-81*, 30 miles off Gibraltar. Hit on 13 November 1941, she was gradually overcome by flooding and sank the following day, with the loss of only one life.
BRIEF DATA (1939) Displacement: 22,000 tons; Dimensions: o/a lgth – 800', b – 94' 9"; Speed: 30.75 knots; Armament: 16 × 4.5" DP gun, 48 × 2pdr AA gun, 32 × 0.5" AA gun, 60 aircraft.

Armed Merchant Cruisers Some 60 passenger liners were taken over by the Royal Navy* from 1939 and converted as Armed Merchant Cruisers, to make good a shortfall in regular light cruisers for trade protection. Given armament (where available) up to light cruiser level and thinly armoured, these relatively slow and bulky vessels fared badly when they came up against true war-ships. Fifteen were sunk before they were phased out of front-line operations. Later in the war, some British merchantmen were converted as fleet anti-aircraft* vessels, armed with the latest relevant weaponry and again compensating for a shortage of real cruisers for the task. See also Hilfs-kreuzer.

Armée de l'Air The French Air Force had remained numerically strong after WW1, while other powers had reduced their in-vestments in military aviation. The transi-tory nature of air power was not, however, well appreciated and the strength of the French Air Force was increased between the wars by stockpiling enormous numbers of increasingly obsolescent aircraft. The quality of its equipment declined sharply in the 1930s relative to the British, Italian and German air arms, which were concen-trating resources on advanced warplanes. Thus although the *Armée de l'Air* possessed over 5,000 aircraft in 1938, only 1,375 of these were front-line machines, the vast majority of them close to or beyond obsol-escence. Its Chief of Staff, General Vuille-min, admitted that he could expect to field no more than 580 aircraft in battle, and that the prospect of war left him 'scared out of his wits', a factor that undoubtedly influenced the French government's atti-tude to German territorial demands.

The situation was little improved by Sep-tember 1939. With a total of only 285 bombers, supported by fighters the best of which lacked performance and firepower, intervention in Poland* was never really an option. New and more effective warplanes had been ordered both at home and in the US, but they were slow to reach squadron service, hampered particularly by the fail-ings of an aviation industry just emerging from the disruption of its recent nationaliz-ation. By mid-1940 French production lines were operating far more efficiently, but on the eve of the German Western Offensive* in May 1940, the *Armée de l'Air* could still field only 740 modern fighters

(most of them underpowered Morane-Saulnier MS406* interceptors) and 140 genuinely effective light or medium bombers.

Most of them were concentrated in the northeast of France, facing Germany. They were under the control of General d'Astier de la Vigerie, but he was restricted by a clumsy command system. Vuillemin, still the overall commander, was a veteran champion of strategic bombing theories, whose preoccupation did not extend to the formulation of modern bombing tactics but did contribute to an almost complete lack of awareness in the field of army/air co-oper-ation. Although the French were re-inforced by some 350 RAF* aircraft, these were almost all obsolescent types and were subject to the same tactical *naïveté*, leaving the defenders outnumbered and outper-formed in May and June 1940 by 3,500 superior Luftwaffe* aircraft primarily dedi-cated to the direct support of the German Army*.

Many records of the *Armée de l'Air*'s losses and achievements during the Battle of France* were destroyed in the chaos of defeat. The figure of over 1,000 combat victories claimed by its pilots is certainly an exaggeration, as are most figures based on pilot claims throughout the war. The Luftwaffe in fact lost 1,095 aircraft to all causes in the whole Western Offensive, up to July 1940. The latest sources put French losses at 757 aircraft.

Such was the improvement in French production output by June that these were being made good, and ten of the impressive new Dewoitine D520* fighters were being delivered every day. This alone did nothing to alter the overall situation and heavy losses of pilots could not be replaced. Vuil-lemin appealed desperately for increased RAF support, but as events on the ground moved swiftly, Britain's home defence fighter strength could be depleted no further. When France surrendered, a few pilots joined General de Gaulle's* Free France* movement and fought in the RAF using British equipment. Others formed the famous 'Normandie Squadron', the only Allied air unit to fight in the Soviet Union, but most remained loyal to the Vichy* government and operated from colonial bases. Bombers of the *Armée de l'Air* (and the French Navy*) twice attacked the British naval base at Gibraltar* in retaliation for the Royal Navy's* attacks on French colonial bases in 1940. The best French aircraft types were put into limited production for Axis use, and some surviving machines were reclaimed for use against German forces in the last stages of the war in Europe.

Armoured Car Wheeled, armoured reconnaissance and support vehicles had been developed since the early years of automotive transport and were used by all the major belligerents in WW2. Armoured cars could be open-topped or turreted and were variously armed – some carrying only light machine-guns* while others mounted anti-aircraft* cannon or field weapons of up to 75mm calibre. From the 1930s, Germany built and employed many types of armoured car, culminating in the advanced eight-wheeled SUKpf 234/2 Puma, a handsome offensive reconnaissance vehicle mounting a fully turreted 50mm gun. Used for command and communications work in the Desert War* and on the Eastern Front*, these were the most famous and effective examples of the type and could be driven backwards or forwards from separate controls. Germany also produced four-wheeled light armoured cars for scouting and liaison work. This type was favoured by the British, who began the war with vehicles improvised from standard car chassis but soon developed specialized models produced by most major British car-makers. Britain also received T17 Staghound four-wheelers from the United States. These were designed in the light of European combat reports and carried a 37mm weapon on a turret. The US Army*, less convinced of the value of armoured cars and preferring the half-track* for support work, opted for the similarly armed six-wheeled Ford M8

Greyhound as standard in May 1942. Japanese ground forces opted almost exclusively for tracked vehicles as light support. The Red Army* had begun the war with a variety of obsolete armoured cars, but developed and mass-produced the light four-wheeled BA-64, which was comparable with German vehicles of the same class.

Armstrong-Whitworth Whitley The ponderous Whitley had joined RAF* Bomber Command in 1937, and six squadrons of the Mark IV variant were ready when war broke out. Too slow for daylight operations, it was used from the start as a night-bomber and remained on operations until April 1942. Until August of that year, Whitleys also flew reconnaissance and anti-submarine* missions for RAF Coastal Command, and they were active as trainers, paratroop transports and occasional leaflet-droppers until the summer of 1943. Before June 1943 1,466 Whitleys were built, and the main production variant was the Mark V, which reached squadrons in August 1940.
BRIEF DATA (Mk V) Type: 5-seat long-range bomber; Engine: 2 × 1,145hp Rolls Royce Merlin; Max speed: 222mph; Ceiling: 17,600'; Range: 1,650m; Arms: 5 × 0.303" mg; Bomb load: 7,000lb.

Arnhem Dutch city on the Neder Rijn (Lower Rhine) whose bridge was one of the tactical objectives of Operation Market-Garden, launched on 17 September 1944, during the Allied offensives in Northwest Europe*. The combined ground and airborne* attack was proposed by Field Marshal Montgomery* (Commander of the 21st Army Group in France) and designed to gain crossings over the large Dutch rivers, the Maas, Waal and Neder Rijn, to aid the armoured advance of his British 2nd Army towards the north German plain before winter halted operations. Despite problems of hasty planning and last-minute intelligence of the presence of two SS Panzer divisions near Arnhem, three divisions of the 1st Allied Airborne Corps under British Lt General Browning (American 101st and 82nd and the British 1st) launched the airborne element of the attack (Operation Market) on schedule.

Successful American landings at Nijmegen and Eindhoven secured those bridges, as the ground attack force, the British 30th Corps, began its companion advance from the Meuse-Escaut Canal (Operation Garden). The British assault force at Arnhem, however, had insufficient time to secure their positions before a German counter-attack pinned them down. Denied relief by the 30th Corps, which was also held up by German counter-attacks and blown bridges, the British airborne division assisted by the Polish Parachute Brigade at Arnhem held out on an ever-decreasing bridgehead until the survivors (some 2,000 out of 9,000) were finally ordered to withdraw across the Rhine to 30th Corps' position on 25 September. The failure of Market-Garden highlighted the still considerable flexibility and sophistication of response of the German forces under Student* and Model* and marked the end of Anglo-American hopes for victory over Germany before the end of 1944.

Arnim, Colonel General Jürgen von (1891 –1971) German soldier who commanded a panzer division and later a corps on the Eastern Front* in 1941–2. In November 1942, he was transferred to take command of Axis forces based on Tunis. The following March he assumed overall control of Axis troops in Africa, when Field Marshal Rommel* returned to Germany. Arnim surrendered his remaining forces to the Allies on 12 May 1943. See also Tunisia.

Arnold, General Henry H. 'Hap' (1886– 1956) One of the first American military aviators, he was taught to fly by the Wright brothers in 1911. Arnold commanded the US Army Air Corps in 1938, and was responsible for the Corp's development from less than 25,000 officers and men with 4,000 aircraft, to a great air force

comprising two and a half million men and 75,000 aircraft. He became Chief of the newly-formed USAAF* in June 1941 and Commanding General in March 1942. An enthusiastic champion of aid to Britain and member of the American Joint Chiefs of Staff and Allied Combined Chiefs of Staff* throughout the war, Arnold was a major Allied decision maker. His insistent support for the Strategic Bombing Offensive* was combined with a great personal involvement with and commitment to the development of the USAAF. When it was granted independent status in 1947, Arnold became its first five-star general.

Arras Town and road junction in northern France, site of a small-scale British armoured counter-attack on German panzer forces (Rommel's* 7th Division and part of the SS Totenkopf Division) at the height of their lightning armoured drive from the Meuse to the English Channel, at the climax of the battle for France (see Western Offensive). The attack itself, on 21 May 1940 by a token force under General Franklyn including the 4th and 7th Royal Tank Regiments and the 6th and 8th Durham Light Infantry, could not be sustained. But the surprise element, which had temporarily persuaded Rommel that he was facing a serious counter-attack by five armoured divisions, may well have been a factor in General Rundstedt's* caution and Hitler's* subsequent hesitation over strategy, as his panzer groups approached the Dunkirk* canal line.

Artillery, Field The two main artillery weapons used for the direct support of ground forces in WW2 were the field gun and the field howitzer. The former fired a relatively light, high-velocity shell at a target up to a range of about 15,000 yards. The short-barrelled howitzer lobbed a weightier, high-explosive projectile onto its target, and was used from closer range. Both needed a forward observer to direct fire at long range. Light howitzers (usually of 105mm calibre) were particularly favoured for their mobility, but all armies also used medium howitzers of up to 155mm calibre.

The economic strictures of the pre-war years had compelled both the British and US Armies to develop dual-purpose gun/howitzers that relied on variable propellent charges to achieve acceptable performances in both roles. Both the British 25-pounder (3.45-inch) and the American 105mm howitzer fell into this category. They formed the mainstays of their respective armies' artillery and could hit targets at about 13,000 yards. Germany had also developed a 105mm gun/howitzer, but equal priority was given to a 75mm field gun. The Japanese also used both 75mm field guns and 105mm howitzers. Although of light-weight design for jungle mobility, Japanese field weapons were generally dated or substandard, and their artillery development languished throughout the war. A long-barrelled 76.2mm gun was the workhorse of the large and varied Soviet artillery forces.

Wartime development was largely a matter of refining existing designs. The US Army* in particular, backed by the vast uninterrupted output of its manufacturing base, produced innumerable versions of its main field weapons, many of which were quickly discarded. A similar diversification of experiment was enthusiastically pursued in Germany, but with less fortunate results. The beleaguered German production industry could ill-afford to waste resources on failed innovations, and periodic mass cut-backs, such as the One Year Plan of 1939, arbitrarily consigned potentially valuable ideas to oblivion. This randomness was particularly dangerous in view of the vast weight of well-organized field artillery massed on the Eastern Front* in support of the Red Army*. During the war Russia produced 85mm and 100mm versions of its field gun, the latter with a range of 23,000 yards. Light and medium howitzers were also deployed in large numbers, but in general Russian operations were supported by anything and everything that could shoot and was available. The stress placed on

artillery by Soviet strategists was demonstrated by the 32,000 guns and mortars that supported the Red Army's crossing of the Vistula in January 1945. In comparison, massed British operations in Northwest Europe* could call on about 2,000 field weapons, a figure considered formidable at the time.

Important wartime advances were made in the areas of mobility and gunnery control. Self-propelled infantry support weapons were built in numbers by all combatants (see Self-propelled Artillery), but the Western Allies also possessed fully mechanized transport for their towed guns. Mechanization in the German Army* hardly extended beyond the armoured divisions, and its field support guns were usually horse-drawn throughout the war. Mobility was further enhanced by the use of radio communications between observers and gunners rather than the more secure but cumbersome telephone system, and sophisticated artillery command structures were evolved to enable either massed attacks or the rapid deployment of independent units. Meteorological, electronic and aerial developments during the war were also harnessed to improve the quality of information available to field artillerymen, although effective gunnery control radar* was not available to any army for ground operations by the end of the war.

Artillery, Heavy As predicted by enthusiasts for mobile ground or aerial warfare, heavy artillery was shown to be obsolete at field level during WW2. Big guns were cumbersome, slow-firing and expensive in both manpower and materials. They had been effective as long-range weapons in the static infantry warfare of WW1, but could not hope to match the range of modern bombers 20 years later. Nor could they be expected to escape, let alone hit, the fast-moving mechanized forces which were to dominate the land battles in Africa and Europe during WW2. Senior planners on all sides had failed to anticipate these changes and the development of bigger and heavier guns continued throughout 1939–45, particularly in Germany, where much time and money was spent on a wide variety of radical schemes to produce long-range artillery. These were frequently intended for the direct shelling of mainland Britain from the French coast, but provided virtually no return on the investment, most of them failing to reach operational status. In general, heavy artillery saw only very limited and ineffective use in the field, usually on railway mounts and against fortified or besieged positions (see Gustav).

Heavy guns were also employed in the protection of important harbours and coastal fortifications against attack from the sea. Here again the improved performance of modern warships and the spectacular growth of air power undermined the value' of static artillery. Coastal batteries failed to defeat any large-scale assaults throughout the war and scored only isolated successes against hostile shipping.

The main use for heavy artillery in WW2 was aboard major warships. Battleships and cruisers traditionally based their strength on big guns, which remained the decisive factor in actions between them. Traditional naval battles themselves became obsolete, however, as aircraft carriers came to dominate the war at sea in all theatres and, although they remained in constant use, heavy naval guns were exclusively employed for coastal bombardment or protection in the later years of the war. See also Anti-aircraft Defence; Field Artillery.

Assault Gun See Self-propelled Artillery.

Athenia British passenger liner sunk with the loss of 128 lives by the *U-30* on the day Britain declared war. Her sinking was in violation of the international 2nd London Naval Treaty of 1936 which stipulated the removal of passengers to safety before attacks on merchant shipping. The same agreement banned the arming of merchantmen, and Germany accused Britain of staging the incident as an excuse for breaking that stipulation.

Atlanta, USS US anti-aircraft' cruiser and Class, the *Atlanta* and her sisters the *Juneau, San Diego* and *San Juan* were completed between December 1941 and February 1942 as an American interpretation of the concept introduced by the British *Dido'* Class. They were smaller than earlier light cruisers and, deployed on the fringes of the Pacific Fleets, they were well armed for their designated air-defence role, although insufficient priority was given to gunfire control. They were not, however, a great success. Too large to use their torpedoes' efficiently with destroyer' flotillas, their limited radius and the relative ineffectiveness of their dual-purpose main batteries in surface action precluded their employment with cruising squadrons.

Both the *Atlanta* and the *Juneau* were sunk during the mêlée off Guadalcanal' on 13 November 1942, and the death of five brothers aboard the *Juneau* was commemorated in a wartime American feature film. A second group of four similar ships was commissioned in 1943–5 and also saw action in the Pacific War'. The type suffered no further losses. A second wartime USS *Atlanta*, a *Cleveland* Class light cruiser, was commissioned in 1944.

BRIEF DATA (Atlanta, 1941) Displacement: 6,000 tons; Dimensions: o/a lgth – 541′ 6″, b – 53′ 3″; Speed: 33 knots; Armament: $16 \times 5''$ DP gun (8×2), $12 \times 1.1''$ AA gun, 8×20mm AA gun, $8 \times 21''$ TT.

Atlantic, Battle of the The bloody and prolonged Battle of the Atlantic was fought for control of the maritime trade routes upon which Britain depended for vital supplies from all over the world. From the start of the war the German Navy' sought with every means at its disposal to destroy enough merchant shipping to force Britain out of the conflict. Surface warships, supported by a network of supply ships, were deployed as long-range commerce raiders, while most of the 46 fully operational U-boats were ranged around the oceanic approaches to the British Isles.

The first surface raiders sank only a few ships in the opening months of the war, for the loss of the *Admiral Graf Spee** at Montevideo in December 1939. They were more of a distraction than a strategic threat, keeping large numbers of Royal Navy* warships busy in exhaustive oceanic searches. At first the Royal Navy also detached groups of warships in search of U-boats, but this policy was abandoned after the early loss of the carrier *Courageous** off Scotland.

For defence against submarines* a convoy* system had been introduced as soon as the war broke out. Protected by escort vessels equipped with the latest ASDIC (sonar) submarine detection system, convoys proved a remarkably effective deterrent. Unfortunately Britain was desperately short of both escort ships and coastal aircraft, forcing many merchantmen to sail without protection. Lack of effective air cover also hampered the efforts of British auxiliary minesweeping fleets, as both sides began continuous and extensive minelaying operations. In 1939, 79 Allied or neutral ships were destroyed by mines*, while U-boats sank 114 merchantmen, all but four of them unescorted. Losses on this scale were not catastrophic and, while nine U-boats had been sunk by the end of the year, over 5,500 convoyed Allied vessels had reached their destinations.

The fall of Norway* and France* in 1940 transformed the strategic situation in the Atlantic. From their newly acquired bases U-boats could threaten all shipping passing south of Ireland, while their range and endurance were greatly extended. The same was true of the surface fleet, which was augmented after April by the first of 11 disguised auxiliary cruisers (*Hilfskreuzer**). At the same time long-range Focke-Wulf Fw200* aircraft began to be used for the bombing and reconnaissance of even the far northwestern approaches.

On the British side, anti-submarine resources were stretched more than ever by the withdrawal of ships and aircraft for defence against an anticipated invasion. In June 1940, convoys received close escort for only about 200 miles west of Ireland (whose coastal bases were denied to British forces throughout the war) and this had only been extended by about 200 more miles at the year's end. By that time the strain had been slightly mitigated by the service entry of 50 old US Navy* destroyers acquired under the Destroyers-for-Bases* deal of September and by new escort corvettes* which were becoming available in numbers. Unfortunately these latter were barely adequate for the task and their ASDIC was virtually useless against the night surface attacks now favoured by U-boat commanders. Worse, long-range RAF* aircraft were increasingly concentrated on Bomber Command, which played a valuable part in the eventual defeat of the German surface fleet, but achieved very little by its repeated attacks on Brest* and other U-boat bases.

The overall effect of these developments was startling. Allied losses soared and almost 3 million tons of shipping was destroyed between June and December 1940. U-boats claimed the lion's share of these, although surface warships, disguised raiders, mines and aircraft all sank significant tonnage. Admiral Dönitz*, in command of the U-boat arm, achieved this with only about 16 boats on station in the Atlantic at any time, and he now pressed Hitler for greater commitment to submarine construction and for more co-operation from a reluctant Luftwaffe*. Fortunately for Britain, neither demand was fully met at this stage.

For the German Navy, 1941 began auspiciously. Allied losses continued at a dangerously high rate, while the number of U-boats in operation began to increase steadily, with 20 new boats a month entering service. By the summer, the U-boats had perfected new 'wolfpack'* tactics, which enabled large numbers of submarines to gather for repeated night attacks on convoys and threw British anti-submarine tactics badly off-balance. The German Navy's surface warships sank 17 ships in January (and a further 17 in March), and aircraft destroyed over 800,000 tons of shipping in the first half of the year. Meanwhile the disguised auxiliaries took a steady toll of surprised merchantmen in the far oceans.

Nevertheless there were signs that the British were capable of fighting back. During 1941 the threat of the surface raiders was virtually removed, and no German warship attempted to reach the Atlantic after the radar-assisted sinking of the *Bismarck** in May. Shortly afterwards most of the supply ships stationed in the Atlantic were rounded up, limiting the potential of the remaining auxiliaries. The mine menace was somewhat curtailed by effective sweeping, and the German High Command failed to follow up the successes of the few Fw200s with any effective commitment to naval aviation.

The value of aircraft was at last being recognized by the defenders. The Admiralty was given operational control of RAF* coastal aircraft on 1 April 1941, and plans were made to build an escort carrier*, along with a new generation of purpose-built destroyer escorts*. Those escorts in service were being more thoroughly trained and fitted with search radar*, while their numbers were bolstered by warships released from anti-invasion duties. By the second half of the year convoys to Gibraltar* and Sierra Leone received continuous close escort from four or five ships. By the autumn, the increasing involvement of the United States and Canada in Western Atlantic convoy protection enabled continuous surface protection to be given to Atlantic crossings as the U-boats spread their attacks further afield.

The US came increasingly to Britain's aid in the Atlantic throughout 1941. In March the Lend-Lease* Act became law in the US and large numbers of escorts were ordered from American boatyards. War materials supplied to Britain that year included valuable long-range Consolidated Catalina* flying-boats. The repair of British ships in the US was approved in the spring, and US forces began taking over former British bases in Argentia and Greenland.

From July US troops took over the garrison of Britain's vital new base in Iceland* and the American escort of all ships to and from the area was announced. Meanwhile a Canadian Escort Force had been formed in June, and took over convoy protection in the West Atlantic from the Royal Navy.

Without air cover, however, these convoys remained intensely vulnerable to 'wolfpack' operations. During 1941, 875 Allied ships (3,295,000 tons) were lost in the Atlantic, and operational U-boat strength increased fourfold. Effective use of intelligence was the major factor in avoiding even greater catastrophe. Both the British Ultra* intelligence unit and the German xB-Dienst 'Observation Service' were able to read a portion of their enemy's naval codes, but in general only about 10 per cent of deciphered information could be disseminated in time for operational use. In the early years of the war the German organization had held an advantage, but in May 1941 the British captured an intact 'Enigma' coding machine from the *U-110**, giving Ultra an edge for the first time. Coupled with a greatly improved rate of passing on information, this breakthrough enabled many Atlantic convoys to be successfully rerouted away from U-boat concentrations. With brief but expensive interruptions for German code changes, Ultra maintained a partial but vital flow of information for the rest of the war. Over the following 18 months it was the Allies' most effective form of defence against U-boats, for although the need for fully co-ordinated escort groups based on air power had been recognized by mid-1941, it was to be almost two years before they were ready in significant numbers.

The first experiments in integrated defence were carried out around the prototype escort carrier *Audacity* in the autumn of 1941, and although the carrier was lost in December the system worked well. Over the last three months of 1941 Allied losses to U-boats fell dramatically. In part this was due to the transfer of submarines to the Mediterranean* imposed on Dönitz by

Hitler, but only 26 Allied ships were sunk by submarines in both theatres during December, an easing of the pressure which owed much to the relative skill and plenitude of Allied escort forces.

The respite was short-lived. In the New Year, all of RAF Coastal Command's heavy bombers were transferred to Bomber Command as the Strategic Bombing Offensive* over Germany was intensified. At the same time US entry into the war was accompanied by the transfer of warships to the Pacific and a crisis on her own Atlantic seaboard. Forced to divide his strength, Dönitz was at first able to spare only five submarines for operations off the American coast, while a further ten or 12 boats could be stationed at sea in the North Atlantic. American anti-submarine techniques proved surprisingly primitive – brightly lit coastlines illuminating un-convoyed shipping, protected by minimal air and surface cover – and between 12 January and the end of June 1942 a total of 492 Allied ships were sunk off the US eastern seaboard. No more than 12 U-boats were ever in the area, supported by two invaluable Milchkuh* supply submarines, and the carnage was ended by the introduction of an efficient convoy system in July.

Dönitz then moved the main focus of his attacks to the mid-Atlantic (where large gaps still existed in Allied air cover), while new 1,600-ton long-range U-boats continued to find easy pickings in the Caribbean and off the coasts of South America and South Africa. New boats held up in training by the foul weather of the winter also began to enter service in large numbers. By November 1942, 42 U-boats were deployed between Greenland and the Azores*, and 39 were active elsewhere in the Atlantic. That month, losses to U-boats peaked at 729,000 tons, and total Allied losses for 1942 reached 1,664 ships (7,790,697 tons), of which 1,160 (6,266,215 tons) were destroyed by U-boats. By the end of the year British oil supplies were perilously low and, with a force much smaller than he believed he needed, Admiral Dönitz had come close to starving Britain into defeat.

In early 1943, Dönitz became C-in-C of the German Navy, while retaining direct control of the U-boat arm. The surface fleet had by now completely lost favour with Hitler, and submarine construction was given full priority as the offensive in the Atlantic resumed after a lull caused by appalling weather in December and January. U-boats sank 108 ships (627,000 tons) in February 1943, and a further 107 ships in the first 20 days of March, during which time a change in their basic weather code fundamentally undermined Ultra's ability to reroute convoys. At this critical point the material and technological strands of Allied anti-submarine development came together to drastically alter the tactical situation at sea.

The requirements recognized in 1941 had at last begun to be met by late 1942. New, fast escorts had been badly delayed by American concentration on the production of amphibious* landing craft, and the first escort-carriers had been needed to cover the Torch* landings in Northwest Africa. These were now becoming available, and their vigorous training as hunter-killer support groups was enthusiastically promoted by Admiral Sir Max Horton*, the expert submariner who had recently become Allied C-in-C for the Western Approaches. RAF Coastal Command also received a higher priority than ever before as it was realized that control of the Atlantic was vital to the supply of any future invasion of Europe.

Bombers already combed the Bay of Biscay for U-boats and, by April 1943, 30 very long-range B24* bombers had become available for mid-Atlantic patrol. These important aircraft had been held back for two years by the rabid demands of heavy bombing strategists, but could now operate with the benefit of centimetric radar*, which became widely available aboard Allied aircraft during 1943. Extremely accurate and undetectable by U-boats, 10cm radar was combined with improved depth-charges, ahead throwing mortars, Talk Between Ships, HF/DF radio direction finders and airborne anti-submarine rockets* to give the new support groups a clear combat advantage over U-boats for the first time (see Anti-submarine Warfare).

The deployment of these resources brought instant success for the Allies. In the last 11 days of March only ten Allied ships were lost in the Atlantic, and total losses were halved in April when five full escort support groups were in operation (although bad weather also restricted U-boat activities). 15 U-boats were sunk that month, followed by 30 more in May. On 23 May, Admiral Dönitz withdrew his submarines from the North Atlantic, concluding that 'the enemy, by means of new location devices . . . makes fighting impossible.' Convoy sinkings ceased completely, and in the Bay of Biscay Coastal Command aircraft fought a fierce campaign in the approaches to the U-boats' bases. Equipped with the new radar and once more guided by efficient information from Ultra, they sank 24 of the 74 U-boats destroyed between June and August 1943. This total included most of the important supply submarines, while only 58 Allied merchant ships were lost in the same period.

In terms of the German Navy's original aims, the Battle of the Atlantic had been decided. There was now no hope of completely paralysing the British war effort. Nevertheless the U-boats fought on until the end of the war, and their numbers continued to grow into 1945. German losses were curtailed by the use of *Schnorchel* breathing devices from early 1944, and new types of U-boat were developed with greater diving capacity, underwater endurance and surface speed. Although U-boat production facilities remained largely operative until the last weeks of the war, training grounds in the Baltic were severely disrupted much earlier, and few of the dangerous new boats reached operational service. Meanwhile Allied anti-submarine capacity grew enormously as the efforts of the US shipping industry transformed the escort situation. U-boat activities were largely confined to British coastal waters for the rest of the war, apart from a brief and ineffective return to the North Atlantic in early 1944. Although their successes were few, the U-boats were never entirely vanquished and 159 submarines surrendered in May 1945, while a further 203 were scuttled.

Over 70 per cent of all U-boat crews operational between 1939–45 were killed, and 47,000 British and Commonwealth naval seamen, along with 30,000 merchant sailors, died in the war with Germany. The majority of these died in the Battle of the Atlantic, and the greater part of the 21,194,000 tons of Allied shipping sunk during the war (14.5 million tons sunk by U-boats) was lost during the same running battle.

Atlantic Charter A joint declaration of peace aims signed by President Roosevelt* and Prime Minister Churchill* in August 1941. The final text, drafted by the two leaders with the close co-operation of Under Secretary of State Sumner Welles and Under Secretary for Foreign Affairs, Sir Alexander Cadogan, enshrined 'certain common principles in the national policies of their respective countries on which they base their hopes for a better future for the world'. The Charter contained eight global principles: no territorial aggrandizement; no territorial changes without the free consent of the indigenous people; self-government (or a return to self-government) for all nations; international economic co-operation for equal access to the world's raw materials and trade opportunities; improved labour standards, economic advancement and social security; freedom from tyranny, fear and want; freedom of navigation on the 'high seas and oceans'; a general disarmament to precede the abandonment of the use of force, to be guaranteed by the establishment of a permanent system of general security. These principles were later endorsed by the Joint Declaration, signed by representatives of 26 nations in January 1942. See United Nations Declaration.

Atomic Bomb Aerial bomb, far more powerful than anything that preceded it, which was first used by the Allies against Japan in 1945, bringing the Pacific War* rapidly to an end. In 1939, atomic physicists in Europe and the US were experimenting to create a new form of energy based on the principle of nuclear fission. British research – aided by German-Jewish and (after 1940) French exiles – was co-ordinated through a centralized body, code-named the Tube Alloys Committee. In the US, progress was boosted in 1940 by a gift from the Belgian Mining Union in the Congo of its entire stock of uranium, a rare fissionable material. The Americans (also helped by European emigrés) held a considerable lead in the practical development of nuclear physics to produce a weapon, which was entrusted to the Manhattan Engineer Project in 1942, under the command of Brigadier General Leslie Groves. The world's first self-perpetuating nuclear reaction, or atomic pile, was demonstrated at the University of Chicago in December of that year.

Anglo-American co-operation in the field was delayed, both sides believing they had a lead to protect, until urgency was added to the debate by news of progress in Germany, led by Werner Heisenberg in Leipzig. A double strategy was agreed after the 1st Quebec Conference* of August 1943 between Roosevelt and Churchill. A Combined Policy Committee was established in Washington for joint research, and steps were taken to disrupt the German nuclear programme.

The essential component of German research was heavy water, and its chief source was the Rjukan nitrates factory in Norway*. The plant had been destroyed by SOE* saboteurs in February 1943, but was back in operation by the summer. In November it was devastated in a low-level daylight raid by 150 US bombers, but underground heavy-water equipment survived. In fact German scientists had taken a wrong turn with heavy water, and had not received the backing for diversified research extended to other experimental fields. When a ferry boat transporting all available supplies of heavy water to Germany was sunk by a Norwegian resistance* group in February 1944, the German nuclear programme lapsed.

By 1945, broader research in the US had produced bombs using uranium and a man-made fissionable material, plutonium. They were designed and built at a desert complex at Los Alamos, New Mexico, under the direction of J. Robert Oppenheimer*, and the first of three completed bombs was tested successfully at Alamogordo, New Mexico, on 16 July. Once informed of the weapon's existence, the new US President, Harry S. Truman*, formed an interim committee of political and scientific advisors to report on its potential uses. Against the wishes of many leading scientists but with the support of the military leadership, Truman decided to use the second bomb to force unconditional surrender on Japan. On 6 August a uranium-based bomb (known as 'Little Boy') was dropped without warning over the Japanese city of Hiroshima*. Its effects were appalling, but the Japanese government did not immediately surrender. Three days later the final, plutonium-based bomb ('Fat Man') was dropped over Nagasaki*, prompting the capitulation of Japan on 14 August.

Atsugi Town in central Honshu. It was the site of the first landing of Allied occupation forces in Japan on 28 August 1945 by a small force of American 5th Air Force engineers ordered to prepare the large airfield there for the arrival of the 11th Airborne Division.

Attlee, Clement (1883–1967) Leader of the British Labour Party from 1935 to 1955 and Churchill's* deputy in the wartime coalition government established in May 1940, Attlee's dry and diffident manner was in contrast to his astute mind and considerable qualities as a statesman. Having served in the British Army in France and the Middle East during WW1, Attlee was elected to Parliament in 1922, and was an outspoken opponent of Fascism and of Neville Chamberlain's* policy of appeasement*, which he furiously, and in a sense accurately, described as a *war* policy. He played a crucial role as wartime deputy, and in the successful management of labour in the wartime economy. His greatest achievements, however, were made as Prime Minister between 1945 and 1950, when he initiated the first important steps towards the decolonization of the British Empire and the creation of the Welfare State in Britain.

Auchinleck, Field Marshal Sir Claude (1884–1981) Arguably one of the least appreciated British commanders of WW2, Auchinleck had been recognized as one of the outstanding officers of his generation during his service with the Indian Army*. He had become Deputy Chief of Staff at Army HQ at Simla when he was recalled, against establishment convention, to command the British Army 4th Corps for the campaign in Norway* in 1940. Returning to India as C-in-C in early 1941, he was chosen by Churchill* to succeed General Wavell* as C-in-C, Middle East during a difficult phase of the Desert War*. Despite growing tension between Auchinleck and Churchill, whose impatience for action in North Africa was at odds with the general's pragmatic and careful approach, Auchinleck succeeded in enforcing the Crusader* offensive in November. The following June he halted the collapse of the British 8th Army after Gazala*, stabilizing the front at Alamein* and laying the crucial defensive groundwork for Montgomery's* subsequent success. Removed from his command by Churchill and replaced by General Alexander* immediately after his important victory, Auchinleck turned down command of Persia* and Iraq* and returned to India, again becoming C-in-C in June

1943. From November he played an important role in Southeast Asia Command (SEAC) under Mountbatten*, and continued to enjoy the considerable respect of colleagues and subordinates. Promoted Field Marshal in 1946, he remained in India until after its independence in 1947.

Audacity, HMS See Escort Carriers.

Aurora, HMS Royal Navy* light cruiser, launched in August 1936, and the last of four *Arethusa* Class ships ordered in 1933. Significantly lighter than earlier British designs, these were primarily intended to protect trade routes against auxiliary cruisers, but were fast enough to double as fleet units. In the event, they were mainly employed with fleets in home waters and the Mediterranean*. Resilient and increasingly well-protected by anti-aircraft* guns, all four performed well in spite of their light main armament and thin deck-armour. The *Aurora* served with the Home Fleet until 1941, when she was transferred to become leader of the light Force K based on Malta*. She remained in the Mediterranean until 1945, surviving mine* and bomb damage. After the war she was sold to the Chinese Nationalists.
BRIEF DATA (1939) Displacement: 5,270 tons; Dimensions: o/a lgth – 506′, b – 51′; Speed: 32.25 knots; Armament: 6 × 6″ gun (3 × 2), 8 × 4″ AA gun, 8 × 0.5″ AA gun, 6 × 21″ TT.

Auschwitz (Oswiecim) The largest and most notorious of the *Vernichtungslager*, or extermination camps, 150 miles from Warsaw, it was first built in May 1940 as a concentration camp for Poles, under the command of Rudolf Höss*. Perhaps a million and a half human beings, mostly European Jews, but also Russian POWs and gypsies, died at Auschwitz. See Concentration Camps; Final Solution; Wannsee Conference.

Australian Forces During WW2 more than 900,000 men and women served in the

Australian armed forces, which reached a peak strength of 642,466 in August 1943. About 560,000 Australians served overseas, the majority of them with the Army, which employed 482,690 personnel at its peak in April 1943. The Royal Australian Navy, a division of the British Royal Navy* until 1942, was the largest of the armed forces in 1939, but grew less rapidly than other services to reach a strength of 40,000 men and women by mid-1945. The Royal Australian Air Force expanded fortyfold during the war and employed 154,000 personnel by VJ day*.

Australian forces were not controlled by an overall general staff, and the individual service commands were largely concerned with the execution of British or US strategy. The Navy and the Air Force fought primarily as components of British or US forces throughout the war. The Army also fought alongside other Allied forces in most of its campaigns, but it was less fragmented than the other services, and Australian leaders were usually consulted before it was deployed. The Army comprised two basic components. The AIF (Australian Imperial Force) was manned by professional soldiers or volunteers and was used for any overseas operations. Conscripts (first called upon in October 1939) were inducted into the militia, which was intended as a partly volunteer force for home defence. Although it became increasingly difficult to keep the militia up to strength as many more men volunteered for the AIF, this 'two army' system remained in operation in Australia throughout the war, such was the strength of popular feeling against conscription for overseas service.

Although, as a Commonwealth state rather than a colony, Australia was not bound to aid Britain in the war with Germany, inter-war governments had loyally followed British foreign policy and Prime Minister Menzies* declared war on Germany on 3 September 1939. Swelled by growing numbers of volunteers (unemployment was over 10 per cent in 1939), most of the Australian Army spent the first year of the war in training and was not in action until early 1941 although 6th Australian Division was in action in N. Africa from December 1941. The Air Force had by that time lost about 100 men in action over Europe with the RAF*, and the Navy had fought with the British in the Mediterranean* from mid-1940, suffering no losses and sinking an Italian cruiser (see Sydney, HMAS). Along with supplies of foodstuffs and raw materials, some weapons were sent to Britain's aid after the fall of France, including 30,000 rifles* and a few medium-heavy anti-aircraft* guns.

By 1941 three divisions of the AIF (6th, 7th and 9th) had joined British imperial forces in the Middle East, and Australian troops took part in the campaigns for Egypt*, Greece*, Crete* and Syria* in the first half of the year. Australian infantry were in the forefront of the early campaigns against Rommel* in the Desert War* and formed the bulk of the garrison of Tobruk* when it was besieged in August (although most Australians had been evacuated by sea before its relief). By the end of 1941 the Army accounted for 90 per cent of all Australian casualties, although the recruitment of RAAF personnel into the RAF was stepped up and the RAN became active in the Far East, attacking Axis merchant shipping and searching for German auxiliary commerce raiders (*Hilfskreuzer**).

The Japanese attack on Pearl Harbor* and the successful offensives which followed posed a direct threat to Australian security and overran Australian mandated territories in the Southwest Pacific. John Curtin*, Prime Minister since October 1941, proclaimed 'Australia's gravest hour' and recalled two divisions of the AIF and all RAN vessels from the Middle East. By March 1942 the only Pacific division of the AIF (8th Division) had been lost at Singapore* along with two warships, while the second class aircraft of the RAAF in the Pacific were being shot down whenever they met Japanese warplanes. Airmen continued to serve with the RAF in Europe, playing a significant part in the growing

Strategic Bombing Offensive*, but the Commonwealth Boomerang* fighter was ordered off the drawing board for home use, as the threat of Japanese invasion became Australia's major preoccupation.

In response to direct appeals for assistance from Curtin, the US began to send reinforcements to Australia in the spring of 1942. US General Douglas MacArthur* arrived on 17 March to command Allied forces in Australia, and Australian forces operated largely as an adjunct in the important US victories later in the year. Few Australian ships and aircraft took part in the Battle of the Coral Sea* in May and none were at Midway* the following month. On land Australian infantry played a large part in the victory in Papua and fought a bitter campaign along the Kokoda trail to protect Port Moresby (see New Guinea). The remaining (9th) AIF division in the Middle East was prominent at the decisive battle of El Alamein* in October and November before it too was recalled, reaching Australia the following February.

Following the Battle of the Bismarck Sea* in March 1943, a victory in which Australian forces again played a marginal role, Australian troops were put into training as part of General MacArthur's preparations for a renewed Allied offensive in the Southwest Pacific. In September the Australian Army began operations on New Guinea, under the direct command of General Blamey*. This was the most complex Australian campaign of the war and the Army spent six months resting and retraining after it ended in May 1944. By the end of October, when Australian Army units were returned to combat, the Allies were close to victory in both Europe and the Pacific. Australian forces were committed to a series of anticlimactic battles against isolated Japanese units, four divisions replacing US troops at Bougainville, New Britain and Aitape. They took part in a series of limited offensives, known as the 'mandate' campaigns, designed to erode Japanese strength yet minimalize their own casualties. Criticized as unnecessary in Australia then and since, they continued until the end of the war by which time only New Britain had been effectively cleared. Following the defeat of Germany in May 1945, the Australian war effort actually grew, although the many airmen still serving with the RAF in Europe were quickly returned home. Two further AIF divisions were landed in Borneo between May and July 1945, and fighting was still fierce along the convoluted front there when Japan surrendered in August. See also Pacific War.

Austria Neighbour of Germany, with whom it had strong historical ties, Austria was forcibly annexed to the German Reich in 1938 under a thin cloak of legality (see Anschluss). Renamed Ostmark, it was absorbed into the German economic system and placed under the leadership of Seyss-Inquart*. Among other appointees to the new government of Ostmark were Austrian-born SS* leaders Ernst Kaltenbrunner*, named Minister of State and SS head, and Odilo Globocnik, Gauleiter of Vienna, whose reputation for brutality led to his transfer to Poland* to run the extermination camps there. On 14 April 1945, following a renewed drive across central Europe, Vienna fell to Russian forces under General Malinovsky* (see Eastern Front). In late April US General Patch* invaded Austria from Bavaria for a strike against the rumoured last-ditch German defence – the 'National Redoubt' – in the Alps and met the British 8th Army advancing from northern Italy. Austria was then occupied by American, British, French and Russian forces. (See Conferences, Potsdam).

Avalanche, Operation Code-name for the Allied landing by the US 5th Army at Salerno* in Italy* on 9 September 1943, at the start of the Allied invasion of Italy.

Avranches See Cobra.

Avro Anson Fragile British civilian light transport, pressed into military service in 1936 under the pre-war RAF* Expansion Scheme. Cheap and easy to build, it remained in continuous production for 17 years. When the war started, Ansons were slowly being replaced by Lockheed Hudsons* for first-line reconnaissance work, but such was the shortage of maritime aircraft available to the RAF that they remained with Coastal Command in dwindling numbers until 1942. For the rest of the war, they were built as light transports, ambulances and (above all) trainers. Including Canadian models and post-war transport versions, 11,020 Ansons were eventually produced.

BRIEF DATA (Mk I) Type: 3-man reconnaissance; Engine: 2 × 350hp Armstrong-Siddely Cheetah; Max speed: 188mph; Ceiling: 19,000'; Range: 790m; Arms: 2 × 0.303" mg.

Avro Lancaster The Lancaster was the last and most successful British heavy bomber to enter the war. Developed initially as a four-engined version of the disappointing Avro Manchester*, it began operations with RAF* Bomber Command in March 1942. During the course of an epic combat career, Lancasters flew 156,000 missions and dropped 608,612lb of bombs, comprehensively outperforming the RAF's other 'heavies' – the Short Stirling* and Handley Page Halifax*. A spacious bomb-bay, inherited from the Manchester, enabled the plane to accommodate bigger and bigger bombs* as they were devised, culminating in the massive 22,000lb 'Grand Slams' of 1945. For these, some Lancasters were built with bulging bomb doors and no radar*. Other versions were tropicalized for the projected bombing of Japan. Although the ventral turret was eventually abandoned, major design changes proved unnecessary, and the main variant, the Lancaster III, supplemented rather than replaced the Mark I and differed from it only in mounting Packard-built Merlin engines. Of 7,377 Lancasters eventually produced, 6,464 were Mark I or Mark III models. Although the plane carried out some famous precision attacks in daylight, it is best remembered as the mainstay of Bomber Command's prolonged night offensive over Germany (see Strategic Bombing Offensive). By March 1945, 56 squadrons of Lancasters were on first-line duty and they remained in service, mainly with Coastal Command, for some years after the war. Production ended in February 1946.

BRIEF DATA (Mk I) Type: 7-man heavy bomber; Engine: 4 × 1,460hp Rolls Royce Merlin; Max speed: 287mph; Ceiling: 24,500'; Range: 1,660m; Arms: 10 × 0.303" mg; Bomb load: 14,000lb (or 1 × 22,000lb bomb).

Avro Manchester British twin-engined bomber designed specifically to take new and unorthodox Vulture engines. The Manchester was a failure, thus stimulating development of the four-engined Avro Lancaster*. First in action over Brest* in February 1941, Manchesters suffered repeated engine trouble in regular raids over Germany, and were withdrawn from service in June 1942. Early models had a triple-fin tailplane, but in the Mark IA, the central fin was removed and the tailspan increased. A total of 209 Manchesters were built, but contracts for a further 300 were cancelled.

BRIEF DATA (Mk I) Type: 7-man medium/heavy bomber; Engine: 2 × 1,760hp Rolls Royce Vulture; Max speed: 265mph; Ceiling: 19,200'; Range: 1,630m (max); Arms: 8 × 0.303" mg; Bomb load: 10,350lb.

Axis Originally a term coined by Mussolini* to describe the alliance, also known as the Pact of Steel, which formalized the mutual military interests of the two major Fascist powers in Europe, signed on 22 May 1939. The Axis more generally describes the series of pacts developed from Hitler's* success with the Anti-Comintern Pact*, signed with Japan in 1936 and Italy in the following year. Japan and the Soviet Union were also involved in negotiations with Germany in the months preceding the signing of the 1939 Pact, though the Soviet Union finally refused to join. Japan's reluctance to accept Hitler's invitation to join the Axis in 1939 was reversed after the outbreak of war, when the fall of France and the Netherlands left Far Eastern colonial territories (Indochina* and the Dutch East Indies*) vulnerable to Japan. Unwilling to risk US counter-action against a projected Japanese invasion of the colonies, Japan sought support from Italy and Germany, signing in September 1940 a tripartite Axis pact which committed the signatories to a 10-year military alliance.

Further, Germany assured Japan in March 1941 that it was prepared to fight on Japan's side in the event of war with the US, a promise which undoubtedly affected Japan's political and diplomatic stance during 1941. Hitler honoured his assurance after the formal declaration of war against Japan by the US and declared war himself on the US, along with Italy, on 11 December 1941. Though there was no subsequent co-ordination of war aims between Germany and Japan, nor any substantial aid given to Japan by Germany, Hitler's declaration of war on the US must, with hindsight, be considered an act of quixotic folly. For Germany, the United States entry into the war was calamitous.

Other countries who joined the Axis were Hungary*, Bulgaria*, Rumania*, Slovakia and Croatia. Spain, though not a belligerent, also sent troops to the Eastern Front*.

Azores Islands in the Atlantic Ocean controlled by Portugal*, which the Allies sought to occupy as a forward base for the defence of shipping against U-boats. Negotiations with the Portuguese government opened in May 1941, but it was not until October 1943 – by which time the crisis had passed in the Atlantic* – that Britain gained the use of an airstrip at Terceira. US Navy* forces joined the British in extending the airfield and occupying the islands the following January.

Azov, Sea of Inland sea bordered by the Crimea* in the west and the Caucasus* in the east, where Soviet forces narrowly missed an opportunity, in January 1943, to entrap the retreating German Caucasus armies, Army Group A, before they reached the railhead at Rostov*. As the final Soviet assault on encircled German forces under General Paulus* at Stalingrad* began on 10 January, Kleist's* rearguards, covered by Field Marshal Manstein's* exhausted Army Group Don, raced the approaching Russians to Rostov. Unable to retain their clear advantage over the snowbound terrain as they moved further and further beyond their railheads, the Russian forces were finally beaten to the tape. Army Group A crossed the Don at Rostov almost at the same moment that Stalingrad was retaken – and Kleist was promoted Field Marshal in recognition of his achievement.

The German Generals' respite was shortlived as General Golikov's* forces launched a new offensive west towards Kharkov* and then southwards through Krasnoarmeisk towards the Sea of Azov. In an alternating pattern of indirect preparatory moves and direct assaults, the Soviet armies wheeled down over the Donetz* towards the Azov Sea and the Dnieper* bend, in an attempt to cut across the German armies' escape corridor west of Rostov. Again, the Soviet armies narrowly lost the race, their advance now stretched further than their supply lines could sustain, and the Germans were able to rally to launch a counter-offensive. By the beginning of March, the German drive had stabilized a wide front around Izyum and cornered a large pocket of Soviet troops south of Kharkov. Belgorod was also taken in March, but the spring thaw brought the German counter-offensive to a muddy halt. See Eastern Front.

B

B-17 Boeing Flying Fortress US heavy bomber developed from a 1934 US Army Air Corps specification calling for a multi-engined coastal bomber, ostensibly for the defensive task of protecting American waters from enemy fleets. Its four-engined design represented an enormous gamble by the Seattle-based Boeing company, but when it entered service as the B-17B in June 1939, it was the most advanced bomber in the world. The B-17C introduced additional gun-mountings, protective armour and self-sealing fuel tanks, but when 20 of these much-publicized weapons were given to the RAF* for combat testing they proved vulnerable to a blind spot in the rear and their guns tended to freeze at altitude. Improved in the light of this experience, the B-17D equipped USAAF* units during the early fighting in the Pacific War*, and this more extensive combat trial led to the introduction of three additional gun turrets and still more armour in the B-17E. From August 1942, this model began the plane's long career as a daylight bomber over Europe with the US 8th Air Force based in England. A plexiglass nose-cone was soon added to the B-17F, but heavy losses to Luftwaffe* fighters over Germany called for increased armament, culminating at the end of the year in the final bomber variant, the B-17G. Equipped with a front turret and extra fuselage guns, these remained in production until April 1945, and comprised 8,630 of the 12,731 Flying Fortresses delivered.

A few of the F and G types served the RAF as Fortress IIs and IIIs, while other variants and modifications included heavily-armed gunships (X13-40), reconnaissance planes (F9), transports (XC-108), air/sea rescue* craft (PB1G), target drones (QB17) and radar* early-warning ships (PB1W). Although much older than the B-24* Liberator, which was generally produced in greater numbers, the Flying Fortress remained the predominant American heavy bomber in the European theatre until the end of the war.

BRIEF DATA (B-17G) Type: 6–10-man heavy bomber; Engine: $4 \times 1,200$hp Wright Cyclone; Max speed: 287mph; Ceiling: 35,000′; Range: 1,100m (full load); Arms: $13 \times 0.5″$ mg; Bomb load: 12,800lb (max).

B-24 Consolidated Liberator This important American bomber was designed in 1939 as an improvement on the B-17* Flying Fortress with increased lifting power and much greater operational range. It was a hugely effective weapon, serving many air forces on every Allied front, beginning in June 1941, with RAF* Coastal Command's few Liberator Is. These were armed with fixed 20mm cannon and carried ASV radar*, but power turrets were added for the B-24C, which joined the USAAF* in November 1941, and fought for the RAF in the Middle East as the Liberator II. The mass-produced B-24D, with turbo-charged engines, greater firepower and many detail changes, was a very long-range (VLR) model capable of filling the mid-Atlantic 'gap' in Allied convoy protection. It was nevertheless held to a strategic bombing role until late 1942, equipping USAAF bomber groups both in Europe and the

Pacific. Production mushroomed with the B-24G, H and J variants (US Navy PB-4Y, RAF Liberator B-VI and GR-VI), all of which mounted a fourth gun turret. Later versions included the B-24L and M (with new tail turrets), the B-24N (with a single tailfin), the F7 photo-reconnaissance plane, the C-109 fuel tanker and a family of C-87 Liberator transports. Production stopped on 31 May 1945 and a total of 19,203 series Liberators were built, more than any other American aircraft in history.

BRIEF DATA (B-24J) Type: 10-man long-range heavy bomber; Engine: 4 × 1,200hp Pratt and Whitney Twin Wasp; Max speed: 290mph; Ceiling: 28,000'; Range: 2,200m (part load); Arms: 10 × 0.5" mg; Bomb load: 8,000lb internal, 4,000lb external.

B-26 Martin Marauder The winner of a 1939 competition for a US Army Air Corps medium bomber, the B-26A entered service in February 1941. Its wing design, which optimized cruising speed, made landing difficult for inexperienced pilots, and the aircraft had a reputation as a 'widow maker' until a revised USAAF* training programme was implemented. Torpedo-armed B-26As were posted to Australia immediately after Pearl Harbor*, and later B-26Bs, modified for long-range operations, saw extensive action in the Southwest Pacific theatre (see Pacific War). From May 1943, the Marauder became the main medium bomber of the US 9th Air Force in southern Europe, where it enjoyed the lowest loss rate of any American bomber.

As armament and armour were progressively increased, so the plane's weight rose; and all but the first 640 B-26Bs were built with enlarged wings and tailfin. Production continued until March 1945, and 5,157 Marauders were delivered, including about 500 used in Italy* by the RAF* and the South African Air Force. In addition, the US Navy* operated several dozen reconnaissance and utility models while about 200 AT-23 trainers were built.

BRIEF DATA (B-26B, enlarged version) Type: 5–7-man medium bomber; Engine: 2 × 2,000hp Pratt and Whitney Double Wasp; Max speed: 310mph; Ceiling: 23,000'; Range: 1,150m (part loaded); Arms: 12 × 0.5" mg; Bomb load: 4,000lb.

B-29 Boeing Superfortress The American Superfortress was the most advanced bomber of the war and set completely new standards for performance and technical achievement. Prototypes were ordered in August 1940, and the B-29 flew its first combat mission in the Pacific in June 1944, after Boeing engineers had overcome enormous difficulties with the plane's basic structure, weight, wing-loading, pressurization and armament to produce a huge and powerful aircraft. Production output, spread over five companies, was equally impressive, and more than 3,000 machines were delivered before the end of the war with Japan, each representing at least five times the industrial effort required to build any previous bomber. By 1945, despite early problems with overheating engines, 500-strong fleets of B-29s, based in the Marianas*, were devastating the Japanese homeland from far above the operational ceiling of most of the defending fighters. It was a Superfortress, the *Enola Gay*, which dropped the first atomic bomb* on Hiroshima* on 6 August 1945. Three aircraft made emergency landings inside Soviet territory and were copied by Russian designer Tupelov as the TU-4 bomber and the TU-70 transport. The B-29 appeared in 19 post-war variants.

BRIEF DATA (B-29) Type: 10–14-man heavy bomber; Engine: 4 × 2,200hp Wright Duplex Cyclone; Max speed: 357mph; Ceiling: 36,000'; Range: 3,250m (half load); Arms: 2 × 20mm cannon, 10 × 0.50" mg; Bomb load: 20,000lb internal, 44,000lb external.

B-32 Consolidated Vultee B-32 Dominator Ordered by the USAAF* in 1940 to the same specification as the B-29*, the B-32 heavy bomber was a relative disappointment. Stability problems and insurmountable difficulties with complex pressurization and remote armament systems seriously delayed development, and the first Dominators were eventually delivered at the beginning of November 1944. Only fifteen of them saw combat in the Pacific War*.

BRIEF DATA (B-32) Type: 10–14-man heavy bomber; Engine: 4 × 2,300hp Wright Cyclone; Max speed: 365mph; Ceiling: 35,000'; Range: 800m loaded, 3,800m clear; Arms: 10 × 0.5" mg; Bomb load: 20,000lb.

Babi Yar A ravine near the Ukrainian city of Kiev*, where more than 30,000 Jews were massacred in September 1941 by SS Einsatzgruppen* in a two-day-long 'reprisal action'. Allegedly a response to the NKVD's* sabotage bombing of Kiev, the action was described in a horrifying account by a German engineer, Gräbner.

Bach-Zelewski, Eric von dem (1899–1972) SS* General and specialist in anti-partisan operations (see Resistance) who served as senior SS and police chief of Army Group Centre area on the Eastern Front* during 1941–2 and later suppressed the Warsaw* rising of 1944. Sentenced to ten years' effective house arrest from which he was released early in 1958, Bach-Zelewski was rearrested and retried on charges associated with his wartime activities, and finally resentenced in 1962 to life imprisonment for murders committed during the mid-1930s.

Bäck, Leo (1873–1956) Jewish scholar and leader of the Jewish community in Berlin. He refused to leave Germany in 1933 and sat on the Jewish Council set up by the Nazis to defend those rights still remaining to German Jews. In 1943 he was sent to Theresienstadt concentration camp* where he became leader of the Jewish elders. In 1945 Bäck defended the camp guards against lynching by prisoners. After the war he lived in London and New York.

Bader, Group Captain Douglas (1910–82) One of the best-known British airmen of WW2, he combined considerable skill with a legendary triumph over disability to regain entry to the RAF*, despite having lost both legs in a flying accident, and then to lead a fighter squadron in the Battle of Britain* from June 1940. Although highly successful in command of 12 Group Wing (with over 60 fighters) during the Battle of Britain, Bader was involved in arguments with Fighter Command over his controversial 'big wing'* fighter formation technique, which ignored the defensive doctrines prevalent in Fighter Command at the time. In August 1941 he was captured after a mid-air collision with an enemy aircraft. His notoriety assured him respectful treatment by the Germans, who even consented to an RAF parachute drop to bring Bader a new set of artificial legs.

Badoglio, Marshal Pietro (1871–1956) Italian soldier and premier of the first post-Fascist government in Italy, he signed the Italian treaty of unconditional surrender to the Allies on 28 September 1943. Badoglio served as an artillery officer in the Italian colonial wars and as a colonel during WW1. An opponent of Mussolini's* regime from the outset, Badoglio nevertheless accepted an appointment as Field Marshal in 1926 and subsequently went as Mussolini's Governor to Libya (1928–34). He later commanded Italian forces in the war against Abyssinia (Ethiopia) during 1935 and served briefly as its Viceroy in 1936. His collaboration with Mussolini ended, however, in 1940 on Italy's entry into the war. He resigned as Chief of Staff four months later, following Italy's disastrous invasion of Greece*.

A conspirator against Mussolini from 1942, Badoglio was called upon by King Victor Emmanuel* to head the new government following the Fascist Grand Council's decision to depose Mussolini in July 1943. During negotiations with the Allies over Italy's capitulation and the planning of the Allied invasion of Italy*, the position of

Badoglio's government remained unstable, attempting to seek terms from the Allies intent on unconditional surrender and increasingly threatened by Germany's reinforcement of mainland Italy (while Hitler personally planned the dramatic rescue of Mussolini from Gran Sasso and his establishment at the head of a puppet republic).

Finally, at Cassibile on 3 September 1943 General Castellano signed the secret armistice on Badoglio's behalf which provided for the unconditional surrender of all Italian forces and the establishment of an Allied administration in Italy. By declaring war on Germany shortly afterwards, on 13 October, Badoglio was able to resolve the ambiguity of his government's position and smooth Italy's path after Germany's surrender, which he now believed was inevitable. He also secured Soviet recognition of his government in March 1944 by winning the support of Palmiro Togliatti, leader of the Italian Communist Party. Marshal Badoglio resigned and was succeeded by Ivanoe Bonomi* after the Allied capture of Rome* in June 1944.

Bagramyan, Marshal Ivan K (1897–?) Veteran of the Russian Imperial Army, and graduate of the Frunze Military Academy in 1934, Bagramyan was appointed Deputy Chief of Staff of Operations for the Kiev* Military District in 1938. In 1941 he was Chief of Staff of the Soviet Southwest Front under General Kirponos*. He later commanded the 16th Army at Kursk*, Bryansk and Kiev. In November 1943, Bagramyan was promoted General and replaced General Yeremenko* as Commander of the 1st Baltic Front*. Forces under his command subsequently took Riga and encircled German Army Group North at Memel. At the end of the war, Bagramyan was appointed Commander of the Baltic Military District and became a Marshal of the Soviet Union.

Bagration, Operation The Soviet campaign to clear Belorussia and destroy German Army Group Centre, begun on 22

June 1944. With his forces depleted by necessary redeployments to Northwest Europe* to fight the Allied advance, German Field Marshal Busch commanded a thinly held front in Belorussia when a four-front Soviet attack was launched around Vitebsk in the north and Bobruisk in the south. In the north, Bagramyan's* 1st Baltic and Chernyakhovsky's* 3rd Belorussian Front* took Vitebsk in five days and Orsha soon afterwards, reclaiming the Moscow–Minsk highway which could now be used to threaten the German rear. In the south, Zakharov's 2nd Belorussian Front simultaneously recaptured Bobruisk, while Chernyakhovsky's mobile forces entered Minsk, trapping 50,000 Germans, on 3 July. Rokossovsky's* 1st Belorussian Front cleared the Pripet marshes, capturing Pinsk and Kovel on 5 July while the main offensive drove on through Baronovichi to the Polish border at Grodno, reached on 13 July. In the north, Bagramyan turned to drive through the Baltic states, taking Vilnyus (Lithuania*) and Daugavpils (Latvia*) on 13 July. The final toll claimed by the Russians in the Belorussian campaign amounted to 158,000 German troops, 2,000 tanks* and 57,000 motor vehicles. The attempt on Hitler's* life at Rastenberg on 20 July (see July Bomb Plot) merely compounded the crisis now faced by Germany and exacerbated the dictator's already fanatical mistrust of his General Staff. As a result of the defeat in Belorussia, Busch was replaced by Model* as commander of Army Group Centre. See Eastern Front. See Map 32.

Bailey, USS The first wartime *Bailey* was a *Clemson* Class destroyer* commissioned in 1919 (see Reuben James, USS). In 1940 she was transferred to the Royal Navy* as part of the Destroyers-for-Bases* agreement, and served in the Atlantic as HMS *Reading*.

A second *Bailey* was commissioned in 1942. A *Benson* Class destroyer, she served in the Pacific and was damaged by 8-inch gunfire off the Komandorski Islands in March 1943. After repairs she returned to

action and was employed in support of amphibious* campaigns for the rest of the war.
BRIEF DATA (*Bailey II*, 1942) Displacement: 1,839 tons; Dimensions: o/a lgth – 348' 4", b – 36' 1"; Speed: 35 knots; Armament: 4 × 5" DP gun, 4 × 40mm AA gun, 7 × 20mm AA gun, 5 × 21" TT.

Balbo, Marshal Italo(1896–1940) Italian soldier and airman, and a long-time Fascist, he contributed greatly to the development of the *Regia Aeronautica* (Italian Air Force*) between the wars. Balbo was Governor-General and C-in-C of Italian forces in Libya when he was accidentally killed over Tobruk* in 1940 by his own anti-aircraft* gunners. He was credited in many quarters with inventing the 'big wing'' fighter formations of four to six squadrons that were used by some RAF* units from 1940.

Balkans, German Invasion of Control over the Balkans was regarded by Hitler as a preliminary to the invasion of Russia (see Eastern Front), originally scheduled for 15 May 1941. His plans for that year envisaged military action only in Greece*, a British ally since Italy's unilateral attack in 1940. The potential threat of a British landing behind the German advance into southern Russia was to be pre-empted by an attack on eastern Thrace from Bulgaria*. Salonika was to be taken, and the coastline occupied. No further incursion into Greek territory was deemed necessary at this stage and the coastal positions were to be held mostly by Bulgarians while German troops (and above all tanks*) rushed to the assault on Russia. Elsewhere in the Balkans, Hitler hoped to dominate by diplomacy.

Hungary* and Rumania* had joined the Axis* in 1940, the latter hastened into friendship with Germany by Soviet territorial demands. On 1 March 1941 Bulgaria also joined, enabling German troops to take up positions for the attack on Greece. Days later a British force, albeit a small one, landed at Salonika and Hitler expanded his invasion plan to include the rest of Greece. When the pro-Axis Yugoslav government signed a pact on 25 March allowing for German troop movements southwards, diplomatic preparations appeared complete.

Two days later, with Field Marshal List's* 12th Army ready to move from Bulgaria, a *coup d'état* in Belgrade deposed Yugoslav regent Prince Paul and reversed his pro-German policy. Angrily, Hitler added the subjugation of Yugoslavia to his immediate plans, an increased commitment of resources which contributed to the postponement of the invasion of Russia at the end of March.

The campaign opened on 6 April. The German 2nd Army (under Weichs) thrust south into Yugoslavia from Austria, while Kleist's* 1st Panzer Group (originally intended for Thrace) pushed towards Belgrade from Bulgaria. The 12th Army attacked Thrace, detaching the 40th Panzer Corps westwards through the Vardar region of southern Yugoslavia, which led to Macedonia and the Monastir Gap. Italian and Hungarian armies operated along the Adriatic coast and in the northwest respectively.

The offensive was completely successful and Yugoslavia, poorly mobilized and barely unified, collapsed in a week. In the north the Croatians mutinied and Weichs met little resistance. In the south the fully mobilized Yugoslav 5th Army was overrun by the panzer divisions. Belgrade was heavily bombed (Operation Punishment*) and Serbia quickly isolated. On 12 April, the Germans met up with Italian forces in the south and moved towards Greece. The next day Belgrade was occupied and three days later an armistice was signed, creating a separate Croatian state under a puppet government and placing the rest of Yugoslavia under martial law.

In Greece, List pierced the Metaxas Line by 9 April and took Salonika, cutting off eastern Thrace and a large part of the Greek Army. In the centre, the lightning advance of the 40th Panzer Corps swept through the strategically important Monastir Gap from Yugoslavia. The British force, some 75,000 men under General Wilson*, was deployed between these forces, guarding the mountain approaches to Greece from Bulgaria, and retreated to a line west of Mount Olympus on 14 April. The Greek 1st Army, fighting in Albania to the west, now found itself surrounded (see Greece, Italian invasion of). Greek C-in-C General Papagos* had ordered its withdrawal on 12 April, but this was too late and it was forced to surrender on 21 April – leaving the Germans free to concentrate on the British. Hounded by the Luftwaffe*, Wilson's force beat a desperate retreat, hoping to reach the ports of southern Greece and avoid capitulation. This was achieved, a stand at the line of Thermopylae* on 24 April allowing evacuations to continue until 27 April. King George* of Greece fled on a British destroyer*, marking the effective close of a campaign which had lasted only three weeks.

For Hitler, the Balkan operation was an unqualified success. His armoured divisions had proved as irresistible as ever, in spite of the mountainous conditions. Of half a million German troops employed, only about 5,500 were killed or wounded, yet they captured about 10,000 British, 90,000 Yugoslavs and 270,000 Greeks. By contrast, the whole episode was damaging to the British. Morale and prestige suffered badly from the defeat, and the redirection of forces from North Africa proved expensive (see Desert War). Some credit for delaying the German invasion of Russia until late June may be due to the Yugoslav rebels, but not to the British government, to whom the equation had not occurred. Most of the British evacuated from Greece were shipped to Crete*, which was taken by German airborne* forces at the end of May 1941 in a dramatic postscript to the campaign that further dented British stature. See also Greece, British occupation of; Balkans, Russian campaign in; Map 26.

Balkans, Russian Campaign in, 1944 In the first weeks of August 1944, the German

Army had all but halted the Russian advance along the main Eastern Front* from the Baltic to the Carpathians. On 20 August, forces of the 2nd and 3rd Ukrainian Fronts* attacked towards Galatz, in the southeast corner of Rumania, from the north and west respectively. The Rumanians, bombed by the Allies since April and tempted by peace overtures from Stalin, overthrew their leader Antonescu* and changed sides on 23 August, after which the Red Army* was able to move swiftly. Tanks* swept through Galatz and headed west, taking the Ploesti* oilfields on 30 August and Bucharest the next day. Within another week they had reached the Yugoslav border at Turnu-Severin, trapping the whole German 6th Army (100,000 men) in Bessarabia. The Rumanian surrender inspired Bulgaria, nervous about Soviet intentions, to sue for peace with Britain and America. Stalin was unimpressed and launched a token invasion across the Danube on 8 September. Unopposed, the Soviet force entered the capital Sofia a week later.

General Malinovsky's* 2nd Ukrainian Front then wheeled north into Hungary* on two fronts – across the mountains from the Ukraine towards Transylvania and, in the wake of a mechanized dash which took Arad on 22 September, from the far northwest of Rumania. Progress was slower, hampered by problems of supply and communication as well as by German delaying tactics – they could muster little more. Cjuj, the capital of Transylvania, fell on 11 October, and a few days later the 4th Ukrainian Front under Petrov* broke through Hungarian lines in the north before turning for Slovakia. Malinovsky's forces reached the suburbs of Budapest in strength on 4 November, but the city was stubbornly defended (see Hungary) – gaining time for the recall of Axis troops from Greece and Yugoslavia.

Considerable German forces remained in Greece, shunning voluntary withdrawal until early November, when they began their long, dangerous retreat. In Yugoslavia, Tolbukhin's* 3rd Ukrainian Front (advancing from the southern wing of the force in Rumania) and Marshal Tito's* partisans found Belgrade grimly defended. The German garrison was finally driven out on 20 October. Tolbukhin's 35 divisions then moved north to support Malinovsky in the investment of Budapest which, though fully encircled by Christmas, held out until mid-February 1945. Post-war Soviet control of the Balkans was confirmed at major Allied conferences* during 1945, apart from Greece* which was designated a British sphere of influence. See Balkans, German invasion of; Greece, British occupation of; Map 26.

Balloon Bomb In November 1944 the Japanese launched the first balloon to carry incendiary or fragmentation bombs* aimed at the North American mainland. About 1,000 balloon bombs eventually reached the Pacific coast of America but they did little damage, although one killed six picnickers in Oregon in May 1945.

Baltic Republics See Latvia; Lithuania; Estonia.

Baltimore, USS US Navy* heavy cruiser and Class of 14 ships completed from 1943–5. After other naval powers had abandoned heavy cruisers, America persevered with the type in the belief that only large size could ensure the radius of action needed for the patrol of her vast oceanic spheres of interest. Although not constructed with the same urgency as the smaller *Cleveland** Class units, seven of the class (beginning with the *Baltimore* in late 1943) saw action in the Pacific War*. With 8-inch main guns and powerful anti-aircraft* defences, they were the finest examples of their type in the world, vulnerable in surface engagement only to capital units. None was lost in combat, although the *Canberra* was badly damaged by aerial torpedo* off Formosa* in December 1944, and the *Pittsburgh* lost her bow in a typhoon the following June.

The (second) *Quincy* was the only ship of the class used in Europe. She covered Allied landings in Normandy* and the Anvil/Dragoon* Operation in southern France before joining her sisters in the last stages of the Pacific campaign.

BRIEF DATA (Baltimore, 1943) Displacement: 13,600 tons; Dimensions: o/a lgth – 673' 6", b – 70' 9"; Speed: 33 knots; Armament: 9 × 8" (3 × 3), 12 × 5" DP gun, 48 × 40mm AA gun, 24 × 20mm AA gun, 4 aircraft.

Ba Maw, Dr (1893–1977) Burmese lawyer first appointed Burmese head of state by the Japanese and subsequently the first Prime Minister of Burma when it gained semi-independence (under Britain's supervision) in 1937. Dr Ba Maw opposed Burma's participation in the war and was imprisoned by the British in 1940. In 1942, however, he escaped from prison to lead a puppet regime under Japanese occupation. His efforts to negotiate for Burmese independence resulted in a nominal independence and an alliance with Japan (August 1943), under which Burma declared war on Britain and the United States. When the British returned to Burma in 1944, Ba Maw fled into hiding, and established a Supreme Defence Council to organize fighting against the Allies. Captured by the Americans and imprisoned in Tokyo from December 1945 until July 1946, he then formed the Maha Bama Party, which he led until his rearrest by the U Nu regime in August 1947.

Banzai Charge A style of attack used by Japanese troops and characterized by a ferocious, frantic and often disorganized charge on enemy lines to the shout of 'Banzai', translated as 'Long Live the Emperor'. A recurrent feature of Japanese fighting used as a final expedient against superior forces, this often suicidal tactic was based on principles of the ancient code of martial conduct, the Bushido* code, which laid down the ultimate duty of the warrior to die in the defence of his country.

Bushido had been revived in part in Prime Minister Tojo's* 'Soldier Code' for the Japanese Army* in 1941. The tactic shocked and mystified Allied troops, whose training did not match the ideological bombardment, physical hardship or simple brutality that was generally endured by the Japanese soldier. See also Pacific War.

Barbarossa, Operation Code-name for the German invasion of the Soviet Union, launched on 22 June 1941. See Eastern Front. See Map 27.

Barbie, Klaus (1914–) A middle-ranking German Gestapo* officer who became notorious as the 'Butcher of Lyons' in the occupied southern part of France in 1942. In 1987 he was the subject of widespread publicity during his trial in the city which he had once terrorized. He was sentenced to life imprisonment for crimes against humanity.

Barham, HMS British battleship of the *Queen Elizabeth* Class, completed in 1915 and – like her sister ship *Malaya* – only partially modernized in time for WW2. With the Home Fleet, the *Barham* was torpedoed off the coast of Scotland in December 1939. After repairs she took part in the abortive attack on Dakar* and was transferred to the Mediterranean Fleet, but was bombed during the British withdrawal from Crete* in May 1941. Again repaired, she was eventually torpedoed and blown up by the *U-331* in the Mediterranean on 25 November 1941. The *Malaya* was a convoy escort in 1939–40, joined Force H* at Gibraltar* in 1941, and at the end of the year returned to the Home Fleet. At the end of 1943 she was disarmed and used as an accommodation ship.
BRIEF DATA (Barham, 1939) Displacement: 31,000 tons; Dimensions: o/a lgth – 643' 9", b – 104'; Speed: 24 knots; Armament: 8 × 15" gun (4 × 2), 8 × 4" AA gun, 16 × 2pdr AA, 16 × 0.5" AA mg, 2 × 21" TT, 1 aircraft.

Bartolomeo Colleoni Italian Navy* light cruiser, completed in 1932. The good-looking, modern Italian cruisers enjoyed a high reputation before the war, based largely on their exceptional speeds. Unfortunately these were derived from trials conducted with ships stripped for maximum performance, and at combat weight they proved no faster than their older British counterparts. The *Bartolomeo Colleoni* was sunk on 19 July 1940 by gunfire and torpedoes* from the cruiser HMAS *Sydney* and her escorting destroyers*.
BRIEF DATA (1940) Displacement: 5,200 tons; Dimensions: o/a lgth – 555' 7", b – 49' 3"; Speed: 37 knots; Armament: 8 × 6" gun (4 × 2), 6 × 3.9" AA gun, 8 × 37mm AA gun, 8 × 13.2mm AA gun, 4 × 21" TT, 2 aircraft.

Bastico, Marshal Ettore (1876–1972) Veteran Italian Army* officer, he was appointed C-in-C of Axis* forces in Libya in July 1941, in which capacity he was Rommel's* official superior. General Bastico had little success imposing his often defensive orders on the aggressive German general, who tended to treat them as 'advice' and usually appealed to higher authorities if he disagreed. In June 1942 Rommel was made a Field Marshal answerable directly to Rome but in November the newly promoted Marshal Bastico regained nominal control, charged with preventing the Afrika Korps* from retreating into Tripolitania. In fact, by February 1943 Rommel had retired west beyond Tripoli, which led an incensed Mussolini* to recall Bastico to Italy.

Bastogne French town and vital road junction defended by US forces against Hitler's Ardennes* offensive in December 1944 (see Battle of the Bulge). The decision, without higher orders, by the acting American commander of the 101st Airborne Division, Brigadier General McAuliffe*, to hold the town against the German advance, and his subsequent reply of 'Nuts!'

to the commander of the surrounding 47th Panzer Corps when he called for McAuliffe's surrender have since become legendary. Holding out for eight days without reinforcements after a 100-mile overnight drive from Rheims, the defence was performed so aggressively that they could not be bypassed, and the arrival of two German reserve divisions also failed to dislodge them. The 101st Division was relieved by General Patton's* 3rd Army on 26 December 1944. See also Northwest Europe, Allied Invasion of.

Bataan Peninsula A small jutting peninsula on the west of the main Philippine* island of Luzon*. The Philippines were among the American island territories invaded in force by Japan following the attack on Pearl Harbor* on 7 December 1941. Caught between two converging Japanese assault forces under General Homma*, the 80,000 American and Filipino troops under General MacArthur* were forced to resort to an earlier defensive plan (War Plan Orange) and fall back to the Bataan Peninsula, designated by MacArthur as the centre of resistance to the Japanese invasion, to fight a brutal and costly siege.

The opposing forces settled initially into a stalemate, both sides suffering heavily from the malarial conditions on the mountainous jungle peninsula. General Homma's forces were further depleted by the loss of 48th Division to Java*, while the Bataan Defence Force positioned on Mount Rosa suffered increasingly from lack of food and medical supplies. Fierce attacks by Japanese forces began again on 9 February, pushing the American troops back to their reserve positions. A decision had already been made in January not to reinforce the peninsula, despite repeated pleas for reinforcements from MacArthur and repeated promises of help from Washington. Heavily besieged, the Allied forces fought on, despite the loss of their overall commander General MacArthur, who was ordered to leave for Australia on 10 March to take over a new command. It was not

until April that a reinforced Japanese offensive forced his successor, General Wainright*, to surrender to avoid a massacre.

In a now infamous act of cruelty, the 70,000 starving survivors were subsequently forced to march 60 miles, from Mariveles to San Fernando, before being transferred to goods trains for transfer to prison camps. The Bataan Death March alone claimed some 14,000 lives.

The final episode in a highly courageous defence took place on the fortified island of Corregidor*, opposite the tip of the Bataan Peninsula, where a garrison of 15,000 men under General Wainright* had withdrawn before the surrender of the Bataan force and survived for a further two months before finally capitulating.

Battleaxe, Operation After the failure of Operation Brevity* to dislodge General Rommel's* forces from the Egyptian frontier in May 1941, General Wavell* planned the more ambitious Operation Battleaxe, an offensive aimed at driving the Axis* forces back beyond Tobruk* (see Desert War). On 12 May a fast convoy, rushed to Alexandria* via the dangerous Mediterranean* route, had arrived with 238 tanks, and this gave Wavell's Western Desert Army a numerical advantage of more than 4 to 1 over his opponent's armoured forces. However, this superiority was undermined by a battle plan calling for the division of the British tanks into separate 'cruiser' and 'infantry' roles (see Tanks).

The original plan was to launch a three-pronged attack on coastal positions near the frontier. Heavily armoured Matilda* tanks would support the infantry, while the 7th Armoured Division (the Desert Rats*) was to drive for Tobruk only after covering the desert flank of the initial advance. Destroying Rommel's two panzer divisions, it would then join the fortress garrison in an exploitative push further westwards.

The Western Desert Army began its coastal attack on 15 June. In the centre Fort Capuzzo was taken quickly, but to the right and left British tanks ran into lethal tank traps laid by Rommel at the Halfaya Pass and Hafid Ridge. Converted 88mm anti-aircraft* guns demolished the infantry tanks at Halfaya and all but destroyed a cruiser tank regiment (with the help of Rommel's forward panzer units) on the desert wing at Hafid Ridge. By the end of the day almost half the British tanks had been lost.

The next day both Rommel's armoured divisions had arrived at the battlefront. One attacked Capuzzo, which held out, while the other worked to cut off the inland section of the British force. Overnight both divisions were switched to an enveloping move towards Halfaya, threatening the British line of retreat, and by mid-morning on 17 June Operation Battleaxe had been abandoned. The British retreated hastily back into Egypt, having lost 91 tanks and destroyed only 12.

After the failure of Battleaxe Wavell was replaced, and supplies were poured into Egypt for the next British offensive (Operation Crusader*). Results of Crusader were to show that many of the tactical lessons of Battleaxe had not been learned.

Baytown, Operation Code-name for the amphibious* landing of the British 8th Army at Reggio di Calabria in the toe of Italy, on 3 September 1943. The operation signalled the start of the Allied invasion of Italy* and was co-ordinated with landings by Allied forces at Salerno* (Operation Avalanche) and Taranto* (Operation Slapstick). It was regarded, even at the time, as ill-conceived and wasteful of resources.

The object of the assault was hazy from the outset and 8th Army Commander Montgomery's* complaints failed to bring a satisfactory clarification from Allied C-in-C Alexander*. In addition, the landing site itself was poorly chosen. Over 300 miles from Salerno, where American forces under General Clark* were due to launch the main attack, the 8th Army faced a difficult route of advance over terrain which heavily favoured the German defenders.

Nevertheless, an overwhelming and, as it turned out, totally unnecessary barrage from British 30th Corps on Sicily* covered the 8th Army's passage across the Straits of Messina and the landings at Reggio by 13th Corps under General Dempsey early on the morning of 3 September. The two divisions assigned to the assault (5th British and 1st Canadian) landed unopposed, pushing five miles inland on the first day without meeting any resistance. Once advancing towards Salerno, however, the 8th Army's drive was continually checked by demolitions expertly executed by the withdrawing German forces. It was not until 17 September that the leading reconnaissance units of the 8th Army made contact with the 5th for the push up the Italian peninsula. See Map 34.

BCRA (Bureau Central de Renseignement et d'Action) The Free French intelligence service, run by André de Wavrin ('Colonel Passy'), which co-operated on resistance* measures with American and British intelligence organizations. See Free France.

Beaverbrook, 1st Baron (William Maxwell Aitken) (1879–1964) Canadian-born British newspaper owner and politician, and long-standing friend of Winston Churchill*. Despite a wilful, driven personality which often aroused disagreement and suspicion, Beaverbrook was appointed by Churchill to lead the newly created Ministry of Aircraft Production in mid-1940. Criticism of his appointment was silenced by his success in achieving and beating production targets for desperately needed fighter aircraft during the Battle of Britain*. Although he received great credit for the trebling of fighter output between May and August 1940, the mechanism for the improvements was already in place when he arrived. His undoubtedly energetic but roughshod approach to the process of reorganization also led to serious shortfalls in the production of other types of aircraft, which proved damaging during 1941. Appointed to the War Cabinet in 1940, Beaverbrook subsequently held appointments as Minister of Supply, Lord Privy Seal, and British Lend-Lease* administrator in the US.

Beck, General Ludwig (1880–1944) A prominent figure in the German Army's opposition to Hitler* (see Resistance: Germany). Chief of the General Staff from 1935, Beck opposed Hitler's war plans and attempted to defend the army against Hitler's takeover. In 1938 he sent General Kleist* to London in an unsuccessful attempt to gain assurances of British military action against Germany if Hitler invaded Czechoslovakia*. He also urged Brauchitsch*, Army C-in-C, to unite with senior army officers in protest against Hitler's plans, but was forced to resign in August when Brauchitsch passed Beck's paper on to Hitler. During the war, Beck remained in contact with others who opposed the war, including Canaris*, Oster*, Hassell and Gördeler*. Although his involvement with the July Bomb* attempt on Hitler's life was only nominal, he tried, unsuccessfully, to take his own life after it failed, and was finally shot by one of his subordinates.

Beda Fomm See Egypt, Campaign for.

Belfast, HMS See Sheffield, HMS.

Belgian Army Under the supreme command of King Leopold III, the conscript Belgian Army had been placed at war readiness in August 1939. General mobilization brought its strength up to 900,000 men at the time of the German invasion in May 1940. Most of the Army consisted of infantry, although there were two cavalry divisions along with motorized and bicycle brigades. There were however no tanks*, few aircraft and serious shortages of anti-aircraft* and anti-tank* guns.

Belgium, German Invasion of See Western Offensive.

Belorussia See Bagration. See also Eastern Front.

Belsen Labour camp in northwest Germany designed originally for political prisoners. Joseph Kramer, its commandant from 1944, was one of the most notorious of camp leaders and known as the 'Beast of Belsen'. Liberated in April 1945 by British troops, Belsen by then had received some 70,000 prisoners evacuated from other camps in the path of the advancing Allied armies; of these some 30,000 were already dead, and had been gathered into heaps or uncovered pits. Kramer was tried and found guilty of war crimes and executed in November 1945. See Concentration Camps.

Belzec Concentration camp* on the Lublin–Lvov railway. Opened in March 1942, it had six gas chambers. An estimated 600,000 people died there.

Beneš, Eduard (1884–1948) Czech statesman and President. A life-long advocate of Czech independence and an ardent supporter of the League of Nations, Beneš served as Foreign Minister from 1918 to 1935, building up a system of central European alliances and establishing ties with the USSR and France. He succeeded President Masaryk* as head of state in 1935. But in 1938, betrayed, as he justifiably felt, by the West and pressurized into resigning as President of Czechoslovakia* by Hitler* after the Munich Agreement*, Beneš went into voluntary exile. After the German invasion of Czechoslovakia, he organized a National Committee and resumed the presidency of the Czech government-in-exile, first in Paris and then in London in 1940, though his government did not receive full recognition by Britain until July 1941.

Beneš later managed to gain recognition from Britain and France that the Munich Agreement was inapplicable to Czech post-war boundaries. During 1942 and 1943, a similar assurance was also given by the Soviet Union, the United States and

Canada. In March 1945, Beneš went for the second time to Moscow, accompanying the Soviet-sponsored Czech Corps back through Slovakia to Prague. Establishing a provisional government, Beneš remained President for three years, until forced to resign in 1948 by the establishment of a Soviet-style political administration.

Benghazi Important northwest Libyan port which changed hands regularly during the Desert War*. A centre of Italian influence before the war, it was taken by the British in February 1941, but recaptured by General Rommel* in April. The British 8th Army again entered Benghazi on Christmas Eve, but withdrew a month later (28 January), before taking the port for the last time on 20 November 1942, when it formed an advance base for the belated pursuit of Rommel after El Alamein*.

Bennett, Air Vice-Marshal Donald (1910 –1988) Australian-born RAF* officer who, in 1942, created and commanded the 'Pathfinder Force'* that flew ahead of bombing forces to pinpoint and mark targets. Along with the Light Night Striking Force of fast de Havilland Mosquito* bombers, which he also helped to found, Air Vice-Marshal Bennett's innovation made an important contribution to the effectiveness of the British night-time area bombing* offensives against Germany (1943–4) and in France during the preparations for the Allied invasion of Normandy*. See also Cheshire, Group Captain Leonard; Strategic Bombing Offensive.

Beresina Nominally a river, the Beresina, east of Minsk in Belorussia, is an extended tangle of streams winding through peat marsh to the northeast of the impenetrable Pripet Marshes. The difficulty of sustaining effective operations in such terrain had been demonstrated 100 years earlier, when Napoleon's retreat had been halted there. During the summer of 1941, the Beresina proved almost as effective in checking the advance of the German invasion forces. In June 1944, when the Soviet armies began a summer offensive against German positions 90 miles east of the Beresina (see Bagration), the German field commander Busch requested permission to withdraw to the river system to throw the Soviet offensive out of gear. Hitler's* refusal, typical of his attitude to such strategic withdrawals, was disastrous to the outcome of the German defence. See Eastern Front.

Beria, Lavrenti P (1899–1953) Successor to Yezhov as Chief of the Soviet Secret Police, the NKVD*, from 1938 until his death, Beria also became a member of the five-man State Defence Committee at the outbreak of war, and provided Stalin with information on the Armed Forces throughout the period. Under Beria, the NKVD carried out a variety of wartime duties and gained a reputation for almost unsurpassed brutality. Its main tasks included large-scale purges in annexed territories, deportations of minority nationalities, control of Soviet partisans and POW camps, and counter-intelligence. An enemy to many people, Beria did not long outlive Stalin. The circumstances of his death in 1953 were never clarified.

Berlin, Battle for, 1945 The closing battle of the war in Europe (see Map 33). In January 1945, the Soviet armies held a front some 300 miles east of Berlin, on the border of East Prussia*, along the Narew River to Warsaw* and following roughly the line of the Vistula* river southwards. Stalin informed his Western Allies of a major new January offensive, involving (according to the *Soviet Encyclopaedia*) over 6 million troops, and to be directed by the three most outstanding Russian field commanders, Konev*, Zhukov* and Rokossovsky*. The announcement apparently failed to impress the Western military commanders – themselves recovering from the shock of Hitler's Ardennes* counter-offensive – and they remained unconvinced about the potential of the new Soviet offensive. But this estimate ignored the steady consolidation of communications and supply lines designed to ensure a sustained momentum for the offensive, the massive build-up of troops and supplies on the front and, most importantly, the steady increase of Russian mobile and armoured corps facilitated by the increasing availability of Soviet tanks* and American vehicles.

During December in Berlin itself, a similar underestimation, dramatically increased in proportion to the dictator's advanced mania, deafened Hitler utterly to the analysis of the military crisis provided by his latest appointment as Chief of the General Staff, General Guderian*. Dismissing military intelligence of the Russian build-up as 'imposture', and ignoring the depletion of Germany's fighting strength, he refused Guderian's request for a withdrawal of troops from the Ardennes to the Eastern Front, and redeployed two desperately needed panzer divisions from Poland for a renewed attempt on Budapest*.

On 12 January, a massive Soviet bombardment preceded the launch of assaults by the three reorganized Russian Fronts* (1st Ukrainian under Konev in the south, 1st Belorussian under Zhukov in the centre and 2nd Belorussian under Rokossovsky in the north) which brought them to the 1939 German–Polish frontier on the Oder before the end of the month. By the beginning of February, Soviet bridgeheads had been established on the east bank of the Oder at Küstrin and Frankfurt. But German counter-attacks along the Stargrad railway in mid-February stalled the westward Russian drive, which now paused to extend its flanks and clear Pomerania and Silesia. Rokossovsky's 3rd Guard Tank Corps spearheaded the push to the Baltic coast, reached on 1 March, and isolated important supply depots at Danzig and Gotenhaven (Gdynia) while a supporting drive under Zhukov reached the coast at Kölberg, which fell on 18 March. Four days later the 1st Belorussian Front launched a flanking attack on Küstrin, which fell on 30 March. In Silesia to the south, Konev's 1st Ukrain-

ian and Petrov's* 4th Ukrainian Front drove towards Grottkau and Moravska Ostrava, clearing all of Silesia except for Breslau during April.

As Marshal Zhukov began to recall his forces to the Oder–Neisse line for the attack on the German capital, the Allied assault on the Rhine* was already in progress and a renewed Allied air assault on Berlin had already further reduced much of the city to rubble (see Strategic Bombing Offensive). Nevertheless, in the fantastic belief that the Allies were incapable of resuming their western offensive after Ardennes, and that fate decreed an imminent change of fortune for Germany not dependent on the actual military situation, Hitler had ordered a stripped-down force to hold the Rhine while regional commissioners were directed to create a 'desert' of destruction in the Allies' path. Concentrating his forces, by now a mixture of regular and *Volksturm* home militia, on the Oder against the Russians, Hitler received the news of President Roosevelt's* death on 12 April as an enigmatic portent of his ultimate victory.

On 16 April, the 1st Belorussian Front under Zhukov attacked Berlin directly from the Küstrin bridgehead, while Konev's forces attacked across the Neisse in three prongs towards Berlin, the Elbe and Czechoslovakia. Bitter defence by German forces under General Heinrici could not stop the breakthrough by Konev's forces which brought them to the Berlin outskirts by 19 April. Linking up with tank spearheads under Sokolovsky west of the city on 25 April, the Red Army completed its encirclement of Berlin. While nearly half a million German troops were isolated in two pockets inside the city and to the west of Berlin, US and Russian troops met at Torgau on the Elbe and house-to-house fighting began in the suburbs of the capital between the eight Russian armies and the now pathetic remnants of SS*, Wehrmacht, Home Guard and Hitler Youth. The Reichstag was stormed on 30 April, the day on which Hitler committed suicide.

On 2 May, the Commandant of Berlin, General Weidling, called upon his troops to surrender. As German men abandoned weapons and uniforms to hide, the women of Berlin faced the first waves of occupying troops. A degree of looting was authorized at the highest command level; every Soviet soldier was to be allowed to send home a limited weight of goods – and rape and murder became a horrendous fact of everyday life. See Germany, Surrender of. See also Western Front; Eastern Front.

Bernhard Line The second of three German defensive lines south of the Liri valley on the Italian peninsula, designed to check the Allied advance in Italy*. It formed a deep chain of defensive positions running from the Adriatic coast to the Sangro river behind heavily mined approaches, slightly forward of the main Gustav Line*.

Best, Werner (1903–) Head of military administration in Paris from 1940 and German Commissioner in occupied Denmark* from 1942. There is evidence that Best made an attempt to alert the Danish resistance* and enable Danish Jews to escape to Sweden*. He was nevertheless found guilty of murder by a Danish court and sentenced to death, though this was commuted to twelve years' imprisonment. He was released in 1951 but heavily fined by a German denazification court in 1958. Arrested again in 1969, and charged with mass murder, he was released on health grounds in 1972.

Beurling, Flight Lieutenant George 'Screwball' (1922–48) Canadian RAF* pilot who was decorated four times between July and October 1942 for missions flown over Malta* when he shot down 27 and damaged eight enemy aircraft.

Biak One of the Schouten Islands to the northwest of Dutch New Guinea*. It was occupied by Japanese forces in April 1942 but largely ignored until late 1943. Though the island housed the veteran 222nd Infantry and became for a few months a major base for Japanese fighter aircraft, a change of strategy decided in mid-1944 moved the main line of Japanese resistance westward, leaving Biak as part of a strategic outpost chain directed to resist for as long as possible. Biak was invaded by units of the American 41st Infantry Division (which included the Hurricane Task Force) under Lt General Fuller on 27 May 1944, but American progress was slowed by the unexpected strength of the opposition and the reinforcement of the Japanese garrison under the Kon Operation, a contingency plan designed to stop the establishment of American airfields on strategic islands. Despite changes in command and the reinforcement of the invasion force by units of the US 24th Infantry Division, organized resistance on Biak did not end until 22 July. Japanese casualties were estimated at 6,000 dead, 460 captured; American casualties were 400 men killed and 2,000 wounded.

Bialystok Russian city west of Minsk and the site of one of the Red Army's* first major defeats at the start of the German invasion (see Eastern Front). Tank* spearheads under Guderian* and Hoth pushed out north and south of Bialystok towards Minsk in late June 1941, taking Minsk at the rear of the salient on 29 June. Although rain and mud slowed the pace of the German encirclement, allowing some troops to escape, 300,000 Russian troops and 2,500 tanks were captured. Russian Western Front commander Pavlov was subsequently arrested and replaced by Marshal Timoshenko*.

Biddle, Francis (1886–1968) American Attorney-General in President Roosevelt's cabinet from September 1941. During 1940, as Solicitor-General, Biddle had been in charge of the operation of the American Alien Registration Act (passed in June 1940 to regulate the status of three and a half million foreign nationals in the US) and had earned a considerable reputation for his wise and moderate approach to this enormously difficult and sensitive task. His protests (which were ignored) against the evacuation of American citizens of Japanese origin and his efforts, which were finally successful, to secure the removal of Americans of Italian origin from the category of enemy aliens, established him as a firm defender of civil liberties. As Attorney-General, Biddle continued his commitment to the just treatment of American citizens of foreign origin, setting up an inter-departmental committee on investigations to improve procedures for the investigation of sedition and forbidding prosecutions for sedition without his personal authority.

After the war, Biddle was appointed by President Truman* (who had initially asked for his resignation) to join the International Military Tribunal*, which tried war criminals at Nuremberg until 1948. Here also, Biddle made a significant contribution, consistently noted for his magnanimity and unequivocal sense of justice. He wrote an autobiographical account of many of the important issues of the period in a book entitled *In Brief Authority*. See also Evacuation of Japanese-Americans.

Big Week Code-name for an intensified series of Allied bombing raids against German aircraft production targets. It began on the night of 19/20 February 1944 with an 800-plane RAF* bomber raid against Leipzig (from which 78 failed to return). Subsequent daylight raids by the US 8th and 15th Air Force B-17s* and B-24s* and night sorties by RAF Bomber Command targeted aircraft manufacturing and assembly plants at Bernburg, Brunswick, Gotha, Regensburg, Augsburg, Stuttgart, Schweinfurt, Rostock, Halberstadt and Steyr. Lasting only six days, Big Week saw over 3,000 8th Air Force sorties from England and over 500 from the Italian-based 15th.

Aircraft production at Leipzig, which had been subjected to a second, even larger raid by the 8th Air Force, was considerably

affected. Production of Junkers Ju88s* halted for over a month, and German production as a whole dropped considerably in the first few months of 1944. Nevertheless, recovery was generally rapid; the Messerschmitt factories at Regensburg, for example, were producing to capacity within four months of a dual strike by Italian- and British-based bombers. Although the Big Week raids achieved their objectives with relatively small overall losses (in the region of 6 per cent), it has since been concluded that the most important blow to German air power was actually the performance of the highly effective Allied fighter escorts, which inflicted enormous damage on intercepting German squadrons. See also Strategic Bombing Offensive.

Big Wing Name given to large formations of fighter aircraft – usually 3–5 squadrons – deployed in mass sweeps against hostile aircraft or positions. Conceived by Italian aerial strategist Italo Balbo*, 'big wings' caused a major controversy within the RAF* during 1940. Fighter Command's defensive strategy in the Battle of Britain*, organized by Dowding*, was to use radar* and intelligence to deploy groups of fighters quickly against definite contacts with approaching Luftwaffe aircraft. One of his Group Commanders – Air Vice-Marshal Leigh-Mallory – nevertheless allowed squadrons to undertake big-wing sweeps in search of possible targets. Leigh-Mallory's No. 11 Group was stationed in eastern England as the tactical reserve for No. 12 Group, which bore the brunt of the Battle of Britain in the south. Although pilots of the big wing (led by Douglas Bader*) shot down many German aircraft, they were not always available when called to an emergency and often only caught bombers returning from their targets. A bitter argument broke out between Leigh-Mallory and the Commander of No. 12 Group, Air Vice-Marshal Park*, whose airfields were being bombed. Dowding failed to impose his authority on the controversy, which festered on into the aftermath of the battle.

In October 1940 Fighter Command was performing ineffectively against night raids by the Luftwaffe, and the Air Council officially endorsed the 'big wing'. The following month Dowding and Park were replaced, with Leigh-Mallory taking the latter's place at No. 12 Group. During 1941 and 1942, Fighter Command aircraft from the south of England were used for mass offensive sweeps against targets of opportunity in the English Channel and northern Europe (see Rhubarbs).

Bir Hacheim See Gazala.

Biryusov, General S. S. (1904–64) Russian commander of 48th Army and chief of staff of the 2nd Guards Army for the Battle of Stalingrad*. Biryosov later commanded the 37th Army in Rumania*, Bulgaria* and Yugoslavia*. After Stalin's death he became Soviet Chief of the General Staff.

Bismarck Ordered in the light of the 1935 Anglo-German Naval Treaty*, the German Navy's* *Bismarck* was ostensibly a 35,000-ton battleship, the maximum permitted under the international limitation treaties to which she was now subject. In fact she greatly exceeded that displacement even before the outbreak of war allowed further weight increases to be made freely. Her design was not particularly advanced, reflecting the inexperience and haste inherent in German pre-war naval construction. Most of her extra weight was invested in armour protection, associated with an immensely broad beam, while her main armament was no more than the equal of other battleships. In addition she retained separate secondary and tertiary batteries for use against light vessels and aircraft, rather than the more economical dual-purpose weapons developed by the Allies. Nevertheless, all her guns were well grouped and sited. Numerous anti-aircraft* mountings were controlled by as many as six gunfire directors, and she possessed a distinct speed advantage over the treaty-bound battleships of other navies. Completed in late 1940, she was hailed as the most powerful warship in the world.

The *Bismarck* was not a component of a coherent battle fleet, but was intended as a giant commerce raider. After a shakedown cruise in the Baltic, she was prepared for a breakout into the Atlantic*. This operation appeared urgent to German planners in early 1941. A distraction was badly needed in the Atlantic both to allow the U-boats a recuperative respite and to divert British forces from the Mediterranean* supply lines of the Afrika Korps*. Meanwhile British advances in tracking radar* and the prospect of US entry into the war were perceived as likely to render Atlantic surface raids impossible in the near future.

The *Bismarck*'s escort for the sortie was to be the new heavy cruiser *Prinz Eugen*. It had been planned to include the battle-cruisers *Scharnhorst** and *Gneisenau**, but both were under repair following Atlantic operations of their own. Their commander, Vice-Admiral Günther Lütjens, took charge on board the *Bismarck*, aware that failure to act quickly had led to the dismissal of his two predecessors as Fleet Commander (Boehm and Marshall). He also knew that, with the *Admiral Hipper**, *Admiral Scheer** and *Lützow* all in hand for refits or repair, and the second giant battleship (*Tirpitz**) months away from operational readiness, he would have to undertake his hazardous mission with only two major warships.

In April 1941, sailing was delayed for a month after the *Prinz Eugen* struck a magnetic mine*, but on 18 May the two ships left Gotenhaven (Gdynia) with their screening destroyers*. British intelligence was quickly aware of their departure and on 21 May they were spotted refuelling in Bergen Fjord, Norway, by aerial reconnaissance. That night they steamed north and west dropping their escorts and heading for the narrow and icy Denmark Straits, speeding to reach their supply ships in the Atlantic and avoid the attentions of the British Home Fleet. This most northerly passage kept Lütjens as far as possible from

Scapa Flow, where his latest intelligence claimed the Royal Navy* was still gathered. In fact Admiral Tovey*, in command of the Home Fleet, knew the *Bismarck* was out of Bergen, had correctly anticipated her course and was calling up every available warship to join the hunt.

On the afternoon of 23 May, the German ships were spotted by the heavy cruiser *Suffolk**, which then shadowed them through fog and foul weather using her newly-installed tracking radar. She was soon joined by her sister, the *Norfolk**, and the two cruisers shepherded their quarry towards the capital ships *Hood** and *Prince of Wales**, which were steaming north to intercept. With the weather clearing slightly, the British engaged early on the morning of 24 May. Before the shadowing heavy cruisers could be brought to bear, Vice-Admiral Holland aboard the ageing *Hood* attacked with the *Prince of Wales* in a head-on charge. His desire to present a small target was understandable – his flagship was notoriously short of deck armour, and the *Prince of Wales* was so new that little could be expected of her inexperienced gunners. Nevertheless this approach masked almost half his ships' main armament and, to make matters worse, the *Hood*, plunging into a blinding swell, mistakenly opened fire on the *Prinz Eugen*, which had overtaken the *Bismarck* since the last British visual report. Although the *Prince of Wales* spotted this error and began firing at the larger ship, her gunners took seven salvoes to find their range and her guns repeatedly failed to function properly. Meanwhile the *Hood* was exposed to a brilliant display of gunnery from both German ships, and she exploded a few minutes later after taking a final straddle from the *Bismarck*'s 15-inch guns. These were promptly turned on the nearby *Prince of Wales* which was damaged and fled, making smoke to cover her escape, The battle had lasted 20 minutes and ended as a stunning German victory. The *Bismarck* had, however, taken two 14-inch hits from the *Prince of Wales*; one hit had ruptured fuel tanks,

reducing her maximum speed and causing a steady leak of priceless fuel oil.

This was a critical time on board the *Bismarck*. Her orders had been specific but they now posed contradictions. Her first task had been to break into the Atlantic, avoiding combat *en route* if possible but fighting to the finish if engaged. Once in the Atlantic, the *Bismarck*'s prime directive was to sink as much merchant shipping as possible. She was to remain at sea for as long as she was fit for combat; and she was to return to a German (rather than a French) port. Lütjens chose to press on into the Atlantic, ignoring those orders which demanded he either finish off the *Prince of Wales* (which he thought was the more experienced *King George V**) or return to Germany. Aware that Admiral Tovey was gathering forces from the Atlantic and the Mediterranean, and convinced that the *Bismarck* would remain in the grip of British radar, Lütjens hoped to lead his pursuers into a submarine ambush before reaching his supply ships.

Early in the evening the *Bismarck* turned and fired briefly on the *Norfolk* and *Suffolk*, opening the range while the *Prinz Eugen* escaped to the south. At sunset, nine Fairey Swordfish* torpedo-bombers attacked the *Bismarck*, somehow got through her immense AA barrage and scored a hit. These were the full complement of the carrier *Victorious**, freighted with fighters for Malta* but held back in the hope of slowing down the German battleship. In fact their 18-inch torpedoes had been unable to dent the *Bismarck*'s belt armour, but within two hours increasing fuel loss had forced Lütjens to change his plan, and he turned his ship south, heading directly for Brest*.

There followed a chapter of accidents on both sides. Shortly after 3 a.m. on 25 May, the heavy cruisers suddenly lost contact with the *Bismarck*. She remained lost for six and a half hours, at which point Lütjens, quite unaware of his freedom, broadcast a long and detailed radio message describing his situation. Miscalculating the information from their radio scanners, the British then wasted hours searching far to the north before realizing their mistake. The *Bismarck*, steaming at moderate speed to conserve fuel and expecting an attack at any moment, was eventually sighted by an RAF* Consolidated Catalina* flying boat at 10.30 a.m. on 26 May. Aircraft then maintained watch until the light cruiser *Sheffield** took over in mid-afternoon, by which time it was clear that only Force H* from Gibraltar, squarely in the *Bismarck's* path, could hope to reach her before she came under the protection of the Luftwaffe*.

Force H included the battlecruiser *Renown** and the aircraft carrier *Ark Royal**. The *Renown* was even less battle-worthy than the *Hood* and so a great deal depended on the carrier's torpedo-bombers. They attacked during the afternoon. The first strike was unopposed, but only because they inadvertently attacked the *Sheffield*, which was able to report the failure of their torpedoes' magnetic detonators. These were replaced with contact detonators for a second strike, which scored two hits on the *Bismarck*. Although neither seemed serious at first, the second jammed her steering gear. This effectively doomed the *Bismarck*. She circled helplessly for a while before fixing herself on a northerly course, straight towards major Royal Navy units which could never otherwise have caught her.

During the night the *Bismarck* was harried by destroyers and the next morning she found herself surrounded by heavy warships. At 8.47 a.m. the battleships *King George V** and *Rodney**, both recalled from Atlantic convoy duty, opened fire from 16,000 yards. With the *Norfolk*, they silenced the *Bismarck's* own guns and reduced her to a blazing wreck within an hour and a half. The cruiser *Dorsetshire** was then called in to finish the job with torpedoes, and the *Bismarck* rolled over and sank at 10.36 a.m., killing all but 110 of her crew. German sources have maintained that her hull was still intact and that she was scuttled. The balance of evidence is against this theory, but in any case the

Bismarck was beyond salvation some time before she went down. Her demise marked the end of the German surface incursions into the Atlantic, and shortly afterwards the Royal Navy hunted down and destroyed nearly all the raiders' supply ships in the Atlantic. The sinking of the *Hood* notwithstanding, the most effective contribution of the world's most feared warship had been as a distraction to the Royal Navy.

BRIEF DATA (1941) Displacement: 41,700 tons; Dimensions: o/a lgth – 822' 9", b – 118' 3"; Speed: 29 knots; Armament: $8 \times 15"$ gun (4×2), $12 \times 5.9"$ gun, $16 \times 4.1"$ AA gun, 16×37mm AA gun, 36×20mm AA gun, 6 aircraft.

Bismarck Islands See Rabaul.

Bismarck Sea, Battle of Site of important American air strikes during 3–5 March 1943 against a 16-ship Japanese troop convoy bound from the major Japanese base at Rabaul* to Lae, on New Guinea's* northeast coast. The convoy had been dispatched under instructions from General Imamura* to reinforce their New Guinea bases but was attacked by low-flying B-17s* and then by an Allied force of Australian Bristol Beauforts* and Bristol Beaufighters*, American B-17s and B-25s* which sank four destroyers, eight transports and forced the surviving Japanese troops (approximately 3,000) to return to Rabaul or land at Kavieng. The American victory effectively isolated the Japanese bases on New Guinea, which could no longer be safely reinforced from Rabaul except by submarine*. It underlined the air superiority which the Allies now commanded over the Bismarck Sea, as well as the quality of American intelligence, which could accurately predict the composition and movements of the Japanese convoys. Finally, it gave the Allied air force an important opportunity to rehearse its tactics for the forthcoming Operation Cartwheel*.

Blackburn Skua The Royal Navy's* first operational monoplane, the Skua was designed to double as a fighter and dive-bomber and joined the Fleet Air Arm* in 1937. Scheduled for replacement just before the war, it proved barely adequate for either task in actions over Norway*, Dunkirk* and Malta*. Only 160 Skuas were built, and they were replaced on British carriers during 1941 by Fairey Fulmars* and modified Hawker Hurricanes*.

BRIEF DATA (Mk II) Type: 2-man carrier dive-bomber/fighter; Engine: 1 × 890hp Bristol Perseus; Max speed: 225mph; Ceiling: 19,100'; Range: 760m; Arms: 1 × 0.5" mg, 4 × 0.303" mg; Bomb load: 500lb.

Blakeslee, Colonel Donald (1918–) One of the best-known of the USAAF* fighter aces. He joined the Royal Canadian Air Force soon after the outbreak of war and first proved himself an outstanding pilot when he was assigned to the 401st (Ram) Squadron in England in May 1941. He then transferred to a US volunteer RAF* squadron, the 133rd (Eagle*), which later went into American service with other similar units as the 4th Fighter Group USAAF*. With Blakeslee as its commander, the Group was responsible for destroying over 1,000 hostile aircraft.

Blamey, General Sir Thomas Albert (1884 –1951) Australia's most important wartime commander. Chairman of the Australian Manpower Committee at the outbreak of war, his appointment to command of Australian* land forces in 1940 surprised most Australians. Blamey's rough, tactless manner and interest in his own aggrandizement, however, were combined with considerable experience in staff work and an ability for administration, developed during WW1. Despite his competitiveness towards rivals and his inability to delegate, Blamey appeared the only practical choice at the time. His lack of combat experience, however, and more particularly the mistakes caused by the monomaniacal exercise of his power at critical moments, was to cause considerable suffering to troops under his command.

Called to take command of Australia's Imperial Force, raised for service in the Middle East in 1940, he held a series of posts in rapid succession. Promoted Lt General in April 1941 and second-in-command to General Wavell*, Blamey directed Australian and New Zealand troops in the fighting and the evacuation of Greece. Posted again to the Middle East, Blamey went to Alexandria to take up his post as Deputy C-in-C Middle East under General Auchinleck*. The appointment, merely a conciliatory gesture towards the Dominion forces, carried little real power, and a rift soon developed between Blamey and Auchinleck.

Recalled to Australia with two divisions after Pearl Harbor*, Blamey was promoted Commander of Allied land forces in Australia under Supreme Commander MacArthur*, and faced with the task of preparing the under-trained and under-equipped Australian forces for battle in the Pacific theatre. More difficult, even, than these practical considerations were the political complexities of Blamey's command. Receiving General MacArthur more or less direct from Corregidor* in March 1942, as the Supreme Allied Commander of the newly-activated Southwest Pacific command, Blamey had no choice but to accept the effective takeover of Australian strategic planning by MacArthur. Prime Minister Curtin's* ready acceptance of MacArthur's dominance in the military sphere galled and frustrated the Australian General, whose main interest remained with his own position.

Nevertheless, in September 1942, Blamey arrived in Port Moresby (New Guinea)* to direct the difficult jungle operations which pushed the Japanese forces back along the Kokoda trail to Buna*, and achieved a hard-won victory in Papua. He exercised personal field command between September 1942 and January 1943, supervising the recapture of Buna, taken on 9 December 1942.

Returning to Australian Army HQ in early 1943, as the focus of fighting shifted to the north and numbers of Australian troops in the area reduced, Blamey's control of Allied land forces was subsequently undermined by the arrival of Lt General Krueger* to lead US land forces, under direct command of MacArthur. From this point, MacArthur's desire to reduce the significance of Blamey's role, and indeed the role of Australian forces in the Southwest Pacific theatre, remained a consistent theme of his strategy and deployments. Despite American criticism of his leadership, Blamey retained his position until the end of the war.

Blitz, The The German air attacks on London, September 1940 to May 1941. See Britain, Battle of.

Blitzkrieg A strategy of 'lightning war' which relied on the independent operation of mobile armoured units striking forward of the main armies to achieve surprise and swift tactical success. The strategy originally developed from the use of shock troops to break through Allied trench lines in the last offensives of WW1. Armed with light machine-guns*, mortars, flame-throwers* and portable artillery weapons, these newly trained units were led by young officers such as Rommel* with great tactical effect. After WW1 the Freikorps added to these tactics the use of armoured cars* and street-fighting techniques. Training in mobile shock tactics was further developed by General von Seekt, post-war commander of the small German Army* (*Reichswehr*); he sent German tank and aircraft crews (forbidden under the Versailles Treaty) to train secretly in Russia. (See Tank; Luftwaffe).

The short-lived but spectacular success in the late 1920s of the British Experimental Mechanized Force (which the German generals had closely followed) foreshadowed the developments in Germany during the 30s. While the British military establishment remained unconvinced about the potential of armoured warfare and ignored the theories being advanced

by its proponents Liddell-Hart and Fuller, Nazi endorsement of the new tank theories was more enthusiastic. General Guderian*, who created the Third Reich's armoured panzer divisions for WW2, was chief of staff to a Freikorps division fighting with these methods in eastern Germany. In planning the attacks on Poland* in 1939 and on western Europe in 1940 (see Western Offensive), the German General Staff made use of this experience. By adding strategic planning, supply systems, the use of air power, as well as the crucial element of political surprise, a new form of offensive was born for which Germany's enemies were unprepared.

The term *Blitzkrieg* was first used by Hitler in a speech at the 1935 Nuremberg Party Rally. The German air attacks on London and other British cities in 1940 were called the Blitz. See also Eastern Front.

Bloch 170 Series The French Bloch 170 had been planned as a bomber in 1937, but was a victim of official indecision, belatedly joining the *Armée de l'Air** in March 1940 as the Bloch 174 reconnaissance-bomber. Only then was its potential as a fast light bomber recognized, and an attack version (Bloch 175) hastily planned. Only 75 of both types were ever delivered, although a further 200 Bloch 175s were on the production line when France surrendered in June 1940.

BRIEF DATA (Bloch 174) Type: 3-man reconnaissance/light bomber; Engine: 2 × 1,140hp Gnome-Rhône; Max speed: 329mph; Ceiling: 36,090'; Range: 800m (max); Arms: 7 × 7.5mm mg; Bomb load: 880lb.

Bloch MB150 Series French fighter, which first flew in 1937. Its development was painfully slow and only 85 of the MB151 and 152 models (none of them fully operational) had reached the *Armée de l'Air* by September 1939. By the following June, however, 593 had been delivered and, although outclassed by Luftwaffe* fighters, they were credited with 180 combat victories during the Battle of France*. Subsequently, surviving aircraft were used both by the Luftwaffe and the Vichy* Air Force, the latter also employing an improved MB155.

BRIEF DATA (MB 152) Type: Single-seat fighter; Engine: 1,080hp Gnome-Rhône radial; Max speed: 323mph; Ceiling: 32,800'; Range: 373m; Arms: 2 × 20mm cannon; 2 × 7.5mm mg.

Blohm und Voss Bv138 Production of this unconventional twin-boomed German flying boat began in 1939 with the Bv138B-1, and the essentially similar Bv138C-1 followed. A total of 279 models were built and they remained operational from 1940 until the end of the war on reconnaissance, escort and submarine* co-operation duties.

BRIEF DATA (Bv138C-1) Type: 5-man reconnaissance flying boat; Engine: 3 × 700hp Junkers Jumo; Max speed: 170mph; Ceiling: 18,700'; Range: 2,000m; Arms: 2 × 20mm cannon, 1 × 13mm mg; Bomb load: 660lb.

Bloody Ridge (Edson's Ridge), Battle of
See Guadalcanal.

Blücher German heavy cruiser completed late in 1939. The *Blücher*, sister ship of the *Admiral Hipper**, was sunk by shore batteries off Oslofjord, Norway*, during her first operation on 9 April 1940. She was one of the few victims of coastal gunfire in WW2 (see Artillery, Heavy).

BRIEF DATA See Admiral Hipper.

Bock, Field Marshal Fedor von (1885–1945) German General of a traditional Prussian military family and described as 'gaunt and hard-bitten' by contemporaries, he commanded Army Groups in Poland* in 1939, in the Western Offensive* in 1940 and on the Eastern Front* from 1941. Made Field Marshal after the capitulation of France, Bock was later relieved of his command in the purge of the German High Command that followed the successful

Russian counter-offensive at Moscow* in December 1941. Briefly reinstated to replace Field Marshal Reichenau* as commander of Army Group South in January 1942, Bock was again dismissed in July and never re-employed. He was killed in an air raid near Kiel in May 1945.

Bodyguard, Operation Generic code-name for a series of elaborate and highly important Allied deception plans, designed to cloak the actual timing and location of the Allied invasion of Northwest Europe* (Overlord) in mid-1944. Originally code-named Jael, Bodyguard included seven major deception operations which it was hoped would force the Germans to disperse their forces throughout Europe. It involved the clandestine co-operation of thousands of resistance* members throughout German-occupied Europe as well as elaborate 'disinformation' operations and the use of dummy installations, weapons, equipment and shipping. Overthrow and Cockade, the first and second deception plans, had attempted to convince Germany of an imminent invasion of France during 1942 and 1943. The other five plans were associated with the actual invasion: two drew German attention to southern France as a landing site; one to the Bay of Biscay; one to the Balkans and the final and most important plan, Fortitude (North and South), to Norway and the Pas de Calais.

An enormous and elaborate deception, which included the high-profile appointment of US General Patton* to command the fictitious US 1st Army Group, apparently targeted on the Pas de Calais, proved central to the success of the Normandy* invasion. When D-Day* came, Hitler and the German High Command's conviction that the main invasion force was still to be launched at the Pas de Calais held up the release of reinforcements to Normandy for several crucial hours. When Ultra* intercepts revealed that the Germans had captured American field orders for Normandy and were now releasing troops, Bodyguard was able to react quickly by passing word through a turned German agent that the captured field orders were themselves part of a deception, and persuade Hitler to rescind the order. By the time Hitler realized that no second invasion was coming, the Allies were established and building up forces quickly to meet the German reserves.

Bofors Gun Light, rapid-firing 40mm anti-aircraft cannon, which had an effective range of about 12,500ft and fired either armour-piercing or high-explosive shell. Developed in Sweden, it was used by many belligerents in WW2, including Poland, France, Britain and the United States. The Germans also employed captured Bofors guns. Produced in air- or water-cooled versions, they were originally drawn on wheeled trailers but were increasingly in demand as self-propelled*, aircraft or naval weapons. The Bofors was the most effective light AA gun of the war, but it was always in short supply and available only to high priority units before 1944. See Anti-aircraft Defence.

Bolero, Operation Code-name for the build-up of American troops and materials in Britain, begun in 1942 in preparation for the Normandy* invasion.

Bomb (conventional) Most bombs dropped from aircraft in WW2 were conventional general-purpose types, which ranged from 100–4,000lb in weight. General-purpose bombs relied on the force of their detonation for destructive effect, and the thickness of their casings was generally reduced as the war progressed. British concentration on strategic bombing led to experiments in heavy bombs resulting in the 12,000lb 'Tallboy' and the 22,000lb 'Grand Slam', which could only be carried by specially adapted Avro Lancaster* bombers. Although considered general-purpose bombs, these were designated DP (deep penetration) by the British because they relied on their great mass to produce underground shock waves. Armour-piercing bombs also relied on deep penetration for

effect. These were always fitted with delayed-action fuses, while general-purpose bombs could also employ impact, timed or proximity fuses (see Anti-aircraft Defence). Relatively small (4–100lb) fragmentation bombs were also dropped, often in clusters, and were deadly against personnel and un-armoured vehicles or structures. These were usually primed to explode just above the ground for maximum effect, as were incendiary bombs. Weighing up to 1,000lb, incendiary bombs were also often dropped in clusters to spread fires after general-purpose bombs had caused initial structural devastation. Filled with highly combustible chemicals such as magnesium, phosphorous or petroleum jelly (napalm), they were known by nicknames in some theatres (e.g. 'Molotov Breadbasket' in Finland, 'Kenney Cocktail' in the Pacific). Incendiary bombs in particular occasioned great loss of life in Germany and Japan in the later years of the war, but no conventional bomb approached the earth-shattering effect of the first atomic weapons. See Atomic Bomb; Guided Bombs; Dambusters.

Bong, Major Richard I (1920–45) See Aces.

Bonhöffer, Dietrich (1906–45) Evangelical Protestant theologian who maintained constant opposition to Nazism. Both his father and brother were committed anti-Nazis. After a period of studying and working in New York and London (1930–35), Dietrich Bonhöffer returned to Germany to work with the non-Nazi Confessional Church. He met and worked with many prominent members of the German opposition to Hitler, including General Beck*, Hans Oster*, Admiral Canaris* and members of the Kreisau Circle*. Between 1939 and 1943 he also made attempts to establish contacts with Britain and the US, although these foundered, as had others, on Allied suspicion and the demand for Germany's unconditional surrender. Bonhöffer was arrested in April 1943 by the SD* with Dohnanyi* and others, held at Buchenwald and finally executed at Flossenburg concentration camp* in April 1945. See Resistance: Germany.

Bonomi, Ivanoe (1873–1951) Italian Socialist and statesman who was premier of a coalition government in Italy from 1921 until Mussolini's* break with the Socialists, when his government fell. Bonomi remained outside Italian politics until recalled to Rome*, liberated by the Allies in June 1944, to become leader of the Committee of National Liberation, a cabinet of men with no Fascist associations. See also Italy, Capitulation of.

Booty, Operation Self-explanatory codename for the dismantling of German factories and the removal of machinery to the Soviet Union. It was begun immediately after the Russian occupation of Germany in 1945.

Bormann, Martin (1900–45?) Senior Nazi Party* figure and head of Hitler's secretariat. A post-WW1 Freikorps and *Frontbann* member, he joined the Thuringian Nazi Party in 1925 after serving a prison sentence for murder, and became Gauleiter in Thuringia in 1928. In the same year his fund-raising skills brought him promotion as party treasurer. From this time on, Bormann stayed close to Hitler*, though he kept a low profile. Among Hitler's entourage he ranked next to Deputy Führer Hess*. When Hess flew to Britain in 1941 (an act that may have been encouraged or facilitated by Bormann), he was promoted Party Minister in charge of Party Headquarters, and from this position was able to control access to Hitler, sometimes blocking contact even with Göring*, Göbbels*, Himmler* and Speer*. Ambitious for power even in the last days of the Reich, Bormann followed Hitler in his retreat to the Bunker, witnessing Hitler's will and marriage, attempting to order Göring's execution, and finally sending Dönitz* news of his succession as Führer. He was never seen alive after the breakout of Hitler's

staff from the Bunker, although persistent rumours have placed him in several countries, usually in South America. The discovery of a skull identified as Bormann's and the subsequent official declaration of his death by the West German government in 1973 represents perhaps the natural desperation of German leaders to stem the disruption to German political life caused by 'Nazi hunts', rather than a conclusive belief that the skull was Bormann's.

Borneo Island in the South China Sea, politically divided between the Dutch and the British, and defended only by a token battalion of Punjabi infantry when it was invaded by Japanese forces on 16 December 1941. In 1945, the Australian 1st Corps under Lt General Morshead* undertook the biggest Australian* operation of the war with the support of the US 7th Fleet when it launched assaults from landings on Sadau Island (30 April), Tarakan (1 May) and Brunei Bay (10 June). Having been refused the use of Philippine* air bases for the launch of an offensive against Singapore*, the British were still developing a base on Borneo when the Japanese surrendered on 2 September.

Bose, Subhas Chandra (1897–1945) Indian Nationalist leader who had been jailed several times by the British since his rejection of the independence movement led by Mohandas Gandhi. He saw the outbreak of war as an opportunity to accelerate the expulsion of the British from India. After escape from imprisonment in India in 1940, Bose managed to reach Berlin, where he organized a small body of Indian volunteers to fight the Allies. Following Japan's entry into the war, he went to Tokyo to announce the establishment of a Provisional Government of Free India and an Indian National Army, recruiting a reasonably large force from Indian Army* troops captured during the Malayan campaign. Though he subsequently led some of his troops in the Japanese offensives at Kohima and Imphal in 1944, the defeat of the Japanese ended his own hope of success. Bose died in a plane crash in 1945. See Indian Nationalism.

Bougainville Island Largest and most westerly of the Solomon* Island group in the Southwest Pacific, it was among the territories occupied and garrisoned by Japanese forces during the first half of 1942 and subsequently became an objective of the American amphibious* advance towards Rabaul* in 1943. In response to the launching of a two-pronged American counter-offensive in the summer of 1943, Japanese Imperial HQ retracted its defensive frontiers, abandoning the Central Solomons and withdrawing to Bougainville. The American landing on 1 November, commanded by Vice Admiral Halsey* with the 3rd Marine Division under General Vandegrift*, aimed to secure the valuable harbours and airfields which had served as advance supply and refuelling bases for Japanese operations in Guadalcanal* and the Central Solomons. Estimates of Japanese strength suggested a force of roughly 40,000, chiefly garrisoned in the south of the island.

The landing at Cape Torokina in Empress Augusta Bay by the 3rd Amphibious Force was preceded by diversionary Allied assaults on Treasury Island, Choiseul and the Shortlands Islands and bypassed the main Japanese troop concentration, securing sufficient land against little opposition in the first two days to build the first airstrip for bombers to begin raids on Rabaul. Two attempts by small Japanese forces on 1 November and 7 November to counter-attack were beaten off and the American presence was firmly established by the end of the year, with four newly built airfields and approximately 40,000 troops. Further unsuccessful attempts were made by Japanese forces to counter-attack during March, with heavy casualties, and the American advance moved on, leaving the southern Japanese garrison to 'wither on the vine'. Mopping-up operations were fought by Australian* troops under General Blamey*

well into 1945 against stranded Japanese survivors who had turned to growing vegetables in order to avoid starvation, and stubbornly defended their cultivated areas against vastly superior forces.

Boulton-Paul Defiant First delivered to the RAF* in December 1939, the Defiant fighter was designed with all its guns concentrated in a hydraulic rear turret. Once Luftwaffe* pilots became familiar with this peculiarity at Dunkirk*, it proved no match for single-seat fighters and was withdrawn from daylight operations. During the Blitz* of 1940–1 Defiants served as night fighters, equipped with early air-to-air radar*. The Defiant II, with a slightly more powerful engine, entered service in February 1941, and the plane ended its career performing target-towing and air/sea rescue* duties at home and in the tropical theatres. A total of 1,064 Defiants were built and production ended in February 1943.
BRIEF DATA (Mk I) Type: 2-man fighter; Engine: 1×1030hp Rolls Royce Merlin; Max speed: 303mph; Ceiling: 30,350'; Arms: $4 \times 0.303''$ mg.

Boyington, Colonel Gregory (1912–?) Colourful US Marine Corps flying ace* credited with the destruction of 28 Japanese aircraft, he had a reputation as an outstanding fighter pilot and squadron commander in combat. Veteran of the American Volunteer Group* (Flying Tigers), Boyington commanded the highly successful 214 Marine Fighter Squadron (known as the Black Sheep) in the Central Solomons area from September 1943 to January 1944, when he was shot down and captured. Following 20 months as a prisoner of war, Boyington returned to America to receive the Medal of Honour and the Navy Cross. He retired in 1947.

Bradley, General Omar (1893–1981) Highly successful American Army Group Commander whose considerable reputation as a strategist and leader was largely forged during the fighting in France in 1944 and

1945, though he had originally been picked out of relative obscurity and without combat experience to serve under Generals Eisenhower* and Patton* in North Africa. Here he replaced Patton (who went to command the 7th Army) as the commander of the US 2nd Corps for Allied operations in Tunisia* during the spring of 1943. On the basis of his combat record here and subsequently during the invasion of Sicily*, Bradley was appointed to command the American landings in Normandy* on D-Day, 6 June 1944, under the overall command of General Montgomery*.

In command of the American 1st Army landings on the Omaha and Utah beachheads, Bradley directed the consolidation and then breakout of his forces through the Mortain–Avranches gap into central France. In command of the one and a quarter million men of 12th Army Group from 1 August, he directed key operations against the West Wall*, in the Ardennes (see Battle of the Bulge) and over the Rhine*. It is a measure of his considerable qualities and popularity as a military leader that Bradley was able to achieve consistent success with such a vast command. Much decorated after the war, Bradley remained best known as the 'GI's General' and received perhaps his greatest acknowledgements from the troops who served under him.

Brandenburgers The special service units of the German Army*, the equivalent of the British commandos* or US rangers*. Brandenburgers were formed into companies in October 1939, and used to seize road and rail bridges ahead of the Army at the start of the Western Offensive* in Belgium and the Netherlands the following year. Later in 1940 the Brandenburgers reached regimental strength. In 1942–3 they guarded the rear of the Army's retreat from the Caucasus* and were used as a long-range patrol in the Desert War*. Trained in both defence and sabotage, the Brandenburgers derived their name from the location of their training area. They were not liked by the SS*, which had its own special

service troops and was careful to ensure that they received maximum publicity.

Brauchitsch, Field Marshal Walther von (1881–1948) Hitler's* chosen successor to Fritsch* as German Army C-in-C (OKH) in 1938, Brauchitsch oversaw successful operations in Poland*, Denmark*, Norway*, the Netherlands, Belgium, France (see Western Offensive) and the Balkans* between 1939 and 1941, despite his opposition to Hitler's initial proposal for an offensive in the west and General Manstein's* plan for the conduct of the campaign. Although Generals Beck* and Halder* and other professional staff officers sought his support against Hitler's war policies, there is no evidence that Brauchitsch was prepared, after this initial protest, to resist the established power in the Third Reich. Promoted Field Marshal following the capitulation of France in June 1940, he was subsequently made principal scapegoat for the German failure to capture Moscow* in 1941 and replaced as C-in-C by Hitler himself (see Eastern Front). Brauchitsch was never recalled to active service and died before the start of his trial for war crimes in 1948.

Braun, Werner von (1912–77) Technical director of German rocket* research at Peenemünde, Braun had been employed by the army on rocket research since the age of 20. At Peenemünde from 1937, he developed the prototype V-2* rocket, but Hitler's lack of interest diverted resources from the project until 1943, when he finally ordered mass production of the V-2. Braun resisted the SS* takeover of his now successful project and was briefly imprisoned in 1944. In March 1945 he evacuated his research group and surrendered with them to the US Army. He continued his research in America, was granted citizenship in 1955 and became a leading figure in the American missile programme.

Brazil Anxious to receive large-scale economic aid from the US, Brazil declared war on the Axis in August 1942, after a U-boat had sunk five Brazilian merchantmen in quick succession in the Atlantic*. Her material contribution to the conflict was negligible, although an expeditionary force of 25,000 men was sent to Italy* in 1944, but the use of Brazilian facilities on the South Atlantic coastline was valuable to the Allies in the war against German U-boats and auxiliary surface raiders (*Hilfskreuzer**).

Brereton, General Lewis Hyde (1890–1967) American General notable for his commitment to Allied and inter-service co-operation, he held USAAF* commands in the Pacific, North Africa and Europe and had served under General 'Billy' Mitchell, a controversial theorist of aerial warfare, during WW1. Commander of Far East Air Forces in the Philippines* under General MacArthur* when America entered the war, Brereton presided over the disastrous loss of American B-17* bombers, his main strike force, destroyed on the ground at Clark Field, Luzon*, on the first day of the Japanese attack on the Philippines. Responsibility for the loss, however, is widely attributed to General MacArthur, who continued to stall Brereton's pleas to get his force into the air while awaiting further intelligence.

In command of the newly formed 10th Air Force in India from February to June 1942, he was transferred to command the Middle East Air Forces. Here Brereton quickly earned the respect of British colleagues, working successfully in co-operation with the RAF*, and, in an early venture in Allied integration, taking command of the US Desert Air Force for the El Alamein* offensive. In 1942 Brereton accepted command of the newly designated US 9th Air Force which played a vital role in the Allied campaigns in North Africa, Sicily* and Italy*, including the attack on the Ploesti* oil refineries on 1 August 1943.

Both before and after the Allied invasion of Northwest Europe*, Brereton's 9th Air Force was indispensable to the Allied effort as one of the most effective tactical units

in operation, raiding selected targets in northern France designed to disrupt the German communications system. Brereton accepted an appointment in August 1944 as first Commander of the 1st Allied Airborne Army which fought at Arnhem* in September.

Brest Port in western France used as a base for both surface warships and submarines* of the German Navy* from mid-1940. Brest was bombed repeatedly throughout the war by RAF* Bomber Command, and important German warships were disabled there. The massively protected concrete submarine pens remained virtually undamaged throughout, however, and the same was true of the other major U-boat base on the French coast at Lorient. Both were heavily defended against the Allied invasion forces in 1944, and when Brest fell to the Americans in September it was not in workable condition, although the facilities had been considered important to the success of Allied operations in Northwest Europe*. Lorient held out to the end of the war.

Bretagne French Navy* battleship completed during WW1 and partially modernized between the wars. The *Bretagne* was with Admiral Gensoul at Mers-el-Kébir* when the Royal Navy* attacked on 3 July 1940. After receiving several 15-inch shell hits, she exploded and went down with 977 of her crew.

Her sister the *Provence*, modernized on a similar scale, was beached during the same action. Refloated, she eventually returned to the French naval base at Toulon, where she was scuttled on 27 November 1942. A third unit, the *Lorraine*, had been more thoroughly rebuilt and was with Admiral Cunningham's* Royal Navy force at Alexandria* in 1940. She was neutralized when France surrendered.

BRIEF DATA (Bretagne, 1939) Displacement: 22,189 tons; Dimensions: o/a lgth – 544' 9", b – 88' 6"; Speed: 21.5 knots; Armaments: 10 × 13.4" gun (5 × 2), 14 ×

5.5″ gun, 8 × 3″ AA gun, 12 × 13.2mm AA mg.

Bretton Woods See Conferences, Allied.

Brevity, Operation Although Rommel* had driven the British back from Tripolitania to the Egyptian frontier by mid-April 1941 (see Desert War), his lightning advance had not taken Tobruk* on the coast. Denied urgently needed reinforcements by the German High Command's preoccupation with the forthcoming invasion of Russia, Rommel's early attacks on Tobruk failed and General Wavell* was encouraged to take the offensive from positions in Egypt. Operation Brevity, launched before the arrival of large-scale reinforcements, was Wavell's first attempt to exploit Rommel's apparent material weakness.

The operation began on the morning of 15 May. Brigadier Gott's* small frontier force – augmented by 56 tanks* – attacked Italian-held coastal positions near the border. After taking the Halfaya Pass, the advance collapsed a little further down the coast under a flanking attack from German units. Both sides withdrew in haste, but Rommel countermanded the Axis retreat and sent up a panzer battalion from outside Tobruk, while Gott fell back before Wavell could reverse the order, leaving only a small garrison at Halfaya. This was picked off by Axis units on 27 May. Equipped with converted 88mm* anti-aircraft* guns (see Eighty-eight), it became one of several devastatingly effective Axis forward tank traps which seriously hampered the larger-scale Battleaxe* offensive in June.

Brewster F2A Buffalo In 1936, this squat aircraft was chosen ahead of the Grumman F4F Wildcat* to be the US Navy's* first monoplane carrier fighter. It took the inexperienced Buffalo company until April 1939 to begin service delivery, and the plane failed to justify the faith shown in it. Although the 43 F2As sent to Finland* fought well in 1940, the 170 delivered as the standard RAF* land-based fighter in the Far East were badly mauled by their more mobile Japanese opponents. All but 11 of the 163 Buffalos used in the Pacific War* by the US Navy (and Marines) were the improved F2A-2 or F2A-3 versions, which introduced self-sealing tanks as well as more engine power, guns and armour but were still no match for the Japanese Mitsubishi A6M Zero* fighters. After failing conspicuously at Midway*, the Buffalo was relegated to training duties and production ended in 1942.

BRIEF DATA (F2A-2) Type: single-seat fighter; Engine: 1 × 1,100hp Wright; Max speed: 300mph; Ceiling: 30,500′; Range: 650m; Arms: 4 × 0.5″ mg.

Brezhnev, Leonid I. (1906–82) First Secretary of the Soviet Communist Party and Chairman of the Presidium of the Supreme Soviet from 1977, Brezhnev's wartime service was as a political commissar (see Red Army). First posted to the Southern Front*, and later chief political administrator to the 4th Ukrainian Front, Brezhnev oversaw operations in the Caucasus*, the Black Sea regions and the Ukraine*.

Brindisi Southern Italian port on the Adriatic coast. It was proclaimed the capital of the 'new Italy' when it became the refuge for the Italian royal family and newly appointed government under Marshal Badoglio*, who had fled Rome after the announcement of Italy's* capitulation to the Allies on 8 September 1943. The city was occupied three days later by the British 1st Airborne Division (8th Army).

Bristol Beaufort The Beaufort entered RAF* service in November 1939, and became Coastal Command's standard torpedo-bomber (superseding ancient Vickers Wildebeest biplanes) until being replaced by the Bristol Beaufighter* in 1943. Beauforts saw action over the North Sea, the English Channel, the Atlantic* and the Mediterranean*. Production ceased in 1944, by which time 2,129 had been built, including 700 in Australia.

BRIEF DATA (Mk I) Type: 4-man torpedo-bomber; Engine: 2 × 1,130hp Bristol Taurus; Max speed: 265mph; Ceiling: 16,500′; Range: 1,035m; Arms: 2 × 0.303″ mg; Bomb load: 1,500lb or 1 × 1,605lb torpedo*.

Bristol Blenheim The Blenheim I light bomber, a handsome all-metal monoplane, joined RAF* Bomber Command in March 1937, and was a massive improvement on its biplane predecessors. By the outbreak of war, it was serving only in Egypt* with Middle East Command, home-based squadrons having been equipped with the more powerful, long-nosed Blenheim IVs. Although very vulnerable to modern fighters, these flew daylight raids over Europe until August 1942, when they were withdrawn and replaced by Lockheed Hudsons* and de Havilland Mosquitos*. Three months later, the tropicalized Blenheim V began operations in North Africa, but it was a conspicuous failure and last saw service in the Far East in August 1943. The Blenheim IF, which had joined squadrons in December 1938, was a specialist night fighter. It pioneered the use of airborne radar* and fought throughout the Blitz* of 1940–1. Some Blenheim IVs were also converted as heavy fighters. Production totals of Blenheims I, IV and V were 1,134, 3,297 and 940 respectively.

BRIEF DATA (Mk IV) Type: 3-man light bomber; Engine: 2 × 920hp Bristol Mercury; Max speed: 266mph; Ceiling: 22,000′; Range: 1,460m; Arms: 5 × 0.303″ mg; Bomb load: 1,060lb internal, 320lb external.

Britain, Battle of The critical air battle fought over southern England in 1940 between the Luftwaffe* and the RAF*, following the fall of Belgium, the Netherlands and France to German forces (see Western Offensive). In June 1940, with his victorious armies on the Channel coast, and no indication from Churchill* that Britain had accepted the obvious fact of her defeat along with her ally France, Hitler* accepted Göring's* assurance that the Luftwaffe could engage and defeat RAF Fighter Command and open the way for a seaborne invasion of Britain, Operation Sealion*, should it prove necessary.

In pilot training and the quality of fighter aircraft engaged, the two sides were fairly well matched, although Luftwaffe pilots often had the edge in combat experience. Their Messerschmitt Bf109* fighters marginally outperformed the RAF's Supermarine Spitfires* and were clearly superior to the more numerous Hawker Hurricanes*. The British had possession of the battleground, which gave RAF interceptors more time over the combat area than their German counterparts and enabled more planes and pilots to be salvaged from operations. Fighter Command also had the benefits of an effective early warning radar* system and the accurate intelligence provided by Ultra*. Its commander, Dowding*, employed a strictly centralized system of controlling his limited resources, using these information services to pinpoint attacks against confirmed hostile aircraft.

The Luftwaffe deployed 2,800 aircraft for the battle in three air fleets stationed in northwest France (Luftflotte III), northern France and the Low Countries (II) and Norway* (V). Although this outnumbered Fighter Command's aircraft by 4 to 1, the German medium bombers – mostly Heinkel He111s* and Dornier Do17s – were too slow and underarmed to escape modern fighters, and needed escort from the Bf109s. The same was soon found to be true of the highly regarded Messerschmitt Me110* twin-engined fighter, and the much feared Junkers Ju87* Stuka dive-bombers had to be withdrawn after catastrophic losses in the opening skirmishes.

The battle opened in July 1940, while a German invasion fleet was prepared, with the Luftwaffe attacking Channel ports and shipping in an attempt to provoke the RAF into a decisive engagement. Fighter Command would not be drawn, and in August Hitler issued the order to concentrate attacks on RAF airfields and aircraft. The effective range limit of the Bf109s on the Channel coast was London, and the battle was therefore fought primarily over southern England, protected by Fighter Command's No. 11 Group (Park*) with No. 12 Group (Leigh-Mallory*) supporting from the eastern counties (see Big Wing).

Helped by the Luftwaffe's unaccountable failure to destroy the fragile radar stations, Fighter Command just survived the onslaught. From 1–18 August it lost 208 fighters and 106 pilots, and by the latter part of the month wastage was outstripping production and training. Many airfields were repeatedly put out of action and by early September fatigue was affecting the combat performance of RAF pilots. Each day, combat statistics were announced by both sides and numbers became the key to the battle as the Luftwaffe anticipated Fighter Command's collapse. Based on pilot claims and invariably wildly optimistic, these figures were a boost to civilian and RAF morale in Britain, but in Germany they led to a fatal misinterpretation of the state of the battle.

In late August, Hitler rescinded an order forbidding attacks on civilian targets. He had been provoked by a small RAF bombing raid on Berlin (itself a reprisal for bombs dropped accidentally on London), but also encouraged by Göring, whose arithmetic showed that Fighter Command was virtually beaten. In fact, although Dowding had run out of reserves and his pilots were exhausted, he still had over 700 aircraft available. With the invasion fleet on stand-by (the German Navy* had asked for ten days notice of Sealion), 300 bombers and 600 escorting fighters raided London in daylight on 7 September. This was expected to force Fighter Command to send up its last few aircraft, but Park's squadrons failed for once to intercept the bombers in strength, thus inadvertently masking their true strength. Day and night attacks on the capital over the next week seemed to confirm to the Luftwaffe that Fighter Command's collapse was imminent.

Hitler brought the date of the invasion forward to 17 September, but the relaxation of pressure on Fighter Command's airfields and production centres at this crucial moment quickly enabled it to regain its vigour. This was revealed to the Luftwaffe on 15 September, when heavy losses were inflicted on another mass daylight operation against London, and German airmen began to doubt that they could after all remove the threat of the RAF. This in turn meant that the Royal Navy* could threaten the approach of the invasion fleet (12 per cent of which had already been destroyed by RAF bombing) with the benefit of an air umbrella. On 17 September, Hitler postponed Operation Sealion indefinitely.

From that point German daylight operations began to tail off. Fighters and fighter-bombers still flew daylight sorties, often against aircraft factories, but the medium bomber fleets were directed against British cities at night. At first attacks were aimed at destroying civilian morale. Up to 400 bombers raided London virtually every night when the weather allowed until mid-November in what became known as the Blitz. Contrary to pre-war theories, British society showed few signs of disintegrating under the onslaught, and on 13 October Hitler postponed Sealion until the following spring. By the end of October, when daylight battles had virtually ceased, the Luftwaffe had lost about 1,800 aircraft and over 2,500 aircrew since July. Fighter Command figures were 1,100 aircraft lost and about 550 pilots killed. From 14 November, when 450 aircraft devastated the city of Coventry*, Luftwaffe night attacks were directed more broadly at strategic targets, particularly against ports, as a contribution to the Battle of the Atlantic*.

The Blitz continued until May 1941, with a lull during foul midwinter weather. After London, the principal targets were Liverpool, Birmingham and Plymouth. Using radio direction-finding devices (e.g. X-Gerät) to locate targets, and suffering far fewer losses to the RAF's primitive night fighting methods, the Luftwaffe dropped a total of 54,420 tons of bombs* (including incendiaries) on Britain during the period. Although most attacks were wildly inaccurate, they killed 40,000 people and injured 86,000. Two million homes were destroyed, 60 per cent of them in London. Nevertheless the Blitz failed seriously to disrupt British industrial production, port operations or internal communications – facts which were glossed over when the RAF began its own Strategic Bombing Offensive* against Germany with a far smaller bomber force.

In the spring of 1941 the attacks on ports, including London, were intensified. The Luftwaffe carried out 61 raids between 19 February and 12 May, using up to 700 bombers at a time. Hitler, however, was planning the invasion of Russia, and bomber groups were secretly being withdrawn eastwards so that, by 21 May, 90 per cent of the Luftwaffe's bombing force had left.

British Army Up to 1939 the British Army was primarily charged with the protection of the Empire, although four divisions had been promised to France in the event of German aggression. Much of the burden of this responsibility was borne by the armies of the British Commonwealth and Empire, and the Regular Army was a small professional force. Its main reserve – the volunteer Territorial Army – was poorly trained and ill-equipped, but was being mobilized when war was declared. With the introduction of limited conscription, British Army strength was brought up to 50 divisions during 1940. Nevertheless only 13 divisions (none of them armoured divisions) had been sent to France as the British Expeditionary Force when Germany invaded in May (see Western Offensive). By the end of June, with the evacuations from Dunkirk* and Norway* complete, total British Army strength stood at 1,650,000 men – but they were desperately short of modern equipment, much of which had been left behind.

After the fall of France, the British land effort was concentrated on North Africa, and the defence of other Imperial strongholds (notably Singapore*) was subordinated to the supply of Egypt*. A small force was sent to Greece* in March 1941, but was soon driven back to Egypt, losing Crete* in the process. After Japan entered the war, British and Empire troops were deployed in numbers in the Far East, where India became the home base for a prolonged campaign in Burma*. In November 1942, British forces in North Africa (see Desert War) were decisively augmented by the British 1st Army in Northwest Africa (see Torch; Tunisia), which included American and later French troops. Subsequently, British Army units took part in Allied invasions of Sicily*, Italy*, Normandy* and southern France (see Anvil/Dragoon). Cooperation between British and US forces at both field and High Command levels was very effective in the later years of the war, if occasionally grudging. Rivalries did however surface, sometimes with far-reaching effects (see e.g. Northwest Europe, Invasion of).

Although British heavy industry was effectively mobilized to answer the Army's quantitative needs after Dunkirk*, the quality of British *matériel* was variable. Adequately equipped with field artillery*, infantry weapons and ammunition, the Army lacked modern medium and anti-tank* artillery, and the quality and deployment of its tank* forces left much to be desired. British infantry held one distinct advantage over other major European armies in that it was almost completely motorized, and Britain led the world in the wartime development of special-purpose* armoured engineering vehicles.

Total British Army strength had reached almost two and a half million men by mid-1941, and it rose steadily to reach 2,920,000 by June 1945. During WW2 144,079 British soldiers were killed, 239,575 were wounded and 152,079 were taken prisoner.

British Broadcasting Corporation Semi-public body which had a monopoly over

British radio broadcasts throughout the war. It was paid for out of Treasury Grant-in-aid, public subscription being abolished during the war years. The BBC employed 4,889 people in September 1939, and this had risen to 11,000 by 1942, remaining at about that level for the rest of the war. Twenty-four transmitters were in operation at the start of the war and 121 in May 1945, in contrast to Germany which never possessed more than 50 broadcast transmitters. Television broadcasting, which was in its infancy, was closed down during the war, and the RAF* used the transmitter to jam Luftwaffe navigational aids in 1940–1.

The BBC's prime wartime functions were the dissemination of government-inspired information to the British people (9.9 million households were licensed radio owners by 1945), and long-range broadcasting to agents and civilians in Asia and Europe. The BBC gained credibility with the British people by unflinchingly reporting the calamitous course of the war in its early years. The accuracy of BBC reporting on foreign affairs often left much to be desired, but the policy of the Corporation, loosely or accidentally arrived at, was to attempt to broadcast the truth. By 1944 it was doing this daily in some 50 languages. In many European countries, particularly Denmark*, the BBC played a leading role in encouraging and informing resistance* movements often through broadcasts from exiled national figures (e.g. de Gaulle*). See also Propaganda.

British Somaliland See East Africa, Campaign in.

Brittany, Campaign in, 1944 Following the American breakout from Normandy* (see Cobra) at the end of July 1944, General Patton* detached the US 8th Corps of his newly operational 3rd Army westwards towards Brest, while the 4th Armored Division drove southwest towards Quiberon Bay, cutting off the peninsula from the mainland. Although the advance was rapid, through countryside already largely

cleared of German troops by the FFI (*Forces Françaises de l'Intérieur*), the capture of the ports of Brest*, Lorient and St Nazaire* was checked by a grimly determined German defence. While the main Allied advance eastward towards the Seine increasingly lured Patton's attention, his orders from Bradley* demanded that Patton stay in place to contain the forces at Lorient and St Nazaire and continue the siege of German garrison commander Ramke's forces at Brest. Nevertheless by early September, the Allied front, including the rest of Patton's 3rd Army, had moved so far to the east that the projected development of Brittany as a major logistical base was no longer feasible, and the Brittany operations came under command of Lt General Simpson's 9th Army. Brest fell on 18 September. Lorient and St Nazaire continued to be contained until the war was ended. See also Northwest Europe, Allied Invasion of.

Brooke, Field Marshal Alan (1st Viscount Alanbrooke) (1883–1963) Successor to Sir John Dill* as British Chief of the Imperial General Staff in 1941, and Chairman of the Chiefs of Staff Committee from June 1942, Brooke was widely regarded as one of Britain's most able strategists and field generals, and played a crucial part in the day-to-day running of the war, providing the British Chiefs of Staff with a clear and cohesive leadership. In 1940, as commander of the 2nd Corps, British Expeditionary Force in France, Brooke was instrumental in directing the defensive actions which secured the escape of the BEF from Dunkirk*. Briefly appointed C-in-C Home Forces before replacing Dill as CIGS, Brooke became Churchill's* principal strategic adviser and one of the few military chiefs who was able to influence and contain Churchill's somewhat impetuous and grandiose approach to military strategy. In the face of considerable pressure, he maintained good relations with both Churchill and most American military leaders throughout the war, though the mutual antipathy felt by Brooke and US General

George Marshall* was a regular feature of the sometimes strained relationships among the Allied Combined Chiefs of Staff*.

Brooke-Popham, Air Chief Marshal Sir Robert (1878–1953) British C-in-C of all land and air forces in Hong Kong*, Malaya* and British Borneo* at the time of the Japanese entry into the war, Brooke-Popham had been recalled from retirement begun in 1937, when he became Governor of Kenya, to command British forces in the Far East, though his replacement, Lt General Pownall, had already been appointed when Japanese forces invaded Siam (Thailand*), as a preliminary to the invasion of Malaya in December 1941. He returned to England on 27 December.

Brooklyn, USS American light cruiser and Class. Commissioned in 1937, the nine ships of the *Brooklyn* Class were the first light cruisers to be built for the US Navy* since the *Omaha** Class of the early 1920s. They were inspired by the Japanese *Mogami** Class of 1935, which packed a large number of 6-inch guns (the maximum allowed for cruisers under the international London Naval Treaty of 1930) onto a heavy cruiser hull. This offered the prospect of an advantage over 8-inch armed vessels at a time when long-range gunnery depended entirely on good visibility. Thus the five triple turrets of the *Brooklyns* were designed to provide a massed broadside at relatively close range. They were armoured on about the same scale as the latest *New Orleans** Class heavy cruisers, with which they were intended to combine tactically.

The *Brooklyn*, *Philadelphia* and *Savannah* served mostly in the Atlantic. They covered Allied landings in Northwest Africa (see Torch), Sicily* and Italy* in 1942 –4, the *Savannah* surviving serious damage from a German guided bomb* at Salerno* in September 1943. The rest of the class spent an arduous war fighting their way across the South and Central Pacific, although the *Boise* was at Sicily in 1943 after repairs to gunfire damage incurred at the Battle of Cape Esperance*. The only unit lost was the *Helena* – torpedoed by Japanese destroyers at Kula Gulf* on 6 July 1943 – although several of the class suffered serious damage. After the war, all eight survivors were retired from US Navy active service, most of them joining South American navies in the early 1950s.

BRIEF DATA (Brooklyn, 1941) Displacement: 9,700 tons; Dimensions: o/a lgth – 608' 3", b – 61' 9"; Speed: 32.5 knots; Armament: 15 × 6" gun (5 × 3), 8 × 5" AA gun, 4 × 3pdr AA gun, 8 × 0.5" AA gun, 4 aircraft.

Brummbar See Self-propelled Artillery.

BT7 Tank The BT series of fast tanks was developed by the Soviet Union in the 1930s for use by independent long-range mechanized divisions. Their speed was derived from a suspension system copied from the American Christie M1931 light tank, later also developed by the British for their Cruiser tanks*. The BT7M, introduced in 1939 and a great improvement on its predecessors, formed the bulk of the Soviet armoured force when Germany invaded in June 1941 (see Eastern Front). Thinly armoured, it was no match for German guns and aircraft, and was quickly superseded by the immensely superior T34*, although surviving BTs remained in service until they wore out.

BRIEF DATA (BT7M) Type: 3-man fast tank; Engine: 500hp diesel; Max speed: 53.4mph; Range: 270m; Arms: 1 × 76.2mm gun, 2 × 7.62mm mg; Armour: max 22mm.

Buchenwald One of the earliest concentration camps* of the Third Reich, located in woods outside Weimar. The camp supplied prisoner labour in 12-hour shifts to local armaments plants. Liberated by elements of the US 80th Division in April 1945, Buchenwald held 20,000 starving and exhausted men and boys. Deaths recorded in the *Totenbuch* averaged 6,000 per month. Even so, Buchenwald was not an extermination camp. Experienced camp inmates declared it to contain more long-term survivors than most.

Budapest See Hungary.

Budenny, Marshal Semion (1883–1973) Flamboyant Soviet Marshal, commander of Soviet armies on the Southwest Front in 1941 when they suffered their most devastating defeats. In 1935, having commanded the 1st Soviet Cavalry Army since 1920, Budenny became one of five marshals of the Soviet Union who were created in that year. He was one of only two marshals (the other Voroshilov*) to survive Stalin's* purges of the Russian officer corps in 1938. Owing his prominence largely, it seems, to his friendship with Stalin and his reputation as an old-school cavalry commander, Budenny was appointed a member of Stavka* and commander of the Southwestern Front in the Ukraine* in July 1941. This sector of the front was given priority in supplies and reinforcements by Stalin, who was determined to hold Kiev at all costs. With overwhelming numerical superiority, but with no ability in modern generalship, Budenny was utterly outclassed by German commanders Rundstedt* and Kleist*. In his disastrous defence of Kiev* and Uman, Budenny lost one and a half million men, (over half the Red Army's* active strength) and was forced to abandon Kiev. Ordered, along with his commissar Khrushchev*, to evacuate industry in the Ukraine, Budenny was responsible for the destruction of the Dnieper dam at Zaporozhe. Replaced by Timoshenko* on 13 September, Budenny was sent to the Reserve Front and became Commander of the Soviet Cavalry in 1943.

Bulganin, Political Marshal Nikolai (1895 –1975) Premier of the Soviet Union during the 1950s, Bulganin began his career in the Cheka (the Soviet secret police later replaced by the NKVD*). As political marshal, Bulganin was a member of the Stavka*, detailed to oversee the activities of the front-line generals. Sent first to the Centre Front* commanded by Timoshenko*, he later participated in the investigations into the failure of Kurochkin's* Northwest Front and then went to the West Front, where he sat as a member of the Military Council there with Generals Konev* and Sokolovsky*. Bulganin was promoted Colonel General in 1944 and was sent as representative to the Soviet-sponsored Lublin Committee* in Poland. He later served as Deputy People's Commissar of Defence, 1944–6.

Bulgaria Slavic state in the eastern Balkans*, ruled until 1943 by Csar Boris III, it had sided with Germany in 1915 and was one of the central European states (the other Hungary*) whose friendship with the Third Reich was acquired by means of a grant of territory belonging to Rumania* (an Axis* partner), formalized in the Vienna Award of August 1940. Having joined the Axis in March 1941, Bulgaria joined Germany in the occupation of Yugoslavia* in 1941, but was not involved in the campaign against Russia. Nevertheless Bulgaria was invaded by Soviet forces in September 1944 and a predominantly communist regime was established under Soviet auspices.

Bulge, Battle of the, December 1944 The largest land battle fought by US armed forces in WW2, so called because of the dangerous bulge which it created in the American lines at a critical stage of the Allied invasion of Northwest Europe*. The Battle was precipitated by the launch of the last major German counter-offensive of the war in the west, through the semi-mountainous, wooded Ardennes* region of northern France. In the lull in fighting which followed Montgomery's* abortive drive to the Rhine* (see Antwerp) and the notorious failure at Arnhem*, Hitler exploited the opportunity to launch an ambitiously conceived counter-offensive stroke which he believed might snatch back the initiative on his Western Front. The attack completely surprised Allied Supreme Commander Eisenhower* and the staff of SHAEF*, whose intelligence assessment had discounted the possibility of German Field Marshal Rundstedt* committing all his reserves to such an ambitious gamble of forces. But Hitler's grandiose plan, to drive quickly to Antwerp, split the British and American forces and stabilize his western front overruled Rundstedt's limited aim of restoring the West Wall* (Siegfried Line) defences and ignored the serious reservations of both Rundstedt and Field Marshal Model*.

Thus, on the morning of 16 December, 25 German divisions (11 armoured) arranged into three armies overran the American lines thinly held by six divisions of resting and newly arrived troops, on a 60-mile front from Monschau in the north to Echternach in Luxembourg. Apart from isolated and courageous attempts to hold the line (notably by the US 7th Armored Division at St Vith and by the 101st Airborne Division at Bastogne*), the initial advance of the Sixth Panzer Army under General Dietrich* on the main front developed steadily, supported by General Manteuffel's Fifth Panzer Army drive on the left flank and General Brandenburger's flanking protection in the south. In addition, Hitler launched deception plan Operation Grief* to infiltrate a brigade of Germans disguised as US soldiers, in stolen uniforms and jeeps, to capture bridges and disrupt communications in the vicinity of the Meuse. Although the deception was uncovered, it clearly added to the confusion and mounting consternation at Eisenhower's SHAEF HQ, which was roused only slowly to the scale of the German offensive, initially assumed to be a local attack at Monschau.

Only a combination of sustained heroism on the part of the scattered defenders (which often included clerks, cooks and other non-combative personnel) and speedy troop reinforcement (of nearly 200,000 men in the first four days), managed to contain the German penetration,

allowing time for the reorganization of Allied forces by Eisenhower and the deployment of the Allied air forces temporarily grounded by bad weather. Although further German advances were checked initially by the shortage of fuel, which halted their drive short of the Meuse, rather than by Allied pressure, heavy fighter-bomber raids on the German columns after 23 December and counter-attacks by elements of the US 1st and 3rd Armies during late December and early January finally persuaded Hitler of the necessity to order a withdrawal from the now decreasing bulge. The short-lived gains of the Ardennes offensive had cost Germany 100,000 casualties, 1,000 aircraft and large quantities of weapons and equipment, which, unlike the United States, Germany was unable to replace quickly. In the same month, Germany faced a crucial test in the greatest Russian offensive of the war on the Eastern Front*.

Buna The eastern terminal of the Kokoda Trail over the Owen Stanley Mountains in New Guinea*. It was occupied by Japanese naval forces on 22 July 1942 and retaken by the Allies after heavy fighting at the beginning of January 1943.

Burke, Captain Arleigh (1901–) Able commander of US Navy* destroyer* squadrons operating in the South Pacific during 1943 and 1944, he developed a distinctive strategy for the independent use of destroyers in night actions. Burke served first in the Solomon Islands* and then as commander of Destroyer Squadron 23 (Little Beavers) covering the American landings on Bougainville* and New Guinea* and fighting actions to prevent the Japanese reinforcement of the islands. From March 1944, he served as chief of staff to Vice Admiral Mitscher*, commander of Fast Carrier Task Force 58, and was Mitscher's chief aide in the Marshalls*, Marianas*, Leyte*, Iwo Jima* and Okinawa* campaigns. After the war Burke was given appointments in Washington, the Mediterranean and Korea, and served as Chief of Naval Operations from 1955 until 1961.

Burma, Campaigns in, 1941–5 Part of the huge British colonial territory in Southeast Asia that was included in Japan's expansionist plan for the Greater East Asia Co-Prosperity Sphere*, Burma was invaded in December 1941 by a relatively small force of 35,000 men of the 15th Army under Lt General Iida* (see Maps 24 and 25). The initial invasion force had been launched almost concurrently with the invasion of Malaya* (see Map 23), with landings by a 15th Army detachment (Southern Army) at Tenasserim on the Kra Isthmus assigned to capture three British airfields and cover the rear of the invasion armies landing at Singora and Patani for the move south into Malaya. The major objective of the campaign was to cut the vital supply line to China*, the Burma Road*, and strangle the Kuomintang's* attempts at further resistance. The relatively small size of the force under Iida was justified by the paucity of Allied defensive deployment in Burma, which had not been considered a likely location for major operations before the start of the Pacific War*. The force consisted of a few small British units and a locally recruited 1st Burma Division which was poorly equipped and inadequately trained, along with a squadron of American Brewster Buffalo* fighters and one fighter squadron of Major General Chennault's* American Volunteer Group, numbering about 30 aircraft in total. Following the decisive Japanese victories in Malaya and the Philippines*, two more Japanese divisions, as well as tank*, artillery and anti-aircraft* units, were allocated to the fighting in Burma. General Obata's 5th Air Division provided air support for the invasion.

The Fall of Burma Air attacks on the capital and major port of Rangoon*, which was the principal port of entry for Allied supplies to China, were launched from Tenasserim and Victoria Point airfields on 23 and 25 December and preceded the Japanese northward advance from Thailand* to Moulmein, which was occupied on 31 December. Attempts by the British commander, General Hutton, to argue for a strategic withdrawal to the Bilin River, were overridden by C-in-C Wavell*, who remained committed to holding Rangoon at all costs. As a result, the defenders, withdrawing along roads and across open, cultivated areas, were consistently outflanked and defeated by Japanese units operating from the cover of the jungle.

The arrival of the 17th Indian Division as reinforcements under General Smyth did little to arrest the momentum of the Japanese advance to the northwest, crossing the Salween and Bilin Rivers and driving the defenders in front of them to the broad Sittang River, where the vital Sittang Bridge was blown up by British engineers, leaving most of Smyth's troops stranded on the eastern bank. By 4 March, the Japanese had exploited their advantage to reach Pegu, where the remnants of Smyth's force was assembling for a final stand in defence of the approaches to Rangoon. Despite the courageous efforts of the 63rd Indian Brigade and the insistence of the newly appointed overall commander General Alexander* that Rangoon could be held, the city was finally abandoned on 6 March, and the remaining British troops narrowly escaped encirclement as they withdrew northward through Prome.

The arrival in Burma of two Chinese armies under US General Stilwell* during mid-March did little to alter the pattern of the Japanese advance. After a period of reinforcement, the Japanese drive continued to push the defenders, now hampered by the presence of thousands of fleeing refugees, northwards through central Burma in a withdrawal that quickly disintegrated into a rout. Abandoning a plan to hold Mandalay*, General Alexander was finally compelled to order a general withdrawal to Assam in India. By 30 April Lashio, the western terminus of the vital Burma Road, had fallen to the Japanese. Steadfast efforts by the Chinese army to hold the central Shan Plateau were abandoned to avoid losing the last line of retreat, and the defence broke up, with Chinese units fleeing north. With little time left before the arrival of the monsoon weather, British General Slim* (in command of the Burcorps since 19 April) supervised the long retreat back to India, with Japanese forces in close pursuit. By the end of May, Burma was entirely in Japanese hands, and the British faced a defeat which had cost over 13,000 lives and left Japan in firm control of British colonial territory in Southeast Asia, at the western limit of their planned defensive perimeter.

The British command in India was now faced with an immensely difficult and complex situation. The task of developing Assam as a major base, constructing airfields, depots, roads, railways and pipelines, to prepare for a counter-offensive planned for November 1942 was hampered by monsoon weather and an inadequate labour force. In addition, General Wavell was forced to fight for shipping to carry all supplies from overseas to a theatre which had low priority in comparison with the major Atlantic, Mediterranean and Pacific war theatres. Logistical problems, including the critical shortage of supplies, equipment and adequately trained troops for the Indian Command was compounded by the political situation in India (see Indian Nationalism). Increasing disorder and civil unrest precipitated by the failure of Sir Stafford Cripps's* mission to placate Gandhi and the Indian Congress with a promise of independence after the war had been won, was exploited by Japan to her advantage. Finally, administrative problems were highlighted by the complexities of the command situation in Southeast Asia and the often conflicting views of Wavell, Chiang Kai-shek* and the American commander of Chinese forces, General Stilwell.

The Arakan Offensive Nevertheless, a limited offensive on the Arakan* coast, launched in December 1942, attempted to recapture the port of Akyab for use as an airfield, with disastrous results. An attempt to retrieve the situation by sending a force of Brigadier Wingate's* guerrillas, the Chindits*, on a raid into northern Burma to disrupt Japanese communications, achieved only limited military success, although it provided a valuable morale boost to flagging British spirits in India.

During the rest of 1943 and early 1944, Allied plans for the reconquest of Burma remained fraught with continual political, military and personal conflicts of interest. The restructuring in August 1943 of the India Command as the Southeast Asia Command (SEAC) under Lord Louis Mountbatten*, with Stilwell as Deputy Supreme Commander, went some way to improve the administrative problems in the theatre. The American airlifts across 'The Hump'* also successfully maintained a vital supply route to China across the treacherous Himalayas. But at Allied conferences* during the period, arguments highlighted the multifarious strategic plans being promoted for Burma, and the differing approaches of the American and British military chiefs. General Stilwell vociferously argued the American unwillingness to countenance any broad campaign designed to recover British colonial territory in Southeast Asia, and insisted on the limitation of the Allied effort to Burma itself, a plan which was finally agreed by the Allies for launch in the dry season of 1944.

Kohima and Imphal Meanwhile, the Japanese reinforced their positions in Burma, improved communications and reorganized their command under Lt General Kawabe*, now preparing for a renewed offensive on the Arakan front designed to forestall the offensive in the same area being prepared by the Allies. Both sides planned limited offensives in the southern region, the Arakan front, as a preliminary to further offensives in the northern and central sectors. Three Japanese armies, the 15th under Lt General Mutaguchi, the 28th under Lt General Sakurai, and the 33rd under General Honda, were positioned on the central, southern and northern sections of the Indian–Burmese border with Kohima* and

Imphal* as their major objectives. The Allied plan, Operation Capital, envisaged a thrust through northern and central Burma supporting a diversionary attack by Wingate's Chindits at Indaw and a secondary attack in the south around Arakan by the 14th Army (comprising General Christison's 15th Corps, General Stopford's* 33rd Corps and General Scoones'* 4th Corps) under General Slim*. The Japanese offensive began on the Arakan front on 3 February, with a strong attack by Sakurai's 28th Army, but the improved tactics and air supply of the British and Indian troops under General Slim enabled 15th Corps to meet the attack and hold its positions, forcing Sakurai to order a withdrawal on 23 February, as an attack was launched by British forces against him.

In the north, General Stilwell took direct command of his Chinese forces and sent an American Chindit-style unit known as Merrill's* Marauders in a general attack behind Japanese lines. On the central front, Wingate's Chindits began the offensive on 5 February, launching extensive long-range penetration operations by air and infiltration across Japanese lines. Nevertheless on 7 March, the Japanese 33rd Division opened their offensive with an advance on Tiddim *en route* for Imphal, supported by drives further north towards Ukrul and Kohima by the 15th and 31st Divisions. Although the moves took British forces by surprise, the new tactics developed by Slim and employed with success on the Arakan front again proved decisive. In the major battle for Burma fought around Kohima and Imphal during the spring of 1944, three Japanese divisions were fought to a standstill by British forces under Generals Slim, Scoones and Stopford. Now with almost complete control of the air, which enabled them to supply their large force at Imphal, Slim's 14th Army launched a counter-attack which decimated Mutaguchi's 15th Army. By 4 July, when Mutaguchi finally ordered the Japanese retreat, only 30,000 of the original force of over 80,000 were still fit for duty.

The Allied Recapture of Burma While General Slim's part in Operation Capital, the Allied overland offensive, had been stalled by the Japanese offensive, the advance of General Stilwell's Northern Combat Area forces, with the Chindit groups as the spearhead, had been largely unaffected by the Kohima and Imphal battles. The plan to capture Myitkyina*, using the Chindits to seize Indaw as a preliminary, was hampered by poor preparation and stubborn resistance from Japanese forces under General Hayashi and the garrison commander at Myitkyina, who held out against Stilwell's forces for over two months. The town was finally entered by Stilwell's forces on 1 August. On the Yunnan front in China, close to the border with Burma, the Chinese 11th and 12th Armies had also gone on the offensive in the late spring, in a drive southwards to open up the Burma Road and join up with Chinese forces under Stilwell. At his wartime capital in Chungking*, Chiang was increasingly reluctant to co-operate with Stilwell, as Japanese attacks on General Chennault's forward air bases in China put pressure on Chiang's forces at home.

By October 1944, when Stilwell was finally recalled to America on Chiang's insistence and replaced by General Wedemeyer*, the British 14th Army had crossed the Chindwin* and driven 140 miles south to approach Mandalay and Meiktila*, while the northern Burmese roads were ordered cleared by Lord Mountbatten for the advance of Stilwell's Chinese New 1st Army. With the reopening of the Ledo–Burma Road at the end of January 1945, secured by the Chinese 11th Army's capture of Wanting, the success of the Allied effort to recapture Burma was more or less assured. British victories on the Arakan front in January and February 1945, most notably in the difficult actions fought in the mangrove swamps and narrow waterways of the western coastal region (sometimes known as the Chaung War), were followed by the capture of Meiktila by General Slim's forces on 4 March and the recapture of Lashio by forces under General Sultan on 7 March. On 3 May, an amphibious landing, code-named Dracula, was combined with a parachute operation for the recapture of Rangoon, and the capital was entered by units of General Messervy's 4th Corps on 6 May, signalling the virtual end to the war in Burma.

Burma Road Vital communications and supply link between Burma* and China*, running over 700 miles as a single-track road from Lashio in northern Burma to Kunming in Yunnan, China, it had been started from Kunming in 1920 and provided Chinese Nationalist leader Chiang Kaishek's* armies with their only overland supply route after 1938 (see Map 11). The road was closed by the Japanese advance through Burma to the Lashio railhead terminus, and retreating Chinese defenders blew up the vital Salween Bridge and a section of the road along the Salween River canyon. Thereafter, Chiang was forced to rely on supplies flown across the towering Himalayas from airfields in India (see Hump), though both he and his military commander, US General Stilwell*, continued throughout 1942 and 1943 to press for an offensive to reopen the key overland supply route. During September 1943, work began on the reconstruction of the road with Chinese and American engineers and thousands of Chinese labourers using primitive equipment. By August 1944, it joined the newly built Ledo Road* through Chineseheld territory, and General Stilwell began the attempt to recapture the Burma Road from Ledo, in Assam. Sending engineers to reconstruct the road ahead of the advance, Stilwell finally linked up with the Burma Road at Lashio in February 1945.

Bush, Vannevar (1890–1974) American scientist and electrical engineer, president of the Carnegie Institute in Washington. He was appointed chairman of the National Defense Research Committee in 1940, an agency designed to supplement the US Army and Navy research into the develop-

ment of war materials, including atomic research. In 1941, Bush also became director of the Office of Scientific Research and Development, which included the NDRC and the Committee on Medical Research. Between 1941 and 1945 OSRD was heavily involved in financing the development of new weapons, including the atomic bomb*. As its director, Bush acted as overall coordinator of American scientific research and development, as well as adviser to the President.

Bushido Code (Warrior Code) Originally a code of conduct for the *samurai* (warrior) class in Japan, it evolved during the Kamakura period (1192–1333) and has been compared with the medieval chivalric code of western Europe. Bushido was deliberately revived and adapted during the Meiji period in Japan in the later nineteenth century as a basis for the philosophy of education for Japanese of all classes and formed a particularly large part of the training and discipline of the Japanese Army* officer class. Incorporating the martial mysticism, stern asceticism and bodily self-denial of Zen Buddhism, the harsh discipline of Bushido and the *samurai* ideal insisted on the absolute loyalty of the Imperial soldier, who was trained to fight to the death in his Emperor's service. It was adapted by Prime Minister Tojo* as the basis for his 'Soldier Code', issued in 1941, which explicitly detailed the soldier's duty to die, if necessary, rather than suffer the ignominy of capture. Penalties for soldiers who failed in this ultimate duty included the removal of their name from official records and the public castigation of their families. Bushido thus formed a key part of the apparently fanatic Japanese fighting mentality which so shocked the inexperienced Allied troops facing them at the start of the Pacific War (see Banzai).

It also accounts in part for the particularly brutal treatment of the 150,000 Allied prisoners who surrendered during the first months of 1942. In the absence of any code of conduct laid down by Tokyo, the handling of captives was left to local commanders, who generally relied on a strict interpretation of Bushido and regarded their captives as contemptible slaves. Although some Japanese commanders treated their prisoners humanely, many POWs were forced to live and labour in appalling conditions which flagrantly contravened the Geneva Convention*. A huge percentage of those held captive by the Japanese did not survive the ordeal, falling victim to starvation, epidemics and the sometimes sadistic regimes of their guard commanders.

Byrnes, James Francis (1879–1972) US Senator and close friend of Franklin Roosevelt*, Byrnes was active in pressing for the Cash and Carry Arms Act to increase aid to Britain at the start of the war and subsequently helped steer the passage of the Lend-Lease* and Selective Service Acts through Congress (see Neutrality, US). Appointed first director of the newly created Office of Economic Stabilization (later changed to the Office of War Mobilization) in October 1942, Byrnes became chief planner and director of the American wartime economy. From 1943 his successful, if sometimes unpopular, policies to hold down inflation and stimulate war production made him an increasingly influential advisor to Roosevelt, who took Byrnes with him to the Yalta Conference in 1945.

After Roosevelt's death, Byrnes resigned but was later recalled by President Truman to succeed Edward Stettinius* as Secretary of State (July 1945) participating in the Potsdam and London post-war conferences as well as at the Paris Peace Conference – see Conferences, Allied. Byrnes was a firm advocate of the use of the atomic bomb* against Japan in August 1945. His contributions to the European peace included the establishment of the UN Atomic Energy Commission. He resigned his office in January 1947 and was succeeded by General George Marshall*.

Bzura River River to the west of Warsaw* in Poland*, where German General Reichenau's* 10th Army established a blocking position ahead of retreating Polish forces during the second week of September 1939. The battle fought there was distinguished by the bravery of the entrapped Polish forces. It was the largest battle of the short-lived German–Polish war. See Poland, German Campaign in.

C

C-46 Curtiss Commando Designed and built as a civil airliner, the Commando first flew in March 1940, and some 3,500 modified versions served the USAAF* between 1943 and 1945. Employed as a troop-transport, cargo freighter, ambulance or glider-tug, the C-46 was prominently involved in the Pacific War* 'island' campaigns but did not appear over Europe until March 1945.
BRIEF DATA (C-46) Type: 5-man transport; Engines: 2 × 2,000hp Pratt and Whitney Double Wasp; Max speed: 265mph; Ceiling: 24,500′; Range: 1,600m (normal); Arms: none; Load: 36–40 passengers or 45,000lb freight.

C-47 Douglas Skytrain (and C-53 Skytrooper) The principal military versions of the famous Douglas DC3 Dakota commercial transport. The C-53, which joined the USAAF* in October 1941, was (as the name implied) primarily a troop carrier and had seats for 28 passengers. The C-47 doubled as a freighter or trooper, and entered service the following January. As a mainstay of both American and British transport units throughout the rest of the war, the DC3 dropped paratroops, handled cargo all over the world, towed gliders and performed as a flying ambulance. The US Navy* operated the plane (as the R4D), and more than 1,200 machines served with the RAF*. Military production reached 10,123, not including civilian models impressed under the designations C-68 or C-89, and the DC3 remained in worldwide use for many years after the war.
BRIEF DATA (C-47) Type: 4-man all-purpose transport; Engines: 2 × 1,200hp Pratt and Whitney Twin Wasp; Max speed: 230mph; Ceiling: 24,100′; Range: 1,350m (normal); Arms: none; Load: 12,000lb.

C-54 Douglas Skymaster Planned, and later famous, as the DC4 commercial transport, the C-54 was adapted to USAAF* requirements during pre-production in 1941, and entered service late the following year. Almost 1,000 Skymasters were built (US Navy* versions were designated RSD) and they were capable of carrying 50 men or equivalent cargo over enormous distances. Principally employed in ferry work across the Atlantic, they also operated over the Himalayas, the Indian Ocean and the Pacific. A few examples were lent to RAF* Transport Command and flew supplies to the Far East. These were returned to the United States after the war, when the plane reverted to its natural commercial role.
BRIEF DATA (C54A) Type: 6-man transport; Engines: 4 × 1,350hp Pratt and Whitney Twin Wasp; Max speed: 275mph; Ceiling: 22,500′; Range: 3,900m; Arms: none; Load: 28,500lb.

Caen City in Normandy, approximately ten miles from the coast at the mouth of the river Orne, the site of prolonged and bitter fighting between German armoured forces and the British 2nd Army under Dempsey* during the attempt to break out of the Normandy beachheads in the summer of 1944 (see Northwest Europe, Allied Invasion of; Map 36). The original plan of exploitation called for the British capture of Caen on the first day of the landing, but delays in getting the advance started and the arrival of the bulk of available German armour checked and then held the British forces. An attempt by overall commander Montgomery* to break the deadlock in July by squeezing a massive tank* attack of three divisions across a small bridgehead over the Orne River (code-named Goodwood) proved a costly mistake. In the stormy period of recrimination that followed, Montgomery persisted in his assertion that the aim of the attack had simply been to hold his position and absorb the brunt of the German effort, in order to facilitate the American breakout on the right flank across the Cotentin peninsula.

Although the evidence clearly suggests that Montgomery's later assertion attempted to conceal a major tactical blunder, the British investment of Caen undoubtedly provided a diversion to enable the American forces under General Patton* to push a spearhead through at Avranches on 31 July (code-named Cobra*). It has also subsequently been pointed out by historians that the prolonged battle of the bridgeheads in Normandy worked to the Allies' final advantage in depleting the limited German forces available to resist their subsequent advance into the French interior.

Caesar Line German defensive line 15 miles south of Rome* which was designed to check the Allied advance in Italy*. The line was breached by the US 36th Division on 30 May 1944 after the successful capture of Velletri on National Route 7 on the approach to Rome. German General Senger und Etterlin's resistance on the more southerly Acre–Ceprano section of the line looked determined for a time to hold off the Allied advance and allow stabilization of a further front south of Rome. But the breakthrough by 36th Division was successfully exploited by General Clark's* forces, who entered Rome on 4 June 1944. See Map 34.

Cairo Conference See Conferences, Allied.

Calabria, Battle of See Giulio Cesare.

California, USS See Tennessee, USS.

Canal Defence Light See Special-purpose Vehicles.

Canaris, Admiral Wilhelm Franz (1887–1945) Head of the Abwehr*, German armed forces intelligence, from 1935 to 1944, Canaris was an important though enigmatic member of the 'Junker' resistance to Hitler (see Resistance, Germany). From a wealthy and well-established military background, Canaris entered the Navy as a cadet in 1905 and saw service on the cruiser *Dresden* at the Battle of the Falklands during WW1. His success in escaping internment after the scuttling of his ship and making his way back to Germany through British controls brought him to the attention of German military intelligence. In 1934 he succeeded Conrad Patzig as head of the Abwehr, then a small though important department which grew significantly once the war began.

A complex and private personality, Canaris's motives for his rejection of Nazism have been attributed to the general and partisan attitude of his class towards National Socialism and its consequences for Germany, rather than to moral objections to national policy, though this may be an unfair interpretation of Canaris's commitment to the resistance movement in Germany. In 1938 Canaris had become involved in the formation of a nucleus of active conspiracy which also included senior army members Beck*, Halder*, and Kleist*. After the invasion of Poland*, warnings of the possibility of invasion by German forces were passed to the Netherlands*, Denmark*, Belgium and Norway*, probably though not conclusively originating from Canaris.

As the war progressed, the Abwehr played a central role in recruitment to the resistance, and provided liaison between civilian and military opponents of the regime, though it was increasingly overlooked by antagonistic SS* and Gestapo* chiefs who saw the Abwehr as a direct challenge to their own power and influence. Afforded the vital cover of Canaris's authority, Abwehr's second-in-command, General Hans Oster*, nevertheless successfully recruited men like Bonhöffer*, Dohnanyi* and Josef Müller, as well as making contacts with ministerial officials, the Army High Command and even the Gestapo and SS. But the risks of resistance, however concealed by the normal functioning of the intelligence service, were bound to increase. Early in April 1943, the Gestapo occupied General Oster's department and arrested his most important collaborators. Although Canaris succeeded in avoiding a trial (which would have endangered the whole opposition) and temporarily covering his own tracks, the suspicious surveillance of the rival SS and Gestapo rendered the Abwehr resistance largely ineffective.

The 1944 attempt on Hitler's life (see July Bomb Plot), in which Canaris was not directly involved, nevertheless sealed his fate. The dictator's close escape at Rastenberg made him ruthless to subordinates whose commitment was anything but fanatical. Among hundreds of others with no direct connection with Stauffenberg's* bomb plot, Canaris was arrested, tried for treachery and imprisoned. Transferred to a series of camps and prisons, the former Abwehr chief was executed at Flossenberg in a final, futile act of SS vengeance, in the last days of the war.

Canberra, HMS See Suffolk, HMS.

Canned Goods A particularly callous code-name referring to the corpses of concentration camp* victims who were used in a deception plan to aggravate the critical relations between Poland* and Germany preceding Germany's attack on 1 September 1939 (see Poland, German Campaign in). The plan involved disguising SS* men as Polish soldiers for an attack on the German radio station at Gleiwitz on 31

August. The corpses were similarly disguised and left behind as 'casualties'. This affair, along with various other incidents staged along the Polish–German frontier on the eve of the pre-planned attack, provided Hitler* with the thin screen of 'legality' which his foreign policy style demanded.

Cant Z-1007 (and Z-1018) First produced in 1939, the Italian trimotor Z-1007 bomber – called the *Alcione* (Kingfisher) – was a land-based development of the Cant Z-506B* seaplane, and was similarly constructed almost entirely of wood. Early models with 950hp engines were too slow, and most of the several hundred *Alciones* built were of the slightly larger and more powerful Z-1007*bis* variant. Although never a match for British fighters, these performed stoically throughout the Mediterranean* (sometimes armed with torpedoes*) and a few even appeared on the Eastern Front*. Development of the type culminated in the all-metal, twin-engined Z-1018 *Leone* (Lion), capable of 320mph in level flight, which entered service in early 1943. A night fighter version of this excellent aircraft was planned but never completed, and few of the bombers had been delivered when Italy surrendered in September 1943.

BRIEF DATA (Z-1007*bis*) Type: 4–5-man medium bomber; Engine: 3 × 1,000hp Piaggio PXI; Max speed: 280mph; Ceiling: 26,500'; Range: 800m; Arms: 2 × 12.7mm mg, 2 × 7.7mm mg; Bomb load: 4,400lb.

Cape Esperance, Battle of, 11 October 1942 One of several important naval engagements fought around Guadalcanal* that tested the newly won American initiative in the Pacific and provided the first tactical victories to bolster American morale during the second half of 1942. Two months after the initial American landing on Guadalcanal in early August 1942, American Rear Admiral Scott's Task Force 64 (including the two heavy cruisers *San Francisco* and *Salt Lake City*, two light cruisers and five destroyers*) was detailed to escort a supply convoy from Noumea to Guadalcanal through the narrow channel between the Eastern and Western Solomons (Ironbottom Sound*), where decoded radio intercepts indicated that a Japanese strike force under Rear Admiral Goto was also escorting a 'Tokyo Express'* reinforcement force.

Warned by American spotter planes of the approach of Goto's force of three heavy cruisers and six destroyers from the northwest, Scott attempted a difficult manoeuvre to deploy his ships across their line of approach in the passage between Savo Island and Cape Esperance. The cruiser *Helena* opened fire at 11.46 p.m., but was immediately ordered to cease firing by Scott, because of communications confusion which made it difficult for both commanders to identify their targets in the dark. An intense gunnery duel nevertheless sank the cruiser *Furutaka** and the destroyer *Fubuki*. Another cruiser, the *Aoba**, was badly damaged. The US destroyers *Duncan* and *Farenholt* were also disabled, having both been hit with American shells in the confusion, which also gave the Japanese opportunity to damage the light cruiser *Boise*. While the action continued, the Japanese reinforcement convoy was able to land some of its cargo of troops, supplies and artillery, and retire safely. Despite the success of the operation for the Japanese and their relatively small losses, the Battle of Cape Esperance was claimed as a significant victory by the Americans, for whom it was the first tactical success of the Pacific War*.

Cape Matapan, Battle of On 16 March 1941, pilots of the Luftwaffe's* Fliegerkorps X, based on Sicily, reported damaging two battleships of the British Mediterranean Fleet. On the basis of this inaccurate information, German pressure was brought to bear on the Italian surface fleet to disrupt convoy supplies for British troops in Greece*, which Hitler had decided to invade. A powerful Italian naval force assembled for the purpose off Sicily on 27 March. Comprising the battleship *Vittorio Veneto**, eight cruisers and nine destroyers*, it set out to surprise shipping to the north and south of Crete under the command of Admiral Iachino.

RAF* strength in the operational area was thought to present the greatest danger, and air cover had been arranged with Fliegerkorps X. These arrangements had been intercepted and quickly deciphered by British intelligence through Ultra*, which had given full details of the plan to Admiral Cunningham*, C-in-C of the Mediterranean Fleet, by 25 March. Successfully concealing his preparations from Italian agents, Cunningham put to sea from Alexandria* on the evening of 27 March, taking three battleships and an aircraft carrier in search of the raiders.

An advance force of British light cruisers made contact with the Italian fleet the following morning. Iachino, aware that he could no longer hope to surprise convoys, pursued them as they fled to the southwest. He mistakenly believed Cunningham's main force to be 170 miles away, a belief which persisted even after torpedo-bombers from the aircraft carrier *Formidable** attacked and damaged the *Vittorio Veneto* in the afternoon. While his main force turned back towards its home base at Taranto*, protecting his limping battleship, a cruiser division remained behind to guard the heavy cruiser *Pola*, which had been stopped by a torpedo* during the air attack. The support promised by the Luftwaffe failed to appear.

Cunningham's battleships ran directly into this remnant during the night as they pursued the *Vittorio Veneto*, which had been wrongly reported dead in the water. The British ships were equipped with radar* and their crews were trained and equipped for night fighting; the Italian cruisers enjoyed neither advantage. The battleships opened fire at 10.30 p.m., supported by destroyers with searchlights and torpedoes. In the mêlée that followed, two Italian heavy cruisers and two destroyers were sunk, while the *Pola* could only watch helplessly and was evacuated and torpedoed the next morning. British losses throughout the battle amounted to one aircraft.

Although the main body of Iachino's fleet was beyond pursuit, the Royal Navy's dominance of the Eastern Mediterranean had been thoroughly confirmed. During the hazardous evacuations of Greece and Crete* in April–May 1941 the Royal Navy, although savagely mauled by the Luftwaffe, was spared the attentions of the Italian surface fleet, which resumed a self-protective posture after Matapan. See Mediterranean Sea; Italian Navy.

Capital Code-name for the Allied offensive across the Chindwin River* from Assam (India) into northern Burma*, launched on 15 October 1944, as part of the Allied effort to recapture Burma from the Japanese.

Caproni Ca133 Italian short take-off and landing general-purpose colonial aircraft, built in large quantities during the late 1930s. In June 1940, they equipped 14 Italian bomber squadrons, mostly in Africa where they worked hard but were utterly outclassed by the RAF*. Later they remained in service as transports and ambulances in the Desert War*, on the Eastern Front* and in Italy* – flying for both sides after the Italian surrender of 1943.
BRIEF DATA (Ca133) Type: 4–7-man medium bomber/transport; Engine: 3 × 650hp Piaggio Stella; Max speed: 174mph; Ceiling: 21,325'; Range: 839m; Arms: 2–4 7.7mm mg; Bomb load: 2,200lb.

Caproni Ca313/314 Multi-purpose twin-engine series of Italian monoplanes which first appeared as the lightly-armed Ca309 desert patrol craft in 1936. Many of its early descendants were exported and some Ca310s briefly saw action in April 1940, as armed general-purpose aircraft with the Norwegian army. The most important wartime models were the glass-nosed Ca313 and the virtually identical Ca314, which

served as torpedo-bombers, convoy* escorts and reconnaissance aircraft with both the *Regia Aeronautica** and the Italian naval air arm. A catapult-launched reconnaissance seaplane, the Ca316, also fought in the Mediterranean*. About 2,400 of all types were built, mostly in the period 1938–42.
BRIEF DATA (Ca313) Type: 4–7-man medium bomber; Engine: 2 × 650hp Isotta-Fraschini Delta; Max speed: 271mph; Arms: 3–5 × 12.7mm mg, 3 × 7.7mm mg; Bomb load: 1,760lb.

Carboni, Major General Giacomo (1889–1973) Italian head of army intelligence from 1939–41, when his opposition to co-operation with Nazism resulted in his removal, Carboni commanded a motorized corps during the defence of Rome*. He participated in the removal of Mussolini* from power in July 1943. See also SIM.

Carlson, Brigadier-General Evans Fordyce (1896–1947) American Marine* Commander who had served two tours of duty in China* during the 1920s and 30s and was ordered back there in 1937 to act as a military observer. An opportunity to watch Chinese Communist guerrilla operations in Shensi province contributed to Carlson's interest in élite commando units, later set out in recommendations made by him in 1941 for the formation of commando*-type units within the Marine Corps. Despite the misgivings of some senior officers about the creation of an élite within what was anyway considered an élite corps, and the mistrust that some felt for his apparently uncritical view of the Chinese Communists, Carlson was given command of the 2nd Raider Battalion (Carlson's Raiders) with President Roosevelt's son Major James Roosevelt as his executive officer. Following a reconnaissance mission on Makin Atoll in the Gilberts* (August 1942), the Raiders landed on Guadalcanal* in November, conducting a 150-mile patrol across difficult terrain and engaging the Japanese in over a dozen actions with minimal casualties to themselves. Though Carlson ended the war as Brigadier-General he was not given another command when his battalion was disbanded and sent as cadres to other units.

Caroline Islands Large archipelago north of New Guinea*, it includes Truk*, site of a major Japanese naval base. See Map 11.

Carpet Bombing See Cobra.

Cartwheel Code-name for Allied operations in the Pacific during 1943, aimed at the seizure of the Solomon Islands*–New Guinea*–New Britain area as the preliminary to the elimination of Rabaul*, Japan's most important military and air base in the Southwest Pacific (see Maps 11 and 17). The American dual offensive was launched in June, under the overall command of Admiral Halsey* and General Mac-Arthur*. Landings on the New Georgia Island* group by Admiral Halsey's forces were carefully co-ordinated with assaults on New Guinea, initially at Salamaua, by MacArthur's troops. The drive by Halsey's forces continued successfully through Vella Lavella*, Choiseul and the Treasury Islands to Bougainville*, largest of the Solomon group. Meanwhile, MacArthur's drive had kept pace with leapfrogging amphibious* assaults moving north along the coast of the Huon Peninsula, which was effectively cleared by the end of the year. As a result of the success of Cartwheel, the American Joint Chiefs decided to bypass the now isolated and evacuated Japanese base at Rabaul altogether and concentrate on a direct northward drive towards the Philippines*. See also Pacific War.

Casablanca The only large and well-equipped port on the Atlantic coast of Vichy* French-held Morocco in Northwest Africa, Casablanca was a primary target for the Allied Torch* invasion of 8 November 1942. The main landings of the Western Task Force, under Major General George Patton* were at Fedala, 15 miles north of the city. Smaller forces were sent to secure the valuable concrete airstrip further north at Mehdia, and to take the harbour at Safi, 140 miles south of Casablanca.

The landings at Fedala achieved such surprise that by dawn on 9 November General Noguès – the French C-in-C for Morocco – had arrested unprepared Allied collaborators and ordered his commanders to fire on what he thought was just a raid. Later in the morning French naval forces under Admiral Mechelier began firing on US Navy* warships off Casablanca. Coastal batteries and the incomplete new battleship *Jean Bart* distracted the American covering group, while smaller warships escaped from the harbour and made for Fedala. Two attempts to reach the fleet of Allied transports were intercepted by US Navy cruisers and destroyers. Only one of eight French destroyers returned to harbour undamaged and four were sunk, but as the *Jean Bart* re-opened fire and fears grew of French warships arriving from Dakar*, Patton's land forces remained bogged down in the administrative chaos of the beachhead well into the next day. Fortunately, by the afternoon of 11 November, Nogués had learned of Admiral Darlan's* negotiations with General Clark* in Algiers*, and he ordered a ceasefire in Morocco pending an armistice. See Torch; Map 8.

Casablanca Conference See Conferences, Allied.

Cassino, Battles of A series of bitter and costly battles fought on the German winter defensive line, the Gustav Line*, south of the Liri Valley on the Italian peninsula in the first half of 1944 (see Map 34). The battles focused on Monte Cassino, the hilltop site of a sixth-century Benedictine monastery, which dominated the heavily defended Gustav Line. Despite the costly failure of Allied attempts to break through at Cassino in December 1943, plans were prepared by Supreme Allied Commander in Italy, General Alexander*, for a renewed Cassino offensive combined with an amphibious* operation at Anzio* and supporting offensives by Allied forces on the east of the Line at the Garigliano River. Unsupported and bloody infantry attacks by the US 2nd Corps in January, and then by the New Zealand 2nd Corps in February and the 4th Indian Division in March, failed to dislodge the élite German 1st Parachute Division from their positions behind the ancient monastery. Massive bombardment (including the controversial destruction of the monastery itself in February) similarly failed to advance the Allied breakthrough at Cassino. The position was not finally taken until mid-May, as part of the major Allied spring Diadem* offensive against the Gustav Line. Even then, the success was achieved after some of the most bitter fighting of the war, in which General Anders'* Polish Corps and General Juin's* French Corps were particularly distinguished. The eventual breakthrough at Cassino reversed the Allied position at Anzio, and enabled them to regain the initiative for an advance on Rome*.

Catania Sicilian coastal town which was occupied by the British 8th Army on 7 August 1943 after bitter fighting against the strongly held Axis* defensive line on the Catania Plain to the south and west of the town. See Sicily, Allied Campaign in.

Catapult Armed Merchantman (CAM) See Escort Carriers.

Caucasus, The Strategically highly important region of southern Russia, between the Black and the Caspian Seas, the Caucasus provided oilfields and a huge pipeline which supplied the Red Army* with fuel. Control of the Caucasus was bitterly disputed between mid-1942 and early 1943, when the Russians counter-attacked against a German offensive to take the oilfields and the city of Stalingrad*. Despite early successes by German Army Group A under List* in July and August at Rostov*, the oil centre at Maikop, and Pyatigorsk and Ordzhonikidze in the south, fuel and supply shortages

combined with the mountainous terrain and the diversion of troops to Stalingrad* to sap the strength of the German Caucasus offensive, giving Soviet forces the opportunity to organize for counter-attacks. Throughout November 1942, with all attention focused on Stalingrad, the action in the Caucasus was effectively halted. But as Russian forces successfully encircled Paulus's forces at Stalingrad, General Vatutin* launched attacks in the Donets* area north of Rostov that threatened to cut off the whole of the German force in the Caucasus. Hitler's grudging approval of a withdrawal on 1 January finally enabled Kleist*, now in command of Army Group A, to attempt a retreat without sacrificing his heavy equipment, but only heroic efforts by forces under Field Marshal Manstein* held the 'Rostov Corridor' open long enough to save the bulk of the 1st Panzer Army. See Azov, Sea of; Eastern Front; Map 28.

Cauldron, The See Gazala.

Cavallero, Count Ugo (1880–1943) Marshal of Italy and Chief of the Italian General Staff from 1940 to 1943, Cavallero served in WW1, abandoning his military career after the war to work for the Pirelli Company until 1925, when he was appointed Under Secretary of War in Mussolini's* government. He succeeded Marshal Badoglio* as Chief of Staff in November 1940, in the final stages of the dismal Italian campaign in Greece*.

An admirer of the efficiency of German war production and military structure, Cavallero's appointment was at first regarded by Germany as a valuable one. He comprehensively reorganized the leadership structure of the Italian Armed Forces*, forged closer co-operation with the German High Command (OKW), pressed the Navy to take action in supplying Libya, and even used his industrial experience to influence the chaotic state of Italian war production.

As C-in-C of Italian Forces in northeast Africa and head of Comando Supremo, however, Cavallero disapproved of German

General Rommel's* aggressive strategies. As Axis* fortunes turned in Africa and Italian casualties mounted (see Desert War; Tunisia), Cavallero's reading of Italy's poor military situation – added to rumours of a planned Fascist take over of the army – convinced him to join with other conspirators against Mussolini's regime. Rumours of the plot in turn reached Mussolini, who replaced Cavallero in January 1943 and ordered his arrest six months later. Though subsequently released after the charge of conspiracy had been dropped, Cavallero committed suicide in the knowledge that his involvement with the conspirators would shortly be made public.

CBI (China, Burma, India Theatre) See Stilwell, Joseph; China Campaigns.

Centaur Tank See Cromwell Tank.

Ceylon (Sri Lanka) Large island off the southeast corner of India, it was thought by the British to be threatened by the Japanese advance through Southeast Asia during early 1942 (see Pacific War). Ceylon was considered of vital strategic importance by British Chiefs of Staff, who saw its potential to the Japanese Navy* as a base to threaten British troop and supply movements to the Middle East, India and Australia, as well as an essential source of rubber. It was reinforced during March for an all out defence against the expected imminent invasion. The Royal Navy* Eastern Fleet (of which four out of five battleships were outmoded and unable to manoeuvre effectively with the one old and two modern carriers) was put under the command of Admiral Somerville* and ordered to expect an attack on 1 April. Though a Japanese naval offensive was being prepared in the area, its aim was a defensive one, to disperse the British Eastern Fleet, and cover Japanese troop reinforcements *en route* for Rangoon*. After three days of fruitless searching for the Japanese fleet in the Indian Ocean, Admiral Somerville received

a report of a sighting 350 miles south of Ceylon. Still 500 miles away, the Eastern Fleet was unable to reach the island before Japan's five-fleet carrier force under Admiral Nagumo* had devastated the port at the capital, Colombo, sunk two cruisers and an old light carrier, and retired. Despite Somerville's efforts to bait the Japanese fleet and draw it into a night action, the two fleets eventually retired without further action. Following on its earlier losses at Hong Kong* and Singapore*, this was another humiliating defeat for the British Navy.

Chaffee (M24) Tank This American light tank was the best of its type of the war, surpassing anything previously seen in its class in armament and protection. It was put into production for the US Army* in July 1944, but relatively few of the 4,070 built over the next year saw wartime action. BRIEF DATA (M24). Type: 4-man light tank; Engine: 2×110hp petrol; Max speed: 35mph; Range: 100m; Arms: $1 \times$ 75mm gun, 1×12.7mm mg, 3×7.62mm mg; Armour: max 38mm.

Chamberlain, Neville (1869–1940) British Conservative Prime Minister from 1937 to 1940, his name is now wholly identified with the policy of appeasement* of the European dictators, in an attempt to maintain peace in Europe by concession. Although Chamberlain had enjoyed a high-level political career in which he had served as Minister of Health and Chancellor of the Exchequer, his political background and lack of knowledge of foreign affairs ill-equipped him to deal with the succession of political crises facing Europe during the late 1930s. In retrospect, the utter failure of Chamberlain's policy to safeguard peace or address the nature and balance of new forces in post-Versailles Europe seems in-built. Under Chamberlain's leadership, Britain was clearly seen from a European perspective to align herself with the aggressor nations, Italy and Germany –

Clement Attlee*, leader of the Labour Party, bluntly described appeasement as a 'policy of *war*' – and to abdicate her powerful position of diplomatic influence. Between 1936 and 1939, Chamberlain often ignored the advice of his foreign ministry officials, in sanctioning first Hitler's* reoccupation of the Rhineland and Mussolini's* expansionist activities in Abyssinia (1936), then the annexation of Austria* by Germany (see Anschluss) and, most notoriously, Hitler's occupation of the Sudetenland in Czechoslovakia* in 1938 (see Munich Agreement). Even after the Anschluss, Chamberlain appears to have been satisfied that he could assuage Hitler's appetite for the 'resolution of legitimate grievances' and ensure 'peace in our time' by conceding foreign territory to the Third Reich.

The part played by Chamberlain in the immediate causes of war in Europe cannot be ignored. Nevertheless, the urgent commitment to peace on which appeasement rested and the apparent moral blindness to the nature of Fascism in Europe and the unacceptable ideologies on which both Hitler's and Mussolini's foreign policies were based were certainly shared by many politicians and ordinary people both in Britain and in France during the period.

Following Hitler's occupation of all of Czechoslovakia in March 1939, Chamberlain finally abandoned appeasement and offered guarantees to Poland* which led to Britain's declaration of war against Germany in September 1939, though Chamberlain continued to dismiss the notion that Britain had submitted to total war. Chamberlain's poor handling of personal and political matters during the first winter of the war raised much criticism. The subsequent loss of parliamentary and public confidence in his authority and the need to co-ordinate efforts for the prosecution of the war were formalized in Chamberlain's resignation on 10 May and the creation of a national coalition government, with Winston Churchill* at its head. Chamberlain continued as Lord President,

member of the War Cabinet and leader of the Conservative Party until shortly before his death in November 1940.

Chance Vought F4U Corsair Easily distinguished by its inverted gull-wing design, the Corsair first flew in May 1940, at which time it outperformed all other American aircraft. Produced as a carrier fighter, it was initially pronounced unsuitable as such by the US Navy*, and first saw action with land-based US Marines* in February 1943. Although it was a success, modifications were soon introduced. The F4U-1A featured an improved cockpit and the F4U-1C was cannon-armed, but it was not until the appearance of the faster F4U-1D fighter-bomber in 1944 that the US Navy used the plane on carriers. Late that year, the even more powerful F4U-1F reached units and it was in widespread use by mid-1945. Hundreds of F4U-1P and 4P photo-reconnaissance models were produced and other versions included the F4U-4E and 4N night fighters. An excellent and rightly famous fighter, the Corsair established Allied air supremacy in the Pacific War* alongside the Grumman F6F Wildcat*. Production continued until 1952, and many of the 12,571 delivered were built on licence by the Brewster (F3A) and Goodyear (FG models) companies. Over 1,000 Corsairs (designated Corsair Mark I to IV) were exported in wartime to the British Fleet Air Arm*, who pioneered their use as carrier planes.
BRIEF DATA (F4U-1A) Type: single-seat naval fighter; Engine: 1 × 2,250hp Pratt and Whitney Double Wasp; Max speed: 395mph; Ceiling: 37,000'; Range: 1,500m (max); Arms: 6 × 0.5" mg.

Channel Dash, The See Scharnhorst.

Channel Islands The only part of Britain to be occupied by the Third Reich. After the fall of France in June 1940, Britain made no attempt to defend the Channel Islands, 80 miles south of England and 40 miles west of Cherbourg, and they were occupied by German troops. The Islands' legislatures continued to function under control of a military commandant. In 1942, the Islands became part of the German Atlantic Wall defences: restrictions were increased and 1,200 people not born in the Islands were interned in Germany. Slave labour came into operation under the German Todt Organization. In 1943 1,000 French Jews were also imprisoned in a work camp established on Alderney. Between July 1940 and December 1943 the British mounted seven commando* raids on the Islands. In March 1945 a German force from the Islands daringly attacked Allied shipping off Granville on the Cotentin peninsula. At the end of the war the German garrison surrendered as part of the general surrender of German forces in the west.

Char B French heavy tank, built in the mid-1930s for use in support of infantry breakthroughs. The Char B (*Char de Bataille*) was a formidable weapon by contemporary standards, and 387 of the heavily armed Char B1-*bis* version were in French Army* service in May 1940. Although it was cumbersome and its performance was further hampered by the use of a one-man turret (the crew as a whole was seriously overworked), it was at least the equal of the German tanks deployed against it in the Battle of France* but was not used with anything like the same concentrated efficiency. The tank later performed in a number of secondary roles for the German Army* (as the PzKpfw B1 or B1-*bis*), a few models being converted for training or flamethrowing duties.
BRIEF DATA (Char B1-*bis*) Type: 4-man medium/heavy tank; Engine: 307hp petrol; Max speed: 17mph; Range: 93m; Arms: 1 × 75mm gun, 1 × 47mm gun, 2 × 7.5mm mg; Armour: max 60mm.

Chaung War See Burma, Campaigns in.

Chelmno The first extermination camp in history, opened in December 1941 with the objective of 'clearing' the 100,000 Jews living in the newly created *Wartheland*, an area of Poland* annexed to the Reich. See Concentration Camps.

Chengtu Capital city of the Szechwan province of China, it was chosen as the site for the principal mainland base for 14th Air Force B-29s* flying missions against the Japanese home islands. The enormous construction work, which employed nearly half a million Chinese civilians working with nothing but hand tools, severely disrupted agriculture in the region. The choice of location by US General Stilwell*, commander of Chinese forces, was thought at the time to be more secure than a site closer to Japan as suggested by 14th Air Force commander Chennault*, but this was proved unjustified by subsequent events. B-29s flew their first operational mission against Japan, from Chengtu in June 1944. The airfields were abandoned before the end of the year, however, in the face of the major Japanese offensive Ichi Go*, which had been launched into Hunan Province in April 1944. By this time, the Marianas*-based B-29s had taken over the brunt of the strategic bombing offensive* against Japan.

Chennault, Major General Claire L. (1890 –1958) Founder of the American Volunteer Group (Flying Tigers) in China* and specialist in fighter tactics, Chennault served between the wars as chief of US Army Air Corps fighter training. In 1937 he accepted an offer to train fighter pilots for the Chinese Government at an aviation school sponsored by Mme Chiang Kai-shek. Recruiting pilots from the US, Chennault formed the Flying Tigers, China's only effective air arm, which he commanded until 1942, destroying an estimated 300 Japanese planes in the fighting over Burma*, Indochina* and China. Though the Flying Tigers exacted heavy losses on Japanese squadrons and played an important part in the defence of the Burma Road*, they were unable to halt the momentum of the Japanese offensive. The

Burma Road was closed by the end of February 1942.

Recalled to active duty and promoted to Brigadier General, Chennault was given command of the China Air Task Force, consisting at first of 34 Curtiss P-40* fighters and seven B-25* medium bombers. He pressed for an increase in China-based air power, which put him in direct opposition to General Joseph Stilwell*, Chiang Kai-shek's* American Chief of Staff, who favoured a build-up of ground forces. By March 1943, the air strength in China had been built up sufficiently to be redesignated the 14th Air Force, functioning independently from USAAF* units in India. Chennault himself became a Major General. B-24* heavy bombers were brought in and Chennault's highly skilled combat squadrons successfully harried Japanese aircraft over China, but supply difficulties in the remote theatre of operations remained a significant disadvantage. In April 1944, a Japanese retaliatory operation (Ichi Go*), provoked by 14th Air Force raids on Japanese shipping, resulted in the loss of his forward base at Kweilin. Full air superiority in the theatre was not achieved until the Japanese withdrew to coastal positions in May 1945. The frustration and difficulty of command in China, exacerbated by local logistical problems, was reflected in the continued bitterness of the clash between Chennault and Stilwell. When Chennault resigned his command on 6 July 1945, in protest at the threatened disbandment of his Sino-American air force, Stilwell had already been recalled.

Cherbourg French seaport on the northern edge of the Cotentin Peninsula, its capture was a primary objective of the US 1st Army following the Allied invasion of Normandy* on 6 June 1944. The city was taken on 27 June but was not fully operational as a major port of entry for supply ships supporting the Allied drive into Northwest Europe* until September. Although the Allied front moved swiftly east towards Germany, Cherbourg continued to handle US supplies for much of the rest of the war.

Chernyakhovsky, General Ivan D. (1906 –45) Soviet commander of the 3rd Tank Division at the time of the German invasion of Russia (see Eastern Front), he distinguished himself early in the campaign during fighting at Novgorod, south of Leningrad*. Chernyakhovsky was appointed to command the 60th Army in July 1942 and fought in the Kursk* offensive in early 1943. On Marshal Zhukov's* recommendation, he was then promoted general in command of the 3rd Belorussian Front* (becoming the youngest front commander) and directed successful offensives against retreating German forces in Belorussia (see Bagration) and East Prussia*. He was killed by artillery fire at Mehlsack near Königsberg in February 1945.

Cherwell, Frederick Lindemann, Lord (1886–1957) Alsatian-born British scientist, nicknamed 'the Prof' by his close friend, Churchill*, under whose influence Cherwell became unofficial scientific adviser and then War Cabinet member as Paymaster General from 1942. A controversial, acid and often disliked figure, Cherwell had achieved significant success in theoretical and practical work both at the Royal Aircraft Factory at Farnborough and at the Clarendon laboratory in Oxford. His unpopularity was later exacerbated by his support for the policy of area bombing* of civilian populations. He minuted Churchill in March 1942 on the effectiveness (much overestimated) of destroying German morale by making large numbers of the population homeless. Cherwell returned to his Chair of Physics at Oxford in 1945. He was also made Chairman of the British nuclear programme by Churchill on his return to power in the early 50s.

Cheshire, Group Captain Leonard (1917 –) Highly distinguished RAF* bomber pilot, commander of No. 617 (Dambusters*) Squadron and holder of the Victoria Cross, the highest British military decoration. Cheshire was a pioneer of target indicator bombing techniques which significantly improved the accuracy of RAF night bombing offensives and enabled Bomber Command to undertake raids on precision targets with some degree of success during 1944. With the support of Donald Bennett*, who had founded the Pathfinder Force*, Cheshire developed his Light Night Striking Force of fast de Havilland Mosquito* bombers as the spearhead of the British bombing offensive, flying missions ahead of the bomber formations, low over the target, to drop visual markers for the following Avro Lancasters*. He later served at Eastern Air Command HQ, Southeast Asia, and in the British Joint Staff mission in Washington. See Strategic Bombing Offensive.

Chi-Ha (Type 97) Tank The Type 97 Chi-Ha replaced the stalwart but ageing Type 89 as the standard Japanese medium tank in 1939. Designed (and mostly built) by Mitsubishi, it represented a great advance over previous Japanese tanks. Its all-round performance was good and, for the first time, its commander was given much-needed help in operating the turret. Early models mounted a short 57mm gun, but a more effective long-barrelled 47mm weapon was adopted from 1941 and the turret redesigned to accept it. This version became the most widely-used Japanese medium tank of the war and was deployed almost exclusively in support of infantry operations. The Chi-Ha chassis was also used as the basis for many self-propelled* guns and special-purpose* vehicles. Later Japanese medium tanks with bigger guns and thicker armour were only built in small quantities, and a medium tank capable of matching the Allied Grants* and Shermans* was never produced. In general the Japanese tank forces had an undistinguished war, and the fixed belief that tanks should be used only for infantry support was instrumental in their demise. BRIEF DATA (Type 97) Type: 4-man medium tank; Engine: 170hp diesel; Max

speed: 24mph; Range: 130m; Arms: 1 × 47mm gun, 2 × 7.7mm mg; Armour: max 25mm.

China, Campaigns in, 1937–45 Although China officially joined the Allies in the war against Japan on 9 December 1941, the two countries had been at war since 1937, provoked by increasing Japanese incursions into Chinese territory since 1931 (see Map 22). Allowed by international agreement to maintain a force in Manchuria* – the Kwantung Army* – to guard the Southern Manchurian Railway, the Japanese government was unable to control the Kwantung Army in its bid to challenge Chinese Nationalist influence in Manchuria. A fabricated incident at Mukden* in September 1931 led to the Kwantung Army's occupation of Manchuria and the establishment of a puppet regime in the now renamed state of Manchukuo*. Further confrontations on Chinese territory between Japanese and Chiang Kai-shek's* Kuomintang* forces during the 1930s, and particularly after 1935, continued to exploit the fragile political situation in China, where Chiang's Nationalist forces and Chinese Communist forces under Mao Tse-tung* were engaged in intermittent campaigns to oust each other from their respective power bases at Nanking* and Kiangsi. During this period, the Kuomintang gave little support to the resistance movement against Japan, Chiang preferring to tackle the domestic battle with Mao as the first priority.
The Fall of Nanking In July 1937 Japanese forces on night manoeuvres clashed with Chinese forces at the Marco Polo Bridge (Lukouchiao) near Peking, and although an attempt was made to come to local agreements to resolve the crisis, further incidents southeast of Peking at Shanghai in August transformed the scale of the conflict into war. Chiang's army and Mao's forces at first collaborated to resist the Japanese, but the Kuomintang's capital at Nanking fell in December (the Nationalist government escaping to Hankow* before

its fall) and much of the eastern seaboard, as well as Hankow, was in Japanese hands by October 1938. Removed to Chungking, west of Hankow, where he established his wartime capital, Chiang faced the loss of all China's great industrial centres and all her major ports to the Japanese. The capture of Nanning in late 1939 also brought the Japanese control of China's last eastern line of communication, the Yunnan–Indochina railway (see Map 10).

The Pacific War Chinese resistance to Japan's conquest continued, and puppet regimes established by the Japanese in occupied areas were unable to gain any real control over local populations, who sustained guerrilla activities on a wide scale. Nevertheless the multiple threats of a clash with Mao's forces based at Yenan, Japanese air superiority and dwindling sources of supplies and revenues (especially from the Soviet Union, which signed a neutrality pact with Japan in April 1941), put Chiang under extreme pressure. In these circumstances, the Japanese attack on Pearl Harbor* in December 1941 and subsequent Far Eastern offensives (see Pacific War), obliged Chiang to seek greater aid from his newest ally, the United States, who had since April been providing the Nationalist government with air power in the form of Colonel Chennault's* American Volunteer Group.

The Fall of Burma On 4 March 1942, in response to a request from Chiang for an American Chief of Staff, Lt General Joseph Stilwell* arrived in Chungking. Simultaneously designated commanding general of United States Forces in the China Theatre, Burma and India (CBI) with headquarters in Karachi, India, and assuming responsibility for all former American Military Mission to China (AMMISCA) personnel, Stilwell's command was an immensely complex one. Charged with a mission to 'increase the effectiveness of US assistance . . . and assist in improving the combat efficiency of the Chinese Army', funded by large injections of American currency, Stilwell was at

first unable to affect the military situation in China. His first active field command, as leader of the Chinese Expeditionary Force (CEF) in Burma*, failed to halt the Japanese invasion forces which pushed the CEF, and the British colonial forces, right out of Burmese territory.

As a result of the loss of Burma, and the last overland Allied supply route to China, the Burma Road*, China's ability to resist the Japanese armies was critically impaired. Although an increasing tonnnage of supplies and equipment was flown over the Himalayas from India (see Hump), Japanese strength in China was increasing throughout 1942 and Chiang's government was receiving less and less support from Chinese Communist forces. Moreover, the withdrawal of aircraft for the launch of the Anglo-American Torch* offensive and Chiang's increasing intractability over his demand for larger numbers of US troops, aircraft and airlifted supplies, put strains on Stilwell and the CBI command structure which undoubtedly affected the efficiency of the US effort in China. Numerous tensions resulted from the low priority given by the Allies to this theatre. Immense difficulties were additionally posed by the broad dispersal of his command, and the complex relationships with Chiang and the new Allied Southeast Asia Command (SEAC), created in October 1943 under the command of Mountbatten* with Stilwell as deputy. Despite the overwhelming problems, however, Stilwell suggested and began implementation of proposals for training forces in China in Yunnan Province and Ramgarh in India (Y-Force and X-Force).

The Recapture of Burma As local air superiority was contested with increasing success by Chennault's air forces (now renamed the 14th Air Force), supply deliveries over the Hump improved, and the route to Yunnan, the Ledo Road*, was reopened, the pace of preparations for a major offensive against the Japanese speeded up. Already, by late 1943, Stilwell's Chinese armies were committed to fighting in Burma (see Burma Campaigns), in operations in the northwest to support British forces fighting in the south. Stilwell himself took direct command of operations in early 1944. With an American Chindit*-style unit known as Merrill's Marauders (see Merrill), Stilwell launched a general attack behind Japanese lines, capturing Myitkyina* in August 1944. But while Chinese divisions were conducting successful operations in Burma, tensions between Chiang Kai-shek and Stilwell reached their peak.

The Ichi Go Offensive The launch of a major Japanese counter-offensive, code-named Ichi Go*, provoked by Chennault's* air offensive against Japan from Chinese bases, led Chiang to identify the assignment of Chinese troops to Stilwell's command in Burma as the reason for the Chinese failure to repel the Japanese offensive. The major Japanese objectives were to forestall US bombing of Japan by destroying 14th Air Force bases in Hunan and Kwangsi provinces and to 'destroy the backbone' of the Chinese Army between the Hwang Ho and Yangtse rivers, as well as seizing the Peking–Hankow rail links.

Operations began with the successful capture by the Japanese 37th Division of seven airfields in Kiangsi and Kwangsi provinces. Dogged Chinese resistance, combined with US and Chinese air support, was still unable to match the Japanese strength and repeated attacks on the Peking –Hankow railway brought it under Japanese control by mid-June. Further operations in Hunan province secured Changsha (18 June) and after bitter resistance by the Chinese 10th Army, an important railhead at Hengyang (8 August). By early 1945, despite determined efforts on the part of the Chinese armies, Japanese forces controlled the Canton–Hankow railway, though extensive damage had by this time rendered it useless. With fresh reinforcements, the Japanese drove on westwards to threaten air bases at Kweilin and Liuchow. In October, Stilwell was finally replaced, on Chiang's insistence, by Major General Wedemeyer*

in command of the renamed China Theater (CT).

The Liberation of China When General Wedemeyer arrived to assume command of the China Theater on 31 October, the situation at Kweilin and the threat to Kunming (at the head of the Burma Road) and Chungking demanded immediate action. With the advantages of Chiang's support and authority to order reinforcements, however, Wedemeyer was able to initiate the strengthening of the Kweiyang area and plan a well-organized defence of Kunming, while training of Chinese divisions continued and planning began for a major offensive effort to recapture China's eastern seaports. By the early summer of 1945, the success of Wedemeyer's efforts to improve the fighting efficiency of the Chinese forces was evident in the military situation in China. In two separate engagements, from April to June in Hunan, and from March to August in the Hunan–Hupeh region, Chinese forces defeated offensives launched by the Japanese China Expeditionary Force. As Chiang Kai-shek's armies gained the initiative for the first time since the start of the Sino-Japanese war in 1937, Japanese forces were ordered to withdraw to home territory. In mid-August, as the Chinese prepared for a new offensive in the Canton–Hong Kong area, Japan accepted the Allies' terms of unconditional surrender, and the Expeditionary Army surrendered to Chiang.

With Chinese casualties estimated at over 3 million by the end of the war, peace in China was to be delayed for a further four years, while Nationalist and Communist forces fought for control of the country in a renewed civil war.

China Incident Japanese euphemism for armed operations in China between 1931 and 1941. See China, Campaigns in; Manchuria; Manchukuo; Mukden.

Chiang Kai-shek (1887–1975) Chinese nationalist general and President of China from 1943, he was also Allied Supreme

Commander of the China Theatre of Operations from the outbreak of the Pacific War*. Having studied for a military career in China and Japan, he served in the Japanese Army from 1909–11 before returning to China to support Sun Yat-sen's Kuomintang* and aid him in his efforts to build up a republican army. When Sun died in March 1925, amid a struggle for the succession, Chiang took over as C-in-C of the revolutionary army and began to consolidate his political position. A campaign against the Chinese warlords during 1926 was followed by a bloody coup in 1927 to oust the communists from the Kuomintang. By late 1928, with Nanking*, Canton and Peking under his control, Chiang's power base was sufficiently consolidated to formalize his presidency – effectively a dictatorship – of the Chinese republic.

Chiang continued to wage intermittent war against Chinese communists as well as against the Japanese after they occupied Manchuria* in 1931. In addition, he was also faced with three major army rebellions in 1930, 1933 and 1936. In December 1936, Chiang's kidnapping in Sian by rebel officers who were in contact with Chinese communists, involved Chou En-lai* (one of Mao Tse-tung's* principal advisers), in negotiations for a settlement of nationalist and communist conflicts. The resulting agreement to form a united front against Japanese encroachments on Chinese territory, however, provoked a swift reinforcement of Japanese military strength on Chinese frontiers. In July 1937 Japan launched a full-scale (though never formally declared) war against the Kuomintang (see China, Campaigns in) which forced Chiang's withdrawal to a wartime capital at Chungking*. Thus, when in December 1941 Japan launched its attack against Pearl Harbor*, Chiang became an American ally, and US military and economic aid (already flowing since 1941 and December 1938 respectively) was stepped up. Chiang was also assigned an American Chief of Staff, Lt General Joseph Stilwell*, at his own request.

Differences of opinion among the Western Allies about the potential contribution of Chiang's forces to the war effort, as well as the political complexities surrounding Chiang's position *vis-à-vis* the Chinese communists, overshadowed relations and much of the fighting in the China–Burma* theatre until the end of the war. In particular, Chiang's developing feud with Stilwell, who disparagingly nicknamed him 'Peanut', received considerable publicity, and finally resulted in Stilwell being recalled to the US in 1944. As the end of the war approached, talks between Chiang and communist leader Mao Tse-tung failed to avert outbreaks of fighting between nationalist and communist army brigades. By 1947, China was again engaged in all-out civil war, and Chiang was eventually forced to abandon his position in the Kuomintang. In March 1950, now established on Formosa (Taiwan) with many of his supporters, Chiang formally resumed the presidency and continued to hope for US military backing for a return to mainland China. Chiang remained as president in Formosa until his death, overseeing the new prosperity developing in Taiwan from its strong economic links with Japan and the US.

Chindit Soldier of Major General Orde Wingate's* Long Range Penetration force originally formed as the 77th Indian Infantry Brigade during the summer of 1942 from British, Burmese and Gurkha units and trained in jungle raiding and guerrilla tactics. By the time of the Second Chindit Expedition in March 1944, the force had grown to become the 3rd Indian Division (six brigades). See also Burma, Campaign in.

Chindwin River Primary tributary of the Irrawaddy river in northern Burma* and a formidable natural barrier that runs parallel to the frontier with India. A planned re-crossing of the river from Assam into Burma by elements of the British 14th Army (Operation Capital*) was accomplished during

November and December 1944 with major assaults on Sittaung and Kalewa against the Japanese 15th Army.

Chiyoda The *Chiyoda* and her sister, the *Chitose*, were flexibly designed Japanese warships like those of the *Shoho* Class. The London Naval Treaty (which restricted international aircraft carrier construction) expired during their construction, enabling them to be completed in 1938–9 as seaplane tenders with a capacity of 24 aircraft. In 1941 this was halved as both ships were modified to carry 12 midget submarines*, but after the Battle of Midway* in 1942 it was decided to reconvert them as light aircraft carriers. Work on the *Chiyoda* was finished by October 1943 and the *Chitose* was ready by the following January.

The two ships formed a Carrier Division at the Battle of the Philippine Sea* in June 1944, after which they were given an additional 18 25mm guns. They formed part of Admiral Ozawa's* decoy force in the Battle of Leyte Gulf*, where they were both sunk by American carrier aircraft on 25 October 1944. Like other converted Japanese carriers, they were given no armour protection.

BRIEF DATA (1944) Displacement: 11,190 tons; Dimensions: o/a lgth – 631' 6", b – 68' 3" (75' 6" FD); Speed: 29 knots; Armament: 8 × 5" AA gun, 30 × 25mm AA gun, 30 aircraft.

Chokai See Takao.

Chou En-lai (1898–1976) Chinese Communist leader who took an active part in the Communist revolution in China, 1919–20, and then joined the revolutionary coalition of the Kuomintang* under the leadership of its founder Sun Yat-sen. Following Sun Yat-sen's death in 1925, however, the rise to power of the nationalist Chiang Kai-shek* changed the complexion of the Kuomintang. Chou escaped arrest by Chiang and joined the Chinese Red Army, now engaged in civil war with

Kuomintang forces. Though the civil war continued throughout the 1930s, Chou continued to press for a united effort against the Japanese incursions into China (see China, Campaigns in). In 1936, when Chiang was kidnapped by a rebel Kuomintang general, Chou and the Chinese Communists were instrumental in securing his release. In September 1937, following the Japanese attack on Shanghai, the warring Communist and Kuomintang forces agreed to an end to hostilities. Under the new united front, Chou became Chiang's military adviser and then political vice-director of the Communist 8th Route Army's military council.

By 1945, though the internecine peace had been short-lived (ended by a Nationalist attack on Communist forces in central China in January 1941), Chou had established his position as effective second-in-command to Mao Tse-tung*. He was active in setting up negotiations for a truce between the Communists and the Kuomintang during 1946, and subsequently served as Prime Minister of the People's Republic, following the Communist victory in China.

Chuikov, General Vasily I. (1900–) Highly able Soviet general who directed the defence of Stalingrad* from September to November 1942, Chuikov had served in the occupation of eastern Poland*, the Russo-Finnish War* and as an adviser to Chiang Kai-shek* in Chungking*, before being appointed to command the 62nd Army from May 1942. Although the German seige of Stalingrad devastated the city and had to be resisted in house-to-house fighting at enormous cost on both sides, Chuikov's tactic of fighting from isolated pockets of resistance exhausted the resources of the German 6th Army under Paulus*, enabling a Soviet counteroffensive to be launched for the recapture of the city on 19 November. Chuikov subsequently commanded the 8th Guards Army on the Belorussian Front and spearheaded the final offensive against Berlin*.

Under Khrushchev*, Chuikov served as C-in-C of Soviet Military Forces in Germany (1949–53).

Churchill, Sir Winston Leonard Spencer (1874–1965) Orator, writer, politician and wartime Prime Minister of Great Britain. Born at Blenheim Palace (the gift of the nation to his ancestor John Churchill, Duke of Marlborough), Winston Churchill was the son of Lord Randolph Churchill and his American wife, Jenny Jerome. Undistinguished at school, Churchill was accepted at the Royal Military Academy, Sandhurst, only at his third attempt. Commissioned as a subaltern, he served in India and the Sudan and was present at the battle of Omdurman (1898). Resigning his commission, Churchill went to South Africa where he was captured whilst reporting the Boer War for the London *Morning Post*. The story of his escape was the basis of much of his early reputation.

On his return to England, Churchill was elected Member of Parliament for Oldham in 1900; critical of the leadership of the Conservative Party, he became a Liberal in 1904 and a member of the government shortly afterwards. During WW1 he served as First Lord of the Admiralty, and Minister of Munitions. Already he was seen to have a certain swashbuckling quality, a willingness to encourage controversial developments (such as the tank*); or ill-conceived strategies like the Dardanelles expedition.

In the post-war years Churchill moved back towards the Conservative Party as a 'constitutionalist' and was finally appointed Chancellor of the Exchequer by Baldwin. It was an unhappy tenure of office. Within a short time it became clear that his independence of mind, or, as some would have it, his reckless aristocratic spirit, did not fit easily into the British party system. In 1931, he resigned from the Conservative Party Shadow Cabinet.

For Winston Churchill the thirties were years of political wilderness. He held no office, and was regarded with suspicion by many members of the Conservative Party.

But he nevertheless took the lead in warning of the menace of Nazism. While Chamberlain* sought peace by appeasement*, Churchill established himself at the centre of another, at that time much smaller, group of Conservatives implacably opposed to Hitler. In 1939, he was invited back to the Admiralty. Eight months later, when the Allied war effort was evidently foundering, Neville Chamberlain resigned and Churchill became Prime Minister.

He assumed responsibility in the most fateful week of the war when the German armies launched their Western Offensive* against the Netherlands, Belgium and France. It was a moment which required, above all, leadership, and Churchill's magnetic personality was able to supply it. His speeches ('All I can offer you is blood, sweat, tears and toil'), were calculated to inspire the British people; but in equal measure to appeal to the fund of pro-British feeling in the United States. In this sense he universalized Britain's war, firmly expropriating right and justice for the British cause, consciously building a view of the struggle which the United States would find it difficult to reject. The Atlantic Charter* is the most notable example of the determination of Churchill, and in this he was fully supported by Roosevelt, to pre-empt the great moral issues of the Allied cause.

During the Battle of Britain* ('Never was so much owed by so many to so few'), Churchill was again speaking to the American people as well as to his own. The London Blitz* which followed gave Churchill further opportunity; his oratory, his eccentricity and his charismatic presence earned him a unique place in the annals of modern warfare. A German general said he was worth to Britain at least 30 mechanized divisions; Ciano, the Italian foreign minister, lamented that every speech by Churchill was the equivalent of a major Italian defeat.

When Hitler attacked the Soviet Union in 1941, few, and certainly not Stalin, imagined that the British Prime Minister would welcome the Soviet Union as an ally and promise all possible aid. When a colleague remonstrated that half of Churchill's life had been spent looking forward to the downfall of the Soviet Union, he replied: 'If Hitler were to launch an attack on Hell itself, I would at least contrive to make a favourable reference to the Devil in the House of Commons.' Thereafter he acted as a loyal but wary ally of the Soviet Union, his thoughts never far from the shape of the post-war world.

Other areas of disagreement existed between Britain and the United States. Pearl Harbor* had not brought about a significant change in Churchill's policy towards the US, although from now onwards he was dealing with an ally rather than a friendly neutral. Roosevelt had early on proclaimed the 'Europe First' strategy which projected the defeat of Germany – as the greatest menace – before the defeat of Japan. Many senior American officers, especially the US Fleet commanders, could not possibly agree with these war aims. Even so, Roosevelt never showed signs of wavering in this promise to Europe, even when the British declared that the invasion of France in 1942, which Stalin* demanded and the American people wanted, would be nothing less than sheer suicidal folly.

The problem that remained, however, was to find a location where United States forces might confront the enemy. It is difficult to see that North Africa was chosen for any other reason than that the British were already there. However unconvincing the military basis of the choice, the Torch* landings had momentous consequences for the strategic development of the conflict, directing the major Allied effort in 1943 towards Sicily* and Italy* (Churchill's preference), rather than to northwest France. Three major wartime conferences at Cairo, Teheran and Yalta settled the subsequent direction the Allied powers were to take, although Churchill continued to have private discussions with Roosevelt, to the frustration of State Department advisers. Churchill also visited Moscow without Roosevelt but with his agreement (see Conferences, Allied).

Despite intense pressure from Stalin, the cross-Channel invasion was delayed until 1944. Churchill was well aware that British manpower resources were inadequate to remount an invasion of France if the first effort failed and the Allies were agreed on the dangers of defeat and the further prolongation of the war. If Britain was to enjoy the political advantages of having played a major part in the fall of the Third Reich, the Normandy* landings would have to be delayed until success was as near certain as possible.

By this stage of the war, the Allied balance of power had turned decisively against Churchill. The Soviet Armies were driving German forces back towards Germany from the east. Both these offensives and the Allied campaigns in Northwest Europe* were fuelled by American productivity now reaching unparalleled heights. As US air and amphibious* operations in the Pacific vigorously drove Japanese forces back out of the vast area of their short-lived empire, Britain was overstretched in Southeast Asia, the Middle East and Northwest Europe. Inevitably, Yalta saw the emergence of two superpowers.

Winston Churchill's Conservative Party was rejected by the people of Britain in the 1945 election. But it was by no means a total rejection of Churchill himself. Despite an undistinguished period as a post-war Prime Minister, he retained the affection of the British people and the regard of the West as an inspired war leader. His funeral in 1965 was one of the great public ceremonies of the post-war world.

Churchill Tank British Infantry tank*. With less than 100 tanks left in the United Kingdom after Dunkirk*, the Vauxhall company were given just a year in which to design, develop and build a replacement for the Matilda II*. By June 1941, the first production Churchills were ready and quantity manufacture soon followed. Rushed into service, the early Churchills inevitably suffered their teething troubles in an operational context, and it took a year of use before the tank's mechanical fragility was overcome.

Its fundamental offensive weakness was a more enduring problem. Early models were armed with the anachronistic 2-pounder gun, supplemented by a 3-inch howitzer mounted on the hull. In March 1942, the British munitions industry at last made a 6-pounder available, and a 75mm gun was mounted on the Churchill the following year. By now the turret, though comparatively roomy and adaptable, had reached the limit of its design, and it was never successfully modified to take the genuinely effective 17-pounder gun. The Churchill was well armoured from the start, and its protection was increased in successive models. Its other main assets were a low silhouette, hydraulically assisted steering and a durable suspension system.

The Churchill's operational début – at Dieppe* in August 1942 – was a complete disaster, and there was talk of halting production the following year. Success with the 1st Army in Tunisia* (particularly its ability to climb hills) earned the tank a reprieve, and it fought in increasing numbers there and in Italy* throughout the war. Some early models were supplied to fight on the Eastern Front*, and several Churchill brigades took part in the Allied invasion of Northwest Europe*. Although outgunned by German heavy tanks in the last years of the war, the strength of their armour stood them in some stead. Churchill chassis were also used for bridging, minesweeping and other specialized tasks, proving particularly successful as flamethrowers*. Altogether 5,640 Churchills were built and they remained in British service into the 1950s. See also Special-purpose Vehicles.

BRIEF DATA (Mk III) Type: 5-man infantry tank; Engine: 350hp petrol; Max speed: 15.5mph; Range: 90m; Arms: 1 × 6pdr gun, 2 × 7.92mm mg; Armour: max 102mm.

Chu Teh, General (1886–1976) C-in-C of the Chinese Red Army from 1937, Chu Teh had served with the Imperial Chinese Army and subsequently with a number of warlords before joining the Communist Party during the 1920s. As a strategist of the Chinese Peoples Liberation Army, he developed a military plan to complement the party's political activities in rural areas of China*. Until 1937, Chu Teh also commanded forces against the Nationalist leader, Chiang Kai-shek*, when the Communist armies were integrated with the Kuomintang* in order to fight Japanese forces in China. Appointed to command the Red Army forces, now renamed the 8th Route Army, Chu Teh directed the successful Battle of Pingsinkuan against Japanese forces in late September 1937, though the tension between Communist and Nationalist forces continued to provoke armed conflict throughout the war.

Ciano, Count Galeazzo (1903–44) Mussolini's* Foreign Minister from 1936–43, Count Ciano was an ambitious convert to Italian Fascism and a participant in the Fascist March on Rome in 1922. He held various diplomatic posts during the 1920s and subsequently guaranteed his career by marrying Mussolini's daughter, Edda, in 1930.

Appointed Foreign Minister in 1936, Ciano firmly advocated an alliance between the two major Fascist powers. The Berlin–Rome Axis*, signed by Ciano in Berlin in October 1936, appeared to cement his ambitions for the recognition of Italian power in Europe. But Germany's initiation of hostilities against Poland* in 1939, launched without consultation with Italy, directly breached the agreement. Ciano's subsequent reversal of attitude towards Germany and his attempts to persuade Mussolini to disentangle himself from Hitler were overtaken by the events of 1940. The fall of France and the consolidation of Germany's earlier successes (see Western Offensive, 1940) rendered her friendship irresistible – and Italy entered the war as Germany's ally on 10 June 1940.

Thereafter, however obvious the failure of his diplomatic skills, Ciano was clearly more able than Mussolini to analyse the course of the war and predict the outcome for Italy. The halting of the German offensive before Moscow* and the US declaration of war in December 1941 convinced Ciano of the need to make a separate peace settlement with the Allies. His arguments, however, served more to increase Mussolini's suspicion of Ciano than convince the dictator of the need for action. In February 1943, Ciano resigned and was exiled to the Vatican as Mussolini's ambassador. Remaining a member of the Fascist Grand Council, he participated in the decision to depose Mussolini in mid-1943 and to call on Marshal Badoglio* to form a new government. Mussolini's rescue by the Germans and temporary re-establishment at the head of the puppet Salo Republic, however, fatally reversed Ciano's fortunes. Already denounced by the new government in Rome on charges of corruption, Ciano was arrested by supporters of Mussolini, along with other members of the Grand Council, sentenced to death at Verona and shot on 11 January 1944.

Citadel (Zitadelle) See Kursk.

Clark, Rear Admiral Joseph (1893–1971) Colourful commander of the American carrier *Yorktown** and later commander of Task Group 58, one of the fast carrier task forces whose striking power played a major part in the operations against the 'Jimas', the Battle of the Philippine Sea*, the capture of Okinawa* and the attacks on the Japanese home islands. After the war, Rear Admiral Clark served as Assistant Chief of Naval Operations.

Clark, General Mark Wayne (1896–1984) Charismatic US general nicknamed 'the American Eagle' by Churchill* and widely regarded as a highly effective field commander. Clark was a West Point graduate who served in WW1 and began WW2 as a

staff officer of Army ground forces. His commitment, ambition and leadership qualities saw him quickly promoted to Chief of Staff, Commander of 2nd Corps, and then deputy to C-in-C Eisenhower for the Torch* invasion of North Africa in November 1942.

Clark was responsible for handling the difficult secret negotiations with French officers over the planning and co-ordination of the Torch landings in North Africa. Immediately preceding the landings, Clark was landed off Algiers by submarine to make contact with Admiral Darlan*, finally securing an armistice with French North African forces three days later, although the involvement with Darlan subsequently caused the Allies significant political embarrassment.

In January 1943, now a Lt General, Clark was given command of the US 5th Army, then a training organization, which was assigned to participate in the Allied invasion of Italy*. He commanded the landings at Salerno* on 9 September 1943, beginning the long campaign in which he gained his reputation as a battlefield commander. Fighting against an exceptional German defence directed by Field Marshal Kesselring* and over terrain which largely favoured the defenders, Clark commanded 5th Army operations (including the unsuccessful Anzio* operation) in the face of political as well as military difficulties. Forcing a slow passage up the toe onto the leg of the Italian mainland, Clark's supply and reinforcement (like Montgomery's*, in command of the British 8th Army) was increasingly subject to the vacillations and disagreements among the Allied leaders and Combined Chiefs of Staff over the status and objectives of the Allied campaign in Italy. Criticism of Clark's leadership of the 5th Army, notably in the winter of 1943–4 and at the Rapido River* battles, should perhaps take into account the significant difficulties of command posed by these factors.

Following the costly Anzio operations and his opportunistic capture of Rome* with the 5th Army, in June 1944, Clark continued to apply himself energetically to success in Italy, despite the drain of men and equipment imposed by the Allied decision to invade Northwest Europe*. From late 1944, commanding the 15th Army Group, one of the most heterogeneous field armies of the war (it included American, British, Italian, French, Polish, Brazilian, New Zealand, African, Canadian and Palestinian troops), Clark directed the gruelling advance of his armies up the narrow Italian peninsula, before accepting the surrender of German forces in Italy under Vietinghoff* (Kesselring's successor) and SS* General Wolff*, on 2 May 1945.

Now a full general, Clark was subsequently posted to Austria to command US forces of occupation there. Afterwards he commanded the 6th Army and, later, UN forces in Korea. In July 1953 he was a signatory of the truce in Korea.

Clark Field See Philippines.

Cleveland, USS US Navy light cruiser and class. The *Cleveland* Class was a development of the last *Brooklyn* Class vessels, similarly armoured but with improved hull structure and anti-aircraft* armament, the latter increased at the expense of a 25 per cent reduction in main armament. American light cruiser design was standardized on the class and no less than 50 units were ordered. Twenty-seven were eventually completed during the war, the biggest single class of cruisers in history, and a further nine were converted as *Independence* Class aircraft carriers. The first two ships – the *Cleveland* and the *Columbia* – were commissioned in June 1942, and 20 were in service by the end of 1944. They operated in the Pacific, mostly as protection for the fast carrier forces and in support of amphibious* landings. Not a single unit was lost during the war, although all were exposed to attack in forward positions and several survived repeated damage. Perhaps the greatest resilience was displayed by the *Columbia*, survivor of two Kamikaze* hits

in four days at Lingayen*, and the second *Houston*, severely damaged by torpedo-bombers off Leyte* on 14 and 16 October 1944.

BRIEF DATA (1942) Displacement: 10,000 tons; Dimensions: o/a lgth – 610', b – 66' 6"; Speed: 33 knots; Armament: 12 × 6" gun (4 × 3), 12 × 5" DP gun, 8 × 40mm AA gun, 13 × 22mm AA gun, 4 aircraft.

Coastwatchers New Zealand and Australian servicemen who worked alone or in small groups in co-operation with local civilians to provide a flow of information on Japanese naval and air movements during the lengthy campaigns to recapture the Solomon Islands* and neutralize the Japanese base at Rabaul*. Using radio transmitters from isolated hidden outposts on islands of the Solomon and Bismarck groups to report Japanese activity, the coastwatchers contributed to the effective use of the United States Guadalcanal*-based air power and played an important role in maintaining the Allied initiative in the Pacific during 1942 and 1943.

Cobra, Operation Code-name for the American breakout from the Normandy* hedgerow country launched from St-Lô* on 25 July 1944. The move was preceded by an enormous preliminary 'carpet-bombing' bombardment by over 500 fighter-bombers of the US 9th Air Force followed by a 2,000-bomber raid (of B-17s* and medium bombers) on German positions around St-Lô. Last-minute postponement of the assault on the target date of 24 July caused confusion which resulted in tragic casualties to American infantry. When the assault was launched on the following day, the later waves of bombers were again confused by obscured target markers and caused a further 600 American casualties. But the devastation to German positions nevertheless enabled the US 1st Army ground-assault troops under General Bradley* to breach the German lines, and Bradley's four divisions reached Avranches, at the base of the Cotentin Peninsula, by 31 July. See Northwest Europe, Allied Invasion of. See Map 36.

Collins, Lieutenant General Joseph (1882 –1963) Aggressive and able commander of the US Army 7th Corps, which fought at Guadálcanal* and went ashore at Utah Beach, Normandy* on D-Day, fighting through the remainder of the campaign in Europe. Initially sent to Hawaii as Chief of Staff of 7th Corps, to reorganize its defences after Pearl Harbor*, Collins then replaced General Vandegrift* as commander of 25th Infantry Division on Guadalcanal, where he earned the nickname 'Lightning Joe' for his aggressive pursuit of the enemy. In February 1944, he assumed command of 7th Corps, and lead the breakout from the Normandy beachhead. Successful operations at Argentan-Falaise, Cherbourg, St Lô, Namur and Aachen (the first major German city to fall to the Allies) – and later Cologne, Remagen and the Ruhr pocket (see Northwest Europe, Invasion of) – earned Collins the deep respect of Allied commanders in the theatre. He was promoted to Lt General in April 1945.

Colmar Pocket See Alsace.

Cologne German city on the Rhine and target of the first 'thousand-bomber raid', mounted by C-in-C RAF* Bomber Command, Air Marshal Harris* as a demonstration and promotion of the controversial policy of 'area bombing'*. Code-named Operation Millenium, the raid drew on every serviceable aircraft available to Harris, as well as some from Flying Training Command and Bomber Command Operational Training units. Refused the use of 250 aircraft from Coastal Command by the Admiralty at the last minute, Harris nevertheless put together 1,050 bombers. On the night of 30 May 1942, the thousand-bomber force attacked the city in a concentrated bombardment lasting less than two hours, heavily damaging about a third of the total area of Cologne. Although

photo-reconnaissance confirmed the devastating potential of massed bomber raids, the bombing of Cologne and the subsequent bombing of many German cities and population centres cannot, in retrospect, be said to have justified the policy on which it was based. See also Strategic Bombing Offensive.

Colorado, USS See Maryland, USS.

Combined Chiefs of Staff The Anglo-American military command committee established at the Arcadia Conference in Washington in December 1941, following the United States entry into the war. The operations body, consisting of American chiefs of staff and representatives of their British counterparts, met regularly in Washington. All service chiefs also met at major conferences* throughout the war.

US Joint Chiefs of Staff: Fleet Admiral William D. Leahy*, *Chief of Staff to the C-in-C of the US Armed Forces (Chairman of the Joint Chiefs of Staff Committee)*; General George C. Marshall*, *Chief of Staff of the US Army**; Admiral Ernest J. King*, *C-in-C of the US Fleet and Chief of Naval Operations*; General Henry H. Arnold*, *Commanding General US Army Air Force**; Brigadier General A. J. McFarland, *Secretary*.

British Chiefs of Staff: Field Marshal Sir Alan Brooke*, *Chief of the Imperial General Staff (Chairman of the Chiefs of Staff Committee)*; Marshal Sir Charles Portal*, *Chief of the Air Staff*; Admiral Sir Dudley Pound* (replaced by Admiral Sir Andrew Cunningham* in October 1943), *First Sea Lord and Chief of the Naval Staff*; General Sir Hastings Ismay*, *Deputy Secretary of the War Cabinet and Chief of Staff to the Minister of Defence*; Major General R. E. Laycock*, *Chief of Combined Operations*; Major General L. C. Hollis, *Secretary*.

British Joint Staff Mission in Washington: *Head of the Mission*: Field Marshal Sir John Dill* (until November 1944); Field Marshal Sir Henry Maitland Wilson* (from January 1945).

Commandos Name given to British units, formed in June 1940 to apply irregular tactics to conventional warfare. Commandos offered a way of striking at Axis-held targets at a time when the British were in no position to mount large-scale European operations. After limited training in Scotland as guerrilla fighters, the first Commandos went into action on the night of 23–4 June 1940, carrying out a small and only partly successful raid on the French coast near Boulogne.

Attacks on the Channel Island of Guernsey, the Lofoten Islands, and Vaagso in Norway followed during 1940–1, and a force of three Commando units – known as Layforce after its commander, Colonel Laycock* – was sent to the Middle East in February 1941. Here they combined with Middle East Commandos also formed in 1940. Layforce saw action in the Desert War*, Crete* and Syria*, its most famous operation being a raid on Rommel's* suspected Libyan headquarters in November 1941, which failed to kill the German general and from which only two men (including Laycock) returned. Throughout 1942, Commandos performed a number of small raids, and units took part in larger attacks on St Nazaire* and Dieppe*. After the Allied Torch* landings in November 1942, they were generally used to spearhead amphibious* operations including those in Sicily*, Italy*, Burma* and Normandy*.

Commando units consisted of some 460 men (all volunteers) divided into six troops and grouped into Special Service (later Commando) Brigades. They came under the overall control of Combined Operations Command, which was directed by Admiral Sir Roger Keyes* from July 1940 to October 1941, when he was succeeded by Lord Louis Mountbatten*. In 1943 Laycock, now a major-general, became Chief of Combined Operations, a position he held until 1947. See also SAS; Rangers; Brandenburgers.

Commonwealth (CA-12) Boomerang When the start of the Pacific War* forced Australia to concentrate on home defence, the Boomerang fighter was hastily designed and built in Melbourne by the Commonwealth Aircraft Corporation. Urgently needed to augment the few Brewster Buffalos* that comprised Australia's modern fighter strength, the CA12 was based on the North American trainer series and used the only powerful engine available. It was in service by August 1942, and proved a resilient, highly manoeuvrable craft capable of holding its own with Japanese fighters despite its inevitable limitations. In all, 250 were built in several slightly different versions and production continued until early 1944.

BRIEF DATA (CA-12) Type: single-seat fighter; Engine: 1 × 1,200hp Pratt and Whitney Twin Wasp; Max speed: 296mph; Ceiling: 29,000′; Range: 930m; Arms: 2 × 20mm cannon, 4 × 0.303″ mg.

Compass, Operation See Egypt, Campaign for.

Compiègne Site of the signing of the armistice after the capitulation of France to Germany in June 1940. Precisely staged by Hitler* to re-enact the signing of the 1918 armistice, it took place in the same railway carriage which was hurriedly brought from a French museum. Hitler's terms were delivered by General Jodl* and signed by the French envoys on 22 June. See also Petain, Marshal; Western Offensive.

Compton, Arthur (1892–1962) American physicist, Nobel Prize winner in 1927, and a leading figure in the development of the first nuclear weapons. He headed the department at the University of Chicago which created the first atomic pile in 1942, became an important member of the Manhattan Engineer Project and directed research into the use of man-made plutonium to create nuclear fission. In 1945 he became President of Washington University, St Louis. See Atomic Bomb.

Concentration Camps The numerous hutted camps for prisoners of the Third Reich used as prisons, as slave-labour reservoirs and as killing sites, so-named from camps set up by the British during the Boer War to 'concentrate' Boer farming families during war operations. The Nazi Party* Boxheim Papers, uncovered in a scandal of 1931, had foretold the creation of special camps to hold enemies of the state. As soon as Hitler* had taken power in German in 1933, SA men acting as 'auxiliary police' began rounding up prisoners into hurriedly constructed camps, first at Esterwegen and Dachau* and soon at other sites. Although some were released by Göring* prior to his handing over of control of camps to Himmler* as head of the SS* in 1934, and many SA 'wild camps' closed down after the first enthusiasm for arrests, the concentration camps, reorganized on the pattern of Eicke's* Dachau administration, soon housed many thousands of political prisoners, freemasons, Jehovah's Witnesses, those known to associate with Jews and countless other 'undesirables'. During the 1930s Eicke's Concentration Camp Directorate trained SS men as guards and administrators, and controlled an increasing number of newly constructed camps designed to house the ever-growing number of Jews, trade unionists, gypsies, homosexuals, Protestants, Catholics, petty criminals and dissenters now subject to *Schutzhaft*, 'protective custody'. Among the more notorious camps opened in this period were Sachsenhausen in 1936, Buchenwald* in 1937, Flossenbürg and Mauthausen in 1938, and Theresienstadt and Ravensbrück, a women's camp, opened in 1939.

After 1939, war changed the nature of the concentration camp system. Many more camps opened in occupied territories to herd together the millions of Jews, political prisoners, Russian POWs and Slavic peoples made victims of the war. The SS-WVHA, responsible for the considerable commercial and industrial interests of the SS, took over administration of the camps from early 1942. New camps were set up to supply the necessary labour to munitions factories, leading to competition in the SS between the extermination and cheap-labour schools of thought, though both styles of camp survived until the end of the war. Satellite labour camps associated with the principal extermination camps, often built by the industries themselves, grew as the system grew, and the SS charged companies 4–8 marks per day for use of prisoners on 12-hour shifts, recouping an average net gain of 1,431 marks per labourer (based on a life expectancy of nine months). Camps also provided the SS with legitimized looting sites. Apart from organizing the deaths of over 700,000 people, Treblinka Commandant Franz Stangl also made SS bank deposits of $2.8 million, £400,000, 12 million roubles, 145 kilograms of gold from rings and 4,000 carats of diamonds.

Following the Wannsee* Conference in January 1942, which sought to systematize the extermination of the Jews, extermination camps were founded in the east. Belzec*, Sobibor, Treblinka (where most Warsaw Jews were taken) and Majdanek all opened in 1942 with a combined planned killing capacity of 60,000 per day. The capacity of Auschwitz* was increased seven times between 1942 and 1944. Other camps, such as Belsen* (Bergen-Belsen) and Natzweiler, caused death by horrific neglect.

As Germany's military effort began to collapse and Russian armies moved into Poland, prisoners were evacuated and marched west, many dying *en route*. It was not until April 1945, however, that relief could begin to be brought to the vast numbers of surviving camp victims. After the war, all surviving concentration camp records were assembled by the Red Cross* at Arolsen, site of their International Tracing Centre. Recent research suggests that between 1933 and 1945, a total of 1.6 million people were sent to work camps, of whom over 1 million died, and that some 18 million more may have gone to extermination camps, at which up to 11 million died. Accurate figures are, however, impossible to obtain. A figure close to 6 million deaths is often acknowledged by historians. See also Anti-Semitism; Final Solution.

Conferences, Allied Conferences, and particularly summit meetings between the leaders of the three major Allied powers – Russia, the US and Britain – were the principal Allied means of establishing combined overall strategy in WW2, and were the medium through which the political structure of the post-war world was deliberated.

Consultations about the war between Britain and the US had begun when Winston Churchill* became Prime Minister in May 1940. Churchill, who had close personal contacts with the US, maintained a candid correspondence with President Roosevelt*, informing him of the progress of the war and eliciting a warmly sympathetic response. Also in 1940, a scientific mission to Canada and the US revealed the secrets of Britain's most advanced war technology, including the proximity fuse for anti-aircraft* shells and the latest radar* research. In January 1941, British and US military staffs agreed in Washington to establish joint planning groups on both sides of the Atlantic to prepare for the possibility of US intervention in the war against the Axis*. During the spring, US involvement in the protection of Atlantic* convoys was stepped up and the German invasion of Russia (see Eastern Front) in June prompted promises of aid to the Soviet Union from both Britain and the US.

Placentia Bay The first wartime meeting between Churchill and Roosevelt took place at sea in Placentia Bay, Newfoundland, in August 1941. Previous agreements were confirmed, and the two leaders issued the Atlantic Charter* – a general declaration of peace aims – which was endorsed by the Soviet Union and various governments-in-exile, but which was less than the firm US commitment to defeating Germany that Churchill had hoped for. Restricted by isolationist opinion and legislation at home (see Neutrality, US),

Roosevelt could only privately confirm that in the event of war, the defeat of Germany would be the first American priority.

The Arcadia Conference Held in Washington between 22 December 1941 and 3 January 1942, the Arcadia Conference was the next Anglo-American summit. The US had entered the war two weeks earlier, and the conference was proposed by Churchill to discuss long-term strategy. The British arrived prepared for a struggle to preserve the 'Germany first' policy, expecting the US to concentrate on defeating Japan. In fact Roosevelt fully intended to honour his commitment, and this was confirmed at the conference. Military co-operation between the two Allies was formalized by the creation of a Combined Chiefs of Staff* committee in Washington, and the principle agreed of appointing an overall Allied commander for each theatre of operations. US Chief of Staff George Marshall* was the moving force behind these developments, and the Americans also agreed to examine British proposals for Allied landings in Northwest Africa (see Torch) against their own plans for attacking mainland Europe. A number of combined economic authorities, including two munitions boards, were established to harness British war experience and US production capacity.

Apart from a boost to Churchill's popularity with the American people, the most visible result of the Arcadia Conference was the Joint Declaration*, drafted by Churchill and Roosevelt and signed on 1 January 1942. This announced an alliance to defeat the Axis* powers and reiterated adherence to the Atlantic Charter. It was signed by 26 nations, including China and the Soviet Union but not France, due to uncertainty over the status of the Free France* movement. A simultaneous visit to Moscow by British Foreign Minister Anthony Eden* revealed that Soviet agreement was conditional on acceptance of her territorial gains in the Russo-Finnish War*, in clear contravention of the renunciation of 'territorial aggrandizement' contained in the Atlantic Charter.

Following visits to London and Washington by Soviet Foreign Minister Molotov* to press for an Allied Second Front in Europe, Churchill again travelled to meet Roosevelt in June 1942. During private meetings at the Roosevelt family home, Churchill stated the British view that a landing in Europe was impossible in 1942 and suggested a revival of previously rejected plans for invading Northwest Africa. The US Joint Chiefs of Staff opposed the project, but the palpable weakness of Britain's military position and Roosevelt's own insistence forced them to reconsider and adopt Operation Torch* the following month.

The Casablanca Conference With the invasion of Africa going well, the next summit was convened in January 1943 to plan the Allies' next offensive. The conference, code-named Symbol, took place near Casablanca in Morocco and Roosevelt was anxious that Stalin* should attend. The Soviet leader refused on the grounds that he was busy with operations around Stalingrad*, but the conference nevertheless centred on the opening of a Second Front in Europe for the relief of Russia. Churchill and the British Chiefs of Staff, supported to an extent by Roosevelt, sought to extend Allied success in Africa to an invasion of southern Europe. American service chiefs, led by Marshall, favoured a cross-Channel invasion of occupied northern Europe in 1943, which the British claimed was premature. US Naval C-in-C Admiral King* in particular favoured deploying all available resources in the Pacific*, if France could not be invaded. Arguments became heated over the ten days of the conference, but the British plan was adopted and the invasion of Sicily* (Operation Husky) was approved. This was the last time that Churchill's close relationship with Roosevelt significantly helped determine overall Allied strategy.

Other important military decisions were taken at Casablanca. Priority was given to defeating the U-boats in the Battle of the Atlantic*, and the combined Strategic Bombing Offensive* over Germany was intensified. Both were measures intended to ease the path of a future invasion of northern France, for which a joint planning group (COSSAC) was set up in April 1943. In the Far East, increased aid to China (a particularly American cause) and a tentative plan to retake Burma* were approved, but Pacific operations were not to interfere with opportunities to defeat Germany. Attempts were also made to bring together General Giraud*, the French commander in North Africa, and the intransigent Free French leader de Gaulle*, who had been excluded from Operation Torch*.

Much of this was overshadowed by Roosevelt's statement on 24 January, promptly endorsed by Churchill, that: '. . . peace can come to the world only by the total elimination of German and Japanese war power . . . [which] means the unconditional surrender by Germany, Italy or [sic] Japan.' Taken as a statement of Allied policy, the words 'unconditional surrender' have been blamed for rendering any early negotiated peace impossible. The Allied demand certainly slowed down negotiations for the Italian capitulation and, thanks to Nazi propaganda, it meant that the German people had nothing to lose by fighting on in the last stages of the war. But its importance is almost certainly overstated in the context of the surrender of Japan (see Pacific War).

Trident and Quadrant The target date for the cross-Channel invasion postponed at Casablanca was set for 1 May 1944. This was agreed at a third Anglo-American Washington Conference (code-name Trident) in mid-May 1943. The US plan for an offensive drive on Japan through the Central Pacific was approved, and the bombing of Germany was confirmed as a necessary preliminary to the cross-Channel invasion. At the first Quebec Conference (code-name Quadrant) in August, the commitment to the May invasion was confirmed, representing US refusal to accept Churchill's conviction that the main Allied offensive should be directed through Italy to the Balkans*. Quadrant also established a combined Anglo-American programme for the development of an atomic bomb*, and created Southeast Asia Command (SEAC) to invigorate the Allied campaign in Burma*. Stalin, still insistent on the urgency of a Second Front, again declined to attend the summit.

Cairo and Tehran Chinese leader Generalissimo Chiang Kai-shek* joined Roosevelt and Churchill at the Cairo Conference (code-name Sextant) during the latter part of November. Largely concerned with China*, in which Churchill had little interest, the meeting also enabled the leaders to prepare for their first conference with Stalin – to take place some days later in the Persian capital of Tehran.

Stalin excluded Chiang Kai-shek from the conference (code-name Eureka) and took care to isolate Churchill by arranging for Roosevelt to be housed in the Russian embassy. He opened the meetings by stating that after the defeat of Germany, for which he gave his support to the projected invasion of Normandy*, the Soviet Union would declare war on Japan. He then gained the approval of his allies for his intended expansion into eastern Poland*, coupled with the extension of Polish borders into Germany. He was categorically opposed to an Anglo-American suggestion that post-war Germany should be partitioned into five autonomous states, and the proposal was never implemented. Other business discussed in Tehran included the potential character of the United Nations Organization*, an agreement to guarantee the independence of Persia* (which was under Allied occupation) and a shift in Allied support to Yugoslavia, where Tito* was belatedly recognized as the major resistance leader.

After Tehran the Western leaders returned to Cairo for further meetings to plan the invasions of Normandy and southern France. Roosevelt had promised Chiang Kai-shek an invasion of the Andaman Islands (Operation Buccaneer) at the first meeting, but dropped the idea when it

became clear that *matériel*, particularly landing craft, could not be spared from Europe.

Quebec and Moscow Before the next meeting of the 'Big Three' at Yalta, Churchill visited Quebec and Moscow. At the second Quebec Conference (code-name Octagon) in September 1944, the main subject discussed was the post-war treatment of Germany, but nothing of long-term significance was agreed and the controversial 'Morgenthau Plan' for the enforced pastoralization of Germany was only briefly considered. Anxious to ensure continued US aid to Britain after the war, Churchill offered to send a British fleet to the Pacific – a gesture which Roosevelt accepted, although the US Navy* tended to regard British involvement as an unnecessary complication. His Moscow discussions with Stalin in October concerned the future of eastern Europe. Less demonstrably anti-Bolshevik than he was soon to become, Churchill agreed that Bulgaria*, Hungary* and Rumania* were to be predominantly Soviet spheres of interest, and that Britain should control the destiny of Greece (see Balkans, Russian Campaign in). The fate of Yugoslavia was left open, and the two leaders parted without resolving which of the two Polish administrations (the London-based government-in-exile or the Soviet-sponsored Lublin Committee*) would control the post-war state.

Bretton Woods and Dumbarton Oaks The practical structure of the United Nations was established during 1944. In July, a multinational monetary and financial conference at Bretton Woods, New Hampshire, agreed to the formation of both the International Monetary Fund and the International Bank for Reconstruction and Development. Between August and October, representatives of the US, Britain and Russia met at Dumbarton Oaks Estate in Washington to discuss the general form of the UN organization, and it was agreed that states who were members of the Security Council should have the power of veto. China, the fourth Security Council member, took Russia's place for the final week of the discussions, which ended with serious differences over procedure unresolved.

The Yalta Conference The second 'Big Three' summit (code-name Argonaut) was held at Yalta in the Crimea, opening on 4 February 1945. After bitter wrangling, short-term solutions were found to arguments over the use of the UN veto and the inclusion of the Soviet Republics of Belorussia and the Ukraine as full members of the United Nations. With Germany clearly on the verge of defeat, Roosevelt was determined to secure Soviet participation in the war against Japan, as he believed it would be of great military value. Stalin restated his intention to declare war on Japan, which he projected for three months after the defeat of Germany. In return Russia received secret territorial concessions some of which infringed Chinese sovereignty, on her Far Eastern frontiers.

The issue of Poland, on which Britain had gone to war, received great attention, but Russian military domination of eastern Europe meant that there was little the Western Allies could do about the accession of a Soviet-sponsored government. 'Unconditional surrender' was again demanded of Germany, which it was agreed to partition. The details were left until later, but the Anglo-American proposal to allocate a zone to France, which was not represented at Yalta, was accepted by Stalin. Apart from confirming the success of arrangements made earlier in Moscow concerning the Balkans, Churchill's role in the proceedings was marginal, a first indication of the downgrading of British diplomatic status *vis-à-vis* the US and the Soviet Union which reflected their respective economic power.

The Potsdam Conference The last major Allied conference of the war (code-name Terminal) took place at Potsdam, near Berlin, in July 1945. Roosevelt had died in office in April and his former Vice-President, Truman*, strengthened his bargaining position with Stalin by delaying the conference until the new atomic bomb* had been tested. Churchill, who had opposed the suggestion that Truman meet Stalin alone, was also present at the meeting. He was defeated in the British General Election and replaced by Socialist leader Attlee* in mid-summit. Although the war with Japan was still in progress, most of the business at Potsdam concerned the reconstruction of Europe.

Germany was not formally partitioned, but the Allies retained sovereign control over their respective Occupied Zones. Although an Allied Control Council was set up to co-ordinate overall policy in Germany, its actions were subject to veto from any one power and so its effectiveness was entirely dependent on goodwill. The principle of reparations, to be paid to the victims of German aggression by the removal of assets, was agreed at Potsdam, but the amount and precise nature of these was again left to individual occupying authorities. A joint body was created for the administration of Berlin; the remains of the German Navy and merchant fleet were divided between the 'Big Three'; and an International Military Tribunal was formed to arrange the prosecution of war criminals*. A broad agreement to treat Germany as 'one economic whole' was never implemented.

The European territorial decisions reached at Yalta were confirmed at Potsdam, and the resettlement in Germany of some 6 million ethnic Germans from Czechoslovakia*, Hungary and Poland was planned. The Polish government was formally recognized after Stalin agreed to broaden its membership to include members of the London-based government-in-exile, but Soviet demands for a trusteeship of Libya and the acceptance of provisional governments in Bulgaria and Rumania were not met. An Allied Council of Foreign Ministers, including French and Chinese representatives, was established to draft peace treaties with Germany and Japan. Japan had already asked Russia to act as a neutral intermediary in seeking peace terms, but Stalin was preparing for brief but profitable participation in the Pacific War and encouraged instead the Potsdam Declaration, which called for the unconditional surrender of Japan without mentioning the new bomb, but threatening the annihilation of the country.

Potsdam appeared at the time to have laid the basis for Allied co-operation in world reconstruction, although it was appreciated in the West that Russian occupation of much of eastern Europe had been accepted after the fact. The political decisions reached by the Allies proved unenforceable, however, and the post-war period was characterized by growing antipathy and suspicion between Russia and the West – much of it centred on the European territories discussed at Potsdam.

Coningham, Air Marshal Sir Arthur (1895–1948) Dynamic New Zealand born RAF* commander, he took command of the British Desert Air Force, a component of Sir Arthur Tedder's* Middle East Air Force, in July 1941 and immediately instituted a system of close co-operation with the ground forces of the 8th Army. RAF doctrine, which stressed the independence of air power, had made little provision tactically or technically for Army/Air co-operation, but the desert provided few targets for strategic bombing and tactical skills had been developed during the campaigns in Egypt* and East Africa*. Coningham now linked air and ground command at every level, sharing army field headquarters and siting forward air bases close to the front lines. In November 1941 he deployed his 27 squadrons (including for the first time Hawker Hurricanes* converted as fighter-bombers) with considerable success in direct support of the Crusader* offensive against Rommel's* Axis forces in Libya (see Desert War).

Supported by Tedder, Coningham refined his system as Allied air strength in the theatre mounted over the next year, and his forces played an important part in the decisive British victory at El Alamein*

in October 1942. During 1943–4 he commanded the combined Allied Air Forces in Tunisia*, Sicily* and Italy*, which were specifically dedicated to tactical support operations. The concept reached its full potential in the highly successful operations of the Second Tactical Air Force, which Coningham commanded in Northwest Europe* in 1944–5.

Consolidated (PBY) Catalina Tough and adaptable long-range flying-boat, which saw distinguished service with US and Allied air forces in every maritime theatre. It was one of the most celebrated aircraft of its time and maintained viable military, naval and commercial careers for many years after the end of the war. It entered the US Navy* in late 1936 as the PBY-1, powered by 825hp engines, which were progressively uprated in subsequent variants. The prominent waist-blisters characteristic of later models were introduced with the PBY-4 in 1938, and major wartime production got underway with the PBY-5 and its amphibian counterpart the PBY5-A. Hundreds of these were built both in the United States and Canada (as the Boeing PB2B1 and the Vickers PBV-1) and from 1940 they were adopted by the RAF* as the Catalina, a name thereafter employed by the US Navy. The PBN-1 was a tall-tailed development with increased range and defensive armament, which also appeared as the amphibious PBY6-A and the Canadian-built PB2B2.

The bulk of the 3,290 Catalinas of all types built in the US and Canada served the US Navy as bombers, torpedo carriers, convoy* escorts, anti-submarine* and air-sea rescue* aircraft. Over 650 of various marks were eventually used by the RAF, while models in Canadian service were known as 'Cansos'. Other examples served the wartime airforces of France, the Netherlands and Australia. In addition, several hundred Catalinas (designated GST) were built under licence in the Soviet Union after 1938.

BRIEF DATA (PBY-5) Type: 8-man patrol and reconnaissance flying boat; Engines: 2 × 1,200hp Pratt and Whitney Twin Wasp; Max speed: 196mph; Ceiling: 25,700'; Range: 3,100m (max); Arms: 5 × 0.5" mg; Bomb load: 4,000lb.

Consolidated (PB2Y) Coronado First flown in December 1937, but subject to prolonged delays in development, the Coronado entered the US Navy* as a patrol bomber at the start of 1941. The major wartime model was the PB2Y-3, which remained in production until the autumn of 1943. A total of 210 were built, along with 32 PB2Y-3R transport and cargo versions. During 1944, Coronados began to be replaced as patrol bombers by land-based US Navy B-24* Liberators (PB4Y), and the later PB2Y-5 model was mostly used for transport and ambulance (5H) work. Ten machines were supplied to the RAF* and served as freighters with Transport Command.
BRIEF DATA (PB2Y-3) Type: 9-man patrol/reconnaissance flying boat; Engines: 4 × 1,200hp Pratt and Whitney Twin Wasp; Max speed: 255mph; Ceiling: 24,100'; Range: 3,705m (normal); Arms: 8 × 0.5"mg; Bomb load: 8,000lb internal, 4,000lb external.

Conti di Cavour See Giulio Cesare.

Convoys A convoy is a group of merchant ships sailing together under the protection of warships. This form of trade defence had been considered anachronistic in 1914, but had proved so effective against German U-boats in the latter part of WW1 that it was adopted universally and immediately by the British Admiralty in 1939, remaining in operation throughout the war.

Without effective protection a convoy, which is forced to travel at the speed of its slowest component, is a large and tempting target for submarines*. Not only were the British desperately short of escorts and air cover for their convoys, but they had prepared primarily against the anticipated threat of surface raiders, relying on ASDIC sound detection equipment to deter submarines. German commanders quickly developed tactics which could defeat the limited ASDIC available, and terrible losses were inflicted on Allied convoys once U-boat operations extended into the Atlantic* after June 1940.

Convoys to and from the Russian port of Murmansk were regarded as a death trip by British merchant seamen, who could expect to survive for only a few minutes in the icy northern waters. These Arctic convoys were twice suspended in 1942 as losses to German aircraft and submarines reached decisive proportions, but the Admiralty kept faith with the system in other waters.

One compelling reason for so doing was the disastrous fate of unconvoyed merchant shipping on trade routes protected by other navies. The US Navy* rejected the use of convoys for its Atlantic coastal traffic early in 1942. The result was a carnage of merchant losses to U-boats that was only ended by the introduction of an effective convoy system in July. Japan, even more reliant on maritime trade than Britain, failed to convoy its merchantmen or make effective escort provision until most of their commercial fleet had been destroyed by US submarines.

The other great virtue of the convoy system was that it gave anti-submarine forces some chance of locating their prey in the years before the advent of accurate airborne search radar*. Early in the war, the Allies attempted to hunt for submarines with warships, and the RAF* repeatedly bombed U-boat pens. Neither approach was even remotely successful, and by mid-1941 the British had realized that the best way to hunt U-boats was to concentrate powerful air and surface forces around bait in the form of a convoy. Once large, well-armed and tactically informed escort support groups appeared from the spring of 1943, the convoy became an offensive weapon capable of defeating any U-boat

pack. See also Anti-submarine Warfare;
Arctic Convoys.

Cooper, Alfred Duff (1890–1954) Influential British politician who opposed the
policy of appeasement* during the 1930s,
resigning from his post as First Lord of
the Admiralty in protest at the Munich
Agreement*. He later invested his considerable energy in overcoming British ambivalence towards the French (and de
Gaulle* in particular). Duff Cooper served
as Minister of Information in 1940–1 and
was Churchill's* representative in the Far
East from April 1941 to January 1942. As
British representative of the French Committee of National Liberation, established
at Algiers*, from October 1942, and then
as British ambassador to Paris from November 1944, Duff Cooper worked hard to
ameliorate the situation in newly liberated
France. His commitment to a close relationship with a strong France, which he
considered crucial to the health of post-war
Europe, was embodied in the Treaty of
Dunkirk, signed in 1947.

Coral Sea, Battle of the, 7–8 May 1942
First of three crucial naval battles fought
between US Navy* and Japanese Navy*
forces in the Pacific during the second half
of 1942, the Battle of the Coral Sea and
the later battles at Midway* in June and at
Guadalcanal* in November were decisive
in arresting the enormous momentum of
Japan's conquests in the first phase of the
Pacific War* (see Map 16). The battle was
triggered by the launch of a renewed Japanese offensive, code-named Operation
Mo, planned as a dual stroke to exploit
earlier gains. The offensive had as one of
its objectives three targets in the Coral Sea:
Tulagi, Port Moresby* and the Louisiade
Islands, which could provide Japan with
bases for air attacks on Queensland, Australia's coastal region bordering the Coral Sea.
    The offensive role of the Japanese fleet
under the overall command of Vice
Admiral Inoue was to draw the US Pacific
Fleet into the Coral Sea and destroy it

between two pincers. US intelligence had
gathered sufficient information, however,
to provide Admiral Nimitz*, Pacific Fleet
Commander, with a reasonable evaluation
of the Japanese plan. Before the Japanese
force was in position, two US carrier forces
joined an Allied task force under US Rear
Admiral Fletcher* and sailed to counter-
attack.
    The Allied fleet included Task Force 17,
under US Rear Admiral Fletcher, Task
Force 11 under US Rear Admiral Fitch*
and Task Force 44 under British Rear
Admiral Crace*. Fletcher's Task Force 17
was based on two carriers, *Yorktown** and
*Lexington**, with eight heavy cruisers and
11 destroyers*. The Japanese carrier force,
under Rear Admiral Goto and Vice
Admiral Takagi*, included three carriers –
*Shoho**, *Shokaku** and *Zuikaku* – along with
six heavy cruisers and seven destroyers.
    Receiving news of the Japanese landing
at Tulagi on 2 May Admiral Fletcher sailed
to intercept, causing slight damage (overestimated at the time by reconnaissance)
before turning south to join up with the
rest of the Allied fleet. Early on 7 May,
Fletcher dispatched Crace, with a task
group of cruisers and destroyers, to the
Louisiades, to intercept any Japanese attempt on Port Moresby. Then, by a series of
errors which had both fleets passing within
range of each other with shots fired, but
without a correct sighting on either side,
the opposing forces finally joined battle in
earnest on 8 May, the fifth day of the
Operation Mo offensive, with almost simultaneous sightings of their fleets and the
launch of immediate air attacks. In a carrier
action which was the first-ever naval engagement fought without coming in sight
of the enemy, both sides suffered important
losses. The *Lexington* had to be abandoned
and the *Yorktown* was also hit, though she
was still able to land and launch aircraft.
The *Shokaku* had to be withdrawn from the
battle with three bomb hits and the light
carrier *Shoho* had already been disabled by
air strikes the day before.
    Despite the loss of a precious fleet carrier,

the Battle of the Coral Sea proved a key strategic victory for American forces in the Pacific. Forced to abandon the invasion of Port Moresby and withdraw the Invasion Group transports, Admiral Inouye had failed to bring Australia within range of Japanese bombers and had also sacrificed many aircraft and two carriers to the tactical victory. The damage to *Shokaku* and the loss of most of the *Zuikaku*'s aircraft was to keep both carriers out of the more decisive Battle of Midway in June.

Corregidor A small fortified island opposite the tip of the Bataan Peninsula* of Luzon, in the Philippines*. American forces under General Wainright* made a courageous final stand here against the invading Japanese forces under General Homma* in the final phase of the defence of the Philippines in 1942.

Constant artillery bombardment and heavy air attacks maintained over the island during April and May increasingly diminished morale and supplies for the 15,000 strong garrison. Finally, a massive bombardment of 16,000 shells on the night of 4 May covered the landing of 2,000 Japanese troops with tank support at Cavalry Bay on the following evening. Breaching the American defences in the Malinta Tunnel area, General Homma was finally in a position to demand the general surrender of the Philippines from the American commander.

Corvette Small escort and patrol vessel built by British and Canadian merchant shipyards from 1940 until the end of the war to an adapted whalecatcher design. The corvette was planned by the British in 1939 as an answer to their desperate shortage of escort vessels and was intended for coastal work. Armed either for anti-aircraft* or anti-submarine* operations, the initial Flower Class, of which 300 were eventually built, displaced less than 1,000 tons and could make 16 knots. Once the U-boat threat in the Atlantic had moved away from coastal areas, anti-submarine

corvettes were used wholly as ocean-going escorts. Although they could cross the Atlantic without refuelling, their speed (slower than a surfaced U-boat) and liveliness at sea were serious combat disadvantages.

The larger and faster River Class was therefore produced from 1942. These were again based on a mercantile design but received the name frigate to distinguish them from their predecessors. By 1944 these had in turn been supplanted by the mass-production Loch (anti-submarine) and Bay (anti-aircraft) Class frigates, while those yards unable to handle the 300ft-long hull of this larger type built an improved corvette, the Castle Class.

In all, 139 River Class frigates were built and 55 Loch/Bay units and 43 Castles entered service with the British and Dominion navies. A few of these small escort ships were lent to the United States in the early years of the war, but American escort destroyer production soon rendered this arrangement unnecessary (see Destroyer Escort). Corvettes and frigates continued to form the bulk of the Royal Navy's* surface escort forces throughout the war, although *Hunt* Class escort destroyers and *Black Swan* Class sloops (the specialist 1,500-ton, 20-knot escorts in production at the start of the war) continued to be built on a relatively small scale. All these types were far more effective in the escort role than the conventional destroyer*, which found its high speed, torpedo* tubes and surface weapons wasted in the war against predatory submarines* and aircraft. See Atlantic, Battle of the; Anti-submarine Warfare.

Cossack, HMS British Tribal Class destroyer, completed in 1938. The Tribals were the Royal Navy's* answer to the large destroyers being built by other powers (see Destroyers). They had double the main armament of their predecessors, improved light weaponry and fewer torpedo tubes. They were employed mostly to protect the fleet in home waters or the dangerous Mediterranean* and only four of the 16-strong class survived the war. By contrast, only one of the nine similar units completed during the war for the Canadian and Australian Navies was lost. The *Cossack* – famous for her rescue of prisoners from the *Altmark** in 1940 – was torpedoed in the North Atlantic on 23 October 1941 and foundered off Gibraltar* four days later. BRIEF DATA (1939) Displacement: 1,870 tons; Dimensions: o/a lgth – 377' 6", b – 36' 6"; Speed: 36 knots; Armament: 8 × 4.7" gun, 4 × 2pdr AA gun, 8 × 0.5" AA gun, 4 × 21" TT.

Courageous, HMS Under the terms of the Washington Naval Treaty (1922), the practically useless WW1 light battlecruisers *Courageous* and *Glorious* had to be either scrapped by the Royal Navy* or converted to another purpose. Built for speed, they were chosen for conversion as aircraft carriers and this was begun in 1924. The *Courageous* was completed in 1928, and the *Glorious* in 1930. They benefited from experience gained in earlier conversions, carrying more aircraft and anti-aircraft* defences than their predecessors. Both were lost, however, to forms of attack against which they remained ill-protected.

The *Courageous* was torpedoed west of Ireland on 17 September 1939 by the *U-29*. She was the Royal Navy's first major loss of the war, a disaster which demonstrated to the Admiralty the folly of hunting submarines* with single warships. Her captain was one of the last to go down with his ship as a matter of traditional duty. The *Glorious* ran into the German battlecruisers *Scharnhorst** and *Gneisenau** on 8 June 1940, while laden with RAF* planes and pilots returning from Norway*. Unable, for reasons never fully explained, to launch a strike by her aircraft, she was sunk (with her two escorting destroyers*) by accurate heavy gunfire. BRIEF DATA (1939) Displacement: 22,500 tons; Dimensions: o/a lgth – 786' 3", b – 90' 6"; Speed: 29.5 knots; Armament: 16 × 4.7" AA gun, 24 × 2pdr AA gun, 48 aircraft.

Covenanter Tank See Crusader Tank.

Coventry English manufacturing centre for armaments, munitions and military vehicles, Coventry was subjected to a heavy Luftwaffe* raid (code-named Moonlight Sonata) by 449 bombers on 15 November 1940. The raid left much of the city destroyed, including the historic cathedral, and casualties of over 1,000 dead or severely injured. The recent charge that the raid had been forecast by Ultra* intelligence but was left unchallenged because of fears of revealing the existence of the Enigma* decoding device remains unproven.

Coventry, HMS Although at the start of the war the Royal Navy* could (and did) claim a strength of 64 cruisers, 27 of these were of WW1 design and not one of the new vessels ordered in 1936 had been completed. Veteran cruisers were generally suitable only for the protection of trade routes, but some of the light 'C' Class vessels were converted as anti-aircraft* ships between 1937 and 1942. The first of these was the *Coventry*, launched in 1917 and sunk by bombing off Tobruk* in September 1942. BRIEF DATA (1939) Displacement: 4,190 tons; Dimensions: o/a lgth – 451' 6", b – 43' 6"; Speed: 29 knots; Armament: 10 × 4" AA gun (10 × 1), 8 × 2pdr AA gun.

Crab See Sherman Tank; Special-purpose Vehicles.

Crace, Rear Admiral Sir John G. (1887–1968) British commander of Pacific Task Force 44, an Australian naval squadron which participated in the important actions in the Coral Sea* in 1942 and patrolled the southeastern tip of New Guinea*, narrowly escaping sinking by Japanese aircraft. Crace retired in the same year, but remained admiral superintendent of HM Dockyard Chatham until 1946. He was promoted to Admiral in 1945.

Crerar, General Henry (1888–1965) Distinguished and highly able Canadian commander of the Canadian 1st Army which fought throughout the Allied campaign in Northwest Europe* during 1944–5. A vociferous opponent of Canadian isolationism and promoter of programmes for the development of Canadian forces based in Britain, Crerar resigned as Chief of the General Staff in 1941 to organize the UK training of 100,000 Canadians of the 1st Canadian Corps. Following active service with the Corps in Sicily* and Italy*, Crerar returned to Britain to form the Canadian 1st Army (which at times included also Dutch, Polish, Belgian, US, British and Czech elements) for the invasion of Normandy* in June 1944. After directing the battle at Argentan-Falaise* and fighting in the Pas de Calais, the Scheldt and in the Netherlands*, Crerar took command of the bulk of the 21st Army Group forces (over 500,000 men) for the offensive against the Lower Rhine, begun in February 1945. He retired in 1946.

Crete, German Invasion of The island of Crete, dominating sea routes to the Eastern Mediterranean and within flying range of North Africa, had been occupied by the British in October 1940 as a forward base for possible operations in the Balkans. After the rout of the British force in Greece in April 1941, large numbers of battle-weary, underequipped troops were evacuated to Crete and General Freyberg*, in command of the island, prepared to meet an anticipated German invasion with a swollen garrison of 28,000 men plus two Greek divisions (see Balkans, German invasion of). With only two dozen fighter planes, the same number of infantry tanks*, scant anti-aircraft* defences and a lack of short-range radios, Crete was ill-equipped to face an attack from the air. Freyberg, however, regarded such an operation as impractical and dispersed his defences to meet a seaborne invasion.

Hitler recognized that Royal Navy* supremacy in the area ruled out an assault by sea, and intended to break off the Balkan campaign at the southern coast of Greece

until General Student* of the Fliegerkorps impressed upon him the feasibility of a purely airborne* operation. The plan was approved on 21 April as Operation Mercury, commanded by General Löhr, and it involved 13,000 paratroops, 9,000 mountain troops, 500 warplanes, 500 transports and 80 gliders.

On the morning of 20 May, after sustained bombing, 3,000 Germans parachuted into Crete, detailed to take the three main airfields in the north (Máleme, Heraklion and Retimo) and secure the nearby beaches. They were to be progressively reinforced by air, and heavy artillery was to arrive by sea. The plan did not go well. Large numbers of men were cut down in the air or killed on landing, the artillery failed to arrive and none of the airstrips were taken on the first day. Nevertheless German airborne reinforcements were poured in, and the quality of those that got through was a telling factor.

The capture of an airfield was vital to the Germans if troop transports were to land before the parachute force was wiped out. Only at Máleme in the northwest had much progress been made by the end of the first day, and there the assault regiment was engaged in fierce fighting with New Zealand troops. On the night of 20–21 May, Student decided to send in his last parachute reserves in an attempt to take the strip. Let down by poor communications, the defenders withdrew to regroup overnight, and the next day the Luftwaffe* was able to start landing reinforcements in quantity – if hardly in comfort.

The capture of Máleme was the decisive moment in the battle. The build-up of German strength in the area soon began to push the British back into the mountains. The Royal Navy struggled to control coastal waters under severe pressure from the Luftwaffe, and was forced to withdraw from the northern approaches on 24 May. Reinforcements could not be spared from the Desert War* in North Africa and on 26 May, with over 20,000 Germans extending their positions on the island, Freyberg decided the position was hopeless and ordered a retreat to the southern port of Sfakia. For four nights from 28 May, the Royal Navy rescued as many of the defenders as possible, suffering heavy losses in the process. Three cruisers and six destroyers were sunk, and 13 other ships badly damaged – including the fleet's only aircraft carrier – and more than 2,000 seamen were killed. About 16,500 men were evacuated, including some 2,000 Greeks, but 12,000 British troops were left behind and captured, with over 4,000 more killed or wounded.

German overall losses were smaller – 4,000 killed, 2,000 wounded and 220 aircraft destroyed – but they were significant, seriously weakening Hitler's only parachute and glider units. General Student's long-cherished plans for a series of similar attacks towards Suez were never sanctioned. Shocked by the audacity of the operation, the British awaited a follow-up in Cyprus*, Malta* or Syria* – but it didn't come. Instead Hitler concentrated on the Eastern Front* and never again attempted a large-scale airborne invasion.

Crimea, The Peninsula of southwestern Russia, strategically important because of its proximity to the Black Sea and the oil-rich Caucasus*, its capture was of primary importance to Hitler at the start of the German invasion of Russia (see Eastern Front). In August 1941, ignoring the exasperated protests of his General Staff, whom he claimed 'knew nothing about the economic aspects of war', Hitler denied the necessity for maintaining sole momentum on the central front aimed at Moscow*, to pursue his obsessional interest in the south, diverting troops and armoured forces from the central advance on the Russian capital to the southern objectives of the Crimea, the Donets basin coalfields and the Caucasus oilfields.

Thus on 20 October 1941, German forces launched an attack on Soviet lines across the five-mile wide gateway to the Crimea, the Perekop Isthmus. Ten days later, Manstein's* 11th Army, consisting of German and Rumanian troops, broke through and poured onto the peninsula, aiming towards the Kerch peninsula in the east and Sevastopol in the southwest. On 17 December, an attack was launched on Sevastapol*, but Soviet amphibious* attacks on Kerch diverted German attention from the city, forcing Manstein to fight a bitter series of battles to clear the Kerch peninsula, which cost the Russians two whole armies and was not completed until mid-May 1942. Detaching a corps to guard the Kerch peninsula, Manstein now turned back to Sevastopol (garrisoned by over 100,000 Soviet troops) with a five-day preliminary air and artillery bombardment followed by a ground attack which made deep penetrations to the north and south of the city by 17 June. Effectively encircled, the Sevastopol forces were withdrawn by evacuation at the end of June. On 4 July, Manstein announced the official occupation of the city, for which he was made a Field Marshal.

In November 1943, following the disastrous German defeats at Stalingrad* and Kursk*, General Tolbukhin's* drive along the northern shores of the Sea of Azov* and the Black Sea cut off German and Rumanian forces in the Crimea. Although Tolbukhin's drive was checked by the narrowness of the approaches, a dual assault by his 4th Ukrainian Front* and Yeremenko's* Coastal Army broke through into the Crimea at the beginning of April 1944. Heavy artillery attacks on the German 17th Army at Sevastopol itself began on 5 May. The sheer power of the attack, using twice the field artillery* employed by the Germans in 1942, resulted in its surrender (against Hitler's orders) on 12 May, with 12 German and Rumanian divisions destroyed and 25,000 prisoners taken.

Cripps, Sir Stafford (1889–1952) British Socialist, Labour Party politician, Ambassador to Russia 1940–2 and Minister of Aircraft Production 1942–5. Cripps had resigned from the Party in protest at

Labour's accession to Chamberlain's* policy of appeasement* of the European dictators, but was recalled by Churchill* to lead a mission to Moscow in 1940. He also led the unsuccessful British mission to India in 1942 to win Indian support for the Allied war effort, in return for promises of full autonomy after the war (see Indian Nationalism). On his return to Britain, he briefly held a post in the War Cabinet before becoming Minister of Aircraft Production. In July 1945 he became Chancellor of the Exchequer in Attlee's* post-war Cabinet.

Crocodile See Special-purpose Vehicles.

Cromwell Tank In 1941 the British Army General Staff ordered a 'heavy cruiser' tank*, to be known as the Cromwell, to replace the vulnerable Crusader*. The Leyland company had planned a tank around the powerful Rolls Royce Meteor, a detuned aircraft engine, and this was accepted for production. Until Meteors could be spared, it was powered by a Liberty engine and named the Cavalier. This entered service in mid-1942, and was then modified as the Centaur. About 950 Cavaliers and Centaurs were built, although some later became Cromwells after engine conversion. Exhaustively tested, the first Meteor-powered Cromwells were finally ready by January 1943.

The opportunity for action did not arise until the invasion of Normandy*, by which time the Cromwell's 75mm gun was outmatched by the best German weapons. Although close support versions of the tank were equipped with a 95mm howitzer, the Cromwell's narrow hull prevented further upgunning. Nevertheless the Cromwell was a fast and agile tank, remarkably easy to maintain. Alongside the American-built Sherman*, it formed the main equipment of British armoured divisions in the last year of the war and was used to exploit Allied infantry breakthroughs in Northwest Europe*. Several thousand Cromwells had been completed when production ended in

1945. A lengthened Challenger version (260 built) could mount a more powerful 17-pounder gun, but its field performance was poor and the genuinely effective Centurion heavy battle tank was not produced in time to see combat.

BRIEF DATA (Mk IV) Type: 5-man heavy cruiser; Engine: 600hp petrol; Max speed: 40mph; Range: 173m; Arms: 1 × 75mm gun, 2 × 7.92mm mg; Armour: max 76mm.

Crossbow, Operation See V-1 Missile.

Crusader, Operation Code-name for the major British offensive in North Africa of November 1941. It was planned by General Auchinleck*, who replaced Wavell* in July as British C-in-C Middle East, and was projected as a large-scale armoured sweep towards Tobruk* from the south, while infantry forces pinned down Axis-held positions on the Libya/Egypt frontier (see Map 7). Since the failure of Operation Battleaxe* in June, resources had been poured into Egypt* by an impatient Churchill at the expense of other theatres, while troops had become available from Greece* and East Africa*. Renamed the 8th Army and commanded by Lt General Cunningham*, the desert force could call on over 700 tanks, almost as many aircraft and plentiful reinforcements.

Axis ground forces commander Rommel*, whose High Command was preoccupied with the invasion of Russia, had only 320 tanks (almost half of them inferior Italian types) and the same number of aircraft. The British advantage was reduced in the planning, however, by the strict tactical separation of 'infantry' and 'cruiser' forces into their respective roles (see Tanks), and further diluted by instructions to forward units to 'seek out and destroy' Rommel's armour, encouraging dispersal in pursuit of targets.

Operation Crusader opened on 18 November and at first achieved complete surprise. Units in the centre of the armoured sweep took the airfield at Sidi Razegh –

only 12 miles from Tobruk – but were not reinforced as armoured brigades to the left and right became bogged down in costly actions at Gabr Saleh and Bir el Gubi. Alerted, Rommel deployed artillery on the road to Tobruk and sent the Afrika Korps* in search of the dispersed British armour. Even without effective aerial reconnaissance, the panzer divisions inflicted heavy defeats on British armour at Gabr Saleh and Sidi Razegh, before Cunningham belatedly brought up infantry units – hitherto held rigidly in their inactive frontier role – on 22 November.

The following day as the battle concentrated around Sidi Razegh, General Cruewell, in command of the Afrika Korps, drove a wedge through the converging British forces. Hampered by the loss of his command HQ early in the day, it was a cumbersome victory, leaving Cruewell with only 90 tanks. While the British armoured force had only 14 per cent of its 500 tanks left, they could be quickly replaced from reserve. On 24 November Rommel therefore changed his tactics and led all his armour east, heading for Egypt and hoping to induce a panic retreat.

Cunningham was ready to withdraw, but Auchinleck flew from Cairo personally to insist that the offensive continue and then replaced Cunningham with Ritchie* on 26 November. The remnants of the advanced British armour pushed on to Tobruk, making contact with the garrison there on 27 November. This was enough to persuade Rommel, whose advance had become bogged down on the Egyptian frontier more through lack of fuel and support than any effective defences, to return his panzer divisions to Tobruk. By 29 November the British had again been swept from Sidi Razegh, prompting another visit from Auchinleck. Recognizing Rommel's underlying material weakness, he ordered a strong armoured force to cut the Axis escape route to the west.

With less than 60 tanks left in action and aware of the threat to his rear, Rommel withdrew the siege of Tobruk on 4 December. By 11 December his forces had safely reached prepared positions at Gazala*. An unsuccessful British attempt to take Gazala by frontal assault resulted in significant losses on both sides. A tentative attempt to outflank the Axis positions was also unsuccessful and Rommel's forces escaped again. On 16 December his mobile forces struck across the desert, while Italian infantry took the coast road, racing towards the bottleneck on the Tripolitanian border. Slow in pursuit, the British failed to catch the infantry, while Rommel's tanks – doubled in number to 60 by last-minute reinforcements from Benghazi – held off their pursuers and inflicted another heavy defeat on an advanced brigade at El Haseiat, before escaping into Tripolitania by the end of the year.

Operation Crusader was a limited success for the British. Although isolated coastal garrisons and an Italian infantry division (stranded in the wake of Rommel's raid on Egypt) raised the bag of prisoners taken, the Afrika Korps was still in being and the 8th Army had lost many of its most experienced fighting men. While Auchinleck deserves credit for his decisive interventions at crucial moments, his army paid a heavy price for the poor disposition of his original plan.

Crusader Tank When considering its future tank* requirements in 1936, the British War Office decided on the development of infantry and cruiser tanks, the former heavily armoured for close support and the latter shell-armed for cavalry operations. As befitted their role, the first cruiser designs, culminating in the Covenanter of 1939, were fast machines, but their light protection and main armament were found to be inadequate in France* and Egypt* during 1940.

The slightly larger cruiser Mark VI Crusader, approved in July 1939, was at least much more effectively armoured than its predecessors, although it was at first plagued by engine unreliability and was always uncomfortable to operate. Its great strength was its speed, which could reach 40mph with field modification, and this was well suited to desert operations. Entering the Desert War* at Tobruk* in June 1941, it became the standard British tank for the remainder of the campaign, although it retained the relatively puny 2-pounder gun until the improved Mark III reached service in mid-1942 mounting a 6-pounder. By the following year this too was outmoded and production was stopped after 5,300 vehicles had been built. Crusader chassis were later used as mine* clearers, bulldozers, anti-aircraft* tanks and in the other special-purpose* functions.

BRIEF DATA (Mk I) Type: 5-man cruiser tank; Engine: 340hp petrol; Max speed: 27mph; Range: 100m; Arms: 1 × 2pdr gun, 2 × 7.92mm mg; Armour: max 40mm.

Cunningham, General Sir Alan (1887–) British soldier (the younger brother of Admiral Sir Andrew Cunningham), he commanded British forces in Kenya in 1940 –1. After leading the successful invasion of Italian Somaliland and Ethiopia (see East Africa, Campaign in), Lt General Cunningham was transferred to the Western Desert in August 1941 to command the 8th Army. Three months later he was replaced by Lt General Ritchie* after a lack-lustre performance in the opening stages of Operation Crusader*, and he spent the rest of the war in home commands.

Cunningham, Admiral Sir Andrew (1883 –1963) The star among Britain's wartime naval leaders, Admiral Cunningham took command of the Mediterranean Fleet (the Royal Navy's* most important overseas force) in 1939. A highly successful destroyer captain in WW1, his approach to high command contrasted aggressively with that of his Italian counterparts. Vastly outnumbered by the Italian Navy* after June 1940, Cunningham immediately went onto the offensive. Using the advantages at his disposal – superior combat expertise, radar, accurate intelligence and naval aviation – he followed a series of coastal bombardment

operations with successful attacks on Italian warships at Taranto* and Cape Matapan*, establishing a dominance over Italian surface forces that he never lost.

From 1941 the Luftwaffe* was a more dangerous threat, inflicting enormous losses on Cunningham's fleet in operations around Greece and Crete*, while multiplying the threat to British convoy routes. Cunningham's effective concentrations of his dwindling resources and imaginative tactical deployments helped his battered ships to maintain supplies to Malta* and North Africa, while inflicting significant losses on convoys destined for the Afrika Korps. The fate of Malta* and the 8th Army in Africa hung in the balance when Cunningham left the Mediterranean in June 1942 for discussions with the Combined Chiefs of Staff* in Washington.

He returned in November as C-in-C of a far larger Anglo-American fleet covering the Torch* landings in Northwest Africa. By May 1943, when fighting ended in Africa, naval superiority had been established in the Mediterranean and Cunningham was responsible for the planning and execution of the amphibious landings in Sicily* and Italy* from his headquarters on Malta. In October 1943, following the death of Sir Dudley Pound*, Cunningham was appointed First Sea Lord, the highest position in the Royal Navy, and was Churchill's principal naval strategist for the remainder of the war. He retired in June 1946. See also Mediterranean Sea.

Curtin, John (1885–1945) Australian Prime Minister from October 1941 until his death. A lifelong pacifist, Curtin had become leader of the Labour Party in 1935, and took power from Arthur Fadden's short-lived United Australian Party government in an atmosphere of disillusion over Britain's treatment of Australian interests since the start of the war. When Japan entered the conflict weeks later, Curtin asked the United States for aid and backed this with an Australian declaration of war which was separate from Britain's.

He remained loyal to the British Commonwealth but argued forcefully that this alone could not stop the Japanese.

Mistrusted in London, Curtin nevertheless sought to balance British and American interests in Australia. In 1942 Australia was desperately short of troops for home defence and Curtin recalled units of the Australian Army* from the Middle East, refusing Churchill's* request to divert them to Burma*. In March, General Douglas MacArthur* became Supreme Commander of the newly activated Southwest Pacific Area, which included Australia. Inexperienced in military planning and anxious to retain American sympathy, Curtin consistently allowed MacArthur unchallenged control over Australian military strategy. Later in the war, however, he pressed for a strong British naval presence in the Far East to counterbalance US influence in the area.

Until the general election of 1943, Curtin's government was in constant danger of defeat, and not until after his landslide victory was he able to risk personal appearances at major conferences abroad. He was meanwhile represented in London by his able and aggressive Minister for External Affairs, Herbert Evatt, whose avowed concern for Australian rather than Imperial interests did not endear him to his colleagues in the British War Cabinet. Curtin himself attended the London conference of Empire Prime Ministers in May 1944, and reaffirmed his faith in the Commonwealth. During his journey home, a fatal illness developed and his health kept him from further involvement in international affairs. He died on 5 July 1945, five weeks before the end of the Pacific War*.

Curtiss SB2C Helldiver The prototype of this American dive-bomber crashed a few days before the attack on Pearl Harbor*, and large-scale modifications introduced in the light of wartime experience further delayed the start of its operational career until November 1943. Despite its late entry, the Helldiver played an important part in the Pacific War* 'island' campaigns, relieving the older Douglas Dauntless* of the main burden of US Navy* dive-bombing operations. The mass-produced SB2C-1 also served as a ground-attack plane with the USAAF* (A-25A), and a few Canadian-built examples flew for the Australians. Engine power and defensive armament were improved before the end of the war – the original 0.5-inch machine guns* were soon replaced by wing cannon and underwing rocket* attachments appeared on the SB2C-4. Helldivers remained with the US Navy until 1949, by which time 7,200 had been completed.

BRIEF DATA (SB2C-3) Type: Two-man carrier dive-bomber; Engine: $1 \times 1,750$hp Wright Cyclone; Max speed: 294mph; Ceiling: 29,300'; Range: (max) 1,925m; Arms: 2×20mm cannon; $1 \times 0.5''$ mg; Bomb load: 1,000lb or torpedo.

Czechoslovakia Republic created in 1918 under a provisional government (the Czechoslovak National Council) led by Jan Masaryk* and Eduard Beneš*, it included the most valuable industrial areas of Austria-Hungary and comprised 7 million Czechs, 2 million Slovaks and three and a quarter million Germans in the Sudetenland, a mountainous region between Bohemia and Silesia. Although Czechoslovakia enjoyed a comparatively high standard of living, the difficulties inherent in drawing new national boundaries around racial groupings and the insecurity which accompanied her proximity to Germany made Czechoslovakia particularly vulnerable to political tensions during the 1930s. Genuine grievances among Sudeten Germans over high unemployment and repressive security measures in the frontier regions were manipulated by Hitler* and his agents in the Sudetenland to support his claim to territorial expansion. A Sudeten Party under Henlein*, sponsored by Berlin, was instrumental in stirring up agitation which forced the issue of the Sudetenland. In a now infamous act of appeasement* of

Hitler's exploitative foreign policy, the Sudetenland was ceded to Germany in an agreement signed by Britain and France at Munich in September 1938 (see Munich Agreement).

After the occupation of all of Czechoslovakia (now under Hacha*) in March 1939, the Czech Army of 35 divisions was disbanded and Germany took control of both its high quality equipment and the highly developed Czech arms industry, greatly increasing the German Army's* strength in tanks*, artillery* and infantry weapons.

After the oubreak of war in September, the Czech National Committee, in exile in France and then in Britain, allied itself to the anti-Nazi resistance* at home and is said to have endorsed the British decision to assassinate the German chief in Czechoslovakia, Reich Protector Heydrich* in 1942, for which Czechoslovaks paid highly in SS* reprisals (see Lidice).

In early 1944, as the Red Army* drove the beleaguered German forces westwards in a final winter offensive, Soviet troops crossed the border in the eastern tip of Czechoslovakia. On the west, Supreme Allied Commander Eisenhower* ordered his forces to stand on the 'Pilsen' line, at the Russian's request, unwilling to commit forces to battle for purely political motives. It was not until October that General Petrov's* 4th Ukrainian Front* invaded eastern Slovakia, joined later by the 2nd Ukrainian Front under Malinovsky*. Little serious resistance held up the Russian advance. On 6 May, Czech partisans staged an uprising in Prague*. Germany surrendered unconditionally on 8 May and Prague was occupied by Russian forces on 11 May. Shortly afterwards a 'National Front' government was restored under Beneš, but, under considerable Russian pressure, electoral successes put communists in a strong enough position to overthrow the democratic government in February 1948. See also Eastern Front; Resistance: Czechoslovakia.

D

Dachau Village close to Munich now notorious as the site of Nazi Germany's first concentration camp*, established in 1933 with Theodor Eicke* as its commandant. Under Eicke, who took overall command of the camp system, Dachau became a model for later camps and by 1943 controlled a vast network of camps stretching into Austria. Despite its furnaces, Dachau itself was not an extermination camp – the administration used sub-camps for this purpose. Nevertheless an unknown number of prisoners were murdered at Dachau, many in the course of medical experiments by doctors like Sigmund Raschler. The camp, whose gate bears the sinister irony of the inscription *Arbeit Macht Frei* (Work Brings Freedom), was liberated by American troops in April 1945. It has been substantially preserved as a museum.

Dakar French naval base, it had by far the best docking facilities on the West African coast. Dakar was attacked on 23 September 1940 by a British and Free French (see Free France) force of 6,400 troops, supported by the warships of Force H* from Gibraltar*. The objective of the action, known as Operation Menace, was to occupy the town as the first stage in the promotion of General de Gaulle* as a rallying point for French colonial forces.

Initial attempts at landings were repulsed in thick fog, and over the next two days British battleships bombarded the town and harbour, which contained units of the French Navy*. Losses were sustained on both sides. The battleship *Barham** was hit and the battleship *Resolution* was torpedoed

and badly damaged by a French submarine* before Churchill ordered the abandonment of the operation on 25 September.

British prestige and Anglo-French relations suffered badly from the episode, and Churchill faced demands from his generals to drop de Gaulle. Dakar and the rest of French West Africa negotiated peaceful terms with the United States in late 1942, after the Allied Torch* landings.

Daladier, Edouard (1884–1970) French radical Socialist and Premier from April 1938, he followed Neville Chamberlain's* appeasement policy* and was a signatory of the Munich Agreement*, which ceded the Sudetenland of Czechoslovakia* to Germany. Resigning as Premier in March 1940 after failing to unite either parliament or the French people behind his cautious approach to mobilization and involvement in the 'Phoney War'*, he was subsequently interned by the Vichy* government and tried in February 1942 for betraying his country. He was deported to Germany and held there until the end of the war, when he successfully returned to French politics.

Dambusters The popular name for the specially trained British 617 Squadron, led by Wing Commander Guy Gibson*, which successfully breached the Mohne and Eder dams in the Ruhr on the night of 16 May 1943. The raid, for which the squadron had trained in precision bombing techniques, formed part of the huge Allied air offensive against Germany's western industrial centre (comprising 43 raids on cities and towns) which was known as the Battle of the Ruhr, and its target was the destruction of five dams on the Mohne, Eder, Sorpe, Lister and Schwelme lakes to disrupt vital water supplies to the Ruhr. Despite its undoubted success, the very low level techniques used in the raid could not be used for regular bombing operations. Seven out of 19 aircraft which took part in the raid were lost and the RAF* could not sustain losses on that scale. In November 1944, 617 Squadron carried out the precision raid on Tromsö (Norway) that sank the German battleship *Tirpitz**.

Danzig (Gdansk) Ancient Baltic seaport at the mouth of the river Vistula*, historically one of the Germanic Free Ports of the Hanseatic League, though subject to the old Kingdom of Poland. After WW1 the Treaty of Versailles, in re-creating the Polish state, tried to solve Danzig's anomalous position by designating it a demilitarized Free City under a League of Nations commissioner (1920). A strip of land with a coastline was given to Poland to assure access to the sea, the so-called 'Polish Corridor'. Though the population of Danzig was largely German speaking, the presence of a vocal Polish minority caused conflict in the area long before the local elections of 1933 gave the indigenous Nazi Party (see NSDAP) control of the city. From early in 1939, Hitler* began to demand the political reunification of Danzig with the Reich. Alternating diplomacy with threats, he finally settled the issue by the invasion of Poland (see Poland, German Campaign in) and the incorporation of Danzig and the Corridor into the Reich. The shelling of the Corridor in support of German troops by the old battleship *Schleswig-Holstein* in Danzig Harbour signalled the beginning of the war. Danzig eventually fell to the Russians on 30 March 1945. See also East Prussia, Fall of.

Darlan, Admiral Jean François (1881–1942) C-in-C of the French Navy* at the start of the war. After the fall of France in June 1940, he assured British Prime Minister Churchill that his ships would never fall into German hands but, instead of delivering them to British ports, he ordered the fleet to colonial bases in North Africa, provoking a series of disabling attacks by the British Mediterranean Fleet. At the same time he accepted the post of Minister of Marine in the Vichy* government, becoming Vice-Premier the following February. Pursuing a policy of limited collaboration with the Axis* while hinting to the Americans that he would welcome strong Allied intervention, Darlan excited the mistrust of both sides. Early in 1942, he was appointed C-in-C of French armed forces and High Commissioner in North Africa.

At the time of the Allied Torch* landings in Northwest Africa, Darlan was in Algiers visiting his sick son. His influence in French military circles was such that he was quickly called to negotiate a cease-fire with General Mark Clark* when it became clear that Allied troops were meeting resistance. Characteristically, Darlan wavered until Hitler occupied Vichy France on 11 November, at which point he came down firmly on the side of the Allies. Two days later he was officially endorsed by General Eisenhower* as the political head of French North Africa. This arrangement was effective in securing French co-operation in the theatre, but provoked public outrage among the Allies, particularly in Britain where de Gaulle* was active in stirring up protest against a man hitherto presented as a pro-Nazi. On Christmas Eve 1942, Darlan was assassinated by a young French monarchist, sparing the Allies further embarrassment and easing relations with French colonial forces.

DD (Duplex Drive) See Sherman Tank; Special-purpose Vehicles.

D-Day The launch date of the Allied invasion of Normandy* on 6 June 1944. See also Northwest Europe, Allied Invasion of.

De Gaulle, General Charles (1890–1970) Controversial French military commander, post-war Prime Minister and President of France, he led the Free France* resistance* movement from his exile in London between 1940 and 1944. Wounded and taken prisoner at Verdun during WW1 when he served under General Pétain*, his release came with the armistice of 1918. During the 1920s and 1930s, de Gaulle attended and graduated from the Ecole Supérieure de Guerre and subsequently held a number of staff posts under Pétain (now a Marshal) whom he greatly admired, as well as serving with the Rhineland Army of Occupation at Trier and in the Lebanon.

As a self-styled military strategist, de Gaulle was highly influenced by his experience of the 'static war' on the Western Front during WW1. As a result he was increasingly critical, during the interwar period, of the conventional doctrines of fortification and firepower which were favoured by the French military establishment. His own strategic arguments, developed in a book entitled Vers l'Armée de Métier (the Army of the Future), called for a highly professional army with mobile armoured units and supporting air capability which paralleled some of the strategic thinking developing in Germany (see Tank). Albeit forward looking, de Gaulle's theories were unrealistic for a nation dependent on a conscript army.

The outbreak of war in 1939 initially saw de Gaulle in command of a tank brigade of the 5th Army in Alsace. Whether prompted by disaffection with the military establishment or an ambition to further his own fervently held beliefs in a different arena, de Gaulle had already made contact with French political circles through Paul Reynaud* as early as 1935. In 1940, as the German invasion armies thundered westward from the Ardennes* towards the northern French coastal regions, de Gaulle (recently given command of an armoured division) was drawn fully into the political sphere and appointed Under Secretary for National Defence. Called to London only three weeks before Reynaud's resignation as Premier (which gave Marshal Pétain the opportunity to form a new government and seek an armistice with Germany), de Gaulle found himself stranded in exile, and tried in absentia for treachery by the new Vichy* government.

His later acknowledgement by the British as leader of the Free France movement and subsequent development of France Combatante (Fighting France) as a political and military entity undoubtedly represents a significant personal and political achivement. But at the time, de Gaulle's now famous radio broadcast to the French immediately before the armistice was not considered important enough by the BBC* to be worth recording – and the message of resistance, however eloquently stated, fell largely on deaf and disbelieving ears in 1940. Neither was there much initial support for Free France among the French African colonies. Moreover, despite his recognition by Britain, de Gaulle's military interventions in Africa were treated with suspicious hostility by both Britain and the US. In 1942, when the Allies were preparing their Torch* invasion of North Africa, the US, which had recognized the Vichy government in France, placed General Giraud* at the head of the French forces in Algeria in place of de Gaulle.

It is arguable that his overweaning confidence, arrogance, and the tailoring of his immense personal ambitions to those of France Combatante were the key to both de Gaulle's failures in relations with the Allies, and to his success (despite his status as a political castaway) in maintaining a feasible alternative to the Vichy government. Crucial also was the recognition and assistance of Russia, whose involvement in the French resistance movement after the German invasion of 1941 was exploited by de Gaulle to strengthen his own position as leader of an expanding and politically heterogeneous resistance movement. It is also likely that, faced with the renewed possibility of a communist leadership in post-war France, Britain and the US looked more favourably on de Gaulle as the war progressed.

In June 1943 he became head of the French Committee of National Liberation in Algiers*. By May 1944, de Gaulle was in a strong enough position to form a provisional government. Winning a final battle against the US by extracting a promise of support for his control over all French liberated territories, de Gaulle entered Paris* in the wake of the American liberation forces on 26 August. The delirious atmosphere of his welcome, however, was soon diluted by the realities of the French post-war economic situation. Although his administration was formally recognized as the government of France by the Allies in October, de Gaulle resigned from the premiership in January 1946, frustrated by the constituent assembly's lack of interest in his proposals for a strong, new American-style presidency for the new Fourth Republic.

His later dramatic re-entrances into French politics – in 1947 at the head of the anti-communist movement, the *Rassemblement du Peuple Française*, again during the crisis in Algeria in 1958 and finally as President of the Fifth Republic from 1959 – continued to be based on a powerful, self-sustained mythology of the intertwined fates of de Gaulle and his country. His claim that *'Je suis la France'* (I am France), first made as early as 1940, was echoed in 1970, when President Pompidou momentously proclaimed his death as the widowing of France.

Degaussing See Mines (naval).

De Havilland Mosquito For more than two years after its introduction in late 1941, this extremely versatile monoplane was the fastest aircraft in the RAF*. Privately designed as an unarmed fast bomber and constructed almost entirely of wood, it was sanctioned with great reluctance as a potential reconnaissance craft by the British Air Staff. When the first prototype flew in November 1941, its performance was so impressive that it was promptly ordered as both a bomber and a fighter.

The bomber prototype joined RAF squadrons as the Mosquito IV in November 1941, and the plane was an immediate success when it became operational in mid-1942. As Bomber Command was almost totally committed to night operations, many Mosquitos served with the Pathfinder* Force, marking targets for heavy bombers (see Strategic Bombing Offensive). Unarmed, but too fast to be intercepted, Mosquitos enjoyed the lowest loss rate of any Bomber Command aircraft. The important Mosquito XI, heavier and mounting the latest avionics, first flew in May 1943, and was modified to carry the new 4,000lb 'Blockbuster' bomb*. During the summer of 1944, they were used to attack V-1* rocket sites and began to operate as mine-layers, by which time the final mass-produced bomber version, the high altitude Mark XVI, was in service.

RAF Fighter Command accepted its first Mosquito IIs in January 1942. Armed and equipped as night fighters, with a strengthened airframe and metric air-to-air radar*, they gradually replaced Bristol Beaufighters* as the standard RAF aircraft in that role. More powerful later versions carried improved radar in place of guns in the nosecone, culminating in the high altitude Mosquito XXX.

The aircraft's performance always suggested an effective ground support weapon, and the mass-produced Mosquito VI fighter-bomber entered service in May 1943. Altogether, 2,584 of these were built and enjoyed brilliant careers as day or night intruders and attack planes, carrying out precision raids in Europe and the Far East as well as defending home airspace against V-1 attacks. From February 1944, rocket-armed Mosquito VIs joined RAF Coastal Command, eventually becoming its principal shipping attack aircraft. A few Mosquito XVIIIs, specifically designed for that purpose, carried a fearsome 57mm gun.

As at first envisaged by the Air Ministry, the Mosquito was an excellent long-range photo-reconnaissance plane. The first Mosquito I flew reconnaissance missions from September 1941, and over 700 P.R. models were used in all theatres. Most were conversions of Mark IX and Mark XVI bombers, but the Mosquito P34 (50 built) boasted a range of 3,500 miles. Total production of all Mosquitos was 7,781 – including some built in Canada and Australia – and the plane served the post-war RAF in all its major roles.

BRIEF DATA (Mk VI) Type: 2-man fighter-bomber; Engine: 2 × 1,230hp Rolls Royce Merlin; Max speed: 380mph; Ceiling: 36,000′; Range: 1,200m; Arms: 4 × 20mm cannon, 4 × 0.303″ mg; Bomb load: 1,000lb internal, 1,000lb external.

De Lattre de Tassigny, General Jean Joseph (1889–1952) French cavalry officer who remained in the Vichy* French 'Armistice Army', the token French force allowed by Germany after the fall of France in 1940. De Lattre de Tassigny was imprisoned in 1942 for his opposition to the German occupation of the southern *zone libre* (free zone) but escaped to England and joined de Gaulle*. He participated in the invasion of southern France (see Anvil/Dragoon) and commanded the French 1st Army during the campaign in Northwest Europe*. After the war he commanded French forces in Indo-China*.

Dempsey, Lieutenant General Sir Miles (1896–1969) Highly respected commander of the British 2nd Army which landed in Normandy* on D-Day and successfully drove the German armies out of northern France during 1944, for which he was knighted. Dempsey had already distinguished himself at Dunkirk*, where he commanded a rearguard action fought by the 13th Infantry Brigade. He also served with the 8th Army in the latter stages of the Desert War* and with Montgomery for the invasion of Sicily* and then Italy*.

DEMS (Defensively Equipped Merchant Ships) British organization set up to provide guns and gun crews for the protection of merchant ships against aircraft and surface attacks from submarines*. Instituted in 1939, it was at first given only surplus or obsolete weapons, and crews were in permanently short supply. By March 1941 almost 4,500 merchantmen had been armed, but even this was seriously inadequate and a system was introduced whereby vessels received temporary armament for journeys through dangerous Atlantic* or Mediterranean* waters. A similar but smaller American organization (the US Navy Armed Guard) was set up in December 1941. See Anti-aircraft Defence.

Denmark Before WW2 the Scandinavian kingdom of Denmark had pursued a policy of almost complete disarmament, and it was occupied in a single day by German forces simultaneously with their invasion of Norway* on 9 April 1940. Unlike other occupied European states, Denmark remained nominally independent. King Christian X stayed in place and a coalition government practised limited co-operation under the threat of civilian bombing by the Luftwaffe*. Allied diplomats were expelled from Denmark as their countries joined the war against Germany; there was strict government press censorship and Denmark signed the Anti-Comintern Pact* in November 1941.

Outside Denmark, many diplomats followed the example of the ambassador to Washington, Henrik Kauffman, in breaking with his government and supporting the Allies. The Danish territories of Greenland, Iceland* and the Faroe Islands were made available to Allied forces, and the Danish merchant fleet responded to calls from London to sail to Allied ports. As a result, 60 per cent of Denmark's 200 merchant ships were sunk by German torpedoes during the war, and some 600 Danish sailors were killed transporting Allied supplies.

The curtailment of trade links with Allied countries, and the strain of supplying German war needs, contributed to a series of economic problems in Denmark. Inflation and rationing, which were acute by 1942, encouraged the Danes to become increasingly defiant. An underground espionage network had been co-operating closely with British intelligence services since 1940, and by 1942 a number of resistance newspapers appeared regularly in Denmark. In October Hitler sent prominent SS* official Werner Best* to Copenhagen as German Commissioner and the exploitation of economic resources was stepped up.

The following May, Prime Minister Stauning died and, although Best seems to have been a relatively lenient administrator, overt resistance in Denmark increased rapidly and relations with Germany worsened. A Freedom Council took shape as the official underground government in 1943, organizing a proliferation of strikes and acts of sabotage. Anti-Semitic legislation was imposed on the Danes in October 1943, but most of the country's 8,000 Jews escaped to neutral Sweden*, aided by Danish authorities and civilians. By 1944 the situation in Denmark was similar to that of other German-occupied states, except that resistance was not hindered by internal factionalism. At the end of the war, the resistance was ready with a contingency plan for a full-scale rebellion, but this was not needed and German forces capitulated in Denmark on 5 May 1945.

Depth Charge See Anti-submarine Warfare.

Desert Rats Nickname of the British 7th Armoured Division in North Africa, derived from the Libyan jerboa which became their emblem. The Desert Rats participated in most of the armoured actions in North Africa (see Desert War). Their reputation was first established during successful British operations against Italian forces in Libya, culminating in the victory at Beda Fomm (see Egypt) in February 1941. They later fought in Tunisia*, Sicily* and Northwest Europe*.

Desert War 1941–2 The fluctuating conflict between Axis* and British forces fought for control of Libya and Egypt. Early in 1941 the war in North Africa appeared virtually over, with the British poised to eject the Italians from Libya (see Egypt). In February Hitler sent the Afrika Korps* – one armoured and one light division commanded by Lt General Erwin Rommel* – to aid the Italians in Tripoli*. Subject to overall control by the Italian High Command (*Commando Supremo*), it was given defensive instructions. The British had similarly discounted the possibility of an Axis offensive in Libya and had suspended the Desert Army's advance at the Tripolitanian border, while experienced units were transferred to East Africa* and Greece* or sent back to Egypt to refit. Nevertheless Rommel went on the offensive even before his divisions were up to strength, attacking British positions at the El Agheila* bottleneck on 24 March 1941 (see Map 7).

Inexperienced British troops fell back from this strongpoint, unleashing the Afrika Korps* into the open desert. The fast-moving German armour provoked a general and confused withdrawal to the Egyptian frontier by the British forces scattered in Cyrenaica, leaving Tobruk* isolated and under siege. With supply lines stretched, Rommel lacked the strength to take Tobruk but defeated two operations (Brevity* and Battleaxe*) mounted for its relief by General Wavell* from Cairo. Wavell's successor, General Auchinleck*, launched a third offensive (Operation Crusader*) in November 1941, with a greatly enlarged force, now renamed the 8th Army. Although heavily outnumbered, Rommel inflicted enormous losses on the British before they eventually reached Tobruk. His own material weakness then persuaded him to withdraw quickly to the Tripolitanian border. The British thus ended 1941 where they had begun it, but with far larger forces committed to the theatre.

As soon as Rommel had been reinforced, he attacked again; and again far larger British forces withdrew in haste. At the start of February 1942, the 8th Army dug itself into positions at Gazala*, but was outmanoeuvred and heavily defeated by the Afrika Korps in June and again retreated from Cyrenaica. Tobruk now fell quickly and the British retreated as far as El Alamein*, 50 miles from Alexandria*. The overrunning of Egypt appeared imminent, but Rommel's force was by now reduced to a few dozen tanks and his first attack on the Alamein Line was defeated by Auchinleck's organized defence at the beginning of July.

Auchinleck was replaced by General Alexander* in August, while Montgomery* took direct command of the 8th Army. As British troops, aircraft and armour arrived in large numbers to reinforce the position, Rommel's second major attack failed at Alam Halfa in August. By October, when the British opened the final Battle of El Alamein, the disparity between the armies was enormous, and Rommel was decisively beaten. Nevertheless his depleted and poorly supplied army evaded all Montgomery's efforts at entrapment during a long retreat. On 8 November, Anglo-American forces invaded Northwest Africa (see Torch) and this was followed by an Axis occupation of Tunisia. By the beginning of 1943, Rommel had withdrawn from Libya altogether and was preparing a co-ordinated offensive against both Allied armies with von Arnim's Tunisian forces (see Tunisia).

The Desert War was dominated by Rommel's tactical brilliance but its outcome was determined by Allied material strength. The geography of the region, a vast expanse of ideal tank country separated from the coastal strip by a steep escarpment, was brilliantly exploited in a series of concentrated armoured thrusts deep into British-held territory. By contrast, the British approach to desert warfare was cautious and at first inflexible. The orthodoxy of separating 'infantry' and 'cruiser' tanks for operational purposes was rigidly upheld, as was the belief that destruction of hostile

armour was a prime strategic aim (see Tanks). This doctrinaire dispersal of numerical superiority enabled Rommel, whose deployment of defensive artillery was highly imaginative, repeatedly to draw British forward units into traps, thus contributing further to their caution.

Morale suffered badly among the multiracial British Imperial forces as losses mounted. Although serious casualties were inflicted on the Axis army, most of the prisoners taken by the Allies were Italian infantry, while they themselves lost experienced tankmen at an alarming rate. Understandably, the men in the field believed that they were facing superior technology, a fiction subsequently maintained by some Allied commentators. In fact Rommel's tank strength consisted primarily of Italian ME* medium tanks and German PzKpfw IIIs*. The former were obsolete and unreliable, while the latter were no more than a match for British 'cruiser' tanks in 1941. By October 1942, the British 8th Army had hundreds of far more powerful American Grants* and Shermans*, while Rommel was never able to call on more than about 40 of the equivalently armed PzKpfw IVs*. Similarly, although the German 88mm* gun was the most fearsome anti-tank gun in Africa, it was never a standard weapon and Rommel's advantage in the field was gained by superior tactics in bringing standard 37mm or 50mm guns to bear from close range.

In matters of supply and reinforcement, however, Axis forces were badly disadvantaged. Rommel envisaged sweeping the British out of the Middle East and meeting up with Axis troops in the Caucasus*, but his High Command was preoccupied with the invasion of Russia and repeatedly denied him the material backing necessary to make such a project viable, seeking to restrain 'this soldier gone mad' on several occasions. Churchill, on the other hand, poured men and equipment into Africa after the collapse in early 1941, and consistently demanded aggression from his commanders. While the British army in Egypt could be supplied, albeit slowly, via the Cape of Good Hope and the Red Sea, Rommel was completely dependent on Mediterranean convoys for the survival of his armies. These were subject to periods of extreme disruption, primarily caused by planes and submarines from Malta*, which was never invaded and survived sustained bombing by the Luftwaffe*. As a result, Axis forces were often desperately short of food, fuel and ammunition, which restricted the scope of operations and encouraged the spread of sickness. By the time of the British victory at El Alamein, Rommel himself was sick and supply shortages were at a critical level. Faced by overwhelming numbers of tanks, guns, aircraft and men, now under the methodical and pragmatic command of Montgomery, Rommel's successful retreat from the desert was as remarkable as his earlier victories.

Destroyer Developed in the late nineteenth century, the Torpedo Boat Destroyer was designed to counter the fast light torpedo* craft then possessed in their hundreds by the world's major navies. By WW1 it was known simply as a destroyer and had evolved into a fast fleet escort, armed with torpedoes for attacking warships and given sufficient surface guns to deal with smaller craft. Their light displacement (seldom above 1,000 tons) and low endurance restricted them to operations inshore or close by the fleet, but larger, more versatile types were developed in the 1920s and 1930s, enabling a considerable expansion of the destroyer's role in WW2.

The main builders of large destroyers between the wars were the French and Japanese navies. The French Navy* built their superb *contre-torpilleurs* to counter Italian light cruisers in the Mediterranean*. They were exceptionally fast – capable of 40 knots in most conditions – and heavily armed, but with only a small radius of action. Japanese Navy* destroyers were even more heavily armed, if rather unstable, and by 1941 possessed the world's

most effective torpedo in the 24-inch Long Lance. Unlike the French ships, they saw extensive combat and proved formidable opponents. Japanese destroyer crews earned a fearsome reputation as aggressive fighters, but much of this large and powerful force was wasted in pointless attacks on well defended targets, and could not be replaced by a crumbling production industry.

British and American destroyer forces at the start of the war were a combination of veteran light boats and more modern designs of around 1,500 tons, half the displacement of the larger Japanese types. The Royal Navy*, which had built a few larger Tribal Class destroyers in 1938 as a response to the 'heavies' of other navies, used its more modern units for fleet protection. Older ships were assigned a multitude of secondary tasks including shore bombardment, anti-submarine* work, minesweeping, coastal patrol and convoy* escort. In the early war years this latter duty took urgent precedence and many British destroyers were pressed into a role for which their armament and emphasis on speed were ill-suited. The smaller, slower Hunt Class of escort destroyers appeared in 1939, and many more purpose-built escorts later took over convoy protection duties, most of them produced in the US (see Destroyer Escorts). British destroyer forces, like their Japanese counterparts, enjoyed a particularly high reputation for skill and aggression.

In the United States, destroyer development had been arrested by the large surplus of WW1 designs ('flushdeckers') which equipped the US Navy* into the 1930s. Many of these very fragile four-stackers were still in service at the start of the war, and 50 were lent to a desperately stretched Royal Navy under the Destroyers-for-Bases* deal of September 1940. The newer American types were of orthodox size and quite heavily armed, with great stress placed upon long range for Pacific operations. Wartime production was standardized on the 1,600-ton pre-war *Benson* Class (see Bailey, USS) and the prolific new *Fletcher* Class (see Heermann, USS). In all, 175 of these were built and they formed the backbone of the US Navy's Pacific Fleets, while older ships served in the Atlantic and on secondary duties. Most of the flushdeckers had been withdrawn from first-line duties by 1943. From 1944, the more heavily armed *Allen M. Sumner* Class entered service and a few longer-hulled *Gearing* Class units saw action before VJ Day. As in other fields, sheer weight of numbers gave US destroyer forces an enormous advantage once mass-production got under way.

Other navies used their destroyer forces with relative lack of success. The German Navy* had begun building destroyers in the 1920s, and from the mid-1930s had produced increasingly heavy ships designed to compensate in quality for inevitable quantitative shortages relative to the British and French fleets. Adequate in speed and firepower, they were given high-pressure machinery which, although it proved unreliable, gave them an impressive operational radius. Destroyers completed during the war were given armament up to light cruiser level and displaced over 2,500 tons, but this made them relatively cumbersome and they were never deployed with great imagination or conviction.

The Italian Navy*, which built some large destroyers but adhered generally to the smaller torpedo-craft concept, committed its forces defensively at first. Later its destroyers suffered heavy losses in the convoy war that developed in the Mediterranean* during 1941–2. The Red Navy* deployed large destroyer forces in the Baltic and the Black Sea, but they were of low technical quality and remained virtually anonymous throughout the war.

By 1945, it was clear that smaller, purpose-built craft were best equipped for most of the secondary duties performed by destroyers. At the same time their prime function of protecting the fleet from surface attack had itself become obsolete, as emphasized by the growing stress on anti-aircraft* armament in most destroyers. In the post-war era destroyers were developed only by the Russians, whose powerful new ships were tactically obsolete before they entered service.

Destroyers-for-Bases Deal By mid-1940 Great Britain was short of funds to buy the war materials she needed from the US, and at the same time the Royal Navy's* lack of convoy escorts had reached crisis point. Prime Minister Churchill* had suggested to Roosevelt* the loan of '40 to 50' old destroyers as early as May 1940, but the US President was bound by law never to dispose of war materials if the defence of the United States was in any way weakened. The Destroyers-for-Bases deal, announced on 2 September 1940 enabled Roosevelt to sidestep isolationist opinion at home by clearly strengthening American defence. In return for 50 utterly obsolete flushdecker destroyers* of WW1 vintage, the US received 99-year leases to British bases in Newfoundland, Bermuda and the Caribbean. This represented an important step towards US involvement in the war against Germany but British authorities were aghast at what was clearly a very bad deal in material terms. Nevertheless they were in no position to argue and the veteran four-stackers were commissioned into the Royal Navy. After overhaul and the installation of sonar*, they were thrown into the Battle of the Atlantic*, where long-range was their most valuable asset. See Neutrality, US.

Deutschland The Versailles Treaty of 1919 had sought to restrict the future German Navy* to a purely defensive capacity. It was allowed to retain six old pre-dreadnought battleships and they could be replaced, but only by ships of no more than 11-inch main armament and 10,000 tons standard displacement. Launched in 1931, the *Deutschland* was the first German warship to be built up to these limits. A genuine *tour de force* for its designers, it successfully circumvented intended restrictions and signalled the revival of German offensive sea power.

In fact the *Deutschland* considerably exceeded the tonnage limit, but this was concealed and she incorporated many weight-saving innovations, including three-gun main turrets and all-welded construction. Her greatest asset was her advanced diesel main propulsion, which extended her operational range to 21,500 miles – ideal for her intended function as a commerce raider. Additional weight was saved by sacrificing thick belt and turret armour, which left her little better protected than the best heavy cruisers, but allowed for powerful main and anti-aircraft* armament as well as a useful turn of speed.

These qualities placed the *Deutschland* in a category expressly forbidden to all the signatories of the Washington Naval Treaty of 1922. This had deliberately and effectively sought to prevent the construction of an intermediate class between battleships and cruisers by applying tonnage restrictions on capital units to all ships of over 10,000 tons, and by restricting all cruisers to 8-inch main batteries. The German Navy was not bound (or even mentioned) by the Treaty and in any case the *Deutschland* was theoretically a capital ship. Faster than contemporary battleships and apparently far more powerful than any cruiser, she was announced as capable of outfighting any ship she could not outrun, a claim challenged only by the eight fragile WW1 battlecruisers divided between the British and Japanese fleets of the day.

The *Deutschland*'s obvious commerce-raiding potential, along with Germany's publicized intention of building the five further units permitted at Versailles, contributed to the international furore that accompanied her appearance. Promptly described as a 'pocket battleship' by the world's popular press, she was classified by the German Navy as a *Panzerschiff* (armoured ship). Still bound by treaty obligations, most other navies did not build in response to the *Deutschland*, although the

French Navy* (in no danger of exceeding its total tonnage limits) briefly revived the hitherto discredited battlecruiser with the *Dunkerque*' Class.

In fact the German Navy completed only two more *Panzerschiffe* (the *Admiral Graf Spee*' and *Admiral Scheer*') and by 1939 the type had lost its air of invincibility. The diesel engines proved disappointing in service and, while battleships had become significantly faster, cruiser tactics had been developed which could exploit the fairly cumbersome main armament of the 'pocket battleships'. The *Deutschland*'s main turrets were in fact ridiculously heavy for sinking merchantmen, but they proved more relevant to some of the varied duties asked of her in a largely disappointing combat career.

At the start of the war the *Deutschland* was at sea in the North Atlantic, and she sank two merchant ships before returning to Germany for machinery repairs in November 1939. In February 1940 she was renamed on Hitler's instructions (to avoid the risk of losing a ship named after the state) and took part in the invasion of Norway* as the *Lützow*. Later she was based in northern Norway as a threat to Allied Arctic* convoys, but on 31 December 1942 she failed (with the *Admiral Hipper*') to disrupt a convoy protected only by destroyers* and a distant shadowing cruiser in what was called the Battle of the Barents Sea. This failure so outraged Hitler that he threatened to disband the surface fleet forthwith, provoking the resignation of Grand-Admiral Raeder* as C-in-C of the Navy. Transferred to the Baltic for training and later used in the Eastern Baltic for army support work, the *Lützow* was badly damaged by air attack in April 1945, and was scuttled on 4 May.

BRIEF DATA (1939) Displacement: 11,700 tons; Dimensions: o/a lgth – 616' 9″, b – 68'; Speed: 26 knots; Armament: 6 × 11″ gun (2 × 3), 8 × 5.9″ gun, 6 × 4.1″ AA gun, 8 × 37mm AA gun, 10 × 20mm AA gun, 8 × 21″ TT, 2 aircraft.

Devers, General Jacob (1887–1979) Popular commander of the US 6th Army Group which fought throughout the Allied campaign in Northwest Europe*, his relaxed style of leadership may have contributed to Supreme Allied Commander Eisenhower's* periodic uncertainty about Devers' judgement. Having acted as Eisenhower's caretaker in command of ETOUSA (European Theatre of Operations, US Army) during 1943, Devers was sent to command NATOUSA (North African Theatre of Operations) and then SACMED (Supreme Allied Command, Mediterranean) before returning to France to command the US 6th Army Group. Although his troops were employed as a subsidiary force to the Army Groups under Bradley* and Montgomery*, Devers' command (US 7th Army and French 1st Army) nevertheless played an important part in the campaign.

Dewoitine D520 French monoplane fighter which entered service in February 1940. It was the best aircraft available to *l'Armée de l'Air** in the Battle of France*, its pilots claiming 147 victories against 85 planes lost. After the French surrender, the Vichy* government maintained limited production and 720 D520s were eventually built, 411 of which were seized by the Germans when they occupied southern France in November 1942. Subsequently some D520s saw action with the Bulgarian and Rumanian Air Forces, and others were recaptured and used against German forces by Free French pilots in 1944.
BRIEF DATA (D520-5) Type: single-seat fighter; Engine: 1 × 910hp Hispano-Souza; Max speed: 329mph; Ceiling: 36,090'; Range: 777m; Arms: 1 × 20mm cannon, 4 × 7.5mm mg.

Diadem, Operation Code-name for the 1944 Allied spring offensive on the Italian peninsula – a final attempt by Supreme Allied Commander Alexander* to break the costly stalemate in Italy* – which had left exhausted Allied forces halted on the Gustav Line* and trapped on the Anzio* beachhead to the north (see Maps 34 and 35). The operation planned to concentrate the entire Allied strength on the Cassino*–Liri Valley sector of the front. Redeployment of the British 8th Army under Leese from the eastern side of the Appenines brought the total number of Allied divisions there up to 12 out of a total of 16. The force comprised two American, four French, four British and two Polish divisions. Air support was provided by Operation Strangle*, which was directed to strike at German supply and communications lines.

Begun on 11 May with a direct assault on the German strongpoint at Cassino* by Polish forces, the breakthrough was made to the west of Cassino by French and Moroccan forces under General Juin* on 14 May, advancing across mountainous terrain beyond the Garigliano river behind the retreating German 71st Division and forcing a corridor near the west coast for the advance of the American 2nd Corps. The collapse of the western flank of the German defence enabled 5th Army units trapped at Anzio to break out of the bridgehead and US General Clark* pushed his forces in a drive towards Rome*, which was entered on 4 June 1944. Thereafter, the Allies pursued the withdrawing German forces to the Gothic Line.

At a cost of 42,000 casualties and the employment of 30 Allied divisions, it is arguable that Diadem proved a poor strategic investment, especially since General Clark's hunger to capture the capital had enabled the bulk of German forces to escape and stabilize their position on the Gothic Line*.

Dido, HMS British light anti-aircraft* cruiser and Class. The first six *Didos* were laid down in 1937 as part of the Royal Navy's* rearmament programme, but they were only completed between May 1940 and June 1941. Armed with dual purpose 5.25-inch guns (whenever sufficient turrets were available) they were the smallest cruisers then under construction but were not noticeably outclassed by their European contemporaries. They gave good service, mostly in the Mediterranean*, but construction of a further ten vessels was much delayed in the post-Dunkirk* period by German bombing, material shortages and a welter of detail modifications. The sixteenth and last of the type (the *Diadem*) was eventually ready in January 1944.

The only *Dido* Class ship to be destroyed from the air was the *Spartan*, sunk at Anzio* by a German guided bomb*, although four units were lost to torpedoes*. Improved light anti-aircraft capacity and radar* installations were fitted as modifications to early vessels and as standard to the later ones.
BRIEF DATA (1940) Displacement: 5,600 tons; Dimensions: o/a lgth – 512', b – 50' 6"; Speed: 33 knots; Armament: 10 × 5.25" gun (5 × 2), 8 × 2pdr AA gun, 8 × 0.5" AA gun, 6 × 21" TT.

Dieppe Raid An amphibious* assault by a small mixed force of 5,000 Canadian and 1,000 British troops on the coast of France in August 1942. The raid was mounted both as an experiment in landing technique, and as a British gesture of good faith, designed to assuage American and Russian suspicions over Britain's unwillingness to open a Second Front in France, repeatedly demanded by Stalin since the German invasion of Russia in 1941.

The objective was to take and briefly hold a port on the French coast. There were no plans for exploitation of the raid, although tanks were part of the equipment necessary to establish a permanent beachhead that was landed on 19 August, amidst heavy German air and sea attacks. Once ashore, the raiders, with only intermittent close air support, came under fierce attack from forces under General Zeitzler*. With communications between the beach and the task force commander lost within the first few hours, the operation swiftly became a disaster. Of 6,000, 3,369 were killed,

wounded or captured, and all seven battalion commanders were casualties. The 'reconnaissance in force' proved beyond doubt the impossibility of capturing port facilities as initial objectives of a continental invasion and the need for more sophisticated amphibious equipment and techniques (see Special-purpose Vehicles).

Dietrich, SS Colonel General Josep (Sepp) (1892–1966) Commander of Hitler's SS* bodyguard and later of an SS Panzer Army. An ex-sergeant major of WW1, Dietrich's early career was typical of the Nazi Party* member. Experience in the *Freikorps*, a period of unemployment and spare time thuggery in the SA preceded his full-time entry into the SS in 1928. He commanded the 1st SS Panzer Division, which had evolved from the *Leibstandarte Adolf Hitler*, the élite personal SS guard, in the Western Offensive* in 1940, the Balkans* and on the Eastern Front* for the invasion of the Soviet Union, where the Waffen SS (Armed SS) speedily developed a fighting reputation. Dietrich later commanded a Panzer Corps of three SS divisions against the Allied invasion of Normandy*.

Though without staff training or the military background of his colleagues, his coarse, foul-mouthed temperament and style of leadership was perhaps well suited to the troops he led. Following the failure of the German offensive in the Ardennes (see Battle of the Bulge) in late 1944, Dietrich's 6th Panzer Army was moved southeast for Hitler's final offensive of the war at Lake Balaton in Hungary*, and was then sent to defend Vienna, where advancing Soviet armies routed his formation. Widely held responsible by the Russians for the murder of Soviet wounded at Kharkov* in March 1943, Dietrich was perhaps more anxious than most to surrender his units to American forces in May 1945. Sentenced to 25 years imprisonment by a US court, he served less than ten. Dietrich could certainly count himself lucky that he never stood trial on Soviet charges. He died, a free man, at Ludwigsburg, although he did serve a further term of imprisonment, having been found guilty by a West German court of taking part in Hitler's purge of the SA in 1934.

Dill, Field Marshal Sir John (1881–1944) Highly respected British commander of 1st Corps, British Expeditionary Force, which he trained and led in France in 1939 (see Western Offensive). Returning from France in April 1940 as Vice Chief of the Imperial General Staff, he succeeded Ironside as CIGS in the following month but was replaced on Churchill's* order at the end of 1941, following a stormy period of conflict between Churchill's impetuous approach and Dill's personal and professional caution. He then accompanied Churchill to Washington as head of the British Joint Staff Mission, and remained there as Senior British Officer on the Combined Chiefs of Staff Committee*, where he enjoyed considerable diplomatic and personal success and established important relationships with Roosevelt*, General Marshall* and Admiral King*. He died in November 1944 and was buried at Arlington National Cemetery in recognition of the affection felt for him by the American military establishment.

Dnieper River Strategically important river 300 miles inside the Soviet Union, running 1,400 miles north from the Black Sea. In the plan for the German invasion of Russia (see Eastern Front), Hitler had hoped to encircle and smash the Red Army* before the Dnieper was reached. In the event, German forces crossed the river in early July 1941. In August 1943, following the defeat of the German Citadel offensive on Kursk*, Russian forces mounted counter-attacks all along the weakening German front (see Map 30). On the Voronezh front, General Vatutin* drove a wedge in the lines of German Army Group South west of Belgorod, adding to the intensifying pressure on Kharkov* (evacuated, despite Hitler's refusal, on Manstein's* orders of 22 August). As the Russian offensive

extended north to the Bryansk Front* under Popov*, the Kalinin Front under Yeremenko* and the Central Front under Rokossovsky*, Hitler finally agreed to a withdrawal to the line of the Dnieper. As the Russian armies rolled forward across the Mius and the Donets* in the south, capturing Taganrog and Stalino in September, Yeremenko's forces in the north recaptured Smolensk*. By the end of the month, Soviet forces stood at the Dnieper from Smolensk to Zaparozhye.

During November, the focus of the fighting was at Kiev*, and at Kremenchung to the south. A Soviet advance west of Kiev following its recapture (6 November) was turned back by a German counter-offensive to capture Zhitomir. But the coming Russian offensive in the Ukraine* was already in preparation. See also Red Navy.

Dohnanyi, Hans von (1902–45) A prominent member of the German opposition to Hitler* and assistant to the President of the German Supreme Court from 1933. Appalled by the Nazi practice of justice, Dohnanyi assembled a dossier of Party misdeeds and later associated with many who opposed Hitler, including his brother-in-law, Dietrich Bonhöffer*, Canaris*, Oster* and Gördeler*. In 1938 he was ready to join in a denunciation of Hitler under Halder's* leadership, but British appeasement* at Munich* removed the opportunity. By the outbreak of war Dohnanyi had secured a position with the Abwehr* (German military intelligence). Following the 1944 July Bomb Plot*, he was one of many suspected of involvement by the Nazis; he was arrested, released and finally rearrested and taken to Sachsenhausen concentration camp* near Berlin. Dohnanyi was indicted and finally executed in April 1945. See Resistance, Germany.

Donets River Russian river running east of Kharkov*, it was a focus of fighting between Soviet and German forces in mid-1942 and early 1943. See Eastern Front.

Dönitz, Grand Admiral Karl (1891–1980) German naval officer and Führer in brief succession to Adolf Hitler*. Commissioned into the German Imperial Navy in 1910, Karl Dönitz was a submariner during WW1, but spent the post-war years in a navy without submarines, rising to the rank of commander aboard surface ships. In September 1935, he was given command of the German Navy's* first flotilla of three new submarines and over the next four years controlled the tactical and technical developments of the U-boat arm. During this period Dönitz was at odds with the 'big ships' policy of the German naval High Command under Raeder*, who also forbade the introduction of 'wolfpack'* tactics which Dönitz strongly advocated. Instead of the 300 U-boats Dönitz claimed he needed to defeat Britain, he went to war in 1939 with 57 – 39 of which were fully operational.

Promoted to Rear Admiral in 1939, he led the U-boat arm with conspicuous success in the early years of the war. Dönitz deployed his forces shrewdly, finding weak spots in Allied defences throughout the Atlantic* and consistently increasing the pressure on trade routes before March 1943. The 'wolfpacks' in particular proved highly effective when they were eventually deployed from late 1940. U-boat crews were superbly trained and their morale was enhanced by Dönitz's personal commitment to his commanders, who responded with panache and daring in the field.

During this period Dönitz argued consistently (but largely in vain) against the dispersal of his forces to other theatres and in favour of greater concentration of production and scientific resources on U-boats. His frankness and technical mastery impressed Hitler, who had become utterly disenchanted with his surface fleet by the end of 1942 and insisted that it was scrapped. Raeder, its champion, was forced to resign. Dönitz was promoted to Grand Admiral and became C-in-C of the German Navy on 30 January 1943.

His first achievement was the reinstatement of the surface fleet, which Dönitz persuaded Hitler to maintain in a limited role. He next secured steel allocations for a building programme concentrating on small craft, particularly U-boats, over which he continued to exercise direct control. His deployment of submarines after their Atlantic defeat in the spring of 1943 was largely defensive pending the development of new weapons to defeat the Allied anti-submarine groups. Acoustic torpedoes, *schnorchel* breathing masts and improved boats were introduced before the end of the war. Losses were curtailed and the U-boat fleet grew steadily throughout 1944 but never again posed a serious threat to Allied convoys*. In early 1945, Dönitz organized the evacuation of troops and refugees from the Russian advance on the Eastern Baltic, perhaps the most successful German surface operation of the war.

Dönitz's unequivocal acceptance of National Socialist Germany had underpinned his command successes. In the final stages of the war, with Göring*, Himmler* and other leaders discredited, Dönitz earned the dubious reward of being the Führer's named successor as head of state, a post he assumed in Schleswig-Holstein at the end of April 1945. The new Führer appointed a cabinet of his choice (not the one willed on him by Hitler), which effectively dismissed the Nazis from government. He negotiated the surrender of the German forces in the west (see Germany, Surrender of) and was arrested by the Western Allies at Flensburg on 23 May. Convicted as a major war criminal at Nuremberg* on charges of planning a war of aggression, he served a ten-year prison sentence in Spandau, Germany. See also German Navy; Atlantic, Battle of; Submarine.

Donovan, William J. (1883–1959) New York lawyer, veteran of WW1 and confidante of President Roosevelt*, who appointed Donovan to head the newly created Office of the Coordinator of Information (COI), (which Donovan had himself suggested) in July 1941. The creation of the COI represented Roosevelt's commitment to agitational propaganda* and psychological warfare, in contrast to the limited information propaganda authorized via the Office and Government Reports and the information division of the Office of Emergency Management. Donovan's clandestine menu of activities included 'black' propaganda (now known as 'disinformation'), the use of rumour, deceptions and lies, which would transform propaganda into 'an attack weapon . . . the arrow of initial penetration . . .' The COI was the predecessor to the OSS*, which Donovan took over at its inception in July 1942.

Doolittle, Lt General James (1896–) US Army Air Force* commander. Doolittle, a businessman and former record-breaking racing pilot, was recalled to active service from the reserve in 1940, to work with industrial leaders at the conversion of the motor industry to aircraft production. He is best known, however, for leading a raid by 16 B-25s* on a spectacular and near suicidal mission from the US Navy* carrier *Hornet** to bomb targets in Tokyo, Yokohama, Yokosuka, Kobe and Nagoya, on 1 April 1942. Though the direct military impact of the 'Doolittle Raid' (also known as the First Special Aviation Project) was limited, the attack greatly boosted American morale and the longer-term strategic implications of the mission proved immensely important to the outcome of the Pacific War*.

The raid also earned Doolittle immediate promotion to Brigadier General and the Congressional Medal of Honour. He subsequently commanded the US 12th Air Force, created for the Torch* operations in Northwest Africa and became Commander of the Northwest African Strategic Air Force the following year. In 1944, now in command of the 8th Air Force in Britain, Doolittle was created an honorary Knight Commander of the Order of the Bath by King George VI. The following year he took the 8th Air Force to the Pacific.

Doorman, Admiral Karel (1889–1942) Admiral of the Royal Netherlands Navy and commander of the combined Dutch, British, American and Australian (ABDA) cruiser and destroyer force which was created on 14 February 1942 to challenge the Japanese advance through the Dutch East Indies*. The force and its commander operated under the greatest possible handicaps, having never worked together as an integrated unit and therefore lacking a common tactical doctrine or communications system. Its first major operation, the Battle of the Java Sea* (February 1942), saw the loss of its flagship, the Dutch light cruiser *De Ruyter*, and its commander.

Dornier Do17 (and Do215) First flown in 1934, the German Do17 'Flying Pencil' was too slender for its planned role as an airliner, but joined the Luftwaffe* as a bomber in early 1937, at which time it was 25mph faster than any operational fighter. The heavier, bulb-nosed Do17Z entered service in January 1939, and its more powerful subvariant, the Do17Z2 was the standard wartime version. Popular with aircrew and reliable, the plane was a great success in Poland*, but was no longer able to outrun modern fighters by 1940 and suffered heavily during the Battle of Britain*. Between late 1939 and the end of production the following July, about 535 Do17Zs were delivered, and a further 101 Do215Bs (a version originally intended for export) were also used by the Luftwaffe. Twelve of these, converted as heavily armed night intruders, operated successfully over RAF* bases in England until withdrawn in October 1941. By that time, Do17s were being phased out of first-line operations, and even those on the Eastern Front* had been replaced by the end of 1942.

BRIEF DATA (Do17Z2) Type: 4-man medium bomber/reconnaissance; Engine: 2 × 1,000hp Bramo; Max speed: 263mph; Ceiling: 26,740'; Range: 721m (part load); Arms: (typical) 6 × 7.92mm mg; Bomb load: 2,205lb.

Dornier Do18 Originally designed as a civilian transatlantic mail carrier for Luft Hansa, this graceful machine entered the Luftwaffe* as the Do18D in 1938. Rearmed and re-engined, the Do18G was used in the first years of the war for reconnaissance and air-sea rescue* work. Seventy-one of this major version were built, production ending just before the start of the war.
BRIEF DATA (Do18G) Type: 4-man reconnaissance flying boat; Engines: 2 × 880hp Junkers Jumo; Max speed: 165mph; Ceiling: 13,780'; Range: 2,175m; Arms: 1 × 20mm cannon, 1 × 13mm mg (provision for 440lb bomb).

Dornier Do24 Trimotor, structurally similar to the Dornier Do18 series, it was first employed by the Dutch government in 1938 as the Do24K. Twenty-five examples had been built by the time the Netherlands was overrun by Germany, after which production continued for the Luftwaffe*, who used the plane in air-sea rescue* (Do24N), reconnaissance (Do24T1) and transport Do24T2) versions. Altogether 250 machines were manufactured in the Netherlands and in France, and after the German withdrawal, 22 Do24s saw service with the French naval air arm (*Aeronavale*).
BRIEF DATA (Do24T1) Type: 4-man reconnaissance flying boat; Engines: 3 × 1,000hp BMW/Bramo Fafnir; Max speed: 211mph; Ceiling: 19,360'; Range: 1,800m; Arms: 1 × 20mm cannon, 2 × 7.9mm mg; Bomb load: 1,320lb.

Dornier Do217 Versatile German bomber, which superficially resembled an outsized Dornier Do17*, but was a completely new aircraft in design and detail. Developed between 1938 and 1940, it reached full production with the Do217E2, which joined the Luftwaffe* in late 1940. Although classified as a heavy bomber, a role for which its defensive armament proved inadequate, it was never intended to be a strategic weapon and performed a number of other functions in many versions. Several types carried radio-con-

trolled guided* bombs, and the strengthened Do217K models, with increased horsepower, armament and wingspan, were particularly successful with these in the Mediterranean* during 1943.
The Do217J was developed as a stop-gap night fighter, often a converted bomber, and the Do217N was a similarly adapted version of the later, 348mph Do217M bomber. Fighter models were heavily armed, often mounting the oblique-firing *Schräge Musik* * installation, but their handling capabilities left much to be desired. A very fast, high-altitude reconnaissance version, the 217P, failed to reach general service before manufacture was stopped in late 1943, by which time 1,366 production bombers and 364 fighters had been built.
BRIEF DATA (Do217E2) Type: 4-man medium/heavy bomber; Engine: 2 × 1,580hp BMW 801; Max speed: 320mph; Ceiling 24,610'; Range: 1,300m; Arms: 1 × 15mm mg, 2 × 13mm mg, 3 × 7.92mm mg; Bomb load: 8,818lb.

Dornier Do335 'Arrow' (Pfeil) Although it never reached combat status, the German *Pfeil* was remarkable for its bizarre design, featuring two power plants in the fuselage driving nose and tail propellers. Apart from a few handling problems this worked well enough, and the plane was developed as both the Do335A fighter-bomber, a few of which joined Luftwaffe* units near the end of the war, and the Do335B two-seat heavy fighter.
BRIEF DATA (Do335A) Type: single-seat fighter-bomber; Engine: 2 × 1,900hp Daimler Benz; Max speed: 413mph; Ceiling: 37,400'; Range: 1,280m; Arms: 1 × 30mm cannon, 2 × 15mm cannon; Bomb load: 1,100lb.

Dorsetshire, HMS Royal Navy* heavy cruiser completed in 1930 which, along with HMS *Norfolk*, formed the final County Class of 10,000-ton British units (see Suffolk, HMS). The *Dorsetshire* served in the East Indies until 1940, when she was transferred to the Atlantic and took part in the

attack on Dakar* in July. In May 1941 she fired the final three torpedoes which sank the *Bismarck* before being transferred back to the Far East, where she was sunk off Ceylon* in April 1942. The *Norfolk* served in the Home Fleet throughout the war, covering the progress of Arctic convoys* and participating in operations against the *Bismarck* and later the *Scharnhorst*. Wartime modifications to the *Norfolk* included the removal of spotter aircraft facilities, rendered obsolete by the fitting of radar*.
BRIEF DATA (1939) Displacement: 9,975 tons; Dimensions: o/a lgth – 630', b – 66'; Speed: 32.25 knots; Armament: 8 × 8" gun (2 × 4), 8 × 4" AA gun, 16 × 2pdr AA gun, 8 × 0.5" AA gun, 8 × 21" TT, 1 aircraft.

Douglas, Air Marshal Sir W. Sholto (1893–1969) Assistant Chief of the British Air Staff at the outbreak of war, Douglas succeeded Dowding* as head of RAF* Fighter Command in November 1940 and switched the operational emphasis of his forces from defence to attack. With the object of drawing Luftwaffe units into battle (particularly important after the German invasion of Russia in June 1941), massed daylight fighter sweeps were undertaken against targets of opportunity along the German-occupied coast of northern Europe which caused considerable local disruption and provided his short-range interceptors with some, albeit strategically marginal, offensive function. Douglas was appointed successively C-in-C RAF Middle East in 1943 and then C-in-C Coastal Command for the invasion of Normandy*. After the war, he became C-in-C and Military Governor of the British Occupation Zone in Germany. See also Big Wing; Rhubarbs.

Douglas DB-7 Series Successful multi-role aircraft, built to a US Army Air Corps attack specification of 1938 but ordered first by the French government in February 1939. Faster and more complex than contemporary European bombers, the plane was diverted to Britain after the fall of

France* in 1940, and over 100 were converted into RAF* 'Havoc' night-fighters. From February 1942, the re-engined and more powerfully armed Boston III models joined the RAF as daylight bombers and intruders over northern Europe, while the similar USAAF* A-20 version was just entering full production. The most important American variant was the formidable A-20G bomber, of which 2,850 were built for the USAAF and US Navy*, but P-70 night-fighter types were also manufactured in quantity. Most of the series featured a solid nosecone packed with guns, but the A-20J and K (RAF Boston IV and V) were glazed-nosed reconnaissance aircraft. Of the 7,385 A-20s produced in total, 3,125 were sent to the Red Air Force* under Lend-Lease*. Production was stopped in September 1944.
BRIEF DATA (A-20G) Type: 2-man intruder or 3-man light bomber; Engine: 2 × 1,700hp Wright Double Cyclone; Max speed: 342mph; Ceiling: 25,300'; Range: 1,000m (loaded); Arms: (typical) 4 × 20mm cannon, 9 × 0.5" mg; Bomb load: 4,000lb.

Douglas (TBD) Devastator All-metal monoplane torpedo-bomber introduced to the US Navy* in late 1937, it supplanted completely obsolete biplanes, but was too slow and cumbersome to avoid modern Japanese naval fighters. Nevertheless it was important in the early stages of the Pacific War* and 125 Devastators saw action, remaining standard equipment aboard US carriers until mid-1942. Heavy losses at the Battle of Midway* in June, attributed to the obsolete performance of the aircraft, hastened the demise of multi-crewed attack planes with the US Navy in favour of single-seat types carrying external ordnance.
BRIEF DATA (TBD-1) Type: 3-man naval torpedo-bomber; Engine: 1 × 825hp Pratt and Whitney Twin Wasp; Max speed: 225mph; Arms: 1 × 0.5" mg, 1 × 0.3" mg; Bomb load: 1,000lb or 1 × 21" torpedo (internal).

Douglas (A-26) Invader Designed as a successor to the Douglas DB7* series of intruder planes, the Invader was ordered in three variously armed prototypes by the US Army Air Corps in early 1941 and first flew in July 1942. A-26B attack models were purchased first and, faster than any tactical bomber except the British de Havilland Mosquito*, they began combat missions over Europe in November 1944. Eventually, 1,355 were delivered, and a further 1,091 glass-nosed A-26C reconnaissance versions saw service from January 1945. Usually equipped with panoramic air-to-ground radar*, these flew as the 'eyes' of heavy blind-bombing formations. The whole production programme was terminated after VJ day, but the plane later saw widespread action in Korea and was back in production by 1963 for operations in Vietnam.
BRIEF DATA (A-26B) Type: 3-man attack bomber; Engine: $2 \times 2,000$hp Pratt and Whitney Double Wasp; Max speed: 355mph; Ceiling: 22,100'; Range: 1,400m (loaded); Arms: $10 \times 0.5''$ mg; Bomb load: 4,000lb.

Douglas SBD Dauntless First built in the summer of 1940 for the US Marine Corps, the aptly named Dauntless joined the US Navy* as the SBD2, and was the mainstay of American air power in the first years of the Pacific War*. Although obsolete by the time of Pearl Harbor* and outclassed by its Japanese counterparts, it gave staunch service both as a bomber and a reconnaissance aircraft, displaying a rugged ability to absorb enemy fire. Production increased for the SBD3 and SBD4 series, which were only minor modifications and which retained a 1,000hp radial engine. This was upgraded in the mass-produced SBD5, which also mounted radar*. Late in its long and varied career, the plane flew anti-submarine* missions armed with depth charges, and was among the first American warplanes to be equipped with rocket* launchers. Although primarily a naval aircraft, the Dauntless was also used by the USAAF*, which employed about 850 machines as A-24s. The programme finally ended with the SBD6 in July 1944, after 5,936 of all types had been built.
BRIEF DATA (SBD5) Type: 2-man naval light bomber/reconnaissance; Engine: $1 \times 1,200$hp Wright Cyclone; Max speed: 255mph; Ceiling: 25,200'; Range: (max) 456m; Arms: $2 \times 0.5''$ mg, $2 \times 0.3''$ mg; Bomb load: 1,000lb.

Dowding, Air Chief Marshal Sir Hugh (1882–1970) Uncharismatic but tactically well-informed Commander of RAF* Fighter Command from 1936–40. Dowding was responsible for the organization of Britain's home defence air force and instituted a strictly centralized control system for the deployment of his numerically stretched forces. In June 1940 he insisted on the retention of his main fighter strength in Britain during the Battle of France*, and the following month his system went into effect in the Battle of Britain*. Based around early warning radar* and the sparing commitment of fighters against definite targets, Dowding's tactics frustrated the Luftwaffe's repeated attempts to force a decisive major confrontation and were the most important factor in enabling Fighter Command's eventual victory. He was nevertheless criticized within the RAF by those, notably Air Vice Marshal Leigh-Mallory*, who sought a more aggressive seek-and-destroy role for Fighter Command (see Big Wing). Despite his victory, Dowding was removed from his post in November 1940, at a time when Fighter Command was having little success against Luftwaffe night bombers, and replaced by Sholto Douglas*. He served for a time on a Ministry of Aircraft Production mission to the US and Canada in 1941 before retiring the following year.

Dracula Code-name for an Allied air and seaborne assault on the Rangoon* area in southern Burma*, in support of the Allied advance southward by General Slim's*

14th Army from Meiktila* and Mandalay* at the start of April 1945.

Dresden, Bombing of See Strategic Bombing Offensive.

Duke of York, HMS British battleship of the *King George V* Class, completed in late 1941. Apart from a spell in the Mediterranean supporting the Torch* landings in Northwest Africa, the *Duke of York* served with the Home Fleet until 1945. On 26 December 1943, she engaged and seriously damaged the German battlecruiser *Scharnhorst** during the Battle of North Cape. When Japan surrendered (15 August 1945) the *Duke of York* was *en route* to join the Pacific Fleet, and was present in Tokyo Bay when the surrender was signed on 2 September.
BRIEF DATA See King George V, HMS.

Dumbarton Oaks (Washington, DC) Country home site of a conference (22 August–28 September 1944) held between representatives of the United States, Britain, the Soviet Union and, in the final week, China, whose brief was to discuss the implementation of the Teheran Declaration's call for a permanent world security organization, the United Nations. See Conferences.

Dunkerque The battlecruiser *Dunkerque*, ordered in 1931, was the French Navy's rather exaggerated response to the shock of the first German *Panzerschiffe*, the *Deutschland**. Her sister the *Strasbourg* was laid down in 1934 once it was known that the Italians were building their *Littorio** Class battleships. The battlecruiser, armed as a capital ship but lightly protected for high speed, had been discredited as a tactical weapon by the end of WW1. Although more powerful than the far lighter *Panzerschiffe*, the *Dunkerques* were no match for true battleships and were excessively vulnerable to other forms of attack.

Both ships were at Mers-el-Kébir* in Morocco when the British attacked in July

1940. The *Strasbourg* escaped unharmed and proceeded to the French naval base at Toulon. The *Dunkerque* was damaged by bombs and a nearby explosion but survived with the loss of 150 lives. Refloated, she returned to Toulon in February 1942. While she was still under repair the Germans occupied southern France, and both ships were among those scuttled on 27 November 1942, to pre-empt German seizure.
BRIEF DATA (1939) Displacement: 26,500 tons; Dimensions: o/a lgth – 702' 4", b – 101' 9"; Speed 29.5 knots; Armaments: 8 × 13" gun (4 × 2), 16 × 5" gun, 8 × 37mm AA gun, 32 × 13.2mm AA mg, 2 aircraft.

Dunkirk Northern French seaport close to the Belgian frontier from which British and Allied troops were withdrawn in a last-minute escape, after the German breakthrough across France in May 1940 (see Western Offensive). Following the unsuccessful counterstroke by British Expeditionary Force Commander General Gort* at Arras* on 21 May, he made the difficult decision, in the light of dwindling supplies and the imminent collapse of the Belgian forces, to withdraw to Dunkirk for an evacuation, holding a final position along the 'canal line' of the Aa, the Scarpe and the Yser rivers. Code-named Operation Dynamo, the evacuation from Dunkirk was organized by Vice Admiral Ramsay*, Commander of Dover.

Beginning on 26 May, a combined British, Dutch, French and Belgian 'fleet' of over 40 destroyers*, with sloops, minesweepers, personnel and patrol ships, and hundreds of privately owned volunteer craft of all types and sizes numbering nearly 900 in total, ferried 338,226 mostly British troops from inlets, jetties and beaches around Dunkirk, while the BEF and elements of the French Army* fought courageous rearguard actions to maintain a defensive perimeter. Maintained until 4 June, the evacuation was a remarkable and heroic, if negative, achievement. But the reprieve of the BEF was attributable in great part to Hitler's last-minute decision to hold back his tank divisions from a drive through the canal line and rely on air attack (agreed with Army Group A Commander Rundstedt* on 24 May), which provided critical days for a defence to be organized around Dunkirk.

Although the reasons for Hitler's 'fatal decision' have been variously interpreted – as an honour accorded Göring's* Luftwaffe* as reward for their part in the Western Offensive, as a way of encouraging Britain to come to negotiated terms, or as a way of preserving his tank force for the coming drive southwest across the 'Weygand Line' – the result was of vital importance to the morale and even, perhaps, the viability of the British war effort.

Dutch East Indies (Indonesia), Fall of, 1942 Large, Dutch-held territories in the Southwest Pacific, and rich in oil, they were a major objective of the Japanese offensive during the first half of 1942 (see Pacific War; Map 11). Projected as a three-pronged invasion, the strike was aimed at southern Sumatra, western Java and North Borneo in the south; East Borneo and then Java* in the centre; and the Celebes and eastern Java in the eastern sector. By the end of 1941, Japanese forces had captured Davao on Mindanao as a springboard for the invasion from the east, as well as Jolo in the central sector and Kuching on the western coast of Sarawak. Under the overall command of Vice Admiral Nobutake Kondo*, the Eastern Force (under Takahashi) and the Western Force (under Ozawa*) were opposed by the newly created Allied force under General Wavell*, ABDA Command. The task of holding what was called the Malay Barrier was given to the ABDA naval command of Admiral Thomas Hart* (C-in-C of the US Asiatic Fleet), who faced acute shortages of naval and air power as well as the problems of differences in *matériel*, language, signals and tactics.

During January, Japanese landings were made on Sumatra, Borneo* and Celebes, at Tarakan, Manado, Kema, Balikpapan, Pemangkat and on Amboina. In February, Japanese forces also captured Bandjermasin and Makassar before moving into Timor and Bali, breaching the line of Wavell's bases. Attempts during January and February to resist the Japanese advance, including the naval engagement in the Lombok Strait (19–20 February) against an Allied force under Dutch Rear Admiral Doorman*, only served to underline the immense advantage in forces and organization maintained by the Japanese Pacific offensive. For the final defence of Java, which now seemed imminent, Doorman's force comprised 2 heavy cruisers (British *Exeter* and American *Houston*), 3 light cruisers (Dutch *De Ruyter* and *Java* and Australian *Perth*), and 5 American, 3 British, and 3 Dutch destroyers. The Japanese forces under Kondo, split into several task groups, comprised 7 carriers, 1 seaplane carrier, 1 battleship, 13 heavy cruisers, 6 light cruisers and 57 destroyers. Ninety-seven ships carried troops in two transport convoys.

At this stage the ABDA Command was dissolved at General Wavell's request, and overall naval command passed to Dutch Admiral Helfrich, who was determined to put up maximum resistance despite the seeming certainty of Japanese victory. On 24 February, a large fleet of Japanese transports was sighted south of the Makassar Strait, escorted by Rear Admiral Takagi's* three cruisers and seven destroyers, on its way to the assault on Java, scheduled for 28 February. Ordered to search out the convoy, Doorman failed to find the Japanese until a sighting on 27 February provoked a hasty attack on Takagi's force, now reinforced with a light cruiser and six destroyers under Rear Admiral Nishimura and sailing into the Java Sea. In the largest surface engagement since Jutland, Doorman's outnumbered ships fought valiantly, but with little hope of success against the superior firepower and manoeuvrability of the Japanese. Lacking spotter planes and confused by a Japanese smoke screen, the Allied force was obliged to take evasive action and was effectively destroyed with a loss of four warships and its commander (see Java Sea, Battle of). Though a few Allied destroyers and smaller ships managed to escape, the Malay Barrier was breached.

On 1 March, the troop transport convoy which Doorman had failed to stop landed at Kragan on the northern coast of Java. Fierce fighting by General ter Poorten's combined British, Dutch and Australian force could not halt the advance of the Japanese 48th Division to Surabaya, Batavia and finally to Bandung where the Allied force fought a final defensive action. On 5 March, General ter Poorten decided that Bandung could no longer be held and the decision to order a cease-fire was finally made by Stilwell on 8 March.

Dynamo, Operation See Dunkirk.

E

Eagle, HMS British aircraft carrier, completed in 1923 after prolonged conversion on the hull of an incomplete Chilean battleship. Advanced in her day, the *Eagle* was the first British carrier fast enough for fleet operations and the first to employ the offset 'island' superstructure later incorporated into most carrier design. Her battleship hull limited aircraft capacity, but she was well-protected and armed, although too slow and vulnerable for surface engagements by 1939. Additional radar* and light anti-aircraft* guns were fitted to the *Eagle* during a wartime career which began in the Far East, escorting Australian troops to Egypt*. From May 1940 she operated with the Mediterranean* Fleet and, after a spell on patrol in the South Atlantic, joined Force H* at Gibraltar* in January 1942. Regularly employed to ferry aircraft and escort convoys to Malta*, the *Eagle* was torpedoed and sunk by the U-73 on 11 August 1942, during Operation Pedestal*. BRIEF DATA (1939) Displacement: 22,600 tons; Dimensions: o/a lgth – 667' 6", b – 105' 3"; Speed: 24 knots; Armament: 9 × 6" gun, 4 × 4" AA gun, 8 × 2pdr AA gun, 21 aircraft.

Eagle Squadrons Name given to three RAF* fighter squadrons composed of American pilots and operative while the US was still a neutral power. No. 71 Squadron was organized during the Battle of Britain* in 1940, and became active the following February. No. 121 Squadron and No. 133 Squadron were in operation later in 1941. All three Eagle Squadrons fought over Europe and the Mediterranean* in 1941–2

equipped with Supermarine Spitfire* single-seat interceptors, which they also employed as short-range bomber escorts and ground-attack planes. In September 1942, they were transferred to the USAAF*, taking their repainted Spitfires with them, having shot down more than 70 Axis aircraft and lost 100 pilots killed, captured or missing while in RAF service.

Eaker, Lt General Ira C. (1898–?) US Commander of Strategic Air Forces in Europe and a firm advocate of strategic bombing, Eaker's first wartime orders were the establishment of the US Army Bomber Command (the nucleus of the US 8th Air Force) in England, which flew its first raids against marshalling yards outside Rouen in August 1942. Appointed commander of the 8th Air Force in December, Eaker's formations continued to provide proof to critics (notably British Air Marshal Harris* and Churchill*) of the effectiveness of daylight precision bombing. This strategy was sanctioned by the Casablanca Conference* (albeit as a complementary strategy to Harris's night area-bombing* rather than an alternative) and designated the Joint Bombing Offensive, also known as the Eaker Plan. Promoted Lt General in June 1943, he succeeded Air Marshal Tedder* as C-in-C Mediterranean Allied Air Forces in 1944, and in August took command of Allied air forces for the invasion of southern France (see Anvil/Dragoon). See also Strategic Bombing Offensive.

East Africa, Campaigns in, 1940–1 When Italy entered the war in June 1940, her potential for colonial expansion jeopardized British interests in East Africa. Italy's East African empire comprised Eritrea, Italian Somaliland and Abyssinia (Ethiopia) – the latter forcibly annexed in 1936. These territories surrounded the small coastal protectorates on the Gulf of Aden of French and British Somaliland which guarded important Red Sea trade routes (see Map 6). Although the Italian empire was itself hedged in by British forces in the Sudan and Kenya, these were minuscule compared with about 200,000 troops massed under the Duke of Aosta* in Ethiopia. A British blockade ensured that these forces – more than half of them local levies – could not easily be supplied or reinforced, but important trade routes between Britain and the Middle East were clearly threatened at a time when the Mediterranean* had become too dangerous for regular traffic.

After a few tentative border incursions into Kenya and the Sudan, the Italians invaded British Somaliland on 3 August, sending 26 battalions against a British garrison of only 1,500 men. Most of these were evacuated from the main port of Berbera after a five-day delaying action, while Italians also occupied French Somaliland, which was undefended. This marked the end of Italian aggression in East Africa.

During the autumn, the British built up strength in Kenya and the Sudan while they planned the removal of the Italian presence in the Red Sea. An initial advance into northern Ethiopia from the Sudan met with heavy resistance in November and General Wavell*, in overall command of the Middle East, intended to wait until the following spring before attempting a major offensive. By the end of the year 75,000 troops were massed in Kenya – most of them East or South Africans – while 28,000 more were in the Sudan. The presence of such a large force, backed up by accurate military intelligence from Ultra*, brought insistent demands for early action from Churchill* and the South African Prime Minister, Smuts*. Thus in the third week of January two Indian divisions under Lt

General Platt invaded Eritrea from the Sudan, while in the south Lt General Sir Alan Cunningham* entered Italian Somaliland in strength on 14 February.

In Eritrea, Platt met well-organized resistance from 17,000 well-equipped Italians under General Frusci who, after falling back at first, held the key mountain stronghold of Keren for 53 days. British tanks eventually broke through their lines on 27 March, opening the way to the capital Asmara which fell on 1 April. The campaign in Eritrea ended a week later when the Italian naval base at Massawa surrendered after a struggle, enabling the removal of the Italian naval threat from the Red Sea.

By this time the invasion force from Kenya had made remarkable progress. Mogadishu – capital and major port of Italian Somaliland – had fallen within 11 days, yielding a valuable haul of captured fuel. Cunningham then turned inland into Ethiopia, where irregular forces were already successfully promoting tribal resistance (see Wingate). By 17 March, the British had advanced some 400 miles to Jijiga, close to the border with British Somaliland, where a small combined force from Aden had retaken Berbera the previous day. Again turning inland, Cunningham marched on Addis Ababa, the capital, which was entered on 6 April. Although some fierce resistance was met on the way, notably at the provincial capital of Harar, many Italians preferred to surrender to the British rather than face the reported atrocities of the Ethiopian irregulars.

Platt's and Cunningham's armies now converged on the demoralized remnants of Aosta's northern army as they retreated south from Eritrea. With only 7,000 men, few guns and limited supplies, the Duke made his last stand at Amba Alagi in the north west of Ethiopia, surrendering on 17 May. This effectively ended the improvised campaign in East Africa. Three British divisions were promptly rushed to Egypt*; Ethiopian Emperor Haile Selassie – returned from exile by the British – re-entered

Munich, October 1938. British Prime Minister Neville Chamberlain inspecting the SS guard of honour with (left) Adolf Hitler and (right) Joachim von Ribbentrop, German Foreign Minister

May 1940. Fort Eban Emael, Belgium, captured during the German Blitzkrieg in the West. The Germans landed airborne forces on the roof of the fort during the assault

LEFT: *The French crew of a Char B1 tank surrender to German infantry, summer 1940*

BELOW: *Dunkirk, 1940. British troops wade out to the waiting rescue ships during Operation Dynamo, the evacuation of the survivors of the British Expeditionary Force from Europe, 30 May – 4 June*

RIGHT: *Marshal Pétain, President, and Pierre Laval, Prime Minister, of Vichy France*

BELOW: *Adolf Hitler jigs happily before the signing of the Armistice with France, 22 June 1940*

Fighter plane vapour trails over St Paul's, London, during the Battle of Britain, summer 1940

Two of the best-known British and German aircraft of World War II: a British Spitfire, back from action, comes in to land; a German Junkers 87, Stuka dive-bomber releasing its bombs

BELOW: A street in Leningrad during the long and bitter siege. Russian-piloted, British-built Hurricane and Spitfire fighter planes helped repel the repeated German assaults

The Battle for Stalingrad,
1942-3:

ABOVE: *The battle rages in a
tractor factory, floor by floor,
November 1942*

RIGHT: *Von Paulus's encircled
army surrenders to the
Russians, February 1943, and
begins the long march into
captivity*

LEFT: *Soviet tanks in action
during the Battle of Kursk,
July 1943, the greatest tank
battle in history*

RIGHT: *Abandoned transport during the German retreat from Moscow*

LEFT: *A smashed German battery near Minsk, Byelorussia, 1944*

RIGHT: *An artillery barrage to protect advancing Russian troops in Byelorussia, 1944*

ABOVE: *SS executioners pose as they kill Russian villagers*

RIGHT: *The hanging of captured partisans by the Germans was common. The notice on the body reads 'I am a partisan'*

BELOW: *An ammunition ship explodes as a Murmansk supply convoy comes under repeated attack from German aircraft and submarines*

his capital at the head of the irregulars on 5 May and isolated Italian units in the hinterland were cleared during the summer and autumn.

Eastern Front, The *The war between Germany and the Soviet Union, 1941–5* Although the timing of the German invasion of Russia, code-named Barbarossa, achieved complete tactical surprise, the reasons for Hitler's* betrayal of his ally and the preparations for the invasion were not as secretive as they appeared to observers, both inside and outside the Soviet Union, when the invasion was launched on 22 June 1941. The Russo-German Pact*, signed in September 1939, had from the outset been founded less on a desire to establish a peaceful long-term relationship than on the need to quell the mutual suspicions and fears of two neighbouring powers whose ideological prejudices had fostered a deep hostility. Aggravated by the political isolation of both powers, for different reasons, from European diplomacy of the 1920s and 30s (see Introduction), Germany and Russia had come to an alliance as a last resort. It was unlikely that any political arrangements between them would be lasting, based on short-term self-interest – an agreement over territorial sharing that was effectively a division of East European spoils.

In addition to political factors, Hitler's economic designs also militated against the maintenance of an alliance. In *Mein Kampf*, he had made it clear that he viewed the raw materials and resources of the Urals, Siberia and the Ukraine as the fuel of the new Germany's prosperity and expansion.

During 1940, though diplomacy between Germany and Russia continued and reassuring communiqués were issued following Soviet Foreign Minister Molotov's* visit to Berlin, culminating in the signing of a new treaty on 10 January 1941, Hitler grew increasingly suspicious of Russian moves into the Baltic* states and Rumania*. While it was becoming clear that Britain 'did not know that it was beaten', and that Germany's Western Front could not be abandoned, it appears that Hitler now preferred to turn his attention to the solution of the Eastern Front as an alternative to pressing for a military victory over Britain. Thus as early as the summer of 1940, plans were being made for the defensive reinforcement of the Eastern Front. By September, the objectives had become offensive: the destruction of the armies in western Russia, and then an advance into the Soviet Union deep enough to secure Germany against the risk of air attack (to the Archangel–Volga line).

On 3 February 1941, Hitler approved the final text of the attack plan, Barbarossa, which had been initiated by Deputy Chief of Staff General Paulus*, and developed by Halder*. The plan called for a short war to 'crush Soviet Russia in a quick campaign before the end of the war against England. The mass of the Russian Army in western Russia is to be destroyed in daring operations by driving four deep wedges with tanks*, and the retreat of the enemy's battle-ready forces into the wide spaces of Russia is to be prevented.' As with Poland* and France*, Blitzkrieg* tactics would spearhead the attack (though the tank* drives were now conceived on a vastly extended front some 1,800 miles long, from the Arctic Ocean to the Caucasus), achieving the swift elimination of the Red Army* in giant encirclements, before the onset of winter. An economic plan, Plan Oldenburg, for the exploitation of conquered Soviet territory, spelled out the implications of commitment to a long war: 'The war can only be continued if all armed forces are fed by Russia in the third year . . . there is no doubt that many millions of people will starve to death in Russia if we take out of the country the things necessary for us.'

Despite the warning explicit in Plan Oldenburg of the dangers involved in failure to achieve a swift victory, Hitler's decisions during March and April to commit Germany to war in Greece and Yugoslavia (see Balkans) forced him to postpone the invasion of Russia from mid-May to late June – this was to have a significant effect on the German forces' chances of achieving their objectives before the onset of winter.

Nevertheless on 6 June 1941, General Keitel* issued the detailed schedule for Barbarossa. The German forces were organized into three Army Groups comprising 117 infantry divisions (12 motorized), 17 Panzer divisions and nine lines-of-communications divisions supported by over 3,000 aircraft. Estimates of Soviet strength by German military intelligence placed great emphasis on the superiority of German equipment against the numerical Russian advantage in tanks and rough parity in infantry. Though all the German leaders agreed that the war hinged on the use of the panzer groups, acting independently ahead of the infantry, Hitler was finally dissuaded by orthodox arguments from adopting the strategy proposed by Guderian*, who called for the deep penetration of Russia by the armoured divisions before wheeling at the Dnieper*. Instead, though the panzer corps remained at the spearhead, they were to be used in closer co-operation with the infantry in battles of the classic encirclement pattern, to net the Soviet forces before the Dnieper could be reached.

Despite the repeated warnings from Britain, whose intelligence had intercepted information of Hitler's intentions, and the evidence of the Soviet press and radio at the time, which made references to precautionary measures and German troop movements from April onwards, Stalin* and the Russian forces on their western front appeared to have been totally surprised when, early on 22 June, Barbarossa launched three great parallel offensives into Soviet-held territory (see Map 27). Although Russia could immediately deploy 158 divisions organized into 'Fronts'*, to meet the attack, along with 54 tank brigades (comprising 200 tanks) and had enormous potential to mobilize reinforcements (300 new divisions were mobilized within six months of invasion), Germany's overweaning power, commanding the resources of 15 European countries, at first appeared formidable enough to achieve its objective.

Barbarossa Preliminary strikes on Soviet air bases devastated the Red Air Force's* fighting strength. Nearly 3,000 Soviet aircraft were lost in the first ten days of fighting. Army Group North under Field Marshal Leeb* crossed the East Prussian* frontier into Russian-occupied Lithuania*, with Leningrad* as its objective. Army Group Centre commanded by Field Marshal Bock*, began a huge advance against the bulging Russian front in northern Poland, to be followed up with a drive along the Minsk–Smolensk* axis towards Moscow. Army Group South, under General Rundstedt* had the Ukraine and Kiev as its objective.

In accordance with the plan's primary objective to smash the Red Army's* resistance, German armoured divisions pierced the Russian lines, cut lines of communication and trapped large bodies of Russian troops in pincer movements which brought massive gains for the North and Centre Army Groups. Leningrad was under attack by German forces within four days of the start of the campaign, and though it did not fall, was invested by 8 September, by which time the rest of the Baltic (Latvia* and Estonia*) had been cleared. In the centre of the front, a 360-mile advance had brought Bock's Army beyond Smolensk by 7 August, with 850,000 Russians under Timoshenko* captured, though the tenacity of the Soviet Army in defence was clearly demonstrated in the two-month battle for its capture. In the south, the concentration of Russian forces behind better-prepared defences under General Budenny* held up the German advance under Rundstedt and Kleist* for two months. The final capture and casualty toll of one and a half million Soviet troops at Kiev* and Uman in the Ukraine*, however, representing half the active strength of the Red Army*, plunged the Soviet military into deep crisis. Meanwhile in the far south, the Crimea* came under attack from General Manstein's* newly formed

11th Army, which successfully sealed off the fortress at Sevastopol. After Kiev, Rundstedt's Army Group South reached the River Don on 15 October to threaten Rostov* and Kharkov*, which fell on 24 October.

The Battle for Moscow But the vast numbers of Soviet deaths and prisoners taken, and the huge territorial gains made by the advancing German armies, belied the real vulnerability of the German positions, now stretching to the limit of their supplies lines and unprepared for the turn in the weather, which was fast transforming the dusty roads to muddy tracks. Nevertheless, on 2 October Hitler launched Operation Typhoon on the central front, for what was expected to be the final drive to Moscow*. In under three weeks the panzer spearheads had again snapped pincers on Soviet pockets at Bryansk and Vyazma, to arrive at Mozhaisk, 40 miles from Moscow, by 20 October. But as the new commander of the Soviet Central Front forces, General Georgi Zhukov*, arrived to organize a new defensive front, the German armies were already losing their advantage. Zhukov's expectation of reinforcements from the Far East, the concentration of most of the surviving Russian warplanes around the city and the certainty of the imminent turn in the weather, rallied the Soviet defence to turn back a German stab at Moscow via Tula on 15 November by Guderian's tank forces and a final attempt on the centre. As Zhukov counterattacked (6 December) and the Red Army launched a counter-offensive to attack Rostov and relieve Leningrad, the German Army Group Centre, though almost in sight of Moscow, could not be reinforced. As temperatures dropped to minus 40 degrees, the invading forces fell back from the Russian capital.

In Berlin, the recriminations were swift and unflinching. By Christmas, Hitler had appointed himself successor to Brauchitsch*, as direct C-in-C of the Army. Between December and January all the Army Group commanders for Barbarossa were removed and 35 generals, including Guderian

and Hopner*, were dismissed. But Hitler's belief in the betrayal of defeatist generals and his supreme self-confidence in his own ability to achieve victory in the east could not fend off the realities of the military situation or the arrival of winter in Russia. In attempting to encircle the Soviet Army, the Germans had been drawn ever deeper into Russia. Though badly mauled, the Soviet armies had not been conclusively beaten. Now with German troops and equipment perishing in large numbers in the bitter cold and atrocious conditions, and supply and communications lines cut or broken down across the vast distances of overrun but not conquered Russian territory, Stavka*, the Soviet High Command, had already seized the opportunity to strike back.

Nevertheless, Hitler planned to continue his conquest of Slav land as *Lebensraum* for the Third Reich. The difficulties were at least now more fully appreciated. Soviet manpower, it was clear, was practically unlimited. Industrially, the Soviet third Five-Year Plan from 1939 had begun to develop resources beyond the Ural mountains. From 1942, Russian production of munitions, tanks and aircraft increased dramatically; by 1943 the Soviets would be producing more tanks and aircraft than Germany. The new Russian tanks had also surprised German commanders in the field, their panzers outgunned and matched by equal or better armour (see T34). Although Soviet aircraft design had been backward, the Ilyushin Il-2* was now converted to a successful Army support ground-attack aircraft and high-performance fighters began reaching units in large numbers. During 1942 American and British aircraft, vehicles and munitions began to reach the Soviet Union in increasing quantity.

Behind the German lines, the Russians had set up partisan groups to harass the enemy. Although these had little effect in 1941, during 1942 partisan activity would keep up to 250,000 second-line troops away from the front. Even so, as the campaigning season of 1942 begun, Berlin still retained the initiative. Repairs were started on the huge power plant at Dnepropetrovsk and supply lines reconstructed to speed the arrival of food and equipment. Huge numbers of conscript Poles and prisoners of war perished when they were put to work building rearward lines of defence, constructed along the Stalin Line* positions and the Bug and Oder rivers. While both sides planned major offensives for the spring, the Russians moved first with an attempt to relieve Leningrad and Sevastopol and recapture Kharkov. Following the failure on each front, which cost the Russians 600 tanks and 250,000 captured troops, the crisis for the Red Army reached a renewed climax.

The German Caucasus Offensive It was in the south that the second major German offensive launched Hitler's *Fall Blaue* operation to drive through the Caucasus* to the Caspian Sea (see Map 28). Objectives of Army Group South under Bock included the Grozny and Maikop oilfields which supplied the Red Army with fuel, but Stalingrad* increasingly became the focus of the offensive, an important industrial and communications centre whose capture obsessed Hitler as operations developed. The strategic importance of Stalingrad, dominating city on the Volga River (route for the northward flow of petroleum from the Caspian Sea), ensured a long and bitter struggle for its control, although it had initially been seen as a secondary objective designed to secure the flank of the Caucasus thrust. The first drive, from Kursk to capture Voronezh* (secured on 5 July), was halted in an attempt to encircle Stalingrad's defenders. Dismissing Bock for the second time, Hitler divided his forces under General Weichs and Field Marshal List*, lengthened the southern front by some 500 miles and ordered drives in the Caucasus to begin on 13 July. Simultaneously, the 11th Army was withdrawn from the south to attack Leningrad. But with only one panzer army under Kleist for the Caucasus drive, little progress could be made. Further

changes to the operational plan at the end of July improved the position of List's Army Group A, which captured Rostov on 23 July and burst across the Don into the Caucasus, capturing Maikop and its oilfields and reaching the Caucasus mountains before the end of August. As the pace of its drive slowed, Army Group B fought to maintain an ever-lengthening front on its northeastern flank, while its main element, the German 6th Army under General Paulus* began its direct attack on the city.

The Battle of Stalingrad The immensely costly partial capture of Stalingrad by General Paulus in November, which had been ferociously resisted by General Chuikov's* 62nd Army contesting every street and building until the city was a devastated ruin, called up a major Russian counter-offensive, begun on 19 November, that was to completely overshadow, in human cost, the price of the initial victory. In what can now be seen as a pivotal battle on the Eastern Front, overall commander Zhukov, in command of four Russian Fronts under Rokossovsky*, Chuikov, Vatutin* and Yeremenko*, launched operation Uranus to retake the city on 19 November. Hitler's order to stand ground, as Russian spearheads joined on the west of the city, trapping 250,000 6th Army troops, consigned the 6th Army to certain annihilation and gravely imperilled the situation of the million troops of the southern armies locked into stalemate in the Caucasus.

An attempt at relief by a hastily constituted force under General Manstein* (Operation Winter Tempest) failed to salvage the situation. On 2 February General Paulus surrendered along with the remnants of 6th Army. The final loss at Stalingrad of 240,000 German troops killed and some 94,000 captured (as well as one Italian, one Hungarian and two Rumanian armies destroyed) could not be compensated by the last minute escape of the German Caucasus armies threatened with entrapment on the southern front (see Azov, Sea of). The decisive defeat at Stalingrad provided the clearest turning point in the war on the Eastern Front.

The Battle of Kursk In the early spring of 1943, despite Manstein's achievement in recapturing Kharkov and Belgorod with his 4th Panzer Army during March, German forces on the vastly extended front looked ill-prepared to reverse the critical loss of initiative. Nevertheless, as summer approached, it was the new German Chief of Staff at OKW, Colonel General Zeitzler*, who proposed a pre-emptive offensive against the Russian salient centred on Kursk*, already threatened from German positions achieved by Manstein in March. Code-named *Zitadelle* (Citadel), the plan projected converging strikes on northern and southern flanks of the salient to achieve a double envelopment. But the quality of General Zhukov's defensive strategy, the lessons already learned by the Russians in fighting Germany, and the extensive intelligence on German intentions available to Stalin, now provided the Soviet High Command with formidable advantages. Redefining strategic objectives in the light of the German build-up around Kursk, the Russian salient was massively reinforced and dug into heavily mined defensive zones swept by anti-tank artillery*. On the eve of Citadel's launch, the total of forces around Kursk amounted to over 2 million men and over 6,000 tanks (see Map 29).

Begun on 5 July, the offensive was quickly brought to an end on the northern flank, where it broke down on Rokossovsky's defences and became vulnerable to counter-attack by Russian armies breaking through north of Orel. In the south on the same day, early gains by German forces pushing deep into the Russian defences culminated in the greatest tank battle of the war. Pulling in reinforcements from Konev's* Steppe Front, Zhukov threw them into the battle without specific orders. On 12 July on the dust-blinded steppe around Prokhorovka more than a thousand tanks of Hoth's 4th Panzer Army and the Russian Fifth Guards Tank Army joined a battle to the finish. The huge losses at Kursk on both sides (of more than 300 panzers and half the Fifth Guards Army) could not easily be made up. As the Russian commanders immediately launched counter-attacks in the north and south, the Germans were utterly unable to staunch the flow of sheer power of the Red Army, now in command of the offensive initiative (see Map 30).

Russian counter-attacks at Orel forced General Model* to withdraw the 11th Army from the Orel salient by 26 July, and Kharkov was yet again recaptured at the beginning of August. Along almost the whole of the Eastern Front, the Russian Fronts rolled forward, breaching the German line at its weak points. In mid-August General Malinovsky's* forces crossed the northern Donets* and Tolbukhin's* Southern Front drove in to threaten an envelopment of the Germany Army Group South, which was saved again by Manstein, against Hitler's orders, by withdrawing behind skilful counter-attacks to the River Dnieper. Through the autumn the Russian drive continued west, recapturing Smolensk on 24 September and Kiev on 6 November. Four days later an advance by the North Caucasian Front destroyed the last German bridgehead in the Caucasus, cutting off the 17th Army.

The year 1943 had ended badly for the German armies. From the beginning, the qualitative improvement in the Red Army was matched by an increase in the supply of *matériel* from beyond the Urals. Tanks, artillery – and particularly rocket* artillery – became increasingly available to Soviet commanders, and problems of mobility were largely overcome by the supply of American trucks. The quality of Soviet leadership had also greatly improved during the year, as younger commanders gained battle experience and took the places of older men killed, captured or purged during the defeats of 1941–2. On the German side, the year's end saw serious shortages of manpower which could not be disguised by fielding divisions at half strength. Nor were these shortages fully compensated for by the supply of the new Tiger* and Panther* tanks to the panzer divisions. However great the qualitative improvement over earlier German tanks, they were still not arriving in sufficient quantity to maintain formations at 1942's fighting strength. Thus while the Red Army was growing, the Wehrmacht was shrinking.

In January 1944, the Russian armies, now renamed to reflect their positions, launched new offensives all along their fronts, including an assault by two Soviet army groups on the German 18th Army besieging Leningrad. The winter offensive in the Ukraine* launched the 1st and 2nd Ukrainian Fronts on a southwestern advance, capturing Zhitomir, Korosten and Korovograd, and encircling 100,000 German troops near Korsun*, before crossing the Bug and Dniester rivers and breaking through into Rumanian territory by 26 March. In the Crimea, Russian forces invested the trapped German troops on 8 April.

The German Retreat More dismissals and replacements from Berlin followed the Russians' success. Southern Army Group commanders Manstein and Kleist were replaced by Model and General Schörner*. Despite the critical new threat posed by the Allied invasion of Normandy*, Hitler continued to order a strategy of no retreat on the Eastern Front. Still able to command a considerable force in the east, with just under 3 million troops, 3,000 tanks and 3,000 aircraft, the dictator ordered a defensive strategy along the thinly spread 1,400 miles of their front, to be based on fortresses and dominating positions. But the size of the Russian forces was much larger again. Still enjoying the advantages of American supply of vehicles and equipment, and able to deploy some six and a half million men and 8,000 tanks with 13,000 supporting aircraft, the Russian High Command launched their summer offensive in 1944 with little doubt about the outcome (see Map 32).

In the north, the Karelian and Leningrad Fronts counter-attacked Army Group North, forcing it back towards the Baltic states. The Finns finally accepted armistice terms on 4 September, when it became clear that German aid was at an end (see Finland). But the major thrust of the offensive came in the centre. In Operation Bagration*, a massive four-front attack punched out north and south of Vitebsk, to Minsk, which was taken on 3 July along with 50,000 German troops, and drove on to the Polish border at Grodno. A complementary Russian drive farther north through Lithuania and Latvia trapped the bulk of Army Group North in a huge Baltic pocket. Despite a check to Rokossovsky's advance east of Warsaw*, the 1st Ukrainian Front forces under Konev captured Lvov and reached the upper Vistula and Baranov by 7 August. While the Polish Home Army rose to claim the liberation of Warsaw and were savagely sacrificed to investing SS troops (see Poland, Russian Campaign in), the focus of the offensive switched back to the Balkans*, where the drive began on 20 August, and ended with the capitulation of Rumania (along with the bulk of the German 6th and 8th Armies), followed in October by the liberation of Belgrade with the help of Yugoslav partisans (see Balkans, Russian Campaign in).

The Fall of East Prussia The fall of Budapest, in February 1945 (see Hungary), became the first major victory of the final Russian offensive launched in January. With the bulk of the effort focused on a drive on the northern front, towards East Prussia*, Silesia and Pomerania, the Russians hoped to achieve penetrations which could be exploited in a drive across Poland to the Oder River (see Map 31).

From the Baltic to the Carpathians, five Russian fronts attacked along a 750-mile stretch of the line, overwhelming the German forces by sheer weight of men and armour (see Map 33). Zhukov reached the Oder at the head of the 1st Belorussian Front on 31 January, having advanced 300 miles in two weeks. In the south, the advance held up by the siege of Budapest was restarted after the failure of a last-ditch

German offensive by the 6th Panzer and 6th Army. Tolbukhin's counter-attack brought to an end the final German offensive of the war. Crossing the Austrian frontier on 20 March, Malinovsky's 2nd Ukrainian Front drove into Vienna on 13 April (see Austria).

The Fall of Berlin The final assault on Berlin*, by three Soviet fronts under Zhukov, Konev and Rokossovsky, was more than a match for the capital's remaining defences. The two and a half million men of the eight Soviet armies broke through to encircle the city by 25 April and fought off the efforts of boys,. old men and the remnants of German forces not retreating . towards the Western Front. On 30 April Russian soldiers entered the Reichstag building. Hitler committed suicide on the same day. On 2 May the Commandant of Berlin surrendered and on 8 May Field Marshal Keitel* signed the document of unconditional surrender, signalling the end of the war in Europe.

Eastern Solomons, Battle of the One of several important naval engagements fought between the Japanese Combined Fleet and the US Pacific Fleet in the disputed waters around Guadalcanal* during the summer of 1942. As part of a series of planned counterstrokes in response to the America landing on Guadalcanal, Admiral Yamamoto*'s Operation Ka-Go was designed to reinforce the island with 1,500 men transported in old destroyers and escorted by a Japanese force under Rear Admiral Tanaka*. This included a strike force based on the carriers *Zuikaku* and *Shokaku** under Rear Admiral Abe and an advance force of six cruisers under the overall tactical command of Vice Admiral Kondo*. The operation envisaged attacks on Guadalcanal by land-based bombers, while the naval strike force covered the troop landings.

In response to traffic analysis and an intelligence summary which suggested the presence of a large Japanese carrier group, US C-in-C Admiral Nimitz* ordered Vice Admiral Ghormley* to concentrate his South Pacific force off the Solomons, while Admiral Fletcher* was ordered to send his Task Force 61 (with three carriers) into the waters east of the Solomon chain. On the morning of 23 August, the Japanese transports were sighted and air strikes launched from the carriers, though a change of course under cover of bad weather made the strike fruitless. The two forces finally made contact on 24 August with a sighting of the light carrier *Ryujo**, which was attacked and sunk by aircraft from the *Enterprise** and *Saratoga** (the third carrier *Wasp** had been sent south to refuel). Meanwhile planes from the two Japanese carriers made a series of strikes on the US carriers. Under heavy attack from US fighters, the Japanese managed to hit but not destroy the *Enterprise*. On the morning of 25 August, Yamamoto called off Operation Ka-Go and the Combined Fleet was ordered back to its anchorage at Truk*, with few losses but having failed to achieve its objective. The Japanese transport force retired to the Shortland Islands where the troops were transferred to destroyers for the 'Tokyo Express'* run three nights later. Sometimes called the Battle of the Stewart Islands, this engagement is known by the Japanese as the Second Naval Battle of the Solomons.

East Prussia, Fall of, 1945 By the summer of 1944, Soviet forces under Chernyakhovsky* were already in position to threaten German positions on their own frontiers in East Prussia. The launch of the first offensive against East Prussia in mid-October, however, was inconclusive and was not restarted until 12 January 1945, by which time it had become one of a series of objectives of a northern flanking drive focused on an advance across Poland towards the Oder River, and Berlin (see Poland, Russian Campaign in). A rapid advance by the 1st Belorussian Front* under Rokossovsky*, spearheaded by a large armoured force, made contact with Marshal Zhukov's* forces on 22 January. Turning together to wheel north towards Danzig*, the Russians aimed to cut off East Prussia and entrap 500,000 men of Army Group North. Although a large number of Germans were successfully evacuated (and a total of one and a half million refugees were rescued by the German Navy before the fall of Danzig) East Prussia was now pressed from Rokossovsky's forces in the south, and by the 3rd Belorussian Front under Chernyakhovsky in the east. Following the surrender of Braunsberg and Danzig on 20 March and Königsberg* on 9 April, resistance effectively came to an end in East Prussia. See Map 31; Eastern Front.

Eben Emael, Capture of Most modern fortress in Belgium and the dominating position on the Albert Canal defence line, it was held by the Belgian Army against the German advance through Flanders in May 1940 (see Western Offensive). The fortress was attacked in a daring and innovative German airborne* operation mounted by a specially trained assault group of 1st Parachute Regiment, carried in ten gliders which crash-landed on and around the fort. It was seized and held by the group commander, Lt Witzig, for 24 hours before its relief by the 61st Infantry Division.

E-boat See Motor Torpedo Boats.

Eden, Anthony (1897–1977) British Foreign Minister in Churchill's War Cabinet, he had also served in the post under Neville Chamberlain*, 1935–8. Eden had earned an international reputation as Minister of League of Nations Affairs, when he championed Ethiopia's cause against Italy in 1935 and later as Foreign Minister, when he worked, increasingly against the flow of appeasement* of the European Fascist dictators, to promote closer international relations, particularly with the Soviet Union. During the war, Eden distinguished himself on numerous missions and at many of the Allied wartime conferences*. After the war, he was actively involved in the establishment of the United Nations,

served again as Foreign Minister under Churchill in the early 1950s and became Prime Minister himself in 1955. He retired after the Suez crisis in 1956.

Egypt, Campaign for, 1940–1 Confrontation provoked by Mussolini's* opportunistic colonial expansionism in North Africa and British determination to protect her vital Middle Eastern supply routes. Italy's declaration of war in June 1940 was followed by a build-up of Italian troops in Libya, threatening Suez and the Nile Delta across 300 miles of the Western Desert. The Italian 10th Army under Marshal Graziani* in Libya had 250,000 Italian and colonial troops, compared to less than 100,000 British Imperial troops in General Wavell's* Middle East command, which had responsibilities from Palestine to the Sudan. Only 36,000 men guarded Egypt. With reinforcements forced to take the long detour round the Cape of Good Hope and in short supply after Dunkirk*, Wavell could only mount a few cross-border harrying operations from his forward base at Mersa Matruh*, 120 miles from the frontier, and await the Italian invasion, which began on 13 September.

After advancing about 50 miles under an air umbrella, the Italian Army stopped at Sidi Barrani and built a chain of fortified camps, which were too far apart to be mutually supporting. They remained there until December when Wavell (who had been reinforced in the interim) launched Operation Compass, a large-scale raid on the rear of the positions under the executive command of Lt General O'Connor*, whose 30,000 men faced 80,000 Italian troops on the Sidi Barrani line. Nevertheless, O'Connor's qualitative and quantitative superiority in tanks, particularly the heavily armoured Matildas*, played an important part in overrunning the Italian positions on 10–11 December. The invasion army then retreated across the frontier to the coastal fortress of Bardia, which was quickly isolated by advanced British armoured units.

Exploitation of this surprising victory was

hindered by the immediate withdrawal of part of O'Connor's force to the Sudan on Wavell's order, while potential reinforcements were held in Cairo as Churchill contemplated intervention in Greece. Nevertheless Bardia fell on 6 January and Tobruk* followed just over two weeks later. O'Connor was given permission to push on for Benghazi*, but soon realized that Graziani had decided to forego its defence and was heading for the El Agheila bottleneck on the Tripolitanian border. While the 6th Australian Division gave chase along the coast road, the somewhat depleted 7th Armoured Division (the Desert Rats*) struck across the desert to block the retreat. On 5 February, after travelling at great speed, elements of 7th Armoured Division arrived at Beda Fomm, just in time to block the Italian withdrawal south from Benghazi. Italian tanks were trapped between skilfully concealed fire positions and by the morning of 7 February the entire army had surrendered. In total, the British offensive had captured 130,000 troops, 845 guns and 380 tanks, while their own losses amounted to less than 2,000 men.

The way was now open for the British to take Tripoli, the last Italian stronghold in North Africa, but on 12 February Churchill instructed Wavell to prepare the largest possible force for Greece, leaving only a small army to defend the conquests in Cyrenaica. On the same day, Rommel flew to Tripoli ahead of German armoured reinforcements for the failing Italians. The opportunity for the British to bring the North African campaign to a speedy end was missed. Emboldened by his opponents' inactivity in Cyrenaica, Rommel went onto the offensive as soon as a few tanks arrived, shattering the illusion of decisive victory over the Italians (see Desert War; Map 7).

Eiche (Oak) Code-name for the German rescue of Mussolini* from the Abruzzi mountains by Otto Skorzeny and a team of German Luftwaffe parachute troops. Deposed and confined by the new Italian government under Marshal Badoglio*, Mussolini was being held at a hotel in Gran Sasso when the snatch squad landed, surprised the guarding *carabinieri* and flew him to safety in a light Fieseler Storch* aircraft.

Eichelberger, General Robert Lawrence (1886–1961) Popular American commander who led many successful operations in the Pacific*. Superintendent of West Point Military Academy at the time of Pearl Harbor*, he was appointed commanding general of the 77th Infantry Division in January 1942, and then commander of 1st Corps, whose staff he took to MacArthur's* Southwest Pacific Area command in Australia in August of that year with orders to turn back the Japanese Papuan offensive. Eichelberg was the only senior US land commander in the Pacific able to maintain good relationships with his Australian colleagues, in sharp contrast to MacArthur. In December Eichelberger was sent to the Buna* front in Papua (see New Guinea) to revitalize the stalled offensive, winning the first small but important victory against Japanese ground forces there before he took the US 1st Corps on through New Guinea to the Huon peninsula and then to the US landings at Hollandia* in April 1944. Operating as the Operation Reckless Task Force, 1st Corps began a lightning campaign from Hollandia which secured a major base site for the support of subsequent Allied operations.

Commander of the newly formed 8th Army from September 1944, Eichelberger was responsible for all US forces in Dutch New Guinea, for the mounting of independent operations in the southern Philippines* and for clearing-up operations on Leyte* and later Luzon*. After fighting in the Philippines ceased, Eichelberger and his command supervised the surrender of over 50,000 Japanese troops from northern Luzon alone. After the Japanese surrender, Eichelberger commanded the first occupation forces in Japan and retired in 1948 as overall commander of Allied ground forces in the Japanese home islands.

Eichmann, Lt Colonel Adolf (1906–62) An SS* officer, head of the 'Jewish Evacuation Department' of the Gestapo*, he planned and oversaw the mass murders of millions of Jews. In 1941, as a Gestapo department head, Eichmann received Himmler's* direct order for *Aktion 14F13*, the killing of Jews in the wake of an attack on Russia. It was Eichmann who summoned the Wannsee Conference* (through his superior, Heydrich*) in January 1942 with the object of systematizing the arrest, transportation and extermination of the Jews. He subsequently travelled throughout Europe to see it carried out. In February 1945, Eichmann vanished from Prague*. He escaped Europe with a Vatican passport in the name of 'Ricardo Klement'. In 1961 Israeli agents tracked him down in Argentina and kidnapped him. He reappeared on trial in Israel, where he was condemned to death and hanged.

Eicke, Theodor (1892–1943) Inventor of the concentration camp* system. Commandant of the newly built camp at Dachau* from June 1933 and Inspector of Concentration Camps from 1934, he commanded the Waffen SS* Totenkopf (Death's Head) Division for the invasion of Poland* in 1939. He was shot down while on a reconnaissance south of Kharkhov* in February 1943.

Eighty-eight One of the most feared guns of the war, the German 88mm high-velocity gun was originally a heavy anti-aircraft* weapon used for static defence. It achieved its reputation after a few were converted as anti-tank* guns and used by Rommel* in the Desert War* during 1941. Its long range and high-velocity, armour-piercing shell combined to give the 88 a long-range destructive power beyond the tolerance of any tank* in the world at the time. Its combat disadvantages were its weight and lack of mobility, along with a high profile that made it a good target for hostile artillery. Specialist anti-tank versions of the gun were produced later in the war which lowered its silhouette. Eighty-eights were never available in great numbers to German forces in Africa, but they nevertheless remained a major threat to Allied armoured forces until the Axis surrender in Tunisia* of May 1943 (see e.g. Battleaxe). On the Eastern Front* and in Europe they were eventually outmatched by Allied tanks and artillery*, particularly the vast array of big guns deployed by Soviet forces.

Einsatzgruppen SS* Special Action Groups. First organized by Himmler* and Heydrich* in 1939 to follow the German armies in Poland*, murdering national leaders and rounding up Jews. When Germany invaded Russia in 1941 (see Eastern Front), the Einsatzgruppen had orders to exterminate all Jews and Soviet political commissars. Huge numbers of people were called together for 'resettlement', transported to a place of execution and shot. In Russia the Einsatzgruppen were divided into four 3,000-man units, with a mission to 'ensure the security of their respective operational zones'. This included preventing resistance from civilians. Gas vans were also used from the end of 1942 for the killing of women and children. Apparently Himmler's sensitivity to watching women shot (as he did at Minsk in 1942 when he ordered a demonstration of the method) provoked the change of tactic. Exact figures of civilians killed are not available, but SS statistician Dr Korherr informed Himmler on 23 March 1943 that 633,000 Jews in Russia had been 'resettled' – the Einsatz groups' term for extermination. Between 1944 and 1945, 100,000 more were murdered. There are no separate figures for numbers of Soviet communists killed.

Eisenhower, General Dwight David (1890–1969) General of the Army and 34th President of the United States and Supreme Allied Commander of the Allied Expeditionary Force in Western Europe from December 1943. A lieutenant colonel during WW1 in which he did not see combat,

Eisenhower had transferred from infantry to tank corps before attending the General Staff School at Fort Leavenworth, from which he graduated first class in 1926. Following a varied and distinguished service in the US and abroad, he attracted the patronage of first MacArthur* and later George Marshall*. He was promoted brigadier general in 1941 and brought to Washington by Marshall immediately after the attack on Pearl Harbor* to head the War Plans Division. Committed to the idea of the soonest possible cross-Channel attack as the most direct route to Germany, rather than spread thinly the limited US resources available at the time, Eisenhower drew up the blueprint for an invasion of Northwest Europe (code-named Roundup) and was sent with Mark Clark* to London to discuss the build-up and future operations. His success with Churchill and other senior officials resulted in his appointment to command US forces in the European Theatre of Operations (ETOUSA) in June 1942.

Already reaping the benefits of the enormous personal charm which was to make him a supreme service diplomat, Eisenhower became the logical choice for promotion to Allied C-in-C for the North African Torch* landings when Roosevelt acceded to Churchill's plan for an invasion of French Northwest Africa as an alternative to a cross-Channel invasion in 1942 (see Conferences). In the Allied Force Headquarters, formed to direct operations, Eisenhower put together an innovative integrated staff, with a British and American officer jointly filling each staff position. Eisenhower's insistence on an Allied approach which dispensed with national interests and outlooks reduced friction to a minimum and produced a highly effective headquarters team.

Nevertheless the political implications of his North African command, specifically *vis à vis* the considerable French colonial forces scattered through the region, could not be so straightforwardly resolved. From 9 November, when the crisis with French forces erupted into fighting around Oran,

until Christmas 1942, when the assassination of Marshall Pétain's deputy, Admiral Darlan*, brought an end to the controversy, Eisenhower faced widespread public criticism in the US and Britain for his involvement (via his representative Mark Clark) with Darlan over French co-operation with the Allied invasion force.

Although the subsequent Allied operations in Tunisia* were fought in the face of considerable disadvantages, Eisenhower's contribution at supreme command level, was an important element in the eventual victories against the Axis* that brought the North African campaign to an end. By this time, however, Eisenhower was already planning for the invasion of Sicily*, agreed by the Allies as a next major strategic step, though not without prolonged controversy (see Conferences).

Eisenhower remained in supreme command of Allied forces in the Mediterranean for the successful completion of the Sicilian campaign and the first phase of the campaign in Italy*, before returning to Washington in January 1944 to discuss the preparations for Operation Overlord, the projected invasion of Normandy* agreed by the Allies in late 1943. Appointed Supreme Allied Commander of the Allied Expeditionary Force in Western Europe, Eisenhower went to London, where he established a headquarters (SHAEF) to oversee and direct the planning, preparation and launch of the D-Day* invasion.

It was in this command that Eisenhower's diplomatic skills were most severely tested, as he attempted to weave the heterogeneous mix of troops and commanders, as well as the complex political elements, into a war-winning operational entity. Even after the successful consolidation of the landings and initial advance into France, Eisenhower displayed remarkable diplomatic as well as strategic skill in maintaining the momentum and achieving the final success of the Allied advance into Germany (see Northwest Europe, Invasion of).

A uniquely respected general and popular hero, Eisenhower was perhaps at his most effective in the face of defeat. At both the Kasserine* Pass and the Battle of the Bulge*, he acted with speed and determination more than sufficient to refute the charges against him that consensus was always his sole aim. After the war he headed the occupation forces until December, when he was appointed Army Chief of Staff and Supreme Commander of the NATO Powers. He was elected President of the United States in 1952 and 1956.

Electronic Countermeasures (ECM) The development of radar* was accompanied by research into ways of jamming or confusing it. Electronic Countermeasures were employed to mask bombing operations, particularly over Germany, and were also used by U-boats to defeat Allied search radar. The first and simplest form of ECM was Window – used originally by the RAF*, but also known in Germany. This consisted of small strips of metal, cut to a particular length for each wavelength and dropped from aircraft to produce an incomprehensible excess of readings on a ground radar screen. This was used by the British from mid-1943, but was not enough on its own. Defenders could simply alter their wavelength, or else night-fighters could wait on patrol and use airborne radar to report genuine bomber positions.

The Allies responded to this by using transmitters to jam defenders' air-to-ground communications. A transmitter which could confuse early warning radar – the Mandrel system – was introduced in time to screen the Normandy* landings of 1944. This could be used from ground stations or from specially equipped B-17* or Short Stirling* bombers, and in conjunction with Window it protected the latter stages of the Allied Strategic Bombing Offensive* over Germany. Less successful was an advanced detection system employed on fast de Havilland Mosquito* light bombers to track down night-fighters. This could not detect the Luftwaffe's latest radar and served only to advertise the position of its user. The primitive nature of Japanese radar defences

meant that ECM were rarely used for Pacific bombing missions, although some Window was dropped.

Search radar played an important role in Allied anti-submarine* warfare, and by late 1942 most U-boats carried Metox receivers which could detect the use of airborne radar from about 30 miles. Metox was outmoded by the widespread introduction of centimetric radar sets to Allied maritime aircraft during 1943. Although the German Navy* developed the Natox-U receiver at the end of the year, which could detect 10cm radar, it was in service too late to prevent heavy U-boat losses to Allied aircraft.

Embry, Air Chief Marshal Sir Basil (1902 –77) Outstanding RAF* bomber pilot and commander of a bomber squadron during the campaign in Norway* and during the German Western Offensive*, for which he received two awards. Shot down in May 1940 over St Omer, Embry escaped at the third attempt and returned in time to serve with night-fighters during the Battle of Britain*. Promoted to command No. 2 Bomber Group (2nd Tactical Air Force) in June 1943, he continued to fly operational missions, including three spectacular precision bombing raids on Gestapo* offices at Aarhus, Copenhagen and Odense. After the war he rose to become C-in-C Allied Forces, Central Europe.

Enfidaville See Tunisia, Campaign in.

England, USS US Navy* *Buckley* Class destroyer escort* commissioned in 1943 and assigned to the Pacific. The *England* became famous when she sank five Japanese submarines in six days during May 1944, and assisted in the sinking of a sixth five days later. The following May she was badly damaged by a Kamikaze* attack off Okinawa* and returned to the United States for repairs.
BRIEF DATA (1943) Displacement: 1,400 tons; Dimensions: o/a lgth – 306', b – 37'; Speed: 23.5 knots; Armament: 3 × 3" gun, 6 × 40mm AA gun, 3 × 21" TT.

Enigma An enciphering machine for radio transmissions invented in the early 1920s and employed commercially in Germany before being adapted for military purposes later in the decade. The machine was copied by Polish cryptanalysts and provided the key to the most important intelligence coup of the war. See Ultra.

Eniwetok See Marshall Islands.

ENSA Entertainments National Service Association. Originally an off-shoot of the British NAAFI, ENSA was formed in September 1939 to provide entertainments for British forces at home and abroad, with Seymour Hicks as Controller and Basil Dean as Director of Entertainments. It was initially privately funded, but was subsidized by the British government after 1942. It gave over two and a half million performances during its existence, at nominal charge, to 300 million military and industrial personnel. Popularly known among British troops as 'Every Night Something Awful', ENSA was disbanded in August 1946.

Enterprise, USS Launched in 1936, as the second ship of the *Yorktown** Class, the *Enterprise* was perhaps the most famous American fighting ship of WW2. Although absent from Pearl Harbor* when the Japanese attacked, some of her aircraft arrived in time to participate in the defence of the base, and she went on to survive almost every major action of the Pacific War*. She was badly damaged by bombs during the Battle of the Eastern Solomons* on 24 August 1942, and again upon her return to action at Santa Cruz* three months later. Although in need of major repairs, she was forced to remain in action for the Guadalcanal* campaign in November, as she was by then the only US Navy* carrier left in the Pacific. From late 1943 she began operations with the carrier task forces and was in the vanguard of the 'island' offensives until April 1945, when she was hit by two Kamikaze* attacks in

three days off Okinawa*. Returned to the US for repairs, she saw no further action and was retired at the end of the war. Sole survivor of her class, she received modern radar* and additional light anti-aircraft* installations during the war.
BRIEF DATA See Yorktown, USS.

Eritrea See East Africa, Campaign in.

Escort Carrier Escort carriers were conceived as a way of providing Allied convoys* with air cover outside the range of shore-based aircraft. The British had considered building aircraft carriers suitable only for trade protection in the late 1930s but, regarding surface raiders as a greater potential threat than air or submarine* attacks, preferred to spend their limited funds on fleet carriers. However, by mid-1940, with German forces in possession of Atlantic bases and Royal Navy* resources desperately stretched, emergency measures were needed to stem the mass slaughter of British merchant shipping by U-boats.

As an interim defence against the Luftwaffe's* long-range Focke-Wulf Fw200* reconnaissance aircraft, much feared as the 'eyes' of the U-boats, Fighter Catapult Ships (FCS) and Catapult Armed Merchantmen (CAM) were introduced. These were fitted with a single fighter aircraft and a catapult but had no flight deck, forcing pilots to ditch in the sea after each mission. The five auxiliaries converted as Fighter Catapult Ships were manned by naval crews with naval aircraft, while the merchantmen were allocated 50 Hawker Hurricane* fighters with specially trained RAF* crews. In spite of heavy losses and the inevitable waste of aircraft, these remained in service until 1943 when large numbers of decked escort carriers became available.

The prototype escort carrier was HMS *Audacity*, a simple conversion of the captured German liner *Hannover*. Her superstructure was replaced by a single wooden flight deck, which carried six Grumman Martlet* naval fighters. Commissioned in

September 1941, she was sunk by a U-boat three months later, but in that time amply proved her worth in convoy battles with submarine 'wolfpacks'*. Plans had by then already been made for five further conversions, while another six were ordered from the United States under Lend-Lease*.

Well informed of British developments, the US Navy* had completed its first conversion, the *Long Island*, even before the *Audacity*, and hulls had already been requisitioned which could be converted to fill the bulk of the Royal Navy's initial order. The sixth unit (HMS *Tracker*) was purpose-built on an incomplete hull to a much improved design and became the lead ship for a class of 20 more ships, equally divided between the US Navy (*Bogue* Class) and the Royal Navy. Equipped to carry both fighter and anti-submarine aircraft, these were of broader operational value than the early conversions and, once convinced of their importance, the United States embarked on a high-priority mass-construction programme which produced 118 escort carriers before production was halted in late 1945. All but the four *Sangammon* Class units (which were converted oilers) were purpose-built and all were similar in aircraft capacity and performance. By far the largest single type was the *Casablanca* Class of which 50 were completed at a phenomenal rate. The first of the class entered service on 8 July 1943 and had been completed in eight months. The final unit was commissioned on the same day the following year and had been built in 14 weeks. Displacing 7,800 tons, they were armed primarily with light anti-aircraft* weapons and could carry 28 aircraft at up to 19 knots. Output slowed with the more refined *Commencement Bay* Class (24 built) as US production priorities switched to more offensively geared *matériel* in 1944.

Thirty-three US-built escort carriers were lent to the Royal Navy who, beset by production shortages, built very few of their own. Those they did build were conversions, mostly on the hulls of refrigerator ships. Larger than their American counterparts, they were more stable at sea but carried fewer aircraft in an enclosed hangar. None of the escort carriers ordered in 1941 were in Royal Navy service before mid-1942, and as they were then employed in support of the Torch* landings in Northwest Africa, a further stop-gap was introduced by the British, the Merchant Aircraft Carrier (MAC). Nineteen grain ships and oil tankers were converted as MACs, their cargo capacity largely unimpaired by the shipping of four anti-submarine aircraft and the decking-over of the superstructure.

Dismissed before the war as a single-purpose weapon, the escort carrier performed valuably in most naval theatres and was also used both as an aircraft transporter and with fleets in offensive operations. However, its major contribution to the Allied war effort remained the fulfilment of its original purpose, the winning of the Battle of the Atlantic. In this its effectiveness was much enhanced by the use of increasingly sophisticated radar*, without which offensive operations against U-boats would have required hundreds more surface ships. The deployment of escort carriers as the basis of convoy protection support groups from the spring of 1943 was a vitally important factor in decisively curtailing the submarine threat to Allied merchant shipping. See Anti-submarine Warfare; Atlantic, Battle of the.

Essex, USS Commissioned into the US Navy in 1943, the *Essex* was the name ship of the most numerous class of fleet aircraft carriers ever built. Unrestricted by naval treaties, they were improved and enlarged versions of the *Yorktown*• Class and retained an open-sided hangar and flight deck design in spite of contemporary British developments (see Illustrious, HMS). Although purpose-built for capacity, they carried no more aircraft than their predecessors but could cope with bigger and heavier types. They had increased anti-aircraft defences and their hulls were well compartmentalized, which greatly aided their survival when hit.

Ten units were ordered in 1940 and a further 16 (of which 14 were eventually built) between the end of 1941 and 1943. The second group were of a slightly modified 'long hull' design, with a fuller bow to restrict weather damage making room for an extra four 40mm guns. Four of these were ready in time to see combat.

The class formed the heart of the fast carrier task forces in the Pacific, beginning with operations against the Gilbert Islands* in November 1943, in which *Essex* and three of her sisters took part. In general they proved remarkably difficult to sink, and not a single unit was lost in combat, although they accumulated a gruesome catalogue of war wounds.
BRIEF DATA (1943) Displacement: 27,100 tons; Dimensions: o/a lgth – 876', b – 93' (147' 6" FD); Speed: 33 knots; Armament: 12 × 5" AA gun, 68 × 40mm AA gun, 52 × 20mm AA gun, 80 aircraft.

Estonia One of three independent republics (see Latvia and Lithuania) on the Baltic Sea that were delimited under the Versailles Treaty after WW1. Historically a 'buffer territory' between the Polish and Russian empires, Estonia was pledged to the Soviet sphere of influence by a secret protocol of the Russo-German Pact* in 1939. After the partition of Poland by Germany and Russia under the terms of the Soviet-German Boundary and Friendship Treaty, Stalin* acted quickly to conclude 'mutual assistance' pacts and garrison key positions in all three buffer states, aiming to secure his flank against potential incursions of his new and uncertain ally before turning his attention to Finland (see Russo-Finnish War).

Early in June 1940, Russia occupied Estonia by force. Compelled to accept a new government under Andrei Zhanov and vote in a 'free election' for incorporation in the USSR, Estonians also suffered large-scale executions and deportations initiated by Stalin. In June 1941, the German invasion

of Russia placed Estonia in the path of the advancing Army Group North whose objective was Leningrad*, and the republic was overrun by the end of August. Estonia remained under a heavily repressive German occupation until 1944 when Govorov's Leningrad Front* forces moved back through Estonia, retaking the capital Tallinn in September. See also Eastern Front.

Ethiopia See East Africa, Campaign in.

Evacuation of Japanese-Americans Demands for action against the *Nisei*, Americans born to Japanese immigrants, mounted sharply following the Japanese attack on Pearl Harbor* in December 1941. Military fears about fifth columnists, evidence from Magic* intercepts during 1941 which indicated the establishment of espionage organizations, and the panic of the civilian population on the West Coast (as well as the pressure exerted by self-interest groups in a position to profit from the property losses of 'JAs') were factors in President Roosevelt's decision to sign Executive Order 9006 on 19 February 1942. The emergency legislation allowed the Secretary of War to exile any or all persons from sensitive military areas. Though couched in these broad terms, the order enabled the military to force 116,000 Japanese-Americans to leave their homes and be interned in ten specially built 'camps', under the supervision of the War Relocation Authority. Forced to live an austere captive existence which directly denied their constitutional rights, the plight of the Japanese-Americans was eventually championed by General George Marshall*, who initiated programs of recruitment and employment from the beginning of 1943 that went some way to compensate for the undeniable constitutional injustice they had suffered. Compensation to evacuees after the end of the war was generally slow and often inadequate. Though investigations into the camps' internees uncovered the presence of a core of 'disloyal JAs' among the *Kibei* (those born in America but educated in Japan), no satisfactory justification of American conduct in this matter has since been argued. Later in the war, a Japanese-American infantry regiment fought with distinction in Italy.

Exeter, HMS See York, HMS.

F

Fairey Albacore Designed as the British Fleet Air Arm's* successor to the Fairey Swordfish* torpedo-bomber, the biplane Albacore was slightly faster and much more comfortable than the famous 'Stringbag', yet never fully replaced it. Entering service in 1940, it was used from shore bases for a year before operating from carriers at the battle of Cape Matapan*. From then until its withdrawal in 1943, it flew anti-submarine* missions over the Mediterranean*, the Atlantic* and the Indian Ocean. A total of 800 Albacores were manufactured.

BRIEF DATA (Mk I) Type: 3-man naval torpedo-bomber; Engine: 1 × 1,065hp Bristol Taurus; Max speed: 161mph; Ceiling: 20,700'; Range: 930m (max); Arms: 3 × 0.303" mg; Bomb load: 2,000lb or 1 × 1,610lb torpedo*.

Fairey Barracuda High-wing monoplane light bomber intended by the British Fleet Air Arm* as a replacement for the Fairey Albacore* and Fairey Swordfish* biplanes, but delayed by engine failures until 1942. The Barracuda operated both from shore bases and carriers, seeing action in the Far East and Norway*, most notably in a carrier attack on the German battleship *Tirpitz** in Altenfjord on 3 April 1944. The final wartime version, the Mark III, was equipped for radar* reconnaissance, and the Barracuda could carry a variety of additional equipment – including personnel pods for inserting agents into German-occupied Europe – under its wings.

BRIEF DATA (Mk II) Type: 3-man torpedo and dive-bomber; Engine: 1 × 1,640hp Rolls Royce Merlin; Max speed: 228mph; Ceiling: 16,600'; Range: 524m; Arms: 2 × 0.303" mg; Bomb load: 1,800lb or 1 × 1,670lb torpedo*.

Fairey Battle The monoplane Battle typified the pre-war weakness of the RAF* in ground-support aircraft. It entered service in May 1937, and although far superior to the biplanes it replaced, proved much too slow and lightly armed to survive in combat. In all, 2,815 Battles were built before production was halted in December 1940, after heavy losses in unescorted daylight raids during the German Western Offensive* in May and June. Surviving aircraft ended their days scattered throughout the British Empire and Commonwealth as trainers and target tugs.

BRIEF DATA (Mk I) Type: 3-man light bomber; Engine: 1 × 1,030hp Rolls Royce Merlin; Max speed: 241mph; Ceiling: 23,500'; Range: 1,050m; Arms: 2 × 0.303" mg; Bomb load: 1,100lb.

Fairey Firefly Carrier aircraft designed to replace the essentially stop-gap Fairey Fulmar* with the British Fleet Air Arm*. Classed as a fighter, but with impressive low-level attack capability, it first saw action in July 1944, and was widely deployed in all theatres, particularly the Far East. The main wartime version was the Mark I, and 805 of these were built, including 346 fitted with radar* for reconnaissance and night work. Thirty-seven Mark II night fighter models were also built, and the post-war Firefly IV survived to fight in Korea.

BRIEF DATA (Mk I) Type: 2-man carrier fighter; Engine: 1 × 1,730hp Rolls Royce Griffon; Max speed: 316mph; Ceiling: 28,000'; Range: 580m; Arms: 4 × 20mm cannon (provision for 2,000lb ordnance).

Fairey Fulmar Hurriedly designed to meet the British Admiralty's urgent need for a modern carrier fighter, the Fulmar joined the Fleet Air Arm* in May 1940. Its specification had called for a navigator's seat in anticipation of long-range open-sea operations, and this made the Fulmar too slow for really effective air-to-air combat. Nevertheless, it was well-armed and resilient, performing successfully against Italian fighters in the Mediterranean*, and protecting Atlantic* convoys aboard catapult-armed merchant (CAM) ships (see Escort Carriers). A Mark II with a 1,300hp engine was put into production, but by 1943 they were being replaced by faster Supermarine Seafires*. The last of 600 Fulmars was delivered in February 1943.
BRIEF DATA (Mk I) Type: 2-man carrier fighter; Engine: 1 × 1,080hp Rolls Royce Merlin; Max speed: 256mph; Ceiling: 22,400'; Range: 830m; Arms: 8 × 0.303" mg (provision for 500lb ordnance).

Fairey Swordfish Open cockpit, biplane torpedo-bomber, it entered the British Fleet Air Arm* in 1936, and remained in action throughout the war, outlasting its intended successors. Its very low speed and light armament were balanced by extreme manoeuvrability, ease of repair and the ability to lift large loads from small decks. Its outdated canvas structure was often its salvation, as shells fitted with contact fuses frequently passed right through the aircraft without detonating. Although famous for carrier-based operations – particularly at Taranto* in November 1940, and against the *Bismarck** the following May – Swordfish were also fitted with floats and used from catapult ships (see Escort Carriers) to protect convoys*. Some 2,400 were eventually built.

BRIEF DATA (Mk I) Type: 2–3-man naval torpedo-bomber/reconnaissance; Engine: 1 × 690hp Bristol Pegasus; Max speed: 139mph; Ceiling: 10,700'; Range: 770m; Arms: 1 × 0.5" mg, 1 × 0.303" mg; Bomb load: 1,500lb or 1 × 1,610lb torpedo.

Falaise Pocket See Northwest Europe, Allied invasion of.

Faïd Pass See Tunisia, Campaign in.

Fiat BR20 An advanced bomber in its day, the BR20 *Cicogna* (Stork) joined the *Regia Aeronautica** in late 1936 and saw extensive action in Spain. By the time Italy entered the war in June 1940, about 250 Storks were in service, including 60 of the strengthened and slightly better-armed BR20M variant. In October 1940, these raided England in daylight, but were badly battered by the RAF*, survivors being transferred to Greece* the following January. In the Mediterranean*, BR20Ms were reduced to training and reconnaissance duties during 1942, and a large force operating on the Eastern Front* incurred heavy losses even when protected from well-defended targets. The much improved BR20*bis* never reached full production.

606 Storks were built and some of the earlier models were exported, most notably to the Japanese Army*, who used their 75 BR20s against China* and in the Pacific War*.
BRIEF DATA (BR20M) Type: 5–6-man medium bomber; Engine: 2 × 1,000hp Fiat; Max speed: 267mph; Ceiling: 22,145'; Range: 1,243m; Arms: 1 × 12.7mm mg, 3 × 7.7mm mg; Bomb load: 3,525lb.

Fiat CR42 Falcon (Falco) The last biplane fighter built by any of the belligerents in WW2, the *Falco* was manufactured between 1939 and 1942 and saw extensive action in the Mediterranean* and North Africa*. Descended from a long line of Fiat interceptors (including the CR32, still active with second-line units in 1940), it remained in operational service throughout the war, and was also used in escort, night-fighter and fighter-bomber roles. Although it was clearly inferior to its monoplane contemporaries, about 1,800 were built, including the ICR42 floatplane version and a CR42B model, powered by a 1,010hp German Daimler-Benz engine.

BRIEF DATA (CR42) Type: single-seat fighter; Engine: 1 × 840hp Fiat; Max speed: 267mph; Ceiling: 32,472'; Range: 480m; Arms: 2 × 12.7mm mg (provision for 220lb bombs).

Fiat G50 Arrow (Freccia) Like the Macchi C200*, which it resembled, the *Freccia* was an attractive and well designed aircraft, let down by light armament and a feeble power plant. The G50 first flew in 1937 and was tested operationally in Spain the following year. Improved in the light of this experience, the G50*bis* began replacing it with the *Regia Aeronautica*∗ shortly after Italy entered the war in June 1940. Although they were never the equal of the best Allied fighters, 350 of these were built, seeing action over Greece* and in the Desert War*. The soundness of the plane's basic design was demonstrated in the 385mph G55 Centaur (*Centauro*), a refinement fitted with a 1,475hp liquid-cooled engine and armed with cannon. This, however, did not enter production until 1943, and only 105 were built, equipping just one operational group for the pro-German government in the north of Italy*.

BRIEF DATA (G50*bis*) Type: single-seat fighter; Engine: 1 × 840hp Fiat; Max speed: 293mph; Ceiling: 35,100'; Range: 420m; Arms: 2 × 12.7mm mg.

Fiat RS14B Handsome floatplane introduced to the *Regia Aeronautica*∗ in 1941. It flew reconnaissance, convoy* escort or coastal patrol missions in the Mediterranean*. Including RS14C air-sea rescue* versions, 150 were built, but only 25 were still in operational service by October 1943.

BRIEF DATA (RS14B) Type: 4–5-man floatplane reconnaissance/bomber; Engine:

2 × 870hp Fiat; Max speed: 242mph; Ceiling: 16,400'; Range: 1,535m; Arms: 1 × 12.7mm mg, 2 × 7.7mm mg; Bomb load: 880lb.

Fido See Torpedo.

Fieseler Fil56 Storch (Stork) Reliable and popular German short take-off and landing light communications aircraft. It entered production in 1937 and served throughout the war as a command liaison plane and ambulance. About 40 captured examples were eventually in use with Allied commanders, reflecting the plane's superiority over other comparable types. Total wartime production of the *Storch* was 2,549 aircraft.

BRIEF DATA (Fil56C3) Type: 2-man short range reconnaissance/liaison; Engine: 1 × 240hp Argus; Max speed: 109mph; Ceiling: 15,090'; Range: 236m; Arms: 1 × 7.9mm mg.

Fighter Catapult Ship (FCS) See Escort Carriers.

Fighting France (France Combattante) See Free France.

Fiji, HMS The *Fiji* Class was the second (heavier) group of cruisers ordered under the pre-war British Re-Armament Programme. Although theoretically limited to 8,000 tons by the 2nd London Naval Treaty of 1936, they carried similar arms and armour to the heavier Town Class cruisers (see Sheffield, HMS). Eleven units were completed between May 1940 and August 1942, and they enjoyed active and largely successful careers both with the Fleet in Home or Mediterranean* waters and on trade routes in the Indian Ocean. Only two vessels were lost. The *Fiji* itself was sunk by bombing off Crete* in May 1941, and a year later the *Trinidad* was destroyed by Luftwaffe* aircraft in the Barents Sea while still weakened from (self-inflicted) torpedo* damage. In 1943–4 two of the class (the *Gambia* and the *Uganda*) were taken over by New Zealand and Canadian forces respectively in an attempt to relieve the Royal Navy's* critical personnel shortage. BRIEF DATA (*Fiji*, 1939) Displacement: 8,525 tons; Dimensions: o/a lgth – 555' 6", b – 62'; Speed: 33 knots; Armament: 12 × 6" gun (4 × 3), 8 × 4" AA gun, 8 × 2pdr AA gun, 16 × 0.5" AA gun, 6 × 21" TT, 2 aircraft.

Final Solution (Endlösung) The systematic annihilation of European Jewry attempted by the Third Reich between 1941 and 1945. The Nazi Party* programme had emphasized a ruthless racism since its formation: 'Citizenship is to be determined by race; no Jew to be a German.' Having allowed many Jews to leave Austria and Germany in the early years of the Reich (often to the considerable profit of Nazi officials), emigration to Palestine was limited after 1936. Moreover, it was becoming more difficult for refugees to find a country to accept them, and poorer Jews had no resources to pay their way to safety. After 1939, war was used to cloak a new ruthlessness towards Jews. Even though there seems little doubt that the term 'Final Solution' meant genocide from its first employment in 1941–2, confusion has continued over the use of cover-names used by senior Nazi officials who were clearly unwilling to describe the process in frank terms. It is still uncertain whether 'resettlement', as widely used in the 1930s, was equally a cover-term for mass murder.

Nevertheless, by early 1942 the Einsatzgruppen*, special squads of mixed SS*, SD* and Gestapo*, had already killed over 500,000 people in Poland*, the Ukraine* and Russia, disposing of them brutally in crudely dug pits near towns, where inhabitants were lined up and shot. It is now generally agreed that the conference held at SS RHSA (Reich Chief Security Office) headquarters in the Berlin suburb of Wannsee* in January 1942 and attended by 15 senior SS and government officials was the key event in the initiation of the Final Solution. The briefing given by Heydrich* as chairman set in train the adminis-

trative processes which established the Final Solution as a formal state policy. Nevertheless, no explicit mention was made of *killing* during the briefing and careful reading of the conference documents suggests the possibility that the SS, represented by Heydrich, favoured the transportation of Jews to the east to form a vast labour pool, at least initially, rather than wholesale extermination at that point. This ambiguity of interpretation, of the primacy of labour or extermination within the Final Solution, was to remain an issue within the SS and the Third Reich until the concentration camp* system itself collapsed.

Deportations to the east were carefully arranged so that victims thought they were being sent to work. This deception was often sustained until the moment of execution – many victims believed they were entering a bath house rather than gaschamber. In Auschwitz* victims were sometimes even lulled by a macabre band of Jewish prisoners playing classical music to the queue. Prisoners were also used to herd in the victims, and pile up the bodies for incineration afterwards. Appalling experiments in mass-execution were tried by the Einsatzgruppen, though most of these failed to dispose of sufficient numbers, and permanent extermination sites were built from early 1942: in Poland at Belzec*, Lublin*, Sobibor, Treblinka, Kulm and Auschwitz*. The SS had estimated the need to kill 11 million Jews. Perhaps over 5 million had been killed before the war ended. Apart from the detailed Korherr report of March 1943, there is no complete record of the slaughter and numbers can only be estimated roughly.

By early 1945, extermination was grinding to a halt and hopeless attempts were made to destroy the abundant evidence of Nazi guilt. It was of course impossible, because the evidence was clear, in the silence of the once Jewish Polish and Russian villages and in the absence of Jewish voices throughout much of post-war Europe. See also Anti-Semitism.

Finland A democratic republic from 1919, Finland's foreign policy between the wars was characterized by frontier disputes with Sweden* and the Soviet Union, with whom Finland went to war in November 1939 over disputed territorial claims (see Russo-Finnish War). In 1941, Finns joined with German troops in the invasion of Russia (see Eastern Front), with the intention of recovering the 16,000 square miles lost to her in the war, although Finnish C-in-C Mannerheim* refused to co-operate with German forces in cutting off Leningrad* in August 1941. By June 1944, Russian advances into the Karelian Isthmus and the capture of Viipuri put the Finns under pressure to accept the armistice terms proposed by Stalin*, but the promises of German aid prompted Finland to refuse the armistice terms until September, when the German retreat was in full swing.

Firefly Tank See Sherman Tank.

First Special Aviation Project See Doolittle, Lt Colonel James.

Fitch, Rear Admiral Aubrey (1883–1978) American commander of Task Force 11, based on the carrier *Lexington**, which fought at the battle of the Coral Sea*. Although the *Lexington* was sunk during the action, lacking sufficient fighters to protect it, Fitch went on to take overall command of land-based aircraft in the South Pacific. During 1943 and 1944, though he attracted little attention, Fitch contributed significantly to the success and the pace of the American offensives, notably in the Solomons*, by employing new offensive strategies for bombardment, invasion and the quick exploitation of captured airfields for further offensives.

Flail Tank See Special-purpose Vehicles.

Flamethrowers The flamethrower as a means of directing a jet of fi.. ~e at an enemy had been introduced during WW1, and the more reliable weapons of 1939–45

used the same basic system. Inflammable liquid was forced through a nozzle under pressure from an inert gas. As it emerged, it was ignited by a spark or a charge, causing a short burst of fire. Separate triggers were needed for fuel emission and ignition.

The most widely used flamethrowers were one-man portable types, but they were limited in capacity and range. The British 'Ack Pack' was typical, and carried 4 gallons of fuel for a maximum of ten 10-second shots to a range of about 50 yards. For greater performance, flamethrowers could be mounted on tanks or amoured vehicles. The German Army converted various vehicles as *Flammpanzers*, but the Allies made the greater use of such devices. The British 'Crocodile', a modification of the Churchill* tank, towed 400 gallons of fuel in a trailer (see Special-purpose Vehicles), and the US Army produced an integrated flamethrower based on its M4 Sherman* tank. Flamethrowers were also placed in some British coastal fortifications, but a US airborne flamethrower was superseded by the development of napalm (see Bomb).

Flasher, USS US Navy* *Gato* Class submarine, commissioned in 1943. The *Flasher* is credited with having sunk 100,231 tons of hostile shipping, the highest total of any US Navy submarine.
BRIEF DATA See Albacore, USS.

Flax, Operation Code-name for the disruption by Allied air forces of Mediterranean supply routes to General von Arnim's* Axis army in Tunis in April 1943. See Tunisia.

Fleet Air Arm The British naval air force in WW2. The Royal Navy* had lost control of its aircraft in 1918, when the Royal Naval Air Service was absorbed into the new RAF*. At the time it led the world in naval aviation, pioneering the basic techniques of shipboard take-off and landing. By 1937, when the Fleet Air Arm was returned to the Royal Navy*, it had slipped to a poor third behind Japan and the US.

Under the aegis of the RAF, which defined itself as an independent strategic bombing force, the FAA had been starved of modern aircraft types, and the development of air-sea tactics had been largely neglected. With little forward planning in hand for future warplanes, the FAA was forced to fight much of WW2 with a combination of outmoded Admiralty designs (e.g. Fairey Swordfish*, Blackburn Skua*), imported American types (e.g. Grumman Martlet*) and converted RAF fighters (e.g. Supermarine Seafire*). Tactical realities were not revealed until the campaign in Norway of 1940, when British preconceptions were undermined by the Luftwaffe's low-level bombing methods. .

The Navy was more successful in quickly replacing the RAF's personnel organization (withdrawn in 1937) than in maintaining sufficient aircraft for its carriers, which were seldom able to carry their full capacity until the later stages of the war. Another disadvantage was the separation of the FAA from the command of shore-based aircraft. Although under the operation control of the Admiralty for the Battle of the Atlantic*, Coastal Command remained under RAF administration throughout the war, receiving a very low priority before 1943.

Despite these weaknesses, the FAA performed valuably in combat. In particular, its ancient Fairey Swordfish torpedo-bombers achieved wonders, delivering many accurate attacks despite a top speed of only 138mph. Carrier operations were a feature of Royal Navy actions in the Mediterranean* and against German capital ships in northern waters (see Bismarck; Tirpitz), although they were on a far smaller scale than those in the Pacific. The world's first carrier offensive was mounted by the FAA in November 1940 against Taranto*, but involved only 21 Swordfish. In Europe, naval battles between carriers were impossible as only Britain possessed any. By the time the FAA was committed to the Pacific War in late 1944, the Japanese carrier fleet had been defeated and the main threat to Allied carriers was the Kamikaze* suicide attack, which British ships were armoured

to defeat. In the battle to protect Allied trade routes, FAA aircraft played an increasingly important role aboard escort carriers* from late 1942 until the end of the war.

Fletcher, Vice Admiral Frank (1885–1973) Winner of a Medal of Honour during WW1, Fletcher commanded carrier-based naval forces in the Pacific during WW2. Chosen to lead the operation to relieve Wake Islands* after the attack on Pearl Harbor*, Fletcher's most distinguished service was given during the crucial naval battles of the summer of 1942, most notably at the Battle of the Coral Sea* and at Midway*. The interception by Fletcher's Task Force 17 of the Japanese invasion force headed for Port Moresby*, which resulted in a four-day air battle (4–8 May), contributed significantly to the crucial Allied tactical victory achieved in the Coral Sea, though Fletcher lost the carrier *Lexington** and suffered damage to his flagship *Yorktown**. After the Midway battle Fletcher was appointed Vice Admiral in command of the expeditionary force to protect operations at Guadalcanal*, fighting at the battle of Savo Island* and finally at the battle of the Eastern Solomons*, where his ship, the *Saratoga** was damaged, and Fletcher himself wounded. He returned to Washington for temporary duty and retired in 1947.

Flying Tigers See Chennault, Major General Claire.

Focke-Wulf Fw189 Originally designed as a light ground-support bomber, but rejected by the Luftwaffe* in favour of the marginally faster Henschel Hs129*, the Fw189A entered production as a reconnaissance aircraft in 1939. A total of 846 of the type was built and production continued until 1944, the plane operating mostly on the Eastern Front* but appearing in all European theatres. Although it proved able to absorb considerable punishment, lack of speed made it a fairly easy target for fighters and it was confined to liaison and training duties in the later years of the war.

BRIEF DATA (Fw189A1) Type: 3-man reconnaissance; Engine: 2 × 450hp Argus; Max speed: 221mph; Ceiling: 27,550'; Range: 430m; Armament: 4 × 7.9mm mg; Bomb load: 220lb.

Focke-Wulf Fw190 Unquestionably the most valuable German fighter aircraft of the war, the Fw190 was conceived as the successor to the Messerschmitt Bf109* as early as 1937, and a prototype flew in June 1939. Incorporating a bulky BMW radial engine into a remarkably clean design, it entered the Luftwaffe* as the Fw190A1 (armed with two cannon) in June 1941, and immediately proved itself a superb combat machine. Fast, highly manoeuvrable and providing an exceptionally stable gun-platform, the 'Butcher Bird' quickly established a clear superiority over the British Supermarine Spitfire V* in cross-Channel operations. In March 1942, the 1,700hp A3 appeared armed with four 20mm cannon and, as production gathered momentum, the A4 reached units in the early summer, fitted with a power-booster enabling it to reach 416mph.

By the end of 1942, production of the Fw190 about equalled that of the Bf109 and, like the older fighter, it was manufactured in a welter of subvariants. The A5, similar to the A4 but with a better mounted engine, was designed with such modifications in mind. It saw extensive service as a night-fighter (Fw190A5, U2) as well as appearing in reconnaissance (A5, U14), ground-support (A5, U3, U16), long-range fighter-bomber (A5, U8, U13) and anti-shipping (A5, U14) versions. Weight increases prompted some structural changes for the A6, first produced in April 1943, and designed primarily for the Eastern Front*. This also existed in many variously armed and applied sub-types, often determined by the use of field modification kits (*Rüscatz*). The A8, introduced in late 1932, was the most common version of the Fw190, and had one extra fuel tank behind

the cockpit, improved machine-guns and new avionics. In the east, faced by a much improved Red Air Force* fighter arm, these were being used almost exclusively as fighter-bombers by early 1944, while in the west their function became increasingly defensive after the Allied landings in Normandy*.

Early in 1944, the projected high-altitude Fw190B was abandoned in favour of the Fw190D ('Dora'). The main production version was the D9 interceptor, which began operations in the autumn. Driven by a 1,776hp liquid-cooled power plant and with a longer nose and tailplane, it was capable of a boosted speed of 428mph and comfortably outclimbed its predecessors. 'Doras' gave good accounts of themselves against numerically superior forces on all fronts until the end of the war, but production was limited by Allied bombing disruption and the plane's effectiveness was diluted by shortages of fuel and pilots.

Purpose-built fighter-bomber and ground-support versions of the Fw190 were manufactured in some numbers during the last two years of the war. The Fw190G could lift a 3,790lb bomb load, and the Fw190F was a heavily armoured attack plane and could carry about 1,000lb of ordnance. Total production of all Fw190s was 20,001.

BRIEF DATA (Fw190A8) Type: single-seat fighter; Engine: 1 × 1,700hp BMW; Max speed: 408mph; Ceiling: 37,400'; Range: 500m; Arms: 4 × 20mm cannon, 2 × 13mm mg.

Focke-Wulf Fw200 Kondor (Condor) German long-range aircraft which had been built purely as a commercial transport since 1937. The following year, a Japanese order for one machine modified for maritime reconnaissance encouraged a similar improvisation for the Luftwaffe* and the resultant Fw200C entered service in the spring of 1940. Over the next three years, Kondors were highly effective as the 'eyes' of U-boats in the Battle of the Atlantic*, and themselves sank significant quantities of Allied merchant shipping. Although prone to catastrophic structural weaknesses and short of protective armour, the plane was much respected by the Allies, who gradually fought back with escort carriers* and long-range aircraft of their own. Faced with airborne opposition, the Kondor was something of a sitting duck, and surviving aircraft had been forced back into transport work by September 1944. In all, 276 of the Fw200C series were built, although operational strength never rose above about 60, and production stopped in February 1944. Late models could launch Hs293 guided* bombs from outboard nacelles.

BRIEF DATA (Fw200C) Type: 7-man maritime reconnaissance/bomber; Engine: 4 × 1,200hp Bramo Fafnir; Max speed: 224mph; Ceiling: 19,030'; Range: 2,206m; Arms: (typical) 2 × 20mm cannon, 1 × 13mm mg, 3 × 7.92mm mg; Bomb load: 4,626lb.

Foggia City on the eastern ankle of Italy, whose nearby airfields were an objective of the British 8th Army, following their landings at Taranto* on 9 September 1943. The airfields were occupied by 13th Corps on 1 October 1943, though there was considerable debate at the time over the actual value of the facilities at Foggia. The major source of argument was the basing of Allied strategic air forces units there. Their targets were not in Italy and the strain on supply services in maintaining them, when they were contributing nothing to the campaign in Italy, was resented by Alexander*. See Italy, Campaign in.

Fokker D21 First produced in the Netherlands in January 1938, this was the standard monoplane fighter of three European nations – the Netherlands, Finland* and Denmark* – at the start of WW2. It was manufactured in all three countries with slightly varying engine and armament capacities. Thirty-eight D21s fought successfully in the Russo-Finnish War* of 1939 –40, and the Luftwaffe* requisitioned eight

of the 10 Danish models in April 1940. The 29 operational Dutch D21s were all lost in the German Western Offensive* the following month.

BRIEF DATA (Dutch version) Type: single-seat fighter; Engine: 1 × 830hp Bristol Mercury; Max speed: 286mph; Ceiling: 36,000'; Range: 590m; Arms: 4 × 7.9mm mg.

Fokker G1 Dutch heavy fighter that entered production in 1937, amid great praise for its novel twin-engined design and its heavy firepower. It was sold to Sweden*, to Denmark* and very nearly to the Spanish. Of all 23 Dutch G1a models ready for action in May 1940, all but one were destroyed in combat by the Luftwaffe*. A similar fate befell the 12 less powerful G1bs intended for Spain that were pressed into battle from Schipol Airport where they stood waiting export.

BRIEF DATA (G1a) Type: 3-man fighter-bomber; Engine: 2 × 830hp Bristol Mercury; Max speed: 295mph; Range: 945m; Arms: 9 × 7.9mm mg; Bomb load: 880lb.

Force 141 Allied headquarters established in January 1943 by General Eisenhower* for the planning of the invasion of Sicily*. Force 141 became an independent operational HQ on 15 May, at the end of the campaign in Tunisia*. Two subsidiary HQs, Force 343 and Force 545, representing Patton's* US 7th Army and Montgomery's* 8th Army, were also set up for the same purpose.

Force H British naval squadron established at Gibraltar* in June 1940, to fill the gap in Mediterranean* defences left by the surrender of French forces. Commanded by Vice Admiral Somerville*, Force H consisted initially of the aircraft carrier *Ark Royal**, the battlecruiser *Hood**, two battleships, three cruisers and escorting destroyers. It was the main Allied task force in the Atlantic* and western Mediterranean, participating in attacks on French colonial bases at Mers-el-Kébir* and Dakar*, the sinking of the *Bismarck**, and the invasions of Madagascar*, Northwest Africa and southern Europe. Force H was also the main escort for convoys* to Malta*. The fighting strength of the squadron fluctuated, but the ships most associated with Force H were the *Ark Royal*, the battlecruiser *Renown** and the heavy cruiser *Sheffield**. Force H was disbanded in October 1943, when Allied naval supremacy in the Mediterrean was no longer in doubt.

Force Z Code-name for the British naval squadron based on the battleship *Prince of Wales** and the battlecruiser *Repulse**, it was sent to the Far East in late 1941, arriving in Singapore* on 2 December, with orders to impede Japanese landings. Despite the lack of air support (a promised carrier, *Indomitable**, had been damaged and was not available in time), the Force Z commander, Admiral Phillips, sailed to Kota Bharu on 8 December, to intercept Japanese transports bound for an assault on northern Malaya*. Protected by bad weather as it sailed out, Force Z was spotted by Japanese aircraft as soon as the weather cleared. Now returning via Kuantan (where there were reports of landings) *en route* for Singapore, Admiral Phillips's fleet was sighted again by submarines and had no protection against the élite Japanese 22nd Air Flotilla bombers that began their attack on the morning of 10 December. Although the force survived the first wave of torpedoes*, subsequent attacks sank the *Repulse* and then the *Prince of Wales*, leaving the escorting destroyers to pick up over 2,000 survivors. The sinking of Force Z, made inevitable by the overwhelming Japanese advantage of air power, was a great blow to British prestige and dramatically highlighted the folly of deploying modern naval forces without air support.

Formidable, HMS Royal Navy* aircraft carrier, completed in December 1940 as the second unit of the *Illustrious** Class.

The *Formidable* first joined the Home Fleet but, after a spell in the South Atlantic hunting German Navy* commerce raiders, she pursued a long and successful Mediterranean* career. Before her transfer to the Pacific in 1945 she saw action at Taranto*, in the battle for Crete*, and in support of Allied landings in Northwest Africa (see Torch) and Italy*. Hit by two Kamikaze* aircraft off Okinawa* in May 1945, she remained operative and, although later badly damaged by a hangar accident, took part in the final attacks on Japan until August 1945.

BRIEF DATA See Illustrious, HMS except – Dimensions: o/a lgth 740' 9".

Formosa (Taiwan) Large island in the China Sea, the Allies considered it as a final stepping-stone to an invasion of Japan. As the campaign in the Pacific developed, however, arguments between the Pacific commanders (notably Admirals Nimitz* and King*, and General MacArthur*) over the direction of the main offensive against Japan held up the development of plans to attack Formosa. The debate was finally resolved on logistic grounds in favour of Luzon* (MacArthur's preference) as the major objective rather than Formosa, though the island was nevertheless subjected to heavy air raids from US carrier forces once they began operating in the China Sea in late 1944. See Map 11.

Fortitude, Operation See Normandy, Invasion of; Northwest Europe, Allied Invasion of.

France, Fall of See Western Offensive.

Franco, General Francisco (1892–1975) Leader of the revolt of officers and soldiers against the Popular Front republican government of Spain. The revolt began in July 1936 and its eventual success put Franco at the head of the Spanish state. Despite the substantial military aid provided by Germany and Italy to Franco's nationalist forces during the Spanish Civil

War, Hitler was unable to bring Franco to terms over Spain's entry into WW2. In October 1940, mutual distrust brought a lengthy meeting at Hendaye in France to an end without agreement over Hitler's requirements or the conditions of Franco's participation. Without it, Hitler could not make the free movements through Spain to Gibraltar* and other major British bases in the Mediterranean* that would otherwise have given Germany an immense advantage in the theatre. One of the few European statesmen who managed to rival Hitler's dominance of the negotiating table, the importance to the Allies of Franco's long-term success in keeping Spain out of the Axis* alliance should not be underestimated.

Frank, Hans (1900–46) German Governor-General of occupied Poland*. Frank saw service in the post-WW1 Freikorps and was an early member of the Nazi Party*, becoming its legal adviser from 1929. Frank was responsible for the drafting of the *Gleichschaltung* legal system and founded and became President of the German Academy of Law. He proclaimed that 'love of the Führer has become a concept in law'.

Following the defeat and occupation of Poland and the seizure of territory by Germany and the Soviet Union, Frank was appointed Governor-General of the remainder. From his headquarters at Wavel Castle in Krakow he operated a brutal and punitive regime of enslavement and extermination, which ended when he fled to Germany before the Russian advance in 1944. Arrested by the Allies after the war, Frank compiled an extensive diary of his work which is a source of much early Nazi history. He was tried as one of the major war criminals at Nuremberg*, pleaded guilty to the charges against him and was hanged in October 1946.

Frank, Karl Hermann (1898–1946) One of the leaders of the Sudeten German Party along with Henlein*. He was made Sec-retary of State of Bohemia and Moravia after Germany's occupation of Czechoslovakia*. He is also said to have directed the 'terror campaigns' instigated in Czechoslovakia by Reich Protector Heydrich*, and to have ordered the Lidice* 'reprisal action' after Heydrich's assassination. He was tried by a Czech court and hanged.

Franklin, USS United States aircraft carrier of the *Essex** Class, commissioned in January 1944. Beginning with the capture of the Mariana Islands*, her career exemplified the resilience of her class. She was slightly damaged by a Kamikaze* attack off Leyte* on 15 October 1944, and two days later a bomb destroyed one of her aircraft elevators. She remained in action for the Battle of Leyte Gulf*, but was hit by another Kamikaze on 30 October that crashed through the flight deck killing 120 men. At last returned to the US for repairs, she was back in the Pacific by March 1945, and took part in strikes on Japan prior to the Okinawa* landing. On 19 March she was hit by two bombs off Kyushu, causing fuel and magazines to explode below decks. Dead in the water and on fire she was saved by the efforts of her crew. Power was eventually restored and the *Franklin* was again under repair when the war ended. BRIEF DATA See Essex, USS.

Free France The movement, founded in London by Charles de Gaulle*, that fought on against the Axis* in defiance of the armistice signed by the French government on 22 June 1940 (see Western Offensive).

De Gaulle had fled to London on 17 June, and the following day he broadcast a dramatic appeal to his countrymen over the BBC*, which Prime Minister Churchill* had put at his disposal. Expressing faith in Britain's ability to continue the war, and in the inevitability and value of US economic assistance to the Allies, de Gaulle claimed that the French cause was not lost. He urged Frenchmen to join him in London and fight for Free France to keep alive 'the flame of French resistance'.

The appeal was not a great success. Few in France actually heard it, and fewer still were impressed by it, understandably in view of the military situation in Europe. By the end of July, only 7,000 volunteers had joined Free France and de Gaulle (branded a traitor by the French government when he ignored an order to return) had failed to attract many prominent Frenchmen to the cause. Nevertheless, Free France was important to the British, who lent crucial early support to the movement. De Gaulle's leadership was formally recognized by Churchill on 28 June, and Free France was permitted to recruit troops from French exiles in Britain and to continue its BBC broadcasts.

In France, however, de Gaulle's dependence on London soon became a major embarrassment for the movement. British attacks on the French Navy* in July (see Mers-el-Kébir) caused great bitterness, hardening anti-British sentiment inside France and in her important North African colonies, which affirmed their allegiance to the Vichy* regime. Although French territories in equatorial Africa followed the lead of Chad's governor (Félix Eboué), who proclaimed his support for Free France in late August, a failed British attack on Dakar* (proposed by de Gaulle) in September caused further deterioration of Anglo-French relations, and ensured French West Africa's loyalty to the Vichy government. Churchill publicly reaffirmed his faith in de Gaulle's leadership on 26 September, but other British leaders – many of whom disliked and mistrusted the aloof and arrogant Frenchman – pressed for his removal. Without a strategically valuable base in French territory, de Gaulle found himself reviled by many Frenchmen and lambasted by the Anglo-American press.

During October and November de Gaulle undertook a tour of French Equatorial Africa, which became the Free French African State, and by the end of the year his standing had somewhat improved. French territories in India, New Caledonia and the New Hebrides joined the movement, while the Governor-General of French Indochina (Georges Catroux) and the military commander of French Somaliland (General Legentilhomme) abandoned their Vichy-controlled posts to follow de Gaulle. Equipped by the British, Free France now began small-scale military operations, beginning in late 1940 with raids from central Africa (under the command of General Leclerc) into Italian-held southern Libya.

During the first half of 1941 Free French forces took part in actions at Sidi Barrani (see Egypt), in Eritrea and in Ethiopia (see East Africa), as well as unsuccessfully attempting a land blockade of Djibouti in French Somaliland. In June and July, 6,000 Free French troops joined British forces in the successful invasion of Syria*, held by some 25,000 Vichy troops, but the victory was soured by de Gaulle's adamant refusal to allow the repatriation (agreed by the British) of the defeated forces. Although Syria and neighbouring Lebanon were eventually granted to Free France as mandated territories, the argument provoked considerable resentment in Britain and Free French military prestige gained little from the episode. Tellingly, de Gaulle was afterwards able to recruit only about 6,000 of the Vichy troops in Syria.

Despite the heroic performance of General Koenig's* Free French unit against Rommel's* forces at Bir Hacheim the following June (see Gazala), the movement remained militarily peripheral throughout 1942. About 100,000 Free French troops were scattered among the French colonies, but they were almost totally dependent on Allied supplies and equipment, as was the small Free French air corps. The Free Frency Navy (FNLF), which comprised fifty ships and some 3,600 seamen, and a merchant fleet of 170 ships and about 5,000 crew, had both played an important role in the Battle of the Atlantic*, but operated only as an auxiliary force to the British fleets.

Politically, the supreme egotism of de

Gaulle and his failure to attract leading compatriots to the cause ensured that the movement remained overwhelmingly dominated by its founder. De Gaulle had established a small but competent personal staff – headed by Geoffroy de Courcel as *chef de cabinet* – at his base in central London, and in September 1941 he created a formal administrative cabinet, the French National Committee. This was recognized by Britain and the Soviet Union (but not the US) as the official government-in-exile. Soviet recognition of Free France and the support of significant communist groups inside France were the tangible results of de Gaulle's overtures to Moscow following the Axis invasion of the Soviet Union in June 1941. In return de Gaulle vociferously supported Stalin's repeated demands for a 'second front' in Europe.

At the beginning of 1942 de Gaulle sent a special emissary, Jean Moulin, into France to work towards the unification under the Free French banner of the growing number of underground resistance* groups. Although de Gaulle faced a challenge to his leadership from his naval commissioner (Admiral Muselier) in the spring, it foundered for lack of support and the political prestige of the movement grew throughout the year as Allied military strength mounted and more Free French agents were dropped into France. In an attempt to further broaden his appeal, de Gaulle changed the name of the movement to Fighting France (*France Combattante*) in July. In acknowledging the change, Moscow proclaimed Fighting France the only authority qualified to guide the French war effort inside and outside France.

Nevertheless, as planning got under way for the Anglo-American invasion of French Northwest Africa in late 1942, acceptance of de Gaulle was by no means universal. Apart from a persistent, if low-key, campaign against him by non-affiliated French exiles in London, he was unpopular in the US. As a neutral power, the US had recognized the Vichy government in 1940. This made any recognition of Fighting France in

Washington politically awkward, besides which de Gaulle's demeanour appeared offensively pompous to many Americans, including President Roosevelt* and Secretary of State Hull*. Anxious to encourage sympathy among Vichy forces in Northwest Africa and aware of the bitterness felt there since the British attacks of 1940, US leaders supported General Giraud* as the leader of pro-Allied French forces in Africa, and de Gaulle was completely excluded from Operation Torch* when it took place in November.

De Gaulle reacted with characteristic hostility when Giraud was appointed commander of French forces in North Africa following the death of Darlan* at the end of the year, and it appeared to most observers that Fighting France must subordinate itself to the wider cause. Initial Allied attempts to reconcile the two leaders met with little success, despite their well-publicized handshake at the Casablanca Conference* in January 1943. To the exasperation of British and US leaders, de Gaulle insisted that all Vichy supporters were traitors and that only he could lead France to liberation. His hand was strengthened in May when Moulin's work in France culminated in the formation of a National Council of Resistance (CRN), which united all the leading underground factions inside France behind Fighting France. Despite Anglo-American support, Giraud proved an ineffective administrator and he was persuaded to invite de Gaulle to his headquarters in Algiers* to share a common authority. The resulting French Committee of National Liberation (created 3 June, with de Gaulle and Giraud as co-leaders) declared itself the administrative authority for France, with the aim of restoring French republican ideals and liberties. Within a few weeks de Gaulle had asserted a thorough personal dominance over Giraud, and in November he formed the Consultative Assembly which, to Anglo-American dismay, rejected the constitution of the pre-war French Third Republic (although the formation of a Fourth Republic was postponed pending the end of Axis occupation).

By 1944 French resistance groups home and abroad were genuinely united behind the Committee in Algiers, and Fighting France was effectively merged into this larger force. Swelled by former Vichy troops, the French armies now numbered about 400,000 men. They were, however, still widely scattered and poorly equipped, with only limited combat effectiveness. By far the largest concentration of French forces (230,000 troops) was based in Algiers, but half of these were committed to the Allied campaign in Italy* and could play little part in the liberation of France itself. De Gaulle himself returned to France for the first time a week after the Allied invasion of Normandy*, appointing a Gaullist local governor during a brief tour of the province. On 3 July the Committee of National Liberation proclaimed itself the provisional government of France, and de Gaulle returned to Normandy on 20 August, after visiting Algiers, Italy and the US. Five days later the French Second Armoured Division under Leclerc entered Paris* and on 26 August, with German gunfire still audible, de Gaulle entered the capital in triumph.

French Air Force See Armée de l'Air.

French Army The standing strength of the French Army in 1939 was about 900,000 men, but peacetime conscription meant that France could slowly mobilize 5 million trained men, or 110 divisions. Although mostly infantry, these included colonial, alpine, motorized, cavalry and fortress divisions. The first armoured divisions were just being formed, and three were ready by the spring of 1940. Some forces defended African colonies and southern France against possible Italian aggression, but the vast majority (100 divisions in May 1940) of the French Army was stationed on the northeastern frontier facing Germany.

Regarded, particularly by themselves, as possessing Europe's most powerful army,

the French based their military thinking on the victory of 1918 and concentrated on firepower at the expense of mobility. Great faith was placed in the formidable static defences of the Maginot Line*. Most artillery was horse-drawn (as was the German Army's) and there were shortages of anti-aircraft* guns and anti-tank mines*, but on the whole the French Army was plentifully equipped with modern weapons. Its tanks* were more powerful if slower than their German counterparts in 1940, while field artillery* and anti-tank* guns were of good quality. Unfortunately this technical strength was poorly applied, being stretched across a static defensive system geared to an infantry war on the WW1 model. It was controlled by a complex and slow moving command structure and little had been done to develop tactical co-operation with the air force (see Armée de l'Air).

Germany's use of concerted armoured force closely supported by air power was fundamental to the defeat of France in June 1940 (see Western Offensive). After the surrender, the victors restricted the Vichy* government to an army of eight small divisions (about 100,000 personnel) with only obsolete weapons. This was formally established in November 1940, but was disbanded two years later when Germany occupied southern France. The colonial army in northwest Africa, a mixture of French and indigenous troops, was of about the same size but remained intact and retained some modern fighting equipment. After putting up brief resistance to the Allied Torch* landings in November 1942, the great majority of these forces joined the Allies and subsequently fought in Tunisia* and Europe with the forces of Free France*.

French Navy During WW1, the French Navy had been given a low military priority and most of its home bases had been unusable. It was thus a backward and demoralized force in the early 1920s. France was a signatory of the Washington Naval Treaty of 1922, which restricted the building of major new warships and set French limits at a much lower level than the quotas permitted Britain, Japan and the US. The French, aware of the need to defend their Atlantic seaboard, felt they should be allowed greater strength than the Italians, but in fact, in an atmosphere of economic restraint and political instability, their reconstruction capacity could barely sustain purely Mediterranean* competition. Conflicts of colonial and commercial interests with the Italians ensured that just such a competition quickly developed.

Initial inter-war building concentrated on producing fast, well-armed but thinly armoured cruisers and flotilla craft for the protection of Mediterranean trade. When Germany announced her return to the ranks of world sea powers with the first 'pocket battleship' (see Deutschland) in 1929, greater interest in capital ships was displayed by the French, who produced their own *Dunkerque* Class battlecruisers. Well within Treaty limits on tonnage and armaments, these were again lightly armoured – such protection as they had being concentrated below the waterline – and very fast, qualities that were carried forward into the 35,000 ton *Richelieu* Class superbattleships, two of which were nearly complete when WW2 began. The impetus for these later investments was provided by Italian plans for new capital ships, and to counter the highly regarded Italian light cruisers, giant *contre-torpilleur* destroyers*, the finest ships of their type in the world, were designed to protect the fleet. Several older warships were completely modernized after international naval treaties lapsed in 1936, and rearmament of the Navy was given full priority from 1938.

By September 1939 the French Navy was a modern force concentrated on the Mediterranean. All the fleet units except two old battleships had been either modernized (three battleships) or built in the previous 13 years (two battle-cruisers, seven heavy cruisers, 12 light cruisers). There were also powerful forces of 71 destroyers and 76 submarines* (including the

famous *Surcouf*) along with a great many smaller craft and auxiliaries. The most glaring of the fleet's inadequacies was a complete lack of aircraft carriers, but it was also seriously deficient in anti-submarine* equipment or expertise. In common with other navies, its ships lacked sufficient quality and quantity of anti-aircraft weapons.

French warships had little opportunity to test their combat strength in WW2. Until the surrender of June 1940, the French co-operated with the Royal Navy*, taking part in the evacuation of Dunkirk*. At the time of the Armistice many French ships escaped to or were in British and French colonial ports. This posed a problem for the British, who were very afraid of French units falling into Axis* hands, and who reluctantly and controversially decided to take pre-emptive action. Ships in British ports were seized on 3 July 1940, and the main French squadrons at Mers-el-Kébir* – who had refused a virtual ultimatum to surrender – were attacked and many ships put out of action. A less successful attack was also attempted on Dakar*. These measures embittered Anglo-French relations for years, but they effectively ended French naval influence in the Mediterranean. Surviving units in the theatre were recalled by the Vichy* government to their main home base at Toulon, and front-line action was subsequently restricted to the colonial squadrons of Africa and Indochina*.

On the same day as the attack on Mers-el-Kébir, the Free French Navy (FNLF) was founded in London. Although this never numbered more than a few thousand men and relied on British equipment, it did play a prominent part in a second attack on Dakar in September 1940 and in the assault on Vichy-controlled Syria* of June 1941.

In November 1942, fighting between French and Allied forces in Northwest Africa (which involved naval units stationed in Morocco) was curtailed by an armistice, and the Allies sought to gain control of the main body of the fleet. The German response, apart from an immediate occupation of Tunisia*, was to occupy southern

France. For a time they made no attempt to enter Toulon, but mined the harbour to prevent any attempt at a breakout. When they occupied the port on 27 November, the French warships – including three battleships, seven cruisers, 29 destroyers and 2 submarines – scuttled themselves. Interned and colonial ships, thus far fiercely loyal to the Vichy government, now joined the FNLF in fighting on the side of the Allies, and this remnant (4 battleships, 9 cruisers and 11 destroyers, bolstered by a few Allied escorts) saw action in the Mediterranean, Indochina* and the Far East before the end of the war.

Freyberg, General Bernard (1889–1963) Colourful British Army* officer, raised in New Zealand, who commanded New Zealand ground forces throughout WW2. After a famous career in WW1, during which he was wounded many times and received the Victoria Cross (highest British award for gallantry), Freyberg retired a popular hero in 1937. In 1939 he returned to the British Army as a major-general and took command of the New Zealand division, which he trained for Imperial service.

Although New Zealand forces* had expected to fight in Europe, the rapid defeat of France in 1940 meant that Freyberg's troops first saw action in the campaign for Egypt* as part of Wavell's* Desert Army. Freyberg later led his forces in Greece*, Crete*, the Desert War*, Tunisia*, Sicily* and Italy*. Freyberg has been criticized for his defence of Crete, where as garrison commander in May 1941 he dispersed his forces to meet an anticipated seaborne attack, and later for his strong advocacy of the bombing attack on the monastery at Cassino*. Taken as a whole, however, his WW2 career was a success, and the New Zealand division was one of the most respected units of the British 8th Army. Freyberg was Governor General of New Zealand from 1946–52.

Frick, Wilhelm (1877–1946) Nazi Party* bureaucrat. Reichstag member from 1924 (when he was associated with Gregor Strasser's radical National-Socialism) and Reichsminister of the Interior from 1933, Frick operated the Enabling Act and drafted the *Gleichschaltung* laws which deprived individual German states of their rights. After the outbreak of war, however, increasing opposition to the wide powers of the SS* led to his displacement as minister by Himmler* in 1943. He was appointed Protector of Bohemia and Moravia, where he remained until the end of the war. At Nuremberg* he was tried as a major war criminal, convicted and hanged.

Friedman, Colonel William Frederick (1891–1969) Chief cryptanalyst of the War Department in Washington between 1941 and 1947, Friedman led the US Army team (the Special Intelligence Service) which broke the major Japanese diplomatic code in 1940 (the Purple Code) and subsequently remained a key member of the Operation Magic teams which decoded Japanese ciphers and enabled American military commanders to read regular intercepts on Japanese military movements. See Magic.

Frigate See Corvette.

Fritsch, General Werner Freiherr von (1880–1939) German Army C-in-C from 1934–8, he supported Defence Minister Blomberg's declaration of direct allegiance of the Army to Hitler after his takeover of power but later questioned Hitler's war plans against Austria* and Czechoslovakia*, as did Blomberg. As a general staff officer of the old school, Fritsch welcomed Hitler's dictatorship but was hostile to the Nazis – and particularly to the SS*. In 1938 he was falsely charged by the SS with homosexuality and cashiered from the Army. Blomberg was similarly forced to resign because of a scandal involving his wife. The removal of both Blomberg and Fritsch enabled Hitler to restructure, and effectively subordinate, his High Command in a new organizational structure, OKW (*Oberkommando der Wehrmacht*).

Fritsch rejoined his artillery regiment as an honorary colonel when a secret military court found him not guilty, and he was killed in action in Poland in September 1939. Blomberg died in 1946 while awaiting trial at Nuremberg* for war crimes.

Front This term, normally describing a strategic line on which advance or defence is based, was used by the Soviets to denote an army group rather than, or as well as, a strategic position. Thus the 4th Belorussian Front was an army group operating in the Belorussian theatre, whose strategic fronts moved as operations developed. In July 1941, the Soviet armies deployed against the Germans were organized into theatres, or groups of fronts: the Northwest Theatre, the Western Theatre and the Southwest Theatre. After May 1942 these temporary groups of fronts were reorganized and renamed, usually as Fronts, to reflect strategic changes, and this process continued throughout the Eastern Front* war. This was the case in early 1945, for example, prior to the final Soviet drive on Berlin*.

Fuchida, Commander Mitsuo (1902–76) Veteran pilot of Japan's war against China*, Fuchida commanded the air strike against Pearl Harbor* in December 1941 and was later involved in the planning for the Battle of Midway*. Unable to pilot his plane during the Midway battle due to illness, Fuchida was wounded on the deck of his flagship Akagi*, when it was attacked by dive-bomber squadrons from the US carriers Yorktown* and Enterprise*. In 1943 –4 he served as a senior staff officer to Admiral Koga*, newly appointed commander of the Combined Fleet. After the war, Fuchida was converted to Christianity and travelled regularly to the United States and Canada to visit Japanese immigrants there. Fuchida became a US citizen in 1966.

Furious, HMS Elderly British aircraft carrier, converted shortly after its completion as a light battlecruiser in 1917. More exten-

sively converted as a true fleet carrier between 1921–5, the *Furious* was thoroughly rearmed and refitted for front-line service in the years before the war. She was kept continuously employed in Mediterranean* and home waters until August 1944, when she was placed in reserve.
BRIEF DATA (1939) Displacement: 22,450 tons; Dimensions: o/a lgth – 786' 6", b – 90'; Speed: 29.5 knots; Armament: 12 × 4" AA gun, 24 × 2pdr AA gun, 33 aircraft.

Furutaka Japanese Navy* heavy cruiser and class, which also comprised the *Kako*. Completed in 1926, they were Japan's first modern cruisers with 8-inch main armament and, using advanced techniques pioneered in the earlier *Yubari**, packed considerable weaponry onto a relatively low displacement. Modernized in 1937–8, they formed part of a cruiser squadron with the South Sea Force in December 1941. Both ships were lost in the Solomons. The *Kako* was sunk by an American submarine at the Battle of Savo Island* in August 1942, and the *Furutaka* was destroyed the following October at the Battle of Cape Esperance*.
BRIEF DATA (*Furutaka*, 1941) Displacement: 9,150 tons; Dimensions: o/a lgth – 602', b – 55' 6"; Speed: 33 knots; Armament: 6 × 8" gun (3 × 2), 4 × 4.7" AA gun, 8 × 25mm AA gun, 4 × 13mm AA gun, 8 × 24" TT, 2 aircraft.

Fuso Veteran Japanese battleship and class. Completed as dreadnoughts during WW1, the *Fuso* and her sister the *Yamashiro* were extensively modernized and reclassed as battleships in the early 1930s, as Japan strove to bring her fleet up to US Navy* standards. They were too slow for fleet operations in the Pacific War* and were mostly confined to home waters, receiving no wartime supplement to their anti-aircraft* defence. Following crippling losses at the Battle of Midway* in 1942, the Japanese Navy* planned to convert them as hybrid aircraft carriers, but this was abandoned after the struggle for the Marianas* had left Japan seriously short of naval aircrew. Both ships were finally thrown into the Battle of Leyte* Gulf and were sunk in the Surigao Strait* by American battleships and destroyers on the night of 24–5 October 1944.

BRIEF DATA (*Fuso*, 1941) Displacement: 34,700 tons; Dimensions: o/a lgth – 698′, b – 100′ 6″; Speed: 24.75 knots; Armament: 12 × 14″ gun (6 × 2), 14 × 6″ gun, 8 × 5″ AA gun, 16 × 25mm AA gun, 3 aircraft.

G

Galland, Lt General Adolf (1911–) An ace* fighter pilot and commander of the Luftwaffe* Fighter Arm from 1942–5. Like other keen young German pilots, Galland practised in gliders during the post-Versailles prohibition on aircraft building and was trained secretly in military techniques while an employee of Lufthansa, the German commercial airline. Transferring to the newly formed Luftwaffe in 1935, he served as a pilot in the Kondor Legion, which fought for the nationalists during the Spanish Civil War. He flew over 300 sorties and developed close support tactics for the new Messerschmitt Bf109* monoplane fighter.

During the Battle of Britain* in the summer of 1940, Galland became recognized as an outstanding fighter leader, scoring top points among the German fighter pilots with 57 credits. In late 1941, as a colonel, he succeeded his close friend Mölders* in charge of Luftwaffe day fighter squadrons and the following year he was promoted Inspector General in command of all fighter aircraft, at 30 the youngest German general.

In spite of his distinguished combat record, popularity and technical innovations, Galland oversaw the gradual failure of the Fighter Arm between 1942 and 1944. Constantly overruled in his advocacy of greater use of defensive fighter forces by Luftwaffe chief Göring*, and by Hitler, Galland was finally made the scapegoat for the Luftwaffe's failures and removed from high command in January 1945. He ended the war commanding a crack squadron of new Messerschmitt Me262* jet fighters, which fought on until grounded by lack of fuel. After the war, Galland went to Argentina as technical adviser to the Argentine Air Force. On his return to Germany he became a consultant to the German aerospace industry.

Galvanic Code-name for the American capture, occupation and development of the Gilbert Islands*.

Gamelin, General Maurice Gustave (1872–1958) One among a number of 'old school', defensively minded military chiefs, whose rigid tactical doctrine proved poor equipment to combat the German Blitzkrieg* invasion of France in May 1940 (see Western Offensive). Gamelin had held a series of political posts since transferring from command of operations at French General Headquarters after WW1 and was acting as Commander of Land Forces at the outbreak of war. Having pre-planned the static deployment of French forces and delegated responsibility to his field general Georges*, Gamelin failed to intervene in the conduct of the battles in May and was replaced by Weygand*, too late to affect the outcome, on 19 May. Gamelin was subsequently among those tried at the Riom* show trial and was later imprisoned in Germany at Buchenwald concentration camp until its liberation in May 1945 by American forces.

Garand Rifle The Garand or M-1 semi-automatic rifle was standard issue to US Army* infantrymen in 1941, although it was by no means universally available when the United States entered the war. First issued in 1936, it remained in production into the 1950s and its success helped convince other armies that the semi-automatic rifle was a viable weapon for foot soldiers. See also Rifles.

Gazala Libyan town on the Cyrenaican coast some 40 miles west of Tobruk*. See Map 7. Gazala stands at the head of a pass offering access to the Libyan inland plateau from the coastal strip that formed a line of defence for both sides during the fluctuating North African campaigns of 1941–2.

German commander Rommel* had quickly abandoned his prepared positions on the Gazala Line in December 1941, as he retreated from the British Crusader* offensive. On 21 January 1942, he launched his own counter-offensive, after reinforcement from Tripoli. Overextended and dispersed across a broad front, British forces fell back quickly. Benghazi* fell on 29 January and British Middle Eastern Commander Auchinleck* ordered a retreat to the Gazala Line. Arriving on 4 February, the 8th Army spent several months establishing a line of 'box' fortifications and minefields extending some 50 miles inland.

Overcoming the resistance of his Italian High Command, Rommel again reached the Gazala Line in early April, and launched an attack on 26 May, pre-empting a planned British offensive. While Italian infantry attacked the front of the line, Rommel drove his armour round the inland edge of the fortifications and made for the coast to cut off supply routes. Delayed by his first encounter with American Grant* tanks, he halted short of his objective after two days and established a defensive position to the rear of the line, on 28 May.

Although Rommel was surrounded, heavily outnumbered in armour and subject to continuous air attack, the 8th Army commander, Lt General Ritchie*, squandered his numerical advantage in a series of disjointed attacks using only part of his armour each time. In defeating these, Rommel was able to seize the line fort of Sidi Muftah and establish supply lines through its adjacent minefields. He also sent a strike force to attack the isolated 'box' at Bir Hacheim on the extreme inland edge of the line. There the Free French garrison held out for ten days, but when they evacuated the fort on 11 June, Rommel was free to launch a full-scale breakout from what had become known as 'the Cauldron'.

Plentiful reinforcements meant that Ritchie could still field 284 tanks, more than double his opponent's strength. Nevertheless, when the panzer divisions struck eastward on 12 June, two of the three British armoured brigades were caught in a pincer movement and badly battered. The following day Rommel turned north, taking the Knightsbridge 'box' before resuming his original drive for the coast. On 14 June, with less than 100 tanks left, Ritchie abandoned the Gazala Line to save its two infantry divisions, which escaped and retreated all the way to the Egyptian frontier. Tobruk was therefore left isolated and scantily defended just at the moment when Churchill ordered it held.

Tobruk fell on 21 June, its supplies fuelling the Axis drive to the Egyptian frontier. When Rommel arrived at the border on 23 June he had only 44 German and 13 Italian tanks left, but he found the position abandoned, Ritchie having fallen back 120 miles to Mersa Matruh*. The 8th Army's line of defence finally stabilized several days later at El Alamein*. See also Desert War.

Gehlen, Reinhard (1902–72) Head of German army intelligence on the Eastern Front from 1942. At the end of WW2 he put his records and contacts in Eastern Europe into American hands and, with US assistance, opened the 'Gehlen Bureau', a major Munich-based intelligence organization.

Geneva Conventions There had been several international conventions agreed at Geneva concerning the conduct of warfare, but that most widely quoted during WW2 was the 1929 Convention Relating to the Treatment of Prisoners of War. This sought to ensure humane care of PoWs and was formally adhered to in Europe and Africa but not by the Japanese or in Russia. Neutral observers visited prison camps and information about individuals was statutorily made available to them.

George II, King of Greece (1890–1947) George II had first come to the throne in 1922, only to be deposed the following year – and then recalled in 1935. In 1940, his popularity reached new heights as the Italians were driven back into Albania. Ever the Anglophile, George fled to London (via Crete*) when Greece fell to the Germans. From there he headed a government-in-exile and used radio broadcasts to urge unity on his turbulent former subjects. In March 1943, his cabinet transferred to Cairo. George Papandreou was brought out of Greece to become Prime Minister, and in May 1944 the warring factions of Greek underground politics assembled in reluctant and short-lived unity behind the Cairo administration. It was Papandreou who took uncertain control in Athens when the British returned to Greece in October, King George agreeing to stay away pending a plebiscite. This was eventually held in 1946, and invited him to return. See also: Greece, Italian invasion of; Balkans, The, German invasion of; Greece, British occupation of.

George VI, King (1895–1952) Popular and self-effacing King of Great Britain and titular head of the Commonwealth and Empire. George VI and Queen Elizabeth ignored contingency plans for their removal to Canada and remained in Britain throughout the war. Their visits to military, naval and air force units, as well as their trips to British cities during the Blitz undoubtedly boosted public morale during the difficult early years of the war.

Georges, General Alphonse (1875–1951) Veteran French soldier, passed over as C-in-C of the French Army* in 1935 and subsequently concerned with the overall review of its tactics. At the start of WW2 he was deputy commander of the Northeast Front (facing Germany) under General Gamelin*. The reorganization of the Army gave him overall command of the Front from January 1940, but Gamelin retained direct control of planning and strategy, leaving Georges in charge of operations and liaison with other Allied forces. When the German Army* attacked westward in May, Georges concentrated on integrating Belgian forces into his defensive system. He was slow to react to the German armoured thrust through the Ardennes, and then failed to attempt a large-scale counter-attack. On 19 May, he was relieved of operational command. Georges played little part in Vichy* affairs and joined de Gaulle* and Giraud* in 1943 as a member of the French Committee of National Liberation established at Algiers*.

Gerard Callenburgh Most of the Royal Netherlands Navy was either scuttled or taken to Britain when Germany invaded the Netherlands in 1940. The *Gerard Callenburgh* was one of four destroyers under construction at Rotterdam and Flushing. Scuttled on 15 May 1940, she was refloated in 1942 and commissioned into the German Navy* as the *ZH 1*. She was sunk attempting to reach Cherbourg shortly after the Allied invasion of Normandy*. One of her sisters, the *Isaacs Sewers*, was towed to England for completion and served with the Royal Navy in the Mediterranean* until she was torpedoed off Oran* in November 1942.
BRIEF DATA (*ZH 1*, 1942) Displacement: 1,922 tons; Dimensions: o/a lgth – 351′, b – 34′ 9″; Speed: 37.5 knots; Armament: 5 × 3.9″ gun, 4 × 37mm AA gun; 4 × 20mm AA gun, 8 × 21″ TT.

German Army The German Army had been rapidly expanded by Hitler* from 1933 beyond the 100,000 figure permitted to it after WW1. This growth was felt in professional military circles to be too fast to allow proper training and, regularly assured by Hitler (even as late as 1938) that a major war was impossible before 1944, the German Army was ill-prepared for it in 1939. Although 98 divisions could be mobilized on the eve of the attack on Poland*, including 9 armoured (panzer) divisions, only 58 (1.5 million men) could be deployed, most of the rest being ill-equipped veteran reservists.

By May 1940 2.5 million men were available for the Western Offensive*, including ten panzer divisions with about 2,500 tanks*. It was the tactical concentration of this fast-moving armour, supported by motorized infantry (Panzergrenadier) units and aircraft, which secured victory. Weapon for weapon the larger French Army* was the superior force, while both sets of regular infantry were largely unmechanized (as the German infantry remained throughout WW2).

A total of about 3 million men, including some 200,000 from Germany's allies and satellites, were used for operations on the Eastern Front* in June 1941. They included 17 panzer divisions (reorganized on a smaller scale and totalling about 4,000 tanks), along with 9 motorized, 3 Waffen SS* (motorized) 3 alpine and 142 infantry divisions. Strength in divisional terms increased steadily thereafter, and 58 divisions (including 10 panzer) were deployed to counter the Allied invasion of Northwest Europe* in June 1944, of which 33 were drawn from second-line (coastal defence or training) strength. By the start of 1945 the German Army included 168 infantry, 10 Panzer Grenadier (the name given to motorized divisions after 1943), 10 airborne*, 4 Luftwaffe* (including the Hermann Göring Panzer Division) and 23 Waffen SS divisions, There were 25 panzer divisions in the regular Army, and 7 of the SS divisions were armoured.

These bare figures are misleading and disguise the virtual disintegration of the German Army as a coherent force during the period. Its training and replacement capacity had already been crucially compromised at the start of WW2 by the absorption of virtually all reinforcement and support units into the front-line field army (*Feldheer*) for the Polish campaign. This process was repeated for all major offensives and, once heavy casualties were sustained in the east, it left the Army dependent on raw recurits as its main reserve by 1943, and as its front-line formations by late the following year.

German Army leaders in 1939 were aware that it was ill-equipped for a long war, and its early victories were achieved quickly with the help of new tactics (see Blitzkrieg) dependent on weapons (above all aircraft) at the peak of their modernity. As enemy *matériel* caught and overtook that of the German Army in both quality and quantity, those same leaders lost all operational and administrative control over the Army to Hitler. Form December 1941, when he became its Commander-in-Chief, Hitler's dominance of the Army was total and disastrous. His increasingly unrealistic strategic plans took little or no account of Germany's fragile manpower and industrial bases, and stretched both to irredeemable levels. Professional Army officers, whom he generally mistrusted, were retained in high command only as long as they remained loyal, optimistic and obedient executives, and they could expect to be blamed for the failure of the Führer's schemes. Operationally, Hitler abandoned the fluid, mobile warfare that had brought success in Poland, in the Western Offensive, in the Balkans* and (initially) in the Soviet Union, enforcing instead a rigid standfast policy that cost the German Army hundreds of thousands of men, lost pointlessly defending ground.

These losses could not be made good after 1942, and in order to achieve even part of the strength required for further ambitious offensives in the east, formations in western Europe and occupying forces in the Balkans and Scandinavia were regularly 'combed out' to provide front-line troops. To increase the number of formations available, divisional establishments within the German Army were greatly reduced, This was particularly true of the panzer and motorized forces. In 1940 an armoured division had 328 tanks, 8 support battalions and 6 artillery batteries, but by 1944 the few full-strength divisions had only 159 tanks and 4 motorized support battalions. Most armoured divisions were in fact far weaker still on the Eastern Front (although SS units were usually kept up to strength) and infantry divisions in the theatre were often down to less than 1,000 combat troops by early 1944. Unwilling to strike destroyed formations (such as the ill-disciplined and ill-led Luftwaffe divisions) form the order of battle, Hitler railed at the incompetence and treachery of his generals while refusing them any leeway to rescue the situation.

With the threat of an Allied Second Front in Europe looming in 1944, the manpower shortage was such that the leaders of the Army's heavily fragmented organizational structures (OKH* for the Eastern Front, OKW* for other theatres, and separate commands for armoured, SS, Luftwaffe and replacement forces – all answerable only to Hitler) were reduced to squabbling over the deployment of single divisions in transit, these representing the sum of German mobile reserves at a time when massive attacks were expected on two widely separated and undermanned fronts. Although economic rationalization under Speer* brought a great increase in German armaments production in 1944, lack of raw materials meant this could not be sustained, lack of fuel meant that new weapons could not be fully deployed, and lack of trained personnel meant they could seldom be used to full effect.

The July Bomb* plot of 1944 destroyed the last vestiges of Hitler's faith in the Army. Army leaders were ruthlessly purged and control over Army formations was concentrated in the hands of the trusted SS. Political commissars, first introduced in late 1943, were henceforward appointed down to battalion level, with orders to root out traitors and dissenters. All senior ground commanders were subject to exhaustive security checks (and, from early 1945, to co-option by the SS), and the families of soldiers were made officially responsible for their actions in the field.

From late 1944 the regular Army was supplemented on both main fronts by units of the *Volkssturm*, a People's Militia created by Hitler which figured prominently in the final defence of Berlin*. Composed largely of those too old, young or infirm for regular service, it was poorly equipped despite attempts to mass-produce cheap submachine-guns* for its use. Its front-line deployment reflected the depth of the manpower crisis facing the German Army after five years of war.

Despite the chaos into which the German Army's high command structure had sunk by the latter part of the war, the German soldier and his regimental officers displayed consistent efficiency to the last. Skilled defensive campaigns in 1944–5, particularly in Italy*, reinforced the fighting reputation of German ground forces as second to none. A training system based on the 'leader concept', whereby each man was trained to assume responsibility two levels up, was one reason why the Army performed so well. Another was the generous treatment in terms of pay and home leave afforded to German troops, which was well in excess of anything Allied or other Axis forces could expect to receive, and remained so almost until the end with salutary effects on loyalty and tenacity. A third factor was the enduring faith of the rank and file in Adolf Hitler. Albeit a deluded strategist and the one man primarily responsible for the overcommitment and destruction of the German Army, Hitler was nevertheless perceived by the rank and file (even in 1945) as the sole instrument of national unity through which victory could be acheived.

In total about 12.5 million Germans served in the Army during WW2, and it is estimated that between 3 and 3.5 million were killed.

German Navy In 1939 the German Navy comprised two old battleships, two battlecruisers, three armoured cruisers (*Panzer-schiffe*), three heavy cruisers, six light cruisers, 22 destroyers*, 59 submarines*, 20 flotilla craft and a powerful force of motor boats for coastal operations. Several major units of an ambitious construction programme were also nearing completion, including two battleships, three heavy cruisers and an aircraft carrier.

This powerful force had emerged from the ruins of 1919, when the Treaty of Versailles had effectively restricted the German Navy to coastal capabilities and had banned the use of aircraft or submarines. Design teams had quickly been re-assembled in the early 1920s. During the Weimar years efforts were concentrated on secret research into submarines, the development of advanced (and uncontroversial) small craft and the production of replacement warships within the numerical and class limits set at Versailles. The warships were usually built in excess of their announced tonnage and this trend culminated in the formidable 'pocket battleships' (*Panzerschiffe*) of the late 1920s and early 1930s, which signalled to the world the re-emergence of German sea power (see Deutschland).

When Adolf Hitler* became Chancellor in 1933, German naval construction took on a new dimension. By the time Hitler denounced the Versailles Treaty in early 1935, two (ostensibly) 26,000-ton battle-cruisers and 36 quite illegal submarines were already on order. In the absence of any sign of coherent international response to Germany's evident naval expansion, Britain chose to unilaterally ensure its limitation by the Anglo-German Naval Treaty* of 1935.

This was in effect a licence to build for the relatively tiny German Navy, which embarked on a ten-year programme (Plan Z), to develop a coherent fleet capable of challenging the Royal Navy*, widely (and after 1937 officially) regarded as the future enemy. Direct confrontation with such a gigantic opponent was out of the question, but by concentrating on fast, powerful sur-face squadrons and a strong submarine arm, the German Navy sought to control Britain's vital trade supply lines. In this area the Royal Navy of 1935 was visibly deficient in protective capacity and had other powerful potential enemies all over the world to cope with.

A major flaw in this ambitious scheme was its failure to allow for Royal Navy expansion, which eventually took place on a scale and at a pace which was never fully appreciated in Germany. Furthermore, the British were responding to what were often no more than paper projects. German ship-yards proved quite incapable of meeting increased demands after 1935 and none of the major warships ordered after that year were ready by 1939. The war in fact came five years before the German Navy planned to be ready for it, forcing it to abandon all hope of building a surface fleet capable of dominating British trade routes. Instead resources were concentrated on submarines and the German Navy set about simply sinking as much trade shipping as possible with the means at its disposal.

This strategy was limited by certain technical deficiencies. German heavy warships benefited from their hidden extra weight but lacked the nautical refinement of their Allied contemporaries. Inexperience and haste were also displayed in the design of the smaller classes and the long-range high-pressure turbine engines fitted to cruisers and destroyers proved notoriously unreliable. In combat the cruisers proved under-protected and the heavy armament of the newer destroyers rendered them cumbersome, often fatally so, in battle. Even the successful U-boat arm suffered from the selection of a 750-ton boat as standard (see U-48). Chosen to extract the highest possible number of submarines from overall total tonnage restrictions imposed after 1935, it proved uncomfortably small for Atlantic* operations. The German Navy had radar*, but only for gunnery control, and an early lead in the field was soon overhauled by the British and American navies. Radar aside, German warships were particularly well protected against air attack, but the German Navy possessed no air arm.

The Luftwaffe* guarded its aircraft and its integrity with equal jealousy, repeatedly blocking developments in naval aviation. One aircraft carrier – the *Graf Zeppelin** – was eventually completed for the protection of commerce raiding forces, but it could never be equipped with sufficient aircraft, and no purpose-built carrier aircraft were ever designed. Politically, the Navy could never match the bombastic central influence of Hermann Göring*. Its own C-in-C from 1933–43, Grand Admiral Raeder*, was an aloof man, ill-suited to the intrigues surrounding Hitler's government, and the Navy's political weakness contributed to its peripheral status in German war plans. Adolf Hitler's personal intrusions into naval affairs mainly served to inhibit operational initiative, while hastening the loss of confidence in major warships, only three of which (the *Bismarck**, *Tirpitz** and *Prinz Eugen**) were completed after 1939.

In the first four months of the war, the U-boats sank over 100 ships (including a battleship and an aircraft carrier) and they remained far and away the most successful arm of the German Navy throughout WW2. During 1941–2 they came close to paralysing Britain's supply lines, but the combination of US shipbuilding capacity and Allied advances in anti-submarine* warfare had effectively defeated the U-boats by mid-1943 (see Atlantic, Battle of the). Considerable effort was devoted to developing a U-boat which could remain submerged for long periods, in the hope of restoring the pre-eminence of the submarine. Unfortunately the fixated enthusiasm of the High Command for the most radical inventions delayed the best of these (the excellent Type XXI) beyond usefulness. Morale remained high nevertheless and, backed by the bulk of Germany's faltering production industry, the U-boats eventually sank a staggering 14 million tons of shipping. A further offensive planned for 1945 was pre-empted by the destruction or

capture of boatyards and submarine pens, and the U-boats themselves survived the war in large numbers.

The other highly successful arm of the German Navy was the light surface force. The superb, diesel-powered motor torpedo boats* (*S-Boote* or E-boats) proved their superiority time and again in hundreds of actions, particularly in British home waters and the Baltic. Although overwhelmed in 1944 by Allied air superiority in the English Channel, they retained the upper hand to the end in their battles with Russian light forces. Their victories could, however, only marginally affect the overall course of the war.

The same was increasingly true of the major surface warships. The 'pocket battleships' *Admiral Graf Spee** and *Deutschland** were at sea in the Atlantic when the war started. Supplied by a pre-arranged network of cargo ships, they sank a few merchantmen before the *Graf Spee* was cornered at Montevideo in December 1939. Her loss was a serious blow to prestige, and Hitler's decision to recall and rename the *Deutschland* (as the *Lützow*) demonstrated early the pessimism which was to characterize German Navy surface operations. Although the fleet played an important part in supporting the successful invasion of Norway*, it suffered serious losses (including three cruisers and ten destroyers) while several other major units were damaged.

Like the U-boats, the warships benefited from new bases in mid-1940. Once released from the proposed invasion of Britain, which the German Navy as a whole regarded as an extremely dangerous venture, they enjoyed their most successful period. Major units completed highly successful Atlantic cruises in late 1940 and early 1941, and 11 disguised auxiliary cruisers (*Hilfskreuzen**), which left French ports from December 1940, sank more than 800,000 tons of shipping over the next two years. The heyday of the surface ships was short-lived, however, and after the sinking of the *Bismarck* in May 1941 it was clear that they could no longer raid the Atlantic with impunity. With French ports under increasing bombardment from the RAF*, the audacious Channel Dash (see Scharnhorst) of February 1942 marked a retreat from the theatre, although it also demonstrated the continued potency of the fleet and was a rare example of effective German air-sea co-operation.

By late 1942, as the relatively marginal Arctic* convoys became the focus of fleet operations, pressure for action from the surface ships was growing from Hitler, who nevertheless expressly forbade the taking of risks. The following January he lost patience completely and ordered the fleet dismantled, prompting the resignation of Raeder, its prime architect. His successor, U-boat C-in-C Karl Dönitz*, managed to save the fleet, but only with the argument that it distracted Allied attention from anti-submarine operations. The battleship *Tirpitz* was then sent to Norway with the enduring *Scharnhorst*, while other surviving units went to the Baltic and were restricted to training duties.

Although their mere presence significantly affected British naval strategy, the big ships achieved little in the North Sea beyond the bombardment of the Spitzbergen weather station. The *Scharnhorst* was lost in a desperately ill-conceived sortie at the end of 1943. The *Tirpitz* remained an entirely passive threat and was gradually pounded to destruction in Norwegian waters by repeated air attacks. Her demise in late 1944 left the Baltic as the sole remaining parish of the German fleet, and its rescue in early 1945 of troops and refugees from the advancing Russians in the Eastern Baltic was its last major operation. Losses, mostly to bombing, remained high, and by the end of the war only the *Prinz Eugen* and two light cruisers (one of them crippled) remained afloat.

Germany, Surrender of By early April 1945, Berlin* was under threat from Allied forces advancing from east and west. While Anglo-American forces continued to advance from the west and Marshal Zhukov's*

Soviet armies prepared for a final assault on the city from the east, secret negotiations were opened between Himmler* and the Allies for an armistice. German forces' commanders, Field Marshal Kesselring* and SS General Wolff*, were also in the process of agreeing a separate capitulation to the Allies in Italy*. At this desperate moment for the Third Reich, Hitler* was totally unprepared to accept the notion of surrender. Unconcerned with the survival of Germans, whom he believed had proved unequal to his leadership, Hitler had already prepared his final strategy – a scorched earth policy to destroy German infrastructure. Deliberately inviting disease and starvation to follow him (though few were now prepared to carry out his demoniacal orders), Hitler denied his responsibility for defeat or the millions of German lives lost in the struggle. Betrayed by the German people, Hitler believed they deserved the future he foresaw for them.

When the dictator shot himself on 30 April, Admiral Dönitz*, his named successor, made an immediate attempt to open surrender negotiations, though he was also anxious to delay long enough to allow the maximum number of civilians to escape across the projected Soviet boundary of occupation (along the Elbe) to the Allied control zone. While troops on the Eastern Front fought a desperate rearguard action, Dönitz opened talks with the Allies for a ceasefire. Subsidiary surrenders came into force in Italy on 2 May and on the north of the Western Front on 5 May, though no delegate arrived at Supreme Allied Commander Eisenhower's Rheims HQ to negotiate for a ceasefire on the rest of the Front until 5 May.

Aware that Dönitz was playing for time, Eisenhower was obliged to request an agreement on immediate unconditional surrender. The arrival of Jodl* to discuss the matter merely exacerbated tension. Eisenhower threatened to close the Elbe to crossings from the east and Dönitz had no choice but to assent to the signing of the surrender document on 7 May. The document was ratified in Berlin, on the insistence of the Russians, on 9 May, although fighting around Prague and in Yugoslavia continued after this date.

Gestapo (GEheimes STAatsPOlizei) The Third Reich's secret police which originated in Prussia (each German state had its own police) under Göring*, who took over the Prussian ministry in 1933. Nazi careerists jockeyed for power within the Gestapo, which came under SS* chief Himmler's* organizational control, with Heinrich Müller at its head. In 1936 the Gestapo was given formal national status and a national headquarters was established at Prinz Albrechtstrasse. In 1939 the Gestapo came under Heydrich* as Department IV of the RSHA (the state security organization), with Müller as operational chief. Essentially policemen, the Gestapo were equally the instruments of Nazi methods and encouraged terror as a weapon to control the state and its people. By 1943 there were 45,000 Gestapo in contact with some 60,000 agents or with the 100,000 informers on SS files.

As Nazi power spread, so did the fearsome reputation of the Gestapo. Backed by the system of concentration camps* and by the right under law to extract confessions by beating, the leather overcoated Gestapo man with snap-brim hat became a figure of terror to Germans and the subject populations of Nazi-occupied Europe. The Gestapo was so thoroughly enmeshed with the whole SS operation that Allied jurists found it difficult at Nuremberg* to identify those Gestapo members responsible for the organization's manifold crimes. Gestapo men denied being other than policemen and sought to hide behind the SD*, the SS intelligence department. They claimed no knowledge of the Einsatzgruppen*, the notorious task forces that moved behind the advancing German armies in Russia and whose officers were often drawn from the Gestapo. Many of the senior Gestapo escaped arrest altogether. 'Gestapo Müller', who undoubtedly knew most about Gestapo

operations, disappeared at the end of the war, having burnt his files and all photographs of himself.

Ghormley, Vice Admiral Robert L. (1883 –1958) Acting as a military observer in London at the outbreak of WW2, Ghormley left his diplomatic posting in March 1942 to fight in the South Pacific, assuming command of the South Pacific Ocean Area after the Battle of the Java Sea*. In the following month he was sent to Auckland in New Zealand to organize the US naval forces under Admiral Nimitz*. Operations organized by Ghormley against the Solomon Islands* (to safeguard communications with Australia) were more successful, despite the American forces' lack of experience, than the initial assaults by American Marines against Guadalcanal* and Tulagi that saw some desperate fighting and were widely judged to have been poorly handled by Ghormley (though he himself had expressed doubts during the planning of the landings). As a result he was replaced in October 1942 by Admiral William Halsey* and returned to Washington to US Fleet C-in-C King's headquarters, where he was subsequently given command of the Hawaiian Sea Frontier defences. After VE day, Ghormley directed the disarmament and demobilization of the German Navy*.

GI Bill of Rights One of the most important pieces of American wartime legislation, it provided special rehabilitation benefits and opportunities to millions of returning American WW2 veterans and had a massive impact on American post-war society as a whole. The Bill was originally framed by President Roosevelt* in a presentation to Congress in October 1943 that contained an outline of proposed educational benefits for veterans. The legislation provided for supported education as well as government-guaranteed life insurance, medical care and rehabilitation benefits, pension rights and re-employment rights. This legislative package was taken further by an American Legion proposal, presented to Congress in January 1944, that also called for the provision of a centralized administration – the Veterans Administration – and of federally guaranteed loans for homes and farms. This omnibus Bill, publicized as a bill of rights for 'GI Joe and GI Jane', was passed unanimously in the Senate in March and, with the important contribution of a Mississippi Democrat, John Rankin, passed through Congress by May.

By 1955, statistics showed how many veterans had taken advantage of the provisions: nearly 4 million people had used the home loan benefits, and over 5 million had used the readjustment allowance. An estimated 7 million veterans had taken education or training opportunities provided for under the Act, including 250,000 blacks who were given the opportunity to go to college for the first time. The social ramifications of the Bill were as sweeping. Apart from establishing the principle of federal involvement in education and housing, the legislation gave literally millions of Americans, especially from the working classes, opportunities for education, home and business ownership that would certainly have been denied them otherwise.

Giap Vo Nguyen (1912–75) Vietnamese communist general who was arrested in Hanoi in 1939, but escaped, along with other communist revolutionaries to southern China*. Between 1942 and 1945 he aided Ho Chi Minh* in organizing resistance to the Japanese and served as Minister of the Interior in Ho's short-lived provisional government of Vietnam. In 1946 he was given command of the Viet Minh.

Gibraltar British naval base on the southern tip of Spain, guarding the narrow entrance to the Western Mediterranean from the Atlantic* Ocean. From 1940 it was the home base of the Royal Navy Force H*, and convoys* for Malta* and Egypt*

were organized from Gibraltar. Frequently bombed by Axis forces, and by the French *Armée de l'Air* in reprisal for the British attacks on the French fleet in July 1940, Gibraltar was regarded as indefensible in the event of aggression by the Spanish. This fear was expressed by US military leaders pressing for the Allied Torch* landings (for which Gibraltar was the command headquarters) to be concentrated on the Atlantic coast of Morocco in 1942. Spanish military support for the Axis never materialized, and after the capitulation of Italy* in 1943 the base was not seriously threatened. See also Mediterranean Sea.

Gibson, Wing Commander Guy (1918–44) Leader of the RAF Avro Lancaster* force from 617 Squadron, he received the Victoria Cross for his leadership of the Möhne dam raid (see Dambusters) and was killed when his plane crashed in the Netherlands, when returning from a raid on Rheydt on 19 September 1944.

Giffard, General Sir George (1886–1964) A successful British commander, Giffard had gained considerable experience in Africa and was Military Secretary of the War Office when war broke out. Appointed GOC (General Officer Commanding) in Palestine and Transjordan early in 1940 and then C-in-C of Western African forces in June, Giffard successfully trained and developed West African regiments and specialist units. As a result of his success, Giffard was sent by General Wavell* to India in 1942 to command the Eastern Army. During 1943, his administrative expertise and experience in specialist tactics contributed to the preparations for the Allied recapture of Burma*. He was appointed to command the 11th Army Group under Lord Louis Mountbatten's* newly organized Southeast Asia Command (SEAC). Dismissed from his post following clashes with Montgomery* and US General Stilwell*, commander of Chinese forces, Giffard was replaced by General Leese* in November 1944.

Gilbert Islands An island group southeast of the Marshalls* in the Central Pacific, the Gilberts had been occupied by the Japanese in 1941 during their initial advance into the Pacific island territories. See Map 10. In 1943, they became the primary objective of the American Central Pacific campaign, code-named Granite, under the overall command of Admiral Nimitz*. The attack force under Vice Admiral Raymond Spruance* was supported by Rear Admiral Pownall's Fast Carrier Force, comprising six fleet carriers, five light carriers, six new battleships and numerous smaller warships. Also in support was the newly developed American Mobile Service Force, a floating maintenance 'train' with full service facilities (including tankers, tenders, barges, minesweepers, ammunition ships, etc.) which significantly improved the range and power of the US fleets in the Central Pacific.

The Gilberts, recently reclassified under Japanese Imperial HQ's 'New Operational Policy' as 'non-essential' territories (see Pacific War), were still awaiting reinforcements when the two most westerly islands, Makin and Tarawa (and the atoll of Apamama) were invaded by units of the US 5th Amphibious Corps under Marine Major-General Holland Smith, on 20 November. The operation, code-named Galvanic, had early success at Apamama, where the Japanese garrison was only 25 strong. The capture of Makin, with a garrison of 800, was achieved after four days and was largely delayed by the inexperience of the American infantry units.

At Tarawa, which was the key to the Japanese defence of the Gilberts and much more heavily garrisoned and fortified, heavy aerial and naval bombardment of Betio in the south of the atoll preceded the landing of 5,000 men of the US 2nd Marine Division which had earned its reputation at Guadalcanal. Problems caused by the encircling coral reef, which made it impossible to use landing craft, forced US Marines to wade ashore under raining Japanese artillery fire from the fortified beach positions.

Although some Marines in Amtracs managed to gain a shallow foothold, many were lost before they gained the beach. A second landing on the second day also incurred heavy losses, but bitter fighting on the beachhead enabled the Marines under Colonel Shoup to relaunch attacks on two fronts, supported by artillery fire from emplacements on Bairiki Island, which had been captured by the 2nd Battalion (6th Marines) the previous afternoon. A final furious Japanese counter-attack threw all the remaining strength against the American forces, but was fought off by the morning of the 23rd, and the island was declared secure on that day. The heavy losses of nearly 1,000 dead and over 2,000 wounded, against fanatically determined Japanese defenders, shocked Americans at home, and Galvanic caused widespread controversy at the time. Nevertheless, by 26 November Spruance's forces were able to retire to prepare the advance to the Marshalls. See also Amphibious Warfare.

Giraud, General Henri (1879–1949) Successor to Corap in command of the French 9th Army which was routed by the German armoured formations in May 1940 (see Western Offensive), Giraud was taken prisoner but escaped German captivity in April 1942. Seen by the Allies, and particularly by the US, as a more acceptable leader of French forces than de Gaulle*, leader of Free France*, Giraud was taken from Gibraltar* to Algiers* by British submarine in November, and appointed High Commissioner for French Africa and French Army C-in-C, following Darlan's* assassination in December. Despite a brief attempt at co-operation as joint heads of the French Committee of National Liberation, de Gaulle's political manoeuvring increasingly cost Giraud his American support. In August 1943 he stepped down as High Commissioner, though he continued to work towards rebuilding the French military forces. In April 1944, his task largely completed, a final confrontation with de

Gaulle resulted in his resignation as C-in-C.

Giulio Cesare Along with her sister the *Conte de Cavour*, this veteran Italian battleship had been almost completely rebuilt from 1933–7. At the Battle of Calabria on 9 July 1940, she was hit by one long-range 15-inch shell from the British battleship *Warspite** and withdrew damaged. This brief action contributed to the poor reputation of the Italian Fleet in the Mediterranean, but the *Giulio Cesare* was acting in accordance with defensive instructions issued by the Italian High Command. Unharmed by the British attack on Taranto* in November 1940, she survived the war and subsequently served in the Red Navy* as the *Novorossiisk* (1948–55). The *Conte di Cavour* was badly damaged at Taranto and was never fully repaired. She was seized by German forces at Trieste in September 1943, but further damaged by Allied air attack in 1945.

BRIEF DATA (*Cesare*, 1940) Displacement: 26,140 tons; Dimensions: o/a lgth – 611' 9", b – 92'; Speed: 27 knots; Armament: 10 × 12.6" gun (5 × 2), 12 × 4.7" gun, 8 × 3.9" AA gun, 8 × 37mm AA gun, 12 × 20mm AA gun.

Gloire French light cruiser and class of six ships, built from 1931–7. The *Gloires* were the best of the French cruisers, achieving a good balance between speed and protection, while possessing an oceanic range rare in French designs. At the start of the war they served on Atlantic* convoy duty, but after the fall of France* the *Gloire* and two of her sisters (the *Georges Leygues* and the *Montcalm*) attempted to reach Vichy* French forces at Dakar*.

On 18 September 1940, the *Gloire* was intercepted by the British and forced to sail to Casablanca, where she was neutralized. The other two ships reached Dakar and joined in defeating the subsequent British attack on the port. The ships were reunited in late 1942 when the French in Northwest Africa joined the Allies after the Torch*

landings, and all three were refitted in the US. Later they were used as bombardment support for the Normandy* and Anvil/Dragoon* landings. The *Galissonière*, *Jean de Vienne* and *Marseillaise* had remained in their home base at Toulon and were all scuttled in November 1942.

BRIEF DATA (*Gloire*, 1939) Displacement: 7,600 tons; Dimensions: o/a lgth – 587' 6", b – 57' 4"; Armaments: 9 × 6" gun, 8 × 3.5" AA gun, 8 × 13.2mm AA mg, 4 × 21" TT, 2 aircraft.

Glorious, HMS See Courageous, HMS.

Gloster Gladiator The last British biplane fighter, the Gladiator was virtually obsolete when it entered service in February 1937. Nevertheless, production continued until April 1940, and Gladiators saw combat with both the RAF* (overseas and with auxiliary forces) and the Fleet Air Arm*. A total of 480 was delivered to the RAF, and 60 slightly slower, carrier-equipped Sea Gladiators were built. These were largely replaced on warships by Grumman Martlets* during 1940, although from June of that year four quaint but stubborn Sea Gladiators became famous in the defence of Malta*. A further 216 Gladiators were exported to 12 countries.

BRIEF DATA (Mk II) Type: single-seat fighter; Engine: 1 × 840hp Bristol Mercury; Max speed: 253mph; Ceiling: 33,000'; Range: 440m; Arms: 4 × 0.303" mg.

Gloster Meteor First flown in March 1943, the Meteor was the only Allied jet fighter to see action in the war. The first Mark Is reached RAF* squadrons in July 1944, in time to join the fight against the V-1* rockets, but only 16 of this version were ever supplied. The Mark II existed only in prototype and the re-engined Mark III, which saw action over Europe in the last weeks of the war, was the first main production model.

BRIEF DATA (Mk III) Type: single-seat fighter; Engine: 2 × 2,000lb thrust Rolls Royce turbojet; Max speed: 493mph; Ceil-

ing: 44,000'; Range: 1,000m; Arms: 4 ×
20mm cannon.

Glowworm, HMS Royal Navy* 'G' Class
destroyer. Completed in 1936–7, the 'G'
and 'H' classes were developments of the
small torpedo-boat destroyer designs produced in the 1920s and early 1930s (see
Destroyers). During the war most of these
were modified to carry increased anti-
aircraft* and anti-submarine* armament
for escort work as more modern destroyers
took over fleet duties. The *Glowworm* contributed to the high reputation enjoyed
by the Royal Navy's destroyer forces by
ramming and seriously damaging the German heavy cruiser *Admiral Hipper** off the
coast of Norway* before sinking on 8 April
1940.
BRIEF DATA (1939) Displacement: 1,345
tons; Dimensions: o/a lgth – 323', b – 32'
3"; Speed: 35.5 knots; Armament: 4 × 4.7"
gun (4 × 1), 8 × 0.5" AA mg, 10 × 21"
TT.

Gneisenau German Navy* battlecruiser,
launched in 1936. The *Gneisenau* was the
sister ship of the *Scharnhorst** and the two
units co-operated in successful operations
in the Atlantic* and off Norway*, culminating in the famous Channel Dash of
February 1942. A few days later the *Gneisenau* was badly damaged in a bombing
raid, and repairs were interrupted by further
serious bomb damage at Kiel in July.
Although she was towed to Gotenhafen
(Gdynia), out of reach of Allied aircraft,
and work was put in hand to up-gun her
main batteries, shortages of labour and materials meant that this was never completed. On 28 March 1945 she was scuttled
at the harbour entrance to deny access to
Soviet forces.
BRIEF DATA See Scharnhorst.

Göbbels, Josef Paul (1897–1945) Chief
propagandist of the Nazi Party* and Nazi
Propaganda Minister from March 1933,
Göbbels developed and demonstrated a
mastery of the techniques of mass com-

munication which served as one of
National Socialism's most characteristic
weapons. A consummately skilled orator,
he used the new media of radio and sound
cinema to advance and sustain the myths
of National Socialism and began the world's
first regular television service in March
1935. Among so much intellectual medioc-
rity in the Nazi leadership, Göbbels was
bound to stand out. He also created a Reich
Chamber of Culture, with chambers and
academies for every field of cultural activity, though most of its highly prescribed
output was dull and sterile, a host of German intellectuals, writers, artists and actors
having been lost to the wave of emigration
from Nazi Germany.
After 1939, Göbbels' key importance
waned. His broadcasting services directed
against Germany's enemies never carried
the conviction of the BBC (see Joyce, William). After the pivotal German defeat at
Stalingrad*, however, Göbbels created a
new role for himself by taking a stand for
total war and calling for full support and
devotion from Germans in a fight to the
death. He fully mobilized German manpower for the first time, as well as touring
bombed cities (which Hitler* never did),
and organizing relief convoys, gaining a
new popularity and prominence within the
party. His efforts, however, could not prevent Germany's ultimate military collapse.
In April he and his family joined Hitler in
the *Führerbunker*. The day following Hitler's suicide, he poisoned his wife and
children and shot himself. See also Propaganda.

Golikov, Colonel General Fillipp I. (1900
–) Deputy People's Commissar of Defence
from 1943–50 and Head of Russian Military
Intelligence, Golikov headed a Lend-
Lease* mission to London and Washington
in 1941 and was one of those who advised
Stalin* against the likelihood of a German
attack. After the German invasion in June
1941, Golikov commanded the 10th Army
and then the Bryansk and Voronezh
Fronts*, but was dismissed following

Marshal Timoshenko's* abortive drive against Kharkov* and the subsequent German advance under General Bock* in May 1942. Reinstated to command the 10th Army at Stalingrad*, forces under Golikov then participated in the recapture of Kursk*, Kharkov and Rostov* in early 1943. Following his appointment as Deputy Defence Minister, Golikov also acted as Chief of the Repatriation Mission in Moscow in 1944–6.

Golovanov, Chief Marshal of Aviation, Aleksandr E. (1903–) Commander of the 81st Long Range Division which supported the Russian defence of Moscow in 1941, Golovanov was promoted general and appointed to command the Air Force for Long Range Operations (ALFRO) in March 1942. Red Air Force* operations were directly under the command of local front commanders; as an adviser to General Zhukov*, Golovanov prepared the joint artillery and air force plans for the campaign in Belorussia* in 1944. He was also responsible for planning the air offensives against Hungary* and Königsberg.

Goodwood Code-name for the controversial British 2nd Army offensive southeast of Caen* (Normandy*) begun on 18 July 1944. See also Northwest Europe, Allied Invasion of.

Gördeler, Carl (1884–1945) German politician and civilian leader of resistance to Hitler in the Third Reich, Gördeler had publicly opposed rearmament and anti-Semitism* and had used his international contacts as overseas representative of the Bosch company to try to warn British, French and US governments about the dangers of Nazism. He met Winston Churchill* in Britain in 1938. After the outbreak of war, Gördeler associated with Canaris* and the older German military leaders, like Beck*, attempting to persuade other senior officers of their duty to oppose Hitler. He was arrested in August 1944 following the failure of the July Bomb Plot*

and executed at Plötzensee, after prolonged interrogations, in February 1945. See Resistance: Germany.

Göring, Reichsmarschall Hermann (1893 –1946) C-in-C of the German Air Force and the most prominent German war leader after Adolf Hitler*. A Bavarian, Göring became a fighter pilot in WW1 after arthritis had made him unfit for infantry service. A well-known ace with 22 combat victories, he was the last commander of the famous Richthofen Fighter Squadron in 1918. Discharged as a captain (and holder of the *Pour le Mérite*, the highest Imperial battle decoration), Göring worked in Denmark and Sweden before returning to Germany in 1923 and joining the new Nazi Party.

His fame and powers of leadership brought immediate success within the party and he soon became commander of the SA (*Sturmabteilung*), its storm-troopers. Göring helped plan the Beer Hall Putsch in Munich in November 1923, and suffered bullet wounds in the thigh and groin when the police opened fire on Hitler's march to the Oldenplatz. He was then taken to Austria by his wife and the couple lived in exile until amnesty was granted to the Beer Hall insurgents in 1926. During this period, Göring became addicted to morphine, which was administered in the treatment of his wounds and of his recurring arthritis.

Rejoining the Nazi Party, he gained a seat in the Reichstag in 1928, becoming its president after the election of 1932. His role within the party was to mediate with powerful nationalists and right-wing industrialists, to whom he was more socially acceptable than other Nazi leaders. In Hitler's first cabinet of 1933, Göring was a minister without portfolio and Prussian Minister of the Interior, the latter appointment giving him control over Germany's largest police force. When the existence of the new German air force – the Luftwaffe* – was announced in 1935, Göring was revealed as its C-in-C.

In the years before the war Göring was

unquestionably Hitler's most important assistant. His power grew in political, economic and military affairs and he amassed a large personal fortune. In 1937 he became Minister of the Economy and the following year was created a field marshal. In 1939 Hitler named Göring as his successor. During this period he performed a number of personal diplomatic missions – most frequently to Italy – and undertook his many administrative duties with vigour and efficiency. Göring's first wife had died in 1931, but he had remarried a well-known actress and they remained a happily devoted couple. The Field Marshal's wealth and vanity were the talk of Germany, but he was a very popular public figure.

Regarded in diplomatic circles as a relative moderate, Göring did not want or expect war as early as 1939. His response to it was, however, characteristically confident. 'Leave it to my Luftwaffe' was his slogan, and in the first year of the war the air arm did much to justify his optimism. 1940 was the high point of Göring's life. The Luftwaffe was the world's largest air force, equipped with aircraft close to their operational peak and manned by pilots with experience of combat in Spain. German land victories in 1939–40 were also acknowledged triumphs for the air force and, when Hitler promoted nine of his generals to the rank of field marshal after the fall of France*, he created the title of Reichsmarschall for Göring.

Göring's career now began a rapid decline. The Luftwaffe suffered its first defeats at Dunkirk* and in the Battle of Britain*. The invasion of Russia in 1941 strained German air resources and did not bring conclusive victory. Overburdened, the German aviation industry lurched into crisis as its opponents began to fully mobilize their own resources. The RAF* began bombing Germany, which Göring had publicly insisted could never happen. The Reichsmarschall withdrew increasingly from the centre of power, neglecting his duties and alienating important lieutenants. Ambitious men like Himmler*, Bor-

mann* and Göbbels* were quick to exploit Göring's demise and erode his relationship with Hitler. Although he still held economic office in 1942 – and took an active interest in the exploitation of Russian conquests – his leading role in the field passed to Speer*.

The Luftwaffe suffered badly for its dependence on Göring for political influence. Its C-in-C was still capable of extreme optimism and the air force had to carry out the disastrous airlift of supplies into Stalingrad* in January 1943 in response to Göring's boast. It had, however, no strong voice to oppose Hitler's obsession with offensive aircraft and neglect of fighter development for home defence. By 1944 Göring was often far from the conduct of the war and its crises, opulently tending his estates and his spectacular fine art collection. His dependence on drugs had increased (along with his girth) and his behaviour became erratic, although seldom introvert.

On 20 April 1945, Göring left the Berlin bunker for the last time after saying goodbye to an indifferent Hitler. He travelled south and three days later telegraphed the Führer confirming his willingness to act as his successor. This was presented to Hitler as a treasonable act by Bormann, and Göring was arrested and stripped of all his ranks. Hitler's will expelled him from the party.

Uneasy under SS guard, Göring put on a special uniform and drove off on 8 May to surrender graciously to American forces. He was imprisoned and taken off drugs, which greatly improved his health. He performed brilliantly when tried as a war criminal at Nuremberg* in October 1946, and was clearly the leader of the defendants. Found guilty of several capital offences, he was sentenced to death by hanging. Göring had refused the option of a firing squad, but was found dead in his cell on the night of 15 October, having bitten a concealed cyanide capsule.

Gorshkov, Admiral Sergei G. (1910–88) Commander of Red Navy* formations in the Black Sea Squadron 1931–44, Gorshkov also commanded the Azov* Military Flotilla which participated in the defence of the Crimea* and the Caucasus* during the Battle of Stalingrad* and later the Danube Military Flotilla (1944). In 1956, Gorshkov was appointed C-in-C of the Red Navy by Stalin's successor, Khrushchev*. He later radically reshaped Soviet naval strategy.

Gort, Field Marshal John (1886–1946) Awarded the Victoria Cross for outstanding gallantry during WW1 when in command of a battalion of Grenadier Guards, he was promoted Chief of the Imperial General Staff (CIGS) in 1937 and went to France in command of the British Expeditionary Force in 1939 (see Western Offensive). Though unable to provide an imaginative challenge to the lightning advance of German forces, Gort was prepared to take the decisions which led to the withdrawal to Dunkirk* and the eventual escape of the BEF from there in May 1940. He was replaced by Dill* in the same month, and later served as Governor of Malta*, where he was instrumental in defending the island against besieging Axis forces, and as High Commissioner in Palestine and Transjordan.

Gothic Line Final German defence line in Italy, north of Florence and the Arno River Line, it stretched from La Spezia in the west to Pesaro on the Adriatic. Operation Olive, a plan devised by Allied Supreme Commander Alexander* and modified by General Oliver Leese*, commander of 8th Army, envisaged a reinforced assault on the eastern stretch of the Gothic Line as a diversionary measure to ease the 5th Army's more central thrust towards Bologna. The operation began on 25 August 1943 with actions by units of the British 8th Army, but the initial advance was halted at the Coriano ridge. It was not until mid-September that the Gothic Line was breached and the direct assault on Bologna resumed. See Italy, Campaign in.

Gott, Lt General William (1897–1942) As a brigadier in May 1941, 'Strafer' Gott led the armoured strike force for Operation Brevity*, General Wavell's* abortive first attempt to relieve Tobruk*. Promoted to Lt General, he took command of the 13th Corps in Cyrenaica (Libya) in 1942 and led it through defeats at Gazala* and Mersa Matruh* in June. Gott's forces performed disappointingly in the offensive follow-up to the first victory at El Alamein*, yet in early August Churchill proposed to give him command of the 8th Army. On the way to Cairo to receive the appointment, Gott was killed in an air crash and Montgomery* was brought out from England to fill the post under General Alexander*.

Goums Moroccan light infantry units, also used as police, originally employed to supplement French units in North Africa, the Goums (consisting of approximately 200 *goumiers*) used mule teams for transportation of mortars and light anti-tank cannon and were incorporated into the French Army* after the outbreak of WW2. The Goums fought some important actions in the Allied campaigns in Italy* and Northwest Europe* between 1943 and 1945. Their experience of combat in mountainous terrain was particularly important during the operations against the strongly held German defensive lines on the Italian peninsula, notably under General Juin* during the fighting on the Gustav* Line in the winter of 1943–4.

Graf Zeppelin Ordered in 1935 and launched in 1938, the *Graf Zeppelin* was the German Navy's* first aircraft carrier, intended to provide air cover for commerce raiding squadrons. The design clearly demonstrated the inexperience of her designers. Her radius was barely up to Atlantic cruising, and her main armament was unnecessarily excessive, wasting weight that could have usefully been invested in more armour protection. Anti-aircraft* guns were poorly positioned for use in conjunction with flight-deck operations, and her aircraft capacity was small for a carrier with an open-sided hangar. The *Graf Zeppelin's* most serious disadvantage was a complete lack of co-operation between the Navy and the Luftwaffe*, the latter jealously holding back its aircraft (which were in any case barely viable as naval types) and refusing to countenance the formation of a naval air arm. Amid much wrangling and indecision over equipment, construction was slowed and then halted in August 1940, with the carrier 80 per cent complete. Re-activated in 1942, the ship was finally suspended in April 1943 and her hull was scuttled two years later at Stettin. A second projected carrier was scrapped on the slipway at Kiel in 1940.

BRIEF DATA (as planned) Displacement: 23,200 tons; Dimensions: o/a lgth – 862' 9", b – 103' 3" (118' 9" FD); Speed: 33.75 knots; Armament: 16 × 5.9" gun (8 × 2), 12 × 4.1" AA gun, 22 × 37mm AA gun, 28 × 20mm AA gun, 40 aircraft.

Granite Code-name for US offensive operations under Admiral Nimitz* in the Central Pacific, it was fully launched in March 1944 with a carrier raid on Truk*, Japanese naval headquarters. See also Admiralty Islands; Marshall Islands; Saipan; Tinian.

Grant (M3) Tank The medium tank in service with the US Army* in September 1939 was the M2A1, armed with a 37mm gun. Although only recently introduced, this was regarded as obsolete in the light of European combat reports, and it was decided to build a medium tank armed with a 75mm weapon. As an expedient, pending the design of a new turret, the gun was to be mounted on the right-hand side of an up-armoured M2A1 hull. The resultant M3 entered mass-production in August 1941, and by the end of its run in December 1942 a total of 6,258 had been completed.

This impressive acceleration in output derived from the full co-ordination of the US automobile industry in the business of building tanks, as supervised by Lt General William S. Knudsen, President of General Motors and a co-opted member of the American National Defense Advisory Committee. He also oversaw the rapid construction of a prolific government-owned (but Chrysler-run) tank arsenal in Michigan, and this ability to gear its manufacturing capabilities to its wartime needs was one of American's great advantages in her conduct of WW2.

The M3 design went through several versions and all later production models carried a long-barrelled version of the 75mm gun. The 1,000 M3s ordered by the British Tank Purchasing Commission in 1941 were equipped with a turret of British design and shipped to North Africa. Known as the Grant tank, it arrived in time for the operations around Gazala* in May 1942, and although its weapons system was far from perfect, it gave the British 8th Army full parity with the German PzKpfw IV*. American M3 types shipped to the British under Lend-Lease* were known as the Lee tank (Marks I–VI), although the final M3A5 version was designated the Grant II. Apart from its successful career in North Africa, the M3 was used in Burma* and on the Eastern Front*. Its replacement, the Sherman*, was in service in 1942, but the Grant was not finally declared obsolete until April 1944.

BRIEF DATA (M3A5) Type: 6-man medium tank; Engine: 340hp petrol; Max speed: 26mph; Range: 120m; Arms: 1 × 75mm gun, 1 × 37mm gun, 4 × 7.62mm mg; Armour: max 37mm.

Graph, HMS On 28 August 1941, the German Type VII submarine *U-570* surfaced beneath an RAF Coastal Command Lockheed Hudson* bomber, was bluffed into surrendering and boarded before she could be scuttled. The Royal Navy* renamed their prize HMS *Graph* and used it to test their own anti-submarine* measures. After a propaganda-inspired patrol off Norway*, she was expended as a target vessel

in 1944, her identifiably German silhouette rendering her an operational liability.
BRIEF DATA See U-48.

Graziani, Marshal Rodolfo (1882–1955)
A soldier since the age of 16, Graziani was appointed C-in-C of Italian forces in Libya in 1940, after serving as Governor of Libya, Viceroy of Ethiopia and Army Chief of Staff in the 1930s. Reluctantly pressed into commanding the invasion of Egypt by Mussolini, Graziani advanced with extreme caution and was replaced in February 1941, after defeats by the British in Cyrenaica (see Egypt). He came out of retirement in September 1943 to serve Mussolini briefly as Defence Minister. In 1945 he was captured by partisans and tried for treason. Sentenced to 19 years in prison, he received amnesty in 1950 and spent his last years in Italian right-wing politics.

Great Marianas Turkey Shoot See Philippine Sea, Battle of.

Greater East Asia Co-Prosperity Sphere
Concept of economic 'autarky' which was a key element in Japan's November 1938 declaration of the creation of a 'New Order'* in Southeast Asia, effectively a blueprint for Japan's political and economic hegemony in East Asia. It was first framed by Premier Fumimaro Konoe* in November 1938 (though based on earlier ideas of pan-Asianism), and used to designate an economically self-sufficient sphere 'of co-existence and co-prosperity' among Japan, China*; Manchukuo* and the former Dutch, French and British colonies in Southeast Asia. The concept was later extended to cover the Philippines and a Greater East Asia Ministry created to promote the idea. Although an amount of economic integration was achieved in the area, attempts by Japan (notably at the Greater East Asia Conference in November 1943) to gain real support for the idea from occupied countries was unsuccessful. See also Pacific War; Map 10.

Grechko, Marshal Andrey A. (1903–76)
C-in-C of Warsaw Pact Armies 1960–7, Grechko began his military career during the Civil War in Russia. A protégé of General Shaposhnikov*, Grechko graduated from the General Staff Academy in 1941. During WW2, he commanded first a cavalry division, then a cavalry corps and was finally appointed to command the 12th Army in April 1942. In that year Grechko participated in the defence of the Transcaucasus and led liberation forces in the Caucasus* and the Tamon Peninsula. In the following year he fought at Kiev*, becoming first Deputy Commander of the 1st Ukrainian Front* and then commander of the 1st Army, with whom he fought in the Carpathians in 1944 and at Mor Ostrava in 1945.

Greece, British Occupation of (1944–5)
Although German forces left Greece in ordered withdrawal during November 1944, the British force which took up positions in their wake faced a local situation fraught with dangers. British support for, and attempts to unite, resistance groups had failed to prevent the chaos of Greek underground politics from degenerating into civil war by October 1943. The Germans had let the Greeks get on with it, and by the time of a British inspired armistice (the Plaka Agreement, 29 February 1944), the communist EAM/ELAS coalition had greatly extended its control over the countryside. During the spring and summer of 1944, Russian support for the EAM/ELAS had replaced that of the British, who sheltered the Royalist government-in-exile. At the same time, the communists had actively consolidated their strength and organization at the expense of rival guerrilla groups, particularly their main opposition the liberal-republican EDES. In September, both the communist leader General Saraphis and Colonel Zervas of EDES had agreed to co-operate with British forces and the following month, in Moscow, Churchill had insisted that Greece be excluded from the agreed Russian sphere

of influence in the Balkans* (see Conferences).

When the British arrived in early October, they installed an all-party government in Athens under George Panandreou, head of the government-in-exile. Over the next few weeks, with Albania*, Yugoslavia and Bulgaria already under communist regimes, the EAM/ELAS tightened its grip on the hinterland and, with the Royalists powerless to prevent it, began an armed takeover in Athens on 3 December.

The British Commander, Scobie, had been reluctant to interfere; but by 4 December British troops were fighting in Athens and Salonika against an enemy internationally regarded as anti-Nazi freedom fighters. The conflict continued until 12 January 1945, with the British gradually forcing back the communists, who received no support from Stalin as agreed at the Moscow conference*. At the time of the ceasefire – which somehow lasted until February 1946 – 75,000 British troops had been employed with 237 killed and about 2,000 wounded. Communist casualties were probably higher, while the liberal EDES was virtually wiped out and replaced as the main anti-communist group in Greece by the extreme right-wing 'X' organization. See Balkans, Russian campaign in.

Greece, German Invasion of, 1941 See Balkans, German invasion of.

Greece, Italian Invasion of By mid-1940, Mussolini's* foreign adventures had garnered rather more humiliation than glory, but he was still jealous of Germany's triumphs, and determined on military expansion. The Italians had successfully occupied Albania* the previous April, and Mussolini regarded Greece as falling similarly within his Mediterranean sphere of influence. In August 1940, after failing to make any impact on the campaign in France*, he decided upon the invasion of Greece. It began from Albanian positions on 28 October and Hitler* was not informed in advance.

Glory did not follow. Despite numerical superiority and complete command of the air, the attack made little progress through the mountainous Epirus region against Greek forces operating with great resilience on familiar ground. In November the Greeks counter-attacked. Large contingents of snow-bound Italians were outflanked and surrounded – the rest were driven back with such success that by the end of the year Greece occupied the southern quarter of Albania.

Early in 1941 the Greek leader, General Metaxas*, felt able to turn down Churchill's excited offer to divert British tanks and artillery *en route* for Egypt*, arguing that a small force could provoke German intervention without having any chance of repelling it. Though logically sound, this was actually irrelevant. Hitler, his fury at Mussolini's independent expansionism only slowly mollified by its undignified progress, had already decided to invade eastern Greece from Bulgaria to secure the flank of the forthcoming invasion of Russia*. Metaxas died at the end of January, and in early March – a few days after German troops entered Bulgaria – British reinforcements began landing at Salonika, causing Hitler to expand his invasion plans to include the rest of Greece.

On 9 March, Mussolini launched a counter-offensive in Albania, but it was abandoned as a failure a week later. Nevertheless, when German forces invaded in April, the Italians were at least keeping the Greek 1st Army committed in the northwest and thus fatally exposed to the rear. Disastrous on its own terms, the main significance of the Italian invasion lies here and in its galvanizing effect on Hitler's Balkan ambitions. See Balkans, German Invasion of; Greece, British Occupation of.

Greer, USS US Navy* *Wickes* Class flush-decker destroyer*, commissioned in 1918 and brought out of reserve as European war approached in 1939. The *Greer*'s well-publicized but inconclusive duel with a U-Boat while on Atlantic* patrol in

September 1941 was followed by President Roosevelt's* open admission of a US Navy 'shoot on sight' policy with regard to Axis submarines and surface raiders in the Atlantic (see Neutrality, US). The *Greer* remained in the Atlantic until early 1944, when she was reduced to secondary duties, and was broken up at the end of the war.
BRIEF DATA (*Greer*, 1941) Displacement: 1,090 tons; Dimensions: o/a lgth – 314′ 4″, b – 30′ 10″; Speed: 35 knots; Armaments: 4 × 4″ gun, 2 × 1pdr AA gun, (*or* (1 × 3″ AA gun), 12 × 21″ TT.

Grenade, Operation Code-name for the US 9th Army's successful offensive in the Rhineland in February 1945, designed to link up with the Canadian 1st Army's Operation Veritable. See Northwest Europe, Allied Invasion of.

Grew, Joseph Clark (1880–1965) American ambassador to Japan from 1932 until the attack on Pearl Harbor* in December 1941, Grew had begun his career with diplomatic postings to Mexico City, Cairo, St Petersburg (Leningrad) and Berlin. A knowledgeable and intelligent observer of Japanese politics, government and culture, Grew was generally sympathetic and conciliatory in his relations with Japan, although he supported the freezing of Japanese assets in 1940 as a valuable show of force and was among the first to warn of the possibility of a pre-emptive strike on American territory by the Japanese Fleet. After the attack on Pearl Harbor, Grew was confined in the Japanese capital for several months before being allowed to return to the United States in exchange for the release of Japanese diplomats. He subsequently became adviser to the State Department on Japanese affairs and Under Secretary of State in 1944. He retired in 1945. See also Pacific War; Introduction.

Grief, Operation Code-name for the unconventional and only partially successful action, Hitler's* own brain-child, that began the German counter-offensive against

Allied forces in the Ardennes* in December 1944 (see Battle of the Bulge). The operation was led by Hitler's protégé, Colonel Otto Skorzeny, who had planned the rescue of Mussolini* from his mountain-top prison a year before. It was conceived as a dual stroke: English-speaking commandos, disguised and travelling in US jeeps, would penetrate the Allied lines, then sabotage local communications and create maximum confusion; this action was to be followed by a similarly disguised tank brigade, detailed to seize bridges over the Meuse. Although most of the American equipment for the operation failed to materialize, and the tank drive had to be delayed and finally abandoned, the 40 jeeps which penetrated the Allied lines caused an immense amount of confusion and disruption, vastly disproportionate to their size or strength. After the first few days, Skorzeny's command reverted to a more conventional role as 150 Panzer Brigade.

Grumman F4F Wildcat Originally conceived as a biplane, the F4F lost a competition to find a US Navy* monoplane fighter in 1936 to the Brewster Buffalo*. Grumman developed the plane independently, and the first production models of the fixed-wing F4F-3 were delivered to the rapidly expanding Navy in February 1940. Folding wings and more armour were added to the F4F-4 version in 1941. Although no match for the Japanese Mitsubishi A6M2* in a dogfight, the Wildcat was a sturdy little aircraft and remained the US Navy's main fighter for two years after Pearl Harbor*. Grumman stopped building the F4F-4 in May 1943, but the plane remained in production – as the FM-1 – at General Motors' Eastern Aircraft Division. The lighter FM-2, with a more powerful engine, entered service that autumn, and 4,777 of this final version were delivered, the last in August 1945. Of the 7,905 Wildcats built, 1,082 served with the British Fleet Air Arm* as Martlets (Marks I to V) and then as the Wildcat VI, and it was the British who pioneered their valuable work from small escort carriers*.

BRIEF DATA (F4F-4) Type: single-seat naval fighter; Engine: 1 × 1,200hp Pratt and Whitney Twin Wasp; Max speed: 318mph; Ceiling: 35,000'; Range: 900m; Arms: 5 × 0.5" mg (provision for 500lb bombs).

Grumman F6F Hellcat Planned as a replacement for the inadequate Grumman F4F Wildcat*, the big F6F fighter was developed quickly and mass-produced in the US with enormous efficiency. Between late 1942 and November 1945, a total of 12,272 were delivered, and they mastered the skies over the Pacific for the Allies. The first service model (the F6F-3) was supplanted in 1944 by the F6F-5, which differed only in refinement, by which time the Hellcat was the US Navy's* principal carrier fighter. The British Fleet Air Arm* employed more than 1,200 F6Fs (as Hellcat Is and IIs) in Europe as well as the Far East. They also received some of an F6F-5N night-fighter version, with centimetric radar* mounted on a wing pod. The Japanese, although they eventually built fighters which could match the F6F's performance, were overcome by sheer weight of numbers, and about 75 per cent of American air-combat victories in the Pacific War* were credited to Hellcats.

BRIEF DATA (F6F-3) Type: single-seat naval fighter; Engine: 1 × 2,000hp Pratt and Whitney Double Wasp; Max speed: 376mph; Ceiling: 37,500'; Range: 1,090m; Arms: 6 × 0.5" mg.

Grumman F7F Tigercat Powerful fighter-bomber, huge by naval standards, it was designed primarily to operate from US Navy* land bases. The first prototype flew in December 1943, but the Tigercat arrived too late for combat, and although fast and well-armed, was cut back after the war as emphasis switched to jet power.

BRIEF DATA (F7F-1) Type: 1–2-man naval fighter-bomber; Engine: 2 × 2,100hp Pratt and Whitney; Max speed: 427mph;

Ceiling: 36,200'; Range: 1,170m; Arms: 4 × 20mm cannon, 4 × 0.5" mg; Bomb load: 2,000lb or torpedo*.

Grumman Martlet British version of the US Grumman F4F Wildcat* naval fighter.

Grumman (TBF) Avenger One of the most successful and widely used torpedo-bombers of the war, the Avenger entered the US Navy* in the spring of 1942 as a replacement for the Douglas Devastator*, and first saw action at the Battle of Midway*. Despite its bulk, it proved easily manageable on carrier decks and was one of the few US production aircraft capable of carrying a 22-inch torpedo*. In 1943, after Grumman had completed 2,311 TBF-1s, production was switched to the Eastern Aircraft Division of General Motors, who built 2,882 redesignated TBM-1 versions and 4,664 TBM-3s. Altogether, 958 of all three types served with the British Fleet Air Arm* (as the Tarpon, Avenger II and Avenger III) and, although incompatible with British torpedoes, they were effectively employed as conventional bombers, minelayers and rocket*-armed attack planes. The final production model was the re-engined TBM-4, which remained in service for many years after the war.

BRIEF DATA (TBF-1) Type: 3-man naval torpedo-bomber; Engine: 1 × 1,850hp Wright Double Cyclone; Max speed: 259mph; Ceiling: 23,000'; Range: 1,020m (normal); Arms: 3 × 0.5" mg, 2 × 0.3" mg; Bomb load: 2,000lb or 1,921lb torpedo.

Guadalcanal Island in the Solomon* group that was the primary strategic objective of the first American Pacific offensive of WW2, code-named Operation Watchtower, and became the focus of a long series of crucial naval and land battles between Allied and Japanese forces during the second half of 1942. See Map 14. The prolonged bitterness of the fighting at Guadalcanal over six months was foreshadowed by the gloomy atmosphere surrounding the launch of the American offensive. Nicknamed 'Operation Shoestring', available resources were limited and planning of the amphibious* landings hastily executed, with much background dispute between the Joint Chiefs of Staff* that had already undermined the morale of the relatively inexperienced troops.

Under the overall command of Vice Admiral Ghormley*, with Rear Admiral Fletcher* as tactical commander and Major General Vandegrift* leading the landing force of 19,000 of the US Marine 1st Division, the first landings were successfully made on Guadalcanal, Gavutu and Tulagi on 7 August 1942, although the progress of debarkation was considerably held up by poor organization and lack of experience. Despite the lack of opposition to the American assault on the Japanese airfield on Guadalcanal, where unarmed Japanese construction workers mostly fled into the jungle, the American force was brought under pressure on the night of 8 August, when a Japanese cruiser force under Vice Admiral Mikawa sailed down the 'Slot' into Sealark Channel to shatter Australian Rear Admiral Crutchley's screening force in the Battle of Savo Island*.

On Tulagi, the Japanese garrison of 4,000 'Special Landing Force' troops held out for two days of bitter fighting against a larger Marine force with massive supporting naval gunpower. It was here that the Marines, spearheaded by 'Edson's Raiders' (see Edson) first experienced the fanatical resistance of the 2,000 Japanese defenders who refused to surrender and held out in caves, without food, water or any hope of relief – a feature which was characteristic of the Japanese fighting mentality (see Bushido). Japanese control of the seas around Guadalcanal continued to press the isolated groups of Vandegrift's forces, until 20 August, when the first American aircraft were landed on the now renamed Henderson Field*.

Under orders from Imperial GHQ to drive the Americans off Guadalcanal, and with command of 50,000 men of the 17th Army based at Rabaul at his disposal, Lt General Hyakutake* ordered a series of day and night bombings of Guadalcanal and sent a small force under Colonel Ichiki to attack the eastern perimeter of the 1st Division on 18 August. The Battle of Tenaru River on the 21st saw the destruction of the whole of Ichiki's small force, which had rushed the American positions on the sand spit at the mouth of the river in the face of point-blank fire and had been savagely cut down.

Thereafter the American build-up of aircraft, combined with the effects of the frequent and sometimes crucial naval engagements fought in parallel (see Torpedo Boats; Eastern Solomons), won the American forces daytime control of the sea and a firm toe-hold on Guadalcanal, though the night-time supply and reinforcement of the Japanese forces from Bougainville, nicknamed the 'Tokyo Express'*, enabled the Japanese to maintain a ferocious resistance. A raid by Marines on the Japanese base at Taivu on 7 September brought intelligence of a planned counterattack on Henderson Field by 3,500 troops of the Japanese 35th Brigade under Major General Kawaguchi. In response, a composite battalion under Colonel Edson took up positions on a ridge south of the airfield, and fought an infamous battle, now called the Battle of Bloody Ridge, under heavy naval bombardment, to effectively destroy the Japanese assault.

Undaunted by the scale of their losses, the Japanese continued the heavy reinforcement of Guadalcanal, landing troops, supplies and equipment at night at Cape Esperance*. During September and October the Japanese force was increased by 20,000 men, while Vandegrift's force was also swelled by the arrival of the 7th Marines and units of the Americal Division. In this hard campaign of attrition, which was increasingly fought for control of the sea, the naval engagements were crucial to the outcome of the efforts on land. Japanese superiority in naval night-fighting techniques continued to be a feature of these engagements. In the major naval battle at Cape Esperance (11–12 October) Ghormley's* naval force failed to stop the landing of the transports carrying a new Japanese force under Maruyama, escorted by Admiral Yamamoto* and the Combined Fleet, and Ghormley was subsequently replaced by Admiral Halsey*. On 23 October a renewed offensive led by Maruyama and Hyakutake, who had arrived with the 17th Army from Rabaul to direct operations personally, was launched across the Matanikau River but was pushed back twice under heavy artillery fire, leaving 3,500 Japanese dead. Meanwhile Admiral Yamamoto's force was lured back to Guadalcanal by false reports of the destruction of Henderson Field and engaged two American task forces under Kinkaid* and Murray in the Battle of Santa Cruz* (26 October).

On 9 November, the Japanese made a final attempt to reinforce Guadalcanal, resulting in the great naval battle there (see Guadalcanal, Naval Battle of). Following this decisive engagement, in which the majority of Japanese troops and supplies destined for Guadalcanal were lost, the Americans had undisputed control of the seas around Guadalcanal. Although Hyakutake managed to evacuate 13,000 men from Cape Esperance, he had lost 25,000 men during the six-month campaign as well as 24 ships. The sometimes desperate struggle at Guadalcanal resulted in the seizure by the US of the initiative in the Pacific War*. For many of the relatively inexperienced American forces, it served as an apprenticeship from which they were quick to learn. With relatively small American losses, the campaign was much covered in the American press and victory gave a highly important boost to American morale.

Guadalcanal, Naval Battle of Climactic naval engagement in the American campaign to capture Guadalcanal* that brought Japanese reinforcement of the island to an end. The action began on 12 November 1942 with a Japanese bomber attack on American transport ships. The attack was beaten off by anti-aircraft* fire, but it was followed up that night by the arrival of a strong Japanese surface force – a 'Tokyo Express'* under Vice Admiral Abe with two battleships, two cruisers and 14 destroyers. Deployed as a bombardment force against Henderson Field*, it was attacked, amidst some confusion over the identity of the ships involved, by two transport escort groups under Rear Admiral Callaghan and Rear Admiral Scott who managed to damage severely the battleship *Hiei** and sink two Japanese destroyers*. Of the American force the cruisers *Atlanta** and *Juneau* were sunk, as well as four destroyers. Both American admirals were also killed in the action. Their action successfully thwarted Japanese attempts to put Henderson Field out of action.

Further Japanese attempts to bombard Henderson Field and land reinforcements were made on 13 November when Admiral Mikawa's flagship *Chokai* (see Takao) with three heavy cruisers and six destroyers arrived off Savo Island, bombarding Henderson Field and destroying 18 aircraft before being attacked by land-based and carrier aircraft from the *Enterprise**. The next day, Rear Admiral Tanaka's* 11 transport convoy sailed down the 'Slot' under intense bombardment by Navy and Marine Corps aircraft, again from Henderson Field and the *Enterprise*. Six of the transports were sunk, although Tanaka landed the surviving troops successfully on Guadalcanal.

Meanwhile, Tanaka's escort bombardment squadron under Vice Admiral Kondo* clashed with Admiral Lee's two battleship force in Ironbottom Sound* after another bombardment attempt on Henderson Field. American destroyers were put out of action, leaving the battleships *Washington** and *South Dakota** without protective screening, but determined action by Lee on the *Washington* caused Kondo to retire with his remaining ships, the battleship *Kirishima* (see Kongo) having been sunk by gunnery fire from the *Washington* and the transports were run aground with a meagre quantity of supplies and men landed. Control of the seas around Guadalcanal now came firmly into American hands.

Guam Central Pacific island in the Mariana* group and American territory, it was captured by a Japanese invasion force with support from Saipan*-based bombers from a small Marine garrison and Insular Guard Force on 8 December 1941, three hours after the attack on Pearl Harbor*. See Map 10. The island was re-invaded by the Marine 3rd Amphibious Corps under Major General Roy Geiger as part of an operation against the Marianas designed to provide air bases for USAAF* B-29s* to fly bombing missions to Japan. The assault was launched on 21 July 1944 after a 13-day pre-invasion naval bombardment. The Japanese force of 19,000 men under General Takashina managed to contain the Marines' advance from two beachheads, but a counter-attack was beaten back and the American assault was renewed. The northern tip of the island, Ritidian Point, was reached by American forces on 10 August, though a Japanese guerrilla campaign continued to be fought until the end of the war with characteristic ferocity (see Bushido). A large American base was subsequently established on Guam with long runways for the American B-29 Superfortresses. See also Tinian; Battle of the Philippine Sea; Amphibious Warfare.

Guderian, General Heinz (1888–1954) A pioneer of tank* warfare and Blitzkrieg* tactics and their most outstanding exponent, Guderian was born in Kulm (Polish Chelmo) and served as a staff officer during WW1. After 1918 he remained in the shrunken post-Versailles *Reichswehr*, posted to a telegraph battalion at Koblenz. Perhaps influenced by his work in communications technology, Guderian was a founder member of a group of young, forward-thinking military strategists who advocated the creation of a fast, independent task force, to be supported by highly mobile infantry and

artillery*. Inspired by British experiments of the late 1920s and early 30s, notably by Captain Liddell Hart and General John Fuller, the German 'tank school' (which also included Thoma, Reichenau* and Lutz) was initially opposed at High Command level by conservative military chiefs. With Hitler's takeover in 1933, however, came an opportunity to demonstrate the new theories in a series of field displays. In 1934, Hitler sanctioned the first Wehrmacht tank battalion.

Guderian gained rapid promotion in the 30s and was appointed General of Armoured Troops in 1938. By the outbreak of war, the German Army* had six panzer divisions operational. In command of the 19th Corps for the invasion of Poland*, Guderian proved and perfected his Blitzkrieg theories. Striking ahead of the main advancing infantry, his self-supporting armoured units achieved deep penetration at incredible speed, succeeding even in apparently tank-proof terrain and creating observable terror among the enemy. The potential value of tactical air support was also demonstrated for the first time in the Polish campaign.

In 1940, when Hitler announced his decision to launch the Western Offensive*, Guderian supported Manstein's* plan for an attack on the west through the Ardennes, using the new tactics (see Manstein Plan). In May, in command of the southern wing of Kleist's* Panzer Army, his 19th Corps smashed through the French forces at Sédan and, in one of the key actions of the offensive, forced the crossing of the Meuse, advancing at astonishing speed across northern France against a now fatally dispersed opposition. After the fall of France in June, Blitzkrieg was established as the orthodoxy of the German High Command and Guderian was promoted to Colonel General.

The opening of the Eastern Front* war against the Soviet Union in June 1941 saw Guderian repeat his triumphs of 1940 at the head of the 2nd Panzer Group, striking first through Belorussia* and then south into the Ukraine*. But the intervention of the Russian winter and the effectiveness of the Soviet counter-attack commanded by Zhukov* early in December brought the long line of Guderian's successes to a halt. On Christmas Day he was relieved of his command for carrying out a withdrawal against Hitler's specific order. Recalled from retirement in March 1943 after the defeat at Stalingrad*, as Inspector of Armoured Troops, Guderian controlled the supply and re-equipment of the panzer divisions, maintaining their effectiveness in the increasingly difficult conditions on the Eastern Front during 1943 and 1944.

Though a blunt and outspoken military critic, Guderian was apparently a model soldier, uninterested in the political conduct of the war. He escaped implication in the July Bomb Plot* in July 1944 and later succeeded General Zeitzler* as Chief of the General Staff, a post he held until dismissed by Hitler for the second time on 28 March 1945.

Guided Bombs Both the US and German air forces enjoyed some success with remote-controlled bombs in the later years of WW2. The USAAF's* VB-1 (AZON) was a general-purpose 1,000lb bomb* with a pair of radio-controlled rudders, which were manipulated by a bombardier in the aircraft after dropping. A flare in the bomb's tail was used to provide visual guidance. The AZON could only be directed laterally, but the later VB-3 (RAZON) could also have its range adjusted by altering the angle of its descent. RAZON bombs were successfully used for precision bombing attacks in the last months of the war.

Development of the German Fritz-X guided bomb (also known as the FX-1400 or SD-1400) had begun in 1939, and the weapon was perfected during 1942. Operating on a similar principle to the American types, it was a modified 3,900lb armour-piercing bomb. The Fritz-X made its operational début against Allied warships covering Operation Avalanche, the invasion of Italy* in September 1943. With

a range of eight miles, it reached its target at a speed too great for anti-aircraft* gunfire or evasive manoeuvre. The most notable victim of the Fritz-X was the Italian battleship *Roma*, sunk by three bombs on 9 September 1943, but several Allied ships were also hit and damaged, including the Royal Navy battleship *Warspite**. Another German remote-controlled bomb was the Heuschel HS293 glider-bomb. This carried a 1,100lb warhead and was launched from its specially modified parent aircraft by an initial thrust from a rocket engine.

Gustav Giant 800mm calibre railroad gun designed and built at the Krupp* works from 1937–42. The largest gun in the world, Gustav weighed over 1,300 tons, was 141ft long and stood 38ft high. It had to be partly dismantled for rail travel, and 4,120 men under a major-general were needed to assemble, operate, maintain and guard Gustav, which fired a 25ft long, 10,500lb shell at a rate of two per hour. Its only recorded appearance in action was at the siege of Sevastopol in 1942 (see Crimea) and (briefly) outside Warsaw* in 1944.

Gustav Line The rearward and most formidable of three German defensive lines (also known collectively as the Winter Line) on the Italian peninsula south of Rome*, to which the German 10th Army withdrew at the start of winter 1943–4 to fortify positions for a prolonged defence. See Map 34. Carefully planned along the Garigliano and Rapido* rivers and pivoted on the dominating Cassino* defile, the Line was fortified heavily with gun pits, concrete bunkers, turreted machine-gun emplacements, barbed wire and minefields. Held by 15 German divisions under the exceptional command of Field Marshal Kesselring*, the Line saw some of the most bitter fighting of the campaign in Italy*. Several abortive efforts were made by the New Zealand Corps, US 2nd Corps and British 10th Corps (5th Army) to breach the western flank of the Gustav Line during early 1944 in support of the 5th Army's landing at

Anzio* (22 January) to the rear of the Line. The successive failures of these operations and the near disaster at Anzio renewed doubts among the American military chiefs about the wisdom of maintaining significant forces in Italy. A compromise gave Allied Supreme Commander Alexander* a final opportunity to launch a renewed offensive, code-named Operation Diadem*, in the spring. The breakthrough on the Gustav Line, supported by a heavy preliminary bombardment and a huge air operation designed to cut the Germans' supply lines (Operation Strangle*) was finally made in mid-May, though at great cost in men killed and wounded.

Guzzoni, General Alfredo (1887–1965) Italian Under Secretary of State for War until 1943, General Guzzoni returned to active service in command of the Italian 6th Army in Sicily* at the time of the Allied invasion in July 1943. Guzzoni was arrested by the Germans in October but subsequently freed.

Gymnast, Operation See Torch, Operation.

H

Hacha, Emil (1872–1945) President of the federal state of Czechoslovakia* from November 1938, Hacha was an international jurist and self-proclaimed reactionary who succeeded Eduard Beneš* as Czech President after his resignation under German pressure in November 1938 (see Munich Agreement). Appointed largely because of his neutral status and conciliatory stance *vis-à-vis* Hitler*, Hacha nevertheless took the decisive step of declaring martial law in response to demands for independence from Ruthenia and Slovakia (largely stirred up by Berlin). Travelling to Berlin in March 1939 to plead for non-interference, Hacha was answered by the announcement that an invasion was already under way. Hacha had little alternative but to sign the surrender document produced by Foreign Minister Ribbentrop* and Göring*.

Ironically invited as a guest of honour to Hitler's birthday celebrations in the following month, Hacha subsequently urged Czechs to collaborate with Germany, and became nominal head of state of Bohemia and Moravia, by then a protectorate of the Third Reich. Hacha died in prison in June 1945, after the Soviet reconquest of Czechoslovakia.

Ha-Go (Type 95) Tank Japanese light tank first used in 1935, at which time it compared well with contemporary vehicles of its class. Like most Japanese armoured vehicles, it was outdated by the start of the Pacific War* and hopelessly obsolete by 1945, at which time it was still in active service. Unimaginatively deployed in small units or in static defence positions, it was adequate as an infantry support weapon only during the early campaigns of the war, when opposition was minimal. Altogether about 1,250 Type 95s were built, and other less important Japanese light tank designs included the Types 3 and 5 (mounting a short 57mm and a high-velocity 47mm gun respectively), and the Type 98, a faster version about 100 of which were completed in 1942 and 1943.

BRIEF DATA (Type 95) Type: 3-man light tank; Engine: 120hp diesel; Max speed: 28mph; Range: 156m Arms: 1 × 37mm gun, 1 × 6.5mm mg; Armour: max 12mm.

Halder, General Franz (1884–1972) Highly capable German general and Chief of the General Staff from 1938, responsible for the military planning (though not the conception) of the German campaign in Poland* in 1939, the Western Offensive* in 1940 and the (abandoned) Operation Sealion*, the planned invasion of England. Much of the early German success in the 1941 invasion of the Soviet Union was due to Halder's preparations, although he was dismissed in 1942 after disagreement with Hitler* over strategic issues (see Eastern Front). Halder's record of anti-Hitler activities seems to have been prompted by doubts about Hitler's military rather than moral leadership. He plotted to arrest Hitler during the Munich* crisis, and approached the Vatican during 1939. After the military successes of 1940, however, Halder appears to have accepted Hitler's authority. His ambivalence about accepting a Nazi head of state is interestingly characteristic of many senior German officers: unable to support Nazi policy, they nevertheless developed a technical loyalty to Hitler that fundamentally ignored the moral issues. Arrested and sent to Dachau* after the failure of the July Bomb Plot* in 1944, Halder survived to be liberated by American troops in 1945. See also Resistance: Germany.

Halfaya Pass See Brevity, Operation; Battleaxe, Operation.

Half-Track As the name suggests, the half-track was a vehicle with wheels in the front and tracks at the back. At the start of the war, Germany led the world in half-track design. A whole family of specialized half-tracks was designed, ranging in weight from 1 to 18 tons, for the mechanized support of armoured divisions. They were built up to tank standards with manganese webbed tracking extending to about 75 per cent of the vehicle's length, torsion bar suspension and an efficient drive system. These served as armoured personnel carriers, anti-aircraft* vehicles, ambulances, flamethrowers*, engineering transports, command and radio cars. Late versions carried 28cm rockets* (on the Eastern Front*) or mounted 75mm field howitzers (see Field Artillery). The 1- and 3-ton models remained in widespread service until the end of the war.

The other major producer of half-tracks was the United States, whose vehicles were by comparison no more than lightly armoured cars with tracks attached. They were built either as gun tractor/munitions carriers (M2, M9) or as armoured personnel carriers (M3, M5), but were widely employed in other utility roles. Their relatively simple design enjoyed one advantage over German vehicles in having a driven front axle, but by the end of the war most of their functions were being taken over by wheeled or fully tracked vehicles. American half-track production tailed off in mid-1944 after more than 40,000 had been built.

Japan produced a small number of half-tracks, but the British relied on small, full-tracked Universal Carrier armoured vehicles to perform many comparable functions.

Halifax, 1st Earl of (Edward Wood) (1881 –1959) Aristocratic and somewhat mannered British Foreign Secretary from 1938 –40 and a principal supporter of Chamberlain's* policy of appeasement*, Halifax was Chamberlain's chosen successor as Prime Minister, though he stood down in favour of Churchill*. Appointed ambassador to Washington by Churchill, the degree of Halifax's success in representing Britain's case and gaining friends in Washington was generally unexpected, given the extreme delicacy of Britain's position *vis-à-vis* the isolationist United States (see Neutrality, US). Halifax nevertheless earned the confidence of Roosevelt*, Cordell Hull* and, during extensive tours of the US, of many ordinary Americans.

Halsey, Admiral William Frederick (1882 –1959) Brusque and dynamic American admiral, an early exponent of the use of naval air power, Halsey won his first carrier command in the mid-1930s after distinguishing himself as a destroyer* commander in WW1 and winning his pilot's wings in 1935. In December 1941 Halsey was at sea in command of a carrier task force under the flagship *Enterprise** and participated in one of the first US Navy* carrier offensives of the Pacific War* against Japanese positions in the Gilbert* and Marshall Islands*.

Aggressive and salty in his approach – he later coined the operational motto for SoPac (US South Pacific forces): 'Kill Japs, kill Japs, kill more Japs!' – Halsey was informal and solicitous with his subordinates, who regarded him highly.

Promoted Commander of Carriers, Pacific Fleet as well as Commander, Carrier Division 2 in the spring of 1942, Halsey was absent from the Battle of Midway* in June due to ill health but returned in the autumn when he replaced Vice Admiral

Ghormley* as Commander of South Pacific Forces. Halsey's fighting reputation and personal flamboyance proved an important tonic to US troops in the South Pacific, although it took nearly two years of hard fighting, from Guadalcanal* through the Russell and Solomon Islands* campaigns, before Halsey, now back at sea in command of 3rd Fleet (June 1944), was able to join up with the 5th Fleet under Spruance* for the start of Central Pacific operations.

In October 1944, Halsey received orders to sail to support General MacArthur's* landing at Leyte* in the Philippines*. His controversial role in the subsequent battle (see Leyte Gulf, Battle of) did little to undermine his overall reputation as an exceptional carrier commander, although the later loss of a number of ships and many lives when his Fleet was hit twice by typhoons in December 1944 and June 1945 resulted in courts of enquiry to establish responsibility for the losses. Despite being held partly culpable and criticized for taking inappropriate action in both cases, Halsey was considered vital to the US efforts in the Pacific and continued to command 3rd Fleet in the final US offensive against the Japanese home islands, launched on 1 July. He was present at the signing of the surrender document aboard the USS *Missouri** on 2 September, and was promoted admiral in December, remaining on active service until 1947.

Hamburg German port city which was subjected to 187 air attacks between 1940 and 1945. The heaviest concentration of Allied bombing, during late July and early August 1943, was known as the Battle of Hamburg. Repeated raids caused a firestorm which resulted in the loss of 50,000 lives and enormous devastation. One million people fled the city in its wake. Hamburg surrendered to British forces in May 1945. See Strategic Bombing Offensive.

Handley Page Halifax The second British four-engined bomber to enter operational service, the Halifax began operations with RAF* Bomber Command in March 1941. Like the Avro Lancaster*, it evolved from a twin-engined design, but, unlike its partner in the prolonged Strategic Bombing Offensive* against Germany, it was also used extensively in other fields.

With Bomber Command, Halifaxes concentrated almost exclusively on night work. At first they were not a great success, but the introduction of a third gun-turret, more powerful engines and improved flight stabilizers in later models made the Halifax a genuinely successful heavy bomber. When it was nearing obsolescence, the Halifax was given a new lease of life in February 1944 with the fitting of much faster engines in the Mark III. After the Allied invasion of Normandy*, this was returned with other 'heavies' to daylight operations, notably against V-1* rocket sites.

As reconnaissance and anti-submarine* planes, Halifaxes served RAF Coastal Command from the end of 1942, operating from Britain and Gibraltar*. Many Halifax Vs (with an extra ventral machine-gun) filled this role, although some also equipped bomber squadrons after April 1943. In addition, the aircraft saw action in Europe as a glider tug, paratroop transport, supply dropper and radio-jammer*. From 1942, a Halifax squadron was stationed in the Middle East and bombed the Afrika Korps* from Egypt*. The long-range Halifax VI, capable of over 300mph, entered service late in the war. Some of these remained with Coastal Command after hostilities ended, when all bombers were immediately withdrawn. Post-war models were built as transports and production ended in 1946, after 6,176 aircraft had been delivered to the RAF.

BRIEF DATA (Mk I) Type: 7-man heavy bomber; Engine: 4 × 1,280hp Rolls Royce Merlin; Max speed: 265mph; Ceiling: 22,800'; Range: 1,860m (part loaded); Arms: 6–4 × 0.303" mg; Bomb load: 13,000lb.

Handley Page Hampden The Hampden looked a good prospect when it reached

RAF* Bomber Command in August 1938. Manoeuvrable and almost as fast as the Bristol Blenheim*, it could carry twice the bomb load almost twice as far. In combat, however, the total inadequacy of its defensive armament was cruelly exposed during the RAF's earliest daylight raids. With increased armament, the Hampden was more successful as a night-bomber, remaining with Bomber Command squadrons until September 1942. As an anti-submarine* patrol aircraft, it operated with RAF Coastal Command until December 1943. Production was stopped in March 1942, when 1,410 Hampdens had been completed, 160 of them built in Canada.

BRIEF DATA (Mk I) Type: 4-man medium bomber; Engine: 2 × 1,000hp Bristol Pegasus; Max speed: 254mph; Ceiling: 19,000'; Range: 1,885m (max); Arms: 6 × 0.303" mg; Bomb load: 4,000lb.

Hankow, Siege of Temporary seat of the Chinese Nationalist government under Chiang Kai-shek* after the Japanese capture of the Nationalist capital at Nanking* in December 1937. Advancing from Hsuchow with greatly reinforced armies, the Japanese devastated Hankow before occupying it on 25 October 1938. The Nationalist government fled to Chungking*, where it remained for the duration of the war. See China, Campaigns in; Map 22.

Harmon, General Millard (1888–1945) American commander of the US 2nd Air Force in 1941–2 and subsequently commander of all US Army air forces on Guadalcanal* and the South Pacific islands. From July 1944 Harmon was USAAF* Commander for the whole of the Pacific area, with primary responsibility for mounting the Strategic Bombing Offensive* against Japan which caused extensive damage to industrial and civilian areas in the final phase of the Pacific War*. Harmon died in February 1945 when his plane disappeared on a routine flight.

Harriman, William Averell (1891–1986) American businessman and diplomat, he acted as President Roosevelt's* negotiator with Stalin*. In 1941, Harriman was put in charge of the Lend-Lease* arrangements in London, where he had built up a solid relationship with Churchill*. In September of that year he accompanied Lord Beaverbrook*, the British Minister of Supply, on a mission to Moscow to establish relationships following the German invasion of Russia (see Eastern Front). A firm advocate of co-operation with Russia, Harriman was appointed ambassador to Moscow in 1943. He was subsequently in direct contact with Stalin, and an important participant in all the major Allied conferences*, including Yalta, where he negotiated with Soviet Foreign Minister Molotov* over the Far East. After the war, Harriman acted as an unofficial foreign policy adviser to the White House.

Harris, Air Chief Marshal Sir Arthur (1892–1984) Most outspoken proponent of the RAF's* controversial policy of area bombing* and C-in-C of Bomber Command from February 1942, Harris had seen distinguished service as a pilot in WW1, and commanded No. 5 Bomber Group in 1939. In 1941 he led an RAF delegation to Washington where he established good relations with US Air Chiefs, including Generals Eaker* and Arnold*, during discussions over air co-operation. Following his promotion to C-in-C Bomber Command, Harris furiously promoted a renewed offensive strategy, area bombing, which focused on civilian targets and the destruction of civilian morale. His immutable advocacy of this policy of terrorization, which reached an early climax in the devastating 'Thousand Bomber Raid' on Cologne* on 30 May 1942, and whose effectiveness was increasingly subject to criticism, characterized Harris's continued approach to the air war.

Suspicious of innovations, such as the Pathfinder Force* which substantially increased the accuracy of bombing raids,

Harris nevertheless presided over significant improvements to the techniques and success of Bomber Command's 50 operational squadrons, which continued to raid Germany in the night-time area bombing offensive during 1943 and 1944, causing unprecedented damage to many regions, particularly the Ruhr, Hamburg and Berlin*. Having retained the endorsement of the British War Cabinet, even after the controversial destruction of Dresden in February 1945, 'Bomber' Harris was promoted Marshal of the RAF after the war and received a baronetcy in 1953. The moral rectitude of Harris's unequivocal commitment to area bombing has since been regularly questioned, but during the war it was generally believed in Britain that the defeat of Nazism (and to a lesser extent the avoidance of a bloody land campaign in Europe) represented a higher moral imperative.

Hart, Admiral Thomas C. (1877–1971) From 1939 until 1942 Hart was commander of the US Asiatic Fleet, which was based near Manila* and comprised one heavy and two light cruisers, 13 destroyers, 29 submarines, six gun-boats, five minesweepers and 32 flying boats. It was no match for the Japanese invasion forces dispatched to the Philippines* at the start of 1942 and was led by Hart to safer waters in the Dutch East Indies*, before he resigned as C-in-C. Briefly appointed General Wavell's* commander of the Allied naval forces in the Far East (ABDA), Hart directed actions in the Makassar Strait off Borneo*, but resigned his command to Dutch Admiral Helfrich immediately before the decisive Battle of the Java Sea* that breached the Allied defence line, the 'Malay Barrier', and won for the Japanese control of Java*.

Haruna See Kongo.

Hatanaka, Major Kenji (1912–45) Leader of the abortive coup on the night of 14 August 1945 that attempted to prevent Japan's capitulation to the Allies. Major Hatanaka shot his commander, General Takeshi Mori, when Mori refused to co-operate and seized the Emperor's Palace with the aid of elements of the Imperial Guards Division. The failure of Hatanaka's plan to capture the tape of the unconditional surrender broadcast recorded by Emperor Hirohito* before its transmission resulted in his suicide in the palace compound before he could be arrested.

Hawker Hurricane (and Sea Hurricane) When it entered RAF* service in December 1937, this famous fighter set new standards for speed and armament. By August 1940, 2,309 had been delivered and Hurricanes formed the backbone of RAF Fighter Command in the first years of the war, outnumbering the more modern Supermarine Spitfire* by almost 2 to 1 at the height of the Battle of Britain*. Punchy enough to be effective against bombers, and manoeuvrable enough to survive against superior Messerschmitt Me109E* fighters, Hurricanes destroyed more German aircraft than all other British types combined during 1940.

From September 1940, the faster Hurricane IIAs joined squadrons, with IIB (12 machine-guns) and IIC (4 cannon) versions becoming available by the following June. These were mostly employed in ground-support work and, as it became outmoded as a dog-fighter, the Hurricane was modified for a number of alternative roles. The first 'Hurribombers' – with two 250lb (later 500lb) bombs under the wings – began anti-shipping operations over British home waters in October 1941. By then Sea Hurricanes, mostly converted Mark Is, were being catapulted from merchant ships to defend convoys in the Atlantic* (see Escort Carriers), and the following year the Mark IID began Desert War* operations as a tank-buster. The last main production Hurricane was the Mark IV, featuring a universal armament wing which could mount guns, bombs or rockets*. This served mainly in North Africa and Burma*.

A total of 2,952 Hurricanes was also delivered to the Soviet Union, and some of them were fitted with skis. The last Hurricane was built in September 1944. Total production in Britain was 12,708 and 1,451 were manufactured in Canada.

BRIEF DATA (Mk I) Type: single-seat fighter; Engine: 1 × 1,030hp Rolls Royce Merlin; Max speed: 318mph; Ceiling: 36,000'; Range: 460m; Arms: 8 × 0.303" mg.

Hawker Tempest British fighter that began life as a modification of the Hawker Typoon*. Attempts to reduce the aerodynamically obstructive thickness of the Typhoon's wing involved so many structural changes that the new plane was renamed. The first of several prototypes to see action was the Tempest V, which reached RAF* squadrons in April 1944. It was immediately effective against flying bomb attacks, Tempests downing 638 V-1* rockets between June and September that year. During the Allied invasion of Northwest Europe*, Tempests flew as ground-attack planes or bomber escorts, and had destroyed 7 German Messerschmitt Me262* jet fighters by VE Day (8 May 1945). When production ended in August 1945, 800 Tempest Vs had been built. A tropicalized Mark VI first flew in May 1944, but development was slow and it missed the war.

BRIEF DATA (Mk V) Type: single-seat fighter-bomber; Engine: 1 × 2,180hp Napier Sabre; Max speed: 427mph; Ceiling: 36,000'; Range: 740m; Arms: 4 × 20mm cannon; Bomb load: 2,000lb.

Hawker Typhoon British fighter designed for the RAF* as one of two big interceptors capable of mounting the latest 2,000hp engines. Its sister project (the Tornado) fell through, and although the first Typhoon flew in February 1940, serious development problems delayed its service entry (as the Mark IB) until August 1941. As a fighter, it was fast enough to catch the German Focke-Wulf Fw190, but its performance at altitude proved disappointing. Moreover,

its undertested Sabre engine was very unreliable, and repeated structural failures at high speeds caused many accidents. There was talk of scrapping the programme, but the Typhoon's exceptional low-level performance mitigated in its favour. Structurally modified and re-engined, it was converted as a ground-attack fighter-bomber from November 1942, and Typhoon squadrons spent 1943 successfully terrorizing German forces in and across the English Channel. In 1944, they formed the offensive backbone of the 2nd Tactical Air Force in Europe, an army support role which they repeated with the final Allied offensives during 1945. Virtually all of the 3,030 Typhoons built were manufactured under contract by Gloster aircraft, and the last were delivered in November 1945.

BRIEF DATA (Mk IB) Type: single-seat fighter-bomber; Engine: 1 × 2,180hp Napier Sabre; Max speed: 412mph; Ceiling: 32,500'; Range: 510m (max); Arms: 4 × 20mm cannon; Bomb load: 1,000lb.

Hedgehog See Squid.

Heermann, USS US Navy* *Fletcher* Class destroyer, commissioned in 1943 (see Destroyers). The *Heermann* was with Rear Admiral Sprague's* Carrier Group off Samar in the Battle of Leyte Gulf*, and with other destroyers fought the giant warships of Admiral Kurita's* 1st Striking Force on 25 October 1942. Although damaged in the action, she returned to the Pacific after repairs and screened US carrier forces until the end of the war.

BRIEF DATA (*Heermann*, 1943) Displacement: 2,325 tons; Dimensions: o/a lgth – 376' 5", b – 39' 7"; Speed: 38 knots; Armament: 5 × 5" DP gun, 4 × 1.1" AA gun, 4 × 20mm AA gun, 10 × 21" TT.

Heinkel, Ernest (1888–1958) German aircraft designer and manufacturer, whose operation was greatly expanded from 1933 as part of the new National Socialist government's plans to revolutionize the German aviation industry. Heinkel's designs formed a vital part of the Luftwaffe's* burgeoning strength in the years leading up to the war, and his He111* medium bomber was one of the most widely used aircraft of the conflict. However, later designs failed badly – notably the important He177* bomber – and Dr Heinkel was suspected of neglecting new types in favour of the profitable He111, which remained in production long after it was obsolete.

During 1942, Heinkel lost the confidence of the Nazi leadership, which he was never slow to criticize. He lost direct control of his factories, and his He280 – the world's first turbojet fighter – was officially ignored. At the end of the war, he was arrested by the Allies, but evidence of anti-Hitler activities led to his acquittal on charges of promoting the Nazi war effort and he returned to the post-war German aviation industry.

Heinkel He59 Designed in 1930 as a torpedo-bomber for the embryonic and secret Luftwaffe*, the biplane He59 was obsolete by the start of the war but was employed for a few months on minelaying and convoy* shadowing missions. A few He59Cs remained active until 1943 on air-sea rescue* duties, although they were seldom granted immunity as such by the RAF* who suspected them of signalling the positions of convoys.
BRIEF DATA (He59C2 ambulance) Type: 4-man rescue floatplane; Engine: 2 × 660hp BMW; Max speed: 137mph; Ceiling: 11,480′; Range: (max) 1,087m; Arms: none.

Heinkel He111 The He111 first entered the Luftwaffe* in 1937 and greatly enhanced the reputation of Germany's medium bomber forces with its successes in the Spanish Civil War. In 1938, the He111P introduced a shorter, glazed nose, and this also characterized the prolific He111H series, which was the Luftwaffe's standard horizontal bomber at the start of WW2. At that time, the *Spateu* (Spade) was marginally superior to its RAF* counterparts, but

it could no longer outrun modern fighters and was therefore seriously underarmed with only three machine-guns. Heavy losses in the Battle of Britain* necessitated increases in defensive armament and protective armour, which called for at least one extra crew member and adversely affected performance, so that by 1942 the plane was an easy target in urgent need of replacement. Such were the delays experienced in developing its successors, that the He111H remained in production until October 1944, and over 7,000 were built, ending with the He111H23. They saw action on all fronts, performing many extra duties as parent craft for various missiles, anti-balloon deflectors and glider-tugs. The bizarre He111Z was built for the latter purpose and comprised two He111s joined by a common wing mounting a fifth engine.
BRIEF DATA (He111H3) Type: 4–5-man medium bomber; Engine: 2 × 1,200hp Junkers Jumo; Max speed: 258mph; Ceiling: 25,590′; Range: 745m (full); Arms: 6–7 × 7.92mm mg; Bomb load: 4,400lb.

Heinkel He115 First produced in 1937 and in operational service throughout the war, the German He115 was one of the best seaplanes used by any of the belligerents. The He115B, an excellent performer on the water, flew reconnaissance, anti-shipping and minelaying missions in the Atlantic*, the Mediterranean*, the North Sea and the Channel (see Torpedo Boats). Better armed He115C models, in service from late 1940, were variously modified for specialist Arctic, minelaying and torpedo-carrying work. With 128 machines delivered, production was stopped at the end of 1940 to make way for land-based aircraft, but surviving He115s continued to give such excellent service that the programme was reinstated and a further 141 were completed in 1944. Two early He115A models, survivors of a batch sold to Norway* before the war, were secretly employed by the RAF* for spy missions.
BRIEF DATA (He115B1) Type: 3-seat all-purpose floatplane; Engine: 2 × 970hp

BMW; Max speed: 203mph; Ceiling: 17,060'; Range: 1,300m; Arms: 2 × 7.9mm mg; Bomb load: 2,750lb or torpedo* or mine.

Heinkel He162 Salamander On 8 September 1944, faced with continuing delays to the Messerschmitt Me262* programme, the Luftwaffe* issued a specification for a high-performance jet fighter to be constructed largely of non-strategic materials and assembled by semi-skilled labour. Sixty-nine days later, the prototype He162 Salamander made its first flight and, by the time the war ended, 116 aircraft had been completed with almost 800 more in advanced stages of construction. Powered by an engine mounted behind the cockpit, the *Volksjäger* (People's Fighter) was an effective design, but only entered limited service amid the chaos of April 1945, and was never in combat.
BRIEF DATA (He162A) Type: single-seat interceptor; Engine: 1 × 1,760hp thrust BMW turbojet; Max speed: 522mph; Ceiling: 39,500'; Range: 410m; Arms: 2 × 30mm cannon.

Heinkel He177 Griffon (Greif) German heavy bomber, it was one of the most significant design failures of WW2. Until war with Britain appeared certain, the Luftwaffe* General Staff showed only sporadic enthusiasm for a strategic heavy bomber, and so the He177 was not officially ordered until November 1939. Even then, the Technical Office under Ernst Udet* held the plane to its 1938 specifications, which called for dive-bombing capability, thus shackling it to a disastrous design feature whereby its four engines were paired-off to drive two propellers. Funds and resources on an enormous scale were committed to the project but, in spite of repeated assurances of imminent success from Dr Heinkel*, almost 50 prototypes were written off in fires or crashes. Although its dive-bombing requirement was eventually abandoned, its engines were retained and when the He177A1 eventually entered service in

March 1942, it was far from combat-worthy, proving unserviceable in the field and self-igniting regularly in the air. A lack of successful alternative designs demanded perseverance and about 1,100 He177s had been built by April 1945 – mostly of the restructured A5 version. Many were never delivered to operational units, but those which saw action fought mostly on the Eastern Front* without ever achieving much beyond a bad reputation.
BRIEF DATA (He177A5) Type: 6-man heavy bomber; Engine: 2 × 2,950hp double Daimler-Benz; Max speed: 303mph; Ceiling: 26,500'; Range: 3,000m; Arms: 2 × 20mm cannon, 3–5 × 13mm mg, 1 × 7.9mm mg; Bomb load: 13,225lb (provision for torpedoes*, guided* bombs).

Heinkel He219 Owl (Uhu) Originally planned as a multi-role fighter, the He219 was developed for the Luftwaffe* from late 1941 as a purpose-built night fighter, amid increasing RAF* night raids on Germany. When it reached operational trials in June 1943, it was an instant and spectacular success against the RAF's Avro Lancaster* heavy bombers, becoming much sought after by Luftwaffe aircrew. Production output was, however, painfully slow and in May 1944, just as the major A7 version was entering full service, the programme was downgraded in favour of the better-established Junkers Ju88G* night fighter. A later order to discontinue production altogether was tacitly ignored, but only 268 series Owls were ever delivered, along with about 20 prototypes. A superb and advanced machine, it was successfully targeted from late 1944 against fast de Havilland Mosquito* attack planes, and outmatched them in all but radar* technology. Late in the war a few B2 versions, with a short-term boosted speed of over 430mph, were also rushed into service, but they proved comparatively underarmed.
BRIEF DATA (He219A7) Type: 2-man night fighter; Engine: 2 × 1,900hp Daimler-Benz; Max speed: 416mph; Ceiling: 41,660'; Range: 960m; Arms: 4 ×

30mm cannon, 2 × 30mm *Schräge Musik* * cannon, 2 × 20mm cannon.

Heinrici, Colonel General Gothard (1886 –1971) Able German general with a considerable reputation in defensive tactics won during his long service on the Eastern Front*. Heinrici commanded the 4th Army under Kluge* from January 1942 and later led the 1st Panzer Army and the Hungarian 1st Army in the retreat to Silesia during 1944. One of the most long-serving of Hitler's wartime generals, he was captured by the Russians after the fall of Berlin*, whose defence he had been appointed to lead. He was repatriated in 1955.

Henderson Field Airfield on Guadalcanal*, it was the focus of bitter fighting between opposing air and ground forces in the first phase of the assault on the island. The value of this airfield was reflected in the decision of American planners to choose Guadalcanal as primary objective of the first American offensive in the Pacific. The airfield had already been largely constructed by Japanese technicians when the American force invaded on 7 August 1942. It was captured by Marines and completed for air operations within a week of the initial landings. See Map 14.

Henlein, Konrad (1898–1945) Czechoslovak pan-German nationalist who served in the Austrian Army during WW1 before becoming a gymnastics teacher and leader of the Czech German Gymnastics Movement, Henlein was the founder of the Sudeten German Party in 1933. Essentially a fifth column, Henlein's party organization and ideology was based on the Nazi Party*, and was financed from Berlin. During the late 1930s, the party was used by the German Foreign Office, with Henlein's full co-operation, to agitate the issues of the Sudetenland and ferment the crises in Czechoslovakia* that reached their climax in 1938 (see Munich Agreement). Between March and September of that year, Henlein travelled regularly to Berlin for instructions. When the Czech government offered to accede to all Sudeten demands, thereby endangering Hitler's plan for the armed annexation of Sudetenland, negotiations were broken off by Henlein on a pretext. The final crisis then developed rapidly. Hitler made speeches threatening violence; Sudetenlanders rose against the Czech government; martial law was declared and Henlein fled to Germany as the German occupation of the Sudetenland began.

In March 1939, when Hitler marched into Czechoslovakia, Henlein was rewarded by being made head of the Civil Administration of Bohemia and Moravia. He committed suicide on 10 May 1945 in a POW camp at Pilsen after being captured by US forces.

Henschel Hs129B By spring 1942, growing Allied tank* strength on the Eastern Front* and in the Desert War* obliged the Luftwaffe* to quickly introduce an anti-tank aircraft. The unpopular and rather puny Hs129B, which had previously been rejected, was therefore sent into action on the Eastern Front in May, and it claimed its fair share of Soviet tanks during the great land battles of 1943. A few were used in Tunisia* in early 1943 but the plane's captured French engines, fragile and unreliable at the best of times, proved quite unserviceable in Africa and it was quickly withdrawn. Slow and extremely uncomfortable to fly, the Hs129B was nevertheless the only German aircraft of WW2 designed specifically for operations against armour and 858 were built before production ended in 1944. Soviet armour continued to improve and the Hs129B appeared in a number of variously armed versions, including a model with a 20ft-long 75mm gun which could knock out a heavy tank with one shot.
BRIEF DATA (Hs129B/R2) Type: single-seat anti-tank plane; Engine: 2 × 700hp Gnome-Rhône; Max speed: 253mph; Ceiling: 29,500'; Range: 348m; Arms: 1 × 30mm cannon, 2 × 20mm cannon, 2 × 7.9mm mg.

Hermes, HMS Completed for the Royal Navy* in 1922, the Hermes was the world's first purpose-built aircraft carrier. Planned before any large carrier conversions (e.g. Furious*, Eagle*) had entered service, and thus in the light of severely limited experience, she was a highly successful innovation in her day. By 1939 she was outmoded – able to carry only a few torpedo-bombers and too slow for fleet operations. Her war modifications were therefore limited to the addition of a few light AA installations. She took part in the abortive attack on Dakar* in 1940 and performed trade protection duties in the Indian Ocean before joining the Eastern Fleet in 1942. On 9 April 1942 she was sunk by a large force of Japanese Aichi D3A* naval dive-bombers off Ceylon.
BRIEF DATA (Hermes, 1939) Displacement: 10,850 tons; Dimensions: o/a lgth – 600', b – 70' 3"; Speed: 25 knots; Armament: $6 \times 5.5"$ gun, $4 \times 4"$ AA gun, 12 aircraft.

Hess, Rudolf (1894–1987) Deputy leader of the Nazi Party until his dramatic personal surrender to the British in May 1941. An ingenuous student of right-wing politics in his youth, Hess became a devoted follower of Adolf Hitler* in the early 1920s. He took part in the Beer Hall Putsch in Munich of 1923, and voluntarily shared his leader's subsequent imprisonment. In Landsberg gaol the two men shared a cell and Hess advised and assisted in the writing of Mein Kampf. After their release, Hess played a leading role in the complete reorganization of the NSDAP, becoming a Reichstag member and a minister without portfolio in Hitler's first cabinet of 1933. By 1939, Hess was one of the most powerful men in Germany. A member of the secret Cabinet Council, and of the Council for Defence of the Reich, he was third in Party hierarchy after Hitler and Göring*.

There is no doubt that the skilled Party organizer was less important to Hitler in wartime than his economic and military strategists, but Hess still retained great pres-

tige. It is also probable that he sincerely believed in Hitler's professed desire for peace with Britain, and he appears to have been making elaborate preparations for a meeting with British contacts in a neutral country. These factors alone do not fully explain the Deputy Führer's astonishing actions on the night of 10 May, when he apparently piloted a twin-engined Messerschmitt Me110* fighter from Augsberg in Germany to Scotland, baled out and surrendered himself as an emissary of peace.

Asking to see the Duke of Hamilton, with whom he claimed a previous acquaintance (a claim denied by the Duke), Hess was promptly taken to London and imprisoned. The British government paid virtually no attention to his peace proposals, and made surprisingly little propaganda* out of their catch. An incensed Hitler stripped Hess of all his titles and declared him insane. For the rest of the war, Hess behaved as though he were insane, claiming amnesia and twice attempting suicide. At the end of the war he was moved to Germany and became a celebrated psychiatric case before his trial at Nuremberg* in 1946. Found guilty of crimes against peace, he received a life sentence and remained in Spandau* prison until his death in 1987. All attempts to secure his release on humanitarian grounds were blocked by Russian veto.

Evidence revealed since his death has cast doubts on the accepted version of these events. An expert pilot (contrary to widely quoted belief), Hess later claimed to have made his flight non-stop and without extra fuel tanks. This was not possible in a 1941 Me110 and it now seems likely that two separate aircraft were involved. Circumstantial evidence suggests that Hess may have been shot down by the Luftwaffe while leaving German airspace, and that British intelligence services were expecting some kind of contact from a leading Nazi. The absence of certain known distinguishing marks on the body of the last prisoner of Spandau have led medical authorities to conclude that he was not Hess. Some kind of conspiracy is suggested but its precise nature and purpose will probably never be known, since those most likely to have known the facts – Bormann* and Göring – are not available for questioning.

Heydrich, Reinhard Tristan (1904–42) Chief of the SS* Reich Security Head Office and Protector of Bohemia and Moravia (governor of occupied Czechoslovakia*). Widely regarded as one of the most ruthless and effective of senior Nazi Party* functionaries, Heydrich's rise through the party was sponsored and encouraged by Heinrich Himmler*, who was impressed by his exceptional organizational abilities, intimidating Nordic appearance, intense anti-Semitism* and utter ruthlessness. Heydrich was also almost certainly of Jewish origin though he had suppressed the facts from early in his career. Himmler's knowledge of this may well have contributed, ironically, to his attraction to Heydrich, confident that the information provided a sure lever of control over his exceptionally talented associate.

Certainly from 1931, when Heydrich joined the Party as an unemployed ex-naval officer (dismissed by an Honour Court for dishonourable conduct towards a young woman), Himmler was prepared to promote Heydrich until he became the second most powerful man in the RSHA (see SS). Having headed the SD* and created the notorious Einsatzgruppen*, Heydrich was appointed Obergruppenführer SS in 1941, by which time it is almost certain that he was already deeply involved in organizing the machinery of genocide of the Jews in co-operation with Eichmann*, described by senior Nazis as the 'Final Solution* to the Jewish Question'.

Appointed Reich Protector of Bohemia to succeed Neurath* in September 1941, Heydrich's regime saw staggering brutality in the early stages, followed by a policy of 'carrot and stick' which divided and neutralized opposition. In circumstances that have remained mysterious and controversial, he was assassinated by a group of Czech soldiers flown in from London (code-named Anthropoids), following a decision made by the British government. Despite requests from the Czech resistance* fearful of massive reprisals to call off the attempt, Heydrich was shot and injured by a hand grenade of 27 May 1942 and died on 4 June in a Prague hospital. Inexplicably, he remained the only Nazi leader whose assassination was plotted by the Allies. In retribution, the village of Lidice* was razed and its inhabitants massacred, thousands of Czechs were deported to Mauthausen concentration camp* and the hostility of Czechs towards their German occupiers was guaranteed.

Hilfskreuzer At the start of the war, the German Navy* began converting 12 fast cargo ships as auxiliary commerce raiders or *Hilfskreuzer*. Their armament (5.9-inch guns and sometimes torpedoes*, reconnaissance aircraft or torpedo boats*) was concealed, and their appearance varied to deceive their victims. From mid-1940 they achieved considerable success and notoriety in their attacks on Allied merchantmen, the *Atlantis* and the *Pinguin* sinking 145,697 and 136,551 tons of shipping respectively before being tracked down and destroyed by British warships in 1941. One auxiliary, the *Kormoran*, even sank a regular cruiser in the Pacific, when her disguise encouraged the *Sydney** to venture too close to her guns and torpedoes in November 1941. By late 1942, most of the *Hilfskreuzer* had been destroyed and the last of them, the *Michel*, was sunk by a US Navy* submarine in October 1943. They had accounted for 830,588 tons of shipping (plus the *Sydney*), far more than German surface warships ever sank. See also Armed Merchant Cruiser; Atlantic, Battle of the.

Himmler, Reichsführer SS Heinrich (1900–45) German head of the SS* from 1929. An early adherent of German nationalist movements, Himmler became a fanatically devoted member of the Nazi Party working as general secretary to Gregor

Strasser and then in the Schutzstaffel body-guard, the nascent SS*. At this time he also devoted his energies to the development of his extraordinary politico-eugenic theories, in breeding experiments carried out on his smallholding chicken farm in Landshut, Bavaria. Between 1929, when he became chief of the SS (then numbering 280 and still a branch of the SA), and 1936 when he assumed control of all the state police forces, Himmler worked assiduously to increase the size and breadth of function of the SS.

After 1936, he developed greater and greater aspirations to power in the Nazi state: by 1942, when Himmler's SS empire reached its zenith, he controlled, in addition to the vast administrative and policing network, the Gestapo*, the concentration camp system*, the feared Einsatzgruppen*, and a vast Waffen SS* army of 40 divisions. In addition the SS had developed a hugely profitable economic section, which owned its own industries, and had embarked on a human breeding programme based on the *Lebensborn* maternity homes serviced by chosen SS men that was designed to perfect a future German élite. From 1941, when Bormann* replaced Hess* as head of Hitler's secretariat, Himmler was Bormann's only real rival for Hitler's confidence.

Aside from Himmler's responsibility for the direction of all instruments and organs of repression in the Third Reich, he was also without doubt the prime mover in the execution of the policy known as 'The Final Solution* to the Jewish Question'. He is almost alone among leading Nazis in unequivocally articulating the concept of the extermination of the Jewish people, recorded in several speeches to concentration camp officers, where Himmler lectured them on their responsibility for destroying a whole people.

After the failure of the July 1944 Bomb Plot*, Himmler reinforced his position by removing rivals such as Abwehr* chief, Admiral Canaris* and by exploiting Hitler's mistrust of his generals to secure

his appointment as C-in-C of the Army reserve. Given command first of Army Group Upper Rhine and then, in January 1945, of Army Group Vistula, Himmler's lack of military experience was disastrous in the face of the Russian advance. As the German Army was discredited in defeat and Bormann took control in Berlin*, Himmler made an initial approach to the Swedish Red Cross representative Count Bernardotte, though Himmler hesitated to commit himself formally when they met in April 1945. Returning to Berlin, Himmler was dismissed from all posts by Hitler, two days before his suicide. The final Dönitz* government saw Himmler as a liability. Hoping to escape arrest, he took the name and documents of a dead village policeman, but was unable to sustain the deception when stopped at a routine check by British military police and admitted his real identity. He was arrested, but took poison before he could be interrogated.

Hirohito, Emperor (1901–89) Emperor of Japan from 1926, generally regarded as a modest and studious man, Hirohito's function in Japanese wartime politics is difficult to assess since he played no direct role in Japanese foreign policy or the conduct of WW2. Though his silent presence was required in order to ratify decisions at all cabinet meetings, and all war orders were issued in his name, the Emperor's divinity, assumed by ancient Imperial tradition, placed him outside the realm of sectional politics. Nevertheless, this traditional transcendental silence on political matters was broken by Hirohito on a number of occasions, notably in 1941 when he issued a caution to the Japanese General Staff about the threat of war and urged renewed negotiations with the United States (see Pacific War). He approved the attack on Pearl Harbor* and subsequently followed the course of the Pacific campaigns closely, but also repeatedly urged Prime Minister Tojo* to seek an end to the war. Ironically, it was in part the General Staff's absolute loyalty to the Emperor, enshrined in the traditions of the Japanese officer class, and fears for his status following a surrender – demanded unconditionally by the Allies at the Casablanca and Potsdam Conferences* – that drove the Japanese military on and prolonged the fighting in the Pacific.

In August 1945, as the first atomic bomb* was released on Hiroshima*, Hirohito actively used his influence to seek peace by urging the acceptance of the Allied surrender demand, despite the threat to his position as Emperor. On 15 August Hirohito addressed his people personally on radio for the first time, to announce the formal surrender of Japan. Hirohito was not tried for war crimes, but he was forced by the Allies to renounce his divine status in a 'non-divinity' proclamation on 1 January 1946 in order to retain his title and function as symbolic head of state.

Hiroshima Port on the southwest coast of Japan, it was the primary target for the USAAF's 509th Composite Group, assigned to drop the atomic bomb*. The bomb, known as 'Little Boy', weighed 9,000lb, and was carried by a B-29* Superfortress, 'Enola Gay', piloted by Colonel Paul Tibbets, who took off from Tinian* early on the morning of 6 August 1945. At 08.15 a.m. the bomb exploded 2,000 feet above the city. A blinding heat flash was followed by the blast, radiating out with devastating effect to a radius of 4,000 yards and flattening 47 square miles of the city. Three days later, a second bomb of a different type was dropped on Nagasaki*. The death toll at Hiroshima and Nagasaki was estimated by Japanese sources as 240,000. Many thousands more suffered appalling injuries and radiation sickness. The long-term effects of the radiation on survivors and children of survivors may make it impossible to produce a final toll of human lives.

Hiryu See Soryu.

Hitler, Adolf (1889–1945) Führer of the Third Reich. The Hitler family origins lay in the Austrian Waldviertel region near the Bohemian border, an area of poor, backward peasants, ignorance and inbreeding. No information is available earlier than 1837 when Maria Anna Schicklgruber gave birth to an illegitimate child, Alois Hitler, later Hitler's father. For reasons never established Alois, by now a relatively prosperous civil servant aged 40, changed his name in 1877 to Hitler, a rustic approximation of his stepfather's name, Georg Hiedler. His son, Adolf, was born to his third wife at Braunau, Austria on 20 April 1889.

The principal source material for Hitler's childhood is the highly unreliable *Mein Kampf*. But it is probable that he grew up, more or less as he describes, the son of an over-indulgent mother and a disciplinarian father. Certainly he was a wilful and resentful child and became, via failures at a monastery school at Lembach and his Gymnasium at Steyr, an arrogant and self-centred adolescent.

There followed in Hitler's youth a series of painful set-backs which seem, if anything, to have increased his particularity, his belief in himself. In 1907 and again in 1908 he failed to gain entrance to the Vienna Fine Arts Academy. By now living in Vienna, he was reading voraciously, but almost certainly cheap, easily digested pamphlets many of which would express strong nationalist and anti-Semitic views (see Anti-Semitism). This is the period which he romanticized as one of great poverty in *Mein Kampf*. The truth is, however, that Hitler received a small allowance from his guardian and in 1909 was left a substantial sum of money by his aunt.

In 1914, having moved to the Bavarian capital of Munich, Hitler volunteered for the German Army and was posted almost immediately to the Western Front. He saw service as a front-line soldier throughout the war and was undoubtedly considerably courageous, though thought odd by his comrades. To the end he believed utterly in a German victory. By 1918 he had been wounded twice and awarded the Iron Cross,

First Class. In 1919 he returned to Munich. Bavaria was in chaos. A Soviet government there had just been dissolved. Politically, it was a land of opportunity.

In February 1919 Hitler, acting for the Army, was sent to investigate a tiny gathering of workmen that called itself the DAP, the German Workers' Party. It was this roomful of right-wing radicals that in 13 years Hitler transformed into the election-winning Nazi Party.

Surviving a ban in Bavaria and the imprisonment of Hitler himself, the National Socialist German Workers' Party (NSDAP) began, after 1924, a period of rapid recruitment. It was by now a national party and by the election of 1930 had polled over 6 million votes, a Reichstag entitlement of 107 members.

The Nazi State was now at hand. Industrialists offered funds; the Army offered covert assistance; the powerful German Communist Party, on Stalin's orders, concentrated its attack on the German Social Democrats. In the election of March 1933, Adolf Hitler and his allies won 51.9 per cent of the vote.

The State now formed was devoted to foreign policy objectives that Hitler had proclaimed throughout his career. Every adult German knew of the 'Versailles Diktat', the unjust peace terms 'dictated' by the Allies at the end of WW1 (see Introduction); every German knew that Nazi foreign policy was aimed at sweeping aside the military restrictions and many of the territorial arrangements imposed by the Allies. Nobody counted on the speed with which Hitler acted.

Within six years, he had occupied the Rhineland, negotiated a favourable Naval Treaty with Britain, introduced conscription, withdrawn Germany from the League of Nations, engulfed Austria*, recovered the Sudetenland, destroyed Czechoslovakia*, signed a treaty with the Soviet Union (see Russo-German Pact) and invaded Poland*. The cost was a declaration of war by Britain and France.

From this point Adolf Hitler ceased to interest himself in domestic policy, party or economic matters. While other Nazi leaders began to develop powerful fiefdoms within the State (see Himmler; Göring), Hitler became supreme warlord of the Third Reich. There were three separate steps. In 1934, on the death of Hindenberg, Hitler had become head of the Armed Forces, a position restrained to an extent by the existence of an Army C-in-C, Fritsch*, and a Minister for War, Field Marshal Blomberg. As the second step to independence from all military guidance, Hitler took direct command of the Armed Forces by removing Fritsch and abolishing the ministerial post. Keitel, an officer totally loyal to Hitler, became Chief of the General Staff of the Wehrmacht (see OKW). With the great crises in the first winter on the Eastern Front*, the final step was taken when the Führer assumed the roles of Supreme Commander, Minister and C-in-C of the Army. From 1941, therefore, Adolf Hitler directed military strategy on each of the Reich's war fronts. The great military decisions of the war had been removed from the jurisdiction of the German Army*.

The reaction of the German officer class was complex. Hitler was first and foremost the man to whom they had sworn a personal oath of allegiance early in the regime. Yet he was also, sometimes to the very same officers, an upstart – the 'Bohemian Corporal'. Moreover, however much his accent and manner grated, he was in a position to confer promotion to the highest rank. At the end of the 1940 Western Offensive* in France and the Low Countries, a host of new field marshals was created and hundreds of senior officers received significant advancement.

Yet there was opposition to Hitler among senior officers even before the war (see Resistance: Germany). In 1938 General Beck* had called for a mass resignation of general officers to prevent the action planned against Czechoslovakia, although he had finally resigned alone. But it was in 1938 that senior German officers began to ride the unedifying see-saw between self-interest on one side and patriotic opposition on the other. Thus Halder*, Chief of the General Staff, plotted to arrest Hitler in 1938. After the victories in 1940, he appears to have accepted that the fate of Germany was – and perhaps should be – in Hitler's hands.

While there undoubtedly were dissenting general officers, most seemed to have served their master from an undecipherable combination of unthinking loyalty and professional contempt, fear and personal profit. Too often the peaks and troughs of opposition coincided with German victory or defeat.

Yet Hitler as warlord was not without some successes. Most military opinion now accepts that his encouragement of armoured warfare (see Blitzkrieg) in 1934 played a decisive part in the successful outcome of the 1940 campaign. Similarly, there is agreement that Hitler's refusal, costly as it was, to allow the German Army to retreat in the first winter of the campaign on the Eastern Front probably averted total devastation of the Wehrmacht.

But on many occasions, in North Africa, Italy, and to an even greater extent in Russia and in Northwest Europe* in 1944, German generals found their room for manoeuvre fatally restricted by the Führer's orders that allowed no withdrawals. To them it was a simple denial of military reality by a commander who rarely visited the front. In the Stalingrad* winter of 1942 –3, Adolf Hitler had nothing to offer his soldiers but a promotion to field marshal for their commander, Paulus*, and a blank refusal of permission to withdraw. It had worked once, but German officers knew that it was no substitute for generalship.

By the spring of 1944 the certainty of an Allied landing in the west was preoccupying the Führer; when and where were the subjects for constant discussion. In the event, Hitler came closer to choosing the Normandy* location for the landings than any of his generals although he persisted in the fatal error of believing in an additional landing at Calais.

Hitler's last major intervention in the war was the Ardennes* counter-offensive of 1944 (see Battle of the Bulge). Its grandiose aims and possibilities were shrouded in a misty unreality, deepened by the desolate fanaticism provoked, at least in part, by the latest attempt on the Führer's life (see July Bomb Plot). Certainly his political objective for the Ardennes assault, the splitting of the West from its Soviet Ally, can never have been less likely than at that moment.

As the end of the Third Reich approached, a new and deadly theatrical element was revealed, or, more likely, resurfaced in his personality. As the ring closed round Berlin*, Hitler had no taste for surrender. Instead he was preparing a new version of the 'Final Solution'*, but this time for the German people. His final orders were to adopt a 'scorched earth' policy that would completely destroy Germany's industrial infrastructure: all electricity manufacture, all coal mines, all water and sewage plants, bridges, factories and rolling stock. Deliberately, he invited disease and starvation to follow him.

As the Soviet Army began to shell Berlin and the Third Reich was overcast by the glow of burning buildings, Adolf Hitler wrote his Testament: he was personally responsible for nothing, neither military defeat nor the deaths of millions of his countrymen and untold millions of others. He had been betrayed. The German people had proved unequal to his leadership. They would deserve the future he foresaw for them.

On 29 April, Hitler married his mistress Eva Braun. They committed suicide together on the following day, their bodies were apparently burned in the Chancellery garden as the Russians shelled the building.

Hiyo Japanese aircraft carrier and class. The *Hiyo* and her sister the *Junyo* were begun in 1939 as luxury liners but completed in 1942 as aircraft carriers. They were similar to the preceding *Soryu** and *Shokaku** Classes, but featured an island superstructure surmounted by the funnel for the first time. Both were in almost constant action in the Pacific War*. The *Hiyo* was sunk by torpedo-bombers from the US light carrier *Belleau Wood* at the Battle of the Philippine Sea* on 20 June 1944. Shortly afterwards the *Junyo's* 25mm armament was further increased and 5-inch rocket* launchers were fitted to her bow. She survived the war, albeit damaged and decommissioned, to be scrapped in 1947. BRIEF DATA (*Hiyo*, 1942) Displacement: 24,140 tons; Dimensions: o/a lgth – 719' 6", b – 87' 9" (89' 6" FD); Speed: 25.5 knots; Armament: 12 × 5" AA gun (6 × 2), 24 × 25mm AA gun, 53 aircraft.

Hobby, Colonel Oveta Culp (1905–) Director of the US Women's Army Auxiliary Corps 1942–3 and subsequently the first member of the newly incorporated Women's Army Corps (WAC) with the rank of colonel. She remained as director until July 1945 and was awarded the Distinguished Service Medal for her services. See also Women.

Ho Chi Minh (1890–1969) Vietnamese communist revolutionary, born Nguyen Van Thanh, his adopted name means 'He Who Enlightens'. In 1940, Ho Chi Minh attempted to organize an uprising against the French in Hanoi and Saigon, but was forced to flee to southern China, where at Changsi he established a coalition of communist and non-communist Vietnamese exiles known as the Viet Minh. On Chiang Kai-shek's* orders, he was imprisoned for much of 1941–2, but returned secretly (with the support of OSS*) to Indochina* in 1943 to encourage resistance to the Japanese. After the Japanese surrender, Ho Chi Minh returned to Hanoi and became leader of the Democratic Republic of Vietnam, though this was short-lived, as British and later French forces moved in.

Hodges, General Courtney Hicks (1887– 1966) Little recognized and self-effacing US general and infantry warfare expert.

Hodges commanded the US 1st Army under General Bradley* for the invasion of Normandy* in 1944 and throughout the Allied drive across Northwest Europe*, directing the 1st Army in some of the campaign's key battles, including the Battle of the Bulge*, at Remagen* and during the encirclement of the Ruhr. After victory in Europe, Hodges went to the Pacific to participate in the battle for Okinawa*.

Hollandia The seat of local government in Dutch New Guinea* before the war, Hollandia was captured by Japanese forces in April 1942, but remained unexploited until the following year when preparations went ahead for the construction of a major Japanese base there. Allied air strikes during March and April 1944 effectively destroyed Japanese air power and subsequent assaults by the 'Operation Reckless Task Force' (US 1st Corps) from landings at Humboldt and Tanamerah bays secured the inland airfield area. Hollandia later became a major air and logistical base for American General MacArthur's* forces in the Southwest Pacific. See Map 15.

Hollow-charge Weapons The armour-piercing potential of a charge with the surface hollowed out had been discovered in the late nineteenth century. It was only developed in earnest by the major powers after the Swiss produced and marketed a workable weapon based on the principle in 1938. As subsequently perfected in Britain, Germany and the USA (among others), the hollow charge became an effective portable anti-tank* weapon.

The hollow-charge shell contains a lining of soft metal. This is rendered molten by the detonation of its casing and a stream of molten metal is created which has impressive penetrative performance against armour. First seen in action with German airborne* troops in 1940, shells were initially manufactured in various calibres for use in conventional guns, giving limited anti-tank capability. Although the hollow-charge effect is not dependent on high velocity, fin-stabilized shells were found to have greater destructive power. This led to the widespread development and use of shoulder-fired rocket launchers such as the German Panzerschreck, the British PIAT and the American Bazooka.

Hollywood Exiles The group of German and Austrian film-makers, directors, producers, cameramen, composers and actors who emigrated to Hollywood when the Nazis came to power. In June 1933, publication of the *Arierparagraph* banned all Jews from the German film industry on explicitly racial grounds. The vast majority went to Hollywood, often via Paris; some of them, like Fritz Lang, despite personal invitations from Hitler to remain. Robert Siodmark, Billy Wilder, Fred Zinnemann, Max Ophuls, Otto Preminger, Peter Lorre, Oskar Homolka and Marlene Dietrich were among those of the German *Filmwelt* to prefer working in the United States. Kurt Weill and Franz Waxman were among the best-known composers.

Holocaust See Final Solution, The; Anti-Semitism; Concentration Camps.

Home Guard British volunteer organization proposed by War Secretary, Anthony Eden in May 1940, to assist the defence of Britain against German invasion. Originally called the Local Defence Volunteers, the organization successfully recruited about 500,000 men aged 17 to 65, equipped with British, Canadian and American weapons. When the likelihood of invasion had decreased, the Home Guard manned anti-aircraft and coastal defences. It was officially dissolved on 31 December 1944.

Homma, General Masaharu (1888–1946) Japanese general with little combat experience before the Japanese declaration of war on the United States, Homma had served as a military observer with British forces in France and later as military attaché in London and in the press section of the Japanese War Ministry. He briefly com-

manded forces in China* in the late 1930s before being appointed Supreme Commander of Japanese Army Forces in the Philippines* in December 1941. Homma led the Japanese surprise assault on the Philippine island of Luzon*, begun on 22 December, that was to develop into the long and immensely costly Siege of Bataan*, involving 74,000 Japanese troops in an extended struggle for control of the peninsula. Though ultimately successful in forcing the beleaguered American and Filipino force to surrender (see Corregidor), Homma was much criticized for his handling of the operation and effectively relieved of command before the surrender. He was nevertheless held responsible by the Allies for the vast number of deaths caused by the Bataan Death March, a forced trek by thousands of Allied troops taken prisoner at the end of the siege, in which over 10,000 are estimated to have died. Homma was arrested in September 1945, convicted of war crimes at Manila*, and executed by firing squad in April 1946.

Hong Kong British Crown Colony and headquarters of the Royal Navy* China Squadron. Its proximity to mainland China made Hong Kong an inevitable early victim of the huge Japanese offensive launched concurrently with the pre-emptive attack on Pearl Harbor* on 7 December, 1941 (see Pacific War; Map 10). Despite the certainty of a Japanese victory, once the attack was launched with nine infantry divisions, 17 artillery battalions and supporting air cover, a surrender was psychologically impossible for British leaders to accept and the small garrison under General Maltby (comprising British, Indian and Canadian regiments with supporting units) withdrew to Hong Kong Island for a keenly fought defence that ended with a surrender on Christmas Day. Resigned to the loss of the Crown Colony, which had been given virtually no air defences, Churchill and the British military chiefs found themselves just as ill-prepared for the speed with which the

Japanese began their subsequent assault on Malaya*.

Hood, HMS British battlecruiser, completed in 1920 as the only unit of the Admiral Class. The *Hood* was the largest warship in the world in 1939 and, huge and handsome, had toured the world between the wars as the major symbol of Royal Navy* power and prestige. Unfortunately her busy public relations career had precluded a major reconstruction along the lines of that accorded the *Renown**, and service opinion had long regarded her as something of a liability. Thus, although the *Hood* entered the war as the fastest British capital ship, her machinery was old and she was badly lacking protection against aerial or long-range attack.

In July 1940, the *Hood* was flagship of Force H* for the bombardment of the French naval base at Mers-el-Kébir, near Oran. Between January and March 1941, she was refitted with new anti-aircraft* armament and gunnery control radar* before joining the Home Fleet. On 24 May 1941, she led the new battleship *Prince of Wales** into action against the *Bismarck** and the *Prinz Eugen** in the North Atlantic. On fire after an 8-inch shell from the latter had hit her boat deck, the *Hood* exploded following a fifth salvo from the *Bismarck* at 16,500 yards. She disappeared in a matter of seconds and only three out of a complement of 1,421 survived. The exact cause of the explosion remains a matter for conjecture, despite the deliberations of two boards of inquiry, but it is certain that the vessel's age and condition contributed to her demise, along with an impressive display of German gunnery. For the British the loss of the *Hood*, embodiment of naval supremacy, seemed nothing less than a national catastrophe. See also *Bismarck*.
BRIEF DATA (1939) Displacement: 42,100 tons; Dimensions: o/a lgth – 860′ 9″, b – 105′ 3″; Speed: 31 knots; Armament: $8 \times 15''$ gun (4×2), $12 \times 5.5''$ gun, $8 \times 4''$ AA gun, 24×2pdr AA gun, $20 \times 0.5''$ AA mg, $4 \times 21''$ TT.

Hopkins, Harry Lloyd (1890–1946) Close and most trusted adviser to President Roosevelt* throughout most of the war, and widely regarded as a man of exceptional courage and talent, Hopkins suffered from chronic ill health which had forced him to resign as Secretary of Commerce in 1941, but was appointed supervisor of the Lend-Lease* Program and Roosevelt's special envoy, travelling to London and Moscow as Roosevelt's representative during 1941, to confer with Churchill* and Stalin* over American support against Germany. Particularly admired by Churchill, Hopkins was also present at the signing of the Atlantic Charter* and subsequently attended all the major Allied conferences*, advising on strategy and supplies. Following the United States' entry into the war, Hopkins was also appointed Chairman of the Munitions Assignment Board, and later member of the Pacific War Council and War Production Board. He also acted as a personal liaison officer between Roosevelt and the US Chiefs of Staff.

In the later stages of the war, after Roosevelt's death, Hopkins made a great contribution to the difficult discussions with Stalin over the Soviet Union's position on Poland* and other contentious issues; he was able to break the deadlock that had developed at the San Francisco Conference and win a commitment from Stalin to a further 'Big Three' meeting, held at Potsdam in July 1945, though ill health prevented Hopkins from attending himself. Among the many tributes paid to Hopkins after his death in January 1946, Churchill's was perhaps the most eloquent: Churchill spoke of 'the priceless work of Hopkins . . . an extraordinary man . . . who played a decisive part in the whole movement of the war . . . with a soul that flamed out of a frail and failing body'.

Höpner, General Erich (1886–1944) Courageous and highly effective German tank commander and a consistent opponent of the Nazi regime, he led a panzer group on the Eastern Front* for the German invasion of Russia in June 1941. Dismissed during Hitler's recriminatory purge of the German High Command after the failure outside Moscow* in December 1941, he was subsequently involved in the July Bomb Plot* against Hitler, in which he was to have taken over as Army C-in-C. He was arrested after the failure of the Plot and executed on 8 August 1944. See also Resistance: Germany.

Hornet, USS The first wartime *Hornet* was a slightly modified *Yorktown** Class aircraft carrier, completed in 1941. At the time of the attack on Pearl Harbor* she was still on her inaugural cruise, and her first mission was to launch the B-25* bombers of the 1st Special Aviation Project (see Doolittle, Lt Colonel James) against Tokyo in April 1942. She later took part in the Battle of Midway*, but was sunk on 27 October 1942 by aircraft and destroyers at the Battle of Santa Cruz*.

A second *Hornet* was commissioned in 1943. An *Essex** Class carrier, she fought successfully in the Pacific until the end of the war.

BRIEF DATA (*Hornet* I, 1941) Displacement: 19,900 tons; Dimensions: o/a lgth – 827', b – 83' (114' FD); Speed: 33 knots; Armament: 8 × 5" AA gun, 16 × 1.1" AA gun, 16 × 0.5" AA gun, 85 aircraft.

Horrified Allied code-name for Sicily*.

Horrocks, General Sir Brian (1895–1985) British field commander who was promoted under General Montgomery* in August 1942 to command 13th Corps, which fought at Alam Halfa and El Alamein*. After recovering from severe wounds suffered at the end of the campaign in Tunisia*, Horrocks followed Montgomery to Europe to command 30th Corps, 21st Army Group for the invasion of Normandy* and the drive across Northwest Europe*.

Horton, Admiral Sir Max (1883–1951) British naval commander. An outstanding submariner in WW1, Horton was in com-

mand of the Royal Navy's* reserve fleet in September 1939. After a brief period in command of the Northern Patrol blockading Germany, he became Flag Officer, Submarines in December. In this capacity he was responsible for training and administration, being promoted to admiral in 1941. His particular skills reached their full potential when he replaced Sir Percy Noble as C-in-C, Western Approaches in November 1942, and took operational control of the battle against U-boats in the Atlantic at a critical moment. His contribution to the Allied victory in the Battle of the Atlantic was enormous. He brought intimate knowledge of submarine warfare and tactics to his command, and above all sponsored the formation of powerful submarine-hunting support groups, bravely withdrawing escorts from convoy service for extended specialized training in the role. From spring 1943 these gained a decisive upper hand in combat against U-boat 'wolfpacks'*. Admiral Horton remained in this post until the end of the war, when he retired. See also Atlantic, Battle of the; Submarine.

Hosho Japan's first aircraft carrier, completed in 1922. Her small superstructure was soon removed, setting the fashion for later designs. Returned to front-line duty at the start of the Pacific War*, the *Hosho* was retired to a training role after the Battle of Midway*.

BRIEF DATA (1941) Displacement: 7,470 tons; Dimensions: o/a lgth – 551' 6", b – 59'; Speed: 25 knots; Armament: 4 × 5.5" gun, 8 × 25mm AA gun, 21 aircraft.

Höss, Rudolf (1900–47) Commandant of Auschwitz* extermination camp. Veteran of WW1 and ex-Freikorps member and an early associate of Martin Bormann*, Höss was invited to join the SS* in 1934, working at Dachau* concentration camp* and Sachsenhausen before transferring to Auschwitz. Noted for his brutal efficiency, Höss was the first to use Zyklon-B gas for extermination. Promoted in 1944 as Deputy Inspector General of concentration camps in the SS WVHA, he avoided arrest in 1945 but was eventually detected. Höss was hanged in Auschwitz by Poles in 1947.

Hotchkiss H-35 and H-39 Accepted by the French cavalry in 1936 as its standard light tank, the H-35 was at first badly underpowered and displayed poor cross-country performance. The H-39 (introduced in 1939) was modified to accept a bigger power plant and had thicker armour. The majority of these were fitted with a long-barrelled version of the 37mm turret gun, but they retained the burden of one-man turret operation. Of about 1,000 H-35/39 series tanks produced, 791 were in service with French tank units in June 1940, and they fought either in the cavalry role or in direct support of infantry. The German Army* took over many H-35 and H-39 tanks after the Battle of France*, and a few were deployed on the Eastern Front* in 1941. Two German self-propelled* guns based on the Hotchkiss chassis were also produced in limited numbers.
BRIEF DATA (H-39) Type: 2-man light tank; Engine: 120hp petrol; Max speed: 22.5mph; Range: 93m; Arms: 1 × 37mm gun, 1 × 7.5mm mg; Armour: max 40mm.

Hotrocks American code-name for Mount Suribachi, on Iwo Jima*, which was the site of the famous flag raising by men of the US 28th Marines Regiment.

Houston, USS See Northampton, USS; Cleveland, USS.

Hu Shih, Dr (1891–1962) Chinese ambassador to the United States from 1939 until 1945, Hu Shih had been educated in the west and became a leading intellectual in revolutionary China*. As ambassador in Washington, his main task was to seek funds to maintain China's war effort.

Huff-Duff See Anti-submarine Warfare.

Hull, Cordell (1871–1955) American senator and Roosevelt's* Secretary of State from 1933–44, Hull had been a committed supporter of Woodrow Wilson and had deplored the American failure to participate in the League of Nations. Appointed in 1933 as Secretary of State for party political reasons rather than for his ability in foreign affairs, Hull's uninformed and blinkered perception of Far Eastern affairs worked against the US State Department's attempts to reach any valuable decisions regarding US Far Eastern policy at a time when the absence of a clear and informed stand greatly exacerbated an already tense and difficult situation. Although Hull was active in developing relations with Latin America (the Good Neighbour Policy) and later in supporting the President's interventionist policies vis-à-vis the war in Europe, he failed to take account of Ambassador Grew's* repeated warnings about political events in Japan and was unable to contribute anything but a crude economic analysis to the developing crisis in the Far East.

Following the Japanese invasion of Indochina*, and the imposition of the US oil embargo, Hull conducted the negotiations with Japan during the late autumn of 1941 that failed to resolve the intransigence of both sides over China* and ended finally in a deadlock which precipitated the attack on Pearl Harbor*. He remained an energetic advocate of the development of the United Nations, playing an active part in international relations throughout the war as leader of the US delegation to the Moscow Conference in 1943 and a major participant at the Dumbarton Oaks Conference (see Conferences). Hull retired in November 1944. For his contribution to the establishment of the UN, he was awarded the Nobel Peace Prize in 1945.

Human Torpedo See Midget Submarines.

Hump, The Allied nickname for the treacherous air route over the Himalayas, (also called the Aluminium Trail because of the littered crashes which marked the route) from the Brahmaputra valley in India to Kunming* in China*. It was flown by American C-47* transports carrying supplies and equipment to the Chinese armies following the closure by Japanese forces of China's vital overland supply line, the Burma Road*. Supply missions began in April 1942 and continued until 1945, by which time larger and more numerous transports (C-87s, C-109 tankers, C-46s* and C-54s*) were carrying an average of 45,000 tons of cargo per month. See also USAAF. See Map 10.

Hungary A signatory of the Axis* pact and, like Bulgaria*, a beneficiary of Hitler's Vienna Award of 1940, in which Rumania* ceded a large part of Transylvania to Hungary. The Czech province of Ruthenia had already been taken by Hungary when Hitler marched in to annex Bohemia and Moravia in March 1939. Under the leadership of Regent Miklós Horthy, Hungary had been befriended by Nazi Germany during the 1930s and allied itself to the Reich after the German invasion of Russia. Based largely on self-interest, the relationship became increasingly strained as Germany's military situation worsened. Following the Soviet reconquest of Rumania in 1944, forces under Marshal Malinovsky* advanced towards Hungary on two fronts, breaking through via Arad on 22 September and joining Petrov's* 4th Ukrainian Front* to launch a strong drive on the capital, Budapest. While Malinovsky's divisions were stalled on the outskirts of Budapest by bad weather, an outflanking manoeuvre by Marshal Tolbukhin's* 3rd Ukrainian Front reached Lake Balaton, encircling the city by 4 December. The German garrison under General Freissner, ordered to defend the capital and the Balaton oilfields until the last man, was forced to mount a series of counter-offensives, despite the surrender of the Magyar government and the refusal of the Hungarian Army to fight a losing battle against two Soviet army groups. But the desperate situation inside the city and the annihilation of 16,000 troops who attempted a retreat

to their lines on 11 February finally resulted in surrender on the following day.

A final attempt to secure the Hungarian oilfields with the 6th Panzer and 6th Army was ordered by Hitler during March, but Tolbukhin's counter-attacks quickly ended it. On 20 March, Soviet forces reached the Austrian border. The capture of Budapest signalled the climax of the Russian campaign in the Balkans*. The sacrifice of Germany's few remaining reserves to the attempt to retake the city merely increased the pace of the Soviet advance into Austria and Germany itself. See Balkans; Eastern Front; Resistance: Hungary.

Huon Peninsula See New Guinea.

Hurley, Major General Patrick (1883–1963) US ambassador to China* after 1944, he saw active service at the start of the Pacific War* in the Philippines* area and subsequently held a variety of diplomatic posts, in New Zealand, as envoy to Moscow and as Roosevelt's representative in China, where he worked to prepare the ground for the meeting of Churchill*, Roosevelt* and nationalist leader Chiang Kai-shek* at the Cairo Conference (see Conferences). Returning to China in August 1944 with a difficult brief to harmonize relationships between Chinese and US military establishments (see Stilwell, Joseph), Hurley also initiated conferences between rival Chinese leaders Chiang Kai-shek and Mao Tse-tung* in an attempt to end the civil war in China. Hurley resigned in November 1945 in protest at what he believed to be State Department sabotage of his efforts to reconcile the communist and nationalist leaders in China.

Husseini, Amin el (1893–1974) Muslim leader and dedicated anti-Zionist who, as Grand Mufti of Jerusalem, organized the Arab revolt in Palestine of 1936. From October 1939, he was in Iraq*, where he was instrumental in the overthrow of the pro-British government in March 1941. Exiled to Germany after the British occupation of Iraq, the Mufti spent the rest of the war as Hitler's preferred leader of the Arab movement, raising Muslim units in Axis-occupied countries.

Hyakutake, Lieutenant General Haruki-chi (1888–1947) Younger of two brothers and well-known Japanese generals, Hyakutake was director of the Hiroshima Military Preparatory School before being appointed to command the Japanese 17th Army based at Rabaul*, after the attack on Pearl Harbor*. During August 1942, Hyakutake took personal command of the Japanese efforts to retain control of Guadalcanal* and the other islands in the Solomon Group*. He landed with his army on Guad-alcanal on 9 October 1942 in an attempt to relieve the stricken and starving troops there and shore up the flagging Japanese defence, but was unable to overturn the American advantage secured by growing US superiority in the seas around Guadalcanal. Following the decisive Battle of Guadalcanal* that finally stifled Japanese reinforcement of the island, and with the Japanese force falling victim to starvation and disease that killed over 100 men every day, Hyakutake made the decision to organize an evacuation from Cape Esperance*. Hyakutake remained based at Rabaul until the end of the war, fighting later with his army on Bougainville* and adjacent islands.

I

I-19 In a rare major success for the Japanese submarine service, the *I-19* sank the US aircraft-carrier *Wasp** off Guadalcanal* on 15 September 1942, after penetrating her destroyer* screen. This left only one American aircraft carrier active in the South Pacific.
BRIEF DATA (1941) Displacement: 2,198 tons (surface); Dimensions: lgth – 356′ 6″, b – 30′ 6″; Speed: 23.5 knots (8 submerged); Armament: 1 × 5.5″ gun, 2 × 25mm AA gun, 6 × 21″ TT, 1 aircraft.

I-156 Japanese Navy* fleet-type submarine*. Although these large vessels proved disappointing in combat, the reconnaissance provided by their seaplanes was sometimes valuable in the Pacific War*. It was the *I-156* that first sighted the capital ships of the Royal Navy's Force Z* in December 1941. In 1944, the *I-156* was overhauled and fitted with two Kaiten* midget submarines in place of her main gun. She rejoined the fleet the following year and survived to be surrendered to the Allies. Most large IJN fleet submarines were disarmed as trainers during the last year of the war.
BRIEF DATA (1941) Displacement: 1,650 tons (surface); Dimensions: lgth – 331′ 4″, b – 26′; Speed: 20 knots (8 submerged); Armament: 1 × 4.7″ gun, 8 × 21″ TT.

Iceland In 1939 Iceland was administered by Denmark*, but after German forces had invaded Scandinavia the following year British troops occupied the island as a base for North Atlantic operations. In July 1941, neutral US forces relieved the British garrison and the American government announced that it would protect all commercial shipping as far east as the area around Iceland. In 1943 Iceland served as the base from which important long-range anti-submarine* aircraft patrolled the mid-Atlantic. The following year the people of the island voted for independence from Denmark and it became a republic. See also Atlantic, Battle of.

Ichi Go Code-name for the Japanese offensive, mounted on 18 April 1944, to consolidate Japanese positions in eastern China* and capture US 14th Air Force bases there (see Chennault, Major General Claire; USAAF).

I-Go Code-name for a major Japanese air counter-offensive begun during April 1943 that combined forces from Rabaul* with Admiral Yamamoto's* Fleet air power from Truk* against the US Pacific Fleet advancing north round Papua (New Guinea*) and the Solomons*. Despite the apparent success of the operation in harrying air power and shipping in the area, the actual Allied losses were small.

Iida, General Shojiro Commander of the Japanese 15th Army for the invasion of Burma* from Malaya* in early 1942. Iida was responsible for establishing a controlling Provisional Administrative Committee under Dr Ba Maw* for occupied Burma.

Illustrious, HMS British aircraft carrier and class. The six *Illustrious* Class units, ordered by the Royal Navy* between 1936 and 1939, complied with the 23,000 ton displacement limit agreed by signatories of the 2nd London Naval Treaty (1935), but were otherwise a radical departure in carrier design. The Pacific powers (US and Japan) were building carriers with large open-sided hangars designed to deploy the maximum number of aircraft, and had independently arrived at their policies of grouping carriers into an offensive strike force. This could, the Americans believed, operate if necessary without the support of a battle fleet, and the aircraft carrier was treated by both powers as the capital unit in naval actions. Britain, partly because she operated three major fleets and partly because of her poverty in naval fighters, envisaged her carriers harnessed in support of more traditional fleet actions, and anticipated major confrontations with the powerful but carrier-free European fleets. The *Illustrious* Class was therefore designed to be impregnably armoured, packed with anti-aircraft* defence against land-based air attack, and relatively free from the fire-hazard implicit in an open-hangared design.

Completed in May 1940, the *Illustrious* was given a fully enclosed and armoured 'box' hangar (with a ventilation system to remove petrol vapour) that housed a reduced number of aircraft. She was followed into service by the *Formidable** in December and the *Victorious** was completed soon afterwards. The fourth vessel, *Indomitable**, was completed late in 1941 and (in response to earlier criticism) had extra space in the hangar at the expense of much of its side armour. This process was extended with limited success in the last two units, the *Implacable* and *Indefatigable*, which were subject to periods of suspension during construction and not commissioned until 1944. By the end of the war, use of deck parks and outriggers meant that these could carry up to 81 aircraft, compared with a maximum of 54 in the earlier units. Other war modifications were generally limited to improving light AA defence and radar capability.

The *Illustrious* was sent straight to the Mediterranean* and was highly successful in operations against Italian shipping, her aircraft carrying out the attack on Taranto* in November 1940. On 10 January 1941, she was hit by six 1,000lb bombs from German Junkers Ju87* dive-bombers and set on fire. Her armour and fire precautions saved her and she limped into Malta*, later undergoing extensive repairs in the United States. Back in service from December 1941, she supported Allied landings in Madagascar* (alongside the *Formidable* and *Indomitable*) and Salerno* before joining the Pacific Fleet in January 1944. Her many Far East actions included strikes on Sumatra, Java* and Formosa* before she was hit by a Kamikaze* attack in April 1945 off Okinawa*. Although damaged and eventually sent home for repairs, she was able to remain operative and, when all five of her sisters survived similar attacks before the end of May 1945, the US Navy* began to revise its own opinion of the armoured aircraft carrier.

BRIEF DATA (*Illustrious*, 1940) Displacement: 23,200 tons; Dimensions: o/a lgth – 743′ 9″, b – 95′ 9″; Speed: 30.5 knots; Armament: 16 × 4.5″ DP gun, 48 × 2pdr AA gun, 8 × 20mm AA gun, 36 aircraft.

Ilyushin Il-2 The product of immense efforts by the Soviet Union to build an effective armoured ground-attack aircraft (called a Stormovik in Russia), the Il-2 entered production in March 1941 and saw service with the Red Air Force* that summer in the initial campaigns against the German invasion of Russia*. Re-engined, just as heavily armoured and mounting improved 23mm cannon, the Il-2M appeared the following year and was a highly successful anti-tank weapon. Its vulnerability to Luftwaffe* fighters was largely overcome in October 1942, when the two-seat Il-2M3 reached full production. With a flexibly mounted rear machine-gun* and increased bomb load, this was a formidable weapon, capable of flying its low-level attack missions without need of a fighter escort. This quickly replaced earlier models and was mass-produced until the summer of 1943, when improved German tank* armours called for a modification with 37mm cannon and a further increased bomb load (which could include 200 light anti-tank bombs). Other production versions included the Il-2U trainer and the naval Il-2T, with provision for one torpedo*.

The Il-2 was one of the most important Soviet weapons of the war, and occupies a vital place in the development of specialized ground-attack aircraft. It pioneered the use of rockets* in its operations, was regarded as vital by the Russians themselves and was even recognized in the West. Manufactured with great dedication and enterprise, the Il-2 was produced in greater numbers than any other wartime aircraft (36,163) and remained in widespread service with the air force of Russia's post-war satellites.

BRIEF DATA (Il-2M3) Type: 2-man ground-attack plane; Engine: 1 × 1,770hp Mikulin; Max speed: 251mph; Ceiling: 19,690'; Range: 475m (normal); Arms: 2 × 23mm cannon, 1 × 12.7mm mg, 2 × 7.62mm mg; Bomb load: 1,321lb or 8 × 82mm (or 132mm) rockets.

Ilyushin Il-4 Produced from 1939, originally as a variant of the DB3 long-range bomber, the lightly armed Il-4 was the mainstay of Russia's medium bomber forces in the first years of the war. Serving both the Red Air Force* and Red Navy*, it was used as a torpedo attacker, close support plane and strategic bomber, visiting Berlin many times. From 1943 Il-4s also towed gliders and flew reconnaissance missions. Production output faltered after the German invasion of Russia*, but new plants were opened in Siberia during 1942 and built thousands of Il-4s with a redesigned airframe, which maximized the use of wood. Manufacture was stopped in 1944, after more than 6,800 had been delivered.

BRIEF DATA (Il-4) Type: 4-man medium bomber; Engine: 2 × 1,100hp M88B; Max speed: 255mph; Ceiling: 32,808'; Range: 1,616m (loaded); Arms: 3 × 12.7mm mg; Bomb load: 2,200lb internal or 3 × 1,102lb torpedo external.

Imamura, General Hitoshi (1886–1968) Widely regarded as one of Japan's most successful generals, Imamura was Vice Chief of Staff of the Kwantung Army* before the start of the Pacific War*. Appointed to command the 16th Army in 1941, he directed the successful invasion of Java*, and subsequently established himself as one of the few Japanese generals who seriously attempted to win local support for Japan's expansionist policies (see New Order). Ordered to new headquarters at Rabaul* in 1943, with command of the 17th and 18th Armies, Imamura directed successful attempts to reinforce and resupply Guadalcanal* against the American assault but was ultimately forced to withdraw. After the war General Imamura was convicted of war crimes and sent to Surigamo prison. He was released in 1954.

Imphal Major town of Manipur province in northeastern India, it was the site of a key battle in the attempted Japanese invasion of India from Burma (Operation U-Go*), in the spring of 1944. See Kohima; Burma, Campaigns in; Map 24.

Independence, USS US Navy light aircraft carrier and class. The nine units of the *Independence* Class were ordered on the incomplete hulls of *Cleveland** Class light cruisers in March 1942, to meet the urgent need for carriers in the Pacific War*. They were all rushed into US Navy* service in 1943, and proved fast and battleworthy adjuncts to carrier task forces for the rest of the war. The *Independence* began her combat career with an attack on Marcus Island in September 1943, but was severely damaged by a torpedo* off the Gilbert Islands* in November. She returned to action in time for the Palau* campaign in the autumn of 1944, and was at the battles of Leyte Gulf* and the Philippine Sea*. She survived the war to serve as a target vessel in 1946. Of her sisters, only the

*Princeton** was lost, although the *Belleau Wood* and *Cabot* were both damaged by Kamikaze* attacks in late 1944.

Later units were completed with 12 more 40mm guns in place of their 5-inch armament, a modification retrospectively applied to the whole class, as was the addition of individual fire-control radar* sets for light anti-aircraft* gunners. When used as aircraft transports, *Independence* Class carriers could haul double their usual load of aircraft, although this made for extremely claustrophobic crew conditions.
BRIEF DATA (*Independence*, 1943) Displacement: 11,000 tons; Dimensions: o/a lgth – 622' 6", b – 71' 6" (109' 3" FD); Speed: 32 knots; Armament: 4 × 5" AA gun, 26 × 40mm AA gun, 40 × 20mm AA gun, 45 aircraft.

Indian Army The Indian Army, whose officers were largely British, numbered 160,000 men in 1939 and was wholly separate from the British Army* in India, which comprised 60,000 whites. Indian forces were efficiently trained but lightly armed, with no tanks* or heavy field artillery and very little available air or naval support. During WW2 India was the major base for British operations in the Far East and the Indian Army underwent an enormous growth in manpower. Over 2 million men eventually served, and Indian divisions played a major part in British campaigns in East Africa*, the Desert War*, Tunisia*, Italy* and Burma*.

Indian Nationalism Opposition to the British Raj in India was encouraged by a decline in the efficiency of the colonial administration during WW2. Shortages of rolling stock and industrial materials contributed to severe economic distress in many parts of the subcontinent, including a major famine in Bengal in 1942–3. Indian nationalist leaders saw the war as an opportunity to speed up the process of independence and, although they were aware that Indian self-determination was in the long run inevi-

table, the British were at pains to suppress any potential disruption of their war effort.

India's major political grouping, the Congress Party, refused to support British viceregal policy over entry into WW2, and its leaders were imprisoned in 1942 after the suppression of a sabotage campaign. Mohandas Gandhi – the most influential single figure in Indian politics – announced a 'quit India' campaign, but he too was arrested. Revolutionary nationalist S. M. Bose* formed an Indian National Army to fight against the British. Drawn from Indian Army* troops captured by the Japanese, it provided about 7,000 troops at Imphal* and Kohima* but never had any great appeal inside India.

The atomized nature of Indian society, compounded by unabated hostility between Hindu and Muslim sections of the subcontinent, led Gandhi to conclude by 1945 that religious partition was inevitable. Not fundamentally anti-British, he co-operated with Wavell* (the last wartime Viceroy) in seeking an independence settlement along those lines. Other Congress leaders were released to join the consultations. Wavell was not able to sanction partition, but his successor – Mountbatten* – was empowered to grant independence to the separate republics of India and Pakistan in 1947.

Indianapolis, USS Commissioned in 1932 –3, the *Indianapolis* and her sister the *Portland* were modifications of the US Navy's* *Northampton** Class heavy cruisers. They were slightly larger and better protected than their predecessors and were designed without torpedoes*, which American naval planners had deemed superfluous in heavy cruisers. Both vessels were kept busily employed in the Pacific War* and received standard electronic and anti-aircraft* modernizations. The *Indianapolis* was with the Pacific Fleet at the time of Pearl Harbor*. Her later career included actions in the Aleutians*, the Gilberts*, the Marshalls*, the Marianas* and at Iwo Jima*, before she was badly damaged by a Kamikaze* attack off Okinawa on 31 March 1945. After repairs she returned to the Pacific, but was sunk by submarine *I-58* while steaming unescorted from Guam* to Leyte* during the night of 29 July 1945. Electrical failure prevented the *Indianapolis* from sending an SOS and her loss went unsuspected for 82 hours. As a result more of the crew died in the water awaiting rescue than were lost with the ship. Out of a complement of 1,199 men, 883 were killed.

BRIEF DATA (*Indianapolis*, 1941) Displacement: 9,950 tons; Dimensions) o/a lgth – 610′ 3″, b – 66′; Speed: 32.75 knots; Armament: 9 × 8″ gun (3 × 3), 8 × 5″ AA gun, 2 × 3pdr gun, 8 × 0.5″ AA gun, 4 aircraft.

Indochina A huge area (approximately 250,000 square miles) in Southeast Asia (see Map 10) including Annam, Tonking, Cambodia and 'Cochin-China' (the region around Saigon), that was colonized by the French in the nineteenth century. In the twentieth century local revolts increasingly challenged French authority. A Vietnamese nationalist party seeking the unified independence of Annam, Tonking and Cochin-China was founded by left-wing exiles from Canton in 1925, attracting revolutionaries like Ho Chi Minh* and Giap*.

With the fall of France in 1940 (see Western Offensive), control of Indochina was contested by Britain and the US against Japan. The Vichy* government of France acceded to Japan's demand to halt the flow of supplies to China* and allow Japanese troops and aircraft to be based in northern Indochina in September 1940. In July 1941, Japan also demanded the use of airfields in the south and an agreement to station unlimited numbers of troops throughout Indochina, resulting in Japan's virtual occupation of the colony. In response, the United States froze all Japanese assets and placed an embargo on oil exports to Japan, an action which, though aimed at inhibiting Japanese expansionist ambitions, actually gave irreversible momentum to the proponents of a Japanese war of

expansion in Southeast Asia (see Pacific War).

Indomitable, HMS British armoured aircraft carrier of the modified *Illustrious* Class, completed in late 1941. Her war career began in the Indian Ocean and later included coverage of the occupation of Madagascar*, the Pedestal* convoy to Malta* and Allied landings in Sicily*. Damaged during both the latter operations, she was subsequently transferred to the Pacific where she served out the war, comfortably surviving a Kamikaze* strike off Okinawa* in 1945.

BRIEF DATA (1941) Displacement: 24,680 tons; Dimensions: o/a lgth – 754′, b – 95′ 9″; Speed: 30.5 knots; Armament: 16 × 4.5″ DP gun, 48 × 2pdr AA gun, 8 × 20mm AA gun, 17 × 0.303″ AA gun, 48 aircraft.

International Military Tribunal The name of two judicial bodies established at Nuremberg* and Tokyo to conduct the trials of accused war criminals after the war. The legal basis for the establishment of the Nuremberg Tribunal, unique in judicial history, was agreed at a conference of jurists from Great Britain, the United States, Russia and France that convened in London in June 1945. A statute, later known as the London Charter, was agreed and signed on 8 August, and subsequently subscribed to by 23 nations, although it attracted criticism, particularly in Germany, by applying a code of law retroactively and nominating judges as accusers.

The Tribunal at Nuremberg, which began sitting on 20 November 1945, was to continue its vast work until 1948, when the German courts were finally authorized to take over the trials of Nazi war criminals. See Nuremberg War Trials.

The International Military Tribunal for the Far East was established following the precedent set by the London Charter and began sitting in May 1946. The principal trials were held at Tokyo under Australian presiding judge, William Webb, but other trials were also held at Singapore, Hong Kong and smaller cities. Lasting for 417 days, the Tribunal of the Far East sentenced over 900 to death, frequently for crimes against the civilian population of occupied areas. Of 25 Japanese military leaders found guilty at Tokyo, seven were sentenced to death, the others to life imprisonment.

International Military Tribunal for the Far East See International Military Tribunal.

Iowa, USS United States battleship and class. Six *Iowa* Class units were ordered by the US Navy* in 1939–40, but only four – *Iowa, New Jersey*, *Wisconsin* and *Missouri* – were ever completed. Free from pre-war treaty limitations on size, they were 10,000 tons heavier and 200ft longer than the preceding *South Dakota** Class, but remained narrow enough to use the Panama Canal. The increases were primarily dictated by the need for enough speed to screen new fast carriers already under construction, a target which was comfortably achieved. Main armament was on the same scale as previous classes, but increased deck space enabled more light anti-aircraft* weapons to be shipped than ever before. They were fitted with simple individual radar* sets, which helped the class to an excellent record as anti-aircraft escorts for Pacific War* carrier and invasion forces.

The *Iowa* was the first to be commissioned. After transporting President Roosevelt* to and from the Tehran Conference* late in 1943, she supported numerous operations against Japanese positions, including Kwajalein (see Marshall Islands), Truk*, the Marianas*, Leyte* and Okinawa*. All four ships were in the Pacific by the end of 1944. They were the last battleships to enter US Navy service and none of them was ever required to fight a surface engagement. After the war, the *Iowa* was decommissioned but was reactivated to serve in Korea before finally retiring in 1958.

BRIEF DATA (*Iowa*, 1943) Displacement: 45,000 tons; Dimensions: o/a lgth – 887' 3″, b – 108' 3″; Speed: 33 knots; Armament: 9 × 16″ gun (3 × 3), 20 × 5″ DP gun, 60 × 40mm AA gun, 60 × 20mm AA gun, 3 aircraft.

Iraq The kingdom of Iraq was an important source of British oil supplies, and the RAF* maintained bases there under a 1930 treaty between the two states. From the start of WW2, growing anti-British feeling in Iraq was encouraged by Amin el Husseini*, the exiled Grand Mufti of Jerusalem, and by German agents in Baghdad. On 3 April 1941, the Anglophile government of Nuri-es-Said was ousted by opposition politician Rashid Ali. He immediately appealed for German aid, but the British reacted quickly. On 17 April, an Indian Army* brigade was sent to secure the Iraq–Haifa oil pipeline and two weeks later hostilities opened between British and Iraqi forces around the RAF base at Habbaniya. By the end of May, the British were in control of Baghdad and Rashid Ali had fled to Persia. Nuri-es-Said and the regent, Emir Abdullah, were reinstated but British troops remained in Iraq for the rest of the war. Iraq declared war on the Axis* in January 1943.

Ironbottom Sound Waters between Guadalcanal* and Florida Island in the Solomons*, so called by the Americans because of the loss there of a significant number of ships in a series of bitterly fought naval engagements.

Ironside, Field Marshal Edmund (1880–1959) Colourful British ex-intelligence officer and Commander of Allied Forces in Russia during 1918–19, Ironside was appointed by War Secretary Hore Belisha to replace Gort* as Chief of the Imperial General Staff in 1939. Disappointed not to have been chosen to command the BEF (Gort's new appointment), Ironside was later, perhaps unfairly, increasingly associated with Britain's poor military performance, and he was replaced by General John Dill* on 27 May 1940.

IS (Iosef Stalin) tank Soviet heavy tank ordered in August 1942, when the Russians became aware of German plans for the powerful new Tiger* tank. A design bureau was established and its first successful response was a much modified version of the KV85* heavy tank, known as the IS-1. With thicker and more sloped armour than its predecessor, but mounting the same 85mm gun, this was accepted for production in the early autumn of 1943. Soon after manufacture began in October, a few prototypes were tried with a 100mm weapon, but before the end of the month the big 122mm L/43 gun had been successfully fitted to the IS chassis. Thus armed, the IS-2 entered production and was the most formidable tank in the world. It was first used in battle the following February, and by the end of 1944 2,250 models had been completed. Work had begun almost immediately on further improving the tank's armour layout, resulting in the radically reshaped IS-3, which joined the Red Army* in January 1945. Low on the ground and contoured for maximum anti-ballistic effect, this nevertheless weighed little more than the relatively primitive German Panther*. Few IS-3s reached combat, and the tank was first revealed to astonished western observers in the Berlin* Victory Parade of September 1945, remaining the yardstick for international tank design for many years after the war.

BRIEF DATA (IS-2) Type: 4-man heavy tank; Engine: 520hp diesel; Max speed: 23mph; Range: 149m; Arms: 1 × 122mm gun, 1 × 12.7mm AA mg, 3 × 7.62mm mg; Armour: max 120mm.

Ise Japanese battleship and class, completed late in WW1 as dreadnoughts. Like other major Japanese Navy* warships, the *Ise* and her sister the *Hyuga* were thoroughly modernized in the mid 1930s. Fifth and sixth turrets were added, as well as the steepling bridge tower characteristic of Japanese battleships in WW2. Both units began the Pacific War* in home waters but during 1943 they were dramatically modified in an attempt to make good the devastating carrier losses at Midway*. Their two rear turrets were removed and replaced by an aircraft deck and hangar, intended to house 22 catapult-launched bomber/seaplanes. Radar*, albeit fairly primitive, was fitted and their anti-aircraft* defence was much improved, secondary armament giving way to eight more 5-inch and a final total of 108 25mm weapons. In September 1944, 180 anti-aircraft rocket* launchers were also added, but these proved valueless in combat. Shortages of specialized aircraft and (above all) of trained pilots meant that neither ship was ever used as an aircraft carrier, but they were among the survivors of Admiral Ozawa's* decoy force in the Battle of Leyte Gulf*. Both were, however, destroyed in the Japanese port of Kure by American carrier aircraft in late July 1945.

BRIEF DATA (*Ise*, 1941) Displacement: 35,800 tons; Dimensions: o/a lgth – 708', b – 104'; Speed: 25.25 knots; Armament: 12 × 14″ gun (6 × 2), 16 × 5.5″ gun, 8 × 5″ AA gun, 20 × 25mm AA gun, 3 aircraft.

Ismay, General Sir Hastings Lionel (1887 –1965) Distinguished 'desk' general and Chief of Staff to Churchill* (in his position as Minister of Defence), he proved an outstandingly successful intermediary between Churchill and the British Chiefs of Staff. Within a framework of recurrent friction between Churchill's eccentric and implacable temperament and the sober pragmatism of the Chiefs of Staff, Ismay managed to establish and sustain close and effective working relationships. His contribution to the development of overall British strategy and to the Allied victory has been widely acknowledged. Ismay later became the first Secretary General of NATO.

Isolationism See Neutrality, US.

Italia See Littorio.

Italian Air Force (*Regia Aeronautica*) Founded by Guilio Douhet, Mussolini's*

Under-Secretary for Air and the world's leading international proponent of strategic bombing theory, the *Regia Aeronautica* was formally established in 1923. By 1933 it boasted 1,200 first-line aircraft and was regarded as one of Europe's most formidable air forces. Italian machines had won the Schneider Trophy for racing seaplanes three times during the 1920s, and commercial aircraft like the Cant Z506 continued to set world records into the 1930s. Tested successfully in support of General Franco in Spain, the *Regia Aeronautica* had grown to an operational strength of almost 2,500 warplanes by the time Italy entered the war in June 1940.

In the immediate pre-war years, however, Italian front-line aircraft had declined in quality relative to those of other, more industrially developed powers. The *Regia Aeronautica* went to war with hundreds of well-designed but obsolete Fiat CR42* biplane fighters, and dependable medium bombers like the Savoia-Marchetti SM79*, advanced in their day but outclassed in 1940. New monoplane fighters coming into service, the Macchi C200* and Fiat G50*, had superb state-of-the-art airframes, but were saddled with weak Italian engines and poor defensive armament. Only with the introduction of imported German engines in 1942–3 was any kind of operational parity with Allied fighters attained, and then the impact of improved aircraft was lessened by the inefficiency of a production industry which completed only 11,000 machines between 1940 and the end of the war. Similarly, the introduction of a modern heavy bomber (Piaggio P108B*) in 1942 was accomplished in only small numbers before the surrender of September 1943.

Operationally, the *Regia Aeronautica* was largely confined to the Mediterranean* and North African theatres, although from October 1940 a short-lived and unsuccessful attempt was made to support Luftwaffe* bombing raids on Britain from bases in Belgium. On the whole, the demise of Italian air power was swift and complete.

Hundreds of aircraft were lost in Egypt*, the Desert War* and East Africa* during 1940–1 to RAF* forces equipped with equally dated warplanes. In the same period Italian bombers failed in their attempt to knock Malta* out of the war at an early stage. With the aircraft industry unable to meet its basic requirements, let alone its losses, and crippled by shortages of fuel and spares, the *Regia Aeronautica* ceased to be a major power after these initial campaigns. The Luftwaffe then took over most offensive operations in the Mediterranean, while Italian units in the theatre concentrated on supply and reconnaissance work. A few squadrons supported the Luftwaffe on the Eastern Front*, mostly in second-line duties.

After September 1943, *Regia Aeronautica* units based in southern Italy formed the Co-Belligerent Air Force and fought with the Allies, equipped with a variety of Italian, British and American aircraft. Those in the German-held north continued to operate as the *Aviazione della Repubblica Sociale Italia* alongside the Luftwaffe, which had long been supplying the Italians with aircraft.

Italian Army The officers and men of the Italian Army were bound by oath to the King, and had played little part in Mussolini's* Fascist takeover. Black Shirt divisions formed out of the Fascist militia fought with the regular Army in Ethiopia and Spain in the 1930s and swore allegiance to Mussolini. By 1940 Fascist Party influence affected all aspects of the Army, and the advancement of officers favoured for their political loyalty to the government lowered the quality of Italian field command and seriously damaged morale among royalist *Comando Supremo* (High Command) officers.

Strategic control over Italian Army operations 1940–3 rested entirely with Mussolini. Senior officers were not consulted when Italy entered the war in June 1940, and the Army was in no way prepared for a major conflict. Although in theory 72 divisions, mostly of unmechanized infantry, were available, only 42 could in fact be mobilized. These were smaller than their official establishment of 13,000 men, and were mostly reserve formations or colonial levies. There were three armoured and three light divisions, but their tanks* and artillery were of inferior quality. Italian heavy industry was incapable of rapidly producing improved weapons, and the Army relied on imported designs, many of them very old, for much of its field artillery and light armament.

Some Italian Army units (notably the six alpine and two motorized divisions) were excellent, but the bulk of the infantry was poorly trained, led, cared for and paid. In Egypt*, Greece*, East Africa* and the Desert War*, Italian troops suffered defeat and deprivation. In support of German operations on the Eastern Front* from 1942, they were completely unacclimatized. When the Allies invaded Italy* in September 1943, only 12 divisions were available for home defence, and many soldiers simply went home after the surrender on 8 September, although some units fought with German forces in the north of the country.

Italian Navy The Italian Navy had been expanded in the inter-war years as a by-product of the colonial aggression inherent in Fascist rule and in direct competition with the French Navy* in the Mediterranean*. The Washington Naval Treaty of 1922 had given the two navies parity in the permitted construction of major warships, and while the Italians strove to match the size of the French fleet, the latter was geared to maintaining a sufficient advantage for the defence of its Atlantic seaboard. Rivalry was exacerbated by clashes of colonial interests in North Africa and by 1939 both powers possessed large, modern and apparently powerful fleets.

The high speed and élan of modern Italian designs, particularly their light cruisers, masked a number of serious operational deficiencies. Although the major warships were certainly fast (if often unable to make their published speeds in combat conditions), they sacrificed range and seakeeping qualities as a result. These were not fatal drawbacks in the relatively small and calm Mediterranean, but a fundamental shortage of armour protection was more dangerous. The Italians knew of radar* but had not developed it and their ships lacked effective anti-aircraft* defences, a deficiency which, unlike Allied navies, the Italian Navy was never able successfully to make good.

Mussolini* had deemed Italy to be one big aircraft carrier and the Italians had no naval air arm. Great reliance was placed on co-operation between naval and air authorities, but this proved badly inadequate and Italian naval air operations remained technically backward throughout the war (see Italian Air Force). Submarines*, motor torpedo boats* and other smaller craft had been built in great numbers, but the development of convoy* escorts was largely ignored. This was an expensive mistake in view of the exposed nature of Italy's North African trade routes, which carried vital supplies to a navy chronically short of fuel. During the war, the oil shortage became critical and ultimately disabling as British forces in the Eastern Mediterranean were able constantly to threaten communications between Italy and colonial bases in Libya and East Africa*.

Another problem was the strained relationship between the Navy and the Fascist government. Although service morale and unity were well maintained throughout the war, command coherence inevitably suffered by the unpopularity and professional inadequacies of some of the more politically motivated naval appointments.

In June 1940, the Italian Navy consisted of four operational battleships, seven heavy cruisers, 14 light cruisers, 119 submarines and one coastal defence ship, along with over 120 destroyers* or smaller torpedo craft. Conditions could hardly have been more propitious for a Mediterranean sea war with the French out of action and the British desperately stretched, but the Italians quickly lost the initiative in the theatre to the Royal Navy's* smaller force of older ships.

From the start of the conflict, the Italian Navy was charged with the passive task of protecting North African trade. The main battlefleet was ordered to remain intact, remaining in the central Mediterranean protected by submarines and aircraft while avoiding major confrontations with the Royal Navy. This reluctance to engage was first demonstrated at the Battle of Calabria in July 1940, along with the ineffectiveness of Italian naval air tactics, providing a useful boost to British morale and earning the Italians a largely unjustified reputation for timidity (see Giulio Cesare).

Other than the benefits of greater operational experience, the Royal Navy possessed only one advantage in the Mediterranean – an aircraft carrier. This they used to great effect in an attack on the main Italian fleet at Taranto* in November 1940 that sank one Italian battleship and badly damaged two others. Italian *matériel* superiority was finally eroded at the Battle of Cape Matapan* the following March, when the only remaining active battleship was damaged and three heavy cruisers were lost.

In the following months the British themselves suffered heavy losses (largely to the Luftwaffe*) off Greece* and Crete*, and by the time Italian human torpedoes* sensationally sank two British battleships at Alexandria* in December 1941 a fierce war of convoy attrition had set in as each side strove to prevent supplies reaching Malta* or North Africa*. During this period the Italian Navy gradually lost ground. The successes of its submarines were few and expensively gained, and the individual exploits of torpedo boat forces could not greatly affect the overall picture. American involvement ensured a progressive increase in Allied strength, but the Italians could rely on Germany only for air support, not for warship production or fuel supplies, both of which began to falter badly.

Any hope of the Italian Navy directly affecting the outcome of the war ended with the Allied Torch* invasion of Northwest Africa in late 1942, and by the time of the landings on Sicily* the following July its influence was no more than that of a fleet in being. When Italy capitulated in September 1943 the fleet steamed to Malta and surrendered to the Allies.

Morale remained high and although most units remained inactive for the rest of the war a few fought with the Allies. A large number of Italian ships under construction or repair were seized by the Germans when they occupied northern Italian shipyards, and Italian forces were particularly active in attacking these. After 7 September 1943, 4,117 Italian sailors were lost, and 24,660 had been killed in the war against the Allies. Official Italian figures record the loss of 904 craft of all types from July 1940 to September 1943, 565 of them merchant marine vessels. See also Mediterranean Sea.

Italy, Campaign in, 1943–5 The Allied campaign in Italy began on 3 September 1943 with a three-pronged invasion of the southern peninsula and ended on 2 May 1945, the date of the German forces' surrender, negotiated by SS General Wolff* and Allen Dulles*, Head of American military intelligence in Europe (see OSS*). See Maps 34 and 35. It has remained a controversial campaign, fought against the background of protracted Anglo-American disagreements on the overall strategic planning of the war following the conclusion of the Allied campaign in North Africa. In particular, argument developed over whether to continue to commit large forces to the Mediterranean theatre (heavily pushed by the British) or divert resources to the earliest possible invasion of France as the decisive theatre, the argument advanced by American chiefs of staff (and repeatedly demanded by Stalin*).

The decision to invade Italy was therefore not an undisputed one. Heavily backed by Churchill*, who keenly desired a large-scale British victory in the Italian theatre, and fought for by him at the Casablanca Conference in January 1943 and the Trident Conference in May 1943 (see Conferences), the impetus arose finally out of circumstances. The fall of Mussolini* in July, the willingness of Sicily* to surrender and Marshal Badoglio's* hints at the possibility of an armistice offered a chance to guarantee Italy's speedy elimination from the war and draw German forces from other theatres.

The Allies resolved to take the opportunity offered them, but resolved nothing else. Having reached an agreement to prepare an invasion force, the Combined Chiefs of Staff* postponed further disputes over the final aim of the attack, which remained undecided and limited. Meanwhile, delays in the progress of negotiations with Badoglio over the unconditional surrender demand (see Italy, Capitulation of), and thus the launch of the invasion, allowed Germany time virtually to occupy Italy. By early September, contingency plans (see Achse; Alarich) had brought eight German divisions to northern Italy, reinforced the Rome* area with two divisions under General Student* (2nd Parachute Division and 3rd Panzer Grenadier), and brought in six divisions as the 10th Army, under Vietinghoff*.

Other advantages were similarly squandered by the Allies during the planning of the invasion. The choice of landing sites within range of the Sicilian air bases was easily predictable by German military intelligence well aware of the Allies' commitment to air support. The resulting failure to achieve surprise at the start of the invasion was, as 5th Army commander General Mark Clark* later described it, very nearly disastrous (see Salerno).

Against this background, the tactical progress of the campaign was to suffer from the outset by resulting delays in exploiting tactical opportunities and from epidemic overcaution among the Allied command,

symbolized by British General Montgomery's* approach but evident in many operations, of which Anzio* is only the most notorious (see, for example, Slapstick). Having confirmed the timing of the Allied invasion of Northwest Europe* for spring 1944 at the Tehran Conference in November 1943, Allied progress in the later stages of the Italian campaign was also hampered by the loss of troops, equipment, and most importantly air support for the Allied operations in France.

Planning for the invasion, begun at the end of July 1943, assigned the British 8th Army under Montgomery and the US 5th Army under Mark Clark to amphibious* landings at three points on the southern peninsula. The 8th was to cross the Straits of Messina for the landing at Reggio* and drive through Calabria to join up with the main landing force of the 5th Army at Salerno. A subsidiary landing by the British 1st Parachute Division was to seize the Italian naval base at Taranto*, and enable the Italian fleet to escape to Malta*. Though the plan was carefully conceived, General Alexander*, commander of the combined 15th Army Group, undoubtedly failed to take adequate account of the terrain. The primary objectives of the landings (Naples* and Foggia*) had been scheduled without regard to the geographical obstacles and limited road systems, which generally favoured a defending force and were ably exploited from the outset by German Field Marshal Kesselring's* defensive strategy. The oversight was to have a costly effect on operations.

Reggio and Salerno On 3 September the invasion was launched by Montgomery's 8th Army on the toe of Italy at Reggio. The landing was scarcely opposed, the German forces there withdrawing slowly; leaving obstructions and demolitions in their wake. On the same day, British warships landed the 1st Parachute Division at Taranto, again without opposition. Then on 9 September, hours before the announcement of the capitulation of Italy* to the Allies, the US 6th Corps and British 10th Corps landed at Salerno. Meeting immediate and heavy resistance from German divisions already concentrating in the area, and lacking adequate shipping to reinforce quickly enough to repel the German counter-attacks, the landing force suffered heavy losses. On 13 September, German counter-attacks threatened to drive the invading force off the Salerno beachhead. It was finally stabilized a week later (20 September) after a ferocious battle, having been reinforced by an American parachute regiment, and supported by a massive naval bombardment of German positions.

The ferocity of the fighting and the skill displayed by the German forces in defence provided a pattern that was to be repeated again and again in the long and sometimes bitter struggle for Italy. Having failed to gain the advantage at Salerno and trap the German divisions retreating from the toe of Italy, the Allied armies were subsequently forced to advance inch by inch up the Italian peninsula. Naples, which had been destroyed by the retreating Germans, was taken by the 5th Army on 1 October. The 8th Army, having crossed over to the east coast, took the Foggia airfields at the same time.

The Gustav Line The primary objectives achieved, Supreme Allied Commander General Eisenhower* directed Alexander to pin down the German forces. But the slow pace of the Allied advance had prompted a change in tactics on the German side. Pressed by Kesselring, Hitler agreed to a plan to hold, rather than merely slow down, Allied progress up the peninsula. Preparations thus began for the construction of a heavily fortified line across the peninsula south of the Liri valley and the approach to Rome*, known as the Gustav Line*. While the Allied armies continued their drive north on either side of the Apennines, both the cost and the pace of their progress was dictated by the exceptional defensive reactions of Vietinghoff's* 10th Army, which drew back slowly across the Volturno River* on the west and the Sangro River* on the east.

Fortifying outpost positions as it withdrew (Barbara and Bernhard Lines), the 10th Army prepared to establish itself across the narrow ankle of the peninsula, along the carefully planned Gustav Line (Winter Line).

Held back by the forward German divisions, and increasingly bogged down by the onset of bitter winter weather, the 8th Army fought for and crossed the Sangro (2 December), only to be pinned down at Ortona. On the west coast the 5th Army seized Mount Camino and Mount San Pietro, crossed the Garigliano, reaching the Rapido River* in January. There, in the shadow of the dominating fortification at Monte Cassino*, the offensive petered out. As the year drew to an end, the barrier between the Allies and Rome appeared to be impregnable. Exhausted and heavily depleted, the armies were withdrawn. Battle losses for the 5th Army alone amounted to nearly 40,000, with 50,000 more casualties of the weather. Commanding General Mark Clark came under heavy criticism for his handling of the Rapido operations, which were denounced as reckless by the divisional commander under him.

Anzio Having committed their armies to Italy, Allied commanders' hopes of an early victory in Italy were utterly frustrated. The only practicable objective at this stage was that of pinning down the German armies as a diversionary measure to aid preparations for the Allied invasion of France. At the Tehran Conference a decision was made to limit the objective in Italy to the capture of Rome and an advance to the Pisa–Rimini Line. To that end, Operation Shingle* projected a major new offensive, combining an amphibious end-run operation at Anzio* to the north of the line, with a renewed direct assault on German positions on the Gustav Line. The plan aimed to hold down the German forces on the Gustav Line and enable a breakthrough at Anzio, which would force a German withdrawal and leave a route open to Rome.

The Anzio operation, one of the most infamous of Allied failures, began according to plan. A renewed offensive against Monte Cassino on the Gustav Line quickly drew German reserves, allowing the Anglo-American force under General Lucas* to get ashore with little opposition. Advised through Ultra* intelligence reports of Hitler's immediate order for the swift reinforcement of the German positions at Anzio, Clark supported General Lucas' recommendation not to risk an advance to the first objective, the Alban Hills, but to dig in for the German counter-attack. Lucas' failure to exploit the establishment of the Anzio beachhead forced the Allies to a bitter fight to save it, leaving their forces trapped by the German counter-attack and pinned down on the beachhead. The repeated Allied failures on the Gustav Line, combined with the failure at Anzio, brought the British military chiefs under increasing pressure from their American counterparts to limit the campaign in favour of Operation Anvil*, a diversionary landing in the south of France in support of the Normandy* landings scheduled for early summer. A compromise gave Field Marshal Alexander a last opportunity to launch a renewed offensive in the spring, code-named Operation Diadem*, that finally broke through the German defensive line and freed Allied forces for the advance on Rome.

The Fall of Rome An opportunity to direct the Anzio forces east to Valmontone, to cut off the escape routes of the 10th Army and bring the campaign to a swift end, now presented itself to Army Group commander Alexander. But Alexander's order to Clark to effect the drive for National Routes 6 and 7 was ignored. Lured by the prize of Rome, Clark detached the bulk of his forces for a direct assault on the capital, leaving a small contingent to race eastwards as ordered. The failure at this point to trap and destroy the withdrawing 10th Army represented yet another significant lost opportunity for the Allies in Italy and General Clark's decision to disregard the order a

costly boost to morale. On the day following the capture of Rome on 4 June 1944, the Allied invasion of Normandy rapidly superseded Italy as the primary front. Resources for the continuance of the Italian campaign were increasingly difficult to assure from this point.

The Gothic Line Nevertheless, following the capture of Rome, Allied forces pursued the German 10th Army north (taking Leghorn, Pisa and Venice), but were again checked by the arrival of winter weather at the final bulwark of the German defence, on the Gothic Line* in the northern Apennines. Before a spring offensive could be launched, General Clark, now 15th Army Group commander (in place of Alexander who had succeeded Maitland Wilson* as theatre commander), had lost a substantial number of troops to Northwest Europe* and had the task of commanding the most heterogeneous field army of the war, comprised of national contingents from over 25 countries.

The relatively swift breakthrough by 5th and 8th Army units (now commanded by Generals Truscott* and McCreery*) to the west and east of Bologna in mid-April 1945, linking up for the final drive through the Po valley was, in the circumstances, a remarkable testament to the commitment of the Allied troops and the abilities of its commanders at all levels. An armistice was granted on 29 April 1945. The treaty of unconditional surrender was signed three days later on 2 May (see Wolff, SS General Karl; Dulles, Allen).

Whether the campaign in Italy was necessary to the Allied victory over Germany, especially after the invasion of Northwest Europe, has continued to be debated. It has been suggested that the campaign was justified by its strategic value as a diversionary focus for German forces in Europe, especially during the Normandy* landings themselves. The lack of good planning, however, and the concomitant problems of fighting across difficult terrain along a chokingly narrow front made it a highly expensive victory, even without taking into account the cost of the Allies' own confusion over its prosecution. It is hard not to conclude also that Churchill's feverish commitment to the campaign was emotional as well as rational, and related to his desire for a major British victory and fear of confronting Germany prematurely. The 'soft underbelly' of Europe had apparently – but erroneously – been regarded as the softer option.

Italy, Capitulation of, 1943 The Allied invasion of Sicily* on 10 July 1943 had provided the final impetus for the Italian Fascist Grand Council to move to depose Mussolini*. On 25 July, called on by the Council, King Victor Emmanuel* authorized Mussolini's arrest and appointed Marshal Badoglio* to head the new government. Badoglio immediately opened secret negotiations for an armistice (though these were held up by Badoglio's attempts to seek terms in the face of the Allies' insistence on unconditional surrender). Meanwhile, the success of the Sicilian campaign and the willingness of Italian forces in Sicily to surrender had somewhat resolved the disagreements between the Allies over the prosecution of the war in the Mediterranean (see Italy, Campaign in).

The 'wait and see' policy gave way to plans for an Allied invasion of Italy. But the necessary delay in signing the formal surrender until 8 September, hours after the first Allied landings began the invasion of the mainland, gave Hitler, already suspicious of the Italians' intentions, the opportunity to mount operations for the effective occupation of Italy by Kesselring's* 10th Army, ostensibly to aid Italians in fighting an Allied invasion.

On 10 September, with the invasion launched, Badoglio and the government were forced to flee Rome* to Brindisi* to set up an administration with Allied support. On 13 October, Badoglio declared war on Germany and Italian forces which had not been disarmed by German commander Kesselring's* troops re-entered the war as 'co-belligerents', now fighting on the side of the Allies. Hence, though Italy's capitulation and change of alliance ensured her a smoother path after Germany's surrender, it did not avoid lengthy combat and heavy losses for the former Axis* power. Fighting ended in Italy in May 1945.

Iwabuchi, Rear Admiral Sanji (1893–1945) Japanese commanding officer of the battleship *Kirishima*, which fought at the Battle of Midway* and at Guadalcanal* before being sunk off Savo Island* in November 1942 (see Kongo). Promoted Rear Admiral in 1943, Iwabuchi was appointed to command the 31st Naval Base Force in Manila* in November 1944 and directed the stubborn defence of the city on the direct orders of Japanese Imperial HQ, following General Yamashita's* decision to abandon it and retreat to Baguio. The defence, fought from house to house, demolished the city and cost Iwabuchi every one of his 15,000-man force. He was killed in action in February 1945 and was posthumously promoted to Vice Admiral.

Iwo Jima A small volcanic island in the Bonin Group, known as 'Japan's unsinkable aircraft carrier', it was the target for a massive amphibious* assault by American forces in February 1945 during the final phase of the Pacific War* and the site of a key strategic battle to gain a forward air base for the projected Allied attack on the Japanese home territories. See Map 11.

Garrisoned by a mixed Japanese force, including 20,000 veterans of the Japanese Special Naval Landing Force under Lt General Kuribayashi, delays in mounting the assault gave the Japanese commander time to construct a massive fortress defence of the island centred on Mount Suribachi, which overshadowed the only southern landing beach. An immense preparatory air and sea bombardment launched by the 5th Fleet under Admiral Spruance* preceded the launch of the American assault on 19 February, for which a 250,000 strong force with over 900 ships in two huge fleets had sailed from assembly areas at Ulithi and Saipan*.

The massive bombardment appeared initially to have achieved its objective. Major-General Schmidt's 5th Amphibious Marine Corps began its landing under heavy shell and mortar fire but with little opposition and prepared to make the two-pronged advance to capture its first objectives, Mount Suribachi and Motoyama No. 1, one of three airstrips on the island. However, the Japanese responded from their entrenched positions with a barrage of mortars, field artillery* and machine-gun* fire that pinned down the attackers and resulted in 2,500 casualties on the first day.

From strongly fortified positions augmented by a system of defensive caves and interconnecting tunnels, deeply excavated and well concealed, the Japanese garrison relied on the sheer entrenchment of their positions to hold out for a total of five weeks against the repeated assaults and yard-by-yard advances of the vastly superior American force. Though Mount Suribachi was captured in three days by a combat patrol of the 28th Regiment led by Lt Harold Schirer (signalling victory by hoisting an American flag from the height, which was later immortalized in photographs taken by Joe Rosenthal of the Associated Press) fierce Japanese resistance stalled the American drive to the north of the island by the 4th and 5th Divisions.

An all-out counter-attack mounted on 24 February won the second airstrip, Motoyama No. 2, four days later. The fighting moved to the fortified hills which formed a defensive chain across the island. The battle here was particularly bitter, and the region was nicknamed 'The Meat Grinder' by US Marines. Though the two key defensive positions were taken by 1 March, fighting continued until the 10th, when organized resistance ended, and then for a further two months of mopping-up operations. Only 216 Japanese prisoners were taken alive from the force of 23,000.

By the end of March, three airfields were ready to receive the vast fleets of American B-29* Superfortress bombers which were to raid Japan in the final phase of the Allied Strategic Bombing Offensive*, but the conquest was a costly one: 5,391 Marines killed, 17,400 wounded. Admiral Nimitz's* ringing tribute to the Americans who fought for Iwo Jima perhaps provides an appropriate epitaph for *all* the participants in the battle: 'uncommon valour was a common virtue'.

J

JAAF (Japanese Army Air Force) The air arm of the Japanese Army, completely separate from that of the Japanese Navy, and committed primarily to operations on the Asian continent rather than in the Pacific. See Japanese Air Forces.

Japanese Air Forces The first Japanese aeroplane factory had been set up by Nakajima and Kawanishi in 1916, and by 1921 the basis for an indigenous aircraft design and construction industry was in place. For another decade, with demand for warplanes constrained by international treaty agreements, Japanese aviation relied largely on imports, licensed designs and copies for its hardware. From the early 1930s, however, the Japanese aero-industry was geared towards self-sufficiency.

Between 1933 and 1936, with new companies being set up, about 900 planes were built each year. The outbreak of war with China* brought further expansion, and annual output jumped to about 3,800 aircraft annually in the period 1937–41. The Japanese built the aircraft they expected to need. Acutely aware of the implications of transoceanic warfare, they built carrier-borne fighters, torpedo-bombers and dive-bombers, along with seaplanes and tactical support craft to protect troop landings. From 1934, the need for long-range conventional bombers was perceived, but the development of purely defensive aircraft lapsed.

The Japanese Army and Japanese Navy controlled separate air arms, and each was a fully integrated part of its parent service. Competition between them was rife and

wasteful throughout the war. Some production companies worked exclusively for one service or the other and, by dictating the flow of precious raw materials, the military authorities exercised some control over production patterns. This haphazard system of patronage severely hindered government attempts, begun tentatively in 1938, to rationalize the distribution of labour and supplies. A Ministry of Munitions was eventually set up in 1943, but indiscriminate conscription had by then decimated the skilled workforce, and a system of supply quotas was implemented far too late to affect substantially the war effort. The Japanese Army, heavily involved in the war with China, initially spared about 700 aircraft for operations in the Pacific, and over 1,500 Navy machines were available.

All of the first-line aircraft operative when the Pacific War* began in December 1941 were based on specifications issued no later than 1937, and many of them were built to operate in temperate or sub-Arctic conditions against China and Russia. Furthermore, all but the ground-support planes were consciously designed to stress range and speed at the expense of armour and protective armament, rendering them comparatively vulnerable to returned fire. Nevertheless, the quantity and quality of these warplanes – particularly the widely used Mitsubishi A6M Zero* fighter – astonished the Western Allies and, boldly deployed against feeble opposition, they contributed enormously to the success of the first Japanese offensives.

In 1942, the strategic decision to secure existing gains by further offensives ensured that aircraft development remained centred on attack planes, although the success of the US 1st Special Aviation Project (see Doolittle) in April should perhaps have alerted the Japanese authorities to the need to defend their own airspace. The loss of four large carriers at Midway* in June was a terrible blow to naval air strength, and repeated military setbacks over the following months brought demands for better long-range aircraft. To some extent these were met by transferring many remaining carrier units to shore bases, but the resultant further losses of planes and experienced pilots gravely weakened Japan's capacity to redeem her situation with a decisive naval victory.

The aircraft industry, which could never hope to match US output, expanded prodigiously in attempting to keep pace with the growing crisis. In 1942, 8,861 planes were built, 16,693 in 1943, and in the peak year of 1944, 28,180 aircraft left the factories. Increasingly outnumbered nevertheless, they were mostly flown by inexperienced crews and were not of the types most needed. The high-altitude fighters and radar*-equipped night fighters urgently required in 1944 and 1945 had not been developed, and modified versions of existing designs were pressed into roles for which they were ill suited. Some good defensive aircraft (e.g. Nakajima Ki-84*) did emerge before the end of the war, but they were too few and too late.

The temporary successes of Kamikaze* suicide attack planes against shipping did not interrupt American bombing raids on Japan; these were the major cause of a dramatic fall in production during the first half of 1945. Once US bases in the Marianas* enabled B-29* bombers to reach the industrial concentrations of Nagoya (hit by an earthquake in late 1944), Tokyo and Osaka, the frightened and exhausted labour force began to disperse, and already acute material shortages worsened. At the last minute, plans to disperse the industry into safer, underground locations were put into operation, but the war ended before these could achieve much beyond further disruption.

Before the war, despite the evidence of observers in China, the Japanese were widely believed to have no warplanes comparable with the best western machines. The events of 1941–2 utterly destroyed that myth, and Japanese aircraft performed impressively throughout the war when used in the roles for which they were designed. Total wartime production amounted to 70,000 plans (50,000 warplanes) and 116,577 aero-engines, of which about 60 per cent were built by the giant Nakajima and Mitsubishi concerns. The bulk of the remainder were produced by Kawanishi, Kawasaki, Aichi, Tachichawa and various government arsenals, although development and construction of individual designs were often spread among a number of companies and many smaller firms made significant contributions.

Japanese Aircraft Designation

Japanese Navy: A letter/number system was applied to all naval aircraft at the detailed design stage. The first letter indicated the plane's function (e.g. A = carrier fighter; K = trainer, etc.) and this was followed by a specification number within the context of that function. The next letter named the design or development company responsible for the aircraft (e.g. N = Nakajima), and variants were assigned a suffix number with, for minor changes, an additional small letter. If a plane's function was altered by modification, the corresponding letter was added as a further suffix.

Once a design was in any form of production, a further official designation was added, consisting of a type number (revealing the year in which production was first authorized), a functional description in words and a model number of two digits (describing changes in the airframe and the engine during series production). Thus, the G4M2 was the fourth type of land-based attack bomber (M) and was in its second major variant. A further slight modification resulted in the G4M2a. The G4M1 had entered service as the Naval Type 1 Attack Bomber, Model 11. (The Navy regarded 1940 as the base year, and thus 1941 was described as Year 1.) A later model with improved engines was the Model 12, while the G4M2 became the Type 1, Model 22, both its airframe and engines differing from the original production.

From 1943, in a gesture to both security and propaganda, type numbers were superseded by official names. Generally, dramatic meteorological phenomena were used to describe fighters, while bombers were named after celestial bodies or mountains, the clouds were invoked for reconnaissance aircraft and trainers became trees or plants.

Japanese Army: After 1932, every specification built for the Japanese Army was allotted a *Kitai* (Ki) number. Until 1944, when anomalies were introduced for security reasons, these were given in simple numerical order. At first gliders were included, but these later received *Guraida* (Gu) numbers of their own. The function and origin of aircraft were not described and variants were indicated by Roman numerals after the Ki number. A small letter suffix indicated minor changes in equipment or armament, while the Kaizo (KAI) symbol was inserted to represent more serious structural alterations.

Once in production, army aircraft were given official designations similar to those of naval planes. Type numbers and functional descriptions were the same as the Navy's (except in 1940, which the Army treated as 'Year 100' instead of 'Year Zero'), and model numbers adhered strictly to the plane's variant suffixes (e.g. Ki-61Ia = Model 1A). Popular names were attached to army types, but they were not based on any system and never replaced year numbers.

Allied Code-names: Unable to identify or classify most Japanese aircraft at the start of the Pacific War*, the Allies instituted their own system of nomenclature in the summer of 1942. Generally, boys' names were used to describe fighters and re-connaissance seaplanes; girls' names covered bombers, flying boats and wheeled reconnaissance aircraft. Transports were given girls' names beginning with the letter 'T', trainers were trees and gliders were birds. These guidelines were not rigidly adhered to, and many already familiar nick-names were incorporated, but they survived throughout the war. About 30 names were erroneously applied to aircraft never used by the Japanese. See Japanese Air Forces.

Japanese Army Since 1900 the Army had held an increasingly powerful political position inside Japan, and by the mid-1920s – when a steady expansion and modernization began – it had become a stronghold of ultranationalist* and militarist values that fuelled aggressive expansionism and brought Japan to war against the United States and Britain in December 1941. The military bureaucracy in Japan had unique and independent control over the armed forces and national security, as well as being able to exert a strong influence over civilian life through active reservist organizations and compulsory military training for civilians (introduced in 1925). As Japanese politics suffered from increasing instability during the 1930s, successive cabinets found themselves wholly dependent for their existence on the Army's willingness to participate in the appointment of a war minister, a position reinforced from 1936 when a law was revived stipulating that only a serving officer could hold the post (see Introduction).

Army control over foreign policy was demonstrated by the independent actions of the Kwantung Army* in Manchuria* from 1931, and after the outbreak of full-scale war with China* in 1937. The Army also exerted a considerable hold over domestic policy through an Imperial headquarters (*daihon'ei*) with nominal responsibility to the Emperor Hirohito*. The culmination of this assertion of power came with the appointment of ex-Kwantung Army General Tojo, who took over from Konoe* as Prime Minister in October 1941 and led Japan into the Pacific War*. Internal dissent and factionalism notwithstanding, Tojo's dominance was not seriously challenged until the closing stages of the war.

Before 1937, the strength of the Japanese Army had peaked at about 300,000 men. War brought rapid expansion and by 1941 it comprised 51 active divisions and various special-purpose artillery, cavalry, anti-aircraft and armoured units – a total of about 1,700,000 men. The bulk of these (38 divisions) were deployed in China and Manchuria at the start of the Pacific War, as was most of the large and well-equipped air arm (see Japanese Air Forces). Of those forces deployed in the first Pacific offensives, armies were assigned to take Hong Kong* (23rd), the Philippines* (14th), Thailand* and Burma* (15th), the Dutch East Indies* (16th) and Malaya* (25th). Even in 1943 there were 41 divisions in China and Manchuria, while only six were available for the defence of the Southwest Pacific against Allied invasion, an indication of how fixedly the Army regarded Asia as its proper sphere of interest and Russia as its principal long-term enemy.

The fighting quality and dedication of the Japanese soldier remained the Army's greatest strength throughout the war (see Bushido), but the Army's technical standard dropped alarmingly. In large part this was dictated by the fragility of Japanese heavy industry, which was not organized for mass-production and which was crucially dependent on imported raw materials. Supply shortages were exacerbated by direct (and often cut-throat) competition for equipment with the Navy, itself a considerable political force. Thus those guns, tanks* and aircraft that had been effective against the Chinese were often still on the production lines after 1943, by which time they were dangerously obsolete. Existing designs were modified and improved to the limits of their potential, but new generations of ground weapons failed to appear and modern aircraft came too late and in insufficient numbers.

Continuous expansion throughout the war meant that by 1945 there were over five and a half million men and almost 200 divisions in the Army. Its most important figures under the Chief of Staff remained the Inspectors General of Military Education and of Aircraft. Beneath the central council resources were organized geographically, defence areas with their own overall C-in-Cs being flexibly created wherever Japanese ground forces were in action. After the war the Army and all institutions associated with it were disbanded by the Forces of Occupation, and the 1947 constitution banned all military forces in Japan.

Japanese Intelligence Agencies From 1938, Japanese gathering of political intelligence overseas was entrusted to individual diplomatic missions. When the Pacific War* started, this system largely collapsed. Counter-intelligence, the detection and suppression of hostile spy networks, was carried out in Japan and Japanese-occupied territories through the Ministry of War. A secret police organization, the *Tokko*, controlled internal subversion. Offensive espionage – subversion and the collection of military information overseas – was the responsibility of Organization F, a branch of the Japanese Army*. Months before the attacks on Indonesia* and Malaysia that opened the Pacific War, Organization F had furnished the Army with detailed reports on its targets from extensive spy networks.

Japanese Navy Since her defeat of the Russian Grand Fleet in 1905, Japan has been acknowledged as one of the world's major sea powers. This was recognized by the Washington Naval Treaty of 1922, which allowed Japan to build three capital ships to every five built by Britain or the United States, with similar ratios in other surface classes. This was more than either Italy or France (the other signatories) were permitted, but was regarded within the Japanese Navy as an insult, an attitude that shaped the characteristics of future

Japanese warships. Determined to compensate for discrepancy in numbers by producing the world's most powerful fighting ships, Japanese designers crammed extraordinarily heavy armament onto the relatively light hulls permitted by the Treaty. Although costly, inclined to instability and often well above their published tonnage, these formidable units impressed naval opinion worldwide. They provoked a general escalation of warship armament, most notably in the United States, which was regarded by the Japanese Navy as its logical enemy.

In December 1941, Japan had the third largest navy in the world, after Britain and the US. In the important field of naval aviation it led the world. It possessed ten aircraft carriers which were equipped with first-class purpose-built aircraft and operated by highly trained, experienced crews. The Navy enjoyed full control over all aspects of its air arm and had evolved tactics based around carriers as capital fleet units and as the main offensive weapon in surface combat. Twelve battleships were also in commission with the giant *Yamato** Class under construction. These were primarily intended to screen and support the fleet carriers, as were the 18 heavy and 18 light cruisers. The more modern components of a force of over 100 destroyers* were large, fast, well-armed ships likewise dedicated to offensive fleet actions. They relied heavily on torpedo armament and achieved considerable success with the oxygen-powered 24-inch Long Lance torpedo*.

No treaty restrictions bound the Japanese in the building of submarines*, and they constructed numerous very large long-range 'cruiser' submarines, again for the express purpose of taking part in major fleet operations. Perhaps the most significant area of Japanese advantage in the early years of the Pacific War* was the priceless benefit of combat experience gained in China* since 1937.

The offensive power of the Navy, enshrined in High Command doctrine, masked a number of serious weaknesses in defensive areas. Few escorts or anti-submarine* weapons of any sort had been built and vital merchant shipping was never efficiently organized into convoys*. In the field of electronics Japan lagged far behind the western democracies. The Navy possessed no operational radar* at the start of the war and only a few primitive sets were used later. The most damaging disadvantages faced by the Japanese Navy in wartime were, however, outside its direct control. In immediate operational terms the breaking of Japanese codes by the US Navy* was of enormous importance (see Magic), and in the long term utter dependence on imported raw materials (especially oil) doomed the Navy to defeat in any prolonged war with the United States.

Both the Naval General Staff and successive Naval Ministers (who were serving officers after 1936) were well aware of the need to protect trade routes from the south and had maintained political pressure for overseas action against the US rather than Russia, the preferred target of the Japanese Army*. While never able to match the dominance of the Army in Japanese political life, naval influence increased steadily from the late 1930s and the two services operated more as rivals than as partners throughout the war. Factionalism was rife within the Navy itself, but in general morale and optimism were high.

In the first months of the Pacific War* the Japanese Navy was enormously successful. The carrier forces gained a momentous triumph at Pearl Harbor*, and the sinking of the British Force Z* demonstrated the comparative innocence of the Royal Navy in air-sea warfare. The turning point came in the summer of 1942 as Japan sought to expand her protective ring of conquests. The crushing defeat at Midway.* in June cost four aircraft carriers. These could be and were replaced by conversions or new fleet units, but their experienced and skilled crews could not. Sufficient aircraft and trained aircrew were never again available for Japanese carrier operations, and the situation worsened steadily until by 1944 vital missions were being entrusted to raw recruits.

As US forces mounted in the Pacific, the fleet policy with submarines proved increasingly disastrous against well-organized anti-submarine defences, and by 1944 active submarine operations had virtually ceased. Meanwhile the toll on Japanese trade exacted by the large and often unmolested force of US submarines was crippling the Navy's war effort. Lack of oil and raw materials meant that shipyards, which had never developed mass-production techniques, were unable to meet repair demands, let alone make good increasing losses.

Anxious to bring the US Navy to a decisive confrontation, which represented the only real chance for any overall victory in the war, the Japanese Navy poured most of its surviving ships into the massive Leyte Gulf* operation of October 1944. Their comprehensive defeat to all intents and purposes ended Japanese sea power, and the remainder of the war was characterized by a grim determination to fight on beyond all hope of victory. The air arm, which had been beyond salvation for some time, signalled its desperation with the fleetingly successful suicide attack campaign from early 1945 (see Kamikaze). The 'last sortie' of the surface fleet in April 1945 was just that – a suicide mission to Okinawa* using all the main surviving units based around the leviathan battleship *Yamato*. When this force was destroyed, long before reaching its destination, the Japanese Navy ceased to exist. Its remnants were either destroyed in their dockyards by Allied aircraft or surrendered (mostly inoperative) at the end of the war. The victorious Allies found the remains of a navy with no oil, few ships and 2 million unemployed sailors awaiting demobilization. See also Japanese Air Forces.

Jassy-Kishinev, Battle of See Rumania.

Java Most heavily populated island of the Dutch East Indies* and a key link in the Japanese defensive perimeter in the Southwest Pacific, it was invaded by units of the Japanese 16th Army under Lt General Imamura* on 28 February (the day after the action in the Java Sea* ended Allied naval resistance in the Dutch East Indies). Java came under Japanese control on 9 March. The island was reoccupied after the end of hostilities in the Pacific, though not without opposition from islanders who contested the reimposition of Dutch rule. See Map 10.

Java Sea, Battle of, February 1942 An important naval engagement fought at the height of the Japanese drive into the Southwest Pacific between an Allied naval force, the Combined Striking Force under Dutch Admiral Doorman* and a Japanese task force under Vice Admiral Takagi*. A clear victory for the Japanese, the action put Japan in control of Java* and thus of the whole of the Dutch East Indies*, breaching the Allied defensive perimeter, the 'Malay Barrier'.

On 27 February, Admiral Doorman received orders while refuelling at Surabaya to sail immediately to intercept a Japanese invasion force in the Makassar Strait off Borneo*, this being part of a large fleet under Admiral Kondo* that Doorman had been hunting with his tiny and exhausted force since the start of the year. With an escort of two heavy and two light cruisers and 14 destroyers under Takagi, the Japanese force was more than a match for Doorman, whose Combined Striking Force comprised two heavy, three light cruisers and nine destroyers.

Drawing the Japanese within range of his light cruisers' guns exposed Doorman's fleet to torpedoes* from the Japanese destroyers* led by the cruiser *Jintsu*. When the Allied cruiser *Exeter*ature was damaged and broke formation, it was followed mistakenly by the *Houston*, *Perth* and *Java*. The communications confusion and an immediate order from Doorman to counter-attack cost him the *Kortenaer* and the Allied force was ordered by Doorman to retreat south to regroup. Forced to detach four American destroyers to refuel and another destroyer to recover survivors of the *Kortenaer*, the remainder of Doorman's force was sighted by the Japanese cruisers *Nachi* and *Haguro* (see Myoko) which immediately opened fire, sinking the *Java* and Admiral Doorman's flagship *De Ruyter*, with him aboard. The two remaining cruisers retired to western Java where they were sunk hours later.

Jean Bart Second of the French Navy's* *Richelieu* Class battleships, the *Jean Bart* was launched in March 1940, but was incomplete when France surrendered in June. She escaped to Casablanca* where she remained throughout the war, firing briefly during the Allied Torch* landings in November 1942, before her one operative gun turret was temporarily knocked out by the US Navy battleship *Massachusetts*. She was returned to France for repair after the war.
BRIEF DATA (1942) See Richelieu except Armaments: $4 \times 15''$ gun, $4 \times 3.5''$ AA gun.

Jodl, General Alfred Josef (1890–1946) Outstanding German staff officer and Hitler's OKW* Chief of Operations from 1939. Jodl had been associated with nationalist and anti-democratic racialist groups during the 1930s and remained, despite a disapproval of Nazism, a loyal and highly skilful technical adviser and executor of Hitler's strategic decisions. He opposed the dismissal of General Halder* and Field Marshal List* in 1942 and asked for a field command, but remained on Hitler's staff. He was injured while standing next to Hitler in the 1944 July Bomb Plot*. In May 1945 Jodl signed the unconditional surrender document on behalf of Dönitz's* government. He was subsequently tried at Nuremberg* as a 'planner of aggressive war', found guilty and hanged.

Johnson, Group Captain James Edgar (1916–) RAF fighter ace*, he served in operations throughout the war (including

the Battle of Britain*, the Dieppe Raid* and the D-Day* preparations) and was the highest scoring pilot of the air war against the Luftwaffe*, with 38 kills. He remained in the RAF after the war, rising to command the Air Forces Middle East during the early 1960s.

Joint Bombing Programme See Strategic Bombing Offensive; Eaker, Ira; Conferences, Casablanca.

Joint Chiefs of Staff The American component of the Combined Chiefs of Staff*, the body charged with the planning and implementation of general Allied strategy. Although this co-ordination of staff commanders across the American services did not end the internecine rivalry of US Army* and Navy*, it did unify strategic planning for American forces far more effectively than had the Army-Navy Joint Board which had existed before 1942. See also Marshall, General George.

Joubert de la Ferté, Air Chief Marshal Sir Philip (1897–1965) Commander of RAF* Coastal Command 1941–3, he initiated a 'planned flying' scheme which considerably improved operations and maintenance co-ordination. In addition, he sponsored operations research and the use of new tools and techniques, including airborne search radar*, which substantially solved the serious deficiencies in anti-submarine* technology that had previously existed in the Command. For most of his tenure Coastal Command was granted a very low priority in the allocation of pilots and equipment, and only became genuinely effective against U-boats when large-scale Allied resources were directed to his successor, Slessor*. In 1943, Joubert was appointed Deputy Chief of Staff for Information and Civil Affairs on Lord Mountbatten's* staff in SEAC.

Joyce, William (1906–46) A British-bred broadcaster who worked in Germany under Göbbels' Propaganda Ministry, his regular radio programmes purported to expose the weakness in the British war effort. Joyce's braying, upper class tones earned him the nickname 'Lord Haw-Haw', a term that suggests the general amusement, rather than the credulity, of British listeners, at the substance of Joyce's exposures.

Born in New York and brought up in England and Ireland, Joyce was a member of the British Fascist Party under Mosley* from 1932. In 1939, immediately before the outbreak of war, he went to Germany to offer his services to the Reich.

Joyce was arrested in May 1945 at Flensberg and returned to Britain to stand trial at the Old Bailey for treason. Although he claimed German (and possibly US) citizenship, his British passport was sufficient to secure his conviction. He was hanged in Wandsworth Prison, London, in 1946. See also Propaganda.

Juin, General Alphonse (1888–1967) Generally regarded as an exceptional field commander, Juin began his military career with the highest achievement record of his class at St Cyr military academy (a class which included Charles de Gaulle*). As commander of the French 15th Motorized Division (1st Army) in 1940, Juin's service in Belgium and northern France (see Western Offensive), where he was captured by German forces, was rewarded by a personal request for his release from Marshal Pétain*, who subsequently offered him the post of War Minister in the Vichy* Government – a post which he refused.

Promoted instead C-in-C of French forces in North Africa, where he replaced Weygand*, Juin's command was initially handicapped by his ambivalence towards Vichy. But separate and secret negotiations between the French Army and the US (notably between Admiral Darlan* and US General Clark*) resulted in the agreement of an armistice in North Africa and Juin brought his forces back into the war on the Allied side in late 1942, serving with distinction in Tunisia* against Rommel's* forces.

Later, in command of the French Expeditionary Corps in Italy* in 1944, Juin again proved his rare abilities in the field, notably at Monte Cassino* during the Allied offensive to capture Rome*, in what was described by an observer as 'one of the most daring and brilliant advances of the war'.

Promoted Chief of Staff of the French National Defence Committee under de Gaulle, Juin was requested to raise four fresh divisions to participate in the liberation of France. Before his death in 1967, Juin held a NATO command. He was buried at Les Invalides.

July Bomb Plot The unsuccessful attempt on 20 July 1944 to take Hitler's life. By early 1944, Hitler had already survived two attempts on his life and the Gestapo* and SD* had succeeded in dispersing much of the anti-Hitler opposition within Germany (see Resistance: Germany). Many of the best known conspirators, including Dietrich Bonhöffer*, Joseph Müller and Hans Dohnanyi* had been arrested or, like Hans Oster* and Admiral Canaris*, had been dismissed from their positions. Count Claus Schenk von Stauffenberg*, the driving force behind the July attempt, had been in touch with various opposition members within the army since the end of 1942, when he had urged Field Marshal Manstein* to join the anti-Hitler conspiracy.

The evasive reactions of Manstein and other senior officers perhaps triggered Stauffenberg's decision to assume a leading role in a new plot against Hitler's life during the second half of 1943. Two immediate objectives of the operation were identified: the assassination of Hitler and the separate seizure of the German state in the face of SS* forces which would be loyal to Himmler*, Göring*, or whichever Nazi leader attempted to assume control. Hence in the summer of 1943, Generals Beck* and Gördeler* asked Stauffenberg to plan for the seizure of Berlin after Hitler's death.

Operation Valkyrie was both a cover-story and a plan for this seizure. Openly, Stauffenberg prepared a contingency plan for Berlin garrisons to seize key government buildings, telephone and signal centres and radio stations in the event of a revolt of foreign slave labourers working in the Berlin region. In reality, however, the plan projected an assault on SS forces stationed there. The Berlin police force under Count Helldorf could be relied on. The Commandant of the City of Berlin, General von Hase, was also a committed anti-Nazi. The major uncertainty lay in the attitude of General Fromm, Commander of the Home Army.

But the key to the conspiracy remained the successful assassination of Hitler. With the recent dismissal of Admiral Canaris* from his Abwehr* post, the conspiracy suffered from lack of information about Hitler's movements, though Stauffenberg's appointment as General Fromm's Chief of Staff at the beginning of July ensured him regular access to Hitler at his headquarters at Rastenberg, known as the 'Wolf's Lair', in East Prussia. As events made it essential to act quickly, Stauffenberg took the opportunity provided by a conference to be attended by Hitler, where Stauffenberg was to report on the state of the Home Army. With a primed time-bomb hidden in his briefcase, he positioned himself as close as possible to Hitler, about 12 feet away, and rested the briefcase against the heavy leg of the oak map table which dominated the room.

The bomb exploded at 12.42 p.m. The tar-paper roof and six windows of the large wooden hut were destroyed immediately. Stauffenberg was already clear of the hut, certain that all at the conference were dead. Only when he arrived in Berlin after 4 p.m. did he realize to his astonishment that Hitler was still alive. The conspiracy now quickly foundered. Göbbels acted with speed in Berlin to control the situation. Fromm had Stauffenberg shot that night, clearly in part in order to allay suspicions of his own involvement. Operation Valkyrie had failed – months of vengeance followed.

Hundreds of suspects were arrested and tortured. Those whose names had been extracted from victims were in turn arrested and tortured. After the trials, held by the notorious Roland Freisler, Judge of the People's Court, sentences were carried out by firing squad, axe and even strangling. It is recorded that Hitler watched 'home movies' of the deaths of the principal conspirators.

Junkers Ju52/3M The box-like *Tante Ju* (Auntie Junkers), constructed of corrugated metal, was one of the most distinctive and widely used Luftwaffe* aircraft of the war. A successful civil airliner in the 1930s, it was tried as a bomber in Spain before settling into a long career as a military transport with the arrival of specialist Dornier Do17* and Heinkel He111* bombers. At the start of WW2 547 Ju52/3M transport models were available to the Luftwaffe and, although used sparingly in Poland*, they played a major part in the invasion of Norway*, pioneering the use of air transport in offensive operations. At the start of the Western Offensive* in May 1940, they were employed as glider tugs, and a year later 493 Ju52/3Ms participated in the expensive airborne* assault on Crete*. On the Eastern Front* they performed a vital supply role for the rapidly advancing German Army*, at the same time remaining the Luftwaffe's all-purpose workhorse in the Mediterranean* theatre and in German-occupied territories.

A genuine sitting duck for opposing fighters and a regular victim of anti-aircraft* fire, the Ju52/3M suffered enormous losses in all its major operations. Attempts to replace the *Tante Ju* were unsuccessful – neither the Ju252 or Ju352 developments were produced in large numbers – but output of the ageing transport remained high almost until the end of the war and 3,500 machines were completed. Only after crushing defeats at Stalingrad* and in Sicily* during 1943 were the Luftwaffe's transport units weakened beyond replenishment, and thereafter reduced numbers of Ju52/3Ms were mostly concerned with ferrying the German Army in retreat, an increasingly hazardous task in the face of total Allied air supremacy.

BRIEF DATA (Ju52/3M) Type: 2–3-man transport; Engine: 3 × 830hp BMW; Max speed: 165mph; Ceiling: 18,000'; Range: 800m; Arms: 1 × 13mm mg, 2 × 7.9mm mg.

Junkers Ju86 The Ju86 was a standard Luftwaffe* bomber of the late 1930s. Many 86D and 86E models saw action against Poland* in 1939, but the type was then withdrawn from bomber groups. The high altitude Ju86P model, first flown in February 1940, was operational over the Soviet Union in 1941 as a reconnaissance bomber, while big-winged Ju86R photo-reconnaissance versions flew over southern England until the security of their high ceiling was pierced by modified Supermarine Spitfires* in late 1942.

BRIEF DATA (Ju86R) Type: 2–4-man reconnaissance; Engine: 2 × 1,000hp Junkers Jumo; Max speed: 261mph; Ceiling: 42,650'; Range: 980m; Arms: usually none.

Junkers Ju87 The Ju87 'Stuka' – a name derived from the German generic term for dive-bomber – exemplified the army support role to which the Luftwaffe* was geared at the beginning of the war. The Ju87A had entered service early in 1937, to be followed in 1938 by the much-improved Ju87B, with 900hp engines, redesigned cockpit, spatted undercarriage and attack sirens (*Jericho-Trompeten*). A few of both types were tested operationally in Spain, and achieved great success and notoriety, confirming the Luftwaffe's faith in dive-bombing to the point of dogma. This faith was well rewarded in the campaigns of 1939 –40 as the ugly and sinister 'Stuka', screaming at its target in a near-vertical dive out of ill-defended skies, came to symbolize both the triumph and the terror of German Blitzkrieg* tactics.

Some 340 Ju87s were deployed at the start of the Battle of Britain* in the summer of 1940, but their reputation for invincibility suffered grievously at the hands of the RAF's* Supermarine Spitfires* and Hawker Hurricanes*. Too slow and cumbersome to cope with these modern interceptors, they were quickly withdrawn to only limited service in the north but were prominent in the Balkans* and the Mediterranean* during 1941, as well as in support of Operation Barbarossa. The Ju87D1, which began replacing the B version on the Eastern Front* at the end of 1941, had increased engine power, armour and payload, and its D3 and D4 successors, built without dive-brakes, marked the effective end of the plane's dive-bombing career. Instead, the 'Stuka' became a specialist ground-attack aircraft, carrying a variety of underwing arms packs or anti-tank modifications and remaining in front-line service long after it was obsolete. In the absence of successful purpose-built replacements, production continued until late 1944, and 5,709 Ju87s of all types were built.

BRIEF DATA (Ju87D1) Type: single-seat dive-bomber; Engine: 1 × 1,400hp Junkers Jumo; Max speed: 255mph; Ceiling: 24,000'; Range: 620m; Arms: 4 × 7.9mm mg; Bomb load: 3,960lb.

Junkers Ju88 The most versatile German aircraft of WW2. Conceived as a fast bomber, it entered Luftwaffe* service as the Ju88A just before war broke out in 1939, and was prominent in strategic, tactical and anti-shipping operations throughout Europe, the Eastern Front* and the Mediterranean*. Speed was intended to be the Ju88's greatest asset but, although it usually flew unescorted during the Battle of Britain*, the 'Wonder Bomber' was never fast enough to outrun wartime fighters. The Ju88A4, improved in the light of combat experience, was better armed, had broader wings and displayed none of its predecessor's teething troubles, but remained inadequate as a strategic bomber. Like the Heinkel He111*, it owed its long service to Germany's inability to find an effective successor.

After the invasion of Russia, Ju88As usually operated in small groups against precision targets on the Eastern Front. The later Ju88P tank-buster (with guns of up to 50mm calibre) and Ju88S tactical bomber were reflections of this changed role. Various torpedo-armed maritime versions were also developed and total production of Ju88 bombers was about 9,000.

The performance of pre-production Ju88As had compared so favourably with that of the best pre-war interceptors that a heavy fighter (*Zerstörer*) version was being tested as early as 1938. It entered full service in mid-1940 as the Ju88C2, a fighter-armed and armoured adaptation, which retained a small bomb capacity and was initially used as a disguised escort among bomber formations. Soon the plane began to be employed as an interim night fighter and for a while in 1941 operated as a night intruder, lurking near British RAF* bases. Ju88Cs appeared in seven major versions and a number of sub-variants, representing frequent changes of armament, repeated attempts to introduce BMW radial engines (always thwarted by supply problems) and various radar* installations.

The Ju88R, packed with radar equipment, appeared in 1943 and, as Luftwaffe night defence tactics reached a high level of sophistication, the definitive Ju88G night fighter became operational in mid-1944. Almost completely redesigned, these were mass-produced using the angular tailfin of the Junkers Ju188* bomber. They inflicted serious losses on the RAF heavy bomber streams (see Strategic Bombing Offensive), but could never match the performance of the British de Havilland Mosquito* night fighters and operated in dwindling numbers as the war came to an end. Over 15,000 Ju88s of all types were produced.

BRIEF DATA (Ju88G7) Type: 4-man night fighter; Engine: 2 × 1,725hp Junkers Jumo; Max speed: 389mph; Ceiling: 28,800'; Range: 1,400m; Arms: 4 × 20mm cannon, 1 × 13mm mg, 2 × 20mm *Schräge Musik** cannon (firing upwards).

Junkers Ju290 Manufactured for two years from October 1942, although never in great numbers, this big German transport was first used by the Luftwaffe* at Stalingrad* and later saw service primarily over the Atlantic* and the Mediterranean* as a maritime patrol aircraft. The Ju290A, which appeared in eight versions, was usually heavily armed. The Ju290B carried radar* and could launch guided* bombs.

BRIEF DATA (Ju290A8) Type: 4–6-man transport/maritime patrol; Engine: 4 × 1,600hp BMW; Max speed: 280mph; Ceiling: 19,700'; Range: 3,785m (max); Arms: 5 × 20mm cannon, 6 × 13mm mg.

Juno Code-name of the central British assault area (the beach at Courseulles-sur-Mer) for the D-Day invasion of Normandy* on 6 June 1944.

K

Kaga The Japanese *Kaga* was originally launched as a battleship in 1921 but was due to be scrapped incomplete under the terms of the Washington Naval Treaty. She was saved and completed as an aircraft carrier when the original choice for conversion, the *Amagi* was wrecked in the great earthquake of 1923. The *Kaga* eventually joined the fleet in 1930 and was refitted in 1935. Her wartime career was brief but eventful. She was in constant action with Admiral Nagumo's* 1st Carrier Division until sunk at the Battle of Midway* on 6 June 1942.
BRIEF DATA (1941) Displacement: 38,200 tons; Dimensions: o/a lgth – 812' 4", b – 106' 9"; Speed: 28.5 knots; Armament: 10 × 8" gun (10 × 1), 16 × 5" gun, 22 × 25mm AA gun, 90 aircraft.

Ka-Go Japanese code-name for an operation to reinforce Guadalcanal*, which resulted in the Battle of the Eastern Solomons*, August 1942.

Kaiten Japanese one-man human torpedo modified from the oxygen-propelled Long Lance 24-inch torpedo*. Operational from 1944, they were carried to within range of a target by a warship (often a submarine) and many Japanese Navy vessels were adapted for the purpose. Most *Kaiten* were Type 1 models, which were produced and used in large numbers. These were over 48ft long, carried a 3,400lb warhead and could make 12 knots at maximum range (under 50 miles). Later models with higher speeds or heavier warheads reached only limited production. The effectiveness of the *Kaiten* is doubtful, American sources disputing Japanese claims of large-scale damage to shipping. See also Midget Submarines.

Kaltenbrunner, Ernst (1903–46) Head of the Austrian SS* before and after the Anschluss* and successor to Heydrich* as Head of RHSA, SS Security, Gestapo* and SD* after the latter's assassination. He also took over control of the Abwehr* (German military intelligence) after the dissolution of Canaris's* command. He was hanged as a major war criminal in 1946, although he protested at his trial in Nuremberg* that he was serving as a substitute for Himmler*, already dead by poisoning.

Kamikaze (Divine Wind) A Japanese tactic of suicidal dive-bombing attack on enemy warships, it was first employed by pilots of the Special Attack Corps in the struggle for the Philippines* during 1944. Inspired by the oath of absolute loyalty to the Emperor and the honour believed to be derived from death as the ultimate service to their country (see Bushido), Japanese pilots first flew suicide missions against the flat-tops of the American carrier forces supporting the invasion of Leyte*. Training in Kamikaze techniques had begun under Admiral Onishi* after the fall of Saipan* in July 1944. Flying Mitsubishi A6M Zero* fighters and Yokusaka D4Y* dive-bombers in intensive training sessions lasting for as little as a week, Kamikaze pilots aimed at the central elevator on carriers and the base of the bridge on large warships, and inflicted considerable damage on the US fleets in the

Philippines. Over 2,000 Kamikaze missions were also flown against the US Fleet at Okinawa*.

During April 1945, Kamikaze pilots under Admiral Toyoda* launched a further 1,400 suicide missions from Kyushu alone, as part of Operation Ten-Go*, a massive air operation in defence of the Japanese home islands, with Allied losses from these raids mounting to 26 ships sunk and 160 damaged. The rate of attrition, however, and the impossibility of improving technique without returning pilots, added to the improving evasion techniques of the American naval forces, dulled the impact of the Kamikaze tactic in the final months of the Pacific War*, although Kamikaze pilots continued to be sent out until the end of the war. See also Japanese Air Forces.

Karlsruhe German Navy* light cruiser launched in 1927. The *Karlsruhe* and her two sisters, the *Königsberg* and the *Köln*, were well-armed and had dual turbine and diesel propulsion systems, extending their operational range for potential Atlantic* sorties. By German standards, however, they were thinly armoured and they did not much exceed their announced 6,000-ton displacement. The *Karlsruhe* alone was refitted before the war, having her keel externally bulged and losing two knots in speed.

The *Karlsruhe* was lost attempting to return from the Norwegian campaign of 1940, sunk by her escorts after being torpedoed by the British submarine *Truant* off Christiansund on 10 April. The next day land-based Fleet Air Arm* Blackburn Skuas* sank the *Königsberg* at Bergen, where she lay after being damaged by the port's shore batteries during the German assault. She was the first major warship to be destroyed by dive-bombers. The *Köln* survived the campaign and was eventually sunk at Wilhelmshaven on 30 April 1945 by carrier aircraft.

BRIEF DATA (*Karlsruhe*, 1939) Displacement: 6,650 tons; Dimensions: o/a lgth – 570′ 9″, b – 54′ 6″; Speed: 30 knots; Armament: 9 × 5.9″ gun (3 × 3), 6 × 3.5″ AA gun, 8 × 37mm AA gun, 4 × 20mm AA gun, 12 × 21″ TT, 2 aircraft.

Kasserine Pass A gap in the Tebessa Mountains of western Tunisia* which became the focus of an Axis attempt to outflank the Allied 1st Army in February 1943. From the east, the pass guards a road junction leading to Tebessa or Thala, both of which were important American supply centres for Tunisian operations. Field Marshal Rommel*, whose forces had retreated into eastern Tunisia after their defeat at El Alamein*, saw the chance to inflict a decisive defeat on the Americans to his rear before he faced the British 8th Army, which was approaching from the west. Rommel's strength was reduced by the diversion of one of his two armoured divisions to the north, where Colonel-General von Arnim* had received High Command backing for a later offensive against much stronger Allied positions (see Map 8).

On 19 February, elements of the Afrika Korps* launched their first attack on the pass, while other units tried to force an alternative passage to the north. The next day Rommel concentrated all his available armour on Kasserine, and by late afternoon a much larger US force had been overrun. A small British detachment sent in support delayed the panzers for a time, but the next morning they moved towards Thala. Rommel's strong preference for an attack on Tebessa, which was much further behind Allied lines than Thala, was overruled by a telegraph from Mussolini. After two days the Afrika Korps was forced to withdraw by the presence of large Allied reserves in the sector, and it returned through the Kasserine Pass in ordered retreat on 23 February. Largely unmolested by the battered US Army 2nd Corps, Rommel drove his forces back to the Mareth Line* and prepared to face the 8th Army. He had failed in his strategic objective of driving the Allies back into Algeria but had inflicted heavy casualties at minimal cost. The reversal at Kasserine was a serious blow to American morale in Tunisia and at home.

Katori Japanese light cruiser and class. Completed in 1941, the *Katori* and the *Kashima* were designed for the ocean training of Japanese seamen, but performed as flagships after the outbreak of the Pacific War*. A third unit, the *Kashii*, was ready in 1942, but a fourth was cancelled at an early stage of construction. They were slow and had no armour protection.

The *Katori* was sunk in the American raid on Truk* of February 1944, after which her sisters were converted as antisubmarine* vessels, a type which, contrary to their expectations, the Japanese found they needed desperately. Torpedo* tubes and aircraft were removed and replaced with additional 5-inch guns and light antiaircraft* defence. The *Kashima* survived the war, but the *Kashii* was destroyed by aircraft off the coast of Indochina* in January 1945.

BRIEF DATA (*Katori*, 1941) Displacement: 5,890 tons; Dimensions: o/a lgth – 425', b – 52'; Speed: 18 knots; Armament: 4 × 5.5" gun (2 × 2), 2 × 5" AA gun, 4 × 25mm AA gun, 4 × 21" TT, 1 aircraft.

Katyn Massacre In the spring of 1943 in Katyn Forest, near Smolensk, Russia, mass graves containing thousands of corpses of Polish officers and troops were discovered and announced by Berlin Radio. Though the actual number murdered is now hard to establish (varying between 1,700 and 4,500), evidence showed that the victims had been shot in the head, almost certainly by Russian NKVD*. Medical examinations of the bodies established the date of the massacre as the spring of 1940. Moreover, a further 10,000 Poles held by the Russians in three camps near Smolensk were also unaccounted for.

While the London-based Polish government-in-exile* attempted to force an investigation of the deaths by the Red Cross* (refused by Moscow), and Berlin energetically exploited the affair as anti-

Russian propaganda, Stalin* used the accusation as a pretext to break relations with the exiled Polish government in April 1943, insisting that the massacre had been committed by Germans after their invasion of Russia in 1941 (see Eastern Front). The political embarrassment for the Allies was intense. Under pressure to remain on good terms with Russia as a major ally, their refusal to support Polish Premier Sikorski* caused much bad feeling. Moreover, it represented the sacrificing of much Allied influence in Poland, over which Britain had originally gone to war against Germany, allowing Stalin a more or less free hand to direct the future for post-war Poland*.

Kawabe, Lt General Masakuzu (1886–1965) Japanese Chief of Staff of Japanese forces in China* in early 1942, he assumed command of the army in Burma* in 1943, and planned the offensive against Imphal* and Kohima* that was part of the unsuccessful invasion of India in 1944. Relieved of command and sent back to Japan to control Japan's Central Area, he was appointed to lead the Army Air Forces in 1945.

Kawanishi H6K Designed after a Kawanishi staff visit to the Short Brothers factory in Britain, 176 of these reliable flying boats were built for the Japanese Navy* between 1938 and 1942, mostly of the H6K4 and H6K5 versions. Primarily reconnaissance aircraft, they were sometimes used as bombers in the first months of the Pacific War*, but were superseded in production by the superior Kawanishi H8K* during 1943. An additional 38 aircraft were built purely for transport purposes (H6K2L and 4L) and these were divided between naval and civilian operations.

BRIEF DATA (H6K5) Type: 9-man flying-boat; Engine: 4 × 1,300hp Mitsubishi Kinsei; Max speed: 239mph; Ceiling: 31,500'; Range: 3,067m; Arms: 1 × 20mm cannon, 4 × 7.7mm mg; Bomb load: 2,200lb or 2 × 1,760lb torpedo*; Allied code-name: Mavis.

Kawanishi H8K Like the Short Sunderland*, which it was specifically designed to outperform, the Japanese H8K was a big, graceful craft, well-armed and notoriously difficult to shoot down. Exceptionally fast for its type, it was also better armoured than most Japanese warplanes, and had partially self-sealing fuel tanks. About 150 were built between 1942 and 1945, mostly of the refined and more powerful H8K2 version, which appeared in 1943. A further 36 H8K2-L 'Clear Sky' (*Seiku*) transport models were produced, exclusively for military use.
BRIEF DATA (H8K2) Type: 10-man long-range flying boat; Engine: 4 × 1,850hp Mitsubishi Kasei; Max speed: 295mph; Ceiling: 29,000'; Range: 4,439m; Arms: 5 × 20mm cannon, 5 × 7.7mm mg; Bomb load: 4,400lb or 2 × 1,760lb torpedo*; Allied code-name: Emily.

Kawanishi N1K1-J Violet Lightning (Shiden) Japanese fighter, developed privately by Kawanishi in 1942 as a modification of the N1K1 *Kyofu*, a Japanese Navy* floatplane designed to support troop landings in remote areas where carrier forces were unavailable or unnecessary. The *Shiden* was a land-based interceptor with a retractable undercarriage in place of floats, and was soon superseded by the refined N1K2-J, designed for ease of construction. This competed successfully with the best American naval fighters in the Philippines* and at Okinawa*, but its performance fell off badly at high altitude against B-29* bombers. Between early 1943 and the end of the war, about 1,400 of both versions were manufactured, along with a few two-seater N1K2-J trainers.
BRIEF DATA (N1K2-J) Type: single-seat naval fighter; Engine: 1 × 1,990hp Nakajima; Max speed: 369mph; Ceiling: 35,000'; Range: 1,065m; Arms: 4 × 20mm cannon (provision for 2,200lb bombs); Allied code-name: George.

Kawasaki Ki-45 Dragon Slayer (Toryu)
After years of development as a long-range

escort fighter, the Ki-45a began full production at the beginning of 1942, and performed a number of functions for the Japanese Army* throughout the Pacific War*. Upon entering service, it proved most effective as a ground-attack plane, and the Ki-45b version was introduced specifically for that role. From 1944, the plane began operations as a home-based night fighter (Ki-45c), but plans to equip it with air-to-air radar foundered and the transition was not entirely successful. All later models were powered by 1,050hp Mitsubishi engines, and weight of armament was steadily increased, culminating in the anti-shipping Ki-45d, which mounted three cannon and one machine-gun. About 1,700 Dragon Slayers were completed before the end of the war.
BRIEF DATA (Ki-45a) Type: 2-man heavy fighter; Engine: 2 × 950hp Nakajima HA25; Max speed: 340mph; Ceiling: 35,000'; Range: 1,400m; Arms: 1 × 20mm cannon, 1 × 12.7mm mg, 1 × 7.92mm mg; Bomb load: 1,100lb; Allied code-name: Nick.

Kawasaki Ki-48 Introduced to the JAAF* in 1940 as a fast day-bomber, the Ki-48I found itself fatally outpaced when it faced modern Allied fighters. The better-armoured and slightly faster Ki-48II fared little better, yet the plane saw widespread service and remained in production until the autumn of 1944. Nearly 2,900 were built, including a Ki-48IIb dive-bomber version.
BRIEF DATA (Ki-48II) Type: 4-man light bomber; Engine: 2 × 1,150hp Nakajima Ha-115; Max speed: 314mph; Ceiling: 33,000'; Range: 1,275m (normal); Arms: 3 × 7.7mm mg; Bomb load: 1,760lb; Allied code-name: Lily.

Kawasaki Ki-61 Swallow (Hien) JAAF* fighter designed around a liquid-cooled engine licensed from Daimler-Benz of Germany, it bore a distinctly European appearance. It fought first in New Guinea* in April 1943, and later operated against

USAAF* bombers over Japan. The Ki-61-I*kai*, a modified version with stronger wings, was produced in quantity, but only a few of the high-altitude, 380mph Ki-61-II*kai* interceptors were completed. Well over 2,500 Swallows had been manufactured by January 1945.

BRIEF DATA (Ki-61-I) Type: single-seat fighter; Engine: 1 × 1,100hp Kawasaki Ha-Ho; Max speed: 368mph; Ceiling: 33,000'; Range: 684m (max); Arms: 2 × 12.7mm mg, 2 × 7.7mm mg (later all 20mm cannon); Allied code-name: Tony.

Kawasaki Ki-100 When American B-29s* began raiding Japan from refuelling points in China* in 1944, only the latest Kawasaki Ki-61* fighter offered the JAAF* the high-altitude performance necessary to intercept them. Burdened by an unreliable liquid-cooled engine, it was stranded in the prototype stage, and so its completed airframe was married to a radial engine to produce the Ki-100. From September 1944, about 375 of these performed reliably in the defence of the homeland, but they were never sufficiently armed and were increasingly entrusted to inexperienced pilots.

BRIEF DATA (Ki-100) Type: single-seat fighter; Engine: 1 × 1,500hp Mitsubishi Ha-112-II; Max speed: 360mph; Ceiling: 36,000'; Range: 870m; Arms: 2 × 20mm cannon, 2 × 12.7mm mg; Bomb load: (optional) 1,100lb; Allied code-name: none.

Kawasaki Ki-102 Designed to succeed the Kawasaki Ki-45* as a ground-support plane for the Japanese Army*, the Ki-102b went into production in October 1944. About 200 were built and some took part in the defence of Okinawa* in April 1945. Fifteen examples of a high-altitude fighter version (Ki-102a) were delivered, but a Ki-102c night fighter variant only reached prototype form.

BRIEF DATA (Ki-102b) Type: 2-man ground-attack aircraft; Engine: 2 × 1,500hp Mitsubishi Ha-112-II; Max speed: 360mph; Ceiling: 33,000'; Range: 1,243m; Arms: 1 × 57mm cannon, 2 × 20mm cannon, 1 × 12.7mm mg; Bomb load: 1,100lb; Allied code-name: Randy.

Kearny USS US Navy* *Benson* Class destroyer, commissioned in 1940. The *Kearny* was damaged by a torpedo* while depth-charging a U-boat in the North Atlantic on 17 October 1941. Although the US was still neutral at that time, President Roosevelt had announced a 'shoot on sight' policy against Axis submarines a few weeks earlier, and US warships had been escorting Atlantic* convoys as far as Iceland* since July. The *Kearny* survived and returned to escort duty. In November 1942 she was part of the screening force for the Torch* landings in Northwest Africa, and later covered the Anzio* and Anvil/Dragoon landings. See also Destroyers; Neutrality, US.

BRIEF DATA (*Benson* Class) Displacement: 1,630 tons; Dimensions: o/a lgth – 348' 3", b – 36' 3"; Speed: 37 knots; Armament: 5 × 5" gun, 10 × 0.5" AA mg, 10 × 21" TT.

Keitel, Field Marshal Wilhelm (1882–1946) Chief of Staff of the German High Command (OKW*) from 1938 with a reputation for subservience to Hitler that earned him the nickname 'Lakeitel', a coinage from 'lackey – Keitel'. Keitel attended all significant German conferences on the conduct of the war and signed operational orders. After the attempt on Hitler's life in July 1944 (see July Bomb Plot), he sat as a member of the 'Court of Honour' which sentenced many high-ranking officers to death. After the war, Keitel was included among the major war criminals tried at Nuremberg*, charged with responsibility for issuing in 1941 the *Nacht und Nebel* decree on Hitler's orders. Notorious among many brutal decrees, it deliberately initiated a new dimension of fear in Germany by declaring that enemies of the state would disappear into 'Night and Fog' and that no information of any kind would be available to friends and relatives of missing persons. Keitel was hanged in 1946.

Kelly, HMS British K Class destroyer, famous for her exploits in the Mediterranean* under the command of Lord Louis Mountbatten*, later to become Supreme Allied Commander, Southeast Asia. In service from 1940, the Royal Navy's* J and K classes were reduced versions of the earlier Tribal Class (see Cossack, HMS), designed to reduce costs while retaining heavy armament. All 16 of the J and K units went to the Mediterranean and only four survived the war. Badly damaged twice during the course of many actions, the *Kelly* was sunk by Luftwaffe* dive-bombers during the British withdrawal from Crete* in May 1941.
BRIEF DATA (*Kelly*, as built) Displacement: 1,695 tons; Dimensions: o/a lgth – 336' 6", b – 35' 9"; Speed: 36 knots; Armament: 6 × 4.7" gun (3 × 2), 4 × 2pdr AA gun; 8 × 0.5" AA gun, 10 × 21" TT.

Kennedy, Joseph (1888–1969) US ambassador to Great Britain from 1937–41. Kennedy was a highly successful business magnate whose view of potential war in Europe was conditioned by his concern for economic stability. He shared this essentially commercial viewpoint with Prime Minister Neville Chamberlain*, and consistently advocated the concession of German territorial demands. Strongly opposed to British entry into the war on Poland's behalf and a committed isolationist ('This war is not our war, and Britain is not fighting our battle'), Kennedy nevertheless supported US aid to Britain in a war he was sure Germany would win. This undoubted sympathy did not extend to the level of support envisaged by the Lend-Lease* Act, which he opposed after his recall to the US early in 1941. The Japanese attack on Pearl Harbor* completely discredited the powerful isolationist lobby inside the US, and Kennedy's political position declined from that point. See also Neutrality, US.

Kesselring, Field Marshal Albert (1885–1960) Arguably the most successful German general in WW2, commanding the German withdrawal up the Italian peninsula that held superior Allied forces for 20 months (see Italy, Campaign in).

A Bavarian-born regular soldier, Kesselring served as an artilleryman and a general staff officer in WW1. In order to take a post as head of administration with the newly formed and still illicit Luftwaffe*, he learned to fly at the age of 48. When the Luftwaffe's first commander, General Wever, was killed in an air crash in 1936, Kesselring took over as Chief of Staff. He commanded Luftflotte I in Poland* in 1939, and in 1940 led Luftflotte II in the campaign in the Low Countries and France (see Western Offensive). During the Battle of Britain* Kesselring directed Luftflotte II in highly effective raids on air bases in south-east England, though it can be argued that he made his only serious tactical error in underrating the RAF's* ability to resist daylight attacks. The advantage gained by Luftflotte II was ultimately wasted by Göring's decision to redirect the Luftwaffe against London.

From the west, Kesselring was transferred with Luftflotte II to the Eastern Front* for six months before his appointment to the Mediterranean theatre (December 1941) as C-in-C South (OB Sud) and subsequently commander of all German forces in the Mediterranean. He jointly directed the campaign in North Africa with General Rommel*, leading the Axis* withdrawal from Tunisia*.

As C-in-C in Italy in 1943 and 1944, Kesselring fought the classic defensive campaign against a stronger, better-equipped enemy on which his reputation as a general rests. In March 1945 he had already opened negotiations with the American intelligence chief, Allen Dulles*, for a separate surrender when Hitler* transferred him to the Western Front to succeed Field Marshal von Rundstedt* as C-in-C West. But by then no generalship of whatever quality could turn the tide of the Allied successes and Kesselring surrendered to American forces on 7 May 1945.

In 1947 a British court found him guilty of ordering the execution of 335 Italian civilians and he was sentenced to life imprisonment. The conviction was in fact an extreme interpretation of the concept of a commander's responsibility for the acts of his troops, notwithstanding the command conditions of the last days in Italy when the campaign was characterized by intense partisan activity and drives by SS formations who were a law unto themselves. Many British jurists and senior officers later became concerned at the court's verdict. Kesselring's British opponent, Field Marshal Alexander*, was among those who expressed serious doubts, as an indirect result of which Kesselring was released from prison in 1952, officially on grounds of ill health. Before his death in 1960, Kesselring was appointed president of the ex-serviceman's association Stalhelm.

Khalkin-Gol, Battle of See Russo-Japanese Border Conflict.

Kharkov Eastern Ukrainian city, fourth largest in the Soviet Union, it was one of a line of bastion towns (including Novgorod, Rzhev, Vyasma, Bryansk, Kursk, Taganrog and Orel) known as 'hedgehogs' and used as winter bases for German forces during the Russian winter counter-offensive in 1941. Outflanking manoeuvres by Soviet forces failed to destroy these fortified points and a renewed attack focused on Kharkov was launched by Timoshenko* on 12 May, after a lull in fighting during the spring thaw. Although his large tank* force quickly drove spearheads behind the German rearward positions across a 70-mile front, a counter-attack by General Paulus's* 6th Army, spearheaded by Kleist's* panzers, trapped approximately 240,000 Soviet troops and 600 tanks in the Izyum salient, and opened the route through the 'Donets corridor' to Stalingrad*.

Nine months later, following the German defeat at Stalingrad, the Russian armies were again threatening General Manstein's* northern flank at Kharkov. It was abandoned by the SS panzer division deployed to hold it on 15 February 1943,

but Hitler ordered that Kharkov was to be recaptured and the attempt was started by General Hoth on the 21st. Aided by the heavy armament of the Tiger* tanks that was effective against the Russian T34* medium tanks, an encircling manoeuvre halted and trapped Bryansk Front* forces under Popov*, Hoth's forces pushed on to the Donets* by the beginning of March. Kharkov was finally recaptured for the Russians in August 1943 following the major German defeat at Kursk* that initiated Soviet offensives along much of the front. See Eastern Front; Maps 27, 28, 29.

Khrushchev, Nikita S. (1894–1971) Post-war Soviet leader from 1953, he became a member of the Politburo in March 1939. Khrushchev was responsible for supervising the annexation of eastern Poland* and subsequently served as political commissar on the Western and Southwest Fronts. Remaining on the Southwest Front following the defeat at Kharkov* and the dismissal of General Timoshenko* in May 1942, Khrushchev was posted to the Ukrainian Central Committee after the liberation of Kiev* in November 1943, and was responsible for the purges of Ukrainian nationalist forces that brought the Ukraine* under Soviet control.

Kiev Capital of the Ukraine* and focus of one of the most overwhelming Soviet defeats of the German campaign in Russia in September 1941, when an estimated 600,000 Russians were killed or taken prisoner. See Budënny, Semion; Eastern Front.

Kimmel, Admiral Husband E. (1882–1968) American veteran of WW1, he was appointed to command the Cruiser Battle Force in 1939. He became C-in-C of the US Fleet (renamed the Pacific Fleet) based at Pearl Harbor* in February 1941 and therefore carried much of the blame for the unpreparedness of US naval forces and the scale of the disaster following the surprise Japanese attack in December. Although he continued in command until the end of the month, Kimmel was eventually replaced by Admiral Nimitz* and charged with derelection of duty by a board of inquiry, as a result of which he retired in 1942. A Congressional Inquiry set up in 1946 to investigate the causes of the tragedy at Pearl Harbor, however, cleared Kimmel of the charge. In 1955 the Admiral published a personal account, entitled *Admiral Kimmel's Story*, of his time at Pearl Harbor.

King, Admiral Ernest Joseph (1878–1956) C-in-C of the US Fleet and Chief of Naval Operations, King was arguably the most important American naval figure of the war and one of the chief architects of the American victory in the Pacific. He served on the Combined Chiefs of Staff* Committee and attended all the major Allied Conferences* throughout the war, gaining a reputation as an abrasive and argumentative, though highly able, strategist and a committed advocate of the United States' special responsibility in the Pacific.

Though criticized early on as a traditional naval strategist, King's background in naval aviation and carrier command prepared him well to salvage the disaster at Pearl Harbor* and recognize, develop and exploit the innovations in naval warfare that were essential to American success in the Pacific. With its increasing emphasis on air power, the carrier and amphibious* warfare (and its concomitant emphasis on logistics), the US Fleet also grew quickly in size and experience under King to become a supremely effective naval force, which in sheer numbers surpassed the combined strength of all other navies by 1945 (see US Navy).

In 1942, however, the huge task of developing the strength of the US Fleet was combined with the immense responsibility for co-ordinating not only joint US forces operations but Allied naval operations as well. King's achievement in directing the huge strategic and logistical scope of the war should not be underestimated. Although he presided over the planning and resourcing of major naval operations in the Atlantic*, North Africa* and Europe, King's primary responsibility (as he saw it) was the Pacific, where his greatest contribution was made. Limited in the early stages by lack of resources to adopting defensive strategies for both ocean theatres, King persistently argued for the direction of American resources to the Pacific, both with the Combined Chiefs and at Allied Conferences (most notably Casablanca), gaining a reputation, particularly among his Allied colleagues, for unbridled chauvinism in his advocacy of the Pacific War*.

Though unable to convince his Allied counterparts, King nevertheless went on to direct American efforts during the second half of 1942 that turned the tide of Japanese conquests in the Pacific (see Coral Sea; Midway) and enabled the US to go on the offensive, scoring some crucial victories with the new tactics of amphibious warfare that pushed Japan decisively onto the defensive. In overall control of deployments in the Pacific Ocean Areas*, King often came into conflict with General Douglas MacArthur*, Supreme Commander of the Southwest Pacific Area, over the assignment of priorities for Pacific offensives. Nevertheless, as US Fleet strength and experience grew steadily, King was increasingly able to count on its strategic and tactical superiority over the Japanese Fleet and establish himself as a pre-eminent figure in the development of modern naval logistics. Promoted a five-star full fleet admiral in December 1944, King received this greatest of many acknowledgements of his contribution with characteristic relish. See also Nimitz, Admiral Chester.

King, William Mackenzie (1874–1950) Canadian Liberal Party Leader and Prime Minister (1921–30 and 1935–48), King's shrewdness and political agility successfully rode the changes in Canadian public opinion over involvement in WW2. Initially a committed isolationist, King successfully appealed to the country to begin conscription after Pearl Harbor*, drawing Canada into the conflict while managing to maintain national unity by avoiding commitment to an 'Imperial War' (a concept favoured by Australian leader John Menzies*) and to over-expenditure of troops overseas. He also played an early, though perhaps overstated, part in establishing relations between Roosevelt* and Churchill*, and subsequently hosted two Allied Conferences* at Quebec in August 1943 and September 1944. By early 1945, increasing casualties and the pressure to provide conscripts for the war in Europe appeared to threaten his credibility, but the resignation of his Defence Minister and the subsequent Allied successes in Europe resolved the problem.

King George V, HMS British battleship and class, it also comprised the *Prince of Wales*, *Duke of York*, *Anson* and *Howe*. Built from 1937 to the 35,000-ton weight limit ostensibly observed by all navies under international treaty agreements, they were given 14-inch main armament (the treaty limit was 16-inch) by a reluctant Admiralty in support of government attempts in 1936 to impose a lower international standard. These efforts conspicuously failed to sway the Pacific powers, but it was too late to change if the new ships were to be ready by 1940–1 as planned.

In the event, they were ready just in time to preserve Britain's slender advantage in capital ships over her European enemies in WW2. The *King George V* was commissioned in late 1940 and the *Prince of Wales* in May 1941. The *Duke of York* followed at the end of the year and the *Anson* and *Howe* in 1942. Apart from the Japanese *Yamato* Class, they were the most heavily armoured warships in the world. They possessed adequate speed and heavy armament but, like most British fighting ships, they were manifestly short of effective light anti-aircraft defence. In the last three units this was augmented during construction, and by 1945 surviving vessels carried a variety of 40mm, 2-pounder and 20mm installations, as well as warning and fire control radar*.

The *King George V* began service as flagship of the Home Fleet, and played an important part in the sinking of the *Bismarck** in May 1941, setting her ablaze with repeated hits from 14,000 yards, before retiring short of fuel. In May 1943 she began operations in the Mediterranean and, along with her three surviving sisters, fought in the latter stages of the Pacific War*. In July 1945, the *King George V* took part in the bombardment of industrial targets on the Japanese mainland, the last British battleship to fire its main armament in anger.

BRIEF DATA (*King George V*, 1940) Displacement: 36,830 tons; Dimensions: o/a lgth – 745', b – 103'; Speed: 29.25 knots; Armament: 10 × 14" gun (2 × 4, 1 × 2), 16 × 5.25" DP gun, 32 × 2pdr AA gun, 16 × 0.5" AA gun; 3 aircraft.

King Tiger Tank (PzKpfw VI-II) Almost as soon as the Tiger* tank entered service, the German High Command (and Hitler in particular) perceived the need for a bigger and better successor. Early in 1942, both the MAN and Henschel companies were asked to build second generation versions of their respective Panther and Tiger designs. The Panther II was never built, although valuable time was wasted attempting to standardize its components with those of the Tiger II, which did not finally reach production until December 1943.

The massive new tank, known as the King Tiger, incorporated many of the best features of both its predecessors and could dominate the battlefield if skilfully handled. Able to outrange and outshoot almost any Allied tank, it was the best protected tank of the war and the heaviest. Inevitably ponderous, it could be left behind in a fast-moving battle, but had the power to knock out large numbers of hostile tanks without damage to itself. In service from May 1944 on the Eastern Front* and three months later in Northwest Europe*, it was deployed (like the Tiger I) in small units of four or five. Only 484 King Tigers – known to the Allies as Royal Tigers – were ever completed, and only one version was produced. Monthly production peaked at 84 in August 1944, the month in which the Tiger II became one of the only two turreted tanks retained in the German rationalization programme. Later it declined as efforts were concentrated on the Panther G*, which could be turned out twice as quickly.

BRIEF DATA (Tiger II) Type: 5-man heavy battle tank; Engine: 600hp petrol; Max speed: 24mph; Range: 68m; Arms: 1 × 88mm gun, 2 × 7.92mm mg; Armour: max 185mm.

King's African Rifles British regiment comprising battalions drawn from the East African colonies of Kenya, Tanganyika, Uganda, Nyasaland and British Somaliland. The KAR served in the Middle East and Madagascar before being transferred to Burma* in 1943 as the 11th East African Division. East Africans then fought in Burma until the end of the war, always under the command of white officers. The British also made extensive use of African labour, transporting volunteer groups to the Middle East but often employing conscription to fulfil the internal needs of individual colonies.

Kinkaid, Vice Admiral Thomas (1888–1972) Highly respected American naval commander of Pacific carrier forces, initially based on the *Enterprise** and *Hornet** which fought several important naval engagements during 1942, including the Coral Sea*, Midway*, Santa Cruz* and Guadalcanal* battles. After the naval battle at Guadalcanal in November, Kinkaid was put in command of a cruiser squadron, Task Force 67, which was assigned to prevent Japanese reinforcement transports from reaching Guadalcanal. In January 1943, Kinkaid was appointed Commander, North Pacific Fleet, but was promoted in November to command the US 7th Fleet, a convoy and support fleet composed of

escort carriers and old battleships, under Southwest Pacific forces commander, General MacArthur*. In October 1944, the 7th Fleet transported the 6th Army for the assault on Leyte*, fighting in the Battle of Leyte Gulf* and covering General MacArthur's campaigns in Leyte and later in Luzon*. He was promoted admiral in April 1945.

Kirishima See Kongo.

Kirponos, Colonel General Mikhail (1892–1941) Russian general who commanded forces on the Northwest Front against Finland* in 1939–40 and was commander of the Kiev* Military District in June 1941 when German forces under Rundstedt*, spearheaded by Kleist's* panzer divisions, approached the city. Forced back from the Polish border to defend Kiev itself in early July, Kirponos died while attempting to lead a breakout of the German encirclement.

Kiska See Aleutian Islands.

Kleist, Field Marshal Paul Ludwig von (1881–1954) Consistently successful German tank* commander, with overall command of two panzer groups for the Western Offensive*, and commander of Panzer Group I on the Eastern Front* for the invasion of Russia in 1941, where he spearheaded the advance of Army Group South towards Kiev*. Kleist earned particular distinction in the Caucasus* during 1941 and 1942 and was promoted field marshal in recognition of his achievements in southern Russia in 1943. Relieved of his command by Hitler* in March 1944, after the German defeats in the Ukraine*, he was captured by British forces in 1945, extradited to Yugoslavia, and turned over to the Russians in 1949. Kleist died in Soviet captivity in November 1954.

Kluge, Field Marshal Günther Hans von (1882–1944) Commander of the German 4th Army for the successful invasion of

Poland* in 1939 and for the Western Offensive* (where he commanded Rommel
as a divisional tank commander) in 1940.
One of 12 promotions to field marshal following the capitulation of France, Kluge
later led the 4th Army for the unsuccessful
attack on Moscow* in 1941 (with Guderian* under his command). He then took
command of Army Group Centre after
Bock's* dismissal in December. Invalided
out of action after a car crash in 1943
following the unsuccessful Kursk* offensive, he did not return to the Eastern Front*
but was sent to succeed Rommel on the
Western Front in July 1944. He was swiftly
relieved of his command in August, however, for failing to warn Hitler of the July
Bomb Plot*. Ordered back to Germany, he
committed suicide by poisoning himself.

Knox, W. Frank (1874–1944) Republican
publisher and politician, he was chosen by
President Roosevelt* as Secretary of the
Navy in 1940 (along with another Republi-
can, Henry Stimson*, who was appointed
Secretary of War) and had considerable
success in overseeing the staggering growth
of the US Navy* between 1941 and 1944.
Despite the criticism he received from Re-
publicans at the time of his appointment,
Knox was described by the official history
of American Naval Operations during
WW2 as 'one of the best secretaries the
Navy ever had'.

Koenig, General Marie-Pierre (1898–
1970) French soldier and one of the few
senior officers to rally to de Gaulle* in 1940
after the fall of France*. General Koenig
commanded the Free French garrison at
Bir Hacheim, which held off an armoured
strike force from the Afrika Korps* for ten
days during the battle for the Gazala* Line
in June 1942. In 1944 he took command
of the French Forces of the Interior (see
Resistance: France) after the landings in
Normandy*. He was military governor of
Paris for a time following the Allied liberation of France, and served briefly as Minister of National Defence in the 1950s.

Koga, Vice Admiral Mineichi (1885–
1944) Successor to Admiral Yamamoto* as
commander of the Japanese Navy* Combined Fleet after the latter's death in April
1943. Koga had previously served with the
Naval General Staff and as commander
of the Yokusuka Naval Station. Koga was
unable to halt the steady tide of American
gains in the Pacific during 1943 (see Pacific
War). His dogged defence of Japanese
conquests was increasingly prey to attrition
by a series of US counter-offensives, and
he presided over the major Japanese withdrawals from Rabaul* and the Gilbert
Islands*. Vice Admiral Koga died in an
air accident as his forces were engaged in
withdrawing to the Philippines* in March
1944.

Kohima Town in the Indian province of
Manipur, close to Imphal* and the Burmese
border, it was the site of a siege during the
attempted Japanese invasion of India early
in 1944 (see Burma, Campaigns in; Maps
24 and 25). Code-named Operation U-Go,
the Japanese offensive against India aimed
in part to forestall the Allied offensive into
northern Burma. With overall command
of three Japanese armies, the 33rd under
General Honda in northern Burma, the
28th under General Sakurai on the Arakan
Front in the south, and the 15th Army
under Mutaguchi, which was assigned to
the capture of Kohima and Imphal. General
Kawabe* opened the offensive with a diversionary attack in Arakan*. Held up by
supply problems, and increasingly pressed
by Christison's 15th Corps, which was being supplied by air, the offensive was called
off on 24 February.

At the beginning of March, Mutaguchi's
three divisions were ordered to make an
ambitious advance in three prongs to
threaten Imphal and Kohima, though this
dangerously extended their lines of supply
and communication. Despite Ultra* intelligence warnings of the Japanese troop
movements, General Scoones* was unable
to withdraw his 4th Corps into defensive
positions around Imphal and was cut off by

the Japanese advance on 14 March. On 29 March, the Japanese 15th Division under Mutaguchi reached the Dimapur–Kohima –Imphal road to the north of Imphal, cutting off the city. This critical situation for the British forces under General Slim* was resolved largely by air supply. Calling in American 'Hump'* and RAF transports, Lord Mountbatten*, Supreme Commander in Southeast Asia, was able to reinforce and supply the besieged garrison of only 500 men at Kohima and the much larger force of 155,000 at Imphal that held out in some of the most bitter fighting of the war in Burma, finally forcing a Japanese retreat.

At Kohima itself, the whole of Mutaguchi's 31st Division was held off by the tiny garrison and the 4th Battalion Royal West Kent Regiment under Colonel Hugh Richards, until it was finally relieved by two brigades of the 33rd Corps under General Stopford*, over two weeks later. Orders for the official retreat of the Japanese forces were given on 4 July, following the arrival of the monsoon.

Koiso, Lt General Kuniaki (1880–1950) Japanese General Staff officer and Minister of War during the 1930s, he retired in 1942 to serve as Governor General of Korea before re-entering Japanese political life in association with Admiral Yonai (and indirectly, Prince Konoe* and Emperor Hirohito*), who were urging peace with the Allies. When Prime Minister Tojo* was finally ousted in October 1944, Koiso replaced him, remaining as premier until his resignation in April 1945, although his cabinet had already suffered a near collapse after the defeats at Leyte* and Iwo Jima*. His attempts to negotiate with Chiang Kai-shek* in order to secure a more favourable peace settlement had also ended in failure. Koiso was convicted of war crimes by the International Military Tribunal* for the Far East and sentenced to life imprisonment.

Kolombangara, Battle of, 12 July 1943 A night surface action fought in the waters of

the Central Solomon Islands* north of Kula Gulf between US Rear Admiral Ainsworth's Task Force 18 (comprising two *Brooklyn*∗ Class light cruisers, *Honolulu* and *St Louis*, New Zealand light cruiser *Leander* and ten destroyers* deployed in two squadrons) and Japanese Rear Admiral Izaki's force (comprising a light cruiser and five destroyers). The Japanese fleet was escorting a four-destroyer troop transport fleet to reinforce the Japanese garrison at New Georgia*, in one of many 'Tokyo Express'* reinforcement missions from Rabaul*. With both forces manoeuvring with the aid of radar*, although Allied equipment was of superior quality, the Japanese force displayed exceptional skill in finding and firing on its targets. Although the cruiser *Jintsu* (see Sendai) was shattered by radar-guided gunfire, Rear Admiral Isaki then took swift advantage of a confusion between the two squadrons of Allied destroyers to salvo his four destroyers' torpedoes* and quickly withdraw, as Rear Admiral Ainsworth relocated the enemy and turned his force broadside to the Japanese ships. *St Louis*, *Honolulu* and the destroyer *Gwin* were all hit, although the cruisers managed to limp back to Tulagi with the previously damaged *Leander*. In the meantime the Japanese transports landed its reinforcements on the far side of Kolombangara. As in the action in Kula Gulf* in the previous week, the Allied naval forces had so far failed to stop the Japanese reinforcement operations.

Kon, Operation Japanese operation for the reinforcement of Biak*, near to northwestern New Guinea* during May and June 1944.

Kondo, Vice Admiral Nobutake (1886– 1953) Commander of the Japanese Navy* 2nd Fleet for the first two years of the Pacific War*, Kondo was in overall command of many operations against the Allied naval forces in the Pacific, including the invasion of the Philippines*, Malaya* and Java*. He commanded the Japanese Southern Force which sank Force Z* in the battle for Singapore* and subsequently provided the main support forces for the invasion of Midway*. Kondo later participated in the fighting for the Solomon Islands*, at the battle of the Eastern Solomons*, Santa Cruz* and Guadalcanal*. The defeat of his strike force during a final attempt to reinforce Guadalcanal on 13 November 1942 enabled the Allies to save the major air base at Henderson Field* and subsequently to threaten New Guinea* and Japanese control in the Southwest Pacific. Kondo was appointed to the Japanese Supreme War Council in May 1945.

Konev, Marshal Ivan Stepanovich (1897 –1973) One of the most outstanding Soviet field commanders of the war, Konev began his military career at 15 as a private in the Tsarist Army and joined the Red Army in 1918 as a member of the Bolshevik Party. A survivor of Stalin's* purges during 1937, he was transferred to command the Kalinin Front Army Group, which played a vital part in holding the Russian northern flank against the German advance on Moscow* in the late autumn of 1941. The subsequent launch of a Soviet counter-offensive saw Konev's armies force the invading German forces 100 miles back from their positions in a year of bitter battles.

But Konev's greatest military achievements were in command of the huge Soviet counter-offensives of 1943 to 1945. Now in command of the 2nd Ukrainian Front, Konev directed the northern assault to link up with Marshal Zhukov's* 1st Ukrainian Front in a giant envelopment of German forces around Korsun*, south of Kiev*. In the first half of 1944, Konev's armies drove on to the Vistula* in Poland*, suffering heavy losses but devastating the German armies in their path (see Poland, Russian campaign in). By early 1945, having crossed the Oder–Neisse* line in mid-February, Konev, now a marshal, prepared to lead the million men of the 1st Ukrainian Front in the Battle for Berlin*, which brought the war in Europe to an end. Twice decorated Hero of the Soviet Union and

awarded the Order of Lenin five times, Konev's contribution to the Soviet victories on the Eastern Front* is undisputed. After the war, Konev replaced Marshal Zhukov* as C-in-C of Land Forces. He was appointed Soviet Minister for Defence in 1955.

Kongo Japanese battleship and class which also included the *Hiei*, *Kirishima* and *Haruna*. They were completed as battlecruisers (to a British design) just before WW1, but were reclassed as fast battleships for carrier escort after extensive modernization during 1930–6. The *Hiei*, demilitarized under the First London Naval Treaty (1930), was rearmed after 1936 and given a more modern internal layout.

All four ships were with Admiral Yamamoto's* main battlefleet in December 1941, and remained in front-line action for most of their careers. The *Hiei* and *Kirishima*, which were with the Southern Force in 1941, were the first to be lost. The *Hiei* was badly damaged by American cruisers off Guadalcanal* on the night of 12 November 1942, and was finished off by aircraft the following day. Two nights later, at the naval Battle of Guadalcanal, the *Kirishima* was the victim of radar*-controlled gunfire from the USS *Washington*, the last battleship to be sunk solely by another in combat. The surviving vessels were later modified in the light of increasing air attacks on warships. By June 1944 both the *Haruna* and the *Kongo* carried about 100 25mm light anti-aircraft* guns and more 5-inch weapons were subsequently added, but it was a torpedo from the US Navy submarine *Sealion II* that sank the *Kongo* off Formosa on 21 November 1944. The *Haruna* survived until July 1945, when she was sunk in Kure dockyard by carrier aircraft.

BRIEF DATA (*Kongo*, 1941) Displacement: 31,720 tons; Dimensions: o/a lgth – 729' 6", b – 95' 3"; Speed: 30.5 knots; Armaments: 8 × 14" gun (4 × 2), 14 × 6" gun, 8 × 5" AA gun, 20 × 25mm AA gun, 3 aircraft.

Königsberg City in East Prussia* (now Kaliningrad, USSR) where retreating German forces fell back to resist the Soviet advance and were invested by the 3rd Belorussian Front* under Bagramyan* in January 1945 (see Map 31). Although the main Soviet effort was then redirected further south under Vasilevsky* during February and March, Königsberg held out until 9–10 April, when an air and artillery barrage ordered by Stalin* and Novikov* forced the German commander, General Lasch, to surrender. The occupation of Königsberg by the Red Army was accompanied by a high degree of barbarism and atrocity. Furious at Lasch's surrender, Hitler* sentenced him to death in absentia and his family was arrested.

Königsberg German cruiser. See Karlsruhe.

Konoe, Prince Fumimaro (1891–1945) Japanese Prime Minister who served three times between 1937 and 1941, Konoe entered politics via a post in the Japanese Home Ministry. Between the wars, Konoe was active in the work to pass a universal male suffrage law, as well as attending the Paris Peace Conference in 1919 as secretary to Kimmochi Saionjii. He subsequently criticized the Conference as an effort by the West to preserve the status quo. Though a supporter of an expansionist foreign policy for Japan, he opposed the extreme militarist and Fascist ideals of the Army factions, and thus came to be seen by many moderates in Japan as an ideal figure to unite the warring political groups in Tokyo.

Asked to form a cabinet in July 1937, Konoe made little effort to stop the spread of hostilities with China* and further undermined efforts to control the conflict by declaring his unpreparedness to deal with the Chinese Nationalist government in January 1938. In November he announced the founding of a 'New Order'* for East Asia (a blueprint for Japanese control of China, Manchukuo* and ex-colonial territories in Southeast Asia) but resigned in January 1939 over the protrac-

tion of the Chinese war. Returning to office in July 1940, Konoe proved unable to control the steady rise in influence of the extreme Control Faction (*Toseiha*) led by General Tojo*, to stop the war with China, or, finally, to avert the war against America (see also Matsuoka).

He was replaced as Prime Minister by General Tojo, who had served as his War Minister, and remained politically inactive throughout much of the war, although from 1944 he was involved in attempts to bring it to an end, and was working on a plan for constitutional reform when he was arrested in December 1945. He committed suicide on learning of the possibility that he would be charged with war crimes, and was condemned posthumously, chiefly on the grounds that he had attended the birth of a totalitarian state in Japan and bore the responsibility of that crime.

Korsun Southwestern Ukrainian town where units of six German divisions were encircled in the 'Cherkassy pocket' in early 1944 by elements of the 1st and 2nd Ukrainian Fronts* and German Field Marshal Manstein* lost an estimated 20,000 men and sacrificed his tank* reserves in an unsuccessful attempt to relieve them. See Ukraine; Eastern Front.

Kos A Greek island in the Aegean Sea, it was occupied, along with Samos and Léros, by British forces on 13 September 1943. The RAF* immediately established an air base there – the only Allied air base in the Aegean. A month later, German forces reinvaded and ejected the British force from its Aegean toeholds.

Kosciusko Division A Russian-trained Polish division under General Berling, drawn from Polish soldiers and civilians who had not been evacuated with General Anders* to Persia (Iran) and the Middle East. The Kosciusko Division first saw active service in the summer of 1943. In 1944 it accompanied the Red Army into Poland. By the latter part of 1944 a larger force, the

1st Polish Army, was serving with the Red Army. See Poland, Russian Campaign in.

Kota Bharu See Malaya.

Kra Isthmus A narrow neck of land in the south of Thailand*, where Japanese divisions landed on 8 December 1941, at the start of the drive to Singapore*.

Krebs, General Hans (1898–1945) The last chief of the German General Staff, appointed on 1 April 1945 as successor to Guderian*. Krebs was sent by Dönitz* to inform the Russians of Hitler's death and negotiate an armistice, but returned to the bunker to report the Russians' unconditional surrender terms and their request that Dönitz come to Berlin to accept it. He committed suicide on about 1 May, the day before Russian forces captured the bunker.

Kreisau Circle See Resistance: Germany.

Kretschmer, Lt Commander Otto (1912 –) The most successful U-boat commander of the war, credited with sinking 313,611 tons of Allied shipping before he was captured and his submarine (U-99) sunk by destroyers on 27 March 1941. Another U-boat ace, Lt Commander Schepke (U-100) was killed in the same convoy action. These losses, coupled with the death of Gunther Prien*, helped convince Admiral Dönitz* that his new boats needed a longer and more thorough training programme before tackling the Allies' improving anti-submarine forces. Kretschmer was a founder member of the postwar Kriegsmarine and rose to the rank of Rear Admiral. See also Atlantic, Battle of the.

Krueger, Lt General Walter (1881–1967) US 6th Army (Alamo Force) commander, he directed operations in the Southwest Pacific and led the reconquest of the Philippines*. Krueger was in command of the US 3rd Army at the start of the Pacific War*.

Ordered to Australia in January 1943 to command the 6th Army, activated in February, Krueger led operations from June of that year under the code-name Alamo Force – essentially a device of General MacArthur's* to take direct charge of the 'special task force' and avoid losing operational control of such a large army to the Australian generals (notably General Blamey* who was MacArthur's Southwest Pacific land forces commander). From June 1943, Krueger commanded almost all Southwest Pacific ground operations – in New Guinea*, the Admiralty Islands*, New Britain and the Philippines*. Handing over control of final operations in Luzon* in July 1945, Krueger was charged with preliminary planning for an amphibious* invasion of Japan. After the Japanese surrender, Krueger went with the 6th Army as part of the US occupation forces in Japan.

Krupp von Bohlen und Halbach, Alfried (1907–67) German industrialist, whose father Gustav had enthusiastically supported Hitler after he became Chancellor in 1933. The Krupp armaments and munitions works was one of the largest and most powerful in the world, and under Alfried Krupp's management (he was its most influential vice-president) the business prospered further during the Third Reich. Alfried formally took control from his ailing father in 1943, but had previously supervised the firm's removal to new factories – often sited near 'known sources of labour', i.e. concentration camps* – in German-occupied territories, using conscripted and slave labour to resource the expansion of the concern. In 1943 he was appointed Minister of War Economy. Between 1943–5 Allied bombing destroyed 70 per cent of Krupp's factories in the Ruhr, and the remainder was confiscated at the end of the war. Alfried stood trial – his father did not because of his age – for war crimes, and was sentenced to 12 years imprisonment and the confiscation of all his property. He was nevertheless released from Landsberg prison in 1951 and most of his vast fortune was returned to him. See also Gustav.

Krylov, General Nikolai (1903–72) Chief of Staff to General Chuikov* in the 62nd Army which fought for Stalingrad* during September 1942, Krylov later commanded the Soviet 5th Army in the 3rd Belorussian Front* and later in the 1st Far Eastern Front which fought the Japanese Kwantung Army*.

Kula Gulf, Battle of, 6 July 1943 Night surface action between a Japanese transport force of ten destroyers* in two squadrons under Rear Admiral Akiyama and an Allied Task Group (36.1) under Rear Admiral Ainsworth comprising three light cruisers and four destroyers, it took place in the Kula Gulf, between Kolombangara* and New Georgia*. The Japanese transport force was carrying troops and supplies to reinforce the garrison at Kolombangara in response to American landings on New Georgia, Rendova and Vangunu.

Arriving off the northern entrance to Kula Gulf, the Japanese commander detached three transport ships to Vila to unload, as American radar* picked up the Japanese support group and Ainsworth deployed his cruisers for radar-controlled firing. Although Aikyama's force was able to regroup, the American guns inflicted heavy damage on the *Niizuki*. Before retreating, two of the Japanese destroyers launched torpedoes* which sank the cruiser *Helena*. All four remaining destroyers of the second transport group, two of which were damaged, turned back to Vila and were able to land their cargoes, although their commander Akiyama was killed.

Kunming Capital city of Yunnan province in China* and the Chinese terminus of the Burma Road* (and later the Hump* air supply route), its various headquarters, training facilities and supply depots provided a crucial centre for China's wartime survival. In late 1944 it became the focus of an Allied defensive plan, code-named Alpha, designed to repel the Japanese threat to the area. See Maps 22 and 11.

Kuma Japanese light cruiser and class of five ships completed in the early 1920s. These and two subsequent classes of 5,000-ton cruisers were developments of the earlier *Tenryu* Class. In December 1941 the *Kuma* was based on Formosa*, while two of her sisters (*Kiso* and *Tama*) were stationed in the North Pacific. The *Kitikami* and the *Oi* meanwhile formed a cruiser squadron with Admiral Yamamoto's* battle fleet.

All five saw a great deal of fighting and four were lost during 1944. The sole survivor was the *Kitakami*, scrapped in 1947. She was also the most modified, eventually carrying four 5-inch AA guns, 67 25mm weapons and eight *Kaiten** submarines.
BRIEF DATA (*Kuma*, 1941) Displacement: 5,870 tons; Dimensions: o/a lgth – 535′, b – 46′ 6″; Speed: 31.75 knots; Armament: $7 \times 5.5″$ gun (7×1), $2 \times 3″$ AA gun, $8 \times 24″$ TT, 80 mines, 1 aircraft.

Kuomintang Chinese 'National People's Party', it controlled much of Chinese political life from 1928 until 1949. It was founded in 1912, from a collection of small revolutionary groups, by Sun Yat-sen and was broadly moderate in character during its early period under his leadership, being based on the tenets of nationalism, democracy and 'people's livelihood'. The later military entanglements of the Kuomintang, however, in civil war against the Chinese communists during the 1930s and subsequently in operations against the Japanese, saw a parallel increase in more extreme nationalist and authoritarian influence, foreshadowed by the rise to power of Chiang Kai-shek* as Sun Yat-sen's successor. Under Chiang's leadership, the communists, who had formed an independent but integral part of the Kuomintang, were ousted from the Party during 1927 and 1928. Many were arrested and imprisoned, and thousands were killed. Survivors escaped on the epic 'Long March' to the remote regions of northwest China.

Between 1937 and 1945, the Kuomintang, with Chiang as its leader, remained fiercely militarist and nationalistic. The acknowledgement of a common enemy did not stop the rival regimes from committing large resources to their internecine struggles. Despite a shortlived truce with the communist Red Army following the Japanese attack on Shanghai in January 1941, and another in 1946 once the war with Japan was over, Chiang's forces continued to fight the communists intermittently until 1949 (both armies heavily supported by American and Soviet aid respectively). The remains of the battered nationalist army finally fled the mainland for Formosa*, renamed Taiwan, and established an island Republic of China. See China.

Kurochkin, Colonel General Pavel A. (1900–) Russian army commander during the Russo-Finnish War* and later commander of the Northwest Front in 1941–4, Kurochkin directed the defence of and breakout from Smolensk* and then took charge of the Northwest Front in the winter of 1941–2 for the first Soviet offensive, which in February succeeded in encircling nearly 100,000 Germans at Demyansk. Promoted to command the 2nd Belorussian Front* in 1944, his failure at Kovel resulted in a transfer to the 60th Army before he was reinstated as commander of the 1st and 4th Ukrainian Fronts. He was awarded the gold star of Hero of the Soviet Union.

Kursk City in the central Soviet Union, it had been captured by German forces in the autumn of 1941 and fortified as part of a defensive system of bases from which to repel the first Soviet offensive in the winter of 1941–2 (see Map 29). After the major German defeat at Stalingrad* in January 1943, Kursk was outflanked and recaptured by Russian forces on 7 February 1943, creating a bulging salient in the German lines between Orel and Kharkov*. A renewed

German offensive in the spring, code-named *Zitadelle*, focused on the Kursk salient with the objective of encircling the defending Voronezh Front* forces and cutting a deep hole in the Soviet central front. German reinforcements during the spring swelled the forces for the offensive to 900,000, with 2,700 tanks and 2,000 aircraft. Forewarned by intelligence, Soviet Marshal Zhukov* had also reinforced the salient, constructed several concentric defensive circles and planned Operation Kutusov, to commit the German forces to its attack before mounting an enveloping counter-attack.

Often described as the largest tank* battle in history (although estimates are exaggerated on both sides), the Battle of Kursk opened on 5 July with the German 9th Army under Kluge* attacking from the north supported by the 4th Panzer Army under General Manstein* attacking from the south. Minor penetrations on the northern flank cost 25,000 casualties within a week. In the south, Manstein's army advanced 25 miles but also at a high cost. On 12 July Soviet forces under Popov* (Bryansk Front) and Sokolovsky* (Western Front) counter-attacked against the Orel salient north of Kursk. Although the German advance was still continuing in the south, the improved tactics and sheer weight of Soviet forces fought off the attacks. By 23 July, the German lines had been pushed back to their earlier positions. As Manstein withdrew his forces to the Dnieper* against Hitler's orders, the Russians moved onto the offensive along the whole front. See Eastern Front; Tank.

Kuznetsov, Admiral Nikolay (1902–74) C-in-C of the Red Navy*, protégé of Stalin* and a beneficiary of his political purges of the late 1930s in Russia, Kuznetsov was a member of Stavka* throughout the war and participated in all planning, though he did not see active service. He was largely responsible for the build-up of the Soviet cruiser and submarine* fleet, which enabled Germany to extend limits on her own submarine construction (see Anglo-German Naval Treaty). Kuznetsov also attended the Potsdam and Yalta conferences* in 1945. After the war he was demoted, his fall in reputation linked to the new regime in Moscow under Khrushchev*, but he was later reinstated by Leonid Brezhnev*.

Kuznetsov, General Vasiliy I. (1894–1964) One of the group of younger generals (which also included Konev*, Rokossovsky* and Govorov*) to emerge during the war from the ranks of the Soviet General Staff, stripped of many members during Stalin's* purges in 1937. Kuznetsov participated in the defence of Kiev* in 1941 and was subsequently held responsible by Russians for the loss of the city, though it is clear that Marshal Budenny* shares responsibility for the Soviet failure. From command of the 1st Guards Army at Stalingrad*, Kuznetsov was promoted Deputy Commander of the Southwest Front*. He later directed forces in Poland* and at the Battle for Berlin*.

KV Tank When it was designed in 1939, this important Soviet weapon was far in advance of any contemporary large tank. The Soviet Union had led the world in the production of heavy tanks, and several multi-turreted designs were tested in the Russo-Finnish War*. A single turret derivation of these, the KV (after Soviet general Klimenti Voroshilov*) was accepted for service on 19 December 1939, simultaneously with the T34* medium tank. The KV was used successfully against the Finns in February 1940, and 636 had been built when Germany invaded Russia in June 1941 (see Eastern Front). Its performance in 1941, seemingly impervious to any anti-tank* artillery, gave a severe jolt to German armoured planning and stimulated a hasty re-evaluation of their future requirements. Output of the KV increased dramatically after the mass transfer in September of the Soviet heavy tank industry to Chelyabinsk, where production facilities were concentrated well beyond the range of German bombers.

Simple, robust and powerful, the original production KV1 was soon joined by a KV2 infantry support model. This mounted a huge 152mm howitzer, but proved cumbersome, unstable and short-lived. The most widely used of several later versions was the KV1C, in production during 1942, which had a single cast turret and even more armour. By the end of the year, it was clear that these were being outpaced on the battlefield and the faster, lighter KV1S was produced for a short while before the heavier version was reinstated. The final KV85 model, operative from the autumn of 1943, mounted an 85mm gun. This was regarded as a stop-gap while the new IS* heavy tank was being developed, and was built in only limited quantities. From February 1943, the KV chassis formed the basis of the mighty SU152 self-propelled* gun, used in large numbers during the great battles around Kursk* later in the year. By the end of the war about 13,500 tanks and self-propelled* guns had been completed on the KV chassis.

BRIEF DATA (KV1C) Type: 5-man heavy tank; Engine: 600hp diesel; Max speed: 22mph; Range: 140m; Arms: 1 × 76.2mm gun, 3 × 7.62mm mg; Armour: max 120mm.

Kwajalein See Marshall Islands.

Kwantung Army (Kantogun) Large Japanese garrison based in southern Manchuria*, originally established in 1907 by international agreement to protect the Southern Manchurian Railway (see Matsuoka, Yosuke) and other Japanese interests in Manchuria. In 1919 the troops in Manchuria were given independent status as the Kwantung Army. Comprising one division as well as military police, the Army was from the outset an important agent in promoting development of Manchuria. Despite its small size, the Army became highly politicized during the 1920s, and attracted the most ambitious of younger officers (e.g.

see Tojo, Hideki). From 1928, with new headquarters at Mukden, the Army played an increasingly assertive role in Japanese policy towards Manchuria. Many officers believed that the promotion of Japanese interests (see Ultranationalism) necessitated the use of force to separate Manchuria from China*. It was the Kwantung Army that assassinated the Manchurian warlord Chang Tso-lin, and fabricated the Mukden* Incident in 1931, resulting in the Japanese occupation of Manchuria, renamed Manchukuo*. The commander of the Kwantung Army became ambassador to Manchukuo, largely free of control from Tokyo.

The strength of the Kwantung Army was increased to five divisions in 1937 and 13 in 1941. Assigned to contain communism, the Army placed its élite units on the Soviet–Manchukuo border, resulting in major clashes at Changkufeng and Nomonhan in 1939 (see Russo-Japanese Border Conflict). Following the German invasion of Russia, the Kwantung Army was prepared for conflict with the Soviet Union, but most of the best forces were gradually moved to the southern front, and the Russian attack of August 1945 met with little resistance. After the Japanese surrender, the Kwantung Army was disbanded with other Japanese forces. See Japanese Army.

L

Lae See New Guinea.

Landing Vehicle Tracked (LVT) An American series of amphibious cargo, troop-carrying and infantry support vehicles developed from the 'Alligator' swamp rescue craft of 1935. The militarized LVT1 was ordered for the US Navy* Marine Corps in November 1940, and the much-improved LVT2 appeared in 1943. The major LVT4 version, of which 8,438 were built, was modified to incorporate a rear ramp, and a few twin-engined LVT3s entered service at the end of the war. Armoured versions, in effect light amphibious tanks, were also produced. The LVT(A)1 was given the turret and 37mm gun of the Stuart Tank*, and the LVT(A)4 mounted a 75mm howitzer from the M18 Hellcat self-propelled* gun. The LVT(A)2 was used solely as a cargo carrier. Propelled through the water by paddles attached to its tracks, the LVT was vital to Allied amphibious operations in all theatres. Although landing vehicles were basic to all Allied offensives in the Pacific War*, priority was given to operations in Europe, where a British Army* version, called the Buffalo, fought alongside US LVTs. See Amphibious Warfare.

Langley, USS The *Langley* was the United States' first aircraft carrier, converted from the collier *Jupiter* in 1922. Used as an aircraft tender from 1937, she was sunk in that capacity by Japanese bombers in the Java Sea on 26 February 1942. The second *Langley* was an *Independence* Class carrier; commissioned in 1943, she fought in the battles of the Philippine Sea* and Leyte Gulf*.

BRIEF DATA (*Langley I*, 1941) Displacement: 11,500 tons; Dimensions: o/a lgth – 542', b – 65' 6"; Speed: 15 knots; Armament: 4 × 5" gun, 55 aircraft.

Latvia Like its sister republics on the Baltic Sea, Estonia* and Lithuania*, Latvia was assigned to the Soviet sphere of influence by a secret protocol of the Russo-German Pact* in 1939. In October it was obliged to sign a 'mutual assistance' pact with Russia, granting the Red Army military bases on Latvian territory. On 16 June 1940, Latvia was invaded by Russian forces and a puppet regime installed under August Kirchensteins. Mass deportations and executions took place here as in the other Baltic republics and Latvia was made a constituent of the USSR in August. After the German invasion of Russia (see Eastern Front), Latvia was occupied by German forces from July 1941 until October 1944. As part of the Reichscommissariat Ostland, which also included Estonia, Lithuania and part of Belorussia, Latvians continued to suffer death and deportation on a massive scale. When the Russians returned to Latvia, further deportations of an estimated 105,000 people preceded its reincorporation in the USSR. See Maps 27 and 32.

Laval, Pierre (1883–1945) Unattractive and controversial French 'nationalist' statesman, best known for his co-authorship of the Hoare–Laval Pact (1935), which sought to appease Mussolini by recognizing his claim to Abyssinia (Ethiopia), and for his collaboration with Germany following the fall of France. Laval had earned a reputation during the 1920s for political agility, and was increasingly criticized during the war for his empirical stance (regarded by Laval as 'practical nationalism') to France's political problems. Having convened the meeting of the National Assembly which made Marshal Pétain* head of the Vichy* government, Laval became his deputy from June to December 1940, when he was instrumental in persuading the Vichy government to ratify the armistice. He assured colleagues that France would thus guarantee her share in the New Order which would follow from Germany's inevitable military success.

Out of favour and office between December 1940 and April 1942, Laval was recalled as premier and continued his policy of collaboration, earning renewed hatred from Frenchmen by agreeing to supply French labour for German factories. Taken to Germany and then Austria in 1945, Laval escaped to Spain, but was returned to France, where he was tried for treason. Vilified by the French public, the Allies and the French resistance* movements, Laval's justification of his role as fundamentally patriotic failed to secure his acquittal. He was executed by firing squad on 15 October 1945.

Lavochkin LaGG-1 (and LaGG-3) Produced by the Soviet Union in great numbers from late 1940, the streamlined monoplane Lavochkin LaGG-1 was an indifferent fighter, most notable for its robustness and the cheap simplicity of its largely wooden structure. The LaGG-3 which superseded it in 1941 was little better in combat and they suffered heavy casualties in the first weeks of the German invasion of Russia*. The last of hundreds of LaGG fighters were delivered to the Red Air Force* in June 1942.
BRIEF DATA (LaGG-3) Type: single-seat fighter; Engine: 1 × 1,240hp Klimov; Max speed: 348mph; Ceiling: 29,527'; Range: 404m; Arms: very varied, typically 1 × 20mm cannon, 2 × 12.7mm mg.

Lavochkin La-5FN (and La-7) Russian attempts to improve on the low performance Lavochkin LaGG-3* fighter led to a faster version, the LaGG-5, which entered production in May 1942. This was soon replaced by a further improvement with a new fuselage, the La-5. Although faster than the German Messerschmitt Bf109G-2* at altitudes below 20,000ft, it could still be outclimbed, a deficiency rectified in the lighter La-5FN, which first appeared in late 1942. Thousands of these fought successfully in the great Eastern Front* battles of 1943. The even more successful La-7 – faster, better armed and beloved of fighter aces* – first saw action in the summer of 1943.
BRIEF DATA (La-5FN) Type: single-seat fighter; Engine: 1 × 1,700hp Shvetson M82FN; Max speed: 403mph; Ceiling: 32,800'; Range: 475m; Arms: 2 × 20mm cannon (provision for 330lb bombs).

Laycock, Major General Robert (1907–68) Commando* leader and British Chief of Combined Operations for the invasion of Northwest Europe* in 1944. Laycock raised a commando unit in 1940 and early in 1941 he took three commando units, including his own, to the Middle East for the projected capture of Rhodes. Now known as Layforce, the force was joined by a locally raised Middle East Commando. Elements of it operated on the Libyan coast, especially Tobruk*, and took part in the invasion of Syria in June 1941. Laycock took half his force to Crete* after the German airborne landings in May 1941 and it covered the withdrawal to the south coast. Only a fraction, including Laycock himself, returned to Egypt. Laycock's force was then disbanded, but partially resurrected at Churchill's insistence and in November 1941 Laycock led a raid on Rommel's* suspected HQ. On this occasion only he and one other got back to safety. Laycock later commanded a commando brigade for

RIGHT: *General Erwin Rommel, Commander of the German Afrika Korps, during the North African campaigns*

BELOW: *British troops in action against the Afrika Korps in the Western Desert*

ABOVE: *The bombing of Cassino, March 1944. Over 2,500 tons of bombs rained down on Cassino before New Zealand troops stormed and captured Castle Hill (top right)*

LEFT: *General Orde Wingate and Colonel Phil Cochrane, USAAF, signalling aircraft to land at a Chindit fortress base behind Japanese lines, Burma, 1943*

ABOVE: *Pearl Harbor, 7 December 1941. Battered by bombs and torpedoes, the battleship* California *settles into the mud, as clouds of black smoke pour from a stricken sister ship*

RIGHT: *Adolf Hitler announced the Declaration of War on the United States in the Reichstag, 11 December 1941*

ABOVE: *Trailing smoke and flame, a Japanese torpedo plane is shot down by fire from a US aircraft carrier*

RIGHT: *A US marine on Saipan helps a Japanese child to safety*

OPPOSITE ABOVE: *General Percival surrenders British forces in Singapore and Malaya to the Japanese, 15 February 1942*

OPPOSITE BELOW: *Japanese dead surround a devastated bunker on Tarawa, 1943*

LEFT: *A US marine receives communion from a Roman Catholic chaplain on top of Mount Suribachi, a Japanese strongpoint on Iwo Jima, captured by assault, February 1945*

BELOW: *General Douglas MacArthur wades ashore on his return to the Philippines, 21 October 1944*

D-Day, June 1944:

RIGHT: *American half-tracks and motorized infantry move inland from Omaha beach*

BELOW: *British infantry landing on Sword beach during the Normandy landings*

ABOVE: *Members of the French Resistance fighting in the streets of Paris before its liberation by the Allies in July 1944*

LEFT: *The people of Brussels give Allied troops a rapturous welcome to the city, September 1944*

the invasion of Sicily* in 1943 and then returned home to succeed Mountbatten* as Chief of Combined Operations, a post which he held until 1947. He was later Governor of Malta.

Leahy, Admiral William Daniel (1875–1959) American ex-Chief of Naval Operations, he was called back from retirement to go to Vichy* France as ambassador in 1940, Leahy was faced with the difficult task of liaising with the Vichy government and avoiding involvement in the war, while attempting to support the efforts of the French resistance* against the German occupation. Leahy's dislike of de Gaulle*, leader of Free France*, however, had a clear effect on his judgement of the situation. He is generally judged to have been a competent but uninspired ambassador. Following his recall to the US in 1942, he became Roosevelt's* personal Chief of Staff and an increasingly important White House figure, acting as presidential liaison with the Joint Chiefs of Staff Committee* and Roosevelt's close adviser and chief source of military information, with authorization to originate messages to the British government. As Chairman of the Joint Chiefs of Staff, Leahy earned a considerable reputation for promoting agreement among the often heatedly opposed service chiefs. When Roosevelt died, Leahy remained at the White House as adviser to President Truman*, taking part in the debate over the use of atomic* weapons against Japan, which Leahy himself opposed.

Ledo Road Major route from Ledo, in Assam, to Bhamo in Burma* that formed part of the vital land supply link with China*, the Burma Road* (see Map 24). Following the Japanese capture in June 1942 of the Burmese section of the Burma Road, which forced the Allies to supply China by air over the treacherous Himalayas (the Hump*), Stilwell* began work on reconstructing the Ledo Road to link up with the Burma Road, reopened in mid-1944. The Ledo Road was officially renamed the Stilwell Road by Chiang Kai-shek* in early 1945.

Leeb, Field Marshal Wilhelm von (1876–1956) Senior German Army officer, he retired after the dismissal of Fritsch* and Blomberg in 1938, but was recalled to command Army Group C for the invasion of Poland*. He subsequently directed Army Group C for the Western Offensive* in 1940 and went to the Eastern Front* in 1941 in command of Army Group North for the invasion of the Soviet Union in June. Leeb was removed in Hitler's* purge of the German High Command after the failure at Moscow* in December.

Leese, General Sir Oliver (1897–1978) Popular and able field commander, Deputy Chief of Staff of the British Expeditionary Force during its escape from Dunkirk* and later protégé of Montgomery* (whom he eventually replaced as 8th Army commander), Leese was promoted under Montgomery to lead the 30th Corps, 8th Army, for the (2nd) Battle of Alamein* and subsequently for the invasions of Sicily* and Italy*. In January 1944, he succeeded Montgomery, but handed over leadership of the 8th Army to McCreery* in November when he was appointed Commander of Allied Land Forces in Southeast Asia.

Legaspi See Philippines.

Leigh-Mallory, Air Chief Marshal Sir Trafford (1892–1944) Ambitious and aggressive head of RAF* Fighter Command from November 1942, he commanded No. 12 Group RAF Fighter Command during the Battle of Britain* and was a firm advocate of the 'Big Wing'* fighter formation tactic against the Luftwaffe*. Although these views brought him into conflict with Park*, No. 11 Group Commander, and C-in-C Fighter Command, Air Marshal Dowding*, Leigh-Mallory was later given the opportunity to initiate offensive tactics when Dowding was replaced by Air Chief

Marshal Douglas*. Appointed head of the Allied Expeditionary Air Force for the coming invasion of Normandy* in late 1943, Leigh-Mallory's dogmatism and bluff manner brought him into regular conflict with the strategic air force commanders, uneasy with Leigh-Mallory's lack of experience of heavy bomber operations. He made a significant contribution to the invasion plans, however, in his support for a concentrated preparatory air assault on communications in Normandy (see Transportation Plan) that was crucial to the success of the D-Day landings. In November 1944, Leigh-Mallory was promoted Air C-in-C, Southeast Asia, but died in an air crash *en route*.

Leipzig City in eastern Germany and site of a large aircraft-production complex. Leipzig was subjected to large-scale air assaults, notably during February 1944. See Big Week. The city fell to US forces after determined German resistance, on 19 April 1945.

Leipzig German Navy* light cruiser, launched in 1929 and a modification of the earlier 'K' class units (see Karlsruhe). The *Leipzig* was one of only three major German surface warships to survive the war (the others were the *Nürnberg** and the *Prinz Eugen**). She was surrendered in a severely damaged condition, having been accidentally rammed by the *Prinz Eugen* and reduced to employment as a shore battery.
BRIEF DATA (1939) Displacement: 6,710 tons; Dimensions: o/a lgth – 580' 9", b – 53' 3"; Speed: 32 knots; Armament: 9 × 5.9" gun (3 × 3), 6 × 3.5" AA gun, 8 × 37mm AA gun, 10 × 20mm AA gun, 12 × 21" TT, 2 aircraft.

Lemay, General Curtis E. (1906–) American pilot who became an expert in air bombardment tactics over Japan and Europe, LeMay earned a considerable reputation as a navigator with the pre-war US Army Air Corps and was sent to England in 1942 in command of the 305th Bomb Group (US 8th Air Force) where he led the campaign of daytime strategic bombing (see USAAF). LeMay's employment of flying-formation (combat-box) tactics introduced a new success rate in American bombing techniques. Chief American proponent of strategic bombing in WW2, LeMay employed pattern bombing techniques with devastating effect against Germany in the last phase of the war, though he had his most dramatic successes as Chief of 21st Bomber Command headquartered at Guam* from late 1944. From here he sent B-29* heavy bombers on missions to Japan. Stripped of their defensive armament, heavily armed instead with incendiary bombs*, and trained in new techniques of low-level attack, the tactic greatly increased the destructive power of the nighttime area bombing raids. See also Strategic Bombing Offensive.

Lend-Lease Act A US statute passed on 11 March 1941, it gave President Roosevelt* unique powers to 'sell, transfer title to, exchange, lease, lend or otherwise dispose of' equipment for the defence of any country upon which the United States' own defence was thought to depend. In effect, the Act allowed Roosevelt to massively extend US involvement in the war without compromising neutrality by direct intervention.

The Act was strongly opposed by isolationist opinion in the US, and was only passed after months of debate. Britain and Greece* were then immediately declared qualified to receive materials under the Act. A sum of $7 billion was appropriated by Congress for Lend-Lease in 1941, followed by a further $26 billion. Congress also authorized $21 billion for assistance from the US Navy* and War Departments. Out of $50 billion actually given in foreign aid to a total of 38 countries, over $31 billion went to Great Britain, with most of the rest going to the Soviet Union, China* and France. Repayments of loans made under Lend-Lease totalled $10 billion in goods and kind. Britain, virtually bankrupt by 1945, was eventually asked to repay $650 million. Lend-Lease ended officially on 14 August 1945. See also Neutrality, US.

Leningrad Second city of the Soviet Union, it was under threat from advancing German forces in mid-August 1941, following the German invasion of Russia in June (see Eastern Front; Map 27). Prepared defences on the Luga River and a last-ditch counter-attack did little to halt the German advance, which closed on the southern approaches to the city by the first week of September. Although an attempt spearheaded by panzer divisions under Reinhardt to take the city was repulsed in bitter street fighting, the German advance continued, cutting Leningrad off from its main supply lines. But the arrival of Marshal Zhukov* on 12 September to direct the defence had stiffened resistance, and both sides dug in to prepare for a siege that was destined to last for 890 days. The extreme difficulties of constant aerial bombardment inside the city were now compounded by the dwindling of vital food and supplies. In November, the situation became critical. Strict rationing was enforced and violators were shot, or sent to the front. A ferrying service by Red Navy* units of the lake flotilla was maintained across Lake Ladoga, providing a thin trickle of supplies to the city.

In the same month, German forces advanced through Tikhvin towards a link up with Finnish troops at the Svir River, further threatening supply of the city and reducing the Leningrad population to literal starvation. When the Soviet winter offensive got under way in December, the assault against the central front was supported by a major operation to relieve Leningrad by Meretskov's* Volkhov Front*, but the assault failed and the siege continued. Although various plans were prepared at German OKH for the seizure of Leningrad, and an attempt was made to relieve it in August 1942, the city continued to receive only intermittent attention from Hitler until early in 1943, when

Russian forces made a renewed attempt (code-named Iskra) to relieve it, and re-opening a supply route to the stricken city.

After a further year of bitter fighting in which German forces contained the breach in their lines around the southern shore of Lake Ladoga, the German 'Northern Wall' defences were finally decisively penetrated and Soviet troops liberated Leningrad on 19 January 1944. The final toll of civilian casualties was enormous – over 600,000 died of starvation and 200,000 in the bombing.

Lexington, USS Two wartime US Navy* aircraft carriers bore the name *Lexington*. The first, completed in 1927, was the sister ship of the *Saratoga**. On 8 May 1942, she was reduced to a wreck by Japanese naval bombers at the Battle of the Coral Sea*, and was sunk by the US destroyer* *Phelps* later the same day. The second *Lexington* was an *Essex** Class carrier and joined the US Navy's Central Pacific Force in 1943. She was torpedoed off Kwajelein (see Marshall Islands) in December 1943, and damaged by a Kamikaze* attack late the following year off Luzon*, but survived and remained in service long after the war. BRIEF DATA See Saratoga, USS; Essex, USS.

Ley, Robert (1890–1945) German head of the Labour Front (DAF), the German trades union movement, his violent anti-Semitism* and dissolute reputation exemplify the coarse, corrupt face of Nazism. He was selected for trial among the major defendants at Nuremberg*, but hanged himself in his cell before the trial began.

Leyte Island of the Visayan group, sited midway between Luzon* and Mindanao, Leyte was the first of the Philippines* islands retaken by American forces at the end of 1944 (see Maps 11 and 19). A two-day naval bombardment preceded the amphibious* landing of Lt General Krueger's* 6th Army on 22 October, accompanied by General MacArthur* and

Philippine President Osmena*. The follow-up offensive pushed the Japanese 35th Army under Lt General Suzuki* out of the central valley onto the mountainous inland backbone of the island. Mopping-up operations brought American control of the south coast of Samar Island* north of Leyte, though bitter Japanese resistance around the port at Ormoc on the west coast forced Krueger to launch an amphibious attack on Japanese positions there on 7 December, securing Ormoc on 10 December. A courageous airborne* attack on American airfields on 6 December failed to retain the initiative for the Japanese, and Suzuki dispersed his remaining troops. Casualties were high, estimated at 3,500 US and 55,000 Japanese dead. See Leyte Gulf, Battle of.

Leyte Gulf, Battle of, 23–6 October 1944
The last, largest and finally decisive naval battle between the US Fleets in the Pacific and the Japanese Combined Fleet (see Map 20). It was fought around the landlocked Gulf of Leyte south of the main Philippine* island of Luzon*, in four major surface actions (the Sibuyan Sea, 24 October; Surigao Strait, 24–5 October; Samar Island, 25 October and Cape Engano, 25–6 October). The battle was triggered by the American reinvasion of the Philippines under the overall command of General MacArthur*, projected to begin with a huge amphibious* assault on Leyte* itself on 22 October. In response to this imminent threat, Japanese naval chiefs initiated a bold and skilfully planned operation (Sho I) to draw the American 3rd Fleet into a decisive battle and save the Philippines.

Forming part of a larger operation (Sho Go), a last ditch effort to maintain the Japanese Empire's defensive perimeter, Sho I called for the deployment of every surviving Japanese Navy* warship in two strike forces under Vice Admiral Kurita and Vice Admiral Shima, with a third decoy force of Japan's four remaining carriers (now carrying a greatly reduced complement of 116 aircraft) under Vice Admiral Ozawa*.

The decoy force was assigned to draw the US 3rd Fleet under Admiral Halsey* away from Leyte, leaving the two surface attacking forces to strike the Allied invasion force. Navy C-in-C Admiral Toyoda* (who had succeeded Koga*) argued that Sho 1 represented Japan's last chance against the now massively superior resources of the US Navy. Chief of Naval Operations, Admiral Nakazawa had pleaded emotionally with the sceptical Japanese generals that the Combined Fleet be given this chance of victory or 'bloom as the flowers of death'.

Meanwhile, General MacArthur's forces were being massed for the invasion of Leyte itself. A huge armada of over 400 transports with 175,000 men of the US 6th Army under General Krueger* was escorted by the 7th Fleet under Admiral Kinkaid*, commanding the naval support and amphibious operations. Distant cover was to be provided by Admiral Halsey's main carrier strike force, the 3rd Fleet, and the flamboyant commander was by now displaying as much determination as Toyoda to eliminate the enemy fleet at the earliest possible opportunity, though his quoted intention to 'completely annihilate the Jap fleet' was a less poetic expression of his commitment to victory than Nakazawa's.

The biggest naval engagement of the war, the action at Leyte Gulf began with the sighting of Kurita's Force A sailing north from Brunei (Kurita had split his force in two, the other under Admiral Nishimura, in order to approach Leyte from two directions) off the treacherous Palawan Island reefs, west of Leyte, on the morning of 22 October. US submarine* attacks sank the cruisers Maya and Atago, and badly damaged the Takao*. This was followed by the first surface action, in the Sibuyan Sea, in which aircraft from Task Force 38 (3rd Fleet) located and attacked Kurita's and Nishimura's forces, sinking the giant battleship Musashi*, while the 3rd Fleet came under heavy attack from Admiral Fukudome's land-based bombers, mortally disabling the carrier Princeton* and damaging a light cruiser and five destroyers.

During the night of 24–5 October, the 3rd Fleet fast carriers moved north from the San Bernadino Strait on the hunt for the Japanese carrier force, as Sho I had predicted, and Kurita's Force A was able to withdraw through the Strait and turn south for Leyte and the American invasion force. On the same night Nishimura's Force C entered the Surigao Strait on course to join Kurita, but was surprised and effectively destroyed by a task force of six old battleships, four heavy and four light cruisers and a screen of destroyers under Rear Admiral Oldendorf, with the loss of Nishimura and his flagship *Yamashiro**. This was the last engagement fought between battleships in WW2.

Nevertheless, the greatest shock was received the next day by Admiral Kinkaid when he was told that Rear Admiral Sprague's Task Group (7th Fleet), off the coast of Samar, was under attack from Kurita's Force. Sinking two Allied escort carriers* and three destroyers* before withdrawing again, in the mistaken belief that he was facing Halsey's carrier force, Kurita lost a unique opportunity to overcome the escort force and destroy the huge Philippine invasion force on the beachhead. Even so, there were bitter recriminations among the American naval chiefs over the loss of Sprague's escort force and the 'near miss' on the Leyte beachhead and Halsey's desertion of the San Bernardino Strait appeared to make him wholly responsible for the near tragedy – though it later transpired that poor communications were at least as much to blame.

Desperate radio signals from Kinkaid finally persuaded Halsey to break off his engagement with Ozawa's decoy force in the vicinity of Cape Engano (having sunk two and damaged the other two Japanese carriers) even though Hasley knew that he would not be able to reach the stricken Task Force in time to affect the outcome. By the time Hasley's fleet got back to Leyte Gulf, however, Kurita had withdrawn and the danger had evaporated. The remnants of the Japanese fleet were finally withdrawing, battling their way back to the safety of Brunei against the final attacks of US shore- and carrier-based aircraft.

The battle of Leyte Gulf marked the end of the Japanese Navy's Sho strategy and the end of the Japanese challenge to American naval superiority in the Pacific. The surviving handful of Japanese warships could no longer protect itself from air attack nor effectively guard the sea approaches to Japan. Once again, the US Navy's* air power had proved the decisive factor.

Liberty Ship Mass-produced cargo vessel built in the United States. The US Maritime Commission produced 5,777 cargo ships from 1939–45 and 2,770 of them were Liberty ships, designed with simple reciprocating engines to save on naval materials. Constructed from prefabricated sections, which could be produced anywhere, not just in dockyards, they were an important boost to US shipbuilding capacity. Variants on the basic type were designed to carry specific loads, and most were operated by civilian carriers. The later Victory ships were faster and built with more of an eye for post-war commercial use, and US manufacture of fuel tankers was standardized on the basic 500ft T2 design.

Lidice Czechoslovakian village which was the scene, in 1942, of a violent reprisal for the assassination of Reinhard Heydrich*. Tenuously connected with the operation by Czech soldiers flown from Britain, the village was razed to the ground and all its inhabitants murdered. Thousands of Czechs were also deported to the Austrian concentration camp* at Mauthausen.

Lingayen Gulf See Philippines.

Liore-et-Olivier LeO-451 The LeO-451 entered service with the *Armée de l'Air** in August 1939, and was by far the best French bomber of WW2. In spite of chaos caused by the recent nationalization of the French airframe industry, 472 were operational by May 1940, and they performed well against mighty odds in the battle for France*. After

the surrender in June, several versions of the aircraft served both the Vichy* Air Force and the Luftwaffe*. Other examples flew as transports for Italy, Britain and the US. Production ended in 1943.
BRIEF DATA (LeO-451) Type: 2–3-man medium bomber; Engine: 2 × 1,140hp Gnome-Rhône; Max speed: 307mph; Ceiling: 29,530'; Range: 1,430m (part loaded); Arms: 1 × 20mm cannon, 2 × 7.5mm mg; Bomb load: 4,410lb.

Lipski, Josef (1894–1958) The Polish ambassador to Berlin from October 1933 until the outbreak of war on 1 September 1939. See Poland.

List, Field Marshal Wilhelm von (1880–1971) Bavarian officer and engineer, he was appointed field marshal following his successful leadership of the German 14th Army in Poland* and of the 12th Army in France (see Western Offensive). List had demonstrated his loyalty to Nazism in 1938, when he supported the forced resignations of Field Marshal von Blomberg and General von Fritsch* on spurious charges initiated by Hitler* for political reasons.

In the spring of 1941, List went to Greece as C-in-C of the invasion forces (see Balkans, German Invasion of). He subsequently commanded Army Group A in Russia (see Eastern Front) in its advance into the Caucasus* (July–October 1942), but was abruptly dismissed by Hitler, following an interview at Hitler's forward headquarters at Vinnitsa in which List revealed his belief that Germany did not have the resources to win the war. He was not among the large number of senior German officers approached by conspirators against Hitler after 1942.

Lithuania One of three independent Baltic republics, the others Estonia* and Latvia*, its fate was tied to the Soviet Union in 1939. Lithuania was assigned to the Soviet sphere of influence by an amendment to the Russo-German Pact* known as the Soviet-German Boundary and Friendship Treaty. In October it was forced to sign a 'mutual assistance' pact with Russia allowing key positions to be garrisoned by Soviet forces. On 15 June, Moscow issued an ultimatum demanding the formation of a government 'friendly to the Soviet Union' and Lithuania was invaded on the same day. A puppet regime was established and a rigged referendum cast Lithuania as a member of the USSR in the characteristic pattern of Soviet subjugation. Although accurate estimates of the executions and deportations that occurred throughout the Baltic states are impossible to gather, it is clear that Lithuanians suffered equally from brutal policies of 'Sovietization', which were then exchanged, after the German invasion of Russia, for the brutal effects of 'Germanization', including the extermination of Lithuanian Jews. It has also been estimated that between 1944, when Soviet forces reoccupied Lithuania, and 1949, some 350,000 Lithuanians were exiled to Siberia. See also Eastern Front; Maps 27 and 32.

Littorio The Italian Navy's* *Littorio* Class battleships were conceived as a reply to the two French *Dunkerque** Class battlecruisers. By the time the first two units were laid down in 1934, France was building its *Richelieu** Class battleships, and two more *Littorios* were begun in 1938. The *Littorio* and the *Vittorio Veneto* were completed in the spring of 1940 and the *Roma* was ready in 1942, but the *Impero* was never completed.

The *Littorio* was sunk in the shallows of Taranto* harbour by Fleet Air Arm* torpedo-bombers on the night of 11 November 1940, but was repaired and returned to serve in April 1941. She was damaged twice more by air attack before her name was changed to *Italia* in celebration of the fall of Mussolini* in July 1943. Meanwhile the *Vittorio Veneto* had been damaged at the Battle of Cape Matapan*, and was torpedoed by the British submarine *Urge* in December 1941. Both ships, along with the new *Roma*, attempted to reach Malta* after the Italian surrender. The *Roma* was hit by two German FX1400 guided bombs* off Cape Corso on 9 September 1943, and exploded before sinking. The *Italia* was slightly damaged in the same attack but again survived to spend the rest of the war interned at Alexandria* with the *Vittorio Veneto*. The incomplete hull of the *Impero* was destroyed at Trieste by USAAF* bombers early in 1945.

BRIEF DATA (*Littorio*, 1940) Displacement: 41,650 tons; Dimensions: o/a lgth – 780' 4", b – 108'; Speed: 30 knots; Armament: 9 × 15" gun (3 × 3), 12 × 6" gun, 12 × 3.5" AA gun, 4 × 4.7" lighting guns, 20 × 37mm AA gun, 30 × 20mm AA gun, 3 aircraft.

Litvinov, Maxim (1876–1952) Native of Russian Poland and an early Bolshevik, Litvinov served as Commissar for Foreign Affairs from 1930 until 1939, when he was replaced by Molotov* in the realignment of Russian foreign policy that resulted in the Russo-German Pact* (August 1939). Having until then been an important advocate of co-operation with the West, Litvinov remained out of favour until the German invasion of Russia in June 1941. He subsequently served as ambassador to Washington, 1941–3, and as Deputy Commissar of Foreign Affairs from 1941–6.

Lockheed Hudson The American-built Hudson was ordered by the British Purchasing Commission in July 1938, and was originally intended as a navigation trainer. With the approach of war, it was diverted to first-line duties as a reconnaissance and anti-submarine* plane with RAF* Coastal Command. Hudsons began replacing Avro Ansons* in this role in the summer of 1939, and saw service in the North Sea, the Atlantic* and the English Channel. From late 1942, as they became obsolete, Hudsons transferred to air-sea rescue* duties, and they returned finally to training and transport squadrons during 1943–4. Early models mounted single-stage Cyclone engines, and the Mark IV was the first version

with faster, supercharged Twin Wasps. Many late Hudson VI models had their gun turret removed for transport duties. Just over 2,000 Hudsons reached the RAF and production ended in June 1943. An additional 418 aircraft, intended for Britain under Lend-Lease*, were seconded to the USAAF* (as the A-29, A-28, AT-18) and the US Navy* (as the PBO-1).

BRIEF DATA (Mk IV). Type: 5-man maritime reconnaissance; Engine: 2 × 1,200hp Pratt and Whitney Twin Wasp; Max speed: 284mph; Ceiling: 24,500'; Range: 2,160m; Arms: 5 × 0.303" mg (provision for depth charges).

Lockheed Ventura (and Harpoon) Developed from the Lockheed Lodestar transport, the Ventura closely resembled its predecessor, the Lockheed Hudson*, and joined the USAAF* (as the B34 bomber) and the US Navy* (as the PV) in late 1942. At the same time, British versions began operations with RAF* Bomber Command in small-scale precision daylight raids over Europe. Altogether, 394 Ventura I and Ventura IIs were exported to Britain, but the aircraft was not a success as a bomber, and was transferred to coastal reconnaissance duties from the autumn of 1943. With the US Navy, hundreds of torpedo*-armed PV-I Venturas flew antisubmarine* patrols until the end of the war. The PV-II, named the Harpoon, mounted additional nose guns, and the PV-III Ventura was the export model as used by the US Navy.

BRIEF DATA (RAF Ventura II) Type: 5-man light bomber; Engine: 2 × 2,000hp Pratt and Whitney Double Wasp; Max speed: 300mph; Ceiling: 25,000'; Range: 1,000m; Arms: 2 × 0.5" mg, 6–8 × 0.303" mg; Bomb load: 2,500lb.

Lockwood, Vice Admiral Charles (1890–1967) US Commander of Submarines Pacific Fleet from 1942, he is credited with the US submarine forces' transformation into a highly effective fighting force. See Submarine.

Long Lance See Torpedo.

Long-Range Penetration Groups See Wingate, Major General Orde.

Longstop Hill Vantage point overlooking the Medjerba Valley on the southwest approach to Tunis, officially known to the Allies as Hill 290. Abandoned by the British during the Axis* counter-attack from Djedeida of December 1942 (see Tunisia), Longstop Hill was a preliminary target for the next Allied offensive on Christmas Eve. After fierce fighting in driving rain, the position was taken but regained the following day by German troops, who renamed it Christmas Hill. The wider offensive was then cancelled and Longstop Hill was only retaken after further attrition in April 1943.

Lord Haw-Haw See Joyce, William.

Los Alamos See Atomic Bomb.

Lübeck, Bombing of See Strategic Bombing Offensive.

Lublin Committee A Soviet-backed Polish provisional government which formed the backbone of the first Polish post-war government (see Poland). Following the break in relations between the Soviet Union and the London-based Polish government-in-exile*, precipitated by the revelation of the Katyn* massacre in April 1943, Moscow developed links with the communist Union of Polish Patriots to ensure a pro-Soviet government body for post-war Poland.

Having successfully defended his claim to territory in east Poland at the first meeting of the 'Big Three' at Tehran, (see Conferences), Stalin* went further by announcing the formation of a communist-dominated National Council for Poland (also comprising members of the Polish Workers' Party) on 1 January 1944. In spite of protests from the Polish government-in-exile, no attempts were made by the Western Allies to force Stalin to step down over Poland. Hence, in July 1944, the Polish Committee of National Liberation – the Lublin Committee – was established by Stalin at temporary headquarters in Lublin, with limited administrative power over Polish territory liberated from the Germans.

In December 1944, the Lublin Committee was reconstituted as the provisional government of Poland, and promptly recognized by Stalin, thus pre-empting Allied discussion of the composition of the Polish government scheduled for the Yalta Conference in February. Lacking any leverage with which to influence Stalin, the Western Allies accepted the claim of the Lublin Committee with the proviso that the postwar Polish government should also include some of the London-based Poles. A committee headed by Russian Foreign Minister Molotov* was formed to supervise its composition. The Polish government was finally formed in June 1945 and officially recognized by the US and Britain.

The town of Lublin was also the location of a concentration camp* (also known as Majdanek) which was fitted with gas chambers in the autumn of 1942. It is believed that 200,000 people were murdered there.

Lucas, Major General John (1890–1949) American staff officer who served as personal deputy to General Eisenhower* in 1943, Lucas commanded the controversial operations following the landing of US 5th Army units (British and American) largely unopposed, at Anzio* on 22 January 1944. Lacking confidence in the operation from the outset, Lucas was judged to have made a timid decision to consolidate the Anzio beachhead rather than strike inland while the German forces awaited reinforcement. Though this decision had the backing of his commander, General Mark Clark* (and subsequent commentators have suggested that a strike inland might have proved an equal tactical error), Lucas was removed from his command. He was succeeded by Major General Truscott*.

Luftwaffe The air arm of the Third Reich was formally established by Hitler and Göring* in March 1935, although plans to create a German air force, independent of the Army, had been secretly under way since 1923. Forbidden under the terms of the Treaty of Versailles to build military aircraft, the then commander of the army, General von Seeckt, and a select group of like-minded officers (including Kesselring* and Stumpf*) set about developing German aviation from the limited resources available.

Civil aviation had continued in Germany almost from the Armistice, and the state-subsidized Luft Hansa airline was formed in 1926. In 1929 Erhard Milch*, a protégé of Seeckt, became its chief executive, leaving a management position with the Junkers production company, which was already building metal transports capable of fairly simple adaptation as bombers. Lufthansa (the name was conjoined in 1934) provided an operational medium for aircrew trained at the Lipetsk flying school, leased secretly from the Russians since 1923. German aviation was further encouraged by the officially sponsored growth of the German Union of Sporting Flying, which had 50,000 members by 1929. The lack of an indigenous aircraft industry and the economic strictures of the Weimar years were overcome by the manufacture of hundreds of elementary gliders, enthusiastically piloted by thousands of 'sportsmen'. By the time the National Socialists came to power in 1933, Air Minister Hermann Göring possessed the effective basis for a military air force, under the able administration of his new deputy, Milch.

The Luftwaffe lost its first Chief of Staff, General Wever, in a 1936 air accident, and with him its leading advocate of long-range strategic bombing. The development of heavy bombers was subsequently neglected in favour of medium and dive-bombers, and the Luftwaffe was geared towards a sophisticated army support role. This was confirmed by the performance of German aircraft in the Spanish Civil War. Specialist fast bombers – the Heinkel He111* and Dornier Do17* – saw service in Spain along with the Junkers Ju87 Stuka* dive-bomber and the superb Messerschmitt Bf109* fighter. By 1939, these had been joined by two new twin-engined designs (Messerschmitt Bf110* and Junkers Ju88*) to form the main strength of the Luftwaffe at the outbreak of WW2. Meanwhile German pilots were sent to Spain on a rota system and gained invaluable combat experience.

Although the Luftwaffe command had planned almost to the last for a war in 1942 or 1943, Germany possessed the most powerful air force in the world by September 1939. Its 3,750 aircraft were superior to those of any European power and in Poland*, Norway* and the Western Offensive* they swept all before them in direct support of German armoured forces. After first establishing air supremacy, the Luftwaffe brought chaos to the infrastructure of its enemies, attacking military targets far beyond the front lines and disrupting any response to the rapid armoured thrusts of the Army. Apart from these triumphant Blitzkrieg* operations, the Luftwaffe carried out virtually unopposed strategic bombing operations against cities that were highly effective and seemed to confirm the value of the medium bomber fleet as an independent strike weapon. Although it failed to finish off the British Army at Dunkirk*, the Luftwaffe's reputation was at its height in June 1940.

As the prelude to an invasion of Britain (see Sealion), 2,800 combat aircraft were then set the task, welcomed by Göring, of destroying the RAF*. Their failure to do so left both the Me110 and the Ju87 discredited as front-line weapons after heavy losses to modern RAF fighters. The medium bombers were shown to be incapable of independently delivering a knock-out blow to a major power, or of surviving unescorted against modern interceptors in daylight. Although the Bf109 retained its combat superiority, new designs were clearly needed (see Britain, Battle of).

Unfortunately the Luftwaffe technical directorate – chaotically administered by Ernst Udet* – had failed to provide a new generation of warplanes, and Germany was forced to fight with refined versions of pre-war designs for most of the war. Most of the types in front-line service in 1939 were still in production in 1944. An excellent new fighter, the Focke-Wulf Fw190*, became available from 1941 but no other entirely successful new designs reached the Luftwaffe until the last months of the war. A jet fighter, the Messerschmitt Me262*, had been conceived as early as 1938, but its development and deployment were confused and its service entry was delayed beyond combat usefulness.

From early 1941, the Luftwaffe took over offensive duties from the Italian Air Force* in the Mediterranean*, and inflicted heavy losses on British shipping in the absence of modern opposition. In June, 2,700 aircraft, out of a total first-line strength of 4,700, were deployed for the invasion of Russia 'see Eastern Front). Once more operating in conjunction with the Army against inferior aircraft, the Luftwaffe almost destroyed the Red Air Force* in the first weeks of the campaign and its pilots registered huge individual scores. The Russian manufacturing industry soon recovered, however, to produce large numbers of viable combat aircraft, and a prolonged air battle developed along the Eastern Front from 1942, largely fought in direct support of ground operations.

The year 1943 marked a watershed in the fortunes of the Luftwaffe. In the west, the Allied Strategic Bombing Offensive* demanded increased commitment to home defence, reducing the Luftwaffe's effectiveness in other theatres. Although interception tactics were developed that inflicted heavy losses on Allied bomber streams, the arrival of long-range Allied escort fighters in early 1944 exposed the obsolescence of German designs. Bombing inflicted further disruption on a production industry which, bolstered since 1938 by the use of occupied or allied factories, now struggled to keep pace with demand. The Luftwaffe's operational strength had fallen below 4,000 aircraft in 1943, while reserves were non-existent and there was a growing shortage of trained aircrew.

The Allied invasion of Normandy* in June 1944 stretched resources still further, and by late 1944 large-scale production of new designs was impossible as the aircraft industry atrophied amid the chaos caused by uninterrupted heavy bombing on a vast scale (see also Northwest Europe). Complete Allied superiority in machines and aircrew was now compounded by acute fuel shortages. Hopeless though the situation had become, morale remained surprisingly high and the last of the Luftwaffe, some 1,500 aircraft, fought on until defeated by lack of fuel and forced to surrender on 8 May 1945.

Throughout the war the basic flying unit of the Luftwaffe was the *Gruppe*, composed of three *Staffeln*, each with about ten planes. Combat units were formed into *Geschwader*, each comprising three *Gruppen*, and the largest formation, the Luftflotte varied in strength between 200 and 1,250 aircraft. The Luftwaffe controlled all of Germany's ground anti-aircraft* defences – radar, searchlights and guns – as well as a parachute division (see Airborne Warfare), 22 field (infantry) divisions and, nominally at least, the 'Hermann Göring Panzer Division'.

Luger See Pistols.

Lützow See Deutschland; Prinz Eugen.

Luzon Largest and most northerly island in the Philippine archipelago and site of two of the largest campaigns of the Pacific War*. See Philippines.

M

M13/40 Series Tanks Short of funds, the Italians had concentrated their armoured development in the 1930s on light tanks* and small tankettes which, while adequate for colonial policing, proved quite useless for the mechanized warfare of WW2. The standard Italian medium tank of 1939 was the M13/39, but only 100 of these were built before they were phased out in favour of the more powerful M13/40. Eventually 799 M13/40s were completed, although only 15 were ready by July 1940, and they were followed by 1,103 M14/41 versions with bigger engines and desert sand filters. These were the only important Italian tanks of WW2, and they served in the Balkans* and the Desert War*. Their thin armour proved very vulnerable to contemporary anti-tank* weapons, and early models were very prone to breakdowns. In early 1943, a faster M15/42 version was introduced but less than 100 had been finished before all Italian tank production was switched to the Semovente, a series of 75mm (and a few 105mm) self-propelled* guns based on the M13/40 series chassis.

BRIEF DATA (M13/40) Type: 4-man medium tank; Engine: 125hp diesel; Max speed: 20mph; Range: 125m; Arms: 1 × 47mm gun, 2 × 8mm mg; Armour: max 30mm.

MacArthur, General Douglas (1880–1964) One of the United States' most brilliant and controversial generals whose commitment to the defence and reconquest of the Philippine* Islands has since become legendary. Son of senior US Army officer Arthur MacArthur, for whom he acted as aide in 1905, MacArthur's career developed meteorically from his exceptional performance at West Point, where he graduated first in his class in 1903. As Chief of Staff and later 42nd Division commander during WW1, MacArthur's reputation grew dramatically. Described by the then US Secretary of War as the United States' best front-line general of WW1, MacArthur accepted an appointment as Superintendent of West Point in 1919, became the youngest US Major General in 1925 and was promoted Chief of Staff of the Army in 1930.

A political conservative, MacArthur achieved some unwanted publicity for his involvement (along with Majors Eisenhower* and Patton*) in the suppression of the Bonus Army in July 1932, at the height of the American Depression. He also set in motion the limited development of tanks* and other armoured vehicles for the US Army*. In 1935 he stepped down as Chief of Staff to accept an appointment as military adviser to Philippine President Manuel Quezon*. Also charged with command of the small (US and Filipino) Commonwealth Army based in the Philippines, MacArthur exaggerated both the importance of his position (for which he chose the title 'Field Marshal' and designed a sharkskin uniform) and the tactical and strategic significance of the Philippine-based force. But the rising tension between Japan and the US during 1941 prompted US Joint Chiefs of Staff* to reverse their strategic policy for Pacific defence, recall MacArthur to the active list in July and provide at least a proportion of the reinforcements and funds he demanded for the Philippines. Despite MacArthur's bold assessment in October that the Philippine forces now represented the key point in the US Pacific defensive strength, the initial Japanese invasion of the islands on 8 December 1941 overran the Filipino and US defence almost immediately, and MacArthur was forced to a last-minute retreat to save his forces from imminent capture.

Having withdrawn with his forces to Bataan*, the southern peninsula of the main island of Luzon, and besieged by the Japanese 14th Army under General Homma, MacArthur endured the same privations as his men and at first refused to contemplate leaving his HQ on Corregidor* to assume another command, as ordered by signal from the President on 22 February. Having finally agreed to leave in his own time, MacArthur delayed a further nine days before escaping at night with his wife and son in a high-speed dash with a party of four PT boats across Manila Bay and 600 miles of ocean to Mindanao. A few days later he landed in Australia by B17 to assume command of all US troops in the Pacific. Arriving at Adelaide, he faced a large group of reporters when he made his famous, Caesarean promise: 'I came through and I shall return.'

As Supreme Commander of the Southwest Pacific Area from April 1942, MacArthur was utterly committed (in contrast to the Combined Chiefs of Staff*) to defeating Japan before Germany. Apparently bound by the grave responsibility of his promise to return, he took for granted the central role of the Philippines in any attacks on the Japanese mainland, and persistently and argumentatively promoted the earliest possible Philippine offensive, often at the expense of good relations with senior US commanders (particularly Admirals King* and Nimitz*). Nevertheless he proposed and planned many of the operations which he commanded, with great courage and skill, against New Guinea*, New Britain (Rabaul*), New Georgia*, the Admiralty Islands* and the Solomon Islands*,

between 1942 and 1944. In this period MacArthur developed the 'leapfrogging' tactics that combined the bold use of sea and air power with skilful amphibious* landings to bypass large Japanese concentrations, allowing them to 'wither on the vine', and concentrate assaults on vulnerable communications lines. The tactic became an increasingly effective characteristic of US offensive strategy in the vast scatters of Pacific island territories as the campaign progressed (see Pacific War).

In early October 1944, after weeks of raging argument which highlighted the personal as well as professional rivalry between MacArthur and the US Navy*, the general was instructed by the Joint Chiefs to proceed with operations against the Philippines. His return was staged on a scale appropriate to MacArthur's histrionic view of his mission. The largest amphibious operation of the war till then, the landings on Leyte* island, launched a campaign that, though ultimately successful, would outlast the war itself. Promoted a five-star general in December and Commander of all US forces in the Pacific in April 1945, MacArthur controlled a huge force of nearly one and a half million men, until transferred to Tokyo in August to accept the Japanese surrender, signed on 2 September. Appointed Supreme Commander of the Allied Powers in Japan (SCAP), which administered and controlled the country after the war, he stayed on in the Far East to command the US and UN forces in Korea until he was recalled because of his support for the use of the A-bomb against China to a belated hero's welcome in 1951. Having failed to secure a nomination for presidential candidate in the election campaign of 1952, MacArthur retired to live in Manhattan.

McAuliffe, General Anthony C. (1898–1975) US Army officer and acting divisional commander of the 101st Airborne Division during the Battle of the Bulge*, he became famous for his spirited reply of 'Nuts!' to the German commander, General Luttwitz, who demanded his surrender, following the German encirclement of the American troops at Bastogne*. McAuliffe was subsequently promoted to Major General. He served as C-in-C, US Army in Europe, during the 1950s.

Macchi C200 Series Descended, like the British Supermarine Spitfire*, from a series of racing seaplanes, the C200 *Saetta* (Dart) was first flown in 1937 and formed the backbone of the *Regia Aeronautica*'s* fighter strength – along with the obsolete Fiat CR42 – when Italy joined the war in 1940. A thousand production C200A1 and A2 models (the latter a fighter-bomber version with strengthened wings) saw action on all Italian fronts. Of excellent airframe design and supremely manoeuvrable, the plane was let down by its relatively weak radial engine. Performance only approached that of the best Allied fighters when liquid-cooled German power plants were fitted to the C202 *Folgore* (Thunderbolt), which was introduced in 1942, and some 1,500 of these were built, serving in the Mediterranean* and on the Eastern Front*. The C205 *Veltro* (Greyhound), a refinement fitted with a 1,475hp German engine, did achieve parity with the American P51D*, but it was not available until early 1943 and only 262 were built. After the Italian surrender of September 1943, a few of these fell into Allied hands but most fought beside the Luftwaffe* in the defence of Northern Italy.
BRIEF DATA (C202) Type: Single-seat fighter; Engine: 1 × 1,200hp Daimler-Benz; Max speed: 369mph; Ceiling: 34,500'; Range: 376m; Arms: 2 × 12.7mm mg, 2 × 7.9mm mg.

McCreery, Sir Richard (1898–1967) An able strategic planner and field commander, McCreery served with the British Expeditionary Force in France and with the Home Forces at the start of the war. In May 1941 he was appointed adviser to General Auchinleck*, then C-in-C in North Africa, but lost his post over disagreements

with Auchinleck about the reorganization of his armoured forces. He was nevertheless appointed Chief of Staff to General Alexander*, who succeeded Auchinleck in August 1942, at a critical point in the Desert War*. Here McCreery earned the great respect of his commander, taking a key role in the planning for the final stages of the Battle of Alamein*, which Alexander later judged crucial to its success.

McCreery commanded the British 10th Corps during the landings at Salerno* in September 1943, at the start of the Allied invasion of Italy*. He subsequently directed his forces in the gruelling campaigns against Kesselring's withdrawing forces on the Italian peninsula, notably at Cassino*. Promoted commander of the 8th Army to succeed General Leese* in November 1944, McCreery saw the campaign in Italy through to its end on 2 May 1945, when German forces in Italy finally surrendered. He is widely regarded as having made an important contribution to that hard-won success.

Machine-guns As an infantry weapon, the machine-gun was the focus around which WW2 ground forces were organized. Light weapons – such as the British 0.303-inch Bren Gun, the Russian 7.62mm Degtyarev DP and various Japanese 6.5mm weapons – were bipod-mounted and comprised the main armament of an infantry section (6 –10 men). The US Army employed its 0.3-inch Browning Automatic Rifle in the role, and similar automatic weapons saw service with the Red Army. Light machine-guns could also be adapted for tank* use, while the French Army fitted its 7.5mm Chatellerault guns to Maginot Line* forts.

Heavier weapons, notably the 0.3-inch version of the US Browning Machine Gun, were sometimes employed at squad level but they were primarily issued to support companies. Weapons like the British 0.303-inch Vickers Gun, the US 0.5-inch Browning and the Soviet 7.62mm SG43 (which eventually replaced the veteran

Maxim Gun*), supplied a relatively sustained and accurate barrage of fire with the aid of a larger, more stable mounting. The Japanese built a standard 7.7mm heavy machine-gun adapted from a French design and, like the Russians, also used 12.7mm weapons. In Germany, no distinction was drawn between light and heavy machine-guns. The rapid-firing 7.92mm Mauser MG34 and its successor, the MG42, were given different mountings for use in either role, a policy that resulted in much waste of ammunition during infantry operations.

Heavy machine-guns were also the principal air-to-air combat weapon of the war, although shell-firing cannon were increasingly preferred for fighter armament. Similarly, rapid-firing cannon were found to be far more effective than machine-guns as standard light anti-aircraft* defence aboard warships. Cannon remained in short supply throughout the war, however, and machine-guns remained in widespread use on smaller craft of all types. Armed merchantmen were often dependent on obsolete types, like the British Lewis Gun, drawn from reserve (see DEMS). All nations fitted machine-guns to tanks and armoured vehicles of all kinds. Usually for anti-personnel use, they were also fitted as AA weapons to most US combat vehicles. See also Submachine-guns.

Madagascar Large island in the Indian Ocean off the coast of East Africa, now the Malagasy Republic. In French hands at the beginning of the war, Madagascar was invaded on 5 May 1942 by a British force comprising three infantry brigades, supported by a large fleet including the capital ships of Force H* from Gibraltar. The attack (Operation Ironclad) was aimed at the naval base of Diégo Suarez to the north of the island, which was regarded as a possible target for Japanese expansion. It was not well handled, and two days of fierce fighting took place after the advantage of surprise had been wasted in some very naive diplomatic approaches to the French commander. Diégo Suarez surrendered on 7

May, but French submarines continued to attack British ships in the harbour until the following day, although they did no damage and two submarines were lost. In the battle 109 British troops and twice as many Frenchmen were killed, and sporadic fighting continued on the island until September, when a further British force was landed and took the capital Antananarivo after only light skirmishes.

Churchill described this expensive sideshow as 'a brilliant action', but with hindsight its only lasting achievement was to help make de Gaulle*, whose Free French forces played a small part in the operation, appear unacceptable as a potential leader of French colonial forces in Northwest Africa at the time of the Torch* landings.

Madang See New Guinea.

Magic Code-name for a joint American Army and Navy operation, first set up in 1939, to break Japanese diplomatic and military codes, Magic provided US military and political chiefs with much important intelligence throughout the war and its contribution to the major operational Allied successes has until recently been largely underestimated. The Navy special intelligence section, the Communications Security Unit, with a staff by 1942 of about 300, worked alongside the Army Signals Intelligence Section (SIS), deciphering and relaying the enormous traffic of coded messages sent by the Japanese Government to their agencies worldwide, and by Imperial Headquarters to their commanders at sea and in the field.

But in 1939 the major task facing both sections (each consisting at this time of a small team of less than a dozen men), was the breaking of the 'Purple' code. A new cipher machine, invented by Captain Jinsaburo Ito, worked on the principle of a telephone switchboard, and, throughout 1939, defied all attempts by the two American teams of cryptanalysts to penetrate it. Nicknamed the Purple Machine, it was finally cracked, after 19 months of exhaustive work, in September 1940 by the Army cryptanalyst Colonel William Friedman*, who suffered a breakdown as a result of his enormous efforts.

Though the success with the Purple Code enabled analysts to penetrate much more deeply into Japanese diplomatic traffic, especially during the tense autumn of 1941, the sheer volume of intelligence being received by Magic, the laboriousness of the procedures involved, and the lack of any centralized system for evaluating the importance of and appropriate destination for the decoded information, substantially reduced the value of the unique efforts being made by the tiny Army and Navy teams. The crucial failure to predict the attack on Pearl Harbor* can be partly assigned to these causes.

Nevertheless, the rapid expansion of Operation Magic following Pearl Harbor enabled the Intelligence teams to penetrate Japanese operational codes and collect intercepts that laid the vital groundwork for many important Allied victories. Probably the single most important contribution made by Magic intelligence to the American victory in the Pacific was the decoding of ciphers that revealed the Japanese attack plan for the Battle of Midway* in mid-1942. Informed in advance of the Japanese objectives, direction of approach and timing of the attack at Midway* by Magic intercepts, Admiral Nimitz* was able to pre-empt the Japanese strategy and fight off a much superior force, decisively halting the thrust of the Japanese offensive in the Pacific. See also Pacific War; OSS; Ultra.

Maginot Line A line of static concrete and steel defences that stretched between Luxembourg and Switzerland along France's border with Germany (see Map 1). The Line had been proposed by Marshal Joffre and built by the French between 1930 and 1935 under the supervision of the then French War Minister, André Maginot, as a supposedly impregnable defence from the threat of German invasion. Since WW1, which had seen a three-year battle, at enor-

mous human cost, to break the German trench line, the French government and people had been convinced of the necessity to create a permanent line of fortifications on its northeastern frontier. Based on three interdependent fortified belts with anti-tank emplacements and pillboxes standing in front of bombproof artillery casements and a rearward line of modern forts, the line cost 7,000 million francs to construct and was regarded at the time as a miracle of military engineering. Although it proved impenetrable, the Maginot Line was not unavoidable, as was to become clear in May 1940, during the German Western Offensive*.

Maisky, Ivan (1884–1975) Widely respected Soviet ambassador to London from 1932 until his recall in 1943 to become Deputy Commissar of Foreign Affairs. As ambassador, Maisky had developed solid friendships in Britain that were to be tested in the difficult autumn of 1939, following the signing of the Russo-German Pact* in August and the opening of the war against Finland*. After the German invasion of the Soviet Union in June 1941, the major issue of Anglo-Russian relations was the opening of a 'Second Front' against Hitler, and Maisky was involved in regular discussions with Churchill* over this issue. He also negotiated with the Czech and Polish governments-in-exile* for mutual assistance agreements, similar to the Anglo-Soviet Mutual Assistance Pact signed with Churchill. His meeting with US emissary Harry Hopkins* and subsequent three-way negotiations resulted in a Lend-Lease* Agreement being reached with Britain and the US that dramatically improved Russia's resources to fight Germany. He later participated in talks with Eden*, Churchill and Molotov* in London (1942) that were formalized in the Anglo-Soviet Treaty, May 1942, before being recalled to his new post. In 1945, Maisky attended the Yalta and Potsdam conferences* and chaired the Allied Commission on Reparations.

Major Martin Fictitious name given to a corpse which was floated off the coast of Spain on 30 April 1943 by the British Naval Intelligence Division as a bait to Nazi agents in Spain. The corpse was identified by fake documents as an officer of the Royal Marines and was carrying a courier's briefcase containing documents designed to convince the Axis* that the Allies planned an invasion of Sardinia and Greece, rather than Italy*, as a follow up to their success in North Africa. The deception, code-named Mincemeat, was accepted by many Axis commanders, including Hitler* himself, as confirmation of their belief that this was indeed the Allied plan.

Makin See Gilbert Islands.

Malan, Group Captain Adolph (1910–63) South-African born RAF* fighter ace*, he joined the RAF in 1936 and subsequently became the third highest scoring RAF pilot of WW2, with 35 kills. He commanded No. 74 Squadron for the Battle of Britain* and received both the Distinguished Service Order and bar, and the Distinguished Flying Cross and bar.

Malaya, Fall of, 1941–2 The most economically productive and strategically important territory of the British Far Eastern Empire, it was guarded at its southern tip by the British fortress at Singapore* and the new Changi naval base. Supplying nearly half the world's natural rubber, and more than half its tin ore, the Malay states were among those valuable territories incorporated into the Japanese plan of expansion in the Greater East Asia Co-Prosperity Sphere*. By the summer of 1941, a secret plan had synthesized the work of hundreds of Imperial agents gathering information on defences, airstrips, landing beaches, etc. and of a small team of detailed planning officers under Colonel Tsuji*, to provide a blueprint for the Japanese conquest of Southeast Asia in a massive sea, land and air offensive. In the meantime, some measures were being taken by the British to prepare a defence of Malaya and Singapore, though the distraction of military developments in the Soviet Union, North Africa and in the Atlantic during 1941 limited the scope of planning and supplying of British forces in Southeast Asia as a whole. Throughout 1940, new airfields along the Malayan coast were constantly under construction, although only 150 RAF aircraft could in the end be spared for reinforcement. Apart from this, Malaya's defence rested on 88,000 troops (Malayan, Indian, Australian and British) under General Percival*, most of whom were poorly trained and equipped, and the historic fortress at Singapore*, with its new naval base, though lacking a fleet to protect it (see Map 23).

Although relatively small and equipped on a limited budget, the invasion force of three divisions under General Yamashita* were among the best in the Japanese Army. Supported by over 200 tanks and 500 aircraft, the attack had been carefully planned to exploit the difficult terrain and weather conditions. On the night of 7 December 1941, a diversionary landing by a regiment (5,500 men) of the Japanese 18th Division at Kota Bharu accompanied the main landings at Singora and Patani. The two forces moved quickly south, pushing units of the 9th Indian Division out of Kota Bharu on the east coast. On the same day, 10 December, the British capital ships *Repulse** and *Prince of Wales** (Force Z*) were sunk off the coast of Malaya, leaving the Japanese fleet in control of the sea. Jitra, on the west coast, was abandoned on the following day in what was to become a continuous pattern of the Japanese advance, infiltrating through the jungle to flank their enemy and 'hook' behind the British forces attempting to block the Japanese advance along the roads. The effectiveness of this tactic, combined with air bombardments, quickly reduced the tactical withdrawal ordered by General Percival to chaos. While Singapore suffered its first air attacks from the Japanese 11th Air Fleet and frantically prepared defences for an imminent invasion, Lt General Heath, commander of the 3rd Indian Division, attempted without success to rally his disintegrating forces to hold the aggressive Japanese advance along a line at the Perak River.

Successive and increasingly futile attempts were made during January 1942 to dig in along the roadways and hold Yamashita's divisions, notably at Kampar by General Heath's 3rd Division, then on the Slim River by the 11th Indian Division and on the Muar River by the 11th Indian with the support of the Australian 8th Division under General Gordon Bennett. Again and again, tank and artillery bombardments preceded the Japanese infiltration of the jungle to the flank and rear of vulnerable British positions and 'hooked' the desperate and demoralized British troops. Unable to counter Yamashita's overwhelming tactical superiority or the ferocity of the Japanese advance through southern Malaya, often borne on a vast fleet of bicycles, and now supported by aircraft from captured airfields, General Percival issued the final order for a general retreat across the Johore Strait to the island of Singapore on 25 January. The lack of any serious landward defences for Singapore, which might have halted the Japanese southward overland drive, made any long-term resistance impossible.

Malaya, HMS See Queen Elizabeth, HMS.

Malenkov, Georgiy M. (1902–) Wartime member of the Soviet State Defence Committee from 1941 (see Stavka), Malenkov was a close associate and collaborator with Stalin* in the Communist Party's general Secretariat and had played a part in the political purges of 1937–8 that had rid Stalin of both real and imagined opposition to his regime. Malenkov also served as political commissar on a number of Russian fronts: at Leningrad* and Moscow* in 1941, and at Stalingrad* and the Don during 1942. From 1943–5 he was Chairman of the Committee for the Restoration of the

Economy in liberated areas of the Soviet Union.

Malinovsky, Marshal Rodion (1898–1967) Post-war Soviet Minister of Defence (1957–67), he first distinguished himself in command of the 2nd Guards Army during the critical battle for Stalingrad*. Promoted to command the Southwest Front* after the Russian victory on the Volga*, he was later transferred to lead the 3rd and 2nd Ukrainian Fronts, and he directed successive Soviet victories in the Donbas, western Ukraine*, Rumania* and Hungary*. Budapest fell to forces under Malinovsky in February 1945. Transferred again to command the Transbaykal Front in August, he directed the successful campaigns against the Japanese Kwantung Army* in Siberia.

Malta The tiny island of Malta was Britain's only military base in the central Mediterranean area. Entirely dependent on seaborne supplies and only 60 miles from Sicily*, it was considered indefensible before the war, and was garrisoned in 1940 by only five infantry battalions and ten obsolete aircraft. The Royal Navy* maintained a base there, but the submarine flotilla stationed in Valetta harbour was not provided with bomb-proof pens. In June 1940, Italy's declaration of war and the fall of France* made the survival of Malta vitally important to the British, as it was the only possible springboard for offensive operations against Italian supply routes to North Africa.

For the next two years Malta was the subject of almost continuous bombing attacks, at first by the *Regia Aeronautica** but primarily by the Luftwaffe* from 1941. Meanwhile the Royal Navy strove to protect convoys to the island with heavy warships from Gibraltar* and Alexandria*. Vital fighter aircraft were flown to the island from aircraft carriers, and offensive operations were able to continue against Axis convoys. Submarines based on Malta took a significant toll of Rommel's* supply ships in 1941, but losses were high and the situation on the island never less than critical.

Matters worsened late in the year. Depleted Royal Navy forces in the Mediterranean now faced increased Luftwaffe activity; U-boats were deployed in the theatre for the first time; the supply of Tobruk* stretched resources still further; and Force K, the group of four light cruisers stationed on Malta in October, was all but destroyed when it ran into a minefield in December.

By early 1942, as the Luftwaffe stepped up its day and night bombing, only fast minelayers and submarines were able to supply Malta. Only two merchantmen reached the island in the first half of the year and both were bombed while unloading. In March the remnants of the submarine flotilla were withdrawn and in April, at the height of the bombing, only six aircraft remained on Malta after a consignment of Supermarine Spitfire* fighters had been destroyed on the ground as soon as they arrived. That month, with many of its starving inhabitants forced to live in caves, the island as a whole was awarded the George Cross by the British King George VI.

The intensification of the bombing campaign against Malta had been intended as the prelude to Operation Hercules, the German airborne* invasion of the island. This never took place, although at the time it would almost certainly have succeeded. Heavy losses in Crete* had dampened Hitler's enthusiasm for paratroop operations, and Rommel's Desert War* offensive towards Suez instead claimed the bulk of the Luftwaffe's attention in mid-1942. The position on Malta gradually improved. Spitfires were successfully deployed there in late May, and in August supplies arrived from the Pedestal* convoy.

By the autumn the position on the island had eased. The 8th Army's final victory at El Alamein* and the Torch* landings in Northwest Africa provided new forward air bases, which enabled the Allies to establish naval air superiority over Mediterranean supply routes. After the defeat of Axis forces in Tunisia* in May 1943, Malta became an important forward base for operations against southern Europe. Admiral Cunningham's* huge amphibious* invasion fleets for these landings were organized from his headquarters on Malta, and the surrender of the Italian Fleet to the Allies took place in Valetta's Grand Harbour in September 1943. See also Mediterranean Sea.

Manchukuo The name given to the puppet regime established by the Japanese in Manchuria* in March 1932 after the Mukden* Incident. With the addition of Jehol Province in 1933, Manchukuo consisted of four provinces with a population of about 30 million. The country was nominally headed by Pu Yi, the last emperor in China, made emperor of Manchukuo in March 1934, but was not recognized by the League of Nations. There was no elected assembly and power was wielded by Japanese in key posts in the administration under the direction of the commander of the Kwantung Army*. Manchukuo was a major source of raw materials for Japan. Economic development, in which a crucial role was played by the South Manchurian Railway, concentrated on large-scale mining and heavy manufacturing. Development was hindered, however, by the war with China*, and the effect of Japan's economic and political policies led to increasing dissent within the country. After 1937 anti-Japanese guerrilla activities increased, often led by local communists. In August 1945, Manchukuo was invaded by Russian troops. The state was disbanded, the area returned to China, and Japanese who had emigrated were repatriated. See Map 22.

Manchuria Northeastern province of modern China* (see Map 22), whose wealth of agricultural products and industrial raw materials were increasingly sought after by Japan in the late nineteenth century. Largely occupied by Russia after the Boxer

Rebellion, it was the site of much of the fighting during the Russo-Japanese War (1904–5). Privileges granted to the Japanese in Manchuria after the war were consistently exploited thereafter to develop Japan's political and economic domination of the area. During the 1920s, Manchuria was increasingly seen by Japan as a source of valuable industrial raw materials, a territorial bulwark against the Soviet Union, and as an emigration destination for the expanding Japanese population. From 1919, it was garrisoned by the Japanese Kwantung Army*, ostensibly as guardian of the leased South Manchurian Railway. In this period, the course of the domestic wars in China between nationalist and communist forces appeared to threaten Japan's expansionist interests in Manchuria. The danger of Chinese unification under Chiang Kai-shek* led members of the highly politicized Kwantung Army to assassinate the Manchurian warlord, Chang Tso-lin, in 1928. Continuing resistance to the Kwantung Army's influence in Manchuria led to the fabrication of an incident by Japanese officers at Mukden* in 1931 and the subsequent establishment of a puppet regime in Manchuria, named Manchukuo*. See also Matsuoka, Yosuke.

Mandalay Second largest city in Burma*, it was stubbornly but unsuccessfully defended by Chinese troops under US General Stilwell* against a Japanese assault at the end of April 1942. The city was retaken by British and Chinese troops under General William Slim* in March 1945. See Maps 24 and 25.

Manhattan District (Project) See Atomic Bomb.

Manila Capital and economic and communications centre of the Philippines* and the focus of American military and naval planning in the Far East before WW2 (see Map 12). In order to avoid the city being taken by force, Manila was declared an open city by Far Eastern forces commander

General Douglas MacArthur* on 26 December 1941, following the Japanese invasion of Luzon* on 22 December. It remained the commercial, political and military centre of the Philippines under Japanese occupation, as well as serving as the major military supply base for Japanese forces in New Guinea*, the Dutch East Indies*, Indochina* and Malaya*. In January 1945, the early recapture of Manila was the focus of MacArthur's strategy for the reconquest of the Philippines. Although MacArthur had hoped to avoid damage to the city, it was eventually recaptured in a costly battle of attrition, fought from house to house against the Japanese Manila Naval Defence Force, that resulted in many casualties and devastated the city, port and harbour. It is estimated that 100,000 Filipino civilians were killed – many of them in brutal atrocities committed in the south of the city – along with 1,000 US and 12,500 Japanese troops.

Mannerheim, Marshal Carl Gustav (1867 –1951) Finnish President and C-in-C of the Finnish Army, Mannerheim was of noble Swedish ancestry and had served in the Imperial Russian Army (while Finland formed part of the Tsarist Empire). He returned to Finland* when it declared its independence in October 1917 to lead the White Guard against the Bolshevik-supported Red Guard in the civil war of 1918. Following defeat in the presidential election of 1919, Mannerheim retired from active politics until recalled in 1931 to head the National Defence Council and reorganize the Finnish Army. He was responsible for the construction of the Mannerheim Line, stretching across 65 miles of Finland's southeastern frontier. In 1939 Mannerheim led the highly courageous but unsuccessful defence of Finland against Russian forces in the Winter War (see Russo-Finnish War) and continued to direct Finnish forces in co-operation with Germany in the 'Continuation War' (1941 –4), which aimed to take back territory lost to Russia in 1940. His skill in negotiations, which had already won Finland reasonable armistice terms from Russia in 1940, again succeeded in achieving favourable terms with Russia in a separately negotiated peace settlement. Mannerheim was subsequently made President of Finland but retired in 1946. See also Paasiviki.

Manstein, Field Marshal Fritz Erich von (1887–1973) Generally regarded by historians as the most outstanding of the Third Reich's military strategists. As major general and chief of staff to Rundstedt* in Army Group South in 1939, he suggested the invasion plan of France which was used by Hitler with spectacular results (see Manstein Plan). In June 1941 in the invasion of Russia, he commanded the 56th Panzer Corps for the advance on Leningrad (see Eastern Front). Later that year he took command of the 11th Army on the southeast front, which cut through the Crimea*, and took Sevastopol.

In July of the next year Manstein was promoted field marshal, and that autumn given command of Army Group Don. He tried unsuccessfully to relieve General Paulus's* 6th Army, nominally under his command, and which was besieged at Stalingrad*. Throughout 1943 on the Eastern Front, Manstein achieved some tactical success, though his strategy at Kursk* in July proved a costly disaster. His successive disagreements with Hitler* eventually led to his dismissal on 25 March 1944. In the same period he may have been involved in an unsuccessful plot originated by General Tresckow* to assassinate Hitler. In the view of war historian Liddell Hart, he was the Allies' most formidable military opponent, combining 'modern ideas of manoeuvre, a mastery of technical detail and great driving power'.

Manstein Plan Most common name for the highly effective German plan for the Western Offensive* in 1940, originally conceived by General Manstein* with the support of his commanding general Rundstedt (Army Group A commander). The plan proposed an alternative to the more conventional original plan, *Fall Gelb*, prepared by Chief of the General Staff, General Halder* and his staff at OKH (German Army HQ) during October and November 1939. Halder's plan (somewhat misleadingly compared with the WW1 Schlieffen plan), projected a major defeat of Franco-British forces in northern France based on an attack by Bock's* Army Group B through the 'Maastricht Appendix' and northern Belgium with the Channel coast as its ultimate objective. In contrast, Manstein's plan placed the main weight of the attack with the centrally positioned Army Group A, with its axis through the Ardennes forest and southern Belgium, splitting the Franco-British forces in a drive to the coast.

Despite a lack of confidence in the *Fall Gelb* plan among the German General Staff, who considered an attack in the west to be premature and militarily reckless, and criticism of its content by Hitler, the alternative plan presented by Rundstedt on Manstein's behalf was initially suppressed by Halder and Brauchitsch*. It was not until February that Manstein was given the opportunity to present his ideas to Hitler, who firmly approved them. A new plan was drafted by Halder at OKH that expanded Manstein's scheme, placing the bulk of the armoured forces with Rundstedt to push a 'Panzer Corridor' from Sédan to Abbeville, on the French coast. The quality of Manstein's original conception was to be dramatically demonstrated in May 1940.

Mao Tse-tung (1883–1976) A founder-member of the Chinese Communist Party in 1921. Between 1931 and 1934 Mao attempted, with Chou En-lai* and Chu Teh*, to establish a revolutionary base on the border of Hunan and a Chinese Soviet Republic in Kiangsi, before being forced by Chinese Nationalists under Chiang Kai-shek* to trek to Shensi on the epic 'Long March'. He collaborated with the Nationalist Kuomintang* against the Japanese between 1937 and 1945. During this period, Mao was based at Yenan, where he developed his political and military theories and instituted a purge of party officials. Following the surrender of Japan in September 1945, Mao resumed the struggle against Chiang's Nationalist forces. See China, Campaigns in.

Maquis, The See Resistance: France.

Mareth Line A slender fortification stretching 22 miles inland from the coast of southeast Tunisia, it was built by the French against any incursions by Italian forces from Tripolitania, 80 miles away (see Map 8). Early in 1943, Rommel's* army had dug into positions around Mareth after retreating from Libya (see Desert War). The British 8th Army's pursuit was delayed by supply shortages, and its anticipated attack on the Line (Operation Pugilistic Gallop) was not ready until 20 March, by which time Rommel had left Africa and an Italian, General Messe*, had assumed command of the defence.

The main weight of the attack was concentrated on a frontal approach near the coast by 30th Corps but after three days this had made little progress against heavily outnumbered defenders. British commander Montgomery* therefore switched his armour to support the newly formed New Zealand Division, which had made good progress on the inland flank, but was blocked in the hills northwest of Mareth. This flexibility of approach brought eventual success, and the renewed attack (Operation Supercharge II) broke through to El Hamma on 27 March. By that time, however, the bulk of Messe's army had escaped to positions behind the Wadi Akarit on the orders of Colonel General von Arnim*, overall Axis commander in Tunisia. See also Tunisia.

Mariana Islands Strategically important island group in the Central Pacific of which the most important islands are Saipan*, Tinian* and Guam* (see Maps 10 and 11). The Marianas had been garrisoned by

Japanese forces at the start of the Pacific War and were the targets of amphibious* assaults by American Marine forces during the summer of 1944. Following their recapture, the Marianas served as bases from which B-29s* could bomb Japan. See Strategic Bombing Offensive. See also Battle of the Philippine Sea.

Market-Garden, Operation See Arnhem.

Marshall, General George Catlett (1880 –1959) An immensely popular and able American general and administrator, chairman of the American Joint Chiefs of Staff* and one of the key Allied strategists of WW2, he made a substantial contribution to the Allied victory in 1945. Marshall had already gained a considerable reputation as a staff officer in France during WW1, then as aide and personal friend of Chief of Staff General John Pershing during the 1920s and later as assistant commander of the infantry school at Fort Benning, when war broke out in 1939. Appointed Chief of Staff and full general by President Roosevelt* on the day of the German invasion of Poland*, Marshall was instrumental in preparing, restructuring and enlarging the small US Army* (of approximately 200,000) for war. He was also responsible between 1939 and 1941, for advising on and explaining his activities to a highly sensitive and divided American Senate (see Neutrality, US).

In addition, Marshall made considerable efforts during 1939 and 1940 to establish close working relationships with British military chiefs, developing strategic plans for the coalition that he saw as inevitable.

After the attack on Pearl Harbor*, Marshall also became a chief architect of American strategic planning. An unshakeable advocate of the earliest possible direct attack on German forces in western Europe, Marshall was the key proponent of the 'Europe First' strategy, fighting against consistent opposition from General MacArthur*, the American naval chiefs (notably Admiral King*) and a large segment of the American public who demanded priority for the Pacific theatre. During 1943, Marshall accompanied Roosevelt to the Casablanca, Trident and first Quebec Conferences* and was instrumental in the planning of the invasion of Normandy*, and it was generally assumed that he would be in overall command of Allied forces (though he finally remained in Washington, persuaded by Roosevelt's uneasiness at losing his most able strategist).

Appointed Secretary of State by President Truman*, the only career Army officer to hold that post, Marshall was responsible for the development of the American aid programme known as the Marshall Plan, designed to shore-up the war-torn economies of western and parts of eastern Europe. He was awarded the Nobel Peace Prize in 1953 for his contribution to the recovery of the European economies.

Marshall Islands Island group in the Central Pacific consisting of two island chains of coral atolls and islets stretching across 400,000 square miles of ocean, and including two groups of atolls that, by late 1943, had become strategically important to the US Central Pacific offensive (see Pacific War; Maps 10 and 11). Mille, Maloelap and Wotje in the Ratak chain, and Jaluit, Kwajalein and Eniwetok in the Ralik chain were the sites of Japanese airfields, and would supply the US Pacific fleets with good anchorages within 1,000 miles of Truk*, headquarters of the Japanese Combined Fleet. Moreover, in September 1943, Japanese Imperial GHQ had redrawn the defensive perimeters of its empire, reducing the garrisons on the Marshalls as outposts to the new line of defence. Hence a complex and skilfully planned amphibious* invasion of the Marshall Islands (code-named Operation Flintlock) envisaged smashing the outer layer of the Japanese defensive perimeter and opening the way for the 1,000-mile advance to the Marianas*, bypassing Truk, Japan's 'Gibraltar of the Pacific'.

During December 1943 and January 1944, while the large invasion force (nick-

named the 'Big Blue Fleet') massed at Pearl Harbor, the Marshalls were subjected to bombardments by planes based on the Gilbert Islands*. The assault force was split into two (the Northern Landing Force – US 4th Marines – and the Southern Landing Force – 7th Infantry Division), the first to attack Roi and Namur, islets off Kwajalein, and the second to attack Kwajalein itself, some 300 miles away. In support of Admiral Turner's 5th Amphibious Force, four fast carrier task forces of the US 5th Fleet under Admiral Spruance*, including Admiral Mitscher's* Task Force 58, were ordered to neutralize the outlying islands and be ready to meet and destroy the main Japanese fleet, should it sail from Truk. A three-day naval and air bombardment from the 5th Fleet pounded the Japanese defences before the landings began on 31 January 1944.

Undefended, the Majuor atoll was captured on the first day. Kwajalein was taken after four days of fierce fighting with the defenders who had survived the massive bombardment. On Roi and Namur, US forces ended any remaining opposition to their capture within two days. While Admiral Mitscher's Task Force broke off to strike at Truk (the attack was brought forward on the basis of the quick success of Operation Flintlock's first stage), Admiral Turner's forces invaded Eniwetok atoll after another ferocious naval bombardment. It was captured in four days by a regiment of the 27th Division.

Martin Baltimore Produced by the American Martin company to British requirements, the Baltimore was a development of the Martin Maryland* light bomber, with more powerful engines and better conditions for the crew. The RAF* used it only in the Mediterranean* theatre, where it operated as both a day and night bomber. Armament was increased in successive versions and Baltimores remained in action with some squadrons until the end of the war. Production ended in July 1944, after 1,575 had been built.

BRIEF DATA (Mk III) Type: 4-man light bomber; Engine: 2 × 1,660hp Wright Double Cyclone; Max speed: 302mph; Ceiling: 24,000'; Range: 950m; Arms: 8–10 × 0.303" mg; Bomb load: 2,000lb.

Martin Maryland The Martin 167, which first flew in February 1939, was designed as an attack bomber for the US Army*, who turned it down. Orders were, however, placed by the French government and, when France* fell in 1940, the 75 undelivered aircraft were shipped to Britain with the name Maryland. They served the RAF* as light bombers or photo-reconnaissance planes in the Mediterranean* and North Africa until late 1941. Marylands also equipped four squadrons of the South African Air Force. A further 225 Marylands were built to British orders, of which 150 were Mark II versions with two-stage supercharged engines.
BRIEF DATA (Mk II) Type: 3-man light bomber; Engine: 2 × 1,200hp Pratt and Whitney Twin Wasp; Max speed: 278mph; Ceiling: 26,000'; Range: 1,210m; Arms: 4 × 0.5" mg, 2 × 0.303" mg; Bomb load: 2,000lb.

Martin PBM Mariner Flying boat designed as a reconnaissance bomber capable of delivering a 2,000lb load. The PBM1 joined the US Navy* in 1940, but major production centred on the improved PBM3 series, introduced in 1942 with a much increased payload. Variants included 478 PBM3C and 3D combat models, which were used mostly for US coastal patrol, 32 PBM3Bs, similarly employed by RAF* Coastal Command, 50 PBM3R transports and 156 PBM3S long-range antisubmarine* versions. The final wartime PBM5, introduced in September 1944, mounted 2,100hp engines, advanced search radar* and eight 0.5-inch machineguns*.
BRIEF DATA (PBM3D) Type: 7–8-man patrol flying boat; Engine: 2 × 1,900hp Wright Cyclone; Max speed: 211mph; Ceiling: 19,800'; Range: 2,420m; Arms: 5 × 0.5" mg, 1 × 0.3" mg; Bomb load: 8,000lb.

Maryland, USS US Navy* battleship and class, which also included the *Colorado* and the *West Virginia*. Commissioned in 1921–3 they were identical to the earlier *Tennessee** Class in all but main armament, which was enlarged to match that of the British *Queen Elizabeth** Class, and they were not modernized before the start of the Pacific War*.

Along with the *West Virginia*, the *Maryland* was at Pearl Harbor on 7 December 1941. Unlike her sister, she was only slightly damaged and so remained largely unaltered throughout the war, except for standard improvements in anti-aircraft* defence and radar*. After a spell on escort and patrol work, she began an arduous career as an offshore bombardment and gunfire support vessel at the Gilbert Islands* in late 1943. Although torpedoed at Saipan in June 1944, and extensively damaged by Kamikaze* attack at Leyte* that November, she survived the war and was decommissioned in 1946.

The *Colorado* was being overhauled in Washington at the time of Pearl Harbor, and later performed a bombardment role in the Pacific offensives with only standard modifications. The *West Virginia* was bombed, torpedoed and sunk in Battleship Row, but was refloated and extensively rebuilt along the lines of the two *Tennessee* Class units. She was not recommissioned until September 1944, but took part (with the *Maryland* and other old battleships) in the night action in the Surigao Strait* the following month. Like her sisters, she then concentrated on shore bombardment until the end of the war.
BRIEF DATA (*Maryland*, 1941) Displacement: 31,500 tons; Dimensions: o/a lgth – 624', b – 97' 6"; Speed: 21 knots; Armament: 8 × 16" gun (4 × 2), 12 × 5" gun, 8 × 5" AA gun, 4 × 6pdr AA gun, 3 aircraft.

Masaryk, Jan Garrigue (1886–1948) Important member of the Czech government-in-exile, a colleague of Eduard Beneš* and highly skilled diplomatist, his work in representing the interests of occupied countries in Europe, and Czechoslovakia* in particular, earned him much respect. Masaryk died in mysterious circumstances on 10 March 1948. It has been suggested that he was murdered by agents of the post-war communist Czech state, who regarded his anti-communist stance as unacceptable.

Maschinen Pistole 38 Often erroneously called the Schmeisser, the MP38 was a 9mm submachine-gun manufactured by 'Erma-Werke' of Erfurt and adopted by the German Army in 1938. An excellent weapon, it saw ubiquitous service with German ground forces until replaced by the MP40, a cheaper, mass-produced version of which over one million were issued after 1940. See also Submachine-gun.

Massachusetts, USS See South Dakota, USS.

Matador Code-name for a British contingency plan to forestall land attacks by Japanese forces into Malaya* by a pre-emptive invasion of Thailand* and the seizure of Singora. Although the invasion began with landings at Kota Bharu, south of Singora, Matador was not authorized by the British Cabinet until it was too late to pre-empt the main Japanese landings at Singora and Patani.

Matilda I Aptly named after a contemporary cartoon duck, the Matilda I was a British tank* firmly rooted in the military concepts of 1919. Designed to support infantry at walking pace, armed with only one machine-gun and built as cheaply as possible, it was almost completely useless in the context of mobile armoured warfare. Between 1938 and August 1940, 139 examples were delivered to the British Army*. They were used by the 1st Tank Brigade in France*, where only the strength of their frontal armour proved adequate. All the Matilda Is in France were lost,

and after Dunkirk* surviving models were relegated to training duties.
BRIEF DATA (Mk I) Type: 2-man light infantry tank; Engine: 70hp petrol; Max speed: 8mph; Range: 80m; Arms: 1 × 0.303" (later 0.5") mg; Armour: max 60mm.

Matilda II The limitations of the Matilda I* were readily appreciated by the British War Office and while it was still in the prototype stage a radically improved new version was ordered. The Matilda II was ready in April 1938. It was heavily armoured and carried a shell-firing gun, but was a difficult machine to mass-produce, particularly in view of Britain's limited capacity to build large castings. Only two were in service by September 1939.

A good tank* by the standards of the day, the Matilda II nevertheless suffered from the common contemporary defects of poor vision and limited mobility. First used in strength during the retreat to Dunkirk* in 1940, the Matilda was a success in the campaign for Egypt* later that year, where it proved virtually immune to any Italian anti-tank weapon. Its armour was less effective against German anti-tank* artillery in the Desert War* during 1941–2, and the powerful 88mm* gun left the Matilda outclassed. It was increasingly replaced by American Grants* and Shermans*, and fought its last action as a battle tank in June 1942 at the first battle of El Alamein*.

Subsequently, Matildas performed in a number of support roles and formed the basis for various special-purpose vehicles*. It was particularly developed as such by the Australian Army (see Australian Forces) who used the tank in the Pacific War*. Other Matildas went to Russia, where their armour was more admired than their weaponry. Production continued until August 1943, and 2,987 were built. A few remained in service, though not as gun-carrying tanks, until the end of the war.
BRIEF DATA (Mk II) Type: 4-man infantry tank; Engine: 2 × 87hp diesel; Max speed: 15mph; Range: 160m; Arms: 1 ×

2pdr gun, $1 \times 0.303''$ mg; Armour: max 78mm.

Matsuoka, Yosuke (1880–1946) Japanese Foreign Minister 1940–1 under Konoe*, Matsuoka had been educated in the United States, graduating from Oregon University in 1900. Following 20 years as a diplomat in China, the US and Europe, during which time he became increasingly associated with the conservative bureaucrats, the *Seiyukai*, and with senior members of the Army and Navy, he became director, vice-president and then president of the South Manchurian Railway Company which was responsible for the economic development of Manchuria*. He was Japan's delegate to the League of Nations in 1933, and his walkout over its refusal to recognize Manchukuo* was followed by Japan's withdrawal from the League.

Described as a 'firebrand nationalist', Matsuoka was chosen as Foreign Minister, along with General Hideki Tojo* who became War Minister, to aid Premier Konoe in his national crusade for a 'New Order'* in East Asia. As Foreign Minister, Matsuoka was responsible for committing Japan to the Tripartite Pact* with Germany and Italy and the neutrality pact with Russia. After the German invasion of Russia in June 1941, Matsuoka advocated war against Russia and continued to oppose negotiations with the US. Alienated from colleagues by his attitudes and ambitions, Matsuoka was left out of the cabinet when Konoe resigned to form a new government. Arrested after the war as a 'Class A' war criminal, Matsuoka died before the completion of the main war crimes trial in Tokyo.

Maxim Gun Water-cooled heavy machine-gun, widely used in WW1 but superseded in most armies by 1939. The exception was the Red Army*, which used a modified – and even more cumbersome – version of their 'Model 1910'. Its replacement, the Goryunov SG43, was developed in 1940, but the Maxim remained in front-line ser-

vice until late in the war. See also Machine-guns.

Médenine See Tunisia, Campaign in.

Mediterranean Sea Before 1939, the Mediterranean Sea was an important sphere of interest for three major naval powers. Italy and France both had Mediterranean coastlines to protect and colonial bases to supply. France also had extensive interests in the Middle East, potentially threatening the passage of Italian oil imports through the Eastern Mediterranean. A fierce naval arms race had developed between the two, while Great Britain (an ally of France) maintained its strongest overseas fleet at bases in Alexandria*, Gibraltar* and Malta* for the protection of its rich Middle and Far Eastern trade, which passed through the Suez Canal.

After Italy's declaration of war and the fall of France* in June 1940, a straight fight developed for control of the Mediterranean between the Italian Navy* and the Royal Navy* with the odds heavily in Italy's favour. Both sides sought to support their land forces in the campaigns in Egypt* and East Africa*, but the Royal Navy's Mediterranean Fleet was outnumbered by faster and more modern Italian warships. With reinforcements unlikely in view of Britain's desperate home position, its commander, Admiral Cunningham*, was also required to provide regular relief to his central Mediterranean toehold in Malta* and to ensure that the powerful French Navy* stayed out of Axis* hands.

His aggressive response to these problems brought gratifying results. The French ships were either neutralized or attacked in their colonial ports (see Mers-el-Kébir), and Cunningham made full use of his few advantages – accurate intelligence, radar*, superior night-fighting techniques and aircraft carriers – to establish a tactical dominance over the Italian surface fleet. Serious losses were inflicted on the Italian Navy at Taranto* in November 1940, and Cape Matapan* the following March. With Italian land forces on the defensive in Africa and Greece*, Cunningham's success was undermined by the entry of Germany into the theatre, and particularly by the arrival of the Luftwaffe* early in 1941.

Unlike the Atlantic* and Pacific* Oceans, the Mediterranean was entirely within the range of land-based air cover. The stationing of Fliegerkorps X (the Luftwaffe's specialist anti-shipping group) on Sicily* from January 1941 greatly increased the pressure on Malta and on Allied shipping in general. The Luftwaffe announced itself by badly damaging the modern aircraft carrier *Illustrious* and then took a heavy toll of British warships during operations off Crete* in May. Although Cunningham retained an undoubted advantage over the Italians, who were reluctant to risk their surface units in action, the success of the Afrika Korps* in the early campaigns of the Desert War* and British involvement in the defence of Greece extended Royal Naval resources still further. Maritime operations in the theatre settled into a costly convoy* war, increasingly dominated by the Luftwaffe as the RAF* lost control of forward bases in North Africa.

The British now relied almost solely on submarines to disrupt central Mediterranean supply routes to Axis forces in Africa. Clear, shallow waters and the omnipresent threat of aircraft made life difficult for submarines in the Mediterranean. Only the smallest coastal boats could operate effectively, and the submarine fleets of both sides suffered heavy losses for very limited returns. Nevertheless British boats achieved valuable results in the summer and autumn of 1941, sinking an important proportion of Rommel's* supply ships. When U-boats reached the Mediterranean in the latter part of the year, they too suffered losses and found conditions difficult for their Atlantic boats. They nevertheless sank three major British warships before the year ended, and with two battleships succumbing to Italian 'human torpedoes'* at Alexandria, the Royal Navy's ability to protect convoys to Africa

and Malta had been critically weakened by early 1942.

The situation in Malta deteriorated with increased Luftwaffe activity in 1942, and the island's submarine flotilla was withdrawn in March. Allied convoy traffic suffered appalling losses in the first half of the year, while supplies poured through to Rommel, whose latest offensive threatened Alexandria. The proposed German invasion of Malta didn't take place at the time of the island's greatest weakness in April. Instead Luftwaffe strength was increasingly concentrated on the Desert War. Rommel's advance was halted at El Alamein* in July, and Malta's supplies were partly replenished by the giant Pedestal* convoy of August.

The decisive British victory at El Alamein in October, quickly followed by the Allied Torch* landings in Northwest Africa, transformed the war in the Mediterranean. Submarines returned to Malta and greatly increased Anglo-American air and surface forces devastated Axis convoys with the help of consistently accurate intelligence from the Ultra* decoding unit in England. On land Axis forces retreated into northern Tunisia*, delivering forward air bases into Allied hands. Axis forces in Tunisia surrendered in May 1943, by which time Allied naval superiority had been re-established in the theatre. Aggressive air and surface patrols were able to ensure that no seaborne evacuations of the defeated forces were possible.

Allied supplies to the Far East could now be routed through the Suez Canal (avoiding the long detour round the Cape of Good Hope) and goods could be shipped to the Soviet Union via Persia*. U-boats remained in the area but their numbers dwindled as the Mediterranean became the medium for the Allied amphibious* invasions of southern Europe, beginning with the landings on Sicily* in July. Surface warships in the theatre were now exclusively used for coastal bombardments, and with the surrender of the Italian Fleet at Malta in September, only the Luftwaffe remained to challenge Allied operations in waters that had been among the most dangerous in the world for three years. See also French Navy; Italian Navy.

Medjez el Bab See Tunisia.

Meiktila Important town and railway junction in central Burma*, it was captured by Japanese troops during their conquest of Burma in 1942 and subsequently retaken by troops of the British 17th Indian Division on 3 March 1945. The Japanese promptly launched a series of counterattacks but fell back at the end of the month as part of a general withdrawal of Japanese forces in the area. See Maps 24 and 25.

Mekhlis, Political General Lev (1889–1953) Mekhlis acted as direct liaison between Stalin and his front-line commanders, investigating military disasters (such as that in the Ukraine* in 1941 and the Crimea* in 1941–2) and sitting on the military councils of Front* commanders. He was responsible for the dismissal of General Tolbukhin* from the Crimea, and of General Petrov* from the Ukrainian Front.

Mengele, Joseph (1911–79?) Notorious Auschwitz* doctor in charge of 'racial experiments' from 1943 to 1945, he escaped to South America after the war and has since been one of the most hunted of war criminals. Confessions by friends and family during 1985 led to an investigation of a man drowned in Brazil in 1979: his remains were judged to be those of Mengele.

Menzies, Sir Robert Gordon (1894–1978) Australian statesman who became Prime Minister in April 1939, after winning the leadership of the liberal United Australia Party. Over the next two years he headed a minority government, devoting his energies to preparing for war, establishing new ministries and introducing conscription. Menzies was actively concerned to support British conduct of the war – troops and

warships were sent to the Middle East, food and raw materials went to Britain. Other members of his cabinet expressed a popular view in doubting Britain's guarantees of Far Eastern security. Menzies' long visit to London from January to June 1941 encouraged the view at home that he was in thrall to Churchill. Faced by revolt in his cabinet, Menzies resigned as Prime Minister in August 1941, and his party fell from power on 6 October. The Labour party under Curtin* then governed Australia for the rest of the war, but Menzies returned to the premiership from 1949 until his retirement in 1966.

Merchant Aircraft Carrier (MAC) See Escort Carriers.

Meretskov, Marshal Kiril A. Soviet Chief of the General Staff at the outbreak of war in 1939, having commanded the 7th Army for the breakthrough of the Mannerheim Line in the Russo-Finnish War*. Meretskov was soon replaced as overall commander by General Zhukov* (January 1941). Meretskov subsequently commanded various Russian Fronts* and was for a time Deputy Commander in Chief of the Russian Western Front, before being transferred to the Far East to command the Far Eastern Front in the offensive against the Kwantung* Army in August 1945. He was awarded the Order of Victory, the most lavish and prestigious honour given to senior Soviet commanders.

Merrill, Major General Frank D. (1903–55) Commander of the US 5307th Composite Unit, better known as Merrill's Marauders, from January 1944. The unit was composed of volunteers in the doctrines of British Brigadier Orde Wingate*, who pioneered the use of long-range penetration tactics in Ethiopia and with Chindit* units in Burma*. Posted to Rangoon* at the outbreak of the Pacific War*, Merrill was retained by Chinese forces commander US General Stilwell* and fought under him with the Marauders during the drive to recapture northern Burma between March and August 1944, playing an important part in operations at Myitkyina. After a short period in hospital due to illness in mid-1944, Merrill returned to become deputy US Commander of the Burma–India theatre and later Chief of Staff of the US 10th and 6th Armies.

Mersa Matruh Small Egyptian port about 120 miles east of the Libyan frontier (see Map 7). Mersa Matruh was fortified and used as a forward base by the British Desert Army in 1940. In June 1942 elements of the British 8th Army made a stand at Mersa Matruh against the numerically inferior Axis forces pursuing them across Egypt after the battle at Gazala*. An encircling move by one depleted panzer division produced a retreat to the area around El Alamein*, and Rommel* took Mersa Matruh on 27 June, capturing 6,000 prisoners.

Mers-el-Kébir French naval base on the coast of Morocco near Oran* into which the main squadrons of the French Navy* were crowded after the Franco-German armistice of June 1940. The British government was prepared to go to great lengths to avoid the dread prospect of French units falling into Hitler's hands. On the morning of 3 July 1940, French ships in British ports were forcibly confiscated, and in the afternoon Operation Catapult was launched against Mers-el-Kébir. The Royal Navy's* newly convened Force H*, under Sir James Somerville*, appeared off the coast and presented Vice Admiral Gensoul in command of French forces with an ultimatum to surrender, scuttle or be attacked. After hours of negotiation, during which Somerville more than once signalled the Admiralty in the hope of changed orders, British capital ships opened fire at 5.40 p.m., sinking one battleship and seriously damaging two more. Not at battle readiness, the French ships were easy targets and 1,147 sailors were killed by the attack.

Early in the morning of 6 July, aircraft from the *Ark Royal** delivered a further attack on Mers-el-Kébir, torpedoeing the battleship *Dunkerque** (which had already been damaged) and strafing survivors, killing 150 more men. The next day the French squadron at Alexandria* surrendered its fuel and ammunition to Royal Navy forces. These incidents contributed to the embitterment of Anglo-French relations evident during the Allied Torch* campaign in Northwest Africa more than two years later.

Messe, General Giovanni (1883–1968) One of the most experienced and successful of the senior Italian commanders, Messe commanded Axis* troops in the Western Desert. A veteran of the fighting in Libya (1911), Ethiopia (1935–6) and Albania (1939), Messe took part in the disastrous invasion of Greece* before being sent to the Eastern Front* in command of the Italian Expeditionary Force at the start of the German invasion of Russia in June 1941. In early 1943, when Rommel's* army was reorganized, Messe returned to Africa as C-in-C of the Italian 1st Army in Tunisia*. Messe surrendered in May 1943, along with over 250,000 troops. He subsequently returned to Italy as Chief of Staff under Marshal Badoglio's government but was replaced in 1945.

Messerschmitt, Professor Willy Emil (1898–1978) German aircraft manufacturer and designer of the Luftwaffe's most enduringly successful fighter – the Bf109*. Later models of the aircraft and Messerschmitt's subsequent designs were given the prefix ME, after he bought out the Bavarian Aircraft Works (Bayerische Flugzeugwerke) and took personal control of the company.

Hitler thought highly of Messerschmitt as did Udet*, the Luftwaffe's Director of Armaments from 1939–41, and the designer was given preferential treatment over major contracts. However, the professor had difficulty harnessing his creative ambitions to the exigencies of war production, and his later projects failed to repeat the success of the 109, which remained in production throughout the war. Udet's successor, Field Marshal Milch*, detested Messerschmitt who nevertheless retained the confidence of the Führer. This contributed to the delay of the important ME262* jet fighter programme and prolonged the life of white elephants like the ME210*. See Luftwaffe.

Messerschmitt Bf109 The Bf109 was built in greater numbers than any other German aircraft and ranks as one of the great fighters of WW2, serving the Luftwaffe* throughout the conflict on all fronts. Flown as a prototype in September 1935, the plane overcame competition and political opposition to win a major production order, and joined units as the Bf109B in early 1937. By September 1939, 1,000 were available to the Luftwaffe, 80 per cent of them 109E models, first introduced in the previous spring. They triumphed easily in Poland*, where only about 200 fighters were used, and enjoyed similar success during the German Western Offensive* of 1940.

In the Battle of Britain*, re-engined 109E3s met their first serious challenge from RAF* Fighter Command. The hitherto undisputed master of the skies proved superior to the British Hawker Hurricanes* and a good match for the more modern Supermarine Spitfires*, outperforming the latter below 23,000ft and in the dive. Its greatest combat disadvantage was its very short operational radius, although a congenitally weak undercarriage also caused many accidents.

The Bf109E Emil series was manufactured in a multitude of subvariants to a pattern repeated in later types. Often these involved minor changes of armament, but the E1/b and E4/b were fighter-bombers, armed with up to 550lb of ordnance, and the E4/n was fitted with a 1,200hp engine. The E5 and E6 were reconnaissance models, and the E/*trop* was given sand filters for Desert War* operations. Long-range (E7), nitrous-oxgyen boosted (E7-2) and armoured ground-support (E7/u2) versions

were also built, with engine power being further increased for the E8 model.

The Bf109F – Friedrich – series was first delivered in the spring of 1941 and entered service on the Channel Coast, re-establishing the plane's combat viability against the improved Spitfire V. With a redesigned fuselage, a new propeller and the 1,300hp engine of the E8, Friedrich had largely supplanted Emil in time for the invasion of Russia (see Eastern Front), and its pilots racked up huge scores early in the campaign. Although over 2,000 Bf109Fs of various types saw service on all fronts, they were phased out in favour of the Bf109G (Gustav) by the end of 1942.

The Gustav had first entered service in May, and its major production model, the G6 was designed to accept a variety of field-conversion weapons packs. Although superb at altitude, the plane's performance suffered from increased weight and drag, an indication that development of the basic design had reached saturation point. Increasingly used to defend Germany against American daylight bombers, the Gustav was underarmed for the task. The use of under-wing rockets* against USAAF* B-17s*, while obviating the need for dangerous head-on cannon attacks, rendered it too slow to cope with the arrival of long range P-51* escort fighters early in 1944.

Production output of the Bf109G series, which appeared in as many variations as its predecessors, was enormous. In 1943 6,418 were built, and 14,212 in 1944, but shortages of pilots and spares left front-line strength hardly altered. From January 1945, the Bf109K was produced alongside the later G-types in an attempt to rationalize the costly proliferation of subtypes into a universal production model. In the hands of an experienced pilot (which generally was rare), this final version could match the Allied Hawker Tempest* and P47* fighters. When the war ended only 754 Bf109Ks had been completed out of a total wartime production of 30,480 Bf109s.
BRIEF DATA (Bf109G6) Type: single-seat

fighter; Engine: 1 × 1,475hp Daimler-Benz; Max speed: 387mph; Ceiling: 38,500'; Range: 450m; Arms: 3 × 20mm cannon, 2 × 13mm mg.

Messerschmitt Bf110 Sleek, twin-finned German aircraft, it was conceived as a heavy escort fighter for a strategic bomber force that was never built. It was first produced in 1938, and about 200 Bf110Cs were in service with the Luftwaffe* in the vague role of Zerstörer (destroyer) in 1939. They achieved some successes against disorganized opposition over Poland* and France*, but were severely mauled by faster British fighters when operating as bomber escorts in the Battle of Britain*. The later 110D, E and F series were mostly armed and employed as ground-attack fighter-bombers. They performed disappointingly, although they became an important part of Germany's emerging night fighter force, first deployed in the summer of 1940.

The failure of the Messerschmitt Me210* project in 1942 lent fresh impetus to production of the ageing Zerstörer, and the much improved and re-engined 110G series began to equip the Luftwaffe at the end of the year. The 110H, with a strengthened fuselage and many detail changes, was built simultaneously and both types concentrated on night work, performing very successfully against RAF* bombers as German tactics and radar* technology were improved. In the second half of 1943, the introduction of upward-firing Schräge Musik* guns increased their effectiveness still further, and deliveries continued until January 1945. Out of a total of 5,762 Bf110s produced, 3,105 were built in 1943 and 1944.

BRIEF DATA (Bf110G4) Type: 3-man night fighter; Engine: 2 × 1,475hp Daimler-Benz; Max speed: 342mph; Ceiling: 26,000'; Range: 1,305m (with drop-tanks); Arms: 2 × 30mm cannon, 2 × 20mm cannon, 2 × 7.9mm mg.

Messerschmitt Me163 Comet (Komet)
Originally designed as a glider, the Luft-waffe's small, tail-less Me163 became the only purely rocket*-powered interceptor to see action in WW2. It first flew in 1941 and, drastically remodelled for combat purposes, the Me163B began to equip two élite home defence units in the summer of 1944, attacking American B-17s* for the first time on 14 August. Taking off into a dramatic climb and jettisoning its undercarriage, the Komet had just enough fuel for one, or at most two passes at its targets, before gliding back to base and landing on its under-fuselage skid at about 135mph. The considerable dangers inherent in this *modus operandi* were greatly exacerbated by the devastatingly explosive instability of the plane's C-Stoff rocket fuel, which accounted for the complete and sudden obliteration of a number of planes and pilots. About 300 Me163s were delivered, but they only ever equipped one fully operational fighter group and destroyed a meagre total of 14 Allied aircraft.

BRIEF DATA (Me163B) Type: single-seat interceptor; Engine: 1 × 3,750lb thrust Walter rocket; Max speed: 596mph; Ceiling: 39,500'; Range: 8 minutes; Arms: 2 × 30mm cannon, 24 rockets.

Messerschmitt Me210 (and Me410) The Me210 was planned as the successor to the Messerschmitt Bf110* heavy fighter as early as 1937, and 1,000 models were ordered from the drawing board by the Luftwaffe*. This turned out to be a very costly error because the plane never overcame catastrophic aerodynamic problems and caused an epidemic of fatal accidents when it was pressed into service in late 1941. At great cost to the German war effort the programme was scrapped in April 1942, after only 200 machines had been built, although a further 152 were later finished off and delivered.

Out of the wreckage of Me210 came the Me410 Hornisse (Hornet), which was preferred for production to a more radical Me310 project favoured by Professor Messerschmitt*. Similar in appearance to its predecessor, but a far superior aircraft free from any aerodynamic caprice, the Me410A reached front-line units in May 1943. It saw action in variously armed light bomber, heavy interceptor, anti-shipping and reconnaissance versions. Although never a match for the best Allied fighters in daylight operations, it proved an effective night bomber over England and home defence night fighter. Production stopped in 1944 after 1,121 Me410s had been completed (108 of them in Hungary), and most surviving examples saw out the war as reconnaissance aircraft.

BRIEF DATA (Me210A1) Type: 2-man heavy fighter; Engine: 2 × 1,395hp Daimler-Benz; Max speed: 385mph; Ceiling: 22,695'; Range: 1,491m; Arms: 2 × 20mm cannon, 2 × 13mm mg, 2 × 7.9mm mg.

Messerschmitt Me262 The Me262A1 reached the Luftwaffe* in April 1944, and was the world's first operational jet fighter, ahead of anything the Allies could then produce. Yet its development had been slow and accorded a relatively low priority by the German High Command. An airframe had been ready for three years, but turbojets were not successfully incorporated until November 1943. At this point Hitler had made clear his firm intention to use the plane as a bomber. His angry insistence on the matter seriously exacerbated production delays while the Me262A2 – with underwing bomb-racks – was perfected. It also meant that the plane's performance strengths were wasted in tactical bombing operations. Only in the last months of the war were Me262s primarily used as interceptors, and even then they were targeted at bombers, which they had to slow down to hit at the expense of their advantage over other fighters. Although 1,433 machines were built, only about 220 were ever used operationally, and of these over 120 were shot down by Allied fighters.

BRIEF DATA (Me262A1a) Type: single-seat fighter; Engine: 2 × 1,980lb Junkers Jumo turbojet; Max speed: 540mph;

Ceiling 37,565'; Range: 652m; Arms: 4 × 30mm cannon, 24 × 5cm rocket*.

Messerschmitt Me321 (and Me323) The giant among German transport gliders, for which the extraordinary Heinkel He111Z* composite aircraft was developed as a tug. Late in 1941, the Me323 version took to the air powered by six engines, and served as a transport, ferrying men and supplies to North Africa. Capable of lifting 130 troops or equivalent freight, the plane was an easy target and, although about 200 (powered or otherwise) were produced, the Luftwaffe* soon recognized the folly of putting so many eggs into such a cumbersome basket.

BRIEF DATA (Me323E) Type: 5–7-man heavy transport; Engine: 6 × 990hp Gnome-Rhône; Max speed: 136mph; Range: 685m; Arms: 5 × 13mm mg.

Messervy, Major General Frank (1893–1974) British Army commander who served in East Africa*, North Africa* and Burma*, where he ended the war in command of 4th Corps.

Messina Port city on the northeast coast of Sicily*, it was the key objective of the Allied Sicilian campaign, code-named Husky. Directly opposite the toe of Italy, across the Straits of Messina, the port was the escape route for Axis* forces withdrawing in the face of the Allied advance. Despite the impressive efforts of General Patton's* 7th Army to catch them up, advancing across the island from the west, most Axis troops had been evacuated, along with a good proportion of their equipment and vehicles, before a combat team of the US 3rd Division entered Messina on 17 August.

Metaxas, General Joannes (1871–1941) Greek military and political leader. An extreme royalist, General Metaxas was appointed Prime Minister by King George II* in 1936 and soon turned his regime into a dictatorship. Although he displayed pro-German sympathies, he successfully united the country against the Italian invasion of 1940. His sudden death on 29 January 1941 removed a formidable obstacle to Churchill's plans to send a British force to Greece. See Greece, Italian invasion of.

Mexico Mexico declared war on the Axis on 30 May 1942, and was one of only two Latin American countries to commit fighting forces to the conflict (the other was Brazil*). From February 1945, a squadron of the Mexican Air Force saw service in the Far East, losing eight men in operations over the Philippines* and Formosa*. Mexican involvement in the war led to a great increase in US influence over the economy.

Michael I, King of Rumania (1921–) The last King of Rumania* and the son of King Carol II, who was forced to abdicate on 6 September 1940. Prince Michael then became regent, as he had been before his father took the throne in 1930, but was obliged to toe the predominant pro-German line. On 23 August 1944, with German seizure of power a possibility and Russian invasion a reality, he overthrew right-wing premier Antonescu* with the help of loyal generals. Rumania immediately sued for peace with the Allies and her forces changed sides. In the confusion that followed, the Red Army swept across the country to threaten Yugoslavia, Bulgaria and Hungary. The official armistice was signed in Moscow on 12 September. After the war, the Russians helped communists to take power in Rumania. King Michael abdicated on 30 December 1947 to make way for a People's Republic. See Balkans, The, Russian campaign in.

Midget Submarines Although both Germany and Japan used miniature submarines during WW2, the Italian and British navies enjoyed most success with the type. In September 1941, the Italians sank three British cargo ships at Gibraltar* with a piloted torpedo* device known as the *Maiale* (Pig). Armed with a detachable 500lb warhead and ridden by a two-man crew,

this weapon was used again to disable the Royal Navy* battleships *Queen Elizabeth* and *Valiant* on 19 December 1941, in Alexandria* harbour. After the Italian surrender in 1943 it was turned on ships of the Italian Navy* that were in German hands.

In 1942, the British developed a human torpedo – the Chariot – modelled on the *Maiale*, but more was achieved with the X-Craft. This was a true midget submarine with a four-man crew, able to stay at sea for several days. Mines* or detachable explosives were fitted to the outside of the hull and modified craft were produced for training and Pacific operations. X-Craft crippled the German battleship *Tirpitz* in 1943 and sank the Italian heavy cruiser *Bolzano* the following February. In the Pacific they blew up the Japanese Navy* heavy cruiser *Takao* at Singapore in July 1945.

After the attack on the *Tirpitz* the German Navy began organizing its own K-Force for small scale underwater operations. The *Niger*, which saw action at Anzio* and Normandy* in 1944, was in fact a one-man surface craft with an underslung torpedo, but the next development, the *Biber*, was a submarine armed with torpedoes. These operated off the coast of northern France and the Netherlands in 1944–5, and were supplemented by the *Seehund* in the last months of the war. Strongly built with direct electric propulsion and two torpedoes, these achieved some success against Allied cargo shipping and were also used to supply beleaguered coastal garrisons. Germany also built more than 400 *Molch* one-man submarines, but they achieved little.

The Japanese used their A-type midget submarines, developed in the mid-1930s, at Pearl Harbor* (where all five used were sunk) and in Sydney harbour early in the Pacific War*. These were short-range, electric-powered, two-man boats, 80ft long and with two 18-inch torpedoes. One of them damaged the British battleship *Ramillies* at Madagascar* in 1942. The 3-man C-Type, introduced after 1943, had a greater operational range, but the 5-man D-Type was far more seaworthy than either of its predecessors and could be easily adapted for suicide missions if torpedoes were unavailable. Known as the *Koryu*, this saw some action in the defence of the Philippines* and Okinawa*. Along with the smaller *Kairyu*, a development of the original A-Type, the *Koryu* was intended for mass-production, but was heavily disrupted by USAAF* bombing. The Japanese Navy also produced five types of one-man human torpedo (see Kaiten).

Midway, The Battle of, 3–6 June 1942 A key naval battle between Admiral Chester Nimitz's* Pacific Fleet and Admiral Isoruku Yamamoto's* Combined Fleet, the US Navy's* victory at Midway successfully challenged Japanese dominance in the Pacific for the first time (see Map 13). Despite the strategic and hard-won victory by the US Fleet at the Battle of the Coral Sea* in early May that had halted the Japanese offensive (Operation Mo) aimed at Port Moresby*, New Guinea* (and hence at Australia), the strategic initiative in the Pacific remained with Japan. Under the direction of Yamamoto, a new and complex plan was devised, splitting the Combined Fleet into eight separate task groups, to make a series of attacks centred on the atoll of Midway, 1,000 miles west of Pearl Harbor*. Though the strategic value of Midway for Japan was limited to an early warning outpost at this stage, Yamamoto believed that the threat to Midway would draw Admiral Nimitz's fleet out from Pearl Harbor, for a decisive sea battle which the Combined Fleet had all the resources to win.

The planning of the Japanese operation was highly skilful. It comprised two expeditionary forces destined for a diversionary attack on the Aleutian Islands*, the Midway occupation force with close cruiser and destroyer support, Vice Admiral Nagumo's* Carrier Striking Force, with carriers *Akagi*, *Kaga*, *Hiryu* and *Soryu*, Vice Admiral Kondo's* Main Support Force,

and finally Admiral Yamamoto's own force of three battleships, including the huge 64,000-ton battleship *Yamato*. Yamamoto did not know, however, that Admiral Nimitz had vital foreknowledge of the planned attack through the intercepts provided by Magic* intelligence. By the time the 165-ship Japanese force sailed from Japan and the Marianas*, Admiral Nimitz had been able to assemble two task forces under Rear Admiral Fletcher* (comprising the carrier *Yorktown*, two cruisers and six destroyers) and Rear Admiral Spruance* (comprising the carriers *Enterprise* and *Hornet*, six cruisers and nine destroyers) to rendezvous north of Midway and await the Japanese attack.

During the night of 3 June, Nagumo's Carrier Force approached Midway from the northwest, unaware of the proximity of Fletcher's Task Force and sent off a strike force of over 100 carrier aircraft for the first attack on Midway. Marine fighters intercepted the force but were heavily outnumbered, and the strike caused extensive damage. A second mission was called for by Nagumo's strike commander and the planes that Nagumo had held in reserve against the possibility of an appearance by a US naval force began to be rearmed with bombs for a second strike. While the laborious process of rearming the aircraft continued, the first Japanese report of a sighting of American ships coincided with the return of the first strike aircraft from Midway. While Nagumo's crews were racing to rearm and refuel the returning aircraft, the first carrier planes from Spruance's Task Force 16 took off to attack them. Although the American strike force of fighters, dive-bombers and torpedo* planes delivered their attack disjointedly, and suffered many losses, it forced Nagumo to manoeuvre to evade torpedoes, delaying the launch of his own air strike until the arrival of dive-bomber squadrons from the *Yorktown* and *Enterprise* which scored immediate hits on *Akagi*, *Soryu* and *Kaga*. The *Hiryu*, under Rear Admiral Yamaguchi, sent out all its available aircraft for a strike on the *York-*

town. Though the American carrier recovered from the first attack, a second strike from the *Hiryu* forced her captain to order the evacuation of the ship. At almost the same moment, dive-bombers from *Enterprise* found *Hiryu*, crippling her and setting her ablaze. She was scuttled the following day. Now without carriers or air support and faced with the intelligence he received during the night of 4–5 June on the remaining strength of the American carrier forces, Yamamoto was forced to retire to safety.

The consequences of the Japanese Navy's* defeat at Midway were deeply felt. Apart from the loss of four of her fleet carriers, Japan had also sacrificed many of her aircraft and her most experienced aircrews as well as the vital strategic initiative. For the American Pacific fleet commanders, a much desired victory was accompanied by valuable lessons on naval air warfare and an emphatic confirmation of the power of the carrier strike force. It also alerted them to the inadequacy of US carrier aircraft (e.g. Douglas Devastator*), which were quickly replaced by superior types. The startling American victory at Midway, made ultimately possible by Magic, was the precursor to the opening of the first American offensive in the Pacific, launched against Guadalcanal* on 12 August 1942. See also Nimitz, Admiral Chester; Japanese Air Forces.

Mihajlovic, General Draza (1893–1946) Yugoslav soldier and leader of the Serbian Chetnik resistance group, which he founded with other officers after the German invasion of April 1941 (see Balkans, German invasion of). With the support of King Peter II's exiled government in London, General Mihajlovic received aid from both Britain and Russia. Strongly royalist and a Serbian nationalist, his aims were incompatible with those of the communist partisans, the other important resistance movement in Yugoslavia, and by November 1941 the two groups were in open conflict. Mihajlovic, anxious to minimize civilian casualties, soon began

co-operating with German and Italian forces against the mutual communist foe, and the partisans did most of the fighting against Axis forces. Mihajlovic nevertheless remained in contact with London, and it was not until mid-1943 that the collaborative leanings of the Chetniks became clear to the British. In November of that year he was warned to stop collaborating and by May 1944 all British missions in Chetnik territory had been recalled. When partisan leader Tito* signed an agreement with Subusic (King Peter's Prime Minister) in June 1944, Mihajlovic was removed from his post as War Minister in the exiled government. By September he had been forced to quit his headquarters in Ravna Gora. After the defeat of Axis forces in Yugoslavia, General Mihajlovic remained hidden in the hills (see Balkans, Russian Campaign in). He was captured on 13 March 1946, tried as a collaborator and executed in July.

Mikolajczyk, Stanislaw (1901–67) Deputy Premier of the Polish government-in-exile* and its Premier from April 1943, when he succeeded General Sikorski*. An able and committed defender of Polish interests, Mikolajczyk was involved in the quarrels with the Soviet Union and the Allies over the post-war boundaries of Poland* and the Katyn* massacre, resigning his post in November 1944 in protest against the Allies' lack of support of Polish Free forces after the disastrous battle for Warsaw* (August –October 1944). Mikolajczyk returned to Poland as Deputy Prime Minister in 1945, one of the few members of the exiled government chosen to join the communist-dominated coalition, the Lublin Committee*. He was purged and forced into exile two years later.

Mikoyan MIG-1 (and MIG-3) Soviet wood-and-metal monoplane which entered production as the MIG-1 in September 1940, less than six months after its prototype flight. Although unsuited for heavy armament and apt to swing dramatically on take-off or landing, it was a competent aircraft and 2,100 are believed to have been built. It was replaced in production by the long-range, aerodynamically improved MIG-3 in about May 1941. Several thousand of these were delivered, but they were never the equal of Luftwaffe* fighters in combat and were relegated to army support duties during 1942. A few, further refined MIG-5s were used by the Red Air Forces*, and a high altitude MIG-7 was produced about which little is known.

BRIEF DATA (MIG-3) Type: single-seat fighter; Engine: 1 × 1,350hp Mikulin; Max speed: 398mph; Ceiling: 39,370'; Range: 776m; Arms: 1 × 12.7mm mg, 2 × 7.62mm mg (provision for rockets* or 440lb bombs).

Milch, Field Marshal Erhard (1892–1972) The prime architęct of the Luftwaffe*. After serving with both air and infantry units in WW1, Milch entered the civil aviation industry as an administrator and rose to become head of the national airline – Deutsche Luft Hansa – in 1929. His outstanding organizational gifts allied to his personal friendship with Hermann Göring*, led to his appointment as Göring's deputy at the Ministry of Aviation in 1933. With the rank of army colonel, he took practical charge of the secret growth of an air force.

When its existence became public in 1935, Milch became Inspector General of the Luftwaffe, and effectively ran the rapidly expanding organization while Göring concentrated on his growing political empire. His efficiency in making the Luftwaffe so powerful so quickly was recognized by Hitler and led to successive promotions. After commanding the air army for the attack on Norway* (Luftflotte V) in 1940, Milch reached the rank of field marshal. During the same period, however, his relations with Göring were cooling, and the latter concentrated greater power in the hands of Udet* from 1939. Although he retained a position of influence, Milch was unable to prevent the chaos that enveloped the German aviation industry under Udet's technical directorship. Two years later, at the end of 1941, Udet's suicide put Milch back in full control of Luftwaffe production and development. He energetically set about reviving industrial output, though he was finally unable to compensate for long-term errors in design selection. Nor was he able to persuade Hitler of the importance of fighter aircraft for home defence – in particular the Me262* jet fighter was miscast as a bomber against his advice.

An ardent supporter of Adolf Hitler, Milch had a Jewish father, but was 'Aryanized' by providing documentary proof that his mother had borne children by another man. Milch suffered from open paranoia in his dealings with other leading figures and his administrative work was punctuated by a series of implacable enmities, often directed against aircraft designers. Arrested by the Allies in 1945, Milch was tried as a war criminal and sentenced to life imprisonment in 1947. He was released on parole eight years later.

Milchkuh Although only ten of these large Type XIV supply submarines* ever saw service with the German Navy*, they were of enormous importance. By providing fuel and supplies they enabled long-range U-boat raiders to remain on station for greatly extended periods. This was most strikingly illustrated in the first half of 1942, when a force of never more than 12 U-boats supplied by two Milchkuh submarines sank over 3 million tons of Allied and neutral shipping off the US Atlantic coast. Too clumsy to avoid radar* directed air attack, all of the Milchkuh were sunk in the second half of 1943, four of them before they ever reached operational areas. This contributed to the success of the RAF* Coastal Command offensive against the home routes of the U-boats in the Bay of Biscay, as boats were forced to return more often through these dangerous waters. See Atlantic, Battle of the.

BRIEF DATA (Type XIV) Displacement:

1,688 tons (surface); Dimensions: lgth – 220' 3", b – 30' 9"; Speed: 14.5 knots (6.25 submerged); Armament: 2 × 37mm AA gun, 1 × 20mm AA gun.

Milne Bay See New Guinea.

Milwaukee, USS One of ten US Navy* *Omaha* Class light cruisers commissioned 1923–8. They were obsolete by 1941, and were not considered worth major modification during WW2, generally operating in less hazardous secondary theatres. All ten vessels survived the war and nine were scrapped in 1946. The *Milwaukee*, which was sent to the Red Navy* under Lend-Lease* and served as the *Murmansk*, returned to be scrapped in 1949.

BRIEF DATA (*Milwaukee*, 1941) Displacement: 7,050 tons; Dimensions: o/a lgth – 555' 6", b – 55' 3"; Speed: 33.75 knots; Armament: 12 × 6" gun (3 × 3, 6 × 1), 8 × 3" AA gun, 2 × 3pdr AA gun, 8 × 0.5" AA gun, 6 × 21" TT, 2 aircraft.

Mines (land) Land mines were the quickest and cheapest way to set up defensive positions and restrict the movements of hostile forces. They were a feature of all land campaigns in WW2, falling broadly into anti-personnel and anti-tank categories. Both were usually laid just under the ground, anti-personnel mines consisting of a few ounces of explosive detonated by light pressure or a trip wire. Anti-vehicle mines were obviously bigger, a metal box containing 3–22lb of high explosive detonated by 300–500lb of pressure from above. Some all-purpose mines existed, but wartime versions of these lacked sufficient power to disable battle tanks*. Material shortages meant that many land mines were improvised in the field, using specially developed fuses and whatever spare explosives were available. See also Special Purpose Vehicles.

Mines (naval) The naval mine had come into its own as a weapon during WW1, and all sides were prepared for its use in 1939.

WW2 mines were of two types: contact or influence. Contact mines were usually anchored to the seabed and floated just below the surface, exploding when touched by a ship's hull. As in WW1, they were swept by a specialist warship which towed a submerged cutting wire. The released mine was usually then destroyed by small arms fire when it floated to the surface. Influence mines were planted on the seabed and were detonated either by sound waves from a passing ship's machinery (acoustic mines) or by the pull of a ship's magnetic field. Both kinds had limited spheres of influence and needed to be laid in shallow waters. They. were swept by the use of noisemaking devices or by the fitting of current-bearing electric coils to neutralize magnetic detonators (degaussing).

Late in the war the Germans developed the pressure (or oyster) mine, which responded to water pressure fluctuations caused by shipping. Although no fully effective defence was developed against these, they were restricted to very shallow waters and appeared too late to significantly affect the course of the war. Controllable mines, detonated from the shore, were also employed in defensive coastal minefields, which were laid to protect strategically important seaways.

Most modern destroyers* in WW2 were capable of minesweeping, but they were mostly deployed with the fleets of major navies. Specialist minesweepers could be small warships of under 1,000 tons (like the US *Auk* Class) or motor boats (like the German R-boats), but hundreds of freighters and trawlers were also requisitioned and fitted out for the task. Casualties among these auxiliaries were high throughout the war.

Aircraft proved the most efficient minelayers during the war, but defensive coastal minefields remained the province of surface ships. Submarines* also performed minelaying duties, but themselves often fell victim to mines laid deep beneath the surface on convoy routes. See also Atlantic, Battle of the.

Mississippi, USS See New Mexico, USS.

Missouri, USS Commissioned in June 1944 as the fourth of the *Iowa** Class units, the *Missouri* was the last battleship to enter service with the US Navy*. Although she saw action at Iwo Jima* and Okinawa*, she is best remembered as the chosen venue for the signing of the Japanese surrender in Tokyo Bay on 9 September 1945. She owed this distinction to the coincidence of her name with the birthplace of the new United States President, Harry S. Truman*. The *Missouri* remained in commission until 1954, seeing action in Korea.
BRIEF DATA See Iowa, USS (except Armament: 80 × 40mm AA gun, 49 × 20mm AA gun).

Mitscher, Vice Admiral Marc A. (1887 –1947) American pioneer naval aviator, expert on naval aviation and Commander of the Fast Carrier Task Force in the Pacific from January 1944, Mitscher commanded the aircraft carrier *Hornet** for the Doolittle* Raid (1st Special Aviation Project) and at the Battle of Midway*. He was next appointed Commander of Fleet Air, Solomon Islands*, headquartered at Guadalcanal* in April 1943 and later, in 1944, commander of Carrier Division 3 (later known as Fast Carrier Task Force 58). Under his leadership, the Fast Carrier Task Force became a highly effective tactical weapon in countless operations, including the key battles of the Philippine Sea*, Leyte Gulf*, and Okinawa*, providing crucial air cover and air strike power to the US Pacific offensives throughout 1944 and 1945. After the war, Mitscher turned down an appointment as Chief of Naval Operations to lead the US 8th Fleet and then the Atlantic Fleet, which he commanded until his death in 1947. See also Essex, USS.

Mitsubishi A5M Manufactured between 1935 and 1940, the A5M was the Japanese Navy's* first monoplane fighter. By December 1941, only a few of the final

A5M4 version were in first-line service aboard the light carrier *Ryujo**, and they were soon replaced. Otherwise the plane spent the war as a trainer.
BRIEF DATA (A5M4) Type: single-seat carrier fighter; Engine: 1 × 785hp Nakajima Kotobuki; Max speed: 270mph; Ceiling: 32,000'; Range: 745m; Arms: 2 × 7.7mm mg (provision for 120lb bombs); Allied code-name: Claude.

Mitsubishi A6M Zero (Reisen) The most famous and successful Japanese aircraft of the war, the Zero entered production as the A6M2 in 1940, and began replacing Mitsubishi A5Ms* in naval service that summer. Typically for Japanese warplanes of the period, its design stressed speed, range and manoeuvrability rather than armoured protection. Although it had been seen in action over China*, the Zero surprised the Western Allies with its performance when the Pacific War* began, and for six months proved more than a match for any fighter in the theatre. Its ascendancy waned after the Battle of Midway* in June 1942, but successive variants remained in widespread front-line service throughout the war, although as Japanese carrier losses mounted they were increasingly restricted to shore-based operations.

All but the earliest A6M2s had folding wingtips, enabling them to fit into the lifts of carriers, but these were omitted from the A6M3, which housed a 1,130hp engine and which fought in the South West Pacific area from the late spring of 1942. The 351mph A6M5, in service from autumn 1943, boasted a stronger wing design, while versions mass-produced during 1944 introduced more powerful machine-guns, increased protective armour and self-sealing fuel tanks. Modified Zeros also saw action from forward bases as A6M2-N floatplanes, while a night fighter version of the A6M5 was built with an obliquely-mounted cannon in the fuselage (see Schräge Musik). The final A6M7, modified as a dive-bomber with a 1,100lb load, entered full production in May 1945, by which time some Zeros

were being used as suicide attack planes. By the end of WW2, 10,938 A6Ms of all types had been delivered, stranding further planned developments in the prototype stage.
BRIEF DATA (A6M2) Type: single-seat carrier fighter; Engine: 1 × 950hp Nakajima Sakae; Max speed: 331mph; Ceiling: 35,000'; Range: 1,166m; Arms: 2 × 20mm cannon, 2 × 7.7mm mg (provision for 260lb bombs); Allied code-name: Zeke.

Mitsubishi F1M The F1M1 prototype of this Japanese single-float biplane flew in 1936, but it eventually entered Japanese Navy* service as the drastically modified F1M2 in 1941. Designed as a catapult-launched reconnaissance plane and gunnery spotter, it also saw action as a fighter, dive-bomber, convoy* escort and offshore patrol. A few were also converted as F1M2K trainers. Slow but highly manoeuvrable, it remained on combat duty throughout the war. Over 1,000 were built.
BRIEF DATA (F1M2) Type: 2-man observation seaplane; Engine: 1 × 875hp Mitsubishi Zuisei; Max speed: 230mph; Ceiling: 31,000'; Range: 460m; Arms: 3 × 7.7mm mg (provision for 132lb bombs); Allied code-name: Pete.

Mitsubishi G3M Production of this long-range Japanese Navy* medium bomber had begun in 1936, and about 200 of the G3M2 variant were in first-line service at the start of the Pacific War*. Armed with torpedoes*, 60 of these took part in the sinking of the British Force Z* on 10 December 1941. Over 1,000 G3Ms reached the Japanese Navy but the aircraft was nearing obsolescence by early 1942. Nevertheless, the G3M3, with 1,300hp engines, was manufactured as late as 1943.
BRIEF DATA (G3M2) Type: 5–7-man land-based naval bomber; Engine: 2 × 1,075hp Mitsubishi Kinsei; Max speed: 259mph; Ceiling: 30,000'; Range: 2,935m; Arms: 1 × 20mm cannon, 4 × 7.7mm mg; Bomb load: 1,760lb torpedo or equivalent bombs; Allied code-name: Nell.

Mitsubishi G4M (and G6M) The G4M was intended to supersede the Mitsubishi G3M* as the Japanese Navy's* main land-based bomber. First delivered in the spring of 1941, it served throughout the Pacific War*. Although successful at first against limited Allied opposition, the plane had been designed without self-sealing fuel tanks in order to increase range, and it soon became notorious as a fire-hazard. The longer-ranged G4M2 proved no less vulnerable, and only about 60 of the safer G4M3s were finished in time to see combat. Many subvariants were produced or projected, with modified engine or armament capacities, but the heavy fighter version (designated G6M1) was developed simultaneously with the first bombers. Too slow for combat effectiveness, these were later built as trainers or paratroop transports. Some 2,500 of all types were manufactured, and further versions were under test when the war ended.
BRIEF DATA (G4M1) Type: 7-man maritime attack bomber; Engine: 2 × 1,530hp Mitsubishi Kasei; Max speed: 266mph; Ceiling: 29,350'; Range: 3,745m; Arms: 1 × 20mm cannon, 4 × 7.7mm mg; Bomb load: 1 × 1,746lb torpedo* or equivalent bombs; Allied code-name: Betty.

Mitsubishi J2M Thunderbolt (Raiden) The Thunderbolt fighter limped into very limited production for the Japanese Navy* in 1942 as the J2M2. Although fast and with an excellent rate of climb, it was dogged by engine trouble and pilots complained of poor cockpit visibility. The better armed J2M3 solved none of these problems, and the plane was only built in numbers from 1944, when B-29* attacks on Japan provoked an urgent demand for high altitude fighters. By this time, the turbo-supercharged J2M5 was in service and it proved an excellent home-defence interceptor. About 470 J2Ms of all types were manufactured by Mitsubishi and an unknown number of J2M5s emerged from the Air Arsenal at Koza.
BRIEF DATA (J2M5) Type: single-seat

fighter; Engine: 1 × 1,820hp Mitsubishi Kasei; Max speed: 372mph; Ceiling: 37,000'; Arms: 4 × 20mm cannon; Allied code-name: Jack.

Mitsubishi Ki-21 When it first appeared in 1937, the Ki-21 bomber was an integral part of the JAAF* revitalization programme. The refined Ki-21Ib was still in service when the Pacific War* began, but had been largely replaced by the more powerful Ki-21IIa as the mainstay of the heavy bomber units. Successful at first against token opposition, the plane soon fell hopelessly foul of modern Allied fighters and heavy losses followed. The addition of a dorsal gun turret in the Ki-21IIb made little or no difference but, although the plane was clearly obsolete, it remained a first-line bomber until 1944. Production only ceased with the belated introduction of the Mitsubishi Ki-67* in September 1944, by which time 2,064 Ki-21s had been built.
BRIEF DATA (Ki-21IIa) Type: 5–7-man heavy bomber; Engine: 2 × 1,450hp Mitsubishi Ha-101; Max speed: 297mph; Ceiling: 32,800'; Range: 1,600m (max); Arms: 6 × 7.7mm mg; Bomb load: 2,200lb; Allied code-name: Sally.

Mitsubishi Ki-46 Japanese Army* spyplane which first flew in November 1939, but entered large-scale production with the Ki-46II in 1941. An aerodynamic masterpiece, the plane relied largely on its turn of speed for protection and was much admired in its allotted role. The Ki-46III, cannon-armed and capable of 391mph, was introduced in 1944. Although this remained primarily a reconnaissance aircraft, some modified versions flew as high-altitude fighters, but were let down by their moderate rate of climb. Ki-46s remained in first-line action throughout the Pacific War* and 1,738 were eventually built.
BRIEF DATA (Ki-46II) Type: 2-man reconnaissance; Engine: 2 × 1,050hp Mitsubishi Ha-102; Max speed: 375mph;

Ceiling: 34,500'; Range: 1,540m; Arms: 1 × 7.7mm mg; Allied code-name: Dinah.

Mitsubishi Ki-51 Japanese Army* ground-support plane designed for landings on short, primitive front-line airstrips, it was produced from 1940 until just before the end of the war. Reliable and manoeuvrable, if lacking in performance, it was built with provision for photo-reconnaissance equipment and was frequently used in that role. About 2,400 were delivered, serving in both China* and the Pacific War*.
BRIEF DATA (Ki-51) Type: 2-man ground-attack plane; Engine: 1 × 900hp Mitsubishi Ha-26; Max speed: 263mph; Ceiling: 27,000'; Range: 660m; Arms: 3 × 7.7mm (later 12.7mm) mg; Bomb load: 440lb; Allied code-name: Sonia.

Mitsubishi Ki-67 Flying Dragon (Hiryu)
Although the Japanese Army* had ordered a new heavy bomber from Mitsubishi in 1941, they failed to settle on a basic production model until early 1944, by which time the need to replace the hopelessly obsolete Mitsubishi Ki-21* bombers was desperate. The resultant Ki-67 Flying Dragon was fast, highly manoeuvrable and better armoured than its predecessors and, although much employed as an overland bomber, also served effectively as a naval attack plane. From October 1944, Ki-67s attacked Allied shipping off Formosa* and later carried out frequent raids on Iwo Jima* and Okinawa*. By far the best Japanese bomber of the war, it appeared in many experimental or specialized variants, including a suicide-attack model and the unsuccessful Ki-109 high-altitude fighter version. In spite of overwhelming production difficulties, 727 Flying Dragons were completed before the end of the war.
BRIEF DATA (Ki-67) Type: 6–8-man heavy bomber; Engine: 2 × 1,900hp Mitsubishi Ha-104; Max speed: 334mph; Ceiling: 31,000'; Range: 2,360m (max); Arms: 1 × 20mm cannon, 3 × 12.7mm mg; Bomb load: 2,200lb or torpedo*; Allied code-name: Peggy.

Model, Field Marshal Walther (1891–1945) German Army* commander, his fierce loyalty to Hitler was the basis of his career and his energy, aggressiveness and frankness earned him a special relationship with the Führer. He was Chief of Staff of the 4th Corps in Poland* in 1939, and of the 16th Army during the Western Offensive* the following year. For the invasion of Russia he was given command of the 3rd Panzer Division, and in 1942 took control of the 9th Army (see Eastern Front). Model remained on the Eastern Front until August 1944, becoming known as the 'Führer's Fireman' as he was switched from one Army Group to another to check Russian offensives. Highly successful in restoring stability to his hard pressed commands, Model's willingness to ignore impossible orders and impose his pragmatism on Hitler did not cost him his position, and he was transferred to France after the Allied invasion of Normandy* as C-in-C of the theatre. With the return of Rundstedt* to command the front in September 1944, Model retained command of Army Group B, then in the Netherlands. Characteristically, he informed Hitler that its position was untenable, but nevertheless organized the successful defence of Arnhem*. After the German defeat at the Battle of the Bulge* and the Allied crossings of the Rhine*, Army Group B was trapped in the Ruhr pocket, and Model disbanded his doomed forces before shooting himself – the traditional response to defeat of a German field marshal – on 21 April 1945.

Mogami Japanese heavy cruiser and class, which also included the *Kumano*, *Mikuma* and *Suzuya*. Completed in 1935–7 as light cruisers with 15 6.2-inch guns, they were designed to be as heavily armed as possible within the international treaty limits on cruiser tonnage and main weaponry. They were also given a new type of sloped armour and, although the first units suffered from top-heaviness at sea until modified, their appearance influenced American designs and signalled the end of British hopes for a general reduction in the size and cost of cruisers. In 1939–40 they were re-armed with 8-inch weapons and their beams were bulged, making them genuine heavy cruisers.

All four units formed a cruiser division with Vice Admiral Kondo's* 2nd Scouting Fleet in December 1941, and were then in action almost continuously. The *Mogami* was badly damaged at the Battle of Midway* in June 1942 (where the *Mikuma* was sunk), just managing to limp back to Kure, where she was repaired and modified. Her rear turrets were replaced by an aircraft deck capable of operating 11 seaplanes (which never became available) and her light anti-aircraft* armament was augmented. None of the class survived the war. The *Mogami* and the *Suzuya* were both lost on 25 October 1944 in the Battle of Leyte Gulf* – the former in the Surigao Strait and the latter off Samar. The *Kumano* succumbed to air attack in the same area a month later.

BRIEF DATA (*Mogami*, 1941) Displacement: 12,400 tons; Dimensions: o/a lgth – 646' 6", b – 66' 4"; Speed: 34.75 knots; Armament: 10×8" gun (5×2), 8×5" DP gun, 8×25mm AA gun, 4×13mm AA gun, 12×24" TT, 3 aircraft.

Mölders, Major General Werner (1913–41) Outstanding German fighter pilot credited with 115 combat victories in Spain, France, Britain and Russia. A skilled tactician and a gifted commander, Mölders was made General of the Luftwaffe* Fighter Arm in 1941, but was killed *en route* to the funeral of another national hero, Ernst Udet*, in November, when his transport to Berlin crashed into a chimney in bad weather.

Molotov, Vyachlesav (1890–1986) Soviet Foreign Minister from 1939 to 1952, described by Churchill as 'totally ruthless'. Replacing Litvinov* as Commissar for Foreign Affairs in May 1939, Molotov figured prominently in the negotiations that led to the Russo-German Pact* and subsequently became executor of Stalin's* labyrinthine wartime foreign policy. During the following year, when German military successes in Europe were placing new strains on the Soviet-German relationship, Molotov discussed a four-power (Germany, Russia, Italy and Japan) pact with Hitler in Berlin. The proposal stumbled, however, on the Soviet requirement of a German withdrawal from Finland*. When the German invasion of the Soviet Union was launched in 1941, it was Molotov who announced the attack to the Soviet people.

The necessary change in foreign policy direction precipitated by the German invasion was steered by the five-man State Defence Committee on which Molotov served throughout the war. Promises of assistance for Russia from the Western Allies was formalized by Molotov in the signing of the Mutual Assistance Pact with Britain (July 1941) and Lend-Lease* agreements with Britain and the US. A 20-year Anglo-Soviet treaty was signed in May 1942, and Molotov also received reassurances about the opening of a 'Second Front' against Germany in the same year, although Churchill* travelled to Moscow in August to explain to Stalin why these promises could not be fulfilled (see Conferences).

Nevertheless, his chairmanship of the Moscow Foreign Ministers' Conference in 1943 laid the groundwork for the Tehran Conference, at which a European invasion date was finally agreed. In 1945, Molotov accompanied Stalin at the major Allied Conferences at Yalta, San Francisco and Potsdam, which were to establish the postwar European (and to an extent global) political structure.

Molotov's long career as Stalin's close associate was ended with the arrest of his Jewish wife. After Stalin's death, Molotov lost favour in the Khrushchev* era. His reputation was not fully rehabilitated until two years before his own death.

Molotov–Ribbentrop Pact See Russo-German Pact.

Moltke, Count Helmut von (1907–45) See Resistance: Germany.

Montgomery, Field Marshal Bernard Law (1887–1976) One of the best known and most controversial of British field commanders and Chief of the Imperial General Staff after the war, his notorious immodesty and poor relations with many of the Allied military chiefs have not detracted from his reputation as a popular and able leader, and skilled self-publicist. In command of 3rd Division during the Battle of France (see Western Offensive), Montgomery was among the last to be evacuated from Dunkirk* and was subsequently promoted to command 5th and 12th Corps. After an important period of troop training he was sent to North Africa to replace the 8th Army commander, General Gott, immediately following the first British check to Rommel's* overstretched eastward advance through Egypt at El Alamein* in August 1942.

Under the leadership of the newly appointed C-in-C, General Alexander*, Montgomery rallied the exhausted 8th Army and directed his most notable victory against the expected Axis* offensive, first at Alam Halfa and then at El Alamein in September and October. Although critics have argued that the record ignores the obvious contribution made by the planning of Alexander's predecessor, Auchinleck*, to Montgomery's autumn victories, the attention to troop morale, cautious preparation, planning and precise execution that were Montgomery's hallmark, certainly contributed to the first great British victory of the war.

In the subsequent Allied Torch* offensives in North Africa, the Allied invasions of Sicily* and Italy* in the following year, and in the invasion of Northwest Europe* in 1944 (for which he commanded overall ground-operations and the 21st Army Group), Montgomery's contribution continued to be competent, though often criticized as overcautious, based on the elements of force, frontal assault and close control, rather than on initiative and manoeuvre. Following the breakout from Normandy (which had been slowed by his expensive failure to capture Caen*), and his failure to make use of his success at Antwerp*, Field Marshal Montgomery came increasingly into conflict with his superior, General Eisenhower, over strategy (see Arnhem). His obsessive rivalry with US General Patton (see Sicily) and his tactless and temperamental attempts during 1944 to press Eisenhower for a single-front strategy, with Montgomery at its head, instead of the co-operative broad-front approach favoured by Eisenhower and General Bradley, were repeatedly criticized.

It is worth noting, nonetheless, that Montgomery displayed a great resilience and consistent commitment to Allied efforts in all the war theatres in which he served, retaining throughout the confidence and loyalty of his subordinates. After VE day, Montgomery commanded the British occupation forces, was named CIGS in June 1946, and later served as Deputy Supreme Allied Commander in Europe (NATO), 1951–8.

Morane-Saulnier MS406 Underarmed and underpowered by contemporary standards, the MS406 interceptor at least had the advantage over most modern French aircraft of being fully operational when war broke out. It entered service with the *Armée de l'Air* in March 1939 and 1,081 had been built by June 1940. In the Battle of France*, they suffered heavy losses against thoroughly superior opponents. Some were later fitted with droptanks by the Vichy Air Force and served in Syria*, while many more fought on skis for Finland*, often with more powerful Soviet engines.
BRIEF DATA (MS406-1) Type: single-seat fighter; Engine: 1 × 860hp Hispano; Max speed: 302mph; Ceiling: 30,840'; Range: 497m; Arms: 1 × 20mm cannon, 2 × 7.5mm mg.

Morshead, Lt General Leslie (1889–1959) Australian soldier who rejoined the army from civilian life in 1939 and commanded the 9th Australian Division in the Middle East. He led his troops through the siege of Tobruk* and the battles around El Alamein* before his forces were recalled to the Far East. He next commanded Australian forces* against the Japanese in New Guinea*, and in 1944 was made GOC of the New Guinea force and Commander of the 2nd Australian Army. He ended the war in control of Allied operations in Borneo*.

Moscow, Battle of, 1941–2 The climactic battle of the first phase of the German invasion of Russia in 1941 (see Eastern Front; Map 27). The launch of the German offensive on Moscow, code-named *Taifun* (Typhoon), on 2 October 1941 followed on from the annihilation of the Soviet armies in the Ukraine*. Army Group Centre, under General Bock*, comprised 18 armoured and eight motorized divisions, striking eastwards in three axes of advance, and capturing more than 650,000 prisoners as the jaws of the pincer snapped closed at Bryansk and Vyazma. With no air cover, and the Soviet armies reduced to improvised battalions, a state of siege was declared in Moscow on 19 October by its new commander, General Zhukov*, as flanking attacks by German panzer divisions under Guderian* and Hoth broke through the Russian lines on the north and south of the capital. Nevertheless, the German advance had begun to show signs of slowing down. As the two main roads to Moscow became increasingly congested, rain turned the small roads to boggy tracks, and the dense forest north of Moscow broke up the advancing panzer formations.

The sudden onset of cold weather froze engine oil, packing grease and firing mechanisms. Lacking winter uniforms, German soldiers began to fall victim to frostbite, and morale sank quickly as the cold appeared to anaesthetize the German offensive. To the south, at Tula, Zhukov's last remaining tank* force under General Katukov stopped Guderian's advance and put the German

4th Panzer Division out of action. To the north, Hoth's Panzer Group continued a creeping advance, though they were now harried by air attack from a hastily reformed Red Air Force*.

On 15 November, Army Group Centre launched a final lunging attack against the city. Frozen roads now aided progress. Although Guderian's forces remained trapped at Tula under attack from Siberian reinforcements, Hoth's 7th Panzer Division broke through at Klin to reach the Moscow–Volga canal line, within 20 miles of the capital, on 28 November. But on 6 December, having persuaded Stavka* to withdraw Russia's eight remaining tank brigades and huge infantry reserves from the Far East, Zhukov launched a counter-attack. With over 155,000 casualties of the drive so far, German Army Group Centre could not repel the attack. Supported by counter-offensives at Rostov* and Leningrad*, the Soviet front began to push back. Literally freezing in its tracks, and unable to reinforce its armies or its positions, the German lines fell away. Despite Hitler's furious order to stand and resist (having dismissed Guderian and Höpner* and appointed himself C-in-C), the German offensive was completely reversed. By the end of January, although all Russian reserves had been used up, the front had been stabilized some 40 miles from Moscow.

Moscow Conference See Conferences, Allied.

Mosley, Sir Oswald (1896–1980) British politician, Conservative and Labour member of Parliament between 1918 and 1930, and founder of the British Union of Fascists in 1932, Mosley's personal charisma and the sweeping, seductive arguments of Fascism combined during the Depression era in England to enlist some 30,000 members of the Fascist Union by 1934. Imprisoned in May 1940, when the Union was disbanded, Mosley was released by Churchill in 1943, on grounds of ill health, amidst a storm of public protest.

Mountbatten, Vice Admiral Lord Louis (1900–79) Highly respected naval commander and Supreme Allied Commander in Southeast Asia from 1943 until his acceptance of the Japanese surrender in that theatre in September 1945. Commander of the 5th Destroyer Flotilla which took command of the evacuation of Norway* in June 1940, Mountbatten was chosen to succeed Admiral Sir Roger Keyes in charge of Combined Operations in 1941. Becoming a member of the Chiefs of Staff Committee in March 1942, Mountbatten planned the Dieppe* and St Nazaire* raids and undertook preliminary planning for the invasion of Northwest Europe* (Overlord) before being selected by Churchill* and Roosevelt* to head the reorganized Southeast Asia Command, as Supreme Allied Commander. In this post, Mountbatten saw his greatest challenge, working in the face of complex political, command and logistical difficulties (see Burma). He subsequently directed the lengthy reconquest of Burma and Singapore*. He was later made Earl Mountbatten of Burma and served as the last supervising Viceroy of India, First Sea Lord, and, in 1959, chairman of the Chiefs of Staff Committee. A first cousin of the Queen, he was killed by a bomb while on holiday in Ireland. See also Kelly.

Mukden Incident (Manshu jihen), 1931
A plot engineered by a group of officers of the Kwantung Army* to provoke an 'incident' that would justify the Japanese occupation of Manchuria*. Despite attempts by the government to halt the operation, an explosion on the Southern Manchurian Railway outside Mukden, purportedly caused by Chinese troops, resulted in the Kwantung Army's occupation of Mukden. Reinforcements brought from Korea (unauthorized by the government in Tokyo) assisted in the subsequent Japanese advance that covered the three eastern provinces of Manchuria by early 1932. Forced to act as an apologist for the actions of the Japanese military in Manchuria, the

Japanese government was in no position to stop the fighting. In February 1932, a puppet 'independent' state of Manchukuo* was established. China's appeal to the League of Nations resulted finally in Japan's withdrawing from the League in early 1933. See also China.

Mulberries Artificial harbours developed from 1942–4 for use in the Allied invasion of Normandy*. Partly sunken ships and concrete caissons were used to form a 200ft breakwater, within which a complex of pontoons and causeways provided mooring facilities. Two mulberries were built in June 1944. The British operated theirs with great success off Arromanches, but the American mulberry off Omaha Beach was virtually destroyed by storms on 19 June. The mulberries transformed the supply situation for the Allied invasion forces and badly upset German defensive calculations.

Munich Agreement An agreement signed in September 1938 by Germany, Italy, France and Britain (but not Czechoslovakia*), it ceded the German-speaking Sudetenland of Czechoslovakia to Germany (as well as providing for a 'settlement of claims' to Czech territory by Poland* and Hungary*). It was the last and most invidious act of appeasement* in the face of a German threat of war.

Hailed by British Prime Minister Chamberlain* (who had originally initiated the negotiations), as a measure that would guarantee 'peace in our time', the agreement dismayed defenders of democratic Czechoslovakia and surprised Hitler* (who had expected a confrontation) by categorically endorsing the blunt tactics of armed diplomacy which had been evolving into Nazi foreign policy.

The roots of the crisis in Czechoslovakia lay in the territorial ambitions that were at the heart of Hitler's foreign policy, and in the principles of nationality and the right of minorities to self-determination, which had been enshrined in the founding of the League of Nations. In direct contradiction

to this fundamental principle, the Versailles Treaty had ceded the German-speaking Sudetenland to Czechoslovakia in order to provide her with a secure buffer territory against Germany. By exploiting the commitment to self-determination of the Sudeten Germans, the Nazi Party in Germany and its agents in Sudeten (notably the Sudeten German Party under Henlein*), were able to initiate, rehearse and stage a diplomatic crisis and then demand a resolution to a problem that they had themselves massively exacerbated, in their own favour.

In August 1938, Hitler had mobilized his army and threatened to attack the Czechs over the pre-fabricated issue of Sudeten self-determination. During two trips to Germany, first to Berchtesgaden and then to Godesberg, Prime Minister Chamberlain listened to Hitler's demands and recommended concessions from the Czechs. Following the second meeting at Godesberg, near Bonn, when Hitler had merely expanded his demands, Chamberlain's appeasement had seemed to fail, though Hitler was drawn back to the negotiating table by Mussolini*, with a suggestion for a further meeting in Munich. Although Germany's demands were only modified rather than withdrawn, both Chamberlain and French Premier Daladier* judged these terms acceptable. Neither Czechoslovakia nor Soviet Russia, bound by treaties to France, were present at the meeting.

Murrow, Edward Roscoe (1908–65) Famous American radio broadcaster who became CBS (Columbia Broadcasting Systems) director of programmes in London in 1937 and made personal reports from London throughout the Blitz*. Murrow also created a staff of radio news correspondents in Europe, before returning to America as CBS vice-president and director of public affairs.

Musashi See Yamato.

Mussert, Anton (1894–1946) Dutch Quisling leader. Founder of the National Socialist movement in the Netherlands*, Mussert was appointed leader of the Dutch people by Berlin in 1942 following the German occupation. In a nation so fiercely anti-Nazi, however, Mussert's following was never large. He was arrested at the end of the war and hanged at the Hague in 1946 as a collaborator. See Resistance: Dutch.

Mussolini, Benito (1883–1945) Italian dictator from 1922–43. Born near Forli in northern Italy and briefly a schoolteacher in his youth, Mussolini moved to Switzerland in 1902 to avoid military service. He returned to Italy two years later, fulfilled his military obligation, and then worked as a manual labourer, developing an interest in socialism. He quickly proved himself an able left-wing agitator and journalist, rising to become editor of the official Socialist Party newspaper, *Avanti*, in 1912. The issue of Italian intervention on the Allied side in WW1, which Mussolini supported as a catalyst to internal change, forced him to resign his post and break with the Socialists in 1915. He later fought in the Italian Army as a corporal, was wounded and returned to civilian life to edit his own right-wing radical newspaper, *Il Popolo di Italia*.

Exploiting post-war fears of a communist revolution and Italian discontent at the terms of the Versailles Peace Treaty, Mussolini organized various right-wing groups which were merged into the Fascist Party – originally the *Fascio di Combattimento*, a Milanese anti-socialist militia – in 1919. The Fascists did well in subsequent elections, and in 1922 Mussolini's demand for a Fascist government to restore law and order was met by King Victor Emmanuel III*. Mussolini became Prime Minister of a right-wing coalition amid widespread social unrest, but what was later glamorized as his March on Rome was in fact a train journey from Milan at the King's invitation followed by a big celebratory parade.

As *Duce* (Leader), Mussolini finalized the character of his new ideology. Fascism – the name derives from a Roman symbol of authority – sought to recreate its leader's personal vision of Italy's imperial past. Pride in the state, martial prowess and obedience to the leader were emphatically stressed; socialism and democracy were regarded with equal contempt. Although Mussolini issued anti-Semitic decrees in 1938, this was rather an imitation of Hitler's* Nazism than a policy that arose from Italian Fascism itself.

Political, legislative and juridical power was concentrated in the person of the *Duce*. A one-party state was fully established by 1929, and a Fascist Grand Council, dominated by Mussolini, took over the functions of the cabinet. Steps were taken to improve relations with the papacy, and a National Council of Corporations controlled industrial relations. The Italian economy appeared to go from strength to strength, and the Italian people displayed few signs of active discontent. Although Mussolini's acheivements were exaggerated by propaganda and mostly superficial, he earned much international admiration and inspired several imitators among Europe's emerging dictators (e.g. Antonescu*) in the 1930s.

Linked, if distinct, ideologies brought Mussolini towards closer contact with National Socialist Germany during the 1930s, although in the same degree, it paradoxically served to feed a jealous distrust of Hitler. An initial meeting in 1934 had not gone well. But Hitler's determination to secure Italian collaboration in sending forces to Spain, and the inevitable similarities in style between the two regimes, helped bring about a non-military alliance in October 1936, known as the Axis*. When the *Duce* was treated to a lavish state visit in Germany the following September, a closer relationship developed between the two men. Hitler was the dominant partner in every way, but in their personal meetings he always treated the older dictator with charm, warmth and respect.

In 1939, Italy annexed Albania* and the Axis partnership was expanded into a full defensive alliance with Germany – The Pact of Steel. Mussolini viewed Germany's conquests in the first year of WW2 with undisguised envy and a sense of his own inaction. His military and economic advisers were aware that Italy was in no position to undertake a major conflict, but they were not consulted before Mussolini's declaration of war with the Allies was announced in June 1940, just in time to share Hitler's glory in the fall of France*. Although extremely anxious about the prospect of a prolonged war with any major power, Mussolini believed – as did most people – that Britain was doomed to a swift defeat and expected quick victories from the Italian invasions of Egypt*, Greece* and East Africa* in 1940. The disastrous course of these campaigns, the defeats suffered by the Italian Navy* in the Mediterranean* and the failure of heavy industry to adapt to a war economy left Italy dependent on German aid by early 1941.

Mussolini's war policies became increasingly fantastic as Italy's military and economic position worsened. He issued direct military orders that bore no relation to the realities of the battlefront and magnified Italy's crisis by sending troops to the Eastern Front* and declaring war on the US. By the end of 1941 Italy was little more than a client state of Germany and Mussolini's role in his personal dealings with Hitler had dwindled to passive insignificance.

The war was never very popular in Italy, even with the predominantly royalist military, and as early as 1942 the King and leading political figures were actively seeking a way out of the conflict. As his armies dwindled, Mussolini remained capable of extraordinary faith in his destiny. In June 1942, when Rommel* appeared to be winning the Desert War*, the *Duce* flew to Tripoli* with a white charger and prepared to lead Axis forces into Cairo. The British victory at El Alamein* and Rommel's rapid retreat into Tunisia* enraged and depressed him, and he saw it as a turning point in his fortunes. Although he issued far-fetched decrees with his customary vehemence, his health failed rapidly and he began to isolate himself, awaiting defeat.

Hitler still courted the ageing dictator. With the Allies poised for the invasion of Italy, the two met in northern Italy in July 1943. On his return Mussolini was presented with a demand from the Fascist Grand Council for his resignation, supported by the King and the veteran soldier Marshal Badoglio*, who was chosen to succeed him as premier. Mussolini was placed under house arrest in the Apennine mountains, apparently resigned to his fate. On 12 September, however, German airborne* troops accompanied by Major Otto Skorzeny rescued Mussolini in a dramatic raid and took him to Germany.

Hitler then set the *Duce* up as the head of the Salo Republic, a Fascist administration nominally in control of German-occupied northern Italy. From his headquarters at Gargagno on Lake Garda, Mussolini passively accepted his puppet status. The most notable act of the regime was the trial and execution of five of those who had voted against Mussolini on the Grand Council, including his son-in-law, Ciano*. In April 1945, with Allied forces approaching and Germany collapsing, he attempted to reach Switzerland with his mistress, Clara Petacci. They were captured on the shore of Lake Como by Italian partisans on 27 April. The next day they were shot, and their bodies displayed for public degradation in Milan.

Mutsu See Nagato.

Myitkyina Northern Burmese town captured by the Japanese on 8 May 1942, it was the site of a bitterly resisted siege during the Allied offensive for the recapture of Burma* during 1944 (see Maps 24 and 25). Located on the Ledo Road*, the western section of the vital land route from India to China*, the Burma Road*, the town was finally recaptured by Chinese forces under US General Stilwell* on 3 August 1944.

Myoko The four ships of the *Myoko* Class, completed in 1928–9, were the first Japanese heavy cruisers built up to the 10,000-ton international limit imposed by the Washington Naval Treaty of 1922. Japanese designers, who tended to regard treaty limits as approximations, used methods pioneered in the experimental cruiser *Yubari** to produce a combination of high speed, heavy armament and increased protection on a displacement not much above that of foreign contemporaries. The class was modernized in 1936 and three units – the *Myoko*, *Haguro* and *Nachi* – formed a cruiser division with Vice Admiral Kondo's* Southern Force on the eve of the Pacific War*. The fourth ship, the *Ashigara* was based on Formosa*. The *Haguro* and the *Nachi* were prominent at the Battle of the Java Sea* in February 1942, and the class as a whole was kept in front-line service until 1944, when they were fitted with simple radar* and additional anti-aircraft* defences in place of half their torpedo* tubes. All four ships were lost in the last year of the war, although the hulk of the *Myoko* was surrendered (inoperative) to the British and scuttled in 1946.

BRIEF DATA (*Myoko*, 1941) Displacement: 13,380 tons; Dimensions: o/a lgth – 661' 9", b – 68'; Speed: 33.75 knots; Armament: 10 × 8" gun (5 × 2), 8 × 5" AA gun, 8 × 25mm AA gun, 4 × 13mm AA gun, 16 × 24" TT, 3 aircraft.

N

Nagara Japanese fast light cruiser and class. The six *Nagara* Class ships were completed in the early 1920s along similar lines to the preceding *Kuma** Class. They were used in the Pacific War* as flagships for cruiser, submarine* or destroyer* flotillas and were all lost in action. The *Yura* was the first to be destroyed, sunk at the Battle of Santa Cruz* in October 1942. The rest of the class were subsequently rearmed with greater stress on anti-aircraft* defence and three times as many torpedo* tubes. Thus equipped, both the *Nagara* and the *Natori* were sunk by American submarines in August 1944. The *Abukuma* and *Kinu* were victims of carrier aircraft at the Battle of Leyte Gulf*. The *Izuzu* survived until July 1945, when she was sunk by American submarines in the Java Sea.
BRIEF DATA (*Nagara*, 1941) Displacement: 5,170 tons; Dimensions: o/a lgth – 535', b – 46' 6"; Speed: 36 knots; Armament: 7 × 5.5" gun (7 × 1), 2 × 3" AA gun, 8 × 24" TT, 1 aircraft.

Nagasaki Final target for the dropping of the second atomic bomb* (nicknamed Fat Man) on Japan on 9 August 1945. While Japanese leaders debated the response to the dropping of the first devastating bomb at Hiroshima* (6 August) and the renewed demand from President Truman* for unconditional surrender, the 10,000lb Fat Man was launched from a B-29 piloted by Major Charles Sweeney. Though originally intended for Kokura, site of a Japanese Army arsenal, the alternate target of Nagasaki was substituted at the last moment because of unfavourable weather conditions

over Kokura. Although broken terrain checked the effect of the blast, and caused less structural damage than at Hiroshima, the number of known dead was nearly 24,000, with as many people injured and numberless victims of long-term radiation. Estimates of total casualties vary extensively.

Nagato Japanese battleship and class, which also comprised the *Mutsu*. Launched in 1919–20, these were the first ships in the world to carry 16-inch guns and the first results of an ambitious Japanese Navy* programme for eight battleships and eight battlecruisers, intended to bring parity with the US Navy* by 1928. The halt in the international battleship race imposed at Washington in 1922 consigned the rest to oblivion, but the *Nagato*s were retained and, much modernized, formed a division of the 1st Battle Fleet in December 1941.

The *Mutsu* was accidentally destroyed by an internal explosion in Hiroshima Bay on 8 June 1943. The cause of the blast remains unknown, but is thought to have occurred in a magazine. The *Nagato*, modernized against air attack in 1944, survived the war and was surrendered damaged at Yokosuka in 1945. She was expended as a nuclear test target for the Americans the following year.
BRIEF DATA (*Nagato*, 1941) Displacement: 39,130 tons; Dimensions: o/a lgth – 738', b – 113' 6"; Speed: 25 knots; Armament: 8 × 16" gun (4 × 2), 18 × 5.5" gun, 8 × 5" AA gun, 20 × 25mm AA gun, 3 aircraft.

Nagoya Japanese industrial city southwest of Tokyo, it was initially a target of the American bombing raid commanded by Lt Colonel James Doolittle* that took place on 18 April 1942. Nagoya was later selected again as a target for the even more devastating raids carried out from the Marianas* by USAAF* B-29* bombers in the Strategic Bombing Offensive* against Japan during early March 1945.

Nagumo, Vice Admiral Chuichi (1887–1944) Commander of the Japanese 1st Air Fleet and strong proponent of the integration of air and sea power, Nagumo was in direct control of the air attacks against Pearl Harbor*, the Dutch East Indies*, northwest Australia, Ceylon* and India during the huge Japanese offensive between December 1941 and May 1942. Following the loss of four aircraft carriers at the pivotal Battle of Midway*, however, Nagumo appears to have suffered from a serious loss of confidence. He was transferred from command of the Japanese carrier force to lead a small naval flotilla in the Marianas* He later organized the defences of Saipan* and committed suicide there in July 1944 during the latter stages of the American conquest of the island.

Nakajima B5N2 The B5N was Japan's first-line naval torpedo-bomber at the start of the Pacific War*, and played a leading part in the attack on Pearl Harbor*. First used in 1937 as the B5N1, it remained in an offensive role until 1944, when it was relegated to convoy* escort duties. The B5N2, introduced in 1939, was only marginally faster than its predecessor but was powered by more reliable engines. Production ended in 1943, after about 1,150 had been built.
BRIEF DATA (B5N2) Type: 3-man carrier bomber; Engine: 1 × 1,000hp Nakajima Sakae; Max speed: 235mph; Ceiling: 27,000′; Range: 607m; Arms: 1 × 7.7mm mg; Bomb load: 1,760lb or torpedo*; Allied code-name: Kate.

Nakajima B6N Heavenly Mountain (Tenzan) Intended to replace the Nakajima B5N2*, which it closely resembled, the B6N1 naval bomber belatedly entered production in early 1943, delayed by serious difficulties with its untried Nakajima engine. This was soon replaced in the more reliable B6N2, of which about 1,000 were built. The plane saw extensive combat against overwhelming numerical odds in the last years of the Pacific War*, and was often used in suicide missions.
BRIEF DATA (B6N2) Type: 3-man carrier bomber; Engine: 1 × 1,850hp Mitsubishi Kasei; Max speed: 299mph; Ceiling: 29,700′; Range: 1,085m; Arms: 2 × 7.7mm mg; Bomb load: 1 × 1,760lb torpedo* or equivalent bombs; Allied code-name: Jill.

Nakajima C6N Painted Cloud (Saiun) The prototype C6N1 first flew in late spring 1943, and production models began long-range naval reconnaissance duties from June 1944. About 460 were built before the end of the war and a few were converted as cannon-armed night fighters (C6N-15).
BRIEF DATA (C6N1) Type: 3-man naval reconnaissance; Engine: 1 × 1,990hp Nakajima Homare; Max speed: 378mph; Ceiling: 35,250′; Range: 1,900m; Arms: 1 × 7.92mm mg; Allied code-name: Myrt.

Nakajima J1N1 Japanese naval authorities deemed this large fighter unsuitable for its planned role as an escort and it entered production in mid-1942 only as a reconnaissance plane. Some were then successfully adapted as night-fighters, with a turret-mounted cannon added to the original single rear machine-gun. From 1943, the J1N1-5 Moonlight (*Gekko*) was built specifically for night fighting, and saw action against American B-29s* over Japan, as well as being used in Kamikaze* attacks. The later J1N1-5A differed only in armament and altogether about 470 J1N1s of all types were delivered before production ended in late 1944.
BRIEF DATA (J1N1-5) Type: 2-man naval

night-fighter; Engine: 2 × 1,130hp Naka-jima Sakae; Max speed: 315mph; Ceiling: 30,600'; Range: 2,346m; Arms: 4 × 20mm cannon; Allied code-name: Irving.

Nakajima Ki-43 Peregrine Falcon (Haya busa) First produced in 1941, this was the JAAF's* most widely built combat aircraft. Early models lacked firepower, protective armament for the pilot and self-sealing tanks, but impressed opponents with their speed and their resemblance to the Mitsubishi A6M* Zero fighter. The later Ki-43II and III variants increased the speed of the plane by 50mph, but only partially overcame its defensive inadequacies. Nevertheless, the Peregrine Falcon remained in front-line action throughout the Pacific War*, and 5,878 of all types were built.
BRIEF DATA (Ki-43III) Type: single-seat fighter; Engine: 1,150hp Nakajima Ha-115; Max speed: 358mph; Ceiling: 37,400'; Range: 1,320m (normal); Arms: 2 × 12.7mm mg; Allied code-name: Oscar.

Nakajima Ki-44 Demon (Shoki) Intended primarily for home defence, the Ki-44Ia was the fastest fighter available to the JAAF* when it reached combat units in 1942. It was quickly replaced by the even faster Ki-44II, about 1,000 of which saw action, mostly against American B-29* bombers in 1944. The Demon conformed to the prevalent Japanese design orthodoxy, in that firepower and protective armour were sacrificed for improved speed and rate of climb, and only a few of the cannon-armed Ki-44IIc and III variants were produced.
BRIEF DATA (Ki-44II) Type: single-seat fighter; Engine: 1 × 1,450hp Nakajima Ha-109; Max speed: 376mph; Ceiling: 1,200'; Range: 805m (normal); Arms: 4 × 12.7mm mg; Allied code-name: Tojo.

Nakajima Ki-49 Storm Dragon (Donryu) Delivered to the Japanese Army* in August 1941, the Ki-49 was a barely adequate replacement for the Mitsubishi Ki-21* heavy bomber. Although faster than its prede-

cessor, it handled badly and could easily be intercepted by hostile enemy fighters. Only 129 were built before it was superseded in the autumn of 1942 by the better-armed Ki-49II. Some 700 of these saw service in the Pacific War*, but after suffering terrible losses during the US offensives of 1944, they were reduced to transport, maritime reconnaissance or suicide attack duties and production ceased.
BRIEF DATA (Ki-49II) Type: 8-man heavy bomber; Engine: 2 × 1,450hp Nakajima Ha-109; Max speed: 306mph; Ceiling: 30,500'; Range: 1,240m (normal); Arms: 1 × 20mm cannon, 3 × 12.7mm mg, 2 × 7.7 mg; Bomb load: 2,240lb; Allied code-name: Helen.

Nakajima Ki-84 Gale (Hayate) The best fighter to be produced in quantity for the Japanese Army* in WW2, the Gale was fast, well armoured and designed with self-sealing fuel tanks. About 3,500 were built between the spring of 1944 and the end of the Pacific War*, mostly of the Ki-84Ia version. These performed well over the Philippines* and later served as fighter-bombers in the defence of Japan. Some aircraft of the Ib and Ic series, constructed partly of wood, also reached service, but projected all-wooden (Ki-106) and all-steel (Ki-113) variants got no further than the prototype stage.
BRIEF DATA (Ki-84Ia) Type: single-seat fighter; Engine: 1 × 1,900hp Nakajima Ha-5; Max speed: 392mph; Ceiling: 34,500'; Range: 1,050m; Arms: 2 × 20mm cannon, 2 × 12.7mm mg (provision for 551lb bombs); Allied code-name: Frank.

Nanking Capital city of China* from 1928 until 1937, when the Chinese Nationalist government under Chiang Kai-shek* withdrew to Hankow* following the capture of the city by Japanese forces (see Map 22). The Japanese conquest, commanded by General Matsui, was accompanied by infamous atrocities in which an estimated 250,000 civilians were murdered. In 1940 Nanking became the seat of the puppet regime established by the Japanese under Wang Ching-wei*.

Naples Southern Italian port city, it was one of the primary objectives of the US 5th Army's landings at Salerno*, at the start of the Allied invasion of Italy* in September 1943 (see Map 34). A determined and effective counter-attack by numerically inferior German forces under General Vietinghoff* forced 5th Army units to fight a ten-day battle for control of the route north from Salerno to Naples through the Sorrento mountain range. It was not until three weeks later (1 October) that the King's Dragoon Guards of the 5th Army entered Naples and Allied engineers under the command of Commodore Sullivan began restoration of the port, German engineers having destroyed as much as possible before their withdrawal from the city. Thereafter the port supplied the invading Allied armies throughout the campaign in Italy.

Narwhal, USS The *Narwhal* and her sister *Nautilus* were large long-range submarines* commissioned by the US Navy* in 1930. Both were used on patrol and reconnaissance duty in the Pacific War*, participating in the Battle of Midway*. From late 1943 they were employed to supply and support the resistance* movement in the Philippines*.
BRIEF DATA (1941) Displacement: 2,730 tons (surface); Dimensions: lgth – 371', b – 33' 3"; Speed: 20 knots (8.7 submerged); Armament: 2 × 6" gun; 6 × 21" TT.

Nazi Escape Organizations Leading Nazis escaped from Germany at the end of the war using SS* funds and helped by a variety of agencies including international business and the Catholic Church. The most notorious escape organization, Odessa, worked alongside others about whom little more than the name is known (*die Spinne, die Schleuse, Still Hilfe, Kreis Rudel*, etc.). Concrete evidence of these SS escape organizations is minimal, though their channels

were sometimes uncovered. Both in southern Germany and Italy, help came from churchmen, some of whom had been appointed to the Vatican during the thirties. Bishop Alois Hudal, for example, Rector of the German church in Rome, undoubtedly helped to issue Vatican passports to war criminals. It is not known to what extent his views were supported by Pope Pius XII*, though the Pope had been responsible for his promotion to bishop. Prominent Nazis like Eichmann* are known to have used the Vatican route. From Italy some Nazis fled to Spain, South America and the Middle East; some Latvian and Lithuanian Fascists found their way to Australia.

Nazi Party The NSDAP*. See Hitler, Adolf.

Nazi–Soviet Pact See Russo-German Pact.

Nelson, HMS British battleship and class. The *Nelson* and her sister ship the *Rodney* were completed in 1927 as the only new battleships permitted to Britain under the Washington Naval Treaty, and were restricted by the Treaty to a displacement of 35,000 tons. To conserve weight, their main armament was all concentrated forward, with machinery and superstructure grouped aft. This was less of a combat disadvantage than it appeared to contemporary observers and, although slow, they were powerful, well-protected vessels with a wide radius of action. They were also the only modern capital units available to the Royal Navy in 1939.

Both served with the Home Fleet until 1942, and the *Rodney* assisted in the final destruction of the *Bismarck** in May 1941. Both ships then joined the escort of the vital Pedestal* convoy to Malta* in August 1942, when the *Nelson* was torpedoed by an Italian bomber. She survived to provide the venue for the signing of the Italian surrender in September 1943, after supporting Allied landings in Sicily earlier in the year (again in the company of the *Rodney*).

Both vessels provided bombardment for the invasion of northern Europe in 1944, and both ended the war in the Far East.
BRIEF DATA (*Nelson*, 1939) Displacement: 33,950 tons; Dimensions: o/a lgth – 710', b – 106'; Speed: 23 knots; Armament: 9 × 16" gun (3 × 3), 12 × 6" gun, 6 × 4.7" AA gun, 32 × 2pdr AA gun, 16 × 0.5" AA mg, 2 × 24.5" TT, 1 aircraft.

Nero Order An order issued by Hitler in the last days of the Third Reich for the destruction of Germany's industrial infrastructure. In his account *Inside the Third Reich*, Armaments Minister Speer* described the chaos of those days, during which he persuaded Gauleiters (District Leaders) to ignore the Nero order and preserve what remained after the Allied bombing as the basis for Germany's post-war future.

Netherlands, The North European monarchy, occupied by German forces from 1940 –5. Although it was a colonial power (see Dutch East Indies), the Netherlands was militarily weak in 1940, with a small conscript home army of nine first-line and five reserve divisions and an air force of only 118 planes, many of them obsolete. It was governed in the thirties by a conservative administration struggling to control the effects of the worldwide economic depression, especially high unemployment. German-style National Socialism had been discredited as a political force in the general election of 1937, but popular opinion favoured the view that Germany's overtly expansionist tendencies could be controlled by appeasement*. Dutch enthusiasm for the Munich Agreement* of 1938 was as profound as that displayed in Britain. When Britain and France declared war on Germany in 1939, the Netherlands remained neutral, and warnings of German invasion plans were not believed by the Dutch authorities until the attack came on 10 May 1940 (see Western Offensive).
Undermined by audacious German airborne* operations and the bombing of civ-

ilians in Rotterdam, Dutch defences (particularly weak in anti-aircraft* artillery) collapsed in five days. Queen Wilhelmina, along with members of her family and the government, managed to escape to London and began a series of radio broadcasts to her subjects, claiming that 'Holland will rise again'. Although these were well-received, the prevailing view among many Dutch men and women at this stage was that Hitler, victorious in France, had won the war. Encouraged by promises of fair treatment from the German Reichskommissar, Seyss-Inquart*, the Dutch accepted conquest with relative acquiescence.
Dutch civilian morale was boosted by the RAF's* victory in the Battle of Britain*, and the will to resist grew with a gradual increase in German oppression. Collaborators among the police and civil authorities began to suffer scathing attacks from a proliferating underground press and from leading Dutch intellectuals, many of whom were arrested. Collaboration in the arrest and deportation of Dutch Jews was particularly reviled. Secret resistance* groups became active in the protection of Jews, and labour organizations in Amsterdam (home of the majority of the 130,000 Dutch Jews) called an anti-persecution protest strike in February 1941. Nevertheless, 100,000 Dutch Jews were murdered in gas chambers during WW2. Thousands of Dutch labourers and technicians were also deported to work in the German war industries, as were students who refused to sign a loyalty oath. Known as *onderduikers* (literally, under-divers), these swelled the ranks of those evading the authorities so that by 1944 they numbered an estimated 300,000.
Efforts by resistance groups to provide safe addresses and economic aid for the persecuted were hampered by worsening food shortages (rationing was based on an identity-card system), but in terms of aid to the Allies the Dutch underground was one of the most effective in Europe. The various Netherlands Interior Forces provided intelligence on German movements and gave direct assistance to Allied pilots

and airborne troops. Often led on the ground by members of the Dutch clergy, the Interior Forces were nominally headed by Prince Bernhard – the German-born husband of Princess Juliana – who worked from London to unify the resistance organizations prior to the Allied invasion of Northwest Europe* in 1944.

The German SD* was active in suppression of Dutch resistance. Those caught harbouring *onderduikers* or running underground presses were usually shot rather than imprisoned, and hostages were similarly treated at random. In October 1944, by which time the southern part of the country had been recaptured by the Allies, the village of Putten in Gelderland was decimated as a punitive gesture.

The failure of the Allied armies to re-conquer the north of the country in the autumn of 1944 (see Arnhem) had terrible consequences for the densely inhabited provinces in the northwest. A railway strike called by the government-in-exile to assist Montgomery's* advance had paralysed the system, and it was not fully reactivated by the Germans after the offensive failed. Vital food supply lines from the eastern provinces were thus cut, bringing a major famine to Amsterdam and the west. While German forces systematically looted the country of rolling stock, vehicles and industrial machinery, thousands died of starvation. Appeals to the Allies and the occupying authorities eventually brought some relief. A short truce, during which desperate civilians watched German anti-aircraft gunners holding fire while Allied aircraft dropped emergency supplies over the city, went some way to alleviating the crisis.

When the north was eventually liberated in May 1945, the exiled government and the royal family returned to a depleted and exhausted country, which they then governed with the help of a council representing the resistance movement.

Nettleton, Squadron Leader John (1917 –43) South-African born RAF* bomber pilot, he was awarded the Victoria Cross for his leadership of an immensely courageous daylight bomber raid on a submarine* engine works at Augsburg in April 1942, from which less than half the aircraft returned. He was killed in action during a raid over Turin in July 1943.

Nettuno Airstrip at the Anzio* beachhead in Italy* where US 6th Corps landed in Operation Shingle on 22 January 1944.

Neurath, Constantin Freiherr von (1873 –1956) An aristocratic career diplomat and German Foreign Minister from 1932, he was one of a small number of German cabinet ministers to retain office after Hitler's takeover of power in 1933, largely in order to boost the Nazi Party's respectability *vis-à-vis* foreign governments. Neurath was removed from his post in February 1938, however, as a result of his public opposition to Hitler's 'Hossbach Conference' revelations in November 1937. The Hossbach Memorandum stunned military and civilian delegates to the conference by outlining Hitler's vision of *Lebensraum*, living space, for Germany and the Germanic peoples, and its fulfilment by way of war on both eastern and western fronts, including Britain and France among the possible belligerents. Neurath was succeeded by the more compliant Ribbentrop*, and subsequently held only titular posts, most notably as Protector of Bohemia and Moravia (Czechoslovakia*) from 1939 to 1941. Neurath was included among the major war criminals tried at Nuremberg* and was sentenced to 15 years imprisonment, but was released in 1954 on health grounds.

Neutrality Acts A series of laws passed by the American Congress during the 1930s that aimed to keep the US out of overseas wars. Successive legislation in 1935, 1936 and 1937 prohibited trading with belligerents and loans to belligerent governments, and required that military equipment be paid for before being received by belligerent nations. This 'isolationist' legislation was progressively eroded, however, by laws initiated by President Roosevelt*. On 4 November 1939 a new law provided for the supply of arms to belligerents (and specifically Britain and France) on a 'Cash and Carry' basis. See Neutrality, US.

Neutrality, US (1939–41) The basis of US neutrality before Pearl Harbor* was isolationism, a policy advocating non-involvement in the affairs of other nations. Isolationism contributed to US rejection of the League of Nations after WW1 and was strong during the Republican Party administrations of the 1920s. When the threat of European war reappeared during the 1930s, isolationist sentiment in the Senate was powerful enough to force a series of Neutrality Acts* (1935–7) on Roosevelt's* Democratic administration. Trade with or loans to belligerent countries were prohibited and all exports had to be paid for before they left the US. Opinion polls showed that in 1939 a staggering 99 per cent of the American people opposed US involvement in a foreign war. By 1940 isolationism was a political movement, sponsored by influential figures like press magnate W. R. Hearst, US ambassador to London Joseph Kennedy* and airman Charles Lindbergh. In September the primarily anti-British America First Committee was founded. By the following spring it had 60,000 members, including leading politicians of both major parties and it remained in the forefront of US domestic affairs until late 1941.

Opinion in favour of aiding the European democracies after the outbreak of WW2 in 1939 was centred on the all-party Committee for Peace Through the Revision of the Neutrality Laws. After the German attack on France*, it was reconstituted as the Committee to Defend America by Aiding the Allies. Its view that Britain and France were on the front line of a battle that must involve the US was shared by President Roosevelt and Secretary of State Cordell Hull*. Hull was largely responsible for a revision of the Neutrality Acts in No-vember 1939 that repealed the embargo on arms sales to belligerents, but retained the 'cash and carry' restriction on exports. Britain and France were now able to rearm with US weapons for as long as their dollar reserves lasted.

Bound by legal restrictions and strongly opposed by isolationists in the Senate and Congress, Roosevelt could not overtly support the Allied cause and his actions in 1940 were ostensibly concerned only with the defence of the US. In July the Two Oceans Navy Bill was passed, allowing for a 70 per cent increase in US naval tonnage and confirming American interest in the Atlantic Ocean. US Navy* warships operated in the Atlantic on Neutrality Patrol, protecting a coastal exclusion zone established around the Americas (except belligerent Canada) by the Panama Conference at the start of the European war. In September Roosevelt announced 'shoot on sight' tactics in operation against Axis submarines (see Greer, USS), using as his medium one of the 'fireside chat' radio broadcasts which he employed to induce pro-Allied sentiments in the American people. Also that month, the Destroyers-for-Bases Deal* was made public. This clearly fulfilled Roosevelt's statutory obligation to only release armaments if American defences were thereby improved. The 50 old destroyers given to Britain were worth far less than the important Caribbean and Atlantic bases gained in return, but possession of those bases drew US forces more directly into the Battle of the Atlantic*.

Roosevelt's election victory of November 1940 strengthened his position considerably and increased his leverage with the isolationist lobby in the Senate. After several months of vigorous debate, the Lend-Lease Act* was passed in March 1941, the culmination of Roosevelt's plan to use the defence of the United States as a basis for aiding the Allies. The Act allowed the President to provide war materials to any country upon which US safety was thought to depend. Britain, now short of dollar reserves, was immediately declared within this category. American involvement in the war grew most obviously in the Atlantic, where US forces took responsibility for the safety of convoys as far east as Iceland*. Isolationist opinion remained strong, although reports of the Luftwaffe's* bombing of British cities in 1940 had encouraged sympathy for the Allied cause. Only the Japanese attack on Pearl Harbor of 7 December 1941 undermined isolationism – and it did so instantly and completely.

Nevada, USS See Oklahoma, USS.

New Georgia Largest of a cluster of islands in the Central Solomons*, it was assaulted in a series of landings by the US 4th Raider* battalion (43rd Infantry) beginning on 21 June 1943, as part of the American Pacific campaign focused on the major Japanese base at Rabaul*. The assault force encountered determined resistance from the 10,000 strong Japanese garrison, reinforced through the 'Tokyo Express'* supply system, and the island was not secured until 25 August.

New Guinea Large island in the Southwest Pacific, it was at the centre of prolonged fighting between US and Japanese Pacific forces from July 1942 until the end of 1944, with isolated Japanese resistance continuing until the end of the war (see Map 15). At the start of WW2 the island was administratively divided between two foreign countries: Dutch New Guinea comprised the western half of the island; Northeast New Guinea and Papua were administered by Australia. Japanese operations began against Northeast New Guinea in March 1942, with amphibious* landings in the Huon Gulf at Lae and Salamaua, where bases were established to protect Rabaul*. But the focus of the Japanese offensive quickly turned to Port Moresby, major port on the southern coast of the Papuan peninsula, as a stepping stone to the isolation of Australia. Delays in launching the Japanese offensive allowed

the Allies time to effect a rapid build-up of Southwest Pacific forces (mostly Australian*, with some American) in Australia under US General Douglas MacArthur*. The first Japanese attempt to capture Port Moresby was repulsed in the Battle of the Coral Sea* in May 1942, imposing the first significant check to the Japanese offensive since the start of the Pacific War*.

The Japanese offensive in New Guinea was not relaunched until after the defeat at Midway* in early June, now under the direction of General Hyakutake*, who had succeeded Admiral Inouye as commander of Rabaul. Although a directive issued by the Joint Chiefs of Staff* on 2 July 1942 had identified New Guinea as one of three main targets for the launch of the first American offensive in the Pacific, the Japanese Operational Plan, (recast following the defeat at Midway as a defensive strategy to secure a perimeter chain of bases and fortified islands against potential Allied attacks), forestalled the Allied assault on New Guinea. On 22 July, a transport convoy from Rabaul carrying a crack Japanese regiment under Major General Horii landed at Sanananda, north of Buna*, eastern terminus of the tortuous, jungle-choked Kokoda Trail, over the Owen Stanley Mountains from Port Moresby.

Forcing their way up the Kokoda Trail against the bitter resistance of the retreating elements of the Australian 7th Division under General Honner, Horii's force advanced to within 30 miles of Port Moresby, but the arrival of Allied reinforcements and air cover at Milne Bay, at the tip of the Papuan peninsula, to counter a second prong of the Japanese offensive launched there on 25 August, brought the Port Moresby offensive to a stop. Without reinforcements, who were now committed to the deepening crisis at Guadalcanal*, the Japanese offensive could not be sustained. A renewed counter-offensive by Allied forces under Australian General Blamey* pushed General Horii's force back down the 'Bloody Track' to Kokoda and then Wairopi, where General Horii drowned.

Mobile reinforcements, the arrival of fresh commanders, notably the popular US Lt General Eichelberger*, and the additional support from newly established air bases at Ponangi and Wanigela, shored up the increasingly exhausted Allied forces under General MacArthur, now angrily impatient for a resolution to the prolonged struggle, which he clearly feared might go the same way as his disastrous defence of the Philippines*. The capture of Buna, Gona and Sanananda after many more weeks of bitter fighting, in January 1943, signalled the end of the Allied Papuan campaign. It remained one of the most costly and bitterly fought of the Pacific War.

While the initiative remained with the Allies in Papua, fierce fighting continued on the Huon Peninsula, concentrated in the Lae–Salamaua–Markham Valley region. The loss of a 3,000-strong reinforcement force in March 1943 (see Bismarck Sea, Battle of) and the failure of a concentrated and costly series of air attacks in an attempt to regain air superiority in April (Operation I-Go*) added to the pressure felt by the Japanese command at Rabaul. By August, when new orders from the Joint Chiefs of Staff concentrated MacArthur's efforts on the northeastern coast of New Guinea, the Japanese air strength in New Guinea had been effectively wiped out. In a series of complex amphibious and airborne* attacks designed to bypass major Japanese troop concentrations, MacArthur's forces first feigned a move against Salamaua, to seize Lae, before jumping immediately to Finschhafen, largest port on the strategic Huon Peninsula.

Now in control of the Huon Peninsula, and with General Blamey headquartered at Port Moresby at the head of the large Allied land forces in New Guinea, General MacArthur prepared for a renewed advance, using the same leap-frogging tactics, up New Guinea's northern coast, for he was anxious to establish a position from which to launch his invasion of the Philippines. Landings were made at Saidor on 2 January 1944 (freeing American amphibious troops

for the daring capture of the Admiralty Islands* in February). While the Australian force advanced from the southwest to entrap the Japanese 18th Army (now under General Adachi*), the US 1st Corps led by General Eichelberger made three amphibious landings on 22 April, at Tanahmerah Bay, Humboldt Bay and Aitape. Meeting with little opposition, they were able to combine to take Hollandia*. The continuing advance of the Australian forces up the coast completed the encirclement of Adachi's 18th Army. Organized resistance on New Guinea ended with a final assault across the Toricelli Mountains to Wewak by the Australian 6th Division in May, although General Adachi and his surviving force of 13,000 men did not surrender until 13 September 1945.

New Jersey, USS United States battleship, second unit of the *Iowa** Class, the *New Jersey* was commissioned in May 1943 and won fame as a flagship in the Pacific War*. From February to April 1944, she was under the flag of Admiral Spruance* and took part in the first raid on Truk*, the Japanese stronghold in the Carolines. After operations off the Marianas, she raised the flag of Admiral Halsey* in August 1944 and screened the raids of the Pacific carrier forces from her base at Ulithi until April the following year (see US Navy). During that time she had become the flagship of Battleship Division 7 and as such took part in the assaults on Iwo Jima* and Okinawa*. She ended the war anchored in Tokyo Bay, once more under Admiral Spruance. Although decommissioned after the war, the *New Jersey* was restored to active duty in Korea, in Vietnam and in the Lebanon (1983–4), making her the last American battleship to see action.
BRIEF DATA See Iowa, USS (except: Dimensions: o/a lgth – 887' 6", b – 108'; Armament: 64 × 40mm AA gun.)

New Mexico, USS United States battleship and Class, which also comprised the *Idaho* and *Mississippi*. Launched in 1917, these were re-engined and extensively re-built during 1930–4, making them the most modern battleships available to the US Navy* until the introduction of the *North Carolina* Class in 1941.

At the time of Pearl Harbor* all three vessels were with the Atlantic Fleet on Neutrality Patrol (see Neutrality, US), but they were soon transferred to redress the balance of capital ships in the Pacific. Given the usual American virtues of power-ful main armament and well concentrated armour protection, they fought largely un-altered in the Pacific for the rest of the war, receiving only standard improvements in radar* and vastly increased anti-aircraft* capability. The growth to pre-eminence of the fast aircraft carrier in fleet actions meant that these older, slower battleships were primarily employed as gun support for amphibious* landings, all three surviving numerous campaigns to take part in the assault on Okinawa* in 1945. The night battle between veteran American and Ja-panese battleships in the Surigao Strait* on 24–5 October 1944 was the swansong of traditional naval warfare, and the final radar-laid salvo from the *Mississippi* into the stricken *Yamashiro* was the last act of battleship against battleship. With no vi-able role left to play, the *New Mexico*s were scrapped soon after the war.

BRIEF DATA (*New Mexico*, 1941) Dis-placement: 33,000 tons; Dimensions: o/a lgth – 624', b – 106' 3"; Speed: 21.5 knots; Armament: 12 × 14" gun (4 × 3), 12 × 5" gun, 8 × 5" AA gun, 4 × 6pdr AA gun, 3 aircraft.

New Operational Policy See Pacific War.

New Order in East Asia (Toa shinchit-sujo) A plan for Japanese expansion into Southeast Asia that formed part of the ideological justification for the Japanese Pacific offensives, launched by the attack on Pearl Harbor* in December 1941. An-nounced by Prime Minister Konoe* in November 1938 – along with the offer of peace terms to China* – it envisaged a co-ordination of military, political and economic activities in China and Manchu-kuo* under Japanese leadership in order to resist the threat of communist and western imperialist encroachment on the region. The idea was broadly based on ideals of Asian self-sufficiency (see Ultranational-ism), stability and isolationism as well as anti-communism. It was rejected categori-cally by China who saw it, accurately, as a blueprint for Japan's political and economic hegemony in East Asia. After the outbreak of war in Europe in 1939 and following increasing calls for Japanese control over the colonies of Southeast Asia, a further declaration by Konoe referred to the 'New Order in Greater East Asia' – the area now incorporated much of Southeast Asia (see Greater East Asia Co-Prosperity Sphere).

Developing from the concept of the New Order was the call from some of Japan's political leaders, including Konoe, for a 'new structure' for the economic and politi-cal life of Japan. The New Structure Move-ment (*shintaisei undo*), envisaged the creation of an 'advanced defence state' able to bring about the new order in East Asia, with a planned economy and the establish-ment of a new one-party movement to 'facilitate communication' between government and people and create a unity of purpose. This plan for a new political structure in Japan became official govern-ment policy in July 1940 and in October the Imperial Rule Assistance Association was created as the core structure, though this was subsequently usurped under Gen-eral Hideki Tojo's* leadership and from July 1942, when it took over responsibility for many national organizations and local government units, it was increasingly used as an instrument of national control. See also Pacific War.

New Orleans, USS Completed during 1934–7, the seven *New Orleans* Class heavy cruisers were the last of the type built for the US Navy* under international treaty limitations. Better protected than their predecessors, with advanced hull design and gunnery control systems, they were at least the equal of any contemporary foreign cruiser. Most of the class spent the war in the Pacific. The *New Orleans* was at Pearl Harbor* in December 1941, and fought at the Battles of Coral Sea* and Midway* before losing her bow to a torpedo* at Tassaforonga* in November 1942. A similar fate befell her sister, the *Minneapolis*, during the same action, and less than three weeks earlier the *San Francisco* had suffered serious damage at the decisive naval Battle of Guadalcanal*. All three vessels survived and returned to support the US 'island' offensives until the end of the Pacific War*.

The *Vincennes* and the *Quincy* were both transferred to the Pacific from Neutrality Patrol in the Atlantic* after Pearl Harbor* (see Neutrality, US). Along with their sister the *Astoria*, the Australian cruiser *Canberra* and a destroyer*, they were sunk by Japanese cruisers at the Battle of Savo Island* on the night of 9 August 1942. All three *New Orleans* Class casualties later gave their names to new wartime heavy cruisers. The only unit to see much service in other theatres was the *Tuscaloosa*. She supported the Allied Torch*, Normandy* and Anvil/Dragoon* landings and operated with the British Home Fleet for a time in 1943. She joined her remaining sisters for the final assault on Japan in 1945. Surviving vessels were fitted with full radar* and many additional light weapons, and were quickly retired after the war.

BRIEF DATA (*New Orleans*, 1941) Displacement: 9,950 tons; Dimensions: o/a lgth – 588′ 3″, b – 61′ 9″; Speed: 32.75 knots; Armament: 9 × 8″ gun (3 × 3), 8 × 5″ AA gun, 2 × 3pdr gun, 8 × 0.5″ AA gun, 4 aircraft.

New York, USS United States battleship and class, commissioned in 1914, the *New York* and her sister *Texas* were the first US Navy* warships with 14-inch guns, and were well-armoured if difficult to handle in rough seas. Extensively refitted in 1926, they were on duty in the Atlantic at the

time of Pearl Harbor*, and their careers were typical of the older American battleships in WW2. At first employed in protection of troops convoys, they were later active in the bombardment role in support of amphibious* landings. Both vessels covered the Torch* landings in Northwest Africa in 1942, and in 1944 the *Texas* operated offshore during the Normandy* and Anvil/Dragoon* invasions while the *New York* was being used for gunnery training. Both survived the campaigns at Iwo Jima* and Okinawa* the following year and were retired after the war. The *New York* was used as a nuclear test target, but the *Texas* was preserved as a relic in Houston.

BRIEF DATA (*New York*, 1941) Displacement: 27,000 tons; Dimensions: o/a lgth – 573′, b – 106′ 3″; Speed: 21 knots; Armament: 10 × 14″ gun (5 × 2), 16 × 5″ gun, 8 × 3″ AA gun, 4 × 3pdr gun, 3 aircraft.

New Zealand As a Dominion of the British Commonwealth and Empire, New Zealand enjoyed *de facto* recognition as an independent state, but had made no attempt to proclaim or assert independence before WW2. Social and economic ties with Britain remained far stronger than emerging links with the US or Australia, and it was generally held by both the ruling Labour Party and the opposition National Party that New Zealand would join any war in which Britain was involved. Thus New Zealand entered the war against Germany in September 1939, although (unlike in 1914) it did so with a declaration separate from Britain's.

Early in the war, volunteer New Zealand troops were sent to the Middle East to be trained for fighting in Europe, but they were in fact deployed in Egypt*, Greece* and Crete* during 1940–1. Some NZ troops later fought in the Southwest Pacific, but their major role remained as a component of Allied forces in Africa and Europe until the end of the war. The New Zealand Division of the Royal Navy* consisted of 2 cruisers and 2 escort vessels in 1939, but took on more cruisers and smaller craft to relieve the chronic British naval manpower shortage and became an independent force in October 1941. New Zealand armed forces contained over 150,000 military personnel at their wartime peak in September 1942, and total wartime casualties were 11,625 dead and a further 17,000 wounded. Despite the efforts of its armed forces, New Zealand's most important contribution to the Allied war effort was the supply of food and wool, primarily to Great Britain but later also to Allied forces in the Pacific.

New Zealand remained under a Labour administration throughout WW2, led by Joe Savage as Prime Minister (until his death in March 1940, and then by Peter Fraser, who won the 1943 general election with a reduced majority. When Fraser sought powers of conscription and sequestration to meet growing war needs after the fall of France in 1940, he faced demands for a share in government from National Party leaders. To accommodate these, a system of tandem cabinets was introduced, with Labour politicians continuing to control domestic affairs, while a coalition sat on the War Cabinet. Apart from an unsuccessful attempt at full coalition in 1942, this system remained in fairly harmonious operation throughout the war.

The indigenous Maori population of New Zealand contributed wholeheartedly to the war effort, despite bitterness caused by the treatment of Maori ex-servicemen after WW1. Over 17,000 Maoris volunteered for combat overseas, and the Maori Battalion fought with distinction in North Africa and Italy*. At home the Maori War Effort organization encouraged tribal participation in recruitment, fund-raising and essential war industries. This participation in national endeavour contributed to a post-war improvement in the status accorded to Maoris in a predominantly white society.

Nimitz, Admiral Chester W. (1885–1966) Popular and astute American Admiral who

succeeded Admiral Husband Kimmel* as the C-in-C of the US Pacific Fleet after the devastating Japanese attack on Pearl Harbor* and was directly responsible for the rebuilding and development of the US Navy*. Gathering a core of highly capable naval commanders to cover the huge expanse of ocean for which he was responsible (including Admirals Mitscher*, Halsey*, Spruance*, Kinkaid* and Turner), Nimitz firmly advocated the use of modern techniques of naval warfare and made the earliest possible use of the air strike power of his carriers (which had survived Pearl Harbor) in operations against Japanese bases on Wake Island*, the Gilbert* and Marshall Islands* and on New Guinea*. His first strategic victory, at the Battle of the Coral Sea* in May 1942, was followed a month later by the crucial victory at Midway*. Exploiting the unique advantage offered him by the intelligence gained through Magic* intercepts, which provided detailed information on the Japanese offensive plan, Nimitz was able to deploy his forces to fight off a superior force and decisively halt the Japanese strategic initiative in the Central Pacific, ending the Japanese threat to Hawaii and the Panama Canal.

By the end of the year, Nimitz had consolidated this achievement with another crucial success at Guadalcanal*. Target for the first American offensive and large-scale amphibious assault of the war, the land and sea battles around Guadalcanal (see Guadalcanal, Naval Battle of) in the second half of 1942 stretched both commanders and troops to the limit of their experience and endurance. The final outcome put the United States in control of sea and air in the Southern Solomons.

During 1943, following the division of the Pacific into two commands under Nimitz (Central Pacific) and General MacArthur* (Southwest Pacific) and the reinforcement of the US Pacific Fleet with new ships and aircraft, Nimitz strongly favoured the development of a Central Pacific island campaign, based on amphibious* assaults, as the most effective way to defeat Japan. Although this approach was in direct contention with General MacArthur's preferred line of attack, via the Philippines, it was agreed by the Joint Chiefs of Staff* and initiated with assaults on the Gilbert Islands (Makin and Tarawa), followed by strikes at Kwajalein, Eniwetok and Truk* early in 1944. Employing his submarine* force to blockade Japanese merchant shipping while his fast carrier task forces opened the way for successive assaults on Saipan*, Guam* and Palau*, Nimitz's forces effectively drove the Japanese forces back to the limits of their defensive perimeter. Working in concert with General MacArthur, whose fanatical insistence had finally persuaded the Joint Chiefs to approve his offensive via the Philippines* in late 1944, Nimitz presided over the major victories at Leyte Gulf*, Okinawa* and Iwo Jima*, which took the US Fleet within striking range of the Japanese home islands. Nimitz was promoted to Fleet Admiral on 19 December 1944.

Following the Japanese surrender, which was formally accepted on board his flagship, the USS *Missouri*, on 2 September 1945, Nimitz succeeded Admiral Ernest King* as Chief of Naval Operations. His contribution to the American victory in the Pacific, as a skilled strategist and a decisive commander, was acknowledged in many decorations and reflected in the immense personal popularity that he enjoyed within the American armed forces.

Nine-Power Treaty One of several important agreements arising from the Washington Naval Conference (November 1921– February 1922) which bound the signatories (US, Britain, Japan, China, France, Belgium, Italy, the Netherlands and Portugal) to 'respect the sovereignty, the independence and the territorial . . . integrity of China'. Ostensibly an international sanctioning of the classical American 'Open Door' policy, the treaty was nevertheless violated by Japan, when she began her assertion of power in the Far East in

the 1930s. See China, Campaigns in; Manchuria.

NKVD (Narodnyi Kommissariat Vnutrennykh Del) Soviet political police and counter-intelligence organization created from OGPU (Unified State Political Administration) in July 1934 under Henrik Yagoda, its multifarious functions before the war included control of the militia (regular police), concentration camps, and maintenance of a huge intelligence network and subversive operations abroad. With the outbreak of war NKVD's activities expanded (now under the leadership of Lavrenti Beria*) to include counter-intelligence operations, conducting political surveillance of military units and searching for deserters and 'draft dodgers'. The NKVD also conducted massive purges of foreign populations considered hostile to the Soviet state. In eastern Poland*, Bessarabia and the Baltic states (Estonia*, Latvia* and Lithuania*) hundreds of thousands of people were executed or deported to Siberia. After the German invasion had begun in 1941 (see Eastern Front), NKVD squads carried out mass executions of political prisoners and were also allocated to fighting units to prevent unauthorized desertions on the front and try deserters at special NKVD tribunals. As the tide of the campaign on the Eastern Front turned against the invaders, many of the NKVD's most brutal operations were conducted in retribution against war criminals and collaborators.

Nomonhan Incident See Russo-Japanese Border Conflict.

Nomura, Admiral Kichisaburo (1877– 1964) One of Japan's most able naval commanders, and a delegate to Versailles and the Washington Naval Conference during the interwar period, Nomura served as Foreign Minister in Abe's cabinet in 1939 and accepted an appointment as ambassador to Washington in 1940. He was thus involved in the difficult and finally abortive negotiations with Cordell Hull* in Washington that preceded the Pearl Harbor* attack. After repatriation to Japan, Nomura resigned from the diplomatic service. See also Pacific War.

Nordwind, Operation See Alsace, German Offensive in, 1944.

Norfolk, HMS See Dorsetshire, HMS.

Normandy, Invasion of, 6 June 1944 (Code-name Overlord) Long-term plans for a cross-Channel invasion of France had been drawn up by British Joint Planning staff as early as September 1941 (code-named Roundup), but serious discussion of the viability of an invasion was brought forward by the American military chiefs after the US entry into the war in December. Early in 1942, a report by Lt General Eisenhower* of the US War Department's Operations Divisions drew attention to the problem facing the United States in fighting in two major war theatres with very limited resources.

Supported by the US Army C-in-C, General Marshall*, a plan to build up US forces in Britain was presented to President Roosevelt*, code-named Bolero, which projected an invasion within a year. An alternative plan, Sledgehammer, covered the possibility of an emergency invasion to establish a beachhead 'Second Front' should Russia show signs of collapse on the Eastern Front*. Marshall persuasively argued with Roosevelt the need to confront and defeat Germany as quickly as possible, in order to concentrate on Japanese forces now scoring successive major victories in the Pacific.

The ferocity of Churchill's opposition to the plan, which he and British military chiefs considered impetuous folly, foreshadowed the Anglo-American conflict over overall strategy in Europe that was to dog Allied relations in the following months (see Conferences).

Despite Roosevelt's decision to back Churchill and support his alternative plan

for an Allied invasion of Northwest Africa (Torch*), the debate continued acrimoniously at the Allied Conference at Casablanca in January 1943, when, with the North African campaign still commanding substantial Allied reserves, it became clear that the continental invasion would have to be postponed further, and could not be mounted before 1944. Nevertheless, a combined Anglo-American headquarters (COSSAC), was established in England in April 1943 under British General Morgan, to co-ordinate planning, and, most importantly, to supervise the immensely complex and widespread deception plans being carried out by Allied and resistance* agents all over Europe. At the Trident and Tehran Conferences during 1943, the combined pressure of Stalin, Roosevelt and the US service chiefs drew a full acceptance of the Normandy invasion plan from Churchill by the end of the year.

Perhaps the single most important factor in the success of Overlord (now with a target date of May 1944) was the deception operations (code-named Jael and later Bodyguard*) themselves crucially dependent on Ultra* information, which enabled the Allies to monitor the German response to their deceptions and adjust their operations accordingly. Meanwhile, the planning for Overlord was handed over to the newly appointed Supreme Allied Commander, General Eisenhower, at his headquarters (SHAEF, Supreme Headquarters Allied Expeditionary Force) in London. At the instigation of General Montgomery* who was to exercise operational command of Overlord, Eisenhower modified the COSSAC plan by increasing the number of ground assault and airborne* divisions for the landings, and postponing the invasion date for one month, thus ensuring sufficient time for operations to reduce the strength of the Luftwaffe*, a vital prerequisite of success.

The choice of location was largely dictated by the need for short-range fighter support. The plan projected assaults on five beaches west of the Orne River near Caen (code-named Sword, Juno, Gold, Omaha and Utah) by the British 2nd Army and the American 1st Army, combined as the 21st Army Group. Follow-up forces included the Canadian 1st Army under Lt General Crerar* and the American 3rd Army under Lt General Patton* (later to join up with the rest of US forces in the 12th Army Group under General Bradley*). Eisenhower's deputy, Air Chief Marshal Tedder* and Leigh-Mallory*, his Air C-in-C co-ordinated the massive strategic and tactical air forces (including over 13,000 American aircraft) assigned to the invasion; Admiral Ramsay* commanded the naval force of 5,000 ships. Once the battle zone had been isolated by the Allied air forces and beachheads had been established, the Allied armies were to be supplied initially from there, using two prefabricated harbours (code-named Mulberries*), until major ports were taken. A 'lodgement area' between the Seine and the Loire was then to be consolidated, before the start of the drive into Germany.

Although the German forces opposing them numbered over 50 divisions (including 10 armoured), Allied air superiority added to the advantage already gained by the success of deception plan Fortitude. By assembling a fictitious army, US 1st Army Group, with dummy installations, radio traffic, etc., the Allies successfully reinforced the view of Hitler and his Western Front commander Rundstedt* that the invasion would be centred on the Pas de Calais. A similar deception, Fortitude North, gave indications of preparations for the invasion of Norway, using the British 4th Army in Scotland. So successful were the deceptions that even after the invasion had begun, Hitler continued to deny Rundstedt reinforcements for Normandy, in the belief that the main invasion was yet to come.

Although stormy weather at one critical point appeared to jeopardize the whole plan, news of a slight improvement, enough to enable the air forces to play their vital part, brought the irrevocable decision to launch Overlord on the night of 6 June. As the airborne landings (by British 6th Division and US 82nd and 101st Divisions) drew two counter-attacking panzer divisions under devastating fire from supporting Allied fighters, the landings themselves began, supported by naval bombardment and heavy bombing attacks along the entire northwestern coast of France (see Transportation Plan). British and Canadian troops stormed ashore with minimal difficulty, making speedy contact with an airborne division, and spared a German armoured counter-attack by the devastating firepower of covering British warships.

On Omaha and Utah, however, the American landings were made in heavy, pitching surf. At Omaha, steep cliffs favoured the defenders, whose artillery rained down on the landing craft and amphibious vehicles, causing 2,500 American casualties. Nevertheless, slow reactions from Hitler's headquarters had held back the two reserve panzer divisions at Rundstedt's disposal for a full day, and Hitler's conviction that the main invasion was yet to come left the German 15th Army's 19 divisions waiting impotently at the Pas de Calais. By the evening of the first day, all five Allied divisions (approximately 150,000 men) were ashore in Normandy, with the flanks already in contact with the airborne units. It represented an enormous achievement for Allied planners, military chiefs and fighting troops and perhaps above all, an outstanding feat of secrecy and deception, Churchill's 'bodyguard of lies', to which Overlord ultimately owed its success. See Northwest Europe, Allied Invasion of; Amphibious Warfare.

North Africa See Egypt, Campaign for; Desert War; Torch; Tunisia, Campaign for.

North American B-25 Mitchell The most produced and most successful American twin-engined combat aircraft of the war, the B-25 Mitchell first flew in 1940 and was ordered into production immediately, seeing action with the USAAF* from the start of the Pacific War*. B-25Bs, which were fitted with an additional gun turret, bombed Japan in April 1942, successfully taking off from the dangerously short runway of the carrier *Hornet** (see Doolittle, Lt Colonel James). The B-25C and D models, with external racks and extra fuel tanks, were supplied to the Red Air Force*, the RAF*, China* and the US Navy*. From August 1942 the B-25G ground-attack version entered US service, mounting a fearsome 75mm field cannon and bristling with machine-guns. The B-25H variant was even more powerfully armed, but cannon were abandoned in the mass-produced B-25J, which operated on all fronts both as a glass-nosed bomber and a solid-nosed attack plane. An F10 photo-reconnaissance version and the A-24 trainer also saw service. The total output of Mitchells was 9,816. Deliveries stopped after August 1945, but the plane served as a post-war transport and remained popular for years with numerous small air forces.

BRIEF DATA (B-25J) Type: 4–6-man medium bomber/attack plane; Engine: 2 × 1,850hp Wright Double Cyclone; Max speed: 275mph; Ceiling: 24,000'; Range: 1,500m; Arms: 13 × 0.5" mg (18 in attack version); Bomb load: 4,000lb.

North Cape, Battle of See Scharnhorst.

North Carolina, USS American battleship and Class. The *North Carolina* and her sister the *Washington* were the US Navy's* first new battleships for 18 years when they were commissioned in 1941. American refusal to compromise firepower or armament in search of speed (experiments in the 1920s with British-style battlecruisers like the *Hood** had been quickly scrapped), left the *North Carolinas* a little slower than their foreign contemporaries, but quite their equal in fighting capability. Deficiencies in light anti-aircraft* defence were soon corrected, and both vessels were crammed with a great many rapid-firing cannon together with the latest in radar* and com-

munications technology by the end of the war.

The *North Carolina* spent 1941 in the Atlantic*, but was transferred to the Pacific the following spring. On 15 September 1942 she was torpedoed by the Japanese submarine *I-15* off the East Solomons* but survived to serve as escort to the fast carrier task forces from late 1943 until VE day. The *Washington* remained in the Atlantic for a time in 1942 with the British Home Fleet before transferring to the Pacific. There she demonstrated her worth at the hard-fought naval battle of Guadalcanal*, sinking the Japanese battleship *Kirishima** on the night of 14–15 November 1942. She, too, spent the last years of the war in support of carriers on Pacific raids and troubleshooting operations. Both ships were decommissioned in 1947.

BRIEF DATA (*North Carolina*, 1941) Displacement: 35,000 tons; Dimensions: o/a lgth – 728' 9", b – 108' 3"; Speed: 28 knots; Armament: 9 × 16" gun (3 × 3), 20 × 5" DP gun, 16 × 1.1" AA mg, 12 × 0.5" AA mg, 3 aircraft.

Northampton, USS US Navy* heavy cruiser and Class, which also comprised the *Augusta*, *Chester*, *Houston* and *Louisville*. Commissioned in 1930–1, they featured more efficiently grouped main armament than their predecessors. The *Northampton* fought at Midway* and Santa Cruz* before being torpedoed and sunk by a Japanese destroyer off Guadalcanal* on 1 December 1942. Two of her sisters were also lost. The *Houston* was one of only two Allied ships to survive the Battle of the Java Sea* in February 1942, but was sunk in Banten Bay, Java*, a few days later. The *Chicago* was torpedoed off Savo Island* in August of that year, but survived and was repaired only to be sunk off Rennel Island immediately after her return to the Pacific War* in early 1943. Both ships later gave their names to new wartime cruisers.

Surviving units were fitted with gunnery and warning radar and the standard proliferation of additional light anti-aircraft* guns. The *Louisville* and *Chester* fought throughout the war in the Pacific, both surviving serious battle damage. The *Augusta* was used to carry President Roosevelt to Placentia Bay in 1941, and President Truman to Potsdam in 1945 (see Conferences). In between she supported major Allied amphibious* operations in Africa and Europe, escorted Atlantic* troop carriers and covered Arctic convoys* from her anchorage in Scapa Flow. Like all pre-war American cruisers, the surviving *Northamptons* were retired at the end of the war.

BRIEF DATA (*Northampton*, 1941) Displacement: 9,050 tons; Dimensions: o/a lgth – 600' 3", b – 66'; Speed: 32.5 knots; Armament: 9 × 8" gun (3 × 3), 8 × 5" AA gun, 2 × 3pdr AA gun, 8 × 0.5" AA gun, 4 aircraft.

Northwest Europe, Allied Invasion of, 1944–5 In retrospect, the successful Allied invasion of France and the subsequent success of the broad-front advance into Germany may appear almost a foregone conclusion. Its well-conceived strategy, careful preparation and sophisticated execution underpin this view. But it is important not to underestimate the tremendous Allied achievement in co-ordinating and sustaining such a vast effort, or ignore some of the vital factors which underscored it. The importance of the part played by the Allied tactical and strategic air forces can hardly be overstated, both in the preparation for the landings (see Transportation Plan) and in maintaining complete air supremacy over the outnumbered Luftwaffe* in support of ground operations throughout the campaign.

Key to the successful landing and establishment of the 150,000 strong invasion force was the maintenance of the Allied deception plans – Churchill's 'bodyguard* of lies' – aided considerably by Ultra*, and the tight secrecy which cloaked its preparation (see Normandy, Invasion of). But other factors also decisively affected the progress of the campaign. Once the Allies

began to move out from their Normandy beachhead positions, they faced an enemy increasingly subject to the remote but fanatical control of Hitler, now directing the defence from his Berchtesgaden retreat. Hitler's continual command changes and his exercise of tactical control, especially during the initial landing stage in Normandy*, decisively disadvantaged the German defence.

Even before the Allied front pushed out towards Paris*, however, disagreement and recrimination also affected the Allied military effort. In particular, the furious competition that developed between Army Group Commander Montgomery*, and US 3rd Army Commander, General Patton* (and which had already been established during the campaign in Sicily*), provoked some costly mistakes that checked the pace of the Allied drive. The over-extension of resources in this race to spearhead the Allied advance and the time lost in correcting earlier mistakes gave Hitler a final opportunity to launch a major counter-offensive in December that severely jeopardized the whole campaign (see Battle of the Bulge; Alsace).

The Breakout from Normandy. (See Map 36.) Vital to the consolidation of the Normandy* landings, which had successfully launched the Allied cross-Channel invasion of France on 6 June 1944, was the maintenance of the Fortitude deception plan (designed to keep significant German forces in the Pas de Calais) and the continued raiding of German positions by the Allied air forces, to harass and delay German troop movements. Of the seven panzer divisions allocated to the defence (since Hitler had ignored Western Front commander Rundstedt's* and General Rommel's* consistent requests for reinforcements), only three were in position to support the German 7th Army's countermoves, while the rest, harried by an air attack, drove from the south of France, the Eastern Front and the Netherlands. Nevertheless, US 1st Army's advance under General Bradley* to cut off the Cotentin Peninsula and isolate Cherbourg* was made with difficulty over marshland and boxed hedgerow country that favoured the German defence. At the same time, the efforts of the British 2nd Army under Montgomery to breakout to Caen were frustrated by German armoured forces deployed against them.

Storms in the Channel between 19 and 22 June halted unloading on the beachheads in a further check to the Allied advance, but the American breakthrough at Cotentin on 18 June, followed by the capture of Cherbourg on the 26th, enabled follow-up forces to gather behind it. By 1 July, the Allies had equalled the German forces in strength, and would soon outstrip them. With almost a million men and 177,000 vehicles now in place, Hitler's decision not to sanction any withdrawals or free the 19 divisions held at the Pas de Calais was suicidal. The crisis faced by Germany was reflected in Hitler's sullen removal of Field Marshal Rundstedt as Western Front commander, and by the increasingly irrational exercise of his supreme command, particularly after the July Bomb* attempt on his life. The new commander, Field Marshal von Kluge* (who had also lost Army Group B commander Field Marshal Rommel*, seriously wounded in a strafing attack), had no alternative but to continue to commit his forces piecemeal.

Following the crucial American breakout at Avranches* on 25 July by six of Bradley's 1st Army divisions – preceded by a massive 'carpet bombing' strike on German positions (see Cobra) – Kluge was finally given leave by Hitler to release the armoured divisions from the Pas de Calais and ordered to concentrate eight of his nine available panzer divisions for a counter-attack on the deep but narrow spearhead of the Allied advance, pushing south from Avranches to Mortain. Although the Mortain counter-attack, launched on 6 August, made early gains of a few miles against the 1st Army (now under Hodges) and those corps of Patton's 3rd Army not fighting in Brittany*, an attack southeastwards by the Canadian 1st Army to threaten Falaise also threatened the envelopment of the whole of the German armoured force in a pocket between Argentan* and Falaise. Caution among the Allied field commanders (notably Montgomery) slowed up the exploitation of this advantage, allowing some 35,000 Germans to escape before the two enveloping pincers finally closed the gap. Nevertheless, as General Model* arrived in France to replace the discredited Kluge, and the news of the Allied invasion of southern France (see Anvil/Dragoon) filtered through the German ranks, the precariousness of the German situation could no longer be ignored. On the way home to Germany, well aware of the sort of reception that awaited him, Field Marshal Kluge committed suicide.

Defence of the West Wall. By 11 September, Paris* had been liberated and forward patrols of the Allied invasion forces that had landed in the south of France made contact with patrols of Eisenhower's northern forces at Dijon (see Map 37). Now reorganized under Lt General Devers* as the 6th Army Group, the southern force came under Eisenhower's direct command for the drive into Germany. Despite the successful advances, overstretched Allied supply lines still ran back to the Normandy beaches, since no Channel ports had yet been secured. The result was a significant loss of momentum at the beginning of September, which enabled German forces to reorganize somewhat for the defence of their homeland. In making the decision to pursue the disorganized German armies east, instead of halting to consolidate the lodgement area around the Seine called for in the original plan, Eisenhower therefore took a calculated risk. In further deciding on a broad-front strategy for the advance, with Montgomery's armies in the north and Bradley's in the south, the Supreme Allied Commander put extra strain on the already stretched Allied supply lines, and provoked increasing arguments with his field commanders, notably Montgomery and Patton, who were anxious to see a concentration of forces behind their respective spearheads for an eastward advance that was fast becoming a race.

Although Eisenhower could not be won over by either commander, he did sanction the controversial operation, code-named Market-Garden, mounted by Montgomery on three important Dutch river positions in September. Despite the serious checks to the Allied advance that had already resulted from Montgomery's tactical oversight at Antwerp*, and the costly failure of Operation Market-Garden (see Arnhem), the two rival commanders continued to stretch their supply lines and demand·reinforcements to support new drives, each aiming to beat the other to the Rhine before the onset of winter.

Meanwhile, the western advance of the Soviet armies into Poland* and the continued Allied bombing of German factories, communications and cities highlighted the desperate situation facing Field Marshal Rundstedt (reinstated as C-in-C in the west on 5 September) and Model (now Army Group B commander) in the autumn of 1944. The defence of Germany's West Wall, which followed the line of Germany's 1939 frontier as far as the Netherlands, was not considered practicable by the German field commanders now gathering their 63 depleted divisions for a stand in compliance with Hitler's orders. The alternative, a retreat to the Rhine*, was not considered by Hitler, who was already planning a major counter-offensive on the US 3rd Army's southern flank.

Correctly assessing the extent to which the Allies had outrun their supply lines, Hitler confidently prepared a December assault through the Ardennes*, where the Allied front was thinly held by reserve troops. While the British in the north fought through October and November to clear the Scheldt estuary, and Patton's 3rd Army pushed through Lorraine in the south to Metz, the US 1st and 9th Armies pushed through to Aachen and the Hürtgen Forest, though difficult terrain, changing weather and stubborn German resistance inhibited

real progress on all Allied fronts. The greatest gains were made south of the Ardennes in Alsace by French and American armies of the 6th Army Group under Devers, who had fought all the way up from the Mediterranean and by December had succeeded in pushing the German defence across the Meuse river line, beyond Strasbourg (captured on 23 November) and into a bridgehead west of the Rhine called the Colmar Pocket. Although Dever's forces were first to reach the Rhine itself, their advance was halted by the launch of Hitler's Ardennes offensive on 16 December.

Battle of the Bulge. There is no doubt that the assault by three German panzer armies on the US 1st Army in the Ardennes completely surprised General Eisenhower and temporarily placed the fate of the Allied campaign in the hands of a small number of highly tenacious American units, before the sheer size and mobility of Allied forces intervened to retake the initiative (see Battle of the Bulge). A subsidiary offensive in Alsace*, code-named Nordwind and designed to stop the movement of American troops to the Ardennes, similarly achieved limited success, and by the end of January 1945 it was clear that the ambitiousness of Hitler's plan had failed to take into account the limitation of German resources.

Crossing the Rhine. Despite pressure from General Bradley, who favoured driving on beyond the Ardennes to the Rhine, Eisenhower turned his attention back to the north as the focus for the main effort, drawing 1st and 3rd Army divisions to reinforce the 9th Army under Montgomery at Aachen. Strong resistance from the largest force still remaining on the German front, Army Group H under General Student*, held up Montgomery's drive until the beginning of March, when the 9th Army reached the Rhine at Düsseldorf and joined up with the Canadian 1st Army.

Despite continued protests from Field Marshal Rundstedt, Hitler refused to allow a withdrawal behind the Rhine. As the bulk of the Allied forces returned to the offensive, clearing the whole Rhineland north and south of the Moselle River by the end of March, General Patton pre-empted Montgomery's set-piece assault across the Rhine, code-named Plunder (and prepared with characteristic caution by the British general) by sneaking a division of his 3rd Army across the river at Oppenheim, while German attention was focused on the Ludendorff railway bridge at Remagen*, the latter discovered undemolished by an American combat patrol scouting ahead of its armoured division. The arrival on 10 March of Field Marshal Kesselring* to replace Rundstedt could not affect the extreme seriousness of Germany's position.

The unqualified success of Montgomery's northern assault on the Rhine signalled the end of effective German resistance to the Allied advance. With the Allied spearhead now in the hands of Bradley's 12th Army Group in the centre of the front, Bradley's 1st and US 9th Armies were allocated to encircle the Ruhr*, trapping German Army Group B and units of Army Group A's Parachute Army in a double envelopment which brought over 325,000 prisoners. Army Group B commander Field Marshal Model, committed suicide on 21 April. In advances which exceeded those made in France, the seven Allied armies moved up to 50 miles a day through undefended countryside, checked only in minute pockets where local resistance vainly engaged Allied units. On 24 April the British 2nd Army reached the Elbe in the north, cutting off the Denmark peninsula and capturing Bremen, Lübeck and Hamburg by 3 May. Fighting in the Netherlands between the Canadian 1st Army and elements of Army Group H was suspended on 22 April when desperate pleas from the German High Commissioner, Seyss-Inquart*, drew attention to the plight of the starving Dutch population, and a truce was arranged to allow supplies and food to be airlifted into the Netherlands.

In the centre of the front, armoured spearheads of the 9th Army reached the Elbe near Magdeburg on 11 April, establishing a bridgehead only 50 miles from the German capital. But with the Soviet armies in position less than 30 miles from the German capital, Eisenhower had already made the decision to halt the 1st and 9th Army drives in that direction and instead to consolidate the central area before driving south to meet a rumoured last-ditch German stand in the Alps, the so-called National Redoubt.

After the fall of Leipzig to the 9th Army on 18 April, forward patrols to the east made first contact with Russian forces and both 1st and 9th Armies neared their final objectives. Further south, the 3rd Army moved alongside the 7th Army for drives into Bavaria, Czechoslovakia* and Austria*. Meanwhile, General Devers' 6th Army Group, swinging southeast from their Rhine bridgeheads, had fought against a firm defence at Heilbronn and Nuremberg, before sweeping through the Black Forest to take Stuttgart on 22 April. Crossing the Danube on the same day, Munich was captured on 30 April and Salzburg on 4 May. The next day an American column crossed the Brenner Pass to make contact with Allied forces in northern Italy. By that time, the final Russian offensive on Berlin* had already begun.

Norway, German Invasion of Hitler's decision to invade the neutral state of Norway in February 1940 was triggered in part by the 'Altmark Incident'*. Outraged by the British action, Hitler's attention was now drawn to the potential benefits to Britain that would result from an occupation of Norway. With major ports on the North Sea, trade and supply routes through the Norwegian Leads (deep sheltered-water passages between the mainland and offshore islands between the Arctic and Stavanger) along which valuable Swedish iron ore was carried from Kiruna, and a strategic position to threaten German control of the Baltic, Hitler was persuaded of the necessity for a pre-emptive invasion. After a month of preparation, overall commander General Falkenhorst launched a series of small simultaneous landings at Oslo, Bergen, Kristiansund, Trondheim and Narvik, with supporting airborne assaults at Oslo and Stavanger airports on 9 April 1940.

The successful invasion was the world's first offensive airborne* operation, troops being ferried into Norway by the Luftwaffe's* transport fleet (see Map 5). It was also the first amphibious* landing of the war, and was carried out despite the nearby presence of a powerful Royal Navy* fleet, which was preparing for Britain's own planned mining of Norwegian waters to interrupt Swedish iron-ore supplies. Although most German Navy units reached Norway in safety, they were caught by the British before they could return. Nine German destroyers and a U-boat were sunk in Narvikfjord by a flotilla led by the British battleship *Warspite*; three cruisers and four more U-boats were lost in other peripheral actions; four major units were also damaged and temporarily out of commission. Although the Royal Navy lost an aircraft carrier and several smaller units, it was far better able to absorb losses than the relatively tiny German surface fleet (see German Navy).

Although the landings at Oslo were delayed long enough to allow the escape of the Norwegian royal family, cabinet and many MPs, and the King courageously rejected Hitler's demand for acceptance of a government under the Norwegian Nazi, Vidkun Quisling*, the largely militia Norwegian Army under Colonel Otto Ruge was unable to challenge the speedy German capture of the coastal cities, nor the decisive effect of German air cover from newly occupied Danish airfields, which enabled German forces to control most of southern Norway by 16 April. An expeditionary force of British and French troops arrived at Namsos and Andalsnes and had initial successes in the Trondheim area, but was finally unable to hold its positions in central Norway, which was also abandoned to German forces at the beginning of May.

In the north at Narvik, which had been captured by the Allies, fighting continued until June, when the crisis in France necessitated the evacuation of the expeditionary force. Resistance formally ended on 9 June, with an armistice signed by Colonel Ruge. For Germany, the victory in Norway had been won at great cost to the Navy, but had provided an early demonstration of the effectiveness of inter-service co-operation that was to be perfected so dramatically in the Western Offensive* which followed it. See also Resistance.

Novikov, Marshal Aleksandr (1900–76) C-in-C of the Red Air Force* from 1942 to 1946, Novikov figured prominently in the reorganization of the Soviet air forces following the German invasion of 1941 (see Eastern Front). Novikov commanded air operations on the Leningrad*, Stalingrad* and Kursk* fronts and during the campaign in Belorussia. In 1944 he became first Russian Marshal of the Air Force.

NSDAP (Nationalsozialistische Deutsche Arbeiterpartei) The Nazi Party. Formed in 1919 by Anton Drexler, Dietrich Eckart and Karl Harrer as the *Deutsche Arbeiterpartei* with Hitler as member number 7. See Hitler, Adolf.

Nuremberg War Trials The International Military Tribunal* which sat in Nuremberg from November 1945 to September 1946 to try the major Nazi figures for war crimes. The legal basis for the establishment of the Nuremberg Tribunal was unique in judicial history. As early as 1943, the United Nations War Crimes Commission had been established in London and British, American and Russian delegates had decided on the need to return Germans charged with atrocious crimes to the countries in which they had been committed. By May 1945, an international tribunal had been agreed on, to consist of American, British, French and Russian judges and prosecutors. Defendants (and organizations such as the Gestapo*) were to be tried on four counts: for crimes against peace (planning and making war); for war crimes (responsibility for crimes during war); for crimes against humanity (to cover racial persecution) and for conspiracy (to commit crimes alleged in other courts).

A shortlist of the most notorious surviving leaders was agreed by the Tribunal, and others were added at individual countries' insistence, though dispute continued on the list of 23 names after its publication in August 1945. The defending lawyers were Germans, and operated under obvious difficulties. Their most effective defence often lay in questioning the precedent for these charges, rather than attempting to prove innocence in specific circumstances. Of 21 senior Nazis that finally stood trial, the verdicts and sentences given were: death for Göring*, Frank*, Frick*, Jodl*, Kaltenbrunner*, Keitel*, Ribbentrop*, Rosenberg*, Sauckel*, Seyss-Inquart* and Streicher*; life imprisonment for Funk, Hess* and Raeder; 20 years for von Shirach* and Speer*; 15 years for von Neurath* and 10 for Dönitz*. Fritsch*, von Papen and Schacht* were found not guilty.

Nürnberg German Navy* light cruiser, launched in late 1934, which survived the war and later served with the Red Navy* as the *Admiral Makarov*.
BRIEF DATA (1939) Displacement: 6,980 tons; Dimensions: o/a lgth – 593′ 9″, b – 53′ 3″; Speed: 32 knots; Armament: 9 × 5.9″ gun (3 × 3), 8 × 3.5″ AA gun, 8 × 37mm AA gun, 4 × 20mm AA gun, 12 × 21″ TT, 2 aircraft.

O

Oboe Navigational aid used by the RAF*
from December 1942, as one of several
methods of improving the accuracy of its
night bombing operations over Germany.
A control station in Britain broadcast a
radar beam in the direction of the target,
and another beam tracked an Oboe-
equipped Pathfinder* bomber. The controller could then guide the aircraft directly
to the target. Although it was more effective than the earlier Gee system (a radio-
based device soon jammed by the Germans)
Oboe had its drawbacks. The curvature of
the earth restricted the range of all land-
based signals, and Oboe was reliant on the
performance of a single aircraft. Airborne
H2S radar* sets were installed in British
bombers for the first time in early 1943,
and they solved these problems. Similar
to the 10cm search radar used by naval
anti-submarine* aircraft, H2S was unable
to provide more than a general picture of
land targets and its success largely depended
on the interpretive skill of its operator. An
improved H2X version was produced in the
US by the end of the year in far greater
numbers than Britain's limited capacity had
allowed, and it was used to guide USAAF*
daylight bombers to German targets in bad
weather. See Strategic Bombing Offensive.

O'Connor, General Sir Richard (1889–
1981) In 1940 Lt General O'Connor was
transferred from Palestine to lead the British Western Desert Force in Egypt. He
commanded it throughout its successful
campaign against the Italian 10th Army
between December 1940 and February 1941
(see Egypt). On 6 April 1941, he was captured by a forward German unit while driving to take control of the British retreat
from Cyrenaica. Held captive in Italy until
his escape in December 1943, O'Connor
returned to action as 8th Corps commander
during the Allied breakout from Normandy*. In January 1945 he became C-
in-C Eastern Command, India.

Octagon Code-name for the second Allied
Conference at Quebec, 12–16 September
1944. See Conferences, Allied.

Oder–Neisse Line The eventual choice for
the western boundary of post-war Poland*
was much disputed by the Western Allies
and the Soviet Union. Two rivers called
Neisse flow into the Oder, one to the east
of Breslau (now Wroclaw, Poland), the
other significantly further to the east. Despite Anglo-American protests, the line
Oder–Western Neisse was finally confirmed as the boundary. See Conferences.

Odessa Black Sea port which served as the
main Russian naval base for the western
Black Sea before WW2. Odessa and the
southern Ukrainian region from Bessarabia
to the Bug River were granted by Hitler to
Rumania* in return for participation in
the war against the Soviet Union, but the
territory (renamed Transnistria by Rumanians) and Odessa itself were reclaimed by
the Soviet Union during the battles in the
Ukraine* in spring 1944.

Odessa See Nazi Escape Organizations.

Oerlikon Gun Swiss 20mm anti-aircraft
gun ordered by the British government in

1939 to ease a desperate shortage of light naval weapons. From 1940 it was manufactured under licence in Britain, demand constantly outstripping production. Shortages of viable alternatives – particularly the 40mm Bofors gun – meant that the Oerlikon gun remained in widespread service throughout the war, although it had been outmoded by the development of heavily armoured strike aircraft. See Antiaircraft Defence.

O'Hare, Lt Commander Edward (1914–43) US Navy* pilot who earned the Medal of Honor for his superb combat flying in a Grumman F6F Hellcat* during an air battle over Bougainville*, in February 1942. 'Butch' O'Hare was killed in action in November 1943 during the Gilbert Islands* campaign. Chicago international airport is named in his honour.

OKH (Oberkommando des Heeres) German Army High Command. See OKW.

Okinawa Island in the Ryukyu group south of Formosa* and the Japanese home islands, and target of the last American amphibious* assault of the war, it claimed the most casualties of any Allied campaign against Japanese forces in the Pacific War* (see Map 11). Chosen in preference to Formosa or the Philippines* as the final springboard for the invasion of Japan, the assault on Okinawa (Operation Iceberg) was a colossal military operation, on a scale comparable with the Allied landings in Normandy*, and projected a landing of 154,000 experienced veterans of the Pacific islands campaign in a five-division assault on the Haguushi beachhead in the southwest of the island. The defence of Okinawa was in the hands of General Ushijima* and 100,000 troops of the 32nd Army, who had constructed a formidable series of defensive lines in three concentric circles, centred on the ancient castle of the Regents of Okinawa at Shuri, in the very south of the island. The heaviest concentration of Japanese artillery of the war was as-

sembled along these defensive lines, dug in along a series of defiles among the hills around Shuri. Ushijima's plan was to abandon the defence of the beachhead and draw the invasion force inland, away from the cover of aerial and naval bombardment, under the enormous firepower of the entrenched Japanese artillery.

Supported by a four-day pre-invasion bombardment, as well as pre-emptive strikes on ships and bases along the Honshu coast of Japan by aircraft from American carrier Task Force 58 and a Royal Navy* carrier force under Admiral Rawlings (both under repeated attack from Kamikaze* raids), the 1,300-ship invasion force manoeuvred into position off the west coast of Okinawa on 1 April 1945. Assigned to a mixed force of Marines and the US 10th Army under the overall command of Lt General Simon Buckner, the assault was to be carried out by 3rd Marines (including the 1st Division) under Major General Roy Geiger and 14th Army Corps (consisting of 7th and 96th Divisions). Two Marine divisions and 27th Army Division were held in reserve.

On the first day 60,000 troops were put ashore against no opposition at Haguushi, while US ships bombarded the island with 100,000 shells and rockets. Two airfields were captured in the American drive to the east coast on 2 April. While the 6th Marine Division broke off to fight northwards up the Motobu Peninsula, the three remaining divisions moved south, reaching the Shuri defences on 4 April. The 24th Corps, first into the bloody battle at Shuri, advanced yard by yard among the forward and reverse emplacements, suffering high casualties, for more than two weeks before the arrival of the 1st Marine Division on their right flank. Reinforced again in early May by the 3rd Amphibious Corps and 6th Marine Division, the invaders managed to repel a ferocious counter-attack by Ushijima on 4 May, but the fighting around Shuri continued to claim large numbers of casualties.

At sea off Okinawa, meanwhile, a 700-plane Kamikaze raid on 6 April sunk and damaged 13 US destroyers*. The remnants of the Japanese Combined Fleet, under Vice Admiral Ito's flagship *Yamato**, had also been ordered out on a similar suicide mission by Admiral Toyoda*. Lacking sufficient fuel for the return journey, the last Japanese battle squadron sailed out towards Okinawa in a final attempt to defend the island. Sighted on 3 April by aircraft of Admiral Mitscher's* strike force, the battleship and her escorts were subjected to successive waves of bomber and torpedo-plane strikes which decimated it within hours (see Japanese Navy).

On 11 May, General Buckner ordered a renewed offensive on the Shuri defences, finally convincing Ushijima to withdraw, followed by the 24th Corps and the 6th Marine Division who demolished one after another Japanese strongpoints as they drove Ushijima back to the southern tip of the island. By 21 June organized resistance had ended and General Geiger (who had succeeded Buckner, killed in action) declared Okinawa secured. General Ushijima was found dead with his Chief of Staff. Both had committed ritual suicide – hara-kiri.

Total American casualties were estimated at 49,000. Japanese casualties, which included many local civilians, were much higher, with over 100,000 killed, nearly 30,000 sealed in caves and 10,000 taken prisoner. While the island was still being developed as a springboard for the invasion of Japan, the two atomic bombs* dropped on Hiroshima* and Nagasaki* brought the war to a sudden end.

Oklahoma, USS United States battleship and Class. Commissioned in 1916, the *Oklahoma* and her sister *Nevada* were the world's first battleships with 'all or nothing' protection, setting the standard for future American designs. All light and medium armour was omitted in favour of much thicker protection for the vital areas of the ships, and weight was saved by grouping part of their main armament in three-gun turrets. They were modernized from 1927 –9 and both were with the Pacific Fleet at Pearl Harbor* when the Japanese attacked in December 1941. Bombed and torpedoed by carrier aircraft, the *Oklahoma* capsized, trapping more than 400 of her crew. Although she was raised at the end of 1943, she proved beyond repair. The *Nevada* was the only American battleship to get under way during the attack, but was severely damaged while heading for the open sea, and beached to avoid blocking the harbour. Refloated, repaired and further modernized (with radar* and scores of light anti-aircraft* cannon), she returned to action in the Aleutians* in 1943, and later supported Allied landings in Europe and the Pacific, surviving a Kamikaze* attack off Okinawa* in March 1945. She ended her days as an atomic-test target ship.

BRIEF DATA (*Nevada*, 1941) Displacement: 29,000 tons; Dimensions: o/a lgth – 583', b – 108'; Speed: 20.5 knots; Armament: $10 \times 14''$ gun (2×2, 2×3), $12 \times 5''$ gun, $8 \times 5''$ AA gun, 4×3pdr AA gun, 3 aircraft.

OKW (Oberkommando der Wehrmacht) German Armed Forces High Command. By 1934, Hitler*, as President and Chancellor of the Third Reich, was nominal head of the armed forces. When War Minister Blomberg and C-in-C Fritsch* were dismissed in 1938, Hitler abolished Blomberg's ministerial post and took personal command. The new organization became OKW, with Keitel* as Chief of Staff and Jodl* as head of operations. Hitler retained OKW as his own planning staff, with OKH for the Army, OKL for the Luftwaffe* and OKM for the German Navy* (*Kriegsmarine*). In 1941, Hitler transferred control of the Eastern Front* to OKH, while OKW continued to command in all other theatres. There were thus effectively two military high commands. In December 1941, after the German defeat at Moscow*, Hitler dismissed Brauchitsch* from OKH and assumed supreme command.

Olbricht, Colonel-General Friedrich (1888–1944) Deputy Commander of the

German Home Army under Fromm from 1940. Associated with Oster*, Gördeler*, Höpner*, and others who opposed Hitler*, Olbricht was involved in the failed attempt on Hitler's life in the July Bomb Plot*, as executive of the planned Army takeover of Berlin after Hitler's death, code-named Operation Valkyrie. Olbricht was among those shot on Fromm's order on the night of the attempt after summary court martial. See also Resistance: Germany.

Olive Code-name for the Allied attack on the German defensive Gothic Line* in Italy*, in August 1944.

Omaha One of two Normandy* invasion beaches, at Colleville and Vierville, which were allocated to US forces for the D-Day landings. US 1st Army forces there met the fiercest resistance of the day. The high casualty rate, acute seasickness and consequent panic among the US 5th Corps nearly cost the Allies a crucial beachhead.

Onishi, Vice Admiral Takijiro (1891–1945) Strong advocate of naval air power and Chief of Staff of the Japanese 11th Air Fleet, he was responsible, along with Commander Minoru Genda, for the early development of the plans for Admiral Yamamoto's* attack on Pearl Harbor*. In late 1944 Onishi was appointed to command the 1st Air Fleet in the Philippines*, where he created the Special Attack Groups of suicide dive-bombing pilots known as the Kamikazes*. One among thousands of Japanese who regarded surrender as an unacceptable betrayal of Emperor and homeland (see Bushido), Onishi committed ritual suicide by sword shortly after the Japanese Emperor Hirohito's* surrender speech was broadcast.

Oppenheimer, J. Robert (1904–67) Established as a leading nuclear physicist before the outbreak of WW2, having received international attention for his work on quantum theory, Oppenheimer was asked to join the project to develop atomic energy for military purposes soon after the outbreak of war. As Director of the laboratories at Los Alamos from 1943, Oppenheimer played a leading part in the race for the development of the atomic bomb*. After the war, Oppenheimer became Director of the Institute of Advanced Study at Princeton University and served as the chairman of the General Advisory Committee to the US Atomic Energy Commission. In 1954, however, Oppenheimer was removed from his position on the basis of allegations of left-wing associations, though the move may well have been provoked by his opposition to the development of the hydrogen bomb.

Oradour-sur-Glâne Village in the Haute-Vienne region of southwestern France, it was the site of one of the most brutal atrocities of WW2. Frustrated by resistance* attacks which checked the progress of the 2nd SS 'Das Reich' Panzer Division towards Normandy in July 1944, its commander ordered the summary execution of all males, burnt all the women and children inside the village church and razed the village, leaving a thousand dead. Among the considerable number of French villages that still maintain memorials to French lives lost to the Germans in WW2, the abandonment of Oradour, left unreconstructed, is one of the most poignant.

Oran Moroccan port which was the target of the American Center Task Force in Operation Torch* on 8 November 1942 (see Map 8). Landings were made to the east and west of the harbour, followed by a light armoured thrust inland to take airfields south of the city. Thus surrounded, the 10,000 French troops in the port could not be reinforced. Apart from the failure of an ill-conceived frontal attack on the harbour by 400 troops in two small British cutters, the operation went well until the afternoon of 9 November, when the converging Americans were halted by growing French opposition. Little progress was made until two days later when infantry attacks from east and west were launched by the American commander, Major General Fredenhall, that distracted the defenders while light armoured columns from the south entered the city almost unopposed. French commanders then agreed to surrender, having already reduced the scale of their resistance in the light of armistice negotiations in progress at Algiers*.

Orzel Submarines* were the most valuable warships available to small navies which could not afford major units. The Polish ocean-going submarine *Orzel* was built by public subscription from 1935–8, and commissioned into the Polish Navy in February 1939. When Germany attacked Poland* in September, the *Orzel* was at sea in the Baltic; but minor damage to machinery and an outbreak of sickness forced her to put into the Estonian port of Tallinn on 15 September. Against international law (and probably due to German pressure) she was immediately interned and deprived of charts, navigational equipment and part of her armament. Nevertheless, the *Orzel* broke out of Tallinn under the nose of an Estonian gunboat on 18 September, and began a solitary and dangerous Baltic patrol as the last Polish Navy warship actively at war with Germany. After an epic and roundabout voyage, avoiding heavy German patrols, she succeeded in joining other surviving Polish warships in Britain, arriving at Rosyth, Scotland, on 14 October. Operating with the Royal Navy*, the *Orzel* was lost – probably to a mine* – in the North Sea in June 1940.
BRIEF DATA (1939) Displacement: 1,100 tons (surface); Dimensions: lgth – 275' 7", b – 22'; Speed: 20 knots (9 submerged); Armament: 1 × 4.1" gun, 2 × 40mm AA gun, 2 × 13.2mm AA mg, 12 × 21" TT.

Osmeña, Sergio (1898–1961) Successor to Manuel Quezon* as President of the Philippines*, Osmena took over the office on Quezon's death in 1944. In October, he returned to the Philippines from Washington, where he had served under Quezon in the Philippine government-in-exile. He was defeated in the first post-war election in April 1946 by Manuel Roxas.

OSS (Office of Strategic Services) American intelligence system created by President Roosevelt* in July 1942 to replace the Office of the Coordinator of Information (OCI) which he rightly judged ineffective. It was staffed by American agents, many of whom, like its director Colonel 'Wild Bill' Donovan*, had studied the British Special Operations Executive, SOE*, which OSS took as its model. OSS was charged with the collection and analysis of foreign information (domestic intelligence was handled by the Office of War Information) as well as special operations under the control of the Joint Chiefs of Staff*. Its major operational areas were black propaganda* (now known as disinformation), intelligence gathering in war theatres where US forces operated and special intelligence operations in guerrilla fighting, demolitions, communications, sabotage and espionage.

Disliked and mistrusted for its independent status and clandestine and unorthodox nature by a number of service and FBI chiefs (including General MacArthur* who refused to allow OSS to operate in the Philippines*), it nevertheless operated worldwide with an active staff at any one time of over 12,000. Integrated in its earliest stages with the British SOE, with whom it was also involved in training and operations, OSS participated in guerrilla and resistance* operations in many major war theatres. Its bureau chief, Allen Dulles*, who operated an OSS mission from Bern in neutral Switzerland, directed one of the most successful espionage organizations of the war, transmitting intelligence on German Foreign Office and Gestapo* activities, as well as negotiating the surrender of German armies in Italy. Though Dulles went on to serve as first director of the Central Intelligence Agency (CIA), OSS was disbanded in October 1945, and its functions and personnel recruited into the US State and War Departments.

Oster, Major General Hans (1888–1945) Chief of Staff to Admiral Canaris*, head of the Abwehr* (German military intelligence) from 1938 to 43. Oster's opposition to Nazism had been cemented from the outset when his superior in the Abwehr, General Bredow, became an early victim of the regime in the 1934 Röhm purge. His opposition was underpinned when Oster was one of those appointed to participate in the shabby manoeuvres which resulted in the dismissal of Defence Minister Blomberg and Army C-in-C Fritsch* in 1938.

Following Canaris's appointment as head of Abwehr in 1935, Oster increasingly became a primary focus of Abwehr's varied resistance activities, acting as his superior's 'front man' in recruitment, information collection and dissemination and planning for Hitler's overthrow. In addition Oster sent a series of warnings of Hitler's intentions towards Czechoslovakia*, Poland*, Denmark*, Norway*, Belgium and the Netherlands*, though these were clearly ignored by their respective governments. He worked closely with other opposition members such as Bonhöffer*, Müller* and Dohnanyi*, narrowly escaping exposure at the time of the latter's arrest in April 1943. Oster was arrested in the aftermath of the July Bomb Plot* in 1944 and, like his superior, underwent interrogations and incarceration until April 1945, when he was hanged with Canaris at Flossenbürg concentration camp. See Resistance: Germany.

Oumansky, Constantine A. (1902–45) Ex-Tass overseas journalist and Soviet ambassador to Washington, 1939–40, he participated in the talks on Allied aid for Russia (Lend-Lease*) in Moscow in November 1941, but was significantly less popular than London Ambassador Maisky*, who had initiated the talks with Harry Hopkins*. In 1943 he became ambassador to Mexico, and played a part in the establishment of relations between the Soviet Union and several Latin American countries. He was killed in an air crash over Mexico City.

Overlord Code-name for the Allied cross-Channel invasion of France in spring 1944 (for which the naval operations were code-named Neptune). See Normandy, Invasion of.

Owen Gun Australian 9mm submachine-gun, produced in 1941 to ease the shortage of British and American weapons. Bulky but reliable, it was preferred to the Austen gun which, as its name suggests, was an Australian copy of the British Sten gun. See Submachine-gun.

Ozawa, Vice Admiral Jisaburo (1886–1966) Promoted Vice Admiral, Ozawa saw his first active fleet command of WW2 in operations against Indonesia (Dutch East Indies*), Malaya* and the Philippines*. He then succeeded Admiral Chuichi Nagumo* as commander of the 3rd Fleet, comprising most of Japan's carrier force, in November 1942 and participated in the major battles of the Philippine Sea* and Leyte Gulf*, where Ozawa's decoy manoeuvring to draw away Admiral Halsey's carrier force nearly cost the Americans a crucial victory. He remained in this post until November 1944. In May 1945, Ozawa was appointed Commander of the Japanese Fleet to replace Admiral Toyoda*, following the latter's failure to prevent the American capture of Okinawa*.

P

P-36 Curtiss Hawk American monoplane fighter which entered service in 1939, but was inferior to German and British fighters developed around the same time. Only a few USAAF* P-36s saw action in the Pacific War*, but the Hawk 75 export version fought for the French *Armée de l'Air** against superior opponents in 1940, and (as the Mohawk) the same model later served the RAF* in Burma*. More than 1,300 P-36s of all types were built before production of the P-40* modification became standard in 1940.

BRIEF DATA (Hawk 75) Type: single-seat fighter; Engine: 1 × 1,200hp Wright; Max speed: 303mph; Ceiling: 30,000'; Range: 680m; Arms: 6 × 0.303″ mg.

P-38 Lockheed Lightning When it first appeared in 1939, this twin-boomed US fighter was a sensation, bristling with innovations and capable of phenomenal speed. It entered USAAF* service, after various setbacks, in June 1941, and fought in every theatre of war in many roles without ever fulfilling its early promise. Of many versions, the first fully combat-worthy was the P-38F, which nevertheless lacked manoeuvrability as a fighter. Engine power was increased in the P-38H and P-38L models, the latter armed as a ground-attack aircraft, and the P38-M was a two-seat night-fighter fitted with radar*. Hundreds of F4 and F5 photo-reconnaissance versions were manufactured. Lightnings also acted as target markers for bomber groups, skiplanes, glider tugs and ambulances. Altogether 9,942 were built and the final batch was delivered in September 1945.

BRIEF DATA (P-38F) Type: single-seat fighter; Engine: 2 × 1,325hp Allison; Max speed: 414mph; Ceiling: 40,000'; Range: 2,260m (max); Arms: 1 × 20mm cannon, 4 × 0.5″ mg (provision for 1,000lb bombs).

P-39 Bell Airacobra Unusual American fighter, first flown as a prototype in 1939, it boasted a nose-wheel undercarriage and an engine located behind the pilot. Though it performed disappointingly as an interceptor, it was a valuable ground-support craft, successfully used as such by the USAAF* in the Mediterranean* and the Far East. Of the 9,588 built, about 5,000 went to the Soviet Union where they were apparently popular with pilots. Production was switched to the P63* Kingcobra in May 1944.

BRIEF DATA (P-39) Type: single-seat fighter; Engine: 1 × 1,325hp Allison; Max speed: 380mph; Ceiling: 35,000'; Range: 1,475m (max); Arms: 1 × 37mm cannon, 2 × 0.5″ mg, 2–4 × 0.3″ mg.

P-40 Curtiss Warhawk A derivation of the P-36* Hawk, the American P-40 fighter entered production in 1939, followed by the more combat-worthy P-40B the following year. The bulk of these and the similar P-40C models were used by the RAF* (as Tomahawks), France and the Soviet Union, but they were produced in relatively small numbers, as was the improved P-40D. Mass production of the type for the USAAF* got under way in 1940 with the more heavily armed P-40E (RAF Kittyhawk IA), and continued through the P-40F, K, L and M variants, all known as Warhawks and mounting various powerplants and gun permutations. The final and most numerous production Warhawk was the P-40N and over 5,000 of these were delivered. Although inferior in performance to many of its European contemporaries, the P-40 formed a substantial part of the USAAF's fighter force in the first half of the war and proved most valuable as a ground-support weapon, seeing service largely in the Pacific. Production continued until December 1944, and a total of 13,738 P-40s were built.

BRIEF DATA (P-40N) Type: single-seat fighter-bomber; Engine: 1 × 1,200hp Allison; Max speed: 343mph; Ceiling: 30,000'; Range: 750m; Arms: 6 × 0.5" mg; Bomb load: 1,500lb.

P-47 Republic Thunderbolt The opportunity to study air combat over Europe in 1940 altered the performance targets of the USAAF*. This was reflected in the Thunderbolt, which flew as a prototype in May 1941, and was a big, chunky fighter – heavily armed and powerfully driven. Entering European service with the US 8th Air Force in 1942, the P-47B was a great success as a long-range bomber escort, especially when droptanks put it within target range. When this role passed to the P-51* in 1944, thousands of P-47Ds rearmed with bombs or rockets* performed devastatingly as ground-attack planes in Northwest Europe* and in the Pacific. Later models included the P-47N, designed for speed to counter V-1* rockets but only ready in time to score successes against German jet fighters in the final weeks of the war. A total of 15,660 Thunderbolts were delivered, including a staggering 12,606 P-47Ds, before production ended in November 1945.

BRIEF DATA (P-47D) Type: single-seat fighter-bomber; Engine: 1 × 2,300hp Pratt and Whitney; Max speed: 428mph; Ceiling: 42,000'; Range: 1,000m; Arms: 8 × 0.5" mg; Bomb load: 2,500lb.

P-51 North American Mustang US fighter designed by the North American company at the behest of the British Air Purchasing Commission. The first of 820 Mustangs reached the RAF* in October 1941, and the USAAF* then adopted 500 P-51 fighters as well as 310 A-36 dive-bomber versions. An effective fighter with a superbly efficient airframe, its weakness at high altitude persuaded the RAF to replace the original Allison engine with a more powerful Merlin in late 1942. The resultant P-51B (RAF Mustang II) was a brilliant aircraft, further refined in the P-51C and P-51D models, which were mass-produced in their thousands. The fastest wartime version, the P-51H, was reshaped, lighter and could reach 487mph.

Mustangs served mainly in Europe, where from early 1944 they escorted heavy bombers all the way from Britain to Berlin and were the vital factor in enabling the USAAF to bomb Germany in daylight (see Strategic Bombing Offensive). They also saw some action as escorts in the Pacific theatre. Total production was 15,586 and the Mustang enjoyed a prolific international post-war career. In 1967, the American Cavalier company put the plane back into production, with the US Air Force among its customers.

BRIEF DATA (P-51D) Type: single-seat fighter; Engine: 1 × 1,520hp Rolls Royce Merlin (US built); Max speed: 437mph; Ceiling: 41,900'; Range: 2,080m (max); Arms: 6 × 0.5" mg.

P-59 Bell Airacomet The first turbojet aircraft built in the United States. The prototype P-59 flew in October 1942, after a Whittle engine and technical crew were sent over from Britain. Quickly produced, its performance never suggested a front-line fighter and the Airacomet served only as a trainer from October 1944.

BRIEF DATA (P-59A) Type: single-seat trainer; Engine: 2 × 2,000lb thrust General Electric turbojet; Max speed: 413mph; Ceiling: 46,200'; Range: 520m (with droptanks); Arms: none.

P-61 Northrop Black Widow Ordered explicitly as a radar*-equipped night-fighter for the USAAF* in 1941, the Black Widow flew for the first time the following year and entered service as the P-61A in May 1944. A big, twin-boomed aircraft, it was surprisingly manoeuvrable as well as fast and, although unable to reach high-altitude bombers, performed with some success in both Europe and the Pacific. The long-range, 3-seat P-61B was fitted with underwing pylons for droptanks or bombs, but the much more powerful P-61C, with an operational ceiling above 40,000 feet, arrived too late to see combat. Total production reached 941 including an F15 photo-reconnaissance version.

BRIEF DATA (P-61A) Type: 2-man night-fighter; Engine: 2 × 2,000hp Pratt and Whitney Double Wasp; Max speed: 366mph; Ceiling: 33,000'; Range: 500m (normal); Arms: 4 × 20mm cannon, 4 × 0.5" mg.

P-63 Bell Kingcobra US fighter, ordered in 1941, it looked like a P-39* but was in fact a completely different and superior design. It was nevertheless obsolete before its service delivery in October 1943, and the USAAF* used Kingcobras only as target planes. Of the 3,303 built, 2,241 went to the Red Air Force* in a ground-support capacity and a further 300 were used by the Free French. The plane appeared in several versions (P-63A to E, RP-63) before production was halted in early 1945.

BRIEF DATA (P-63C) Type: single-seat fighter-bomber; Engine: 1 × 1,325hp Allison; Max speed: 410mph; Ceiling: 38,000'; Range: 2,575m (max); Arms: 1 × 37mm cannon, 4 × 0.5" mg; Bomb load: 1,500lb.

Paasiviki, Juho K. (1870–1956) Finnish statesman who played a key role in armistice negotiations to end the Russo-Finnish War*, after which he served as ambassador to Moscow. He also negotiated the peace treaty with Russia that ended the 'Continuation War' in 1944 and became Prime Minister in November of that year. In March 1946 he replaced Mannerheim* as President of Finland*.

Pacific Ocean Areas In April 1942, American command of the huge Pacific area was divided into two. The first, Pacific Ocean Areas (abbreviated POA and including North Pacific, South Pacific and Central Pacific areas) was placed under the command of Admiral Chester Nimitz*, already C-in-C of the US Pacific Fleet (CINCPAC). Individual area commanders in these three zones operated under Nimitz's orders. The second area, Southwest Pacific Area, SWPA, was commanded by General Douglas MacArthur*. From the inception of the command areas, its two overall commanders were regularly in disagreement over the best broad strategy for offensive operations against Japan. See Pacific War; Map 11.

Pacific War, 1941–5 Initiated by the Japanese attack on Pearl Harbor* on 7 December 1941, the Pacific War was a separate conflict in many fundamental respects from that developing in Europe, North Africa and the Soviet Union at the same time (see Introduction). Although the broad background to the Pacific conflict was partly laid in the previous century by European and American imperial impulses in the Far East – notably towards China – and there are many obvious parallels in the political, economic and social experience of Europe and Japan in the 1920s and 1930s, a key to the Pacific conflict lies in Japan's particular expansionist ambitions. Focused initially on China* and Manchuria*, but spreading out across the Far Eastern colonial territories as far as the Philippines during 1940–1, the 'New Order'* for East Asia, first framed by Prime Minister Konoe* in November 1938, envisaged effective political, economic and military control for Japan over much of Southeast Asia – an empire which would guarantee Japan's security and end her dependence on imports of raw materials from overseas.

When Britain and France went to war in 1939, Japan's militarist political leaders, headed by General Tojo* (see also Kwan-tung Army), saw an impelling opportunity to conquer their own markets as well as sources of food and raw materials, as Britain and France had done in the two preceding centuries. Though the Far Eastern colonial possessions of Britain and France were now completely vulnerable, the military prob-lem rested on whether Japan could take on the US, whose territories she also coveted, and win.

A three-phase plan was developed by the Japanese Imperial Command. It called first for a pre-emptive strike on the forward US Fleet at Pearl Harbor as the vital prelimi-nary to a massive Pacific offensive reaching out to Wake Island*, through the Gil-berts*, New Guinea*, Dutch East Indies*, through to Burma* and the frontier with British India. The second phase called for the fortification of this perimeter. The third phase projected the deflection of counter-attacks sufficient to force the enemy to concede defeat and acknowledge Japanese dominion over what was now also called the 'Greater East Asia Co-Prosperity Sphere'*.

The view – held at the time even by some senior Japanese statesmen and mili-tary leaders – that Japan's attempt to take on the US was 'suicidal' is hard to dispute with hindsight, though it provides a poor framework for analysis of the conflict. Para-doxically, the Japanese mistake appears not so much in the scope of these expansionist strategies as in their limited objectives. The assumption that the Allied govern-ments would quickly be prepared to accept a peace settlement after the successful con-clusion of the offensive was seemingly not questioned – (although C-in-C of the Japanese Combined Fleet, Admiral Yama-moto* was not alone in regarding the possibility of ultimate Japanese victory as an illusion).

As a result, therefore, no plan was pre-pared to exploit these offensives to destroy the military forces of the nations opposing them. The Japanese commitment to a 'grand design', combined with her categori-cal belief in her mission in Southeast Asia (amply sustained by Japan's religious, cul-tural and political experience), ignored the bald statistics of the United States' massive potential fighting strength. Moreover, re-cent research is beginning to establish the supreme importance to the American effort in the Pacific of Magic* intelligence inter-cepts. The achievement of American cryptanalysts in cracking the Purple Code and the later successes with Magic provided the US with a decisive strategic advantage (see, for example, the Battle of Midway*), which Japanese leaders could not have fore-seen.

Pearl Harbor Nevertheless, in a lightning series of offensives in late 1941 and early 1942, the Japanese drove out to their planned perimeter (see Map 10). The at-tack on Pearl Harbor on 7 December 1941 was followed by seven other simultaneous attacks on US, British and Dutch con-trolled territories. On the same day (8 De-cember in the Far East time zone), Japanese forces invaded Malaya* and Thailand*, and made their first landing on Philippine* soil at Bataan Island*, north of Luzon*. Most US aircraft were caught on the ground in an airstrike on Clark Field in the Philip-pines.

The following day Japanese forces occu-pied Bangkok (Thailand*) and invaded the Gilbert Islands*. Further landings on the Philippines, at Aparri and Vigan on the 10th coincided with the surrender of the small US garrison at Guam* and the sinking of the British capital ships *Prince of Wales** and *Repulse** off the coast of Malaya (see Force Z). Burma was invaded on 11 December and Borneo* in the East Indies on the 13th. Wake Island* fell to the Ja-panese on 23 December, Hong Kong* sur-rendered on Christmas Day, with the loss of its 12,000 strong garrison. In mid-January further landings began in the East Indies. By the end of January, the American forces under General MacArthur* in the Philip-pines, on which the American defence against Japan in the Far East had been hinged (see Philippines), had been pinned down and besieged in the Bataan peninsula, and the Japanese had secured a vital base at Rabaul* on New Britain.

During February and March, the pattern continued. Singapore* fell with 138,000 British and Empire troops, and Malaya was by now under Japanese control. Pushing on through Bali and Timor, Japanese forces began landings on the most important of the East Indies, Java*, on 1 March, having already crushed a combined Dutch, US and British fleet in the Battle of the Java Sea* on 27 January. On 9 March, the Dutch East Indies formally surrendered and the Japanese 1st Air Fleet sailed into the Indian Ocean, sinking the British carrier *Hermes* along with other major warships off Ceylon*. Having occupied Thailand, the Japanese 15th Army advanced rapidly into Burma*, occupying Moulmein*, Sittang, and finally the capital Rangoon*, which had been abandoned by the British on 7 March.

By May 1942, most of Burma was in Japanese hands and the British pushed back to the Indian border. Meanwhile Japanese landings in New Guinea*, firstly at Lae, Salamaua and Finschhafen, and then on the Admiralty Islands*, to the north of eastern New Guinea, brought Japanese forces to the edge of their planned defensive perimeter on the southeast. Between the attack on Pearl Harbor and the final US surrender in the Philippines at Corregidor* on 6 May, the Japanese advance had achieved staggering territorial gains over a vast area, at astonishing speed and a relatively low cost in men, machines and warships. The Japanese advantages in aircraft quality, naval and military techniques, highly trained troops and sheer quantity of aircraft carriers was at this stage decisive (see Japanese Air Forces; Japanese Navy; Japanese Army).

Although the areas of natural resources and the defensive island barrier had been conquered as dictated by the strategic plan, the response of the United States and Britain was not the one expected. Pearl Harbor had shocked the world, but the US carrier

force and the vital oil supplies held at Pearl Harbor had remained intact. Moreover, the scheduled 50 days for the conquest of the Philippines had stretched into months and the campaign in Burma had also overrun. American forces had also begun to establish and protect a line of communications across the South Pacific to Australia. Unless halted, the Allies seemed determined to develop Australia as a major base for future operations. As early as April 1942 it was clear to the Japanese that their newly conquered empire would not remain unchallenged. The Doolittle* Raid against Tokyo on 18 April was a direct statement of American intent. Finally, while the dispersion of Japanese forces at far distant targets had initially thrown Allied defensive forces off balance, the subsequent failure of the Japanese High Command to concentrate their forces and pursue a single strategy for the protection of their territory was to be a crucial factor in maintaining the initiative in the face of the American build-up in the Pacific.

Midway (see Map 13). By May 1942, disagreement dividing the Japanese Army and Navy command over the next move to make ended in a plan for the extension of the defensive perimeter in a number of widely separated operations. Two naval task forces were assigned to the capture of Port Moresby*, in order to guarantee protection of the newly drawn southern perimeter. The developing line of Allied communications between Hawaii and Australia was to be eliminated by the capture of New Caledonia, the Fiji Islands and Samoa; protection for the northern perimeter was to be secured by seizing the Aleutian Islands* and, in the central area, by the occupation of Midway* Island. Though the Aleutians fell easily to Japanese forces in early June, the progress of the dual offensive for Port Moresby was frustrated by the Battle of the Coral Sea* on 7–8 May and perhaps even more significantly by defeat at Midway, which Admiral Yamamoto had chosen to see as a unique opportunity to draw and defeat the US Pacific

Fleet at one stroke. Though the defeat at Midway on 5 June was followed up with a series of successful landings in the Solomon Islands*, her loss of all four carriers at Midway cost Japan her naval superiority and the vital initiative in the war in the Pacific.

Rabaul and New Guinea (see Map 15). The defeat at Midway nevertheless left Japan in control of the chain of islands running to the north of Australia including half of New Guinea and the Eastern Solomons*. Between May and July 1942, land operations under General Miamura and fleet actions commanded by Admiral Mikawa from their headquarters at Rabaul attempted to push the defensive perimeter to the southeast, consolidating an air base at Guadalcanal* in the Southern Solomons and by moving again on Port Moresby in southern Papua across the Owen Stanley mountain range. Meanwhile Allied operational command in the Pacific was handed over to the Americans, divided into General MacArthur's Southwest Pacific Command (with headquarters in Australia) and Admiral Nimitz's* Central Pacific Command (see Map 11). While Allied leaders and the Combined Chiefs of Staff* upheld their commitment to a 'Europe First' strategy (see Conferences), thereby limiting the scale of operations in the Pacific, a planned three-phase offensive by MacArthur's Southwest Pacific forces, code-named Operation Watchtower* was being prepared. Dubbed 'Operation Shoestring' by critical American military chiefs, it aimed to secure communications with Australia, take the Solomon Islands and New Guinea and reduce the important Japanese base at Rabaul, though there was considerable background disagreement between the two Pacific commanders and among the Joint Chiefs of Staff* over the overall strategy for the main direction of effort for the first American offensive of the war. MacArthur was personally committed to a rematch on the Philippines. Nimitz favoured a drive through the Central Pacific as the most direct route to the enemy's home territory. *Guadalcanal* (see Map 14). The ultimate

objective for Watchtower, however, was Rabaul, key Japanese military and air base on New Britain in the Solomons. Between March 1942 and the end of 1943, fighting in the Pacific was concentrated on this centre, with Japanese forces on the offensive attempting to push their southeastern perimeter line while US and Australian forces under General MacArthur (and later Admiral Halsey* and Australian General Blamey*) launched repeated attacks on key targets. Landings at Guadalcanal* and Tulagi opened MacArthur's part in the first Allied offensive on 7 August 1942, though control of Guadalcanal was viciously disputed until February 1943, with an enormous cost in casualties in at least ten pitched land battles and seven major naval engagements (including the Battles of Savo Island*, Cape Esperance*, Eastern Solomons*, Santa Cruz* and Guadalcanal*). Meanwhile the clearance of Papua and New Guinea, with large-scale operations at Port Moresby, Buna* and Gona was similarly achieved at high cost, with the pattern of fanatical Japanese resistance (at first so shocking to Allied troops in the Pacific) being repeated again and again. Nevertheless, the initiative gained in the crucial naval battles of the Coral Sea and Midway was underpinned by the hard-won American successes in the Solomons (notably at Guadalcanal), proving also the newly won superiority of the US Pacific Fleet over the Japanese surface forces (see US Navy).

In March 1943, following the US victory in the Bismarck Sea* and the isolation of the Japanese bases in New Guinea, the Joint Chiefs of Staff revised their strategic aims for the Southwest Pacific forces, bringing in Admiral Halsey's 3rd Fleet from the Central Pacific Command to participate in a two-pronged operation which opened in July. Admiral Halsey's drive through the Solomons to Bougainville*, code-named Operation Cartwheel*, culminated successfully in the major engagement at Empress Augusta Bay in November. Meanwhile, MacArthur's leapfrogging advance in New Guinea kept pace, so that by the end of 1943, the Huon Peninsula had been cleared and Japanese strength at Rabaul was sufficiently reduced (most air and naval forces having been withdrawn to Truk*) that it could safely be bypassed altogether. The isolation of Rabaul by June 1944, and the consolidation of the Solomons, effectively ended combat operations in the South Pacific theatre – Halsey's fleet was returned to Nimitz's command. The disagreement between Nimitz (supported by Admiral King*) and MacArthur over the direction of the main spearhead of attack had remained unresolved during 1943. But the American successes, supported by the continued build-up of superior equipment (see, for example, Radar) and new forces, made it possible to support both drives by the end of the year.

Central Pacific Hence a second prong of the offensive, launched from the Central Pacific (where Nimitz now commanded a formidable force including Admiral Spruance's* 5th Fleet, Halsey's 3rd Fleet, 7th Army Air Force based at the Ellice Islands and 100,000 combat troops), began on 20 November 1943 with the seizure of Makin* and Tawara* (where the fighting was particularly bitter) by units of the 5th Amphibious Corps. This was followed up with the capture of the Marshall Islands*, which freed Admiral Mitscher's* Fast Carrier Task Force to threaten Truk itself. Though the heavily fortified Japanese base held out against repeated attacks, the American forces were able to isolate it using the characteristic bypassing tactic used in the South Pacific, and leave it to 'wither on the vine', speeding up the tempo of their main advance westward.

Meanwhile, General MacArthur matched the pace of the Central Pacific advance with a daring operation in February 1944 that led to the capture of the Admiralty Islands, followed by a series of successful amphibious* landings with carrier support at Hollandia*, Aitape*, Wakde and Biak*. Under threat from the converging US drives, the Japanese fleet under Vice Admiral Ozawa* sailed to challenge Nimitz's forces, suffering another crushing defeat in the Battle of the Philippine Sea* (also known as the Great Marianas Turkey Shoot), which cost the Japanese Navy two carriers and 346 aircraft. Once again, the American carrier strike force proved itself as the decisive weapon in the Pacific War. Following three weeks of bitter fighting to capture Saipan*, Nimitz's forces proceeded to Guam* and Tinian*, from which point the two Allied drives quickly converged. In the ten months of the Central Pacific drive Admiral Nimitz had advanced 4,500 miles, from Hawaii to the Palau* Islands. By mid-September, preparations were underway for re-entering the Philippines.

Leyte Gulf and the Philippines (see Maps 17 –21). The continuing debate over strategy, now focused on Admiral King's advocacy of an attack on Formosa* rather than Luzon*, in the Philippines, was decided in General MacArthur's favour on logistical grounds. Since Formosa could not be assaulted until the new year, a major assault was planned against Leyte*, begun on 20 October 1944 with a landing by General Krueger's* 6th Army, which though successful, was quickly overshadowed by the naval battle for Leyte Gulf*, the largest naval engagement in history. Realizing that the establishment of American air bases on Leyte would guarantee the conquest of Luzon, Japanese Chief of Naval Staff Admiral Toyoda* determined to engage in a decisive battle. Though a decoy Japanese carrier force under Ozawa managed to lure Admiral Halsey's forces away from Leyte, the result was a decisive defeat for Japan, who lost four carriers, three battleships and ten cruisers, finally expending in one battle what remained of her mobile fleet and naval air force strike power. Despite this shattering defeat, the 60,000 troops under General Yamashita* on Leyte fought ferociously in a struggle to the death, with a final Japanese death toll of 48,000.

The Luzon campaign began on 15 December, as part of the continuing two-prong strategy, with Lingayen Gulf as the main target of the US 6th Army under MacArthur. A fighting withdrawal by Japanese troops under Yamashita held back US troops, reinforced by a landing at Subic Bay of a fresh corps, for the large part of the year. While MacArthur continued to reinforce his troops in Luzon, increasingly isolating the Japanese forces in pockets, the semi-starved Japanese resisters continued to fight on, until the declaration of unconditional surrender was formally signed by the Japanese in September 1945. In this, as in the rest of the successful operations in the Philippines island group, Filipino guerrilla units played a vital role. In May 1945, Australian forces began the last offensive in the South West Pacific with a series of landings on Borneo.

The strategy debate meanwhile continued unabated. Despite the vast stretch of American and Allied successes in the theatre, Japan remained in control of Burma, the East Indies and a huge area of China, Korea and Manchuria, where the million-strong Kwantung Army* was still garrisoned. Moreover the strategic bombing offensive* by B-29s* from Marianas* bases against the Japanese mainland was not proving decisive, despite the great superiority of the new bombers over Japanese air defences. However inevitable the eventual Japanese defeat, it was becoming clear to some at least of the Joint Chiefs of Staff that the ultimate assault on Japan, from whatever direction it came, would be appallingly costly to the Allies.

Iwo Jima and Okinawa The attacks on Iwo Jima*, launched on 19 February, and on Okinawa*, launched on 1 April, saw a climax to the bitter fighting against the fatalistic and unflinching courage of the Japanese forces. Supported by the concentrated assaults of Kamikaze* planes (in Operation Ten-Go*) on Allied naval forces supporting the Okinawa landings, 117,000 Japanese defenders under Lt General Ushijima* fought on from prepared cave and tunnel defences with a final loss of 130,000 men killed. American losses were 12,520. But the possession of air bases on Okinawa

now brought American bombers and fighters within easy reach of the Japanese mainland. From March 1945 a new phase of strategic bombing opened with the devastation of 15 square miles of Tokyo* in a firestorm raid. Subsequent raids escorted by P-47* and P-51* fighters destroyed the industrial areas of Tokyo, Nagoya, Kobe, Osaka and Yokohama. Operating from forward anchorages in the Ryukyus, the Pacific fleet remained in continuous action against Japan, launching 1,000-plane carrier attacks, with the help of a British carrier force. Estimated deaths from the low-level saturation raids of the B-29s were 260,000, with a further 9.2 million left homeless.

Though the loss of Okinawa was an unavoidable signal of defeat for the Japanese, the Allied insistence on an unconditional surrender, underlined by the Potsdam Declaration of 26 July 1945, clearly ignored the militarist and fanatic ideology that had sustained the Japanese defensive efforts throughout the war in the Pacific. Though advanced planning was underway for Operation Olympic, the invasion of Kyushu, and Operation Coronet, the invasion of Honshu, the alternative course of reducing Japan in one blow by using the newly developed atomic bomb* and thus avoiding further large-scale Allied casualties was supported by most of President Truman's* military and civil advisers. On 6 August, the first atomic bomb was dropped on Hiroshima*. On the 9th, the Soviet Union declared war òn Japan and began an invasion of Manchuria. On the same day a second bomb was delivered on Nagasaki*. The following day the Japanese offered to surrender if Emperor Hirohito* could be retained. On 2 September, aboard Admiral Nimitz's flagship, the USS *Missouri**, General MacArthur received the official Japanese surrender.

Pact of Steel The Berlin–Rome Axis. See Axis.

Palau Islands Island group in the Central Pacific, east of the Philippine* Islands, it formed an important link in the Japanese defensive line flanking the American Central Pacific advance towards the Philippines during 1944 (see Map 11). Although the Japanese Navy* Combined Fleet's advance HQ had been withdrawn to Davao earlier in the year, Operation Stalemate assigned the 3rd Marine Amphibious Corps to an assault on Peleliu, ringed with mangrove swamps inside a coral reef and dominated by a long, steep, jungle-choked ridge (see Amphibious Warfare). Strong Japanese defences at Peleliu were organized by Lt General Inone with 6,000 Japanese combat troops. On 15 September 1944, the US 1st Marine Division landed on the southwest corner of Peleliu, suffering heavy casualties on the first day of fighting against a well-defended beachhead. Though they subsequently took the airfield in the southern part of the island, the American drive northwards was halted by heavy artillery bombardment from the Umurbrogol ridge, pinning US troops down for over a month of bitter fighting in what came to be called the Battle of Bloody Noose Ridge. Organized Japanese resistance formally ended on 13 October, although Peleliu's mangrove swamps and caves continued to harbour many Japanese soldiers, some of whom held out for years, not believing that the war was over.

Palermo Sicilian port on the Tyrrhenian Sea, it was occupied by General Patton's* 7th Army on 22 July 1943, too late to intercept the eastern withdrawal of Axis* forces towards Messina*. The drive from their landings on the southern coast and the occupation itself nevertheless provided a significant morale victory for the newly activated 7th Army. See Sicily, Campaign in.

Panther Tank (PzKpfw V) By autumn 1941, the performance of the new Soviet T34* tank on the Eastern Front* had rendered the Panzerkampfwagen IV*, hitherto Germany's heaviest tank, completely obsolete. The speed, manoeuvrability

and sloped armour of the T34 redefined the combat requirements of the German High Command and a new specification was issued in January 1942. The design chosen for production incorporated all the major features of the Russian machine, while stopping short of direct copying, and was subject to a highly intensive development programme. The first production PzKpfw V Panther was completed at the start of 1943 and output quickly gathered pace.

Problems with engine transmission, cooling and suspension had not, however, been fully overcome when the Panther was first thrown into combat at Kursk* in July, and the results were disastrous. Most of the new tanks broke down before they reached the battlefield, and the few survivors from the first day were immediately withdrawn for reconstruction. Once these faults had been corrected the Panther became a highly successful weapon, popular with its crews and feared by its opponents. Its long 75mm gun could pierce 120mm of armour from over 1,000 yards and, although maintenance was difficult in frozen conditions, the Panther was more than a match for any Allied tank* until the last stages of the war.

The initial production Panther D, of which over 600 were built, was followed late in 1943 by the Panther A with changes to the cupola and the hull machine-gun. As production requirements mounted, many simplifications were imposed on the third and final G model, which also had a new hull front and sides. By the end of the war over 5,000 Panthers had been built for the German Army and they were finally defeated by Allied aerial rather than armoured supremacy.

BRIEF DATA (PzKpfw VD) Type: 5-man heavy tank; Engine: 700hp petrol; Max speed: 28mph; Range: 110m; Arms: 1 × 75mm gun, 2–3 × 7.92mm mg; Armour: max 100mm.

Panzerkampfwagen I In December 1933 the German Army* issued an order for three prototypes of a light training tank*, to be used by the new armoured divisions pending the development of heavier, standard types. The successful design, disguised as the Krupp 'Agricultural Tractor', entered production as the Panzerkampfwagen (PzKpfw) IA the following year. This was soon superseded by the re-engined and much improved PzKpfw IB, still intended only as a stop-gap trainer. Though barely combat-worthy, IBs saw action in Spain from 1936, surviving largely because effective anti-tank* weapons did not yet exist. Of over 2,000 IBs eventually built, 1,445 were still in service when Poland* was invaded and they fought, mostly as reconnaissance tanks, in all the German offensives up to and including the invasion of Russia*. In July 1941, 800 remained active, although by now they were highly vulnerable to any light artillery and were soon afterwards returned to training duties or converted to self-propelled* gun carriages.

BRIEF DATA (PzKpfw IB) Type: 2-man light tank; Engine: 100hp petrol; Max speed: 25mph; Range: 87m; Arms: 2 × 7.92mm mg; Armour: max 13mm.

Panzerkampfwagen II In 1934 the German Army Weapons Office, recognizing delays in the development of battle tanks for its proposed armoured divisions, issued a specification for a 10-ton light tank*. The first production models, designated Agricultural Tractor 100 for camouflage purposes, appeared in 1935. Only about 100 were built before 1937, when production was stepped up for the Panzerkampfwagen (PzKpfw) IIC version, which had thicker front armour and a redesigned suspension system. All secrecy was dropped in 1938.

Only slightly better armed than the Panzerkampfwagen I*, and burdened with similarly poor turret visibility, the PzKpfw II was never originally intended for combat use. Nevertheless, it was an agile machine, usually equipped with radio, and came to form the backbone of German armoured strength in the first years of WW2. In

September 1939, 1,226 PzKpfw IIs equipped combat divisions, a figure reduced to 955 by May the following year. Successful against light or ill-deployed opposition in the early campaigns, the design was clearly outmoded by 1941. The more heavily armed and armoured IIF version failed to significantly improve its battle performance and they suffered heavy losses in the Desert War* and on the Eastern Front*. Nevertheless, 860 PzKpfw IIs were still in service (mainly for reconnaissance work) in April 1942, and production continued until the end of the year, by which time over 3,500 of all types had been built. Late models were produced specifically for fast reconnaissance work and remained in service until the end of the war. The basic chassis was used for a number of flame-throwers* and self-propelled* artillery pieces.

BRIEF DATA (PzKpfw IIF) Type: 3-man light tank; Engine: 130hp petrol; Max speed: 25mph; Range: 124m; Arms: 1 × 20mm gun, 1 × 7.92mm mg; Armour: max 35mm.

Panzerkampfwagen III In 1935, the German Army Weapons Office began issuing specifications for its main battle tanks*. The principle armoured combat vehicle was to be the Panzerkampfwagen III, and Daimler-Benz was given the order to produce a machine weighing no more than 24 tons (in token deference to the tolerance of German road bridges) and equipped with the 37mm anti-tank* gun then entering service with the infantry. A large turret ring was incorporated into the design to allow for easy up-gunning. Development was slow, and the first major production version, the PzKpfw IIIE, was accepted for service only in September 1939. Spread among several inexperienced companies, manufacturing output of the PzKpfw III never matched German expectations, but 98 machines were available for the invasion of Poland* and about 350 participated in the Western Offensive* of 1940.

Adequately powered and easy to handle

compared with other contemporary tanks, the PzKpfw III was fitted with a 50mm gun after operations in France and the Desert War* had exposed the ineffectuality of the smaller weapon. Armament and weight were then regularly increased in successive models, and extra armour plate was fitted to many of the later types. By June 1941, nearly 1,500 PzKpfw IIIs were in German service, and they were highly successful on the Eastern Front* until the arrival of the Soviet T34* and KV* tanks left them fundamentally outclassed. They remained effective in other theatres, however, and output reached 2,600 machines in 1942. By the end of the year the final version, the PzKpfw IIIN, carried a low-velocity 75mm gun to provide support fire for new heavy battle tanks. The PzKpfw III was finally withdrawn from service in 1943, after 5,664 vehicles had been built, although the chassis remained in production as a basis for self-propelled* artillery.

BRIEF DATA (PzKpfw IIIE) Type: 5-man battle tank; Engine: 300hp diesel; Max speed: 25mph; Range: 109m; Arms: 1 × 50mm gun, 2 × 7.92mm mg; Armour: max 90mm.

Panzerkampfwagen IV Of the two main battle tanks planned by Germany in 1935, the Panzerkampfwagen IV was the infantry-support model, to be armed with a large-calibre gun and firing a high-explosive shell. Intended to be less numerous (by 3 to 1) than the Panzerkampfwagen III* battle tank, its specification called for a very similar vehicle, and the two tanks were in fact much alike in both appearance and function. Contracts were placed with a number of companies but development and refinement of the various designs delayed quantity delivery until 1939, when the PzKpfw IVD appeared. This fought in Poland* and the Western Offensive* with conspicuous success, but experience in the early Eastern Front* campaigns of 1941 showed that improvements were urgently needed.

Thicker armour was added to the IVE

model, and the IVF and IVG were fitted with a long-barrelled 75mm gun. Both these latter versions were produced in large numbers from mid-1941, and began to take over the main fighting role from the PzKpfw III on all fronts. Formidable weapons, they gave German forces a clear advantage when they appeared in the Desert War* and were useful on the Eastern Front, although a refined version of the 75mm gun was needed in 1943 to maintain any sort of viability against the Soviet T34*. The final model, the PzKpfw IVJ, appeared in 1944 and its simplified design reflected increasing shortages of raw materials. Nevertheless, it was the same basic machine that had entered the war in Poland, and the PzKpfw IV was the only German tank* to remain in production throughout the war. It was also the most numerous German tank in service and over 8,000 had been delivered by 1945 along with several types of self-propelled* gun based on the PzKpfw IV chassis.

BRIEF DATA (PzKpfw IVD) Type: 5-man medium tank; Engine: 300hp diesel; Max speed: 25mph; Range: 125m; Arms: 1 × 75mm gun, 2 × 7.92mm mg; Armour: max 90mm.

Papagos, General Alexander (1883–1955) C-in-C of Greek forces when the Italian invasion of Greece from Albania began on 28 October 1940, he succeeded in driving the Italian invasion forces back into Albania. When the Greek Army was forced to capitulate to the Axis following the German invasion from Bulgaria and Yugoslavia in April 1941, Papagos was arrested by the new military leader, General Tsolacoglou, and handed over to the Germans. He was taken to Germany in 1943 and imprisoned until his liberation from Dachau* concentration camp by the Americans in 1945. See also Greece, Italian invasion of; Balkans, The, German invasion of.

Paris, Liberation of, 25 August 1944 Disputes over the liberation and control of Paris (captured intact by German forces in

1940; see Western Offensive), following the Allied invasion of Normandy* and successful advance into the French interior in 1944, involved both elements of the French resistance* (communist under Colonel 'Rol' Tanguy, and Free France* forces under de Gaulle*), as well as the German garrison commander General Choltitz and the Allied Supreme Commander, General Eisenhower*. Ordered by Hitler to hold the city or see it in ruins, Choltitz uncomfortably awaited reinforcements, but was preempted on 19 August by a communist uprising led by Tanguy. Unwilling to destroy the city despite his orders, Choltitz arranged a temporary truce with the Gaullist resistance. When the uneasy truce foundered, and Choltitz ordered tanks to the city, the communist resistance appealed to the Allies. Eisenhower, who had planned to bypass Paris to avoid a costly battle, was persuaded to dispatch General Leclerc's 2nd Free French Armoured Division. Receiving intelligence via Leclerc from inside the city on the size of German forces there, Eisenhower finally ordered the city taken on 23 August. Supported by the US 4th Infantry Division, Leclerc broke into the city on the 25th with de Gaulle following him the next day. Choltitz ignored Hitler's orders and surrendered the city intact. See also Northwest Europe, Allied Invasion of; Free France.

Park, Air Marshal Keith (1892–1975) Air Officer Commanding No. 11 Group RAF* Fighter Command during the Western Offensive* and the Battle of Britain*, Park shares with the commander of RAF Fighter Command, Dowding*, much credit for the successful evacuation of Dunkirk* and the subsequent victory over the Luftwaffe*. He was nevertheless criticized by colleagues, as was Dowding, for the conventional defensive doctrine which underpinned the tactical deployment of his formations and both Park and Dowding were replaced immediately after the Battle of Britain, a decision which Park bitterly resented (see Leigh-Mallory, Air Chief Marshal Sir Trafford;

Douglas, Air Marshal Sir W. Sholto). Transferred to a training group in December 1940, Park resumed active service as AOC Allied HQ in Egypt* in the autumn of 1941, and then went as AOC to Malta* in July 1942. Here Park initiated offensive tactics to disrupt Axis* supply lines to North Africa and provided air support for Operation Torch* in November. His squadrons later provided substantial support for the Allied landings in Sicily* and Italy* in 1943. In 1944 Park took command of RAF forces in the Middle East, later transferring to command Allied Air Forces in Southeast Asia for the campaigns in Burma*.

Patch, General Alexander (1889–1945) Commander of land forces which won the first land victory of the Pacific War* for the United States at Guadalcanal* in early 1943, Patch went on to command the Desert Training Center and later the US 7th Army, which was assigned to the invasion of southern France (Operation Anvil/Dragoon*) in August 1944. Forces under his command fought up the Rhone Valley into northern Alsace and the Saar. In late April 1945, Patch's forces made a hurtling advance into southern Germany to prevent the formation by Germany of a 'national redoubt', though this last-ditch threat to the Allied advance in Northwest Europe* later proved to be fictional.

Pathfinders Elite RAF* night-bomber squadrons, whose crews were selected for their navigating skills. Their task was to be first over a target and drop accurate markers (flares and incendiaries) to assist the aim of the main bombing force. Pathfinders were first used as part of the Strategic Bombing Offensive* in August 1942, but they were not particularly accurate and results were disappointing. Fast de Havilland Mosquito* light bombers or heavy Avro Lancasters* were the usual equipment of the Pathfinders, and with experience they helped improve the RAF's poor record in finding targets at night. They formed No

8 (Pathfinder Force) Group under Air Vice Marshal Bennett*.

Patton, General George Jnr (1885–1945) Flamboyant and hard-driving American field commander, among the first American converts to the new theories of armoured warfare, he had demonstrated the effectiveness of tank* warfare under his own dynamic leadership as early as 1917, when he commanded the 304th Tank Brigade in the WW1 Meuse–Argonne offensive. Despite the difficulties imposed by his unguarded egotism and ruthless, iconoclastic temperament, Patton was quickly promoted, once war broke out, to divisional commander, 2nd Armored Division and then, in July 1942, to command the Western Task Force for the Allied invasion of Northwest Africa, Operation Torch*. He then took over the US 1st Corps in Tunisia after the disaster at Kasserine* in February 1943.

His dashing command of the US 7th Army for the invasion of Sicily* established Patton as a popular hero and an immensely competitive personality. Characteristically, service in Sicily also nearly cost him his career, when an over-publicized incident in which he impatiently slapped a young battle-fatigued soldier resulted in his humiliating relegation until January 1944, when he was assigned to prepare for the coming Normandy* invasion, playing a major part in the deception plans for it as the notional commander of the US 1st Army Group.

Allocated command of the US 3rd Army as a follow-up force to the cross-Channel invasion in June 1944, under Supreme Allied Commander Eisenhower*, Patton's orders were to land behind the US 1st Army under General Bradley* (who was also Patton's superior as commander of the 12th Army Group). His forces did not become operational until late July, when an explosive breakout from the Normandy beachhead at Avranches (Operation Cobra*) and a lightning advance into the French interior as far as Lorraine again proved Patton's outstanding abilities.

He was once more at the centre of argument with British General Montgomery* – whose cautious systematic methods were in dramatic contrast to his own – when opposing strategies and logistical factors brought the two commanders into direct competition for supplies (see Northwest Europe, Allied Invasion of). Nevertheless, Patton's contribution to the Allied military effort is hard to overstate. His total self-certainty and its effect on the contribution of troops under his command played a key part in sustaining Allied pressure on German forces through the autumn of 1944 and in the defeat of the German Ardennes counter-offensive (see Battle of the Bulge) in December. In April and May 1945 he overtook the main Allied advance in the fastest and most penetrating drive southeastward into Germany, halting, on Russia's request, over the borders of Czechoslovakia*. General Patton was killed in a car accident near Mannheim in December 1945.

Paulus, Friedrich von (1890–1957) Promoted field marshal just before he surrendered his army to the Russians at Stalingrad* in January 1943, Paulus was a regular officer in WW1 and served both Weimar and Nazi governments. During the first part of the war, he was Deputy Chief of Staff to Halder* and responsible for much of the planning for the invasion of Russia (see Eastern Front). In 1942 he was given command of the 6th Army, poised to attack Stalingrad, and took the city, but his forces were themselves encircled by the end of the year. Forced to surrender on 31 January 1943, Paulus was publicly vilified by Hitler. Later in the war Paulus broadcast for the Russian National Committee for Free Germany and was used by the Soviet Union as a prosecution witness at Nuremberg*, where he confirmed the complicity of the German General Staff in the attack, invasion and colonization plans for Russia. Released from prison in Russia in 1953, he died in East Germany in 1957.

Pearl Harbor American naval base since the early twentieth century and a good natural harbour on the island of Oahu, in the Hawaiian Islands, Pearl Harbor was the headquarters of the US Pacific Fleet in 1941. It was attacked without warning by Japanese carrier aircraft on 7 December 1941, precipitating the US entry into WW2 and opening the Pacific War*. In April 1940 the US Fleet had been sent to Pearl Harbor as part of an effort to deter aggressive moves by Japan in the Pacific. In January 1941, C-in-C of the Japanese Combined Fleet, Admiral Isoruku Yamamoto*, issued the first directive for the development of plans for a surprise attack on the US Fleet (now renamed the Pacific Fleet) at Pearl Harbor. Increasingly convinced that Japan did not have the resources to win a prolonged war against a fully mobilized United States, Yamamoto envisaged the pre-emptive destruction of the US Fleet and its headquarters in one crushing blow, using a carrier strike force launched from long range to achieve maximum surprise. Though Japanese military chiefs were initially opposed to the plan and unprepared fully to accept Yamamoto's concern over the potential power of American war production, the plan was finally agreed by the Japanese Imperial staff in the autumn and the striking force under the command of Vice Admiral Nagumo*, with six carriers, two battleships and escorting cruisers and destroyers, sailed from the Kurile Islands on 26 November.

Although American intelligence (see Magic) had collected much information that suggested the imminent possibility of some 'surprise aggressive movement' by Japan on American territory, during the tense autumn when diplomatic negotiations with Japan over China were clearly breaking down, lack of adequate staff and any effective co-ordination of information handling and assessment meant that nothing had yet been revealed to indicate Pearl Harbor as the target. Moreover, military intelligence was substantially limited by the inability of the Army and Navy cryptanalysts to crack the Japanese Army and Navy codes before December 1941. Thus, when the American Secretary of State, Cordell Hull* rejected the latest proposals offered by Japanese diplomats in Washington on 26 November (the same day that Nagumo's force set sail for Pearl Harbor), bringing tension between the two countries to a new climax, Admiral Kimmel*, C-in-C of the Pacific Fleet, received a warning from Washington that could still only guess at Japan's immediate intentions: 'This dispatch is to be considered a war warning . . . An aggressive move is expected within the next few days . . . organization of naval task forces indicates an amphibious* expedition against either the Philippines, Thai or Kra peninsula or possibly Borneo. Execute appropriate defensive deployment . . .'

Nevertheless, several clear warning signals of the approach of the Japanese strike force in the final few hours before the launch of the attack were ignored or ineptly handled by American military and diplomatic staff, who were still psychologically as well as practically unprepared for war. Two intercepted Purple ciphers sent by Tokyo to Japanese Ambassador Nomura* on the eve of the attack indicating an imminent assault, probably on Pearl Harbor, were passed on by the Army and Navy intelligence to American Chief of Naval Operations, Admiral Stark. With a now inconceivable lack of urgency, a cable to Pearl Harbor to alert them to the threat was eventually drafted, but then held up by a communications bungle until it was too late. Meanwhile, an American private, who was manning the Oahu radar* station and spotted the Japanese aircraft coming in and reported them, was reassured that they were not significant. The sighting and sinking of a Japanese midget submarine* outside Pearl Harbor similarly failed to produce an alert.

Now in position 275 miles north of Oahu, and armed with 104 high-level bombers, 135 dive-bombers and 81 fighter aircraft, Nagumo launched the first wave of the assault at 6 a.m. local time; they dropped their first bombs on the primary target of American battleships, anchored, without torpedo netting, along Ford Island at 7.55 a.m. Against almost no opposition from the shocked and still sleepy pilots and anti-aircraft* gunners, the first-wave torpedoes hit the *Arizona**, *Oklahoma**, *West Virginia** and *California**, sinking all four. American aircraft parked wing-to-wing on the five Oahu airfields were almost completely wiped out. Although the second-wave assault, launched 45 minutes later, was hampered by smoke and unable to inflict as much damage as the first, not one of the eight American battleships escaped damage. In all, 18 warships, 187 aircraft and 2,400 servicemen were lost in an attack lasting no more than two hours. In that time it appeared to the appalled survivors that the entire strength of the US Pacific Fleet had been lost.

Key survivors of the surprise carrier air attack, however, were the harbour installations and oil supplies, and, most importantly, the fleet's three aircraft carriers, *Enterprise**, *Lexington** and *Saratoga**, which were all at sea. This was to prove of vital significance later on, when the US Pacific Fleet sought to challenge the Japanese initiative in the Pacific. Calling 7 December 'a date which will live in infamy', President Roosevelt* was able to call on a united US Congress to declare war on Japan the following day.

Since December 1941, attention has been focused less on the details of the attack than on the reasons why the Americans were so poorly prepared. Immediate recriminations after the disaster at Pearl Harbor identified Admiral Kimmel* and Major General Short (commander of Army operations at Oahu) as scapegoats and they were both relieved of their command by superiors who were perhaps anxious to apportion blame in order to exonerate themselves. Some members of the Joint Committee of Investigation set up by Congress at the end of the war and historians

writing during the 1950s attempted to implicate President Roosevelt in the tragedy, claiming that he had provoked and concealed warnings of the impending attack in order to draw the isolationists into the war (see Neutrality, US), though no hard evidence was ever found to support the theory. Recent revelations that British naval cryptanalysts had broken the Japanese naval code before Pearl Harbor and knew of Japanese attack plans have yet to be analysed. Most recent studies of the mass of declassified intelligence files pertaining to Pearl Harbor, however, agree broadly with the final report of the Joint Committee, which published the conclusions of its exhaustive nine-month long hearings in September 1945. There now seems little doubt that the responsibility for the disaster at Pearl Harbor was a collective one, shared ultimately by American political, diplomatic and military leaders at the highest levels. See also US Navy.

Pedestal, Operation Code-name for a major Allied convoy* of 14 fast merchant ships which left Gibraltar* for the relief of Malta* on 10 August 1942. With Royal Navy* resources boosted by the suspension of Arctic* convoys, a massive escort of three aircraft carriers, two battleships, four cruisers and 14 destroyers was provided, and a decoy fleet of empty merchantmen sailed from Alexandria* at the same time. Attempts to supply Malta with convoys earlier in the year had been comprehensively thwarted and the Pedestal convoy was subjected to almost continuous heavy attacks from Axis bombers, submarines and motor torpedo boats* based in southern Europe. Nine merchantmen were sunk before the convoy reached Malta, and the Royal Navy lost the aircraft carrier *Eagle**, three cruisers and a destroyer. The five surviving merchantmen included the oil tanker *Ohio*, and despite the appalling cost in lives and materials, Malta's immediate crisis was averted.

Peirse, Air Chief Marshal Sir Richard
(1892–1970) British C-in-C of RAF*
Bomber Command 1940–2 and subsequently Commander of Allied Air Forces
in Southeast Asia under Mountbatten* following the Allied defeat in Burma*, Peirse
was responsible for organizing the Allied
air forces for its recapture, as well as for
airlifting supplies from India to China*
over the Hump*. His air force made a
significant contribution to the Allied victory in Burma in 1944, maintaining supply
missions for the invading 14th Army. Peirse
retired in November 1944.

Peniakoff, Vladimir (1897–1951) Founder
and commander of 'Popski's Private Army',
a British raiding force which operated in
North Africa* and Italy*. Of Belgian-
Russian parentage, Peniakoff studied as an
undergraduate at Cambridge University before joining the French Army at the start
of WW1. Becoming a sugar manufacturer
in Egypt between the wars, Peniakoff travelled extensively in the desert where he
learned vital navigation skills. Commissioned in the Libyan Arab Force (British
Army) at the outbreak of WW2, he formed
a small force, known at first as No. 1 Long
Range Demolition Squadron, which carried out reconnaissance and assault duties
behind the enemy lines. It was later officially referred to as PPA – Popski's Private
Army.

Pennsylvania, USS United States battleship and Class. Commissioned in 1916,
Pennsylvania and her sister ship *Arizona*
matched the armament of their bigger,
heavier Japanese contemporaries, and
shipped more internal and underwater protection than their *Oklahoma** Class predecessors. Both were extensively modernized
from 1929–31 and were with the Pacific
Fleet at Pearl Harbor on 7 December 1941.
The *Arizona* was one of two battleships
irretrievably lost during the Japanese attack. Her magazine exploded and she went
down with the loss of 1,103 lives, remaining on the harbour floor as a war memorial.

The *Pennsylvania* was only slightly damaged
and returned to service the following
August, after repair and further modernization. Back in the Pacific, she fought in support of American landings from the
Aleutians* to Okinawa*, and took part in
the last battleship confrontation of the war
in the Surigao Strait* in October 1944. Her
war modifications were typical for old American battleships. Secondary armament was
removed, and a battery of dual-purpose air–
surface guns installed, as well as numerous
light anti-aircraft* mountings and radar*
sets. On 12 August 1945, the *Pennsylvania*
was badly damaged by an aircraft torpedo*
off Okinawa. Her repairs were cut short by
the end of the Pacific War* and she was expended as a target vessel.
BRIEF DATA (*Pennsylvania*, 1941) Displacement: 33,100 tons; Dimensions: o/a
lgth – 608', b – 106' 3''; Speed: 21 knots;
Armament: $12 \times 14''$ gun (4×3), $12 \times 5''$
gun, $8 \times 5''$ AA gun, $4 \times$ 3pdr AA gun, 4
aircraft.

Pensacola, USS United States heavy
cruiser and Class. The *Pensacola* and her
sister the *Salt Lake City* were the first American cruisers designed under the 10,000-
ton, 8-inch gun limitations imposed by the
Washington Naval Treaty of 1922. Completed in 1929–30, they benefited from late
entry into the international race to build
up to these limits and were the best balanced ships of their breed. They were
matched only by the Japanese *Myoko**
Class, which considerably exceeded treaty
regulations whereas, partly thanks to an
innovatory arrangement of mixed twin and
triple gun main turrets, the *Pensacolas* were
completed 900 tons under the limit.

Both ships served throughout the Pacific
War* and both survived, although not un-
scathed. *Pensacola* was severely damaged by
torpedoes at Tassafaronga* late in 1942,
and the *Salt Lake City* was hit at Cape
Esperance* that October, and suffered
further damage off Komandorski Island in
the North Pacific the following March.
Both cruisers then took part in the Central

Pacific offensives from late 1943 until the end of the war, and were later expended as nuclear-test targets.

BRIEF DATA (*Pensacola*, 1941) Displacement: 9,100 tons; Dimensions: o/a lgth – 585' 9", b – 65' 3"; Speed: 32.5 knots; Armament: 10 × 8" gun (2 × 3, 2 × 2), 8 × 5" AA gun, 2 × 3pdr AA gun, 8 × 0.5" AA gun, 4 aircraft.

Percival, Lt General Arthur (1887–1966) British commander of forces in Singapore* at its surrender to the Japanese in February 1942, Percival had taken command of British forces in Malaya* in July 1941, having previously served in France as Chief of Staff of General Dill's* Corps and been a divisional commander in Britain. When three divisions of crack Japanese troops landed in northern Malaya and Siam (Thailand*) at the start of an offensive directed against Singapore in December 1941, Percival was faced with the practically hopeless task of holding off the Japanese advance southwards through Malaya with two and a half unreinforced and poorly prepared divisions and virtually no air cover. Having sunk the two British battleships, *Repulse* and *Prince of Wales*, which had been sent to defend Singapore and challenge any attempted landing of Japanese troops on the Malay peninsula, Japan's control of the seas around Malaya was undisputed. The resulting costly and chaotic retreat of British forces in Malaya that culminated in the defence of Singapore and the final surrender of Percival and some 130,000 troops to Japanese General Yamashita* was blamed on Percival's poor generalship at the time. The responsibility for the ignominious British defeat must be shared, however, by complacent British military and political leaders who had continued, without justification, to view the conquest of Singapore as impossible. He survived Japanese captivity and was present at the signing of the Japanese surrender in Tokyo Bay.

Pershing (M26) Tank American heavy tank* which entered full production early in 1945 (despite doubts concerning the value of such a weapon) after 20 examples had undergone successful operational testing in Northwest Europe*. The Pershing arrived too late to make any real contribution to the war, although it was at Okinawa*, but remained in post-war production and fought in Korea.

BRIEF DATA (M26) Type: 5-man heavy tank; Engine: 500hp petrol; Max speed: 30mph; Range: 100m; Arms: 1 × 90mm gun, 1 × 12.7mm mg, 2 × 7.62mm mg; Armour: max 102mm.

Persia For many years a source of conflict between the British and Russian empires, Persia (Iran) became an important supply route once the Soviet Union entered the war against Germany in June 1941. When the Persian government refused to expel German agents, British and Soviet forces jointly entered and occupied the country in August/September, meeting little resistance and forcing Shah Reza Pahlevi to abdicate in favour of his son. The following January Britain and Russia signed a treaty agreeing to withdraw within six months after the end of the war, provided Persia remained neutral. The US was included in this agreement after the Tehran Conference* of December 1943, and Persia remained open for the transit of western aid to the Soviet Union throughout the war.

Petacci, Clara (1912–45) Benito Mussolini's* mistress from 1936 until their deaths in 1945. Clara Petacci became Mussolini's favoured companion from the time of their first meeting, in spite of his reputation as a notorious womanizer. She joined Mussolini at Gargano after he was deposed, and was shot with him by the partisan leader Walter Audisio on 28 April 1945.

Pétain, Marshal Henri Philippe (1856–1951) French military hero of Verdun (1916), post-WW1 commander of the French Army and highly influential military figurehead and strategist of the conservative school, Pétain acted as head of state of Vichy* France from 1940–4. Brought into the French cabinet by Premier Paul Reynaud* in 1940 while German forces advanced through Belgium, Pétain, like Laval*, was influenced by Hitler's grandiose claims to be midwife to a new era and a new order in Europe. Adamantly opposed to any military union with Britain, which he had already prejudged as doomed to defeat, Pétain had a majority of cabinet support in pressing Reynaud for an armistice with Germany, following the German invasion and occupation of Paris on 14 June. Reynaud's commitment to carry on the war effort from Africa and the French Empire (with the aid of Admiral Darlan* and General de Gaulle*) resulted in his resignation as premier, to be replaced by Pétain.

The surrender terms dictated to the French at Compiègne on 22 June divided France in two zones, northern (occupied) and southern (unoccupied). Formally self-appointed head of the new *Etat Français*, by powers given him by the French National Assembly in July, Pétain's leadership of Vichy France (whose government was divided between Catholic conservative and extreme right-wing members) was authoritarian and collaborative (although he rejected German pressure to enter the war against Britain despite his deputy Laval's urgent recommendations). Although the new constitution of France was never completed, Pétain envisaged a state based on 'work, family and fatherland' that broadly echoed Fascist ideology. Following the Allied Torch* invasion of Northwest Africa, however, and Hitler's occupation of the 'free zone' in early 1942, old age and compromise increasingly undermined Pétain's authority.

Arrested by the Germans in August 1944, Pétain chose to return to France to face trial in April 1945. Convicted of collaboration and sentenced to military degradation and death, his penalty was commuted by General de Gaulle to life imprisonment.

Petlyakov Pe-2 Series Designed as a high-altitude fighter and tested as a high-altitude bomber, the Pe-2 entered Soviet service in August 1940 as a dive-bomber and ground-support plane. It was one of the outstanding Allied combat aircraft of the war and, continually modified, remained in front-line action along the whole Eastern Front* until the German surrender.

A fighter version, the Pe-3*bis*, appeared in 1941 without dive-brakes but with additional 20mm and 12.7mm guns. During 1942, the plane's armament was further increased, and self-sealing tanks, improved aerodynamics and extra protective armour were introduced. From 1943, new 1,600hp engines gave the Pe-21 interceptor a top speed of 408mph, and tripled the load capacity of bombers. Numerous other versions included the P2R long-range reconnaissance version, the P2UT trainer and a P2VI high-altitude fighter. Production appears to have ended in early 1945, with just over 11,400 built.

BRIEF DATA (Pe-2) Type: 3–4-man attack-bomber; Engine: 2 × 1,100hp Klimov; Max speed: 336mph; Ceiling: 28,870'; Range: 746m; Arms: 4 × 7.62mm mg; Bomb load: 2,200lb.

Petlyakov Pe-8 Russian concentration on twin-engined tactical bombers meant that the Pe-8 was the only strategic heavy bomber built by the Soviet Union in WW2. Although the plane was fast and reliable, only a few hundred were built between 1940 and 1944, beginning major operations over Berlin* in mid-1941 and flying many long-range missions to Germany, Hungary* and Rumania*. From 1943, 1,630hp Shetzov engines were used in the Pe-8, raising its ceiling to 29,000ft, its range to over 3,000 miles and its bomb load to 11,600lb.

BRIEF DATA (Pe-8) Type: 9-man heavy bomber; Engine: 4 × 1,300hp Mikulin; Max speed: 276mph; Ceiling: 23,000'; Range: 2,321m; Arms: (typical) 2 × 20mm cannon, 2 × 12.7mm mg, 2 × 7.62mm mg; Bomb load: 8,800lb.

Petrov, General Ivan Y. (1896–1950) Soviet commander of the Special Maritime Army which defended the Black Sea port of Odessa in 1941. In the following year Petrov took command of the Black Sea Front and the defence of Sevastopol*, which fell to German forces in July 1942. Transferred to command the North Caucasus Front in 1943, he directed operations in the Kerch peninsula and the Crimea*, but was removed from his command. He was also removed, on the recommendation of Political General Mekhlis*, from command of the 2nd Belorussian Front*, and was later dismissed as commander of the 4th Ukrainian Front, after the failed offensive on the Carpathians.

Philippine Sea, Battle of the, 19–20 June 1944 Last of the large-scale carrier force battles of the Pacific War*, precipitated by the launch of the American assault on Saipan* in the Mariana Islands* by Admiral Spruance's* 5th Fleet, which included Admiral Mitscher's* Fast Carrier Strike Force (Task Force 58), on 15 June 1944 (see Map 18). The assault prompted Admiral Toyoda*, C-in-C of the Japanese Navy* Combined Fleet, to put Operation A-Go* into effect. The plan aimed to relieve Saipan (of vital strategic importance to Japan's defence since it was within bombing range of Japan's home islands) and entrap the US Fleet between Admiral Ozawa's* 1st Mobile Fleet and land-based air power from Guam*. The nine-carrier force, including three fleet carriers Shokaku*, Zuikaku and Taiho*, was deployed in two principal groups (with a Van Force under Vice Admiral Kurita) and prepared to launch a 300-plane strike against Task Force 58, spotted by seaplanes on 19 June, lacking the information that the supporting air power from Guam had been reduced to a fraction by heavy carrier air strikes from the powerful US carrier fleet with a strike force of about 1,000 aircraft.

The first two waves of aircraft sent off by Ozawa were intercepted 50 miles ahead of the US Fleet by Mitscher's aircraft and only 20 planes got through to inflict minor damage on two US ships. By the end of the day, in a spectacular series of air actions, 240 Japanese planes had been lost and two carriers sunk, including Admiral Ozawa's flagship, Taiho.

In the late afternoon, when Ozawa ordered a retirement in order to refuel and prepare for a renewed attack in the morning, Admiral Mitscher made the decision to risk a night-time return and recovery for his aircraft in order to chase the Japanese fleet. Launching a 216-plane strike just after 4 p.m., Mitscher's pilots found and sank the carrier Hiyo*, damaged the Zuikaku and the Chiyoda*, the battleship Haruna* and sank two Japanese oilers. Although the Americans lost 80 planes, which crashed into the sea or onto carrier decks in the returning darkness, most of the pilots and air crew were retrieved, and Ozawa's force was decisively beaten.

Known as the 'Great Marianas Turkey Shoot', this substantial American victory brought the threat of a major Japanese countermove in the Pacific to an end and clearly demonstrated the now vast superiority of the American Pacific forces. When General MacArthur* launched the reinvasion of the Philippines* at Leyte* four months later, only a battered remnant of the Japanese Combined Fleet could be assembled to meet it. See Japanese Air Forces.

Philippines, The Large archipelago in the Southwest Pacific (see Maps 12, 18–21) it was the site of two major campaigns in the Pacific War*: first, the Japanese conquest of the islands from 8 December 1941 to 7 May 1942; then the American reconquest, begun on 17 October 1944 and still being contested at the end of the war. Historically linked as a colonial territory to the United States since 1898, though with independent commonwealth status since 1934, the Philippines had been of great strategic importance to US Pacific defence policy since the first decade of the century. War Plan Orange, the United States' defensive strategy against a Japanese attack finalized in 1911, positioned the Philippines' garrison as the bulwark of Far Eastern defence against Japanese attack until the arrival of the US fleet. With the rising threat of war in Europe during the late 1930s, however, and despite the equally ominous implications of Japanese expansionism in Southeast Asia, the US Joint Chiefs of Staff* drastically revised their military strategy, on the fundamental premise that Germany and the Axis* now represented the greatest evil, and the greatest danger to US security.

The new Rainbow defence plans, initiated from mid-1939, redrew the defensive boundaries in the Pacific. The aim was now drastically limited – to hold Hawaii, at the certain cost of the Philippines if the Japanese attacked. In 1941, however, the growing threat to the Philippines from the increase of Japanese forces in Formosa* and movement south towards Indochina* again forced a change of strategy. The appeals to Washington by Philippine President Manuel Quezon* for funds to mobilize the Commonwealth Army were persistently echoed by his military adviser and Field Marshal of the Commonwealth Army, Douglas MacArthur*. Although MacArthur's grandiose title (and equally grandiose ambitions for the Commonwealth Army) were not matched by his actual strength – less than 4,000 regular troops, 20,000 barely trained irregulars and a small number of obsolete fighters and medium bombers – his insistence on the need to reinforce the Philippines was soon borne out by events.

The breakdown of negotiations between Japan and the US in June, followed by the US freezing of assets in July (on the same day that Japan moved into advance bases in Indochina) gave irreversible momentum to the military and political arguments for an increase of defensive strength in the Philippines. Recalled to active duty as a major general, with $10 million from the President's Emergency Fund to mobilize the Philippine Army, MacArthur was also promised a large force of over 100 B-17* Flying Fortresses, the long-range heavy

bomber with an immense reputation (despite the contradictory evidence provided by their performance with the RAF* in August 1941). Not only MacArthur and American Air Corps enthusiasts but also US Chief of Staff Marshall* continued to believe that the B-17 would revolutionize warfare and open up a whole new range of strategic options for the US in the Far East.

Strongly backed by Churchill*, who saw it as a way to fulfil his earlier promise to defend 'kith and kin' in Australia, and by Australians, who were increasingly concerned about the worth of that promise (see Menzies, Robert and Curtin, John), the American build-up in the Philippines continued during mid-1941. By October, MacArthur felt sufficiently confident of progress to send a triumphant memorandum to Marshall, describing his 227 assorted fighters, bombers and reconnaissance aircraft (including only 35 B-17s) as a 'tremendously strong offensive and defensive force' and the Philippines as 'the key or base point of the US defence line'. In the same month a similarly complacent assessment of US strength in the Philippines was provided by the Joint Chiefs* for Churchill and Roosevelt*.

Ignoring the relentless timetable for offensive action imposed on Japan by the US oil embargo, American military and political leaders felt confident that the deterrent effect of the embargo and the Philippine build-up would be decisive in avoiding war with Japan. In Tokyo, meanwhile, with 12,000 tons of oil consumed from national reserves every day, the Japanese military leaders won their case for a deadline on negotiations with the US. In early September the Japanese government formally resolved to complete preparations 'to wage war if necessary against the United States, Britain and the Netherlands'.

On the eve of the Japanese invasion (see Pacific War), MacArthur commanded roughly 135,000 troops in the US Army Forces Far East (USAFFE), deployed for the defence of the main island of Luzon*, the second major island of Mindanao, and the vast scatter of 7,000 islands between Luzon and Mindanao known collectively as the Visayans. Although on full war alert from 27 November and forewarned of the attack on Pearl Harbor* some hours before local attacks began, the initial Japanese attack was completely successful.

Japanese air strikes from Formosa destroyed half of MacArthur's air force (including two squadrons of B-17s) on the ground on 8 December (local time), despite requests from US Far East Air Forces commander General Brereton* to launch a pre-emptive strike on Formosa and evacuate the B-17s to Mindanao. The air strikes were followed up on 10 December by air attacks on Manila* by the 11th Air Fleet that also destroyed Philippine torpedo* reserves and advance landings by elements of General Homma's* 14th Army, all effectively unopposed, to capture air bases at three points in northern Luzon. Subsidiary landings at Legaspi in the south were similarly unchallenged.

The main 14th Army landing at Lingayen Gulf, north of the capital, Manila, on 22 December, completely overran the inexperienced Filipino troops deployed around the Luzon coastline. Relying on superior air power as an offensive back-up to ground operations, the relatively small Japanese force (of 57,000 men in total, with limited tank*, field artillery* and anti-aircraft* support) made quick advances. Within two days the veteran superiority of Japanese forces combined with the poor defensive positioning of MacArthur's tactical deployments, with American divisions guarding the interior and Manila, and half-trained Filipino units charged with coastline defence, forced a decision on a change of tactic. After much preliminary agonizing, MacArthur was obliged to accept the stark military position and resort to the old War Plan Orange option of a general retreat to the Bataan* peninsula. At the last possible moment he radioed his commanders to begin the withdrawal, hurriedly gathering scattered food, ammunition and supplies for the defence, as Man-

ila was declared an open city and evacuated. The Northern Luzon Force, commanded by General Wainright*, was ordered to hold a series of defensive lines while the Southern Luzon Force retreated to the southern peninsula of Bataan.

By 7 January 1942, all USAFFE troops on Luzon had withdrawn to a partially prepared battle line on Bataan. Continuous Japanese assaults pushed the US defensive line back and depleted much of its already limited supplies. Although General Homma was forced to call off assaults on the line at the end of February, the condition of the US troops, the lack of food, medicines and ammunition put the eventual outcome of the siege beyond doubt. Ordered back to Australia to assume command of Allied Southwest Pacific forces at the beginning of March, MacArthur made an emotional departure from his HQ on the fortified island of Corregidor*, leaving Wainright in command, and Major General King with operational control of the peninsula. By mid-March, Homma had been sufficiently reinforced to increase air and artillery bombardment as a prelude to a major assault on 3 April that shattered the right flank of the line and sent Japanese units streaming southwards down the peninsula. Under orders to attack, General King nevertheless made a decision to surrender the Luzon forces six days later. Although General Wainright's garrison of 11,000 on Corregidor continued to hold out, with exceptional courage and under appalling conditions, until the beginning of May when Homma landed a battalion on the fortified island, the Philippines were already conclusively lost.

Between mid-1942 and the beginning of October 1944, when General MacArthur was finally ordered to prepare his return to the islands, the broad strategic role of operations aimed at the reconquest of the Philippines was more or less constantly under discussion by the US Joint Chiefs of Staff. The arguments between MacArthur (and later US Pacific Commander Admiral Nimitz) on one side, and Chief of Naval

Operations, Admiral King, on the other, centred on what was the most effective strategy for victory against Japan, and how best to achieve it. The status of the Philippines within this strategy was subject to regular alteration – the opinions of the Joint Chiefs changed as their Pacific offensives gathered momentum (see Pacific War). MacArthur, however, remained unwavering in his commitment to the reconquest of the entire archipelago, continually stressing the importance of the United States' prestige in Asia which he understood to demand a total victory in the Philippines. Finally, in October 1944, he was instructed to proceed with operations.

Operations against Leyte Island, which opened the US campaign in the Philippines, involved the creation of the largest amphibious* force yet used in the Pacific. Ground forces under 6th Army commander Krueger* were provided with land-based air support under Far East Air Forces commander Lt General Kenney*. Naval support and amphibious operations were provided by Vice Admiral Kinkaid* and the US 7th Fleet. Admiral Halsey's* 3rd Fleet contained the main naval strike force assigned to eliminate any Japanese fleet which engaged it, under overall command of Admiral Nimitz. General MacArthur had overall control of the rest of naval, air and ground forces.

Although the US invasion transports arriving at Leyte initially came under a serious surprise threat from Japanese Admiral Kurita's Centre Task Force, the main landings on the east of the island by four infantry divisions on 20 October met only limited resistance, and important air bases near Tacloban and Dulag were captured within four days. In a final attempt to reverse the momentum of the American offensive, the Japanese Navy* (whose remaining carriers by now lacked more than a token complement of aircraft) initiated a daring plan (Operation Sho-I) to draw the US naval forces into a decisive battle using a decoy force under Ozawa* and eliminate the invasion force with a striking group under Kurita. The Battle of Leyte Gulf* was the largest naval battle of all time, involving nearly 300 vessels and many more aircraft. The final failure of the Japanese battleships to reach the invasion force effectively ended any threat still posed by the remains of the Imperial Japanese Navy.

Nevertheless, reinforcement of Japanese forces on Leyte by order of Imperial GHQ – against the advice of Philippine forces' commander Yamashita* who wished to preserve strength for the inevitable struggle for Luzon – had increased the garrison from 15,000 to 60,000. Resistance to the American advance south stiffened but by 2 November Marines controlled the Leyte Valley from Carigara in the north to Abuyog on the east coast. Although heavy rainfall halted operations for several weeks, American forces threatened the Japanese base at Ormoc on the west coast by mid-November and Yamashita was forced to concede the certain loss of Leyte and the probable loss of Luzon to MacArthur's forces soon afterwards. His decision to adopt a defensive strategy, to tie down the maximum possible enemy forces, successfully delayed the launch of the Luzon offensive (scheduled for 20 December 1944 but begun on 9 January 1945), though it could not pose any real threat to the vast command of nearly one and a half million men under MacArthur's leadership now poised to clear the archipelago and transform the Philippines into the 'England in the Pacific', in preparation for the invasion of mainland Japan.

The Luzon campaign began with the rapid capture of air bases on Mindanao, 150 miles south of Manila, as a preliminary to the main landings at Lingayen Gulf on 9 January. Within a month American forces had driven across the Central Plain, albeit against strong resistance, to threaten Manila. While Yamashita withdrew his forces to the mountains, a house-to-house struggle for the city was fought against the 31st Naval Base Force under the independent command of Rear Admiral Iwabuchi*.

Manila fell on 4 March having cost 16,000 Japanese lives. Meanwhile secondary landings at San Antonio and Mariveles to prevent Japanese withdrawals to Bataan, combined with a difficult landing on Corregidor with heavy losses, succeeded in opening up Manila bay to shipping by mid-March, although extensive repairs were necessary before the harbour was fully operational again. The capture of Yamashita's mountain HQ at Baguio on 27 April by a combined force of Filipino units and the US 33rd and 37th Divisions proved the final blow to the Japanese defence. Although MacArthur's forces were in practical control of Luzon by June, the substantial remains of Yamashita's forces continued to tie down four divisions from isolated mountain positions, though by this time they were semi-starved.

While the major battles continued on Leyte and Luzon, Lt General Eichelberger* had led the US 8th Army, supported by Filipino guerrilla units, in a drive to clear the southern Philippines, starting with a landing at Palawan on 28 February, followed by an amphibious assault on Mindanao on 10 March and other landings in rapid succession on Panay, Cebu, Negros, and Bohol. Further landings at Mindanao were co-ordinated with an American drive southwest down the Sulu archipelago towards Borneo in April. Mopping-up operations continued into July. On 2 September General Yamashita surrendered with roughly 50,000 men. The Luzon campaign alone exceeded in scale and cost the entire American involvement in either Italy or North Africa.

Phoney War (Sitzkrieg) The phrase applied first by American journalists and later by the British to the relatively calm period in northwestern Europe between September 1939 and May 1940. With their principal formations engaged in Poland* and a period of refitting and redeploying necessary before any new offensive could be undertaken, the reasons for German inactivity need little analysis. It is more difficult to account for the inactivity on the British and French side, although the 'Maginot mentality', which called for defence at all costs, provides an immediate answer. It has recently been suggested, however, that the tactic of defence from prepared positions followed logically from the political tactic of appeasement*, and was in effect its military extension. The phoney war ended dramatically on 10 May 1940 when Germany launched its Western Offensive*.

Piaggio P108B The P108B was the only production version of Italy's first heavy bomber. First flown in 1939, it entered service in 1942 and, although only 163 were completed, was used extensively in both the Mediterranean* and the Eastern Front*. The most interesting of its many advanced design features were the two-gun remote turrets attached to its outer engine nacelles.

BRIEF DATA (P108B) Type: 7-man heavy bomber; Engine: 4 × 1,500hp Piaggio; Max speed: 270mph; Ceiling: 21,000'; Range: 1,550m; Arms: 8 × 12.7mm mg; Bomb load: 8,000lb.

Pips, Battle of the A surface action fought by an American naval force against what appeared to be a Japanese naval force south of the Aleutian Islands, in July 1943. Some, though not all, of the American ships' radar* sets showed a group of 'pips', which seemed to manoeuvre like a formation of Japanese ships. Two battleships and four heavy cruisers fired at the positions from long range for half an hour before the pips disappeared. Later reconnaissance of the area revealed no sign of Japanese ships, however, and the cause of the 'ghost' images was never explained beyond the relative inexperience of the US Navy* with the then new radar equipment.

Pistols During WW2, pistols were issued to serving officers, airmen, military police and the crews of large weapons or tanks*. The most famous types were the American

Browning Colt 0.45-inch, and the German 9mm Luger, although the latter had been superseded as standard issue from 1938 by the 9mm Walther P38. These were all semi-automatic weapons, as was the standard Russian 7.62mm Tokarev pistol, but the British 0.38-inch Service Pistols were revolvers. Undoubtedly the worst pistol adopted by a major belligerent was the hopelessly unreliable Japanese 8mm Type 94, which shared widespread service with the more efficient Taisho 14 Nambu pistol.

Pius XII (Eugenio Pacelli) (1876–1958) Elected Pope in March 1939, having served as Papal Nuncio in Berlin from 1920–9, Pacelli had been a chief adviser to his predecessor, Pius XI, during the negotiations for the Concordat between the Roman Catholic Church and the Nazi state, signed in July 1933. In November 1939, Pius XII assured Josef Müller, a representative of the Abwehr*-centred anti-Nazi conspirators meeting secretly with him, of his preparedness to act as intermediary between the British and any new government formed in Germany. In the absence of any coup, however, Pius XII seems to have become reluctant to involve himself on either side.

Many attacks have been made on Pius XII for his failure to condemn Nazi atrocities (while he remained unhesitating in his condemnation of communist misdeeds). His declaration to the College of Cardinals in June 1943 that public condemnation of mass genocide of the Jews might cause more harm than good was undoubtedly seen as a betrayal of many Catholics who believed that the Pope's power of excommunication might well have disrupted the practical execution of that policy. See also Nazi Escape Organizations.

Placentia Bay (Newfoundland) Conference See Conferences, Allied.

Ploesti Centre of the great Rumanian oilfields, which were capable of producing 7 million tons a year. Rumanian oil was vital to Germany's war effort and Hitler spared nothing in his protection of Ploesti. In June 1940, the implied threat of Soviet seizures in Bessarabia and Bukovina was met by a build-up both of German forces in nearby Poland and of Hitler's mistrust of Stalin. The German invasion of Russia* was in part prompted by the need to secure oil supplies, and after 1941 the Ploesti fields were strongly defended in the face of repeated Allied bombing attacks.

In June 1942, days after declaring war on Rumania, the United States sent a detachment of 12 B-24* Liberators to bomb the refineries from North Africa (the Halverson Project). They did little damage and merely alerted the defenders to the possibility of an attack from that quarter. On 1 August the following year, 177 USAAF* B-24s raided Ploesti from Libyan bases in Operation Tidal Wave. Fifty-four bombers were lost and, although extensive fires were started, the oilfields kept functioning. Subsequent attacks failed to shut down the refineries until August 1944, by which time Allied aircraft were landing on Russian airfields and bombing Ploesti again on the way home. On 30 August, the Red Army* occupied the ruins. Overall, more than 350 bombers were lost in operations against the oilfields.

Point-blank See Strategic Bombing Offensive.

Poland In 1918 a Polish republic was formed out of the Polish-speaking parts of Russia, Austria and Germany, which, however, included large areas of minority groups, most notably German. After the Treaty of Brest-Litovsk (imposed by Imperial Germany on Russia in March 1918), the area was fought over in 1918 and 1920, with German Freikorps on one side and Soviet Russians on the other. A particular point at issue was the 'Danzig* Corridor', land between the Baltic Sea and the centre of landlocked Poland, established by the Treaty of Versailles. Poland thus relied greatly on the political support of Britain, and more particularly France, which saw her as a counterbalance to a possible German resurgence.

In 1934, Hitler* signed a ten-year non-aggression pact with Poland, loosening the Franco-Polish alliance. In 1938, when Germany took the Sudetenland from Czechoslovakia*, Hitler tolerated Poland's opportunistic annexation of a small corner of Czechoslovakia. But early in 1939, following Germany's occupation of all Czechoslovakia, Hitler extended his demand to Danzig and the Polish Corridor. Emboldened by the Soviet Union's final reassurance of her support (see Russo-German Pact), Hitler felt sufficiently confident to challenge the last-minute British guarantee of Polish independence (see Anglo-Polish Alliance) and commit Germany to war. Poland was invaded by the Germans on 1 September 1939 and by the Russians on 17 September (see Poland, German Campaign in).

Within three weeks the Polish armies had collapsed in the face of a ferocious German assault based on modern theories of warfare already considerably advanced in Germany (see Blitzkrieg) and was occupied within the month by German and Russian troops in accordance with the secret protocols of the Russo-German Pact (and its revisions in the Soviet–German Friendship Treaty). The Polish government fled to Rumania* and then in 1940 to Britain, where it was recognized as the Polish government-in-exile*. In western Poland, Poles were expelled from their lands which were then resettled by Germans and renamed the Warthegau.

In the Polish regions that remained following the seizure of territory by both Germany and Russia, Hans Frank's* appointment as Governor-General saw the start of a brutal policy of national destruction and degradation zealously pursued in accordance with the Nazi theory of race. From his palace at Krakow, Frank set about the systematic murder and removal of Polish nationalists, intellectuals and professionals that aimed to reduce the population of Poland to a slave society. From 1940 to 1944, Frank was responsible for the transportation of tens of thousands of Poles to forced labour, and for the deaths of 3 million Jews (see Warsaw, Uprisings in). Poland suffered a higher percentage of deaths during the war than any other country.

Following the recapture of Poland by Russian armies in early 1945 (see Poland, Russian Campaign in), the Western Allies failed to support the claims of the exiled Polish government against Russian pressure. The Yalta Conference (see Conferences), held in February 1945, recognized the Russian-backed communist-led Polish provisional government, known as the Lublin Committee*, which, as Moscow's protégé, accepted Russia's claim to territory assigned by the Russo-German Friendship Treaty. (Poland was to be compensated by moving her frontier with Germany westwards to the Oder–Neisse line*.) Thereafter, despite the temporary inclusion of a few members of the Polish government-in-exile in the coalition, and promises of free elections in the future, Poland had little hope of maintaining her sovereignty. Already wholly within the Russian military sphere, Poland was now effectively brought under her political control.

Poland, German Campaign in, 1939 Hitler had made the decision to attack Poland* several months earlier than the actual date of the invasion. His efforts to isolate Poland diplomatically, which reached a climax in the few days before the attack, were countered at the last minute by Britain's decision to commit herself to Poland's interests against European aggressors, even though the promise was untenable without Soviet support. Unwilling to believe that Britain would actually fight a European war over Poland and prepared, with Soviet support, to risk a short decisive war which he hoped would not reverse Britain's earlier commitment to the maintenance of peace in Europe, Hitler* issued the first directive for the conduct of the war on 31 August 1939 and the German armies crossed the frontier on 1 September.

Despite the speedy victory, achieved within a month and spearheaded by the spectacular success of General Guderian's* Panzer Corps, the retrospective appearance of certainty of the outcome is not supported by the facts. In 1939 the German Army* was not fully prepared for war. Of a total of 98 divisions mobilized in 1939, 46 were reserve divisions, many of them short of artillery* and other weapons. No heavy tanks* were available. The majority of tanks employed in Poland were light and thinly armoured. Numerically strong enough therefore to resist the attack, with 30 active and ten reserve divisions, Poland was nevertheless at a significant disadvantage both technically (see Polish Army) and tactically. The new theories of warfare, which were being both propounded and essentially ignored in Britain and France, and were not entertained among the antiquated military thinkers of the Polish High Command, had been enthusiastically developed in Germany (see Blitzkrieg). It was General Guderian's bold plan for the independent deployment of the 14 available armoured divisions, in deep spearheading advances far ahead of their infantry, that was decisive for the outcome of the campaign.

Organized in two Army Groups, North and South under Bock* and Rundstedt*, the Germans deployed five armies attacking in three thrusts. First from East Prussia (3rd Army, General von Kuchler); second from Pomerania (4th Army, General Kluge*); third from Silesia (8th, 10th, 14th, under Blaskowitz, Reichenau* and List*). Facing them were 30 divisions of Polish forces under Smigdly-Rydz*, positioned along the country's frontiers to protect its industrial region, with the greatest concentration in or near the Danzig* Corridor. The choice of forward position without the mobile forces to quickly check the advance of Germany's mechanized columns reflected an emotional rather than a tactical commitment to the country's most prized territor-

ies. The German attack was able to profit from it.

Although many of the more modern Polish aircraft had been moved to new, secret airstrips, technical inferiority and lack of fuel nevertheless severely limited their effectiveness. The breakthrough on the German–Polish border came within the week and Bock's Army Group North overran the Corridor by 5 September, moving southeast. By 7 September, 10th Army had advanced northeast to within 30 miles of Warsaw and succeeded in cutting off Polish forces before they could reach the Vistula*, in the first move of a double pincer envelopment. On 10 September, Smigdly-Rydz ordered retreat to southeast Poland. The 3rd Army completed the northern pincer movement on 15 September, and 4th and 14th completed the encirclement from the east on 17 September. Only at Kutno did the Germans face any serious counterattack. But the Kutno force was overwhelmed by 19 September, and surrendered with 100,000 men. Called the Battle of the Bzura River*, this was the largest engagement of the campaign.

The invasion on 17 September by the Russians could not be resisted. On 18 September, the Polish government and High Command fled to Rumania, though Warsaw* resisted until the 27th. Polish prisoners of the campaign amounted to roughly 700,000, with 66,000 killed and 200,000 wounded. German losses were estimated at 14,000 killed, 30,000 wounded. See also Polish Government-in-exile.

Poland, Russian Campaign in, 1944–5

On 4 January 1944, Russian mobile forces of the 1st Ukrainian Front (Army Group), driving westward from the junction at Novigrad Volynsk, crossed the pre-war Polish frontier as part of a winter offensive that had swept the German forces hundreds of miles west, across the Dnieper and out of Leningrad*. By mid-June, when the Russians launched a major new offensive in Poland* (see Map 31), they had reorganized and reinforced their forces along a broad front between the Baltic Sea and the Pripet Marshes. Meanwhile, for the Germans, the interval between the winter and summer offensives had seen an increase of pressure on their communications lines from Allied shuttle bombing attacks in the Balkans*.

The summer offensive was aimed at the German Army Group Centre, commanded by Busch (who had replaced Kluge*). Other drives to the north and south would begin, in accordance with the now characteristic Russian tactic, once the German reserves were committed to that sector of the front. With a battle strength of 166 divisions, the Russian offensive was carried out by four of the seven available fronts*: the 1st Baltic Front under Bagramyan*, the 3rd Belorussian Front under Chernyakhovsky*, the 2nd Belorussian under Zakharov and the 1st Belorussian under Rokossovsky*. Hampered by Hitler's insistence on no strategic withdrawals, which had already cost German forces huge casualties, and forced to maintain its defence across a wide front with shrinking reinforcements, the German forces were unable to check the sweeping Russian advance which followed the breakthrough on the northern flank to Polotsk, Vitebsk and Stolbtsy.

With the Allied invasion of France (see Northwest Europe, Allied Invasion of) now well established, and enjoying the advantage of American supply of motorized equipment, the Russians maintained their vast offensive effort. In the north, the 2nd and 3rd Belorussian Fronts joined to take Bialystok on 18 July. South of the Pripet Marshes, Rokossovsky's 1st Belorussian Front crossed the Bug River near Kovel on 22 July outflanking Lvow, which was taken by Konev's* forces on 24 July, and driving north to take Brest-Litovsk on 28 July. Konev's forces then built spearheads across the San River at Jaroslaw and Przemysl. By 2 August, a bridgehead was established by the 1st Ukrainian Front over the Vistula at Baranow. The capture of Lublin to the north, on 28 July by Rokossovsky's left wing, brought the Russians within 30 miles of the Vistula* at this point, and only 100 miles southeast of Warsaw. Mobile units of the 1st Belorussian Front sent forward met stiff resistance and were checked at Siedlce, but on 31 July one of Rokossovsky's columns reached Praga on the outskirts of Warsaw.

On 1 August, as German forces, now under General Model*, began to retreat across the Vistula bridges into the city, the Polish underground leaders gave the signal for the second rising of Warsaw* (see Polish Home Army). Although much of Warsaw fell quickly to the Polish free forces in the first few days and Model's forces appeared on the brink of a final rout, the Russian advance was not pushed beyond the Vistula. Now at the furthest stretch of its communications lines, the Russian army groups were met with a massed bombardment from air and ground, and the arrival of three SS panzer divisions drove a wedge into the Russians' northern flank. In the city, the Polish forces were ferociously repelled by special SS* units under SS General Bach-Zelewski*. Charges made against Stalin that he held back his forces in order to ensure the destruction of the Polish free forces at the hands of the Germans have some evidence to support them. There is little doubt, however, that military factors were at least as decisive as political ones in the halting of the Russian offensive. The offensive was not resumed until January 1945.

On 12 January 1945, the Russians launched the last great offensive on a 750-mile front with heavy reinforcements and new armour. German General Guderian*, who had been appointed Chief of the General Staff in July 1944, was unable to persuade Hitler to reinforce the 'gateways' into Germany, or to transfer troops from the Ardennes* in support of the Eastern Front. Blind to the possibility of failure, even at this desperately late stage, Hitler concentrated his attention on the offensive edge he believed had been regained in the west. Thus, when the Russian offensive began, Guderian had actually lost two panzer divisions to Hungary* and was left with a force largely composed of 50 weak infantry divisions, stretched out across the main front.

Konev's armoured spearheads crossed the Vistula at Baranow, thrusting out in two drives for Krakow and Oppeln, and cutting off Upper Silesia by the end of the month. Konev's northern flank joined with Zhukov's* 1st Belorussian Front, which had crossed the Vistula (14 January), outflanked Warsaw and had reached Poznan. Although the city did not fall until 23 February, the achievement of this objective brought Zhukov to the 'Brandenburg Frontier' – 100 miles from Berlin*. To the north, Rokossovsky's 2nd Belorussian Front had also achieved its objectives, breaking through to the Baltic west of Danzig, trapping German forces in East Prussia. Within a month, the Red Army had swept through Poland, to regroup on the Oder in preparation for the final assault on Berlin. See also Eastern Front.

Polikarpov I-16 Rotund little monoplane that put the Soviet Union briefly at the forefront of world fighter design when it appeared in 1935. By 1937, the I-16 (Type 10) was still superior to the early German Messerschmitt Bf109* fighters it met in Spain, but soon found itself outperformed by the much improved Bf109E variant. Urgent efforts to improve performance led to the introduction, in 1939, of the re-engined I-16 Types 18 and 24, which formed about 65 per cent of Soviet fighter strength at the time of the German invasion of Russia in June 1941. By now quite obsolete, they suffered enormously in the first stages of the campaign, but remained in front-line service until the spring of 1943, latterly achieving a measure of success as rocket*-armed ground-attack planes. Total production of single-seat models reached 7,005, while the simultaneous manufacture of 1,639 two-seat trainer versions reflected handling difficulties beyond the skill of inexperienced pilots.
BRIEF DATA (II-16 Type 24) Type: single-seat fighter; Engine: 1 × 1,000hp

Shvetsov; Max speed: 326mph; Ceiling: 29,530'; Range: 250m; Arms: 2 × 20mm cannon, 2 × 7.62mm mg (provision for 6 rockets).

Polikarpov I-153 Manoeuvrable Soviet biplane fighter that entered the Red Air Force* as the I-15 in 1934. By 1937, it was being superseded by the bomb-armed I-15bis and about 250 of the two types saw action in Spain. The final I-153 fighter-bomber version, of which thousands were built, was first delivered in 1939 and was still a mainstay of the Russian fighter force in June 1941. All three major variants fought and suffered against the Luftwaffe*, whose estimates claim 2,200 I-15s of all types destroyed in the first week of the German invasion of Russia. Far better Soviet designs were, however, already in production.
BRIEF DATA (I-153) Type: single-seat fighter-bomber; Engine: 1 × 1,000hp Shvetsov; Max speed: 267mph; Ceiling: 35,100'; Range: 293m; Arms: 2–4 7.62mm mg; Bomb load: 220lb or 6 rockets*.

Polish Army In 1939 the Polish Army comprised 30 active and 10 reserve divisions, along with 12 large cavalry brigades. Including trained conscripts, its potential strength was almost two and a half million men. Only one of the cavalry brigades was motorized, however, and there were no armoured divisions, few modern aircraft or tanks* and shortages of modern artillery* and anti-tank* weapons. Moreover, Polish commanders believed that the cavalry charge was an effective tactic against modern weapons. In the event this primitive thinking and the Army's lack of mobility utterly outweighed any potential numerical superiority over the German forces of invasion, and the confidence in it displayed by Western as well as Polish political leaders proved thoroughly misplaced. Notwithstanding this misjudgement at high command level, Polish soldiers displayed conspicuous bravery and panache throughout the brief campaign against Germany and reconvened Polish ground forces later fought alongside the Allies in both Western and Eastern Europe. A Polish army using British and American equipment performed with great distinction under General Anders*. A Russian-sponsored 1st Polish Army also fought on the Eastern Front*, re-occupying Warsaw* in 1944. See Poland, German campaign in; Polish Home Army.

Polish Corridor See Danzig.

Polish Government-in-exile Following the German invasion of Poland* in 1939, a government-in-exile was established in London under the leadership of President Wladyslaw Raczkiewicz, Premier Wladyslaw Sikorski* and Vice Premier Stanislaw Mikolajczyk*. The government was recognized by the British and succeeded temporarily in gaining some concessions from the Soviet Union following the German invasion of Russia in 1941. In June 1941 an important agreement was reached with Moscow that invalidated the Russo-German partition of Poland and offered an amnesty to Polish POWs in Russia. But the later discovery of the mass graves of Polish officers at Katyn lead to a political crisis which was to be disastrous for the Polish government-in-exile.

Using the accusations against her as a pretext, Russia accused the Polish government-in-exile of exploiting an atrocity committed by the Germans for propaganda purposes. Despite the medical evidence which clearly established the date of the deaths before the German invasion of Russia, Stalin* broke off relations with the Polish government-in-exile in April 1943. The Allies' embarrassed refusal to challenge Stalin's denials and support Premier Sikorski's furious demands for investigation into the massacre at Katyn undermined the tenuous influence of the exiled government as certainly as the Russian rejection.

Subsequently, though it continued to have nominal support from the Western Allies, the government-in-exile, now under the leadership of Prime Minister Stanislaw Mikolajczyk, was levered out of power by Russian diplomacy abroad and the increasing influence at home of the Russian-backed communist National Committee, which had the support of the other communist groups in Warsaw* (see Polish Home Army). By the time the Allies met at Yalta (see Conferences), to discuss the composition of the post-war Polish government, Stalin, who already had effective military control in Poland, was able to force the Allies' acceptance of a coalition government for post-war Poland that would give effective control to the communist provisional government (the Lublin Committee*) and ensure Russia's hegemony in Poland.

Polish Home Army Polish underground army formed in 1939 under General Sikorski*, it was involved in the resistance* to German occupation in Poland* throughout the war. The position of the Home Army was complicated by its allegiance to the London-based Polish government-in-exile*. Following the break in relations between the exiled government and Russia over the Katyn Massacre*, the communist-led PPR and Polish Peoples' Army, heavily backed by Russia, emerged as the controlling faction of the underground forces in Poland. Though Home Army C-in-C Bor-Komorowski* made contact with and supported the Red Army* in operations against German forces in eastern Poland at the beginning of 1944 (see Poland, Russian Campaign in), Home Army units were poorly treated. Frequently disarmed after engagements, their leaders arrested or killed, Home Army units were often impressed into the Red Army.

Hence in August 1944, General Bor-Komorowski led an independent attack on German forces in Warsaw*, in order to pre-empt Russian occupation. This second uprising of Poles in Warsaw, in which civilians fought alongside underground forces, was ferociously repelled by German forces with a huge cost in Polish casualties. The Russian forces grouped nearby in the eastern suburbs of Warsaw were ordered not to lend support. It was not until the city had been razed and evacuated by the Germans and the Home Army decimated, that the Russian-sponsored 1st Polish Army entered the city.

During 1945, under the leadership of Colonel Okulicki, the Home Army engaged in anti-Russian operations for which they were denounced as traitors by the newly created communist provisional government. In March 1945, 16 underground leaders were trapped and arrested in Poland and sent for trial to Russia where they were convicted of sabotage. The Polish government-in-exile could do nothing to influence their fate. The Home Army was formally disbanded in July 1945.

Popov, General Markian M. (1902–69) Soviet Front* commander who fought with distinction at Leningrad* and Stalingrad* and commanded the Bryansk Front (north of Kursk*) during the Russian counter-attack in July 1943, though it appears that he did not have Stalin's* confidence. In command of the 2nd Baltic Front during 1944, Popov was replaced by Yeremenko* when his forces failed to take Riga.

Port Moresby. Administrative centre of the Australian territory of Papua New Guinea with minor port and air facilities, it was identified by the Japanese as having important potential as a military base and was a focus of their Second Operational Phase offensives from May 1942. See New Guinea.

Portal, Air Marshal Sir Charles (1893–1971) British air leader, and a committed supporter of strategic heavy bombing as the RAF's* prime function. Portal became head of Bomber Command in April 1940, and was Chief of the British Air Staff from October 1940 to December 1945. As Air Member of the Chiefs of Staff Committee, Portal directed RAF policy and played an important role in shaping wartime Allied air strategy. A firm advocate of the policy of area bombing* for much of the war, Portal came into conflict with the American strategic bombing chiefs who favoured precision bombing as a more effective strategy. A compromise arrangement to continue separate daylight and night bombing, agreed at the Casablanca Conference*, was modified by Portal, who was convinced of the need to combine Allied operations against chosen targets and establish a higher level of co-operation with the USAAF*. Early in 1944, increasingly impressed by the effectiveness of precision bombing, Portal ordered experimentation by the RAF in night-time precision raiding against the oil targets on which US daylight attacks were concentrated. The subsequent diversion of part of Britain's strategic bombing force to the pre-invasion precision bombing of German communications and supply lines in France, known as the Transportation Plan*, was highly successful, although it strained relations with Harris*, C-in-C Bomber Command, who deplored any distraction from the mass area bombing of German cities and offered to resign in January 1945, an offer rejected by Portal. See also Strategic Bombing Offensive.

Portugal Portugal remained neutral throughout the war, though the Portuguese Pacific territory of East Timor 400 miles north of Australia was attacked by Japanese forces in February 1942 and finally occupied in December of that year. The Portuguese governor, however, remained nominally in charge. In August 1943 Portugal was chosen as the location for initial meetings between representatives of the Allies and envoys of Italy's new government under Marshal Badoglio, to begin negotiations for surrender. The choice was made by default – Allied representatives at the Vatican, the obvious channel of communication, were unable to provide a secure code for secret communication with either London or Washington. After long negotiations, Portugal finally allowed the Allies to use its territories in the Azores* for Atlantic* operations in October 1943.

Potez 630 Series First produced in February 1938 as a heavy fighter for the French *Armée de l'Air*, the Potez 630 suffered serious engine problems and was soon withdrawn. The re-engined Potez 631 was more successful, and 208 were delivered, performing mostly as night-fighters in the Battle of France*. Produced in many versions, the plane was widely exported, particularly the Potez 633 fighter-bomber version, which fought for Greece* against Axis forces and for Rumania* on the Eastern Front*. The Potez 637 and 63.11 reconnaissance versions were also produced in large numbers. They were used by the Luftwaffe* and by both the wartime French air forces. Over 1,300 of all Potez 630 types were built. BRIEF DATA (Potez 631). Type: 2–3-man day and night fighter; Engine: 2 × 700hp Gnome-Rhône; Max speed: 273mph; Ceiling: 32,800'; Arms: 2 × 20mm cannon, 6 × 7.5mm mg.

Potsdam Conference See Conferences, Allied.

Pound, Admiral Sir Albert Dudley (1877 –1943) British First Sea Lord. A flag captain at the Battle of Jutland in 1916, Pound alternated between sea and staff commands after WW1 and was a full admiral in command of the British Mediterranean Fleet when he was recalled to fill the post of First Sea Lord (Chief of Naval Staff) early in 1939. Although a fine fleet tactician, his methods in this high office – which was combined with the chairmanship of the British Chiefs of Staff Committee until 1942 – provoked considerable criticism. Regarded as too old for the job by the press, his personal concern with the direct running of operations led to unjustifiable interventions on several occasions (e.g. the dispersal of Arctic* convoy PQ17), resulting in serious overwork and the eventual failure of his health. Nevertheless, his grasp of overall strategy proved to be accurate

and by the time he collapsed from a brain tumour at the first Quebec Conference* of August 1943, the Royal Navy* had all but mastered its European enemies. Pound died in London on 21 October 1943, and was replaced by Admiral Cunningham*.

Poznan, Fall of See Poland, Russian Campaign in.

PQ17 See Arctic Convoys.

Prague, Uprising in, 1945 With Allied and Russian forces converging from west and east on the Czech capital in the spring of 1945, Czech partisans rose against Reich Protector Frank* and the German occupying forces under General Toussaint in an attempt to oust the Germans, and prevent them from destroying property, before the arrival of the Allies to liberate the city. Beginning on the night of 1–2 May, bridges were blown up and the radio station barricaded against German attack while it broadcast the news of the uprising to the world. Pleas from Czech Foreign Minister in exile, Hubert Ripka, and from Churchill* himself to Supreme Allied Commander Eisenhower* to send in Patton's 3rd Army before the Soviet Ukrainian Front* forces under Konev* reached the city were ignored. With US Chief of Staff Marshall's* approval, Eisenhower had already made the decision to comply with the Soviet request to hold his forces on the 'Pilsen' line. With German reinforcements arriving in Prague even as Germany formally capitulated on 8 May, the Revolutionary Czech National Council approached the commander of the Russian Army of Liberation (ROA*), Lt General Andrei Vlassov*, who had 20,000 troops stationed at Beroun to the west of the city. The ROA arrived in Prague on 8 May, fought off the arriving German reinforcements and cleared the city of Germans before themselves withdrawing. On the following day, Konev's forces of liberation arrived in the capital already cleared of Germans, although German Army

Group Centre did not surrender to the Russians in Czechoslovakia until 11 May.

Prien, Lt Commander Gunther (1908–41) Commander of the submarine *U-47*, Prien became a German national hero after successfully penetrating the Royal Navy* anchorage at Scapa Flow and sinking the battleship *Royal Oak** on the night of 13–14 October 1939. The *U-47* was sunk in the Atlantic* in March 1941, killing Prien. See also Kretschmer, Otto; Atlantic, Battle of the.

Prince of Wales, HMS British battleship of the *King George V** Class completed in 1941. The *Prince of Wales* had a short but eventful career. She was barely in commission (and not at full fighting efficiency) in May 1941, when she joined the battlecruiser *Hood** in action against the *Bismarck** and *Prince Eugen**. Hit seven times by German 5- and 8-inch shells, she scored two vital hits on the *Bismarck* before being forced to withdraw. In August, she delivered Prime Minister Churchill to the Arcadia Conference (see Conferences) off Newfoundland with United States President Roosevelt that produced the Atlantic Charter* declaration.

The *Prince of Wales* was then sent to Singapore*, with the obsolete battlecruiser *Repulse**, to act as a deterrent force. Both ships were sunk on 10 December 1941 by a large force of Japanese dive- and torpedo-bombers. The loss of such a modern unit, at a time when Britain's relative strength in capital ships was at its nadir, occasioned an intensive search for attributable design defects. Although it was noted that the *Prince of Wales* lacked sufficient anti-aircraft* defence, the prime cause of her demise was lack of fighter protection. See also Bismarck: Force Z.
BRIEF DATA See King George V, HMS.

Princeton, USS US Navy* *Independence* Class light carrier commissioned in 1943. The *Princeton* operated in the Pacific with the carrier task forces and took part in the Battle of the Philippine Sea*. On 24 October 1944, during the Battle of Leyte Gulf*, she was destroyed after a single bomb exploded below decks, setting off fires and detonations that went out of control and culminated in a final, massive blast which sent her to the bottom.
BRIEF DATA See Independence, USS.

Prinz Eugen The heavy cruiser *Prinz Eugen* was the most enduringly successful component of the German Navy's* surface fleet and was regarded as its 'lucky ship'. Apart from a slight increase in all-round size and displacement, she was similar in design to the earlier *Admiral Hipper** and *Blücher**. She entered service late in 1940 and took part in the *Bismarck** sortie of May 1941, surviving to make port in Brest*. From there she took part in the equally dangerous Channel Dash the following February (see Scharnhorst). Again she escaped serious damage, although two weeks later she lost her stern to a torpedo. From 1943 she was sent to the Baltic for training duty and in support of land operations, accidentally ramming and severely damaging the light cruiser *Leipzig** in October 1944, but remaining relatively undamaged herself. She was eventually surrendered intact to the Allies at Copenhagen in May 1945. The *Prinz Eugen*, the only major German warship still afloat at the war's end, finished her career as a nuclear test target in the Pacific.

Two sisters were planned for the *Prinz Eugen*, but neither was ever completed. The *Lützow* was sold incomplete to the Russians in 1940, and later abandoned by the Red Navy*. The *Seydlitz* was chosen in 1942 for conversion as an aircraft carrier, but was scuttled incomplete at Königsberg* in April 1945.
BRIEF DATA (1940) Displacement: 14,800 tons; Dimensions: o/a lgth – 689', b – 71' 6"; Speed: 32 knots; Armament: 8 × 8" gun (4 × 2), 12 × 4.1" AA gun, 12 × 37mm AA gun, 8 × 20mm AA gun, 12 × 21" TT, 3 aircraft.

Propaganda Modern propaganda techniques were first widely employed by the opposing combatants in WW1, to convince doubters of the rectitude of their respective causes and spread tales of alleged atrocities to denigrate opponents. The major instruments of propaganda in this period were the popular press and the use of leaflets dropped from aircraft. The effectiveness of propaganda in WW1 – which included the successful involvement of the US in the war, attributed at least in part to the British Ministry of Information's efforts – was from the outset a controversial issue among liberal-minded observers. Although its early success encouraged the development of new techniques during the 1920s and 30s in many countries (notably the Soviet Union, Italy and Germany), some British, French and American opinion viewed the manipulative power of propaganda as practised between 1916–18 with great suspicion. Many believed that propaganda 'threatened the very existence of democratic societies'.

Among the one-party state systems, however, and particularly in Germany and Italy, the advent of new technologies of sound cinema and radio, which revolutionized the potential for influencing mass electorates, were enthusiastically exploited, both domestically and internationally. Although the press remained the primary propaganda tool during the 1930s, cinema steadily became the prime information media during WW2. As early as 1935, Leni Riefenstahl's *Triumph of the Will*, which was distributed and shown throughout Germany, had shown military leaders and film-makers all over the world how film could be used to unify the beliefs of whole populations. US General George Marshall* was a strong proponent of film propaganda, commissioning a well-known series of films called *Why We Fight*, which justified the American entry into the war and told the story of WW2 in dramatic instalments (simplified as a tale of right and might in a world divided between freedom and enslavement).

Wartime propaganda in Britain was coordinated by the Ministry of Information (MOI) and the Political Warfare Executive, established in August 1941. Basing their work on the belief that the average Briton, and particularly the middle classes, were insufficiently psychologically prepared to fight a 'total war', the MOI launched a large scale 'Anger Campaign', which was intended to frighten, as well as impassion, the British worker, secretary or civil servant. Learning from the material and methods of Göbbel's* Propaganda Ministry, the MOI enlisted journalists to launch an unofficial campaign of 'disinformation', which it was hoped would galvanize the British fighting mentality. 'White' broadcasts by the BBC*, which reported accurate information about the non-Nazi world's efforts to remain free, balanced the 'black' broadcasts to Germany by over 60 stations that used propaganda inventions peppered with intelligence culled from Ultra* to present lurid reports on the private lives of Third Reich personalities.

By contrast, the United States was the only major power without a propaganda agency at the start of WW2. The Office of Government Reports (OGR), created by President Roosevelt* in late 1939, and the CIAA, created in August 1940, began by acting as clearing houses for information about the defence programme, using a strategy of 'informational propaganda', which disseminated accurate neutral information in a reassuring context. Much of the US propaganda effort at this stage went into straight reporting, particularly from the European battlefields before Pearl Harbor*. It was not until August 1941 that Roosevelt demonstrated his commitment to 'agitational propaganda' by setting up the Office of the Coordinator of Information (COI), the precursor to the OSS*, which controlled 'black' and 'grey' broadcasting after the US entry into the war (see Donovan, William).

But by far the most powerful agency for propaganda in the US was the motion picture industry. Until August 1940, when Germany and Italy banned Hollywood from their cinema screens, removing the key export market pressure to produce inoffensive subject matter, Hollywood's output remained firmly neutral. Unprepared to risk their foreign profits, which were often decisive profit- or loss-makers, Hollywood executives effectively censored themselves, and went along with the edicts of the 'Hays Office' (and Hay's subordinate Breen's Production Code Administration) to produce bland and uncontentious material. Only a few attempts were made in this period to tackle the war as a subject, backed by emigré production staff (see Hollywood Exiles) and writers greedy for good stories. The 1939 Warner Brothers production, *Confessions of a Nazi Spy*, which boldly depicted Germany aiming at world domination, and Nazism as a threat to American security, got through Breen's Production Code on a technicality.

But after mid-1940, Hollywood was increasingly interventionist in temperament. The Jewish lobby, in particular, was less and less prepared to ignore the moral issues raised by the fight against Nazism. *The Mortal Storm*, produced by Metro in 1940, was the first Hollywood essay on the Jewish question. As the US defensive build-up continued, feature films began to review home defence issues and the armed forces, lending an added glamour to military subjects, though they lacked any specific propaganda content. By mid-1941, however, Hollywood was frustrating isolationist sentiment by producing heavily interventionist features. *A Yank in the RAF*, *International Squadron* and *Sergeant York* (premiered in July 1941) contained an unequivocal message. After December 1941, Hollywood could volunteer unparalleled resources for the US wartime propaganda effort.

In general, however, the task of co-ordinating the wartime propaganda activities of the democratic agencies, especially where Allied 'volte-faces' like the Darlan* affair called for a reversal of position, was an immensely complex one. The Allied leaflet raids, in which US and British bombers dropped nearly 6 billion pieces of propaganda between 1939 and 1945, mostly originating from the Psychological Warfare Division of SHAEF*, was one of the more straightforward of Allied propaganda efforts.

By contrast, in Italy, Germany, Japan and particularly the Soviet Union, no such complexity existed. Schooled since the 1920s to accept the Party's interpretation of events – Stalin* himself had trained in propaganda techniques at Tblisi – Russians accepted the Party's ideologically laden definition of the nation's war aims – the concept of the 'Great Patriotic War' – as it was projected in newsreels, feature films and documentaries. All film was propaganda in Russia, although until the ban on Hollywood products in the 1920s Russians also watched American feature films.

In Germany, Propaganda Minister Göbbels made particular use of radio and newsreel for propaganda purposes. Apart from obvious exceptions such as the films of Leni Riefenstahl, state propaganda ministry features (*Staatsauftragsfilms*) tended to contain latent rather than active propaganda content. Escapist in subject, they nevertheless constantly rehearsed the social and moral values prescribed by Nazi ideology. Göbbels' pre-eminent role in the Third Reich actually declined somewhat after 1939, and his external broadcasts (see Joyce, William) never carried the same conviction as those of the BBC. The propaganda concept of 'Total War' and a fight to the death, created by Göbbels after the decisive German defeat at Stalingrad*, was as much a tool for his personal re-aggrandizement as it was an effective propaganda weapon.

In Japan, propaganda and educational broadcasting had played an important part in civilian life since the early 1920s. In 1926 the Japanese Broadcasting Association (Nihon Hoso Kyokai – NHK) was created from a number of licensed radio stations with a monopoly on all radio broadcasting. The NHK, controlled by the Japanese Communications Ministry, was a central propaganda weapon throughout the war, with a noted strength in co-ordinating elaborate propaganda campaigns to promote particular aspects of the Japanese struggle, using a rich mixture of songs, literary works, drama, talks and symposia – often transmitted in a single day.

During the 1920s and early 30s, Japanese activities in Manchuria* and China* gave a great stimulus to broadcasting. From the beginning of 1942, the Cabinet Information Board controlled the content of broadcasts and the press, although Army GHQ continued to have its own information issuing service. Radio Tokyo, a branch of NHK, was the main propaganda voice from Pearl Harbor* onwards. Much of the propaganda was aimed at the US (especially after the end of 1942 when Britain had been driven out of Southeast Asia – see Tokyo Rose) and at the subject peoples of Japan's conquered Southeast Asian territories, attempting to win their co-operation for a new economic zone under Japanese leadership (see New Order). By 1944, however, the serious propaganda direction of Radio Tokyo had been modified with lighter entertainment and cultural broadcasts to raise morale. Towards the end of the summer, when the first B-29s* attacked Tokyo* from bases in the Mariana Islands*, the NHK network's main function was as the air-raid warning system. As such it was no longer a propaganda tool, but a key to survival.

Proximity Fuse See Anti-aircraft Defence.

PT Boats See Torpedo Boats.

Puller, Lt General Lewis (1898–1971) One of the most often decorated US Navy* Marines and commander of the 7th Marines, and the 1st Marine Division, he was twice awarded the Navy Cross (his third and fourth) during the fighting on Guadalcanal* and Cape Gloucester.

Punishment, Operation Code-name for the German bombing of Belgrade in April 1941. The operation was outstandingly effective, devastating the city on its first night and destroying vital government buildings. Its title aptly reflects Hitler's fury at the sudden switch in Yugoslav allegiance following the *coup d'état* led by General Simovic* on 27 March – only two days after the government of Prince Paul had guaranteed German troop passage for the imminent invasion of Greece. Reacting with characteristic speed and certitude, Hitler expanded his Greek plans and attacked Yugoslavia from Austria* and Bulgaria* on 6 April, marginally assisted by Hungarian and Italian forces. Only partly mobilized and plagued by provincial separatism, Yugoslavia lasted less than a week. Belgrade fell on 12 April, having lost 17,000 dead in the bombing. The entire conquest cost only some 500 German lives. See Balkans, German invasion of the.

Pyle, Ernest Taylor (1900–45) Best known and best loved American journalist of WW2, he followed American armed forces from 1942 until 1945 through all the major war theatres in Europe, North Africa and the Pacific, reporting on the experiences of the troops in his own personal and informal style. Although on friendly terms with many high-level US military commanders, including Generals Eisenhower*, Doolittle* and Bradley*, Pyle was little interested in overall campaign strategy and execution. Instead, he concentrated on capturing the individual experiences of servicemen, uniquely conveying the atmosphere of the front to his readers. He was immensely popular on both sides of the Atlantic. In the United States he contributed six columns a week, printed in over 300 newspapers. In 1941 Pyle was reporting from London during the Blitz*. He later wrote vivid accounts of the Allied campaigns in North Africa*, Sicily*, Italy* and Northwest Europe*, winning the Pulitzer Prize in 1943. Reporting from the Pacific during the Iwo Jima* and Okinawa* campaigns, Pyle was killed by Japanese machine-gun* fire on Ie Shima Island off Okinawa* on 18 April 1945.

PZL P11 This ageing monoplane had been a distinguished success for the Polish National Aero Factory (PZL) in the mid-1930s, when Poland's* air force was a much admired weapon. It was produced in many versions, but 12 squadrons of P11c fighters comprised the bulk of Poland's fighter defence against Germany in 1939. They were comprehensively defeated by the Luftwaffe*, and the only operational model of their intended successor – the PZL P50 – was accidentally shot down by defenders unused to the sight of a modern Polish aircraft.

BRIEF DATA (P11c) Type: single-seat fighter: Engine: 1 × 645hp PZL Mercury; Max speed: 242mph; Ceiling: 36,000'; Range: 503m; Arms: 4 × 7.7mm mg (provision for 54lb bombs).

PZL P23 Carp (Karas) A fine attack bomber when it first flew in the mid-1930s, Poland's* *Karas* was obsolete by 1939 but equipped 12 squadrons against the German invasion. They were soon overwhelmed, although a few survivors later fought for Rumania* on the Eastern Front* in 1941. About 50 of a more powerful P43 version were exported to Bulgaria* just before the war.

BRIEF DATA (P23b) Type: 3-man reconnaissance/bomber; Engine: 1 × 680hp PZL Pegasus; Max speed: 217mph; Ceiling: 24,600'; Range: 410m; Arms: 3 × 7.7mm mg; Bomb load: 1,500lb.

PZL P37 Elk (Los) Delivered to the Polish Bomber Brigade in 1938, the P37 was a fine bomber and excited great international interest. Its service career was badly disrupted by political opposition from the Polish Army* and only 36 (of about 100 built) were fully operational in September 1939. The Elk proved very effective in the few days of Polish resistance, and most escaped to Rumania* to be flown against the Russians in 1941.

BRIEF DATA (P37b) Type: 4-man medium bomber; Engine: 2 × 925hp PZL Pegasus; Max speed: 273mph; Ceiling: 19,700'; Range: 1,616m; Arms: 3 × 7.7mm mg; Bomb load: 5,700lb.

Q

Quebec Conferences See Conferences, Allied.

Queen Elizabeth, HMS British battleship and Class, which also comprised the *Barham**, *Malaya**, *Valiant* and *Warspite**. When completed, these WW1 veterans were fast and powerful fighting units, but they were kept almost constantly in commission in the post-war years, and by 1939 only the *Warspite* had been fully modernized. The *Barham* and *Malaya* remained only partly refitted and were particularly vulnerable in the vital areas of anti-aircraft* defence and armour protection. The *Valiant* and the *Queen Elizabeth* were undergoing major reconstruction when the war broke out. With dual-purpose air–surface secondary armament and improved deck armour, they were ready in 1940 and both joined the Home Fleet before transfer to the Mediterranean*. While lying in Alexandria* harbour on 19 December 1941, the two battleships were badly damaged by Italian human torpedoes (see Midget Submarines). Sunk upright in the shallows, they were eventually refloated and repaired, the *Valiant* reappearing in the Mediterranean in time to support Allied landings at Salerno* in 1943 before completing her service in the Far East. The *Queen Elizabeth* was moved to the Indian Ocean and employed first as a convoy* escort and later in bombardment operations off Burma*.
BRIEF DATA (*Queen Elizabeth*, 1939) Displacement: 31,585 tons; Dimensions: o/a lgth – 643' 3", b – 104'; Speed: 24 knots; Armament: 8 × 15" gun (4 × 2), 20 × 4.5" DP gun, 32 × 2pdr AA, 16 × 0.5" AA mg, 3 aircraft.

Queen Mary The British *Queen Mary*, which had broken the North Atlantic crossing speed record in 1938, and her sister the *Queen Elizabeth* were giant 80,000-ton passenger liners converted as troopships. From August 1942, they were used to transport more than 15,000 US and Canadian troops at a time across the Atlantic. They sailed independently, relying on their speed (over 28 knots) and efficient re-routing for protection, before being met in the approaches to Britain. This calculated risk paid off and neither was ever caught. Four other ships – the liners *Aquitania*, *Mauretania*, *Ile de France* and *Nieuw Amsterdam* – were used in the same role as over 2 million men were transferred to Europe within a few months.

Quezon, Manuel (1878–1944) President of the Philippines* Commonwealth from its foundation in 1935 and constant ally of the United States, Quezon fled the capital, Manila*, with American forces, on the recommendation of his military adviser, General MacArthur*, following the Japanese invasion in December 1941. His second term as president was actually inaugurated in an air-raid shelter on Corregidor*, where the besieged American forces had withdrawn from Luzon*, and Quezon subsequently went to Australia and then to the United States to plead his country's cause. In May 1942, Quezon established a government-in-exile in Washington but died of tuberculosis three months before the

American reinvasion of the Philippines, launched by General MacArthur at Leyte* in October 1944. He was succeeded by Sergio Osmena*.

Quincy, USS See New Orleans, USS.

Quisling, Vidkun (1887–1945) Unattractive and unsuccessful Norwegian politician and founder of the Norwegian Fascist Party (Nasjonal Samling), whose failing political fortunes were briefly revived by his association with various Nazi leaders, including Hitler*, who approved Quisling's formation of a pro-German government after the German invasion of Norway* in April 1940. Widely vilified as a traitor (for which his name has become an often-used synonym) and highly ineffective as a leader, Quisling was removed from office, and then reinstated by Berlin as Minister President of the State Council in 1942, although power was actually wielded in Norway by German Reichskommissar, Josef Terboven. Quisling was tried and executed in 1945, after voluntarily surrendering to the newly restored Norwegian government.

R

Rabaul Australian base with two harbours on the eastern peninsula of New Britain in the Southwest Pacific, it was captured at the end of January 1942 by Japanese forces landing at Rabaul and Kavieng (New Ireland) (see Map 10). Control of both gave Japan the advantage of dominating the New Guinea*/Solomons* region as well as threatening Australia and her lines of communication. Recovery of Rabaul became a prime objective of Allied planning for the Pacific War*. By mid-1943, Rabaul had been developed as the core of Japan's base system, supported by two carrier air groups based at Truk*, 790 miles to the east. In September, on the eve of the Allied offensive against Rabaul, the Japanese 11th Air Fleet based there comprised roughly 300 planes and 10,000 men.

Considered too strongly defended to be assaulted by amphibious* operation, an air offensive was launched in October 1943, coinciding with the successful culmination of a drive to Bougainville*, and a landing at Empress Augusta Bay in November which put Rabaul within US fighter range. A staggering number – approximately 30,000 – sorties were flown against Rabaul, and the tonnage of bombs dropped reached a similar figure. Approximately 90,000 Japanese troops in the area finally surrendered on 6 September 1945.

Radar Radar stands for *radio detection and ranging*, a system derived from the principle of bouncing a radio wave against an object and measuring its travel to provide targeting information. Equipment for this had been simultaneously and secretly developed before the war in Britain, Germany and the United States, but it was the British who led the field in 1939. Their land-based Chain Home early warning radar system was installed 1937–9 and played a crucial defensive role in the Battle of Britain* in 1940.

Radar equipment was used during WW2 for land-based, shipboard and airborne detection, and the substantial Allied lead in the field was of enormous value throughout. Although the Germans had good radar by 1940 and made widespread use of it, they were never equipped with the variety of sets available to the Allies. Radar was known but not developed in Italy, and the Japanese lagged far behind in the field. They had only poor equipment available at the start of the war and never used radar effectively.

Early operational radar was restricted to large, unwieldy sets transmitting broad metric wavelengths. Size was dictated by the high power required to achieve viable range, but the British invention of the Magnetron cavity resonator in 1940 enabled more accurate centimetric waves to be transmitted. It also allowed more compact high-frequency sets to be built which could then be fitted to aircraft.

Airborne radar was initially fitted to night-fighters for target detection, but later a series of reflections from the ground displayed on a cathode-ray screen was also able to provide bombers with navigation and bomb-aiming information (see Oboe). In a naval context airborne radar enabled Allied aircraft to locate and attack surfaced U-boats. Early sets could be detected by submarines*, allowing them to dive in time to escape, but this was not true of ASV-3 10cm radar, introduced in 1941 to ships and increasingly carried by Allied anti-submarine* aircraft from 1943. Developed in Britain but largely manufactured in the US, this major breakthrough was a vital factor in the defeat of U-boats in the Atlantic*.

US early warning radar technology was first used operationally in predicting the Japanese attack on Pearl Harbor* almost an hour before the event. Unfortunately the warning was ignored with very expensive consequences. From 1942, when the German equivalent of Chain Home – the Kammhuber Line – became operational against bombers from southern England, sophisticated land-based radar was standard equipment for both Allied and German anti-aircraft* defences, providing early warning and fire control information. By the end of the war Allied AA gunners could track and sight a target automatically with 'auto-follow' radar, enormously improving their chances of hitting a fast target. Coastal heavy artillery* could be similarly directed and, although attempts to use radar with field artillery* were beset by technical problems, it was valuable in the calculation of hostile mortar positions (by the measurement of shell trajectories).

On ships, radar was widely used for both early warning defence and gunnery control. German radar development had concentrated on the latter field. They had a set installed in the *Admiral Graf Spee* by 1936 and, although Britain and the US soon followed, German superiority in the field was demonstrated in the early sea battles of the war. The vital area of air defence, upon which British and American research was largely focused, was neglected by Germany. The first Air Warning sets had been fitted to Royal Navy* ships in 1938 and the British made rapid advances in the field, all of which were shared with the US Navy*. Well before the end of the war, Allied warships carried a large and complex array of radar equipment, capable of controlling even light gunfire and of detecting hostile activity at various ranges and in all forms, both above and on the surface. See also Electronic Countermeasures.

Raeder, Grand Admiral Erich (1876–1960) C-in-C of the German Navy* from 1935. Raeder oversaw the growth of the *Kriegsmarine* from a tiny coastal force into a powerful, modern fleet in the 1930s. He at first hoped to build up a large, coherent battlefleet, but accepted a commerce-raiding strategy as war approached more quickly than the German naval staff had imagined likely. He nevertheless remained associated with the building of big warships in preference to small craft and submarines. Highly professional, aloof and a strict disciplinarian, Raeder became less and less comfortable in his relations with Hitler as the latter's faith in surface warships was progressively eroded in the first years of the war. Disagreements over strategy came to a head when Hitler determined to scrap the surface fleet altogether in early 1943 and Raeder retired on 30 January. He was sentenced to life imprisonment at Nuremberg*, but was released in 1955.

RAF (Royal Air Force) The British air force became an independent service on 1 April 1918, when the Royal Flying Corps and the Royal Naval Air Service were merged to form the RAF. Between the wars it was developed as a strategic bombing force. This role stressed the independence of the RAF, exploited a generally held belief in the invincibility of the bomber and offered a relatively cheap alternative to the demands of other services.

The RAF was expanded and modernized from the mid-1930s to match the numerical strength of the new Luftwaffe*, and its dedication to long-range bombing reached dogmatic proportions. A fleet of light and medium monoplane bombers was developed – the best of them the Vickers Wellington* – along with two fast, heavily armed interceptors (the Hawker Hurricane* and Supermarine Spitfire*) for home defence against bombers. Other important areas of military aviation were neglected. No modern aircraft was ordered for ground-support work, military transport, photo-reconnaissance or coastal operations, and overseas commands remained short of equipment. Naval aviation was allowed to stagnate and the Royal Navy faced an enormous task when it regained control of shipboard aircraft in 1937 (see Fleet Air Arm).

Overall control of the RAF was vested in the Air Council, a body which included senior political and military figures, headed by the Air Minister and the Chief of Air Staff (CAS). Beneath this, the RAF divided its home air force into functional commands from 1936, and they reflected its prejudice against co-operation with other services. Its main component was Bomber Command, which in theory consisted of 55 squadrons (920 aircraft) by August 1939. In fact only about 350 front-line bombers were available, most of them unsuited for long-range operations. Fighter Command's 39 squadrons (600 aircraft), by no means all of which were equipped with the new interceptors, were committed to the defence of Great Britain. Although fighter production had recently been given higher priority, important targets like Belfast and Scapa Flow still had no air cover when the war started. The smallest and least impressive major operational component was Coastal Command, which protected Britain's ports and ocean approaches. Most of its equipment was obsolete and the RAF had only 96 reconnaissance aircraft in September 1939.

Tactically, the RAF entered the war intent on long-range daylight bombing by small groups of unescorted aircraft. This proved quite untenable in practice. Many important targets in Germany could not be reached and daylight bombing proved virtually suicidal against modern fighters. Experience quickly showed that the RAF had neither the training nor the technology for accurate night operations, and Bomber Command was soon primarily concerned

with the support of other services – minelaying, attacks on German naval targets and co-operation with ground forces in Norway* and France* during 1940.

The importance of air superiority to land operations was demonstrated in the battle for France. By the end of the campaign the RAF had lost more than 900 aircraft, mostly light bombers and fighters overwhelmed by the pace of the land battle and the army support skills of the Luftwaffe. Only the Spitfires could match the performance of the best German aircraft, and they were held back until the Dunkirk* evacuation as Fighter Command prepared to defend its home bases.

The Battle of Britain* was a narrow victory for Fighter Command. Much credit must go to its commander, Dowding*, whose strictly centralized control of his limited resources – founded on the use of early warning radar* and accurate intelligence – frustrated the Luftwaffe's desire to force a decisive aerial confrontation. The Blitz* followed, exposing Fighter Command's weakness in night operations but not significantly disrupting Britain's war effort.

As the Luftwaffe's attacks tailed off in 1941, the RAF again sought an offensive role. Fighter production had received ruthless priority from late 1940, but the short-range interceptors were of limited value beyond home airspace. Fighter Command began to be used for mass sweeps against cross-Channel targets, sometimes escorting light bombers (see Rhubarbs). These costly exercises, designed to draw the Luftwaffe into combat, were of peripheral strategic value but at least encouraged the development of ground-support fighter-bombers. Coastal Command remained distinctly undernourished, while the scale of its task had multiplied with the threat of invasion and the expansion of U-boat activities. The submarine* was its prime target, but Coastal Command aircraft sank no U-boats before 1942, mainly because the long-range machines it needed went to Bomber Command. Only in 1943, when American long-range aircraft and improved anti-submarine* technology became widely available, was Coastal Command capable of a genuine offensive (see Atlantic, Battle of the).

Sir Charles Portal* – a strong supporter of long-range bombing – had become CAS in October 1940, and resources were again concentrated on Bomber Command, which seemed to offer the only means by which Britain could directly threaten Germany in 1941. For the rest of the war the bulk of Bomber Command's effort was committed to the Strategic Bombing Offensive* over Germany. By this the RAF sought to shatter German war production or civilian morale, but until 1944 the main tangible benefit of the policy was the large-scale diversion of Luftwaffe resources to home defence.

Although the scale of attacks over Germany was steadily increased from 1941, Bomber Command losses were high and its expansion was slow. The basic problems of its inaccuracy in night operations and the inadequacy of its aircraft were not solved until 1943. Then the widespread availability of a genuinely successful heavy bomber, the Avro Lancaster*, combined with navigational aids (e.g. Oboe*), improved bombs* and the use of Pathfinder* squadrons enabled the RAF to find and devastate a general target area such as Hamburg* or Berlin*. German defences continued to inflict insupportable losses, however, and when the USAAF* joined the offensive over Germany in strength in 1943, its daylight raids were soon suspended because of heavy casualties. The Luftwaffe was overcome the following year. The excellent American P-51B* fighter, which thoroughly outperformed all Axis types, began escorting bombers all the way to their targets, and the Allied Pointblank offensive concentrated operations against airfields and the aviation industry. Above all the Allied invasion of Normandy* in June seriously diluted Luftwaffe strength on the home front. Portal and Sir Arthur Harris*, C-in-C Bomber Command from February 1942, were slow to recognize the potential for daylight operations of long-range escort fighters and argued consistently throughout against any deviation from heavy night bombing priority.

Allied bombers were able to operate over Germany with relative impunity from mid-1944, and they caused great devastation and loss of life. They also at last inflicted massive and irreparable damage on the German war economy, which had atrophied by early 1945. Attacks on oil resources were particularly effective, and by the spring lack of fuel had virtually grounded the Luftwaffe.

RAF overseas commands had mixed fortunes. British Far Eastern interests were dangerously underdefended in the air, and the few obsolete aircraft available were overwhelmed wherever the Japanese attacked in 1941–2. Later in the war, the RAF in the Far East was primarily deployed in support of the prolonged campaign in Burma* where ground forces came to rely on air resupply. In the Mediterranean* the vital base on Malta* was heavily bombed for two years from mid-1940. It barely survived and needed constant reinforcement with both fighters and bombers. Middle East Command was the largest overseas component of the RAF, and like the others it consisted largely of second-line biplanes when the war started. Based in Egypt*, it gained supremacy over numerically stronger but similarly obsolete Italian Air Force* units in Libya and East Africa* during 1940–1.

Rapidly shifting lines of battle and a shortage of suitable targets for strategic bombing encouraged Middle East Command to develop effective ground co-operation tactics. These were refined during the Desert War* and backed by increasing numbers of modern British and American-built aircraft, mostly fighter-bombers and medium bombers. The decisive British victories at El Alamein* in 1942 featured complete qualitative and numerical superiority over the Luftwaffe, and this was emphatically maintained throughout the later campaigns in Tunisia*, Sicily* and Italy*. Strong USAAF forces were committed to the Mediterranean theatre from late 1942, and they co-operated closely with the RAF in perfecting the organization and *matériel* needed by a tactical air force.

For the invasion of Normandy*, the 2nd Tactical Air Force (TAF) was formed in late 1943. It temporarily absorbed Fighter Command, but its most valuable aircraft were fast multi-purpose types like the the de Havilland Mosquito* and the Hawker Typhoon*. Operations in Northwest Europe* began with an attack on the railway system in northern France (the Transportation Plan*), which was enthusiastically supported by Air Chief Marshal Tedder*, who was in overall command of Allied air forces in the theatre and had been prominent in the development of army–air and inter-Allied co-operation in the Mediterranean. Second TAF operations in support of Allied ground offensives for the rest of the war in Europe were characterized by efficient co-ordination on both levels. Harris opposed the use of Bomber Command resources for these tactical operations but was overruled.

Short-range interceptors were still needed both for aerial combat with the Luftwaffe in Northwest Europe and as a means of defeating V-1* flying-bomb attacks on English targets in 1944. A turbojet fighter, the Gloster Meteor*, joined the RAF in time to test its speed against the V-1s, which were a more potent enemy by 1945 than any Axis air force.

During the war the RAF reached a total strength of 1,208,843 men and women (185,595 aircrew), compared with 175,692 (20,033) in September 1939. Figures include large numbers of personnel from Canada, South Africa*, Australia, New Zealand* and other parts of the British Commonwealth and Empire. Many of these were recruited through the highly successful Empire Training Scheme, started in 1940, and over 130,000 pilots from the Dominions fought for the Allies either with their national air forces or within the RAF.

Some 30,000 aircrew from Britain's defeated European allies also joined the RAF during the war. A total of 70,253 RAF personnel were lost on operations in WW2 – 47,293 from Bomber Command. See also Strategic Bombing Offensive.

Raiders See Carlson, Brigadier General Evans.

Ram Cruiser Tank The Canadians' first experiment in tank construction was to build 1,420 British Valentines*, and in 1940 they began work on a medium tank of their own to replace the obsolete American vehicles of the Canadian Armoured Corps. The result was the Ram I, which entered production in late 1941 and was based on the hull of the American Grant/Lee* medium tank, modified to take a turret mounted 2-pounder gun. Only 50 of these were built before the Ram II appeared, but its 6-pounder was already obsolete and it was used only for training in Britain and Canada. Production was stopped in July 1943, after 1,899 Ram IIs had been completed.

With its turret removed, the Ram was widely used by the British as the Kangaroo Armoured Personnel Carrier, and from May 1943, 2,150 chassis were built as the important Sexton self-propelled* gun.
BRIEF DATA (Ram I) Type: 5-man cruiser tank; Engine: 400hp petrol; Max speed: 25mph; Range: 144m; Arms: 1 × 2pdr gun, 3 × 7.62mm mg; Armour: max 87mm.

Ramsay, Admiral Sir Bertram (1883–1945) British naval officer. Ramsay was recalled from the Royal Navy* retired list in 1939 to act as Flag Officer, Dover, and was thus responsible for the evacuation of the British Expeditionary Force from Dunkirk*. He subsequently commanded the Allied naval forces for the amphibious* landings in North Africa (Operation Torch*) and in Sicily*. In 1943 he was appointed naval C-in-C under Eisenhower* to plan and direct the highly successful Operation Neptune, the naval element of Operation Overlord, the Allied invasion of Normandy* in June 1944. Ramsay was killed in an air crash in January 1945 while *en route* to a conference at Montgomery's* 21st Army Group HQ.

Ranger, USS US Navy* aircraft carrier, commissioned in 1934 as an experimental 'small carrier'. Speed, armament and protection were sacrificed for maximum aircraft capacity on a displacement well below the limit imposed by contemporary naval treaties (22,000 tons). The *Ranger* served in the Atlantic* from 1941–2 but was recognizably below combat standard and was often used as an aircraft transport before her relegation to training duties.
BRIEF DATA (1941) Displacement: 14,500 tons; Dimensions: o/a lgth – 769', b – 80' (109' 6" FD); Speed: 29.25 knots; Armament: 8 × 5" AA gun, 1 catapult and 86 aircraft.

Rangers US Army special service units, trained and equipped for raids behind hostile lines and to lead amphibious* assaults. Six battalions of Rangers, all volunteers, were formed in 1942–4. The first unit trained in Scotland alongside their British counterparts, the Commandos*, and most Ranger operations were carried out in the northwest African and European campaigns. Only the 6th Battalion fought in the Pacific, seeing action in the Aleutians*, New Guinea*, Leyte* and Luzon*. See also: Merrill, Major General Frank; Carlson, Brigadier General Evans.

Rangoon Capital city of Burma* and important port which served as the Allies' principal entry point for supplies bound for China*, until its demolition and evacuation by Allied troops under General Hutton and its subsequent occupation by Japanese 15th Army units on 6 March 1942 (see Maps 24 and 25). After the reoccupation of most of central Burma by the British 14th Army under General Slim* in a long and difficult campaign during 1944 and 1945, the capture of Meiktila* and

Mandalay* in March 1945 opened the route south to Rangoon. Sending a small motorized force from General Messervy's* 4th Corps along the central railroad to cut off any Japanese escape route to the Sittang region, General Slim also ordered General Stopford's* 33rd Corps to drive south down the Irrawaddy. A plan for an amphibious landing, code-named Dracula, on Rangoon by General Christison's 15th Corps was awaiting launch in support of the 4th Corps, should it prove necessary.

Advancing steadily on both fronts until the beginning of May, when early monsoon* weather slowed the pace of the drive, Slim made the decision to launch Dracula on 27 April, and one Gurkha battalion of the British 26th Indian Division was dropped by parachute at Elephant Point, later re-embarking to land nearer to Rangoon when they discovered that the Japanese forces had already evacuated the area. At the end of an advance of over 300 miles lasting 26 days, General Messervy's 4th Corps crossed the Pegu River and entered the Burmese capital on 6 May, signifying the effective end of the war in Burma.

Rapido River The site of some of the most bitter fighting between Allied and German forces during the Allied campaign in Italy*. One of the tributaries (Liri the other) of the Garigliano River flowing past the foot of Monte Cassino*, the Rapido River formed a natural part of the formidable German defensive deployments on the Gustav Line*, roughly 80 miles south of Rome*, where German forces entrenched during the winter of 1943–4 (see Map 34). In January 1944 repeated Allied assaults attempted to cross the Rapido and Garigliano, both swollen by heavy rainfall, in a diversionary operation to support the Allied landing at Anzio*, behind the Gustav Line. Two divisions of the 5th Army (French and British) managed to gain temporary footholds inside the line, but these were abandoned following the failure of the main assault on 20 January by US 2nd

Corps, whose 36th Division suffered particularly heavy casualties. The Rapido River battle was later the subject of an inconclusive Congressional investigation, the division commander having accused commanding US General Clark* of 'recklessness' in pursuing the operation. The Rapido River was finally decisively crossed by British 13th Corps on 11 May, on the first day of a heavily reinforced spring offensive against the Gustav Line, codenamed Diadem*.

Red Air Force The Russian air arm was not an independent service but was controlled by the Red Army* and Red Navy*. Naval air forces were commanded directly by the People's Commissar of the Navy but, like the parent service, were subdued and rather anonymous throughout the war. The much larger Army service had its own air commander, subject to the People's Commissar for Defence, and was used primarily as a tactical weapon in support of ground operations.

In 1933, the Army's Air Brigades had been grouped together to form an Air Corps, which became the 1st Air Army in 1936. By then the Russian manufacturing industry was completing about 3,500 aircraft a year, and the Polikarpov I-15* and I-16* fighters, along with the Tupolev SB-2* medium bomber, were highly regarded internationally. Further restructuring of the air force took place in 1940, when air armies – composed of air regiments, each with about 60 planes – were allotted to front commanders on the ground. By the spring of 1941, the Red Air Force possessed a total of 18,000 aircraft (59 per cent of them fighters) and employed 200,000 personnel (including 20,000 pilots). By June 7,500 first-line machines were available to face about 2,700 Luftwaffe* warplanes.

Once the German invasion of Russia began (see Eastern Front), the air armies were confined to ground-support operations as directed by the front commanders. A fighter command and a long-range strategic

bombing unit were also formed – the latter being sent by the High Command to operate under the jurisdiction of whichever front was deemed needful of strategic bombing support. The basic unit remained the air regiment, containing five squadrons (four for fighters) of 12–15 aircraft, and several regiments comprised a division. Local air defence regiments were assembled under their own air commanders and were separate from the air armies.

In spite of its numerical superiority, the Red Air Force was surprised and outperformed by the Luftwaffe, which had planes and pilots of far superior quality, and which destroyed about 3,000 Soviet aircraft in the first ten days of the campaign. Such resistance as materialized was mostly in direct support of Army units, and few fighters met the German bombers over Moscow* in late July and August. The aviation industry was saved by a huge and highly efficient relocation of production facilities to sites beyond the Urals and outside the range of German bombers.

From mid-October Russian air strength was massed on Moscow, maintaining at least local air supremacy, and by December about 1,000 aircraft were grouped around the capital. Modern types began to enter Soviet service in numbers, reducing the technical advantage held by the Luftwaffe, which was experiencing its first Russian winter. The Red Air Force substantially outnumbered the Luftwaffe by the following spring, as the quality of German planes and pilots available on the Eastern Front slowly began to deteriorate, and in July some 2,500 Luftwaffe machines faced three times as many opponents (with four times as many fighters). The German technical and tactical edge was soon eroded by the arrival of the Lavochkin La-5* fighter in August, and by Russian development of efficient low-level tactics with heavily armoured ground-attack planes like the Ilyushin Il-2* and the Petlyakov Pe-2*. Alexander Novikov*, commander of the Red Air Force since May, personally supervised the destruction of hundreds of German aircraft at Stalingrad* at the turn of the year.

From early 1943, with each ground army now boasting an air army of 700–800 machines, air supremacy on the Eastern Front passed finally to the Red Air Force. Increasingly committed to the defence of its home airspace against Anglo-American bombing raids, the Luftwaffe nevertheless mounted a massive operation in support of the German Army's Kursk* offensive in July, but Soviet numerical superiority was emphasized in a counter-attack employing 60 per cent of all first-line air strength, which now approached 10,000 aircraft in the theatre. By early 1944, armed with new fighters (e.g. Yakovlev Yak-3*) that consistently outperformed their opponents, the Red Air Force had reduced German bombers to the relative safety of very short-range night operations (Soviet night-fighters had no radar*). Later in the year, as Luftwaffe strength dwindled rapidly, Soviet long-range strategic units began bombing Axis-held targets in central Europe. Although direct support of the Army remained the air arm's prime function in the last year of the war, 800 heavy bombers joined the four air armies (7,500 aircraft) that converged on Berlin in April 1945. On 9 May, the Red Air Force performed its last act of the European War, when German surrender documents were flown to Moscow.

Russian warplanes were mostly constructed of cheap materials, designed for ease of assembly and able to operate in conditions far beyond the tolerance of many German types. Most Red Air Force operations took place at very low altitude and at very short range and its new aircraft were specifically designed for the task, making particularly widespread use of air-to-ground rockets*. Its potentially cumbersome integrated command system was also well-suited to very short-range operations, and the quality of Soviet aircrew, some of whom were women, improved dramatically after 1941. A total of 45,000 Russian aircraft were destroyed by the Luftwaffe on the Eastern Front, yet supply – bolstered by some 18,000 British and American machines – more than kept up with demand after the opening months of the campaign. The enormous output of the Soviet aircraft industry during 1942–5 was the single most important factor in enabling the Red Air Force to hold and ultimately overwhelm the Luftwaffe.

Red Army The ground forces of the Soviet Union during WW2. Founded in 1918 to defend the infant Bolshevik revolution from the Central Powers in WW1, the Red Army was at first little more than a reconstituted rump of the Tsarist Imperial Army, using the same equipment, peasant conscripts and often the same officers. Much of its early history is shrouded by the subjectivity of Soviet accounts, but its first campaigns – in the Russian Civil War (1918 –21) and against invading Polish forces in the Ukraine (1920) – were little short of disastrous, although the strikingly similar White Army was narrowly defeated in the Civil War.

During the 1920s and 1930s the Red Army was regarded by informed foreign observers as a second-class force. It had inherited many of the faults traditionally associated with its Tsarist predecessor – an ill-trained and barely competent officer class, an unwieldly centralized command structure, ramshackle supply and communications systems and an almost slavish (if imperfect) imitation of the military doctrines of other European armies. The German Army*, with which there was important collaboration in the post-Versailles period, was particularly admired and copied.

Apart from the use of egalitarian forms of military address (which was later abandoned), the main Bolshevik innovation had been the introduction of political commissars to oversee Army field command at all levels. Usually accompanied by highly active secret police, the commissars were the eyes and ears of the central government, intended to ensure obedience and weed out anti-revolutionary elements. In fact, their presence created an inefficient duality of field command and stifled any combat initiative among professional officers. Although commissars were not a permanent feature of the pre-war Red Army and their influence varied according to local conditions, they were at the height of their disruptive power in the months after the German invasion of 1941.

It was universally recognized that the Soviet Union possessed enormous manpower resources, and that the Russian infantryman was a resilient and obedient fighter dependent on good leadership, which was manifestly lacking in the Red Army. By the 1930s the Red Army had also amassed huge stockpiles of equipment, particularly small arms, artillery* and ammunition, but many of its numerous tanks* and aircraft (see Red Air Force) were seen to be obsolete or obsolescent by the end of the decade. At high-command level observers noted the absolute personal dominance of Stalin* over all Red Army leaders after the late 1920s.

Stalin's intense interest in the development of the Red Army took in every aspect of military life, from equipment specification and allocation to the formulation of tactics and the appointment of relatively junior commanders. Coupled with the violent repression characteristic of Stalin's regime this dominance meant that Soviet commanders were generally regarded as obedient mediocrities even before the terrible purges of the 1930s deprived the Red Army of almost all its experienced leaders (only Marshals Voroshilov* and Budenny*, Stalin's henchmen, survived of the high command) and left important gaps in its organizational structure. Nevertheless Stalin was similarly responsible for the great investment in arms production that emerged from his first Five Year Plans, for the intensive development of new and superior guns and tanks during the late 1930s, and for the creation of a vast heavy industrial complex in the Urals – deep in the Russian hinterland – that was crucial to the Red Army's survival in 1941.

Soviet military tactics under Stalin remained a hotch-potch of borrowed ideas, despite extravagant claims for their originality by Soviet writers. The Red Army's only acknowledged contribution to interwar military development was Marshal Tukhachevsky's demonstration of airborne* warfare techniques in 1927, but the innovation was not effectively pursued and its originator was later purged. Soviet response to new theories of armoured and mobile warfare was confused. Armoured forces were repeatedly reorganized on either the French (infantry support) or the German (independent divisional) model, culminating in the hasty re-formation of independent armoured corps after the fall of France in 1940. Though sufficient in numbers (the Red Army possessed about 10,000 tanks of all types and ages by 1941), Soviet tank forces lacked the training, the leadership or the radio sets to carry out Blitzkrieg*-style operations, while the air arm was not equipped to perform the disruptive role behind enemy lines perfected by the Luftwaffe*.

In the Russo-Finnish War* of 1939–40, an apparently inept performance in difficult conditions reinforced the international conviction (shared by Stalin at this stage) that the Red Army was unfit to fight a major war. Nevertheless by early 1941 it boasted a total strength of some 300 divisions, of which over half (about 3 million men) were stationed in the west, facing smaller German forces. Most were unmechanized rifle divisions, organized along conventional European lines and grouped into corps, which were themselves grouped into armies (see Front). This infantry was supported by horse-drawn artillery and cavalry divisions, while the new tank corps each consisted of two tank divisions (700–1,000 tanks) and one motorized infantry division.

The inferiority of Soviet forces in all but numbers was decisively demonstrated after the German invasion of June 1941. Although the attack was not unexpected, the Red Army suffered a series of staggering defeats in the months before winter halted the German advance. Stalin's unquestioned enforcement of a rigid standfast policy worsened the disaster, and by October the Red Army had lost about 1.5 million men in prisoners alone and some 5,000 tanks. Desertion was becoming rife and many Soviet troops simply fled into the forests, not at this stage to become resistance* fighters but merely to escape the enemy.

Soviet propaganda* concealed the full extent of the defeat from its own people and from the foreign press. Heroic defensive actions were invented (e.g. the defence of Brest-Litovsk) and chosen regiments were arbitrarily designated as heroes and given the honorific title 'Guards'. Stalin, however, recognized the need for drastic action. Immediately after the invasion he began a search for traitors and incompetents within the Army, and tightened his personal control over the conduct of the war, setting in motion an anarchic period of constant command and field structural changes, dependent entirely on the whim of the dictator.

Stalin officially became C-in-C of all Soviet armed forces in July 1941 (only a week after appointing Timoshenko* to the post), and the army general staff became no more than a strategic advisory body, harangued by the dictator but otherwise largely ignored. Politically, Stalin controlled the war effort through a number of committees of which he was *de facto* head, notably a defence committee (GKO) primarily concerned with political and industrial affairs, and STAVKA*, a small group of top military advisers. With all administrative functions of the Red Army thus concentrated in the person of Stalin, field operations came to be conducted by terrified men, whether officers or commissars (given military rank from 1942), who received their volatile and often unrealistic orders directly from the C-in-C via the notoriously unreliable wire telephone system.

Nevertheless, much of the Soviet armaments industry was already operative in the Urals by the autumn of 1941, and the winter respite enabled some re-equipment. By November 2,000 guns and 300 tanks (all desperately needed) had reached the front around Moscow, and 15 divisions had been transferred to the west from Siberia. More reinforcements followed from the Far East after the Japanese attack on Pearl Harbor*, and conscription was rapidly stepped up. Stalin, although he continued to sponsor regular rounds of arrest and execution, regained some faith in the Army and began to believe that it was ready for a major counter-offensive. Timoshenko's ambitious plan for a spring attack in the Ukraine was duly undertaken. Despite the arrival of superior KV* and T34* tanks in numbers, the ill-prepared Soviet forces were ineptly handled and the offensive failed with the loss of 2,000 guns, 1,200 tanks and 200,000 troops taken prisoner. German forces then advanced to the Don, where another large Red Army force was decisively defeated.

By late 1942, however, the process of rebuilding was more nearly complete, while the German Army was weakening. Helped by aid from Britain and the US (particularly the supply of vehicles and radio sets), Soviet industry was transforming the quality and quantity of Red Army equipment, and its field organization had begun to adapt realistically to its needs. The rifle division (reduced in strength) still formed the basic infantry unit, now grouped directly into Fronts as the corps system had fallen into disuse. Within divisions, each infantry regiment was centred around its own artillery unit, giving local commanders the benefit of immediate supporting fire at all times. The infantry nevertheless retained many of the characteristics of a medieval horde, and its operations still appeared utterly chaotic to observers.

The large tank corps of 1941 had been abandoned soon after the invasion for lack of tanks, and were re-formed as independent tank brigades of about 90 tanks. Well-suited to the improvised nature of many

Red Army operations, these remained the basic Soviet armoured formation for the rest of the war. By late 1942 numbers of tanks were sufficient to allow the additional creation of experimental tank corps (each comprising one motorized infantry and two tank brigades) modelled on contemporary panzer divisions, and the following year new mechanized corps formations (75 per cent motorized infantry) began to appear. These relatively small armoured groupings were used to exploit gaps created by the massed infantry (still supported by cavalry units) and by a huge barrage of artillery, which was deployed as a centrally controlled mobile reserve to be concentrated wherever needed. By 1943 the armoured, motorized and air forces of the Red Army were élites, far better trained, led and equipped than the infantry.

Although Stalin still completely dominated the Army, his relations with his High Command improved slightly, as the situation at the Front began to conform to his offensive plans. Moreover, Stalin's absolute certainty of purpose and organizational gifts were crucial to the successful harnessing of the Soviet economy to the war effort. In contrast the deteriorating relationship between Hitler and the German Army, which was occupying far more ground than it could hold, resulted in the same refusal to countenance withdrawals that had undermined the Red Army in 1941. Having mastered the German tactics of encirclement, Soviet forces could attack weak points in the static Axis* line almost at will.

In contrast to the failures of the spring and summer, Red Army offensives in late 1942 and early 1943 were brilliantly successful. A series of operations, aimed primarily at areas held by the forces of Germany's allies, cut off and virtually destroyed the Axis salient in the south. In July a massive German counter-offensive around the Kursk* area was demolished by a well prepared Red Army concentration of some 3,000 tanks with powerful air support. Henceforward it was the German Army

which, outnumbered and exhausted, fought a hopeless defence from static positions against the superior guns, tanks and aircraft of a tactically cohesive enemy.

Steady Soviet advances along the Eastern Front in the first half of 1944 were accelerated from midsummer by a series of major Red Army offensives launched to coincide with the Allied invasion of Northwest Europe*. All along the Eastern Front, beginning in the north and working southwards, these campaigns further demonstrated the Red Army's new mastery of large-scale armoured and artillery operations, and Axis forces were effectively beaten long before the end of the European War in May 1945. Huge and terrible, with a massively powerful tank arm, the Red Army (renamed the Soviet Army in 1946) still suffered from its old organizational and command weaknesses, but these were not seriously tested as it took firm military control of Eastern Europe and came to overshadow all immediate post-war European politics.

Following the defeat of Germany, the Red Army prepared for war with Japan. The 30 divisions in the Far East were brought up to a claimed strength of 1.5 million men, 5,000 tanks and 4,000 combat aircraft, and an invasion of Japanese-held Manchuria* was planned. By the time war was declared, on 9 August 1945, Japan had been attacked with US atomic* bombs and was ready to surrender, and the Soviet invasion was no more than a rapid occupation.

The total number of men and women employed by the Red Army in WW2 is incalculable, but its active strength peaked at about 12.5 million men and women. Its casualty figures also remain a matter for speculation. Although certainly less than the 20 million dead claimed by the Soviet Union after the war, they were undoubtedly many times larger than those of any other Allied nation. See also Eastern Front.

Red Cross An international humanitarian agency established in 1865, the Red Cross provided medical care for military and civilian casualties on both sides during WW2. It also operated field canteens, instigated relief campaigns in refugee areas and oversaw the treatment of prisoners in Europe and Africa.

Red Navy At the beginning of 1939 the Red Navy possessed large fleets in the Baltic and the Black Sea as well as forces of destroyers* and submarines* in the Pacific and Arctic Oceans. It was an ill-organized and largely unmodernized service, which had been seriously affected by the purges of the 1930s. Only when Admiral Kuznetzov* became Commissar of the Navy in April 1939 was any coherent attempt made at reform and reconstruction, but in October 1940 all capital ship construction was suspended to conserve steel for tanks* and aircraft, and little was ever achieved. Meanwhile, the Navy's inept performance in the Russo-Finnish War* (1939–40) against a force ten times smaller had served only to emphasize its professional weakness (although Russian fleets had traditionally never fought in winter). Nevertheless, in June 1941 the Red Navy had two battleships and two cruisers in the Baltic, as well as a battleship and five cruisers in the Black Sea. Both fleets were backed up with large numbers of submarines and flotilla craft of various types, and a force of 15 submarines, seven destroyers and smaller vessels was stationed in the Arctic. A much larger force of small ships in the Pacific was never able to reach the European theatres.

In the first six months of the war on the Eastern Front*, to which the German Navy* contributed only a few light units, Soviet naval strength was decimated by the Luftwaffe*. By late 1941 most of the Baltic Fleet still afloat formed part of the defensive artillery of Leningrad* and most of its crews fought ashore as infantry. A similar fate befell the Black Sea Fleet, which was subject to absolute German air superiority. Most Soviet naval aviation was destroyed in the first weeks of the invasion, and surviving aircraft were then transferred to fight with the land forces (see Red Air

Force). This was a considerable blow to any hopes of conventional offensive action, and major units remained tied to port defence duty (with its attendant anti-aircraft* cover) or coastal support of land operations until late 1945, a situation that further encouraged the consistent subordination of naval forces to local army commanders.

The main burden of the surface war at sea therefore fell on the 'Mosquito fleets' of motor torpedo boats*, minesweepers, submarine chasers and numerous small conversions or auxiliaries. Soviet submarines were also very active, but were not particularly effective. The quality of both boats and crews left much to be desired, and losses were high (107 sunk), mostly to mines*. Perhaps the most successful components of the Red Navy were the river flotillas that patrolled inland waterways. Often improvised, these forces gave important assistance to land operations and protected both the transport of supplies and the transfer of warships along the major rivers.

Soviet naval production was heavily disrupted by the German invasion of 1941. Black Sea shipyards were lost, those in Leningrad blockaded, and no large warships were laid down from 1942 to 1945. Output was restricted to 29 submarines and a few small vessels, along with about 900 motor boats of various types. These could be completed only thanks to engines delivered under Lend-Lease*, which also provided a Royal Navy* battleship, a US Navy* cruiser and numerous smaller craft as well as mines, torpedoes*, ammunition, sonar (see Anti-submarine Warfare) and radar*.

The Soviet Navy claimed to have destroyed 614 warships of all sizes and 676 merchantmen during WW2; the majority of them by air attack, with submarines and torpedo boats sharing most of the rest. Western estimates have suggested figures as many as ten times smaller. What is clear is that the Red Navy fought a highly unorthodox war. Its fleet units were employed consistently as part of the land army and, although they eventually put to sea in support of a few late amphibious* operations, its crews distinguished themselves as ground troops. Forty-nine regular and several independent brigades of naval infantry saw combat, particularly in the defence of Leningrad.

Reggiane Re2000 Series Beaten by the Macchi C200* in the 1938 competition for a new Italian fighter, the Re2000-1 was produced for export, and 170 were sold to Sweden* and Hungary*. The Italian Navy* did operate a few of the improved Re2000-3 model, but it was not until the Re2001 (with a German engine) was developed in 1941 that the type was ordered for the Italian Air Force*. This was capable of 350mph but only a few were delivered before the Italian surrender, and the plane subsequently served as a night-fighter, armed with two underwing cannon, in the defence of German-held northern Italy. The heavily armed Re2005, a strengthened and slightly smaller version, appeared in 1943. About 300 were built and almost all of them fought for pro-German units in the last years of the war, seeing action in northern Italy, Hungary and Germany.
BRIEF DATA (Re2005) Type: single-seat fighter; Engine: 1 × 1,475hp Daimler-Benz; Max speed: 390mph; Arms: 3 × 20mm cannon, 2 × 12.7mm mg.

Reggio di Calabria Site of the landing of Montgomery's* 8th Army on 3 September 1943 that signalled the start of the Allied invasion of Italy*. See Baytown.

Reichenau, Field Marshal Walther von (1884–1942) An ambitious German career officer who followed General Blomberg into the German War Ministry in 1933, co-operating fully with the Nazis. Reichenau commanded the 10th Army for the invasion of Poland* in 1939, and the 6th Army for the Western Offensive* in Belgium and France in 1940. Promoted field marshal, he was sent to command first 6th Army and later Army Group South in place of Rundstedt*. He was responsible for issu-

ing orders of extreme brutality, including the 'Severity Order' which prescribed the vicious treatment of Russian prisoners and for which Reichenau would undoubtedly have been brought to trial had he survived the war. He died of a stroke in 1942.

Reitsch, Hanna (1912–79) German pilot and the only woman in the war to receive the Iron Cross, which she was awarded First and Second Class. She had been a champion glider pilot in the 1930s and was well-known as a skilled and daring flyer. Reitsch test-piloted the V-1* rocket before its adoption as an unmanned bomb. Personally devoted to Hitler, she flew to the Bunker in April 1945, taking General Griem* to receive his appointment as C-in-C of the Luftwaffe*. After avoiding Russian anti-aircraft* guns and escaping from Berlin, Reitsch was captured by the Americans. She was released without trial in 1946 and resumed her international flying career.

Remagen Site of a bridge (the Ludendorff Bridge) over the Rhine*, which was brilliantly seized by a reconnaissance patrol of the US 1st Army, just as German engineers prepared to blow it up on 7 March 1945. Following the explosion, which damaged the bridge but left it standing, American riflemen reached the east bank and established the first Allied bridgehead across the Rhine. See also Northwest Europe, Allied Invasion of.

Renault R-35 The most numerous French tank* at the start of the war, the R-35 was accepted by the infantry as its standard light tank in 1935, after favourable comparison with the Hotchkiss H-35*. It was also exported to Poland, Yugoslavia, Turkey and Rumania, total production exceeding 1,600. About 945 R-35 and R-40 tanks, the latter a version with improved suspension, equipped the French Army* in May 1940, and they were used in support of infantry. Too slow for mobile strategic operations, the R-35's effectiveness was further reduced by the stress placed on its commander, who had also to act as gunner, loader and, when one was fitted, operator of the radio. As the PzKpfw R-35, about 200 machines were later used by Germany for reconnaissance on the Eastern Front*. The chassis was also used for towing German artillery, transporting ammunition or mounting a variety of self-propelled* weapons.

BRIEF DATA (R-35) Type: 2-man light tank; Engine: 82hp petrol; Max speed: 12.5mph; Range: 87m; Arms: 1 × 37mm gun, 1 × 7.5mm mg; Armour: max 45mm.

Renown, HMS Royal Navy* battlecruiser and Class. Completed in 1916, the two ships of the *Renown* Class (the other was the *Repulse*) were extreme examples of the contemporary Admiralty 'speed is armour' policy and were therefore dangerously under-protected. The *Renown*, however, was one of only two British capital ships to be completely modernized before 1940 and was adequately armoured (at least against air attack) for carrier or convoy* escort. She was active throughout the war, most notably during the campaign in Norway* and as the flagship of Force H*, based on Gibraltar*. Standard radar* installations were added to the *Renown* early in the war, and the removal of her aircraft in 1943 hastened a steady increase in light armament. In 1944 she served in the Far East but was replaced early the following year by more modern units. In the absence of German capital ships to threaten home waters, she was retired and plagiarized for carrier armament.

BRIEF DATA (1939) Displacement: 31,988 tons; Dimensions: o/a lgth – 794' 3", b – 102' 9"; Speed: 29 knots; Armament: 6 × 15" gun (3 × 2), 20 × 4.5" DP gun, 24 × 2pdr AA gun, 16 × 0.5" AA gun, 8 × 18" TT, 4 aircraft.

Repulse, HMS British battlecruiser of the *Renown** Class, completed in 1916. The *Repulse* had only been partially modernized before the war and was by no means fit for front-line service in 1939. After a period

as an Atlantic* escort, she was ordered to Singapore* with the *Prince of Wales** in advance of a major refit planned for late 1941 (see Force Z). Whether the intended reconstruction of her wholly inadequate anti-aircraft* defences would have saved the *Repulse* is debatable, and she was sunk by Japanese torpedo- and dive-bombers off the coast of Malaya on 10 December 1941.

BRIEF DATA (1939) Displacement: 32,000 tons; Dimensions: o/a lgth – 794' 3", b – 90'; Speed: 28.5 knots; Armament: 6 × 15" gun (3 × 2), 9 × 4" gun, 6 × 4" AA gun, 24 × 2pdr AA gun, 8 × 0.5" AA gun, 8 × 18" TT, 4 aircraft.

Resistance Opposition to the authorities of occupying powers was not entirely confined to countries overrun or threatened by Axis* forces, although it was most widespread and prominent in those states. In the Middle East and India, for example, British regimes were subject to organized unrest (see Indian Nationalism; Iraq). Resistance took many practical forms: guerrilla forces of all sizes fought military actions against Axis troops; clandestine civilian organizations performed acts of sabotage or espionage; labour or religious groups led acts of civil disruption and protest, often in support of persecuted minorities or at the behest of Allied strategists; underground presses and outspoken public or academic figures spread prohibited ideas and information; exiles and diplomats worked to encourage unity of purpose and supervise Allied support; myriad escape routes were established inside occupied countries to aid captured Allied military personnel or to protect persecuted groups from the authorities; and countless individual, often unchronicled acts of defiance further helped ensure significant diversion of Axis resources to the control of conquered territories.

Although active and successful opposition groups fought the Japanese in China* and the Far East and the Italians in Africa, Europe was the real hotbed of resistance activity in WW2. Generally, the make-up of European resistance movements reflected the political atomization or unity of their respective home states. Thus the coalition of resistance elements behind straightforward nationalist ideals and generally recognized governments-in-exile was more evident in the conquered democracies of northern Europe and Scandinavia than in the strife-torn states of eastern Europe and the Balkans*.

Communist organizations were important to resistance throughout occupied Europe, particularly in the east, where relative proximity to sponsorship from Moscow, difficult (often mountainous) terrain and the conflicts of local interest groups contributed to the growth of revolutionary communist partisan armies. Throughout pre-war Europe, communists had been trained and organized for underground warfare and,once the German invasion of the Soviet Union formally released them into temporary alliance with other groups, they became a dedicated and formidable force for resistance. Nevertheless, extreme political differences and mutual mistrust could and did lead to open conflict with local nationalist resistance groups, notably in Greece and Yugoslavia.

Allied political and material support to western European and Scandinavian resistance groups was largely based in London, with a constant flow of supply, intelligence and personnel traffic crossing British home waters. Further afield in Europe, Anglo-American attempts to sponsor active resistance were generally channelled through the Middle East, with Cairo as the main focus of activity. The Soviet Union certainly maintained close intelligence links with Comintern-affiliated communist groups, and ran extensive NKVD* spy networks throughout Europe, although details of their activities are unavailable. For much of the war, however, Soviet attempts to supply or actively direct resistance operations outside Russia were hampered by the all-consuming need to concentrate resources on the Eastern Front*.

In the Far East, Allied contact with resisters was more limited. Espionage activities were restricted by obvious racial differences between Allied agents and their hosts, while the supply of resisters was subject to enormous distances and lack of accurate local information. The US Navy* was able to provide some long-range supply facilities to resisters in the Phillipines, and the USAAF* flew materials across the Himalayas to Chinese nationalist forces (see Hump). Otherwise there was little that the major Allied powers could do to directly influence resistance to the Japanese. The most successful guerrilla army in the Far East operated quite independently in China under Mao Tse-tung*, and other oriental resistance groups occasionally offered useful intelligence to the Western Allies but received little in return.

Internal activity against Axis governments, especially in Germany, also constituted resistance, bearing in mind the attitude of the totalitarian regimes to their real or imagined opponents. In Japan seditious opposition was effectively silenced by internal intelligence agencies. In Italy the survival of the monarchy gave legitimate focus to a broad spectrum of resistance groups, which later emerged as a powerful force against the German occupation of the north. In Germany, isolated pockets of determined, active opposition had little Allied or popular support and found expression primarily in a series of failed *coups d'état*.

In occupied countries, the anti-resistance work of security organizations like the German SD* was often crucially augmented by that of local police forces (e.g. in Vichy*, France) or para-military collaborationist groups, which were a small but effective minority in most occupied countries. The fate of most of those caught or suspected of resistance activity anywhere was death, and the additional threat of large-scale, brutal reprisals against civilian hostages was ever-present in occupied territories. In German-occupied territories, particularly, these factors were less of a deterrent to large-scale resistance as the war progressed and the prospect of German

Men of the British 1st Parachute Battalion take cover in a shell hole at Arnhem during the disastrous Operation Market Garden, September 1944

American tanks moving into the attack during the German Ardennes counter-offensive launched on 19 December 1944

Hitler's 'miracle weapons' which were unleashed in mass attacks against Southern Britain in the summer and autumn of 1944:

OPPOSITE: the V2 rocket, seen just after firing

RIGHT: the V1 flying bomb, known as the 'Doodle Bug'

BELOW: Dresden, the German city devastated by relentless Allied area bombing 14 February 1945. The air raid was one of the most controversial Allied actions of the whole war

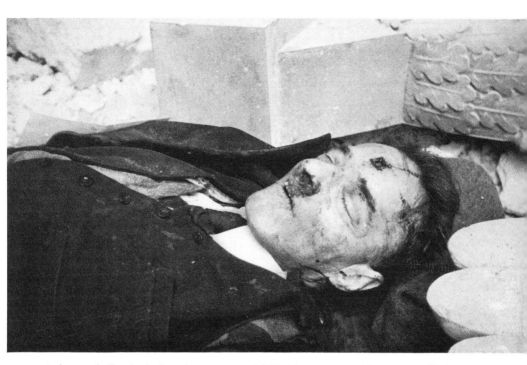

ABOVE: *A photograph alleged to be that of Hitler's corpse, Berlin 1945*

RIGHT: *Soviet troops raise the flag of victory over the Reichstag in Berlin, April 1945*

OPPOSITE ABOVE: *Benito Mussolini, his mistress Clara Petacci and other fascist functionaries hanging ignominiously by their feet in the Piazzale Lorelo, Milan, after being executed by partisans, April 1945*

OPPOSITE BELOW: *Field Marshal Bernard Montgomery accepting the surrender of the German Forces in North-West Europe at Lüneburg Heath, April 1945*

General Dwight D. Eisenhower, Supreme Commander-in-Chief of the Allied Expeditionary Forces, North-West Europe. He later became President of the United States of America

General Douglas MacArthur, Commander-in-Chief of Allied forces in the Pacific

The mushroom cloud from the atomic bomb rises over the Japanese city of Nagasaki, 9 August 1945. The destruction with atomic weapons of the cities of Hiroshima (6 August) and Nagasaki brought about the surrender of Japan on 14 August and the end of the Second World War, 1939-1945.

victory (understandably perceived as inevitable to many in 1940–1) receded. Revulsion towards the Nazi regime also grew universally throughout the war: the relatively well treated 'Aryan' peoples of northern Europe unanimously rejecting the persecution of Jews and other minorities, and the despised Slavic races reversing their initial anti-Russian enthusiasm when subjected to ruthless and appallingly brutal exploitation.

The following outlines some of the most important or successful examples of resistance to Axis powers:

Albania. Albanian resistance to Italian occupation was dominated by the communist Worker's Party, formed by Enver Hoxha after the German invasion of the Soviet Union in 1941. Modelling his movement on the partisans of neighbouring Yugoslavia, Hoxha gathered forces in the mountains and organized the National Liberation Army (LNC – a coalition of resistance groups, including the National Front of conservative local chieftains), which began orchestrating attacks on Axis garrisons from 1943. The collapse of Italy in September provided Hoxha with a significant haul of abandoned arms, and although the subsequent German occupation granted Albania nominal independence, the LNC intensified its activities during 1944. When German forces began their withdrawal from the Balkans* late in the year all major Albanian towns were under Hoxha's control. Despite the defection of many right-wing elements from his coalition, and an almost total lack of contact with Anglo-American agencies, Hoxha was recognized by all the Allies as head of state, and established a post-war dictatorship in Albania along strictly Stalinist lines. He remained in absolute power until his death in 1986. See also Albania, Italian invasion of.

Belgium. Although Belgium, like other northern European states, contained some elements that welcomed German occupation, the great majority of Belgians viewed Nazism with increasing horror. Oc-cupied by Germany during WW1, Belgium possessed an abundance of resisters experienced in the mechanisms of clandestine warfare. The heavily fortified Belgian coastline was of little use for sea escapes, but the country was a fertile source of intelligence for the Allies, and Belgians were highly active in the shelter of Jews from the Nazi authorities. Militarily, an insurgent guerrilla force was set up to seize power in Belgium (pending the return of the government-in-exile) but it was not called upon to fight, instead performing valuable work maintaining law and order in the aftermath of the German retreat, and preventing destruction of valuable installations, such as the port facilities at Antwerp*. A total of 17,000 Belgian resisters were killed during WW2.

Bulgaria. Traditionally an ally of Russia, Bulgaria did not declare war on the Soviet Union in 1941 and maintained diplomatic contacts with Moscow until 1944. Nevertheless, the pro-German government was primarily concerned with repressing small-scale communist partisan activities in the first years of the war, and western attempts to stimulate resistance activity elicited little response. As the Red Army* gained the upper hand on the Eastern Front* during 1943, partisan groups received greater encouragement and direction from the Soviet Union, and acts of anti-government sabotage rose from 12 in January to 280 in November. An insurrectionist Fatherland Front was set up by the communists in the same year, and the death of King Boris III in August contributed to a significant destabilization of the country by the time Soviet forces launched an invasion of Bulgaria a year later. The invasion was supported by a well organized Fatherland Front uprising, and after an easy conquest the Red Army was joined by 450,000 Bulgars in the fight against Germany. Exiled communist Dimitrov, brought from Moscow, headed a post-war government purged of non-communist influences.

Czechoslovakia. Equipped with a first-class intelligence service, the Czech government was well prepared to conduct resistance from exile after 1939, and German occupation was beset from the first by a wave of sabotage activity coupled with civil disobedience at all levels of society. In September 1941 the Nazi governor Neurath* was replaced by Reinhard Heydrich*, who instituted a policy of brutal repression, which included the rounding-up and shooting of most Czech communists – hitherto spared in deference to Germany's alliance with the Soviet Union. Heydrich's assassination the following May, by a team of Czech agents flown from Britain, provoked a massive outburst of retaliatory repression (most famously the massacre of Lidice*) which effectively destroyed organized subversion in Czechoslovakia. Czechs nevertheless continued to display antipathy towards the occupiers and to pass intelligence to the Allies, while the government-in-exile under Benes* in London sought unification with Czech communists exiled in Moscow.

The puppet state of Slovakia, separated from Bohemia and Moravia by partition after the German occupation, remained relatively passive until August 1944, when an uprising in support of the approaching Red Army* was put down within a few weeks by German forces and driven into the hills. A unified government-in-exile entered Czechoslovakia with the Red Army the following year, and in April 1945 a Czech/Slovak National Front was formed to govern the country after the defeat of Germany. The people of Prague* rose against the German garrison on 5 May, sustaining 2,000 fatal casualties in heavy street-fighting before the Red Army entered the city on 9 May. During WW2 about 350,000 Czechs were deported to concentration camps*, 100,000 of whom survived to return. See also Czechoslovakia.

Denmark. See Denmark.

Ethiopia. Nationalist tribesmen had been fighting Italian occupation since 1936 and they received support from a special British unit (Mission 101 under Brigadier Sandford) six months before the British offensive in East Africa*. The restoration of exiled Emperor Haile Selassie was a prime aim of Ethiopian nationalism, and the British flew him into the country to encourage revolt in the wake of their invasion. Such was the impact of tribal unrest on Italian forces that mass surrenders to the British were attributed to fear that the rebels might get them first. Ethiopian rebels were vigorously assisted throughout the campaign by the Gideon Force, a British guerrilla unit under Orde Wingate*.

France. Resistance to German occupation in France began spontaneously in 1940 in the assistance of escaping Allied airmen and French Jews, and by the end of the year underground publications had begun appearing exhorting action against German control. Many Frenchmen nevertheless accepted the authority of the Vichy* government, and appeals by de Gaulle* for Frenchmen to join him in London were not well received at first. Britain's survival into 1941 and clear signs of German intent to loot and Nazify the occupied north encouraged the growth of internal resistance, but opposition to the German authorities was all that united the many widely disparate factions of the movement. Russia's entry into the war brought French communists into active organized opposition to Axis forces. The communist National Liberation Front was formed in 1941, with a military wing, the *Francs-Tireurs et Partisans Français.*

Acts of sabotage, the escape of Allied PoWs and information gathering were organized with help from British special service units, and spy traffic flowed regularly across the English Channel (see SOE; Westland Lysander), but central organization was lacking and casualties were high, often due to betrayal. During 1942 the build-up of US military strength and Soviet successes on the Eastern Front* added credibility to de Gaulle's continued appeals from London, and agents of his Free France* movement began infiltrating northern France in order to promote unity among the underground factions.

By the start of 1943 Germany had occupied southern France and the Allies were in control of much of French West and Northwest Africa. The resistance inside France had broadly coalesced behind three overseas authorities. De Gaulle's supporters (his Secret Army) suffered the loss of most of its leadership to German counterespionage but joined forces in the spring with the Army Resistance Organization (ORA), which supported the leadership of General Giraud*, the US-sponsored French leader in Africa. These formed the National Council of Resistance (CNR), which claimed central control of all resistance activity in France. The CNR announced its support for de Gaulle's overall leadership in May 1943, but the communists kept their military forces separate from the Council despite their nominal acceptance of Moscow's instruction to back de Gaulle.

The prospect of Allied reinvasion of France added greater unity of purpose to resistance activity during 1944. Well organized underground operations paralysed German communications throughout Brittany in May, as a rehearsal for the Allied Transportation Plan*, and resistance units fought valuable harassment actions in support of Allied invasion forces in the north and south of the country (see Northwest Europe; Anvil/Dragoon). See also Free France.

Germany. The scope and style of resistance to Nazism inside Germany was necessarily different in character to that practised in German-occupied territories. In March 1933 the Enabling Act had destroyed what still remained of the German constitution, making opposition to Hitler high treason. Nevertheless pockets of resistance forming across the political spectrum were never entirely suppressed by the apparatus of Nazism. Before and after 1939 active opposition to Hitler was centred on the Army, though it also included state officials, churchmen, and a few highly important Nazi officials like Admiral Canaris*, head of German military intelligence, the Abwehr*. Often nourished by resentment and fear of Hitler's crude and dangerous militarism, as well as by an instinctive disdain for Nazism characteristic of the 'Junker' class, a core of opposition which included high ranking officers such as Chief of the General Staff Beck*, General Halder*, Head, Admiral Canaris and his subordinate Oster*, as well as civilians still in official positions like the lawyer Dohnanyi* and Gördeler*, Mayor of Leipzig until 1937, discussed plans to oust Hitler before a war broke out.

Representatives of the opposition including Adam Trott zu Solz* and Dietrich Bonhöffer* travelled to Washington and London on a number of missions in the two years preceding the outbreak of war (and continued to do so until 1943) to try to establish contacts for a resistance, and to convince British and US governments of the need to support the resistance as a serious alternative to Nazism in Germany.

In 1938 Beck, Halder and Kleist* conspired with other senior army officers to arrest Hitler, and Kleist was sent as emissary to London to obtain British support for a coup. But Prime Minister Chamberlain's* commitment to appeasement* of Hitler paralysed Britain's response and undermined Kleist's efforts. The outbreak of war in 1939 added a further burden to the efforts of German resisters. Although opposition was widespread, in groups and cells based around universities, churches, or factory sites, and a growing active core of resistance was recruited and protected under the umbrella of the Abwehr* by its enigmatic leader Canaris* it cannot be said that the thousands of arrests and deaths for anti-Nazi activities, which ranged from the armed opposition of MAN (relatively rare in Germany) to the distribution of anti-Nazi newsletters and leaflets and maintenance of information networks, had any effect on the grip of the regime.

Nevertheless, resistance groups survived. Aristocratic anti-Nazis formed groups such as the Solf Circle and the better known Kreisau Circle, founded by the aristocratic

Graf Hemlut von Moltke*. As the war progressed and German fortunes waned, prominent Germans were drawn into increasingly radical discussions of the path to a post-Hitler Germany. Underground groups based on the Social Democrats such as the Eilbeck Comrades and New Beginnen continued to publish anti-Nazi material and maintain courier services to other parts of Europe. Among young people in Germany, all compulsorily obliged to join Nazi youth organizations from early teenage, there was extensive though unquantifiable opposition to Hitler throughout the Nazi period. A dedicated department of the RSHA (Reichs Security Department under Heydrich* which controlled the SD* and Gestapo*) investigated the activities of the youth resistance groups and a youth concentration camp was established at Neuwied. Countless groups were infiltrated, broken up and re-formed.

White Rose, organized in Munich University under the leadership of Hans and Sophie Scholl, was probably the most significant youth opposition group, operating from 1939 until early 1943. In these years their activities expanded from printing and distributing anti-Nazi material at the University to gathering and disseminating material on some of the regime's more brutal and inhuman activities to towns all over central Germany. In early 1943, however, the Scholls abandoned their clandestine methods and openly distributed leaflets around the university. They were arrested immediately, tried and executed in Stadelheim prison in February 1943.

After mid-1940, no more worthwhile Army support was available for recruitment to the opposition. Further missions by Trott zu Solz and others had failed to bring any firm support from authorities in London or Washington. The demand for Germany's 'unconditional surrender' seemed a further rejection by the Allies. Constantly subject to the energetic activities of the Gestapo*, many prominent members of the opposition had been arrested or dismissed from their positions by mid-1943. Increasingly deadly

rivalry between Admiral Canaris and RSHA head Kaltenbrunner* progressively endangered the activities of the Abwehr-based resistance.

In March 1943 a conspiracy (Operation Flash) involving General von Tresckow*, Gördeler, Generals Olbricht and Schlabrendorff unsuccessfully attempted to murder Hitler during a visit to army headquarters in the Smolensk area of the Eastern Front*. By mid-1944 further arrests (among the Moltke) and the disbanding of the Abwehr were further blows to opposition. In July 1944 a planned takeover, to be triggered by another bomb attempt on Hitler's life, failed but with far wider consequences. Involving the covert co-operation of many that were unprepared to act themselves, but developed by Count von Stauffenberg* and a core of co-conspirators, the failure of the July Bomb Plot* at Rastenberg sealed the fates of many more resistance members. Hundreds were arrested; all direct and some suspected conspirators were brutally executed. Many who had not been involved but whose loyalty was insufficiently proven became victims of Hitler's vicious retributive actions. What remained of the resistance to Nazism by the summer of 1944 was forced to await the Allied invasion of Europe and final military defeat to see the end of Hitler's regime.

Greece. Although a multitude of organized underground and political factions were active in Greece after the German invasion of 1941, they were concerned as much with local conflicts as with the removal of Axis forces, and a situation close to civil war existed throughout the German occupation. The German authorities were generally content to let the Greeks fight among themselves, although evidence of close co-operation with the Allies (sometimes exaggerated in reports by the BBC*) brought savage reprisals. In fact, the Greek underground resisted all Allied (mainly British) efforts to bring it together as a viable opposition to Axis forces, and after the voluntary withdrawal of German troops in late 1944 the Greeks fought on, against the

British force which then entered the country and against each other. See Greece, British occupation of.

Italy. Political opposition to Italy's participation in WW2 and to Mussolini's* Fascist government mounted from 1940. Less effectively and savagely repressive than Nazi Germany, Mussolini's regime left room for legitimate political overthrow and although there were plots to remove the Duce among royalist officers and politicians he was deposed by peaceful and legal means in July 1943.

The subsequent German occupation of northern Italy provoked considerable partisan activity in the area. The partisan movement in Italy had its roots in anti-Fascist groups formed in the 1920s and, led by former Socialist premier Ivanoe Bonomi, these were unified into the Committee of National Liberation (CLN) and its military arm the Resistance Army during late 1943 and early 1944. Apart from harassing the rear of German defensive positions, Italian partisans were sufficiently co-ordinated to call a general strike in the north on 1 March 1944, and they maintained close and efficient links with nearby Allied forces for the rest of the war in Europe.

Hungary. Under Admiral Horthy* revisionist Hungary benefitted initially from its co-belligerent relationship with Germany. Territorial acquisitions, a booming war economy and the sense of being on the winning side meant that hardly any resistance activity took place before 1944. A few communists, survivors of the most thorough persecution practised by Horthy's government, organized strikes and demonstrations against the government in 1943, but their numbers only began to swell after the German occupation of Hungary in March 1944. When Horthy's government collapsed in October no resistance group was sufficiently organized to take power, which remained in the hands of the Fascist Szalisi until the Red Army* arrived and imposed a left-wing provisional government on an anarchic political situation.

Netherlands. See Netherlands, The

Norway. Following the German invasion of 1940 the Norwegian government fled to London, retaining the enthusiastic support of almost the entire population. No prepared underground organization existed to fight the occupation government (led first by the collaborator Quisling* and later by *Reichskommissar* Terboven), but Milorg, a clandestine group of servicemen dedicated to preparing for an Allied counter-invasion, quickly expanded to a membership of some 32,000. While Milorg planned meticulously for the future, it was not prepared to risk reprisals against civilians by undertaking terrorist activities. Nevertheless, Norway's long coastline and proximity to Britain made it a fertile area for British intelligence agencies, who found no shortage of willing agents and contacts in Norway, and whose plans for direct offensive action were sanctioned by Milorg despite the certainty of reprisals.

While ordinary citizens kept up a campaign of disobedience to the new regime (schoolteachers, for example, refused to implement a Nazified history syllabus), British commando* and SOE* missions performed regular raids and sabotage operations from 1941, most significantly against important heavy water installations (see Atomic Bomb). Allied aircraft also dropped arms and supplies to the potential insurgents of Milorg, while both the long frontier with Sweden* and the Shetland Bus boat shuttle to Britain provided reliable escape and communications routes.

These activities contributed to Hitler's expectation of a major Allied offensive in Norway, and 17 divisions of the German Army were held there in the summer of 1944, their movements severely restricted by railway sabotage. The following spring, as German forces retreated, Milorg went into action to protect resources from destruction and looting. Although unsuccessful in protecting the far north of the country, Milorg (aided by British agents) then took political control of Norway pending the return of the popular legitimate government.

Philippines. Many Filipino troops did not surrender to Japanese forces in 1942 but instead withdrew to the interior of various islands and formed the nuclei of guerrilla forces which kept up a running campaign against Japanese garrison troops throughout the occupation. Filipino guerrillas included stranded American officers (such as Lt-Colonel James Cushing, who commanded resistance forces on the island of Cebu), who were frequently in direct radio contact with US commands. US attempts to supply resistance forces were inevitably hampered by the vast distances involved, but by 1944 large ocean-going submarines (e.g. USS *Narwhal**) were being used successfully for the task. By March 1945, the island of Negros in the Visayan group boasted a resistance army of 14,000 guerrillas (about half of whom were armed), and they helped US troops overcome a 15,000 strong Japanese garrison. Filipino guerrillas also gave valuable support to US operations on Luzon and in the South Philippines in April and May 1945 (see Pacific War).

Poland. See Anders, Lt. General Wladyslaw; Bor-Komorowski, Tadeusz; Polish Home Army; Warsaw uprisings.

Thailand. Despite the uneasy alliance between the Thai government and Japan, the Thai people were generally anti-Japanese and a well-organized, well-led underground kept in close touch with the Allies. Many government officials also co-operated with Allied agencies and the view in the US was that the Thai people sought liberation from Japanese influence. Thailand was therefore not treated as an opponent of the Allies after WW2.

USSR. Resistance to Axis occupation of Soviet territory began immediately after the German invasion of June 1941. Bands of partisans, guerrilla groups of local civilians, began using their knowledge of the inhospitable countryside to cut the German Army's supply lines and raid the rear of its advance. At first Communist Party and NKVD* attempts to impose a central organization on the partisans met with little success, and resistance groups remained small, isolated and ineffectual during 1941.

Many partisans on the Eastern Front* fought to protect their homeland rather than out of loyalty to the Soviet regime, but confidence in central government increased significantly after the first Soviet winter offensive of 1941–2. Resentment of German occupation grew as acts of brutality became widespread and Nazi plans for the economic exploitation of the country began to unfold. By the summer of 1942 there were an estimated 150–200,000 partisans fighting the invaders, with bands sometimes numbering over 1,000 men and women each. Increasingly trained and supplied by the Soviet government, they became a serious threat to German rear columns.

Although they operated all along the Eastern Front, Soviet partisans were most heavily concentrated against the German Army Groups North and Centre, and were particularly effective in the Bryansk Forest area. By January 1944 they had established direct radio links with Red Army* commands, which further increased their efficiency and led to the formation of special Red Army staffs to co-ordinate operations. Partisans killed thousands of German troops and captured thousands more, and they were taken very seriously by the German Army*, which had not expected resistance on such a scale and which made some efforts to win over local opinion and (more successfully) to recruit local forces as Osttruppen.

Vietnam. The only popular anti-Japanese resistance movement of any consequence in WW2 was the Viet Minh, a coalition of Vietnamese (anti-French) nationalist and communist groups formed in 1941. Primarily organized by Ho Chi Minh*, who emerged as its leader by the end of the war, the Viet Minh undertook small-scale raids against Japanese forces and supplied occasional intelligence to the Allies.

Yugoslavia. Pre-war Yugoslavia was an uneasy federation of Balkan states, and the German occupation of the country in 1941 brought its virtual disintegration. Military action by Serbian resistance groups – the liberal monarchist chetniks and the communist partisans – was balanced by collaboration in Croatia and to a lesser extent in Montenegro. Resistance activity was further undermined by a series of bitter clashes between the fervently anti-communist chetniks and the partisans. Eventually the chetniks began collaborating with Italian forces, leaving the communists besieged in the hills as the only force in Yugoslavia fully committed to fighting the Axis, a fact only belatedly recognized in London and Washington. Their achievement in liberating Yugoslavia by their own military actions, after a long and at times desperate struggle, was unique among resistance groups in WW2. See Mihajlovic, General Draza; Tito, Josip Broz.

Reuben James, USS US Navy* destroyer of the *Clemson* Class. These distinctive four-stacked flushdeckers had been laid down late in WW1 but many remained in active service throughout 1939–45 in both ocean theatres. A number of *Clemsons* served with the Royal Navy* under the destroyers-for-bases* deal of 1940. On 31 October 1941, the *Reuben James* was escorting a British convoy* west of Ireland with four other US Navy destroyers when she was torpedoed by the *U-562*, becoming the first American ship of the war to be sunk by hostile fire. As the United States was still a neutral power, the loss of 115 lives in the incident caused considerable public outcry. A second *Reuben James*, a destroyer escort*, was commissioned in 1943.
BRIEF DATA (1941) Displacement: 1,190 tons; Dimensions: o/a lgth – 314' 6", b – 31' 9"; Speed: 35 knots; Armament: 4 × 4" gun; 1 × 3" AA gun; 12 × 21" TT.

Reynaud, Paul (1878–1966) French politician who succeeded Edouard Daladier* as premier, 21 March 1940, and was a strong advocate of resistance to the German Western Offensive*, launched in May 1940. His support for Churchill's* proposal for an Anglo-French Union caused the 'defeatists' led by Pétain* to unite to force his resignation on 16 June 1940. Reynaud was arrested by Pétain's Vichy* government in September and was later one of the accused in the notorious Riom Trial* of 1942.

Rhine, River Great natural defensive frontier separating Germany from western Europe, it provided the Allies with their final major obstacle of the campaign in Northwest Europe* in early 1945. Following the failure of Hitler's ambitious counter-offensives against the Allied front in the Ardennes (see Battle of the Bulge) and in Alsace in December 1944, Crerar's* Canadian 1st Army advanced to the Rhine from the Netherlands in Operation Veritable, beginning on 9 February 1945. A complementary advance, code-named Grenade, projected the 9th Army's advance to the Rhine and the capture of Cologne, reached on 5 March. Patton's 3rd Army, attacking through Eifel, was slower to reach the Rhine (22 March) but inflicted heavy casualties and achieved a surprise crossing at Oppenheim on the night before the main Allied attack got underway.

Meanwhile the 7th Army had cleared the Saar and reached the Rhine by 10 March. Although the first crossing of the river itself was made at Remagen* on 7 March, the main Allied assault on the Rhine was commanded by General Montgomery* in Operation Plunder, a large-scale set-piece offensive, preceded by a two-week-long preparatory air bombardment. Begun on 23 March, crossings were made by the British 2nd Army between Xanten and Rees and by the US 9th Army south of Wesel. On the following morning, one US and one British airborne* division landed on the east bank in Operation Varsity and made speedy contact with ground forces, establishing a strong bridgehead by the end of the day. The success of the operation was the signal for the other Allied armies to move forward. Beyond the Rhine, Germany now lay undefended.

Rhubarbs Massed attacks by RAF* fighter aircraft against German targets in occupied northern France. Begun in January 1941 as an attempt by RAF Fighter Command to take the offensive after the Battle of Britain*, Rhubarbs were costly and only superficially effective, revealing the extent to which German early warning radar* had improved since 1939. 'Circuses' – similar operations including a few otherwise obsolete light bombers – were marginally more effective. The German invasion of the Soviet Union in June prolonged the experiment, as Rhubarbs were wrongly credited by RAF leaders with forcing the Luftwaffe* to divert large-scale resources from the Eastern Front*. They did, however, deter the Luftwaffe from further reinforcing the Eastern Front from units still based in Northwest Europe. See Douglas, Air Marshal W. Sholto.

Ribbentrop, Joachim von (1893–1946) German Foreign Minister from 1938, an effective functionary, though generally not the initiator of most of the diplomacy in which he was involved. Founder of the 'Ribbentrop Bureau' under Hess's* Party secretariat in 1933, which rivalled the functions of the German Foreign Ministry, Ribbentrop's duplicate organization sought to prove the superiority of Nazi methods over the traditional foreign service (a strategy for usurping traditional state power bases that became common Nazi practice – see SS). His success was demonstrated by the independent conclusion of the Anglo-German Naval Treaty* in May 1935, and the addition of Japan's signature to the Anti-Comintern Pact* in 1936. Finally, in February 1938, Hitler dismissed the Foreign Minister, von Neurath* and Ribbentrop succeeded to the high Nazi aristocracy, acting as Hitler's adjutant for the period of armed diplomacy which immediately preceded the outbreak of war. Ribbentrop subsequently retained his status, though war had superseded diplomacy. He was arrested in June 1945 and tried at Nuremberg* with the major defendants. Like others,

he claimed ignorance of concentration camps*, racial extermination policies and other Nazi crimes. He was found guilty and hanged.

Riccardi, Admiral Arturo (1878–1966) Chief of the Italian Naval Staff and Under Secretary of State for the Navy 1940–3.

Richelieu French battleship and Class which also included the *Jean Bart**. Ordered in 1935, the *Richelieu* was almost complete when France* fell in June 1940. She steamed to Dakar* and was actively involved in resisting British attacks on the port, suffering bomb damage during the first of these in July. After the Torch* invasion of Northwest Africa in late 1942, she joined the Allies, and was refitted in the US before serving during 1944–5 with the British Indian Ocean Fleet.
BRIEF DATA (1940) Displacement: 35,000 tons; Dimensions: o/a lgth – 814', b – 108' 6"; Speed: 30 knots; Armaments: 8 × 15" gun (4 × 2), 9 × 6" gun, 12 × 4" gun, 16 × 37mm AA gun, 28 × 13.2mm AA mg.

Rifles The rifle was the standard weapon of the WW2 infantryman. Most front-line troops used hand-operated repeater designs which stressed ease of manufacture and robustness. These could be modified for specialist tasks such as airborne* or jungle warfare and sniping. The best of the type was on balance the German Army's* standard 7.92mm Manser Kar 98. Immensely strong and reliable, it was far more accurate than the comparable British Lee-Enfield 0.303-inch rifles, which nevertheless maintained a superior rate of fire. Both the Russian 7.62mm Mosin-Nagant and the 7.7mm Arisaka rifle of the Japanese Army* were rugged, simple and reliable weapons, although the manufacturing quality of the latter dropped markedly late in the war. The French Army* of 1940 was largely equipped with various models of the 7.5mm Berthier rifle, but most other armies relied, like the Italians, on adapted or developed versions of imported designs. The exception to this general orthodoxy was the US Army*, which officially adopted a gas-operated semi-automatic weapon as standard issue in 1940. Although the excellent 0.3-inch Garand* (or M1) rifle was not universally available when the US entered the war, its success helped demonstrate the practicability of the automatic rifle to other forces, particularly the Red Army*. See also Submachine-guns.

Riom Trial An attempt by the Pétain government in February 1942, with Nazi sponsorship, to organize a show trial, with specially picked members of a special 'court', for those like Paul Reynaud* accused of leading France unprepared into war against Germany. Among the accused were Léon Blum, Edouard Daladier*, Paul Reynaud, Air Minister Pierre Cot and General Gamelin*. Repeated and vociferous challenges to the legitimacy of the proceedings led to their suspension in April.

Ritchie, Lt General Sir Neil (1897–1983) On 26 November 1941, Ritchie was given command of the British 8th Army, replacing Sir Alan Cunningham* in the midst of the major Crusader* offensive against Rommel's* forces in Libya. He had been Assistant Chief of Staff to General Auchinleck* in Cairo and had little experience of combat command, but was appointed as the executor of his chief's determination to continue the faltering offensive. His tenure was not a great success. Following defeat at Gazala* and the fall of Tobruk* in June 1942, his army was in disorderly retreat when General Auchinleck took over personal command in the field. Ritchie's planned full-scale defence of Mersa Matruh* was then abandoned in favour of a further withdrawal to El Alamein*. In 1944 Ritchie returned to combat as a corps commander in Northwest Europe*.

River Plate, Battle of See Admiral Graf Spee.

ROA (Russkaya Osvoboditelnaya Armiya) The Russian Liberation Army, organized in Germany in November 1944 by Lt General Andrei Vlassov*. It was envisaged as the potential core of a free Soviet Army under a non-communist Russian government, and approaches were made to anti-communist groups in the Ukraine and other eastern European countries. But the opposition of Berlin, as well as the difficulties of establishing relations with other national groups in wartime, made such a movement practically impossible. The ROA's only major independent military action was in Prague* in 1945. ROA forces who surrendered to US Army forces were mostly returned to Russia.

Roatta, Lt General Mario (1887–1968) Italian staff officer who became military attaché in Berlin in 1939, and Chief of the Italian General Staff in March 1941. Roatta commanded the Italian 2nd Army during the Balkan* campaign, and was Chief of Staff when Mussolini was overthrown in July 1943. His association with Fascism resulted in his dismissal in November 1943 and his trial by an Italian court in 1945, though he escaped before the sentence of life imprisonment was passed on him. The sentence was overturned by appeal in 1948.

Rockets Rocket development was taken up in Germany during the 1920s and other powers began experimenting in the 1930s with rocket-powered warheads as anti-tank or anti-aircraft weapons. They were generally very inaccurate and only blanket fire was thought to be effective. The first multiple rocket projector to reach combat service was the Soviet Katyusha: used against German forces from July 1941, it fired a bank of 16 warheads to a range of some 6,500 yards. The German Nebelwerfer followed, a six-barrelled weapon with slightly longer range; it was used on the Eastern Front* in late 1942. The success of these weapons prompted both armies to introduce larger and more powerful versions, although German rocket development concentrated on the V-1* and V-2* missiles along with a number of less successful projects. British, US and Japanese forces also used rockets for land bombardment, and with limited success for anti-aircraft* defence on land or sea. Rockets were too inaccurate to be an effective naval weapon but an increasing number of fighter aircraft were fitted with wing-mounted rockets for anti-submarine* or ground-attack operations. The Red Air Force*, which was largely committed to army support work, made particularly extensive use of air-to-ground rockets. See also Hollow-charge Weapons.

Rodney, HMS See Nelson, HMS.

Rokossovsky, Marshal Konstantin K. (1896–1968) Highly regarded Soviet front commander, he was conscripted into the Tsarist Army at the outbreak of WW1 and imprisoned during the Stalinist purges of 1937–8 but was reinstated as a corps commander in the Kiev* Military District under General Zhukov* in the spring of 1940. After the German invasion of Russia (see Eastern Front), Rokossovsky fought under Zhukov first at Kiev and then in the Battle for Moscow* in December 1941, where he commanded the 16th Army with distinction. Transferred to Stalingrad*, Rokossovsky directed the decisive breakthrough on that front which led to the encirclement of Paulus's* 6th Army, and accepted the German general's surrender. He later commanded the Central Front* during the Battle of Kursk* and the 1st Belorussian Front which pushed the German centre forces across the Polish frontier, taking Lublin* and Brest-Litovsk in 1944, although his advance was halted in July, and held up for six months outside Warsaw*. His otherwise impressive record bears the stigma of events in Warsaw, where the Soviet armies encouraged and then failed to support the local uprising, brutally crushed by German forces in a barbarous

campaign costing some 300,000 civilian lives. After the reorganization of Soviet forces for the final offensive launched at the start of 1945, Rokossovsky led the 2nd Belorussian Front in the drive north to Danzig*. After the war, Rokossovsky went to Poland* where he served as Minister of National Defence.

Roma See Littorio.

Rome Following the Allied invasion of Italy* in September 1943 and the broadcast of the Italian capitulation* to the Allies, German forces under General Student* in the Rome area made a preliminary attack on the Italian General Headquarters at Monterotondo. The Italian commanders responded with an immediate withdrawal to Tivoli, leaving the capital in the hands of the Germans. Against Hitler's specific order, however, a capitulation agreement suggested by German Field Marshal Kesselring* offered the five Italian divisions in the area the option of going home rather than fighting for the capital. Further, Kesselring undertook to declare Rome an open city, occupied only by police units to guard communications. The Italians agreed and dispersed.

On 4 June 1944, 5th Army divisions under US General Mark Clark* entered the city after a bitter struggle to breach the German defensive positions on the Gustav Line*, south of the Liri Valley and Rome. Ignoring Allied C-in-C Alexander's* orders to cut the escape routes of the German 10th Army withdrawing from the Gustav Line, General Clark's forces at Anzio* turned the axis of his advance towards Rome, thereby allowing Kesselring's forces to withdraw and retrench. Thus, the capture of the Italian capital was won at the expense of extending the struggle for Italy.

Rommel, Field Marshal Erwin (1891–1944) Outstanding German field commander, adored by the German public and respected by the Allies for his many spectacular successes. Although ultimately never tested at High Command level, his rise to prominence was meteoric. He had a distinguished infantry career in WW1 but was a relatively obscure military instructor when Hitler made him commander of his personal headquarters on the outbreak of WW2. After the campaign in Poland*, Rommel asked for, and was given, a panzer division (the 7th 'Ghost' Division) for the 1940 Western Offensive*. The crossing of the Meuse and the subsequent drive to the Channel established him as a bold and inspiring armoured leader, and early in 1941 he was named commander of the Afrika Korps* – two mechanized divisions sent to aid the Italians in Libya (see Egypt).

Lt General Rommel quickly made his name as an armoured strategist in North Africa, where conditions were well suited to his fast-moving and aggressive tactical approach. Ignoring instructions to prepare a defensive campaign in Tripolitania, Rommel went immediately onto the offensive, bewildering British commanders with the pace and variety of his manoeuvres, and driving them back to the Egyptian border within two weeks of his opening attack on 31 March. Over the next 18 months he retained the upper hand over ever-growing British forces in the desert, consistently upsetting the 8th Army's cautious approach by a combination of superbly organized defences and bold armoured thrusts deep beyond the front line.

Regarded as a 'clean' fighter (prisoners were generally well treated in North Africa) Rommel was viewed with awed respect by the British. Churchill described him as a great general, while Auchinleck* went to the trouble of officially discouraging the idea that he was more than mortal. Certainly Rommel led a charmed life in the desert, usually driving his troops hard from the front and several times narrowly avoiding capture in forward positions. In Germany his elevation to hero status was encouraged by Hitler, who saw in him no political ambition, and after the capture of Tobruk* in June 1942, Rommel was made a field marshal.

Even at the height of his success, Rommel was not without his critics. Senior officers in the German Army* did not share his vision of an armoured sweep through the Middle East, and were dismayed by his unpredictability. Relations between the Afrika Korps and its direct control, the Italian High Command, were exacerbated by Rommel's roughshod disregard of Italian interests and his habit of sacrificing Italian infantry. Rommel has since been accused of fatally overextending his resources and supply lines in the Desert War*, but bearing in mind that enormous British reinforcements in North Africa were by no means matched by the Axis, modern commentators agree that extreme boldness represented his only hope of decisive victory.

When forced to retreat by the overwhelming strength of the 8th Army in late 1942, Rommel's reputation with the dictators declined rapidly, although the extrication of his army to Tunisia* was itself a considerable achievement. Rommel was not at first given overall command of Axis forces in Tunisia, and his characteristically aggressive campaign was diluted by disagreements with von Arnim* and Kesselring* over choice of targets. By the time he was given full control he had become convinced that North Africa should be evacuated, but this view found no favour with Hitler and Rommel – by now a sick man – was recalled from Africa in March 1943.

Rommel's faith in Hitler was badly shaken by the Führer's refusal to contemplate strategic withdrawal in Africa, and was further undermined by conditions as he found them in Germany during his convalescence. He nevertheless accepted command of Army Group B in January 1944, charged with defending France from the expected Allied invasion (see Northwest Europe). Rommel's overall commander Rundstedt disagreed with his planned concentration of defence on the coastline and his armoured effort was again diluted when the assault came. Shortly afterwards both commanders urged Hitler to withdraw from the unequal struggle in France, but to no effect. On 17 July Rommel's staff car was strafed by a British fighter and he suffered a fractured skull. He was in hospital when the abortive attempt was made on Hitler's life (see July Bomb Plot), but his frequent contacts with the plotters became known to the Führer and he was given the option of standing trial or taking poison. He poisoned himself on 14 October. Rommel was given a state funeral and his death ascribed to his earlier wounds.

Roosevelt, Franklin Delano (1882–1945) Wartime American leader and thirty-second president of the United States. Born into a prominent New York family, Roosevelt attended Harvard and Columbia University Law School at the turn of the century. In 1910 he entered political life as New York State Senator for the Hudson River District, and within three years he had been appointed Assistant Secretary to the Navy in the Wilson Administration. In 1920, his political ambitions well advanced, he stood as running mate to the unsuccessful Democratic candidate, James Cox. In the following year, Roosevelt suffered a severe attack of polio which left him partially paralysed. Not until 1928 was he sufficiently recovered to re-enter politics, gaining the important governorship of New York.

As Democratic candidate in the presidential election of 1932, F.D.R. campaigned and won on a New Deal platform designed to revive the economy. He was to be re-elected in 1936, 1940 and 1944.

During the 1930s US naval power was fundamental to the preservation of American Pacific interests in the face of Japanese military expansion. Although the US Navy* was a force to be reckoned with, events in Europe in 1940 not only prevented Dutch, French and many British forces from defending their own Far East interests but increased the pressure on the US to defend her Atlantic* seaboard (see Introduction). Roosevelt's avowed policy of flexible neutrality in foreign affairs, never

sufficient to contain an increasingly expansionist Japanese foreign policy, was rendered impractical by what the President saw as the necessity to aid Britain on one side of the world and contain Japan on the other. At this time, in 1940, the US Army* was still a small peacetime force and its air corps had not yet been unified to form the USAAF*. Roosevelt energetically set in motion an unprecedented expansion of all arms of the military.

Meanwhile, Great Britain alone was engaged in a European war which, if lost, would leave Germany dominant on the European continent and in the Atlantic. The powerful isolationist lobby in the US preferred to see this as a strictly European problem posing no threat to American interests (see Neutrality, US). Unable to support Britain with an open declaration of war, Roosevelt now embarked on a campaign of the utmost political duplicity. In 1940, he fought and won the presidential campaign on a platform which promised to keep the United States out of the European war. It is inconceivable that he believed it possible. Within months of his election he had secured the passage through Congress of the Lend-Lease* legislation, which harnessed the US economy to the long-term support of the European Allies.

The issue of peace or war was decided by the Japanese attack on Pearl Harbor* on 7 December 1941. American isolationism disappeared overnight and opposition to supporting Britain dissolved with Adolf Hitler's* precipitous declaration of war on the US.

What might have seemed to Americans as the simple pursuit of a war until victory, however, was decidedly not. The Atlantic Charter*, a joint declaration of global intent signed by Churchill* and Roosevelt in August 1941, had embraced a world view which divided the globe in terms of democracies and tyrannies. Similar principles formed the basis of US war aims until 1945, and were fundamental to the eventual formation of the United Nations. Yet the war had already joined the US and the Soviet

Union as allies, and over the next four years the realities of global alliance forced Roosevelt to repeatedly compromise the Charter's well-meaning manifesto for good against evil.

From June 1941, when Germany invaded the Soviet Union, Roosevelt assumed an international role as one of the leaders of an alliance against Hitler that encompassed vastly different interpretations of the conflict. With Winston Churchill, the President shared a common language, broadly similar democratic political antecedents, and (initially at least) some personal regard. None of these advantages existed in his relationship with Stalin, but Roosevelt was soon forced to recognize that each leader was battling for a different version of the peace, based primarily on the post-war ambitions of their own countries.

Nevertheless, he maintained his commitment to the prime aim of defeating Germany in the face of increasing pressure (particularly from the Navy) to concentrate resources against Japan. Roosevelt ensured that Britain's war in Africa and the Allied invasions of Europe were supplied by the full weight of US industry and included a large US military contingent. Despite vast ideological differences with the Russians, the USSR was furnished with huge quantities of war supplies by British Arctic* convoys and via the land route through Persia*.

Perhaps because he saw the role of the United States as a defender of democracy and the democracies, not as a prop to the threatened British and French empires, Roosevelt came to believe that he had more to be wary of from Churchill than from Stalin in planning the shape of the post-war world. In the major Allied conferences* at Tehran and Yalta, he acted in the belief that it was only the exclusion of the Soviet Union before the war that had created the political paranoia from which the Russian leadership appeared to suffer. He believed he could treat Stalin as he might a wayward American politician, and neutralize him by bringing him into the fold. The political

arrangements of post-war Europe proved that he could not.

At home he presided over a massive growth in the American economy and the recruitment of American armies unequalled either before or since. It was Roosevelt's decision to establish the Manhattan Project, although it fell to his successor, Truman*, to decide where and when to use the atomic bomb*. Roosevelt died in April 1945 after winning an unprecedented fourth term as president. His contribution to the salvation of the West is incalculable. His commitment to the support of democracy has never been questioned and, although his judgement in geopolitical matters can be criticized, he was supremely efficient at marshalling the vast resources of the US to its defence.

Rosenberg, Alfred (1893–1946) An early Nazi anti-Semitic ideologue, he came from Russian Estonia to Munich after the Russian Revolution to write for extreme nationalist and anti-Semitic publications. Rosenberg joined the early Nazi Party* and was given a Party rather than a national post in 1933. In 1940 he set up a task force to collect and loot art treasures from conquered Europe, and in 1941 became Minister for the occupied eastern territories. He was arrested by the British in 1945 and included among major defendants at the Nuremberg Trials*, found guilty of crimes committed in eastern Europe, and hanged.

Rostock, Bombing of See Strategic Bombing Offensive.

Rostov Russian city on the River Don, known as the 'Gateway to the Caucasus'* and the site, in November 1941, of the first major Soviet victory since the German invasion in June 1941 (see Eastern Front; Maps 28 and 30). Although the turn in the weather slowed the advance of German Field Marshal Rundstedt's* armies, already exhausted by the campaign in the Ukraine*, Rostov was taken by a direct attack by Kleist's* armoured divisions on 21 November. Nevertheless, a counter-attack by elements of the Soviet 9th and 37th Armies under Timoshenko* ousted Rundstedt's forces. The significance of the German defeat at Rostov was the indication it provided of the overstretching of German forces. Rundstedt's defeat at Rostov was a clear demonstration of Hitler's strategic error in deciding to halt his direct central advance on Moscow in August in order to detach forces to clear the Ukraine and the Caucasus in the south. As a result, pressure was relieved on the Moscow front at a critical moment, and Rundstedt, ordered not to withdraw, felt it necessary to resign over the issue.

In July 1942, German forces again attacked Rostov and took the city on 23 July, in the build-up to the major engagement at Stalingrad*. Several Russian field commanders were executed on Stalin's orders following the defeat. But after the Russian victory at Stalingrad, Soviet forces again recaptured the city in February 1943, narrowly missing the opportunity to trap the 1st Panzer Army retreating from the Caucasus with the rest of Army Group A.

Rote Kapelle See Resistance: Germany.

Roundup Code-name for various cross-Channel attack plans, and in particular the projected assault on the Continent with a 1943 target date. It was superseded by Overlord*.

Royal Navy The British naval forces were the largest in the world in 1939, despite ground lost during the inter-war years to the US Navy* and the Japanese Navy*. They were built around a total strength of 15 capital ships, 15 heavy cruisers and 46 light cruisers. The partly self-imposed limitations of the Washington and London Naval Treaties, as well as the severe economic restraints of the Depression era, meant that many of these ships were distinctly elderly. Only about half had been modernized, and even they were seriously deficient in horizontal armour (for protection against modern, long-range shell-fire) and were less prepared for anti-aircraft* defence than their foreign contemporaries. New ships were immediately ordered when the treaties expired in 1936, but none were ready when the war started.

In the field of naval aviation Britain stood a poor third behind the USA and Japan. Although the Royal Navy had pioneered the construction of aircraft carriers and possessed seven at the outbreak of the war, it had lost control of its aircraft, aircrew and land bases during 1918–37 to the independent RAF*. Relations between the services were harmonious by international standards, but the application of air force priorities had resulted in poor naval aircraft and relatively primitive operating techniques (see Fleet Air Arm). The British aircraft carrier was not elevated to the capital status accorded it by the Pacific powers, and was seen as an important support for fleet actions rather than as their main offensive weapon, a view encouraged by the shorter distances and lack of other carriers in the potential European war zones.

The newer components of a force of 118 destroyers* were to be used for fleet protection while older ships were intended for convoy* escort. In addition, 54 specialized escort ships were in service, with many more escort corvettes* on order. Britain possessed a large and varied collection of smaller craft and auxiliaries for laying or sweeping mines*, anti-aircraft, anti-submarine* and supply work. The submarines* in service were of similar quality and quantity to their German counterparts but their role was comparatively uncertain.

The Royal Navy's greatest assets were the quality of its personnel, the seaworthiness of its ships and the soundness of its administrative structure. Once the new, better protected warships ordered under the pre-war rearmament programme were ready, and full radar* became operational on most units, the military qualities of its ships were able to match the tactical skill and aggression that earned its seamen a fighting reputation equalled only by the Japanese.

When the war started the Royal Navy's main striking force was stationed at Scapa Flow, off the north coast of Scotland. From there it could menace both the North Atlantic and the North Sea, although the anchorage was vulnerable to German submarine attack at the very beginning of the war, and the battleship *Royal Oak** was torpedoed there. A force of battleships and cruisers was based at Portsmouth on the southwest coast of England, with a smaller one stationed at the mouth of the River Humber to the east. The major overseas fleet was in the Mediterranean* and included a carrier and a battleship along with many smaller units. Squadrons of cruisers and destroyers were based in the North and South Atlantic, the West Indies, the United States, the East Indies and China* – the latter also being given submarines.

The Royal Navy's basic strategy at the start of the war was to blockade Germany from the North Sea and to protect Britain's vital ocean trade routes. At first this worked well enough, and ships were recalled from the Far East to join the blockade, but from 1940 the Royal Navy was forced onto the defensive. The German invasion of Norway*, well within range of the Home Fleet, demonstrated the importance of air power in dictating naval operations. New German bases in the fjords compelled the British to keep powerful warships in the area. The fall of France* was catastrophic, extending the German Navy's* commerce war far into the Atlantic* and exposing Britain's quantitative weakness in anti-submarine weapons. At the same time Italy entered the war, leaving the Royal Navy outnumbered and without an ally in the Mediterranean. Capital ships were sent to Gibraltar*, but the imminent prospect of a German invasion of Britain meant that potential convoy escorts for the Atlantic were held in home waters.

The wastage of Allied merchant shipping in the Atlantic ran at critical levels throughout 1941–2, as US aid and new anti-submarine weapons reached the Navy in insufficient numbers to offset the sophisticated commerce raiding tactics of the German Navy. The Mediterranean fleet, under Admiral Cunningham*, established a decisive superiority over the larger Italian Navy*, but suffered heavy losses to the Luftwaffe*, particularly during the evacuation of Crete*. With Malta* and British forces in the Desert War* to supply and the Italian fleet still in being, the Navy fought a convoy* war in the theatre until late 1942.

From September 1941, the Royal Navy's responsibilities included the protection of Arctic* convoys carrying aid to Russia. In the Far East, a naval task force (Force Z*) sent to relieve Singapore was destroyed by Japanese aircraft, an object lesson in the vulnerability of capital ships to air attack. Against these difficulties, the German surface fleet had at least been kept subdued and its finest unit, the *Bismarck**, destroyed.

The material benefits to the Royal Navy of US entry into the war began to be fully felt after the Torch* landings in Northwest Africa of November 1942. The armada of British and American warships that protected the invasion convoys, along with a reversal of air supremacy in the Mediterranean, enabled an almost completely successful blockade of the North African coast in 1943, which went some way towards ensuring the eventual collapse of Axis forces in Tunisia*. From mid-1943, Allied warships had almost complete control of the Mediterranean. The Royal Navy's main role in the theatre for the remainder of the war was the coastal support of Allied ground operations. The Italian fleet surrendered in September, after which the main threat to Allied shipping was the steadily diminishing Luftwaffe.

In May 1943, the German Navy's threat to Britain's trade routes diminished with the withdrawal of U-boats from attacks on convoys. The vast increase in escort shipping and aircraft that enabled Allied victory in the Battle of the Atlantic was the product of American industry, but their efficient tactical application was perfected by the Royal Navy (see Horton, Admiral Sir Max). The German surface fleet remained elusive but ineffectual. Most of its losses were to bombing but, after Royal Navy units sank the *Scharnhorst** at the end of the year, surface actions between the two navies were restricted to British coastal waters, where motor torpedo boats* and other small craft fought a constant running battle.

The Royal Navy was again primarily concerned with coastal bombardment during the last phases of the war in Europe, while major warships were prepared for transfer to the Far East to fulfil Churchill's offer of increased naval commitment to the Pacific War* (see Conferences). Most British naval involvement in the Far East since 1942 had been restricted to the Indian Ocean, supporting the prolonged ground campaign in Burma* and protecting convoys. From late 1944, however, Royal Navy battleships and carriers joined the US Navy's offensives against Japan. The most effective warships built in Britain during the war were heavily armoured aircraft carriers like the *Illustrious**, which proved more able to survive Kamikaze* attack than their US counterparts. Other wartime production was concentrated on smaller craft – escorts, coastal forces and submarines – and only those battleships and cruisers well advanced in 1940 were completed by 1945.

Beset by material and labour shortages, the Royal Navy was fortunate in having the world's most efficient producer as its major ally. A chronic naval manpower shortage was partly alleviated by the contribution of the British Commonwealth and Empire. The Royal Australian and Canadian Navies manned several cruisers and destroyers throughout the war, as did the New Zealand Division of the Royal Navy (which became an independent Navy in October 1941). In 1941 the Canadians formed an Escort Force, which relieved the Royal Navy of responsibility for convoys in the Western Atlantic. The Royal Navy lost 9.3 per cent of its personnel in action during WW2, the highest proportion among the British services, and 427 ships, excluding small boats and rescue craft. See also Atlantic, Battle of the; Mediterranean Sea.

Royal Oak, HMS British battleship of the *Royal Sovereign* Class, completed in 1916. Had war not intervened these veteran units, smaller and slower than the preceding *Queen Elizabeth** Class, would have been withdrawn on completion of the new *King George V* Class, and they were not thought worth the expense of pre-war modernization. Ill-equipped to deal with air attack or long-range surface engagement, they were retained in the hope of numerically containing the German and Italian battlefleets in the first years of the war.

On 14 October 1939, the *Royal Oak* was torpedoed by the *U-47* inside Scapa Flow anchorage and exploded with the loss of 833 lives. The rest of the Class were luckier. The *Royal Sovereign* served in the Atlantic* and the Mediterranean* (on escort duty) until 1942, when she joined the Far East Fleet. In 1944 she was handed over to the Red Navy*, and survived the war as the *Archangelsk*. The *Resolution* – badly damaged by shore batteries at Dakar* in 1940 – and the *Revenge* were retired in mid-1944. The *Ramillies* participated in operations against Madagascar in 1942 at the end of which she was badly damaged by a Japanese midget submarine*. She was retained until the end of 1944 to support the Allied Normandy* and Anvil/Dragoon* landings.

BRIEF DATA (*Royal Oak*, 1939) Displacement: 29,500 tons; Dimensions: o/a lgth – 620' 9", b – 102' 6"; Speed: 22 knots; Armament: 8 × 15" gun (4 × 2), 12 × 6" gun, 8 × 4" AA gun, 16 × 2pdr AA, 1 aircraft.

Ruhr, The Valley of the Ruhr River, the centre of the German iron and steel industry, which was a principal target of Allied ground and air operations, and in particular of RAF* Bomber Command under Air Marshal Harris*. See Strategic Bombing Offensive; Area Bombing; Dambusters.

Rumania A proclaimed neutral state in 1914, Rumania had been induced to enter WW1 on the Allied side by promises of considerable territorial gains. Under the terms of the Versailles Treaty, Rumania was thus granted Transylvania, Bessarabia and much of the Hungarian plain. Although a member of the 'Little Entente' of central European states that sought to maintain the status quo in central Europe and the Balkans*, Rumania's foreign policy, like those of other signatories Yugoslavia* and Czechoslovakia*, was increasingly tied to the Nazi regime in Germany during the 30s and a strong Fascist party, the Iron Guard, emerged during this period. Although Rumania ceded much of its territorial gains to the Soviet Union, Hungary* and Bulgaria* in 1940, it remained allied to the Axis* (which coveted its vast oilfields at Ploesti*) through the Tripartite Pact* and under Antonescu*, participated in the German invasion of Russia (see Eastern Front), suffering heavy casualties (see Crimea). When Russian forces reached the Rumanian frontiers in the spring of 1944, King Michael I* of Rumania declared war on Germany (25 August). A predominantly communist government was installed under Soviet supervision in November 1945. Rumania was declared a People's Republic in 1947. See Map 26.

Rumyantsev Code-name for the Russian counter-offensive at Kursk*.

Rundstedt, Field Marshal Karl Rudolf (1875–1953) German forces commander for the Western Offensive* in 1940 and for the German defence against the Allied landings in Normandy* in 1944 (see Northwest Europe, Invasion of). Promoted general in 1927 after service in France and Turkey during WW1, Rundstedt had become one of the most senior German Army commanders when he was sent into retirement in 1938 following Hitler's purge of the High Command (see Fritsch, Werner von). Recalled for the planning of the invasion of Poland*, he was given command of Army Group South in August 1939 and later led the invasion of France in 1940 with command of Army Group A. It was on his orders that German armoured forces halted behind Dunkirk*, ostensibly to allow the Luftwaffe the finishing blow to British forces withdrawing there, thus providing the opportunity for the British evacuation.

Promoted field marshal after the victory in France and named commander of Army Group South for the invasion of Russia (see Eastern Front), Rundstedt was dismissed in November 1941 for directing his forces in a tactical retreat at Rostov*, and later reinstated to command Army Group West in France in March 1942. Remaining in command to face the Allied invasion of Normandy in June 1944, Rundstedt was again removed from command for suggesting that the war should be ended, briefly arrested in the purges following the July Bomb Plot* against Hitler's life, and then had to preside over the Court of Honour established to discuss the involvement of Army officers in the Bomb Plot. He was again reinstated to direct the retreat to the Rhine* and the last Ardennes offensive in December (see Battle of the Bulge). He retired from active service in March 1945. A British prisoner of war, he was generally regarded by them as a professional who had maintained some distance from the excesses of other Third Reich generals, although there were discussions about bringing him to trial for war crimes after the war.

Russell Islands Two large islands (Pavuvu and Banika) lying 35 miles northwest of Cape Esperance on Guadalcanal*, they were taken by the US 43rd Infantry Division on 21 February 1943 immediately after Guadalcanal was secured by American forces. Banika became a US supply base and Pavuvu the 'home' of the US 1st Marine

Division, from which it staged its landings at Peleliu (see Palau) and Okinawa*.

Russia, German invasion of, 1941 See Eastern Front.

Russo-Finnish War, 1939 Secret negotiations between the Soviet Union and Finland* had begun at Helsinki in 1938 to discuss joint security measures against a third power. Following the partition of Poland* by Russia and Germany, Russia was anxious to safeguard its Baltic* flank, and in particular Leningrad*, from the possibility of an attack by Germany. On 14 October, Russia formulated its demands for an agreement proposing an exchange of territory including the cession to Russia of the Karelian isthmus and the Rybachi peninsula and several islands as well as leasing the port of Hango for 30 years. Though territorial compensation for these losses was considerable, it was nevertheless difficult for the Finns to accept all the Soviet terms. Despite the refusal of diplomatic support from the other European powers, Finland refused to accede to the Russian demand for Hango, and the agreement faltered. On 28 October, Stalin* broke off the non-aggression pact signed with Finland in 1932 and Red Army* units attacked Finland on a broad front, with its main drive on the Karelian isthmus.

The check imposed by Marshal Mannerheim's* Finnish troops to the Russian advance at Kemijarvi, Suomussalmi and most spectacularly in the south at the Mannerheim Line on the Karelian isthmus, was a great surprise to observers and a costly embarrassment for the Russians. While plans were prepared to send an expeditionary force from Britain and France, Hitler occupied Norway* to forestall the sudden danger of an Allied move into Scandinavia. The Red Army's strength and efficiency was cast in great doubt at this stage, with enormous casualties suffered during the six-week battle to breach the Line. It was not until 1 March 1940 that the massively reinforced Northwest Front* (7th and 13th Armies) under General Meretsokov*, again with heavy losses, broke through the Finnish defences, with heavy air and naval support, to capture Viipuri.

A second assault by Soviet forces across the frozen Gulf of Finland forced a passage behind the Finnish lines that put the eventual outcome beyond doubt. Unable to wait for the arrival of the promised expeditionary force and refused aid by the rest of Europe, Finland was forced to send a delegation to seek peace terms from the Russians that were finally accepted on 13 March.

The demonstrated weaknesses of the Red Army in fighting the Finns were registered by everyone including Stalin himself. The war had cost the Russians 200,000 men, nearly 700 planes and 1,600 tanks*, against Finnish losses of 25,000. The result was miscalculation – by Germany, Britain and Stalin* – of the fighting potential of the Red Army. The real problems, the purge of officers that had removed so many experienced commanders and the poor logistical support, which had failed to forecast the supply needs of the Russian forces, were at this point largely ignored. A year later, Hitler's optimism about the possibility of destroying the Red Army must have been based on this evidence. Although a radical reorganization of the Red Army was set in motion following the Russo-Finnish war, the process was still incomplete when Hitler invaded in 1941 (see Eastern Front).

Russo-German Non-aggression Pact, August 1939 The pact between Nazi Germany and communist Russia that appeared to guarantee the Soviet Union's security on her western and Baltic front and enabled Hitler to exercise Nazi aggression by risking war with Britain and France on the issue of the invasion of Poland*. The diplomatic background to the signing of the pact lies in the effective collapse of the Versailles security system in Europe during the 1930s (see Introduction). Aware of Russia's enormous weaknesses and of the growing threat of Japan in the Far East, Stalin* watched Hitler's moves to rearm Germany, and the success of his armed diplomacy in the Rhineland (1936), Austria (1938) and the Sudetenland (1939), with increasing nervousness (see Anschluss and Czechoslovakia).

Nevertheless, Stalin's suspicion of *all* the imperialist powers, combined with marked Anglo-French reluctance to accommodate Soviet political and strategic interests in eastern Europe or to commit themselves to multilateral treaties with the Soviet Union, lent increasing weight to the idea of some rapprochement with Germany.

The crude Anglo-French assumption that Russia's ideological incompatibility with Nazi Germany guaranteed Stalin's *de-facto* partnership with the West without formal alliance was not shared by Stalin, who noted the widespread conservative sympathy for German expansionism in Britain and France, as well as the diplomatic efforts both countries made to appease Fascist Italy. Employing his own style of appeasement with some skill, Stalin observed the development of the 'crisis' over Hitler's demand for the Danzig Corridor*, and signalled his preparedness to treat with Hitler by replacing Litvinov* with Molotov* in May 1939. While low-level negotiations with British and French delegates during the spring had only served to underline the Western Allies unpreparedness to commit themselves to joint action with the Soviet Union against possible Nazi aggression (and the Polish government remained unprepared to open negotiations with the Soviet Union), Stalin was increasingly in a position to place leverage on Hitler, as the diplomatic crisis over Poland developed.

In August, with the German attack on Poland set for 1 September, it became imperative for Hitler to have an assurance of non-interference from Russia. German Foreign Minister Ribbentrop's* overtures to Molotov on 15 August stressed the urgency of negotiations but were at first stalled by Moscow. Requesting a trade and credit agreement as a preliminary to the signing of the pact, Molotov also referred to the need for a special 'protocol' with regard to mutual interests in the Baltic states (Latvia*, Lithuania* and Estonia*). Impatient with the progress of negotiations, Hitler intervened on 20 August with a personal telegram to Stalin. The resulting meeting in Moscow on 23 August, between Ribbentrop, Molotov and Stalin produced an agreement within 24 hours. The details of the pact were: (*i*) neither party would attack the other; (*ii*) should one become the object of belligerent action by a third power, the other would not lend its support to the third power; (*iii*) neither Germany nor Russia would join any grouping of powers that aimed directly or indirectly at the other party. The secret protocol requested by Russia (still unacknowledged by Soviet historians) provided for the effective partitioning of eastern Europe. In the Baltic, the northern frontier of Lithuania provided the dividing line between Soviet and German spheres of interest. In Poland, the approximate boundary followed the Narew, Vistula and San river lines. Despite the undoubted triumph of diplomacy for Russia, the signing of the pact contributed directly to the exercise of Nazi aggression, to which the Soviet Union in its turn would fall victim in June 1941.

Russo-Japanese Border Conflict, 1938–9

A series of incidents triggered by tension between the Soviet Union and Japan resulting from Japanese incursions into Russian Far Eastern territory and Manchuria* during the 1930s. Since 1931, when the Kwantung Army* had occupied Manchuria, their exploitation of the fighting in China* between the nationalist Kuomintang* and the Chinese communists under Mao Tsetung* to extend their military presence in China had been seen as a serious threat to Russia's Far Eastern territories. When in July 1938, Japanese regiments attacked Soviet positions at Lake Khassan near Vladivostock (see Map 10) and began construction of fortifications, the newly created Russian Independent Eastern Army counter-attacked, forcing the Japanese back into Manchuria. A renewed assault was also beaten off by the superior Soviet forces, but further Japanese border raids in the vicinity of Nomonhan in January and February 1939 reopened hostilities.

In May, the Kwantung Army attacked Mongolian border troops and Russia sent in massive reinforcements under General Zhukov*. In August, the Japanese 6th Army was decisively beaten at the Battle of the Khalkin-Gol, suffering some 50,000 casualties. As a result of this defeat (and perhaps the conclusion of the Russo-German Pact* on 22 August), Japan signed an armistice with Russia that established a joint border commission, and ended further hostilities in Soviet Far Eastern territory until 1945. See also Russo-Japanese Neutrality Pact; Pacific War.

Russo-Japanese Neutrality Pact Signed in Moscow on 13 April 1941 after protracted negotiations over Japan's intentions regarding China*, the pact provided for neutrality in the case of an attack by a third power, for the maintenance of peaceful and friendly relations, and for the guarantee of Manchukuo* and Mongolia's territorial integrity. The term of the agreement was initially for five years. For both powers the pact offered short-term security. Japanese Foreign Minister Matsuoka* had decided that a Soviet –German war was unlikely and was keen to resolve the situation in the north before Japan's plans for expansion southward were launched (see Pacific War). On the Soviet side, increasing nervousness about the possibility of an attack from the west made Stalin anxious to secure at least an interim agreement with Japan. Despite the agreement, Japan continued to maintain the Kwantung Army* in Manchuria* (Manchukuo). The collapse of Germany in 1945, however, enabled the Soviet Union to eliminate the Japanese threat by denouncing the pact and, with the Allies' approval, declaring war on Japan

on 9 August and invading Manchuria. See also Russo-Japanese Border Conflict, 1938–9.

Rybalko, General Pavel S. (1894–1948) Russian Marshal of the Tank Corps under Marshal Konev* during the last stages of the war, Rybalko saw active service for the first time in 1942 when he was appointed to command the 5th Tank Army, and later the 3rd Tank Army. He participated in operations at the Don and the Dnieper*, as well as in Poland*, Germany and Czechoslovakia*.

Ryujo Japanese light aircraft carrier completed in 1931. The *Ryujo* benefitted from design experience gained in the building of the *Agaki** and *Kaga**, but was found, like many other Japanese Navy* warships, to be top-heavy at sea. During 1934–5 this was rectified by the removal of four of her 12 5-inch guns, the fitting of a heavier keel, and improvements to her superstructure, which were later incorporated into the design of the *Soryu** Class. The *Ryujo* saw a great deal of action during the first months of the Pacific War*, launching the first strike on the Philippines* on 8 December 1941. She took part in the Battle of Midway* and in the Battle of the Eastern Solomons*, where she was sunk by aircraft from the USS *Saratoga** on 24 August 1942.
BRIEF DATA (1941) Displacement: 10,600 tons; Dimensions: o/a lgth – 590' 4", b – 68' 3"; Speed: 29 knots; Armament: 8 × 5" AA gun (4 × 2), 4 × 25mm AA gun, 24 × 13mm AA gun, 48 aircraft.

Ryukyu Islands (Nansei Shoto) Island chain stretching between the Japanese home islands and Formosa*, of which Okinawa* is the most important (see Map 10). The Ryukyus appeared to be of vital strategic importance to the US in the later stages of the war as forward and air bases for a possible attack on Japan, and Okinawa was taken by American forces in the last and one of the most costly battles of the

Pacific War*, fought between April and June 1945. The victory finally proved unnecessary, however. The dropping of two atomic bombs* on Hiroshima* and Nagasaki* brought the war to an end while Okinawa was still being developed.

S

Safford, Captain Laurence (1894–1973) Assistant director of American naval communications for cryptographic research during WW2, Safford was one of the pioneers of the work on Japanese codes and worked alongside Colonel William Friedman* in Operation Magic*.

St Lô Fortressed French town in Normandy on the Vire River, it was an important communications centre (as well as German 84th Corps HQ) and one of the first objectives of invading US forces moving out from their beachheads after the Allied cross-Channel invasion of Normandy*, 6 June 1944. In July, St Lô was the springboard for the break-out of Allied forces under Bradley*. See Northwest Europe, Allied Invasion of; Cobra, Operation; Map 36.

St Nazaire French port situated on the Atlantic coast 150 miles south of Brest*. St Nazaire was a U-boat base from 1940 and also possessed a dry dock capable of mooring the giant German battleships *Bismarck** and *Tirpitz** should they venture into the Atlantic. On the night of 27–8 March 1942, a spectacular combined operations attack by Allied forces disabled the dry dock by ramming its gates with the old flushdeck destroyer* *Campbeltown*, which was packed with 3 tons of explosives timed to detonate later. Meanwhile commandos* destroyed the winding gear which operated the gates and attempted unsuccessfully to attack the U-boat pens. A motor torpedo boat* destroyed the lock gates of the St Nazaire basin, again using delayed action

fuses. Both major explosions took place the following day, killing a number of senior German officers who were inspecting the wreck of the *Campbeltown*. The operation, known as Chariot, was a success inasmuch as the *Tirpitz* was unable to contemplate a trip to the Atlantic, but British losses were high, partly because a heavy air-raid planned as a distraction failed to take place in bad weather, leaving all of the port's guns free to concentrate on the small raiding party.

Saipan Island of the Mariana* group in the Central Pacific, of great strategic importance to the American Central Pacific advance during 1944, Saipan was the first objective of the American amphibious* offensive against the Marianas, designed to provide bases from which to launch B-29s* to bomb mainland Japan (see Strategic Bombing Offensive) and secure advance bases for operations against the Philippines* (see Map 11). The landings, by US 2nd and 4th Marine Divisions of General Holland Smith's* 5th Amphibious Corps (with 27th Infantry Division in reserve), were made on the extreme south of the island under heavy Japanese fire on 15 June 1944. By nightfall there were 20,000 troops ashore.

While the Marines advanced north, suffering heavy casualties from Japanese fire from the controlling heights near Garapan, the 27th Infantry Division landed in the south to take Isley airfield. On the night of 16–17 June a heavy Japanese counter-attack led by tanks* failed to stop the Marines' advance, though progress was slow and the cost in casualties was very high. Army and marine units then joined up, on the 23rd, for a drive towards the northern tip at Marpi Point to clear the island of Lt General Saito's 30,000-strong garrison, though interservice rivalry contributed to the dismissal of the army commander, Major General Ralph Smith, for failing to maintain a sufficiently speedy advance.

As the American forces pressed the attack to the very north of Saipan, Saito and Admiral Nagumo*, the titular head of the garrison, committed suicide as a final encouragement to their troops, who then launched suicidal counter-attacks which left less than 1,000 survivors. In a ghastly footnote to the battle, the civilian population of Saipan also committed mass suicide on 9 July. Egged on by Japanese soldiers, whole families threw themselves off the cliffs at Marpi Point. An estimated 22,000 civilians died in this way. US casualties were also high, with 3,500 killed and many more thousands injured. The loss of Saipan, combined with the Japanese defeat at the Battle of the Philippine Sea* on 19 June, provided a grim foretaste of the even more bitter losses that were to follow for the Japanese Pacific forces. The most immediate result, however, was the fall of Premier Tojo's* government in Japan, forced to resign on 18 July. See also Tinian; Guam.

Salerno Port on the western ankle of Italy, south of the main port city of Naples, it was the site of landings by the US 5th Army under General Mark Clark* on 9 September at the start of the Allied invasion of Italy* (see Map 34). Code-named Avalanche, the landing was conducted by a joint British and American naval force, and formed part of a three-pronged invasion plan co-ordinated with landings by Montgomery's* 8th Army at Reggio de Calabria* and Taranto*. The choice of Salerno as the 5th Army landing site was both predictable and cautious, though the need for land-based air cover was a crucial factor in planning. Chosen in preference to a port

on the Adriatic coast that could not be provided with Allied air cover from its Sicilian bases, the landing lacked surprise and was very nearly disastrous.

Despite objections raised at the time by the naval task force commander, US Vice Admiral Hewitt, General Clark relied on tactical surprise for the success of the landings, with the result that heavy casualties were suffered, both on the beachheads and during six days of heavy fighting inland against German counter-attacks. Both the US 6th Corps under General Dawley and the British 10th Corps under General McCreery* suffered heavily under raining fire and counter-attacks by German tank groups (29th Panzergrenadier and 16th Panzer Divisions). An urgent request from General Clark for preparations for an evacuation of part of his forces brought a swift reinforcement of the troops on shore and additional support from US 82nd Airborne Division. Even more effective was the heavy naval bombardment of German advance positions by Allied battleships, cruisers and destroyers that halted and finally turned back the German attacking forces.

Contact was finally made with forward units of the British 8th Army moving up from their landing sites at Reggio di Calabria on 15 September. Apart from heavy casualties on shore, the naval force also suffered damage from the first attacks by German FX1400 radio-guided gliding bombs, which disabled the British cruiser *Uganda* and the American cruiser *Savannah* as well as heavily damaging the British battleship *Warspite** (see Guided Bombs).

Salmon, HMS This small British S Class submarine* enjoyed a remarkably successful blockade patrol in December 1939, sinking the German U-36 from a range of 5,000 yards and a few days later torpedoing and severely disabling the cruisers *Leipzig** and *Nürnberg**.
BRIEF DATA (S Class) Displacement: 640 tons (surface); Dimensions: o/a lgth – 208′ 9″, b – 24′; Speed: 13.75 knots (8.5 sub-

merged); Armament: 1 × 3″ gun, 1 × 0.5″ mg, 6 × 21″ TT.

Salo Republic Title of the Italian socialist republic established by Mussolini* at Gargagno on Lake Garda, following the coup which deposed and arrested him, and his dramatic rescue by German airborne* troops from Gran Sasso. Mussolini's republic was effectively a German puppet, supported by the Germans who also denied it power.

Samar Island, Battle of See Leyte Gulf, Battle of.

Sangro River Italian river north of Termoli, it formed part of a natural line of defence (with the Rapido and Garigliano rivers and the Apennines) against the Allied advance up the mainland of Italy*, just forward of the main German defensive line, the Gustav Line*. German forces withdrew to the Sangro at the beginning of November 1943. An assault by Montgomery's* 8th Army (with five divisions and two armoured brigades) against a much smaller German force was launched on 28 November. Two days later bridgeheads had been established across the Sangro, but the offensive was checked at Moro and then at Ortona and finally halted at Riccio in late December, called off by General Montgomery in the face of heavy losses and exhausted troops. See Italian Campaign; Map 34.

Santa Cruz, The Battle of One of a series of important naval engagements in which Japanese and American forces contested control of the seas around Guadalcanal* during the second half of 1942. Both forces had the advantage of land-based air cover. The Japanese force under Vice Admiral Kondo* (with Vice Admiral Nagumo* in charge of the carrier striking force) included an advance force of one carrier, *Junyo* (see Hiyo), two battleships, five cruisers and 14 destroyers*, with a strike force (under Nagumo) of two carriers, *Shokaku** and *Zuikaku*, a light carrier and battleship, five cruisers and 15 destroyers. The US force involved in the action was Rear Admiral Kinkaid's* Carrier Task Force 61 which included Admiral Murray's Task Force 17. The Japanese objective was to drive US forces from Guadalcanal.*

Admiral Yamamoto's* orders directed Kondo and Nagumo to hold the approaches to Guadalcanal and be ready to occupy Henderson Field*, which was to be recaptured by General Maruyama's ground forces on Guadalcanal. Confused by an incorrect report on the status of the battle at Guadalcanal, the Japanese fleet was forced to change course as it arrived northwest of the Santa Cruz islands early on 25 October, having been spotted by sea planes from the US carrier *Enterprise**.

With orders to patrol north of the Santa Cruz islands before turning south to intercept any Japanese force approaching Guadalcanal, Rear Admiral Kinkaid's Carrier Task Force 61, supported by Rear Admiral Murray's Carrier Task Force 17, turned northwards to chase the Japanese fleet, sending aircraft ahead to intercept them. Although the carrier aircraft failed to find the Japanese fleet that day, both carrier groups were sighted by their respective scout planes on the following day, 26 October, and air strikes were launched from both fleets, causing damage to the Japanese light carrier *Zuiho** and the American carrier *Hornet**. A second American strike seriously damaged the *Shokaku* and damaged the cruiser *Chikuma*. The Japanese second wave then struck at the *Enterprise* Task Force, though it inflicted mostly minor damage. The *Enterprise* recovered the majority of her aircraft and withdrew, leaving the badly damaged *Hornet* still on fire, to be sunk by Japanese destroyers before withdrawing. Although a tactical victory for the Japanese, the Battle of Santa Cruz sacrificed many pilots and aircraft and failed to halt the tide of hard-won American successes on Guadalcanal.

Saratoga, USS American aircraft carrier and Class. This famous ship and her sister the *Lexington** were the second and third carriers completed for the US Navy*. Their appearance in 1927 enabled the Americans to develop air-sea tactics and techniques that were to prove invaluable during WW2. Converted on the incomplete hulls of battlecruisers cancelled under the Washington Naval Treaty, they could sustain a high speed and had a large aircraft capacity, remaining the world's largest carriers when WW2 began.

The *Saratoga* survived a particularly arduous combat career. Sent from San Diego to the Pacific after the attack on Pearl Harbor*, she was torpedoed off Hawaii on 11 January 1942. While under repair she missed the Battles of the Coral Sea* and Midway*, but returned to action in time to be torpedoed again off Guadalcanal* on 31 August. By November she was fit again and took part in operations against Bougainville*, Rabaul*, the Gilbert Islands* and Eniwetok*, joining the British Fleet in the Indian Ocean for a time in 1944. At Iwo Jima* on 21 February 1945, *Saratoga* was severely damaged by a Kamikaze* attack and returned to the US for repairs, taking no further part in the war. She was expended as a nuclear test target in July 1946 at Bikini Atoll.

BRIEF DATA (1941) Displacement: 33,000 tons; Dimensions: o/a lgth – 888', b – 130' (105' 6" FD); Speed: 33.25 knots; Armament: $8 \times 8''$ gun (4×2), $12 \times 5''$ AA gun, 90 aircraft.

Sardinia Once considered as a target for an Allied invasion (Operation Brimstone), after the successful conclusion of the Torch* campaigns in North Africa, the plan was dropped, following the success of the Allied invasion of Sicily*, in favour of landings on the mainland of Italy*. The threat of an Allied invasion of Sardinia was kept alive, however, by an ingenious British disinformation plan, based on the 'discovery', by German agents in Spain, of the body of a British officer carrying documents apparently relating to Allied plans for an invasion of Sardinia and the

Balkans (see Major Martin). Sardinia was captured without a shot being fired on 18 September 1943 by a token force embarked in two British torpedo boats.

Sauckel, Fritz (1894–1946) Reich Director of Labour from 1942 to 1945, by whose orders 5 million people were deported from occupied Europe to work as slaves in Germany. One of the early members of the Nazi Party*, Sauckel was given responsibility for mobilization of labour to support Speer's* armaments and munitions production programme in a Hitler decree of March 1942. Teams under his direction abducted men and women from all over Europe, including allied Italy. He was found guilty of crimes against humanity at Nuremberg* and hanged.

Savo Island, Battle of First of the series of important naval engagements that were fought off Guadalcanal* in the second half of 1942. During the night of 9 August 1942, a Japanese force under Vice Admiral Mikawa surprised an Allied cruiser force under Rear Admiral Crutchley, stationed off Savo Island to protect transports. Unaware that Admiral Fletcher's carrier force had been withdrawn, and fearing an air strike, Mikawa concentrated his fire on the Allied cruisers, hitting the Australian cruiser *Canberra** and the American *Chicago*, before illuminating the *Astoria*, *Vincennes** and *Quincy*, sinking all three ships with a final casualty total of 2,000. The Japanese force then withdrew to protect itself from counter-attack. Later referred to as the 'Battle of the Five Sitting Ducks', the engagement lasted only half an hour with a loss of four Allied cruisers and a destroyer*. Despite the disastrous outcome, the American commander, Rear Admiral Turner, later became one of the better known practitioners of amphibious* warfare.

Savoia-Marchetti SM79 Sparrowhawk (Sparviero) Disguised at first as a civilian transport, the trimotor SM79I entered the

Regia Aeronautica in late 1936 and enjoyed a successful career in the Spanish Civil War, both over land and as a torpedo-bomber. The re-engined SM79II, first delivered in October 1939, undertook both tasks with similar success in WW2. Robust and easy to handle, it performed doughtily in difficult conditions and was undeserving of the Allied scorn to which it was subjected. Production continued until early 1944, and the final version was the SM79III, which mounted an additional 20mm cannon above the pilot. About 1,200 *Sparvieros* of all types served with the *Regia Aeronautica*, and just over 100 more were exported. Most of these were slower, twin-engined SM79B versions, but the Rumanian-built SM79JR was driven by two 1,220hp Junkers engines and fought on the Eastern Front* during 1941–4.

BRIEF DATA (SM79II) Type: 4–5-man medium bomber; Engine: 3 × 1,000hp Piaggio; Max speed: 270mph; Ceiling: 23,000'; Range: 1,243m; Arms: 4 × 7.7mm mg; Bomb load: 2,200lb or 2 × 1,000lb torpedo*.

Savoia-Marchetti SM81 Bat (Pipistrello)
In service since 1935, the Bat was a military version of the SM73 airliner, and was nearing obsolescence when Italy entered the war in June 1940. Nevertheless, this versatile and serviceable utility plane saw action in every Italian theatre of war. Production ended in 1941, but the SM81 remained as a first-line night-bomber in the Eastern Mediterranean until the following year, later becoming the most numerous (although not the most efficient) Italian transport aircraft.

BRIEF DATA (SM81) Type: 5-man medium bomber/transport; Engine: 3 × 700hp Piaggio; Max speed: 211mph; Range: 930m; Arms: 6 × 7.7mm mg (typical); Bomb load: 2,200lb.

Schacht, Dr Hjalmar (1877–1970) German economist and Reichsbank President from 1929 to 1939, Schacht recruited bankers and industrialists for financial sup-

port for the Nazi Party* and, as Minister of Economics after 1933, invented financial devices to conceal the inflationary effect of rearmament. Never totally committed to the Nazi programme, he resigned his office in 1937 and was replaced by Dr Funk. Gaoled in 1944 after the July Bomb Plot*, he narrowly eluded the hangman. Acquitted of war crimes at Nuremberg*, Schacht resumed an international banking career, becoming adviser to Colonel Nasser of Egypt in the 1950s.

Scharnhorst In 1933, with the support of the new militarist government, the German Navy* decided to expand its fourth projected 'pocket battleship' (already surpassed by developments abroad) into a 26,000-ton battlecruiser, the *Scharnhorst* (see Deutschland). A second unit, the *Gneisenau* * was ordered the following year. The two ships were built in secret as long as they remained in violation of the shipbuilding limits imposed at Versailles. By the time both were launched in late 1936, the Anglo-German Naval Treaty* had rendered these limits meaningless, but the new battlecruisers nevertheless greatly exceeded their announced displacement.

Built for speed, battlecruisers traditionally carried heavy armament but were virtually without armour protection. The *Scharnhorst* and her sister reversed this (largely discredited) trend by retaining 11-inch main turrets, which were within Versailles limits and were already in production for the 'pocket battleships'. Instead, weight was invested in increased protection and an unprecedented concentration of heavy anti-aircraft* batteries. Their designers were under no illusions concerning the frailty of this armament against true battleships and provision was made for up-gunning at a later date. Large long-range diesel engines could not be developed in time for the battlecruisers and so they used conventional steam-turbine propulsion, which nevertheless gave them an impressive 10,000-mile cruising radius.

Both ships operated successfully together

as Atlantic* raiders at the beginning of WW2, sinking the British armed merchant cruiser* *Rawalpindi* on 23 November 1939. Both also took part in the Norwegian campaign of 1940, and destroyed the carrier *Glorious** off Vestfjord on 9 June. They remained in tandem in early 1941 and sank 22 ships (115,622 tons) in the Atlantic* before docking at Brest* in February, where they remained for a year and were the targets of repeated bombing attacks. On 12 February 1942, the two ships fled Brest with the *Prinz Eugen** in broad daylight and, protected by the Luftwaffe*, ran the gauntlet of the English Channel to reach Wilhelmshaven in Germany virtually undamaged by the end of the day. The success of the 'Channel Dash', officially named Operation Cerberus, was a blow to the prestige and self-esteem of Britain's surprised coastal defences, but the potential German surface threat to Atlantic shipping was greatly reduced by what was in effect a retreat.

After minor repairs, the *Scharnhorst* was sent to Norway to join the *Tirpitz** as a powerful but largely inert threat to Allied Arctic convoys*. Amid growing pressure from the High Command for action by the surface fleet, these two ships bombarded Spitzbergen in September 1943, and in late December the *Scharnhorst* launched an attack on Arctic convoys JW55B and RA55A. British naval intelligence had decoded her orders and on 26 December the *Scharnhorst* found herself in single-handed combat with a powerful Royal Navy* force (including the battleship *Duke of York** and a strong complement of cruisers and destroyers*) off Norway's North Cape. Repeatedly hit by gunfire and torpedoes, she finally went down to a torpedo* from the cruiser *Jamaica* with the loss of 1,864 lives. There were 36 survivors.

BRIEF DATA (1939) Displacement: 31,800 tons; Dimensions: o/a lgth – 771', b – 100'; Speed: 32 knots; Armament: 9 × 11" gun (3 × 3), 12 × 5.9" gun, 14 × 4.1" AA gun, 16 × 37mm AA gun, 6 × 21" TT, 4 aircraft.

Schirach, Baldur von (1907–74) Head of the Hitlerjugend (Hitler Youth) from 1933 to 1940 and subsequently Gauleiter (District leader) of Vienna. He escaped capture for a time at the end of the war but was finally arrested and charged along with the major war criminals at Nuremberg*. He was sentenced to 20 years imprisonment.

Schörner, Field Marshal Ferdinand (1892 –1973) Hitler's last appointment as field marshal and the man chosen to command the Army in Hitler's last political testament, made only ten days before his suicide. Schörner's non-aristocratic background and ostentatious acceptance of Nazism won him rapid promotion during the war. In March 1944 he was sent to the Eastern Front* and given command of Army Group South in the Ukraine* and later Army Group North and Army Group Centre in January 1945, by then a largely fictitious army. He accepted his final promotion and command of the non-existent army before fleeing to escape the US Army. Handed over by them to the Russians, he was imprisoned for ten years. He was subsequently sentenced to a further term by a West German court, on charges of harsh disciplinarianism, which had included the summary execution of German soldiers.

Schräge Musik Literally translated as 'slant music', the German term for jazz, this was a fixed twin 30mm cannon installation which fired obliquely upwards and was fitted behind the crew compartment of Luftwaffe* night-fighters. The Japanese employed a similar device from 1944. *Schräge Musik* was highly successful against RAF* bombers over Europe and remained a mystery to the Allies until after the war.

Scoones, General Sir Geoffrey (1893– 1975) British commander who directed Allied forces in Burma* through bitter fighting in the campaign to recapture Indian and Burmese territory from Japanese forces during 1944. A member of the General Staff at Allied headquarters in India be-

428 . *SD (Sicherheitsdienst)*

tween 1939 and 1941, Scoones was next appointed Director of Military Operations and Intelligence. Transferring in July 1942 to command the 4th Corps at Imphal* in Assam, near the Burmese border, Scoones came under the command of US General Stilwell* in the newly organized Southeast Asia Command (SEAC) at the end of 1943. In January 1944, a planned offensive by 4th Corps across the Chindwin River* into central Burma had to be hurriedly revised when intelligence indicated an imminent Japanese offensive there. In a courageous plan to defuse the assault, Scoones (with the aid of his superior General Slim*) made a dramatic and dangerous strategic withdrawal of his forces to the Imphal plain, where they made a convincing stand against Mutaguchi's 15th Army. After five weeks of dogged and ferocious fighting during March and April 1944, the 15th Army was forced to withdraw from lack of supplies. This success made a firm contribution to the later, decisive Allied victory in the Imphal offensive. In December, Scoones was appointed GOC (General Officer Commanding) Central Command, India and was knighted for his services, along with Generals Christison, Slim and Stopford*.

SD (Sicherheitsdienst) The Nazi Party's own intelligence and security body, created by Himmler* and led by Heydrich* from August 1931. The SD was kept distinct from the uniformed SS* and the Party's foreign intelligence unit which was under Party ideologue Alfred Rosenberg* and was itself brought under SD control in 1934. After Adolf Hitler* became German Chancellor in 1933, the SD's role expanded significantly – enemies of the Party were now enemies of the State – and in 1936 Heydrich took over the Gestapo* as well as the SD, formalizing his empire in 1939 in a new structure, the Reich Security Administration (RHSA). Working without uniforms in a wide variety of intelligence and security functions, the SD was involved in arms negotiations in Argentina, plotting

unsuccessful revolts in Rumania and Iraq, kidnapping (British agent Payne-Best was taken from the Netherlands) and killing. The SD headed the Einsatzgruppen* – the special action, or extermination, squads operating in eastern Europe and on the Eastern Front*.

After Heydrich's assassination in 1942, Himmler ran the RHSA and SD until January 1943, when he handed them over to Kaltenbrunner*. In June 1944, Kaltenbrunner's organization finally absorbed its rival, the Abwehr* (military intelligence, formally under Canaris*). The SD was declared a criminal organization at the Nuremberg* Trials (as was the Gestapo) and members were liable to prosecution.

SEAC – Southeast Asia Command Allied command for the Burma*–Malaya*–Thailand*–Singapore* theatre, with headquarters in India, established on 15 November 1943 under supreme command of Admiral Mountbatten*. US General Stilwell* was chosen as Deputy Supreme Commander. See also CBI; China, Campaigns in.

Sealion (Seelöwe) Code-name for the German invasion plan against England called for in Hitler's* much-quoted War Directive No. 16, issued on 16 July 1940, which cited Britain's stubbornness in refusing to recognize 'her hopeless military situation' following the fall of France as the reason for mounting 'an invasion . . . to eliminate the English homeland as a base for the prosecution of the war . . .' Vital to the invasion plan, however, were several essential preconditions which included the destruction of British air power, the sweeping of mine-free corridors across the Channel which was to be blocked by German mines at either end, and the diversion of the Royal Navy* to other theatres. Two variants of the invasion plan were discussed during the summer of 1940 that projected a first-wave assault by nine divisions on a stretch of coastline between Worthing and Dover, to be followed up with a second wave of seven divisions allocated to hold a lodgement area while the third-wave force was assembled and transported.

Despite Luftwaffe* commander Göring's unequivocal assurance to Hitler of the first condition, however, the final planning for the invasion awaited the outcome of the Battle of Britain* and strong evidence suggests that, by August, Hitler had already secretly decided on an alternative invasion of the Soviet Union. Historians have since commented on Hitler's apparent disinterest in finalizing plans for Sealion. Certainly it is arguable that Hitler continued to hope for a negotiated settlement with Britain, which enjoyed a curiously elevated status within Hitler's world-view.

But the successive defeats exacted by the RAF* on the Luftwaffe during September were finally to decide the question. The invasion fleet, which had assembled from throughout northern Europe, had been harried by RAF attacks and was dispersed in the same month. Increasingly obsessed with Barbarossa, the plan for war on his Eastern Front*, Hitler issued orders in October that preparations for Sealion were to be limited to sustaining diplomatic and military pressure on Britain. When in January it became clear that Luftwaffe air superiority was unattainable, all preparations were finally discontinued.

Self-propelled Artillery This is a general term covering artillery pieces mounted on tracked, half-tracked or wheeled vehicle chassis. Self-propelled weapons were built in large numbers by all the main belligerents in WW2 and can broadly be divided into assault guns, for the close support of infantry, and tank destroyers.

The idea of the assault gun had been an integral part of German planning for armoured warfare, and the Sturmgeschütz III series of armoured infantry support vehicles first appeared in 1940. Armed with a short-barrelled, limited traverse 75mm gun, they were built onto the chassis of the Panzerkampfwagen III* battle tank, and over 10,000 had been produced by the end

of the war. The use of tank chassis for gun carriages became standard practice in the German Army*, production outstripping that of more complex tanks as the need for defensively deployed armoured vehicles mushroomed in 1944–5. From 1942, 105mm howitzers were fitted to PzKpfw III chassis and other German close-support weapons included two 150mm self-propelled howitzers, built onto the Panzer-kampfwagen IV* (Brummbar) and a composite PzKpfw III/IV (Hummel) chassis. Self-propelled tank destroyers were also used by the German Army. The 75mm Marder III and Hetzer guns greatly prolonged the useful life of the Czech PzKpfw 38t light tank; heavier 75mm and 88mm guns used more modern chassis. The 88mm Jagdpanther and 128mm Jagdtiger were built in conjunction with their Panther* and Tiger* battle tank counterparts.

Similar in concept and performance to the German assault guns, the Semovente series of (usually) 75mm SP guns were the most valuable Italian fighting vehicles of the war. Based on the chassis of the M13/40* medium tank series, the Semovente replaced all Italian tanks in production by early 1943, and almost 900 were eventually built.

The Allies were quick to follow the German lead in self-propelled weapons. After early experiments with wheeled and half-track* vehicles, American policy was generally to standardize on tank chassis. The 105mm M7 Howitzer Gun Carriage – a close support weapon based on the Grant/M3* medium tank – entered service in 1942 and remained in action throughout the war. The 76mm M18 and 90mm M36 Gun Motor Carriage were tank destroyers based on the Sherman*. Less heavily armoured but more nimble than their German counterparts, these American guns were fitted with full turrets (fully traversable in later models) which gave them an offensive combat value close to that of a battle tank, but made them more difficult to conceal in defensive positions.

British and Commonwealth forces in the

Desert War* were at first equipped with the hastily designed Bishop 25-pounder, which used a Valentine* tank chassis. This was replaced by the US M7 (known as the Priest to British forces), and later the Sexton 25-pounder on a Ram* tank chassis became the principal British SP support weapon. A further Valentine-based British gun – the rearward-firing Archer – saw action in Europe from 1944.

The Soviet Union produced large numbers of reliable and powerful SP weapons on all their main tank chassis in both anti-tank and infantry-support versions. The SU85 and SU122 were 85mm high-velocity and 122mm close-support weapons mounted on the chassis of the T34* tank. This pattern was repeated on the KV* (SU122 and 152) and IS* (ISU 122 and 152) chassis, late models giving a performance comparable with battle tanks and often being deployed integrally within heavy tank regiments. Japanese SP artillery was largely restricted to a 75mm anti-tank gun and a 150mm support howitzer, both based on the ubiquitous Chi-Ha* medium tank, but both with their guns mounted in a very limited traverse. See also Anti-tank Artillery, Field Artillery.

Semovente See Self-propelled Artillery.

Sendai Name ship of the third and final Class of light cruisers built by Japan in the early 1920s. Six units were laid down in 1922, but only the *Sendai*, *Jintsu* and *Naka* were completed, the rest being cancelled after the signing of the Washington Naval Treaty in 1922. They were modernized in 1940 and employed as flagships for destroyer flotillas at the start of the Pacific War*, receiving urgently needed extra anti-aircraft guns after the Battle of Midway*. None of the Class survived the war. The *Jintsu* was destroyed at the Battle of Kolombangara* in July 1943, a notable victim of radar*-controlled cruiser gunfire. American cruisers also accounted for the *Sendai* at Empress Augusta Bay, off Bougainville* in November, and the *Naka* was a victim of the US Navy's* carrier raid on Truk* of 17 February 1944.
BRIEF DATA (*Sendai*, 1941) Displacement: 5,195 tons; Dimensions: o/a lgth 534', b – 46' 6"; Speed: 35.25 knots; Armament: 7×5.5" gun (7×1), 2×3" AA gun, 8×24" TT, 1 aircraft.

Senger und Etterlin, Fridolin Rudolf von (1891–1963) Highly educated German tank* commander (a Rhodes scholar), Senger served in WW1 and was head of the German delegation at the meeting of the Franco-Italian armistice commission in 1940. In 1942 he was sent to the Eastern Front* in command of a panzer division and was put in command of the Italian forces in Sicily* a year later. He later commanded the 14th Panzer Corps, which fought at Monte Cassino*.

Serov, General Ivan A. (1908–) Prominent member of the Russian secret police, he was responsible for the brutal 'sovietization' of the Baltic states of Estonia*, Latvia* and Lithuania* after the signing of the Russo-German Pact* in September 1939. In 1940 he headed the NKVD* in the Ukraine*. He was promoted Deputy Minister of State Security after the German invasion in June 1941. During 1943–4, Serov oversaw the mass deportations of racial minorities from the Soviet spheres of influence. In 1945, Serov became Deputy Supreme Commander of Soviet forces in Germany.

Servizio Informazione Militare (SIM) Italian Army* intelligence organization responsible for gathering information on foreign armed forces and for counter-espionage ahead of Italy's own military operations. During WW2, SIM provided detailed information on the forces of France, Greece, Yugoslavia, Russia and the British in Africa that was either ignored or misinterpreted by the Italian High Command (*Comando Supremo*). In 1940 SIM operated alongside autonomous naval and air force intelligence groups, and an independent special services organization also performed espionage work. Repeated wartime restructuring failed to bring effective co-ordination between these networks.

Sevastpol See Crimea. See also Eastern Front.

Sexton See Self-propelled Artillery.

Seyss-Inquart, Arthur. (1892–1946) Viennese lawyer, covert supporter of the Austrian Nazi Party and advocate of the Anschluss*, he acted as a German 'Fifth Column' from his position as Austrian state councillor, not emerging publicly as a Nazi supporter until appointed Minister of the Interior by Chancellor Schuschnigg in 1938 on Hitler's* insistence. After the Anschluss, Seyss-Inquart served as Chancellor of the now renamed state of 'Ostmark'. His last service to the Nazi state was as Reichskommissar for the Netherlands, where he earned the hatred of the Dutch peoples for the brutality of his regime. Repenting after 1945 the 'fearful excesses' of Nazism, he was nevertheless sentenced to death and hanged at Nuremberg* on 16 October 1946. See Austria; the Netherlands.

SHAEF Acronym for Supreme Headquarters Allied Expeditionary Force, the Allied force which fought in western Europe from the Normandy* invasion in June 1944 until Germany's surrender. SHAEF succeeded COSSAC, which had conducted the early planning of Overlord. SHAEF moved to Granville in France on 1 September 1944 (and then to Versailles on the 20th with an advanced HQ at Reims) when General Eisenhower* took direct command of Allied forces in France. It was from the advance HQ at Reims that the Allies accepted the German surrender on 7 May 1945. See Northwest Europe, Allied Invasion of.

Shaposhnikov, Marshal Boris (1882–1945) Highly regarded Russian military theorist and member of Stavka*, he was thought to have been Stalin's chief military adviser before the war, and as such one of the few high-ranking officers to survive the purges of 1937–8. Appointed Chief of the General Staff in 1937, Shaposhnikov was forced to resign, apparently due to ill health, in 1940 (though this may have resulted from a disagreement with Stalin over defensive strategy). Reappointed to the post in July 1941 following the German invasion, his recommendations of withdrawal were unwelcome to Stalin. In November, he was replaced by General Vasilevsky*, and ill health now prevented him from further active involvement in the war, although he remained as Commandant of the Voroshilov Military Academy until his death.

Sheffield, HMS British cruiser, completed in 1937 as the third of the Royal Navy's* Town Class vessels. The 1930 London Naval Treaty had imposed an international moratorium on heavy cruisers armed with larger than 6.1-inch guns. Japan and the United States had responded with their *Mogami** and *Brooklyn** Classes, which were essentially 10,000-ton designs armed with multiple 6-inch weapons, retaining a marked superiority over the less expensive light cruisers to which Britain was committed. Revised Royal Navy plans then called for a similar British Class to enable the delivery of a massed broadside from relatively close quarters. Five were completed in 1937 and a further three (with improved protection and firing systems) in 1938–9. A final group of two modified and slightly enlarged units were handed over to the Royal Navy in the summer of 1939.

The entire Class saw strenuous war service, mostly with the fleet in Arctic or Mediterranean* waters, and the *Sheffield* was one of the most famous and active fighting ships of the war. In 1939–40 she was with the Home Fleet and fought in actions off Norway* before her transfer to the Mediterranean. As part of the Force H* (with the *Renown** and the *Ark Royal**),

she was involved in bombardment operations against Italian positions and in the
interception of the *Bismarck** in May 1941.
Later she distinguished herself in the Barents Sea protecting Arctic convoys*
against German Navy* 'pocket battleships'
(see Deutschland), and took part in the
sinking of the *Scharnhorst** in December
1943. Barely scratched throughout, the
Sheffield survived to be broken up in 1967.

None of the other nine ships escaped
damage and four, the *Southampton, Gloucester, Manchester* and *Edinburgh*, were sunk.
The final unit of the Class, the *Belfast*,
survives as a museum ship in the Pool of
London. Small-scale modifications were
made regularly to wartime British cruisers.
Typically the *Sheffield* in 1945 had no aircraft catapult or 0.5-inch machine-guns,
but carried multiple 40mm and 20mm
anti-aircraft* cannon along with extensive
gunnery control and early warning radar*.
BRIEF DATA (1939) Displacement: 9,100
tons; Dimensions: o/a lgth – 591' 6", b –
64' 2"; Speed: 32 knots; Armament: 12 ×
6" gun (4 × 3), 8 × 4" AA gun, 8 × 2pdr
AA gun, 8 × 0.5" AA gun, 6 × 21" TT, 2
aircraft.

Sherman (M4) Tank The most produced,
most used and most important US tank of
the war. Inferior to the best German and
Soviet tanks in armament and protection,
it was supreme in terms of reliability, serviceability and cost-effectiveness. It was
employed by every Allied army on every
battlefront and in every possible role.

As soon as the design of the Grant/
M3* was finalized in March 1941, work
commenced in the US on a new medium
tank, to be armed with a 75mm gun in a
fully traversable turret. In September, a
design based on the M3 chassis but with a
completely new cast or welded hull was
adopted as the Sherman/M4, and it was
phased into production from March 1942.
By the end of the year, the Sherman had
fully supplanted its predecessor at a dozen
automobile or tank factories, and it went
on to become the most prolific tank in

history, production reaching 49,320 before
it ended in 1946.

The Sherman was developed in dozens of
subtypes, often occasioned by the perpetual
shortage of its standard 353hp Wright-built
Continental engines, which were needed
for aircraft. Construction details were
varied according to the mass-production
requirements of individual factories. All
later models mounted a long-barrelled
76mm weapon, and the tank's suspension
was redesigned and improved in late 1944.

Although relatively palatial in terms of
crew comfort, early Shermans suffered a
reputation as 'Ronsons' because of their
incendiary tendencies. Protection was
given to later models (given the suffix 'wet')
in the form of ammunition stowage racks
surrounded by water jackets. Over 4,600
close-support versions of the M4 and M4A3
were built, mounting a powerful 105mm
howitzer, and the British developed a conversion ('Firefly') armed with a 17-pounder
gun which took part in the invasion of
Normandy*. By April 1943, the Duplex
Drive flotation device had been successfully
fitted to the M4, and Sherman DDs were
used in Normandy and the Rhine* crossing.
The outstanding ruggedness and simplicity
of the Sherman encouraged its use for a
number of other special-purpose vehicles*
and self-propelled* guns. First used operationally at El Alamein* in 1942, the Sherman was the mainstay of Allied offensive
operations in Africa and Europe for the rest
of the war and remained in widespread
service all around the world for decades
afterwards.
BRIEF DATA (M4A3 Sherman IV) Type:
5-man medium tank; Engine: 500hp petrol;
Max speed: 26mph; Range: 100m; Arms:
1 × 75mm gun, 1 × 12.7mm mg, 2 ×
7.62mm mg, 1 × 2" smoke mortar; Armour: max 100mm.

Shigemitsu, Mamoru (1881–1957) Experienced Japanese diplomat and politician
who served on the 'surrender cabinet' and
in Prince Higashikuni's first post-war cabinet. Japan's ambassador to China from

1931 to 1933, Shigemitsu served as Vice Minister of Foreign Affairs from 1933 to 1936 and then went to Moscow as ambassador until 1938, when he was appointed ambassador to London. Shigemitsu's undoubtedly sincere attempts to reassure British political leaders that Japan's alliance with Germany in the Tripartite Pact* did not represent a threat of war between Japan and the Allies were totally undermined by the Japanese attack on Pearl Harbor*, which pre-empted further discussion. Two days after the attack, Shigemitsu was sent to Nanking* as ambassador to the puppet regime led by Wang Ching-wei*.

Shigemitsu was a firm opponent of the colonization of China*. Preferring a 'good neighbour' policy based on mutual co-operation rather than military occupation, he sought to persuade Japanese political leaders to abolish the unequal treaties with Nanking and offer economic aid without restrictions. His influence with the Japanese Premier Tojo* led to his recall to Tokyo to become Foreign Minister in April 1943, where he continued to campaign for political freedom for the nations of East Asia.

Following Japan's surrender, which Shigemitsu signed as head of the delegation aboard the USS *Missouri** on 2 September 1945, he was convicted of war crimes by the International Military Tribunal* for the Far East and served seven years imprisonment. Shigemitsu later served again as Foreign Minister (1954–6) and helped to negotiate Japan's entry into the United Nations.

Shinano The *Shinano* was conceived as a Japanese super-battleship of the *Yamato** Class but was converted as an aircraft carrier while under construction. Like the *Taiho**, she had an armoured flight deck and was otherwise well protected although her hangar was open-sided. She was intended for use as a giant floating air-base and carried relatively few aircraft of her own, leaving space for supply and repair facilities. Completed in November 1944,

she was promptly sunk by the US submarine *Archerfish* while *en route* from Yokosuka to another naval yard for final fitting out.
BRIEF DATA (1944) Displacement: 64,800 tons; Dimensions: o/a lgth – 872' 9″, b – 119' 3″ (131' 3″ FD); Speed: 27 knots; Armament: 16 × 5″ AA gun (8 × 2), 145 × 25mm AA gun, 47 aircraft.

Shingle Code-name for the Allied amphibious* landing at Anzio* in Italy*, begun on 22 January 1944.

Shinyo Formerly the German liner *Scharnhorst*, the *Shinyo* was rebuilt as a carrier for the Japanese Navy* and commissioned in December 1943. Well armed, but without protective armour, she was sunk by the US submarine *Spadefish* in the South Yellow Sea on 17 December 1944.

A similar conversion was carried out on the smaller Japanese liner, *Argentine Maru*, which was completed as the carrier *Kaiyo* in November 1943. With a capacity of 24 aircraft she was used mostly as a transport and for pilot training. *Kaiyo* was sunk by aircraft in Beppu Bay in August 1945.
BRIEF DATA (*Shinyo*, 1943) Displacement: 17,500 tons; Dimensions: o/a lgth – 650' 6″, b – 84' 9″ (80' FD); Speed: 22 knots; Armament: 8 × 5″ DP gun, 42 × 25mm AA gun, 33 aircraft.

Sho-Go (Victory Operation) Code-name for a Japanese plan, developed after the fall of the Marianas* to American forces in 1944, to defend the inner Empire against invasion. Since Japanese intelligence services* had little clear idea of American intentions, Sho-Go projected four area plans of which one only was to be designated the 'theatre of decisive battle', once the American invasion objective was revealed. Sho-Go called for the concentration of all available Japanese forces in this decisive theatre to counter-attack. Thus Sho-Ichi-Go (Sho No. 1) provided for the defence of the Philippines*, which the Japanese rightly considered the most likely target; Sho-Ni-Go covered the defence of the Ryukyus* and Formosa*; Sho-San-Go provided for the defence of the Japanese home islands; Sho-Yon-Go projected the defence of the Kuriles and Hokkaido. When it became clear that the Philippines were to be the next target for invasion, Imperial Headquarters called Sho-Ichi-Go into effect. It was the general plan under which the Battle of Leyte Gulf* was fought.

Shoho Japanese light aircraft carrier and Class, which also included the *Zuiho**. The *Shoho* was originally launched in 1935 as the proposed high-speed oiler *Tsurugisaki*, but had been designed for easy conversion as a submarine tender or aircraft carrier in order to circumvent international treaty limitations on those types. It was as a submarine tender that she was completed in 1938, but at the beginning of 1941 she was recalled for conversion as an aircraft carrier. On joining the Combined Fleet a year later, she was deployed with the 4th Carrier Division and renamed, but was sunk at the Battle of the Coral Sea* on 8 May 1942. Like other converted Japanese carriers, she had no armour protection.
BRIEF DATA (1942) Displacement: 11,262 tons; Dimensions: o/a lgth – 712', b – 59' (75' 6" FD); Speed: 28 knots; Armament: 8 × 5" AA gun (4 × 2), 15 × 25mm AA gun, 30 aircraft.

Shokaku Japanese aircraft carrier and Class. The *Shokaku* and her sister the *Zuikaku* were the first Japanese carriers planned after the lapse of the naval limitation treaties of the 1920s and 30s. They were launched in 1939 as bigger versions of the well-tried *Soryu** design, with a strengthened flight deck, a redesigned bow, higher speed and a wider operational radius.
The two ships formed the 5th Carrier Division of the Japanese Navy* in December 1941, and took part in most major Pacific War* naval engagements, missing the Battle of Midway* only because of damage and crew shortages after the Battle of the Coral Sea*. Their light anti-aircraft*

defence had been doubled by the time of the Battle of the Philippine Sea* in June 1944, in which the *Shokaku* was sunk by the US Navy* submarine *Cavalla*. After the battle, the *Zuikaku* was fitted with 180 5-inch rocket* launchers and her given additional 25mm armament. She was part of Admiral Ozawa's* lightly equipped decoy force for the Battle of Leyte Gulf*, in which she was sunk off Luzon* on 25 October 1944.
BRIEF DATA (*Shokaku*, 1941) Displacement: 25,675 tons; Dimensions: o/a lgth – 844' 9", b – 85' 4" (95' FD); Speed: 34 knots; Armament: 16 × 5" AA gun (8 × 2), 36 × 25mm AA gun, 84 aircraft.

Short Stirling The Stirling was the only British four-engined bomber of the war to be specifically designed as such, and was the first to reach service. Stirling Is made their RAF* operational debut in March 1941, and the aircraft was in the front-line of the Strategic Bombing Offensive* against Germany throughout the next two years. Although well armed and able to deliver previously unheard of loads, the bomber was not a success. Its narrow wingspan, dictated by the width of pre-war hangar doors, severely restricted the Stirling's operational ceiling and range, while its bomb-bays were divided into compartments unsuitable for the bigger bombs* then being developed. Stirlings were already proving obsolete by the time the most prolific model, the Mark III, entered service in late 1942. From the middle of 1943, they were confined to attacking fringe targets, mine-laying and radar*-jamming. Later they were retained largely as glider-tugs or transports, and the Mark IV and V versions represented a progressive conversion to purely transport duties. Before production ended in November 1945, 2,381 Stirlings were built.
BRIEF DATA (Mk III) Type: 7–8-man heavy bomber; Engine: 4 × 1,650hp Bristol Hercules; Max speed: 270mph; Ceiling: 17,000'; Range: 590m (full); Arms: 8 × 0.303" mg; Bomb load: 14,000lb.

Short Sunderland Stately, but bristling with defensive firepower, the Sunderland flying boat was RAF* Coastal Command's main front-line patrol plane for 17 years from 1938. It served throughout the war on convoy* escort and anti-submarine* operations in the North Sea, the Atlantic*, the Mediterranean* and the Indian Ocean, demonstrating remarkable powers of self-preservation. As a rescue plane, it won great fame during the evacuations of Norway*, Greece* and Crete*.

Early Sunderlands mounted 1,065hp Pegasus engines and manually operated beam guns. These guns were replaced by a turret in the Marks II and III, which were the standard wartime models, but they were restored to the more powerful Sunderland V, which joined squadrons in February 1945 and was the RAF's last production flying boat. Altogether, 739 Sunderlands were built in Britain by the Short and Blackburn companies, the last in June 1946. In addition eight Seafords, the name given to the short-lived Sunderland IV, saw brief service late in the war.

BRIEF DATA (Mk V) Type: 13-man patrol flying boat; Engine: 4 × 1,200hp Pratt and Whitney Twin Wasp; Max speed: 213mph; Ceiling: 17,900'; Range: 2,980m; Arms: 2 × 0.5" mg, 12 × 0.303" mg; Bomb load: 2,000lb.

Shtemenko, General Sergei M. (1907–76) A 1939 graduate of the Frunze Military Academy and member of the Moscow General Staff throughout the war, he was appointed Chief of Operations in May 1943. Shtemenko ended the war as Soviet Deputy Chief of the General Staff.

Sibuyan Sea, Battle of See Leyte Gulf, Battle of.

Sicily, Allied Campaign in The Allied invasion of Sicily, code-named Husky, was launched on the night of 10 July 1943. Numerically the greatest amphibious assault of the war in terms of initial assault strength, Husky involved nearly half a million men deployed in eight divisions.

The decision to invade Sicily had been taken at the Casablanca Conference* in January 1943. A compromise strategy, unaccompanied by any clear plan for its exploitation, it highlighted the fundamental differences of approach between British and American Chiefs of Staff. Strategically the British view was based on resistance to any American inclination towards an immediate attack on German forces in France, which Churchill* and the British military chiefs regarded as dangerously premature. An invasion of Sicily satisfied the more direct strategic ambitions of the US. Seen as a means to clear the Mediterranean for Allied shipping, divert German pressure from the Eastern Front* and intensify pressure on Italy to get out of the war, it was acceptable to both.

The operation was placed under the supreme command of General Eisenhower*. British General Alexander*, Eisenhower's deputy, was given direct control of ground operations as Commander of the 15th Army Group (comprising Patton's* 7th Army and Montgomery's* 8th Army), Admiral Sir Andrew Cunningham* took command of naval operations, while Air Marshal Tedder* was chosen as air commander.

The outline plan for Husky was significantly modified by changes sought by Montgomery before its final approval on 13 May, a week after the final collapse of Axis forces at Tunis in North Africa (see Tunisia). Montgomery's main alteration to the plan concentrated the Allied assault in the southeast of the island over two 40-mile strips. Though strategically justifiable, the change was characteristically overcautious. In retrospect it is arguable that had Patton's 7th Army landed, as originally planned, in the northwest of the island near the port of Palermo, the Allies would not have forfeited the opportunity to cut off the evacuation of the four German divisions from Messina, opposite the Italian mainland. Undoubtedly the subsequent campaigns in Italy* would have been much less costly.

Nevertheless, the Allied achievement in successfully planning, co-ordinating and conducting an operation of this scale must not be underestimated. In transporting and assembling the men and equipment necessary for the invasion, two huge task forces, the Eastern Naval Task Force under British Vice Admiral Ramsay* and the Western Naval Task force under American Vice Admiral H. Kent Hewitt, were assembled from units brought from Britain and the United States as well as from all over the Mediterranean*. The vastly superior Allied air cover (4,000 aircraft operational in comparison with 1,500 Axis aircraft) was so effective that most of the convoys were not even sighted as they arrived at their assembly areas east and west of Malta* during 9 July and began their final approach to Sicily. Even more significantly, the air cover enabled the huge armada to remain anchored without serious harassment while the 15th Army Group established itself ashore.

Despite the sudden onset, during the evening of 10 July, of high winds and difficult seas, the landings by the 8th Army at five points on the south-eastern tip of the island and by the US 7th Army at three beaches to the west of the British forces were remarkably successful, aided considerably by the employment of several new landing craft (see Landing Vehicle Tracked). The worst casualties of the weather were the Allied airborne units, whose assault was intended to capture key bridges and road junctions ahead of the main forces. Significant numbers of the British 1st and American 82nd Airborne divisions were dropped far from their targets – 47 out of 137 British gliders came down in the sea and American parachute troops found themselves scattered over a 50-mile-wide area.

These problems were offset, however, by the decoying effect of the weather on the dispirited Sicilian coastal defence units, who easily convinced themselves that the Allied assault would not come that night. Only one serious counter-attack,

mounted by the hastily rebuilt Hermann Göring Panzer Division, which had arrived in Sicily at the end of June, threatened seriously to halt the establishment of the American 1st Infantry Division at Gela during 11 and 12 July. Preceded by a courageous spearhead action by an Italian tank unit that broke through the American outposts, the German tanks succeeded in reaching the sand dunes above the beach at Gela before the attack was broken up by skilfully directed naval gunfire. Meanwhile the British forces, whose landing points were less exposed, were more quickly established. Within three days Augusta and Syracuse had been taken and the 8th Army had cleared the south-eastern corner of the island. On the basis of this speedy progress, Montgomery ordered a major advance for the night of 13 July to break through into the Plain of Catania, with an airborne assault on the key position at the Primasole Bridge over the Simeto River. By a coincidence the British parachute brigade landed almost simultaneously and in the same position as German airborne troops dropped behind the Axis line to reinforce it, and it was not until three days later that, having lost the position to the 1st Parachute Division, the bridge was retaken and the way opened to Catania. The delay had cost Montgomery the initiative and he was forced to shift the weight of his advance westward into the hilly interior round Mount Etna across the line of Patton's flanking advance. The change of tactic left the 7th Army temporarily stranded without a clear path of advance, but with the approval of General Alexander, General Patton drove rapidly north and west to take Palermo before turning east along the northern coast of the island towards the ultimate objective, the port of Messina. The success of the 7th Army's drive thrust it out of its subsidiary role into the spearhead of the assault. While the 8th Army was held up by the able defensive withdrawal of German forces under Field Marshal Kesselring* across mountainous terrain which favoured the retreating armies, Patton pushed on towards Messina attempting several forward amphibious assaults at Sant' Agata, Brolo and Spadafora to cut off the German withdrawal. None of these actions, however, nor the British landing at Scaletta were successful in stopping the evacuation of the Axis forces across the Messina Straits to the Italian mainland.

The effectiveness of the evacuation, which over six days brought more than 40,000 German and 60,000 Italian troops, as well as nearly 10,000 German vehicles, 47 tanks and thousands of tons of supplies to safety, did little at the time to diminish the victorious atmosphere of the US entry into Messina. On 17 August, the leading US patrol entered the city, cheerfully deriding the British troops arriving later that day as 'tourists'. With hindsight, however, it is clear that the Allied failure to capture the Axis forces at Messina was a significant lost opportunity.

There is no argument for challenging the basic success of this vast and logistically complex operation in achieving its primary objectives, though subsequent critics have suggested that its cost was never justified in terms of broad strategy. Nevertheless, the capture of Sicily made it possible to clear the Mediterranean for Allied shipping and gave the final impetus to the fall of Mussolini* and the capitulation of Italy*. On 25 July the Fascist Grand Council called for Mussolini's resignation. Less than a month later, Marshal Badoglio* began discussions with the Allies on the terms of Italy's surrender.

There is a footnote to be written on the rivalry which developed between Generals Montgomery and Patton during the Sicilian campaign. It would be difficult to find two men who spoke the same language, supposedly shared common aims and served the same profession yet who were at the same time so deeply opposed in personality and background. The rivalry that developed between them in the 'race' to Messina was reproduced and exacerbated in France a year later and made heavy demands on the

Alliance and the skills of the Supreme Commander, Dwight Eisenhower*.

Sidi Barrani See Egypt, Campaign for.

Sidi Razegh See Crusader, Operation.

Sikorski, General Wladyslaw (1881–1943) Polish general and statesman, Premier of the Polish government-in-exile* and C-in-C of Free Polish forces. A leader of the Polish nationalist movement before WW1, Sikorski served as Premier, Interior Minister and War Minister of Poland* during the 1920s. When Poland was invaded by Germany and the Soviet Union in September 1939, Sikorski was refused a command by the military regime in Warsaw under Smigdly-Rydz*, who had inherited his predecessor Pilsudski's distrust of Sikorski.

Following the collapse of Poland, however, Sikorski was named Premier of a Polish government-in-exile in Paris, where he recruited approximately 100,000 Polish troops to join Allied forces fighting in various theatres. After the fall of France in 1940, the exiled government based itself in London. From here, in June 1941, Sikorski was responsible for the negotiation of a collaboration agreement with the Soviet Union that won important concessions for Poland, including the invalidation of the Russo-German partition of Poland and an amnesty for Polish prisoners in Russia.

The granting of the amnesty, however, gave Polish General Anders* freedom to find and recruit a Polish army from the Polish POWs in Russian labour camps. Ander's investigations focused attention on the enormous number of Polish losses in Russia, and particularly on the fate of 14,500 Poles, including 8,000 Polish officers, who had been held by the Russians in three camps near Smolensk since 1939, and of whom nothing had been heard since April 1940. Sikorski's request to Churchill* for an investigation was refused even after evidence had been found to suggest that the prisoners had been murdered by the Russians (see Katyn Massacre). Stalin* exploited the instability of the situation by accusing the Polish government-in-exile of advancing Nazism by spreading anti-Russian propaganda*. In April 1943 Russia broke off relations with the exiled government. Sikorski was killed three months later, on 4 July 1943, in an air crash at Gibraltar.

Sikorsky R-4 Developed from Igor Sikorsky's VS300, demonstrated in 1939, the American R-4B became the world's first production helicopter in 1943. Altogether, 127 of the type were built and they performed reconnaissance and rescue work for both the USAAF* and the US Navy* (as the HNS-1). Improved R-5 and R-6 designs were in advanced development when the war ended.

BRIEF DATA (R-4B) Type: 2-man helicopter; Engine: 1 × 200hp Warner driving 38ft rotor; Max speed: 82mph; Range: 130m; Arms: none.

Simovic, General Dusan (1882–1962) Yugoslav soldier, politician and Serbian nationalist. In 1940 he was Chief of the Yugoslav Air Force and his headquarters at Zenum became a focus for anti-German activities in the Balkans. In February 1941 he warned the Regent, Prince Paul, against bowing to pressure from Hitler to join the Tripartite Pact*. On 27 March, two days after the Yugoslav government had signed an agreement with the Axis, Simovic led a bloodless overnight coup in Belgrade, installing King Peter II on the throne. Germany invaded on 6 April, and armed resistance collapsed in a few days. Simovic fled with the King, and became head of the exiled royal government in London, a position he resigned in 1942. In early 1945, Tito* vetoed his appointment to the proposed regency council and in May of that year Simovic returned to retirement in Yugoslavia. See Balkans, The, German invasion of.

Singapore, Fall of, 1942 Originally chosen by Admiral Jellicoe as the main base and bastion of the British Far Eastern Fleet in 1919 and commonly regarded as Britain's 'Gibraltar of the Far East', it was taken in a week by three Japanese divisions under General Yamashita*, following his lightning conquest of Malaya* in the previous two months. British expenditure (which finally reached a staggering £60 million) on the fortress at Singapore had become a focus of political debate during the 1930s. Work on its construction had stopped and restarted several times before the final completion of the Changi naval base in 1938. Despite the warning about its potential vulnerability to overland attack, through the 'back door' from Malaya* over the Johore Strait, set out in a report sent to British Chiefs of Staff by a local army commander in 1937, Changi's defence remained based on massive emplacements of 15-inch guns firing armour-piercing shells, on the assumption of a seaborne rather than land assault. Moreover, even in the autumn of 1941, Singapore still awaited the arrival of a Royal Navy battle fleet, without which, as Admiral Jellicoe had already warned, the base was merely a haven.

At dawn on 1 February 1942, the last remnants of exhausted British and Empire troops completed General Percival's* order for a general retreat from Malaya, issued a week before, crossing the causeway over the Johore Strait to Singapore itself. The defence of the island was split into three sectors, western, northern and southern areas, allocated to the Australian 22nd Brigade, the 3rd Indian Corps and the Singapore garrison respectively. On 8 February, following artillery and air bombardments, 13,000 assault troops of Yamashita's 5th and 18th Divisions landed in darkness on the northwest corner of the island, forcing the withdrawal of the Australian troops. On the next day, a further 17,000 Japanese troops were landed on the western sector, penetrating quickly inland, and forcing General Percival to order the abandonment of a defensive line across the interior (the Jurong Line) to establish a final defence of the city on the southern tip of the island. With the Japanese divisions pressing their attack on all sides, and lacking adequate supplies and no water, Percival judged a siege to be impossible, a major factor being the plight of one million civilians on the island, and surrendered on 15 February, with 130,000 men. The ignominious loss of Singapore was described by Churchill as the 'greatest disaster and capitulation in British history'.

Slapstick, Operation Code-name for the Allied landing at Taranto* on the heel of Italy on 9 September 1943, it had originally been envisaged as a possible primary objective of the Allied invasion of Italy*. The original plan had been rejected, despite its strategic value, on the grounds that Taranto was out of the range of Allied air cover (a decision which critics have since argued was shortsighted and over-cautious). The occupation of Taranto was finally revived as a subsidiary operation to ensure adequate supply of the invading armies landing at Salerno* and Reggio di Calabria*. It was achieved without opposition by the British 1st Airborne Division, carried by five cruisers and a minelayer from Bizerta in Tunisia. But an opportunity to exploit Slapstick as the basis for a quick advance up the east coast, to seize the initiative while Allied troops were bogged down on the west coast at Salerno, was entirely missed by Allied commanders (notably Montgomery*) unwilling to move without planning and preparation. Instead, German General Vietinghoff* was able to make use of the delay to reinforce the German 1st Parachute Division and hold Montgomery's 8th Army on the first of many defensive lines across the Italian peninsula.

Sledgehammer, Operation See Normandy, Invasion of.

Slessor, Air Marshal Sir John (1897–1979) British Air Ministry Director of Plans at the outbreak of war, Slessor took part in the Anglo-American staff discussions in Washington in 1941 that first formulated the 'Europe First' strategy in the event of American entry into the war (see Conferences). After commanding the No. 5 Bomber Group he became AOC-in-C RAF* Coastal Command, working closely with the Royal Navy* and US naval forces to improve decisively the effectiveness of his forces against German U-boats in the Battle of the Atlantic*. From January 1944, Slessor commanded RAF units in the Mediterranean* with equal ability, and later became Deputy C-in-C Allied Air Forces in that theatre. In 1950 Slessor became Chief of the Air Staff.

Slim, Field Marshal Viscount (1891–1970) Highly respected and able British field commander. Slim commanded a brigade in Sudan and Eritrea before being wounded. On his return to active duty he was transferred to command 10th Indian Division for the Iraq* revolt and the campaign in Syria*. Promoted to lieutenant-general in 1942, he was appointed by General Wavell*, Commander in Chief India, to command the 1st Burma Corps (Burcorps) at the height of the Japanese offensive to capture Burma*. After attempting unsuccessfully to regain the offensive in central Burma during April, Slim managed against all the odds to withdraw his depleted and demoralized forces 900 miles back into India, where he was transferred to command 15th Corps, directing intensive training in guerrilla and jungle tactics, as well as morale building.

Appointed commander of SEAC's (Southeast Asia Command) newly formed 14th Army in October 1943, Slim made a significant contribution to the achievement of the Allied victory in Burma. On the offensive from December 1944 in Operation Capital*, Slim's 14th Army crossed the Chindwin River* and fought steadily south with extraordinary tenacity, against fanatical resistance from defending Japanese forces. Early in 1945 the 14th Army advanced across the Irrawaddy, taking Mandalay* by late March and the capital,

Rangoon*, in May. In the retreat, Japanese forces lost nearly 350,000 men. Considered by some historians as the greatest land victory achieved against Japanese forces during WW2, the 14th Army's victory in Burma led to Slim's appointment as C-in-C of Allied Land Forces in Southeast Asia and his promotion to full General in August 1945, just before the Japanese surrender. Appointed Chief of the Imperial General Staff after the war (he had already been knighted in December 1944), Slim later served as Governor-General of Australia.

Smigdly-Rydz, Marshal Edward (1886–1943?) Polish statesman and general who succeeded Josef Pilsudski as virtual ruler of Poland* in 1935 and hence directed the brief war against the Germans in September 1939. He was strongly criticized for poor deployment of forces and an anachronistic attachment to the use of cavalry, though no quality of leadership of the war in Poland would have withstood the decisive impact of German Blitzkrieg* tactics and the speed of the German advance. Following the Russian invasion of eastern Poland on 17 September, Smigdly-Rydz escaped to Rumania* and was interned there with the Polish government. Dismissed from his post *in absentia* by the Polish government-in-exile*, he escaped to Poland in 1941 to join the underground. He is believed to have been killed by the Germans in 1943. See Poland, German Campaign in.

Smith, Major General Holland (1882–1967) Marine commander of the US 5th Amphibious Corps and widely regarded as one of the founders of the American system of amphibious* warfare, 'Howlin' Mad' General Smith was a tough and uncompromising commander who led successful Marine island assaults throughout the Pacific War*. The headquarters of the redesignated 5th Amphibious Corps (VAC) was set up at Pearl Harbor* in September 1943 under General Smith and planning for the invasion of the Gilberts*, the Marshalls*, Saipan*, Tinian* and the Marianas* was directed by him from there. During the Saipan operation, Smith earned unfavourable notoriety as the initiator of a bitter controversy between the Army and Marine Corps by dismissing the 27th Infantry Division commander, Ralph Smith, for poor performance.

In August 1944, he took over command of the newly established Fleet Marine Force with nominal authority as Pacific Fleet Commander Admiral Nimitz's* chief Marine adviser. In July 1945 he was recalled to the United States to a training command, and retired in May 1946.

Smolensk Russian city and communications centre on the upper Dnieper* River, the focus of a crucial battle between German invading forces and Russian defenders attempting to arrest the German drive into central Russia during July 1941 (see Eastern Front). The German plan projected a pincer movement across the Dnieper River behind General Timoshenko's* strong western front forces, with panzer divisions under Hoth and Guderian* striking ahead of the 20th and 9th Field Armies, held up in the rear by bad roads and mud. Although known as the Battle of Smolensk, the action began on 9 July when German spearheads breached the Russian defensive line, the Stalin Line*, west of Smolensk from Vitebsk to Rogachev. The large concentration of Russian forces in the area, including the 21st Army south of Smolensk, the 20th between Vitebsk and Smolensk, the 16th to the east of the city and the 19th to the west, presented an opportunity to the German High Command to win a decisive victory and destroy a huge enemy force as a precursor to a direct offensive against Moscow.

On 16 July, German forces entered Smolensk, with the panzer divisions already pushing ahead eastwards to threaten the Russian Bryansk Front* at Roslavl. But Russian counter-attacks kept the focus of fighting at Smolensk, reaching a peak between 21 July and 7 August. Although encircled, local successes by units of the

Russian 16th and 20th Armies threatened to bog down the German offensive. At Yartsevo a renewed drive to reduce the city by the 17th and 20th Panzer Divisions was repulsed by units under General Rokossovsky* with heavy German casualties. Nevertheless, by 5 August, resistance in the pocket around Smolensk had been broken and over 300,000 Russian troops were trapped, along with over 3,000 tanks, before Reserve Front forces, under the newly appointed overall commander General Zhukov*, could be brought forward from their positions around Moscow to relieve them. Smolensk was recaptured by a vast seven-army force under Marshal Sokolovsky*, at enormous cost in casualties, on 25 September 1943.

Smuts, Field Marshal Jan Christian (1870–1950) South African soldier and statesman who had become a convinced supporter of the British Commonwealth and Empire after leading Boer commandos against the British in his native Cape Colony at the turn of the century. Smuts had served in the Imperial War Cabinet in the last years of WW1 and was Prime Minister of the Union of South Africa 1919–24. He returned to the office in 1939 on the issue of immediate entry into WW2, which he supported while the previous Prime Minister (General Herzog) remained committed to neutrality.

South African support was of great value to the British war effort. Units of the South African Army – in which all combat troops were whites – fought in East Africa*, the Desert War*, Tunisia* and Italy*. The South African Air Force, British equipped, played a significant army support role in East Africa (see RAF). Despite active and growing opposition to the war at home, Smuts himself retained his long-standing intimacy with Winston Churchill and exercised considerable influence in London over African strategy. He was created field marshal in 1941, and visited Britain four times during the war, as well as taking part in the Cairo Conference* on November 1943. At the end of the war he played a major role in the drafting of the UN Charter at the San Francisco Conference*. He was the only man to take part in the peace conferences at the end of both world wars. Smuts was also a respected botanist and philosopher, becoming Chancellor of Cambridge University in England after his defeat in the South African elections of 1948.

Snowflake A powerful illuminant rocket flare fired by Allied merchantmen to counter night attacks by surfaced U-boats in the Atlantic. Naval escort vessels used Starshell for the same purpose, but neither guaranteed the detection of such a small attacker. See Atlantic, Battle of the.

SOE (Special Operations Executive) British organization established in July 1940 to direct and supply resistance* organizations throughout occupied Europe. Its agents operated wherever resistance movements arose, in the Balkans, the Baltic, Italy, Scandinavia, the Netherlands, Belgium, France and central Europe. Close links with the French resistance were augmented after 1943 by amalgamation with the Special Operations section of the American OSS* (Office of Strategic Services). The activities of the SOE varied greatly in type and effectiveness, depending largely on local geographic and political factors. It was unable, for instance, to forestall the penetration of the Dutch resistance movement by the Gestapo* (where over 20,000 people lost their lives) but was considerably more successful in aiding the efforts of the partisans fighting guerrilla actions against German forces in the Yugoslav mountains (see Tito, Josip). Its major sphere of operations, however, was France. Although accurate figures were never available, the scale of resistance in France was clearly greater than elsewhere in Europe. It is estimated that some 75,000 members of the French resistance and a further 20,000 *maquisards* lost their lives during the German occupation. In their support of the French resistance, SOE lost almost 200 agents, apparently executed in two waves during September 1944 and March 1945. At the end of the war only about 30 of the 200 survived.

Sokolovsky, Marshal Vasili D. (1897–1968) Commander of Soviet forces in Germany after the war, Sokolovsky was Chief of Staff of the Russian Western Front* under Konev* 1941–3 and Chief of Staff of the 1st Ukrainian Front 1944–5.

Solomon Islands Large island group in the Western Pacific, east of New Guinea*. The group includes Guadalcanal*, Bougainville* and New Georgia*, all of which were important strategic objectives of the American offensives focused against Rabaul*, Japan's major military base, during late 1942 and 1943. See also Tulagi; Vella Gulf; Vella Lavella; Pacific War; Map 11.

Somerville, Admiral Sir James (1882–1949) British naval officer who had been invalided out of the Royal Navy* in 1939 while serving as C-in-C, East Indies. Fully recovered and unemployed, he assisted Admiral Ramsey* at Dover in a voluntary capacity during the evacuation of Dunkirk*, and in June 1940 took command of Force H* based on Gibraltar*. He remained in this demanding post until March 1942, when he was transferred to command the hastily created Eastern Fleet in the Indian Ocean. Somerville was a highly successful surface commander, but retired from active service in 1944 when he became head of the British naval mission in Washington, a post he held as an Admiral of the Fleet when the war ended.

Somua S-35 Intended for use by French cavalry units, this highly regarded medium tank* was introduced in 1935. The first tank to be assembled entirely from precast sections, it was well-armoured, mobile and hard-hitting but suffered operationally from the burden placed on its commander, who as sole occupant of the turret was also the gunner and loader. By June 1940 about 500 S-35s had been built, and they were more than a match for anything they met in the Battle of France*. Poor French armoured tactics and communications gave them little opportunity to prove their worth. After the fall of France, Germany used S-35s (as PzKpfw 35C 739(f)) on the Eastern Front* as well as for crew training and internal security. Production of an improved model, the S-40, was begun in 1940. This had a more powerful 220hp engine and modified suspension, but few had been completed when France fell.

BRIEF DATA (S-35) Type: 3-man medium tank; Engine: 190hp petrol; Max speed: 23mph; Range: 160m; Arms: 1 × 47mm gun, 1 × 7.5mm mg; Armour: max 56mm.

Sonar See Anti-submarine Warfare.

Sorge, Richard (1895–1944) German journalist and spy for the Soviet Union. Entering the Soviet Secret Service in the 1920s, Sorge first travelled extensively as a Comintern agent, with assignments in Europe and Asia. In 1933 he went to Japan under cover as a loyal German correspondent for the *Frankfurter Zeitung*, gaining the confidence of the German ambassador, whose embassy became a key source, and passing secret German and Japanese strategic information to his Red Army superiors over a period of eight years. Sorge was able to inform Stalin* of the impending German invasion and, perhaps even more importantly, of the improbability of a Japanese incursion into Siberia, allowing troops to be withdrawn in 1941 for the pivotal defence of Moscow*. Sorge was arrested on 16 October 1941, to the obvious surprise of German embassy staff, interrogated at length, and finally hanged by the Japanese in 1944.

Soryu Japanese aircraft carrier and Class. Completed in 1937, the *Soryu* was an enlargement of the *Ryujo** design and set the pattern for later carriers. Her sister, the *Hiryu*, entered service two years later and was built without treaty restrictions. She was slightly larger and heavier, with a superstructure modified for improved seaworthiness. The two ships formed the 2nd Carrier Division of the Japanese Navy* Combined Fleet in December 1941, and took part in the attack on Pearl Harbor*. Both were lost at the Battle of Midway*, where they were part (with the *Akagi*￼* and *Kaga*￼*) of Admiral Nagumo's* ill-fated striking force. The *Soryu* was fatally damaged by dive-bombers from the USS *Yorktown*￼* on 4 June 1942 and was finished off by the submarine *Nautilus*. Although the *Hiryu* later put the *Yorktown* out of action, she was herself set upon by aircraft from the USS *Enterprise*￼* and fatally damaged. Japanese destroyers sank her next day.

BRIEF DATA (*Soryu*, 1941) Displacement: 15,900 tons; Dimensions: o/a lgth – 746' 6", b – 70' (85' 6" FD); Speed: 34.3 knots; Armament: 12 × 5" AA gun (6 × 2), 28 × 25mm AA gun, 73 aircraft.

South Africa As a dominion of the British Commonwealth and Empire, the Union of South Africa enjoyed the theoretical right to remain neutral in the event of Britain going to war. In 1939 the Union was governed by a coalition dominated by the National Party under Prime Minister Herzog and Jan Smuts'* South Africa Party. Both leaders were committed to integration and co-operation between South Africa's English and Afrikaner communities, but the predominantly Afrikaner Nationalists (and right-wing breakaway groupings like Dr Malan's Purified Nationalists) were generally far more anti-British than their leader. Herzog had therefore pursued a policy of neutrality in the event of European war, but his motion reaffirming this was defeated in Parliament on 4 September; Smuts, supported by the minority Labour and Dominion Parties, formed a new government two days later that brought South Africa into the war.

Smuts, deeply concerned about the threat to Europe from both Hitler* and Stalin*, devoted his attention to the conduct of the war, while his cabinet carried on normal domestic government in the face of increasingly volatile public opinion. Afrikaner cultural and political groups flourished and remained determinedly anti-British, with extreme racialist elements finding much to imitate and admire in Nazi Germany. Smuts' United Party (UP) government took a generally soft line towards opposition to the war at home, although the War Measures Act of 1940 gave it arbitrary powers to control supplies of raw materials, possession of firearms and industrial unrest. Although the UP was returned to power with a massive majority in the general election of 1943, Afrikaner politics during WW2 were characterized by increasing radicalism and unity of purpose, which was to bring Dr Malan to power in 1948 with a government composed entirely of Afrikaners.

South African participation in WW2 brought considerable industrial expansion (particularly in the mining, steel and textile industries), and South African factories produced armoured cars*, artillery, munitions, boots and uniforms for the Allied war effort. In order to meet wartime production targets, a great increase in black, unskilled labour employed in South African factories took place.

Militarily, South Africa's first responsibility to the Allies was the defence of the important Cape sea route, but otherwise Smuts at first cast the Union in a passive role. Although the armed forces were strengthened, the South African Defence Act legally restricted them to operations in southern Africa until 1940, when volunteers were allowed to fight anywhere on the African continent. All South African forces were volunteers, but only white troops were allowed into combat, blacks and coloureds performing auxilliary and labour duties only.

Union forces later fought in East Africa* and Madagascar*, and three volunteer divisions fought alongside British forces in the Desert War* (one, 2nd Division, was captured by Rommel* at Tobruk*). The 6th South African Armoured Division was prominent at the climactic battle of Alamein in 1942, and took part in the rest of the war in Africa before fighting in Italy* as part of the US 5th Army (its members having volunteered to fight anywhere in the world).

The South African Air Force enjoyed a particularly distinguished war. Using obsolete British aircraft, the SAAF performed maritime and anti-submarine* duties along coastal trade routes from 1939. In East Africa the SAAF pioneered close support tactics with Imperial ground forces, and South African units were at the forefront of the army–air co-operation developed during the Desert War (see RAF). By 1943 sixteen squadrons of the SAAF were serving in the Middle East, and units also fought in Sicily* and Italy. Total wartime SAAF strength peaked at 35 squadrons with 45,000 personnel (6,500 of whom were women), and many more South Africans also served within the RAF.

In all, about 200,000 volunteer South Africans fought in uniform during WW2, and almost 9,000 were killed.

South Dakota, USS Name ship of a Class of four battleships commissioned in 1942 and including the *Indiana*, *Massachusetts* and *Alabama*. They were the last capital ships designed for the US Navy* under the constraints of the pre-war naval limitation treaties, and were armed on the scale of the preceding *North Carolina** Class. By compressing the superstructure amidships, a saving of some 50 feet in overall length was achieved, allowing for greater weight of protective armour and incidentally offering improved manoeuvrability at sea.

The *South Dakota* demonstrated the value of her protection early in her career. She was damaged by a bomb at the Battle of Santa Cruz* in October 1942, and less than three weeks later survived as many as 42 hits from Japanese warships after a power failure put her out of action at the climactic naval battle of Guadalcanal*. After a spell with the Royal Navy* Home Fleet, she returned to the Pacific in late 1943 to join the fast carrier task forces. Packed with anti-aircraft* weapons, she escorted the lightly armed carriers in numerous operations from the Gilbert Islands* until the end of the Pacific War*. Her three sisters all saw some service in the Atlantic* or Mediterranean* (the *Massachusetts* fought French Navy* units at Casablanca* in November 1942) before themselves joining the Pacific carrier groups in 1942–3.

BRIEF DATA (1942) Displacement: 35,000 tons; Dimensions: o/a lgth – 680', b – 108' 3"; Speed: 28 knots; Armament: 9 × 16" (3 × 3), 16 (others 20) × 5" DP gun, 68 (others 56) × 40mm AA gun, 40 × 20mm AA gun, 3 aircraft.

Spaatz, General Carl (1891–1974) Eminent US air commander who held high command positions in both the Pacific and European theatres. American Chief of the Air Staff when Japan attacked Pearl Harbor*, Spaatz had been an official air observer in London during the Battle of Britain* and was appointed to command the 8th Air Force there in June 1942. While the 8th Air Force flew daytime bombing missions as part of the Strategic Bombing Offensive* from January 1943, Spaatz's command was extended first to the 12th Air Force fighting in the Desert War* and then to command of the Northwest African Air Forces which supported the Allied offensives in Tunisia*, Sicily* and Italy*.

Promoted lieutenant general in March 1943, Spaatz became Deputy Commanding General, Mediterranean Allied Air Forces for a short period before returning to Britain in January 1944 to co-ordinate the 8th Air Force, based in England, and the 15th Air Force, based in Italy under the aegis of the newly formed USSAFE (US Strategic Air Forces in Europe).

With the planning for the invasion of Normandy*, Operation Overlord, now well advanced, Spaatz came into conflict with Leigh-Mallory*, Commander of the Allied Expeditionary Force, and Air Marshal Tedder*, Eisenhower's* deputy, over the strategic role of the Allied air forces for the coming invasion of Northwest Europe*. Nevertheless, his formations played an important part in the success of the air offensives against German communications and installations in the second half of 1944.

Returning briefly to the United States to collect his fourth star, Spaatz was transferred to Guam* to command US Strategic Air Forces Pacific (8th and 29th Air Forces) and directed the final stages of the bombing offensive against Japan that culminated in the missions on Hiroshima* and Nagasaki*.

Special Air Service British special operations unit formed in 1941 to carry out independent sabotage missions behind Axis lines in the Desert War*. In 1943–5 two SAS regiments fought in Italy* and Northwest Europe*, while a third (the Special Boat Service) operated in the Aegean. See also Commandos.

Special Attack Corps See Kamikaze.

Special-purpose Vehicles The British were the outstanding contributors to the development of specialized armoured vehicles in WW2. Adaptations of tanks* for mine clearing were first developed during the Desert War*. Flail tanks, fitted with heavy chains on a revolving drum that beat the ground in front of the vehicle, were the most effective device of the war for clearing land mines*. Initially attached to Matilda*, Crusader* and Grant* tanks (as the Baron, Scorpion I and II), the flail system was latterly most used on the Sherman* Crab, with the rotor powered by a take-off from the main engine.

The failure of the Allied raid on Dieppe* in August 1942 demonstrated the effectiveness of German beach defences and provided the catalyst for a wide variety of imaginative modifications to tank chassis. Most were based on the British Churchill* tank. Three hastily modified Mark IIs had taken part at Dieppe as flamethrowers* but none survived the landing. A more satisfactory system was developed as the Churchill Crocodile, which carried the fuel for its flame projector (sited in place of hull machine-guns) in an armoured trailer. About 800 of these were built in the last two years of the war. Some 700 assorted Churchill AVRE (Assault Vehicle Royal Engineers) conversions were fitted with a mortar instead of a conventional tank gun and carried a variety of engineering fittings on hull brackets, including box bridges, rolls of 'carpet' for soft beach operations and recovery cranes. The Churchill Ark could position a 60-ton bridge with the help of hydraulics in the crew compartment.

The American Duplex Drive (DD) flotation system, a tent-like device for amphibious* landings, was first applied to the British Valentine* tank in 1942, but was fitted to the Sherman for operational use in Northwest Europe*. The Canal Defence Light, a searchlight dazzling device, was mounted on the small central turret of some Grant medium tanks in 1944. A closely guarded secret, it was eventually employed in the Rhine* and Elbe crossings.

The Japanese also produced a wide variety of specialized armoured vehicles, usually on the chassis of the ubiquitous Chi-Ha* medium tank. Flail tanks, bulldozers, jungle cutters, bridge-layers and recovery vehicles were all developed, although only the light amphibian Ka-Mi 2 appears to have seen much action.

Speer, Albert (1905–82) Reich Minister for Armaments and Production 1942–5 and one of the most able men to serve Hitler, Speer was trained as an architect, joined the Nazi Party in 1932 (see Hitler) and the SS* shortly afterwards. He first attracted Hitler's attention for the technical arrangements he made for a Berlin Party rally in May 1933. Asked to provide a spectacle for the 1934 Nuremberg Rally, his success resulted in his appointment to Deputy Führer Hess's staff where his main responsibility was to design the 25 'reconstruction cities' in the Reich. He also worked with

Hitler on grandiose schemes for the Reich Chancellery in Berlin and the Party Palace at Nuremberg. Speer's celebrated metamorphosis into Armaments Controller resulted from the death of the Minister, Dr Todt, in February 1942. Appointed in his place, Speer proved himself an exceptional administrator, raising production levels to previously unattained heights.

By 1944, however, Speer's commitment to Nazism had declined and he had realized, like other senior Nazis, that an end to the war must now be sought. Nevertheless, he remained in his post until April 1945. Arrested by the British at Flensburg in May, Speer stood trial at Nuremberg*, pleading guilty to charges of war crimes and crimes against humanity (committed against the slave labour used for his production programmes), for which he was sentenced to 20 years imprisonment. During his imprisonment Speer wrote his autobiography, *Inside the Third Reich*, published in Germany in 1969, and in English in 1970. It still provides one of the most complete and authoritative descriptions available of the processes of government in the Nazi state.

Sperrle, Field Marshal Hugo (1885–1953) A German flight commander in WW1, Sperrle had remained in the post-Versailles German Army* and was transferred to the newly formed Luftwaffe* in 1935. The following year he was the first commander of the Luftwaffe force sent to aid the nationalist side in the Spanish Civil War. From January 1939, as a Lt General, he commanded Luftflotte III – the air army stationed in Northwest Europe – which he led through the Battle of Britain* in 1940, gaining promotion to field marshal. Apart from a spell in North Africa, Sperrle remained in western Europe until he was retired in 1944, after the Allied invasion of Normandy* had overrun Luftflotte III. Although he knew of the July Bomb Plot* against Hitler that year, and was in Paris at the time, he was not suspected of complicity with the conspirators. Hitler liked to have Sperrle present at difficult meetings

as one of his 'two most brutal looking generals' (the other was Reichenau*), and the veteran airman was generally respected more for his intimidatory qualities than for any great military acumen. Sperrle stood trial for war crimes at Nuremberg*, but was acquitted and eventually freed in November 1948.

Spruance, Vice Admiral Raymond A. (1886–1969) Widely regarded as one of the most effective admirals of WW2, Spruance was in command of a cruiser division in the Central Pacific at the outbreak of the war with Japan and fought his first action of WW2 at the Battle of Midway*. Assuming tactical command of the US Navy* forces there after the flagship *Yorktown** was severely damaged, Spruance deployed the available American strength with great effectiveness against the much larger Japanese force, to gain one of the key victories of the Pacific War*. Awarded the Distinguished Service Medal for his efforts at Midway, Spruance was appointed Chief of Staff to US Pacific Fleet Commander, Admiral Nimitz*, and played a vital role in the planning of operations in the Solomon Islands* and the Central Pacific.

In command of the US 5th Fleet from August 1943, Spruance directed the naval operations in the Gilbert Islands*, the Marshall Islands* and the Carolines (at Truk*) that proved decisive in defeating the Japanese in the Pacific. A full admiral from February 1944, Spruance led the 5th Fleet, including Admiral Mitscher's* Fast Carrier Task Force, in actions against New Guinea*, the Palau Islands* and then in the large-scale assaults on the Mariana Islands*, where units under Spruance successfully protected the invasion of Saipan*. Spruance also directed operations at the Battle of the Philippine Sea* and during the assaults on Iwo Jima* and Okinawa*. His ability to develop and direct amphibious* warfare, which was the key to American success in the Pacific, earned him great respect and many subsequent decorations, including an honorary British decoration as Companion of the Order of the Bath. After the war he briefly succeeded Admiral Nimitz as Commander of the Pacific Fleet, before his appointment as President of the US Naval War College.

Squid Squid was by far the best of the ahead-throwing depth-charge mortars devised by the Allies to deal with the submarine* menace in the Atlantic*. Squid was a triple 12-inch mortar firing three 390lb bombs in a triangular pattern at about 275 yards mean range ahead of its parent ship. Depth-determining sonar was vital to its operation, as charges were automatically preset to the depth reading given. The first production Squid was completed in September 1943, and by the end of the war between 60 and 70 ships had been equipped. More than 500 vessels were also fitted with the less effective Hedgehog system, first used in 1941 but ill-suited to deep water operations. See Anti-submarine Warfare; Atlantic, Battle of the.

SS (Schutzstaffel – Defence Unit) Originally the personal guard of Adolf Hitler, it was transformed by Heinrich Himmler* into a unique independent organization – effectively a state within a state, an army within an army. From 1936, when Himmler combined the offices of Reichsführer SS and chief of all German police under his control, the SS began to develop as a unique independent power in the German state, with new branches and associated organizations proliferating throughout the war. Separate SS offices, established between 1931 and 1942, co-ordinated the vast range of SS operations, from Reich Security (RHSA), to SS Business Enterprises (WVHA), to the Race and Resettlement office (RuSHA), which established standards of entry into the SS and prepared plans for resettlement of occupied lands with the pure Aryan stock whose membership the SS encouraged. Entry standards were based largely on racial appearance, good physical condition and general bearing. No defined intellectual attainment was

required. The marriages of SS men were vetted before approval by the RuSHA.

The core of the SS in the early stages, however, were the armed units formed in 1925 and operating alongside the SA (Brownshirts) and the security and concentration camp* functions established in 1931 and 1933 respectively. First, Sepp Dietrich* was given command of an expanded bodyguard, the Leibstandarte Adolf Hitler, formed from the armed groups of the general (Allgemeine) SS. Himmler then proposed to enlarge military SS units to three divisions. A Hitler decree of August 1938 assigned the SS military units (SS-VT* –Verfügungstruppe) a clear wartime role, as well as an internal political function. In March 1939, the Waffen SS (armed SS) were formed from the SS-VT and the SS Death's Head Units, the 3,500 strong concentration camp guards under Eicke*. During the mid-1930s Himmler also took control of both ORPO (Ornungspolizei), the regular uniformed police, and SIPO (Sicherheitspolizei), the security police. From this base he was able to take over the Gestapo* as a national organization, and centralized the national police system under his control.

The Waffen SS, the SS army, numbered 39 divisions at its peak strength. Formed in 1939 from the SS-VT and enlarged by the inclusion of the Death's Head Units in 1940, the Waffen SS was not at this time a favoured body. The army discouraged recruitment to it and numbers had to be made up with *Volkdeutsche*, men of German origin living outside Germany and not liable for German conscription. With expansion in 1942–3, however, volunteers for the oversubscribed Luftwaffe* and German Navy* were directed into the SS. Expansion continued, more and more members coming from outside Germany, until it was calculated that of 900,000 men who served in the Waffen SS half were non-German. Whole divisions were raised outside Germany, from Belorussia, the Ukraine, France, the Netherlands, Belgium and Scandinavia. The quality of Waffen SS divisions varied greatly. Seven (including SS Panzer Leibstandarte, Das Reich, Totenkopf, Viking – a Scandinavian division – and Hitler Jugend) were top-class fighting formations who, after their successes on the Eastern Front*, received preference in equipment and were used by Hitler as his élite army. Among the best of Third Reich soldiers, these units often contained the worst in character. The atrocities committed inside the concentration camps by the Totenkopf division, the activities of the Einsatzgruppen* and independent actions such as the massacre of an entire village population at Oradour* in 1944 serve as more than adequate testament to the bestial character of some members.

Apart from the armed SS, under Hans Jüttner, and the huge SS security and intelligence function, the RHSA under Heydrich* – which included the Gestapo* and the SD* – the SS also developed a massive structure of business enterprises under Oswald Pohl and co-ordinated by the SS WVHA office. As well as controlling 20 concentration camps and 165 labour camps, the WVHA also owned four major businesses in 1939: an excavation and quarrying company, a marketing company for products made in concentration camp workshops, a foodstuffs, estates, forestry and fishery company and a textile and leather company based on Ravensbrück women's concentration camp.

In addition the SS controlled most of the Reich's soft drink and mineral water factories based on takeovers in the Sudetenland (see Czechoslovakia), a huge furniture-making complex derived from former Jewish and Czech companies, and cement, brick and lime companies mostly from Poland and often using Jewish slave labour. All these enterprises had their own subsidiaries, ranging from jam-making to shale-oil production. WVHA gradually enlarged its activities with contracts for building armament factories, underground hangars and even, after July 1944, for the building of V-1* and V-2* weapons. Added to the profits from looting, the leasing of

slave labour (see Concentration Camps) and huge loans at low interest from the Dresdner Bank and the Reichsbank, the wealth derived from these businesses was enormous. The disappearance of much of it at the end of the war has never been satisfactorily explained.

Stalin, Joseph Vissarionovich (1879–1953) General Secretary of the Communist Party (1941–53), Prime Minister (1943) and Generalissimo of the Soviet Union (1945). Born Joseph Vissarionovich Dzhugashvili in Gori, Georgia, Stalin, like Hitler, was directed by his mother towards the priesthood. In 1890, however, he was expelled from the seminary at Tiflis for subversive views and joined the Bolsheviks in 1903. He was imprisoned (and escaped) several times in the next ten years but in 1913 he was exiled to Siberia where he remained until released by the Revolution in 1917. Appointed Commissar of Nationalities after the October Revolution, he defended Tsaritsyn during the Civil War and the city was subsequently renamed Stalingrad after him.

In 1924 he succeeded Lenin as Chairman of the Politburo and assembled enough support to crush his rivals. By now uncontested dictator, he initiated in 1928 the first five-year plan for industry and the collectivization of agriculture.

As real or imaginary opposition arose, Stalin destroyed it by show trials and arbitrary arrests. In 1938, his purge of the Red Army* deprived the Soviet Union of some 10,000 senior officers.

Before 1939, there is little doubt that Stalin was prepared to initiate an anti-Fascist alliance with the West. In retrospect it is hard to ignore the final result of blinkered French and British lack of interest in any collective security arrangements that included Soviet Russia. The dramatic change of Russian policy enshrined in the Russo-German Pact* of August 1939 testified to the isolation of Russia from any other system of alliances than that of the Axis*. The full significance of the pact, which was in effect a division of eastern European spoils, was not revealed until Russia's occupation of east Poland* in September 1939. In the months before the German attack on Russia, Stalin, with German encouragement, signed a non-aggression pact with his long-term rival, Japan (see Manchuria; Russo-Japanese Border Conflict). It was a treaty as vital to Stalin as to the Japanese Army*, now in control in Tokyo and pressing for an aggressive expansionist drive south from Japan's northwestern frontier with the USSR.

In June 1941, when Hitler launched his attack on the Eastern Front*, Stalin became Prime Minister (Chairman of the Council of People's Commissars) and took command of the Soviet Armed Forces (see Stavka). Though certainly not blind to the possibility of German aggression, he seems to have been totally surprised by its timing. His first reaction was the historic appeal to the Soviet people to leave the invader nothing but scorched earth. But the scale of the early defeats of the Soviet armies appears to have created panic in the Kremlin. Rumours circulated that Stalin had left the capital. Not until the Soviet stand at Moscow* had he clearly reasserted his authority.

It will probably never be possible to establish precisely Stalin's military contribution to victory in what came to be called in the Soviet Union the Great Patriotic War. From the Zhukov* counter-attack, which drove German forces from the gates of Moscow in December 1941, to the final battle for Berlin*, Stalin was served by an increasing number of generals (including Konev*, Rokossovsky*, Timoshenko*) distinguished in their own right. Certainly the initial lack of readiness of the Soviet Army was in large part the result of earlier Stalin purges; equally Stalin learnt, or at least appreciated, the art of generalship as the war progressed.

To the Nazis he showed himself an implacable enemy; to Britain and the United States he was often a querulous and demanding ally. He attended the Allied Conferences* at Tehran in 1943, Yalta in 1945 and Potsdam in the same year, emerging from his negotiations with Churchill* and Roosevelt* as a dominant figure on the world stage.

In the area of military diplomacy, his immediate objective was the earliest possible Anglo-American involvement in the war on land against Germany. As an army commander, he believed, or perhaps claimed to believe, that only by the diversion of German divisions from the Eastern Front would Britain and the United States make a serious contribution to victory. To this end he used argument, sneers and sometimes even encouragement to persuade Churchill and Roosevelt to initiate an early 'Second Front' in Northwest Europe. But his demands for a landing in France in 1942 fell on deaf ears. In the event, even his veiled threats of an 'understanding' with Germany could not draw a firm commitment to an Allied cross-Channel assault before 1944.

Joseph Stalin died in 1953, a dictator deeply feared by his associates and the upper echelons of Soviet society, though greatly admired by the Soviet people. Since then, the dismantling of the cult of personality has left only one public statue of Stalin in the Soviet Union, at his birthplace in Georgia, and has led to a rejection of the role in WW2 claimed for him during his lifetime. Even Stalingrad is now renamed Volgograd, finally obliterating, if only officially, the association of Joseph Stalin with his earliest success and the Soviet Union's greatest military victory.

Stalin Line Russian defence line running from the Gulf of Finland through Pskov and Mogilev, turning southwest north of Kiev, then southeast to follow the Dniester River line to the Black Sea. During the 1930s a fortified line was envisaged along this axis, inspired by the Maginot Line*, and consistent with the largely defensive conventional military doctrine of the time.

Under the supervision of Marshal Tukhachevski, from a combination of concrete field works, tank traps, natural obstacles and minefields used in conjunction with lakes and marshes, engineers and labourers created an impressive, though by no means unbroken defensive line. After Russia's occupation of Poland*, Bessarabia and the Baltic* states in accordance with the secret protocols of the Russo-German Pact*, the Stalin Line was superseded as the main defensive frontier and troops were moved from the line to forward positions on the frontiers of occupied territories. The Stalin Line was easily penetrated by the German armies in 1941.

Stalingrad, Battle of, 1942–3 The decisive battle of the war on the Eastern Front*, and the first indication to the rest of the combatants in WW2 that the Third Reich could be defeated. Having failed to win a decisive victory against the Soviet Union in 1941, Hitler returned to the offensive in the following year. In July he moved to headquarters at Vinnitsa in the Ukraine to supervise the southern advance of his armies to the Volga River and into the Caucasus*. Nevertheless, when the command was given to 6th Army commander, General Paulus*, to attack Stalingrad, key point on the Volga controlling the rail and waterway communications of southern Russia, it was still unclear whether this assault was secondary to the main Caucasus offensive or a primary objective in itself.

The attack began on 19 August 1942 with a pincer assault by 6th Army from the northwest and the 4th Panzer Army attacking from the southwest. Although mobile German units reached the Volga above Stalingrad, breaking into the northern suburbs within a few days, the Russian 66th Army forces under General Chuikov* kept the two arms apart. In a bitter war of attrition, concentrated attacks met concentrated defence. By 12 September, the Soviet forces had been squeezed inside a 30-mile perimeter. As German troops entered the suburbs and

Paulus's forces attacked again directly from the west, the city was completely destroyed by bombardment, though paradoxically the heaped rubble that remained was easier for Chuikov's forces to defend than the city intact. Nevertheless, the effective capture of the city – it was never totally secured – was finally achieved at enormous cost to Paulus's armies.

On 19 November, a Russian counterattack, code-named Uranus and conceived by Stalin*, Zhukov and General Vasilevsky*, was launched by Southwest Front* forces under Vatutin* from north of the Don River. Within five days, attacks on the north supported by attacks by Yeremenko's* Stalingrad Front forces from the south of the German salient at Stalingrad had eliminated any hope of a withdrawal by the German 6th Army. In an attempt to break through the circle from the south, Field Marshal Manstein* launched Operation Winter Storm in December, but his Army Group Don was checked by the Russian 2nd Guards Army and 7th Tank Corps, newly arrived on the front, some 25 miles from the city. Supply was now the crucial factor in the battle. Denied permission to surrender his forces trapped inside the devastated city, Paulus was forced to rely on Göring's* promises to supply 700 tons a day by air. Within days, the promise was reduced to 300, but even this could not be maintained in the Russian winter and the Luftwaffe's invaluable transport fleet was decimated. In January 1943, the Russians offered surrender terms to the Germans, but Hitler ordered his army to fight on and a renewed offensive against Paulus's beleaguered forces, now commanded by Rokossovsky*, reduced the 6th Army to a fraction of its original strength. When Paulus, who had been promoted to field marshal on 30 January, finally surrendered to General Shumilov, more than 94,000 troops surrendered with him, but more than 200,000 men had already been lost in the battle, including two Rumanian, one Italian and one Hungarian army completely destroyed.

Although the fighting at Stalingrad enabled Kleist's* 4th Panzer Army to escape the Caucasus before the Soviet counter-offensives were fully under way, the scale of the German defeat at Stalingrad could not be compensated. The German armies in Russia were now to be forced into retreat.

Starvation Code-name for an American operation to plant minefields around the Japanese home islands in the final months of the war. Over 10,000 mines* were planted by American submarines* and aircraft before the Japanese surrender in August 1945.

Stauffenberg, Colonel Count Claus von (1907–44) The officer who placed the bomb for the attempt on Hitler's life at Rastenberg on 20 July 1944. Fiercely anti-Hitler in his views, Stauffenberg joined the opposition through the Kreisau Circle (see Resistance: Germany). But by early 1944, Stauffenberg was exasperated by the lack of action among the many groups that comprised the aristocratic and military opposition to Hitler and assumed a leading role in a new plot to take the dictator's life that was to combine an assassination with a military takeover of Berlin code-named Operation Valkyrie. The failure of the July Bomb Plot* in 1944 resulted in Stauffenberg's execution by shooting after summary court martial on the evening after the explosion.

Stavka (Soviet High Command) In 1934, the Russian Military Soviet had consisted of 80 members. Following Stalin's* purges in 1937–8, only five remained. On the date of the German invasion of the Soviet Union in June 1941, there were few experienced military leaders, no surviving military district commanders and no High Command at all for the commissariats of Defence and the Navy. On 23 June 1941, the day after the launch of Barbarossa*, a Soviet High Command, known as Stavka, was established under General Timoshenko*. Seven days later, the system was altered by Stalin's establishment of a five-man State Defence Committee (GKO), including himself, Molotov*, Malenkov*, Voroshilov* and Beria*. Stavka remained to direct military operations, though it was also reorganized with Stalin as Chairman, and Molotov, Budënny*, Timoshenko, Voroshilov, Shaposhnikov* and Zhukov* as members. Finally, on 8 August, Stalin named himself Supreme Commander of the Soviet Armed Forces in place of Timoshenko. The resulting effect on early tactical deployments, the disastrous battles of the Fronts in the first stages of the German campaign, the chaos caused by lack of contingency plans and the virtual destruction of the Red Air Force* were symptomatic of this organizational monomania.

Sten Gun See Submachine-gun.

Stettinius, Edward Reilly Jr (1900–49) American industrialist who succeeded Cordell Hull* as Secretary of State in December 1944. Appointed chairman of the War Resources Board at the start of the war, Stettinius became Director of the Office of Production Management from January 1941, where he was responsible for the conservation of raw materials for war production. Later in 1941 he was appointed administrator of the Lend-Lease Program* and was subsequently President Roosevelt's* special adviser on war production. In October 1943, Roosevelt appointed Stettinius Under Secretary of State. In this office he was largely responsible for the organization of the Dumbarton Oaks Conference*, which brought together delegations from Britain, Russia and China to discuss proposals for a world-wide organization, later called the United Nations. Secretary of State from November 1944, Stettinius acted as President Roosevelt's chief adviser at the Yalta Conference and attended the San Francisco Conference as chairman of the delegation. In July 1945, he became first US delegate to the United Nations.

Stilwell, General Joseph W. (1883–1946) US commander of American and Chinese troops in the China, Burma, India Theatre of operations (CBI – see China). A staff instructor at West Point from 1906 to 1917, Stilwell was sent to France on the United States' entry into WW1 to serve as a Combat Intelligence Officer with the American Expeditionary Force. After the war, Stilwell took the unusual decision to study Chinese and spent three years in Peking in the early 1920s and a further three years at Tientsin. Between 1933 and 1939, Stilwell was again in China as Military Attaché. Immediately after Pearl Harbor*, General Marshall*, impressed by Stilwell's command of the language and understanding of China's difficulties, appointed him to command US troops in China, Burma and India with an urgent brief to improve the training of Chiang Kai-shek's* Chinese forces.

Stilwell's personality was complex and abrasive, and in his relations with the British (whom he generally disliked) and the Chiang Kai-shek leadership circles (which he generally despised) Stilwell fully earned the name the US press accorded him of Vinegar Joe. Yet to the British he was a loyal and effective ally and his belief in the qualities of the Chinese soldier sustained him through long periods of defeat and withdrawal.

Acting as the nationalist leader Chiang Kai-shek's chief of staff, Stilwell, newly promoted lieutenant general, commanded the 5th and 6th Chinese Armies attacking north and central Burma* in an attempt to stem the rapid Japanese advance in early 1942. Despite some local successes, Stilwell was unable to hold Lashio*, southern terminus of the Burma Road*, the logistic lifeline to China. Though the Allies would later construct a bypass link, the loss of Lashio forced British and Stilwell's Chinese forces to fall back into India and Yunnan.

In October 1942, a reorganization of the command structure in Southeast Asia (SEAC*), called upon Stilwell to act simultaneously in several roles. He was at the same time a US general responsible to the US Chiefs of Staff, principal adviser and 'minder' of Chiang Kai-shek and deputy to the Supreme Allied Commander in Southeast Asia, Lord Louis Mountbatten*. The conflict of responsibilities thus imposed upon him was a dilemma he was unable to resolve. Frustrated by the labyrinthine intrigues of the Chinese leadership as well as the appalling logistical and communications difficulties imposed by the remoteness of the Chinese theatre, Stilwell was increasingly at odds with Chiang, as well as other colleagues such as Major General Chennault*. In 1944, Stilwell's Chinese command and a small US force, known as Merrill's* Marauders, made a successful advance on the Japanese-held airfield at Myitkyina* in northern Burma, but Chiang's intrigues were by now bearing fruit. In October 1944 Stilwell was recalled to Washington on Chiang's insistence.

It is unlikely that Vinegar Joe Stilwell will ever be considered a great commander, but his political contribution to keeping China in the war was crucial and his abilities as a training general were fully realized between 1942 and 1944 in his reorganization of the Chinese armies under his command. He died on 12 October 1946, embittered at what he considered lack of official recognition for his efforts in Southeast Asia.

Stimson, Henry Lewis (1867–1950) American Secretary for War under President Roosevelt and leading member of the New York Republican establishment, his appointment in July 1940 (at the age of 72) was his third cabinet office. A strong advocate of aid to Britain and Lend-Lease*, Stimson was highly influential in nudging American public opinion away from its commitment to non-involvement with the European war. After 1941, Stimson remained as overseer of mobilization, training and later military operations, took part in all the major Allied Conferences and was an early supporter of the development of atomic power. He was among those who recommended the use of the atomic bomb* against Japan in 1945.

Stopford, General Sir Montagu (1892–1971) Highly regarded British commander from 1943 of the 33rd Indian Corps, which participated in some of the most important and difficult fighting in India and Burma* between 1943 and 1945. Having advanced from Dimapur to raise the siege of Kohima* (Assam) in April 1944, 33rd Corps then drove on at great speed through monsoon weather to join up with troops of 4th Corps under General Scoones* and reopen the road to Imphal*. Pressed on by Stopford, 33rd Corps then pursued Japanese forces over mountainous terrain to central Burma, taking part in the recapture of Meiktila* and Mandalay* in March 1945.

Strangle, Operation Code-name for an Allied air operation against German forces in Italy*, begun in March 1944, designed to support the Allied ground forces' spring offensive on the Gustav Line*, scheduled for May. Its objective was the disruption of German supply lines so as to 'make it impractical for him to maintain and operate his forces in Italy'. The operation drew support from all Allied air forces in the theatre, co-operating in heavy and widespread attacks on German commander Kesselring's* rail and road networks. Raids concentrated on marshalling yards, bridges and other key points were supported by heavy bomber attacks against inshore shipping by Vickers Wellingtons*, B-25s* and Bristol Beauforts* supplied by the Allied Coastal Air Force. The operation did not, however, seriously disrupt Germany's communication and supply system which was maintained by impressing Italian vehicles and supplies and by moving at night. Strangle nevertheless encouraged the Allies to adopt the Transportation Plan* in preparation for the invasion of Northwest Europe*.

Strasbourg See Dunkerque.

Strategic Bombing Offensive
Germany: the Anglo-American air attacks 1939–45 The doctrine of strategic heavy bombing had developed in Europe at the end of WW1, and was adopted by the RAF*, in part as a justification for its independence from the British Army* and the Royal Navy*. By the 1930s it was widely believed in Europe and the US that mass long-range bombing raids were unstoppable and could deliver a 'knock-out blow' to a hostile power. Nevertheless, in 1939, none of the European powers possessed bombers capable of carrying out such operations. The Luftwaffe* had abandoned plans for heavy bombers to concentrate on army support operations. The RAF had ordered heavy types but none were ready and it relied, like the French Air Force (*Armée de l'Air*)*, on twin-engined bombers with moderate range and payload. The four-engined B-17* was in service in the US, but was designed for coastal patrol work.

Both sides' air forces went to war in 1939 with a strict policy of attacking military targets only. Britain began the air war by launching a series of daylight raids on German coastal targets, but these were extremely costly and largely ineffectual. RAF Bomber Command was forced to concentrate on night operations, which were stepped up as the RAF sought an offensive role in late 1940, after the Battle of Britain*. Poorly trained in night bombing, which it had not expected to perform, Bomber Command lacked efficient bombs and navigational aids for the task. By the end of 1941, Bomber Command had dropped 45,000 tons of bombs over military targets in Germany, but most of its attacks were wildly inaccurate and achieved little of strategic value. The RAF therefore adopted a policy of 'area bombing'*, the less discriminate bombing of entire cities and towns, known by the Germans as 'terror bombing'. In spite of the failure of the Luftwaffe seriously to disrupt Britain's war effort by its night attacks on cities during 1940, 'area bombing' was championed by the British Air Staff, led by Sir Charles

Portal*, as a quick means to bring about the collapse of civilian morale in Germany.

In February 1942, Air Marshal Harris*, a single-minded and aggressive proponent of long-range bombing, became head of Bomber Command. With the support of Portal, he further increased the scale of area-bombing operations. Raids were launched against broad targets in northern Germany, particularly the heavy industrial centres of the Ruhr*, using incendiary bombs* to illuminate targets. Photographic evidence still showed that only a small percentage of bombs were being dropped anywhere near their designated targets. In late March and April, partly as a demonstration to doubters in Parliament and the Air Council (the RAF's overall controlling authority), Harris launched massed incendiary raids against the small coastal cities of Lübeck and Rostock. Hailed as great victories in the British press, the attacks wiped out large parts of the ancient towns but only briefly interrupted civilian life and had little effect on the German economy. Their main attractions as targets were their coastal location (which made them easier for aircraft to find), the fact that they largely consisted of closely packed wooden buildings and their low-priority anti-aircraft* defences.

Only 24 RAF bombers were lost in the coastal raids on Lübeck and Rostock, but Bomber Command lost 150 aircraft overall in April. Proposed expansion was further slowed by a shortfall in bomber production and the operational failure of the first new heavy bombers, the Short Stirling* and the Avro Manchester*. When Harris launched the first 1,000-bomber raid on Cologne* in May, he used every conceivable aircraft available, but the mainstay of his force was still the pre-war Vickers Wellington*.

In the second half of 1942, a genuinely successful heavy bomber – the Avro Lancaster* – at last became widely available to the RAF. The Lancaster, in combination with Pathfinder* target-marking squadrons and improved navigational devices based on radar* (e.g. Oboe*), increased Bomber Command's hitting power. The new high-speed de Havilland Mosquito* offered greater scope for precision attacks and high-altitude photo-reconnaissance. Nevertheless, Bomber Command lost 1,400 aircraft in 1942, mostly to Luftwaffe night-fighters, and by the end of the year the offensive was adding to a critical strain on Britain's oil supplies. Although the German High Command appears to have been badly dismayed by the bombing, war production and civilian morale showed no sign of flagging.

In August 1942, the USAAF* brought its B-17s to Britain and began daylight raids (with fighter escorts) on precision targets in German-occupied Europe. Denounced by Harris for raiding 'panacea targets', the US 8th Air Force under Spaatz* refused to be absorbed into the RAF's night operations. Harris and Portal remained convinced that area bombing would render an Allied invasion of occupied Europe unnecessary, and pressed for a (largely American) combined force of 4,000–6,000 heavy bombers by 1944 to bring the German people to its knees. With prospects of an Allied invasion of northern Europe in 1943 receding, the need for co-ordination of the two air forces was recognized and discussed at the Casablanca Conference* of Allied leaders in January 1943, which established priorities for a Joint Bombing Programme. Primary German targets were defined in order of importance as submarine yards, the aircraft industry, transportation and the oil industry. This clear emphasis on precision targets – inspired by the new 8th Air Force commander, Major General Eaker* – was not, however, made explicit and Harris was able to interpret the conference as an endorsement of his strategy.

Throughout 1943, the RAF bludgeoned German cities at night while the USAAF extended its precision daylight operations to German targets. Huge night offensives were conducted against the Ruhr, Hamburg*, where an incendiary attack caused a firestorm in August and 45,000 people died, and Berlin*. American bombers suffered heavy losses to Luftwaffe fighters and after the second of two disastrous raids on the manufacturing centre at Schweinfurt (14 October), daylight operations over Germany were suspended pending the arrival of a long-range escort fighter. By the end of 1943, the Allied Air Forces had dropped a total of 200,000 tons of bombs on Germany, but the most tangible strategic benefit of the offensive remained the distraction of large-scale Luftwaffe resources from other theatres.

The 'Pointblank' Directive of June 1943 recognized the need for both air forces to subdue the Luftwaffe's fighter arm. Harris and Portal regarded the development of escort fighters as an unnecessary deviation from bomber production, but the USAAF introduced the long-range P-51B* Mustang fighter to its daylight operations early in 1944. This excellent aircraft could escort bombers all the way to targets deep inside Germany and was far superior in combat to any German aircraft in service. With its arrival the USAAF's bombing force dominated aerial combat over Europe and Luftwaffe losses soared.

The Allied invasion of Normandy* in June further diluted German air defences. Despite strong opposition from Harris, Eaker and Spaatz, bombers were diverted to carry out the Transportation Plan*, aimed at destroying German communications beyond the Allied front. Over Germany, the 8th Air Force, supported by American units in the Mediterranean, systematically attacked German oil production and supply lines and British commanders, Harris apart, also began favouring oil targets. By September, the Luftwaffe's fuel supply had been reduced to 10,000 tons of octane out of a monthly requirement of 160,000 tons.

In the last three months of 1944, the Allies enjoyed complete air supremacy in Northwest Europe*. Purely military targets could now be destroyed almost at will and the German economy began to atrophy. By this time Portal and the Air Staff preferred the precision tactics used by the Americans

yet Harris, at the height of his prestige, still directed much of his effort against cities – over 40 per cent of the 344,000 tons of bombs dropped on Germany by the RAF between October 1944 and the end of the war. From February 1945, raids on cities were carried out by both air forces at Russian request to block German troop movements. Berlin, Chemnitz, Leipzig and Dresden were among selected targets. On 3 February, 1,000 US bombers killed an estimated 25,000 Berlin civilians in a single day. In raids on Dresden from 13–15 February, RAF and USAAF combined to create a firestorm which killed between 30,000 and 60,000 civilians. The morality of the Allied massacre of German civilians – particularly late in the war by the RAF – has been subject to vigorous criticism ever since.

Japan USAAF strategic area bombing went into operation against Japan in late 1944, when the new B-29* Superfortress heavy bombers began operating from bases in the Mariana Islands* under General LeMay*. Precision bombing had been tried at extreme range from Chinese bases earlier in the year but was abandoned in favour of incendiary attacks on whole cities. When high altitude incendiary strikes failed to bring about a surrender, General LeMay, exploited Japan's poor night defences to bomb from low altitude at night. On the night of 9–10 March 1945, a raid left much of Tokyo devastated and initiated a series of similar missions against other Japanese cities. The predominance of wood in the construction of most buildings made these fireraids particularly destructive. Although by the time the attacks began, Japan's military effort was almost at a standstill, further attacks with incendiaries, followed by the dropping of two atomic bombs* were considered necessary to force Japan's acceptance of unconditional surrender.

Streicher, Julius (1885–1946) A coarse and brutal early Nazi and violently anti-Semitic propagandist, he created and edited the notorious and obscene anti-

Semitic newspaper *Die Stürmer* between 1922 and 1933. Disliked and mistrusted by most Nazi leaders (though Hitler retained a curious attachment to his earliest supporters), Streicher was dismissed in 1940 from his post as Gauleiter of Franconia for various miscreant activities. Streicher was tried at Nuremberg* and sentenced to death.

Strydonck de Burkel, General Victor van (1876–1961) Belgian general who commanded the Free Belgian Forces from Britain, having escaped Belgium when it fell to the Germans in May 1940 (see Western Offensive). In September 1944 he returned to lead the Belgian military mission.

Stuart (M3/M5) Series Tank Less than 40 tanks were built in the United States from 1920 to 1935, but in 1932 the new Army Chief of Staff, General MacArthur* had ordered the development of light reconnaissance tanks for the infantry and similar 'Combat Cars' for the cavalry. A series of these were developed with strictly limited financial resources in the late 1930s, culminating in the M2A4 light tank, designed in the spring of 1939.

The outbreak of hostilities in Europe enabled the US Army* to re-evaluate its combat needs, and the M2A4, with armour up to 25mm and a 37mm turret gun, was put into large-scale production in April 1940, In all, 375 were built as standard US Army equipment before March 1941, when the more heavily armoured M3 entered mass production. The M3 underwent numerous modifications during a production run of over 13,000 vehicles that lasted until late 1943, and these were standardized into two main improved versions – the M3A1 and M3A3. From mid-1942, the tank's closely related successor, the twin-engined M5, was in full production and remained in front-line service until the end of the war.

They were all reliable and nimble vehicles similar in performance and weight to the contemporary British Cruiser tanks*,

and were widely used by Allied forces on all fronts. A few M2A4s had fought in the early Pacific War* campaigns but most, including some delivered to the British, were used for training. In 1941 and 1942, the M3 was supplied to the British Army as the Stuart I and it was used with some success as a battle tank in the Desert War*. A batch of M3s fitted with diesel engines conformed to the British Stuart II, and the later M3/M5 models (British Stuart III–VI) saw action in all theatres, including the Eastern Front*. In the Pacific their light weight was valuable in amphibious* operations and they remained in fighting units until the end of the war. In Italy* and Northwest Europe*, where they were outclassed in battle by heavy German weapons, they continued to be useful for armed reconnaissance and training.

BRIEF DATA (M3) Type: 4-man light tank; Engine: 250hp petrol; Max speed: 36mph; Range: 70m; Arms: 1×37mm gun, 5×7.62mm mg; Armour: max 51mm.

Student, Colonel General Kurt (1890–1978) The leading German paratroop commander of WW2, Student had joined the Luftwaffe* upon its establishment in 1935 and was charged with the formation of an airborne division. At the start of the German Western Offensive* in May 1940, his troops achieved remarkable success in Belgium and the Netherlands*. Using gliders and specially developed lightweight weapons, they were dropped behind the defenders' lines, spreading great confusion and securing vital bridges before they could be destroyed. Student was one of the few casualties of the operation. He was wounded in the head and put out of action for the next eight months.

The following May, Student commanded 11,000 parachute and mountain troops in the audacious airborne capture of Crete*, but heavy losses sustained in the operation dampened Hitler's enthusiasm for offensive actions using paratroops. Student had originally proposed the attack

on Crete and subsequently pressed for
further assaults on Mediterranean* targets,
particularly Malta*, but none was ever
sanctioned. Instead, his forces were used
as a highly mobile tactical reserve in the
defence of Sicily*, Italy* and Northwest
Europe*. Respected by Hitler, to whom he
was unswervingly loyal, Student became an
important commander of ground forces,
leading Army Group G (comprising the
1st Parachute Army and the regular 15th
Army) in the defence of Belgium and Germany in 1945. See also Airborne Operations.

Stummpf, General Hans-Jürgen (1889–
1968) Luftwaffe* officer and its Chief of
Staff 1937–9. In 1940 he commanded air
operations against Norway*, becoming C-
in-C for the area in May of that year. His
Air Fleet, Luftflotte V, based in Norway,
participated briefly but unsuccessfully in
the Battle of Britain*. Later in the war
Stummpf commanded Germany's home defence air force.

Subasic, Ivan (1892–1955) Yugoslav politician chosen by King Peter as his representative in the formation of a Yugoslav
government with Tito* as Premier in early
1945.

Submachine-guns Millions of submachine-
guns were manufactured during WW2 as
hand weapons, usually for special-purpose
troops (e.g. commandos*) or vehicle crews.
In great demand, they needed to be produced quickly and cheaply, these being the
criteria by which the many competing designs were judged. Thus the utterly reliable
0.45-inch Thompson* submachine-gun
was replaced in US service by the less
impressive but far less expensive 0.45-inch
M3 'Grease Gun', while the British mass-
produced the universally despised but functional 9mm Sten gun. The Soviet Union
standardized on the 7.62mm PPSU41 as a
way of quickly rearming troops shorn of
equipment by the German invasion of
1941, and in Germany the ubiquitous 9mm

Maschinenpistole MP38* (sometimes
wrongly called a Schmeisser) was replaced
by the equally excellent but cheaper MP40.

Submarine Developed as a naval weapon
at the turn of the century, the submarine
proved its military worth during WW1. By
1939, all the world's major navies possessed
large submarine fleets, although even the
most modern boats were essentially surface
vessels, powered by a diesel-electric motor
and usually capable of under 20 knots.
Using batteries, they could travel underwater at about half speed for a few hours
at a time. Most attacks on shipping were
carried out on the surface, and guns, rather
than expensive torpedoes, were used whenever possible to effect sinkings. No navy
possessed a significant technological lead
in the field, but each built the submarines
it expected to need in terms of size, range
and weaponry.

The German Navy* had enjoyed great
success with its U-boats as commerce
raiders in WW1 and when German submarine construction recommenced secretly in
the mid-1930s, it was geared to the same
role. In 1939, Admiral Dönitz's* small (55
boats) but highly professional force was
primarily equipped with the general purpose 750-ton Type VII boat (see U-48),
which was chosen for economy and proved
rather small for Atlantic operations. Larger
long-range types were later introduced with
increased diving depth and operational endurance was further enhanced by the use
of Type XIV Milchkuh* supply submarines
in 1942. From 1940–3 the U-boat arm,
superbly organized and led, took an enormous toll of Allied shipping, primarily in
the Atlantic, but also in the Arctic* and,
to a lesser extent, the Mediterranean.

From mid-1943, however, the combined
growth of all forms of Allied anti-
submarine* warfare decisively outpaced the
tactical and technological development of
the U-boats. In May they retired from the
Atlantic as losses soared and successes
dwindled. Although more submarines were
built than ever before, new types of boat

were needed that could submerge almost indefinitely and travel fast enough underwater to avoid the new generation of Allied escorts. From 1943 the adaptation of a Dutch breathing mast – the *Schnorchel* – enabled U-boats to recharge their batteries at periscope depth, but this only curtailed losses away from combat areas. Much time and energy were wasted on a radical but unworkable Walter submarine design, and only three of the more conventional but excellent Type XXI boat were in operational service when the war ended. By May 1945, the U-boats had been overwhelmed by advances in anti-submarine technology and although more than 350 boats (of 1,160 boats built during the period) were still in service at the end, they had ceased to be a major threat to Allied supply lines. See Atlantic, Battle of the.

Ultimately the most successful submarine fleet of the war belonged to the US Navy*, which had 112 boats in service at the start of the Pacific War* with a further 65 on order. Over half of these were training boats of WW1 vintage, and a few large and cumbersome fleet submarines from the 1920s remained active. Newer boats were smaller 1,500-ton designs, which had been standardized by 1941 on the excellent and prolific Gato Class (see Albacore, USS). Eventually, 195 of these all-welded, long-range boats were built and they remained in standard production throughout the war.

Like the U-boats, American submarines were directed primarily against the commerce of an enemy (Japan) wholly dependent on ocean-going trade. At first, hampered by operational inexperience and hopelessly inefficient torpedoes, results were disappointing. Once these problems were corrected under the vigorous command of Admiral Lockwood*, the weakness of Japanese anti-submarine warfare and the effectiveness of Allied naval intelligence in the theatre offered the Pacific submarine fleet enormous opportunities. Almost 1,000 Japanese merchantmen were sunk by American submarines, paralysing vital oil supplies from the East Indies. They also sank about a third of all the Japanese warships lost in the Pacific War*, establishing a virtual stranglehold on all maritime surface movement before the end of the war. By the end of 1944, 43 US Navy submarines had been lost but, operating in 'wolfpacks'* like their German counterparts, they were never subject to the same intense countermeasures and were able to make an enormous contribution to the collapse of Japan's war effort.

By contrast, the large and powerful Japanese submarine force had virtually self-destructed by 1944. Alone among the leading navies, the IJN had persisted with huge cruiser submarines into the late 1930s. These 3,000-ton giants were armed with powerful surface weapons and often carried seaplanes. Outpaced by modern warships and too cumbersome to avoid depth-charge attack, they proved a bad investment. Nevertheless, with a total strength of 112 boats – including medium I-type and small coastal RO-type submarines – manned by experienced and well-trained crews, the Japanese Navy was in a position to threaten Allied commerce throughout the Pacific and Indian Oceans. In the 21-inch Type 95, they also possessed the best underwater torpedo, but the rigid command policy of deploying submarines with the main battle-fleet was disastrous. Opportunities for easy mercantile pickings were missed early in the war, and combat with US fleet forces increasingly equipped for anti-submarine warfare resulted in few successes and heavy losses. The submarine force dwindled as production failed to keep pace with losses and the Army took over an increasing number of boats as the only means of safely supplying remote or threatened garrisons. By 1944, the submarine service had been virtually eliminated and only four boats remained active by the time it gained its last success, the torpedoing of the USS *Indianapolis** in the closing weeks of the war.

The Royal Navy*, predominantly concerned with trade protection, was uncertain of the role of its submarine force, which comprised 56 boats in 1939. Most of these were of the T (see Tally Ho, HMS) and S (see Salmon, HMS) types which remained standard for most of the war. About 50 of each were built, and the designs were regularly refined. The heavier T boats lacked the range of their US Navy counterparts and operated with only limited success in the Indian Ocean, and the S Class proved too large for inshore or Mediterranean work. A third type – the U Class of small boats intended only for training – was therefore put into combat production and 46 of these were built, followed by the slightly larger V Class of which about 20 reached active service. In total British submarines sank 1,800,000 tons of Axis merchant shipping during the war, along with six cruisers and 17 destroyers. Seventy-seven boats were lost, most of them to mines*. They operated mostly in exceptionally dangerous conditions in the Mediterranean* – where they inflicted vital losses on Axis supplies to North Africa – and in northern waters.

A variety of Dutch, Polish, French and Norwegian submarines operated alongside British boats after the defeat of their respective countries, and some French Navy* submarines fought (to little effect) against Allied attacks on French colonial bases. The large and modern Italian submarine force (115 boats in 1940) suffered heavy losses in the Mediterranean theatre, and made only a brief and minimal contribution to the Battle of the Atlantic.

The largest submarine fleet in the world in 1939 belonged to the enigmatic Red Navy*. By June 1941, it had 210 boats (some of them very old) on active service, including 65 in the Baltic and 44 in the Black Sea. Although one of the most active arms of the Navy, the submarine service was of poor technical, training and command quality. Altogether 107 Soviet boats were lost in the wars with Finland and Germany, many of them to mines, and they appear to have achieved relatively little. Eastern and western estimates of tonnage sunk by Russian boats differ wildly, but they

at least forced the German Navy to convoy Baltic shipping in 1942 and enjoyed some success in the Arctic Ocean.

Throughout the war submarines, particularly those of the US Navy, were active in other types of service including minelaying, reconnaissance, air-sea rescue* and supply. By 1945 it was clear that the submarine was fatally disadvantaged in direct combat by advances in naval aviation and radar, and its post-war development was concentrated on submarines for reconnaissance and conveyance of long-range missiles. See also Anti-submarine Warfare.

Sudeten See Czechoslovakia.

Suffolk, HMS Completed in 1927, this was one of five *Kent* Class heavy cruisers built for the Royal Navy*. They established a short-lived British lead in the design of 10,000-ton cruisers armed with 8-inch guns, the maximum standard displacement and weaponry of a cruiser as defined by the Washington Naval Treaty of 1922. Other powers, notably Japan and the United States, soon developed faster and better protected units, but Britain built six basically similar *London* and *Dorsetshire** Class vessels (all three types were known collectively as County Class) before abandoning heavy cruiser development in favour of cheaper light cruisers for the protection of her vast trade network. In spite of extensive modernization in the mid-1930s, British heavy cruisers were still old, slow and lacked sufficient deck armour against air attack at the start of WW2. Their strengths lay in their seaworthiness and the extent of their operational radius, and so the *Kent* Class was mainly employed by the Royal Navy for trade protection. Typically, their anti-aircraft* defences were steadily improved throughout the war, reconnaissance aircraft giving way to additional radar* and gun mountings.

The *Suffolk* was damaged in action off Norway* in 1940, and later operated in the far north as cover for Arctic convoys*. In May 1941 she participated in the action against the *Bismarck**, but was transferred to the Indian Ocean in 1943, remaining there until 1945. Of her sister ships, only the *Cornwall* was sunk – by Japanese carrier dive-bombers off the coast of Ceylon in April 1942. Two more *Kent* Class vessels were built for Australia. The HMAS *Canberra* was torpedoed by Japanese surface forces off Savo Island in August 1942*, and was eventually scuttled. The HMAS *Australia* served throughout the Pacific War* but was damaged by Kamikaze* attack at Lingayen Gulf* in January 1945.

BRIEF DATA (*Suffolk*, 1939) Displacement: 10,800 tons; Dimensions: o/a lgth – 630', b – 68' 5"; Speed: 31.5 knots; Armament: 8 × 8" gun, 8 × 4" AA gun, 8 × 2pdr AA gun, 8 × 0.5" AA gun, 3 aircraft.

Sugiyama, General Hajime (1880–1945) Japanese Army field marshal and Army Chief of Staff from 1940 until 1944, Sugiyama was one of the group of Japanese militarists involved in the political machinations that brought Japan to war with the United States (see Ultranationalism). He subsequently directed overall Army strategy until February 1944, when, following the devastating Allied raid on Truk*, he was dismissed by Premier Tojo*, who assumed the command for himself. After the fall of Tojo's government in July, Sugiyama became War Minister in Koiso's* newly formed cabinet until its resignation in April 1945. Appointed commander of the 1st Imperial Army with responsibility for Japan's home defence in the last, desperate stages of the Pacific War*, Sugiyama committed suicide with his wife in September 1945, at the start of the American occupation.

Suicide Boat As well as the more famous air and underwater craft, the Japanese Navy* employed small surface boats on suicide missions. Packed with explosives, these 1 –3-man craft attacked US shipping at both Lingayen Gulf* and Okinawa* in 1945. See also Kamikaze; Midget Submarines; Yokosuka MXYZ.

Sunrise Code-name for secret negotiations with the German Command (including SS General Wolff*) in Italy* that brought about the surrender of German forces there in May 1945. (Also code-named Crossword by Winston Churchill*.)

Supercharge, Operations 1 and 2 See Alamein, El (1); Tunisia, Campaign in (2).

Supermarine Seafire The British Fleet Air Arm* was without an adequate carrier fighter at the start of the war, and RAF* fighters were modified as stop-gaps while specialist designs were sought. The 166 Seafire IBs were hastily converted Supermarine Spitfire VBs* but the more extensively modified Seafire IIC joined FAA squadrons in time for Operation Torch* in November 1942. They were of fixed-wing design, but the difficulty of folding such slender wings was overcome in the Seafire III, which fought at Salerno* in September 1943, and later saw action in Northwest Europe* and Burma*. The Seafire XV – a cross between a Seafire III and a Spitfire XII with a more powerful Griffon engine – was just entering service when the war ended. A total of 2,556 Seafires were produced, including post-war versions.

BRIEF DATA (Mk III) Type: single-seat carrier fighter; Engine: 1 × 1,585hp Rolls Royce Merlin; Max speed: 352mph; Ceiling: 33,800'; Range: 465m; Arms: 2 × 20mm cannon, 4 × 0.303" mg (provision for 500lb ordnance).

Supermarine Spitfire British monoplane fighter, descended from the Supermarine racing seaplanes of the late 1920s and early 1930s. The famous Spitfire was the RAF's* most modern warplane at the start of WW2 and was the only British aircraft to remain in production throughout the war. It joined the RAF as the Spitfire I in June 1938 and was soon given increased armament and its standard 'bubble' cockpit canopy. Hundreds of Spitfires fought successfully in the Battle of Britain*, proving marginally faster at high altitude and considerably more manoeuvrable than the German Messerschmitt Bf109E*.

Altogether, 21 versions of the Spitfire saw action in the war. Spitfire IIs, with a new propeller and a bigger engine, entered RAF Fighter Command from August 1940. The even more powerful Spitfire V, delivered in February 1941, was the standard RAF fighter over Europe in 1941–2. Like its predecessor, it came in machine-gun (VA) and cannon/machine-gun armed versions (VB). There was also a VC model with a 'universal armament' wing, and this fighter-bomber type comprised 2,447 of the 6,749 Spitfire Vs built. Marks VI, VII and VIII were high-altitude developments, but progress on the latter was interrupted by the appearance of the superior German Focke-Wulf Fw190* in early 1942. The Mark IX, with a 1,660hp engine, was hastily produced as a stop-gap response, yet over 5,500 were eventually built and it appeared in low (LF), medium (F) and high-altitude (HF) versions. The last main version to use Merlin engines (Mark XVI) entered service in 1944, but operational parity with German fighters was only fully re-established when a Griffon engine – first used in the low altitude Mark XII – was matched with a redesigned airframe in the Mark XIV. This was able to use its increased speed against V-1* rockets in the summer of 1944. The formidable Griffon-powered Mark XVII, capable of 463mph, was just coming into service at the end of the war.

Apart from home defence duties, Spitfires fought in Europe, Africa and the Far East. Many were tropicalized, and many more were built for photo-reconnaissance (Marks IV, XI, XIII, XIV). Several post-war types were produced and a total of 20,334 Spitfires were manufactured up to October 1947. As the Supermarine Seafire*, the plane enjoyed a full and separate naval career.

BRIEF DATA (Mk VB) Type: single-seat fighter; Engine: 1 × 1,440hp Rolls Royce Merlin; Max speed: 374mph; Ceiling: 37,000'; Range: 470m; Arms: 2 × 20mm cannon, 4 × 0.303" mg.

Supermarine Walrus Spectacularly ungainly British amphibian, it first flew in 1933. Its appearance belied the effectiveness of its design, and it performed every conceivable task in every theatre with the Fleet Air Arm* in the first years of the war, although it remained primarily a reconnaissance plane. With the RAF*, the Walrus served as an air-sea rescue* craft, and a Mark II version with a wooden hull (safe from magnetic mines*) was built for that purpose. Before production ended in January 1944, 741 Walruses were built.

BRIEF DATA (Mk II) Type: 3–4-man general-purpose amphibian; Engine: 1 × 775hp Bristol Pegasus; Max speed: 135mph; Ceiling: 18,500'; Range: 600m; Arms: 2 × 0.303" mg (provision for one light bomb).

Surcouf Most major navies had experimented with large cruiser submarines* during the 1920s, but the French Navy's* *Surcouf* was the most extreme example of the type. Intended as a long-range commerce raider, she was given heavy-cruiser surface armament and had a waterproof seaplane hangar. In 1939 she was the largest submarine in the world.

When France fell, the *Surcouf* was at Brest* for overhaul. She escaped to Plymouth, England, and was recommissioned into the Free French Navy in August 1940. At first intended for Atlantic* convoy duty, she had been refitted for the Pacific and was *en route* for the Panama Canal when she was rammed by the US freighter *Thompson Lykes* on the night of 18–19 February 1942. This has been assumed to be the cause of her loss, with all 207 of her crew, which was announced the following April amid apparently groundless rumours that she had been working for the Germans.

BRIEF DATA (1939) Displacement: 3,304 tons (surface); Dimensions: lgth – 361', b – 29' 6"; Speed: 18 knots (8.5 submerged); Armaments: 2 × 8" gun, 2 × 37mm AA gun, 6 × 21" TT, 4 × 15.75" TT, 1 seaplane.

Surigao Strait, Battle for See Leyte Gulf, Battle of.

Suzuki, Admiral Kantaro (1867–1948) C-in-C of the Japanese Combined Fleet and Chief of the Japanese Navy* General Staff in the early part of the century, Admiral Suzuki was an independent-minded political moderate who was appointed Grand Chamberlain and privy councillor to Emperor Hirohito* in 1929 and miraculously escaped an assassination attempt during the coup by Army extremists in 1936 that resulted from his anti-militarist stance. In August 1944 Suzuki was appointed President of the Privy Council. In the following year he was increasingly drawn into the political arena as an influential advocate of peace and was asked to form a cabinet in 1945. Suzuki became Japanese Prime Minister in April, taking over the difficult responsibility of bringing the war to an end while maintaining control over the Japanese armed forces. He resigned as Prime Minister on 15 August, following the Emperor's broadcast surrender to the Allies.

Sweden Unlike other Scandinavian countries, Sweden was able to maintain a policy of independent neutrality throughout WW2 and was neither occupied nor became a belligerent. Although tolerating voluntary aid to the Finns in 1940, the coalition government of Per Hannsonn avoided direct entanglement in the Russo-Finnish War*. After the German invasion of Denmark* and Norway*, however, the government was compelled by economic dependence on trade with Germany tangibly to compromise Sweden's independence.

A Transit Agreement was signed in July 1940, allowing the use of Swedish railways for German troop movements, and supplies of vital industrial materials were guaranteed to Germany at prices fixed by Berlin. A few Allied commodities were imported through the port of Gothenburg, but Sweden's only real contribution to the Allied cause was the leasing of 500,000 tons of merchant shipping (60 per cent of Sweden's fleet) to Britain, about half of which was sunk during the war.

Swedish public opinion was manifestly anti-Nazi throughout the war, and Swedish diplomats in German-occupied Europe – notably Raoul Wallenberg in Hungary – were often very active in their opposition. Sweden provided sanctuary for 5,000 Danish Jews in 1943, and for resistance* groups from other Scandinavian countries. As German strength waned, the government (which was still in office at the end of the war) was able to adopt a more pro-Allied stance. The Transit Agreement was terminated in August 1943, and trade with Germany declined under growing pressure from the Allies until it had virtually ceased by late 1944.

Sword Beach Code-name for the British assault target, the Lion-sur-Mer beach, on the left flank of the Allied line in the Normandy* invasion, 6 June 1944.

Sydney, HMAS British-built light cruiser, one of three completed between 1935 and 1937 and then transferred to the Royal Australian Navy. The *Sydney* sank the Italian cruiser *Bartolomeo Colleone** off Crete in July 1940, but was herself dispatched by a German auxiliary *Hilfskreuzer** (the *Kormoran*) in the Southwest Pacific in November 1941. Her sister ship, HMAS *Perth*, also saw early action in the Mediterranean and was sunk in the Far East by torpedoes from Japanese warships (March 1942). The third unit, HMAS *Hobart*, operated throughout in the Pacific, taking part in the Battle of the Coral Sea* and the Guadalcanal* campaign, and survived to be sold for scrap in 1962.

BRIEF DATA (*Sydney*, 1939) Displacement: 6,830 tons; Dimensions: o/a lgth -- 555', b – 56' 8"; Speed: 32.5 knots; Armament: $8 \times 6''$ gun, 4 (others 8) $\times$ 4" AA gun, $12 \times 0.5''$ AA gun, $8 \times 21''$ TT, 1 aircraft.

Syria The French-held territory of Syria remained under Vichy* control after the defeat of France* in June 1940, but its position on the Eastern Mediterranean coast made its future a matter of strategic concern for Britain and Germany. With German influence apparently rife in Syria, and further Axis expansion expected after the campaigns in Greece* and Crete*, British and Free French forces (see Free France) entered the country on 8 June 1941, from Iraq* (which Britain had just occupied) and Palestine. After meeting tougher resistance than expected from Vichy forces, the Free French entered Damascus on 17 June and an armistice was signed on 12 July. Pro-British regimes were maintained in Syria and neighbouring Lebanon (also a French mandated territory) for the rest of the war.

T

T34 Tank Descended from the BT* series of fast tanks, the Soviet T34 was probably the most important tank* of the war. At the start of 1937, the Komintern factory at Kharkov began planning a 'shellproof' medium tank based on the chassis of the BT7M. The first design, the A20, proved incapable of mounting more than a 45mm gun, but the enlarged A30 – later called the T32 – could carry a 76.2mm weapon. With minor modifications this was accepted by the Red Army* as the T34 on 19 December 1939. By the following February, the first completed models were being tested, and mass production got under way during June. When Germany invaded Russia* a year later, 1,225 had been built.

Distinguished by its shaped armour, which greatly improved resistance to shellfire, the T34 was simple and tough. Although hardly designed for crew comfort, it was easy to mass-produce and maintain. Its all-round performance was superb and its heavy main armament was a formidable innovation in a medium battle tank. The T34's existence remained a well-kept secret from the Germans, who were unpleasantly surprised by its apparent invincibility and immediately set about trying to imitate it.

In mid-1941, a longer-barrelled 76.2mm gun was adopted on the T34, and this was used on the T34/76 until December 1943, when the T34/85 was approved. This featured a new turret already designed for the KV85* heavy tank and mounted a big 85mm gun, essential at a time when German 75mm and 88mm weapons were appearing in growing numbers on the Eastern Front*. By the end of 1944, 11,283 of these had been completed out of a total wartime production estimated at 40,000 T34s. Also built as two important self-propelled* guns, the T34 remained in production until the mid-1950s and with many armies on active service into the 1970s.

BRIEF DATA (T34/76) Type: 4-man medium tank; Engine: 500hp diesel; Max speed: 30mph; Range: 188m (with aux. tanks 280m); Arms: 1 × 76.2mm gun, 2–3 × 7.62mm mg; Armour: max 45mm.

T60 and T70 Tanks The Red Army* produced a series of light tanks* for armoured reconnaissance, beginning with the T38 in the early 1930s. In June 1941 the T40 light amphibious tank was in service and this was replaced by the heavier, land-based T60 in November. Armed with a rapid-firing 20mm gun, it was used for infantry support as well as reconnaissance. Over 6,000 T60s were built before they were replaced in production by the more powerful T70, which first appeared in January 1942. Although the combat value of light tanks was by now questionable, they could be produced cheaply and quickly, reaching units that would otherwise have no armour. The T70A version, with slightly more armour and engine power, was the last Russian light tank used for reconnaissance, and production of the T70 was stopped in the autumn of 1943 after 8,226 had been delivered. Later, the T70 chassis was produced as the basis for a number of self-propelled* artillery pieces.

BRIEF DATA (T70) Type: 2-man light tank; Engine: 2 × 70hp petrol; Max speed: 32mph; Range: 277m; Arms: 1 × 45mm gun, 1 × 7.62mm mg; Armour: max 60mm.

Tacloban Capital of Leyte* island in the Philippines*, it was retaken by the US 6th Army on 21 October 1944. A few days later a ceremony in the capital officially restored the civil government of the Philippines under President Sergio Osmena*.

Taiho Japanese aircraft carrier begun in 1941 but much delayed and not completed until March 1944. The *Taiho* had an armoured flight deck and, to lower her centre of gravity, she was built with one less deck overall than earlier carriers. Upon completion, she joined the 1st Carrier Strike Force as flagship but was sunk in her first action at the Battle of the Philippine Sea* in June 1944. Torpedoed by the US submarine *Albacore**, she erupted into flames after concentrated oil vapour from her aircraft had ignited in the hangar.
BRIEF DATA (1944) Displacement: 29,300 tons; Dimensions: o/a lgth – 852', b – 90' 9" (98' 6" FD); Speed: 33 knots; Armament: 12 × 3.9" AA gun (6 × 2), 51 × 25mm AA gun, 53 aircraft.

Taiyo Japanese Navy aircraft carrier and Class. Completed in 1941–2, the *Taiyo* and her sisters the *Chuyo* and *Unyi* were the first Japanese merchant ships to be converted as carriers. They were larger, faster and carried more aircraft than Allied escort carrier* conversions, but lacked important handling facilities and proved unsuitable for their intended fleet role, being used mostly for pilot training and ferry work. All three were war losses. The *Chuyo* was sunk by the US submarine *Sailfish* on 4 December 1943. Both the *Taiyo* and the *Unyi* were given additional light antiaircraft* weapons the following year, before they too succumbed to submarines on 18 August and 16 September respectively.
BRIEF DATA (*Taiyo*, 1942) Displacement: 17,830 tons; Dimensions: o/a lgth – 591' 4", b – 73' 9" (77' FD); Speed: 21 knots; Armament: 4 × 4.7" AA gun (others 8), 8 × 25mm AA gun, 27 aircraft.

Takagi, Sokichi Japanese Navy* officer and research expert whose research into Japanese shipping and air losses after 1943 convinced him of the need to make peace with the Allies. He was among the group of naval officers, including Admirals Yonai and Inouye, at the centre of the moves to oust Ultranationalist Premier Tojo* and the subsequent efforts to bring the Pacific War* to an end.

Takagi, Vice Admiral Takeo (1892–1944) One of the most effective Japanese naval commanders of the war, Takagi commanded supporting forces during many of the most important Japanese Pacific offensives, including the invasions of the Philippines*, Port Moresby*, Java* and Midway*. Takagi was instrumental in achieving the early tactical victories against US Navy* forces in the battles of the Java Sea* and the Coral Sea*. In 1943 he was posted to Saipan* to command the 6th Submarine Fleet and was killed in action in July 1944.

Takao Japanese heavy cruiser and Class of four ships completed in 1931–2. They were slightly improved versions of the *Myoko* Class, with increased armour protection and an enlarged bridge structure, which housed all their fire control and communications systems. The *Takao* and the *Atago* were modernized in 1939–40 but the *Chokai* and the *Maya* entered the war with their original 4.7-inch secondary armament and only eight torpedo tubes. The *Chokai*, which was regarded as an élite ship within the Japanese Navy*, received no war modifications, but the *Maya* was eventually rearmed in 1943.
At the beginning of the Pacific War* the whole Class formed the 4th Cruiser Squadron based on Hainan under Vice Admiral Kondo*. The four ships were involved in the naval Battle of Guadalcanal* and fought many other actions before all were hit at the Battle of Leyte Gulf* in October 1944. Only the *Takao* survived,

and she limped back to Singapore where she was sunk in the harbour by British X-Craft midget* submarines on 31 July 1945.

BRIEF DATA (*Takao*, 1941) Displacement: 13,160 tons; Dimensions: o/a lgth – 663' 9", b – 68'; Speed: 34.25 knots; Armament: 10 × 8" gun (5 × 2), 8 × 5" AA gun, 8 × 25mm AA gun, 4 × 13mm AA gun, 16 × 24" TT, 3 aircraft.

Tally Ho, HMS This British T Class submarine*, commissioned in 1942, had a particularly distinguished record in the Indian Ocean, operating out of Ceylon*. Her largest victim was the Japanese cruiser *Kuma*, sunk on 11 January 1944.

BRIEF DATA (T Class submarines) Displacement: 1,090 tons (surface); Dimensions: o/a lgth – 275', b – 23' 9"; Speed: 15 knots (9 submerged); Armament: 1 × 4" gun, 1 × 20mm AA gun, 3 × 0.5" mg, 11 × 21" TT.

Tanaka, Vice Admiral Raizo (1892–1969) Widely regarded as one of Japan's most gifted naval commanders, Tanaka commanded escort forces for the invasions in the southern Philippines*, Ambon, Timor and Java* as well as a transport force during the Battle of Midway*. Tanaka is best known, however, for his contribution to the struggle for Guadalcanal*. Though an early advocate of the abandonment of Guadalcanal, which severely drained Japanese naval and air resources, Tanaka commanded repeated operations under Admiral Mikawa during the second half of 1942 to reinforce the Japanese garrison there. In November he decisively defeated a superior US naval force at the battle of Tassafaronga*, the last major naval engagement in the Solomons*. His criticism of the co-ordination of air and sea operations during Guadalcanal resulted in the loss of his command, however, and he remained out of favour for the duration of the war.

Tang, USS US Navy* *Gato* Class submarine, completed in 1943. The *Tang* sank a record number of ten ships on one patrol in June 1944, and she was the second most successful American boat in terms of overall tonnage sunk. Her commander (Richard O'Kane) was the leading American ace*. The *Tang* accounted for seven ships on her final patrol in 1944, but in attempting to finish off an eighth, she was destroyed by the last of her own torpedoes*, which circled back and struck her. Only eight men survived, including O'Kane.

BRIEF DATA See Albacore, USS.

Tank Like the machine-gun in WW1, the tank dominated military tactics in virtually every ground operation from 1939 to 1945, apart from those in the jungles of the Far East. During WW2, tank design made more progress than it had done in the previous 30 years of its development. Its operational role in WW1 trench-warfare had been as an infantry support 'crawler', immune to cratered terrain and massed machine-gun fire. In the large-scale demobilizations that followed the Armistice further development had been largely ignored, and the economic crises of the 1920s and early 30s precluded the adequate funding of armoured experiment. There were those, notably the British theorists Liddell-Hart and Fuller, who predicted the mechanized nature of future warfare, but the view was still widespread that fast-moving cavalry would always triumph over the lumbering tank.

It was thus against a background of establishment opposition that a British Experimental Mechanized Force (EMF) was organized in 1927. This was a self-sufficient unit of little more than brigade strength containing all the major components of future armoured divisions: tanks, armoured reconnaissance vehicles, infantry, artillery and air support. Though short-lived, the EMF was a resounding success in test manoeuvres and demonstrated to the world the potential of independent offensive armoured divisions. Of equal long-term significance was the appearance in the United States of the revolutionary Christie tank in

1928. Although hamstrung by defects and subsequently developed only slowly, this light machine featured a revolutionary suspension and track design, which was to set new performance standards for tanks in the late 1930s.

In Germany, the success of the Experimental Mechanized Force was well noted by armoured strategists like Guderian* and Seeckt. Forbidden to build tanks by the Treaty of Versailles, they at first used cardboard models to perfect tactics, but found the concept of armoured (panzer) divisions enthusiastically endorsed when the National Socialists came to power in 1933. A rationally planned series of tanks was then developed to equip a full-scale armoured force, beginning with the interim PzKpfw I* and PzKpfw II* light tanks, which were intended for training or reconnaissance. Although these were used extensively in the early campaigns of the war, the principal weapons of the panzer divisions were the PzKpfw III*, intended for the anti-tank role, and the close support PzKpfw IV*. To these were added a fifth tank, the excellent Czech LT38 light tank of 1938, which served the German Army in large numbers as the PzKpfw 38(t) and was later built as the basis for several self-propelled* weapons.

In Japan a Mechanized Combined Brigade was formed for operations in Manchuria* in the early 1930s, and the United States, which built almost no modern tanks before 1939, attempted trials with a mechanized force in 1928. By contrast the French, who could field 3,100 tanks by 1939, many of them well-armed and armoured modern types, remained firmly rooted in the tactical atmosphere of 1918. Scattered in support of infantry units, unco-ordinated and largely without radio communication, good designs like the Somua S-35* were wasted in the Battle of France* and defeated by armoured vehicles of generally inferior quality.

In Britain, armoured development was a painstaking affair. In 1934 the Army General Staff called for two types of tank – heavily armoured infantry tanks in the traditional, tortoise-paced support role, and fast cruiser tanks which could roam the battlefield and take on other tanks. Developed slowly, these new types were only just entering service when war broke out, and the British Army* in 1939–40 relied on lightly armed and armoured machines suitable for colonial patrol work but outclassed in France. When they did become operative in the Desert War*, the new tanks were held rigidly to their designated tasks and the lack of heavy firepower intrinsic to the support designs was quickly exposed. The cruisers meanwhile lacked the range or protection of their German opponents, although the fast Crusader* tank, using a modified version of the Christie suspension system, gained some success. Despite a growing numerical superiority in North Africa, the British generally achieved operational parity with German tanks only when US-built vehicles became available in quantity from late 1941.

Later in the war, the British developed reliable and effective infantry (Churchill*) and fast cruiser (Cromwell*) tanks, with which to support offensive operations in Northwest Europe*, and were at the forefront in the design of special-purpose tank conversions for varied and vital tasks such as bridge-laying and minesweeping.

When the war in Europe started, the United States was ill-equipped for armoured warfare, but rearmament gathered pace urgently during 1940. The lessons of German success were thoroughly absorbed in the planning of a combined armoured force and in the specifications of the new medium tank just entering production. This stop-gap series of Grant/Lee* tanks, much exported under Lend-Lease*, achieved parity with the German PzKpfw IV and gave US forces in the Pacific an early ascendancy over Japanese armoured units, which were deployed solely in support of infantry. The speed and efficiency with which the vast American automobile industry was harnessed to the production of the Grant/Lee was carried over to its successor, the Sherman*, which was the most widely used tank of the war. It was outperformed by the best tanks of other armies but dominated the ground war by force of numbers. Like most US armoured vehicles, its greatest assets were serviceability and reliability.

The Red Army* possessed more tanks than any other power in 1940. Able to test their weapons in Manchuria and later in Finland*, the Russians had vacillated between French and German style organizational systems, opting for the latter system by 1941. Nevertheless, the T70* and BT7* machines with which they faced the German invasion in 1941 were obsolete and suffered enormous losses. New designs just coming into Russian service, however, changed the face of the tank war on the Eastern Front* and shook the confidence of the German High Command in the long-term viability of their own panzers. The KV* heavy and T34* medium tanks were masterpieces of design, firepower and functionalism, and the Germans quickly designed bigger, heavier tanks in response.

For the rest of the war the Eastern Front was the main catalyst to tank development, which was characterized by a race to build heavy weapons with bigger guns and thicker armour. The Germans produced the Panther*, Tiger* and King Tiger* tanks, mounting 75mm and 88mm guns to counteract the 76mm weapon carried by the T34/76. The Russians responded by upgunning both the KV and T34 series to 85mm, and eventually produced the IS (Iosef Stalin)* tank which, while weighing no more than its major opponents, mounted a huge 122mm weapon. British and American tanks, operating in less open European terrain, were not upgunned beyond about 75mm, apart from the 17 pounder Sherman 'Firefly' conversion. Although the Americans did produce a heavy tank (the Pershing*) at the end of the war, both armies relied on thousands of their more nimble and reasonably effective medium tanks, aided by tactical develop-

ments designed to exploit the cumbersome performance of the German heavyweights. Narrowly outgunned in the east and outmanoeuvred in the west, German tank forces were heavily outnumbered on both fronts long before the war ended. In the period 1939–44 Germany built less than 25,000 tanks, compared with over 28,000 produced in Britain, 76,000 in the US and about 83,000 in Russia. See also Self-propelled Guns; Special-purpose Vehicles.

Taranto Situated off the Ionian coast of southern Italy, Taranto was the main base of the Italian Navy's* battlefleet. On the night of 11 November 1940, it was the subject of Operation Judgement – the world's first carrier-based air attack. Conceived as part of the offensive strategy of Admiral Cunningham*, in command of the British Mediterranean Fleet, the operation was brilliantly successful, although tiny by later standards. Twenty-one slow but resilient Fairey Swordfish* biplane torpedo-bombers from the new carrier *Illustrious* flew 150 miles at low level to attack warships in the harbour, and all but two returned having disabled three Italian battleships with a total of 11 torpedoes. With only one Italian battleship now operational, the material balance of naval power in the Mediterranean* was redressed in Britain's favour. The attack also contributed to the reluctance of the Italian fleet to challenge the Royal Navy's* supply lines to troops in Greece* the following year. The success of Operation Judgement was observed with great interest by the Japanese Navy*, which was good at learning offensive tactics and possessed large, well-equipped aircraft carriers. See also Slapstick, Operation.

Tarawa See Gilbert Islands.

Tassafaronga, Battle of, 30 November 1942 Final naval engagement in the struggle for Guadalcanal*, it was precipitated by the arrival of Admiral Tanaka's*

2nd Destroyer flotilla, attempting a supply run through Savo Sound to Tassafaronga, on the northwest coast of Guadalcanal. Although the patrolling US cruiser and destroyer* force under Rear Admiral Wright opened fire first, and managed to sink the *Takanami* and prevent the landings, Japanese attacks using superior 'Long Lance' torpedoes* severely damaged the cruisers *Pensacola**, *New Orleans**, *Northampton** and *Minneapolis*. The *Northampton* sank on the following day, while the Japanese flotilla retired with little damage.

Tautog, USS US Navy* *Tambor* Class submarine* completed in 1940 and credited with sinking more ships (26) than any other American submarine in the war. She survived to be scrapped in 1960.
BRIEF DATA (*Tambor* Class) Displacement: (surface) 1,475 tons; Dimensions: o/a lgth – 307' 3", b – 27' 3"; Speed: 20 knots (8.7 submerged); Armament: 1 × 5" gun; 1 × 40mm AA gun; 10 × 21" TT.

Tedder, Air Marshal Sir Arthur (1890–1967) British deputy to Supreme Allied Commander Eisenhower between December 1943 and the German surrender in May 1945. Widely regarded as an able strategist and outstanding wartime Allied commander, Tedder began the war as Director General of Research and Development at the Air Ministry. In 1941 he succeeded Air Marshal Longmore as AOC-in-C Middle East and directed the development of pattern bombing techniques (the 'Tedder carpet') and air-ground force co-operation during the Desert War*. Recognizing the decisive effect of air superiority on ground operations, which was not accepted by official RAF* doctrine, Tedder worked with Air Vice Marshal Coningham* to reduce enemy airfields and installations and to vastly improve inter-service co-ordination in the theatre. Appointed Air C-in-C of the newly formed Mediterranean Air Command responsible to Eisenhower in early 1943, Tedder further

developed techniques of long-range strategic bombing to isolate battlefields to tactical advantage, and achieved a highly effective integration of RAF and USAAF* forces.
As Eisenhower's deputy from December 1943, Tedder's commitment to inter-Allied co-operation forged a highly effective Allied air arm from diverse and sometimes antagonistic components. His resolute advocacy and direction of the Transportation Plan*, the preparatory bombing of enemy communications in support of the Allied invasion of Normandy*, contributed significantly to the success of the operation. See RAF.

Tehran Conference See Conferences, Allied.

Tenaru River, Battle of See Guadalcanal.

Ten-Go Code-name for a Japanese plan for air operations over the East China Sea in defence of their home territories in the last few months of the war. Ten-Go, issued on 2 February 1945, projected a decisive air attack on advancing Allied forces, but the loss of her air power reduced Japan's plan to a series of small-scale strikes that proved ineffective against the by then overwhelming superiority of the US Pacific Fleet (see Japanese Air Forces).

Tennessee, USS American battleship and Class. The *Tennessee* and her sister, the *California*, were commissioned in 1920–1 and were virtual repeats of the earlier *New Mexico** Class. Before WW2 they received only minor modernization but were both extensively rebuilt after the attack on Pearl Harbor*, which left the *Tennessee* seriously damaged and the *California* sunk in the shallows of Battleship Row. Given a new streamlined superstructure, improved hull protection, modern radar* equipment and vastly improved anti-aircraft* capability (16 5-inch dual-purpose guns and at least 90 light weapons) they re-emerged as virtually new ships.

The *Tennessee* returned to service in 1943, beginning a long sequence of Pacific War* shore-bombardment operations at Kiska* in August. The *California* re-entered the fray at Saipan* in the summer of 1944, and both vessels took part in the last battleship confrontation of the war, at Surigao Strait in October of that year (see Leyte Gulf, Battle of). Support of amphibious* landings had become their only viable combat role, however, and after Iwo Jima* and Okinawa* they were retired from active service.
BRIEF DATA (*Tennessee*, 1941) Displacement: 32,000 tons; Dimensions: o/a lgth – 624' 6", b – 97' 3"; Speed: 21 knots; Armament: 12 × 14" gun (4 × 3), 12 × 5" gun, 8 × 5" AA gun, 4 × 6pdr AA gun, 3 aircraft.

Tenryu Japanese Navy* light cruiser and class of two ships. Completed soon after WW1 along similar lines to the British C class cruisers (see Coventry, HMS). They were too old to merit major modification in the Pacific War* and both were lost to submarines*. The *Tenryu* was sunk by the American *Albacore*erican in Madang* harbour on 18 December 1942, and her sister the *Tatsuta* was torpedoed off the coast of Japan in March 1944.
BRIEF DATA (*Tenryu*, 1941) Displacement: 3,230 tons; Dimensions: o/a lgth – 468', b – 40' 6"; Speed: 33 knots; Armament: 4 × 5.5" gun (4 × 1), 1 × 3" AA gun, 2 × 13mm AA gun, 6 × 21" TT.

Terauchi, Field Marshal Count Hisaichi (1879–1945) Son of Masatake Terauchi, former Governor of Korea and Prime Minister of Japan. Terauchi served in various important army posts, and as War Minister in the Ultranationalist* Hirota cabinet (dominated by the *Toseiha* militarist faction) during 1936–7, before being transferred to command Japanese forces in northern China* in 1937, following the outbreak of full-scale war between the two countries. In November 1941, Terauchi was given command of the Southern Army,

with Yamashita* and Homma* in command of forces under him. The invasions of Indochina*, Siam (see Thailand), Malaya* and Java* were successfully completed under his direction, from headquarters in Saigon. He also directed the construction of a 250-mile Burma Road* by Allied POWs during which thousands died in brutal conditions.

After the fall of General Tojo's* government in July 1944, Terauchi was one of those considered to replace him, but remained in command of the Southern Army during 1944 and 1945 for the ultimately unsuccessful defence of the Southwest Pacific, including New Guinea*, the Dutch East Indies* and the Philippine* Islands. Terauchi formally surrendered to the Allied command in Saigon in November 1945, having been absent from the surrender at Singapore* in September due to a stroke.

Texas, USS See New York, USS.

Thailand Japanese troops landed on the southeast coast of Thailand (Siam) on 8 December 1941. Giving permission for these forces to cross Thailand *en route* to Burma* and Malaya*, the sympathetic Thai government became, officially, an ally of the Axis*, although the Thai ambassador to Washington refused to deliver the war declaration to the government. During the war a well organized resistance* and many Thai officials maintained close contact with the Allies. Thailand was not seen as an Allied opponent after the war ended.

Thermopylae A pass about three miles wide in southern Greece. It was the site of a valuable defensive action by British Army troops – mostly from Australia and New Zealand – in late April 1941. Outflanked and forced into headlong retreat by invading German 2nd and 12th Armies, the British force in Greece (some 60,000 men) was threatened with encirclement and capture. The holding of the line based on Thermopylae until the night of 24–5 April enabled evacuation to continue from southern Greek ports until 27 April, by which time about 45,000 troops (but very little equipment) had escaped, mostly to Crete*. See Balkans, German invasion of the.

Thoma, General Witter Wilhelm (1891 –1948) German soldier who commanded German ground forces in the Spanish Civil War and was a tank commander under Guderian* in the battle for France*. In 1942 he briefly commanded the Afrika Korps* but was captured by the British during the climactic Battle of El Alamein* in October.

Thompson Submachine-gun American-built infantry weapon. Heavy and expensive to make, the famous 0.45-inch 'Tommy Gun' was utterly reliable and much admired by those US, British and French troops equipped with it. The gun had first appeared in 1928 and almost 1,400,000 were eventually produced. Although cost per unit was steadily reduced during the war, less expensive weapons were preferred for mass Allied issue. See Submachine-gun.

Thunderclap, Operation Code-name for the Allied bombing of Dresden, February 1945. See Strategic Bombing Offensive.

Thursday Code-name for an operation mounted in northern Burma* by Orde Wingate's* Chindits* behind Japanese lines in March 1944.

Tiger Tank (PzKpfw VI) As early as 1937, work had begun on the development of a heavy German 'breakthrough' tank* to lead the assaults of armoured divisions, but the project had lapsed in an atmosphere of confidence in the long-term success of the Panzerkampfwagen III* and IV* types. This confidence was dented by the tank-for-tank performance of the panzers against British and French armour in 1940, and completely shattered the following year by serious defeats at the hands of Russian T34* and KV* machines. In autumn 1941, therefore, the

heavy tank specification was urgently revived.

Production of the PzKpfw VI Tiger E began in August 1942. At the time of its introduction, the Tiger was the most powerful tank in the world. Its formidable 88mm main armament could pierce 112mm of armour at about 1,400 yards, and its own frontal armour was impervious to any artillery attack. Nonetheless, it had its weaknesses. Its engine and gearbox needed careful maintenance and, although offering light and easy handling, produced an unspectacular performance that undermined attempts to use the Tiger in its planned breakthrough role at Stalingrad* and Kursk*. Furthermore, its smooth and distinctive suspension system, formed by overlapping roadwheels, froze solid during Russian winter nights. When used defensively or in an ambush, however, the Tigers were supremely effective in all theatres and they took a particularly heavy toll of the comparatively vulnerable Allied Shermans*.

The original 642hp power plant was uprated after 250 completions, but later modifications were mostly intended to reduce the time and cost of construction. As the more nimble Allied tanks developed the tactic of outmanoeuvring the Tiger and attacking its more vulnerable rear, the number of well-trained German crews capable of efficiently maintaining and using it declined sharply, and the Tiger was phased out of production when new heavy designs became available. At first only 12 Tigers a month were delivered and, although output improved, a modest 1,335 had been completed when production stopped in August 1944.
BRIEF DATA (PzKpfw VI Tiger E) Type: 5-man heavy tank; Engine: 692hp petrol; Max speed: 24mph; Range: 62m; Arms: 1 × 88mm gun, 2 × 7.92mm mg; Armour: max 110mm.

Timoshenko, Marshal Semion (1895– 1970) Russian cavalry officer and personal friend of Stalin* before the war, Timoshenko served in Bessarabia during the Russo-Finnish War* and was subsequently made a marshal and appointed Commissar of Defence, charged with improving the organization and training of the Red Army* (whose relative impotence in the face of the minute Finnish forces had accelerated the demand for change). Although severely hampered by lack of modern equipment, Timoshenko introduced harsh discipline and training techniques for the armies of the Central Soviet Front. The process of replacing the traditional horse-mounted cavalry with light tanks was speeded up, though it was still far from complete when the German invasion of the Soviet Union was launched in June 1941 and Timoshenko was appointed a member of Stavka*.

Assaulted by 55 German divisions along a 300-mile front, Timoshenko's 47 divisions were forced back 600 miles, losing roughly 400,000 men and over 4,000 tanks. Transferred to the Southwest Front in September 1941, there was again little that Timoshenko could do to salvage the disastrous defeats suffered by forces under his predecessor, Marshal Budënny*. In May 1942, under pressure from Stalin, Timoshenko planned an offensive against Kharkov*, unaware of the build-up of German forces there for their own assault. The outcome appears to have influenced Stalin's view of Timoshenko's abilities. Transferred to the Northwest Front, he played a limited role as Stavka representative in the Baltic and Balkans*, and in operational planning, though he was nominally in overall command of the 2nd and 3rd Ukrainian Fronts* under operational control of Generals Malinovsky* and Tolbukhin*. Timoshenko's early setbacks made him to some extent the scapegoat for Soviet lack of preparedness in 1941. His relative lack of high decorations is a measure of his eclipse in Soviet military iconography. See also Eastern Front.

Tinian Geographically central island of the Mariana* Group in the Central Pacific, it was chosen, along with Saipan* and Guam*, as an American strategic objective in the last phase of the Pacific War* because it could provide air bases from which to launch B-29* bombers against Japanese home territory (see Map 11). Tinian held three good airfields, with a fourth under construction, and was assaulted from Saipan (which had just been taken by US Marines) on 24 July 1944, after a ferocious pre-invasion bombardment. The 4th Marine Division, the first to land, took Admiral Kakuda's 9,000-strong garrison by surprise and established a beachhead, which was consolidated the next day and joined by the 2nd Marine Division on the 26th. Fighting in the north and the south, the 4th and 2nd Marines drove back Japanese counter-attacks that resulted in enormous Japanese casualties, but the island was secured by 1 August, when all organized resistance ceased. US casualties were relatively small by amphibious* standards, with 300 marines killed in comparison with the Japanese figure of nearly 5,000.

Tirpitz The *Tirpitz* was the second of the German Navy's* giant battleships and was virtually identical in all but subsidiary armament to her sister the *Bismarck*. On 16 January 1942, she sailed from Wilhelmshaven for Norway* where she spent her entire career. She never took part in any surface action, but instead lurked in the fjords as a constant threat to Allied Arctic convoys*. As such, she caused considerable disruption by her very existence, the mere suggestion of her movement provoking the fatal scattering of convoy PQ17 in July 1942. Obliged to maintain a strong fleet to guard the area against her, the British launched repeated air attacks on the *Tirpitz*, most of which failed against strong anti-aircraft* defences in the restricted approaches to the fjords.

On 6 September 1943, the *Tirpitz* ventured out (with the *Scharnhorst* and ten destroyers) to bombard Spitzbergen weather station, but on 20 September she was badly damaged in Altenfjord by Royal Navy* X-Craft midget* submarines. She was never again an active threat. Barely had her damaged machinery and main armament been repaired, when she was bombed by Royal Navy carrier aircraft on 3 April 1944. In September a force of Avro Lancaster* bombers armed with 12,000lb 'Tallboy' bombs* caused further serious damage that could not be repaired so far north. The *Tirpitz* was then moved south to Tromsö for use as a floating coastal battery, where three 'Tallboys' from another force of Lancasters sank her on 12 November 1944.

BRIEF DATA (1942) Displacement: 42,900 tons; Dimensions: o/a lgth – 882' 9", b – 118' 3"; Speed: 29 knots; Armament: 8 × 15" (4 × 2) gun, 12 × 5.9" gun, 16 × 4.1" AA gun, 16 × 37mm AA gun, 70 × 20mm AA gun, 8 × 21" TT, 6 aircraft.

Tito, Josip Broz (1892–1980) Leader of the successful partisan resistance* in Yugoslavia and a national hero. Tito had been General Secretary of the Yugoslav Communist Party since 1937. He was prompted to organize an armed movement against Axis forces occupying Yugoslavia by appeals for assistance from Moscow after the German invasion of Russia* (see Balkans, German invasion). He took field command of his troops – named partisans after irregular units which had fought Napoleon – in August 1941, and enjoyed immediate success. By mid-September, his forces controlled a large part of western Serbia, which they administered on the Soviet model.

At this stage, the Serbian nationalist Chetniks were receiving material and propaganda support from London. Negotiations between Tito and Chetnik leader Mihajlovic* foundered on the latter's deep hatred of communism, and in November the Chetniks openly attacked the partisans. The clashes which followed allowed the Germans to reclaim all of Serbia by December, and the depleted partisans withdrew to the mountains of East Bosnia. From there Tito founded the 1st Proletarian Brigade, and gradually fought his way north

towards Croatia during 1942. In the autumn of that year he established a political organization – the Anti-Fascist Council of National Liberation of Yugoslavia (AVNOJ) – and in November the partisans took Bihac on the Croatian border.

The Chetniks, although they were still supplied from Britain, had begun collaborating with Axis forces. In January 1943, they joined with Italians and Montenegrins in a German offensive that all but trapped Tito in Montenegro. In May, the partisans again narrowly escaped encirclement and, shortly after the Italian surrender of September, the Germans launched Operation Thunderbolt – a major onslaught that drove Tito back into the Bosnian hills by February 1944.

In 1943, there had been only four lightly equipped partisan divisions, and the alpine geography of Yugoslavia had been their main protection against much larger German forces. In the summer, a British mission had reached Tito and realized that London was supplying the wrong army. The latter part of 1943 saw an important increase in British support, and Anglo-American aid began arriving in quantity after the Tehran Conference* at the end of the year. Tito had become Premier of a cabinet formed out of AVNOJ in November and, at the time of his last enforced change of headquarters in May 1944, his army was 250,000 strong and bolstered by Allied officers and equipment.

Throughout 1944, Tito strengthened his diplomatic and military positions. Pressure from the British forced the exiled King Peter II to recognize the partisans and AVNOJ in June, and in November a power-sharing agreement between Tito and the Royalist Prime Minister, Subasic, reflected the communists' refusal to countenance the immediate return of the King. Tito had met Stalin* for the first time in August, and by the end of that month the Germans were on the retreat. On 20 October, he led his victorious army into Belgrade alongside the Soviet 3rd Ukrainian Front*.

It was not until May 1945 that the partisans met up with the British 8th Army in Trieste, but at Yalta in February all the Allied powers had acknowledged Tito's position. In March he set up a provisional government with Subasic representing the royalist minority as Foreign Minister. In the elections that followed, Tito received a full vote of confidence and in November 1945 the constituent assembly declared Yugoslavia a republic. See Balkans, Russian campaign in.

Tobruk Important Libyan port situated some 300 miles east of Benghazi*. In 1940 it was held by the Italians, who had heavily fortified its landward perimeter, but it fell to the British on 22 January 1941, becoming a vital forward supply base for Allied desert operations (see Egypt; Map 7). Tobruk was defended in isolation when the British retreated before the first Axis offensive, commanded by Lt General Rommel* in April 1941, and it remained under siege for the next six months, threatening the rear of the Axis advance. Although Rommel's attacks on the fortress were repulsed by the garrison under General Morshead*, British land operations to relieve Tobruk also failed, and its survival depended on the depleted Mediterranean Fleet which protected seaborne supplies. Rommel abandoned the siege of Tobruk on 4 December 1941, when the British Crusader* offensive forced his retreat from Cyrenaica.

After his victory at Gazala* in June 1942, Rommel found Tobruk less adequately defended. It fell in a single day – 21 June – resulting in the surrender of 35,000 British troops and a priceless haul of supplies. Tobruk changed hands for the last time on 13 November 1942, abandoned by Rommel in his rapid retreat after El Alamein*. See Desert War.

Togo, Shigenori (1882–1950) Japanese diplomat with considerable experience in European politics, Togo had served first as secretary to Japan's Berlin and Washington embassies during the 1920s and early 30s, and was later appointed ambassador to Berlin (December 1937) and then to Moscow (October 1938–August 1940). From October 1941, Togo worked in Premier Tojo's* cabinet as Foreign Minister, though his serious attempts to find grounds for settlement of the disputes between Japan and the United States were hindered rather than aided by the increasingly inflexible demands of Tojo and the militarist cabinet. A firm opponent of the surprise attack on Pearl Harbor* and the increasingly dictatorial policies of Premier Tojo, Togo eventually resigned his office in September 1942 in protest at the establishment of the Greater East Asia Ministry (see Greater East Asia Co-Prosperity Sphere), but was reappointed Foreign Minister by Kantaro Suzuki* in April 1945, and charged with seeking a peace settlement with the Allies. He resigned in August 1945 and was later sentenced to 20 years imprisonment for 'crimes of conspiracy against peace' by the International Military Tribunal* for the Far East. He died in 1950 in an American military hospital.

Tojo, General Hideki (1884–1948) Extreme nationalist Japanese Prime Minister, in office from October 1941 to July 1944, Tojo had risen from military police chief of the Kwantung Army* in 1935 to its chief of staff in 1937 and deputy War Minister in 1938. A leader of the extreme militarist group *Toseiha* (see Ultranationalism), in a period when the Japanese Army* was beginning to force government policy, Tojo was well-positioned to exploit the destabilization of Japanese domestic politics, and first entered the government as deputy War Minister in 1938. A direct and uncomplicated personality, Tojo was unequivocal in his belief about the legitimacy of the use of force to guarantee Japan's security. The declaration by Prime Minister Konoe* of the 'New Order for East Asia*', in reality a model for the assumption of political and economic control in China* and Manchukuo* by Japan in November 1938, was fully supported by him.

As War Minister from 1940 to 1941,

Tojo persistently refused to sanction the withdrawal of Japanese troops from China, and regarded war with the United States as inevitable. This attitude contributed to the crisis in negotiations with the US and the subsequent downfall of Konoe, whom Tojo replaced in October. After the outbreak of war, Tojo concentrated on centralizing control inside Japan and reinforcing public support behind the war effort, by using such measures as 'recommended' candidates in the 1942 election. He established the Greater East Asia Ministry (see Greater East Asia Co-Prosperity Sphere) to unify administration of colonies and occupied territories, attempting unsuccessfully to gain their support by such measures as the Greater East Asia Conference. Essentially a dictatorship of the Supreme Command, Japan's Premier controlled the cabinet by monopolizing all important posts. In February 1944 Tojo appointed himself Chief of Staff in order to direct war planning more closely. But unable after 1942 to adjust his policies to the worsening war situation, Tojo was finally forced to resign in July 1944. After an unsuccessful suicide attempt in September 1945, when American forces occupied Tokyo, Tojo was tried as a class A war criminal and executed by hanging in December 1948.

Tokyo Express American nickname for the Japanese seaborne shuttle of supplies and reinforcements for their forces on Guadalcanal*, during the campaign for control of the island in the second half of 1942. Originally called the 'Cactus Express' by American forces in the area, derived from the code-name for Guadalcanal, the term 'Tokyo Express' was substituted later.

Tokyo Fire Raid See Strategic Bombing Offensive.

Tokyo Rose (Mrs Iva Ikuko Toguri D'Aquino) (1916–) An American citizen of Japanese parents, she transmitted daily radio broadcasts from Tokyo that were designed to demoralize Allied troops in the Far East. Caught in Japan on a family visit at the outbreak of war, Mrs D'Aquino worked for the Japanese Broadcasting Corporation (NHK), where she was trained by an American POW. Her broadcasts included reports of Japanese victories and the lack of interest of Americans at home in the plight of their troops overseas. Her nickname was coined by American troops who actually enjoyed her programmes, which also featured contemporary music. After the war, Mrs D'Aquino was convicted of treason and sentenced to 10 years imprisonment, of which she served six. Some 30 years later, she sought to prove her innocence, claiming that she had been coerced into broadcasting for the Japanese and had been one of a number of women known as 'Tokyo Rose'. In January 1977, she was pardoned by US President Gerald Ford on his last full day in office. See also Propaganda.

Tolbukhin, Marshal Fyodor I. (1894–1949) Soviet commander of the 57th Army which figured prominently in the encirclement of the German 6th Army inside Stalingrad* in early 1943. In 1944 Tolbukhin was appointed to command the 4th Ukrainian Front* for the drive to recapture the Crimea*. Promoted to marshal, he subsequently directed operations in the Ukraine*, Bulgaria*, Rumania*, Austria* and Hungary*. In 1945–6 Tolbukhin was Supreme Commander of Soviet forces in Bulgaria and Rumania.

Tone The two *Tone* Class ships – the other was the *Chikuma* – were designed for the Japanese Navy* as fast, well-armed light cruisers along the lines of the *Mogami* Class, but the expiry of the London Naval Treaty in 1936 allowed their completion as heavy cruisers with 8-inch main armament. This was all mounted forward of the bridge leaving the quarterdeck free for the deployment of five reconnaissance aircraft. Both ships were ready just before the war and formed Cruiser Squadron 8 with Admiral Yamamoto's main strike force in December

1941. After almost three years of combat, during which both units were given an extra 45 25mm anti-aircraft* guns, the *Chikuma* was sunk by carrier aircraft off Samar at the Battle of Leyte Gulf*. The *Tone* was sunk by air attack in the shallows of Kure dockyard the following July, and was scrapped after the war.
BRIEF DATA (*Tone*, 1941) Displacement: 11,215 tons; Dimensions: o/a lgth – 661′ 6″, b – 63′ 6″; Speed: 35 knots; Armament: 8 × 8″ gun (4 × 2), 8 × 5″ DP gun, 12 × 25mm AA gun, 4 × 13mm AA gun, 12 × 24″ TT, 5 aircraft.

Torch, Operation Code-name for the Anglo-American invasion of French Northwest Africa in November 1942. Throughout the year pressure had mounted from Stalin for the Allies to open a 'Second Front' to relieve Russia, and President Roosevelt was committed to targeting the first major US land offensive against Germany. US service chiefs favoured an early invasion of mainland Europe but, after the collapse of the British 8th Army in Cyrenaica (see Desert War), they were persuaded to the British view that this was impossible. A proposal to expand Operation Gymnast – the British contingency plan for an invasion of Northwest Africa – had been rejected by American planners after the Washington Conference* at the start of the year. In late July this was revived and adopted as Operation Super-Gymnast. For dramatic effect, the name was changed to Operation Torch.

Over 100,000 Vichy* French troops were stationed in Northwest Africa – scattered around Morocco, Algeria and Tunisia – and the Allies made great efforts to secure at least a passive response to the projected invasion. British attacks on French colonial bases since 1940 had caused great antagonism. General de Gaulle*, whose Free French forces had taken part in some of them, was excluded from the operation and Torch was given a pronounced American appearance. An American C-in-C (Eisenhower*) was chosen for the operation, most of the advance landing parties were to be US troops and all forward shipping was to display the Stars and Stripes. Secret negotiations took place between US officers and sympathetic French officers in Northwest Africa to prepare the way for collaboration and a Vichy officer with known anti-Nazi views, General Giraud*, was chosen to act as a rallying point for friendly French forces after the landings.

The location of the landings provoked some argument among the Allies. The British, anxious to surround Rommel* in Libya before the arrival of Axis reinforcements, wanted to invade as far east as was feasible, on the Mediterranean coast of Algeria. US planners preferred the Atlantic coast of Morocco, avoiding the hazards of the Mediterranean* and any threat of French (or Spanish) aggression at their rear. The eventual result was a compromise. One purely American convoy of 102 ships sailed from the US for Casablanca* with 24,500 troops. The Royal Navy* escorted another 250 ships from Britain with two landing forces – 18,000 Americans for Oran* in Morocco and an Anglo-American group of similar strength for Algiers*. All the landings were synchronized to take place at 1 a.m. on 8 November.

The giant convoys reached Africa on time with the loss of only one transport and the main landings went off successfully. Subsidiary frontal attacks on the harbours at Algiers and Oran met with resistance, however, and confused traffic jams soon built up on the other beachheads, slowing moves towards the cities themselves. The slow pace of events undermined the efforts of poorly informed local collaborators, whose broadcast appeals in the name of Giraud had little effect, and fighting broke out, particularly around Oran. Thus on the afternoon of 9 November, Eisenhower's deputy, Mark Clark*, began negotiations for a ceasefire with Admiral Darlan*, overall C-in-C of Vichy forces, by chance in Algiers visiting his sick son.

By that night Hitler had pressured the Vichy government into accepting German 'support' in Tunisia. Its leader, Marshal Pétain*, was manoeuvring to prevent the German occupation of southern France. He sent a series of vague and contradictory instructions to Darlan, who delayed a ceasefire agreement until 11 November, when German forces entered Vichy France. The half-hearted fighting in Morocco then ceased, but Darlan's writ failed to secure the active support of French officers in Tunisia, who retreated into the hinterland as Axis forces stepped up their airlift into Tunis.

Darlan was now officially endorsed by Eisenhower as French commander in Northwest Africa. He organized the co-operation of Vichy forces in Dakar* and West Africa, but the overall situation remained confused and definite instructions failed to reach Toulon and the French Fleet, which delayed sailing to Africa and scuttled itself on 27 November (see French Navy), a serious blow to the Allies as they pushed east into Tunisia*. Darlan, until now portrayed by Allied propaganda as a pro-Nazi, rapidly became a major public relations problem. To quell outrage in Britain and the US he was publicly described as a 'temporary expedient', which did little to stabilize the situation in Northwest Africa. Darlan was assassinated on Christmas Eve and Giraud temporarily took his place. The assault on Tunisia – by now heavily reinforced with Axis troops – was able to proceed without further delays.

Torpedo A self-propelled projectile carrying a warhead which detonates against a ship's side below the waterline, the torpedo was the most destructive naval weapon of WW2, as it had been in WW1. By 1939 torpedoes were considered superfluous to cruiser armament by most navies but they remained the standard weapon of the submarine*, the destroyer* and various smaller boats. They were also used by naval aircraft and proved the most successful aerial anti-shipping weapon of the war.

Conventional torpedoes had changed little in 40 years and were powered by air

or steam. During the 1930s both Germany and Japan had developed battery-powered electric torpedoes. The Japanese had abandoned these by 1939, but the German Navy* used its electric torpedoes to good effect in the Atlantic* early in the war. The great advantage of these was that they left no visible trail in their wake, but they lacked the speed, range or reliability of the air-steam types which were still used for most attacks on merchant ships. In 1944 Germany introduced the T7 *Zaunkönig* acoustic torpedo for use against convoy* escorts. This homed in on the sound of a heavy ship's propellers and was answered by Allied 'Foxer' noisemaking devices, which were towed at a safe distance behind a ship to confuse the torpedo.

Early Allied torpedoes were all of the air-steam type and the US Navy* in particular suffered an excess of malfunctions in its standard Mark XIV torpedo. An American electric torpedo was completed, with help from salvaged German models, in late 1943 and became available in large numbers the following year. The Allies also developed the valuable 'Fido' anti-submarine homing torpedo, which was delivered by naval patrol craft.

By far the best torpedo of the war was the Japanese Navy's* 24-inch 'Long Lance', which was fitted to their cruisers and all but the oldest destroyers in 1941. This oxygen-powered weapon could deliver a 1,000lb warhead at 49 knots over almost 11 miles, giving IJN units a distinct advantage in surface combat. The standard 21-inch torpedo used by Japanese submarines was also an excellent and reliable weapon. See Submarines; Midget Submarines.

Torpedo Boats Fast, light boats armed with torpedoes had been built in large numbers by the world's major navies before and during WW1. Although great claims had been made for the potential of massed torpedo boat attacks on major warships, the craft themselves were inevitably difficult to control in open waters and the theory remained unproven in the 1930s when large-scale construction of the type recommenced after a post-war lapse.

The German Navy* led the way with their formidable *Schnellboote*, known to the Allies as E-boats. These were fast, with relatively powerful surface armament, superb diesel engines and a good purpose-designed hull. Their low silhouette was valuable in pre-radar* warfare and they were the most successful arm of the German Navy along with the U-boats. Used to harass shipping in countless actions off the south and east coasts of Britain, they remained a considerable thorn in the side of the Royal Navy* until 1944, when losses mounted in the face of growing Allied radar and air superiority. In the Baltic and the Black Seas they were the German Navy's main weapon, fighting a fierce and very successful campaign against Russian light forces.

The British placed large orders for a new Motor Torpedo Boat (MTB) in 1935. Less expensively researched than their German counterparts, they relied on more flammable petrol engines, were slower and had less surface armament. Once it became clear that their main adversaries would be the E-boats, against which torpedoes were useless, the design was produced as a Motor Gun Boat (MGB), armed for surface engagement with small craft. By 1944 a combined MTB/MGB was in service that could effectively attack both blockaded shipping and E-boats.

The US Navy* had regarded torpedo boats as generally unsuitable for Pacific warfare, and had acquired only about 70 craft of various types from 1939 to 1941. Three major models were mass-produced after 1941: the 78ft PT71 Class, the 80ft PT103 Class and the British-designed PT368 Class of 70-ft length. They carried two to four torpedoes* and were also produced in gunboat, depth-charge and smoke-making modifications. In the 'island' campaigns they proved highly effective, particularly in the restricted waters around Guadalcanal*, but, like European boats, they were never able successfully to take on major warships.

The Japanese built torpedo boats in numbers from 1940, designed with the aid of a British boat captured at Canton in 1938. About 250 were built by the end of the war, along with over 100 Motor Gun Boats intended to escort torpedo craft in offensive operations. A number of captured steel-hulled Dutch boats were also employed and the Japanese Navy* built more than 100 smaller armed launches, mostly for river work in China* or for training.

The Mediterranean powers used large numbers of small torpedo boats, which were well suited to the calm waters of the theatre. Activities of French units were inevitably restricted, but the Italian MAS boats were highly regarded within the naval service, and achieved many individual wartime successes, without significantly affecting the broader strategic picture.

Virtually the whole of the Red Navy's* surface war was fought by its 'Mosquito fleets' of torpedo boats and other small craft. In June 1941, 269 MTBs were in Russian service (although half of these were in the Pacific and could never reach European waters), and 180 more were built during wartime. These were largely made possible by Lend-Lease* supplies of US engines and they represented – along with about 700 other small craft – almost the only Soviet warship production of the period.

The main scourge of the torpedo boat in WW2 was the destroyer*, which had been developed originally as the Torpedo Boat Destroyer and possessed both the speed and the armament for the task. In practice, however, destroyers were usually needed for fleet or convoy protection and the light craft frequently fought out their own almost private wars punctuated by interference from aircraft.

Toulon Main French naval base in the Mediterranean*. See French Navy.

Tovey, Admiral Lord John (1885–1971) British naval officer who began the war as

Rear Admiral, Destroyers with the Royal Navy's* Mediterranean Fleet. In 1940, he was promoted and given command of the Home Fleet based at Scapa Flow in the Orkney Islands. In this important post he organized the protection of convoys* and maintained the successful blockade of German ports. He also had overall command of the operation to find and sink the *Bismarck** in 1941, and later advocated an attack on the *Tirpitz** in Norwegian waters. The Admiralty preferred him to concentrate on convoy protection, and Tovey's last wartime position – in charge of naval forces in eastern England from 1943 – also involved protecting supplies, this time for offensive operations in Northwest Europe* following the Normandy* landings in June 1944.

Toyoda, Admiral Soemu (1885–1957) Commander of the Yokosuka Naval Base and the Kure Naval District from September 1941 until his appointment succeeding Admiral Koga* as C-in-C of the Combined Fleet in 1944, Toyoda was faced with the task of designing a strategy to halt the American advance, now almost within striking range of Japanese home territory. His plan, Operation A-Go*, which anticipated drawing the US Pacific Fleet away from the Marianas* for a final engagement, was founded on the traditional concept of the 'decisive battle', though it also had to take into account the limited remaining resources of the Combined Fleet, which were insufficient to support any large-scale counter-offensive. The defeat of his fleet in the resulting Battle of the Philippine Sea*, and later at Leyte Gulf*, saw the virtual destruction of Japan's remaining air and naval power (see Japanese Navy).

Despite the apparent hopelessness of Japan's position in mid-1945, Toyoda was a strong supporter of the Army extremists, General Anami* and General Umezu*, from the time of his appointment as Chief of the Naval General Staff in May, and continued to oppose unconditional surrender. Toyoda was later acquitted of war crimes by the International Military Tribunal* for the Far East.

Transportation Plan Successful though controversial scheme for air operations designed to isolate the Normandy* battle zone by heavy preparatory bombing of communications, including railways, bridges and roads, by combined Anglo-American air forces during the spring of 1944. The plan was strongly promoted by SHAEF* and by Deputy Supreme Allied Commander Tedder*, although it faced substantial opposition from US and British bomber commanders who resented the diversion of resources from German targets (see Strategic Bombing Offensive). Pressed for personally by Supreme Allied Commander Eisenhower*, and endorsed by the commander of French resistance forces, General Koenig*, the plan was put into effect during May. By D-Day*, rail traffic in the region had been halved and all routes over the Seine north of Paris had been closed. See Northwest Europe, Allied invasion of.

Tresckow, Major General Henning von (1901–44) Senior German operations officer of Army Group Centre on the Eastern Front*, serving as Chief of Staff to Kluge*, Bock* and Manstein*, with whom he apparently planned to end the war by assassinating Hitler. Tresckow was the originator of Operation Flash, which involved planting a bomb in Hitler's personal aircraft in March 1943. After the failure of the operation – the bomb did not detonate – he collaborated with Stauffenberg in Operation Valkyrie (see July Bomb Plot) to overthrow Hitler. On the day after the attempt failed, Tresckow killed himself.

Tripoli Major Libyan port used as a supply centre for Axis forces in North Africa. The British Compass offensive of early 1941 (see Egypt) had been ordered to a halt short of Tripoli and General O'Connor's* forces were diverted to Greece. Tripoli was eventually taken by the 8th Army on 23 January 1943. The entry was unopposed (to the relief of a British force critically short of supplies) but military facilities had been disabled by Rommel's* retreating forces and required extensive repair, delaying the 8th Army's advance to Tunisia*.

Trott zu Solz, Hans Adam von (1909–44) German Foreign Office official and prominent member of the Kreisau Circle of anti-Nazi German aristocrats and Christians. Between 1938 and 1942 Trott zu Solz made a number of trips abroad in an attempt to establish contacts with the Allied Authorities. In 1938 a visit to State Department officials in Washington was unsuccessful in convincing the US of the need to support a German resistance to Hitler. In the following year Trott zu Solz approached senior Oxford contacts, originally made during his time there as a Rhodes Scholar, but again failed to convince the British government of the seriousness or viability of an organized German alternative to Hitler's regime. In 1942, meetings with US intelligence chief Allen Dulles* in Switzerland were again inconclusive.

After the failure of the July Bomb Plot* in 1944, Trott zu Solz was among the hundreds arrested. He was tried, found guilty of treason and executed by hanging (with piano wire) on 26 August. See Resistance: Germany.

Truk Island group in the central Carolines (Central Pacific), naturally defended by an encircling reef with only four navigable passages whose chief town, Truk, on Doublon Island, served as a major headquarters and base of the Japanese Navy* Combined Fleet (see Map 10). Its location and strength threatened Allied advances in the Central and South Pacific areas and the presence there of the giant battleship, the *Musashi**, rendered it a formidable obstacle in the eyes of the American Pacific commanders who argued over the best strategy for neutralizing it during 1943. By early 1944, however, the sophistication of the American bypassing tactic and the clear superiority of the American naval forces in

the Pacific (see Pacific War) had sealed the fate of Truk. Subjected to ferocious air and naval bombardment from Admiral Mitscher's* Fast Carrier Task Force 58 during February 1944, it was left to 'wither on the vine' as the American 5th Fleet continued its advance through the Central Pacific. See also Marshall Islands.

Truman, Harry S. (1884–1972) Thirty-third American President who took over from Roosevelt* after his death in April 1945, Truman had been elected Vice President only five months previously and was thus little prepared for the enormous tasks facing him, as the war reached its climax. Nevertheless, Truman's record as a senator, and notably as Chairman of the Special Committee Investigating National Defense (also called the Truman Committee) which sat from February 1941 as watchdog and guardian of the United States' large-scale military and industrial expansion, had already earned him considerable respect in American political circles. Though unable to contain Stalin's* imperialist appetites in eastern Europe (see Conferences) during the final phase of the war, and obliged to tackle weighty international issues such as the establishment of the UN Organization and the employment of the atomic bomb*, Truman impressed Allied leaders meeting him for the first time at the San Francisco and Potsdam Conferences.

Advised by an expert committee of politicians and scientists in a report of June 1945 on the desirability of using the newly tested atomic bomb quickly, Truman was responsible for the final decision to use the bomb against Japan to bring the war to a speedy end, a decision which he continued to defend throughout his political career. Winning election to the presidency in his own right in 1948 following a high-profile campaign, Truman appeared to have established himself as an able president. In foreign policy, Truman evolved the doctrine of supporting 'free peoples who are resisting subjugation by armed minorities . . .' known as the 'Truman

Doctrine', which he followed up with support for the Marshall Plan and the Berlin airlifts. He also brought the United States into its first peacetime military alliance – NATO. Nevertheless, from 1947 onwards, Truman's authority was weakened by the anti-communist hysteria embodied in 'McCarthyism' and the last two and a half years of his presidency were overshadowed by the Korean War. Truman retired from politics in 1953 at the end of his term of office.

Tsuji, Colonel Masanobu (1902–68?) An important Ultranationalist* Japanese Army* staff officer who served with the Japanese Expeditionary Force in northern China*, the Kwantung Army* and in Malaya*, the Dutch East Indies*, Guadalcanal*, the Philippines* and Thailand*. He was involved in much of the planning for the Japanese campaign in Malaya and Singapore in 1941. Escaping to China after the war, Tsuji served as an adviser to Chiang Kai-shek*. He returned to Japan in 1949. Tsugi disappeared in North Vietnam in 1961. He was declared dead in 1968.

Tunisia, Campaign in, 1942–3 Final campaign of the war in Africa (see Map 8). If French forces had immediately co-operated with the Allied Torch* landings on 8 November 1942, combined landings deep into Tunisia would have followed within a few days, with the object of preventing large-scale Axis reinforcements from using the major supply ports of Tunis and Bizerte. Instead French opposition to Torch, mainly in Morocco, delayed Allied plans. Unopposed Allied landings nevertheless took place at the western Algerian ports of Bougie and Bône, followed by a limited advance into Tunisia as far as Souk el Arba, 80 miles from Tunis. This was completed by 16 November, but the main striking force then paused to await reinforcements from General Anderson*, Allied Commander in Algiers. The tiny German forces already in Tunisia counter-attacked, occupying important points on the roads south to Libya and defeating a much larger combination of French and forward Allied forces at Medjez el Bab, 35 miles west of Tunis. By the time Anderson's major push from Souk el Arba got underway on 25 November, 24,000 Axis troops occupied most of northern Tunisia.

The three-pronged Allied offensive, which included American armour brought all the way from Morocco, suffered heavily from German air supremacy, but pursued the outnumbered defenders to within 12 miles of Tunis, before again pausing to concentrate strength after being checked at Djedeida. In early December Nehring, the local Axis commander, counterattacked with all his armoured strength (only about 40 tanks, but including the first two Tigers*), driving the Allies back to positions around Medjez el Bab with heavy losses.

Anderson attempted another offensive on 24 December, but this was quickly abandoned in foul weather after preliminary attacks had failed to hold important hill vantage points (see Longstop Hill). Colonel General von Arnim* had by now arrived to take command of Axis forces in Tunisia and, with the weather precluding further Allied operations towards Tunis, large-scale reinforcements reached him across the short Mediterranean route from Sicily, most of them by air.

Meanwhile Field Marshal Rommel's* army was retreating towards Tunisia, pursued by the British 8th Army under Montgomery* (see Desert War). By the turn of the year Rommel was at Beurat, less than 300 miles from the border. The British had paused to prepare an assault on the position, but when this came in mid-January, it failed to trap Rommel, who made a quick, planned withdrawal after sending one panzer division ahead to counter any threat from American forces in southern Tunisia. His retreat bypassed Tripoli*, where port facilities were blown up by departing Italians on 22 January, and stopped at the Mareth Line*, 80 miles inside Tunisia. A further withdrawal to stronger positions behind the Wadi Akarit was vetoed by Mussolini who, furious at the loss of Tripoli, informed Rommel of his pending replacement by an Italian, General Messe*.

While Montgomery, his supplies exhausted, spent several weeks at Tripoli, both German commanders planned attacks on the 1st Allied Army in Tunisia. Rommel saw the opportunity to threaten vital Allied supply lines by breaking through the Faïd Pass, guarded by inexperienced American forces on the Allied southern wing. Von Arnim*, who commanded most of the 100,000 Axis troops then in Tunisia, also got High Command backing for an ambitious offensive in the north aimed at Medjez el Bab and then Beja, for which he claimed the majority of the available armour. As a result of this division of aims, both attacks were heavily outnumbered.

The assault on Faïd Pass got fully underway on 14 February, after a preliminary attack had been misinterpreted by the Allies as a feint, and had advanced 25 miles to Sbeitla within three days. Meanwhile a combat group sent from the Mareth Line had swung up from the southeast and arrived 35 miles further west. On 19–20 February these forces concentrated to attack the Kasserine Pass*, which guarded the road junction to Allied supply centres at Thala and Tebessa. It fell on the second day and Rommel moved north towards Thala, but was forced to withdraw from 22 February by the presence of strong Allied reserves. As the panzers retreated to face Montgomery at the Mareth Line, the Americans delayed any counterstroke in ignorance of his true weakness.

Rommel was now given full command of all Axis forces in Africa and General Alexander* arrived to oversee Allied operations. Full local control was given too late to Rommel. Heavy Allied losses in the south had not produced a general retreat and were offset by the costly defeat of von Arnim's northern offensive which opened on 26 February. Losses and delays there

forced Rommel to postpone until 6 March a planned attack on the 8th Army, now facing the Mareth Line at Médenine. Given time to build up his strength and his defences, Montgomery took a heavy toll of the panzers on the first day of the assault, prompting Rommel to call it off at once. By now a sick man, Rommel left Africa on 9 March, urging retreat on an unresponsive Hitler on the grounds that the two Allied armies could not now be kept apart. Von Arnim now regained overall command in Tunisia.

The Allies next concentrated on isolating Rommel's army, now commanded by Messe, at the Mareth Line*. The US 2nd Corps, on the southern edge of the 1st Army, began a diversionary move towards the coast north of the Line on 17 March, and the 8th Army's frontal assault opened three days later. The British eventually penetrated behind the Line to El Hamma on 27 March, but not before the bulk of Messe's army had withdrawn safely to hill defences behind the Wadi Akarit. With two-thirds of Messe's armour busy keeping 2nd Corps from the coast, the 8th Army broke through at Wadi Akarit on the night of 5–6 April, but they were slow to exploit their victory and the quarry escaped again – this time 150 miles north to another bottleneck at Enfidaville. The two halves of von Arnim's army were now linked in the defence of a 100-mile arc across northeast Tunisia.

The next Allied offensive was focused once more on Tunis and Bizerte, where the more open country increased the value of numerical strength. The US 2nd Corps was transferred north for the operation (its command passing from Patton* to Bradley*) and began a slow advance with massive air and artillery support on 23 April, along a 40-mile front stretching to the coast. This was preceded by strong subsidiary drives from British 1st Army units further south and a diversionary attack by the 8th Army on Enfidaville. In total the Allies enjoyed a six-to-one advantage in troops (300,000), a 15-to-1 superiority in tanks (610) and similarly overwhelming strength in guns and aircraft.

The increased effectiveness of the Allied blockade in the Mediterranean Sea* had by this time virtually halted the flow of supplies to von Arnim's army, and it was critically short of fuel, ammunition and food. Although all the Allied advances had been halted by 25 April, the effort virtually exhausted Axis resources. As the 2nd Corps renewed its progress in the north, Alexander suspended Montgomery's expensive assault on Enfidaville and transferred two armoured divisions to the 1st Army for a renewed attack on Tunis from the south west, up the Medjerda valley. By the time this offensive (Operation Vulcan) was launched on 6 May, pulverizing most of the remaining German armour under a massive air and artillery bombardment, any other defence had all but disintegrated. The next day, 1st Army armoured cars* drove unopposed into Tunis, while US Forces in the north found Bizerte similarly abandoned. The defenders at Enfidaville, stranded without fuel, were quickly surrounded and by 13 May all Axis forces in Tunisia had capitulated. A few hundred men escaped by air to Sicily*, but over 150,000 were taken prisoner.

Tupolev SB-2 First used by the Red Air Force* in 1936, the SB-2 was superior to the RAF's* comparable Bristol Blenheim* bomber and was a success in the Spanish Civil War. It was obsolete by June 1941, but production continued into 1942 and the plane saw widespread action against German forces until 1943, mostly as a night-bomber. Over 6,000 were built, some of which were exported to China* in the late 1930s.
BRIEF DATA (SB-2, late model). Type: 3-man light bomber; Engine: 2 × 1,000hp Hispano-Souza; Max speed: 280mph; Ceiling: 35,000'; Range: 994m; Arms: 4 × 7.62mm mg; Bomb load: 1,210lb.

Tupolev TU-2 Soviet ground-support bomber which entered production in August 1942 as an intended replacement for the Petlakyov PE-2*. It was a formidable and reliable ground-support plane, yet the PE-2 continued to be built at ten times the rate of its successor and, although the TU-2 enjoyed a long post-war career, it saw only limited action before 1945.
BRIEF DATA (TU-2). Type: 4-man attack bomber; Engine: 2 × 1,850hp Shvetsov; Max speed: 342mph; Ceiling: 31,168'; Range: 1,553m (part loaded); Arms: 2 × 20mm cannon, 3 × 12.7mm mg; Bomb load: 5,000 lb.

Tupolev TU-25 Initial production models of this Soviet bomber were tested operationally in the autumn of 1942, and over 1,000 were delivered between early 1944 and the end of the war. They were deployed in ground-support and attack-bomber roles during the final Red Army* offensives on the Eastern Front*, and they continued in production and service with the post-war Polish and Chinese Air Forces.
BRIEF DATA (TU-25). Type: 4-man medium bomber; Engine: 2 × 1,850hp Mikulin; Max speed: 340mph; Ceiling: 31,170'; Range: 1,243m; Arms: 2 × 20mm cannon, 3 × 12.7mm mg; Bomb load: 6,600lb.

Turbulent, HMS Royal Navy T Class submarine* commanded by Lt Commander J. Linton, who specialized in attacking ships from virtually point-blank range. Based on Malta* and engaged in harassing Axis supplies to Tripoli* during 1942, the *Turbulent* was very successful, sinking four cargo ships and a destroyer* in one raid, and later sinking two ships and a destroyer in a night operation. *Turbulent* went down with all hands after being mined in March 1943.
BRIEF DATA (T Class) Displacement: 1,090 tons (surface); Dimensions: o/a lgth – 275', b – 26' 6"; Speed: 15.25 knots (9 submerged); Armament: 1 × 4" gun, 3 × 0.5" mg, 11 × 21" TT.

Tuscaloosa, USS See New Orleans, USS.

Twining, General Nathan Farragut (1897 –) Chief of Staff of US Army Air Forces

(USAAF*) in the South Pacific in 1942–3, and subsequently commander of the US 13th Air Force and US Air Forces in the Southwest Pacific, Twining directed the increasingly effective air operations against Japanese forces which were crucial to the eventual outcome of the war in that theatre. Transferred to Italy* for a time in 1944–5 to command the 15th Air Force as well as Allied Strategic Air Forces in the Mediterranean, Twining participated in the US Strategic Bombing Offensive* against Germany and eastern Europe before returning to the Pacific to command the 20th Air Force in B-29* bombing offensives against Japan itself.

Typhoon (Taifun) Code-name for the projected decisive German attack on Moscow*, September 1941. See Eastern Front.

U

U-48 The highest scoring U-boat of WW2. A Type VIIb submarine*, the U-48 sank 51 ships (310,407 tons) between the start of the war and June 1941. Type VII submarines were ocean-going boats built to meet minimum size requirements so that maximum numbers could be built under pre-war tonnage restrictions (see Anglo-German Naval Treaty). The first Type VIIa boats were launched in 1936 and the design remained in production until 1945, undergoing many minor modifications. The Type VIIb and the more heavily armed Type VIIc boats were the German Navy's* standard operational U-boats in the first years of the war, and hundreds were mass-produced. Like other surviving Type VII boats, the U-48 was reduced to training duties long before she was scuttled at the end of the war.

BRIEF DATA (Type VIIb) Displacement: 753 tons (surface); Dimensions: o/a lgth – 218′ 3″, b – 20′ 3″; Speed: 17.25 knots (8 submerged); Armament: 1 × 3.5″ gun, 1 × 20mm AA gun, 5 × 21″ TT.

U-110 Type IXb U-boat, it was sunk southwest of Ireland by Royal Navy* escort warships on 9 March 1941. Damaged by depth charges, the U-110 was abandoned by her crew and her captain – Lt Commander Lemp – set scuttling charges. These failed to detonate and before the U-110 was fatally rammed by the destroyer HMS *Broadway*, the Royal Navy captured an Enigma* cypher machine, which gave British intelligence priceless access to the German Navy's codes (see Atlantic, Battle of the). The Type IX U-boat was the German Navy's* standard long-range submarine* for much of the war. It was larger than the Type VII (see U-48) which was produced in greater numbers. Altogether, 370 Type IX submarines were built before production was stopped in favour of the greatly improved Type XXI in the last year of the war.

BRIEF DATA (Type IXb) Displacement: 1,051 tons (surface); Dimensions: o/a lgth – 251′, b – 22′ 3″; Speed: 18.25 knots (7.25 submerged); Armament: 1 × 4.1″ gun, 1 × 37mm AA gun, 1 × 20mm AA gun, 6 × 21″ TT.

Udet, Colonel General Ernst (1896–1941) Famous WWI flying ace and sometime companion of Hermann Göring*, Udet was appointed head of the Luftwaffe Technical Office in 1936 and three years later was given control of the new and powerful Office of Air Armament. A sparkling socialite and a good judge of fighter aircraft, Udet was a startlingly incompetent and lazy administrator, wholly unqualified for the tasks of overseeing all aspects of Luftwaffe development. Under his loose supervision the German aircraft industry descended into chaos. Resources were squandered on new designs sanctioned virtually at random, while production and development estimates were based largely on optimistic guesswork. In the labyrinthine confusion of Udet's vast offices, accurate information was quite lost to the High Command, who knew more about American production than their own by 1941. As existing aircraft were being phased out, their replacements often either failed to function or failed to appear at all. This was particularly disastrous for Germany's bomber programme which, additionally hamstrung by Udet's personal enthusiasm for dive-bombers, ground to a complete standstill, leaving the Luftwaffe stranded with obsolete types for the rest of the war.

Although Göring continued to support his long-time comrade almost to the end, the realities of German aircraft production impressed themselves on other Luftwaffe leaders during 1941. In despair and panic, Udet shot himself in November, and Erhard Milch* took over the bloated shambles of his bureaucracy. His death was officially ascribed to a plane crash and he was given a hero's funeral. Obsolete aircraft remained in production pending rationalization. See Luftwaffe.

U-Go Code-name for the attempted Japanese invasion of India from Burma* in March 1944.

Ukraine Country in the southwestern Soviet Union, with Kiev* as its capital, it was the primary objective of Field Marshal Rundstedt's* Army Group South in the German Barbarossa plan for the invasion of the Soviet Union (see Eastern Front). Initial resistance to Rundstedt's advance was led by General Kirponos*, commanding the Kiev Military District forces, who successfully checked Kleist's* and Reichenau's* armoured forces on the Polish border. But in early July Kirponos was forced back on Kiev and lost his life in an attempt to break out of a threatening encirclement. Forces in the region, one and a half million men in two concentrations at Kiev and to the south at Uman, were now renamed the Southwest Front* and put under command of Marshal Budënny. In mid-July Kleist's forces managed to drive a wedge between the two Soviet armies, and intercepted communications indicating the launch of a Russian counter-attack. Budënny's failure at this point to make a tactical withdrawal to the Dnieper* river to avoid encirclement resulted in one of the most notorious Soviet defeats of the war.

Counter-attacks mounted from Uman could not halt the German armoured encirclement of the Uman pocket by Kleist, Manteuffel and Schobert. Taking Novo Ukraina and Kirovograd on 25 and 30 July, the Germans closed the pincers on 8 August, with all resistance ended by the 22nd. Now advancing in concert with Guderian's* tank forces, moving south from Gomel, Kleist broke through the Russian 38th Army's defences on 12 September, and General Model's* panzers made contact with Guderian's force east of Kiev, completing the encirclement by the 16th. Denied permission to withdraw by Stalin, the Kiev army of over 600,000 men surrendered after five days of resistance. The magnitude of the German success in the Ukraine can only be balanced in retrospect. It is now generally agreed that Russian resistance* here contributed significantly to the failure of the German forces on the centre front to reach Moscow* before General Zhukov* and the winter halted their offensive.

Following the decisive Russian victories at Stalingrad* and later at Kursk* in late 1942 and 1943, new offensives were initiated all along the Soviet front. In the northern Ukraine, Vatutin's* 1st Ukrainian Front began by recapturing Zhitomir, Korosten and Novigrad Volynsk, to cross into Polish territory by 4 January. Despite the appalling weather, Vatutin's forces linked up with Konev's* 2nd Ukrainian Front to trap ten German divisions at Korsun. An attempt by Field Marshal Manstein* to use his tank forces to relieve the trapped divisions foundered against the overwhelming firepower of the Russian T34* tanks and cost an estimated 20,000 lives. In the southern Ukraine, Tolbukhin's 4th Ukrainian Front drove south towards the Crimea*, while Malinovsky's* 3rd Ukrainian Front recaptured Krivoi Rog on the west bank of the Dnieper* on 22 February.

As Zhukov (replacing Vatutin who had been fatally wounded) signalled the launch of the spring offensive with an outflanking manoeuvre on the German lines along the Bug River, the Russian front line rolled forward, supported by Konev's drive from Uman. By the end of March the two armies were joined at Jassy on the Prut. In the south, Malinovsky's drive kept pace, to take Kherson and then Nikolayev on 28 March. In the face of the German defeats in the Ukraine, Hitler replaced Southern Army Group commanders Manstein and Kleist with Model and Schörner. Model launched a counter-offensive along the Dniester south of Lvov, managed to stablize the front but forced a Russian switch to the south, with Konev's and Malinovsky's forces combining to concentrate the fighting on Odessa*. A stalemate dragged out the battle for possession of the Ukraine for several more months. It was not resolved until mid-summer, when a dual attack towards Lvov and Lublin* by Konev's forces combined with a renewed attack by the 4th Ukrainian Front under Petrov* on the German positions on the River Dniester between Jassy and Kishinev in August, to finally break German resistance, and open the way for the centre drive on Poland*.

Ultra Special security classification for information obtained from the Enigma radio enciphering machine, and a designation of the intelligence obtained from it. The Enigma enciphering machine for radio transmissions was modified and adopted for military purposes in Germany in the late 1920s. An electro-mechanically operated computer which generated apparently random number groups, the Enigma machine was copied by Polish cryptanalysts, and two copies each were presented to the British and French just before the outbreak of war in 1939. With daily code changes, and numerous different codes employed by different services, the Germans remained convinced of the security of information passed by Enigma, although British cryptanalysts had constructed a primitive but effective deciphering machine, known as 'Colossus' early on in the war, and thus had access to almost all radio transmissions between the German High Command and field headquarters until very near the end of the war.

Allocated a special security classification, 'Ultra', which was also the designation of the information obtained, the Enigma intercepts were of invaluable assistance to Allied leaders and senior field commanders, particularly during the Battle of Britain*, in North Africa, during the naval war in the Mediterranean* (notably at Cape Matapan*), and throughout the critical phase of the Battle of the Atlantic* from 1940–3. Ultra also informed the Allies of German reactions to the preparations for D-Day and, in particular, their response to the various deception plans which were so crucial to the success of the Normandy* invasion (see Bodyguard). The Allied failure to predict the German Ardennes offensive (Battle of the Bulge*) in 1944 was blamed on Ultra, although indications of an offensive were left uninvestigated by sceptical Allied intelligence staffs. The importance of Ultra, along with other Allied intelligence gathering systems (see Magic), is hard to overstate.

Ultranationalism Japanese political ideology originating in the 1880s as a response to what many saw as excessive westernization, it concentrated on notions of national essence, *kokusuishugi*, and Japanism. Earlier nationalist societies had often emerged directly out of opposition to contemporary governments, though during the Meiji period (from 1890 onwards), there was also increasing opposition to modernization and all its implications. The preoccupations of nationalist groups of the 1920s and 30s were centred on traditionalism and anti-foreignism, although by this period the term included a highly disparate range of ideologies from conservatives to genuine social revolutionaries, from both established societies and newly formed extremist groups. In this period also, much ultranationalist thinking found fertile ground in the Japanese Army*: two factions, the

Toseiha and the Kodo factions, dominated the army during the 1930s. Less concerned with internal reconstruction than the Kodo faction, the Toseiha (Control Faction) envisaged the creation of a 'defence state' under military control and geared to war and expansion in Manchuria and China for economic gain. The continuing dominance of the Toseiha over the Kodo faction and the unique political powers vested in the Japanese Army culminated finally in the premiership of General Tojo* in October 1941. See also Kwantung Army; New Order; Pacific War.

Umberto, Prince (1904–83) Son of King Victor Emmanuel* of Italy, he became king for a short 35-day reign after his father's abdication in May 1946. Umberto commanded the Italian Army of the Alps in France in 1940. Until 1943 he was a public supporter of Mussolini's* regime and encouraged by him to associate closely with German political leaders. In June 1944, after the fall of Rome* to the Allies, Umberto became Regent, with the title Lieutenant General of the Realm. By August he was commanding Italian troops on the Allied front. On 9 May 1946, King Victor Emmanuel abdicated in favour of his son, now King Umberto II. His reign was cut short, however, by a referendum which voted to abolish the Italian monarchy less than six weeks later.

Umezu, General Yoshijiro (1882–1949) Japanese staff commander and Vice Minister of War from 1936 until 1939, Umezu was involved with the Toseiha (Control Faction) Group, of whom Hidecki Tojo* was a prominent leader and was therefore highly influential in promoting their interests during the 1930s, when the Japanese Army* began to force government policy in Japan. Appointed commander of the Kwantung Army* in Manchukuo* (Manchuria*) in September 1939, Umezu became probably the most powerful Japanese figure in China* until 1944, when he replaced General Tojo as Army Chief

of Staff. Despite his militarist commitment, Umezi was persuaded to accept the Potsdam Declaration and was one of the signatories of the surrender document on the USS *Missouri**, in September 1945. Umezi was subsequently sentenced to life imprisonment for war crimes.

Unicorn, HMS British aircraft carrier, designed to maintain and repair fleet aircraft in the field. The *Unicorn* entered Royal Navy* service in 1943 and was used as an operational carrier until the end of the year, before adopting her designated role to good effect with the British carrier squadron in the Pacific.
BRIEF DATA (1943) Displacement: 16,150 tons; Dimensions: o/a lgth – 646', b – 90' 3"; Speed: 24 knots; Armament: 8 × 4" AA gun, 12 × 2pdr AA gun, 12 × 20mm AA gun, 36 aircraft.

United Nations Declaration A statement (also known as the Joint Declaration) signed at the White House on 1 January 1942 by representatives of 26 countries. The United States, Great Britain, Russia, China, Australia, Belgium, Canada, Costa Rica, Cuba, Czechoslovakia, the Dominican Republic, El Salvador, Greece, Guatemala, Haiti, Honduras, India, Luxembourg, the Netherlands, New Zealand, Nicaragua, Norway, Panama, Poland, South Africa and Yugoslavia were the initial signatories, followed by Bolivia, Brazil, Chile, Colombia, Equador, Egypt, Ethiopia, France, Iceland, Iraq, Lebanon, Liberia, Mexico, Paraguay, Persia, Peru, the Philippines, Saudi Arabia, Syria, Turkey, Uruguay and Venezuela. The statement declared the creation of an alliance against the Axis* powers. The Declaration endorsed the Atlantic Charter* and pledged military and economic co-operation against the Axis, with no separate agreements to be made with any Axis power. This wartime coalition provided the basis for the establishment of the United Nations Organization* in 1945. See also Conferences.

United Nations Organization The international body established by the coalition of signatories to the United Nations Declaration* in January 1942, with the primary aim of preserving world peace, it was formally established at the United Nations Conference on International Organization (known as the San Francisco Conference) which met on 25 April 1945 and sat until the end of June. Initial qualification for membership was the declaration of war against the Axis powers by 1 March 1945. See Conferences.

Unryu Japanese Navy aircraft carrier and Class. Six of these ships, similar to the *Hiryu* (see Soryu), were laid down in 1942 –3. Only the *Unryu*, *Amagi* and *Katsuragi* were completed before the end of the war, and by the time they entered service Japanese naval aviation had virtually ceased to exist. Although they carried radar* and were later packed with additional light anti-aircraft* weapons, they were never able to call on experienced or well-trained aircrews. The *Unryu* was sunk by the American submarine *Redfish* in the East China Sea on 19 December 1944, and the *Amagi* was destroyed by carrier aircraft in Kure dockyard the following July (along with the incomplete hulls of two of her sisters). The sole survivor was the *Katsuragi*, scrapped in 1947.
BRIEF DATA (*Unryu*, 1944) Displacement: 17,150 tons; Dimensions: o/a lgth – 741' 6", b – 72' (88' 6" FD); Speed: 32 knots; Armament: 12 × 5" AA gun (6 × 2), 51 × 25mm AA gun, 65 aircraft.

Upholder, HMS One of the most famous British submarines* of the war. *Upholder* was a small U Class boat, well-suited to the shallow waters of the Mediterranean* where she pursued her combat career as part of the Royal Navy's 10th Flotilla based on Malta* in 1941–2. This represented the only real threat to Rommel's* supply lines to North Africa after the fall of Crete*. Although forced by bombing to remain submerged when in Valetta harbour, the flotilla was the outstanding wartime success of the British Submarine Service. *Upholder* sank over 60,000 tons of Axis shipping between September 1941 and her own destruction by an Italian motor torpedo boat* on 14 April 1942.
BRIEF DATA (U Class) Displacement: 540 tons (surface); Dimensions: o/a lgth – 191' 6", b – 16'; Speed: 11.75 knots (9 submerged); Armament: 1 × 3" gun, 3 × 0.5" mg, 6 × 21" TT.

Uranus Code-name for the Soviet counter-offensive at Stalingrad*, November 1942.

US Army In 1939 the US Army was a small professional force (175,000) with little modern equipment, such peacetime resources as were available having been devoted largely to the development of air and sea power. Under the supervision of General George Marshall*, who became Chief of Staff on the day Germany invaded Poland*, the mass-production capacity of American heavy industry was efficiently organized to provide modern weapons on a vast scale. Although these were still in short supply when the US entered the war, within a year the Army was receiving high performance tanks*, field artillery* and infantry weapons in enormous quantities.
The call-up of the volunteer reserve National Guard and the introduction of selective conscription in 1940, the first peacetime draft in US history, brought US Army strength up to 1,400,000 men by mid-1941. A similar transformation was effected in American air power. Established in June 1941, the USAAF* grew rapidly and remained under Army jurisdiction throughout the war. Including air forces, the US Army employed 10,420,000 men and women during WW2. This is a relatively small figure – Germany used more soldiers from a smaller population – and reflects American concentration on technological strengths in artillery* and aerial warfare, as opposed to reliance on massed infantry. A total Army establishment of

105 divisions (8,250,000 men) was planned in 1942, but the following year this was scaled down to 90 divisions (7,700,000) plus 283 combat air groups (2,300,000). In actual fact 100 divisions were raised during WW2, of which 76 were infantry, 16 armoured, 5 airborne*, 2 cavalry and one alpine. Thirteen divisions did not serve overseas, and two of those sent abroad saw no action before VE day (8 May 1945). Overall casualties were 234,874 dead, 701,385 wounded and 124,079 imprisoned.

The US Army's first major combat experiences were against Rommel* in Tunisia* and the Japanese at Guadalcanal*. Both revealed serious shortcomings in organization and technique, but these were quickly corrected as US forces and commanders learnt swiftly from experience and the weight of American *matériel* mushroomed from late 1942. In the Pacific War*, US forces completely dominated the Allied war effort after the swift demise of ABDA* Command, but in Africa and Europe US forces formed a major component of combined Allied armies from 1942–5. The effective, if sometimes strained, co-operation between the British and American armies owed a great deal to the diplomatic gifts of General Eisenhower*, Supreme Allied Commander in Europe, but their ultimate victory was primarily based on the strength and plenitude of US *matériel*. See also Torch; Tunisia; Sicily, Campaign in; Italy, Campaign in; Northwest Europe, Campaign in.

US Marines See US Navy.

US Navy The pre-war US Navy bore the stamp of the international naval limitation treaties of the period 1922–36, which recognized the US and Great Britain as the world's major maritime powers but restricted the size and number of new warships constructed. Parity with the Royal Navy* was maintained in the larger Classes, but from the mid-1920s attention focused increasingly on the Japanese rather than the British as a potential major threat (see Introduction). The Japanese Navy* was generally restricted to three warships to every five operated by the US, but was clearly intent on maximizing its offensive capability in direct competition with the US Navy. US development of smaller types and coastal craft was therefore allowed to lapse and resources concentrated on large, long-range ships for use in the Pacific.

The fleet of 1939 was based on a line of 15 battleships, supported by five aircraft carriers, 18 heavy and 19 light cruisers. Many were old ships, modernized to circumvent treaty restrictions, but those built under the treaties were among the best in the world. Heavily armed and protected to match their Japanese counterparts, the battleships and cruisers had greater operational range than most European warships. Less concerned with high speed than other navies, the US Navy was able to keep them inside treaty tonnage limits and within the dimensional restraints of the Panama Canal. Although the aircraft carriers were still regarded as support for the battleships rather than as capital units, the US was the only power capable of rivalling Japan in the field of naval aviation. The techniques and offensive potential of carrier warfare had been well examined and rehearsed once large *Lexington** Class carriers, purpose-built for maximum aircraft capacity, became available after 1927. The Navy maintained full control over its air forces and had developed specialist monoplane carrier aircraft (e.g. Douglas Devastator*) by the late 1930s. Although far superior to any European types, these were less effective than modern Japanese designs.

Japanese enthusiasm for submarine* construction had prompted extensive development of modern US submarine types. With military funding strictly limited, however, these were not built in any numbers until after 1939, and the US entered the war still seriously short of modern boats. US Navy destroyer* forces were numerically strong but technically less impressive. Large numbers of veteran flushdeckers designed in WW1 were still in front-line service, and the newer ships, though given Pacific range and adequate armament, were less powerful than their Japanese counterparts and carried vastly inferior torpedoes*. In the building of smaller, special-purpose craft, the Americans lagged behind other navies. Although light landing craft had been developed for amphibious* operations (see Landing Vehicle Tracked), US planners perceived little need for torpedo boats* or specialized convoy* escorts in a Pacific context and built few anti-submarine* craft of any sort.

The vital step in transforming this powerful but conventional navy into the vast and complex carrier-based force that finally swept the Imperial Japanese Navy from the seas was the passing of the Two Oceans Navy Bill in July 1940. This recognized the need for naval expansion to protect US interests on both seaboards and allowed for the building of 1,325,000 tons of new warships. It emphasized US sympathies with the British in the European War and geared American shipyards to a war footing at an early stage, allowing the benefits to be felt shortly after the US entered WW2. In the meantime, repair work carried out for Allied navies and operational experience culled from trade protection patrols in the Atlantic were put to good use in the design and formulation of future requirements.

The fruits of this expansion were not available by December 1941, but some major warships had been added to the strength and fleets were deployed in the Atlantic (eight battleships, four aircraft carriers, one escort carrier*) and in the Pacific (eight battleships, three aircraft carriers) along with smaller forces in the South Atlantic, California, and the Philippines*. When the Japanese opened the Pacific War* by attacking the bulk of the Pacific Fleet at Pearl Harbor*, all three of its carriers were absent and survived. The virtual destruction of its battleship line (along with supporting cruisers) and the unqualified success of Japanese tactics encouraged the US Navy to place increased stress on naval

aviation. As the Two Oceans Bill was superseded by a full emergency war building programme, an unprecedented number of large, fast Essex* Class aircraft carriers were put into production, 16 of which were in commission by VJ day*. Nine smaller Independence* Class carriers (conversions on cruiser hulls) and dozens of escort carriers were also produced, an output well in excess of all other WW2 navies combined.

Aircraft development kept pace with this upsurge. War experience quickly alerted US designers to the failings of their slow and bulky carrier fighters and dive-bombers, and their replacements – notably the Grumman F6F Hellcat* and the Chance-Vought F4U Corsair* – reversed the air supremacy of the Japanese in the Pacific after 1942. Produced in enormous numbers, they overwhelmed the Japanese Navy's air arm, which relied on depleted forces of increasingly obsolete aircraft (see Japanese Air Forces). Over 50,000 combat aircraft were delivered to the US Navy from July 1940 to the end of the war, in which time its aviation personnel strength rose from 10,923 to 437,524.

Despite the increasing predominance of air power at sea, ten US Navy battleships were also built during WW2 (although five more were cancelled), along with large classes of heavy and light cruisers. Their role was primarily to protect aircraft carriers in the Pacific and to provide gun support for amphibious* operations in all theatres. More versatile destroyers and submarines were given high priority and mass-produced to standard Pacific designs which were logical modifications of pre-war Classes tried and tested in early combat. At the start of the Pacific War urgent steps were taken to make good the shortage of anti-submarine vessels. Failure to appreciate this need before the war resulted in the extraordinary spectacle of the US Navy borrowing escorts from Britain in 1941–2, but destroyer escorts*, escort carriers, patrol boats and auxiliaries soon poured off US production lines to meet the twin threats of U-boats in the Atlantic and the Japanese fleet submarines. By early 1943 these were available in large numbers in both theatres and the progressive erosion of the submarine threat released production facilities for the vast armadas of amphibious craft of all sizes that were needed for landings in Europe and the Pacific Islands.

At the start of the war the US Navy possessed some radar* and sonar equipment and (in parallel with the Royal Navy) its electronic search and gunnery control facilities mushroomed during the war years. The significant lead in these fields enjoyed by the Western Allies was magnified in combat with the Japanese Navy, which was (and remained) a virtual non-starter in radar technology. The quality and quantity of American guns and ammunition also became more of an advantage as the war progressed, initial problems with faulty torpedoes notwithstanding, and in the '5-inch 38' dual purpose air/surface mounting the US Navy developed the world's most economic and versatile naval artillery piece.

Although the US Navy appreciated and fulfilled its production needs with awesome efficiency, it was nevertheless underequipped and on the defensive in the first year of the Pacific War. After Pearl Harbor, Admiral Ernest King* became C-in-C of the Navy, and he remained in charge of naval operations throughout the war. Reorganization was forced on King by the initial Japanese onslaught. The small US Asiatic fleet based on the Philippines ceased to exist, while battleships and cruisers were quickly transferred from the Atlantic Fleet to restore the balance in the Pacific. Coastal defences were immediately placed under US Navy Sea Frontier Commands and during 1942 operational commands were established in the South Pacific (later called the 3rd Fleet), the Central Pacific (5th Fleet) and the Southwest Pacific (7th Fleet). Nevertheless, none of the new carriers ordered were ready in time for the battles of the Coral Sea* and Midway* in 1942, and the vital strategic victory at the latter owed more to the constructive use of intelligence than to quality of technique or equipment (see Magic). At this stage the Japanese Navy held a definite edge in direct combat in the Pacific. It possessed the devastating Long Lance torpedo, superior aircraft and more experienced crews. Only the use of radar enabled US Navy warships to hold their own.

By late 1942, when the Americans were able to go onto the offensive at Guadalcanal*, the *Enterprise** was the only US Navy aircraft carrier left in the Pacific, and the hard-won capture of the island confirmed the widely held view that much remained to be learned in the art of amphibious assault. By mid-1943 – when amphibious operations had been largely perfected in the Solomons and New Guinea* – the new ships and planes of the war programme were becoming available in large numbers. These enabled the establishment of Fast Carrier Task Forces in the Pacific, which provided direct and long-range support for the amphibious drive through the Central Pacific beginning at the Gilbert Islands* late in the year. Backed up by independent supply groups, they gave the US Navy the power to reach out and devastate targets of choice, isolating important Japanese garrisons by circumventing them in a push towards the homeland.

The 5th and 3rd Fleets were in effect unified throughout the offensive, and were designated according to an alternating command system. Under Admiral Spruance*, the 5th Fleet took part in operations against the Gilberts, the Marshalls*, New Guinea* and the Marianas* in 1943–4. In September 1944 command passed to Admiral Halsey*, and the force became the 3rd Fleet for the rest of the Philippines campaign. This process was later repeated – the 5th Fleet participating at Iwo Jima* and in the early stages of the campaign for Okinawa*, the 3rd supporting the final drive towards Japan.

The Japanese battlefleet, which had become more and more strategically reliant on a decisive naval confrontation, found that the US Navy had become unbeatable by the time the climactic battles came in

1944. While Japanese Navy resources had dwindled and its technology had remained relatively static, the US Navy – which had invested heavily in sophisticated training programmes – won its decisive victory at the Battle of the Philippine Sea* in June with hundreds of modern aircraft on new carriers manned by highly skilled crews. In the 'Great Marianas Turkey Shoot' which followed the battle, 30 Japanese naval aircraft were shot down for every US plane lost, effectively ending the contest for Pacific air superiority. Later in the year, the bulk of the Japanese surface fleet was knocked out by vastly superior US Navy forces in the actions around Leyte Gulf*. Meanwhile the US submarine fleet, deployed in a predatory role against poorly defended shipping, was fighting the most successful undersea campaign in history and had virtually paralysed all Japanese surface movement by the end of the year. By contrast the Japanese fleet submarines had suffered appalling losses to the increasingly sophisticated anti-submarine forces which guarded major US Navy fleet units.

In the final stages of the Pacific campaign, particularly at Okinawa, Kamikaze* attacks took an enormous toll of American shipping. Losses, which briefly threatened even American replacement capacity, were soon contained by improved defensive techniques and anti-aircraft* weapons, while the sophisticated hull design of modern US warships enabled most of them to survive grievous damage without sinking. On the other hand, the policy of designing aircraft carriers for maximum offensive capacity rather than maximum protection was called into question by the relative immunity to Kamikaze attack of armoured British ships. By this time the strangulation of Japanese trade and the destruction of her Navy had made her defeat inevitable and the Kamikaze campaign was an act of desperation. The seaborne invasion of Japan itself, a huge operation projected as the US Navy's final effort of the war, was rendered unnecessary by the dropping of two atomic bombs* by the USAAF*.

In other theatres the US Navy played a less pivotal but nonetheless important and successful role. In close co-operation with the Royal Navy, US naval forces, particularly escort vessels and long-range coastal aircraft, maintained ocean supply lines to Britain in the Battle of the Atlantic*. A 4th Fleet was established for operations in the South Atlantic, and a shore-based 10th Fleet supervised anti-submarine warfare in the Atlantic theatre. The 8th Fleet was formed in 1942 as support for the Allied Torch* landings in Northwest Africa, and as the submarine threat receded, the 12th Fleet supported the subsequent invasions of mainland Europe. Neither was required to fight major surface actions, and their main opponents were hostile aircraft defending coastal positions.

Between July 1940 and September 1945, the US Navy completed or acquired 5,788 warships of all types along with more than 3,000 'district craft' for US shipyard use and over 66,000 landing vessels of various types and sizes. Its personnel strength multiplied from 203,127 in mid-1940 to 486,226 by December 1941, and 4,064,455 by 31 August 1945. This figure includes the US Marine Corps and US Coastguards. The Marine Corps, the US Navy's land army, was primarily employed as the spearhead of amphibious operations in the Pacific. It had grown to a strength of some 66,000 men by the time of Pearl Harbor, having tripled with the call-up of both its land and air reserves in November 1940. Both its land and air sections grew in parallel, and the first two marine divisions and their supporting air wings reached authorized strength in time for the Guadalcanal campaign.

The Marine divisions – six were established by the end of the war – came under the administrative control of the 1st Marine Amphibious Corps (IMAC) from October 1942. Although it exercised no tactical control over marine units in the field, IMAC became the planning agency for the US Navy's amphibious offensives in 1943. From September it was supplemented by

V Amphibious Corps (VAC), which was initially responsible for training but which took direct control of Marine operations in the Gilberts and the Marshalls. IMAC was renamed III Amphibious Corps (IIIAC) in 1944 and the two Corps shared responsibility for the assault stages of the Marianas campaign. A higher command – Fleet Marine Force, Pacific – was established under General Holland Smith* in September 1944 and retained overall control of marine warfare for the rest of WW2.

By 1945 the Marine Corps employed a force of over 450,000 men, of whom about 125,000 were on the aviation strength (10,412 pilots), which was supplied and supervised by Aircraft, Fleet Marine Force, Pacific, throughout the Pacific War. Of five marine air wings activated during the war, four were combat groups while the 9th Wing remained in the US as a training unit.

The United States Coastguard had been administered by the Treasury in peacetime but came under the wartime jurisdiction of the US Navy. In 1940 it comprised 13,756 persons, but by 1945 had grown to a force of 171,192 personnel manning coastal stations, 1,677 seacraft of its own, several hundred Navy or Army craft and 165 aircraft (operating from nine US coastal air stations). Its functions were broad: Coastguards regulated merchant shipping and protected coastal shipping, harbours and wharfage. They performed onshore lookout and patrol duties and even manned landing craft in combat operations. Coastguard aviators flew convoy coverage, antisubmarine, search and rescue missions under the overall control of US Navy Sea Frontier commanders.

USAAF (United States Army Air Forces)
In 1920, amid wholesale military cuts, the US Army* set up an Air Service under its jurisdiction. In competition with the US Navy*, who established their own Bureau of Aeronautics the following year, and in the face of calls for independence from among its airmen, this infant force slowly

equipped itself with post-war machines. By the mid-1930s it was able to call on advanced types, provided by a manufacturing industry kept buoyant by overseas orders. Numerically, however, US air forces remained relatively weak at the outbreak of the war in Europe.

In 1940 the new US Secretary of War, Henry Stimson*, with the co-operation of Army Chief of Staff George Marshall*, appointed as his Air Assistant Robert Lovett, who was charged with increasing aircraft production and reorganizing the air arm. Thus, as strength in machines and pilots developed more quickly, the Air Corps (hitherto responsible for training and procurement) and the Air Force Combat Command were unified under General Henry Arnold* as the United States Army Air Forces on 20 June 1941. Although remaining part of the Army until 1947, the Air Forces enjoyed considerable autonomy throughout the war. Arnold was backed by an air staff and was responsible directly to the Army Chief of Staff. In March 1942, the USAAF became one of three co-equal commands within the Army alongside ground and supply forces.

The USAAF entered the war with 25,000 personnel and about 4,000 aircraft. The strength of its manufacturing base, already geared to high output by the demands of the Lend-Lease* Act of March 1941, enabled it to triple its aircraft strength in the year after Pearl Harbor*, and the types available compared favourably on the whole with the best aircraft produced elsewhere. B-17* bombers, already being complemented by even more effective B-24s*, formed the only four-engined strategic bombing force in the world in 1941, and the USAAF possessed modern and enduringly successful twin-engined designs like the B-25*. Only its fighters suffered by comparison with the best of their opponents, the P-36* and P-40* proving no match for the Japanese Navy's Mitsubishi A6M Zero* Fighters.

Wartime aircraft developments kept pace with increasing output. The P-47* and P-51* fighters, produced in vast numbers, changed the balance of air power in Europe after 1943. The success of the P-51 as a long-range escort, capable of protecting heavy bombers all the way to targets deep inside Germany, restored the feasibility of B-17 operations at a time when losses, always high in spite of enormous increases in defensive armament, threatened to cripple the daylight operations over Germany. These improved fighter types also enjoyed great success in all theatres as tactical support aircraft, and modification of US twin-engined attack planes, latterly supplemented by the powerful Douglas A-26*, maintained their combat effectiveness throughout the war. From mid-1944, the introduction of the awesome B-29* elevated the USAAF's strategic bombing capacity to war-winning status.

Structurally, the USAAF was reorganized and redirected in the wake of Japanese advances after Pearl Harbor. In February 1942, the remnants of the US Far East Air Forces, based in the Philippines*, were reconstituted in Australia as the 5th Air Force. At the same time the Hawaiian Air Force became the 7th Air Force, and both campaigned across the 15,000,000 square miles of the Pacific theatres throughout the war. In December, units that had been rushed to the South Pacific to meet Japanese offensives in the Solomon Islands* were formed into the 13th Air Force, the 'Jungle Air Force', which then supported the advance from the Solomons to the Philippines. This was joined with the 5th Air Force in June 1944, to form Far East Air Forces under General Kenney*, which co-ordinated subsequent strategic bombing operations on Japan, Java* and Borneo*, and which absorbed the 7th Air Force in the summer of 1945.

The few US bombers available in India at the end of February 1942 formed the nucleus of the 10th Air Force which, quickly reinforced, began operations against the Andaman Islands and Burma*. It also protected the trans-Himalayan supply route to the China Air Task Force

(the Hump*), the official successor to the 'Flying Tigers' American Volunteer Group*, who had fought the Japanese in 1941. Established in July 1942, with only 41 aircraft, this had become powerful enough by March 1943 to gain independence as the 14th Air Force. Hampered in its efforts to disrupt Japanese supply lines by its own remoteness and the unreliability of Chinese ground forces, the beleaguered 14th was only able to dominate the theatre after Japanese forces were withdrawn to the coast in May 1945. In the north, the Alaskan Air Force had been renamed the 11th Air Force, and after campaigning against Japanese forward positions at Kiska and Attu (see Aleutians), commenced the bombing of the Kurile chain of islands north of Japan in July 1943, and maintained its attacks for the rest of the war.

The 8th Air Force was dedicated from its inception to the strategic bombing of German-held territory in Europe. Based in southern England and an administrative component of Eisenhower's* European Theatre of Operations, it flew its first mission (against railway yards in Rouen) in August 1942. Supported by a fighter command and a service command, its heavy bombers (mostly B-17s) flew daylight raids over Germany from January 1943 until the end of the war (see Strategic Bombing Offensive). Units of the 8th Air Force were detached to North Africa in 1942 as US Middle East Air Forces, and these were joined by 23 B-24s (diverted *en route* to China) to create the 9th Air Force. Reinforced by fighters and medium bombers, this supported Allied operations in the Desert War*, the Mediterranean* and Italy*, as well as bombing the Rumanian oilfields at Ploesti*. The 9th Air Force rejoined the 8th Air Force in October 1943, as the tactical arm of United States Army Air Forces in the United Kingdom, in preparation for the invasion of Northwest Europe*. The following January the 15th Air Force, formed three months earlier to bomb German-held targets from captured bases in southern Italy, was also absorbed to form the United States Strategic Air Forces in Europe under the command of Lt General Spaatz* and Major General Doolittle* in London.

Doolittle had been the first commander of the 12th Air Force, created in August 1942, to support the Allied Torch* invasion of Northwest Africa with some 500 aircraft. Its strength had doubled by the time it joined RAF* units in February 1943, to form Northwest African Air Forces, itself a division of Mediterranean Air Forces, which became operational at the same time and embraced several RAF Commands as well as (at first) the 9th Air Force. Triumphant in Tunisia*, the 12th then participated in Allied offensives in southern Europe, maintaining bombing and tactical support operations against German-held northern Italy until the end of the war.

The 4th Air Force, which had seen combat in the North Pacific area, was generally charged with the defence of the US Pacific coast. Based in San Francisco from 1943 onwards, it performed extensive training duties, as did the 6th Air Force (although in a tropical context) from its bases in the Caribbean where, apart from protecting the Panama Canal, it assisted the Navy in anti-submarine* patrols.

Commanded directly from Washington, the 20th Air Force was created for the strategic bombing of Japan with B-29s. Of its two components, XX Bomber Command saw action first, attacking Japanese targets in Thailand* from bases in India from June 1944, with generally disappointing results. XXI Bomber Command, initially based in China, began operations from the Marianas* in November. It enjoyed much greater success in reaching important targets and, once devastating low-level incendiary attacks had replaced inaccurate high-altitude raids, the outcome was no longer in doubt. As the war ended, with the dropping of atomic bombs* on Hiroshima* and Nagasaki*, General Spaatz (fresh from Europe) was in the process of co-ordinating B-29 operations with those of Far East Air Forces.

The part played in maintaining the war effort by Air Transport Command, the USAAF's worldwide supply airline, should not be overlooked. Formed in June 1942, from Ferrying Command (the organization responsible for delivering American-built aircraft to Britain in 1941), its C-46*, C-47* and C-54* aircraft (the most commonly used types) hauled cargo and personnel around a 40,000-mile network, including the famous trans-Himalayan 'Hump' route. Expanded throughout the war, Air Transport Command eventually employed a staff of almost 200,000 and 3,700 aircraft, reducing the civilian share of War Department transport work from 88 per cent in 1941 to 19 per cent by the end of the war.

The peak wartime strength of the USAAF as a whole was 75,000 aircraft and 2,411,294 officers and unenlisted personnel. Between 1 July 1940 and 31 August 1945, the US Army accepted a total of 229,554 machines and total wartime casualties amounted to 115,382 (52,173 dead).

Ushijima, Lt General Mitsuru (1887–1945) Commandant of the Japanese Military Academy in 1942, Ushijima subsequently served on Iwo Jima* and then as commander of the 32nd Army on Okinawa*, where he was charged with the defence of the island against the enormous American invasion force which began its landings there on 1 April 1945. The last and most costly island battle of the Pacific War*, the battle for Okinawa saw a skilled defensive campaign conducted by Ushijima. He was nevertheless unable to affect the final outcome and committed ritual suicide, along with his chief of staff, General Cho on 22 June.

Utah Code-name for beach area south of Les Dunes de Varreville on the right flank of the Allied line, allocated to the American assault forces for the Normandy* invasion, June 1944.

V

V-1 Missile The first and most effective of the German secret weapons planned as revenge for the bombing of Germany. Officially known as the F2G-76, this pilotless monoplane was also called the flying bomb, buzz bomb or doodlebug. Developed between June 1942 and the end of 1943, the V-1 was powered by a pulse-jet motor and carried a 1-ton warhead. It was launched from a fixed ramp and travelled at about 350mph and 4,000ft to a preset target at a maximum range of 150 (later 250) miles.

In mid-1943, accurate photo-reconnaissance intelligence led the Allies to divert forces from the Strategic Bombing Offensive* against Germany in an attempt to destroy V-1 production and launch sites (Operation Crossbow). Beginning with a raid on the rocket plant at Peenemünde in August, the Allies dropped 36,000 tons of bombs on identified V-1 sites, mostly on the French Channel coast, before the invasion of Normandy*. The operation was not given priority over the strategic bombing of Germany, however, and V-1s began hitting London from portable launch sites in mid-June 1944. Even after Allied ground forces overran coastal launching sites, V-1 missiles continued to be fired from modified Heinkel He111* bombers.

About 35,000 missiles were mass-produced in 1944–5, of which 9,521 were fired on southern England. Of these 4,621 were destroyed by anti-aircraft* fire or by the RAF's* fastest fighters. The other major target was Antwerp, which had no fighter cover, but where anti-aircraft gunners knocked out 2,455 of the 6,551 missiles fired. Although their margin of accuracy could best be measured in miles rather than yards, the V-1 missiles loomed large in the lives of civilians within their range and proved a more destructive reprisal weapon than the later V-2* rocket.

V-2 Rocket The second of Adolf Hitler's secret weapons to be unleashed, partly in reprisal for the Allied bombing of Germany. The V-2 (or A4) rocket was less damaging to Allied civilian morale than the V-1*, but still caused a great deal of damage and killed thousands of people.

A liquid-fuel rocket with a 1-ton warhead, the V-2 was 46-foot long and weighed 13 tons. Capable of supersonic speed and often flying at an altitude of over 50 miles, it could not be effectively stopped once launched. However, many rockets suffered mechanical failure and many more did most of their damage deep underground, such was their speed of impact. About 5,000 V-2s were fired between September 1944 and the end of the following March, mostly aimed at London, Antwerp and Liège. See Braun, Werner von.

Valentine Tank Plans for this privately designed British infantry support tank* were submitted to the War Office by the Vickers company on 14 February 1938. Its turret was justifiably seen as unacceptably small and orders were not forthcoming until July 1939, when the need for new tanks was desperate. Using major components from its earlier Cruiser Mark II design, Vickers were then able to build the Valentine quickly and with a faster road performance than its predecessor, the Matilda II*.

Production deliveries had begun by May 1940, and some Valentines were used as stop-gap cruisers before they joined infantry tank brigades in the Desert War* from June 1941.

Eleven battle tank versions of the Valentine appeared before production ceased in early 1944, by which time 8,275 had been built in Britain and Canada. All but the Mark I used diesel engines, which were easy to maintain, and the tank's main armament was eventually enlarged – to a 6-pounder in the Mark VIII, and a 75mm gun in the final Mark X. The small turret meant that with these larger guns crew conditions were extremely cramped.

During WW2, 2,720 Valentines were sent to the Soviet Union. The Russians regarded the 2-pounder gun as completely useless, but liked the Valentine's engine, which also earned a great reputation for reliability throughout the desert campaigns. A few Valentines also fought in Burma* and with New Zealand* forces in the Southwest Pacific. By 1944 they had been replaced as gun tanks, but formed the basis of many special-purpose* vehicles.
BRIEF DATA (Mark II) Type: 3-man infantry tank; Engine: 131hp diesel; Max speed: 15mph; Range: 90m; Arms: 1 × 2pdr gun, 1 × 7.92mm mg; Armour: max 65mm.

Vandegrift, Lt General Alexander (1887 –1973) Commander of the US 1st Marine Division from March 1942, Vandegrift was responsible for the division's combat training in preparation for its assignment to the South Pacific as the first marine division to go into combat against an enemy. Arriving in New Zealand in June 1942 with only part of his division and with little useful intelligence of the current situation, Vandegrift nevertheless conducted successful amphibious* landings at Guadalcanal* at the beginning of August, in the first large-scale offensive against the Japanese of the Pacific War*. For the initial assault and for the subsequent remarkable occupation and defence of the island, during which Vande-

grift contributed great leadership of the courageous but inexperienced American troops, he was awarded the Navy Cross and the Medal of Honor. 1st Marine Division was relieved by General Patch's 14th Corps in December, Vandegrift was given command of the 1st Marine Amphibious Corps in July 1943, directing the operations at Bougainville* in November. He was subsequently recalled to Washington to assume overall command of the Marine Corps, and was the first marine officer on active duty to become a four-star general.

Vasilevsky, Marshal Aleksandr M. (1895 –1977) Soviet Deputy Chief of Operations from 1941 to January 1942 and subsequently Chief of the General Staff, Vasilevsky had served in the Imperial Army before the revolution but had been rapidly promoted through the ranks of the Red Army. As Chief of the General Staff he spent most of his time in the field as the representative of the Soviet High Command (see Stavka) rather than in a supervisory capacity, and communicated regularly with Stalin* through his Moscow liaison, Antonov*. Vasilevsky also participated in the planning of the fronts at the Battle of Stalingrad* and subsequently coordinated the activities of the 2nd and 3rd Belorussian Fronts* in Belorussia* and East Prussia*. In 1945 he was temporarily appointed C-in-C of Soviet Armies in the Far East, and stood in as Stalin's deputy during his absence at the Yalta Conference*.

Vatutin, General Nikolai F. (1901–44) Soviet Head of General Staff Operations in 1941, and deputy to Vasilevsky, Vatutin was also a highly able Russian field commander who served with distinction at the Battle of Moscow* in 1941 and later at Stalingrad*, where he led the newly formed Southwest Front* against the German 6th Army under Paulus*. In the later Kursk* offensive, Vatutin's forces halted Field Marshal Manstein's* advance, counterattacking to take Kharkov*. In December 1943, forces under his command retook

Kiev* in the Ukraine*. Vatutin was fatally wounded, apparently by Ukrainian nationalist partisans, in a car ambush on 29 February 1944.

VE day Victory in Europe day. The date of the formal end of the war in Europe, 8 May 1945. See Germany, surrender of.

Vella Gulf, Battle of, 6–7 August 1943 Night surface action fought by two US destroyer* divisions under Commander Frederick Moosbrugger against a Japanese 'Tokyo Express'* supply convoy with four destroyers in Vella Gulf in the central Solomon Islands*. The Japanese ships under Captain Kaju Sugiura, carrying troops and supplies to Kolombangara Island, had been spotted by search plane and were attacked by Moosbrugger's first division, sailing a parallel but reciprocal course out of visible range, using radar* to aim their torpedoes*. Hits on three of the Japanese destroyers were quickly exploited with a supporting barrage from Moosbrugger's second division, which had sandwiched the Japanese force in a similar parallel course. The three Japanese destroyers were sunk, while the fourth retired, believing itself to be under US air attack. The success of the American destroyer attack, operating at night, independently of a cruiser force, finally made it impossible for the Japanese to continue their 'Tokyo Express' reinforcements in the Solomon Islands campaign.

Vella Lavella, Battles of, 17–18 August and 6–7 October 1943 An island of the Solomon* group, northwest of Kolombangara, Vella Lavella was the site of two night surface actions fought between US and Japanese destroyer* forces during 1943. The first action was triggered by the amphibious* landing, on 15 August of a US Army combat team supported by army, navy and marine units (later augmented by the 14th New Zealand Brigade), and the subsequent landing of a small Japanese force, screened by four destroyers under Rear Admiral Ijuin. In the ensuing engagement between

Ijuin and four American destroyers under Captain Thomas Ryan, two of the Japanese ships were damaged, though the landing barges and small craft managed to get ashore.

The larger October engagement, triggered by the Japanese attempt to evacuate the small Vella Lavella garrison landed in August with a screening force of six destroyers, again under Ijuin, was a clear tactical victory for the Japanese. Two patrolling US destroyer groups which converged on the Japanese force were skilfully outmanoeuvred by the Japanese commander and the evacuation was successfully completed, with one American destroyer sunk and two others damaged. The strategic result of this and other evacuations of the Solomon Islands (most notably of Kolombangara*), however, brought American forces closer and closer to their ultimate objective of Rabaul*.

Vian, Admiral Sir Philip (1894–1968) Outstandingly successful British naval commander, who was captain of the *Cossack** during the Altmark Incident* and subsequently commanded a destroyer flotilla in many dangerous and unorthodox Royal Navy* operations in northern waters, including the evacuation of British troops from Namsos in Norway and the hunt for the *Bismarck**. Given command of a cruiser squadron in the Mediterranean as a Rear Admiral, he fought against Italian warships threatening supplies to Malta*. Vian, who was knighted in 1942, commanded an aircraft carrier force which supported the Salerno* landings for the Allied invasion of Italy* in September 1943, before being transferred to Britain to command the Eastern Task Force in Operation Neptune, the naval element of the Overlord* plan for the Allied invasion of Normandy* in June 1944. After VE day, Vian and the Eastern Task Force were transferred to the Pacific, where they participated in the battle for Okinawa*. After the war Vian commanded the Royal Navy Home Fleet.

Vichy A spa town in central France which gave its name to the French government formed after France's defeat by Germany in 1940. On 10 July, the French National Assembly voted full power to Vichy's leader, Marshal Pétain*, who functioned as head of state. Pierre Laval*, who had been heavily involved with the establishment of the collaborationist regime, acted as head of the government, though he was dismissed by Pétain in December 1940, and was succeeded briefly by Flandin and then by Admiral Darlan*. In April 1942, Berlin directed Laval to return to his post and Pétain withdrew from the administration of Vichy. Laval remained as head of the government until the dissolution of Vichy in mid-1944, following the successful Allied invasion of Northwest Europe* in June 1944. Vichy had, however, effectively ceased to rule unoccupied France since the end of 1942, when Germany, in response to the Allied Torch* invasions of North Africa, occupied the southern French 'free zone'. See also Weygand, Maxime.

Vickers Warwick British bomber, first flown in 1939, that was intended as a replacement for the structurally similar Vickers Wellington*. Development was plagued by engine problems, and Warwicks belatedly reached RAF* squadrons in the summer of 1943. By that time it was outdated as a bomber, and saw out the war as a transport and air-sea rescue* plane. About 600 wartime Warwicks were built, but their intended Bristol Centaurus engines were available only for the last 133 Warwick IIs. BRIEF DATA (Warwick I) Type: 6-man air-sea rescue; Engine: 2 × 1,850hp Pratt and Whitney Double Wasp; Max speed: 224mph; Range: 2,150m; Arms: 8 × 0.303″ mg.

Vickers Wellesey The first RAF* aircraft to employ the light, sturdy geodesic structure devised by British inventor Sir Barnes Wallis*. It entered Bomber Command in 1937, and saw action as a ground-support bomber in East Africa* during 1940–1.

Before being retired in 1941, 176 were built.
BRIEF DATA Type: 2-man light bomber; Engine: 1 × 925hp Bristol Pegasus; Max speed: 228mph; Ceiling: 33,000′; Range: 1,110m; Arms: 2 × 0.303″ mg; Bomb load: 2,000lb.

Vickers Wellington British medium bomber, it joined the RAF* in October 1938. At the start of the war the Wellington IC formed the backbone of Bomber Command operations over Europe. RAF tactical orthodoxy at first condemned the Wellington to unescorted daylight raids, but they were disastrously expensive and from December 1939 the plane began a long and successful career as a night bomber (see Strategic Bombing Offensive). Largely because of their latticed, geodesic structure – first pioneered in the Vickers Wellesey* – Wellingtons were able to withstand extensive anti-aircraft* bombardment and, although eventually withdrawn from home-based operations in August 1943, they remained in front-line service overseas until 1945. Several bomber variants saw action, the most widely produced being the Wellington III, with extra tail guns and more powerful Hercules engines, and the further refined Mark X, which joined squadrons in 1943.

Wellingtons also enjoyed a varied and successful career with RAF Coastal Command. Converted Mark ICs had performed occasional maritime duties since 1940, and the first of five versions designed as general reconnaissance planes, the Wellington VIII, joined squadrons in the spring of 1942. Equipped with air-to-surface radar*, and later with searchlights, Wellingtons performed anti-submarine* duties in all British theatres of operations until the end of the war. They also acted as mine-layers, photo-reconnaissance planes, trainers and transports. Altogether, 11,461 Wellingtons were built and the design stayed in production until 1945.
BRIEF DATA (Mk IC) Type: 6-man long-range bomber; Engine: 2 × 1,000hp Bristol

Pegasus; Max speed: 235mph; Ceiling: 18,000'; Range: 1,200m; Arms: 6 × 0.303" mg; Bomb load: 4,500lb.

Victor Emmanuel III (1869–1947) King of Italy from 1900 to 1946 when he abdicated in favour of his son, Umberto*, Victor Emmanuel endured a sickly childhood and an austere education. He spent the last months of WW1 at the front among his troops fighting alongside the British and French.

Lacking, perhaps, a political perspective that could interpret the developments in Europe after WW1, Victor Emmanuel appeared narrowly concerned with the continuance of the Savoy monarchy. He responded to the rise of Fascism in Italy by concession. Following the Fascist 'March on Rome', Victor Emmanuel resolved his position by attaching the monarchy to the new regime. He accepted the Axis* agreement between Hitler* and Mussolini* in May 1939 and abdicated his scant authority to Mussolini's threats after a final attempt at opposition to Italy's entry into the war.

Victor Emmanuel was, nevertheless, charged by the Fascist Grand Council, who voted in mid-1943 to depose Mussolini, to authorize the dictator's arrest and appoint the premier to succeed him. The new government under Marshal Badoglio* sought immediate negotiations for an armistice with the Allies and a treaty of unconditional surrender was signed by Victor Emmanuel on 28 September 1943. Now established at Brindisi* where the Allies supported his government as an alternative to establishing a military administration, Victor Emmanuel urged a declaration of war against Germany (announced by Badoglio on 13 October). But his position, and that of the monarchy, was enfeebled by exile from German-occupied Rome, and compromised by his long liaison with Mussolini.

Following the liberation of Rome* in June 1944, the King named his son regent, and abdicated in his favour two years later.

He spent the last months of his life in exile in Egypt.

Victorious, HMS Royal Navy* armoured aircraft carrier of the *Illustrious* Class completed in early 1941. Her aircraft assisted the Home Fleet in the hunt for the *Bismarck* in May, and she later saw action in the Mediterranean*. Returning to home waters in 1944, she scored several hits on the German battleship *Tirpitz* when her aircraft attacked Altenfjord in April. The *Victorious* was sent to the Pacific for the final onslaught on Japan, surviving a Kamikaze* strike.

BRIEF DATA See Illustrious, HMS.

Victory Ship See Liberty Ship.

Vietinghoff Gennant Scheel, General Heinrich Gottfried (1887–1952) Successor to Field Marshal Kesselring* as German C-in-C in Italy* for the last few months of the war in Europe. Vietinghoff commanded a panzer division in Poland*, a corps in the Western Offensive* and an army on the Eastern Front* before being promoted colonel general in command of the German 10th Army in southern Italy in mid-1943. Vietinghoff's particular contribution to the exceptional and prolonged defensive campaign in Italy directed by Kesselring – against larger and better equipped Allied forces – is widely acknowledged. In March 1945, he replaced Kesselring, who had been transferred to the Western Front, as C-in-C. Along with General Karl Wolff*, Italian military governor and head of the SS* in Italy, Vietinghoff was involved almost immediately in secret negotiations with OSS* Bureau chief Allen Dulles* for the capitulation of German forces in Italy. The talks culminated in the surrender of Vietinghoff's forces six days before the general armistice in Europe was declared.

Vincennes, USS See New Orleans, USS.

Vishinsky, Andrei (1883–1955) Soviet

Vice-Commissar of Foreign Affairs with a particular reputation for coercive and unscrupulous diplomacy, Vishinsky supervised the formation of the provisional government in Latvia* in 1940, and was Soviet Representative on the Allied Mediterranean Commission from 1943–5. As Foreign Minister Molotov's* spokesman on policy towards Poland*, Vishinsky was responsible for denying the use of Soviet airfields to British and American aircraft to support the Warsaw* Uprising. In 1945 he went to Rumania* and oversaw the dissolution of Radescu's all-party government in favour of a communist administration.

Vistula River Site of the launch of the major offensive against Germany, over its bridgehead at Baranow, by the Russian 1st Ukrainian Front* under Marshal Konev* on 12 January 1945. See Poland, Russian Campaign in. See also Eastern Front.

Vittorio Veneto See Littorio.

VJ day Victory over Japan day, formally marking the end of the Pacific War*. This is usually taken as 15 August 1945, the day after the Japanese acceptance of Allied surrender terms, but 2 September (the day Japan signed the surrender) is sometimes also called VJ day in the US. The former date is referred to throughout this volume.

Vlassov, Lt General Andrei A. (1900–46) Anti-Stalinist and anti-Soviet Russian general who had served as an adviser to Chiang Kai-shek* 1938–9 and commanded the 20th Army at the Battle of Moscow* in 1941, for which he was awarded the Order of the Red Banner. Vlassov was captured in May 1942 at Sevastopol and was subsequently exploited by the Germans as a figurehead for the Russian Liberation Army (see ROA), allowed to make propaganda broadcasts expressing the Red Army's* distrust of Stalin* and recruit soldiers from POW and forced labour camps, although Hitler's personal opposition largely limited

the scope of Vlassov's activities to auxiliary functions. After his successful defeat of the SS garrison at Prague* in 1945, the ROA's only major action, Vlassov surrendered to the US 7th Army but was handed back to the Russians in accordance with an agreement made at Yalta*. He was hanged, along with six other generals, in August 1946.

Volga River See Stalingrad; Eastern Front.

Volturno River River on the west of the Italian peninsula north of Naples* where three German divisions held a defensive line against the advance of the US 5th Army during October 1944. The 5th Army drew up to the Volturno line on 16 October, by which time the German forces had withdrawn to another improvised line on the Garigliano River, slightly forward of the heavily fortified Gustav Line*. See Italy, Campaign in.

Voronezh Important Russian city north of Stalingrad, it fell to the German 4th Panzer Army on 6 July 1942. On 22 January 1943, following the German defeat at Stalingrad*, Russian Voronezh Front* forces attacked the German salient on the east bank of the River Don at Voronezh, recapturing the city on 25 January. See also Eastern Front.

Voronov, General Nikolai N. (1899–1968) Russian Marshal of Artillery who was appointed as adviser to the Soviet High Command (see Stavka) and figured prominently in operational planning and the reequipment and tactical deployment of artillery* throughout the war. Marshal Zhukov* referred to the important part played by Voronov in planning the Soviet counter-offensive at Stalingrad*.

Voroshilov, Marshal Kliment E. (1881–1969) Post-war Soviet President (1953–60), an early associate of Stalin and Commissar for Defence from 1934 to 1939, Voroshilov became Deputy Premier in the reshuffle of positions which followed the

Russo-Finnish War*, and later, in July 1941, Deputy Chairman of the State Defence Committee (see Stavka) and Stavka representative on the northwest front at Leningrad*. Following the failure on that front to check the German advance, to which his lack of modern military expertise certainly contributed, Voroshilov was recalled to Moscow and subsequently held staff appointments for the rest of the war.

As a member of the Defence Committee, Voroshilov attended several Allied Conferences*, including Tehran in November 1943. He also contributed to the military talks with Generals Brooke* and Wavell* during Churchill's* meeting with Stalin* in Moscow in August 1942. After the war Voroshilov became head of the Soviet Control Commission in Hungary*, and later President of the USSR.

W

Wacht am Rhein (Watch on the Rhine)
Code-name for the German counter-offensive in the Ardennes* in December 1944 that resulted in the Battle of the Bulge*.

Waco CG-4A Throughout the US during the war, 13,909 of these gliders were built, the largest production run of any glider of the period. Capable of accommodating 15 fully equipped troops (including crew) at a maximum towing speed of 150mph, it was usually drawn behind a C-47* or C-46* transport. The later, larger CG-13A and CG-15A developments – with a C-54* as their usual tug – were built in relatively small numbers. See Airborne Operations.

Wadi Akarit See Tunisia, Campaign in.

Waffen SS See SS.

Wainwright, Major General Jonathan
(1883–1953) Much revered US Army* officer posted to the Philippines* in September 1940, he was ordered by his commander, General Douglas MacArthur*, to command the defence of northern Luzon* against the Japanese landings at Lingayen Gulf. Forced to fall back to the Bataan* peninsula in order to avoid being cut off, Wainwright was left in command of the besieged American and Philippine forces on Luzon after MacArthur was ordered out in February 1942. Promoted to Lt General in the field in March 1942, Wainwright commanded the courageous resistance on Bataan and Corregidor* before being obliged to surrender to Japanese

General Homma* four months later, in May 1942. One of the thousands of prisoners on the forced march known as the Bataan Death March, Wainwright was subsequently transported to Manchukuo*, where he remained as a POW until the end of the war. He was, nevertheless, present at the signing of the Japanese surrender in Tokyo Bay in September 1945.

Wake Island An atoll consisting of three islands in the Central Pacific, it was projected as a forward base for the US Pacific Fleet submarines* during 1941. The naval base under Major James Devereux was still under construction when the first Japanese air raids were launched against the island on 7 December 1941. The island finally fell to troops of the Japanese Special Naval Landing Force on 23 December and survivors were evacuated to Japanese POW camps. See also Pearl Harbor; Pacific War.

Wallace, Henry Agard (1888–1965) Controversial American politician, wartime Vice President and close adviser to President Roosevelt*, Wallace held many important posts, including Chairman of the War Production Board, and later Secretary of Commerce, though he was replaced as Roosevelt's running mate in the 1944 campaign by Harry Truman*, because of his radical views on the Soviet Union and post-war American policy. In 1948, he ran for president as a Progressive Party candidate.

Wallis, Sir Barnes Neville (1887–1979) British aeronautical engineer who pioneered the geodesic system of airframe construction, which was light but exceptionally resilient and enabled aircraft to withstand considerable gunfire damage. His greatest success with the system was the Vickers Wellington*, which was the RAF's* main front-line bomber 1939–41. Wallis later designed some of the most notable bombs* of WW2, including the Grand Slam and Tallboy superheavy deep penetration bombs and the skip (bouncing) bombs which were used in the spectacular Dambusters* raid on the Ruhr in May 1943.

Wang Ching-wei (1884–1944) Former associate of Sun Yat-sen, the Chinese nationalist revolutionary who founded the Kuomintang*, Wang Ching-wei attempted to negotiate a peace between Chiang Kaishek* and Japan in 1938 during its war against China*. Wang later became a Japanese puppet ruler at Nanking*.

Warsaw, Uprisings in Capital city of Poland, the site of two heroic acts of resistance to German occupation, the first in April–May 1943 and the second during the summer of 1944.

By the end of 1940, the German occupiers in Warsaw had removed 80,000 Gentile Poles from the walled Jewish quarter of the city, replaced them with some 150,000 Jews who had been living in other parts of the city, and sealed the ghetto, closing its 22 entrances. Contact with the German authorities was maintained by the Judenrat, the 24 members of the Jewish Council who maintained order through their own police and organized the labour battalions demanded by the Germans.

From the beginning of the ghetto, Jews had maintained underground activities, newsletters and an 'Anti-Fascist Block' (destroyed in 1942) as well as links with other surviving ghettos (such as those in Bialystok, Vilna and Kovno). The Farband (Jewish Military Union) formed in 1939 also had links with the underground Polish Home Army*, from whom they received arms. A communist 'Jewish Fighting Or-

ganization' (ZOB) was set up in late 1942 and it also received arms from the London-based Home Army.

Between 1940 and 1942 an estimated 100,000 Jews died from starvation, disease or execution. In July 1942, a sweep of the ghetto rounded up a further 300,000 Jews for transportation. Most went to the extermination camp at Treblinka (see Concentration Camps). In January 1943, Himmler ordered a swift end to the 'resettlement' programme – the SS* planned to make the city 'Jew-free' by Hitler's birthday, 20 April. Two thousand Waffen SS, supported by artillery and sappers from three army divisions, 200 German and 350 Polish police, some Jewish ghetto police and 300 Ukrainian and Latvian SS auxiliaries, were assembled with a further 7,000 in reserve. The Jews, armed with some machine-guns, pistols, rifles and homemade incendiaries, were determined to resist.

The conclusion to the first day's fighting on 19 April 1943 brought heavy casualties to SS Brigadeführer Stroop's SS and auxiliary forces. Tanks and armoured vehicles were countered with 'Molotov cocktails'. The Germans were forced to retreat without their weapons or their dead. In the ensuing 20 days, Jews fought Germans for every inch of the ghetto, Stroop's force now supported by artillery and aircraft which progressively reduced the area to burning ruins. In a month's fighting, some 60,000 Jews perished.

On 16 May, Stroop reported that 'the former Jewish quarter of Warsaw is no longer in existence'. The Tlomacki synagogue was destroyed and the ghetto overwhelmed, though reports and incidents continued until July to indicate the survival of a few isolated fighting groups. It is believed that only some 100 Jews survived the ghetto rising.

An inevitable tactical defeat, the rising nevertheless represented a powerful moral victory. Similar uprisings subsequently took place in Vilna, Krakow, Lodz and other Polish cities. In 1944, when Soviet General Rokossovsky's* army reached the Vistula* and the Germans appeared to be routed, the Polish Home Army commanded by General Bor-Komorovski* independently attacked German forces in Warsaw on 1 August 1944, determined to win back their city, with the reasonable assumption of support from the Red Army* across the Vistula.

The outcome of this second battle for Warsaw, in which civilians fought alongside the Home Army, has remained one of the most controversial tragedies of the war. Despite initial success in capturing a large portion of the city in the first few days, the Polish forces were decimated by SS detachments under SS General Bach-Zelewski* that were savagely deployed to pursue them. Atrocities committed by the SS during the battle equalled any previous actions. Meanwhile, the Russians looked on from their positions over the Vistula, refusing permission to the Allies to supply the Poles from bases in Russian territory, and even disarming Home Army troops on their way to Warsaw. Demands by Stalin for Polish recognition of his puppet-government, the 'Lublin Committee'*, and transparent excuses for the Red Army's inaction held up support from the Russians until September, by which time the Polish force was effectively beaten and the outcome was no longer in doubt. By January 1945, when the Red Army finally entered the city, most of it had been razed to the ground by the evacuating Germans and over a million of its pre-war population was dead. With hindsight it is difficult to avoid the conclusion that Russia had seen the value for its own political ambitions in the destruction of the only organized Polish force which might have opposed its occupation.

Warspite, HMS British battleship of the *Queen Elizabeth** Class, completed in 1915 and fully modernized 1934–7. Famous since the Battle of Jutland in 1916, the *Warspite* began WW2 with the Home Fleet, leading the force of destroyers* which sank nine German destroyers and a submarine in Nar-

vikfjord in April 1940. Transferred to the Mediterranean as Admiral Cunningham's* flagship, she damaged her Italian counterpart the *Guilio Cesare** with a 15-inch shell from 14 miles range off Calabria in July. *Warspite* was badly damaged by Luftwaffe* dive-bombers off Crete* in May 1941, and needed extensive repairs in the United States before returning to the Mediterranean* in 1943. While supporting Allied landings at Salerno she was almost sunk by two German guided bombs*, but was towed to port and again returned to front-line action after repairs. With one main turret still out of action and capable of only 21 knots, she was employed in off-shore support of the Normandy* landings. Further damaged by a magnetic mine* in the English Channel, she was once more patched up and, further slowed, resumed bombardment duties. After a final operation against the island of Walcheren, the famous old battleship was pensioned off into reserve early in 1945.

BRIEF DATA (1939) Displacement: 36,000 tons; Dimensions: o/a lgth – 643' 9", b – 104'; Speed: 25 knots; Armament: 8 × 15" gun (4 × 2), 8 × 6" gun, 8 × 4" AA gun, 32 × 2pdr AA gun, 16 × 0.5" mg, 3 aircraft.

Washington Conference, Second See Conferences, Allied.

Washington, USS See North Carolina, USS.

Wasp, USS US Navy* aircraft carrier, completed in 1940. Her displacement was arbitrarily fixed by the 135,000-ton limit on total American carrier tonnage imposed by the Washington Naval Treaty, yet she carried as many aircraft as her larger predecessors and great emphasis was placed on their rapid deployment. Sacrifices were made in speed, protection and radius of action, but she was otherwise a generally similar diminutive of the *Yorktown** Class.

With the Atlantic Fleet in December 1941, the *Wasp* was transferred to the Pa-

cific in mid-1942 after ferrying two loads of RAF* Supermarine Spitfires* to Malta*. She covered the landings at Guadalcanal* in August but was torpedoed by the Japanese submarine *I-19*￮ on 15 September while escorting a troop convoy to the island. Fatally damaged, she was later sunk by torpedoes* from the US destroyer *Lansdowne*. A second *Wasp* was commissioned in 1943. An *Essex*￮ Class carrier, she fought in the Pacific War* until bomb-damaged in March 1945.
BRIEF DATA (1941) Displacement: 14,700 tons; Dimensions: o/a lgth – 741' 3", b – 80' 9" (109' FD); Speed: 29.5 knots; Armament: 8 × 5" AA gun, 16 × 1.1" AA gun, 24 × 0.5" AA gun, 84 aircraft.

Watchtower Code-name for the first US offensive of the Pacific War*, the invasion of Guadalcanal* and Tulagi in August 1942.

Watson-Watt, Robert (1892–1973) British government scientist whose research into radio-wave direction-finding was crucial to the development of the 'Chain Home' early warning radar system, installed in southern England just before the war. The first working aircraft detection radar* in the world, it contributed significantly to the defeat of the Luftwaffe* in the Battle of Britain* in 1940. Watson-Watt spent the war successfully extending and adapting his invention to a multitude of important military tasks.

Wavell, Field Marshal Sir Archibald (1883 –1950) British Viceroy of India from June 1943. Wavell had tours of duty in South Africa* and India before seeing active duty in France as a brigade commander during WW1. Appointed C-in-C Middle East in July 1939, Wavell proved himself an imaginative and thoughtful commander as well as a talented administrator of the enormous command area under his control, which included North Africa, East Africa* and the eastern Mediterranean*. Despite limited resources and operational problems

which were largely ignored by London, Wavell launched small-scale offensive operations against the Italian 10th Army's advance into Egypt* (including launching the first Long Range Desert Groups) that drove the numerically superior Italians back across the frontier.

Subsequent successes at Beda Fomm in February 1940 (a victory followed by the 6th Australian Division's capture of Benghazi* to put the Allies in control of Cyrenaica) and at Addis Ababa, where Italian forces surrendered to Wavell's forces on 6 April, were nevertheless overshadowed by the arrival in North Africa of the Afrika Korps*. Forced to commit a large part of his force to Greece*, Iraq* and Syria*, Wavell was unable to counter Rommel's* first offensive of the Desert War*, which reached the Egyptian border on 11 April. The defeat of the Allied offensive to recapture Tobruk*, code-named Battleaxe*, confirmed Churchill in his inclination towards a change of command, and he replaced Wavell with Auchinleck* in July.

Transferred to India as C-in-C in November 1941, Wavell was appointed Supreme Commander, Far East shortly after Japan's entry into the war. He thus presided over the Allied defeats in the Dutch East Indies*, Malaya*, Singapore* and Burma* before returning dejectedly to India to marshal Allied efforts for an offensive against Japanese forces in Burma.

A limited offensive on the Arakan* front launched by Wavell in December 1942 was beset with the familiar problems of inadequate forces, training and equipment and ended in failure. Faced with complex command problems unique to the Southeast Asia theatre, as well as enormous logistical and supply handicaps (see Burma and China), Wavell was increasingly pessimistic about the Allies' ability to recapture Burma by an overland offensive, although this was strongly favoured by Chinese Nationalist leader Chiang Kai-shek* and his American Chief of Staff, General Stilwell*. American complaints about Wavell's lack of motivation encouraged Churchill to make another command change, and Wavell was replaced again in June 1943 and made Viceroy of India, a political appointment which ended his involvement with military planning, though it proved no less difficult a job, coinciding with the climax of political unrest and demands for self-government in India (see Indian Nationalism). Wavell returned to England in 1947.

Wedemeyer, Major General Albert Popular American general who succeeded Stilwell* as Chiang Kai-shek's* Chief of Staff and Commander of US forces in the China* theatre. Wedemeyer began WW2 at the War Department, where he was regarded as an expert in war plans. In September 1943 he was promoted US Deputy Chief of Staff to Lord Mountbatten*, Supreme Commander of the newly created Southeast Asia Command (SEAC). In October, as a major general, Wedemeyer was sent to China to take over General Stilwell's command (now split into China and India–Burma theatres) and serve as Chiang's Chief of Staff. Here his mission included repairing relations between Chiang and the US, encouraging co-operation between Chiang and the communists under Mao Tse-tung*, and directing air operations from China against Japan. Among his notable achievements were improvements in the training, operational quality and general conditions of the Chinese Army. He continued to serve there until 1946, when he returned to the United States to command the 2nd Army.

West Virginia, USS See Maryland, USS.

West Wall (Westwall) A three-mile deep series of fortifications with pillboxes, troop shelters, command posts and anti-tank obstacles, also known as the Siegfried Line, along Germany's western frontier opposite the French Maginot Line*. Construction was still unfinished at the start of the war and the major defence of the West Wall was conducted on Hitler's order in 1944

and early 1945, in the face of the advancing Allied invasion armies. See Northwest Europe, Allied Invasion of.

Western Offensive, The, 1940
The Battle of France and the Low Countries
The dramatically successful German campaign in western Europe that was fought through the Netherlands, Belgium and France in the spring of 1940 resulted in the German occupation of northern France (see Maps 1–4). The campaign has been aptly described by the historian Liddell Hart as 'one of history's most striking examples of the decisive effect of a new idea, carried out by a dynamic executant'. Fought according to a bold plan refined by OKH (German Army HQ) but suggested by General Rundstedt* and his Chief of Staff General Manstein* (see Manstein Plan), the overwhelming success of the campaign was based not on the numerical superiority of German forces and equipment (which they actually achieved only in airpower), but on the dramatic efficacy of a new strategy for tank* warfare adopted in the Manstein Plan and developed and perfected by the Panzer Group Commander, General Guderian*.

In the battle of France, Guderian's Panzer Group was to give a decisive demonstration of the weapon of Blitzkrieg* – the deep strategic penetration by independently operating armoured forces, with tactical air support, to cut the main arteries of the opposing forces far behind its front, and make it vulnerable to encirclement. In contrast, the orthodoxy of British and French military thinking still favoured static deployments with armoured support. Wholly unprepared for Blitzkrieg, the Belgian and Anglo-French plans and deployments for the defence of northwestern Europe (Plan D), made by Allied C-in-C Gamelin* and endorsed by the Allied Supreme Council in November 1939, played exactly into Germany's hands (see also Maginot Line).

The opposing forces in the campaign were of roughly equal strength, with German forces of two and a half million men in 128 divisions (of which 104 were infantry), arranged in three army groups, A, B and C, under Rundstedt, Bock* and Leeb*. They faced 100 French divisions deployed on France's northeastern border with the support of 11 British, 22 Belgian and 10 Dutch divisions (148 in all). The Anglo-French forces were disposed in three army groups, of which the best were allocated to First Army Group under Billotte, to cover the exposed Belgian frontier (see Map 1). Although the two sides also employed roughly the same number of armoured vehicles (about 4,000), many of the Allied tanks were slow and unmanoeuvrable. In aircraft, the Luftwaffe* had a qualitative as well as quantitative advantage and, most importantly, was organized to support the Army's tactical operations, in contrast to the tactical role of Allied airpower, which was reliant on outmoded aircraft and largely limited to reconnaissance and air defence.

The key units, however, were Germany's ten tank divisions, each comprising about 325 mixed armoured vehicles with motorized infantry, artillery and support units. The final OKH plan called for the three divisions of Bock's Army Group B to spearhead the rapid breach of Belgium's prepared defences on the Albert Canal and Meuse River lines (including the major fortress at Eben Emael*), where Belgium's conscript army of 900,000 was concentrated to hold a central delaying position with the support of Anglo-French divisions, advancing into northern and central Belgium to counter any German invasion. Concentrated to the south, in the centre of the front across the barely defended Ardennes* forest, Army Group A's 5th and 7th Panzer Divisions (under Rommel*), the Kleist* Armoured Group (with 19th Corps under Guderian) and the 6th and 8th Panzers under Reinhardt were poised to take advantage of this diversionary attack. The plan projected a strike through the ravined and forested Ardennes (believed 'untankable' by most Allied military chiefs), behind the main concentration of Belgian and Allied forces

and a race to the undefended Channel coast, before turning to complete the encirclement.

The Fall of the Netherlands The German assault began on 10 May, with extensive air attacks on Dutch and Belgian airfields and the seizure of vital Dutch river crossings by paratroops at Moerdijk and Rotterdam. As Bock's 9th Panzer Division drove into the Netherlands towards the densely populated 'Fortress Holland' region (where the conscript Dutch Army had concentrated behind inundated water lines), and the French 7th Army raced across northern Belgium to aid the Dutch, the major Belgian fort of Eben Emael fell to glider troops and Belgian troops began to fall back to the Dyle line. In response, Allied C-in-C Gamelin ordered mobile units of the French 1st Army and BEF to advance into Belgium to hold the line on the Dyle.

Although the Netherlands collapsed on 14 May under threat of aerial bombardment and the outlying Belgian defences at Liège, Maastricht and along the Albert Canal fell rapidly to German airborne* and armoured forces, the Allied armies initially seemed firmly established in their central delaying position, between Antwerp* and Namur, by 15 May. But the German trap had already been set. On the central front, defended by four light cavalry divisions, the Chasseurs Ardennais, and ten hurriedly prepared infantry divisions of the 2nd and 9th Armies, the main German blow was delivered by Kleist's two panzer corps. Beginning on 10 May, seven panzer divisions pushed through the Ardennes and across the Meuse with almost no losses, supported by dive-bomber attacks on French artillery positions. By the 13th, the Army Group A Panzer Corps under Hoth, Reinhardt and Guderian had smashed through the Meuse River defence line at Dinant, Montherme and Sédan, along a 50-mile front.

Having routed the French 9th Army under Corap by the 15th, the German armour's subsequent advance towards the Channel (along a 'Panzer Corridor' called for in the OKH plan) was largely unchallenged, except for two unsupported attacks by French and British armour (the former, Brigadier General de Gaulle's* 4th Armoured Division) from Laon and Arras. The spearheads of Guderian's 19th Corps, which had crossed the Meuse on the 14th, hesitated at Rethel on Kleist's order, and then drove on in a 'reconnaissance in force', to reach the Channel at Abbeville on the 20th. Hoth's Panzer Group, spearheaded by Rommel's 7th Panzer Division, was counter-attacked at Arras*, and made slower progress. In Belgium, the home armies were forced back from the Dyle River line to the line of the Escaut and then the Lys on 20 May. Attempts in the last week of May by Allied forces, now under the overall command of General Weygand*, to mount flank attacks against the 'Panzer Corridor' spearheaded by Guderian ended in failure.

The Fall of Belgium and France As the BEF withdrew behind the Belgians towards Dunkirk* to the north of the 'Panzer Corridor', and Hitler halted Rundstedt's armoured divisions on the edge of the pocket held by the BEF, the Belgian army was cut off and encircled. Under the terms insisted upon by Germany, Belgium surrendered unconditionally on 28 May. In the following days, the German success was dramatized by the last-minute evacuation of the BEF and some French units from Dunkirk. Switching their panzer divisions south, to the Aisne and the Somme fronts respectively, Army Groups A and B, spearheaded by armoured attacks under Guderian and Kleist, attacked southwards towards Paris on 5 June. Against the numerous but ill-equipped and dispirited remnants of the French Army*, who had been gathered to defend a notional 'Weygand Line' in defence of Paris and the interior, Bock's Army Group B were first to drive through to the Seine, below Paris, four days later. Local French resistance held up Army Group A's attack until the 12th, when it broke through at Chalon, spearheaded by Guderian, and forced the French to abandon Paris and much of the Loire line by

the 13th. Paris was entered on the 14th, and the French 3rd, 5th and 8th Armies (with 400,000 men), trapped to the east on the Maginot Line*, were effectively bypassed and surrendered on 22 June.

Requests for an armistice by Marshal Pétain*, supported by General Weygand, were granted by the Germans on the same day. Under the terms of the armistice, northern France and the regions north and west of Vichy came under German occupation (see Compiègne). The French government, removed to Vichy*, remained at liberty, along with the fleet and an 'Armistice Army' of roughly 100,000 men. Comparative losses reflected the enormous scale of Germany's military success. Total casualty figures for French, Belgian, British and Dutch amounted to roughly 390,000, with nearly 2 million Frenchmen taken prisoner. German deaths were estimated at 30–40,000. It has since been persuasively argued that it was only Churchill and Britain's blind stubbornness that now sustained the Allied war effort, against an enemy which had effectively already won the war.

Westland Lysander The high-wing monoplane Lysander began army co-operation duties with the RAF* in 1938. Operating as an artillery spotter, reconnaissance or liaison plane, it fought with the BEF in France* during 1940, and later saw service in Egypt*, Greece*, Palestine and India. From 1941, home-based Lysanders, used for transporting SOE* agents to and from occupied northern Europe, were superseded by American P-40* Tomahawks, but they remained active as air-sea rescue* craft or target tugs. British production ended in January 1942, after 1,425 had been built. A specialist, long-range spy-dropper version – the Lysander III – flew over 400 missions between August 1941 and the end of 1944. BRIEF DATA (Mk I) Type: 2-man army co-operation; Engine: 1 × 840hp Bristol Mercury; Max speed: 219mph; Ceiling: 26,000'; Range: 600m; Arms: 6 × 0.303" mg (provision for light bombs).

Westland Whirlwind Handsome, twin-engined fighter developed for the RAF* as a long-range high performance escort fighter. Engine problems delayed its service entry until June 1940, and persisted thereafter, forcing the RAF to cancel the last 88 of its initial order for 200 aircraft. Most Whirlwinds were converted to fighter-bomber duties and flew opportunist sorties across the English Channel until withdrawn in 1942.

BRIEF DATA (Mk I) Type: single-seat fighter; Engine: 2 × 885hp Rolls Royce Peregrine; Max speed: 360mph; Ceiling: 30,000'; Range: 800m; Arms: 4 × 20mm cannon.

Weygand, General Maxime (1867–1965) Recalled from retirement to command the French Near East Theatre of Operations in 1939, Weygand replaced Gamelin* as Allied Commander of Land Forces at the critical stage of the German invasion of France in May 1940 (see Western Offensive). In the face of imminent collapse on his front, a final attempt by Weygand to rally forces along a defensive line on the Somme and Aisne rivers (the Weygand Line), between the advancing German front and the French capital, had no serious hope of success. After this failure, Weygand joined with Marshal Pétain* in demanding an early armistice and rejecting French Premier Reynaud's* suggestions for a union with Britain to maintain a fighting front against Germany with French colonial forces.

Following a brief period as Defence Minister in the Vichy* government of unoccupied France, Weygand was sent as Delegate-General to North Africa, but the pressures of maintaining independence from Axis* and Allied influence there resulted in his forced resignation. Weygand was arrested after the German occupation of the Vichy 'free zone' in November 1942 and imprisoned in Germany until the end of the war.

Whipcord Code-name for an early British plan for the invasion of Sicily*.

White Rose See Resistance, Germany.

Wilson, Field Marshal Henry Maitland (1881–1964) A strategist and administrator rather than a field commander, this successful British soldier oversaw the early campaigns in the desert as GOC-in-C for Egypt* and then for Cyrenaica under General Wavell*. In March 1941, he led the ill-fated British expedition to Greece (see Balkans, Invasion of), but returned to more bureaucratic commands in Palestine/Syria and Persia/Iraq before his promotion to C-in-C Middle East in February 1943, when Alexander* took over front-line forces in Tunisia*. The following year Wilson took over Eisenhower's* (largely political) role as Supreme Allied Commander, Mediterranean, and was promoted to field marshal. In November 1944, 'Jumbo' Wilson was transferred to Washington, where he headed the British Joint Staff Mission until 1947.

Winant, John Gilbert (1889–1947) Widely experienced liberal Republican politician and popular American ambassador to London from 1941, when he succeeded Joseph Kennedy*, Winant was active in improving Anglo-American relationships, involved in the arrangements for Lend-Lease* and was also an important figure in the establishment of the European Advisory Committee which apportioned Germany and Berlin for post-war occupation. Winant also attended the Casablanca and Tehran Conferences*, and was the American representative at the first meeting of the United Nations.

Wingate, Major General Orde (1903–44) An unconventional man and controversial commander, Wingate pioneered new forms of guerrilla warfare for use against the Japanese in Burma*, having gained experience and a considerable reputation in guerrilla operations and intelligence in Palestine, the Sudan and particularly Ethiopia (see East Africa), where he led the guerrilla unit 'Gideon Force' in 1940. Wingate's success in facilitating the British conquest of Ethiopia had earned him rapid promotion from captain to lieutenant colonel. Following convalescence from malaria and severe depression, which led to an attempted suicide, Wingate was called to India by C-in-C General Wavell* in the spring of 1942, to develop a guerrilla force based on 'Long Range Penetration' tactics, which he had learnt from the Jewish insurgents in Palestine and pioneered successfully against the Italian Army* in Ethiopia.

Exploiting the possibility of air supply and long-range radio communication, Wingate created and trained the 77th Indian Infantry Brigade from a mixed force of 3,000 British, Gurkha and Burmese troops for jungle operations behind the Japanese lines. Known as 'Chindits' after Chinthe, the stone carved creatures which guarded Burmese shrines, Wingate's force launched its first operation on 8 February 1943, from Imphal*, the major British base in Assam, crossing the Burmese border in a two-column drive over the Chindwin River* to disrupt Japanese communications and supply lines between Myitkyina* and Mandalay*. Initial successes encouraged Wingate to advance to the open plain across the Irrawaddy River to rendezvous with his southern force, where, out of range of air supply and unprotected by the 'green hell' jungle terrain for which his men were trained, the Chindits were open to fierce counter-attacks from Japanese patrols. Of the 3,000-strong force, just over 2,000 managed to escape back over the Irrawaddy in small groups to Assam at the end of March, though 600 were too debilitated to be employed on active service again.

Despite the high cost of the mission, Wingate's bizarre personal and military style had caught the imagination of both Churchill* and the British public. Hailed as a hero, Wingate was invited to accompany Churchill to the Quebec Conference* in 1943, where he persuaded Churchill and Roosevelt* to authorize a large-scale Long Range Penetration offensive in Burma, under the overall command of Lord Mountbatten*, Supreme Commander in Southeast Asia, though his fanaticism and his mercurial, uncooperative temperament made him a difficult subordinate and unpopular colleague.

In February 1944, the second Chindit operation was launched as part of the Allied campaign for the recapture of Burma. Though this larger force of 9,000 men played an indirect part in saving Kohima* and overturning the Japanese offensive in northern Burma under General Lentaigne, Wingate himself was killed in an air crash over the jungle on 24 March.

Witzleben, Field Marshal Erwin von (1881 –1944) One of the 12 new German field marshals promoted after the fall of France for which he had commanded the 1st Army, Witzleben was a consistent opponent of Nazism and was in touch with many of the senior army conspirators against Hitler throughout the war. During 1941–2 he served as C-in-C West, but was invalided. Witzleben, who would have been the conspirators' choice for Army C-in-C had the July Bomb Plot* been successful, was among those tried afterwards by Freisler's People's Court. He was executed by strangulation in August 1944. See Resistance.

Wolff, General Karl (1906–84) SS* adjutant to Himmler* from 1935 to 1943 and his close confidant throughout the period, Wolff was also Himmler's liaison officer with Hitler* from 1939. He was promoted SS general in 1942 and went as military governor and SS chief to northern Italy* after the Italian capitulation* to the Allies, where he also acted as liaison between Hitler and Mussolini*. Once convinced that Germany had lost the war, and against Hitler's specific orders, he arranged secret negotiations with the Allies via Allen Dulles*, American head of intelligence at the Office of Strategic Services (OSS*) in Switzerland. German forces in Italy finally capitulated on 2 May 1945, six days before VE day. Wolff was sentenced to four years imprisonment by a German court after the war, but was arrested again in 1962 on charges relating to genocide and sentenced to 15 years imprisonment. He was finally released in 1971.

Wolfpack The term used to describe groups of U-boats deployed simultaneously against convoys. The wolfpacks operated with growing proficiency from late 1940, fulfilling a tactical doctrine propounded by U-boat C-in-C Admiral Dönitz* before the war but rejected by his High Command. A number of submarines*, as many as 20 boats in the later years of the war, were ranged along anticipated convoy* routes. The first to make contact with a convoy, often with the help of a long-range Focke-Wulf Fw200* aircraft, would shadow it on the surface at a safe distance, radioing its position to the shore HQ, which would in turn direct the other U-boats to the scene. Gathering on the surface (where they were faster than most Allied escorts before 1943) U-boats would slip between the lines of a convoy at night and wreak utter havoc from close range on the surface, where sonar equipment could not detect them. Faster Allied escorts, radar* technology and the increased provision of air cover defeated the wolfpacks in 1943, but they maintained the German Navy's* advantage in the Battle of the Atlantic* for over two years (see Anti-submarine Warfare).

Women The political and social status of women all over the world changed most markedly in the early twentieth century where democratic and/or socialist principles framed the political organization. In many countries (though not in Japan or France for example), women were enfranchised between WW1 and WW2, and opportunities to engage in political activity, to enter certain professions previously barred to them, or to become financially independent of men (mostly by working in the vastly expanding service sectors of 'advanced' economies), greatly increased.

In Europe, socialist feminism was dominated by Germany from the late nineteenth century onwards. In the Soviet Union, the Bolshevik Revolution initially supported the development of feminist politics. In 1919 the 8th Congress established the Zhenotdel women's section as part of the Central Committee. But by the mid-1920s the Bolshevik government was increasingly concerned to suppress the 'women question' as a factional issue.

In Japan, where women had few statutory political rights at the start of the twentieth century, the Seitosha (Bluestocking Society), an intellectual middle-class women's association founded in 1911, dominated the women's protest movement until government and Army-sponsored organizations began to challenge the anti-government groups and reassert the traditional status of Japanese women in the late 1920s.

Despite fundamental changes in political status, however, women, even in the advanced democracies of Britain and the United States, were still generally regarded as servants of the kitchen and the typing pool in 1939. The occasional exceptions, such as Amy Johnson, the pioneering female aviator, or her American counterpart, Amelia Earhart, were revered as heroine idols by their generation, but did not substantially affect the canon of social dogma relating to the role of women in western society.

The outbreak of war, however, propelled women – in Europe, in the Soviet Union, in the US and Japan – into a variety of new and indispensable roles, from which they were to emerge with substantially different experiences and expectations. Apart from combat experience, which was limited to partisan activities in all major war theatres except the Eastern Front*, the active contribution of women on their home fronts was considerable. In addition to the Allied and Axis bombing strategies, which placed women on the front line wherever air attacks were launched against areas of civilian population, the economic exigencies of war called women into action as a key element in national survival. British labour policy made more extensive use of women than any other combatant country in WW2 except the USSR. All unmarried women between 17 and 45 were conscripted, either into the auxiliary fighting forces (Women's Royal Naval Service, Women's Auxiliary Army Corps and Women's Auxiliary Air Force) as clerks, drivers, nurses, machine operators, or drafted in as munitions and armaments workers, or to help in agriculture as part of the Women's Land Army. A corps of women of the Auxiliary Territorial Service (ATS) served as volunteers with the Army from September 1938 until given full military status in July 1941. Hundreds of thousands of British women also joined the Women's Voluntary Service (WVS) to help in supplying a wide variety of emergency services at home. As the war progressed, women in Britain also took over a large part of the responsibility for anti-aircraft defences.

In the Soviet Union women fought as partisans, snipers and regular combat forces on the Eastern Front. The Red Air Force* included a women's Bomber Regiment, and women operated anti-aircraft* defences, made munitions, filled and laid sandbags, cleared ruins and participated in much heavy manual labour on an equal level with men, though few went to the battlefields on the Eastern Front*. In France, women were largely responsible for food production after the German occupation in 1940, as Frenchmen were conscripted into service for the Third Reich. In the United States, women had a substantial (though not compulsory) role in the armed forces. Organizations included the Women's Reserve, US Marine Corps (created in 1943), the Women's Airforce Service Pilots (created after Pearl Harbor* to ferry and deliver aircraft inside the US) and the Women's Army Auxiliary Corps. In all, over 300,000 women were employed in the US forces, as well as playing an important part in war production as industrial workers. After the war, American trade unions were quick to demand their expulsion from the labour market.

In Germany under Hitler*, the overriding ideological framework of Nazism demanded a highly specific role for women. The Nazi state specifically excluded women from politics (as did the Japanese state), from the army and from the administration of justice. The Party programme saw women's role in motherhood and the family – in the maintenance of the Aryan race. After 1933, the Party actively sought to exclude women from the labour market and from the universities. From 1936, girls from the age of 14 to 21 were organized in the Bund Deutscher Mädel. From 1939 a year's labour service, mostly in agriculture, became compulsory for all women unmarried and under 25. In 1943 the change to a war economy resulted in a significant increase in the mobilization of women. By 1945 over seven and a half million women were mobilized for labour service and air defence. Only a few women achieved prominence in Nazi Germany, most notably Leni Riefenstahl*, the film director, the aviator Hanna Reitsch* and Hitler's personal secretaries, Gerda Daranowski Christian and Gertrud Hump Junge.

In February 1942, the Greater Japan Women's Association (Dainihon Fujinkai) was created as a powerful tool for state control of women's political and social activities. Created from the amalgamation of a number of state-sponsored women's organizations, notably the army-sponsored Greater Japan National Defence Association (Dainihon Kokubo Fujinkai), membership was made compulsory for all married women and unmarried women over 20. The activities of the membership, claimed to be 19 million in March 1943, included civil defence and savings programmes. In June 1945, it was reorganized as a people's volunteer force and subsequently disbanded.

On the war's home fronts, particularly in Britain and France, women increasingly took over functions from men killed, deported or desperately needed to maintain front-line strength on the battle fronts, as well as serving in resistance* and partisan

activities. Over a quarter of the SOE's*
members were women. Apart from those
whose contribution to clandestine operations subsequently became famous (such
as Violette Szabo, Marie-Madeleine Four-
cade or Odette Churchill), many participated anonymously and with enormous
courage in the secret war against the Axis*.
As men and nations in the post-war era
sought to re-orientate themselves in the
light of their unique experiences, women
were bound to do the same.

X

Xb-Dienst See Atlantic, Battle of.

X-Craft See Midget Submarines.

Y

Yakovlev Yak Series The most important Russian fighter design of WW2. The Yak series was begun in 1939, when the I-36 fighter prototype designed by Alexander Yakovlev was accepted for production. It entered the Red Air Force* as the Yak-1 in July 1941, and was far superior to the ageing Polikarpov I-16s* that it replaced. Lightly armed in typical Soviet style to increase manoeuvrability, it was a solid, easily maintained machine, and about 500 were in action by the end of 1941. A Yak-7V trainer had also been developed since the summer of that year and from it evolved the improved Yak-7A and Yak-7B fighters, which took over first-line duties in early 1942.

The Yak-9, which began operations in October 1942, was essentially a long-range version. It appeared in many forms – including the 9D (long-range), 9DD (very long-range), 9T (heavy, ground-support), 9B (bomber) and 9K (cannon-armed) – and accounted for more than half the Yak fighters produced in the war. The combat-based Yak-3 was developed in parallel with the Yak-9. More powerful and streamlined, it was operational from August 1943, and outperformed the German Messerschmitt Bf109G* and Focke-Wulf Fw190* fighters at altitudes below about 15,000ft. In the second half of 1944 the all-metal, re-engined Yak-9U entered service, giving dramatically improved performance comparable with the best contemporary British and US fighters and thoroughly superior to that of its Luftwaffe* opponents.

Over 37,000 Yak series fighters were built by the Soviet Union during WW2, and they were in constant action throughout the Eastern Front*. They appeared small and rather primitive by western standards, but were carefully designed to suit the working conditions they faced. Made of comparatively cheap materials, they were easy to mass-produce, resilient and above all capable of consistently outperforming their enemies.

BRIEF DATA (Yak-3) Type: single-seat fighter; Engine: 1 × 1,225hp VK105; Max speed: 404mph; Ceiling: 35,450'; Range: 506m; Arms: 1 × 20mm cannon, 1–2 × 12.7mm mg.

Yalta Conference See Conferences, Allied.

Yamamoto, Admiral Isoroku (1884–1943) Highly effective C-in-C of the Combined Fleet, the Japanese Navy's front-line battle force, 1939–43 and principal architect of Japanese naval strategy during the period, Yamamoto had been largely responsible for the development of Japan's naval air forces between the wars and had also studied and seen diplomatic service in the US before 1935, when his intransigent opposition to the extension of limitations on the Japanese fleet at the London Naval Conference brought him into the international limelight. As deputy Navy Minister from 1937, Yamamoto became politically unpopular for his opposition to the idea of armed conflict with the United States, the Soviet Union or Britain. He also opposed Japan's joining the Axis* during 1938.

Nevertheless appointed to command the Combined Fleet in 1939, Yamamoto was the originator of the plan for the attack on Pearl Harbor*, although he continued to agree with a number of senior naval officers who doubted Japan's ability to win a full-scale war against the huge resources of the United States. After the US entry into the war, Yamamoto continued to direct Japan's naval and air strategies, albeit with an increasingly fatalistic pessimism. Even after the decline in Japan's fortunes following Midway*, Yamamoto retained his great reputation, both at home and among Japanese forces. It was therefore a great blow to Japan's strategic direction as well as to morale, when Magic* intelligence intercepts revealed Yamamoto's movements during April 1943, and his aircraft was ambushed by raiding P-38* fighters while on an inspection tour in the Solomons*. See also Japanese Navy; Pacific War.

Yamashiro See Fuso.

Yamashita, Lt General Tomoyuki (1885–1946) Highly regarded Japanese general, with a considerable reputation as a strategist, he served in the Russo-Japanese War, WW1 and the Sino-Japanese War (see China) before being appointed Inspector-General of Japanese aircraft in 1940. At the end of the year he was sent by General Tojo* on a special military mission to Rome and Berlin, where he met Mussolini* and Hitler*. His conclusions, hardly welcomed by the extreme militarist Tojo, warned against a war with Britain or the US until Japan's Army* and Air Forces* could be modernized. When war in the Pacific* was declared in December 1941, Yamashita was in command of the 25th Army, with orders to invade Malaya* and capture Singapore*. The decisive success of the Japanese campaign in Malaya and Singapore, which fell on 15 February 1942, earned Yamashita the nickname 'Tiger of Malaya' though his transfer to command of the 1st Army Group in Manchukuo* kept him away from the Pacific campaigns of 1942.

After the fall of General Tojo's government in July 1944 (Tojo had considered

Yamashita a threat), Yamashita was recalled to command Japanese forces in the Philippines*. Charged with the defence of the extensive archipelago against a very large Allied Southwest Pacific force under General MacArthur*, his flexible tactics and tenacious resistance were finally unsuccessful and Yamashita was forced to surrender first the island of Leyte* (December 1944) and then the major island of Luzon* (though the capital, Manila*, did not fall until February 1945). Yamashita himself surrendered on 2 September at Baguio, with the remains of his army. After the war, Yamashita was brought before a court in Manila, convicted of war crimes (though he denied his complicity in atrocities committed under his command) and was hanged in February 1946. This has been the subject of controversy ever since.

Yamato The *Yamato* and her sister the *Musashi* were giant Japanese battleships completed in 1941 and 1942. Design work had begun in 1934 on a class of superbattleships intended comprehensively to outfight any other warship and to compensate in size for the numerical superiority enjoyed by the Americans, who were committed to building ships small enough to pass through the Panama Canal. Ignoring treaty limitations, the Japanese built in secret, and produced the two largest, most heavily protected and armoured battleships in the world. Further units were planned but were all cancelled for economic reasons, apart from the *Shinano** which was later completed as an aircraft carrier. Although the Western Allies remained unaware of their true dimensions, the *Yamato*s were rendered obsolete before they reached service by the predominance of the aircraft carrier in the Pacific War*.

The *Yamato* was at the Battle of Midway* and the Battle of the Philippine Sea*, where she was joined by her sister. Both ships were part of Vice Admiral Kurita's* Force A (the *Yamato* as flagship) at the Battle of Leyte Gulf*, where the *Musashi* was sunk by aircraft from the US carriers

Intrepid and *Cabot* on 24 October 1944. By that time they each carried over 100 light anti-aircraft* guns with some warning and gunnery radar*. The *Yamato* eventually fielded 147 25mm guns and 24 5-inch weapons. She was sunk on 7 April 1945, overwhelmed by aerial bombs and torpedoes while *en route* for a suicide mission on Okinawa* – the 'last sortie' of the Imperial Japanese Navy*.
BRIEF DATA (*Yamato*, 1941) Displacement: 64,170 tons; Dimensions: o/a lgth 863', b – 127' 9"; Speed: 27.5 knots; Armament: 9 × 18" gun (3 × 3), 12 × 6.1" gun, 12 × 5" AA gun, 24 × 25mm AA gun, 4 × 13mm AA gun, 6 aircraft.

Yeremenko, Marshal Andrei I. (1892–1970) Soviet front commander who first saw service as a cavalry officer with the Tsarist armies in WW1 and entered the Red Army* in 1918. Yeremenko commanded the 6th Cossack Division for the occupation of Poland*, served in the Far East in 1940–1 and was then transferred to the Bryansk Front in August 1941 after the German invasion (see Eastern Front). He and Konev* were criticized by Marshal Zhukov* for their failure to hold their common front against the German drive on Moscow* in October, and Yeremenko, who had been wounded, was relieved of active command for a year. In August 1942 he was appointed to command the Southeast Front (later enlarged to include the Stalingrad* Front) and directed the encirclement of the 6th Army there. Yeremenko subsequently commanded the Kalinin and 2nd Baltic Fronts.

Yokosuka D4Y Designed to serve as a dive-bomber from Japanese Navy* light carriers, the D4Y1 first saw action as a reconnaissance plane in late summer 1942. The first bomber version entered production in March 1943, but its lack of protection for crew and engine was reflected in enormous losses. This remained true of the more powerful D4Y2, but the air-cooled D4Y3 was both more reliable and better armoured. Some 300 of these were modified as suicide bombers and designated D4Y4, while the D4Y5 was a night-fighter version introduced in 1945. Total production of all types was about 2,000.
BRIEF DATA (D4Y1) Type: 2-man carrier bomber; Engine: 1 × 1,200hp Aichi Atsuta; Max speed: 344mph; Ceiling: 32,500'; Range: 2,415m; Arms: 3 × 7.7mm mg; Bomb load: 1,234lb; Allied code-name: Judy.

Yokosuka MXYZ Cherry Blossom (Ohka) Japanese Navy* piloted flying-bomb, powered by rockets* and designed to be launched from a modified Mitsubishi G4M2* bomber. About 750 were built between September 1944 and March 1945, but they were not a great success, most being released prematurely by their ponderous and harassed parent aircraft. A turbojet version failed to reach full production before the war ended, and several alternative launching methods were projected but never used in action.
BRIEF DATA Type: 1- or 2-man 1,760lb bomb; Engine: 3 solid-fuel rockets; Allied code-name: Baka.

Yokosuka P1Y Japanese Navy* bomber which became active as the P1Y1 in the spring of 1944, although the first months of its service were disrupted by engine failures and manufacturing difficulties. By the time it was fully operational in the autumn, some were being modified as night-fighters, reflecting Japan's urgent need for defensive aircraft. As a bomber it was known as the Milky Way (Ginga). It operated largely from home bases in an anti-shipping role, but was also employed as a suicide-attack plane at Okinawa*. It was not a success as a home-defence fighter, and although a specialized P1Y2-5 night-fighter model was produced with upward-firing fuselage cannon, many of these were in turn modified as P1Y2 bombers. Altogether 1,002 P1Y1s were built alongside about 100 P1Y2s, and advanced versions were being planned when the war ended.

BRIEF DATA (P1Y1) Type: 3-man naval attack bomber; Engine: 2 × 1,820hp Nakajima Hamare; Max speed: 339mph; Ceiling: 30,800'; Range: 1,191m; Arms: 2 × 20mm cannon; Bomb load: 2,200lb or 1 × 1,760lb torpedo*; Allied code-name: Frances.

York, HMS British heavy cruiser, completed in 1930 as an alternative to the costly and oversized County Class ships, which had typified international efforts to build up to (or over) the cruiser limits imposed by the Washington Naval Treaty of 1922 (see Suffolk, HMS). Eight-inch guns were retained, but one turret was removed, making the *York* a better balanced and more compact vessel than its predecessors. It was no faster, however, and achieved only insignificant reductions in cost and complement. A second ship, the *Exeter*, was completed in 1931 but, amid general British condemnation of the bigger 10,000-ton heavy types, the experiment was dropped in favour of light cruisers with 6-inch armament.

The *York* served with the Home Fleet until transferred to the Mediterranean* in 1940. On 26 March 1941, she was hit by an Italian exploding motor boat while at anchor in Suda Bay, Crete*. Beached for repairs, she was blown up when the British abandoned Crete in May. The *Exeter* was the main target of the *Admiral Graf Spee*'s* 11-inch guns at the Battle of the River Plate in December 1939. Badly damaged, she survived and later joined Allied operations in the Dutch East Indies*. She was sunk by gunfire from Japanese warships in the South Java Sea on 1 March 1942. Neither vessel was ever significantly modified, although additional light anti-aircraft* guns and standard radar* equipment were fitted during repairs to the *Exeter*.
BRIEF DATA (*York*, 1939) Displacement: 8,250 tons; Dimensions: o/a lgth – 575', b – 57'; Speed: 32.25 knots; Armament: 6 × 8" gun, 4 × 4" AA gun, 2 × 2pdr AA gun, 6 × 21" TT, 1 aircraft.

Yorktown, USS US Navy* aircraft carrier and Class, which also included the *Enterprise* and later the *Hornet**. The first two ships of this famous group were launched in 1936 and were much-improved developments of the earlier *Ranger**. The principle was maintained that large numbers of aircraft, rapidly deployed, were a carrier's best offensive and defensive weapon, but more realistic priority was now given to performance and hull protection. The hangar deck was also armoured, but its sides remained open to maximize capacity and the flight deck was still made of wood. Early in the Pacific War*, anti-aircraft* armament was augmented by the addition of numerous 20mm guns.

The *Yorktown* was with the Atlantic Fleet when the Japanese attacked Pearl Harbor* but was quickly transferred to the Pacific. Bomb damaged at the Battle of the Coral Sea*, she returned to Pearl Harbor for repairs and was back at sea after only three days – in time for the Battle of Midway*. There, on 4 June 1942, she was hit by three bombs and two torpedoes from Japanese carrier aircraft. Attempts to save her were cut short by two more torpedoes from the submarine *I-168* on 6 June, and she sank the next morning. The second *Yorktown* – an *Essex** Class aircraft carrier – was commissioned in 1943, and fought through the Pacific 'island' campaigns to the end of the war.
BRIEF DATA (*Yorktown*, 1941) Displacement: 19,800 tons; Dimensions: o/a lgth – 809' 6", b – 83' (109' FD); Speed: 33 knots; Armament: 8 × 5" AA gun, 81 aircraft.

Yubari Completed in the mid-1920s, the Japanese Navy* light cruiser *Yubari* was an important experimental design. New techniques, employed to give her relatively heavy armament on a very small displacement, were later used to keep large, heavily armed cruisers to within internationally acceptable tonnage limits. Rearmed as an anti-aircraft* vessel in 1943, the *Yubari* was sunk in April 1944 by the US submarine *Bluegill* off the Caroline Islands.

BRIEF DATA (1941) Displacement: 2,890 tons; Dimensions: o/a lgth – 463', b – 40'; Speed: 35.5 knots; Armament: 6 × 5.5" gun (2 × 2, 2 × 1), 1 × 3" AA gun, 2 × 13mm AA gun, 4 × 24" TT, 34 mines.

Yugoslavia See Balkans; Tito; Simovic; Mihajlovic.

Z

Zeitzler, General Kurt von (1895–1963) German Chief of Staff at OKH* from 1942 to 1944, he had distinguished himself by his effective logistical planning for the Western Offensive in 1940 and was credited by Hitler with repelling the Anglo-Canadian Dieppe* Raid. In September 1942, when Hitler dismissed Halder* over his criticism of the Stalingrad* campaign, Zeitzler was promoted over the heads of more senior officers to replace Halder as Chief of the General Staff. He was instrumental in persuading Hitler to launch the offensive against Kursk* in the summer of 1943, but, following its failure, Zeitzler was no longer involved in the initiation of operations. Zeitzler progressively adopted a novel form of resistance to Hitler's military planning by reporting himself unwell and ceasing to carry out his duties. Dismissed from the army in July 1944, after several unsuccessful attempts to resign, Zeitzler survived the war.

Zhukov, Marshal Georgi (1896–1974) Highly regarded C-in-C of the Red Army* from October 1941. Zhukov had already distinguished himself during the Khalkin-Gol offensive in Mongolia (see Russo-Japanese Border Conflict, 1939), where his forces had decisively defeated the Japanese 6th Army. Appointed Chief of Staff in the final stages of the Russo-Finnish War*, Zhukov was sent to assist Marshal Voroshilov* on the northern front, replacing him on 11 September (after the failure at Smolensk*) to take over the defence of Leningrad*. In October he was recalled to Moscow to receive his promotion to C-in-C of the whole Russian western front. Of his subsequent achievements, the most famous was the defence of Moscow* during December 1941 and the successful counter-offensive which drove the German front 40 miles back from the Soviet capital.

Although historians have since suggested that the German failure at Moscow was largely due to the onset of 'General Winter' rather than Zhukov's leadership of the defending Soviet armies, he went on to oversee successful counter-offensives at Stalingrad* (November 1942), at Kursk* (July 1943) and in the Ukraine*. In all these actions, Zhukov's primary tactic was to deliver a series of continuous blows along the vast stretch of the Soviet front, supported by huge concentrations of armour, and effectively without any consideration of the cost in human lives. During this period Zhukov spent much of his time at Supreme Headquarters in Moscow, advising Stalin on strategic plans for the war. In general, he allowed his Front commanders independence of action within the broad strategy, only occasionally interposing his personal command in local areas.

Returning to a field command at the head of the 1st Ukrainian Front* in March 1944, Zhukov's forces met little resistance in their fast-paced drive to the frontier with Hungary*. Transferred to the 1st Belorussian Front in the early summer, Zhukov directed the advance on Warsaw* (see Poland, Russian Campaign in) and, in April 1945, ordered the launch of the final offensive against Berlin*, that resulted in the capitulation of the Third Reich on 2 May.

Generally regarded by both Allied and Soviet observers as a highly effective commander, it is also clear from contemporary accounts that Zhukov was a keen self-publicist, prepared to take credit for Soviet victories without reference to other Red Army generals. Although he commanded the Soviet Control Committee in Germany until 1946, his popularity in the Red Army appears to have aroused Stalin's mistrust, and Zhukov was given command of a relatively small military district. On Stalin's death in 1953, Zhukov became Soviet Minister of Defence.

Zuiho Japanese light aircraft carrier of the *Shoho** Class. Of the same versatile design as her sister, the *Zuiho* had been started as the submarine tender *Takasaki* but was completed as an aircraft carrier in December 1940. She was with the Southern Force of Admiral Nagumo's* Carrier Fleet a year later and served with distinction in the Pacific War* for almost three years. During 1944 her light anti-aircraft* defences were augmented, her flight deck extended forward and 168 anti-aircraft rocket* launchers fitted in six batteries. She was sunk as part of Admiral Ozawa's* decoy fleet at the Battle of Leyte Gulf* on 25 October 1944.
BRIEF DATA See Shoho.

Zuikaku See Shokaku.

APPENDIX I
Chronology of the Pacific and the Far East

1931	Sept.	19	Japan invades Manchuria.
1933	March	27	Japan withdraws from the League of Nations.
1934	Dec.	29	Japan renounces the Washington and London Naval Treaties.
1935	April	1	First US Neutrality Act.
1936	Nov.	25	German–Japanese Anti-Comintern Pact signed.
1937	July	7	Japanese large-scale invasion of China.
	Aug.		Sino-Soviet Non-aggression Pact.
	Dec.	13	Japanese sack Nanking.
1938	Feb.	14	Opening of British naval base at Singapore.
	July	28	Clashes between Japanese and Soviet forces in Manchuria.
	Oct.	21	Japanese capture Canton.
	Nov.	3	Japanese announce the 'New Order' for Southeast Asia.
1939	May	28	Soviet–Japanese clash at Khalkin-Gol.
	Aug.	23	Japan withdraws from Anti-Comintern Pact following Russo-German Non-aggression Pact.
	Sept.	15	End of Soviet–Japanese Border Conflict.
1940	March	30	Japanese set up puppet Chinese government at Nanking.
	July	12	Japanese demands lead to British closure of Burma Road. China now isolated.
	Sept.	16	Conscription begins in US.
		22	Japanese troops occupy northern Indochina.
		27	Japan signs Tripartite Pact. Formation of Rome–Berlin–Tokyo Axis.
	Oct.	18	British reopen Burma Road with support of US.
1941	April	13	USSR and Japan sign Neutrality Pact.
	July	26	US freezes all Japanese assets.
		28	Japanese landings in Indochina.
	Aug.	5	Britain and the Netherlands impose embargoes in support of US action.
	Sept.		Flying Tigers begin operations in China.
	Oct.	17	Tojo succeeds Konoe as Japanese Premier.
	Dec.	7	Japanese attack Pearl Harbor.
		8	Japanese land in Malaya. US declares war on Japan.
		9	China declares war on Japan and Germany.
		10	Sinking of the Repulse. Japanese invade Guam and land on Luzon.
		11	Japanese attack Wake Island and start invasion of Burma.
		16	Japanese land in Sarawak. Nimitz becomes C-in-C, US Pacific Fleet.
		20	King appointed C-in-C US Fleet.
		23	Fall of Wake Island.
		25	Surrender of Hong Kong to Japanese.
1942	Jan.	2	Japanese take Manila and

		Cavite.	*May*	1	Japanese take Mandalay.
	3	Japanese land on Borneo.		3	Japanese take Tulagi.
	4	Japanese air raids on Rabaul.		4	Japanese invasion fleet leaves Rabaul for Port Moresby. Battle of the Coral Sea begins.
	7	Siege of Bataan begins.			
	11	Japanese invade Dutch East Indies.		5	British landings on Diego Suarez, Madagascar.
	21	Stilwell appointed Chief of Staff to Chiang Kai-shek.		7	US surrender at Corregidor.
	23	Japanese landings on New Guinea and the Solomon Islands.		10	Surrender of US forces on Mindanao.
	24	Battle of Makassar Strait.		14	British forces and Chinese forces under Stilwell retreat from Burma to Assam.
	30	British withdraw from Moulmein, Burma. Amboina falls to Japan.			
	31	British retreat from Malaya to Singapore completed.		15	General Alexander moves HQ to Imphal.
Feb.	15	Surrender of Singapore to Japanese.		18	Chinese retreat from Myitkyina.
	19	Battle of Lombok Strait. Japanese bomb Darwin, Australia.		20	Japanese complete conquest of Burma.
			June	4	Battle of Midway begins.
	22	MacArthur ordered to leave Philippines.		7	Japanese invade western Aleutian Islands, Kiska and Attu.
	23	US bombers raid Rabaul from Australia.			
	27	Battle of Java Sea begins.		9	Japanese complete conquest of Philippines.
March	1	Japanese occupation of Java.	*Aug.*	7	US landings at Guadalcanal.
	2	Japanese take Batavia (Djakarta).		8	Tulagi retaken by US forces. Battle of Savo Island.
	5	General Alexander assumes command in Rangoon.		9	Civil disobedience campaign begins in India.
	7	Japanese landings in New Guinea. Evacuation of Rangoon.		13	Further Japanese landings on New Guinea.
	11	MacArthur leaves Luzon.		24	Battle of Eastern Solomons begins.
	19	Slim assumes command of British troops in Burma.		26	Japanese advance on Port Moresby.
	23	Japanese occupy Andaman Islands.		29	Japanese begin landings on Guadalcanal.
April	5	Japanese carrier raids on Colombo, Ceylon.	*Sept.*	7	Japanese defeated by Australian forces at Milne Bay.
	9	Surrender at Bataan.			
	10	Royal Navy leaves Indian Ocean.		14	Australian counter-attacks from Port Moresby begin.
	18	Doolittle Raid on Tokyo.		29	19,000 US troops on Guadalcanal.
	29	Japanese take Lashio.			

Oct.	11	Battle of Cape Esperance.
	26	Battle of Santa Cruz.
Nov.	1	US Marines begin offensive on Guadalcanal.
	12	Naval Battle of Guadalcanal begins.
	24	Japanese forced back to Gona – Buna – Sanananda triangle.
	30	Battle of Tassafaronga.
Dec.	10	Fall of Gona.
	13	Japanese abandon Buna.
	14	Japanese reinforcements land in New Guinea.
	17	Indian troops advance into Arakan region, Burma.
	28	Japan withdraws from 'the Triangle' in New Guinea.
1943 Jan.	2	Japanese resistance in Buna collapses. Japanese forces ordered to evacuate Guadalcanal.
	6	Renewal of Arakan offensive in Burma.
	14	Casablanca Conference.
Feb.	4	New Delhi Conference.
	8	Wingate's Chindits enter Burma.
	9	Japanese resistance ends on Guadalcanal.
	14	Chindits cross Chindwin River.
	21	US landing on Russell Islands.
March	3–5	Battle of the Bismarck Sea.
	8	Japanese forces cross Yangtse on 'Rice Offensive' raids.
	24	Wavell recalls the Chindits. Battle of Komandorski Islands.
April	5	Japanese advance on Mayu peninsula towards India.
	7	Large-scale Japanese air raids on Guadalcanal.
	18	Yamamoto shot down and killed.

	21	Admiral Koga succeeds Yamamoto as C-in-C Combined Fleet.
May	11	US forces begin recapture of Aleutian Islands with a landing on Attu.
	12	Arakan campaign ends in stalemate.
	30	Japanese resistance ends in Attu.
June	3	End of Japanese 'Rice Offensive'.
	30	Start of Operation Cartwheel in Central Solomons.
July	5	Battle of Kula Gulf.
	12	Battle of Kolombangara.
Aug.	6	Battle of Vella Gulf.
	15	US landings on Vella Lavella. US and Canadian troops take Kiska, Aleutians.
	24	End of Quebec Conference. Plans made for Pacific and Burma campaigns. Mountbatten appointed Supreme Allied Commander of Southeast Asia (SEAC).
	28	US landings in Ellice Islands.
Sept.	4	Australian offensive against Lae begins.
	6	US paratroops land at Nazdab.
	15	Japanese abandon Lae.
	28	Japanese evacuate Kolombangara.
Oct.	2	Australians take Finschhafen.
	6	Battle of Vella Lavella.
Nov.	1	US landings on Bougainville.
	2	US air raids on Rabaul. Battle of Empress Augusta Bay.
	12	Japanese withdraw aircraft from Rabaul.
	20	Launch of Operation Galvanic in the Gilberts.

			US landings on Tarawa and Makin.			on Eniwetok.
		23	Fall of Tarawa and Makin.		24	'Merrill's Marauders' advance on Myitkyina.
		23–6	First Cairo Conference. Decision to recapture North Burma.		29	US landings on Admiralty Islands (los Negros).
		30	Tehran Conference begins.	March	8	Japanese counter-attacks on Bougainville. Opening of Japanese offensive on Kohima and Imphal.
	Dec.	4	Second Cairo Conference.			
		15	US landings on New Britain.		15	More US landings on Admiralty Islands.
1944	Jan.	2	US landings on Saidor, New Guinea.		22	Japanese forces close on Imphal.
		6	Transfer of landing craft from Far East to Europe. Cancellation of landings in Burma.		24	Wingate killed in an air crash.
					31	Japanese besiege Imphal.
				April	4	Japanese surround Kohima.
		8	US requests continued Allied action in Burma to draw Japanese forces from the Pacific.		17	Renewed Japanese offensive in China.
					22	US landings at Hollandia, New Guinea.
		9	British take Maungdaw on Arakan front.		28	Chinese and US troops begin offensive on Myitkyina.
		13	Chinese successes in northern Burma.			
		14	Roosevelt demands more co-operation from Chiang in Burma.	May	17	US attack on Wakde, New Guinea. Merrills Marauders capture airfield at Myitkyina.
		31	US invasion of Marshall Islands begins. Landings on Majuro, Roi and Namur.		18	US operations end in Admiralty Islands.
	Feb.	1	US troops land on Kwajalein. Chinese attacks in northern Burma at Taihpa Ga.		20	Wakde secured.
					27	US landings at Biak, New Guinea.
		2	Roi and Namur secured.	June	2	Siege of Myitkyina begins. Allied counter-offensive begins at Kohima and Imphal.
		4	End of Japanese resistance on Kwajalein. Japanese attack on the Arakan front, Burma.			
		5	2nd Chindit Operation begins in Burma.		17	US 23rd Infantry Division land on Saipan, Marianas. First B-29 raid on mainland Japan.
		10	US and Australian troops make contact in New Guinea.		19	Battle of the Philippine Sea.
		15	New Zealand troops land in New Ireland.		22	Japanese withdraw from Kohima/Imphal.
		17	US assaults on Eniwetok. Bombardment of Truk.	July	9	US forces secure Saipan.
					18	Tojo resigns as Japanese Premier.
		21	Japanese resistance ceases		21	US marines land at Guam.

24 US marines land at Tinian.

30 US troops land at Sansapor, New Guinea.

Aug. 1 Japanese resistance ends on Tinian.

3 Myitkyina falls to US–Chinese forces.

8 Japanese take Hengyang, China.

10 Organized resistance on Guam ends.

19 Japanese forced out of Assam.

20 US operations completed at Biak, New Guinea.

Sept. 12 Second Quebec Conference.

15 US landings at Peleliu, Palau Islands. US landings on Morotai.

28 British offensive against Japanese in Arakan begins.

Oct. 9 Japanese advance on US air bases in China continues.

12 US air raids on Formosa begin.

15 British and US–Chinese offensive in northern Burma.

19 British troops take Mohnyin, Burma.

20 US landings begin on Leyte, Philippines.

23–6 Battle of Leyte Gulf.

Nov. 3 Chinese forces reach the Irrawaddy, Burma.

6 Japanese besiege Kunming.

10 Japanese forces overrun US air bases at Kweilin and Liuchow.

19 Indian troops cross the Sittang and Chindwin rivers, Burma.

Dec. 12 Allied offensive on coastal area of Arakan begins.

15 US troops land on Mindoro, Philippines.

1945 Jan. 4 British forces take Akyab on Arakan coast.

9 US troops land in Lingayen Gulf, Luzon.

15 First convoy along new Burma Road reaches Myitkyina from Ledo.

27 Japanese blockade of China broken. Burma Road reopens.

Feb. 2 Resistance to Japanese in Indochina begins.

3 Japanese capture Nanyung, China.

4–11 Yalta Conference.

19 US forces land on Iwo Jima.

25 US firebombing of Tokyo.

26 US troops recapture Corregidor.

March 3 All Japanese resistance ends in Manila, Luzon. US troops land on Palawan.

4 Indian troops take Meiktila, Burma.

7 Chinese troops take Lashio, Burma.

8 Japanese resistance ceases on Palawan.

9 Allied troops reach outskirts of Mandalay, Burma. Massive incendiary raid on Tokyo.

10 US troops land on Mindanao.

21 Japanese resistance ends in Mandalay.

26 Fighting ends on Iwo Jima. US landings on Cebu.

April 1 US troops land on Okinawa.

6 Japanese begin large-scale Kamikaze attacks on Okinawa invasion fleet.

7 Japanese superbattleship *Yamato* sunk.

12 US President Roosevelt dies. Indian troops take Kyaukpadaung, Burma.

13 Japanese open offensive on Chihchiang, China.

	17	US landings on Mindanao.
	28	Recapture of Arakan completed.
May	3	Fall of Rangoon.
	11	Australians take Wewak, New Guinea.
	20	Japanese begin to withdraw from China.
June	10	Australian troops begin recapture of Borneo.
	18	Japanese cease organized resistance on Mindanao.
	22	All Japanese resistance ends on Okinawa.
	30	Luzon campaign officially ends.
July	1	Chinese forces liberate Liuchow.
	13	Italy declares war on Japan.
	16	First atomic bomb is successfully tested at Alamagordo, New Mexico.
	17	Potsdam Conference opens. Terms of surrender given to Japanese.
	25	Organized Japanese resistance ends on Mindanao.

	27	Chinese forces enter Kweilin.
	30	Japan rejects Potsdam ultimatum.
Aug.	6	Atomic bomb dropped on Hiroshima.
	8	USSR declares war on Japan.
	9	Atomic bomb dropped on Nagasaki. Russians commence offensive against Japan in Manchuria.
	10	Japan accepts terms of surrender.
	14	Soviet advance to occupy Manchurian territory, Sakhalin and the Kuril Islands.
	20	Japanese fighting in China ends.
	24	USSR and China sign a treaty of alliance.
	29	Mountbatten accepts surrender of Japanese forces in Southeast Asia and Singapore.
Sept.	2	MacArthur accepts surrender of Japanese in Tokyo Bay.

APPENDIX II
Chronology of the Campaigns in Sicily and Italy

1943 May	11	End of fighting in Africa.
	26	Air attack on Pantellaria begins.
June	11	Surrender of Pantellaria.
July	3	Allies begin air attacks on Sicilian airfields.
	9	Airborne forces seize Ponte Grande near Syracuse.
	10	Allied invasion of Sicily begins.
	11	British forces take Syracuse.
	13	British forces take Augusta.
	14	British paratroops capture Primasole Bridge.
	16	Churchill and Roosevelt appeal to Italians to surrender.
	19	US air raids on Rome marshalling yards.
	23	Patton's 7th Army captures Palermo.
	25	Fall of Mussolini. Badoglio forms new government.
Aug.	5	British forces enter Catania.
	13	USAAF raids on Rome.
	16	US forces advance on Messina.
	18	German resistance ends in Sicily.
	19	Heavy Allied air raids on Avellino, Foggia and Salerno.
	20	Allies insist on unconditional surrender of Italy.
	26	Air raids on Italian centres continue.

Sept.	1	Italy secretly accepts an armistice.
	3	Allied invasion of Italy begins with 8th Army landings at Reggio.
	8	Italy surrenders to the Allies.
	9	US 5th Army landings at Salerno. British airborne attack on Taranto.
	10	German troops occupy Rome.
	12	Mussolini liberated from Gran Sasso.
Oct.	1	US forces capture Naples.
	2	Battle of Termoli begins.
	12	US 5th Army attacks across Volturno River.
	13	Italy declares war on Germany.
	15	US and British forces attempt advances towards Rapido and Garigliano rivers.
	24	US 34th Division captures Sant' Angelo.
Nov.	1	German strategic decision to concentrate efforts for a defence on the Gustav Line.
	5	US 5th Army attacks on the Bernhard Line.
	16	British forces establish bridgeheads over the Sangro River.
	25	Plans approved for Operation Shingle.
Dec.	1	Allies begin assaults on the Gustav Line.
1944 Jan.	5	Allies attempt drives to the Rapido River.

	22	5th Army landings at Anzio.
Feb.	15	Allies bomb monastery at Monte Cassino.
	16	Germans counter-attack at Anzio.
	18	Further Allied attacks on Monte Cassino.
May	11	Allies launch new offensive on the Gustav Line.
	18	Monte Cassino falls to Polish troops.
	23	5th Army breaks out of Anzio beachhead.
June	5	5th Army enters Rome.
	6	Allied invasion of Normandy begins.
	10	US forces reach Cittavecchia.
	16	German forces complete withdrawals to Gothic Line.
	22	8th Army breaks through Trasimene Line.
July	3	US forces advance towards Leghorn.
	12	Operation launched to destroy Po River bridges.
	15	5th Army attacks Arno Line.
	19	US forces take Leghorn.
	23	Fall of Pisa.
Aug.	4	8th Army takes Florence.
	15	Launch of Allied Operation Anvil/Dragoon.

	25	British, Canadian and Polish troops attack Gothic Line.
	30	8th Army launches attacks on Gothic Line.
	31	US troops cross Arno Line.
Sept.	8	Allied advance on Rimini stalls.
	12	Battle of Gothic Line begins in earnest.
	21	Canadian and Greek troops enter Rimini.
	24	Allies advance north of Gothic Line. 5th Army offensive towards Bologna begins.
Dec.	3	British 8th Army offensive towards Bologna.
	5	Canadian troops occupy Ravenna.
	15	Germans counter-attack at Lucca.
1945 March	23	Vietinghoff succeeds Kesselring as C-in-C in Italy.
April	9	Allied spring offensive launched in Italy.
	21	Polish forces capture and US forces occupy Bologna.
	26	Fall of Verona and Genoa. Collapse of German resistance.
	27	5th Army reaches Genoa.
	29	Murder of Mussolini.
May	2	Formal surrender of German forces in Italy.

APPENDIX III
Chronology of the African and Mediterranean Campaigns

1935	Oct.	3	Italian forces invade Abyssinia.
1936	May	9	Abyssinia annexed by Italy.
	Nov.	1	Formation of Rome–Berlin Axis.
1939	April	7	Italians invade Albania.
	May	22	Signing of the Pact of Steel.
1940	June	10	Italy enters the war.
		11	Italian aircraft attack Malta.
	July	3	British neutralize French Fleet at Mers el Kébir.
		4	Italians invade British Somaliland.
	Sept.	13	Italian forces advance into Egypt.
	Oct.	28	Italians attack Greece.
	Nov.		British forces sent to Crete.
		4	Greek counter-attacks on Albanian front.
		11	British attack Italian fleet at Taranto.
	Dec.	9	British counter-attack in Egypt.
		11	British forces capture Sidi Barrani.
1941	Jan.	19	British advance into Abyssinia and Eritrea.
		22	Allies capture Tobruk.
		29	British forces enter Italian Somaliland.
	Feb.	7	Italians surrender at Beda Fomm.
		8	Royal Navy bombards Genoa.
		12	Rommel arrives in Tripoli.
		25	British forces take Mogadishu.

	March	7	British troops arrive in Greece.
		9	Italians attack Greece.
		16	British forces retake Berbera, Somaliland.
		24	Rommel takes El Agheila.
		25	Yugoslavia signs Tripartite Pact.
		27	Prince Paul of Yugoslavia overthrown.
		28	Battle of Cape Matapan.
	April	1	Rashid Ali coup in Iraq.
		6	Germans attack Yugoslavia and Greece. Italians surrender at Addis Ababa.
		8	Fall of Salonika. Fall of Massawa.
		9	Axis forces capture Bardia.
		10	Axis siege of Tobruk begins.
		13	Fall of Belgrade.
		17	Yugoslavia capitulates.
		18	British forces land at Basra, Iraq.
		24	Greek Army surrenders.
		25	German forces enter Athens. Axis occupies Halfaya Pass.
		28	British forces complete withdrawal from Greece.
	May	5	Emperor of Abyssinia restored to his throne.
		15	Launch of Operation Brevity.
		18	Duke of Aosta capitulates at Amba Alagi.
		20	German forces land on Crete.
		30	Rashid Ali flees Iraq.
	June	1	British forces complete

		evacuation of Crete.
	8	British and Free French forces invade Syria.
	15	Allied Battleaxe offensive in Western Desert begins.
	17	British forces withdraw in Western Desert.
	18	Germany and Turkey sign treaty of friendship.
	21	Free French forces take Damascus.
July	12	Vichy French surrender in Syria. Allies occupy Syria and Lebanon.
Aug.	25	British and Russian troops enter Persia.
Nov.	18	Allies open Crusader offensive.
	30	8th Army links up with Tobruk garrison.
Dec.	10	Siege of Tobruk lifted.
	11	Germany and Italy declare war on the US.
	19	Italian frogmen damage Royal Navy ships at Alexandria.
	24	British forces enter Benghazi.
1942 Jan.	17	Allies capture Halfaya garrison.
	21	Rommel advances to Gazala Line. Agedabia retaken.
April	16	Malta awarded George Cross.
May	27	Rommel attacks Gazala Line.
June	10	Free French forces evacuate Bir Hacheim.
	17	British forces withdraw from Libya. Tobruk isolated.
	21	Fall of Tobruk to Rommel.
	23	Axis troops cross Egyptian frontier.
	29	Axis takes Mersa Matruh.
July	1	Start of first battle of El Alamein.
	27	End of first battle of El Alamein.

Aug.	13	General Alexander made C-in-C Middle East. Montgomery takes over 8th Army.
	30	Battle of Alam Halfa begins.
Sept.	2	Alam Halfa battle ends.
Oct.	23	Second battle of El Alamein.
Nov.	4	Second battle of El Alamein ends.
	8	Allied Torch landings in Northwest Africa.
	9	German troops land in Tunisia.
	11	Vichy French forces cease resistance in Northwest Africa. Patton takes Casablanca. Allies retake Bardia.
	13	Allies retake Tobruk.
Dec.	13	Axis forces retreat from El Agheila.
	24	Darlan assassinated in Algiers.
1943 Jan.	14	Casablanca Conference begins.
	15	Allies advance on Tripoli.
	23	Fall of Tripoli.
Feb.	19	Axis forces break through at Kasserine Pass.
March	6	Rommel stalled at Médenine.
	9	Rommel replaced by von Arnim as Axis C-in-C in Africa.
	26	Allies break through on Mareth Line.
April	7	American forces contact 8th Army near Gafsa.
	19–21	Battle of Enfidaville.
May	7	Allies take Tunis and Bizerte.
	11	Axis forces surrender in Tunisia.
Sept.	13	British forces invade Kos.
Oct.	3	German forces retake Kos.
	16	Allies driven out of remaining Aegean positions.

1944 Oct.   4   Allies land in Greece.
           13   Allies retake Athens.
    Dec.   3   Civil war breaks out in
                 Athens.

APPENDIX IV
Chronology of the Western Offensive and the Battle of Britain, 1940

1939 Sept. 3 Britain, France, Australia and New Zealand declare war on Germany.

11 Hitler meets with Quisling.

Oct. 16 First German air raid on Britain.

1940 Feb. 16 The Altmark Incident.

April 8 Germans overrun Denmark. German forces land in Norway.

10 Denmark capitulates.

15 British, French and Polish troops land near Narvik.

16 British troops land at Namsos.

18 British forces land at Aandalasnes.

19 British troops occupy the Faroe Islands.

May 2 British forces evacuate Aandalasnes and Namsos.

10 Germany invades the Low Countries. Churchill becomes Prime Minister.

13 German armies cross the Meuse.

14 Rotterdam bombed. Netherlands surrenders. Queen Wilhelmina flees to Britain.

20 Fall of Amiens. German forces reach the Channel at Abbeville.

21 Allied counter-attack at Arras.

24 German armoured divisions halt before Dunkirk.

25 Fall of Boulogne.

27 Fall of Calais. Evacuation begins from Dunkirk. Belgium capitulates.

28 Allies capture Narvik.

29 Fall of Lille, Ostend and Ypres.

June 4 Final evacuations from Dunkirk.

7 King of Norway flees to Britain.

8 Allies evacuate Narvik.

9 Norway surrenders.

10 Italy enters the war.

14 Fall of Paris.

22 French sign armistice with Germany.

25 Hostilities end in France.

30 German forces occupy Channel Islands.

July 3 British destroy French naval squadron at Oran.

10 Beginning of the Battle of Britain.

Aug. 13 Mass air attacks begin on British airfields, factories and docks.

15 Further mass Luftwaffe raids over Britain.

25 RAF bombs Berlin.

Sept. 6 RAF bombs Berlin.

7 Start of London Blitz.

17 Operation Sealion postponed.

Oct. 12 Sealion abandoned.

APPENDIX V
Chronology of the Battle in the Atlantic

1939 Sept.	3	Britain declares war on Germany. Sinking of the *Athenia*.		Oct.	17	US destroyer *Kearney* torpedoed off Iceland.
Oct.	14	*Royal Oak* sunk in Scapa Flow.			31	US destroyer *Reuben James* torpedoed.
Nov.	3	US Congress passes 'Cash and Carry' amendment.		1942 Jan.	14	*Tirpitz* arrives in Trondheim.
Dec.	13	Battle of the River Plate.		Feb.	12	*Scharnhorst*, *Gneisenau* and *Prinz Eugen* pass through Straits of Dover to Germany.
	17	*Graf Spee* scuttled in River Plate.				
1940 July	6	German submarine base established at Lorient.		June	18	Churchill arrives in Washington.
Sept.	2	Anglo-American Destroyers-for-Bases deal.		July	4	Convoy PQ17 attacked.
				Dec.	31	Battle of the Barents Sea.
Nov.	5	*Admiral Scheer* attacks Convoy HX84.		1943 Jan.	30	Dönitz becomes C-in-C of German Navy.
Dec.	24	*Hipper* attacks Convoy WS5A.		March		Worst month for Allied shipping losses to U-boats.
1941 March	8	US Senate passes Lend-Lease Bill.		May		Lull in U-boat attacks following Battle with RN Convoy ONS-5. Forty-one U-boats sunk.
	12	British ships begin to be 'degaussed' against magnetic mines.				
April	10	US establishes protectorate over Greenland.			22	Dönitz withdraws U-boats from the Atlantic.
May	24	The *Hood* sunk.		Sept.	22	British midget submarines attack *Tirpitz*.
	27	*Bismarck* sunk.		Dec.	26	*Scharnhorst* sunk off North Cape.
July	7	US troops occupy Iceland.				
Aug.	12	Churchill and Roosevelt sign Atlantic Charter.		1944 April	3	British air attack on *Tirpitz* in Altenfjord.
Sept.	4	US destroyer *Greer* attacked by U-boat.		June	6	D-Day.
				Nov.	12	RAF bombers sink *Tirpitz*.
	28	First Arctic convoy to Russia leaves Iceland.		1945 May	7	Hostilities cease in the Atlantic.

APPENDIX VI
Chronology of the Allied Campaign
in Northwest Europe 1944–5

1940 June 24 British raid near Le Touquet.

July 14 Commando raid on Guernsey.

1941 March 4 Commando raid on the Lofoten Islands.

1942 March 27 Raid on St Nazaire.

May 30 Thousand-bomber raid on Cologne.

Aug. 14 Allied raid on Dieppe.

1943 May 12 Trident Conference in Washington fixes date of D-Day for 1 May 1944.

July 24 Allied air raids on Hamburg begin.

Nov. Rommel takes over command on French coast.

1944 Jan. 16 Eisenhower becomes Supreme Commander, Allied Expeditionary Force.

Feb. 20 Start of 'Big Week' intensive bombing campaign on Germany.

May Allies begin air attacks on Continent.

June 6 D-Day. Allied landings in Normandy.

11 Normandy beachheads linked.

13 First V-1 missile lands on Britain.

19 Great storm for three days in the Channel.

27 Allies capture Cherbourg.

July 3 Battle of the Hedgerows begins in Normandy.

9 Allies capture Caen though not yet totally secured.

18 Allies capture St Lô.

20 Bomb Plot against Hitler's life fails at Rastenberg.

Aug. 7 German counter-attack at Avranches.

12 Avranches counter-attack fails.

15 Allies land in southern France (Anvil/Dragoon).

21 German forces trapped in Argentan-Falaise pocket.

25 Liberation of Paris.

28 Liberation of Marseilles and Toulon.

Sept. 3 Liberation of Brussels and Lyons.

4 Liberation of Antwerp.

8 First V-2 rocket lands on Britain. Liège and Ostend recaptured.

11 Allied forces from Normandy and southern France make contact near Dijon.

17 Operation Market-Garden begins.

18 Capture of Boulogne and Brest.

Oct. 2 US troops attack the West Wall defences.

21 US troops take Aachen.

Nov. 23 US 7th Army enter Strasbourg.

Dec. 13 US troops take Metz.

16 German counter-offensive in the Ardennes.

26 Relief of Bastogne.

1945 Jan. 1 Germans launch Nordwind offensive.

16 Allies counter-attack in the Ardennes.

Feb.	9	French victory at Colmar in Alsace. Allies reach the Rhine.
	13	The Dresden raid.
March	6	Allies take Cologne.
	7	US troops cross the Rhine at Remagen.
	22	US troops cross the Rhine at Oppenheim.
	23	British forces cross the Rhine at Rees.
	27	Last V-2 lands in England.
April	1	Allied troops encircle the Ruhr.
	13	Liberation of Belsen and Buchenwald concentration camps.
	18	US troops enter Czechoslovakia.
	23	Himmler offers to surrender to Western Allies.
	25	Liberation of Dachau camp.
	30	Hitler commits suicide.
May	7	Unconditional surrender of all German forces.
	8	VE day.

APPENDIX VII

Chronology of the Eastern Front War 1941–5

1939 March 15   German forces enter
Prague. Czechoslovakia
dismantled.

Aug. 23   Russo-German Pact
signed.

Sept. 1   German invades Poland
and annexes Danzig.

17   Russia invades eastern
Poland.

24   Soviet–German Boundary
and Friendship Treaty
signed.

27   Fall of Warsaw.

Nov. 30   Russia invades Finland.

1940 March 12   Finland capitulates.

Oct. 7   German troops enter
Rumania.

20   Hungary signs Tripartite
Pact.

23   Rumania signs Tripartite
Pact.

24   Slovakia signs Tripartite
Pact.

1941 Jan.   Germany builds up forces
in Rumania.

March 1   Bulgaria signs the
Tripartite Pact.

24   Yugoslavia signs the
Tripartite Pact.

April 6   Germans invade
Yugoslavia.

13   Occupation of Belgrade.

June 22   Barbarossa. Germany
invades the Soviet Union.

24   German forces take
Brest-Litovsk.

July 3   Stalin orders 'scorched
earth' policy.

9   German forces take
300,000 prisoners near
Minsk.

25   German forces reach
Smolensk.

27   Tallinin, capital of Estonia
captured.

Aug. 5   Russian resistance ends in
Smolensk.

12   German forces advance on
Leningrad.

25   British and Soviet troops
occupy Persia.

Sept. 15   German forces encircle
Leningrad.

19   Fall of Kiev.

Oct. 6   Germans launch offensive
towards Moscow.

7   Germans trap 650,000
Soviet troops at Vyazma.

15   German Army Group
South reaches the Don
River.

19   Stalin announces state of
siege in Moscow.

24   Fall of Kharkov.

27   German forces defeat
Soviet armies in the
Crimea although
Sevastopol does not fall.

Nov. 20   Fall of Rostov.

29   Soviet forces retake
Rostov.

Dec. 5   Hitler abandons Moscow
offensive for the winter.

6   Soviet forces under
Zhukov begin
counter-attack before
Moscow.

14   German forces retreat
before Moscow.

19   Army C-in-C Brauchitsch
relieved of command.
Hitler takes personal

		command of the German Army.
1942 Jan.	18	Soviet counter-attack in the Ukraine.
	29	USSR and Britain sign treaty with Persia.
May	8	German forces launch spring offensives.
	12	Soviet forces open Kharkov offensive.
	18	German counter-attack at Kharkov.
	28	Soviet forces defeated in Battle of Kharkov.
June	28	German armies launch summer offensive in the Caucasus.
July	2	Fall of Sevastopol.
	6	Fall of Voronezh.
	23	Fall of Rostov.
Aug.	12	First Moscow Conference begins.
	24	German investment of Stalingrad begins.
Sept.	10	German forces enter Stalingrad.
Nov.	19	Russians open Stalingrad counter-offensive.
	23	Russians encircle Stalingrad.
Dec.	12	German attempt to relieve Stalingrad forces.
1943 Jan.	3	German retreat from the Caucasus.
	14	Soviet forces defeat Hungarian forces on the Don. Russians break the encirclement of Leningrad.
Feb.	2	German forces surrender at Stalingrad.
	8	Russian forces retake Kursk.
	14	Soviet forces retake Rostov.
April	19	Jewish ghetto uprising in Warsaw begins.
May	16	Warsaw uprising brutally suppressed.
July	4	Battle of Kursk begins.

	12	Soviet counter-offensive launched from Smolensk to the Black Sea.
Aug.	5	Soviet forces recapture Kharkov.
Sept.	25	Russian forces retake Smolensk.
Oct.	25	Soviet forces retake Dnepropetrovsk.
Nov.	6	Russian forces liberate Kiev.
	28	Tehran Conference begins.
1944 Jan.	19	Soviet forces retake Novgorod.
	26	Leningrad liberated.
March	20	German forces occupy Hungary.
April	2	Soviet forces enter Rumania.
	8	Russian offensive in the Crimea.
May	12	Russians retake Sevastopol.
June	22	Russians open massive offensive on central front. Operation Bagration.
July	4	Soviet forces retake Minsk.
	28	Soviet forces retake Brest-Litovsk.
Aug.	1	Start of second Warsaw uprising.
	7	Russians reach the Vistula River.
	20	Russians invade Rumania.
Sept.	5	Soviet Union declares war on Bulgaria.
	7	Bulgaria declares war on Germany.
	19	Fighting ends between Russia and Finland when armistice is signed.
Oct.	2	Warsaw uprising viciously crushed.
	20	Soviet and Yugoslav forces retake Belgrade.
	23	Soviet forces enter East Prussia.
Dec.	24	Russians encircle

			Budapest.		16	Assault on Berlin begins.
1945	*Jan.*	12	Soviet winter offensive		25	Soviet and US troops meet
			opens.			near Torgau, joining the
		17	Warsaw falls.			fronts in Northwest
	Feb.	4	Yalta Conference			Europe.
			begins.	*May*	2	Fall of Berlin.
		13	Soviet forces take		7	Formal surrender of all
			Budapest.			German forces.
	March	30	Soviet forces take Danzig.		13	Soviet armies overcome
	April	13	Vienna captured by Soviet			remaining resistance in
			forces.			Czechoslovakia.

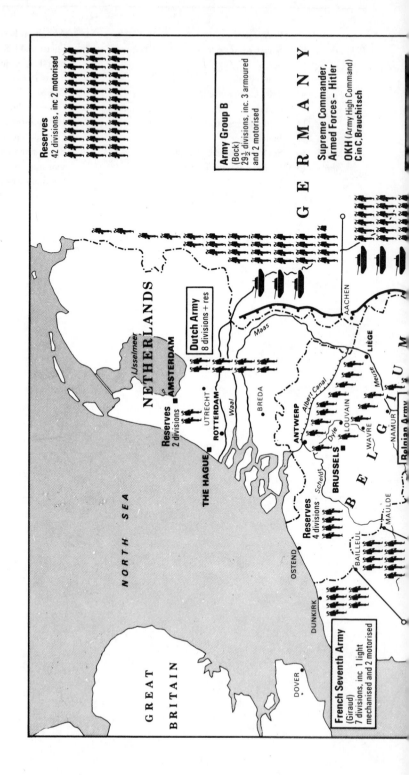

Reserves
42 divisions, inc 2 motorised

Army Group B
(Bock)
29½ divisions, inc. 3 armoured and 2 motorised

G E R M A N Y

Supreme Commander, Armed Forces – Hitler

OKH (Army High Command)
C in C, Brauchitsch

N E T H E R L A N D S

IJsselmeer

Dutch Army
8 divisions + res

AMSTERDAM

UTRECHT

Waal

Reserves
2 divisions

ROTTERDAM

Maas

AACHEN

BREDA

Meuse

THE HAGUE

N O R T H   S E A

ANTWERP

Albert Canal

LIÈGE

Scheldt

LOUVAIN

B E L G I U M

Dyle

WAVRE

NAMUR

BRUSSELS

Belgian Army

Reserves
4 divisions

OSTEND

MAULDE

G R E A T
B R I T A I N

BAILLEUL

DUNKIRK

DOVER

French Seventh Army
(Giraud)
7 divisions, inc 1 light mechanised and 2 motorised

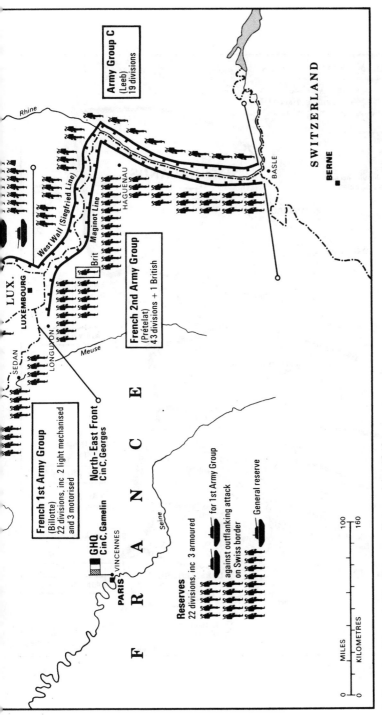

1. Opposing Forces in Northwestern Europe, May 1940

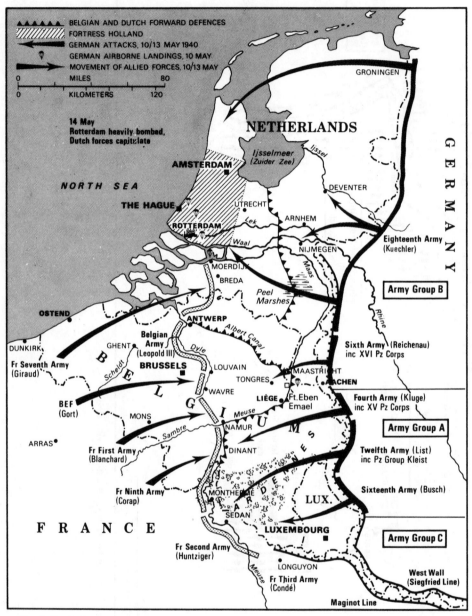

Map legend:

- Belgian and Dutch forward defences
- Fortress Holland
- German attacks, 10/13 May 1940
- German airborne landings, 10 May
- Movement of Allied forces, 10/13 May

MILES 0 — 80
KILOMETERS 0 — 120

14 May
Rotterdam heavily bombed,
Dutch forces capitulate

GRONINGEN

NETHERLANDS

GERMANY

Ijsselmeer
(Zuider Zee)

Ijssel

AMSTERDAM

NORTH SEA

DEVENTER

THE HAGUE

UTRECHT

Lek

ARNHEM

ROTTERDAM

Waal

NIJMEGEN

MOERDIJK

Maas

Eighteenth Army
(Kuechler)

BREDA

Army Group B

OSTEND

Peel
Marshes

Rhine

ANTWERP

Albert Canal

DUNKIRK

Belgian
Army
(Leopold III)

GHENT

Dyle

B E L

Scheldt

Sixth Army (Reichenau)
inc XVI Pz Corps

Fr Seventh Army
(Giraud)

BRUSSELS

LOUVAIN

G I U M S

MAASTRICHT

TONGRES

AACHEN

WAVRE

LIÈGE

Ft. Eben
Emael

Fourth Army (Kluge)
inc XV Pz Corps

BEF
(Gort)

MONS

Meuse

NAMUR

Army Group A

Sambre

ARRAS

Fr First Army
(Blanchard)

DINANT

Twelfth Army (List)
inc Pz Group Kleist

A R D E N N E S

Fr Ninth Army
(Corap)

MONTHERME

LUX.

Sixteenth Army (Busch)

SEDAN

F R A N C E

LUXEMBOURG

Army Group C

Fr Second Army
(Huntziger)

LONGUYON

West Wall
(Siegfried Line)

Meuse

Fr Third Army
(Condé)

Maginot Line

2. The Fall of Belgium, May 1940

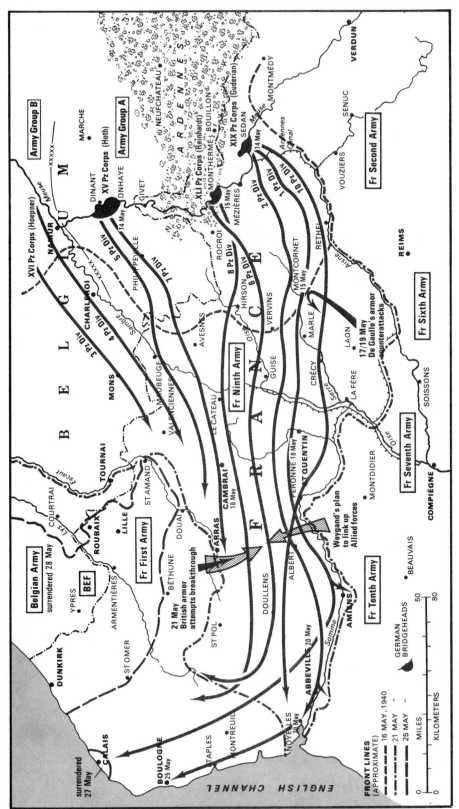

3. The German advance through Northern France, May 1940

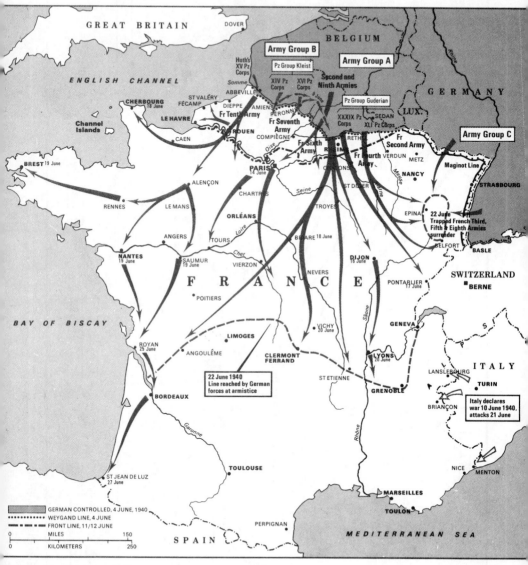

The Battle of France, 1940

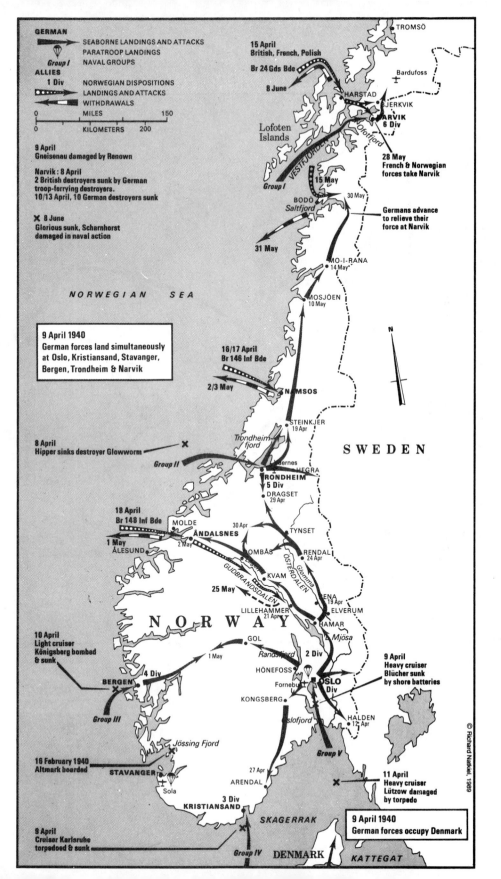

GERMAN
→ SEABORNE LANDINGS AND ATTACKS
↓ PARATROOP LANDINGS
Group I NAVAL GROUPS
ALLIES
1 Div NORWEGIAN DISPOSITIONS
→ LANDINGS AND ATTACKS
← WITHDRAWALS

0 ___ MILES ___ 150
0 ___ KILOMETERS ___ 200

9 April
Gneisenau damaged by Renown

Narvik : 8 April
2 British destroyers sunk by German
troop-ferrying destroyers.
10/13 April, 10 German destroyers sunk

✗ 8 June
Glorious sunk, Scharnhorst
damaged in naval action

TROMSÖ

15 April
British, French, Polish
Br 24 Gds Bde

8 June
HARSTAD
Bardufoss
BJERKVIK
NARVIK
6 Div

Lofoten
Islands
VESTFJORDEN
Group I
15 May
BODÖ
Saltfjord
30 May

28 May
French & Norwegian
forces take Narvik

Ofotfjord

Germans advance
to relieve their
force at Narvik

31 May

MO-I-RANA
14 May

NORWEGIAN   SEA

MOSJÖEN
10 May

9 April 1940
German forces land simultaneously
at Oslo, Kristiansand, Stavanger,
Bergen, Trondheim & Narvik

16/17 April
Br 146 Inf Bde

2/3 May
NAMSOS

STEINKJER
19 Apr

8 April
Hipper sinks destroyer Glowworm
Group II

Trondheim
fjord

SWEDEN

Vaernes
HEGRA
TRONDHEIM
5 Div

DRAGSET
29 Apr

18 April
Br 148 Inf Bde

MOLDE
ÅNDALSNES
30 Apr
TYNSET

1 May
ÅLESUND
2 May

DOMBÅS
KVAM

RENDAL
24 Apr

GUDBRANDSDALEN
ÖSTERDALEN
Glomma

25 May

ENA
19 Apr
ELVERUM

LILLEHAMMER
21 Apr

N O R W A Y

HAMAR

Mjösa

GOL

10 April
Light cruiser
Königsberg bombed
& sunk

1 May

Randsfjord

2 Div

HÖNEFOSS

9 April
Heavy cruiser
Blücher sunk
by shore batteries

4 Div
BERGEN
✗

Fornebu
OSLO
Div

Group III

KONGSBERG

Jössing Fjord

16 February 1940
Altmark boarded

Oslofjord
HALDEN
12 Apr

Group V

11 April
Heavy cruiser
Lützow damaged
by torpedo

STAVANGER

27 Apr
ARENDAL

Sola

3 Div
KRISTIANSAND

9 April
Cruiser Karlsruhe
torpedoed & sunk

Group IV

SKAGERRAK

DENMARK

9 April 1940
German forces occupy Denmark

KATTEGAT

© Richard Natkiel, 1989

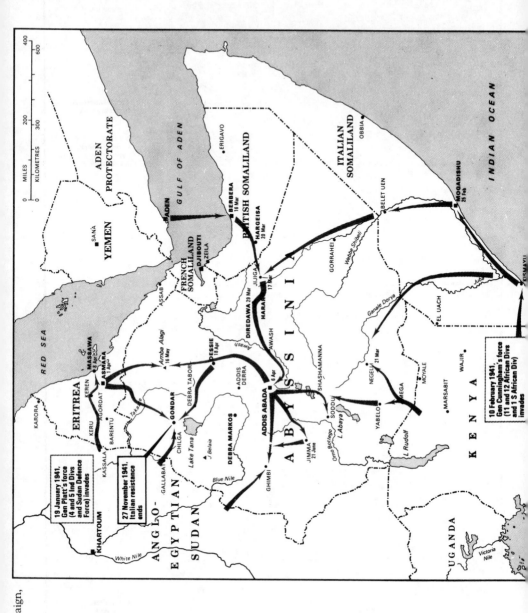

6. The East Africa Campaign, 1940–1

19 January 1941, Gen Platt's force (4 and 5 Ind Divs and Sudan Defence Force) invades

27 November 1941, Italian resistance ends

10 February 1941, Gen Cunningham's force (11 and 12 African Divs and 1 S African Div) invades

RED SEA

ADEN PROTECTORATE

YEMEN
• SANÁ

GULF OF ADEN

ADEN

FRENCH SOMALILAND
DJIBOUTI
ZEILA

BRITISH SOMALILAND
BERBERA 16 Mar
HARGEISA 20 Mar
• ERIGAVO

ITALIAN SOMALILAND
OBBIA •

INDIAN OCEAN

JIJIGA 17 Mar
HARAR
DIREDAWA 29 Mar

GORRAHEI •
Webbe Shibeli

BELET UEN

MOGADISHU 25 Feb

ERITREA
MASSAWA
ASMARA 1 Apr
KEREN 8 Apr
KERU
AGORDAT
BARENTU
KASSALA

KARORA •

Amba Alagi 16 May
DESSIE 18 Apr

DEBRA TABOR
ADDIS DERRA •

AWASH

SHASHAMANNA

Ganale Dorya

EL UACH •

Juba

KISMAYU

ANGLO-EGYPTIAN SUDAN

KHARTOUM

White Nile

GALLABAT
CHILGA
GONDAR
Lake Tana
J Belaia
Blue Nile

DEBRA MARKOS

ADDIS ABABA 6 Apr

GHIMBI •

A B Y S S I N I A

JIMMA 21 June
Omo Bottego
SODDU
L Abaya
YABELO
L Rudolf

NEGELLI 21 Mar
MEGA
MOYALE •

MARSABIT •

WAJIR •

K E N Y A

UGANDA

Victoria Nile

MILES
KILOMETRES
0   200   400
0   300   600

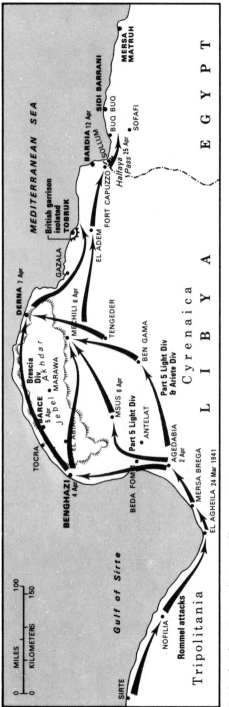

7. North Africa: Rommel's First Offensive, 1941

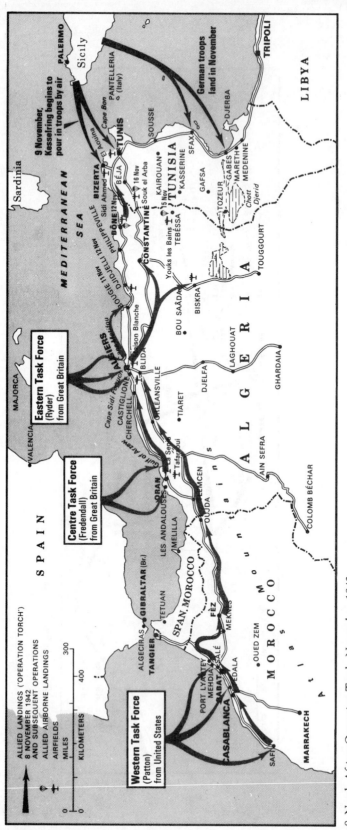

8. North Africa: Operation Torch, November, 1942

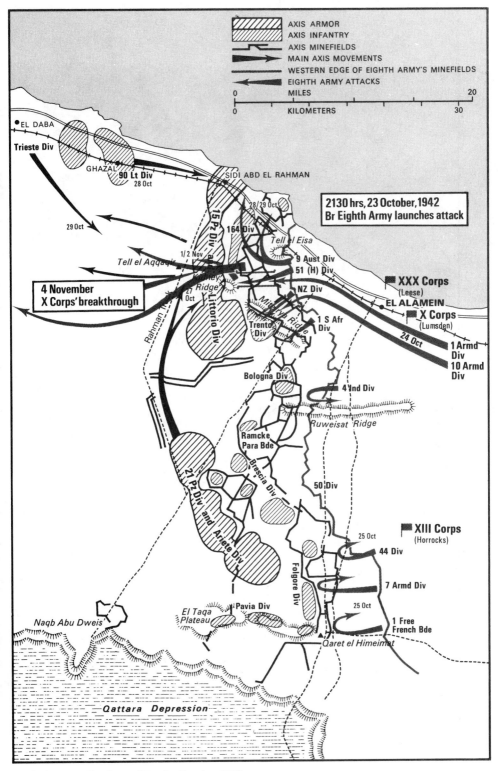

Legend:
- AXIS ARMOR
- AXIS INFANTRY
- AXIS MINEFIELDS
- MAIN AXIS MOVEMENTS
- WESTERN EDGE OF EIGHTH ARMY'S MINEFIELDS
- EIGHTH ARMY ATTACKS

0 MILES 20
0 KILOMETERS 30

2130 hrs, 23 October, 1942
Br Eighth Army launches attack

EL DABA

Trieste Div

GHAZAL
90 Lt Div
28 Oct

SIDI ABD EL RAHMAN

28/29 Oct

29 Oct

15 Pz Div

164 Div

Tell el Eisa

9 Aust Div

51 (H) Div

Tell el Aqqaqir

1/2 Nov

Kidney
Ridge

27 Oct

Littorio Div

NZ Div

XXX Corps
(Leese)

EL ALAMEIN

4 November
X Corps' breakthrough

Rahman Track

Miteirya Ridge

Trento
Div

1 S Afr
Div

X Corps
(Lumsden)

24 Oct

1 Armd
Div

10 Armd
Div

Bologna Div

4 Ind Div

Ruweisat Ridge

Ramcke
Para Bde

Brescia Div

50 Div

21 Pz Div and Ariete Div

XIII Corps
(Horrocks)

25 Oct

44 Div

7 Armd Div

Folgore Div

25 Oct

1 Free
French Bde

Naqb Abu Dweis

El Taqa
Plateau

Pavia Div

Qaret el Himeimat

Qattara Depression

9. El Alamein: The Second Battle, October 1942

JAPANESE EMPIRE, 1933
OCCUPIED BY JAPAN, JULY 1937/DECEMBER 1941
MILITARY BASES ESTABLISHED BY JAPAN, SEPTEMBER 1940

MERCATOR'S PROJECTION

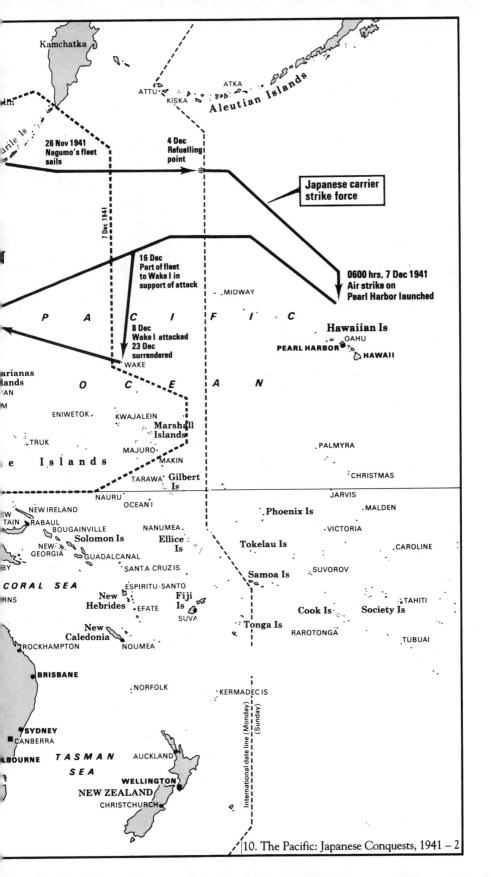

Kamchatka

ATTU
KISKA
ATKA
Aleutian Islands

Kurile Is

**26 Nov 1941
Nagumo's fleet
sails**

**4 Dec
Refuelling
point**

7 Dec 1941

**Japanese carrier
strike force**

**16 Dec
Part of fleet
to Wake I in
support of attack**

MIDWAY

**0600 hrs, 7 Dec 1941
Air strike on
Pearl Harbor launched**

P   A   C   I   F   I   C

**8 Dec
Wake I attacked
23 Dec
surrendered**
WAKE

Hawaiian Is
OAHU
PEARL HARBOR
HAWAII

arianas
lands
AN
M

O   C   E   A   N

ENIWETOK
KWAJALEIN
**Marshall
Islands**

TRUK
MAJURO
MAKIN
TARAWA
**Gilbert
Is**

e   Islands

PALMYRA

CHRISTMAS

NAURU
OCEAN I
JARVIS

NEW IRELAND
TAIN RABAUL
BOUGAINVILLE
NANUMEA
Solomon Is
NEW
GEORGIA
GUADALCANAL
**Ellice
Is**
SANTA CRUZ IS

Phoenix Is
MALDEN

VICTORIA

Tokelau Is
CAROLINE

BY

CORAL SEA
RNS

ESPIRITU-SANTO
**New
Hebrides**
EFATE
**Fiji
Is**
SUVA

Samoa Is
SUVOROV

**New
Caledonia**
NOUMEA
ROCKHAMPTON

Tonga Is
RAROTONGA

Cook Is
Society Is
TAHITI

TUBUAI

BRISBANE
NORFOLK

KERMADEC IS

SYDNEY
CANBERRA
LBOURNE

**TASMAN
SEA**
AUCKLAND

International date line (Monday)
(Sunday)

WELLINGTON
NEW ZEALAND
CHRISTCHURCH

10. The Pacific: Japanese Conquests, 1941 – 2

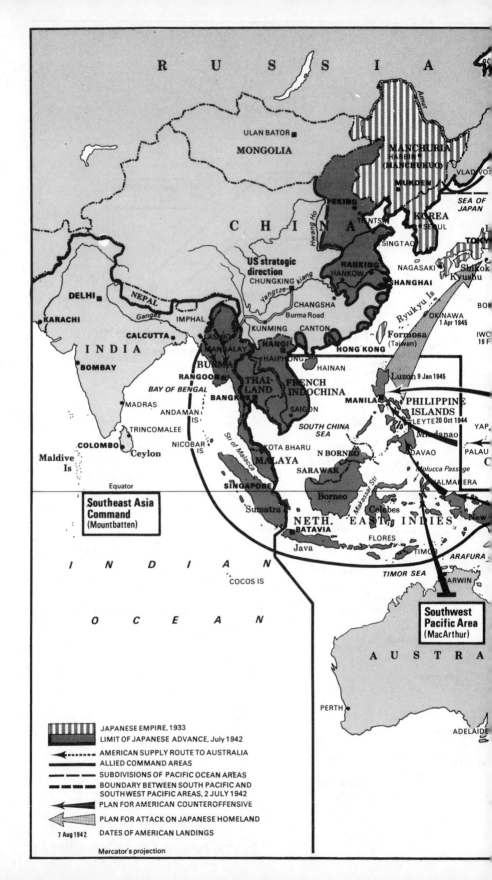

JAPANESE EMPIRE, 1933

LIMIT OF JAPANESE ADVANCE, July 1942

AMERICAN SUPPLY ROUTE TO AUSTRALIA

ALLIED COMMAND AREAS

SUBDIVISIONS OF PACIFIC OCEAN AREAS

BOUNDARY BETWEEN SOUTH PACIFIC AND
SOUTHWEST PACIFIC AREAS, 2 JULY 1942

PLAN FOR AMERICAN COUNTEROFFENSIVE

PLAN FOR ATTACK ON JAPANESE HOMELAND

7 Aug 1942   DATES OF AMERICAN LANDINGS

Mercator's projection

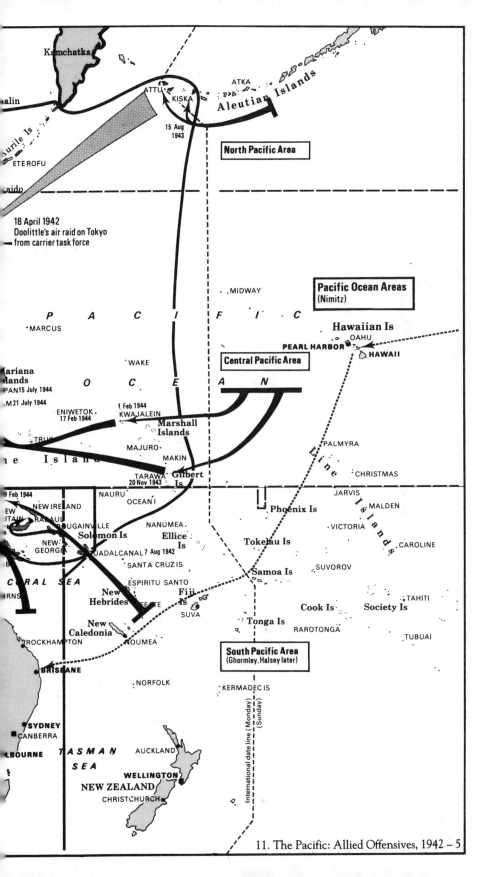

11. The Pacific: Allied Offensives, 1942 – 5

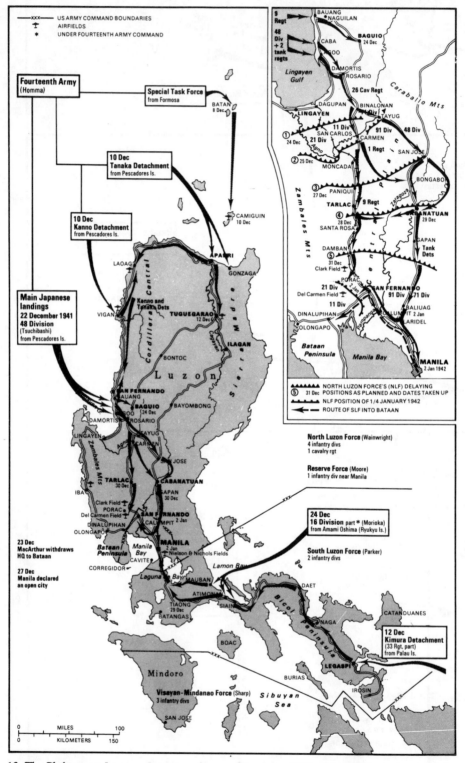

12. The Philippines: Japanese Invasion of Luzon, December 1941 – May 1942

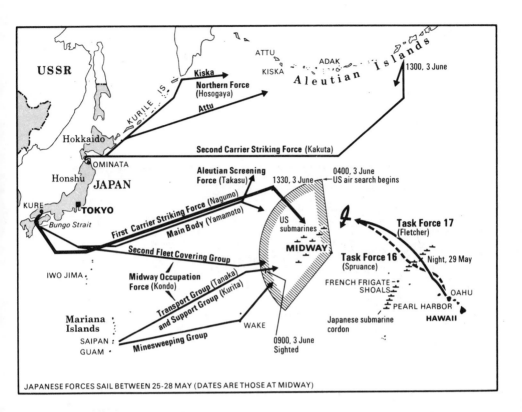

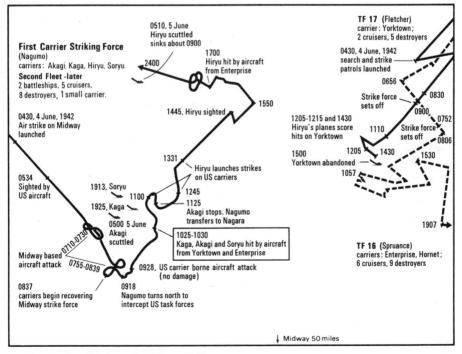

13. The Battle of Midway, 3 – 5 June 1942

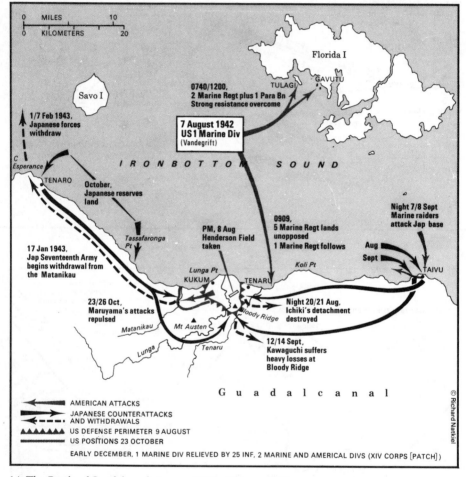

Florida I

Savo I

0740/1200,
2 Marine Regt plus 1 Para Bn
Strong resistance overcome

TULAGI   GAVUTU

1/7 Feb 1943,
Japanese forces
withdraw

7 August 1942
US 1 Marine Div
(Vandegrift)

C
Esperance

I R O N B O T T O M   S O U N D

TENARO

October,
Japanese reserves
land

Night 7/8 Sept
Marine raiders
attack Jap base

Tassafaronga
Pt

PM, 8 Aug
Henderson Field
taken

0909,
5 Marine Regt lands
unopposed
1 Marine Regt follows

Aug

Sept

TAIVU

17 Jan 1943,
Jap Seventeenth Army
begins withdrawal from
the Matanikau

Lunga Pt
KUKUM

Koli Pt

TENARU

23/26 Oct,
Maruyama's attacks
repulsed

Bloody Ridge

Night 20/21 Aug,
Ichiki's detachment
destroyed

Matanikau   ▲ *Mt Austen*

Lunga   *Tenaru*

12/14 Sept,
Kawaguchi suffers
heavy losses at
Bloody Ridge

G u a d a l c a n a l

AMERICAN ATTACKS

JAPANESE COUNTERATTACKS
AND WITHDRAWALS

▲▲▲▲▲▲ US DEFENSE PERIMETER 9 AUGUST

US POSITIONS 23 OCTOBER

EARLY DECEMBER, 1 MARINE DIV RELIEVED BY 25 INF, 2 MARINE AND AMERICAL DIVS (XIV CORPS [PATCH])

0   MILES   10
0   KILOMETERS   20

14. The Battle of Guadalcanal, August 1942 – January 1943

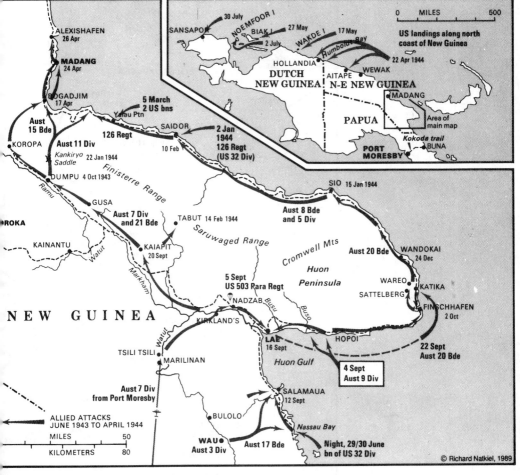

New Guinea Campaigns, 1943 – 4

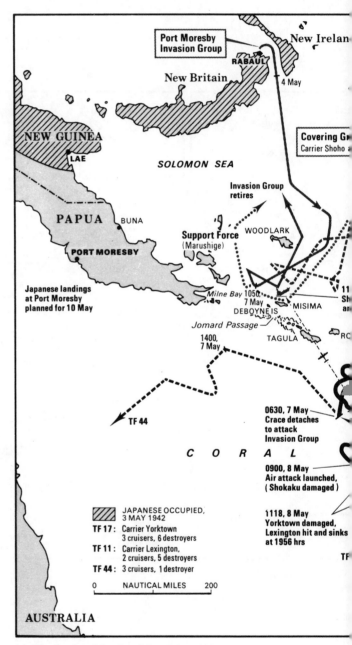

16. The Battle of the Coral Sea, May 1942

ese Carrier Striking Force (Takagi)
s Zuikaku and Shokaku

from Truk

inville

Choiseul

2400,
5 May

S O L O M O N

Santa
Isabel

ased
Shoho

Georgia

I S L A N D S

0010,
5 May

3 May
Japanese land,
establish sea-
plane base

0815, 4 May
First US air strike
on Tulagi

TULAGI

0200, 9 May

Malaita

FLORIDA
IS

Guadalcanal
0930, 6 May

San Cristobal

0630,
4 May

RENNELL

2400,
7 May

2400,
6 May

0010,
5 May

2400,
6 May

1755,
6 May

1930,
6 May

S E A

0930,
6 May

osho

0700,
3 May

Task Force 17
(Fletcher)

y
eosho bombed.
Neosho damaged,
May

Task Forces 11 (Fitch)
and 44 (Crace) **join TF 17**

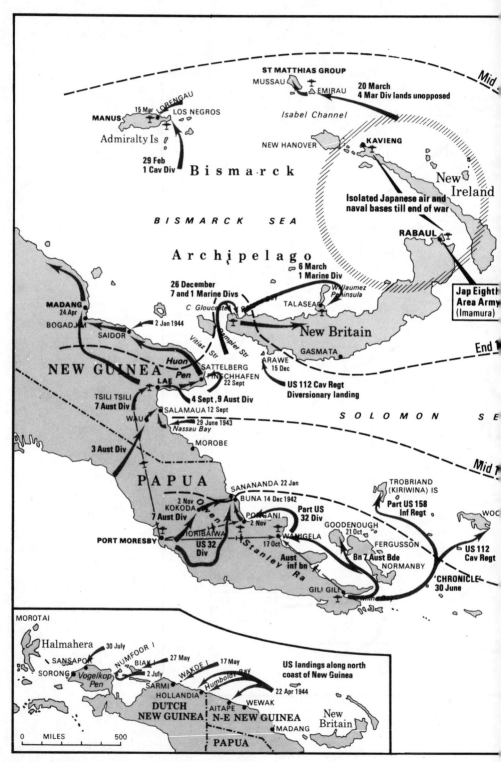

17. Southwest Pacific Theatre Campaigns, 1942 – 4

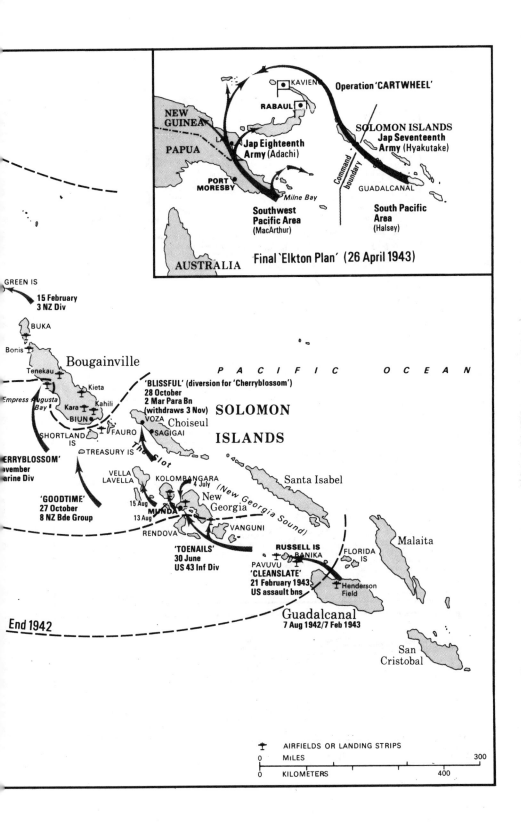

Operation 'CARTWHEEL'

NEW GUINEA

KAVIEN

RABAUL

SOLOMON ISLANDS
Jap Seventeenth Army (Hyakutake)

PAPUA

Jap Eighteenth Army (Adachi)

PORT MORESBY

Milne Bay

Command boundary

GUADALCANAL

Southwest Pacific Area (MacArthur)

South Pacific Area (Halsey)

AUSTRALIA

Final 'Elkton Plan' (26 April 1943)

GREEN IS

15 February 3 NZ Div

BUKA

Bonis

Tenekau

Bougainville

Kieta

P A C I F I C   O C E A N

Empress Augusta Bay

Kara   Kahili

BIUN

'BLISSFUL' (diversion for 'Cherryblossom')
28 October 2 Mar Para Bn (withdraws 3 Nov)

VOZA

SOLOMON

SHORTLAND IS   FAURO

SAGIGAI   Choiseul

ISLANDS

TREASURY IS

The Slot

ERRYBLOSSOM' ovember arine Div

VELLA LAVELLA

KOLOMBANGARA

4 July

(New Georgia Sound)

Santa Isabel

'GOODTIME' 27 October 8 NZ Bde Group

15 Aug

New Georgia

13 Aug

MUNDA

RENDOVA

VANGUNI

'TOENAILS' 30 June US 43 Inf Div

RUSSELL IS
BANIKA

FLORIDA IS

Malaita

PAVUVU

'CLEANSLATE' 21 February 1943 US assault bns

Henderson Field

End 1942

Guadalcanal
7 Aug 1942/7 Feb 1943

San Cristobal

✈ AIRFIELDS OR LANDING STRIPS

| 0 | MILES | | 300 |

| 0 | KILOMETERS | | 400 |

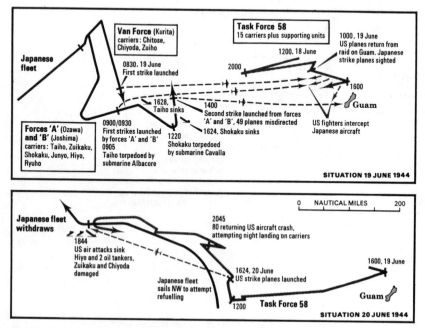

18. The Battle of the Philippine Sea, 13 – 16 June 1944

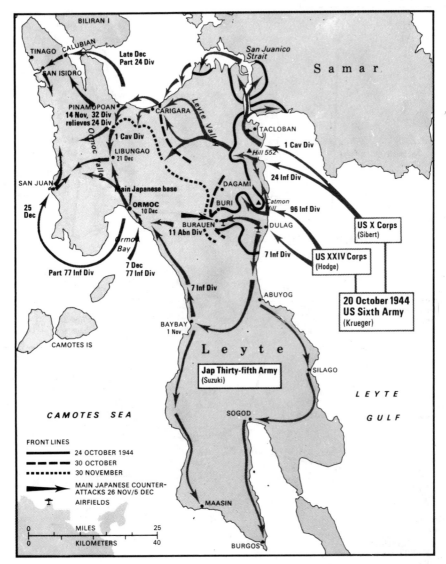

19. The Philippines: US Invasion of Leyte, October – December 1944

POSITIONS OF US CARRIER TASK GROUPS, 0600, 24 OCTOBER
TIMES ARE THOSE FOR 24 OCTOBER UNLESS OTHERWISE INDICATED

0   NAUTICAL MILES   300

Carrier 'Decoy' Force (Ozawa)   0100
0000, 25th
0600, 25th
1140
Group 'A' (Matsuda)
2000
0822, 25th
2241

Task Force 38 (Halsey's Third Fleet) steams north to engage Ozawa's force

Second Striking Force (Shima)

C.Engaño

Luzon

TG 38.3 (Sherman)

Clark Field

0935 Carrier Princeton hit, sinks at 1630

PHILIPPINE ISLANDS

MANILA

Princeton

2345

2000

1200, 23 Oct

Mindoro

TG 38.2 (Bogan)

1026/1530 US air strikes. Battleship Musashi sinks at 1935, cruiser Myoko retires damaged

Sibuyan Sea

1000

San Bernardino Str

0600, 25th

CALAMIAN GROUP

Masbate

Samar

TG 38.4 (Davison)

1200, 23 Oct

Panay

Leyte   0400, 25th

US Seventh Fleet (Kinkaid)

Force 'A' (Kurita)

Cebu

0632, 23 Oct US Submarines sink cruisers Atago and Maya, Takao retires damaged

Negros

Bohol

Surigao Str

1000

Palawan

2000

2330

TG 38.1 (McCain) to Ulithi

0918

1000

Force 'C' (Nishimura)

1200, 23 Oct

Mindanao

Sulu   Sea

First Striking Force (Kurita)

BRITISH NORTH BORNEO

Sails 22 Oct

BRUNEI

20. The Philippines: The Battle of Leyte Gulf, 23 – 25 October 1944

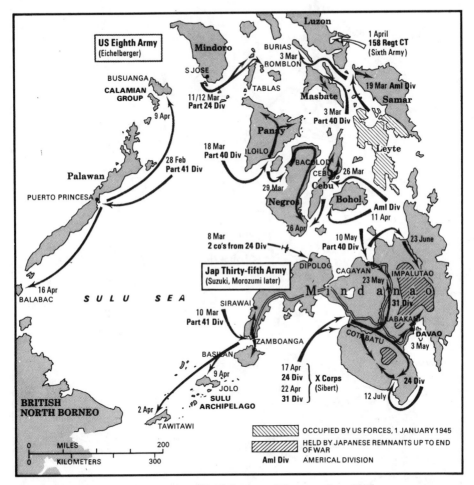

21. The Philippines: US Forces secure the Philippines, February – June 1945

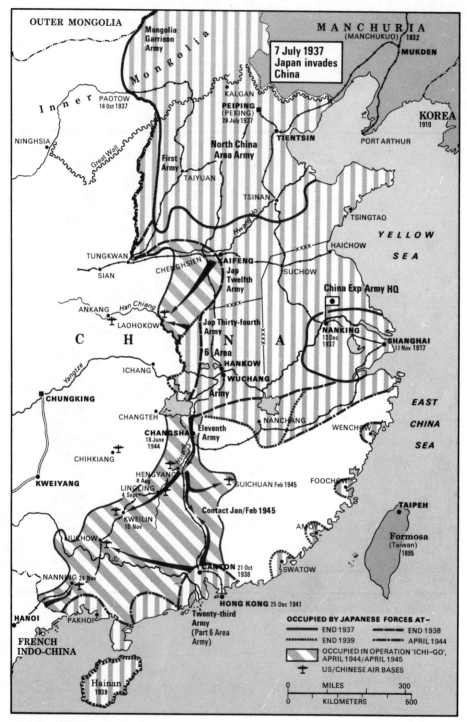

22. China, 1937 – 45

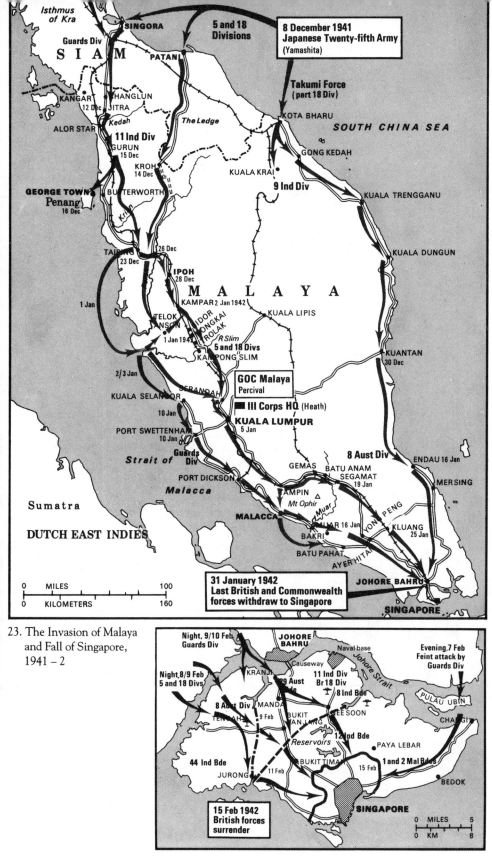

23. The Invasion of Malaya and Fall of Singapore, 1941–2

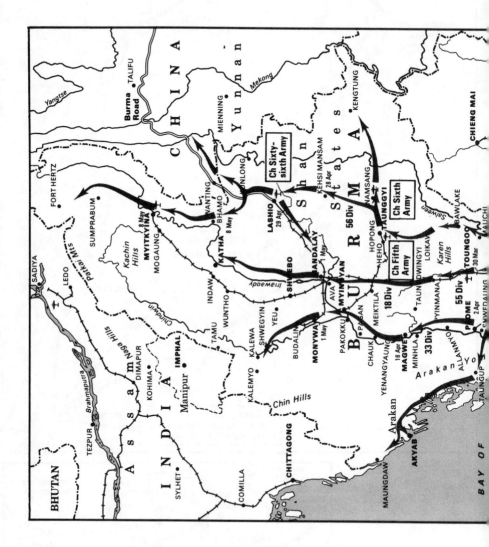

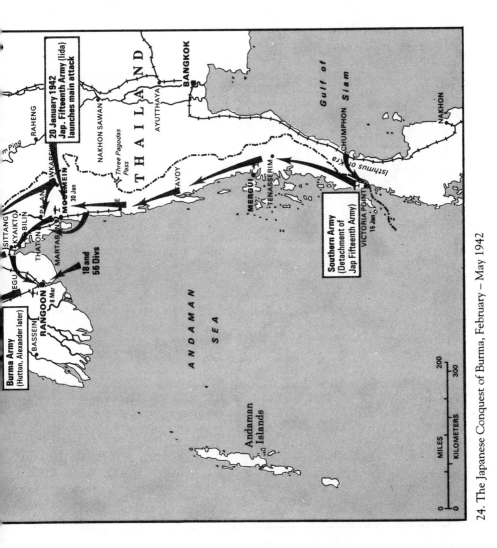

24. The Japanese Conquest of Burma, February – May 1942

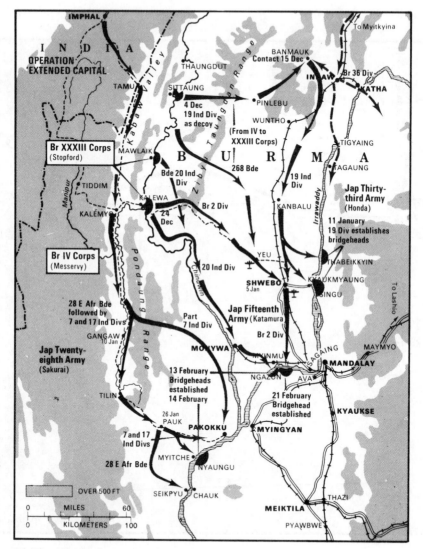

25. The Allied Advance in Burma, 1944 – 5

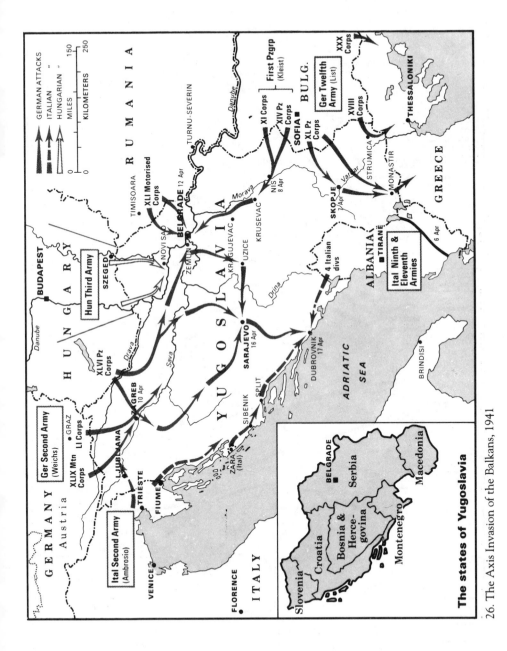

26. The Axis Invasion of the Balkans, 1941

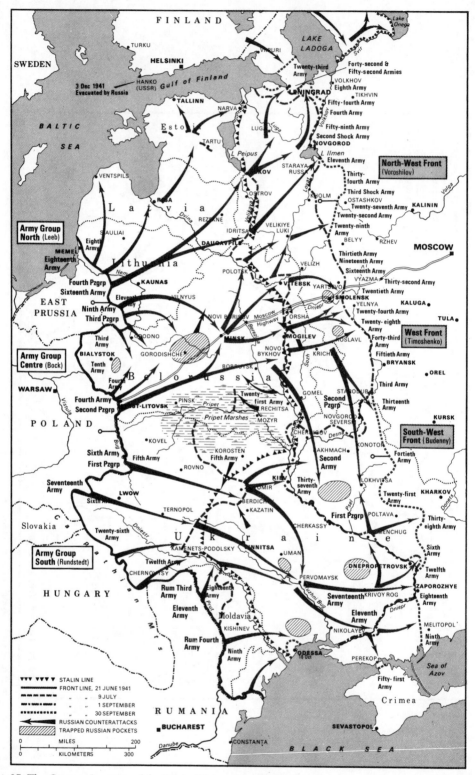

27. The German Invasion of the Soviet Union, June 1941

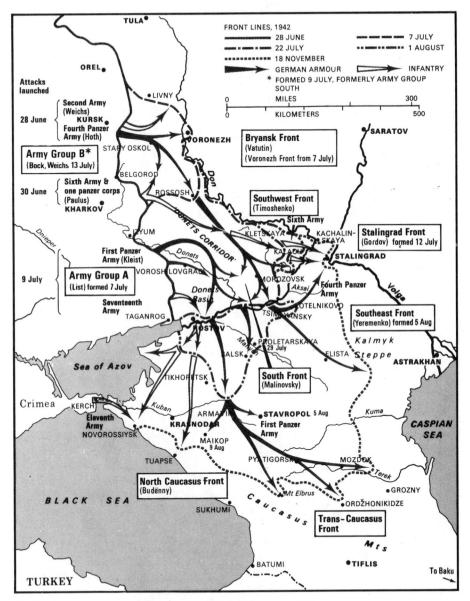

28. The German Summer Offensive towards the Caucasus, 1942

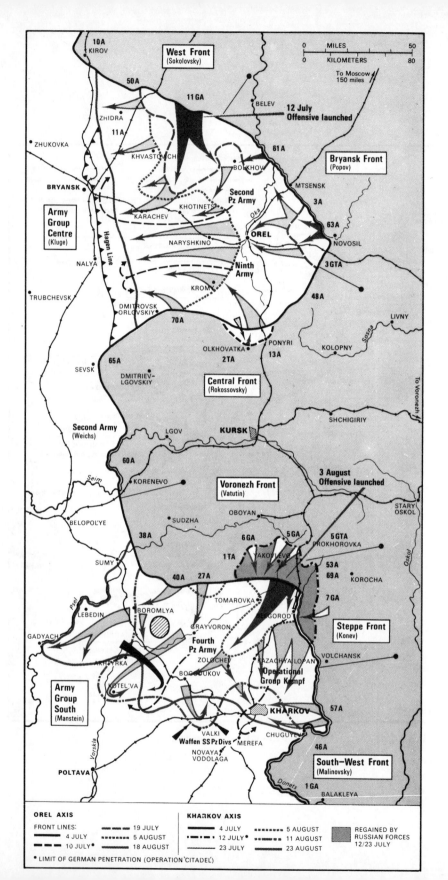

MILES 0 50
KILOMETERS 0 80

To Moscow
150 miles

West Front
(Sokolovsky)

10A
KIROV

50 A

11 GA

ZHIDRA

11 A

ZHUKOVKA

KHVASTOVICH

BELEV

**12 July
Offensive launched**

61 A

BOLKHOV

Bryansk Front
(Popov)

MTSENSK

3 A

**Second
Pz Army**

BRYANSK

**Army
Group
Centre**
(Kluge)

KHOTINETS

KARACHEV

Oka

OREL

63 A

NOVOSIL

NARYSHKINO

3 GTA

NALYA

**Ninth
Army**

Hagen Line

TRUBCHEVSK

KROMY

48 A

LIVNY

DMITROVSK
ORLOVSKIY

70 A

OLKHOVATKA

PONYRI

KOLOPNY

Sosna

65 A

SEVSK

DMITRIEV-
LGOVSKIY

2TA

13 A

Central Front
(Rokossovsky)

SHCHIGIRIY

Second Army
(Weichs)

LGOV

Seim

KURSK

To Voronezh

60 A

KORENEVO

Voronezh Front
(Vatutin)

**3 August
Offensive launched**

BELOPOL'YE

SUDZHA

OBOYAN

STARY
OSKOL

38 A

6 GA

5 GA

5 GTA
PROKHOROVKA

SUMY

40 A

27 A

1TA

YAKOVLEVO

53 A

69 A

KOROCHA

Psel

LEBEDIN

BOROMLYA

TOMAROVKA

7 GA

Oskol

GADYACH

GRAYVORON

BELGOROD

Steppe Front
(Konev)

**Fourth
Pz Army**

ZOLOCHEV

AKHTYRKA

BOGODUKHOV

KAZACHYA LOPAN

**Operational
Group Kempf**

VOLCHANSK

**Army
Group
South**
(Manstein)

KOTEL'VA

KHARKOV

57 A

Vorskla

VALKI

Waffen SS Pz Divs

MEREFA

CHUGUYEV

NOVAYA
VODOLAGA

46 A

POLTAVA

South-West Front
(Malinovsky)

Donets

1 GA

BALAKLEYA

OREL AXIS

FRONT LINES:
——— 4 JULY
━━━ 10 JULY •
━ ━ 19 JULY
········ 5 AUGUST
═══ 18 AUGUST

KHARKOV AXIS
━━━ 4 JULY
—·—·— 12 JULY •
——— 23 JULY
········ 5 AUGUST
———— 11 AUGUST
═══ 23 AUGUST

REGAINED BY
RUSSIAN FORCES
12/23 JULY

• LIMIT OF GERMAN PENETRATION (OPERATION 'CITADEL')

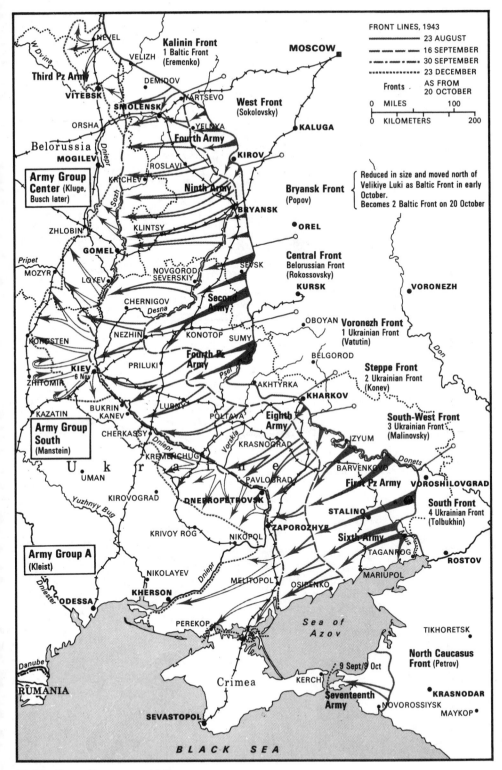

30. The Soviet Resurgence, 1943

29. The Battle of Kursk, July 1943

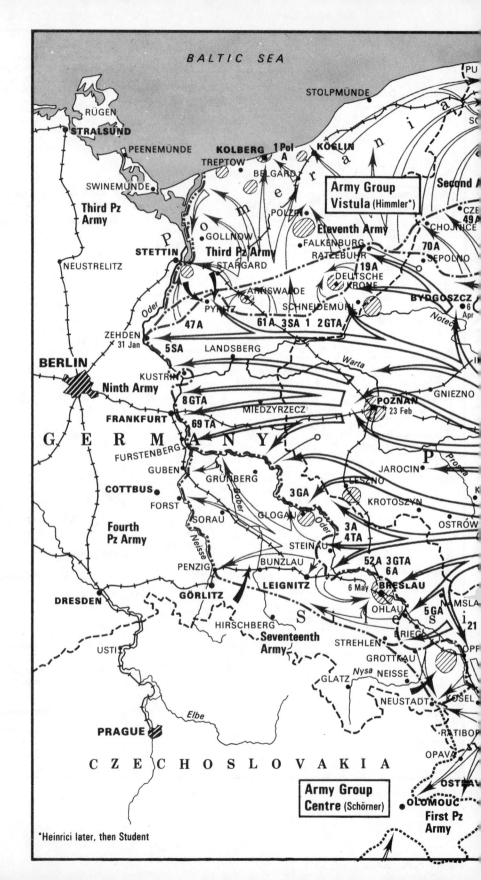

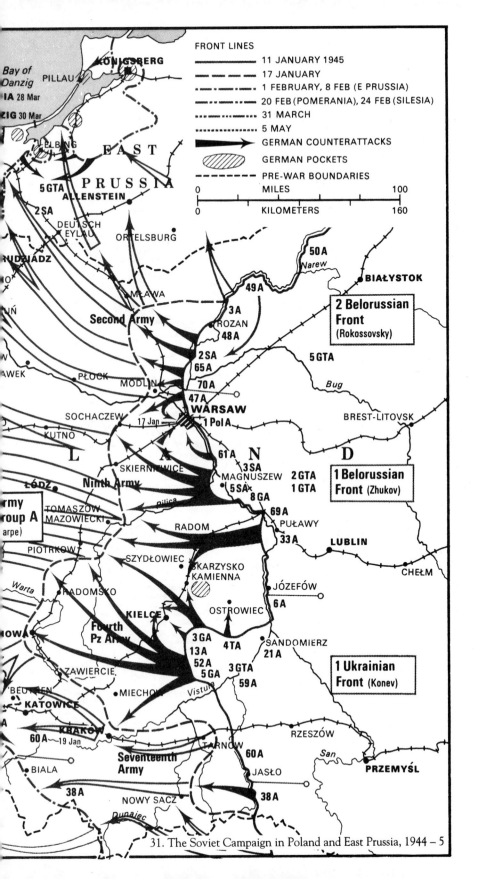

31. The Soviet Campaign in Poland and East Prussia, 1944 – 5

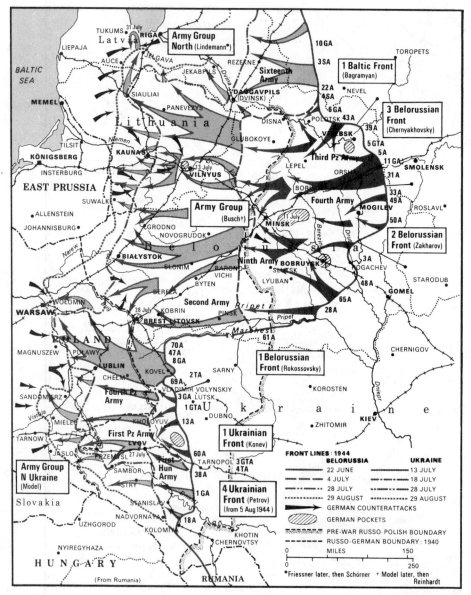

32. The German Retreat from the Soviet Union, 1944

on Berlin, 1945

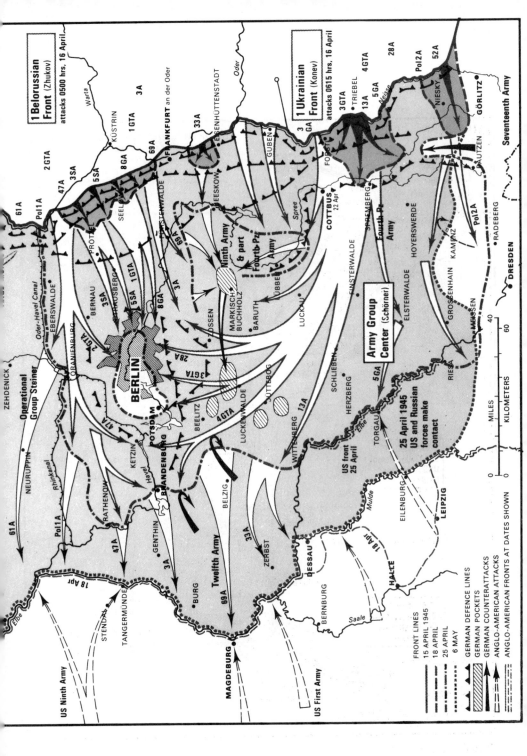

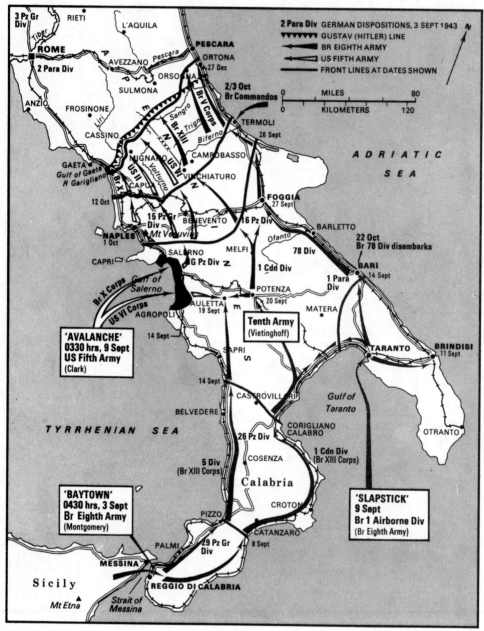

34. Italy, September 1943

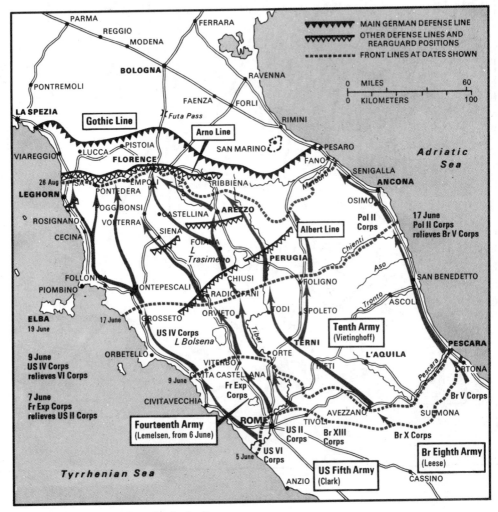

35. Italy: The Allied Push to the Gothic Line

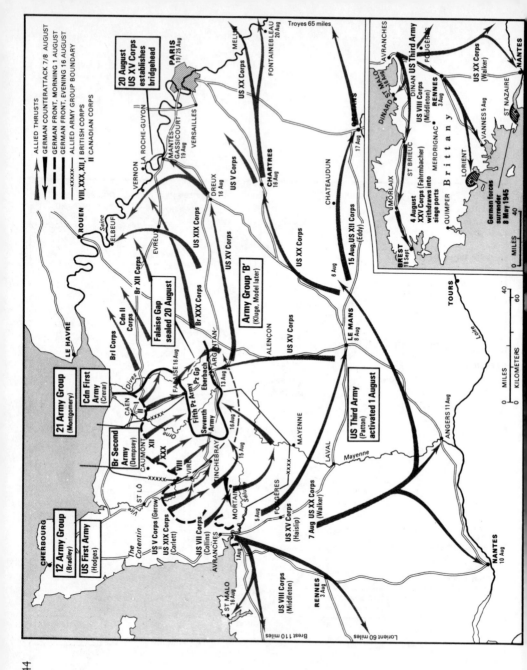

36. The Breakout from Normandy, 1944

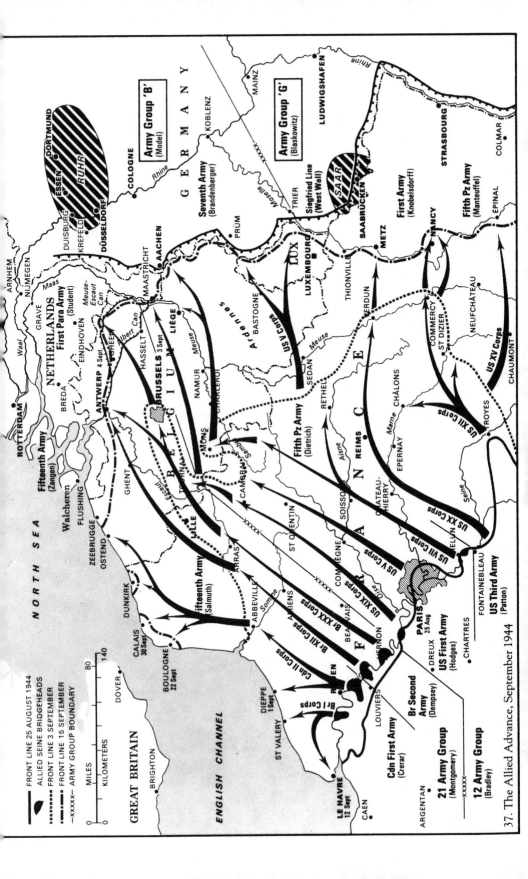

37. The Allied Advance, September 1944

Photo credits

Section I

Munich, October 1938 *Hulton Deutsch Collection*
Fort Eban Emael, Belgium *Bundesarchiv*
French crew surrender to German infantry *Military Archive and Research Services*
Dunkirk, 1940 *Popperfoto*
Marshal Pétain and Pierre Laval *Associated Press*
Adolf Hitler, 22.6.1940 *Imperial War Museum (IWM)*
Vapour trails over St Paul's *IWM*
Spitfire and Junkers 87 Stuka *IWM*
Street in Leningrad *Novosti Press Agency (NPA)*
Battle for Stalingrad – tractor factory *NPA*
Von Paulus's army begins march into captivity *NPA*
Battle of Kursk *NPA*
Abandoned transport *NPA*
Smashed German battery *NPA*
Artillery barrage *NPA*
SS executioners killing Russian villagers *NPA*
Hanging of captured partisans *NPA*
Ammunition ship explodes *IWM*

Section II

General Erwin Rommel *IWM*
British troops in the Western Desert *IWM*
Bombing of Cassino *IWM*
General Orde Wingate and Colonel Phil Cochrane *IWM*

Pearl Harbor *IWM*
Adolf Hitler, 11.12.1941 *IWM*
General Percival surrenders to the Japanese *IWM*
Japanese dead *IWM*
Japanese torpedo plane shot down *IWM*
US marine with Japanese child *IWM*
US marine receiving communion *IWM*
General Douglas MacArthur *IWM*
D-Day – American motorized infantry move inland *IWM*
British infantry landing on Sword Beach *IWM*
Members of the French Resistance *IWM*
People of Brussels welcoming Allied troops *IWM*

Section III

1st Parachute Battalion *IWM*
American tanks moving into the attack *IWM*
V2 rocket seen after firing *IWM*
V1 'Doodle Bug' *IWM*
Dresden *IWM*
Mussolini and his mistress hanging in Milan *IWM*
Field Marshal Montgomery accepting German surrender *IWM*
Photograph of Hitler's alleged corpse *NPA*
Soviet troops raising flag *NPA*
General Dwight D. Eisenhower *IWM*
General Douglas MacArthur *IWM*
G. K. Zhukov *NPA*
Field Marshal Montgomery *IWM*
Mushroom cloud over Nagasaki *IWM*